Human Beliefs and Values

Human Beliefs and Values

*A cross-cultural sourcebook based
on the 1999-2002 values surveys*

Edited by

RONALD INGLEHART, MIGUEL BASÁÑEZ,
JAIME DÍEZ-MEDRANO,
LOEK HALMAN *and* RUUD LUIJKX

siglo veintiuno editores, s.a. de c.v.
CERRO DEL AGUA 248, DELEGACIÓN COYOACÁN, 04310, MÉXICO, D.F.

siglo xxi editores, argentina, s.a.
TUCUMÁN 1621, 7 N, C1050AAG, BUENOS AIRES, ARGENTINA

Cover design: Bi Puranen and Peter Welander
1st edition: March 2004
2nd edition: August 2004

© Siglo XXI Editores, S.A. de C.V.
© Fundación BBVA
© The authors: Ronald Inglehart, Miguel Basáñez,
             Jaime Díez-Medrano, Lock Halman,
             Ruud Luijkx

ISBN: 968-23-2541-2

Contents

List of tables

SECTION F: RELIGION AND MORALE

Foreword

Romano Prodi,
President of the European Commission

Each day, the geographical, economic and political boundaries that once divided the world into isolated compartments, crumble a little more. One example of this trend is the fact that, as this book is being published in 2004, the European Union is bringing the peoples of ten new countries into closer economic, social and political interaction with the peoples of the 15 countries that already are members. Countries that once seemed immensely distant from each other can be contacted almost instantly today. But the cultural diversity among the peoples of the world (and even within the 25-nation European Union) remains great, as this book demonstrates. What people believe and value, and what they want out of life, varies from country to country.

The growing globalization of the world makes it increasingly important to understand this cultural diversity. People with widely varying beliefs and values can live together and work together productively, but for this to happen, it is crucial to understand and appreciate their distinctive worldviews.

This book provides the reader with rich insight into the basic values and attitudes of the peoples of more than 80 societies on all six inhabited continents. It examines what people believe and value concerning politics, economics, religion, sexual behavior, gender roles, family values, communal identities, civic engagement and ethical concerns, and such issues as environmental protection, scientific progress and technological development and human happiness.

I recently pointed out the need for scientific measurements of basic cultural values that would make it possible to compare the cultural values of Europeans with those of other countries. These surveys represent a major step in that direction. They provide data from representative samples of the publics of societies containing 85 percent of the world's population and covering the full range of variation, from the richest countries on earth to some of the poorest, and examining societies that were historically shaped by a wide variety of religious, political and cultural traditions. These surveys were carried out in 36 European countries, including all 25 members of the European Union. They also cover 45 additional countries, making it possible to interpret the beliefs and values of any given society in a genuinely global context. In this broader global context, we find evidence of a "European culture," reflecting relatively similar beliefs shared by European publics—but we also find that certain basic values are widely shared by publics throughout the world. Thus, in every country surveyed, most people consider the family to be the most important aspect of their lives; and the desire for freedom and human liberty is universal.

This sourcebook enables the reader to compare the responses to hundreds of questions across societies from all over the world. It also enables the reader to examine the differences between the responses of men and women in each society; and to examine differences between the worldviews of older and younger generations; it enables one to quickly and conveniently examine differences linked with education and income, and to examine the changes that took place from 1990 to 2000.

Human Beliefs and Values is a valuable tool for understanding how social, political, economic and cultural attitudes differ from one society to another—and how they are changing, with economic and technological development. It provides a wealth of data that will be useful to social scientists, journalists, business executives and policy-makers working in an increasingly global context.

Acknowledgements

This sourcebook reflects the combined efforts of a network of social scientists in more than 80 societies, on all six inhabited continents. For creating and sharing this dataset, we owe a large debt of gratitude to the following people who carried out the World Values Survey and European Values Study: Anthony M. Abela, Atanas Atanasov, Abdel-Hamid Abdel-Latif, Q.K. Ahmad, Ali Aliev, Rasa Alishauskene, Helmut Anheier, Wil Arts, Jose Arocena, Soo Young Auh, Taghi Azadarmaki, Ljiljana Bacevic, Miguel Basanez, Olga Balakireva, Josip Baloban, Nilufur Banu, Kosta Barjaba, Elena Bashkirova, Abdallah Bedaida, Jorge Benitez, Jaak Billiet, Alan Black, Ammar Boukhedir, Fares al-Braizat, Augustin Canzani, Marita Carballo, Henrique Carlos de O. de Castro, Pi-Chao Chen, Pavel Campeanu, Pradeep Chhibber, Mark F. Chingono, Hei-yuan Chiu, Margit Cleveland, Andrew P. Davidson, Juan Díez Nicolas, Jaime Díez Medrano, Herman De Dijn, Karel Dobbelaere, Pieter Drenth, Javier Elzo, Yilmaz Esmer, Pol Estgen, Tony Fahey, Nadjematul Faizah, Georgy Fotev, Aikaterini Gari, James Georgas, Chris Geppaart, Renzo Gubert, Linda Luz Guerrero, Peter Gundelach, Jacques Hagenaars, Loek Halman, Sang-Jin Han, Mustafa Hamarneh, Stephen Harding, Mari Harris, Bernadette C. Hayes, Camilo Herrera, Virginia Hodgkinson, Nadra Muhammed Hosen, Ronald Inglehart, Simon Hug, Kenji Iijima, Ljubov Ishimova, Wolfgang Jagodzinski, Aleksandra Jasinska-Kania, Fridrik Jonsson, Stanislovas Juknevicius, Jan Kerkhofs , Johann Kinghorn, Joanna Konieczna, Zuzana Kusá, Michel Legrand, Noah Lewin-Epstein, Ola Listhaug, Hans-Dieter Klingemann, Hennie Kotze, Marta Lagos, Bernard Lategan, Carlos Lemoine, Jin-yun Liu, Ruud Luijkx, Brina Malnar, Mahar Mangahas, Mario Marinov, Mira Marody, Kostas Mylonas, Felipe Miranda, Robert Mattes, Carlos Matheus, Mansoor Moaddel, Jose Molina, Rafael Mendizabal, Alejandro Moreno, Gaspar K. Munishi, Elone Nwabuzor, Neil Nevitte, Nhu-Ngoc Ong, Stefan Olafsson, Francisco Andrés Orizo, Abdullah al-Otaiby, Merab Pachulia, Dragomir Pantic, Juhani Pehkonen, Paul Perry, Thorleif Pettersson, Pham Minh Hac, Pham Thanh Nghi, Gevork Pogosian, Lucien Pop, Tony Proudian, Bi Puranen, Ladislav Rabusic, Alice Ramos, Angel Rivera-Ortiz, Catalina Romero, David Rotman, Andrus Saar, Rajab Sattarov, Pascal Sciarini, Sandeep Shastri, Shen Mingming, Renata Siemienska, Jose Simeon, Richard Sinnott, John Sudarsky, Tan Ern Ser, Toru Takahashi, Farooq Tanwir, Jean-Francois Tchernia, Kareem Tejumola, Larissa Titarenko, Miklos Tomka, Jose Torregrosa, Alfredo Torres, Niko Tos, Jorge Vala, Andrei Vardomatskii, Manuel Villaverde Cabral, Malina Voicu, Alan Webster, Friedrich Welsch, Christian Welzel, Toru Takahashi, Seiko Yamazaki, Ephraim Yuchtman-Yaar, Brigita Zepa, Josefina Zaiter, Catalin Zamfir, and Paul Zulehner.

This project would not have been possible without the encouragement and generosity of many sponsors. We have been fortunate to have the support of many countries' national social science research councils and a number of charitable trusts and foundations, companies, church organizations, and private individuals, which worked to make our enterprise a success. It would be impossible to mention all organizations, enterprises, and individuals who have contributed to the project, not only because they are too numerous, but also because some of them prefer to be anonymous. Therefore we can only express our appreciation in a general way for their help in enabling us to conduct these surveys. Most of these surveys were supported by sources within the given country, but where such funding was not available, support for surveys and for central coordination was provided by the National Science Foundation, the Ford Foundation, the Bank of Sweden Tercentenary Foundation, the Swedish Agency for International Development, the Fondation Meditel, the Volkswagen Foundation, the Berlin Social Science Research Center, and the BBVA Foundation.

The World Values Surveys grew out of a study launched by the European Values Systems Study Group (EVSSG) under the leadership of Jan Kerkhofs and Ruud de Moor, with a steering committee consisting of Heinz Maier-Leibnitz, Karl Foster, Jacques Rabier, Pierre Delooz, and Mark Abrams, and a technical group consisting of Gordon Heald, Meryl James, Elisabeth Noelle-Neumann, Renate Köcher, Jean Stoetzel, Helene Riffault, Juan Linz, and Stephen Harding. In 1981, the EVSSG carried out surveys in ten West European societies; it evoked such widespread interest that it was replicated in 16 additional countries. Findings from these surveys suggested that predictable cultural changes were taking place: many variables showing large intergenerational differences, and were strongly correlated with Postmaterialist values. To monitor changes, successive waves of surveys were carried out in 1990-91, 1995-96 and 1999-2001, with input from participants from all six inhabited continents. An additional wave of surveys is scheduled for 2005. These surveys are coordinated by the World Values Survey Association, based in Stockholm, and the European Values Study group, at Tilburg University, The Netherlands.

The data from the World Values Surveys were assembled and processed at the ISR in Ann Arbor by Karen Long, Gabriela Catterberg and Zhengxu Wang. They were then cleaned and documented at JD Systems in Madrid by Miluka Galán-Moreno, Pilar Bustos and Mari Cruz Carbajo, under the direction of Jaime Díez-Medrano. Cleaning, documenting and distributing the data from the European Values Study was done in collaboration with Hermann Duelmer, Evelyn Brislinger and Wolfgang Zenk-Moeltgen, at the Zentralarchiv (Cologne), and Helga van Gelder, Cor van der Meer, and Berry Feith from the Netherlands Institute for Scientific Information Services (NIWI) in Amsterdam (see also Halman, 2001). We are indebted to these people, and to Josette Gevers, Carla Janssen, Marit Beijers, Godelief Mars, Helmine Roodenburg, Kim Colaris, Eefje Strijbosch, Maike van Damme, Jorn van der Zanden, and Jolanda van Sluijs from Tilburg University, who assisted in processing the data. We are grateful to the data archive of the Zentralarchiv für Empirische Sozialforschung at the University of Cologne, and to the Work & Organization Research Centre of the Faculty of Social and Behavioral Sciences at Tilburg University for supporting the European Values Study project in numerous ways. Juan Balderas and Dolores de los Rios of Global Quality Research in Mexico City developed a program that produced the hundreds of tables in this book and checked for accuracy and spelling. Ruud Luijkx (Tilburg University, The Netherlands) and Jaime

Díez Medrano (JD Systems and ASEP in Madrid), constructed an integrated data file containing the 1999-2001 European Values Study and World Values Surveys. The results of their efforts are presented in this book and the attached CD-ROM.

For more information about the World Values Survey, see the WVS web site http://www.worldvaluessurvey.org. For more information about the European Values Study, see the EVS website http://www.europeanvalues.nl and http://www.gesis.org/za

The Editors,
Ronald Inglehart, Miguel Basáñez, Jaime Díez-Medrano,
Loek Halman *and* Ruud Luijkx

Introduction

Ronald Inglehart, Loek Halman and Christian Welzel

This book gives insight into the basic values and attitudes of the peoples of more than 80 societies around the world. Using data from the World Values Survey and European Values Study Surveys, it examines standardized cross-cultural measures of human values and goals concerning politics, economics, religion, sexual behavior, gender roles, family values, communal identities, civic engagement and ethical concerns, and such issues as environmental protection, scientific progress and technological development and human happiness. For information about the origins of the Values Surveys and how they are organized, see Harding, Phillips and Fogarty, 1986; Barker, Halman and Vloet, 1992; Ester, Halman and de Moor, 1994; Inglehart, Basáñez and Moreno, 1998; Halman, 2001. Further information including some recent publications, a list of more than 300 earlier publications, news about conferences, and other information, can be found on the World Values Survey web site, http://www.worldvaluessurvey.org and the European Values Study website, http://www.europeanvalues.nl.

These surveys cover a broader range of variation than has ever before been available for analyzing the belief systems of mass publics. They provide data from representative national samples of the publics of 81 societies containing 85 percent of the world's population and covering the full range of variation, from societies with per capita incomes below $300 per year, to societies with per capita incomes of more than $35,000 per year; from long-established democracies to authoritarian states; and from societies with market economies to societies that are in the process of emerging from state-run economies. They cover societies that were historically shaped by a wide variety of religious and cultural traditions, from Christian to Islamic to Confucian to Hindu; and from societies whose culture emphasizes social conformity and group-obligations, to societies where the main emphasis is on human emancipation and self-expression.

The 1999-2001 Values Surveys were carried out in Albania, Algeria, Argentina, Austria, Bangladesh, Belarus, Belgium, Bosnia, Britain, Bulgaria, Canada, Chile, China, Croatia, Czech Republic, Denmark, Egypt, Estonia, Finland, France, Germany, Greece, Hungary, Iceland, India, Indonesia, Iran, Ireland, Israel, Italy, Japan, Jordan, Latvia, Lithuania, Luxembourg, Macedonia, Malta, Moldova, Montenegro, Morocco, Northern Ireland, Netherlands, Nigeria, Pakistan, Peru, Philippines, Poland, Portugal, Puerto Rico, Romania, Russia, South Africa, South Korea, Serbia, Singapore, Slovakia, Slovenia, Spain, Sweden, Tanzania, Turkey, the U.S., Uganda, Ukraine, Venezuela, Vietnam and Zimbabwe. In order to broaden the range of comparisons, this sourcebook also presents data from the following countries that were not surveyed in the 1999-2001 wave, but were included in the 1995 wave of the World Values Surveys: Armenia, Australia, Azerbaijan, Brazil, Colombia, Dominican Republic, El Salvador, Georgia, New Zealand, Norway, Switzerland, Taiwan and Uruguay.

This sourcebook enables the reader to compare the responses to hundreds of questions across societies from all over the world covering the full spectrum of economic, political, and cultural variation. It also enables the reader to examine the differences between the responses of men and women in each society; and to examine generational differences; and differences linked with education and income, and according to whether the respondent has "Materialist," "Mixed," or "Postmaterialist" values (these categories are explained below). And it makes it possible to examine the changes that took place from 1990 to 2000, for the countries that were surveyed at both times. Finally, we show the relative ranking of each society, in response to each question.

In order to present this material concisely, the responses to each question are dichotomized, with only the percentage ranking "high" being shown (missing data is excluded from the percentage base). For example, one of the first tables presented in our data section shows the responses to the question, "How important is religion in your life?" This table A006 is reproduced here to illustrate the overall pattern. As the reader will note, only the percentage saying that religion is "very important" is shown here. The first column in this table shows the name of a given country. The next set of columns compares the results from 1990 with the results from 2000 survey. Reading down one finds that in the 2000 survey in Albania, 28 percent of the public rated religion as "very important": the remaining 72 percent rated it as either "fairly important," "not very important," or "not at all important." In the 1990 Survey, Albania was not included and data is not available ("na")

The table doesn't show the breakdown among the other three categories. If the reader wishes to examine these details (or to run any number of additional cross-tabulations) is invited to use the CD ROM included with this book, which contains the raw data for all of the variables presented here, and a number of additional ones. This book shows only one response category for each variable. This sacrifice of detail brings a huge gain in conciseness: if we were to report every response category for every variable, it would be necessary to expand the hundreds of pages of tables and figures presented here into several thousand pages (this book sums up the results of more than 100,000 cross-tabulations).

This mode of presentation facilitates cross-cultural comparisons. One can simply scan down the columns in each table in order to compare the proportions in each country that consider religion "very important." The countries are listed alphabetically in each table, but they are also ranked from the highest-ranking country to the lowest-ranking country on the given variable, in the right-hand column of each table. When we scan down this column of our sample table A006, we find that Indonesia tops the list, with fully 98 percent of the public saying that religion was very important in their lives—while, at the other extreme, in China only three percent of the public considered religion to be very important in their lives. This illustrates one of the most striking findings from the Values Surveys: there is enormous cross-cultural variation in people's beliefs and values. This finding appears repeatedly throughout this book: what people believe and what they want out of life varies immensely from one society to another. To assume that everyone sees the world as you, yourself, see it, would be extremely misleading.

A006) RELIGION IMPORTANT

For each of the following aspects, indicate how important it is in your life: religion.

Very important (%) (WVS: V9; EVS: V6)

Country	Wave 1990	Wave 2000	Male	Female	16-29	30-49	50+	Education Lower	Education Middle	Education Upper	Income Lower	Income Middle	Income Upper	Mat	Mixed	Postm.	RANKING Country	2000
Albania	na	20	24	32	23	24	38	35	24	21	30	27	27	29	26	32	Indonesia	98
Algeria	na	92	91	92	89	92	96	94	90	92	91	91	91	90	92	93	Egypt	97
Argentina	40	47	39	53	36	45	58	51	40	41	54	50	36	53	48	38	Jordan	96
Armenia	na	27	20	33	23	28	31	32	26	25	23	30	27	23	31	23	Morocco	94
Australia	na	23	19	28	16	22	31	27	21	23	29	23	16	23	25	19	Nigeria	93
Austria	25	20	16	24	7	17	30	23	16	21	28	20	17	22	20	20	Algeria	92
Azerbaijan	na	30	26	34	32	27	36	36	28	33	29	34	28	28	32	54	Bangladesh	88
Bangladesh	na	88	88	88	84	89	94	92	82	83	91	85	90	93	85	79	El Salvador	87
Belarus	12	12	7	17	7	8	22	21	9	7	16	12	6	14	10	7	Philippines	87
Belgium	15	18	14	22	11	11	27	25	16	17	28	20	9	17	18	18	Tanzania	85
Bosnia and Herz.	na	34	31	37	37	32	35	38	33	34	40	31	34	30	35	32	Pakistan	82
Brazil	57	65	60	69	59	68	69	65	65	61	70	65	59	67	65	58	Turkey	81
Bulgaria	12	17	12	21	15	13	21	22	13	14	23	15	12	14	18	15	Iran	80
Canada	31	30	22	38	19	28	40	39	28	27	37	32	22	31	33	24	Zimbabwe	78
Chile	51	47	40	53	41	44	55	56	42	41	55	40	43	50	48	36	Puerto Rico	76
China	1	3	2	4	2	4	1	2	3	5	3	2	3	2	3	na	Uganda	74
Colombia	na	49	43	55	43	50	59	53	50	42	51	53	43	48	47	47	South Africa	70
Croatia	na	26	18	33	20	24	32	31	23	23	33	27	21	31	27	15	Mexico	68
Czech Republic	11	7	6	8	5	3	12	8	6	9	9	6	5	8	7	10	Malta	66
Denmark	9	8	7	9	6	5	12	7	3	10	11	6	5	3	9	5	Brazil	65
Dominican Rep.	na	51	45	56	55	46	46	59	54	50	55	50	42	54	51	55	Venezuela	64
Egypt	na	97	97	98	97	97	99	97	98	99	98	96	98	97	97	98	United States	57
El Salvador	na	87	84	89	84	89	89	88	87	86	88	87	81	na	na	na	India	57
Estonia	5	6	4	7	3	3	9	8	5	4	9	6	4	5	5	na	Peru	53
Finland	15	14	11	17	7	9	21	15	11	16	18	14	10	12	14	17	Dominican Rep.	51
France	14	11	9	13	6	9	16	13	8	9	15	10	8	12	11	8	Romania	51
Georgia	na	49	42	56	57	50	40	51	47	56	51	47	49	47	50	63	Georgia	49
Germany	16	9	5	12	8	7	12	10	8	7	7	12	10	7	11	8	Colombia	49
Great Britain	16	13	10	15	9	9	19	10	13	16	11	13	11	na	na	na	Macedonia	48
Greece	na	33	28	36	25	34	48	60	40	22	42	29	29	37	33	26	Chile	47
Hungary	23	20	14	25	10	13	32	22	14	18	24	21	16	23	16	5	Argentina	47
Iceland	24	19	16	22	6	19	31	24	16	15	25	18	12	20	19	19	Poland	45
India	49	57	55	59	54	57	60	61	55	50	61	59	54	64	51	49	Singapore	36
Indonesia	na	98	98	98	98	98	98	98	98	99	98	98	99	98	98	100	Moldova	35
Iran	na	80	78	83	78	82	86	87	80	72	82	82	75	88	76	71	Bosnia and Herz.	34
Ireland	48	32	25	39	6	25	59	50	24	20	51	29	20	31	34	26	Italy	33
Israel	na	na	na	na	na	na	na	na	na	na	na	na	na	na	na	na	Greece	33
Italy	34	33	24	41	20	29	44	39	27	31	41	30	27	43	32	27	Ireland	32
Japan	6	7	6	9	1	8	10	10	8	4	9	7	7	7	7	9	Canada	30
Jordan	na	96	94	98	96	96	97	97	96	94	96	97	96	96	96	93	Azerbaijan	30
Korea, South	26	23	19	28	21	23	27	36	23	22	22	23	24	23	24	22	Serbia	29
Latvia	7	11	6	14	6	5	17	20	8	9	15	10	5	11	10	6	Northern Ireland	28
Lithuania	16	14	7	21	7	6	27	31	7	13	27	14	9	17	14	9	Portugal	27
Luxembourg	na	16	14	17	9	12	23	20	12	15	19	17	12	15	15	14	Slovakia	27
Macedonia	na	48	45	51	51	49	43	60	43	37	53	44	45	45	48	58	Armenia	27
Malta	na	66	58	74	44	65	82	82	61	53	75	68	53	73	64	53	Croatia	26
Mexico	34	68	60	75	59	70	77	75	60	57	70	67	61	70	67	62	Australia	23
Moldova	na	35	29	40	24	32	48	54	31	24	48	31	30	41	30	32	Korea, South	23
Montenegro	na	19	18	20	16	18	23	23	18	15	19	14	21	18	20	18	Uruguay	23
Morocco	na	94	93	96	93	95	98	96	91	85	97	94	91	97	93	88	Ukraine	22
Netherlands	19	17	14	19	10	11	26	20	14	16	22	16	11	23	15	17	Austria	20
New Zealand	na	19	16	22	19	15	23	19	20	19	24	20	12	23	18	15	Hungary	20
Nigeria	85	93	92	94	93	92	96	93	93	92	93	93	93	93	93	93	Montenegro	19
Northern Ireland	34	28	25	30	18	20	40	32	22	28	27	30	24	30	27	28	New Zealand	19
Norway	15	12	9	15	11	10	16	12	10	14	na	na	na	7	13	13	Iceland	19
Pakistan	na	82	79	85	78	85	81	88	76	71	87	81	76	85	77	75	Spain	19
Peru	na	53	48	57	46	56	60	57	54	47	53	53	50	55	52	51	Belgium	18
Philippines	na	87	85	89	88	86	88	90	87	84	88	87	85	87	87	87	Netherlands	17
Poland	53	45	38	51	45	37	54	51	40	29	51	41	37	51	42	42	Bulgaria	17
Portugal	17	27	21	33	13	24	38	33	16	14	43	27	13	31	27	13	Luxembourg	16
Puerto Rico	na	76	70	78	60	74	84	91	76	72	80	77	71	76	76	73	Switzerland	15
Romania	42	51	40	62	37	45	64	68	47	30	65	55	38	59	45	32	Lithuania	14
Russian Fed.	12	12	7	16	8	10	17	23	11	10	16	11	9	14	10	11	Finland	14
Serbia	na	29	26	32	28	26	33	34	27	28	38	29	24	31	28	24	Taiwan	13
Singapore	na	36	34	38	33	38	38	38	35	34	45	37	31	42	34	32	Great Britain	13
Slovakia	na	27	19	35	16	20	44	41	21	24	39	26	21	30	25	26	Slovenia	12
Slovenia	17	14	10	14	5	10	20	23	9	7	16	16	5	13	11	15	Belarus	12
South Africa	66	70	59	83	68	69	77	72	67	69	71	73	66	74	68	66	Norway	12
Spain	21	19	12	25	7	14	29	24	12	14	24	16	15	27	16	11	Russian Fed.	12
Sweden	10	11	8	14	9	9	14	11	9	14	13	10	8	14	10	11	France	11
Switzerland	24	15	12	18	9	13	20	21	13	16	22	17	9	20	15	10	Latvia	11
Taiwan	na	13	11	14	4	14	16	17	14	9	13	12	10	11	13	11	Sweden	11
Tanzania	na	85	82	89	85	85	84	87	85	80	85	87	81	86	87	92	Vietnam	10
Turkey	61	81	79	83	78	81	86	89	77	51	89	79	63	87	82	68	Germany	9
Uganda	na	74	69	78	71	75	82	70	76	66	78	60	80	71	72	86	Denmark	8
Ukraine	na	22	13	29	15	19	28	40	19	18	25	18	21	24	18	29	Czech Republic	7
United States	53	57	49	66	48	58	65	64	58	54	61	57	53	60	58	53	Japan	7
Uruguay	na	23	15	29	16	19	30	26	19	19	25	21	23	25	23	19	Estonia	6
Venezuela	na	64	60	68	59	66	70	67	64	61	63	65	62	63	65	61	China	3
Vietnam	na	10	8	12	8	11	10	14	6	3	9	7	13	8	11	4		
Zimbabwe	na	78	67	87	76	80	78	79	77	60	75	80	79	73	81	85		
Total	27	40	36	44	42	39	41	47	36	38	46	40	36	44	39	33	Total	40

In our sample table, for example, the publics of the poorest societies tend to place the greatest emphasis on religion. But it is also clear that societies with an Islamic cultural heritage are particularly likely to attach great importance to religion. Thus, Indonesia, Egypt, Jordan, Morocco, Nigeria, Algeria and Bangladesh rank highest in the importance they place on religion. All of them except Nigeria have overwhelmingly Islamic populations, and about half of the Nigerian public is Islamic.

This book mainly focuses on the results from the 2000 wave of surveys, but it also permits the reader to examine changes that took place from 1990 to 2000, for those countries that were surveyed at both times. The second set of columns in this table compares the results from 1990 with the results from 2000. The Values Surveys have expanded their coverage steadily from one wave to the next, so data are available for a considerably larger number of societies in 2000 than in 1990. Nevertheless, time series data are available for a sizeable number of countries, making it possible to examine trends. In the present case, we find that the percentage saying that religion was very important in their lives, increased in about as many countries as it declined—but the pattern varies strikingly according to level of economic development. Emphasis on religion declined in most of the advanced industrial societies, such as Austria, Canada, France, Germany, South Korea, Poland, Spain and the United Kingdom. But it increased in most of the developing countries such as Bangladesh, Brazil, India, Mexico, Nigeria and South Africa (there was also a slight increase in the U.S.). But the developing countries have much higher population growth rates than the advanced industrial societies. Consequently, although secularization seems to be taking place in most rich countries, the number of religious people seems to be increasing in the world as a whole.

The third set of columns in our sample table A006 compares the responses given by women and men. It reveals an interesting point: despite trends toward gender equality in many aspects of life, women remain more religious than men. In every one of the 80 societies for which we have data, women are at least as likely as men to say that religion is very important in their lives—and in most countries they place more emphasis on religion. We do not find a single society in which men place more emphasis on religion than women.

The age differences shown in the next set of columns of this table are also interesting. Although everyone has heard anecdotes to the effect that people get more religious as they age, we find no support for this claim. It is true in some countries but not in others. Overall, the young are about as likely to say that religion is very important in their lives, as are the old. Indeed, in some societies, the younger respondents attach more importance to religion than the older ones (for examples, see the Dominican Republic, Georgia, Macedonia and Tanzania); and in many other societies, strong emphasis on religion is virtually universal, being about as strong among the young as among the old (see Egypt, Indonesia, Jordan, Morocco, Nigeria and the Philippines). We do find large differences between younger and older generations in the importance attached to religion in some countries—with those aged 50 and over being two to four times as likely to say that religion is very important in their lives than it is to those under 30 years of age. But this pattern in mainly found in advanced industrial societies such as Austria, Belgium, Canada, France, Iceland, Italy, the Netherlands, Slovenia, Spain, the United Kingdom and the United States. This suggests that an intergenerational shift toward a more secular outlook is occurring in these societies. But there is no universal tendency for the old to be more religious than the young.

The more educated and the higher income groups tend to place less emphasis on religion than the less educated and lower income groups, as our sample table indicates. But this pattern mainly applies to advanced industrial societies. In less affluent societies, the more educated and upper income groups are as likely—and sometimes even likelier—to say that religion is very important in their lives, as are the poor and less educated (see Algeria, Brazil, Egypt, El Salvador, Georgia, Indonesia, Jordan, Nigeria and South Africa).

There is evidence of an intergenerational shift from Materialist to Postmaterialist value priorities in advanced industrial societies, as a result of rising levels of existential security (this evidence is discussed below). Because Postmaterialists take survival for granted, they are less likely to rely on religion for reassurance in the face of insecurity. On the whole, Postmaterialists place significantly less emphasis on religion than do Materialists—but this applies mainly to postindustrial societies. In low-income societies, Postmaterialists generally are a very small minority, and their numbers may be too small to provide reliable figures.

Most of the findings will seem intuitively plausible to the reader. For example, these tables show that religion tends to be considered much more important by the publics of low-income societies than by those of economically highly developed societies. These findings support the secularization thesis—and though this thesis is hotly debated, it is widely known, so the finding may not seem surprising. Nevertheless, there are some striking deviant cases, with the peoples of both the United States and Ireland showing a much more religious outlook than their economic levels would predict.

We will not pursue our interpretation of this table any farther (for a more detailed discussion of religious attitudes around the world, see Norris and Inglehart, 2004, forthcoming). This discussion is simply intended to illustrate some of the many possible types of cross-cultural comparisons that this sourcebook facilitates. The reader will find a good deal of fascinating material in the hundreds of tables presented in the data section below. An almost unlimited number of additional analyses can be carried out using the data on the attached CD-ROM.

The breakdowns presented in this sourcebook were chosen because they capture some of the most important and most theoretically interesting bases of variation. They reflect the concerns of modernization theory, a body of social thought that has been influential throughout the past two centuries. Modernization theory has been controversial since its inception, and the Values Surveys provide a massive body of new evidence with which to test its claims. As the reader will note, we consistently observe large and systematic differences between the values and attitudes found in rich and poor societies. Economic development seems to make a great deal of difference in what people value and believe. But, although we very often find strong and statistically significant relations between levels of economic development and beliefs and values, these relationships are almost never monotonic: we almost always find deviant cases, sometimes dramatic ones. Though economic development tends to push socio-cultural change in a predictable direction, each society remains unique. This reflects the fact that cultural variation reflects the entire historical experience of given peoples, including political, social, technological, geographic, and other factors and not just economic influences (Inglehart and Baker, 2000; Arts and Halman, 2004).

Implications of Modernization Theory and Human Development

The central claim of modernization theory is that economic, cultural, and political change tend to go together in a coherent pattern, with modern societies showing fundamentally different characteristics from those of pre-modern societies. The two most influential proponents of modernization theory, Karl Marx and Max Weber, agreed on this point. They disagreed profoundly on why economic, cultural, and political changes go together. For Marx and his disciples, they are linked because economic and technological change determines political and cultural changes. For Weber and his disciples, they are linked because culture helps shape economic and political life.

Modernization theory gave rise to heated debate that stimulated influential subsequent work by Deutsch, Lerner, Inkeles and Smith, Bell, Toffler, Nolan and Lenski and many others. Still more recent work analyzing evidence from the Values Surveys, suggests that the central claim of modernization theory is largely correct: economic change, cultural change, and political change are closely linked (Inglehart, 1997, Inglehart and Baker, 2000). More specifically, Welzel (2003), Welzel, Inglehart and Klingemann (2003) and Inglehart and Welzel (2004) demonstrate that the common theme underlying all these economic, cultural and political changes is "human choice," which tends to grow as people gain more material and intellectual resources, place more emphasis on self-expression and obtain democratic rights. Economic prosperity, rising emphasis on self-expression values and the strengthening of democracy, form a coherent syndrome of Human Development. Though we cannot predict exactly what will happen in a given society at a given time, major trends in Human Development are predictable in broad outline. When given processes of change reshape one aspect of this syndrome, other aspects are likely to emerge in the long run. Growing human choice in economic, cultural, and political aspects of life tend to go together.

While conceding an important role to cultural factors, modernization theorists such as Bell (1973) viewed changes in the structure of the work force as the leading cause of cultural change. For Bell, the crucial milestone in the coming of "Postindustrial society" is reached when a majority of the work force is employed in the tertiary sector of the economy, producing neither raw materials, nor manufactured goods, but offering services. This is paralleled by a massive expansion of formal education, driven by the need for an increasingly skilled and specialized work force. Other writers such as Lerner (1958) and Inkeles and Smith (1974) and Inkeles (1983) emphasized the importance of mass communications and formal education as key factors shaping a "modern" worldview. Still others, such as Ember and Ember (1994) and Nolan and Lenski (1998) see the key factor as the individualizing trend in postmodern service economies, based on the fact that service professions require individual judgment, self-reliance, initiative and intellectual creativity—factors linked with human autonomy and choice. And Inglehart (1971, 1977, 1990, 1997), Welzel (2003), and Inglehart and Welzel (2004, forthcoming) emphasize the role of economic security in reducing existential constraints on human choice, giving rise to emancipative values that emphasize human self-expression.

Though any simplistic linear version of modernization theory has long since been refuted, we do find strong empirical evidence that some scenarios of social change are far more probable than others. The Values Surveys show coherent and far-reaching cultural patterns that are closely linked with economic development. In the long term, across many societies, once given processes are set in motion, certain important changes seem likely to happen. Industrialization, for example, tends to bring increasing urbanization, growing occupational specialization and higher levels of formal education in any society that undertakes it. These are core elements of a trajectory called "Modernization."

This trajectory also tends to bring less obvious but equally important long term consequences, such as a shift from traditional religious values toward rational-bureaucratic norms; an increasing emphasis on economic achievement; rising levels of mass political participation and major changes in the types of issues that are most salient in the politics of the respective types of societies.

The modernization trajectory is linked with many other cultural changes. As this sourcebook shows, a wide range of cultural values are closely linked with a given society's level of economic development. For example, the sharply contrasting gender roles that characterize all preindustrial societies tend to give way to increasingly similar gender roles in advanced industrial societies.

The Postmodern Shift

Economic development is linked with social change—but the process is not linear. Though a specific modernization syndrome becomes increasingly probable when societies move from an agrarian mode to an industrial mode, no trend goes on in the same direction forever. It eventually reaches a point of diminishing returns. Modernization is no exception. In the past few decades, advanced industrial societies have reached an inflection point where they begin moving on a new trajectory that Inglehart (1997) describes as "Postmodernization." Inglehart and Welzel (2004, forthcoming) find that this stage brings a pervasive shift in value orientations linked with increasing emphasis on human choice in all aspects of people's lives—including mate selection, gender roles, child rearing goals, working habits, religious orientations, consumer patterns, civic action and voting behavior.

The process of economic development leads to two successive trajectories, Modernization and Postmodernization. Both of them are linked with economic development but Postmodernization represents a later stage of development that emphasizes very different beliefs from those that characterize Modernization. These belief systems are not mere consequences of economic change, but shape socioeconomic conditions as well as being shaped by them, in reciprocal fashion. At the heart of the postmodern shift lies a change of value orientations linked with increasing emphasis on human choice and self-expression. This reflects a change in which authority shifts from religious to secular institutions and ideologies, but authority remains external to the individual. At the peak of modernity, rational science has almost the same absolute authority as religion in premodernity. Postmodernity erodes the absoluteness of all kinds of external authority, whether religious or secular: authority becomes internalized.

Why Is the Postmodern Shift Occurring?

This is not the first major cultural shift in human history. The transition from agrarian society to industrial society was facilitated by a Modernization shift, from a worldview shaped by a steady-state economy, which discourages social mobility and emphasized tradition, inherited status, communal obligations, and absolute religious norms— to a worldview that encourages economic achievement, individualism and innovation, with increasingly secular and flexible social norms. Today, some of these trends have reached their limits in advanced industrial society, where change is taking a new direction.

This change of direction reflects the principle of diminishing marginal utility. Industrialization and modernization required breaking the cultural constraints on accumulation that are found in any steady-state economy. In West European history, this was achieved by what Weber described as the rise of the Protestant Ethic. If it had occurred two centuries earlier, it might have died out. In the environment of its time, it found a niche: technological developments were making rapid economic growth possible and the Calvinist worldview complemented these developments beautifully. These elements created a cultural-economic syndrome that accelerated the rise of capitalism and eventually, the industrial revolution. Once this had occurred, economic accumulation (for individuals) and economic growth (for societies) became top priorities for an increasing part of the world's population, and are still the central goals for much of humanity. Economic growth came to be equated with progress and was seen as the hallmark of a successful society. But eventually, diminishing returns from economic growth lead to a Postmodern shift.

Advanced industrial societies are now changing their basic value systems in a number of related ways. Growing material wealth reduces the basic existential constraints on human choice. The rise of a knowledge-based economy makes people intellectually independent, widening the areas in which people have to rely on their own choices. In that sense, the broadening of human choice is the most pervasive undercurrent of postmodern society.

In postmodern society, the emphasis on economic achievement as the top priority is now giving way to an increasing emphasis on the quality of life. In a major part of the world, the disciplined, self-denying and achievement-oriented norms of industrial society are yielding, leaving an increasingly broad latitude for individual choice of life styles and individual self-expression. The shift from "Materialist" values, emphasizing economic and physical security, to "Postmaterialist" values, emphasizing individual self-expression and quality life concerns, is the most amply documented aspect of this change, but it is only one component of a much broader syndrome of cultural change.

The theory of an intergenerational shift from Materialist to Postmaterialist value priorities is based on two key hypotheses (Inglehart, 1977):

1. A Scarcity Hypothesis. An individual's priorities reflect the socioeconomic environment: one places the greatest subjective value on those things that are in relatively short supply.

2. A Socialization Hypothesis. The relationship between socioeconomic environment and value priorities is not one of immediate adjustment: a substantial time lag is involved because, to a large extent, one's basic values reflect the conditions that prevailed during one's preadult years. This gives rise to substantial differences between the values of older and younger generations—so that cultural change largely takes place as one generation replaces another in the adult population.

The recent economic history of advanced industrial societies has significant implications in the light of the scarcity hypothesis. For these societies are a striking exception to the prevailing historical pattern: they still contain poor people, but most of their population does not live under conditions of hunger and economic insecurity. This has led to a gradual shift in which needs for belonging, esteem, and intellectual and esthetic satisfaction became more prominent. Other things being equal, we would expect prolonged periods of high prosperity to encourage the spread of Postmaterialist values; economic problems, stagnation and welfare state retrenchment would have the opposite effect, re-strengthening Materialist values.

The socialization hypothesis implies that neither an individual's values nor those of a society as a whole will change overnight. For the most part, fundamental value change takes place as younger birth cohorts replace older ones in the adult population of a society. Consequently, after a long period of rising economic and physical security, one should find substantial differences between the value priorities of older and younger groups: they have been shaped by different experiences in their formative years.

Materialist/Postmaterialist values have been measured in every wave of the Values Surveys. Materialist priorities are tapped by emphasis on such goals as economic growth, fighting rising prices, maintaining order and fighting crime; while Postmaterialist values are reflected when top priority is given to such goals as giving people more say on the job or in government decisions, or protecting freedom of speech or moving toward a less impersonal, more humane society. Analyses by Abramson and Inglehart (1995) indicate that these items tap a meaningful and comparable dimension across virtually all types of societies.

The shift toward Postmaterialist values is only one aspect of a much broader Postmodern trend toward values that emphasize human choice and emancipation. This shift from survival values towards self-expression values involves changing political, religious, sexual, and other norms. The rise of Postmodern values manifests itself in a gradual intergenerational shift, as younger, more Postmaterialist birth cohorts replace older, more Materialist ones in the adult population. The orientations that are linked with this Postmodern shift are characterized by their age-related differences and their linkages with Materialist/Postmaterialist values, both of which are shown in the following tables.

Changing Moral Orientations, Gender Roles, and Sexual Norms

Postmaterialist values developed in the environment of the historically unprecedented economic growth and the welfare states that emerged after World War II. And they are part of a Postmodern shift that is reshaping the political outlook, religious orientations, gender roles, and sexual norms of advanced industrial society.

The Postmodern shift involves an intergenerational change in a wide variety of basic social norms, from cultural norms linked with ensuring survival of the species, to norms linked with the pursuit of individual well being. For example, Postmaterialists and the young are markedly more tolerant of homosexuality than are Materialists and the old. This is part of a pervasive pattern. Postmaterialists have been shaped by security during their formative years, and are far more permissive than Materialists in their attitudes toward abortion, divorce, extramarital affairs, prostitution, and euthanasia. Materialists, conversely, tend to adhere to the traditional societal norms that favor childbearing, but only within the traditional two-parent family—and that heavily stigmatized sexual activity outside that setting.

Traditional gender role norms from East Asia to the Islamic world to Western society discouraged women from taking jobs outside the home. Virtually all preindustrial societies emphasized child-bearing and child-rearing as the central goal of any woman, her most important function in life, and her greatest source of satisfaction. In recent years, this perspective has been increasingly called into question, as growing numbers of women postpone having children or forego them completely in order to devote themselves to careers outside the home. The sharply differentiated gender roles that characterize virtually all preindustrial societies, give way to increasingly similar gender roles in advanced industrial society.

As Table C001 in the data section demonstrates, we find enormous differences in attitudes toward equal employment opportunity for women. In Egypt, 90 percent of the public agrees that men have more right to a job than women, while in Sweden only 2 percent agree. The publics of rich countries are much more supportive of gender equality than the publics of low-income societies. Outside of advanced industrial societies, much of the world still takes it for granted that practically everyone lives in a traditional family, with a male as their principal provider. People who see the world from this perspective are willing to accord men preferential employment opportunities. Thus in Africa, Asia, and above all, the Islamic countries, pluralities or even absolute majorities of the public feel that men have more right to a job than women. In Catholic Europe and Latin America, by contrast, solid pluralities of the public feel that men do not have more right to a job than women; in the U.S., Canada, and Northern Europe, support for gender equality is overwhelming: less than one in five agree that men have more right to a job than women.

The differences linked with Materialist/Postmaterialist values are also strong: Materialists are more than twice as likely as Postmaterialists to feel that men have more right to a job than women. The more educated, and the upper income groups are also more supportive of gender equality than the less educated and lower income groups. The overall picture strongly suggests that economic development is conducive to increasing support for gender equality (see Inglehart and Norris, 2003).

Not surprisingly, women are more likely to favor equal employment opportunity than are men—the only surprising finding is the fact that the overall gender gap amounts to only 6 percentage points. Across these societies, 38 percent of the men feel that their sex has more right to a job, while only 32 percent of the women agree. But we find relatively large gender differences in the less developed societies. In the ten richest societies, on the other hand, there is a broad consensus favoring equal rights, and a gender gap of only two points.

Changing Values and Changing Political Cleavages

The pervasive cultural changes linked with Postmodernization have brought about a gradual shift in the issues underlying political cleavages in advanced industrial society.

The political agenda is moving it away from an emphasis on economic growth at any price, toward increasing concern for its environmental costs. The shift toward Postmodern values has also brought a shift from political cleavages based on social class conflict toward cleavages based on cultural issues and quality of life concerns. Economic conflicts are likely to remain important. But, while in the past they dominated the scene to such a degree that many influential thinkers accepted the Marxist view that economics was virtually the whole story, this now seems much less plausible. Today, economic conflicts are increasingly sharing the stage with new issues that were almost invisible a generation ago: in advanced industrial societies, environmental protection, abortion, ethnic conflicts, women's issues, and gay and lesbian emancipation are heated issues today—while the classic Marxist prescription, nationalization of industry, is virtually a forgotten cause.

As a result, a new dimension of political conflict has become increasingly salient. It reflects a polarization between modern and postmodern issue preferences. This new dimension is distinct from the traditional Left-Right conflict over ownership of the means of production and distribution of income. A new Postmodern political cleavage pits culturally conservative, often xenophobic parties, disproportionately supported by Materialists; against change-oriented parties, often emphasizing environmental protection, and disproportionately supported by Postmaterialists.

A Cultural Map of the World

Figure 1 below shows where each of the 81 societies examined here falls on the two main dimensions of cross-cultural variation just discussed, which are linked with the processes of "Modernization" and "Postmodernization" respectively (for a detailed discussion of these dimensions and how they were derived, see Inglehart and Baker, 2000; for a similar type of analysis applied to the European context, see Hagenaars, Halman and Moors, 2003).

These two broad dimensions reflect a large number of the key values examined in the Values Surveys. Since hundreds of questions were asked in these surveys, it would not be feasible to compare the values of each public on each topic separately. Figure 1 compares the orientations of these publics on two important dimensions that sum up the cross-national variation on scores of narrower values. These two dimensions tap:

1. Traditional authority vs. Secular-Rational authority. This dimension is based on a large number of items that reflect emphasis on obedience to traditional authority (usually religious authority), and adherence to family and communal obligations, and norms of sharing; or, on the other hand, a secular worldview in which authority is legitimated by rational-legal norms, linked with an emphasis on economic accumulation and individual achievement.

2. Survival values vs. Self-Expression values. This reflects the fact that in postindustrial society, historically unprecedented levels of wealth and the emergence of the welfare states have given rise to a shift from scarcity norms, emphasizing hard work and self-denial, to postmodern values emphasizing the quality of life, emancipation of women and sexual minorities and related Postmaterialist priorities such as emphasis on self-expression.

The two respective phases of modernization—industrialization, and the emergence of the knowledge society— each give rise to a major dimension of cross-cultural variation. This makes it possible to locate any society in the world on a two-dimensional map of cross-cultural variation. Figure 1 show this map. The Traditional/Secular-rational values dimension constitutes the vertical axis: as one moves from south to north, one moves from societies that emphasize Traditional values to those that emphasize Secular-rational values. The Survival/Self-expression values dimension constitutes the horizontal axis: as one moves from left to right, one moves from societies that emphasize Survival values to those that emphasize Self-expression values.

Figure 1 sums up an immense amount of information. It reflects the responses to scores of questions, given by over 200,000 respondents in 80 societies. There is a great

Figure 1. Cultural map of 81 societies, with economic zones superimposed. Cultural locations reflect each society's factor scores on two major dimensions of cross-cultural variation. Economic zones are from World Bank, World Development Indicators, 2002.

Source: R. Inglehart and C. Welzel. 2004. *Modernization, Cultural Change and Democracy: The Human Development Sequence.* (forthcoming).

deal of constraint among cultural systems. The first two dimensions that emerge from the principal components factor analysis depicted in Figure 1 account for over half of the cross-national variation among ten key variables. Additional dimensions explain relatively small amounts of variance. And these dimensions are robust, showing little change if we drop some of the items, even high-loading ones.

The Traditional/Secular-rational values dimension reflects the contrast between societies in which religion is very important and those in which it is not— but deference to the authority of God, Fatherland and Family are all closely linked. In traditional societies, a main goal in most people's lives is to make their parents proud; they idealize large families, and have large numbers of children. They also have high levels of national pride, favor more respect for authority, and reject divorce, abortion, euthanasia, and suicide. Societies with secular-rational values have the opposite preferences on all of these topics.

The Survival/Self-expression dimension taps a syndrome of tolerance, trust, subjective well-being, political activism and self-expression that emerges in postindustrial societies with high levels of existential security. People in societies shaped by insecurity tend to emphasize economic and physical security above all, and feel threatened by foreigners, by ethnic diversity and by cultural change— which leads to intolerance of gays and other outgroups, insistence on traditional gender roles and an authoritarian political outlook. Societies that emphasize survival values show relatively low levels of subjective well-being, report relatively poor health, are low on interpersonal trust, relatively intolerant of outgroups, and low on support for gender equality. They emphasize economic and physical security more than autonomy and self-expression, have relatively high levels of faith in science and technology, are relatively low on environmental activism, and relatively favorable to authoritarian government. Societies high on Self-expression values tend to have the opposite preferences on all of these topics.

Each individual's score on the Traditional/Secular-rational values dimension and on the Survival/Self-expression dimension is included as a variable on the accompanying CD ROM (they appear near the end of the file, with the names "Tradrat5" [factor score on Traditional/Secular-rational values] and "SurvSelf" [factor score on Survival/Self-expression values]).[1] Each person's score on Materialist/Postmaterialist values is also available.

Economic development and cultural change

As modernization theory implies, these two major dimensions of cross-cultural variation are strongly linked with a society's level of economic development. As Figure 1 demonstrates, the value systems of richer countries differ dramatically and systematically from those of poorer countries. All of the "High Income" societies (as defined by the World Bank), rank relatively high on both dimensions, falling into a zone near the upper right-hand corner. Conversely, all of the "Low Income" societies, without a single exception, fall into a cluster at the lower left of Figure 1. All of the Middle Income societies fall into an intermediate cultural-economic zone. One rarely finds such a striking and consistent correspondence between an objective independent variable such as GNP per capita, and subjective values and attitudes as is found here. Economic development seems to push societies in a predictable common direction, regardless of their cultural heritage.

---

[1] If one of the ten questions used to construct them was not asked in a given country, these dimensions can not be constructed for that sample. The individual-level scores are not directly equivalent to the national-level scores shown on Figures 1 and 2. If one wishes to plot given groups on these maps, the individual-level scores can be converted into a close approximation of the national-level scores by multiplying Tradrat5 by 1.56 and by multiplying Survself by 1.76.

Figure 2. Cultural map of 81 societies, with cultural zones superimposed. Cultural locations reflect each society's factor scores on two major dimensions of cross-cultural variation.

Source: R. Inglehart and C. Welzel. 2004. *Modernization, Cultural Change and Democracy: The Human Development Sequence.* (forthcoming).

The persistence of Cultural Traditions

Figure 2 shows the location of these same 81 societies on our two main dimensions of cross-cultural variation. But this time, instead of showing their economic zones, we show how they fall into coherent cultural-historical zones. The boundaries around groups of countries in this figure are drawn using Huntington's (1993, 1996) cultural zones as a guide. This cultural map resembles an earlier one by Inglehart (1997:334-337) based on the 1990-1991 Values Surveys. Although Figure 2 is based on a factor analysis that uses less than half as many variables and almost twice as many societies as were analyzed by Inglehart (1997), the locations of the respective societies are strikingly similar to those on the cultural maps he generated from earlier surveys. The same cultural zones appear, in similar locations, but some of them now contain many more societies. The similarity between this map and the earlier ones reflects the fact that these two key dimensions of cross-cultural variation are robust.

The maps show consistent cultural clusters based on religion. For example, the historically Protestant societies tend to rank higher on the Survival/Self-expression dimension than the historically Roman Catholic societies. Conversely, all of the former communist societies rank relatively low on the Survival/Self-expression dimension. The historically Orthodox societies form a coherent cluster within the broader ex-communist zone—except for Greece, an Orthodox society that did not experience communist rule, and ranks substantially higher on Self-expression values than the other communist societies. The Islamic societies fall into two clusters: a larger group containing the mainline Islamic societies (Indonesia, Iran, Bangladesh, Pakistan, Turkey, Morroco, Algeria, Jordan and Egypt) constitutes a relatively compact group in the Southwest quadrant of the map; while the Islamic societies that experienced communist rule (Azerbaijan and Albania) are much more secular than the rest of the Islamic societies. Differences in levels of economic development have important influences on prevailing worldviews, as Figure 1 demonstrated, but historical cultural influences persist. The classic version of modernization theory must be supplemented by taking into account the persistence of cultural factors.

This is evident even within European context, where a rich variety of cultures exist. This variety reflects the distinctive religious, cultural, economic and social heritage of each society. Countries and their populations have remained unique in many ways and nation states remain important sources of differences in people's attitudes, values, beliefs and behaviors (Arts and Halman, 1999; 2004 forthcoming; Hagenaars, Halman & Moors, 2003)

The influence of colonial ties is apparent in the existence of a Latin American cultural zone. The Philippines could also be placed in this zone, reflecting the fact that despite their geographical remoteness, the Philippines and Latin America share the imprint of Hispanic colonial rule and the Roman Catholic Church. Former colonial ties also help account for the existence of an English-speaking zone containing Britain and the other English-speaking societies. All seven of the English-speaking societies included in this study show relatively similar cultural characteristics. Geographically, Australia and New Zealand are half-way around the world, but culturally they are neighbors of Great Britain and Canada. The impact of colonization seems especially strong when reinforced by massive immigration from the colonial society—thus, Spain, Portugal, Italy, Uruguay, Chile and Argentina are all relatively near each other on the border between Catholic Europe and Latin America: the populations of Uruguay, Chile and Argentina are largely descended from immigrants from Spain and Italy.

These maps indicate that the U.S. is not a prototype of cultural modernization for other societies to follow, as some postwar modernization writers assumed. In fact, the U.S. is a deviant case, having a much more traditional value system than any other advanced industrial society. On the traditional/secular dimension, the U.S. ranks far below other rich societies, with levels of religiosity and national pride comparable to those found in some developing societies. The phenomenon of American Exceptionalism has been discussed by Lipset (1990, 1996), Baker (2004) and others. The U.S. does rank among the most advanced societies along the Survival/Self-Expression dimension, but even here, she does not lead the world. The Swedes, the Dutch and the Australians are closer to the cutting edge of cultural change than the Americans.

Religious traditions have an enduring impact on the contemporary value systems of these societies, as Weber, Huntington and others have argued. But a society's culture reflects its entire historical heritage, including its colonial history. We have already noted the existence of Latin American and English-speaking cultural zones. The impact of another type of colonial empire is also evident. A central historical event of the 20th century was the rise and fall of a communist empire that once ruled a third of the world's population. Communism has left a clear imprint on the value systems of those who lived under it. All of the societies that experienced communist rule, fall into a larger cluster in the upper-left quadrant of the map. East Germany remains culturally close to West Germany despite four decades of communist rule, but her value system has been drawn toward the communist zone. And although China is a member of the Confucian zone, she also falls within a broad communist-influenced zone.

The ex-communist societies tend to emphasize secular-rational, rather than traditional-religious authority. This is far from surprising. Their people have lived for decades under regimes that systematically repressed religion, and in which it was natural to consider the state important because it dominated economic life, cultural life, and even one's chances of survival. Thus, almost all of the ex-communist societies fall into the upper left-hand quadrant: these societies are characterized by (1) survival values, and (2) a strong emphasis on state authority, rather than traditional authority. Poland is an exception, distinguished from the other socialist societies by her relatively strong traditional-religious values. Adherence to the Catholic church has been a mainstay of the Polish struggle for independence from Russia since 1792. The church continued to play a vital role in this struggle throughout the 1980s, revitalizing religion in the national culture.

The most secular societies in the world are Japan, China, Germany, Sweden and Norway. This seems to reflect a combination of three historic factors: (1) The relatively secular-bureaucratic Confucian tradition; (2) the secularizing impact of communism; and (3) the secularizing impact of affluent postindustrial societies when they are accompanied by an advanced welfare state.

China and the other Confucian-influenced societies have had predominantly secular cultural systems for many centuries; and bureaucratic authority developed within the Confucian system long before it reached the West. Thus China and the Confucian-influenced societies of East Asia have had one major component of modern culture for a very long time. Until recently, they lacked the emphasis on science and technology, and the esteem for economic achievement that are its other main components; but their secular, bureaucratic heritage may have facilitated rapid economic development once these were attained. China's traditional low emphasis on religion and high emphasis on the state was almost certainly accentuated by four decades of socialism. Japan, another Confucian-influenced society, and both East and West Germany are also characterized by relatively strong emphasis on secular-rational authority.

Institutional Determinism?

As we have seen, the historically Protestant countries of both Northern Europe and North America tend to cluster together to form one large group; similarly, the historically Roman Catholic countries of Western Europe, Latin America, Eastern Europe, Sub-Saharan Africa, the Islamic world, South and East Asia tend to cluster together, forming another broad but reasonably cohesive cluster. Despite the enormous recent changes linked with economic and social modernization, and despite the tremendous sociopolitical changes brought by communist domination of five of these societies throughout the Cold War, the historically Catholic societies still manifest cultural values that are relatively similar to each other in global perspective—as do the historically Protestant societies.

If institutional determinism is taken to mean simply that a society's institutions are among the factors that help shape its culture, the claim is undoubtedly correct. But institutional determinism is often pushed to a much more extreme claim than this: it is taken to mean that institutions alone determine a society's cultural values, so one needn't really take cultural factors into account: if one changes the institutions, the culture automatically changes accordingly. If one examines the evidence more closely, it is clear that this position is untenable.

The former West German and East German regions of Germany were still independent states when they were first surveyed, and they were sampled separately even after reunification, to examine the degree to which they continue to display distinctive cultures. Though West Germany falls into the upper right-hand quadrant of Figures 1 and 2, with the other West European societies, and East Germany is somewhat more secular and lower on Self-expression values, the two societies are relatively close to each other on the two main cultural dimensions. This is significant. From 1945 to 1990, the communist regime made a massive effort to reshape East German culture to support a Marxist and atheistic authoritarian regime; while the Western powers launched an equally massive effort, continued by the West German authorities, to remake political culture to support a market-oriented Western liberal democracy. The evidence indicates that 45 years under radically different regimes had some impact: in 1999, the two societies were still rather distinct. But even more impressive is the fact that, in global perspective, the basic cultural values of the two societies were still relatively similar. This natural experiment indicates that, even when it makes a conscious and concerted effort to do so, the ability of a regime to reshape its underlying culture is limited. Though they can reshape it to a limited extent, institutions do not determine culture. After 45 years under diametrically opposite political and economic institutions, East Germany and West Germany remained more similar to each other than the United States and Canada.

There are tremendous cultural differences between Protestant and Catholic societies, but for the most part they do not reflect the direct influence of the Catholic and Protestant churches today. For the direct influence of the church today is very slight in many of these countries. Though church attendance remains relatively high in Poland and Ireland (and the United States, to a lesser degree), it has fallen drastically in most of the historically Catholic countries of both Western and Eastern Europe; and it has fallen even more drastically in most of the historically Protestant societies—to the point where some observers now speak of the Nordic countries as post-Christian societies. Traditionally Catholic and Protestant societies still show very distinct values—even among segments of the population who have no contact whatever with the church. But these values persist as part of the cultural heritage of the given nations, and not through the direct influence of the religious institutions.

This point becomes vividly evident when we examine the value systems of such societies as The Netherlands and Germany—both of which were historically predominantly Protestant societies, but (through the effects of different birth rates and different rates of religious erosion) now have about as many practicing Catholics as Protestants. Despite these changes in their religious makeup today, both The Netherlands and Germany show typically Protestant value systems. Furthermore, the Catholics and Protestants within these societies do not have markedly different value systems: the Dutch Catholics are more Dutch than Catholic in most of their social norms, and have very distinctive values from those of Catholics in traditionally Catholic societies.

There is a remarkable degree of coherence. As we have seen, all of the high-income societies rank relatively high on both of our two major dimensions of cross-cultural variation, and all of the low-income societies rank relatively low on both dimensions. Furthermore, the 80 societies fall into compact and historically meaningful clusters, such as Protestant Europe, Catholic Europe, Latin America, the ex-communist zone, sub-Saharan Africa or the Confucian zone. As the reader examines the following tables, he or she will find that again and again, across scores of variables, the societies that are located near each other on Figures 1 and 2 show relatively similar values and beliefs; while those that are far apart on this figure show dissimilar values and beliefs.

The foregoing provides only a brief overview of the complex but coherent pattern of cross-national differences revealed in the Values Surveys. The tables in the data section enable one to delve into the rich body of evidence provided by these surveys in much greater detail, and to explore the implications of cross-cultural variations and their linkages with economic development and education; one can also explore the extent to which men and women have different beliefs and values; the intergenerational differences or life cycle differences linked with age groups, and the many cultural differences linked with Materialist/Postmaterialist values.

Human beliefs and values are not just an epiphenomenon that is shaped by a society's economic infrastructure. The fact that the Values Surveys cover more than 80 societies, makes it possible to carry out statistically significant cross-level analyses, examining the impact of individual-level values and beliefs on societal-level phenomena such as fertility rates or political institutions. The results indicate that cultural factors play a major role in shaping the societal-level characteristics of given societies.

Moreover, an analysis of the empirical linkages between culture and democracy demonstrates that democracies have strikingly different political cultures from authoritarian societies. Almost without exception, stable democracies rank high on self-expression values, and authoritarian societies rank low on them. These linkages persist when we control for economic level and social structure: a pro-democratic political culture seems to play an important role in sustaining democratic institutions over the long term (Inglehart, 1997).

Welzel (2002), Welzel, Inglehart and Klingemann (2003), and Inglehart and Welzel (2004) have demonstrated that economic development, rising self-expression values, and democratic institutions are so closely linked with each other that these three phenomena reflect a common underlying dimension—human development—to which each of these three components contributes in improving people's ability to exert autonomous choices. These three components occur in a specific causal sequence in which economic development tends to give rise to self-expression values, which in turn tend to promote democracy. Thus, self-expression values were a decisive factor in the Third Wave of Democratization, influencing significantly to which extent formerly non-democratic societies changed into full-fledged democracies. Self-expression values help to strengthen democracy in a number of ways: for example, they lower elite corruption, fuel "good governance" and have a strong tendency to promote gender equality.

The evidence suggests that the remarkably strong linkage found between political culture and democracy is more a matter of culture contributing to democracy, than of democracy determining culture. With economic development, cultural patterns tend to emerge that are increasingly supportive of democracy.

This Introduction is followed by the tables section, which is the heart of this book: it presents hundreds of data tables, interspersed with graphs that place these detailed tables in their broader context. Next, is a section that discusses survey methodology and cross-cultural comparisons, followed by the technical section, which provides information about the dates of fieldwork, sample sizes, data cleaning and archiving procedures, and the people who conducted the surveys in the respective countries. The English-language version of the questionnaires used in the 1999-2001 Values Surveys appears next, providing the exact text of the questions asked in the surveys. The variable numbers from these questionnaires (WVS and EVS) appear near the upper right-hand corner of each table. The text of the questionnaires used in each country can be found in the CD ROM at the back of this book. Finally, the appendix lists variables on the CD ROM, but not in the Source Book, and the Index section helps finding tables easier by a variety of entries.

The authors hope that this sourcebook will be a useful tool to anyone concerned with the role of human values and beliefs in contemporary society. Those who wish to carry out more detailed analyses can analyze the original data, which is provided on the CD ROM that accompanies this sourcebook.

REFERENCES

Arts, Wil and Loek Halman 1999. "New Directions in Quantitative Comparative Sociology." International Journal of Comparative Sociology XL: 1-12.

Arts, Wil and Loek Halman 2004. "European Values at the Turn of the Millennium: An Introduction." In Wil Arts and Loek Halman (Eds.) *European Values at the End of the Millennium*. Leiden and Boston: Brill.

Arts, Wil and Loek Halman. 2004. "European Value Change in the Second Age of Modernity." In Wil Arts and Loek Halman (Eds.) *European Values at the End of the Millennium*. Leiden and Boston: Brill.

Baker, Wayne E. 2004. *America's Crisis of Values: Perceptions and Realities*. Princeton: Princeton University Press.

Barker, David, Loek Halman and Astrid Vloet 1992. *The European Values Study 1981-1990: Summary Report*. London: Gordon Cook Foundation.Basanez, Miguel. 1993. "Protestant and Catholic Ethics: An Empirical Comparison." Paper presented at conference on Changing Political and Social Values, Complutense University, Madrid, September 27-October 1.

Ester, Peter, Loek Halman and Ruud de Moor (Eds.). 1994. *The Individualizing Society. Value Change in Europe and North America*. Tilburg: Tilburg University Press.

Hagenaars, Jacques, Loek Halman and Guy Moors. 2003. "Exploring Europe's Basic Values Map." In Wil Arts, Jacques Hagenaars and Loek Halman (Eds.), *The Cultural Diversity of European Unity: Findings, Explanations and Reflections from the European Values Study*. Leiden and Boston: Brill. Pp. 23-58.

Halman, Loek. 2001. *The European Values Study: A Third Wave*. Tilburg: EVS, WORC, Tilburg University.

Harding, Stephen, David Phillips with Michael Fogerty. 1986. *Contrasting Values in Western Europe: Unity, Diversity and Change*. London: MacMillan.

Inglehart, Ronald. 1997. *Modernization and Postmodernization: Cultural, Economic and Political Change in 43 Societies*. Princeton: Princeton University Press.

Inglehart, Ronald and Wayne E. Baker. 2000. "Modernization, Cultural Change, and the Persistence of Traditional Values," *American Sociological Review* 65 (February): 19-51.

Inglehart, Ronald, Miguel Basáñez and Alejandro Moreno 1998. *Human Values and Beliefs*. Ann Arbor: The University of Michigan Press.

Inglehart, Ronald and Pippa Norris. 2003. *Rising Tide: Gender Equality and Cultural Change around the World*. New York and Cambridge: Cambridge University Press.

Inglehart, Ronald and Christian Welzel. 2004. *Modernization, Cultural Change and Democracy: The Human Development Sequence*. New York: Cambridge University Press.

Lipset, Seymour Martin. 1990. "American Exceptionalism Reaffirmed." *Toqueville Review* 10.

Lipset, Seymour Martin. 1996. *American Exceptionalism*. New York: Norton.

Norris, Pippa and Ronald Inglehart. 2004. *Sacred and Secular: Religion and Politics around the World*. New York: Cambridge University Press.

Welzel, Christian. 2002. *Fluchtpunk Humanentwicklung: Die Grundlagen der Demokratie und die Ursachen ihrer Ausbreitung*. Opladen: Westdeustcher Verlag.

Welzel, Christian, Ronald Inglehart and Hans-Dieter Klingemann. 2003. "The Theory of Human Development: A Cross-Cultural Analysis. *European Journal of Political Research*, 42 (April).

Tables and figures

TABLE OF FREQUENCIES

Each cell shows the actual number of respondents ("n") in a given country (row) by each breakdown (column).
In some cases the number of respondents is small. When analyzing those cases, the specific "n" must be taken into account.

Country	Wave 1990	Wave 2000	Gender Male	Gender Female	Age 16-29	Age 30-49	Age 50+	Education Lower	Education Middle	Education Upper	Income Lower	Income Middle	Income Upper	Values Mat	Values Mixed	Values Postm.
Albania	na	1000	495	505	258	448	294	425	411	164	355	304	332	436	467	39
Algeria	na	1282	650	632	547	477	258	307	555	415	445	303	289	454	642	119
Argentina	1002	1280	597	683	394	457	429	757	402	121	381	514	385	235	683	325
Albania	na	1000	940	1060	771	748	481	168	1415	417	786	638	449	891	964	107
Armenia	na	2000	940	1060	771	748	481	168	1415	417	786	638	449	891	964	107
Australia	na	2048	995	1053	577	792	679	526	810	680	686	623	508	158	1152	704
Austria	1460	1522	659	863	260	588	674	789	544	189	335	445	434	118	920	420
Azerbaijan	na	2002	981	1021	731	937	333	112	1251	639	531	717	490	1205	681	68
Bangladesh	na	1499	828	671	606	745	142	794	403	289	426	619	434	578	799	76
Belarus	1015	1000	449	551	274	382	344	270	583	147	351	447	194	461	415	56
Belgium	2792	1912	886	1026	363	766	776	402	834	647	415	545	581	371	1022	426
Bosnia and Herz.	na	1200	573	627	356	486	358	204	753	243	253	612	276	364	744	53
Brazil	1782	1149	572	577	451	474	224	507	500	142	425	275	401	351	656	134
Bulgaria	1034	1000	428	572	158	362	480	268	457	275	328	270	345	415	469	29
Canada	1730	1931	780	1151	374	785	764	514	906	499	604	562	548	161	1181	544
Chile	1500	1200	566	634	331	513	356	435	552	211	466	404	279	330	645	202
China	1000	1000	494	506	194	572	234	418	539	43	375	345	234	424	405	32
Colombia	na	6025	3071	2954	2188	2833	992	2323	2231	1411	2089	2121	1700	835	2010	485
Croatia	na	1003	428	575	318	424	261	143	637	223	150	418	403	132	601	216
Czech Republic	1396	1908	913	995	384	632	886	887	752	264	557	656	509	453	1193	184
Denmark	1030	1023	504	519	209	415	399	540	146	271	301	405	202	80	708	151
Dominican Rep.	na	417	170	245	260	141	11	32	101	277	130	123	85	77	250	66
Egypt	na	3000	1540	1460	1020	1320	656	1516	927	555	934	702	1042	1285	1484	164
El Salvador	na	1254	591	663	481	472	301	665	345	242	313	522	213	0	0	0
Estonia	1008	1005	464	541	266	343	396	292	524	189	208	314	362	385	534	26
Finland	588	1038	503	533	287	406	324	549	330	134	312	295	319	256	625	109
France	1002	1615	806	809	320	684	611	935	324	356	386	528	378	431	863	278
Georgia	na	2008	901	1107	643	768	597	294	1300	414	892	479	588	930	978	75
Germany	1336	2036	877	1159	326	753	955	923	876	214	768	548	238	597	1078	291
Great Britain	1484	1000	437	562	232	393	346	397	399	135	246	215	225	0	0	0
Greece	na	1142	475	664	479	438	194	101	472	567	305	341	313	203	693	180
Hungary	999	1000	474	526	198	379	421	591	297	109	192	407	367	468	455	22
Iceland	702	968	483	485	259	407	302	396	371	188	269	344	290	204	644	99
India	2500	2002	1137	865	543	957	494	1040	487	466	416	749	818	778	850	45
Indonesia	na	1004	500	500	181	423	396	247	412	334	357	392	138	383	534	28
Iran	na	2532	1361	1171	1276	793	463	765	998	661	852	546	849	639	1012	246
Ireland	1000	1012	465	544	184	388	414	198	491	312	272	285	309	193	652	127
Israel	na	1199	540	659	413	418	360	255	559	378	330	316	317	186	899	43
Italy	2018	2000	959	1041	445	738	817	873	829	298	527	474	512	267	1086	537
Japan	1011	1362	633	729	249	514	599	142	855	319	467	391	399	225	829	128
Jordan	na	1223	595	628	486	515	222	623	329	269	422	425	286	495	621	72
Korea, South	1251	1200	604	596	314	619	267	56	681	463	456	321	423	556	572	68
Latvia	903	1013	461	552	185	373	455	234	597	174	459	209	286	341	589	47
Lithuania	1000	1018	511	507	249	412	357	166	591	261	189	252	407	245	628	60
Luxembourg	na	1211	581	630	387	475	349	418	550	201	211	231	180	209	672	178
Macedonia	na	1055	548	507	270	459	326	350	507	198	388	374	260	360	589	49
Malta	na	1002	483	519	220	361	421	300	597	105	240	232	245	350	574	74
Mexico	1531	1535	748	787	557	639	334	717	524	288	373	397	442	365	842	210
Moldova	na	1008	440	568	272	400	336	239	495	273	252	329	342	461	410	53
Montenegro	na	1060	525	530	248	412	398	428	440	187	235	261	332	492	460	62
Morocco	na	2264	1113	1150	1088	904	269	1738	366	160	334	469	583	851	1127	156
Netherlands	1017	1003	491	510	134	486	382	308	351	344	289	363	282	113	658	220
New Zealand	na	1201	539	653	181	496	502	468	271	413	340	367	381	107	628	235
Nigeria	1001	2022	1032	990	1096	782	144	769	775	470	733	663	542	715	1126	173
Northern Ireland	304	1000	468	532	166	351	448	475	354	166	308	221	199	249	534	152
Norway	1239	1127	549	578	269	481	377	339	428	354	0	0	0	152	843	126
Pakistan	na	2000	1041	959	678	972	350	1083	626	289	601	792	477	1153	806	12
Peru	na	1501	733	768	605	635	261	318	707	472	641	514	346	307	941	216
Philippines	na	1200	600	600	402	528	270	362	465	372	317	489	386	472	647	74
Poland	938	1095	495	600	169	472	454	615	322	156	461	443	165	407	565	74
Portugal	1185	1000	386	614	223	303	474	523	376	101	144	295	237	335	523	105
Puerto Rico	na	720	255	458	146	250	319	71	219	421	194	266	226	85	457	157
Romania	1103	1146	557	589	244	424	478	410	527	201	334	297	428	480	508	75
Russian Fed.	1961	2500	1037	1463	457	1026	1017	334	1645	521	847	732	763	1278	1075	36
Serbia	na	1200	571	624	228	462	510	414	508	271	381	286	355	573	529	71
Singapore	na	1512	722	790	694	589	229	549	814	148	475	537	416	409	978	112
Slovakia	na	1331	647	684	337	536	458	377	837	117	364	409	459	557	614	50
Slovenia	1035	1006	459	547	258	389	357	278	574	151	260	213	175	160	638	152
South Africa	2736	3000	1500	1500	1071	1243	685	1691	1168	141	921	639	992	1154	1587	196
Spain	4147	2409	1172	1237	575	836	998	1237	810	360	599	635	430	576	1286	387
Sweden	1047	1015	505	510	240	382	393	226	481	308	363	324	286	63	703	218
Switzerland	1400	1212	609	603	253	515	436	255	842	111	290	328	349	188	770	193
Taiwan	na	780	381	399	121	473	186	291	176	311	244	217	260	352	344	37
Tanzania	na	1171	648	509	395	534	217	620	358	173	462	380	223	369	696	24
Turkey	1030	4607	2305	2302	1803	2048	752	2516	1385	470	1721	1827	831	1001	2558	865
Uganda	na	1002	502	500	540	409	53	250	674	71	217	128	205	318	577	103
Ukraine	na	1195	437	758	242	485	468	164	733	297	461	387	319	500	552	37
United States	1839	1200	508	692	306	524	370	236	356	604	429	401	299	114	771	295
Uruguay	na	1000	410	590	218	347	435	563	268	168	290	311	330	162	525	252
Venezuela	na	1200	605	595	496	470	234	306	636	258	321	301	383	296	722	171
Vietnam	na	995	489	506	226	469	298	534	380	67	199	413	361	195	608	84
Zimbabwe	na	1002	501	501	469	364	169	583	413	6	349	312	177	403	527	55
Total	56056	118519	56888	61573	35324	48421	34479	43434	49734	24329	35549	36184	31823	33927	61203	12820

RANKING

Country	2000
Colombia	6025
Turkey	4607
Egypt	3000
South Africa	3000
Iran	2532
Russian Fed.	2500
Spain	2409
Morocco	2264
Australia	2048
Germany	2036
Nigeria	2022
Georgia	2008
Azerbaijan	2002
India	2002
Armenia	2000
Italy	2000
Pakistan	2000
Canada	1931
Belgium	1912
Czech Republic	1908
France	1615
Mexico	1535
Austria	1522
Singapore	1512
Peru	1501
Bangladesh	1499
Japan	1362
Slovakia	1331
Algeria	1282
Argentina	1280
El Salvador	1254
Jordan	1223
Switzerland	1212
Luxembourg	1211
New Zealand	1201
Bosnia and Herz.	1200
Chile	1200
Korea, South	1200
Philippines	1200
Serbia	1200
United States	1200
Venezuela	1200
Israel	1199
Ukraine	1195
Tanzania	1171
Brazil	1149
Romania	1146
Greece	1142
Norway	1127
Poland	1095
Montenegro	1060
Macedonia	1055
Finland	1038
Denmark	1023
Lithuania	1018
Sweden	1015
Latvia	1013
Ireland	1012
Moldova	1008
Slovenia	1006
Estonia	1005
Indonesia	1004
Croatia	1003
Netherlands	1003
Malta	1002
Uganda	1002
Zimbabwe	1002
Albania	1000
Belarus	1000
Bulgaria	1000
China	1000
Great Britain	1000
Hungary	1000
Northern Ireland	1000
Portugal	1000
Uruguay	1000
Vietnam	995
Iceland	968
Taiwan	780
Puerto Rico	720
Dominican Rep.	417
Total	118519

TABLE OF PERCENTAGES

Each cell shows the actual percentage in a given country (row) by each breakdown (column).

In some cases the number of respondents is small. When analyzing those cases, the specific "n" must be taken into account.

Country	Wave 1990	Wave 2000	Male	Female	16-29	30-49	50+	Lower (Edu)	Middle (Edu)	Upper (Edu)	Lower (Inc)	Middle (Inc)	Upper (Inc)	Mat	Mixed	Postm.	RANKING Country	2000
Albania			50	51	26	45	29	43	41	16	36	31	34	46	50	4		
Algeria			51	49	43	37	20	24	44	33	43	29	28	37	53	10		
Argentina			47	53	31	36	34	59	31	10	30	40	30	19	55	26		
Armenia			47	53	39	37	24	8	71	21	42	34	24	45	49	6		
Australia			49	51	28	39	33	26	40	34	38	34	28	8	57	35		
Austria			43	57	17	39	44	52	36	12	28	37	36	8	63	29		
Azerbaijan			49	51	37	47	17	6	63	32	31	41	28	62	35	4		
Bangladesh			55	45	41	50	10	53	27	19	29	42	29	40	55	5		
Belarus			45	55	27	38	34	27	58	15	35	45	20	50	45	6		
Belgium			46	54	19	40	41	21	44	34	27	35	38	20	56	23		
Bosnia and Herz.			48	52	30	41	30	17	63	20	22	54	24	31	64	5		
Brazil			50	50	39	41	20	44	44	12	39	25	36	31	58	12		
Bulgaria			43	57	16	36	48	27	46	28	35	29	37	46	51	3		
Canada			40	60	19	41	40	27	47	26	35	33	32	9	63	29		
Chile			47	53	28	43	30	36	46	18	41	35	24	28	55	17		
China			49	51	19	57	23	42	54	4	39	36	25	49	47	4		
Colombia			51	49	36	47	17	39	37	24	35	36	29	25	60	15		
Croatia			43	57	32	42	26	14	64	22	15	43	42	14	63	23		
Czech Republic			48	52	20	33	47	47	40	14	32	38	30	25	65	10		
Denmark			49	51	20	41	39	56	15	28	33	45	22	9	75	16		
Dominican Rep.			41	59	63	34	3	8	25	68	39	36	25	20	64	17		
Egypt			51	49	34	44	22	51	31	19	35	26	39	44	51	6		
El Salvador			47	53	38	38	24	53	28	19	30	50	20	0	0	0		
Estonia			46	54	27	34	39	29	52	19	24	36	41	41	57	3		
Finland			49	51	28	40	32	54	33	13	34	32	34	26	63	11		
France			50	50	20	42	38	58	20	22	30	41	29	27	55	18		
Georgia			45	55	32	38	30	15	65	21	46	25	30	47	49	4		
Germany			43	57	16	37	47	46	44	11	49	35	15	30	55	15		
Great Britain			44	56	24	41	36	43	43	15	36	31	33	0	0	0		
Greece			42	58	43	39	18	9	41	50	32	36	33	19	64	17		
Hungary			47	53	20	38	42	59	30	11	20	42	38	50	48	2		
Iceland			50	50	27	42	31	42	39	20	30	38	32	22	68	11		
India			57	43	27	48	25	52	24	23	21	38	41	47	51	3		
Indonesia			50	50	18	42	40	25	42	34	40	44	16	41	57	3		
Iran			54	46	50	31	18	32	41	27	38	24	38	34	53	13		
Ireland			46	54	19	39	42	20	49	31	31	33	36	20	67	13		
Israel			45	55	35	35	30	21	47	32	34	33	33	17	80	4		
Italy			48	52	22	37	41	44	41	15	35	31	34	14	58	28		
Japan			47	54	18	38	44	11	65	24	37	31	32	19	70	11		
Jordan			49	51	40	42	18	51	27	22	37	38	25	42	52	6		
Korea, South			50	50	26	52	22	5	57	39	38	27	35	47	48	6		
Latvia			46	55	18	37	45	23	59	17	48	22	30	35	60	5		
Lithuania			50	50	25	41	35	16	58	26	22	30	48	26	67	6		
Luxembourg			48	52	32	39	29	36	47	17	34	37	29	20	64	17		
Macedonia			52	48	26	44	31	33	48	19	38	37	25	36	59	5		
Malta			48	52	22	36	42	30	60	11	34	32	34	35	58	7		
Mexico			49	51	36	42	22	47	34	19	31	33	37	20	59	18		
Moldova			44	56	27	40	33	24	49	27	27	36	37	50	44	6		
Montenegro			50	50	23	39	38	41	42	18	28	32	40	49	45	6		
Morocco			49	51	48	40	12	77	16	7	24	34	42	40	53	7		
Netherlands			49	51	13	49	38	31	35	34	31	39	30	11	66	22		
New Zealand			45	55	15	42	43	41	24	36	31	34	35	11	65	24		
Nigeria			51	49	54	39	7	38	39	23	38	34	28	36	56	9		
Northern Ireland			47	53	17	36	46	48	36	17	42	30	27	27	57	16		
Norway			49	51	24	43	34	30	38	32	0	0	0	14	75	11		
Pakistan			52	48	34	49	18	54	31	15	32	42	26	59	41	1		
Peru			49	51	40	42	17	21	47	32	43	34	23	21	64	15		
Philippines			50	50	34	44	23	30	39	31	27	41	32	40	54	6		
Poland			45	55	15	43	42	56	30	14	43	41	15	39	54	7		
Portugal			39	61	22	30	47	52	38	10	21	44	35	35	54	11		
Puerto Rico			36	64	20	35	45	10	31	59	28	39	33	12	65	23		
Romania			49	51	21	37	42	36	46	18	32	28	40	45	48	7		
Russian Fed.			42	59	18	41	41	13	66	21	36	31	33	54	45	2		
Serbia			48	52	19	39	43	35	43	23	37	28	35	49	45	6		
Singapore			48	52	46	39	15	36	54	10	33	38	29	27	65	8		
Slovakia			49	51	25	40	34	28	63	9	30	33	37	46	50	4		
Slovenia			46	54	26	39	36	28	57	15	40	33	27	17	67	16		
South Africa			50	50	36	41	23	56	39	5	36	25	39	39	54	7		
Spain			49	51	24	35	41	51	34	15	36	38	26	26	57	17		
Sweden			50	50	24	38	39	22	47	30	37	33	29	6	71	22		
Switzerland			50	50	21	43	36	21	70	9	30	34	36	16	67	17		
Taiwan			49	51	16	61	24	37	23	40	34	30	36	48	47	5		
Tanzania			56	44	35	47	19	54	31	15	43	36	21	34	64	2		
Turkey			50	50	39	45	16	58	32	11	39	42	19	23	58	20		
Uganda			50	50	54	41	5	25	68	7	40	23	37	32	58	10		
Ukraine			37	63	20	41	39	14	61	25	40	33	27	46	51	3		
United States			42	58	26	44	31	20	30	51	38	36	27	10	65	25		
Uruguay			41	59	22	35	44	56	27	17	31	33	35	17	56	27		
Venezuela			50	50	41	39	20	26	53	22	32	30	38	25	61	14		
Vietnam			49	51	23	47	30	54	39	7	21	42	37	22	69	10		
Zimbabwe			50	50	47	36	17	58	41	1	42	37	21	41	54	6		
Total			48	52	30	41	29	37	42	21	34	35	31	31	57	12		

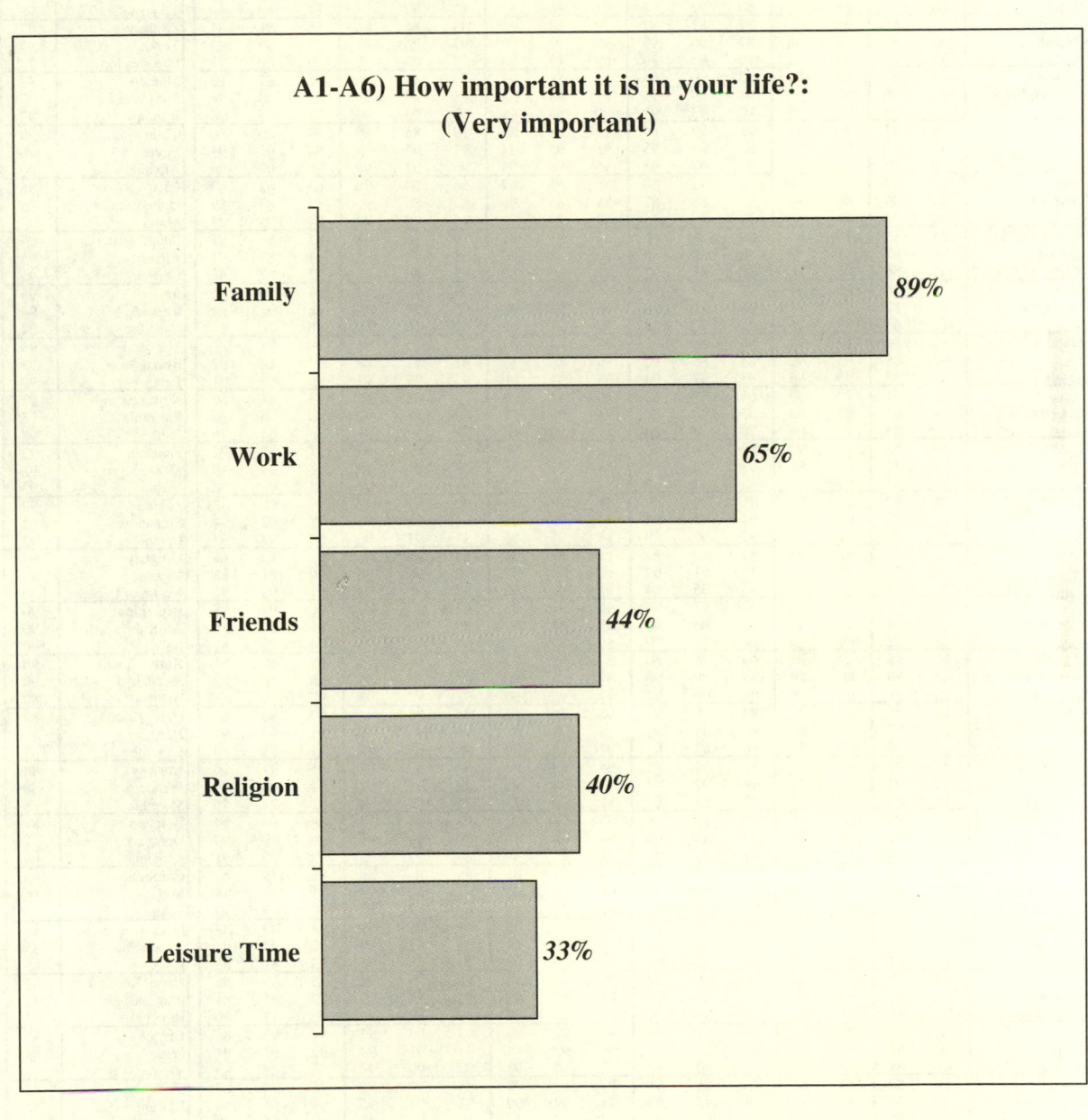

A1-A6) How important it is in your life?:
(Very important)

Family 89%

Work 65%

Friends 44%

Religion 40%

Leisure Time 33%

A001) FAMILY IMPORTANT

For each of the following aspects, indicate how important it is in your life: family.

Very important (%)

(WVS: V4; EVS: V2)

Country	Wave 1990	Wave 2000	Gender Male	Gender Female	Age 16-29	Age 30-49	Age 50+	Education Lower	Education Middle	Education Upper	Income Lower	Income Middle	Income Upper	Values Mat	Values Mixed	Values Postm.
Albania	na	96	94	98	92	97	99	94	97	98	97	95	97	97	96	97
Algeria	na	95	94	95	95	94	96	95	94	95	94	96	94	94	95	98
Argentina	91	90	88	92	86	93	92	90	91	93	90	91	90	87	92	90
Armenia	na	86	85	88	80	91	88	83	86	88	89	86	85	85	88	84
Australia	na	90	87	94	87	93	91	90	92	89	89	92	91	89	91	89
Austria	86	89	85	93	80	92	91	91	88	85	83	92	91	87	89	90
Azerbaijan	na	85	86	84	82	87	87	90	84	86	85	86	86	86	86	84
Bangladesh	na	97	96	98	97	96	99	98	97	93	97	96	97	99	95	97
Belarus	77	79	74	82	79	83	74	69	82	83	77	80	78	79	80	77
Belgium	84	87	84	91	87	90	85	82	88	91	79	88	92	88	87	88
Bosnia and Herz.	na	99	99	99	98	99	99	97	99	100	98	99	99	99	99	98
Brazil	91	93	92	93	92	93	92	90	94	96	91	96	93	92	93	96
Bulgaria	76	83	80	86	75	86	84	85	81	85	78	83	86	84	80	96
Canada	92	94	92	96	88	96	95	91	95	94	92	95	95	94	95	91
Chile	86	96	96	97	98	97	95	96	96	98	95	97	97	96	97	96
China	62	61	61	60	57	62	60	56	64	67	56	60	70	63	62	63
Colombia	na	86	86	86	83	88	87	84	85	90	83	86	90	84	87	89
Croatia	na	79	74	83	79	81	76	78	79	79	74	80	83	84	75	87
Czech Republic	86	85	78	91	80	86	86	82	87	91	79	86	88	82	86	85
Denmark	88	87	81	93	80	89	88	86	85	90	81	90	93	81	87	91
Dominican Rep.	na	86	86	86	86	88	82	87	84	87	83	86	92	82	87	86
Egypt	na	96	96	97	95	98	96	96	97	97	96	96	98	97	96	95
El Salvador	na	97	97	97	96	97	98	96	97	98	95	97	100	na	na	na
Estonia	69	68	59	75	61	72	68	59	73	69	62	70	74	68	70	66
Finland	84	80	77	84	80	85	76	77	84	85	72	83	86	79	81	81
France	82	88	83	92	83	85	92	90	86	83	87	87	88	91	88	82
Georgia	na	95	95	95	93	97	94	95	94	96	93	97	95	95	95	91
Germany	85	81	78	83	65	87	82	80	81	88	74	86	85	83	81	80
Great Britain	89	89	85	93	87	90	89	91	90	85	89	88	91	na	na	na
Greece	na	83	78	86	78	84	89	87	80	84	78	82	86	85	84	79
Hungary	89	89	85	92	85	90	90	88	88	92	82	91	90	91	87	92
Iceland	91	94	91	98	93	96	92	94	94	96	89	96	98	98	94	89
India	77	93	93	93	92	93	92	93	91	94	91	92	94	93	92	98
Indonesia	na	99	99	99	100	99	99	98	99	99	99	99	99	99	99	100
Iran	na	95	95	94	94	95	94	94	96	94	94	95	95	97	93	94
Ireland	91	92	91	92	91	95	89	88	93	95	87	91	96	87	93	93
Israel	na	na	na	na	na	na	na	na	na	na	na	na	na	na	na	na
Italy	88	90	87	93	86	91	92	91	90	88	90	90	90	90	91	88
Japan	78	93	93	92	84	95	94	91	93	92	92	95	93	91	93	92
Jordan	na	97	98	96	97	97	96	96	97	98	97	97	96	96	97	98
Korea, South	93	90	90	90	83	93	90	93	89	89	88	91	90	91	89	87
Latvia	73	72	69	75	64	79	70	65	73	77	69	75	76	74	72	62
Lithuania	65	66	60	70	60	76	60	57	68	72	56	66	75	69	66	51
Luxembourg	na	88	86	89	83	89	90	87	88	88	82	85	89	90	88	82
Macedonia	na	98	98	99	98	99	97	97	98	99	98	97	99	98	99	100
Malta	na	95	93	97	97	98	96	96	96	93	95	98	94	97	95	92
Mexico	85	97	96	97	96	98	96	96	99	97	93	98	99	97	97	99
Moldova	na	86	85	87	86	88	84	82	85	90	86	85	88	87	85	89
Montenegro	na	92	89	96	86	93	95	94	90	93	96	93	92	95	91	86
Morocco	na	93	92	94	94	92	93	93	94	95	89	95	92	94	93	94
Netherlands	82	80	76	83	70	83	82	81	80	78	70	83	84	81	81	76
New Zealand	na	93	90	95	89	93	94	93	93	92	90	96	93	88	94	94
Nigeria	94	99	99	99	98	100	99	99	99	100	99	99	99	99	99	99
Northern Ireland	94	90	88	93	87	91	91	91	91	89	89	92	95	92	90	91
Norway	88	88	84	92	83	92	85	84	91	88	na	na	na	83	89	87
Pakistan	na	93	90	96	91	93	95	94	92	88	94	92	93	91	94	100
Peru	na	83	82	83	80	83	87	81	81	86	82	82	84	82	83	79
Philippines	na	99	99	99	98	98	100	99	98	99	99	99	98	98	99	100
Poland	91	92	92	92	92	92	91	90	96	91	92	92	93	92	92	91
Portugal	65	84	83	85	86	85	83	84	83	90	73	85	92	83	87	83
Puerto Rico	na	96	97	95	94	96	97	97	93	97	93	95	98	96	95	97
Romania	83	85	83	87	76	89	86	82	87	88	82	85	90	87	85	81
Russian Fed.	79	76	73	79	73	83	70	63	77	79	69	80	80	76	77	70
Serbia	na	92	90	95	88	92	94	93	92	90	93	94	92	92	93	89
Singapore	na	92	91	93	90	94	92	91	92	94	91	91	93	92	92	91
Slovakia	na	88	84	91	82	90	88	85	89	91	82	90	91	87	89	83
Slovenia	81	82	77	87	76	85	84	79	82	88	78	87	85	78	82	87
South Africa	90	95	96	94	96	95	93	94	97	99	93	98	96	94	96	96
Spain	82	86	83	89	76	87	91	89	83	81	87	86	86	89	86	78
Sweden	87	90	83	96	79	93	93	93	87	91	83	92	95	85	91	87
Switzerland	88	81	78	84	72	83	85	88	79	84	76	85	82	86	82	78
Taiwan	na	78	78	78	79	83	65	68	82	86	76	77	84	79	80	76
Tanzania	na	93	93	92	90	94	95	93	93	92	93	94	93	96	92	92
Turkey	87	97	97	98	97	98	97	98	97	96	97	98	97	98	98	96
Uganda	na	91	88	94	91	90	95	87	93	89	85	85	93	90	91	97
Ukraine	na	82	76	88	73	87	83	80	83	81	82	83	82	83	81	87
United States	92	95	94	97	94	95	97	94	97	95	93	97	98	96	97	91
Uruguay	na	91	91	91	84	95	92	90	94	93	87	95	93	88	92	93
Venezuela	na	98	98	98	97	97	100	96	98	98	98	97	99	98	98	98
Vietnam	na	82	83	81	80	84	81	79	86	85	82	78	87	82	81	87
Zimbabwe	na	97	97	97	96	98	100	97	97	100	98	98	98	98	97	97
Total	83	89	87	91	87	91	88	88	89	90	87	90	91	89	89	88

RANKING

Country	2000
Nigeria	99
Bosnia and Herz.	99
Indonesia	99
Philippines	99
Macedonia	98
Venezuela	98
Zimbabwe	97
Turkey	97
El Salvador	97
Mexico	97
Bangladesh	97
Jordan	97
Chile	96
Egypt	96
Albania	96
Puerto Rico	96
United States	95
Malta	95
South Africa	95
Algeria	95
Georgia	95
Iran	95
Iceland	94
Canada	94
Morocco	93
Brazil	93
Japan	93
New Zealand	93
Tanzania	93
India	93
Pakistan	93
Montenegro	92
Serbia	92
Poland	92
Singapore	92
Ireland	92
Uruguay	91
Uganda	91
Northern Ireland	90
Argentina	90
Australia	90
Italy	90
Korea, South	90
Sweden	90
Austria	89
Great Britain	89
Hungary	89
Luxembourg	88
Norway	88
France	88
Slovakia	88
Belgium	87
Denmark	87
Armenia	86
Colombia	86
Moldova	86
Spain	86
Dominican Rep.	86
Azerbaijan	85
Romania	85
Czech Republic	85
Portugal	84
Bulgaria	83
Greece	83
Peru	83
Vietnam	82
Slovenia	82
Ukraine	82
Switzerland	81
Germany	81
Finland	80
Netherlands	80
Croatia	79
Belarus	79
Taiwan	78
Russian Fed.	76
Latvia	72
Estonia	68
Lithuania	66
China	61
Total	89

A002) FRIENDS IMPORTANT

For each of the following aspects, indicate how important it is in your life: friends.

Very important (%)

(WVS: V5; EVS: V3)

Country	Wave 1990	Wave 2000	Gender Male	Gender Female	Age 16-29	Age 30-49	Age 50+	Education Lower	Education Middle	Education Upper	Income Lower	Income Middle	Income Upper	Values Mat	Values Mixed	Values Postm.	RANKING Country	RANKING 2000
Albania	na	32	36	28	34	28	37	30	31	43	29	29	38	32	32	26	Uganda	75
Algeria	na	36	41	31	40	35	28	29	38	39	34	34	38	35	36	40	Georgia	74
Argentina	51	50	50	50	52	47	53	45	57	60	49	49	54	44	50	55	Turkey	74
Armenia	na	45	52	38	48	44	40	41	44	49	49	43	40	40	49	45	Sweden	71
Australia	na	63	60	66	61	63	64	62	61	66	63	62	64	58	63	65	Bosnia and Herz.	71
Austria	35	44	47	42	67	39	39	42	45	46	43	40	47	49	41	47	Northern Ireland	65
Azerbaijan	na	35	39	32	48	29	27	27	32	43	32	34	40	32	40	54	El Salvador	65
Bangladesh	na	32	37	26	31	33	37	32	30	34	32	29	37	33	33	24	United States	64
Belarus	37	27	30	24	40	26	18	17	31	29	29	25	30	22	31	45	Nigeria	64
Belgium	46	48	46	50	64	45	44	40	47	57	45	44	51	41	49	53	Australia	63
Bosnia and Herz.	na	71	72	69	74	70	69	68	70	75	74	72	67	67	72	74	Ireland	61
Brazil	57	58	56	60	50	61	65	58	54	67	59	53	59	59	56	63	Netherlands	60
Bulgaria	38	37	43	32	51	39	29	29	42	41	34	39	35	33	39	52	Canada	60
Canada	51	60	58	63	66	57	61	59	60	63	54	62	64	59	60	61	Norway	59
Chile	19	29	29	30	36	27	26	20	30	49	23	30	38	26	29	37	Switzerland	59
China	22	20	21	19	26	20	16	17	21	49	15	23	26	19	23	25	Great Britain	58
Colombia	na	34	34	34	32	33	38	31	34	37	31	35	36	29	30	30	Uruguay	58
Croatia	na	36	36	37	43	34	35	37	36	38	36	32	44	35	35	42	Brazil	58
Czech Republic	27	27	25	29	39	21	25	26	27	29	27	27	26	23	27	35	Serbia	58
Denmark	53	55	49	61	69	49	54	56	58	53	61	53	50	55	56	55	Indonesia	56
Dominican Rep.	na	36	38	34	37	31	46	23	36	36	36	34	35	34	36	39	New Zealand	55
Egypt	na	37	43	31	43	35	34	31	42	47	38	35	37	32	42	47	Denmark	55
El Salvador	na	65	64	66	64	61	71	64	65	66	64	63	71	na	na	na	Venezuela	53
Estonia	23	26	26	26	43	21	22	28	27	22	24	25	28	22	28	42	Finland	51
Finland	43	51	47	56	72	48	44	49	58	43	54	55	41	52	50	59	Argentina	50
France	41	50	50	49	61	47	47	45	54	59	49	46	54	42	51	58	France	50
Georgia	na	74	80	69	80	74	66	70	73	79	69	73	81	71	76	80	Macedonia	50
Germany	34	48	48	49	58	49	43	41	54	54	40	50	50	48	48	52	Belgium	48
Great Britain	48	58	56	60	67	52	58	57	57	60	51	61	56	na	na	na	Japan	48
Greece	na	42	41	43	54	33	35	26	37	50	35	41	50	41	41	49	Germany	48
Hungary	28	34	37	31	47	25	34	34	31	37	35	33	34	33	36	30	Iceland	48
Iceland	49	48	43	52	62	40	46	48	50	43	50	47	46	45	48	51	Jordan	47
India	30	40	46	32	43	40	37	33	45	50	39	39	41	41	42	53	Luxembourg	47
Indonesia	na	56	63	49	63	61	48	46	56	64	55	59	52	56	58	57	Korea, South	45
Iran	na	30	30	29	33	29	23	25	32	32	26	28	33	27	32	25	Armenia	45
Ireland	55	61	57	65	68	57	59	57	60	70	55	59	65	61	60	66	Austria	44
Israel	na	na	na	na	na	na	na	na	na	na	na	na	na	na	na	na	Spain	43
Italy	38	36	37	34	51	35	28	28	42	41	32	36	40	28	34	43	Montenegro	43
Japan	34	48	45	51	66	49	40	39	48	54	48	46	49	41	48	62	Greece	42
Jordan	na	47	52	43	50	44	49	47	43	54	43	53	46	48	46	55	Morocco	42
Korea, South	52	45	46	43	60	41	36	42	42	49	46	43	45	42	46	57	Slovenia	42
Latvia	16	25	22	27	28	21	26	24	24	27	28	24	21	25	24	26	India	40
Lithuania	19	17	19	16	28	16	11	8	20	24	13	13	17	19	16	13	Singapore	40
Luxembourg	na	47	46	47	60	46	39	41	46	58	41	42	47	45	45	51	Ukraine	39
Macedonia	na	50	51	48	53	44	54	47	50	52	47	49	54	43	54	58	Mexico	38
Malta	na	32	33	31	38	27	33	29	32	40	29	30	31	31	33	28	Egypt	37
Mexico	25	38	37	40	39	34	45	36	38	49	38	37	39	44	36	39	Bulgaria	37
Moldova	na	35	43	28	41	31	35	29	39	35	30	34	43	35	37	34	Philippines	37
Montenegro	na	43	46	40	52	42	39	36	47	51	34	36	49	39	46	50	Croatia	36
Morocco	na	42	46	38	47	41	32	40	44	59	30	42	45	43	42	39	Algeria	36
Netherlands	63	60	52	69	74	57	57	56	60	66	62	58	59	55	61	60	Dominican Rep.	36
New Zealand	na	55	48	61	59	51	58	54	54	58	55	53	58	51	56	59	Italy	36
Nigeria	53	64	67	60	66	61	60	64	65	61	67	61	63	62	65	62	Moldova	35
Northern Ireland	53	65	65	66	70	60	68	67	66	62	65	65	55	71	64	65	Azerbaijan	35
Norway	68	59	51	67	67	61	52	55	59	63	na	na	na	54	59	66	Zimbabwe	35
Pakistan	na	20	20	19	26	15	19	19	19	23	21	18	18	21	18	na	South Africa	34
Peru	na	25	24	26	26	22	27	25	24	26	26	21	28	25	23	33	Hungary	34
Philippines	na	37	38	35	38	32	45	39	33	40	33	36	42	37	37	40	Slovakia	34
Poland	23	27	26	29	35	22	29	28	27	26	28	29	25	26	27	28	Colombia	34
Portugal	20	30	35	27	39	26	30	26	39	43	17	30	37	28	32	36	Puerto Rico	33
Puerto Rico	na	33	30	34	27	29	37	46	32	30	37	33	28	29	35	30	Albania	32
Romania	25	26	30	23	36	22	25	24	29	24	26	26	26	25	26	27	Bangladesh	32
Russian Fed.	29	27	28	27	36	27	23	16	28	33	24	29	29	25	30	32	Malta	32
Serbia	na	58	61	54	65	58	54	54	58	63	56	58	56	55	60	62	Tanzania	32
Singapore	na	40	42	37	47	35	27	33	43	46	29	39	47	28	43	49	Portugal	30
Slovakia	na	34	35	32	45	31	28	31	34	40	33	28	37	32	37	38	Iran	30
Slovenia	38	42	41	43	54	32	43	42	43	35	43	41	43	43	41	45	Chile	29
South Africa	23	34	36	32	38	31	36	31	39	37	31	29	44	31	35	51	Taiwan	29
Spain	45	43	45	42	50	41	41	41	44	51	40	43	48	43	43	45	Poland	27
Sweden	69	71	66	75	81	70	65	61	73	76	74	68	69	67	70	75	Russian Fed.	27
Switzerland	52	59	54	63	75	57	51	55	60	54	59	59	63	50	58	68	Belarus	27
Taiwan	na	29	28	30	37	28	28	24	37	30	27	25	34	29	31	27	Czech Republic	27
Tanzania	na	32	35	29	29	33	34	32	33	29	35	30	33	27	34	39	Estonia	26
Turkey	55	74	74	73	73	75	73	72	75	80	72	74	78	73	75	73	Romania	26
Uganda	na	75	79	71	76	74	76	77	74	76	77	71	81	70	77	80	Latvia	25
Ukraine	na	39	40	38	45	39	36	31	40	42	33	38	48	40	39	47	Peru	25
United States	54	64	61	68	59	62	72	58	64	67	59	66	68	62	64	65	Vietnam	21
Uruguay	na	58	59	58	59	56	60	53	64	68	53	59	62	59	56	62	China	20
Venezuela	na	53	52	53	52	49	62	58	49	54	51	52	55	52	53	51	Pakistan	20
Vietnam	na	21	24	18	23	20	22	17	28	19	22	19	23	14	26	22	Lithuania	17
Zimbabwe	na	35	34	36	36	34	34	33	38	48	38	32	33	37	33	35		
Total	40	44	44	43	49	41	42	40	44	48	42	42	45	39	45	51	Total	44

A003) LEISURE TIME

For each of the following aspects, indicate how important it is in your life: leisure.

Very important (%) (WVS: V6; EVS: V4)

Country	Wave 1990	Wave 2000	Gender Male	Gender Female	Age 16-29	Age 30-49	Age 50+	Education Lower	Education Middle	Education Upper	Income Lower	Income Middle	Income Upper	Values Mat	Values Mixed	Values Postm.	RANKING Country	2000
Albania	na	14	16	12	23	12	9	11	14	22	10	16	16	10	19	5	Venezuela	66
Algeria	na	24	25	24	31	22	13	16	27	26	29	20	23	25	24	24	El Salvador	62
Argentina	40	36	37	35	38	38	32	36	36	35	34	35	38	33	35	38	Brazil	54
Armenia	na	24	25	22	26	24	19	17	24	26	22	26	20	20	27	22	Sweden	54
Australia	na	45	45	45	41	50	43	41	46	46	40	45	51	44	43	48	Chile	54
Austria	37	39	41	38	54	37	34	39	41	34	33	41	41	46	38	39	Netherlands	53
Azerbaijan	na	30	28	32	40	26	22	21	26	40	24	27	39	28	34	30	Puerto Rico	53
Bangladesh	na	23	25	22	23	24	25	21	26	27	20	23	28	22	24	30	Nigeria	52
Belarus	37	25	29	22	35	25	18	18	28	27	26	26	23	23	26	30	Great Britain	51
Belgium	41	40	39	40	44	41	36	34	40	44	37	39	42	37	40	43	Mexico	51
Bosnia and Herz.	na	44	44	44	49	44	37	39	44	46	44	43	44	41	44	43	Malta	50
Brazil	52	54	54	54	54	56	52	56	52	57	54	51	56	53	54	58	Uruguay	47
Bulgaria	36	23	26	20	31	28	15	14	28	28	16	23	26	20	26	29	Northern Ireland	46
Canada	42	38	38	39	36	39	38	37	38	40	30	37	43	31	38	42	Switzerland	46
Chile	33	54	57	51	58	55	49	49	55	63	55	51	57	49	56	58	New Zealand	45
China	14	7	8	6	10	6	8	6	7	23	5	8	11	7	7	22	Australia	45
Colombia	na	40	39	40	38	42	38	33	41	49	33	43	45	33	34	39	Uganda	45
Croatia	na	25	27	22	41	21	18	25	23	28	15	22	33	16	24	36	Denmark	45
Czech Republic	30	21	22	21	27	19	19	23	20	17	19	23	20	25	20	22	Japan	44
Denmark	48	45	46	43	46	47	41	46	43	44	43	47	42	46	45	53	Bosnia and Herz.	44
Dominican Rep.	na	31	31	31	34	24	50	36	35	29	32	30	32	35	33	23	Greece	43
Egypt	na	9	11	8	12	8	8	7	10	14	9	9	10	7	10	15	Turkey	43
El Salvador	na	62	62	62	61	60	67	62	62	62	62	63	63	na	na	na	United States	43
Estonia	25	19	18	20	33	15	14	19	20	16	14	17	21	14	21	23	Macedonia	42
Finland	47	39	43	36	50	42	30	38	42	37	38	40	38	39	37	46	Ireland	41
France	31	37	39	35	46	39	30	33	39	46	32	36	43	34	35	46	Morocco	40
Georgia	na	36	39	34	45	37	26	36	35	40	33	38	40	34	38	44	Colombia	40
Germany	36	32	34	31	44	33	26	27	37	34	26	31	33	31	32	37	Belgium	40
Great Britain	45	51	57	45	54	54	49	50	52	48	42	53	60	na	na	na	Austria	39
Greece	na	43	44	41	53	38	30	29	38	49	41	40	46	38	42	53	Finland	39
Hungary	32	31	36	27	44	32	24	30	35	29	27	33	33	27	37	20	Norway	39
Iceland	36	34	32	36	32	34	35	35	31	35	34	34	33	33	34	38	Canada	38
India	17	29	31	26	30	28	29	25	30	36	26	27	32	27	30	31	Luxembourg	38
Indonesia	na	17	18	16	25	19	11	11	16	24	18	17	15	18	18	21	France	37
Iran	na	30	27	33	34	29	21	24	29	36	25	29	32	26	31	37	Georgia	36
Ireland	32	41	42	39	43	41	38	35	42	46	33	44	45	44	39	43	Argentina	36
Israel	na	na	na	na	na	na	na	na	na	na	na	na	na	na	na	na	South Africa	36
Italy	33	29	31	28	42	32	20	23	35	33	25	27	33	24	28	34	Spain	35
Japan	24	44	40	48	61	47	34	33	44	51	40	43	46	46	44	47	Iceland	34
Jordan	na	17	16	19	19	19	11	13	17	27	13	19	21	15	19	24	Slovenia	33
Korea, South	25	24	23	24	31	22	20	27	20	29	24	20	27	21	25	41	Slovakia	32
Latvia	21	17	18	16	18	16	17	15	17	17	16	20	16	18	16	15	Germany	32
Lithuania	17	16	15	16	22	15	11	11	17	17	12	15	15	16	15	18	Dominican Rep.	31
Luxembourg	na	38	43	33	46	39	31	36	38	37	35	37	35	36	35	45	Hungary	31
Macedonia	na	42	44	39	44	44	37	34	43	51	40	44	43	36	45	39	Serbia	31
Malta	na	50	54	40	50	19	44	42	53	49	49	49	50	44	54	41	Azerbaijan	30
Mexico	28	51	50	51	47	53	53	49	52	55	51	54	50	31	54	49	Iran	30
Moldova	na	25	26	24	30	22	24	20	28	25	21	23	32	23	28	35	Italy	29
Montenegro	na	25	25	24	36	24	18	17	29	32	16	15	33	23	24	34	India	29
Morocco	na	40	41	39	44	39	32	37	50	51	31	40	41	38	43	41	Zimbabwe	28
Netherlands	51	53	50	57	59	52	51	56	54	50	54	52	53	54	53	54	Singapore	26
New Zealand	na	45	45	45	48	48	41	44	47	45	39	42	55	50	47	47	Taiwan	26
Nigeria	68	52	53	50	55	50	36	48	53	57	51	52	53	50	52	57	Belarus	25
Northern Ireland	31	46	51	42	57	43	42	43	51	46	46	40	44	51	43	50	Ukraine	25
Norway	42	39	43	35	36	44	35	34	39	43	na	na	na	33	41	37	Moldova	25
Pakistan	na	5	7	3	7	4	4	4	6	6	5	5	7	5	5	6	Poland	25
Peru	na	23	23	23	22	24	24	22	23	23	23	24	22	27	22	21	Croatia	25
Philippines	na	15	17	14	15	15	16	14	16	15	17	12	18	16	15	10	Montenegro	25
Poland	35	25	24	26	29	27	19	22	28	30	22	27	25	21	27	28	Algeria	24
Portugal	16	20	22	19	25	22	16	15	27	38	11	18	25	18	20	30	Korea, South	24
Puerto Rico	na	53	51	53	50	57	50	48	46	57	47	53	55	52	53	53	Armenia	24
Romania	25	24	25	23	33	26	17	17	28	26	17	22	30	22	24	21	Romania	24
Russian Fed.	29	20	22	18	28	20	14	12	20	23	18	18	22	18	21	28	Bangladesh	23
Serbia	na	31	33	29	41	36	22	25	35	34	27	31	32	29	32	39	Peru	23
Singapore	na	26	25	28	28	25	26	26	26	29	24	25	30	22	27	38	Bulgaria	23
Slovakia	na	32	33	31	45	31	24	26	35	37	28	30	34	29	36	36	Czech Republic	21
Slovenia	28	33	31	34	44	31	26	29	34	32	27	34	34	29	31	40	Portugal	20
South Africa	29	36	41	30	41	33	30	30	43	46	25	32	50	32	38	41	Russian Fed.	20
Spain	38	35	38	33	46	38	26	29	38	47	28	37	43	32	35	41	Estonia	19
Sweden	55	54	50	58	57	54	53	55	54	53	54	53	57	55	53	58	Jordan	17
Switzerland	47	46	48	43	60	48	34	42	48	40	43	47	47	43	47	46	Indonesia	17
Taiwan	na	26	26	26	32	27	19	20	27	31	21	24	31	25	27	43	Latvia	17
Tanzania	na	12	11	12	10	11	16	11	12	13	13	10	13	9	13	17	Lithuania	16
Turkey	24	43	41	45	47	40	39	40	46	49	40	44	50	42	44	44	Philippines	15
Uganda	na	45	44	46	49	41	40	39	48	42	38	39	51	40	43	65	Albania	14
Ukraine	na	25	25	25	31	24	22	16	26	28	22	26	28	23	27	35	Tanzania	12
United States	43	43	41	44	43	43	43	46	39	43	40	42	48	49	41	43	Egypt	9
Uruguay	na	47	50	46	47	51	45	46	49	52	44	48	48	47	44	54	China	7
Venezuela	na	66	66	65	64	68	65	65	65	70	60	64	70	64	66	67	Vietnam	7
Vietnam	na	7	8	6	6	7	9	6	8	11	6	7	7	5	9	6	Pakistan	5
Zimbabwe	na	28	25	29	28	29	25	27	28	38	30	27	28	30	26	29		
Total	35	33	34	33	38	33	29	30	34	37	30	32	36	28	34	41	Total	33

A004) POLITICS IMPORTANT

For each of the following aspects, indicate how important it is in your life: politics.

Very / Rather important (%)

(WVS: V7; EVS: V5)

Country	Wave 1990	Wave 2000	Gender Male	Gender Female	Age 16-29	Age 30-49	Age 50+	Education Lower	Education Middle	Education Upper	Income Lower	Income Middle	Income Upper	Values Mat	Values Mixed	Values Postm.
Albania	na	32	42	21	19	34	39	28	32	39	28	32	35	31	32	37
Algeria	na	52	56	48	48	56	53	42	48	64	49	56	52	45	57	61
Argentina	31	24	24	24	21	23	28	18	29	42	18	23	30	18	24	29
Armenia	na	50	60	42	43	55	54	49	48	57	47	52	52	47	56	27
Australia	na	50	51	49	36	52	60	40	46	62	48	50	55	44	48	55
Austria	35	41	46	37	36	41	44	35	43	60	38	39	47	29	38	52
Azerbaijan	na	37	44	31	36	37	39	32	33	47	34	40	40	30	49	57
Bangladesh	na	51	62	36	50	50	59	48	50	59	39	52	59	46	54	55
Belarus	37	30	38	23	29	30	29	20	32	38	26	29	37	27	32	48
Belgium	26	32	36	27	26	34	32	19	29	45	24	31	41	20	30	51
Bosnia and Herz.	na	36	43	29	29	35	44	32	34	45	37	35	38	32	37	33
Brazil	42	51	51	52	52	51	52	43	53	76	47	54	55	43	52	71
Bulgaria	46	31	34	29	27	35	31	23	33	42	27	37	33	25	38	44
Canada	48	41	41	40	29	41	47	37	36	53	36	38	47	32	38	48
Chile	31	31	36	26	30	33	29	21	34	41	24	35	36	27	30	39
China	59	68	72	63	70	65	72	64	70	67	68	68	65	68	70	75
Colombia	na	32	35	30	31	33	34	32	27	41	33	28	38	30	38	35
Croatia	na	29	37	23	24	28	35	23	31	41	24	24	37	29	29	32
Czech Republic	36	31	33	30	23	29	38	26	35	46	33	32	30	21	34	45
Denmark	43	42	43	40	33	41	47	34	44	55	41	40	50	25	41	60
Dominican Rep.	na	39	39	39	38	41	50	50	32	40	45	34	37	39	39	34
Egypt	na	50	55	45	47	49	56	43	53	65	46	50	56	46	54	56
El Salvador	na	38	42	35	44	34	34	29	43	55	30	37	50	na	na	na
Estonia	42	21	26	16	13	17	29	19	18	32	23	20	22	15	24	20
Finland	26	20	21	19	18	17	23	20	17	29	19	19	22	13	21	31
France	33	35	40	31	31	32	42	28	40	52	29	34	46	22	36	53
Georgia	na	47	51	43	34	50	56	38	47	52	50	46	43	46	47	53
Germany	57	39	44	36	35	40	41	28	45	70	28	38	44	33	40	49
Great Britain	43	34	38	31	28	32	41	28	34	54	25	34	38	na	na	na
Greece	na	36	43	32	33	36	43	36	32	41	30	40	41	38	35	45
Hungary	26	18	19	18	12	19	22	15	21	32	15	20	19	14	22	30
Iceland	26	36	34	38	33	36	39	32	34	49	35	33	42	27	37	48
India	40	40	50	26	41	40	40	32	44	52	36	37	46	43	45	38
Indonesia	na	39	47	31	52	37	36	28	40	47	33	42	42	37	41	62
Iran	na	44	47	41	49	45	30	30	43	59	40	44	49	31	51	59
Ireland	28	32	37	27	27	31	37	28	30	43	26	34	37	28	32	41
Israel	na	na	na	na	na	na	na	na	na	na	na	na	na	na	na	na
Italy	31	34	40	28	34	34	34	27	37	46	28	35	39	25	32	43
Japan	54	68	70	67	44	64	82	77	68	65	72	67	69	68	69	74
Jordan	na	47	46	48	48	50	40	34	55	63	37	51	56	40	51	66
Korea, South	71	51	52	51	44	52	58	53	52	50	53	47	53	50	53	54
Latvia	44	24	27	21	15	17	33	20	21	35	24	26	23	23	23	32
Lithuania	51	41	44	38	30	38	50	38	39	56	38	44	43	33	45	38
Luxembourg	na	41	43	40	32	44	44	30	44	54	40	42	46	35	42	50
Macedonia	na	36	42	31	26	38	43	36	35	41	35	34	42	38	37	37
Malta	na	38	42	34	25	36	48	42	37	31	41	36	38	37	38	36
Mexico	41	46	48	44	46	46	47	41	48	65	42	49	54	44	48	51
Moldova	na	36	40	32	28	41	37	28	34	48	33	38	40	31	42	46
Montenegro	na	28	37	19	22	29	31	23	31	33	32	24	32	26	30	41
Morocco	na	25	30	20	28	25	16	19	42	63	27	27	29	15	31	47
Netherlands	53	57	56	56	49	56	61	50	54	66	55	56	60	46	56	64
New Zealand	na	42	40	44	29	43	46	42	42	43	47	38	43	42	39	52
Nigeria	39	52	58	45	53	52	46	51	52	53	51	53	51	48	54	57
Northern Ireland	28	36	46	26	30	35	39	37	31	42	29	35	40	30	36	53
Norway	50	45	45	45	35	51	44	35	44	56	na	na	na	27	47	56
Pakistan	na	14	24	3	13	14	17	14	15	14	12	18	13	15	12	25
Peru	na	44	47	41	47	42	42	37	43	51	42	42	50	35	47	46
Philippines	na	55	57	53	60	52	54	57	53	55	54	52	61	54	56	57
Poland	42	30	32	29	27	28	35	28	30	39	29	32	31	25	32	45
Portugal	22	22	22	22	33	26	24	26	26	36	15	27	31	21	27	39
Puerto Rico	na	40	36	41	31	40	43	41	35	42	37	43	40	35	41	38
Romania	21	25	31	20	16	28	28	20	26	32	23	24	28	22	29	24
Russian Fed.	37	38	43	34	29	38	44	31	35	52	33	38	43	35	42	49
Serbia	na	25	30	20	24	25	25	18	26	31	21	23	33	19	30	31
Singapore	na	47	51	43	51	45	36	44	49	44	41	48	46	39	49	57
Slovakia	na	29	35	24	24	31	31	23	31	40	29	27	32	22	35	51
Slovenia	25	15	18	12	10	10	23	13	16	12	15	16	12	13	16	13
South Africa	59	50	55	45	47	55	46	51	50	40	55	53	43	46	54	55
Spain	22	22	25	19	18	25	22	18	22	35	17	23	29	18	21	32
Sweden	45	55	52	58	50	55	58	47	51	67	51	53	63	53	51	69
Switzerland	41	38	41	36	29	37	45	30	38	61	35	36	44	28	40	42
Taiwan	na	44	47	41	37	47	40	37	52	46	42	43	47	40	50	54
Tanzania	na	71	71	71	65	71	82	76	64	69	72	70	73	71	71	63
Turkey	28	40	43	38	41	40	38	35	45	58	34	42	54	36	40	51
Uganda	na	55	69	43	52	59	57	54	54	75	62	56	62	53	55	62
Ukraine	na	38	43	34	32	38	41	28	37	48	34	39	44	34	41	64
United States	52	57	56	57	52	53	66	53	53	61	55	59	58	60	56	60
Uruguay	na	36	39	34	32	38	37	30	43	52	31	34	45	29	38	41
Venezuela	na	34	37	32	36	31	38	29	36	38	34	29	38	35	34	36
Vietnam	na	78	83	74	68	80	83	75	82	88	79	72	85	73	85	80
Zimbabwe	na	42	43	41	41	43	42	46	36	15	53	38	36	40	41	59
Total	39	39	43	36	37	40	41	34	40	49	38	39	43	34	41	48

RANKING

Country	2000
Vietnam	78
Tanzania	71
Japan	68
China	68
United States	57
Netherlands	57
Uganda	55
Philippines	55
Sweden	55
Algeria	52
Nigeria	52
Brazil	51
Korea, South	51
Bangladesh	51
Armenia	50
South Africa	50
Egypt	50
Australia	50
Jordan	47
Singapore	47
Georgia	47
Mexico	46
Norway	45
Iran	44
Taiwan	44
Peru	44
New Zealand	42
Zimbabwe	42
Denmark	42
Austria	41
Luxembourg	41
Lithuania	41
Canada	41
India	40
Turkey	40
Puerto Rico	40
Germany	39
Dominican Rep.	39
Indonesia	39
Switzerland	38
Russian Fed.	38
El Salvador	38
Ukraine	38
Malta	38
Azerbaijan	37
Greece	36
Macedonia	36
Uruguay	36
Iceland	36
Moldova	36
Bosnia and Herz.	36
Northern Ireland	36
France	35
Venezuela	34
Great Britain	34
Italy	34
Colombia	32
Ireland	32
Belgium	32
Albania	32
Czech Republic	31
Bulgaria	31
Chile	31
Poland	30
Belarus	30
Croatia	29
Slovakia	29
Montenegro	28
Portugal	27
Romania	25
Morocco	25
Serbia	25
Argentina	24
Latvia	24
Spain	22
Estonia	21
Finland	20
Hungary	18
Slovenia	15
Pakistan	14
Total	39

A005) WORK IMPORTANT

For each of the following aspects, indicate how important it is in your life: work.

Very important (%)

(WVS: V8; EVS: V1)

Country	Wave 1990	Wave 2000	Gender Male	Gender Female	Age 16-29	Age 30-49	Age 50+	Education Lower	Education Middle	Education Upper	Income Lower	Income Middle	Income Upper	Values Mat	Values Mixed	Values Postm.	RANKING Country	2000
Albania	na	82	85	80	75	89	79	78	86	87	80	84	84	84	81	92	Tanzania	96
Algeria	na	93	95	91	92	94	92	92	93	93	91	95	92	93	93	93	El Salvador	95
Argentina	76	74	76	72	69	80	73	78	67	75	75	76	70	75	73	73	Philippines	93
Armenia	na	67	73	62	60	74	67	67	66	72	69	65	68	63	71	62	Algeria	93
Australia	na	51	55	47	51	55	48	53	51	51	49	52	55	48	53	50	Venezuela	93
Austria	62	66	68	64	61	67	67	67	65	63	66	69	65	74	68	60	Bangladesh	92
Azerbaijan	na	54	61	47	53	57	50	53	51	60	57	56	53	51	60	71	Zimbabwe	90
Bangladesh	na	92	93	91	89	93	96	93	91	91	93	91	93	94	89	92	Morocco	89
Belarus	55	49	49	48	48	55	42	37	53	54	45	53	43	47	52	61	Indonesia	89
Belgium	58	63	65	61	59	63	65	64	64	61	64	65	62	62	65	57	Nigeria	89
Bosnia and Herz.	na	75	79	71	76	83	63	56	78	80	70	75	79	74	75	72	Mexico	87
Brazil	82	84	86	83	85	85	80	82	86	84	85	85	83	82	85	89	Brazil	84
Bulgaria	57	62	63	60	58	68	58	58	62	68	55	66	65	62	64	48	Albania	82
Canada	59	52	55	49	48	58	49	57	53	47	55	55	50	59	52	51	South Africa	80
Chile	75	76	79	73	74	79	73	79	78	64	84	71	71	81	78	63	Iran	79
China	64	50	54	46	51	51	47	48	50	61	54	48	48	52	49	56	Uganda	79
Colombia	na	72	75	69	69	74	72	68	73	76	68	74	75	68	68	70	Poland	78
Croatia	na	48	52	45	45	52	46	47	48	51	40	50	54	58	47	47	India	78
Czech Republic	56	53	54	52	42	54	58	55	50	52	52	57	50	52	54	47	Macedonia	76
Denmark	51	40	45	34	39	37	43	38	42	42	42	36	44	39	41	38	Chile	76
Dominican Rep.	na	66	71	63	67	65	73	62	74	64	64	66	63	62	68	67	Malta	76
Egypt	na	72	88	55	70	75	70	67	76	78	72	74	73	69	74	77	Bosnia and Herz.	75
El Salvador	na	95	95	95	93	97	96	95	95	96	97	95	96	na	na	na	Turkey	75
Estonia	32	51	53	50	42	58	51	45	53	58	51	51	52	50	53	61	Puerto Rico	74
Finland	54	52	50	54	42	55	55	55	49	48	51	51	57	54	53	48	Argentina	74
France	61	69	69	69	69	65	73	74	68	57	71	71	64	77	70	54	Egypt	72
Georgia	na	58	65	53	49	69	55	58	56	67	60	60	56	60	57	57	Colombia	72
Germany	61	45	54	38	43	51	39	37	48	67	37	48	46	37	49	46	Uruguay	71
Great Britain	51	42	51	33	44	45	36	43	43	37	39	49	46	na	na	na	Romania	71
Greece	na	59	58	60	57	59	62	56	56	62	57	58	64	61	60	58	Latvia	70
Hungary	59	57	58	56	53	60	56	57	57	57	55	58	57	55	60	59	France	69
Iceland	56	54	58	50	39	56	65	57	50	56	55	53	57	53	55	51	Peru	69
India	86	78	81	73	79	80	73	74	83	81	76	79	78	81	79	84	Armenia	67
Indonesia	na	89	94	84	87	90	89	87	90	90	91	88	88	88	90	93	Austria	66
Iran	na	79	82	75	80	80	74	74	80	82	79	79	78	77	80	76	Dominican Rep.	66
Ireland	65	51	61	42	56	54	44	47	54	51	40	52	58	52	50	56	Jordan	65
Israel	na	na	na	na	na	na	na	na	na	na	na	na	na	na	na	na	Belgium	63
Italy	62	62	66	57	57	61	65	65	60	58	65	62	58	67	61	61	Korea, South	62
Japan	41	49	54	45	39	50	53	64	48	46	52	50	48	50	48	45	Ukraine	62
Jordan	na	65	86	45	70	63	59	61	64	75	63	69	68	61	70	68	Italy	62
Korea, South	69	62	66	58	61	63	63	55	62	64	64	61	62	61	64	63	Slovenia	62
Latvia	33	70	71	69	55	73	73	66	71	70	70	72	69	70	71	60	Bulgaria	62
Lithuania	42	54	57	52	58	66	40	32	61	67	47	47	66	53	56	51	Slovakia	62
Luxembourg	na	53	54	51	53	53	51	58	49	52	56	53	53	57	55	42	Pakistan	61
Macedonia	na	76	79	74	68	84	73	72	78	79	75	76	79	76	79	56	Spain	59
Malta	na	76	81	71	75	79	73	70	79	69	72	77	77	72	78	70	Greece	59
Mexico	67	87	90	84	83	90	86	87	86	89	82	90	88	89	86	89	Norway	59
Moldova	na	43	45	41	47	44	39	35	41	54	41	40	54	40	48	38	Russian Fed.	59
Montenegro	na	59	62	55	59	62	54	55	59	64	57	58	68	63	59	36	Montenegro	59
Morocco	na	89	94	85	92	89	83	88	94	91	88	92	89	89	91	91	Georgia	58
Netherlands	49	48	53	43	56	48	45	48	48	48	44	52	48	48	49	47	Portugal	58
New Zealand	na	45	50	41	35	46	48	50	46	38	47	42	48	51	45	40	Hungary	57
Nigeria	94	89	90	87	88	90	87	86	91	89	91	88	88	88	89	92	Vietnam	57
Northern Ireland	57	42	47	38	47	51	33	37	48	44	31	48	47	40	41	52	Serbia	55
Norway	73	59	62	56	54	61	60	56	60	60	na	na	na	55	60	60	Iceland	54
Pakistan	na	61	67	54	55	63	67	59	62	64	62	61	59	63	58	42	Sweden	54
Peru	na	69	71	66	66	70	72	75	66	69	70	68	67	70	69	67	Lithuania	54
Philippines	na	93	95	92	95	95	89	93	94	94	93	95	92	93	94	96	Azerbaijan	54
Poland	70	78	82	75	81	80	74	77	79	79	81	78	73	77	77	83	United States	54
Portugal	35	58	60	57	62	61	53	58	59	56	46	59	68	51	63	63	Czech Republic	53
Puerto Rico	na	74	78	73	72	79	71	73	71	76	70	75	77	69	76	73	Luxembourg	53
Romania	69	71	72	69	59	73	75	67	71	78	67	76	73	72	71	73	Singapore	53
Russian Fed.	46	59	61	56	57	71	45	37	60	65	52	61	63	58	60	74	Canada	52
Serbia	na	55	59	51	47	62	52	45	60	60	55	56	58	51	60	54	Finland	52
Singapore	na	53	60	46	43	63	57	57	54	37	60	56	46	53	52	56	Estonia	51
Slovakia	na	62	64	60	58	67	57	54	64	71	58	63	67	62	64	49	Australia	51
Slovenia	73	62	59	64	49	61	71	66	60	62	69	58	58	69	61	55	Ireland	51
South Africa	79	80	84	76	82	83	67	83	77	72	83	85	72	83	79	76	China	50
Spain	66	59	60	59	59	63	57	59	61	58	58	60	63	60	59	60	Japan	49
Sweden	67	54	51	58	54	56	53	47	54	61	51	56	57	58	55	51	Belarus	49
Switzerland	52	47	51	44	44	52	45	44	48	52	41	52	53	42	48	47	Croatia	48
Taiwan	na	45	51	38	37	51	35	45	42	46	45	47	45	46	46	41	Netherlands	48
Tanzania	na	96	95	96	96	97	94	95	97	98	94	97	98	97	96	100	Switzerland	47
Turkey	59	75	82	67	77	76	63	71	81	80	73	75	77	73	75	80	New Zealand	45
Uganda	na	79	82	75	76	86	66	80	78	79	84	80	89	76	81	76	Germany	45
Ukraine	na	62	66	59	63	76	48	31	66	67	57	63	67	57	66	76	Taiwan	45
United States	62	54	58	50	60	55	46	65	57	48	59	53	48	48	56	50	Moldova	43
Uruguay	na	71	70	72	64	75	71	71	71	73	69	72	73	69	72	67	Northern Ireland	42
Venezuela	na	93	94	91	93	94	91	91	94	91	90	92	94	93	93	92	Great Britain	42
Vietnam	na	57	61	53	60	59	51	54	61	60	57	49	65	48	65	60	Denmark	40
Zimbabwe	na	90	90	90	89	91	92	91	89	92	90	92	92	87	92	92		
Total	60	65	69	62	66	68	61	65	65	65	65	66	66	66	66	61	Total	65

A006) RELIGION IMPORTANT

For each of the following aspects, indicate how important it is in your life: religion.

Very important (%) (WVS: V9; EVS: V6)

Country	Wave 1990	Wave 2000	Male	Female	16-29	30-49	50+	Lower	Middle	Upper	Lower	Middle	Upper	Mat	Mixed	Postm.	RANKING Country	2000
Albania	na	20	24	32	23	24	38	35	24	21	30	27	27	29	26	32	Indonesia	98
Algeria	na	92	91	92	89	92	96	94	90	92	91	91	91	90	92	93	Egypt	97
Argentina	40	47	39	53	36	45	58	51	40	41	54	50	36	53	48	38	Jordan	96
Armenia	na	27	20	33	23	28	31	32	26	25	23	30	27	23	31	23	Morocco	94
Australia	na	23	19	28	16	22	31	27	21	23	29	23	16	23	25	19	Nigeria	93
Austria	25	20	16	24	7	17	30	23	16	21	28	20	17	22	20	20	Algeria	92
Azerbaijan	na	30	26	34	32	27	36	36	28	33	29	34	28	28	32	54	Bangladesh	88
Bangladesh	na	88	88	88	84	89	94	92	82	83	91	85	90	93	85	79	El Salvador	87
Belarus	12	12	7	17	7	8	22	21	9	7	16	12	6	14	10	7	Philippines	87
Belgium	15	18	14	22	11	11	27	25	16	17	28	20	9	17	18	18	Tanzania	85
Bosnia and Herz.	na	34	31	37	37	32	35	38	33	34	40	31	34	30	35	32	Pakistan	82
Brazil	57	65	60	69	59	68	69	65	65	61	70	65	59	67	65	58	Turkey	81
Bulgaria	12	17	12	21	15	13	21	22	13	14	23	15	12	14	18	15	Iran	80
Canada	31	30	22	38	19	28	40	39	28	27	37	32	22	31	33	24	Zimbabwe	78
Chile	51	47	40	53	41	44	55	56	42	41	55	40	43	50	48	36	Puerto Rico	76
China	1	3	2	4	2	4	1	2	3	5	3	2	3	2	3	na	Uganda	74
Colombia	na	49	43	55	43	50	59	53	50	42	51	53	43	48	47	47	South Africa	70
Croatia	na	26	18	33	20	24	32	31	23	23	33	27	21	31	27	15	Mexico	68
Czech Republic	11	7	6	8	5	3	12	8	6	9	9	6	5	8	7	10	Malta	66
Denmark	9	8	7	9	6	5	12	7	3	10	11	6	5	3	9	5	Brazil	65
Dominican Rep.	na	51	45	56	55	46	46	59	54	50	55	50	42	54	51	55	Venezuela	64
Egypt	na	97	97	98	97	97	99	97	98	99	98	96	98	97	97	98	United States	57
El Salvador	na	87	84	89	84	89	89	88	87	86	88	87	81	na	na	na	India	57
Estonia	5	6	4	7	3	3	9	8	5	4	9	6	4	5	5	na	Peru	53
Finland	15	14	11	17	7	9	21	15	11	16	18	14	10	12	14	17	Dominican Rep.	51
France	14	11	9	13	6	9	16	13	8	9	15	10	8	12	11	8	Romania	51
Georgia	na	49	42	56	57	50	40	51	47	56	51	47	49	47	50	63	Georgia	49
Germany	16	9	5	12	8	7	12	10	8	7	7	12	10	7	11	8	Colombia	49
Great Britain	16	13	10	15	9	9	19	10	13	16	11	13	11	na	na	na	Macedonia	48
Greece	na	33	28	36	25	34	48	60	40	22	42	29	29	37	33	26	Chile	47
Hungary	23	20	14	25	10	13	32	22	14	18	24	21	16	23	16	5	Argentina	47
Iceland	24	19	16	22	6	19	31	24	16	15	25	18	12	20	19	19	Poland	45
India	49	57	55	59	54	57	60	61	55	50	61	59	54	64	51	49	Singapore	36
Indonesia	na	98	98	98	98	98	98	98	98	99	98	98	99	98	98	100	Moldova	35
Iran	na	80	78	83	78	82	86	87	80	72	82	82	75	88	76	71	Bosnia and Herz.	34
Ireland	48	32	25	39	6	25	59	50	24	20	51	29	20	31	34	26	Italy	33
Israel	na	na	na	na	na	na	na	na	na	na	na	na	na	na	na	na	Greece	33
Italy	34	33	24	41	20	29	44	39	27	31	41	30	27	43	32	27	Ireland	32
Japan	6	7	6	9	1	8	10	10	8	4	9	7	7	7	7	9	Canada	30
Jordan	na	96	94	98	96	96	97	97	96	94	96	97	96	96	96	93	Azerbaijan	30
Korea, South	26	23	19	28	21	23	27	36	23	22	22	23	24	23	24	22	Serbia	29
Latvia	7	11	6	14	6	5	17	20	8	7	15	10	5	11	10	6	Northern Ireland	28
Lithuania	16	14	7	21	7	6	27	31	7	13	27	14	9	17	14	9	Portugal	27
Luxembourg	na	16	14	17	9	12	23	20	12	15	19	17	12	15	15	14	Slovakia	27
Macedonia	na	48	45	51	51	49	43	60	43	37	53	44	45	45	48	58	Armenia	27
Malta	na	66	58	74	44	65	82	82	61	53	75	68	53	73	64	53	Croatia	26
Mexico	34	68	60	75	59	70	77	75	60	57	70	67	61	70	67	62	Australia	23
Moldova	na	35	29	40	24	32	48	54	31	24	48	31	30	41	30	32	Korea, South	23
Montenegro	na	19	18	20	16	18	23	23	18	15	19	14	21	18	20	18	Uruguay	23
Morocco	na	94	93	96	93	95	98	96	91	85	97	94	91	97	93	88	Ukraine	22
Netherlands	19	17	14	19	10	11	26	20	14	16	22	16	11	23	15	17	Austria	20
New Zealand	na	19	16	22	19	15	23	19	20	19	24	20	12	23	18	15	Hungary	20
Nigeria	85	93	92	94	93	92	96	93	93	92	93	93	93	93	93	93	Montenegro	19
Northern Ireland	34	28	25	30	18	20	40	32	22	28	27	30	24	30	27	28	New Zealand	19
Norway	15	12	9	15	11	10	16	12	10	14	na	na	na	7	13	13	Iceland	19
Pakistan	na	82	79	85	78	85	81	88	76	71	87	81	76	85	77	75	Spain	19
Peru	na	53	48	57	46	56	60	57	54	47	53	53	50	55	52	51	Belgium	18
Philippines	na	87	85	89	88	86	88	90	87	84	88	87	85	87	87	87	Netherlands	17
Poland	53	45	38	51	45	37	54	51	40	29	51	41	37	51	42	42	Bulgaria	17
Portugal	17	27	21	33	13	24	38	33	16	14	43	27	21	31	27	13	Luxembourg	16
Puerto Rico	na	76	70	78	60	74	84	91	76	72	80	77	71	76	76	73	Switzerland	15
Romania	42	51	40	62	37	45	64	68	47	30	65	55	38	59	45	32	Lithuania	14
Russian Fed.	12	12	7	16	8	10	17	23	11	10	16	11	9	14	10	11	Finland	14
Serbia	na	29	26	32	28	26	33	34	27	28	38	29	24	31	28	24	Taiwan	13
Singapore	na	36	34	38	33	38	38	38	35	34	45	37	31	42	34	32	Great Britain	13
Slovakia	na	27	19	35	16	20	44	41	21	24	39	26	21	30	25	26	Slovenia	12
Slovenia	17	12	10	14	5	10	20	23	9	7	16	16	5	13	11	15	Belarus	12
South Africa	66	70	59	83	68	69	77	72	67	69	71	73	66	74	68	66	Norway	12
Spain	21	19	12	25	7	14	29	24	12	14	24	16	15	27	16	11	Russian Fed.	12
Sweden	10	11	8	14	9	9	14	11	9	14	13	10	8	14	10	11	France	11
Switzerland	24	15	12	18	9	13	20	21	13	16	22	17	9	20	15	10	Latvia	11
Taiwan	na	13	11	14	4	14	16	17	14	9	13	12	10	11	13	11	Sweden	11
Tanzania	na	85	82	89	85	85	84	87	85	80	85	87	81	86	87	92	Vietnam	10
Turkey	61	81	79	83	78	81	86	89	77	51	89	79	63	87	82	68	Germany	9
Uganda	na	74	69	78	71	75	82	70	76	66	78	60	80	71	72	86	Denmark	8
Ukraine	na	22	13	29	15	19	28	40	19	18	25	18	21	24	18	29	Czech Republic	7
United States	53	57	49	66	48	58	65	64	58	54	61	57	53	60	58	53	Japan	7
Uruguay	na	23	15	29	16	19	30	26	19	19	25	21	23	25	23	19	Estonia	6
Venezuela	na	64	60	68	59	66	70	67	64	61	63	65	62	63	65	61	China	3
Vietnam	na	10	8	12	8	11	10	14	6	3	9	7	13	8	11	4		
Zimbabwe	na	78	67	87	76	80	78	79	77	60	75	80	79	73	81	85		
Total	27	40	36	44	42	39	41	47	36	38	46	40	36	44	39	33	Total	40

A007) SERVICE TO OTHERS

For each of the following aspects, indicate how important it is in your life: service to others.

Very important (%) (WVS: V10)

Country	Wave 1990	Wave 2000	Gender Male	Gender Female	Age 16-29	Age 30-49	Age 50+	Education Lower	Education Middle	Education Upper	Income Lower	Income Middle	Income Upper	Values Mat	Values Mixed	Values Postm.
Albania	na	20	19	21	18	21	20	19	18	25	17	20	22	21	20	9
Algeria	na	45	46	43	47	42	45	41	46	47	49	41	39	46	44	43
Argentina	na	57	50	63	52	55	62	59	55	48	60	56	54	55	58	55
Armenia	na	na	na	na	na	na	na	na	na	na	na	na	na	na	na	na
Australia	na	na	na	na	na	na	na	na	na	na	na	na	na	na	na	na
Austria	na	na	na	na	na	na	na	na	na	na	na	na	na	na	na	na
Azerbaijan	na	na	na	na	na	na	na	na	na	na	na	na	na	na	na	na
Bangladesh	na	47	50	43	45	45	61	51	42	45	42	42	57	49	47	34
Belarus	na	na	na	na	na	na	na	na	na	na	na	na	na	na	na	na
Belgium	na	na	na	na	na	na	na	na	na	na	na	na	na	na	na	na
Bosnia and Herz.	na	18	17	18	14	16	23	18	16	21	20	17	15	14	19	21
Brazil	na	na	na	na	na	na	na	na	na	na	na	na	na	na	na	na
Bulgaria	na	na	na	na	na	na	na	na	na	na	na	na	na	na	na	na
Canada	na	42	38	47	37	42	46	47	42	39	48	44	37	38	44	41
Chile	na	53	49	58	53	52	57	56	49	60	60	46	54	49	58	48
China	na	16	14	17	16	17	11	17	14	21	16	15	15	15	14	19
Colombia	na	na	na	na	na	na	na	na	na	na	na	na	na	na	na	na
Croatia	na	na	na	na	na	na	na	na	na	na	na	na	na	na	na	na
Czech Republic	na	na	na	na	na	na	na	na	na	na	na	na	na	na	na	na
Denmark	na	na	na	na	na	na	na	na	na	na	na	na	na	na	na	na
Dominican Rep.	na	na	na	na	na	na	na	na	na	na	na	na	na	na	na	na
Egypt	na	62	60	64	60	63	63	60	63	66	63	65	63	63	63	60
El Salvador	na	na	na	na	na	na	na	na	na	na	na	na	na	na	na	na
Estonia	na	na	na	na	na	na	na	na	na	na	na	na	na	na	na	na
Finland	na	na	na	na	na	na	na	na	na	na	na	na	na	na	na	na
France	na	na	na	na	na	na	na	na	na	na	na	na	na	na	na	na
Georgia	na	na	na	na	na	na	na	na	na	na	na	na	na	na	na	na
Germany	na	na	na	na	na	na	na	na	na	na	na	na	na	na	na	na
Great Britain	na	na	na	na	na	na	na	na	na	na	na	na	na	na	na	na
Greece	na	na	na	na	na	na	na	na	na	na	na	na	na	na	na	na
Hungary	na	na	na	na	na	na	na	na	na	na	na	na	na	na	na	na
Iceland	na	na	na	na	na	na	na	na	na	na	na	na	na	na	na	na
India	na	47	48	44	46	47	45	44	49	49	44	48	47	50	45	53
Indonesia	na	36	40	33	38	41	31	30	34	45	32	41	36	35	39	52
Iran	na	62	60	65	58	65	69	63	62	58	63	64	59	67	59	58
Ireland	na	na	na	na	na	na	na	na	na	na	na	na	na	na	na	na
Israel	na	na	na	na	na	na	na	na	na	na	na	na	na	na	na	na
Italy	na	na	na	na	na	na	na	na	na	na	na	na	na	na	na	na
Japan	na	9	7	10	5	6	13	15	9	5	10	8	7	5	8	12
Jordan	na	67	64	70	60	73	70	69	68	63	68	66	69	71	66	67
Korea, South	na	11	10	12	8	11	14	18	12	9	12	12	9	9	12	15
Latvia	na	na	na	na	na	na	na	na	na	na	na	na	na	na	na	na
Lithuania	na	na	na	na	na	na	na	na	na	na	na	na	na	na	na	na
Luxembourg	na	na	na	na	na	na	na	na	na	na	na	na	na	na	na	na
Macedonia	na	16	17	12	11	14	19	16	15	12	18	11	16	13	16	15
Malta	na	na	na	na	na	na	na	na	na	na	na	na	na	na	na	na
Mexico	na	64	60	67	58	65	69	66	59	66	62	65	63	65	65	66
Moldova	na	32	30	34	32	30	36	35	33	28	34	31	35	32	34	28
Montenegro	na	13	13	14	12	11	16	12	13	15	11	9	15	14	13	12
Morocco	na	72	72	72	72	73	70	72	73	66	65	64	75	75	72	62
Netherlands	na	na	na	na	na	na	na	na	na	na	na	na	na	na	na	na
New Zealand	na	na	na	na	na	na	na	na	na	na	na	na	na	na	na	na
Nigeria	na	62	64	60	62	62	63	59	64	65	60	62	65	62	62	65
Northern Ireland	na	na	na	na	na	na	na	na	na	na	na	na	na	na	na	na
Norway	na	na	na	na	na	na	na	na	na	na	na	na	na	na	na	na
Pakistan	na	33	34	33	31	35	34	37	30	26	36	33	29	32	35	42
Peru	na	49	46	52	46	51	53	52	50	47	50	48	51	51	49	52
Philippines	na	58	60	55	52	59	63	56	57	60	55	56	62	56	58	65
Poland	na	na	na	na	na	na	na	na	na	na	na	na	na	na	na	na
Portugal	na	na	na	na	na	na	na	na	na	na	na	na	na	na	na	na
Puerto Rico	na	78	73	80	66	77	84	93	75	77	87	74	76	79	79	76
Romania	na	na	na	na	na	na	na	na	na	na	na	na	na	na	na	na
Russian Fed.	na	na	na	na	na	na	na	na	na	na	na	na	na	na	na	na
Serbia	na	38	36	39	33	39	40	35	40	39	42	41	36	33	42	53
Singapore	na	16	16	16	16	15	17	15	17	15	17	15	18	14	16	19
Slovakia	na	na	na	na	na	na	na	na	na	na	na	na	na	na	na	na
Slovenia	na	na	na	na	na	na	na	na	na	na	na	na	na	na	na	na
South Africa	na	49	45	54	53	48	46	44	56	67	42	55	52	49	51	47
Spain	na	30	27	34	25	28	35	32	28	27	34	26	31	36	28	25
Sweden	na	37	29	46	40	37	36	31	36	45	40	32	37	46	35	42
Switzerland	na	na	na	na	na	na	na	na	na	na	na	na	na	na	na	na
Taiwan	na	na	na	na	na	na	na	na	na	na	na	na	na	na	na	na
Tanzania	na	59	58	59	58	57	64	63	54	55	66	57	52	62	58	58
Turkey	na	na	na	na	na	na	na	na	na	na	na	na	na	na	na	na
Uganda	na	48	50	46	50	48	39	45	50	41	53	44	54	45	49	54
Ukraine	na	na	na	na	na	na	na	na	na	na	na	na	na	na	na	na
United States	na	51	43	60	42	52	59	54	51	51	54	53	46	48	51	52
Uruguay	na	na	na	na	na	na	na	na	na	na	na	na	na	na	na	na
Venezuela	na	68	64	72	64	69	73	69	66	69	67	65	70	62	69	74
Vietnam	na	16	17	15	15	16	17	13	20	19	22	16	13	14	18	17
Zimbabwe	na	62	59	65	67	63	50	61	64	92	60	64	67	61	62	76
Total	na	43	42	45	44	42	43	46	40	45	44	41	43	42	44	48

RANKING

Country	2000
Puerto Rico	78
Morocco	72
Venezuela	68
Jordan	67
Mexico	64
Iran	62
Zimbabwe	62
Nigeria	62
Egypt	62
Tanzania	59
Philippines	58
Argentina	57
Chile	53
United States	51
Peru	49
South Africa	49
Uganda	48
Bangladesh	47
India	47
Algeria	45
Canada	42
Serbia	38
Sweden	37
Indonesia	36
Pakistan	33
Moldova	32
Spain	30
Bosnia and Herz.	18
Vietnam	16
Singapore	16
China	16
Macedonia	15
Montenegro	13
Korea, South	11
Japan	9
Total	43

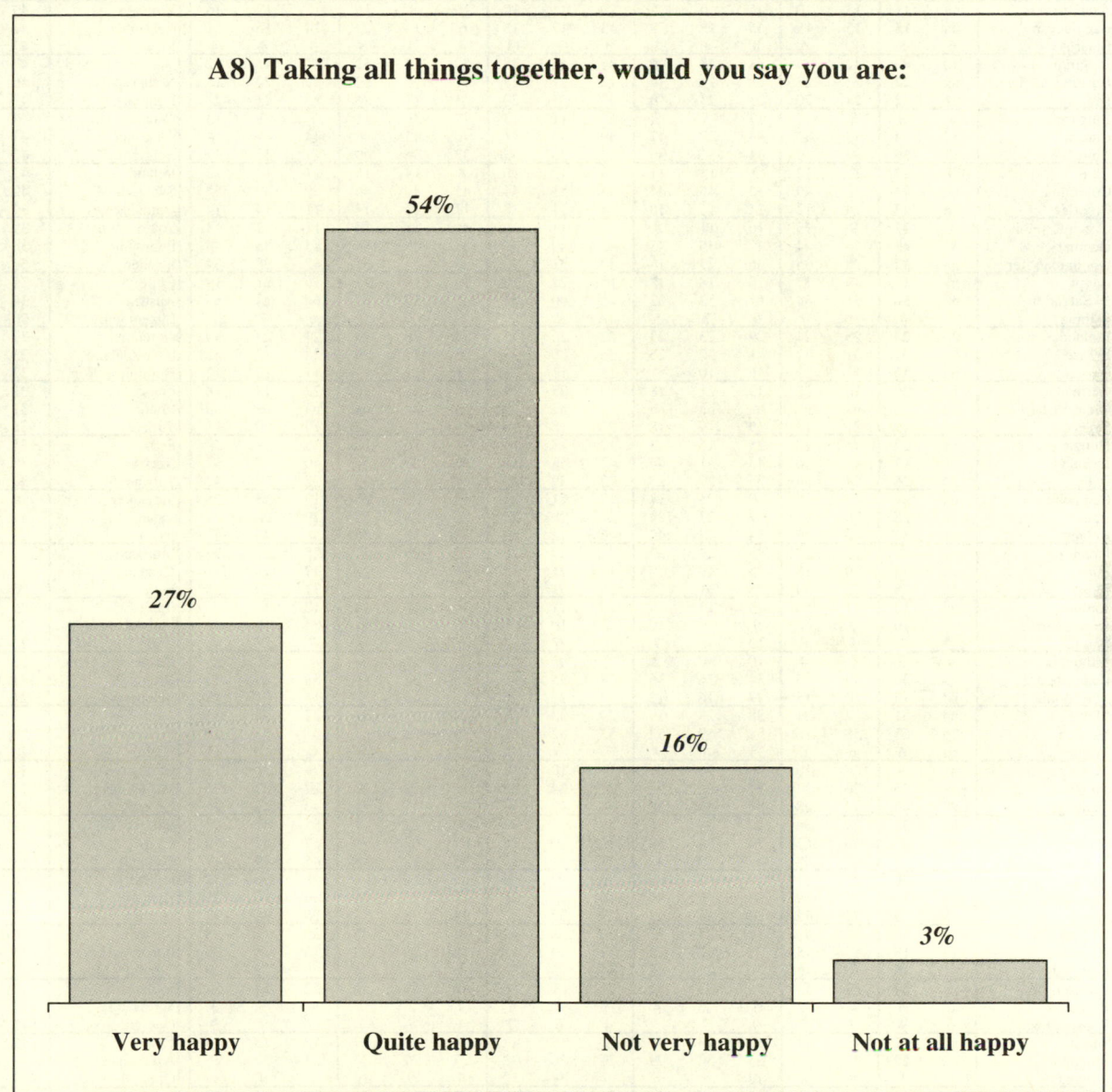

A8) Taking all things together, would you say you are:

27% — Very happy
54% — Quite happy
16% — Not very happy
3% — Not at all happy

A008) FEELING OF HAPPINESS

Taking all things together, would you say you are:

Very happy (%)

(WVS: V11)

Country	Wave 1990	Wave 2000	Gender Male	Gender Female	Age 16-29	Age 30-49	Age 50+	Education Lower	Education Middle	Education Upper	Income Lower	Income Middle	Income Upper	Values Mat	Values Mixed	Values Postm.
Albania	na	10	10	10	11	11	7	6	9	20	7	9	14	8	11	13
Algeria	na	17	14	19	16	18	15	14	18	18	15	15	21	18	15	23
Argentina	33	33	31	35	39	33	28	30	37	37	31	33	37	28	35	33
Armenia	na	6	6	6	6	7	5	5	6	9	7	4	9	7	6	4
Australia	na	43	40	46	43	44	42	41	47	40	38	44	45	46	44	41
Austria	30	36	35	37	45	36	31	36	37	34	29	32	44	33	37	34
Azerbaijan	na	11	13	10	15	10	7	20	11	10	10	9	16	11	12	16
Bangladesh	na	15	15	15	15	13	22	13	17	18	6	12	27	14	15	11
Belarus	6	5	4	6	8	4	4	3	7	5	4	6	8	4	8	4
Belgium	40	43	42	44	48	43	40	35	44	48	29	43	52	37	45	42
Bosnia and Herz.	na	22	22	22	28	21	17	17	21	28	17	20	32	22	22	15
Brazil	21	22	24	20	23	23	19	23	21	20	21	19	26	25	21	21
Bulgaria	7	8	8	8	17	7	5	2	11	13	4	9	11	7	9	13
Canada	30	44	43	46	43	42	47	49	43	41	40	45	46	44	44	44
Chile	33	36	34	39	44	32	36	33	36	43	33	36	40	41	35	32
China	28	12	11	12	9	13	11	12	12	5	8	14	15	11	11	13
Colombia	na	47	45	49	52	45	44	44	51	44	45	49	46	50	49	52
Croatia	na	13	14	12	21	11	10	14	11	18	11	14	14	11	14	14
Czech Republic	5	11	9	13	16	11	8	10	11	16	8	11	13	11	11	13
Denmark	43	45	46	44	47	46	43	45	40	48	37	49	55	43	46	46
Dominican Rep.	na	32	28	35	36	27	18	32	31	33	38	25	37	42	28	34
Egypt	na	18	19	17	18	18	18	15	22	20	16	18	21	16	21	19
El Salvador	na	56	58	54	61	53	52	51	60	63	45	57	67	na	na	na
Estonia	3	7	6	7	9	7	5	6	7	8	5	7	7	6	7	na
Finland	20	24	25	24	29	23	23	22	26	29	17	26	33	24	23	30
France	25	31	31	32	41	32	26	30	36	31	25	30	39	28	33	32
Georgia	na	12	11	12	16	10	9	13	11	13	9	12	14	11	12	12
Germany	14	20	16	22	19	21	18	13	23	29	15	21	26	22	19	18
Great Britain	38	na	na	na	na	na	na	na	na	na	na	na	na	na	na	na
Greece	na	19	21	18	19	19	18	25	18	19	19	13	24	19	20	15
Hungary	11	17	16	18	25	16	13	17	18	16	12	16	23	15	19	13
Iceland	41	47	44	50	43	51	44	43	48	52	33	50	57	50	47	37
India	24	26	27	24	25	27	23	22	29	30	24	19	33	23	33	42
Indonesia	na	21	18	24	19	25	17	17	21	24	17	23	25	19	23	25
Iran	na	25	20	31	27	23	24	24	28	23	20	24	31	29	25	22
Ireland	44	42	40	45	34	47	42	45	42	40	32	48	46	38	43	43
Israel	na	28	25	30	35	24	22	24	29	28	22	26	27	25	28	23
Italy	16	18	19	18	25	19	15	16	21	18	15	17	22	17	18	19
Japan	18	29	22	34	28	31	27	25	31	27	27	29	31	31	29	25
Jordan	na	13	11	15	13	13	14	12	11	16	14	10	16	12	14	5
Korea, South	10	10	9	10	9	10	10	7	10	9	8	9	11	9	10	9
Latvia	2	7	5	8	12	4	7	7	6	9	6	7	9	7	7	4
Lithuania	4	5	6	4	10	4	2	2	5	9	2	6	6	1	4	25
Luxembourg	na	36	39	33	34	36	36	34	35	39	36	37	39	38	35	40
Macedonia	na	10	20	18	27	16	17	13	22	25	12	20	29	18	21	18
Malta	na	31	32	31	38	28	29	29	33	30	28	35	34	25	34	33
Mexico	26	57	58	56	58	59	52	53	62	61	49	64	61	55	58	64
Moldova	na	6	6	6	11	4	4	5	6	7	4	5	9	6	7	11
Montenegro	na	9	7	10	8	10	8	7	10	10	5	8	12	8	9	13
Morocco	na	26	26	27	27	26	25	27	24	28	17	21	26	27	27	25
Netherlands	48	46	44	48	55	49	38	44	49	44	34	46	55	46	47	44
New Zealand	na	33	29	36	27	34	35	31	38	32	30	27	41	31	32	32
Nigeria	40	67	66	67	70	64	58	62	70	70	61	67	74	67	67	69
Northern Ireland	37	47	45	48	47	50	47	41	52	52	35	52	58	46	49	47
Norway	29	30	29	31	34	31	26	26	29	36	na	na	na	28	30	31
Pakistan	na	20	21	19	27	19	8	16	23	26	15	20	26	20	20	25
Peru	na	31	29	32	33	31	27	29	30	33	28	33	33	25	31	38
Philippines	na	38	37	40	45	37	32	35	38	42	30	38	47	35	41	38
Poland	10	18	18	18	27	17	13	17	20	13	12	20	23	16	18	25
Portugal	13	18	19	18	30	21	8	14	25	27	4	19	24	9	23	20
Puerto Rico	na	54	57	51	55	53	53	51	51	56	46	59	56	52	54	52
Romania	6	4	4	4	5	2	4	5	4	1	7	2	2	4	3	3
Russian Fed.	6	6	7	5	9	7	3	4	6	7	4	7	7	5	7	9
Serbia	na	12	13	11	12	13	12	9	15	12	9	11	17	12	13	16
Singapore	na	29	27	31	25	33	29	27	28	38	27	27	34	24	31	25
Slovakia	na	8	8	8	12	8	5	6	9	10	4	9	10	6	10	6
Slovenia	9	16	16	15	20	17	11	11	18	16	11	19	21	12	17	17
South Africa	24	39	35	43	39	36	45	35	43	37	31	37	49	39	40	25
Spain	20	20	21	19	23	20	18	19	22	21	16	20	21	21	20	18
Sweden	41	37	33	40	35	36	38	44	33	37	27	41	44	41	37	34
Switzerland	36	40	37	43	44	38	40	40	41	35	35	41	41	41	41	37
Taiwan	na	30	26	33	28	33	22	25	37	30	22	31	36	31	32	28
Tanzania	na	57	57	58	66	50	58	57	60	48	59	53	55	52	60	67
Turkey	29	31	26	36	30	31	32	34	27	27	31	31	31	32	32	27
Uganda	na	26	26	26	29	24	25	22	27	35	32	28	31	21	27	37
Ukraine	na	6	7	6	10	6	4	2	6	10	3	5	10	4	7	14
United States	41	39	37	42	38	36	44	42	36	41	35	41	43	37	39	40
Uruguay	na	21	17	24	24	20	20	20	22	21	16	19	28	19	21	19
Venezuela	na	57	57	57	59	55	56	50	58	62	49	56	64	52	59	57
Vietnam	na	49	49	50	46	53	47	47	54	43	42	50	52	52	51	49
Zimbabwe	na	20	18	22	25	16	15	18	24	10	17	21	24	19	20	27
Total	23	27	26	27	30	26	23	25	26	30	22	27	30	21	28	31

RANKING

Country	2000
Nigeria	67
Tanzania	57
Mexico	57
Venezuela	57
El Salvador	56
Puerto Rico	54
Vietnam	49
Colombia	47
Iceland	47
Northern Ireland	47
Netherlands	46
Denmark	45
Canada	44
Australia	43
Belgium	43
Ireland	42
Switzerland	40
United States	39
South Africa	39
Philippines	38
Sweden	37
Chile	36
Austria	36
Luxembourg	36
Argentina	33
New Zealand	33
Dominican Rep.	32
France	31
Malta	31
Turkey	31
Peru	31
Norway	30
Taiwan	30
Singapore	29
Japan	29
Israel	28
Morocco	26
Uganda	26
India	26
Iran	25
Finland	24
Brazil	22
Bosnia and Herz.	22
Uruguay	21
Indonesia	21
Zimbabwe	20
Pakistan	20
Spain	20
Germany	20
Macedonia	19
Greece	19
Italy	18
Egypt	18
Portugal	18
Poland	18
Hungary	17
Algeria	17
Slovenia	16
Bangladesh	15
Croatia	13
Jordan	13
Serbia	12
Georgia	12
China	12
Azerbaijan	11
Czech Republic	11
Korea, South	10
Montenegro	9
Slovakia	8
Bulgaria	8
Estonia	7
Latvia	7
Armenia	6
Moldova	6
Russian Fed.	6
Ukraine	6
Belarus	5
Lithuania	5
Romania	4
Total	27

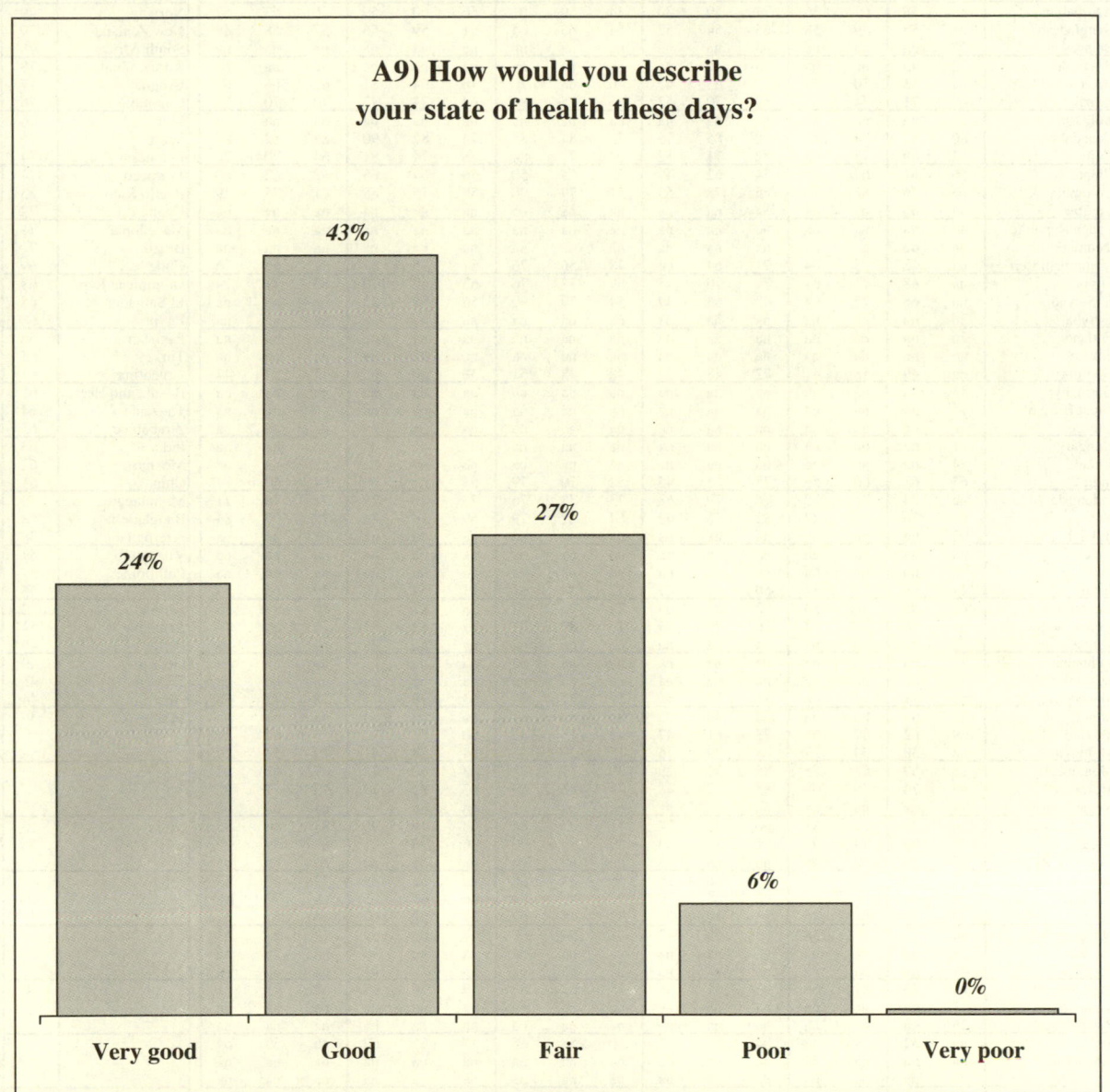

**A9) How would you describe
your state of health these days?**

43%

27%

24%

6%

0%

Very good   Good   Fair   Poor   Very poor

A009) STATE OF HEALTH

All in all, how would you describe your state of health these days? Would you say it is…

Very good / Good (%)

(WVS: V12)

Country	Wave 1990	Wave 2000	Gender Male	Gender Female	Age 16-29	Age 30-49	Age 50+	Education Lower	Education Middle	Education Upper	Income Lower	Income Middle	Income Upper	Values Mat	Values Mixed	Values Postm.
Albania	na	75	76	74	87	83	52	64	81	89	65	78	83	70	79	90
Algeria	na	44	45	42	47	48	28	33	45	50	37	45	51	39	48	45
Argentina	60	65	67	63	71	68	56	60	72	75	58	64	73	59	65	68
Armenia	na	51	54	48	70	45	28	39	51	53	62	44	39	51	49	66
Australia	na	80	79	80	83	85	70	70	81	87	70	82	89	76	80	80
Austria	62	na	na	na	na	na	na	na	na	na	na	na	na	na	na	na
Azerbaijan	na	58	61	56	71	59	30	34	59	61	56	60	59	56	63	57
Bangladesh	na	58	59	58	65	54	52	54	63	64	51	59	66	57	58	69
Belarus	27	na	na	na	na	na	na	na	na	na	na	na	na	na	na	na
Belgium	72	na	na	na	na	na	na	na	na	na	na	na	na	na	na	na
Bosnia and Herz.	na	65	70	59	82	65	47	46	68	70	46	64	81	62	66	62
Brazil	69	71	74	67	80	70	52	63	75	80	64	71	77	70	70	75
Bulgaria	51	na	na	na	na	na	na	na	na	na	na	na	na	na	na	na
Canada	80	82	84	80	90	85	75	75	84	86	74	82	90	83	82	83
Chile	54	69	73	65	82	71	52	52	77	84	58	74	81	64	70	76
China	56	61	63	60	74	62	49	58	65	50	56	64	65	62	62	69
Colombia	na	76	81	70	85	78	53	51	79	90	58	75	88	71	75	79
Croatia	na	na	na	na	na	na	na	na	na	na	na	na	na	na	na	na
Czech Republic	44	na	na	na	na	na	na	na	na	na	na	na	na	na	na	na
Denmark	78	na	na	na	na	na	na	na	na	na	na	na	na	na	na	na
Dominican Rep.	na	68	75	64	71	64	64	48	56	76	57	75	87	61	68	76
Egypt	na	68	71	64	79	70	45	59	77	76	63	67	70	63	71	74
El Salvador	na	68	72	64	83	63	49	54	79	90	56	68	85	na	na	na
Estonia	36	na	na	na	na	na	na	na	na	na	na	na	na	na	na	na
Finland	76	na	na	na	na	na	na	na	na	na	na	na	na	na	na	na
France	66	na	na	na	na	na	na	na	na	na	na	na	na	na	na	na
Georgia	na	49	58	41	72	48	24	48	48	51	38	50	62	45	53	44
Germany	55	na	na	na	na	na	na	na	na	na	na	na	na	na	na	na
Great Britain	75	na	na	na	na	na	na	na	na	na	na	na	na	na	na	na
Greece	na	na	na	na	na	na	na	na	na	na	na	na	na	na	na	na
Hungary	31	na	na	na	na	na	na	na	na	na	na	na	na	na	na	na
Iceland	74	na	na	na	na	na	na	na	na	na	na	na	na	na	na	na
India	63	63	66	59	75	65	45	52	70	79	54	61	69	64	67	71
Indonesia	na	74	77	72	76	79	68	73	73	76	73	76	73	71	76	71
Iran	na	76	75	77	82	73	62	64	82	79	69	76	83	75	77	84
Ireland	82	na	na	na	na	na	na	na	na	na	na	na	na	na	na	na
Israel	na	na	na	na	na	na	na	na	na	na	na	na	na	na	na	na
Italy	55	na	na	na	na	na	na	na	na	na	na	na	na	na	na	na
Japan	44	55	55	54	60	61	47	52	54	61	51	54	60	59	55	54
Jordan	na	83	84	83	92	85	63	74	90	94	78	83	91	80	88	80
Korea, South	na	78	78	77	76	79	75	43	80	78	71	82	81	76	80	74
Latvia	32	na	na	na	na	na	na	na	na	na	na	na	na	na	na	na
Lithuania	43	na	na	na	na	na	na	na	na	na	na	na	na	na	na	na
Luxembourg	na	na	na	na	na	na	na	na	na	na	na	na	na	na	na	na
Macedonia	na	71	74	68	85	74	56	59	77	77	63	76	77	72	73	68
Malta	na	na	na	na	na	na	na	na	na	na	na	na	na	na	na	na
Mexico	69	62	67	56	73	61	47	49	75	84	50	70	71	57	64	74
Moldova	na	30	34	27	48	29	15	18	29	43	24	28	41	29	33	29
Montenegro	na	59	63	55	85	71	29	39	71	78	43	60	72	49	67	82
Morocco	na	74	79	68	85	72	48	71	85	84	63	81	77	72	77	82
Netherlands	74	na	na	na	na	na	na	na	na	na	na	na	na	na	na	na
New Zealand	na	79	77	81	86	81	74	71	83	86	68	79	90	83	80	83
Nigeria	78	90	88	91	91	89	83	89	89	90	86	93	91	89	89	93
Northern Ireland	77	na	na	na	na	na	na	na	na	na	na	na	na	na	na	na
Norway	75	79	81	77	87	86	66	66	83	88	na	na	na	75	80	83
Pakistan	na	66	66	67	92	65	20	52	83	84	46	67	85	64	70	100
Peru	na	49	54	45	55	49	37	33	45	67	37	52	67	44	51	52
Philippines	na	57	57	58	63	58	47	51	54	69	47	63	59	57	58	54
Poland	38	na	na	na	na	na	na	na	na	na	na	na	na	na	na	na
Portugal	44	na	na	na	na	na	na	na	na	na	na	na	na	na	na	na
Puerto Rico	na	73	81	68	93	81	58	45	62	83	59	76	85	62	75	71
Romania	47	na	na	na	na	na	na	na	na	na	na	na	na	na	na	na
Russian Fed.	26	na	na	na	na	na	na	na	na	na	na	na	na	na	na	na
Serbia	na	52	59	46	84	58	32	36	58	65	37	51	62	46	59	64
Singapore	na	na	na	na	na	na	na	na	na	na	na	na	na	na	na	na
Slovakia	na	na	na	na	na	na	na	na	na	na	na	na	na	na	na	na
Slovenia	43	na	na	na	na	na	na	na	na	na	na	na	na	na	na	na
South Africa	68	78	83	72	82	81	60	72	85	94	73	76	86	78	79	77
Spain	57	76	80	72	94	84	57	67	87	88	52	80	83	67	78	86
Sweden	80	na	na	na	na	na	na	na	na	na	na	na	na	na	na	na
Switzerland	81	85	85	85	94	91	73	76	88	85	72	89	92	82	84	91
Taiwan	na	48	52	43	60	51	32	36	49	57	43	51	53	48	49	62
Tanzania	na	64	64	64	65	68	52	58	68	77	59	64	73	63	64	79
Turkey	60	65	68	62	73	65	49	61	71	67	63	66	72	63	65	70
Uganda	na	72	75	70	75	72	57	59	76	89	69	77	84	69	74	73
Ukraine	na	na	na	na	na	na	na	na	na	na	na	na	na	na	na	na
United States	79	84	86	82	84	87	80	81	82	86	77	88	91	85	84	83
Uruguay	na	77	82	73	93	83	65	70	85	91	66	84	84	63	78	85
Venezuela	na	na	na	na	na	na	na	na	na	na	na	na	na	na	na	na
Vietnam	na	57	62	53	74	62	38	54	61	66	52	56	62	61	58	56
Zimbabwe	na	63	65	62	74	60	44	56	73	60	57	59	75	60	66	66
Total	59	67	70	64	77	69	52	58	69	75	58	68	74	62	69	74

RANKING

Country	2000
Nigeria	90
Switzerland	85
United States	84
Jordan	83
Canada	82
Australia	80
Norway	79
New Zealand	79
South Africa	78
Korea, South	78
Uruguay	77
Colombia	76
Iran	76
Spain	76
Indonesia	74
Morocco	74
Puerto Rico	73
Uganda	72
Macedonia	71
Brazil	71
Chile	69
Dominican Rep.	68
El Salvador	68
Egypt	68
Pakistan	66
Turkey	65
Argentina	65
Bosnia and Herz.	65
Tanzania	64
Zimbabwe	63
India	63
Mexico	62
China	61
Montenegro	59
Bangladesh	58
Azerbaijan	58
Vietnam	57
Philippines	57
Japan	55
Serbia	52
Armenia	51
Peru	49
Georgia	49
Taiwan	48
Algeria	44
Moldova	30
Total	67

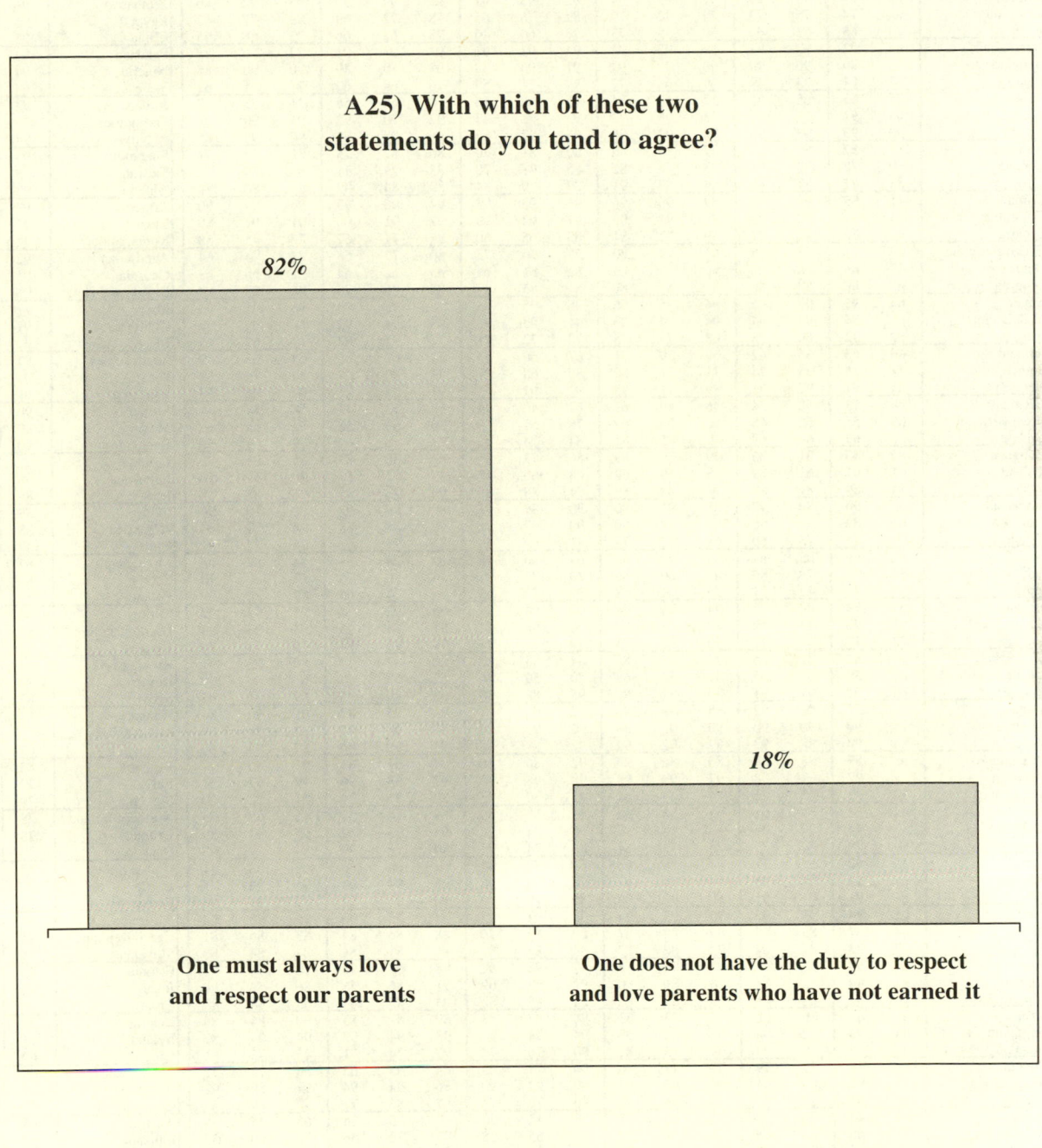

A25) With which of these two statements do you tend to agree?

82%

18%

**One must always love
and respect our parents**

**One does not have the duty to respect
and love parents who have not earned it**

A025) RESPECT PARENTS

With which of these two statements do you tend to agree? A. Regardless of what the qualities and faults of one's parents are,

One must always love and respect them (%)

(WVS: V13; EVS: V162)

Country	Wave 1990	Wave 2000	Gender Male	Female	Age 16-29	30-49	50+	Education Lower	Middle	Upper	Income Lower	Middle	Upper	Values Mat	Mixed	Postm.
Albania	na	87	86	88	84	88	88	84	88	89	85	85	91	88	86	87
Algeria	na	93	92	94	93	91	97	95	93	92	93	94	91	93	93	91
Argentina	75	88	88	88	83	89	92	90	86	79	91	88	85	93	90	81
Armenia	na	93	95	91	91	93	94	95	93	91	92	94	92	95	92	80
Australia	na	74	75	73	72	72	79	82	76	65	78	72	69	83	77	67
Austria	75	65	61	69	60	59	73	73	60	46	73	68	60	72	68	55
Azerbaijan	na	92	92	91	89	93	94	94	92	91	91	93	91	92	90	88
Bangladesh	na	90	90	90	90	90	92	91	90	88	93	89	89	90	90	85
Belarus	83	71	73	69	69	68	77	77	71	59	76	69	67	73	71	62
Belgium	77	65	65	65	57	60	74	75	66	56	72	68	58	71	65	58
Bosnia and Herz.	na	91	91	91	88	93	92	93	92	87	92	90	92	94	90	93
Brazil	90	93	93	93	92	92	96	95	92	87	96	95	89	96	93	85
Bulgaria	83	82	81	83	77	80	86	90	81	70	86	82	75	86	78	71
Canada	69	78	77	78	73	76	82	85	78	70	83	79	71	84	80	71
Chile	88	87	87	87	84	87	91	87	89	84	89	84	89	89	86	86
China	75	95	95	94	89	96	96	96	93	93	94	96	93	94	94	90
Colombia	na	91	90	92	91	91	93	91	92	90	92	91	90	91	91	89
Croatia	na	72	72	71	59	71	81	83	65	60	81	71	67	72	75	58
Czech Republic	67	74	73	75	63	73	80	77	70	73	80	73	68	77	74	64
Denmark	47	na	na	na	na	na	na	na	na	na	na	na	na	na	na	na
Dominican Rep.	na	86	82	88	85	87	82	81	85	87	87	86	78	86	87	83
Egypt	na	95	95	95	94	95	96	95	95	95	95	96	96	96	95	93
El Salvador	na	94	93	94	94	94	93	94	93	93	93	94	93	na	na	na
Estonia	62	72	69	75	68	71	75	72	72	71	77	72	67	77	69	65
Finland	40	63	65	62	59	59	71	67	60	55	63	62	65	63	65	59
France	77	75	75	74	71	71	80	80	68	67	77	80	69	84	76	58
Georgia	na	91	92	91	89	91	95	92	91	92	91	91	91	92	91	93
Germany	76	53	52	54	46	49	61	62	46	44	60	53	45	58	54	44
Great Britain	68	65	65	65	66	60	69	78	57	60	70	63	56			
Greece	na	69	69	69	59	75	81	84	74	63	73	68	69	79	69	58
Hungary	81	81	81	85	79	79	89	86	73	81	87	80	83	85	81	72
Iceland	61	61	63	59	55	59	68	68	60	48	55	67	57	70	59	50
India	84	89	89	89	90	88	89	91	88	85	90	93	85	91	85	88
Indonesia	na	90	88	92	88	91	90	90	89	92	89	89	93	90	90	96
Iran	na	89	89	90	89	89	90	90	87	91	90	88	88	94	87	84
Ireland	78	71	73	69	68	67	78	81	69	59	80	71	63	76	72	57
Israel	na	na	na	na	na	na	na	na	na	na	na	na	na	na	na	na
Italy	84	79	79	80	67	80	86	86	75	71	86	80	76	88	80	72
Japan	79	72	72	71	55	71	78	81	72	65	76	74	66	72	70	69
Jordan	na	94	93	95	94	94	94	96	94	90	96	92	94	95	93	92
Korea, South	94	92	93	92	87	93	97	96	93	91	91	94	93	93	93	84
Latvia	72	77	78	77	72	82	75	79	77	76	78	79	74	75	79	74
Lithuania	80	83	81	85	79	83	85	84	83	82	82	87	79	80	83	91
Luxembourg	na	59	63	55	52	54	69	70	56	46	62	63	45	67	60	40
Macedonia	na	91	91	91	89	89	96	95	89	89	92	89	93	89	92	92
Malta	na	91	91	92	85	90	96	97	90	81	93	95	87	95	90	84
Mexico	78	90	90	90	90	91	89	90	91	87	90	91	91	92	91	89
Moldova	na	90	88	93	87	92	92	92	91	88	93	90	89	89	92	85
Montenegro	na	87	85	89	80	86	93	92	86	80	94	91	81	91	86	77
Morocco	na	97	97	98	97	98	98	98	96	94	97	98	96	99	97	91
Netherlands	38	32	33	31	24	27	41	45	30	21	39	31	24	51	32	20
New Zealand	na	62	64	61	62	56	68	69	62	55	69	64	52	65	60	55
Nigeria	87	94	94	95	93	95	97	96	94	94	95	95	92	95	94	89
Northern Ireland	80	78	79	77	75	73	84	84	74	71	80	78	79	87	79	62
Norway	45	52	53	51	44	48	63	61	53	42	na	na	na	60	52	41
Pakistan	na	94	94	95	94	94	97	95	93	96	95	94	94	95	94	100
Peru	na	91	91	91	89	92	90	89	90	93	90	91	92	89	91	94
Philippines	na	94	92	95	95	93	94	92	94	95	94	95	92	95	93	92
Poland	84	87	85	88	82	88	87	89	87	76	88	86	84	88	86	81
Portugal	77	83	81	84	79	80	87	83	83	82	86	81	84	84	84	80
Puerto Rico	na	98	98	97	95	96	100	97	98	97	98	98	96	98	97	97
Romania	83	84	82	85	76	81	90	92	83	69	91	86	78	86	82	68
Russian Fed.	76	84	84	85	79	85	86	84	85	82	84	85	84	85	84	83
Serbia	na	87	86	88	81	83	93	90	87	83	89	87	85	90	84	88
Singapore	na	93	92	94	94	93	93	94	94	91	93	94	93	94	94	87
Slovakia	na	74	70	77	64	73	82	80	70	74	75	74	71	75	73	61
Slovenia	82	78	77	79	72	75	86	90	77	63	84	85	65	86	77	72
South Africa	87	91	91	91	90	92	88	90	92	90	86	94	94	93	89	92
Spain	80	83	82	85	74	81	91	90	78	73	87	86	77	89	86	68
Sweden	51	44	50	38	33	43	51	59	43	33	49	45	36	65	45	35
Switzerland	70	66	68	65	58	64	75	76	65	55	73	72	56	70	69	57
Taiwan	na	93	91	95	91	94	94	94	90	94	93	95	91	93	93	94
Tanzania	na	91	90	91	91	89	95	90	92	90	90	90	93	91	91	96
Turkey	83	86	85	87	83	87	89	92	81	69	91	85	74	89	87	78
Uganda	na	90	91	89	90	90	89	85	91	96	85	94	93	94	91	75
Ukraine	na	86	84	87	84	83	90	93	85	85	88	83	84	85	87	89
United States	75	77	77	78	77	78	77	82	81	73	80	79	74	81	79	72
Uruguay	na	78	75	80	69	75	84	82	74	65	79	78	78	84	77	74
Venezuela	na	94	93	95	93	95	94	94	95	93	95	92	95	94	94	93
Vietnam	na	99	99	99	100	99	99	99	100	100	99	99	100	100	99	100
Zimbabwe	na	96	97	96	95	97	98	96	97	100	97	96	97	98	95	99
Total	74	82	82	82	81	82	84	86	81	77	85	83	80	87	81	71

RANKING

Country	2000
Vietnam	99
Puerto Rico	98
Morocco	97
Zimbabwe	96
Egypt	95
China	95
Pakistan	94
Nigeria	94
Venezuela	94
Jordan	94
Philippines	94
El Salvador	94
Singapore	93
Taiwan	93
Algeria	93
Armenia	93
Brazil	93
Korea, South	92
Azerbaijan	92
Georgia	91
Bosnia and Herz.	91
Malta	91
Colombia	91
Macedonia	91
South Africa	91
Peru	91
Tanzania	91
Moldova	90
Mexico	90
Bangladesh	90
Uganda	90
Indonesia	90
Iran	89
India	89
Argentina	88
Chile	87
Montenegro	87
Serbia	87
Poland	87
Turkey	86
Dominican Rep.	86
Ukraine	86
Russian Fed.	84
Romania	84
Spain	83
Hungary	83
Lithuania	83
Portugal	83
Bulgaria	82
Italy	79
Slovenia	78
Northern Ireland	78
Uruguay	78
Canada	78
United States	77
Latvia	77
France	75
Australia	74
Czech Republic	74
Slovakia	74
Estonia	72
Japan	72
Croatia	72
Belarus	71
Ireland	71
Greece	69
Switzerland	66
Belgium	65
Great Britain	65
Austria	65
Finland	63
New Zealand	62
Iceland	61
Luxembourg	59
Germany	53
Norway	52
Sweden	44
Netherlands	32
Total	82

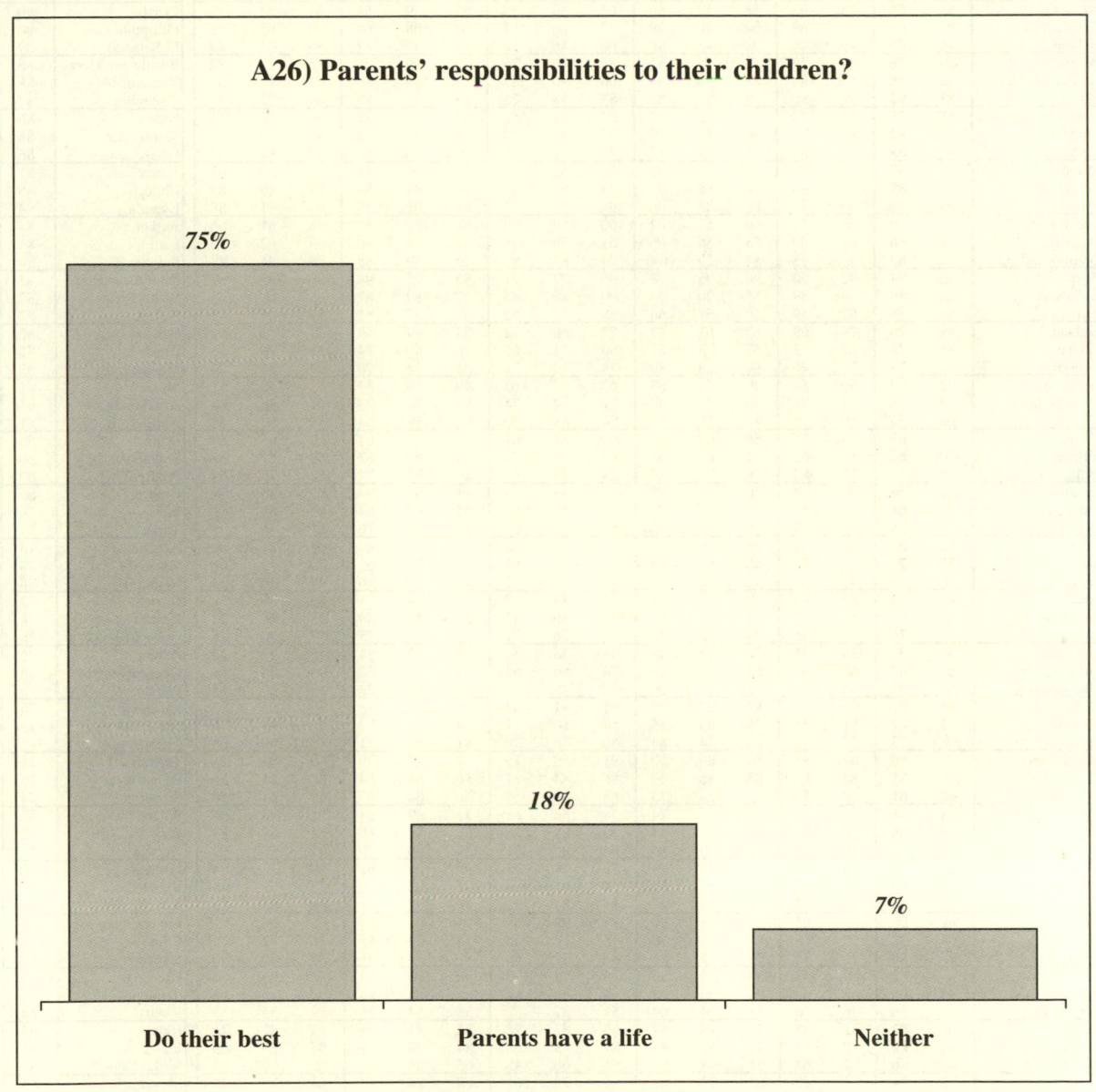

A26) Parents' responsibilities to their children?

75%

18%

7%

Do their best   Parents have a life   Neither

A026) PARENTS RESPONSIBILITIES

Which of the following statements best describes your views about parents' responsibilities to their children?

Do their best for their children even at the expense of their own well-being (%)

(WVS: V14; EVS: V163)

Country	Wave 1990	Wave 2000	Gender Male	Gender Female	Age 16-29	Age 30-49	Age 50+	Education Lower	Education Middle	Education Upper	Income Lower	Income Middle	Income Upper	Values Mat	Values Mixed	Values Postm.	RANKING Country	2000
Albania	na	76	75	76	68	76	82	75	76	74	75	76	76	79	74	69	Egypt	94
Algeria	na	78	79	78	74	80	84	78	80	77	80	79	72	79	78	74	Pakistan	93
Argentina	79	81	81	80	75	82	84	84	74	80	85	80	77	85	82	73	Puerto Rico	92
Armenia	na	64	63	66	55	67	75	66	65	61	63	66	67	68	62	57	Malta	91
Australia	na	75	75	75	73	76	77	81	75	70	77	75	74	76	77	72	Zimbabwe	91
Austria	61	71	72	69	68	67	76	75	68	61	81	76	61	78	71	66	Venezuela	91
Azerbaijan	na	59	55	63	58	59	60	63	59	58	65	59	56	64	53	39	Croatia	90
Bangladesh	na	68	69	68	64	70	79	72	66	61	69	68	69	74	65	52	Philippines	90
Belarus	46	49	49	48	39	45	60	60	46	38	53	47	44	55	46	29	El Salvador	89
Belgium	64	78	77	79	75	75	81	83	76	76	79	79	76	85	77	72	Bosnia and Herz.	88
Bosnia and Herz.	na	88	87	89	88	88	89	90	90	83	88	89	86	91	88	83	Vietnam	88
Brazil	81	82	83	80	74	86	89	87	78	75	83	83	80	84	82	78	Colombia	87
Bulgaria	58	75	72	77	63	72	82	87	72	58	83	68	72	80	70	45	Nigeria	86
Canada	67	82	84	80	86	83	79	83	83	79	85	81	82	85	84	77	Montenegro	86
Chile	80	85	85	86	86	84	87	88	85	80	89	80	86	87	84	87	United States	86
China	61	67	61	74	47	70	79	78	62	33	71	69	61	71	60	63	Morocco	85
Colombia	na	87	88	86	84	88	91	88	89	84	86	89	85	84	89	85	Chile	85
Croatia	na	90	90	91	86	88	96	93	90	83	92	91	90	95	91	88	Uganda	84
Czech Republic	41	60	60	59	59	57	62	60	59	60	68	59	55	58	61	66	Jordan	84
Denmark	52	60	61	60	58	56	65	61	56	59	63	58	60	63	62	55	Peru	84
Dominican Rep.	na	83	83	83	84	79	100	94	83	82	85	79	85	86	81	88	Indonesia	84
Egypt	na	94	92	96	90	95	98	96	92	91	95	95	94	96	93	87	Dominican Rep.	83
El Salvador	na	89	89	89	85	90	93	90	89	86	90	89	87	na	na	na	South Africa	82
Estonia	55	58	57	59	58	51	66	58	61	52	57	59	61	57	61	49	Serbia	82
Finland	49	70	70	69	67	67	73	72	66	72	74	69	69	73	71	61	Canada	82
France	81	75	77	73	67	73	81	80	71	66	76	80	73	82	76	66	Brazil	82
Georgia	na	76	75	76	69	78	80	79	76	71	81	74	70	77	75	76	Macedonia	82
Germany	72	59	59	58	49	55	67	62	54	62	59	59	57	65	58	51	Mexico	81
Great Britain	74	76	74	78	70	71	83	78	74	74	83	76	73	na	na	na	Argentina	81
Greece	na	57	59	55	44	60	79	73	61	50	61	58	54	58	57	52	Northern Ireland	81
Hungary	62	65	66	65	56	63	73	67	62	61	63	66	64	67	65	54	Spain	80
Iceland	50	64	67	61	62	66	63	63	65	64	61	67	63	59	67	57	Singapore	80
India	78	79	77	82	78	78	83	84	79	67	84	84	72	84	74	64	Portugal	80
Indonesia	na	84	84	84	76	85	87	87	83	84	81	85	89	82	86	78	Uruguay	80
Iran	na	61	63	59	57	61	73	73	56	54	65	60	61	63	60	51	India	79
Ireland	73	76	75	77	69	74	86	82	76	67	85	75	70	81	75	73	Turkey	79
Israel	na	na	na	na	na	na	na	na	na	na	na	na	na	na	na	na	Algeria	78
Italy	79	72	72	72	56	67	83	79	67	61	77	72	65	79	72	68	Tanzania	78
Japan	40	40	42	39	32	39	45	44	41	37	42	40	40	47	40	34	Belgium	78
Jordan	na	84	85	83	79	87	88	86	84	79	87	84	81	82	86	78	Norway	77
Korea, South	38	51	55	47	32	54	65	71	56	41	55	47	49	55	50	24	Ireland	76
Latvia	51	76	77	75	70	73	81	79	76	71	76	78	75	77	76	78	Great Britain	76
Lithuania	38	39	38	41	32	35	48	44	38	34	45	42	34	46	37	23	Latvia	76
Luxembourg	na	68	68	68	64	63	75	74	66	61	74	68	62	75	68	59	Georgia	76
Macedonia	na	82	83	81	77	81	86	90	79	73	88	80	73	76	84	85	Albania	76
Malta	na	91	91	92	87	92	93	95	91	83	95	92	88	95	91	83	Moldova	75
Mexico	74	81	81	81	76	83	85	84	80	71	82	82	77	83	81	76	Australia	75
Moldova	na	75	75	76	69	74	83	80	76	70	81	76	71	71	80	65	France	75
Montenegro	na	86	84	88	80	86	90	91	83	79	92	87	79	89	83	76	Taiwan	75
Morocco	na	85	84	87	83	86	92	86	84	81	86	83	84	86	85	76	Bulgaria	75
Netherlands	62	61	69	54	53	54	73	68	59	57	66	64	53	69	61	58	Slovenia	74
New Zealand	na	68	70	67	60	66	74	74	66	61	71	69	64	74	68	64	Poland	72
Nigeria	89	86	86	87	87	85	87	83	88	88	83	88	89	88	86	83	Italy	72
Northern Ireland	82	81	80	81	73	79	85	84	80	71	86	80	70	91	80	69	Austria	71
Norway	73	77	78	76	74	78	78	76	79	75	na	na	na	79	77	74	Finland	70
Pakistan	na	93	92	95	93	93	96	94	92	94	93	92	94	93	93	100	Bangladesh	68
Peru	na	84	84	84	80	86	87	87	84	82	88	82	79	82	85	85	New Zealand	68
Philippines	na	90	88	92	88	91	90	88	92	89	91	91	87	90	90	91	Luxembourg	68
Poland	63	72	76	68	62	71	78	78	67	58	74	72	65	70	72	71	China	67
Portugal	84	80	76	83	73	77	86	83	77	60	87	75	78	86	76	70	Sweden	67
Puerto Rico	na	92	89	93	89	92	93	90	92	92	90	94	92	91	93	90	Hungary	65
Romania	85	na	na	na	na	na	na	na	na	na	na	na	na	na	na	na	Armenia	64
Russian Fed.	51	56	56	56	48	54	64	59	57	52	58	54	56	59	53	58	Iceland	64
Serbia	na	82	82	83	77	79	87	86	82	78	84	81	81	85	81	71	Ukraine	63
Singapore	na	80	79	81	77	83	85	89	78	68	84	79	78	83	80	69	Iran	61
Slovakia	na	60	57	63	55	58	67	65	60	48	63	61	60	62	60	39	Netherlands	61
Slovenia	72	74	76	72	63	73	82	82	73	61	80	74	64	84	72	71	Slovakia	60
South Africa	88	82	80	85	83	81	83	83	81	76	82	88	77	80	85	78	Denmark	60
Spain	75	80	79	82	68	78	91	88	74	68	87	80	75	89	80	68	Czech Republic	60
Sweden	63	67	71	64	75	66	64	65	69	67	69	66	68	68	67	67	Azerbaijan	59
Switzerland	69	59	59	59	49	57	67	67	56	61	57	63	55	65	61	48	Switzerland	59
Taiwan	na	75	75	76	50	79	82	83	79	65	84	77	66	77	72	78	Germany	59
Tanzania	na	78	79	76	74	79	82	79	75	80	75	79	80	81	77	71	Estonia	58
Turkey	67	79	78	80	75	80	85	85	75	61	85	78	66	82	79	71	Greece	57
Uganda	na	84	84	84	83	87	82	79	86	90	78	85	93	86	87	70	Russian Fed.	56
Ukraine	na	63	62	63	54	60	69	70	64	55	67	61	61	62	63	63	Korea, South	51
United States	75	86	86	85	91	83	84	82	89	85	87	85	87	87	85	86	Belarus	49
Uruguay	na	80	78	81	75	77	84	83	77	68	83	79	77	86	80	74	Japan	40
Venezuela	na	91	91	90	89	92	93	93	93	83	94	92	89	87	92	92	Lithuania	39
Vietnam	na	88	86	89	80	88	93	89	87	81	86	89	86	87	88	76		
Zimbabwe	na	91	92	90	92	92	87	90	93	100	90	91	94	92	90	93		
Total	65	75	75	75	71	74	79	80	73	70	77	75	72	77	74	70	Total	75

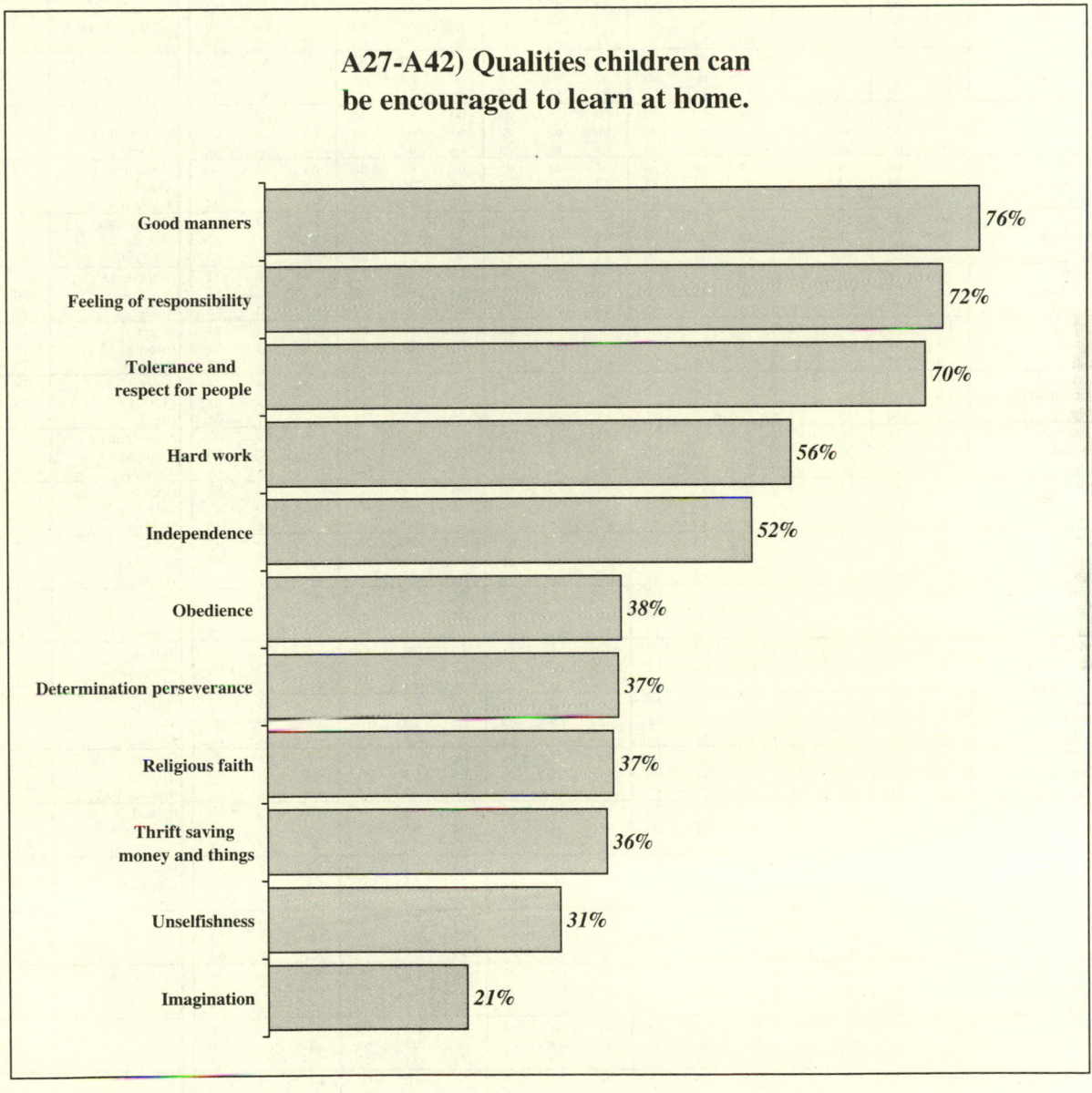

A27-A42) Qualities children can be encouraged to learn at home.

Quality	Percent
Good manners	76%
Feeling of responsibility	72%
Tolerance and respect for people	70%
Hard work	56%
Independence	52%
Obedience	38%
Determination perseverance	37%
Religious faith	37%
Thrift saving money and things	36%
Unselfishness	31%
Imagination	21%

A027_1) CHILD QUALITIES: GOOD MANNERS

Here is a list of qualities which children can be encouraged to learn at home.

Which, if any, do you consider to be especially important?

Good manners (%)

(WVS: IV15; EVS: V164)

Country	Wave		Gender		Age			Education			Income			Values		
	1990	2000	Male	Female	16-29	30-49	50+	Lower	Middle	Upper	Lower	Middle	Upper	Mat	Mixed	Postm.
Albania	na	na	na	na	na	na	na	na	na	na	na	na	na	na	na	na
Algeria	na	83	83	83	81	84	85	82	84	82	83	86	81	84	82	80
Argentina	78	83	83	83	82	81	85	89	76	69	90	83	75	88	85	73
Armenia	na	76	71	80	74	77	79	74	78	72	77	75	79	79	73	75
Australia	na	80	81	80	80	78	84	90	84	68	86	80	73	91	84	73
Austria	78	78	78	78	76	76	81	86	72	64	77	79	78	89	83	66
Azerbaijan	na	53	49	57	56	51	52	38	50	62	44	47	67	53	53	53
Bangladesh	na	na	na	na	na	na	na	na	na	na	na	na	na	na	na	na
Belarus	71	60	53	66	67	62	53	51	63	67	60	59	65	58	66	59
Belgium	72	78	77	79	79	76	79	87	81	67	83	80	73	88	81	58
Bosnia and Herz.	na	na	na	na	na	na	na	na	na	na	na	na	na	na	na	na
Brazil	77	52	56	49	57	51	47	52	56	40	56	52	51	55	53	45
Bulgaria	72	69	69	70	72	69	69	66	73	67	66	77	68	69	72	52
Canada	75	na	na	na	na	na	na	na	na	na	na	na	na	na	na	na
Chile	90	na	na	na	na	na	na	na	na	na	na	na	na	na	na	na
China	53	na	na	na	na	na	na	na	na	na	na	na	na	na	na	na
Colombia	na	84	84	85	85	83	87	87	88	72	88	86	77	88	85	84
Croatia	na	97	97	97	95	98	97	99	96	95	98	97	97	99	97	94
Czech Republic	86	87	86	87	83	87	89	89	86	83	89	87	85	89	87	79
Denmark	66	72	71	74	71	67	79	84	61	54	75	74	61	84	76	47
Dominican Rep.	na	85	84	85	84	87	55	94	90	81	90	81	80	88	84	80
Egypt	na	78	79	77	78	77	79	78	79	78	78	81	77	79	78	71
El Salvador	na	82	83	82	82	82	82	82	85	78	83	84	80	na	na	na
Estonia	74	78	76	80	78	77	80	83	78	73	80	78	77	80	77	84
Finland	82	90	88	92	80	90	95	93	87	82	90	89	89	91	91	84
France	53	69	69	69	70	65	71	75	64	57	72	72	60	79	69	51
Georgia	na	61	57	65	62	63	58	61	60	65	59	60	67	64	59	67
Germany	67	64	64	63	51	61	72	69	59	58	66	65	62	73	64	44
Great Britain	89	92	90	94	87	94	93	94	92	87	94	91	94	na	na	na
Greece	na	76	75	77	75	76	81	87	79	72	75	78	75	81	77	65
Hungary	77	71	74	69	71	67	76	73	71	64	77	68	71	74	69	80
Iceland	90	74	76	73	75	70	80	82	76	56	76	78	67	81	76	50
India	94	na	na	na	na	na	na	na	na	na	na	na	na	na	na	na
Indonesia	na	85	86	86	79	85	89	94	85	80	86	84	83	87	84	86
Iran	na	89	89	89	88	89	91	91	90	84	89	87	90	91	89	83
Ireland	75	87	86	89	92	83	89	92	88	78	89	90	82	92	86	86
Israel	na	77	79	75	74	75	82	88	77	68	83	78	69	78	76	81
Italy	79	75	75	74	76	70	79	83	73	56	80	77	67	86	76	67
Japan	83	na	na	na	na	na	na	na	na	na	na	na	na	na	na	na
Jordan	na	95	96	94	93	96	97	98	91	95	96	96	94	97	94	94
Korea, South	93	na	na	na	na	na	na	na	na	na	na	na	na	na	na	na
Latvia	53	72	71	72	68	67	77	81	71	60	76	71	68	73	71	64
Lithuania	35	34	29	38	42	37	24	27	34	41	29	24	44	36	32	38
Luxembourg	na	83	86	81	85	81	85	93	82	68	87	82	75	89	87	64
Macedonia	na	na	na	na	na	na	na	na	na	na	na	na	na	na	na	na
Malta	na	82	79	84	82	80	83	81	84	73	86	77	77	85	81	72
Mexico	73	na	na	na	na	na	na	na	na	na	na	na	na	na	na	na
Moldova	na	na	na	na	na	na	na	na	na	na	na	na	na	na	na	na
Montenegro	na	na	na	na	na	na	na	na	na	na	na	na	na	na	na	na
Morocco	na	91	89	92	89	91	94	91	91	91	93	93	88	94	88	80
Netherlands	80	81	78	83	83	76	85	94	81	67	83	82	75	92	84	66
New Zealand	na	77	77	76	76	77	76	83	78	68	77	80	74	79	78	69
Nigeria	97	95	95	94	95	95	90	95	95	93	94	95	96	95	95	93
Northern Ireland	95	89	89	89	91	88	89	89	91	84	92	92	84	90	88	88
Norway	77	75	72	77	73	72	80	83	76	65	na	na	na	84	78	47
Pakistan	na	67	65	69	55	71	80	76	59	51	73	66	62	69	64	83
Peru	na	na	na	na	na	na	na	na	na	na	na	na	na	na	na	na
Philippines	na	na	na	na	na	na	na	na	na	na	na	na	na	na	na	na
Poland	na	58	60	56	66	56	54	57	58	58	53	63	58	58	58	51
Portugal	82	77	76	77	72	77	79	79	76	63	75	78	76	80	77	63
Puerto Rico	na	na	na	na	na	na	na	na	na	na	na	na	na	na	na	na
Romania	92	80	79	81	85	84	74	67	86	91	68	81	88	80	83	76
Russian Fed.	57	58	57	59	65	60	53	51	58	62	56	61	59	59	58	62
Serbia	na	na	na	na	na	na	na	na	na	na	na	na	na	na	na	na
Singapore	na	na	na	na	na	na	na	na	na	na	na	na	na	na	na	na
Slovakia	na	73	70	75	65	74	77	74	73	67	72	74	72	76	70	67
Slovenia	89	78	77	78	76	74	83	91	77	56	88	76	65	84	77	70
South Africa	81	na	na	na	na	na	na	na	na	na	na	na	na	na	na	na
Spain	80	86	85	88	84	84	90	90	85	81	90	85	83	92	88	76
Sweden	78	70	70	71	69	66	75	84	72	57	73	71	64	83	77	47
Switzerland	59	66	67	66	67	62	72	80	65	48	68	68	63	77	69	56
Taiwan	na	70	67	72	73	70	68	63	69	76	68	68	77	71	69	70
Tanzania	na	na	na	na	na	na	na	na	na	na	na	na	na	na	na	na
Turkey	92	93	93	93	91	94	98	97	91	78	97	94	83	94	94	90
Uganda	na	na	na	na	na	na	na	na	na	na	na	na	na	na	na	na
Ukraine	na	56	52	59	58	57	54	47	56	60	53	57	58	57	58	45
United States	76	na	na	na	na	na	na	na	na	na	na	na	na	na	na	na
Uruguay	na	81	81	81	74	78	86	88	75	55	86	78	77	87	86	64
Venezuela	na	na	na	na	na	na	na	na	na	na	na	na	na	na	na	na
Vietnam	na	na	na	na	na	na	na	na	na	na	na	na	na	na	na	na
Zimbabwe	na	na	na	na	na	na	na	na	na	na	na	na	na	na	na	na
Total	76	76	75	76	76	75	77	80	74	71	77	76	74	76	77	67

RANKING

Country	2000
Croatia	97
Jordan	95
Nigeria	95
Turkey	93
Great Britain	92
Morocco	91
Finland	90
Northern Ireland	89
Iran	89
Ireland	87
Czech Republic	87
Spain	86
Indonesia	85
Dominican Rep.	85
Colombia	84
Luxembourg	83
Algeria	83
Argentina	83
El Salvador	82
Malta	82
Uruguay	81
Netherlands	81
Australia	80
Romania	80
Egypt	78
Estonia	78
Belgium	78
Austria	78
Slovenia	78
Israel	77
New Zealand	77
Portugal	77
Armenia	76
Greece	76
Italy	75
Norway	75
Iceland	74
Slovakia	73
Denmark	72
Latvia	72
Hungary	71
Sweden	70
Taiwan	70
Bulgaria	69
France	69
Pakistan	67
Switzerland	66
Germany	64
Georgia	61
Belarus	60
Russian Fed.	58
Poland	58
Ukraine	56
Azerbaijan	53
Brazil	52
Lithuania	34
Total	76

A029) CHILD QUALITIES: INDEPENDENCE

Here is a list of qualities that children can be encouraged to learn at home.

Which, if any, do you consider to be especially important?

Independence (%)

(WVS: V15; EVS: V165)

Country	Wave 1990	Wave 2000	Gender Male	Gender Female	Age 16-29	Age 30-49	Age 50+	Education Lower	Education Middle	Education Upper	Income Lower	Income Middle	Income Upper	Values Mat	Values Mixed	Values Postm.
Albania	na	57	59	56	67	55	52	49	62	65	57	60	55	53	61	69
Algeria	na	26	27	24	24	29	24	24	24	29	27	22	29	25	25	30
Argentina	43	36	31	41	39	37	33	29	43	62	28	33	50	27	33	50
Armenia	na	32	37	27	36	34	23	28	30	40	37	31	25	26	36	44
Australia	na	53	47	59	53	57	48	46	52	60	46	55	59	33	52	59
Austria	63	71	66	74	83	74	60	63	76	81	58	70	77	54	68	82
Azerbaijan	na	60	62	58	63	59	54	50	59	62	60	62	57	60	60	65
Bangladesh	na	78	81	74	75	80	81	75	80	82	76	78	79	77	79	72
Belarus	31	32	39	25	39	34	23	24	35	34	27	32	38	27	35	54
Belgium	36	41	42	40	45	45	35	28	41	50	34	38	48	33	39	54
Bosnia and Herz.	na	56	58	55	61	58	50	47	55	69	51	56	61	53	58	53
Brazil	27	20	18	22	21	19	18	16	20	32	16	18	26	15	19	39
Bulgaria	62	42	48	37	49	52	31	34	45	53	33	46	47	35	48	67
Canada	44	62	60	64	59	68	58	55	64	66	58	60	69	50	62	68
Chile	31	53	54	52	58	57	42	46	57	58	49	54	56	54	50	60
China	84	74	77	71	78	77	63	61	84	88	66	75	87	78	77	91
Colombia	na	27	26	28	26	29	25	18	25	45	19	25	40	21	26	31
Croatia	na	85	85	86	90	89	79	83	86	89	86	83	88	81	85	92
Czech Republic	21	69	70	68	68	74	66	67	70	73	66	68	74	61	71	74
Denmark	81	81	76	85	78	83	80	77	83	91	78	80	92	75	81	91
Dominican Rep.	na	40	36	42	39	43	36	9	32	46	34	42	47	34	38	52
Egypt	na	73	72	73	76	72	69	69	77	75	72	73	73	70	74	76
El Salvador	na	36	36	35	36	38	32	30	38	47	31	37	47	na	na	na
Estonia	43	22	21	22	28	24	17	17	22	29	18	14	27	16	26	39
Finland	57	58	56	59	61	64	50	53	65	62	53	62	61	57	57	62
France	27	29	29	29	36	36	20	21	41	41	26	30	35	13	29	53
Georgia	na	51	54	48	56	52	44	47	50	57	46	52	58	50	51	64
Germany	67	70	70	71	83	74	62	62	78	77	62	68	77	63	72	80
Great Britain	43	53	52	55	58	59	43	47	57	56	45	60	62	na	na	na
Greece	na	58	55	61	64	60	39	39	50	69	51	56	65	52	57	69
Hungary	70	71	72	70	73	79	62	66	77	84	67	72	73	66	75	76
Iceland	89	76	72	80	82	81	66	71	77	86	73	75	82	73	77	86
India	30	56	59	53	60	56	53	51	58	65	48	54	62	49	64	84
Indonesia	na	76	73	80	75	78	76	75	77	78	77	76	78	76	77	71
Iran	na	53	53	53	59	49	45	43	54	64	51	49	58	45	57	66
Ireland	43	51	51	50	49	59	42	46	51	56	45	50	57	49	50	52
Israel	na	69	67	70	67	72	67	64	66	76	60	66	81	74	68	70
Italy	31	41	41	41	49	48	31	32	45	56	36	40	46	35	39	49
Japan	65	82	83	81	79	84	81	74	82	85	81	82	83	83	81	91
Jordan	na	22	26	19	23	22	20	19	24	28	19	24	25	21	23	31
Korea, South	54	77	78	77	76	79	74	68	77	79	77	79	76	77	78	74
Latvia	73	51	51	51	51	58	45	33	54	64	46	47	57	48	51	70
Lithuania	81	77	79	75	81	83	68	62	82	83	74	79	82	74	79	85
Luxembourg	na	49	47	51	56	53	40	42	51	54	46	44	58	49	45	62
Macedonia	na	59	57	60	59	62	53	43	64	74	50	59	71	56	61	56
Malta	na	31	33	28	37	33	24	23	33	37	23	31	39	26	32	40
Mexico	47	42	39	45	45	45	33	38	44	60	39	44	52	39	44	55
Moldova	na	56	60	52	59	58	51	47	56	65	50	60	61	51	61	66
Montenegro	na	59	62	56	66	63	51	47	64	75	52	61	65	57	61	66
Morocco	na	34	37	32	39	34	22	32	41	47	36	38	40	30	38	48
Netherlands	51	53	50	57	57	57	48	45	50	65	53	54	57	52	48	70
New Zealand	na	54	47	59	49	60	50	51	51	59	44	54	63	54	51	64
Nigeria	16	26	28	23	26	26	24	24	26	28	26	25	28	22	27	41
Northern Ireland	37	51	47	54	52	53	48	48	52	58	53	46	56	47	50	58
Norway	86	89	85	92	89	93	83	84	89	93	na	na	na	84	89	94
Pakistan	na	13	16	9	21	11	1	4	18	33	4	13	22	11	15	8
Peru	na	39	37	40	39	40	33	33	40	41	36	38	45	33	40	38
Philippines	na	66	66	65	61	67	69	68	65	64	70	64	64	66	66	65
Poland	na	22	25	20	22	24	21	22	22	26	21	22	27	18	25	22
Portugal	24	22	25	20	31	21	18	18	29	44	22	20	29	13	28	31
Puerto Rico	na	51	51	52	61	56	43	48	42	57	45	52	55	54	49	58
Romania	24	30	33	27	40	36	19	18	36	37	20	29	37	26	33	49
Russian Fed.	29	31	36	26	40	32	24	21	30	39	27	26	38	27	33	60
Serbia	na	61	59	63	71	67	51	46	64	79	52	63	70	52	68	85
Singapore	na	75	74	76	75	77	69	76	74	73	72	76	74	75	74	80
Slovakia	na	61	64	59	67	64	53	50	66	70	54	61	66	60	63	70
Slovenia	33	70	69	71	73	75	63	65	72	76	67	72	71	73	70	74
South Africa	16	63	65	60	67	62	52	57	68	80	54	68	68	59	65	66
Spain	37	39	42	37	49	45	29	32	43	55	29	41	46	28	41	53
Sweden	36	69	60	77	66	75	65	58	69	77	65	65	78	55	66	82
Switzerland	42	42	41	44	54	44	35	33	44	47	40	41	45	35	39	60
Taiwan	na	66	67	65	79	69	50	52	64	81	58	66	77	64	71	68
Tanzania	na	42	45	38	43	41	44	39	45	49	40	39	53	37	46	42
Turkey	19	71	71	71	67	73	77	73	68	66	76	70	63	77	70	67
Uganda	na	31	30	33	29	34	29	30	32	26	29	29	29	35	30	28
Ukraine	na	32	37	28	41	32	27	20	30	43	28	33	36	27	38	41
United States	52	61	57	66	62	63	58	65	60	60	62	60	60	66	60	63
Uruguay	na	49	48	50	51	60	40	38	61	76	36	54	58	36	48	68
Venezuela	na	45	45	45	46	45	42	35	44	58	39	48	47	46	45	42
Vietnam	na	56	59	53	49	57	60	56	55	69	48	56	62	59	56	62
Zimbabwe	na	26	29	24	29	25	21	22	32	18	25	25	28	25	27	27
Total	47	52	52	51	53	55	46	45	53	60	47	51	57	46	53	62

RANKING

Country	2000
Norway	89
Croatia	85
Japan	82
Denmark	81
Bangladesh	78
Korea, South	77
Lithuania	77
Iceland	76
Indonesia	76
Singapore	75
China	74
Egypt	73
Turkey	71
Hungary	71
Austria	71
Germany	70
Slovenia	70
Czech Republic	69
Sweden	69
Israel	69
Taiwan	66
Philippines	66
South Africa	63
Canada	62
Slovakia	61
United States	61
Serbia	61
Azerbaijan	60
Montenegro	59
Macedonia	59
Greece	58
Finland	58
Albania	57
Bosnia and Herz.	56
India	56
Vietnam	56
Moldova	56
New Zealand	54
Netherlands	53
Great Britain	53
Iran	53
Australia	53
Chile	53
Puerto Rico	51
Latvia	51
Georgia	51
Northern Ireland	51
Ireland	51
Uruguay	49
Luxembourg	49
Venezuela	45
Switzerland	42
Mexico	42
Bulgaria	42
Tanzania	42
Italy	41
Belgium	41
Dominican Rep.	40
Spain	39
Peru	39
Argentina	36
El Salvador	36
Morocco	34
Armenia	32
Ukraine	32
Belarus	32
Uganda	31
Russian Fed.	31
Malta	31
Romania	30
France	29
Colombia	27
Zimbabwe	26
Nigeria	26
Algeria	26
Portugal	22
Jordan	22
Poland	22
Estonia	22
Brazil	20
Pakistan	13
Total	52

A030) CHILD QUALITIES: HARD WORK

Here is a list of qualities that children can be encouraged to learn at home.

Which, if any, do you consider to be especially important?

Hard work (%)

(WVS: V16; EVS: V166)

Country	Wave		Gender		Age			Education			Income			Values		
	1990	2000	Male	Female	16-29	30-49	50+	Lower	Middle	Upper	Lower	Middle	Upper	Mat	Mixed	Postm
Albania	na	64	63	64	54	65	70	72	61	50	65	64	62	67	61	51
Algeria	na	67	69	65	68	69	62	59	69	70	68	70	65	66	69	67
Argentina	53	57	58	56	50	54	66	63	46	52	67	54	50	67	55	52
Armenia	na	84	85	82	80	86	85	83	84	82	82	88	83	87	81	79
Australia	na	36	42	30	34	34	40	42	35	34	34	37	36	38	38	31
Austria	14	10	12	8	8	9	12	12	9	5	15	8	10	15	10	7
Azerbaijan	na	77	76	79	73	78	84	78	76	79	76	75	77	78	76	68
Bangladesh	na	59	62	56	55	63	55	61	54	60	55	65	54	58	61	53
Belarus	80	92	91	93	86	92	96	96	90	91	94	91	90	92	93	88
Belgium	36	38	39	37	36	33	43	48	36	33	44	39	30	42	37	30
Bosnia and Herz.	na	54	55	53	47	53	62	61	56	42	59	52	55	55	53	45
Brazil	52	47	49	46	45	46	55	58	41	34	55	47	41	53	48	33
Bulgaria	91	86	84	88	74	84	94	94	84	77	93	85	80	88	84	83
Canada	35	53	61	45	53	50	55	55	51	54	48	51	57	55	53	50
Chile	12	26	27	25	19	23	36	33	22	20	25	24	30	31	26	17
China	65	86	86	85	81	89	82	84	87	88	83	88	89	90	86	88
Colombia	na	18	20	16	18	17	19	23	13	18	19	16	18	24	20	18
Croatia	na	95	95	95	92	95	97	98	93	91	98	94	94	97	95	94
Czech Republic	85	73	73	73	59	72	82	76	71	73	79	74	68	80	73	62
Denmark	2	2	3	1	2	2	2	3	3	1	2	2	1	1	2	1
Dominican Rep.	na	50	51	49	49	51	55	56	52	48	48	46	52	49	50	53
Egypt	na	38	44	33	36	40	41	39	38	39	38	39	37	35	41	40
El Salvador	na	38	38	39	35	38	44	47	29	27	50	35	30	na	na	na
Estonia	92	82	79	85	65	82	92	85	81	80	86	88	77	86	82	52
Finland	6	12	14	10	11	8	16	14	9	10	12	15	11	20	9	8
France	53	50	54	47	41	46	59	57	42	41	52	52	44	59	52	35
Georgia	na	82	81	83	72	85	89	86	80	84	83	79	82	84	80	77
Germany	16	23	28	18	11	18	32	30	16	21	28	23	21	29	21	19
Great Britain	29	39	45	33	40	38	40	38	40	39	41	39	40	na	na	na
Greece	na	31	30	32	27	30	44	27	29	34	27	32	33	38	30	32
Hungary	70	71	72	69	61	70	78	76	62	60	70	72	69	77	67	43
Iceland	78	44	50	39	37	41	56	49	41	41	47	41	44	48	45	30
India	67	85	85	85	86	84	86	87	79	86	83	84	86	86	84	82
Indonesia	na	66	73	60	61	66	71	73	68	62	63	69	68	68	65	79
Iran	na	62	63	61	61	63	64	63	62	61	64	60	61	66	61	60
Ireland	28	37	41	33	35	33	44	42	32	38	36	40	36	42	36	31
Israel	na	24	31	19	27	20	26	26	22	25	24	26	26	24	24	16
Italy	27	36	38	35	29	29	46	46	29	28	45	33	29	46	37	30
Japan	31	27	30	24	13	22	37	32	25	28	27	24	32	35	27	13
Jordan	na	45	49	41	41	46	51	47	41	44	47	45	41	45	45	43
Korea, South	64	72	76	67	68	70	79	68	72	71	73	72	70	74	71	63
Latvia	91	85	82	87	75	82	91	86	84	87	87	89	83	89	85	60
Lithuania	92	86	89	85	78	85	94	92	85	84	92	91	85	86	88	88
Luxembourg	na	58	60	56	50	53	68	65	55	51	68	58	44	72	58	42
Macedonia	na	37	39	35	33	38	38	51	28	35	37	41	29	36	36	50
Malta	na	42	42	42	31	41	51	60	35	38	52	38	38	47	39	13
Mexico	23	30	33	28	25	28	41	37	22	21	37	27	22	38	25	24
Moldova	na	87	87	88	81	89	91	92	88	82	90	86	86	89	87	85
Montenegro	na	82	82	83	69	83	90	87	79	79	87	79	83	85	81	79
Morocco	na	70	72	68	69	69	74	71	63	68	76	68	68	69	69	73
Netherlands	13	14	17	12	18	11	17	21	13	10	19	11	13	28	15	8
New Zealand	na	37	46	30	41	34	38	39	40	33	33	38	39	41	37	33
Nigeria	82	80	79	81	81	79	79	81	79	82	80	81	79	81	80	80
Northern Ireland	29	41	45	37	42	37	43	45	38	37	44	42	34	42	42	36
Norway	7	11	14	8	8	8	16	12	11	9	na	na	na	12	12	5
Pakistan	na	56	56	56	52	57	63	60	54	45	60	57	52	57	55	67
Peru	na	59	62	57	58	59	64	63	63	52	63	57	56	65	58	61
Philippines	na	74	75	73	71	76	74	78	72	72	76	71	75	77	73	67
Poland	na	86	88	84	81	86	88	88	84	77	89	85	81	89	85	85
Portugal	67	69	68	70	62	64	78	74	62	52	83	63	63	78	65	65
Puerto Rico	na	52	54	50	54	52	51	59	51	51	56	47	53	65	51	48
Romania	71	82	82	82	72	81	88	89	80	72	85	86	77	86	81	63
Russian Fed.	93	91	89	92	82	92	95	97	90	89	93	91	88	92	89	85
Serbia	na	75	77	73	63	73	81	80	76	65	75	82	73	79	73	59
Singapore	na	64	68	60	56	67	81	73	60	54	69	64	58	67	62	63
Slovakia	na	75	73	77	65	75	83	81	73	70	80	74	74	77	76	63
Slovenia	32	29	30	29	21	23	42	36	26	29	35	25	22	29	30	26
South Africa	30	75	74	77	75	75	76	76	74	79	77	79	69	73	76	81
Spain	48	45	45	45	43	42	49	51	36	43	42	54	46	54	44	37
Sweden	5	4	5	3	4	4	4	3	4	3	4	3	4	7	4	3
Switzerland	36	40	39	40	32	36	48	48	38	31	43	38	36	52	39	32
Taiwan	na	42	43	40	26	36	66	58	34	31	55	39	34	46	36	43
Tanzania	na	83	85	81	81	82	91	85	80	84	85	80	85	84	83	88
Turkey	73	74	75	73	69	76	81	80	68	60	80	72	63	79	74	66
Uganda	na	86	85	86	84	86	90	87	85	85	83	85	85	87	84	89
Ukraine	na	89	88	89	80	93	90	91	89	86	92	88	86	91	88	73
United States	49	61	68	53	68	58	58	65	61	59	60	60	62	66	59	62
Uruguay	na	29	30	28	31	25	31	30	28	24	27	33	27	29	32	20
Venezuela	na	27	29	24	27	25	30	31	26	22	28	26	28	37	24	22
Vietnam	na	75	73	78	74	73	80	79	70	76	78	77	73	80	76	64
Zimbabwe	na	85	85	86	84	85	88	87	83	82	86	88	81	87	85	74
Total	48	56	58	54	53	55	60	60	56	50	59	57	55	67	54	42

RANKING

Country	2000
Croatia	95
Belarus	92
Russian Fed.	91
Ukraine	89
Moldova	87
Lithuania	86
Bulgaria	86
China	86
Poland	86
Uganda	86
Zimbabwe	85
India	85
Latvia	85
Armenia	84
Tanzania	83
Montenegro	82
Estonia	82
Georgia	82
Romania	82
Nigeria	80
Azerbaijan	77
Vietnam	75
South Africa	75
Slovakia	75
Serbia	75
Philippines	74
Turkey	74
Czech Republic	73
Korea, South	72
Hungary	71
Morocco	70
Portugal	69
Algeria	67
Indonesia	66
Singapore	64
Albania	64
Iran	62
United States	61
Peru	59
Bangladesh	59
Luxembourg	58
Argentina	57
Pakistan	56
Bosnia and Herz.	54
Canada	53
Puerto Rico	52
France	50
Dominican Rep.	50
Brazil	47
Spain	45
Jordan	45
Iceland	44
Malta	42
Taiwan	42
Northern Ireland	41
Switzerland	40
Great Britain	39
El Salvador	38
Egypt	38
Belgium	38
New Zealand	37
Ireland	37
Macedonia	37
Italy	36
Australia	36
Greece	31
Mexico	30
Slovenia	29
Uruguay	29
Japan	27
Venezuela	27
Chile	26
Israel	24
Germany	23
Colombia	18
Netherlands	14
Finland	12
Norway	11
Austria	10
Sweden	4
Denmark	2
Total	56

A032) CHILD QUALITIES: FEELING OF RESPONSIBILITY

Here is a list of qualities that children can be encouraged to learn at home.

Which, if any, do you consider to be especially important?

Feeling of responsibility (%)

(WVS: V17; EVS: V167)

Country	Wave 1990	Wave 2000	Gender Male	Gender Female	Age 16-29	Age 30-49	Age 50+	Education Lower	Education Middle	Education Upper	Income Lower	Income Middle	Income Upper	Values Mat	Values Mixed	Values Postm.
Albania	na	68	71	66	67	68	70	64	68	79	69	67	68	69	67	72
Algeria	na	58	55	62	62	58	51	51	57	64	60	58	59	54	60	61
Argentina	80	77	77	77	77	78	76	72	85	81	73	75	82	71	77	83
Armenia	na	69	67	70	67	70	70	63	67	77	70	67	70	68	69	66
Australia	na	66	65	67	58	71	69	63	63	73	64	67	69	67	63	71
Austria	85	86	86	86	86	90	83	82	91	88	79	88	87	78	86	89
Azerbaijan	na	66	66	65	69	65	61	55	65	69	65	64	69	66	66	65
Bangladesh	na	53	54	53	51	55	52	56	50	52	59	50	54	53	54	47
Belarus	82	77	77	76	75	81	73	69	79	85	72	79	80	74	81	79
Belgium	72	80	80	80	78	83	79	74	80	86	76	78	84	75	81	86
Bosnia and Herz.	na	74	72	75	75	74	73	65	76	76	68	75	74	75	73	64
Brazil	72	65	64	65	67	65	58	54	70	85	56	66	72	58	66	75
Bulgaria	68	76	74	77	81	75	73	73	76	80	74	75	77	77	77	66
Canada	75	77	74	80	69	76	83	75	79	76	77	78	77	79	77	77
Chile	88	84	85	84	86	86	80	78	88	88	80	85	90	85	82	90
China	67	64	65	62	72	63	59	56	69	74	58	62	73	65	69	66
Colombia	na	77	79	75	75	80	74	70	77	88	73	75	85	74	75	77
Croatia	na	94	93	95	96	95	91	93	94	95	96	92	94	91	94	98
Czech Republic	65	66	65	66	63	69	65	61	69	76	59	67	69	61	67	70
Denmark	86	81	82	81	76	79	86	79	82	87	80	82	85	75	82	87
Dominican Rep.	na	84	85	85	85	83	100	81	81	87	82	86	88	81	85	89
Egypt	na	51	50	51	53	51	49	49	50	58	49	47	54	47	54	59
El Salvador	na	67	70	64	68	65	69	60	72	79	59	69	76	na	na	na
Estonia	76	79	77	80	82	79	77	76	80	79	71	81	84	76	80	80
Finland	83	86	86	87	86	88	84	83	89	91	83	88	87	86	86	84
France	72	74	70	77	70	74	75	72	74	77	74	73	78	70	75	77
Georgia	na	68	66	69	64	71	68	68	66	73	65	70	69	70	66	59
Germany	84	84	84	84	83	88	80	78	89	87	79	82	85	80	85	89
Great Britain	48	56	55	58	50	61	55	57	55	57	55	62	59	na	na	na
Greece	na	83	82	84	86	82	77	66	82	87	76	85	85	78	84	87
Hungary	66	73	74	73	73	78	69	71	80	71	71	74	76	69	76	100
Iceland	94	81	78	84	79	81	83	81	78	88	79	80	84	80	81	87
India	60	68	69	66	70	68	65	65	66	76	64	62	75	61	76	82
Indonesia	na	82	83	81	80	85	80	79	84	82	83	82	80	79	84	71
Iran	na	72	72	72	73	73	66	66	71	79	73	73	71	70	74	76
Ireland	61	53	56	51	49	56	52	51	54	57	50	52	57	60	51	50
Israel	na	66	62	68	63	69	64	49	69	72	54	63	74	70	66	58
Italy	82	82	80	83	84	82	80	77	84	88	78	83	83	73	84	83
Japan	84	91	91	91	92	90	91	90	91	92	91	89	93	91	92	85
Jordan	na	65	65	66	67	65	63	62	64	73	66	62	69	65	66	57
Korea, South	91	92	92	93	94	92	90	89	92	94	94	91	92	92	93	87
Latvia	75	74	76	73	75	75	74	71	75	78	70	74	82	73	75	79
Lithuania	72	77	77	76	81	80	70	68	79	83	73	76	79	75	79	70
Luxembourg	na	78	75	82	76	80	79	78	78	84	72	78	80	75	79	84
Macedonia	na	74	76	73	75	72	76	62	80	81	72	73	82	74	76	62
Malta	na	77	77	76	82	79	70	70	77	90	66	79	82	74	78	82
Mexico	77	77	78	75	77	79	73	72	83	85	66	83	84	75	79	86
Moldova	na	83	82	84	81	86	80	77	82	88	80	85	82	85	81	86
Montenegro	na	68	68	68	69	69	66	61	69	80	63	74	68	63	73	71
Morocco	na	63	65	61	65	63	59	62	66	72	58	67	60	61	65	66
Netherlands	85	87	86	89	86	88	87	80	91	90	82	88	94	75	88	91
New Zealand	na	59	57	61	53	62	58	58	58	60	57	59	63	53	58	61
Nigeria	36	33	34	32	34	32	31	32	33	36	35	31	33	30	35	33
Northern Ireland	38	54	54	53	45	53	58	54	49	61	51	47	53	52	53	56
Norway	90	92	91	94	91	93	93	91	92	94	na	na	na	91	93	90
Pakistan	na	50	49	52	49	51	51	53	48	45	54	49	46	51	49	50
Peru	na	79	79	79	78	81	77	77	78	82	76	82	80	76	78	86
Philippines	na	65	66	63	70	61	65	57	63	77	61	66	68	62	65	78
Poland	na	73	73	73	69	77	71	67	77	89	70	74	78	74	73	76
Portugal	77	60	59	61	74	59	53	55	67	84	43	53	66	52	64	69
Puerto Rico	na	74	75	74	76	76	72	65	71	77	68	75	80	69	75	76
Romania	56	62	64	60	69	67	53	46	69	77	52	58	73	56	68	85
Russian Fed.	70	76	76	75	78	77	73	70	75	82	69	78	81	75	78	82
Serbia	na	72	73	71	72	74	70	63	73	83	67	72	76	69	75	78
Singapore	na	84	82	85	80	87	87	83	84	84	83	83	85	79	86	85
Slovakia	na	67	67	66	68	70	63	59	69	81	59	67	74	64	70	68
Slovenia	71	76	76	76	76	78	74	67	77	90	67	76	87	70	78	79
South Africa	45	59	61	58	59	58	64	58	61	68	56	51	72	64	57	53
Spain	75	83	82	83	86	84	80	80	84	86	82	81	85	81	82	89
Sweden	89	87	86	88	83	88	88	87	85	90	85	87	90	75	88	85
Switzerland	77	80	81	80	82	80	80	78	80	87	81	77	83	72	82	84
Taiwan	na	81	82	80	86	83	72	71	84	89	75	84	86	80	84	81
Tanzania	na	41	43	40	34	44	50	41	39	53	39	39	56	42	42	38
Turkey	66	63	64	61	67	62	55	53	73	82	51	69	79	60	63	72
Uganda	na	52	55	51	54	53	45	51	53	52	51	56	52	52	54	46
Ukraine	na	75	74	76	78	75	74	68	76	77	74	74	78	73	77	90
United States	72	72	70	74	66	71	78	72	70	73	71	71	75	72	71	74
Uruguay	na	81	82	81	76	85	81	78	86	85	74	85	87	74	82	86
Venezuela	na	88	86	90	88	88	86	82	88	94	84	89	88	86	87	93
Vietnam	na	70	74	66	70	70	71	68	74	73	69	73	68	72	71	75
Zimbabwe	na	48	51	45	50	45	48	44	53	57	45	45	57	47	48	55
Total	73	72	72	72	71	73	72	66	74	79	68	72	76	68	74	78

RANKING

Country	2000
Croatia	94
Korea, South	92
Norway	92
Japan	91
Venezuela	88
Netherlands	87
Sweden	87
Finland	86
Austria	86
Dominican Rep.	84
Chile	84
Germany	84
Singapore	84
Greece	83
Moldova	83
Spain	83
Indonesia	82
Italy	82
Uruguay	81
Denmark	81
Taiwan	81
Iceland	81
Switzerland	80
Belgium	80
Peru	79
Estonia	79
Luxembourg	78
Canada	77
Colombia	77
Belarus	77
Mexico	77
Argentina	77
Lithuania	77
Malta	77
Slovenia	76
Russian Fed.	76
Bulgaria	76
Ukraine	75
Puerto Rico	74
Latvia	74
Macedonia	74
Bosnia and Herz.	74
France	74
Hungary	73
Poland	73
Iran	72
United States	72
Serbia	72
Vietnam	70
Armenia	69
Albania	68
Montenegro	68
Georgia	68
India	68
El Salvador	67
Slovakia	67
Australia	66
Czech Republic	66
Azerbaijan	66
Israel	66
Jordan	65
Philippines	65
Brazil	65
China	64
Morocco	63
Turkey	63
Romania	62
Portugal	60
South Africa	59
New Zealand	59
Algeria	58
Great Britain	56
Northern Ireland	54
Bangladesh	53
Ireland	53
Uganda	52
Egypt	51
Pakistan	50
Zimbabwe	48
Tanzania	41
Nigeria	33
Total	72

A034) CHILD QUALITIES: IMAGINATION

Here is a list of qualities that children can be encouraged to learn at home.

Which, if any, do you consider to be especially important?

Imagination (%)

(WVS: V18; EVS: V168)

Country	Wave 1990	Wave 2000	Gender Male	Gender Female	Age 16-29	Age 30-49	Age 50+	Education Lower	Education Middle	Education Upper	Income Lower	Income Middle	Income Upper	Values Mat	Values Mixed	Values Postm.
Albania	na	29	31	27	34	32	21	26	27	42	22	31	34	28	31	26
Algeria	na	12	13	12	14	10	11	9	13	13	15	15	7	12	12	14
Argentina	31	24	25	22	31	22	18	21	25	34	20	24	27	22	24	24
Armenia	na	16	16	16	17	16	13	14	14	22	20	14	9	12	19	14
Australia	na	26	27	26	30	31	18	18	24	37	24	28	31	15	25	31
Austria	24	24	26	22	31	30	14	14	28	51	16	24	29	10	19	38
Azerbaijan	na	14	14	14	15	14	12	10	14	15	13	17	12	11	19	19
Bangladesh	na	36	35	36	41	33	25	32	37	43	28	41	35	29	40	45
Belarus	7	10	12	9	15	9	7	6	11	16	9	9	15	9	9	25
Belgium	18	23	26	21	30	25	18	12	22	33	19	22	27	13	21	36
Bosnia and Herz.	na	27	28	26	26	31	22	19	26	37	27	27	26	26	27	30
Brazil	12	8	10	6	8	9	4	7	8	10	9	6	9	7	8	10
Bulgaria	16	19	24	16	27	24	12	13	21	27	14	22	23	16	23	31
Canada	23	33	36	31	46	36	22	23	33	42	28	32	39	22	29	43
Chile	32	36	38	34	42	38	26	27	38	47	30	36	44	31	30	60
China	27	35	39	32	43	38	22	28	40	49	33	35	39	36	40	47
Colombia	na	19	22	16	19	20	16	15	18	27	15	18	24	16	19	20
Croatia	na	72	71	73	74	76	66	69	73	76	75	71	71	73	70	79
Czech Republic	7	7	8	6	9	7	5	6	7	12	5	9	7	4	7	14
Denmark	37	37	39	35	43	42	28	27	50	51	34	36	50	22	35	58
Dominican Rep.	na	13	16	10	12	14	na	13	12	13	7	15	18	9	14	12
Egypt	na	15	17	13	17	15	13	14	18	16	14	16	16	16	15	17
El Salvador	na	10	13	8	12	9	10	9	12	14	8	10	15	na	na	na
Estonia	13	11	15	7	19	12	6	9	10	15	7	10	12	8	12	20
Finland	26	28	26	30	39	30	21	23	32	40	31	23	30	19	29	38
France	23	18	21	16	20	24	13	13	24	28	18	16	22	9	16	39
Georgia	na	10	12	9	14	9	8	7	11	11	10	10	11	9	11	16
Germany	28	30	27	32	46	35	17	19	38	39	26	29	29	20	28	48
Great Britain	18	38	41	36	44	45	30	30	44	53	35	46	41	na	na	na
Greece	na	22	24	21	26	20	18	10	18	28	20	22	22	14	20	36
Hungary	9	11	14	8	13	14	7	7	16	18	8	9	13	9	12	32
Iceland	49	18	19	18	23	21	10	13	18	31	15	17	23	7	19	36
India	22	28	28	28	32	27	27	25	28	35	25	23	34	26	33	31
Indonesia	na	29	33	25	20	32	30	29	31	26	33	28	28	27	30	25
Iran	na	11	11	11	12	11	8	9	11	13	10	12	12	7	12	13
Ireland	14	26	27	24	34	29	17	17	28	36	19	20	37	24	25	30
Israel	na	23	24	22	28	21	19	13	21	32	20	21	30	21	23	30
Italy	15	13	14	12	16	14	9	9	14	19	12	13	15	9	11	18
Japan	24	35	41	29	52	38	25	31	32	43	33	36	33	27	35	50
Jordan	na	5	6	5	7	5	3	5	7	6	5	6	5	3	6	15
Korea, South	6	33	36	30	33	34	33	21	30	39	34	32	33	29	37	37
Latvia	11	7	8	6	10	8	5	4	8	10	7	6	9	5	7	13
Lithuania	6	5	5	5	11	4	1	2	5	9	4	3	7	6	4	12
Luxembourg	na	25	28	22	26	30	20	20	26	35	23	23	37	19	22	41
Macedonia	na	13	12	14	17	14	8	6	17	16	10	16	15	15	13	17
Malta	na	7	9	5	9	7	5	4	7	10	4	6	9	5	7	14
Mexico	31	24	25	24	29	23	21	22	25	34	25	22	25	25	26	22
Moldova	na	26	29	24	34	26	21	18	27	33	27	27	28	24	28	42
Montenegro	na	12	12	11	22	12	6	6	13	22	6	11	15	8	15	21
Morocco	na	9	10	8	11	9	5	8	13	12	7	8	12	8	10	15
Netherlands	24	32	34	30	34	40	22	19	29	47	30	35	35	18	28	49
New Zealand	na	28	29	27	45	33	16	19	28	37	19	31	36	18	26	40
Nigeria	6	11	11	11	10	13	10	11	11	11	13	8	11	11	10	18
Northern Ireland	14	31	32	30	34	39	23	24	34	46	32	36	34	20	30	43
Norway	31	37	33	40	47	42	22	26	38	46	na	na	na	25	36	60
Pakistan	na	7	7	7	13	6	2	5	10	12	5	7	9	6	9	na
Peru	na	23	26	20	24	23	21	24	22	24	22	25	22	21	23	25
Philippines	na	14	15	12	12	14	14	14	13	14	11	14	17	12	15	13
Poland	na	13	16	11	21	12	9	11	14	18	12	13	16	9	16	13
Portugal	20	15	16	14	17	18	12	13	18	24	12	16	18	11	16	20
Puerto Rico	na	19	24	16	18	21	18	24	18	18	19	18	19	19	18	19
Romania	17	14	17	10	17	18	8	8	15	20	7	16	18	13	15	18
Russian Fed.	11	7	7	7	11	8	3	3	7	10	6	6	9	6	8	11
Serbia	na	10	12	9	12	14	6	6	11	16	9	8	13	9	11	25
Singapore	na	14	14	13	15	13	8	13	12	22	11	12	17	8	15	21
Slovakia	na	3	3	2	3	3	2	2	3	4	3	3	2	2	2	13
Slovenia	10	12	16	9	16	12	10	8	12	21	8	11	22	7	13	15
South Africa	8	20	21	19	22	18	21	22	17	30	22	22	16	18	20	22
Spain	34	29	32	27	39	32	21	22	33	43	25	26	36	21	29	45
Sweden	40	40	41	40	49	45	31	29	44	44	41	37	43	31	36	54
Switzerland	30	23	27	19	27	26	17	14	23	41	18	20	31	15	20	36
Taiwan	na	15	19	12	15	16	13	12	14	19	17	11	17	15	17	16
Tanzania	na	61	64	58	54	68	61	57	61	76	58	63	70	63	62	54
Turkey	23	22	26	19	24	22	18	17	26	43	19	23	31	18	22	30
Uganda	na	11	16	7	12	10	10	12	11	10	15	10	12	9	11	21
Ukraine	na	11	10	11	13	13	8	7	11	11	10	13	10	9	12	6
United States	27	30	33	28	36	30	25	24	25	35	30	30	31	17	29	36
Uruguay	na	31	33	30	36	37	24	23	42	45	23	34	38	26	29	40
Venezuela	na	24	26	22	23	22	28	20	24	28	18	24	26	24	23	28
Vietnam	na	20	22	19	24	20	17	19	21	22	16	23	21	11	23	19
Zimbabwe	na	11	13	10	10	11	13	11	12	na	10	11	13	9	13	12
Total	21	21	23	19	23	23	16	17	21	27	19	21	23	16	22	32

RANKING

Country	2000
Croatia	72
Tanzania	61
Sweden	40
Great Britain	38
Denmark	37
Norway	37
Chile	36
Bangladesh	36
China	35
Japan	35
Korea, South	33
Canada	33
Netherlands	32
Northern Ireland	31
Uruguay	31
United States	30
Germany	30
Spain	29
Albania	29
Indonesia	29
Finland	28
India	28
New Zealand	28
Bosnia and Herz.	27
Australia	26
Moldova	26
Ireland	26
Luxembourg	25
Mexico	24
Austria	24
Venezuela	24
Argentina	24
Switzerland	23
Belgium	23
Peru	23
Israel	23
Turkey	22
Greece	22
Vietnam	20
South Africa	20
Bulgaria	19
Colombia	19
Puerto Rico	19
France	18
Iceland	18
Armenia	16
Egypt	15
Portugal	15
Taiwan	15
Azerbaijan	14
Philippines	14
Romania	14
Singapore	14
Macedonia	13
Poland	13
Dominican Rep.	13
Italy	13
Slovenia	12
Algeria	12
Montenegro	12
Uganda	11
Zimbabwe	11
Iran	11
Nigeria	11
Ukraine	11
Estonia	11
Hungary	11
El Salvador	10
Serbia	10
Belarus	10
Georgia	10
Morocco	9
Brazil	8
Pakistan	7
Latvia	7
Russian Fed.	7
Czech Republic	7
Malta	7
Jordan	5
Lithuania	5
Slovakia	3
Total	21

A035) CHILD QUALITIES: TOLERANCE AND RESPECT FOR OTHER PEOPLE

Here is a list of qualities that children can be encouraged to learn at home.
Which, if any, do you consider to be especially important?

Tolerance and respect for other people (%) (WVS: V19; EVS: V169)

Country	Wave 1990	Wave 2000	Gender Male	Gender Female	Age 16-29	Age 30-49	Age 50+	Education Lower	Education Middle	Education Upper	Income Lower	Income Middle	Income Upper	Values Mat	Values Mixed	Values Postm.	RANKING Country	RANKING 2000
Albania	na	80	77	83	83	80	78	79	80	84	82	78	80	81	82	69	Croatia	93
Algeria	na	54	52	56	56	53	52	57	54	52	57	53	51	52	56	50	Sweden	93
Argentina	78	70	69	72	67	74	70	70	70	73	69	70	72	67	69	76	Netherlands	91
Armenia	na	48	45	52	45	48	55	51	49	45	46	50	54	49	49	36	Denmark	87
Australia	na	81	78	83	76	83	82	77	81	84	80	80	83	76	81	83	France	85
Austria	66	71	70	73	71	79	65	65	76	86	61	75	77	55	69	82	Iceland	84
Azerbaijan	na	59	59	59	58	59	61	68	63	50	66	58	55	61	58	50	Tanzania	84
Bangladesh	na	71	70	72	70	71	75	70	73	70	73	68	74	76	67	76	Great Britain	84
Belarus	80	72	69	75	69	72	75	73	71	74	71	74	70	74	71	68	Belgium	83
Belgium	69	83	80	86	80	84	83	79	82	87	80	83	85	81	85	87	Finland	83
Bosnia and Herz.	na	72	71	72	72	73	70	70	72	72	74	71	70	69	73	76	Israel	82
Brazil	66	59	54	65	61	58	59	57	60	65	58	61	60	57	60	66	Australia	81
Bulgaria	52	59	58	60	56	62	59	58	60	60	51	62	65	59	62	57	Canada	81
Canada	80	81	78	83	81	80	81	79	79	84	78	80	83	76	80	84	Poland	80
Chile	79	76	73	78	74	80	72	75	77	75	75	76	79	78	75	75	Albania	80
China	62	73	76	70	75	74	67	62	81	79	67	76	78	73	77	72	Spain	80
Colombia	na	68	67	70	68	69	68	64	67	77	66	68	73	62	67	69	Venezuela	80
Croatia	na	93	91	96	95	94	91	93	94	92	95	92	95	91	93	96	United States	80
Czech Republic	64	63	57	68	65	65	61	60	66	70	62	66	62	53	65	67	Switzerland	79
Denmark	81	87	85	90	87	91	84	85	90	91	84	89	93	84	87	93	Zimbabwe	78
Dominican Rep.	na	68	64	70	67	67	82	75	66	68	72	64	67	70	67	71	Luxembourg	78
Egypt	na	65	63	66	64	64	66	67	64	61	68	64	63	66	63	67	Moldova	78
El Salvador	na	59	58	59	59	59	59	58	61	57	54	59	60	na	na	na	New Zealand	78
Estonia	70	71	68	74	69	75	69	64	74	77	71	70	74	69	73	84	Chile	76
Finland	79	83	78	87	83	84	81	80	87	87	81	80	85	74	86	84	Macedonia	75
France	78	85	83	87	85	87	84	84	86	87	85	86	85	85	85	87	Ireland	75
Georgia	na	54	51	57	51	54	58	58	54	52	56	59	48	53	56	49	Italy	75
Germany	74	73	71	75	77	76	68	66	77	86	66	71	79	69	72	83	Northern Ireland	75
Great Britain	79	84	81	86	78	85	88	85	84	85	83	83	85	na	na	na	South Africa	74
Greece	na	53	52	53	52	50	56	63	53	50	54	52	49	53	55	44	Germany	73
Hungary	62	66	61	69	67	66	64	61	72	79	60	67	68	64	66	70	China	73
Iceland	93	84	81	88	86	84	83	80	87	90	78	89	87	82	85	89	Peru	73
India	59	63	63	64	62	65	62	61	61	71	54	64	67	59	70	76	Belarus	72
Indonesia	na	63	63	63	60	62	66	64	65	60	66	61	60	58	65	61	Bosnia and Herz.	72
Iran	na	59	57	61	57	63	57	58	61	56	60	57	58	54	60	59	Austria	71
Ireland	76	75	76	74	74	78	73	71	75	82	71	75	76	73	74	81	Estonia	71
Israel	na	82	79	85	81	84	81	82	82	81	79	80	83	87	81	93	Japan	71
Italy	66	75	72	78	78	78	71	68	80	82	71	76	79	64	76	80	Bangladesh	71
Japan	60	71	69	74	76	72	69	66	72	72	70	72	73	67	74	75	Mexico	71
Jordan	na	67	67	68	65	69	69	72	66	60	69	69	61	68	68	57	Argentina	70
Korea, South	55	65	63	67	75	65	53	61	62	69	58	70	68	63	64	85	Slovenia	70
Latvia	70	70	68	71	62	71	71	69	69	73	70	69	70	69	70	68	Singapore	70
Lithuania	57	58	52	62	58	61	54	53	58	67	56	68	58	53	60	68	Uruguay	70
Luxembourg	na	78	77	80	78	80	76	73	79	86	70	83	86	71	81	83	Latvia	70
Macedonia	na	75	74	77	75	80	70	75	75	78	73	73	81	76	75	69	Colombia	68
Malta	na	61	62	60	59	62	61	58	61	67	60	60	61	56	64	67	Vietnam	68
Mexico	64	71	70	71	74	70	67	66	76	79	64	74	76	69	73	78	Dominican Rep.	68
Moldova	na	78	77	79	75	82	76	80	76	80	79	77	77	79	77	74	Jordan	67
Montenegro	na	57	58	57	60	56	57	52	60	62	56	59	58	57	58	61	Russian Fed.	67
Morocco	na	65	63	67	64	63	71	66	63	63	69	67	56	66	66	59	Norway	66
Netherlands	87	91	88	94	92	92	90	88	93	93	88	93	92	87	92	92	Hungary	66
New Zealand	na	78	74	81	80	78	77	75	79	80	75	80	80	78	80	78	Ukraine	66
Nigeria	75	59	59	59	59	60	58	53	61	66	59	59	60	61	58	57	Portugal	65
Northern Ireland	80	75	73	77	66	75	80	75	75	75	76	78	79	71	80	69	Morocco	65
Norway	64	66	61	70	65	71	61	54	65	79	na	na	na	44	67	87	Korea, South	65
Pakistan	na	53	54	52	59	51	45	42	64	72	42	52	70	49	59	67	Egypt	65
Peru	na	73	72	73	73	73	72	70	73	74	71	74	75	69	74	73	Serbia	65
Philippines	na	60	59	62	56	62	63	58	59	64	59	63	57	60	60	64	India	63
Poland	na	80	79	81	84	82	76	76	84	89	78	81	84	76	81	91	Czech Republic	63
Portugal	69	65	65	66	77	65	59	64	68	73	49	63	65	65	65	70	Indonesia	63
Puerto Rico	na	61	55	64	63	64	57	51	61	63	55	61	66	57	61	63	Turkey	63
Romania	56	58	56	60	58	60	57	56	59	62	56	62	58	58	58	63	Malta	61
Russian Fed.	70	67	64	70	66	66	70	69	66	69	68	67	67	68	68	64	Puerto Rico	61
Serbia	na	65	64	65	71	68	59	48	71	79	56	66	74	57	71	79	Philippines	60
Singapore	na	70	71	69	70	72	63	63	70	86	66	70	75	69	70	71	Brazil	59
Slovakia	na	57	55	59	60	60	51	50	59	65	54	55	63	50	61	70	Bulgaria	59
Slovenia	75	70	67	73	70	72	68	68	71	72	68	73	75	68	71	68	Taiwan	59
South Africa	61	74	74	74	72	77	71	74	73	87	73	71	81	71	77	72	Azerbaijan	59
Spain	71	80	80	80	84	82	75	76	82	86	78	80	82	74	82	84	Nigeria	59
Sweden	91	93	90	95	92	93	93	89	92	96	90	91	97	94	92	93	Iran	59
Switzerland	77	79	76	83	78	83	76	72	82	79	76	83	83	75	78	87	El Salvador	59
Taiwan	na	59	61	58	72	61	48	51	63	65	53	61	64	60	61	62	Romania	58
Tanzania	na	84	84	84	85	82	84	87	81	79	87	83	82	85	83	75	Lithuania	58
Turkey	69	63	61	64	63	62	62	61	62	66	62	63	64	59	62	66	Montenegro	57
Uganda	na	57	59	55	59	56	52	51	59	61	48	52	64	52	61	53	Slovakia	57
Ukraine	na	66	65	66	60	70	65	67	67	62	66	63	68	64	66	79	Uganda	57
United States	71	80	77	82	78	78	84	77	81	80	78	77	84	82	80	78	Georgia	54
Uruguay	na	70	71	69	67	73	68	69	69	73	68	72	69	58	73	71	Algeria	54
Venezuela	na	80	76	83	78	81	80	77	80	82	76	80	85	73	81	86	Pakistan	53
Vietnam	na	68	72	64	68	72	63	67	70	67	69	69	68	55	74	68	Greece	53
Zimbabwe	na	78	76	80	79	78	78	78	79	86	79	76	82	78	78	79	Armenia	48
Total	71	70	68	72	69	71	70	68	71	72	68	71	72	66	72	76	Total	70

A038) CHILD QUALITIES: THRIFT SAVING MONEY AND THINGS

Here is a list of qualities that children can be encouraged to learn at home.
Which, if any, do you consider to be especially important?

Thrift saving money and things (%)

(WVS: V20; EVS: V170)

Country	Wave		Gender		Age			Education			Income			Values		
	1990	2000	Male	Female	16-29	30-49	50+	Lower	Middle	Upper	Lower	Middle	Upper	Mat	Mixed	Postm.
Albania	na	55	53	57	43	60	58	61	54	42	57	57	51	59	51	39
Algeria	na	18	17	19	18	16	21	18	16	20	20	18	17	20	16	19
Argentina	15	15	16	14	14	13	19	16	14	11	17	15	13	19	15	11
Armenia	na	38	38	39	36	37	44	44	40	30	35	41	41	46	30	42
Australia	na	19	19	19	19	16	23	24	19	14	22	18	15	29	21	14
Austria	55	48	45	50	35	40	61	63	39	16	61	46	41	68	54	30
Azerbaijan	na	59	59	60	56	62	60	68	61	55	65	58	57	66	50	47
Bangladesh	na	57	52	64	57	58	54	59	58	53	66	57	51	57	57	63
Belarus	53	46	46	46	41	43	54	60	44	28	51	44	42	51	43	27
Belgium	36	43	41	46	44	37	49	57	44	33	50	46	34	55	45	27
Bosnia and Herz.	na	37	39	36	35	37	39	44	38	30	35	38	35	40	36	30
Brazil	29	39	39	38	33	38	52	46	34	30	41	39	36	42	38	31
Bulgaria	39	39	38	41	31	32	49	48	37	27	49	36	34	44	34	26
Canada	21	27	26	28	18	23	37	38	27	18	33	26	22	39	29	20
Chile	29	34	34	35	31	32	41	42	32	28	37	31	35	37	36	24
China	56	57	58	57	57	55	64	62	56	33	59	62	49	60	55	53
Colombia	na	25	27	24	24	25	26	30	25	19	29	24	22	33	28	26
Croatia	na	85	83	87	77	87	88	88	83	84	91	82	87	91	86	81
Czech Republic	48	32	31	32	32	28	36	35	31	18	38	32	28	47	27	19
Denmark	19	10	10	10	3	5	18	15	3	2	14	9	5	22	10	2
Dominican Rep.	na	11	12	11	10	11	36	22	17	8	8	14	12	18	11	8
Egypt	na	8	9	7	9	9	6	9	8	5	9	7	7	7	9	9
El Salvador	na	30	29	31	27	30	33	33	29	22	29	31	25	na	na	na
Estonia	35	45	44	45	40	43	49	46	47	37	49	46	42	52	40	30
Finland	38	23	23	23	12	17	33	27	18	15	24	21	20	31	21	16
France	36	38	36	39	35	32	45	45	30	25	40	40	29	49	38	20
Georgia	na	32	32	32	25	33	37	32	35	23	34	32	29	35	31	23
Germany	58	37	38	36	24	33	48	48	29	25	46	41	33	47	37	24
Great Britain	26	33	33	33	24	31	38	37	27	32	35	36	30	na	na	na
Greece	na	30	31	29	30	30	33	40	33	25	33	30	30	35	30	27
Hungary	49	42	42	41	34	36	51	49	29	26	47	41	38	47	37	17
Iceland	69	21	22	19	15	17	30	28	18	11	29	16	18	27	19	15
India	24	62	61	63	60	63	61	66	63	52	58	65	62	67	59	42
Indonesia	na	52	54	50	39	50	60	56	55	46	59	49	53	50	53	43
Iran	na	30	33	25	28	28	37	31	28	32	31	28	30	28	29	24
Ireland	22	21	25	19	16	18	29	32	18	12	33	23	14	25	21	14
Israel	na	20	20	19	18	18	24	29	19	15	26	21	15	17	20	21
Italy	29	35	34	35	28	28	44	45	29	20	45	35	24	55	36	22
Japan	40	48	41	55	45	48	49	64	49	38	52	50	42	48	47	36
Jordan	na	19	18	21	17	21	21	21	17	18	19	21	19	21	19	14
Korea, South	53	68	64	71	62	68	73	75	73	59	70	66	66	71	66	52
Latvia	46	45	44	46	44	43	48	53	43	44	44	54	41	48	45	38
Lithuania	37	42	43	42	36	39	50	53	41	28	40	48	40	49	43	20
Luxembourg	na	49	47	50	49	44	54	58	45	39	61	57	32	59	50	32
Macedonia	na	40	38	42	33	41	43	45	39	31	43	39	36	40	41	36
Malta	na	54	54	54	46	52	60	69	51	31	62	55	45	57	53	40
Mexico	33	39	41	38	37	42	70	45	33	26	42	41	32	46	38	34
Moldova	na	42	40	44	47	39	41	43	40	45	41	37	47	47	40	25
Montenegro	na	38	35	42	24	37	49	53	31	24	50	30	26	45	34	19
Morocco	na	37	38	35	37	37	36	37	35	30	38	33	38	38	38	20
Netherlands	28	22	20	23	19	15	29	38	17	11	28	20	13	33	21	18
New Zealand	na	25	26	24	16	22	31	32	28	15	29	24	20	25	26	18
Nigeria	8	10	10	10	11	10	6	9	12	9	10	10	10	7	12	15
Northern Ireland	25	26	25	27	25	20	30	30	22	21	29	22	22	29	25	23
Norway	22	13	14	12	6	8	25	21	12	7	na	na	na	26	12	7
Pakistan	na	56	55	56	54	57	56	65	47	38	68	56	36	59	50	50
Peru	na	24	24	23	18	27	28	31	22	21	27	22	19	27	23	22
Philippines	na	45	45	46	43	46	47	45	47	44	45	45	46	47	45	37
Poland	na	38	37	40	30	36	46	44	33	26	43	36	31	43	37	23
Portugal	31	36	30	41	23	34	45	43	22	15	49	40	35	40	36	18
Puerto Rico	na	24	24	24	19	24	26	32	25	21	28	21	25	28	23	25
Romania	37	31	33	28	28	27	36	36	28	29	33	35	28	35	29	18
Russian Fed.	61	51	49	53	46	50	56	60	54	37	55	55	45	56	48	34
Serbia	na	31	30	31	16	27	40	45	27	17	40	26	25	38	26	13
Singapore	na	44	43	44	38	46	58	51	42	35	51	46	37	51	42	30
Slovakia	na	39	38	39	37	36	44	47	37	21	43	43	32	46	33	22
Slovenia	58	35	38	33	31	30	44	42	36	23	40	35	23	43	34	32
South Africa	17	37	37	37	43	34	31	38	38	25	41	41	28	39	36	39
Spain	18	32	32	32	27	29	38	37	29	23	37	32	31	41	32	20
Sweden	48	31	32	29	20	24	44	48	26	24	33	32	26	56	32	19
Switzerland	42	35	35	35	28	32	43	45	34	26	39	37	29	47	38	21
Taiwan	na	49	48	50	41	47	61	60	47	41	51	53	43	48	50	32
Tanzania	na	54	55	52	51	53	62	58	46	56	57	52	60	56	53	54
Turkey	36	29	28	30	27	31	29	31	28	24	28	30	29	36	30	21
Uganda	na	11	13	9	12	9	12	13	9	19	12	8	11	9	10	15
Ukraine	na	50	49	52	42	52	54	64	51	42	54	51	46	52	52	27
United States	29	23	24	22	20	23	25	29	24	20	25	25	17	28	25	17
Uruguay	na	27	27	27	24	24	30	32	20	17	28	29	24	31	28	20
Venezuela	na	39	40	38	37	42	39	39	40	36	45	39	36	40	39	36
Vietnam	na	48	49	48	37	49	57	51	50	22	64	44	45	49	47	39
Zimbabwe	na	21	20	21	20	21	22	23	17	22	21	25	13	22	20	14
Total	37	36	36	36	31	35	42	41	36	27	40	37	33	43	35	24

RANKING

Country	2000
Croatia	85
Korea, South	68
India	62
Azerbaijan	59
Bangladesh	57
China	57
Pakistan	56
Albania	55
Malta	54
Tanzania	54
Indonesia	52
Russian Fed.	51
Ukraine	50
Taiwan	49
Luxembourg	49
Vietnam	48
Japan	48
Austria	48
Belarus	46
Philippines	45
Latvia	45
Estonia	45
Singapore	44
Belgium	43
Lithuania	42
Moldova	42
Hungary	42
Macedonia	40
Mexico	39
Bulgaria	39
Venezuela	39
Brazil	39
Slovakia	39
Poland	38
Montenegro	38
Armenia	38
France	38
Bosnia and Herz.	37
South Africa	37
Germany	37
Morocco	37
Portugal	36
Slovenia	35
Switzerland	35
Italy	35
Chile	34
Great Britain	33
Spain	32
Georgia	32
Czech Republic	32
Serbia	31
Romania	31
Sweden	31
Greece	30
El Salvador	30
Iran	30
Turkey	29
Canada	27
Uruguay	27
Northern Ireland	26
Colombia	25
New Zealand	25
Puerto Rico	24
Peru	24
United States	23
Finland	23
Netherlands	22
Ireland	21
Iceland	21
Zimbabwe	21
Israel	20
Jordan	19
Australia	19
Algeria	18
Argentina	15
Norway	13
Dominican Rep.	11
Uganda	11
Nigeria	10
Denmark	10
Egypt	8
Total	36

A039) CHILD QUALITIES: DETERMINATION PERSEVERANCE

Here is a list of qualities that children can be encouraged to learn at home.

Which, if any, do you consider to be especially important?

Determination, perseverance (%)

(WVS: V21; EVS: V171)

Country	Wave 1990	Wave 2000	Gender Male	Gender Female	Age 16-29	Age 30-49	Age 50+	Education Lower	Education Middle	Education Upper	Income Lower	Income Middle	Income Upper	Values Mat	Values Mixed	Values Postm.	RANKING Country	RANKING 2000
Albania	na	53	53	53	58	53	49	47	56	59	51	53	56	51	55	51	Croatia	93
Algeria	na	18	17	18	18	17	18	17	15	22	19	15	18	16	18	22	Japan	69
Argentina	29	22	25	20	23	26	17	15	31	37	14	23	29	18	20	31	Armenia	57
Armenia	na	57	64	51	57	61	51	49	56	66	60	57	54	56	57	69	Tanzania	57
Australia	na	36	38	35	41	38	30	26	33	49	29	39	47	33	35	40	Bulgaria	56
Austria	39	36	36	35	32	40	33	29	38	53	29	36	41	30	35	38	Greece	54
Azerbaijan	na	47	51	43	51	47	38	41	49	44	44	49	46	45	49	52	Slovenia	54
Bangladesh	na	36	36	36	39	34	35	34	37	39	31	40	34	33	38	53	Albania	53
Belarus	40	49	59	42	54	51	44	42	50	60	44	53	53	48	49	61	Finland	50
Belgium	39	44	47	41	42	49	40	34	44	50	36	40	52	36	45	53	Estonia	50
Bosnia and Herz.	na	46	48	45	50	47	41	40	45	55	38	47	50	40	49	47	Vietnam	50
Brazil	26	35	36	33	37	36	26	25	40	51	27	28	47	24	37	52	Belarus	49
Bulgaria	41	56	58	54	66	58	50	44	61	65	48	48	67	56	57	64	Canada	48
Canada	38	48	50	46	53	52	41	33	49	60	48	48	54	44	46	53	Switzerland	48
Chile	31	44	45	42	43	46	41	34	46	57	32	48	58	37	44	54	Azerbaijan	47
China	45	16	15	17	21	15	14	12	18	35	12	16	23	18	17	16	Germany	47
Colombia	na	20	23	17	20	20	17	16	20	35	15	21	28	16	20	26	India	46
Croatia	na	93	93	93	95	95	90	93	93	93	96	91	93	86	95	96	Ukraine	46
Czech Republic	42	29	32	26	38	32	21	24	33	35	22	27	38	26	29	36	Bosnia and Herz.	46
Denmark	30	32	32	32	33	34	29	28	35	40	30	30	39	19	33	35	United States	45
Dominican Rep.	na	27	28	27	25	32	36	6	19	33	19	28	40	18	30	29	Venezuela	45
Egypt	na	9	10	8	10	9	9	8	9	12	9	10	9	7	11	9	Montenegro	44
El Salvador	na	14	15	13	19	12	9	9	14	28	7	14	22	na	na	na	Belgium	44
Estonia	51	50	54	46	58	54	41	47	48	59	42	44	56	43	54	73	Chile	44
Finland	38	50	52	49	54	49	49	50	50	52	51	49	51	49	53	41	Indonesia	44
France	39	38	42	35	41	41	34	31	44	52	30	39	50	30	39	52	Macedonia	43
Georgia	na	37	43	32	40	35	34	35	37	36	34	39	39	34	39	48	Korea, South	42
Germany	54	47	51	44	46	47	46	41	49	62	41	48	55	49	43	53	South Africa	42
Great Britain	31	41	42	39	48	41	35	34	46	49	31	47	50	na	na	na	Uruguay	42
Greece	na	54	57	52	61	53	42	41	53	58	51	53	59	55	54	58	Russian Fed.	41
Hungary	12	29	30	28	37	35	17	22	38	46	27	26	32	24	33	36	Great Britain	41
Iceland	75	29	28	31	26	33	27	22	31	41	25	29	34	22	30	42	Serbia	41
India	28	46	48	45	51	46	43	40	50	56	36	46	52	45	50	47	Singapore	40
Indonesia	na	44	47	41	34	42	50	44	47	40	47	43	44	39	47	25	New Zealand	39
Iran	na	28	29	28	31	27	24	21	29	36	25	33	30	27	27	32	Luxembourg	39
Ireland	26	28	29	27	30	30	23	16	32	40	22	24	33	26	29	22	France	38
Israel	na	31	32	30	35	30	26	24	32	33	29	31	35	24	33	26	Philippines	37
Italy	27	34	35	33	36	37	31	28	37	45	28	37	39	31	34	38	Georgia	37
Japan	59	69	69	69	75	67	68	70	70	67	70	72	65	64	70	66	Australia	36
Jordan	na	17	18	16	22	15	11	10	21	25	14	15	22	15	17	29	Latvia	36
Korea, South	31	42	46	39	49	41	38	46	43	41	46	37	43	42	42	46	Bangladesh	36
Latvia	40	36	41	32	41	41	30	27	37	47	31	35	43	33	36	47	Austria	36
Lithuania	34	35	40	31	44	40	25	21	39	43	23	35	39	30	37	43	Norway	36
Luxembourg	na	39	37	41	38	45	33	28	44	49	31	39	52	31	38	54	Uganda	35
Macedonia	na	43	44	41	37	46	43	31	46	54	38	41	53	45	45	29	Lithuania	35
Malta	na	17	19	15	29	15	11	8	18	36	8	17	26	12	18	31	Zimbabwe	35
Mexico	37	33	38	29	34	34	31	24	43	51	24	32	45	31	33	45	Poland	35
Moldova	na	33	34	33	35	35	30	32	30	41	32	33	39	36	29	43	Brazil	35
Montenegro	na	44	47	41	52	43	40	33	47	63	37	44	51	39	49	55	Netherlands	35
Morocco	na	16	17	16	17	17	11	14	23	28	13	18	15	16	18	13	Taiwan	34
Netherlands	30	35	38	31	27	37	37	27	36	40	25	34	43	24	34	40	Italy	34
New Zealand	na	39	39	39	50	41	34	32	36	50	35	39	46	36	39	50	Northern Ireland	34
Nigeria	21	23	23	22	22	23	29	18	26	27	21	22	25	26	21	23	Peru	34
Northern Ireland	18	34	33	35	33	35	33	33	31	42	36	33	34	34	31	44	Moldova	33
Norway	33	36	40	31	34	38	33	31	36	39	na	na	na	24	36	44	Mexico	33
Pakistan	na	29	29	30	37	29	17	17	42	48	17	31	45	26	35	25	Denmark	32
Peru	na	34	36	31	34	34	31	31	30	41	30	33	41	27	35	36	Israel	31
Philippines	na	37	37	37	42	36	33	31	40	41	35	40	35	37	37	39	Pakistan	29
Poland	na	35	34	35	37	36	32	30	39	45	34	35	39	27	38	53	Sweden	29
Portugal	23	24	29	21	37	27	15	19	33	41	12	22	34	20	26	28	Iceland	29
Puerto Rico	na	24	31	20	27	23	23	24	23	24	22	23	26	22	22	27	Spain	29
Romania	40	19	23	15	25	22	12	8	21	33	10	14	27	14	23	26	Czech Republic	29
Russian Fed.	40	41	48	34	51	44	30	23	40	50	32	39	49	37	44	55	Hungary	29
Serbia	na	41	42	39	52	45	32	32	41	53	33	45	45	38	42	47	Iran	28
Singapore	na	40	42	38	48	33	30	31	45	44	30	38	50	34	41	52	Ireland	28
Slovakia	na	25	29	21	29	27	20	17	27	39	19	26	27	20	28	40	Dominican Rep.	27
Slovenia	42	54	57	52	59	58	45	44	55	69	42	51	66	49	54	63	Slovakia	25
South Africa	28	42	40	45	42	43	41	36	47	69	39	42	47	40	43	48	Portugal	24
Spain	22	29	31	27	30	34	24	26	31	35	25	29	34	25	29	36	Puerto Rico	24
Sweden	33	29	29	30	22	33	30	22	27	38	25	29	35	17	28	34	Nigeria	23
Switzerland	na	48	49	47	54	48	44	37	50	51	36	48	55	43	48	51	Argentina	22
Taiwan	na	34	37	32	38	38	23	24	38	42	28	32	44	29	41	38	Turkey	21
Tanzania	na	57	57	57	56	58	56	58	54	58	57	56	66	62	56	54	Colombia	20
Turkey	20	21	21	21	22	20	20	16	25	36	15	23	29	18	20	28	Romania	19
Uganda	na	35	44	28	39	29	42	32	37	28	32	43	38	36	36	31	Algeria	18
Ukraine	na	46	50	43	58	50	36	28	46	58	41	53	46	42	49	57	Malta	17
United States	36	45	50	41	52	46	40	40	42	49	44	45	50	28	47	48	Jordan	17
Uruguay	na	42	41	42	44	45	38	33	53	57	38	41	49	35	41	52	China	16
Venezuela	na	45	49	41	42	48	45	41	45	49	41	40	50	41	45	50	Morocco	16
Vietnam	na	50	50	49	54	50	47	47	53	55	45	47	55	48	52	51	El Salvador	14
Zimbabwe	na	35	34	36	33	37	36	34	36	38	35	34	42	37	33	41	Egypt	9
Total	36	37	39	35	39	39	34	30	40	44	33	37	43	34	38	43	Total	37

A040) CHILD QUALITIES: RELIGIOUS FAITH

Here is a list of qualities that children can be encouraged to learn at home.

Which, if any, do you consider to be especially important?

Religious faith (%)

(WVS: V22; EVS: V172)

Country	Wave 1990	Wave 2000	Gender Male	Gender Female	Age 16-29	Age 30-49	Age 50+	Education Lower	Education Middle	Education Upper	Income Lower	Income Middle	Income Upper	Values Mat	Values Mixed	Values Postm.
Albania	na	36	32	41	32	33	46	42	33	30	35	41	34	36	35	41
Algeria	na	77	76	78	76	77	78	77	74	80	78	79	73	75	78	76
Argentina	28	44	39	48	37	47	46	44	42	43	47	46	37	43	48	35
Armenia	na	12	9	15	11	11	16	16	13	10	10	16	11	8	16	10
Australia	na	21	20	23	16	20	28	25	20	20	26	22	14	27	23	16
Austria	23	20	20	21	13	19	26	21	20	21	23	21	17	24	21	19
Azerbaijan	na	19	18	20	19	17	24	29	18	18	20	23	14	16	20	34
Bangladesh	na	70	70	71	71	67	80	72	72	62	77	67	68	77	66	53
Belarus	6	12	7	16	6	8	22	23	8	8	18	10	6	16	8	7
Belgium	16	14	13	15	13	11	16	17	12	13	16	13	11	15	14	12
Bosnia and Herz.	na	25	22	27	27	23	24	29	24	24	25	26	21	21	25	30
Brazil	46	57	53	60	50	61	61	58	56	56	58	60	54	59	56	52
Bulgaria	11	15	14	16	8	12	21	21	12	12	22	12	11	16	14	11
Canada	31	31	26	36	20	30	38	41	29	25	36	33	23	37	33	26
Chile	54	40	35	45	32	42	46	46	38	34	48	35	37	37	43	36
China	1	na	na	na	na	na	na	na	na	na	na	na	na	na	na	na
Colombia	na	42	38	47	40	42	48	47	42	34	48	39	39	48	47	44
Croatia	na	84	80	87	78	85	87	89	82	72	89	83	81	91	83	81
Czech Republic	15	7	6	7	6	4	9	8	5	7	9	6	4	10	5	6
Denmark	9	8	7	10	5	5	13	8	7	7	9	6	8	9	8	6
Dominican Rep.	na	59	59	60	62	53	64	66	61	58	61	63	49	62	58	62
Egypt	na	87	85	90	84	88	91	88	85	89	88	87	89	89	86	87
El Salvador	na	67	65	69	67	66	69	66	68	69	69	65	63	na	na	na
Estonia	3	6	5	7	4	5	9	9	5	6	10	6	4	6	6	4
Finland	13	16	14	17	11	11	22	20	11	12	18	15	14	13	16	21
France	13	8	7	8	6	7	10	8	6	8	9	9	6	9	9	4
Georgia	na	31	28	34	35	33	24	32	30	34	31	32	29	29	32	39
Germany	16	14	11	15	12	12	16	15	13	9	14	13	14	10	15	16
Great Britain	19	18	20	17	12	16	23	15	21	21	17	23	20	na	na	na
Greece	na	39	37	40	32	39	53	60	47	28	45	41	32	48	40	28
Hungary	24	19	14	24	11	14	28	22	12	17	20	20	16	21	17	na
Iceland	50	11	10	11	4	11	16	12	8	12	11	11	8	13	10	7
India	29	47	44	51	44	46	51	54	45	31	50	50	43	50	40	27
Indonesia	na	93	92	94	92	94	93	92	94	93	94	94	98	92	93	96
Iran	na	71	69	73	69	72	74	77	68	67	73	72	67	79	68	58
Ireland	57	38	34	42	20	36	55	50	32	32	48	36	32	50	36	30
Israel	na	29	27	31	29	33	25	46	29	19	38	31	17	25	29	28
Italy	37	31	28	35	21	31	38	36	28	26	41	30	26	44	32	24
Japan	7	7	6	7	2	7	8	9	7	3	6	7	7	8	7	6
Jordan	na	84	81	87	83	85	84	84	84	84	86	82	84	83	86	75
Korea, South	19	21	19	24	16	22	25	21	22	20	18	20	25	21	21	21
Latvia	9	12	8	15	10	11	14	15	11	11	15	10	10	11	12	11
Lithuania	21	22	20	24	14	12	38	42	15	18	34	19	18	30	19	15
Luxembourg	na	17	18	17	13	13	26	24	11	20	23	16	16	17	19	15
Macedonia	na	27	27	27	34	26	23	40	21	20	29	25	24	26	27	38
Malta	na	56	51	62	45	54	67	67	52	54	58	57	53	59	56	47
Mexico	40	53	48	58	45	54	63	57	50	46	58	51	51	56	54	48
Moldova	na	43	41	44	37	45	44	51	43	34	55	36	38	42	46	31
Montenegro	na	22	20	24	16	22	25	28	20	12	27	18	20	24	19	21
Morocco	na	78	77	80	74	80	87	80	72	69	88	82	66	80	77	73
Netherlands	13	9	8	10	7	7	13	13	9	7	14	8	6	18	9	5
New Zealand	na	16	14	17	16	13	18	14	17	17	19	16	13	19	17	13
Nigeria	74	68	66	69	67	69	67	73	65	63	68	68	67	67	69	61
Northern Ireland	44	40	39	41	34	34	48	44	34	42	42	35	34	41	40	39
Norway	14	12	10	13	9	11	15	12	11	13	na	na	na	11	12	11
Pakistan	na	86	86	87	80	87	95	93	79	76	93	87	79	88	84	75
Peru	na	56	51	60	50	58	63	60	60	45	57	59	49	59	56	50
Philippines	na	59	55	64	63	58	57	58	60	61	55	62	60	58	60	70
Poland	na	40	35	45	39	39	50	51	36	24	46	41	36	53	36	40
Portugal	25	25	22	27	14	26	30	28	18	17	31	30	21	28	24	17
Puerto Rico	na	69	61	73	57	72	72	63	70	69	69	67	71	66	69	68
Romania	43	59	49	69	48	53	71	75	54	42	70	62	49	66	55	36
Russian Fed.	8	9	6	11	4	7	13	16	8	7	12	7	6	9	8	5
Serbia	na	21	20	21	22	18	23	27	19	16	24	18	17	22	20	13
Singapore	na	30	31	29	31	31	26	28	31	30	36	33	27	37	28	26
Slovakia	na	33	25	40	24	29	46	46	28	25	43	32	28	36	31	26
Slovenia	21	18	18	18	16	16	21	29	14	13	24	17	10	18	17	16
South Africa	50	61	55	69	60	61	69	62	61	50	62	62	62	70	58	49
Spain	23	20	15	25	12	14	30	26	15	15	27	18	16	30	18	10
Sweden	6	5	4	6	4	5	6	6	4	6	5	5	4	2	6	3
Switzerland	24	21	17	24	14	20	26	27	19	19	25	27	12	22	20	18
Taiwan	na	9	9	9	5	9	9	10	11	6	8	10	7	9	9	8
Tanzania	na	75	75	76	78	73	77	71	80	81	74	74	82	77	76	88
Turkey	44	47	45	49	45	46	55	57	37	20	57	43	30	49	48	36
Uganda	na	69	61	76	68	69	70	66	69	75	63	65	65	69	69	64
Ukraine	na	18	15	21	10	20	20	33	16	16	21	15	16	18	17	28
United States	55	52	43	61	40	55	58	45	57	53	50	53	54	57	53	49
Uruguay	na	17	11	22	12	16	21	19	15	16	19	14	20	20	17	17
Venezuela	na	45	41	48	46	44	44	48	45	38	51	48	39	45	47	35
Vietnam	na	8	7	9	8	9	8	11	5	5	6	5	12	6	9	7
Zimbabwe	na	74	68	79	74	76	70	72	77	90	67	77	74	72	74	86
Total	26	37	34	39	38	36	36	42	33	34	41	37	33	40	36	30

RANKING

Country	2000
Indonesia	93
Egypt	87
Pakistan	86
Jordan	84
Croatia	84
Morocco	78
Algeria	77
Tanzania	75
Zimbabwe	74
Iran	71
Bangladesh	70
Puerto Rico	69
Uganda	69
Nigeria	68
El Salvador	67
South Africa	61
Philippines	59
Dominican Rep.	59
Romania	59
Brazil	57
Malta	56
Peru	56
Mexico	53
United States	52
Turkey	47
India	47
Venezuela	45
Argentina	44
Poland	43
Moldova	43
Colombia	42
Chile	40
Northern Ireland	40
Greece	39
Ireland	38
Albania	36
Slovakia	33
Italy	31
Georgia	31
Canada	31
Singapore	30
Israel	29
Macedonia	27
Bosnia and Herz.	25
Portugal	25
Lithuania	22
Montenegro	22
Australia	21
Korea, South	21
Serbia	21
Switzerland	21
Austria	20
Spain	20
Hungary	19
Azerbaijan	19
Great Britain	18
Ukraine	18
Slovenia	18
Luxembourg	17
Uruguay	17
Finland	16
New Zealand	16
Bulgaria	15
Belgium	14
Germany	14
Armenia	12
Belarus	12
Latvia	12
Norway	12
Iceland	11
Netherlands	9
Taiwan	9
Russian Fed.	9
Denmark	8
Vietnam	8
France	8
Czech Republic	7
Japan	7
Estonia	6
Sweden	5
Total	37

A041) CHILD QUALITIES: UNSELFISHNESS

Here is a list of qualities that children can be encouraged to learn at home.

Which, if any, do you consider to be especially important?

Unselfishness (%)

(WVS: V23; EVS: V173)

Country	Wave		Gender		Age			Education			Income			Values				Country	2000
	1990	2000	Male	Female	16-29	30-49	50+	Lower	Middle	Upper	Lower	Middle	Upper	Mat	Mixed	Postm.		**RANKING**	
Albania	na	12	14	10	14	11	11	12	12	11	12	12	12	10	15	3		Croatia	90
Algeria	na	17	18	15	17	16	17	16	19	14	19	17	15	15	16	29		Great Britain	60
Argentina	5	13	14	11	8	16	14	11	15	14	10	14	14	10	13	15		Denmark	56
Armenia	na	31	32	29	30	34	26	26	32	29	30	28	35	31	31	18		Uruguay	55
Australia	na	40	38	42	42	40	38	39	41	39	37	40	39	39	40	41		Japan	53
Austria	7	5	7	4	7	4	6	5	6	3	6	6	5	7	5	6		Venezuela	53
Azerbaijan	na	17	18	15	17	16	18	24	18	13	19	17	14	16	18	16		Peru	50
Bangladesh	na	16	17	14	18	14	14	13	18	19	11	15	21	16	15	21		Northern Ireland	50
Belarus	27	17	16	18	19	18	15	13	19	18	18	17	17	16	18	14		Mexico	50
Belgium	27	29	29	29	29	28	30	22	27	37	29	28	28	20	29	41		Ireland	49
Bosnia and Herz.	na	38	38	37	40	38	35	31	39	40	36	38	36	35	39	34		Israel	49
Brazil	28	32	28	37	34	33	28	25	38	37	28	39	34	29	33	39		Indonesia	47
Bulgaria	22	14	13	15	17	15	13	10	16	19	12	16	16	16	13	16		Macedonia	47
Canada	42	45	45	45	50	44	44	44	46	44	45	47	46	46	46	45		Malta	46
Chile	8	34	33	35	37	35	30	32	34	40	33	32	40	29	35	39		Tanzania	46
China	31	37	37	37	38	40	29	33	40	35	37	37	39	40	38	41		Canada	45
Colombia	na	37	36	39	40	35	37	44	38	25	45	37	28	43	41	39		Italy	41
Croatia	na	90	88	91	92	91	87	87	91	90	87	91	90	85	90	93		France	40
Czech Republic	38	37	37	37	41	37	34	37	37	36	31	38	39	31	39	40		Portugal	40
Denmark	50	56	54	58	63	59	49	56	57	54	53	59	52	66	54	64		Montenegro	40
Dominican Rep.	na	12	18	9	13	11	18	19	13	11	15	12	11	13	9	20		Australia	40
Egypt	na	22	20	24	22	22	20	21	22	24	20	21	25	22	22	22		Philippines	39
El Salvador	na	28	27	29	28	29	27	29	26	27	30	28	24	na	na	na		Vietnam	39
Estonia	25	17	17	17	14	16	18	16	16	20	16	16	18	18	15	11		United States	39
Finland	21	21	23	19	27	22	16	13	30	33	19	24	21	15	22	28		Pakistan	38
France	40	40	37	44	43	42	38	37	42	49	43	38	42	38	38	50		Bosnia and Herz.	38
Georgia	na	20	19	20	20	19	20	15	20	21	19	23	18	19	20	19		Slovenia	38
Germany	9	7	8	7	7	7	8	8	7	5	9	8	7	10	7	5		Colombia	37
Great Britain	57	60	61	59	59	63	57	55	62	69	53	63	62	na	na	na		China	37
Greece	na	26	24	27	26	28	24	23	30	23	31	23	24	19	26	29		Czech Republic	37
Hungary	26	21	24	19	26	20	20	17	28	34	17	21	24	19	25	37		India	37
Iceland	75	35	33	36	42	34	30	34	39	29	36	36	35	36	34	39		Iceland	35
India	32	37	37	36	40	37	33	35	41	37	34	37	38	37	38	29		Serbia	34
Indonesia	na	47	49	46	40	46	52	48	52	42	52	45	47	41	51	39		Chile	34
Iran	na	29	31	26	31	27	28	26	28	33	28	29	30	28	28	28		Zimbabwe	33
Ireland	53	49	50	49	54	52	44	40	55	51	45	51	51	47	49	51		New Zealand	33
Israel	na	49	47	51	52	50	44	42	50	52	48	48	51	49	49	47		Sweden	33
Italy	39	41	39	44	47	46	34	34	45	53	39	41	48	31	39	53		Brazil	32
Japan	44	53	55	51	51	58	50	43	53	61	50	55	57	58	53	59		Jordan	32
Jordan	na	32	30	34	33	32	28	31	34	32	30	31	34	29	33	45		Uganda	31
Korea, South	11	15	14	16	16	15	12	14	13	17	14	15	15	13	15	25		Armenia	31
Latvia	16	12	10	13	15	11	11	8	12	14	12	10	13	9	13	19		Switzerland	30
Lithuania	33	29	28	29	29	29	28	26	30	25	31	34	25	21	30	34		Singapore	30
Luxembourg	na	26	23	29	25	27	24	29	21	29	27	29	28	25	25	27		South Africa	29
Macedonia	na	47	48	46	49	49	43	44	47	52	44	50	47	47	46	72		Belgium	29
Malta	na	46	48	44	51	50	39	44	47	44	46	44	51	44	46	55		Iran	29
Mexico	11	50	47	52	55	49	42	49	53	40	50	53	52	46	56	47		Lithuania	29
Moldova	na	12	15	8	13	10	13	12	12	11	10	13	12	11	14	11		Puerto Rico	28
Montenegro	na	40	40	40	44	40	37	35	43	42	46	40	36	39	41	44		Netherlands	28
Morocco	na	10	10	10	9	11	9	10	11	13	5	9	15	8	11	15		El Salvador	28
Netherlands	22	28	32	24	34	29	24	19	33	30	25	30	29	27	29	28		Greece	26
New Zealand	na	33	33	32	35	33	32	31	34	34	32	32	35	33	32	36		Luxembourg	26
Nigeria	17	23	24	23	24	21	28	27	22	20	25	24	21	24	23	21		Nigeria	23
Northern Ireland	49	50	50	51	50	54	47	49	51	51	56	57	50	42	55	46		Turkey	22
Norway	10	11	13	9	15	11	10	7	10	18	na	na	na	7	11	18		Egypt	22
Pakistan	na	38	39	38	42	39	30	32	43	54	29	39	49	36	42	42		Taiwan	21
Peru	na	50	49	52	55	49	43	52	47	54	52	52	45	45	51	55		Hungary	21
Philippines	na	39	39	40	41	36	44	47	41	29	43	37	39	39	40	36		Finland	21
Poland	na	12	11	14	17	13	8	7	17	24	9	13	16	12	12	15		Russian Fed.	21
Portugal	28	40	39	41	44	38	40	39	41	46	38	40	44	39	39	50		Georgia	20
Puerto Rico	na	28	35	25	40	23	27	27	25	31	26	26	33	28	29	27		Slovakia	19
Romania	20	7	8	6	13	6	4	2	8	12	4	7	8	7	7	10		Belarus	17
Russian Fed.	24	21	21	20	19	20	22	18	21	24	23	20	19	20	22	19		Azerbaijan	17
Serbia	na	34	35	35	39	35	32	29	38	36	30	34	40	33	37	34		Algeria	17
Singapore	na	30	30	29	35	26	22	26	31	35	23	29	33	26	31	32		Estonia	17
Slovakia	na	19	19	19	23	20	13	13	20	28	17	19	21	17	19	29		Bangladesh	16
Slovenia	33	38	34	41	37	40	35	29	40	44	34	38	49	38	37	40		Ukraine	15
South Africa	20	29	30	29	28	29	31	28	30	47	28	30	28	31	29	22		Korea, South	15
Spain	12	12	12	12	11	10	14	14	10	10	10	14	14	14	12	9		Bulgaria	14
Sweden	29	33	35	31	48	35	21	22	36	36	35	31	31	28	31	41		Argentina	13
Switzerland	37	30	29	31	28	29	32	23	31	38	30	28	32	26	30	36		Dominican Rep.	12
Taiwan	na	21	22	21	20	22	21	20	21	24	23	19	22	26	19	19		Poland	12
Tanzania	na	46	46	46	44	48	46	42	49	53	42	46	57	45	48	33		Albania	12
Turkey	28	22	21	23	25	21	15	17	27	31	19	22	30	20	22	25		Spain	12
Uganda	na	31	23	39	30	31	39	39	28	31	26	35	28	33	31	29		Latvia	12
Ukraine	na	15	14	17	13	16	17	15	14	19	18	16	11	13	17	24		Moldova	12
United States	37	39	38	40	40	38	39	39	41	37	38	42	38	40	38	42		Norway	11
Uruguay	na	55	57	53	58	51	56	57	51	53	56	54	55	56	55	58		Morocco	10
Venezuela	na	53	51	55	56	51	51	61	51	48	58	52	50	51	54	51		Germany	7
Vietnam	na	39	39	39	45	40	33	34	45	51	40	44	35	48	38	42		Romania	7
Zimbabwe	na	33	33	33	30	37	33	33	33	53	28	37	36	30	36	28		Austria	5
Total	28	31	31	31	32	31	29	29	32	32	30	32	32	27	32	36		Total	31

A042) CHILD QUALITIES: OBEDIENCE

Here is a list of qualities that children can be encouraged to learn at home.
Which, if any, do you consider to be especially important?

Obedience (%)

(WVS: V24; EVS: V174)

Country	Wave		Gender		Age			Education			Income			Values		
	1990	2000	Male	Female	16-29	30-49	50+	Lower	Middle	Upper	Lower	Middle	Upper	Mat	Mixed	Postm.
Albania	na	54	55	53	54	54	54	53	54	57	52	52	57	50	55	77
Algeria	na	56	54	58	57	54	59	62	56	53	56	54	56	58	54	61
Argentina	32	37	37	38	44	36	32	43	32	20	41	39	30	45	40	24
Armenia	na	18	15	21	16	18	22	24	19	11	15	15	25	22	15	13
Australia	na	29	30	28	35	25	28	33	34	20	32	28	24	38	32	24
Austria	25	17	18	16	18	12	21	23	13	5	25	17	12	37	18	8
Azerbaijan	na	25	25	25	19	27	31	33	24	24	21	26	26	23	29	21
Bangladesh	na	19	21	18	20	17	27	17	21	24	18	17	24	20	18	17
Belarus	23	34	32	36	31	29	42	46	32	20	41	32	26	39	29	18
Belgium	37	43	43	43	49	38	45	57	46	28	47	47	35	54	44	23
Bosnia and Herz.	na	44	42	45	40	44	47	55	46	28	48	47	35	48	41	38
Brazil	41	59	61	58	61	58	56	65	58	40	67	63	48	68	60	34
Bulgaria	19	16	15	17	9	13	21	24	12	9	21	15	13	17	15	13
Canada	28	30	30	29	31	29	30	42	30	19	38	30	23	37	33	22
Chile	52	55	51	58	55	55	55	58	54	51	60	55	45	64	54	40
China	9	15	14	16	9	16	16	22	11	2	19	14	11	14	14	13
Colombia	na	43	42	44	47	39	45	51	44	27	53	42	31	47	48	44
Croatia	na	86	84	88	84	87	86	89	87	77	94	84	84	92	87	80
Czech Republic	28	17	19	16	17	16	19	23	12	6	22	16	14	26	15	13
Denmark	20	14	16	13	14	13	17	20	7	7	20	14	7	25	15	6
Dominican Rep.	na	51	51	50	49	53	64	63	57	47	65	52	37	53	54	35
Egypt	na	53	51	56	52	53	56	58	52	43	56	57	49	59	49	45
El Salvador	na	62	62	63	62	64	61	68	61	50	71	63	53	na	na	na
Estonia	19	29	31	27	28	24	33	38	26	19	32	33	23	35	24	15
Finland	25	30	33	28	27	31	30	37	22	18	31	33	26	39	29	16
France	53	36	37	34	34	34	37	44	29	20	36	38	29	48	36	17
Georgia	na	23	22	24	22	21	26	23	26	13	28	19	19	23	23	16
Germany	24	12	11	12	7	10	16	17	8	4	18	14	7	19	11	3
Great Britain	39	49	48	51	44	47	54	59	44	39	55	57	42	na	na	na
Greece	na	11	13	9	9	12	14	25	12	7	15	10	11	11	12	7
Hungary	45	33	32	35	30	30	39	40	22	23	41	33	29	38	30	9
Iceland	68	17	19	16	21	20	11	19	20	9	18	21	15	26	17	3
India	56	56	54	58	57	55	56	58	58	50	57	56	55	59	50	53
Indonesia	na	53	57	49	44	54	57	59	56	47	57	51	54	51	53	46
Iran	na	41	42	41	42	40	42	43	39	40	43	41	44	41	39	44
Ireland	35	47	45	50	48	44	50	54	46	39	57	49	39	46	48	44
Israel	na	16	18	15	17	15	18	23	18	10	22	22	6	19	16	16
Italy	34	28	29	27	24	25	33	38	22	15	38	25	19	44	29	18
Japan	10	4	3	5	5	4	5	5	5	3	5	4	3	4	5	2
Jordan	na	46	45	47	48	44	48	49	51	36	49	46	44	53	42	40
Korea, South	18	13	14	13	8	12	21	23	14	10	15	14	11	15	12	9
Latvia	15	20	22	19	28	17	20	35	18	9	21	22	18	22	20	19
Lithuania	25	20	18	21	12	18	27	29	18	11	29	13	13	23	19	10
Luxembourg	na	26	27	26	27	23	29	38	24	10	43	27	16	34	27	14
Macedonia	na	11	12	11	14	10	11	16	9	8	15	10	8	11	10	29
Malta	na	41	39	43	42	39	44	38	46	24	48	42	33	42	42	30
Mexico	45	60	56	63	62	57	60	61	60	49	64	60	54	63	61	51
Moldova	na	41	43	40	36	40	47	50	42	32	45	37	42	42	40	38
Montenegro	na	47	42	51	37	46	54	62	41	25	54	45	41	53	39	37
Morocco	na	53	49	57	49	52	64	56	43	31	58	51	51	55	51	43
Netherlands	33	26	26	26	27	24	26	38	26	14	29	25	21	29	29	13
New Zealand	na	22	21	22	21	22	22	25	24	17	25	22	18	29	24	13
Nigeria	71	73	71	75	72	72	76	78	71	66	70	76	72	77	71	67
Northern Ireland	56	58	59	56	65	50	60	61	58	47	58	58	56	60	61	45
Norway	31	26	28	24	24	25	29	39	29	10	na	na	na	42	26	6
Pakistan	na	44	44	45	38	44	59	54	37	27	55	44	30	48	39	33
Peru	na	61	61	61	61	61	63	71	61	54	66	62	50	65	60	59
Philippines	na	44	45	44	42	46	44	47	46	39	47	46	40	46	45	36
Poland	na	33	32	33	29	31	37	40	28	14	38	30	26	36	31	25
Portugal	45	39	36	41	30	38	45	41	37	25	43	45	28	46	33	43
Puerto Rico	na	56	52	58	56	56	56	51	58	56	56	57	55	54	55	61
Romania	20	19	17	21	14	15	25	30	16	5	28	21	11	24	15	7
Russian Fed.	26	34	31	36	29	30	42	49	36	19	43	35	23	37	30	6
Serbia	na	32	32	33	28	27	39	50	29	13	40	30	25	41	25	11
Singapore	na	47	43	51	46	47	51	51	48	34	52	46	42	48	48	33
Slovakia	na	26	28	25	27	23	30	34	24	14	32	28	21	29	24	20
Slovenia	40	25	27	24	24	24	28	36	24	9	33	23	16	23	26	20
South Africa	42	52	53	50	51	51	59	57	46	41	55	55	45	53	53	44
Spain	42	49	48	50	43	47	54	54	47	37	54	52	39	55	51	35
Sweden	25	13	15	11	11	10	17	22	13	6	15	16	7	24	14	4
Switzerland	20	24	25	23	21	25	25	33	24	7	25	30	17	38	24	13
Taiwan	na	33	30	36	25	32	42	49	33	19	40	36	22	35	30	22
Tanzania	na	76	77	76	77	76	71	78	76	71	77	74	78	77	77	79
Turkey	31	42	40	44	41	41	46	49	36	21	50	38	30	45	42	35
Uganda	na	72	68	75	73	69	78	74	71	69	71	61	74	75	72	61
Ukraine	na	35	32	38	30	36	44	44	37	27	40	32	33	41	30	32
United States	39	32	32	32	33	34	29	35	37	28	36	33	25	43	34	24
Uruguay	na	29	29	29	28	27	30	34	23	14	31	24	31	40	27	26
Venezuela	na	51	52	50	54	49	51	60	51	41	58	52	47	51	52	52
Vietnam	na	56	52	60	57	54	59	59	51	54	57	57	54	71	49	58
Zimbabwe	na	68	63	73	67	70	69	70	66	53	72	67	61	67	69	64
Total	33	38	37	38	39	36	38	46	35	28	42	38	32	42	36	28

RANKING

Country	2000
Croatia	86
Tanzania	76
Nigeria	73
Uganda	72
Zimbabwe	68
El Salvador	62
Peru	61
Mexico	60
Brazil	59
Northern Ireland	58
Algeria	56
Vietnam	56
Puerto Rico	56
India	56
Chile	55
Albania	54
Egypt	53
Indonesia	53
Morocco	53
South Africa	52
Venezuela	51
Dominican Rep.	51
Great Britain	49
Spain	49
Ireland	47
Singapore	47
Montenegro	47
Jordan	46
Pakistan	44
Philippines	44
Bosnia and Herz.	44
Belgium	43
Colombia	43
Turkey	42
Iran	41
Moldova	41
Malta	41
Portugal	39
Argentina	37
France	36
Ukraine	35
Belarus	34
Russian Fed.	34
Hungary	33
Taiwan	33
Poland	33
Serbia	32
United States	32
Finland	30
Canada	30
Australia	29
Uruguay	29
Estonia	29
Italy	28
Slovakia	26
Luxembourg	26
Norway	26
Netherlands	26
Slovenia	25
Azerbaijan	25
Switzerland	24
Georgia	23
New Zealand	22
Latvia	20
Lithuania	20
Bangladesh	19
Romania	19
Armenia	18
Iceland	17
Czech Republic	17
Austria	17
Israel	16
Bulgaria	16
China	15
Denmark	14
Korea, South	13
Sweden	13
Germany	12
Macedonia	11
Greece	11
Japan	4
Total	38

...of often you do various things? Spend time socially with colleagues from work or your profession

(WVS: V29; EVS: V49)

...e a month (%)

2000	Male	Female	16-29	30-49	50+	Lower	Middle	Upper	Lower	Middle	Upper	Mat	Mixed	Postm.
	Gender		**Age**			**Education**			**Income**			**Values**		
57	69	45	63	61	45	50	57	74	54	59	58	51	61	71
54	64	43	52	58	50	41	60	55	52	55	57	50	57	52
37	50	26	46	40	27	33	42	48	32	35	46	29	38	45
na	na	na	na	na	na	na	na	na	na	na	na	na	na	na
na	na	na	na	na	na	na	na	na	na	na	na	na	na	na
36	45	28	54	44	19	34	37	42	26	35	43	26	37	38
na	na	na	na	na	na	na	na	na	na	na	na	na	na	na
62	74	45	50	68	72	61	60	66	67	61	58	64	60	56
56	65	49	70	58	41	42	61	61	50	58	65	49	60	81
35	34	35	54	33	23	24	32	42	33	33	35	30	35	36
51	57	44	50	65	33	29	53	62	30	55	59	53	48	53
na	na	na	na	na	na	na	na	na	na	na	na	na	na	na
57	63	52	76	71	34	38	61	73	35	64	71	53	63	52
42	47	36	58	45	29	31	41	51	34	42	48	44	39	46
34	38	31	49	29	29	25	36	49	34	31	38	27	36	40
73	76	69	73	77	62	69	75	84	69	76	78	75	74	75
na	na	na	na	54	38	37	58	65	44	54	54	36	55	63
53	62	42	71	54	38	39	41	48	33	39	49	35	42	51
41	45	36	58	44	28	39	41	48	33	35	40	44	36	41
37	38	36	56	37	24	32	42	42	37	35	40	na	na	na
na	na	na	na	na	na	na	na	na	na	na	na	na	na	na
70	76	49	66	75	64	63	75	76	68	75	73	68	73	71
na	na	na	na	na	na	na	na	na	na	na	na	na	na	na
42	40	43	61	43	25	40	43	41	43	37	43	40	43	50
47	50	45	68	50	33	44	50	51	52	45	48	45	49	44
31	36	27	50	32	21	25	37	41	28	30	32	21	31	46
na	na	na	na	na	na	na	na	na	na	na	na	na	na	na
38	40	37	53	43	23	30	45	42	27	43	48	38	39	38
43	49	37	72	41	24	31	49	57	34	39	54	na	na	na
56	56	56	68	51	44	41	53	61	49	57	63	62	55	57
na	na	na	na	na	na	na	na	na	na	na	na	na	na	na
40	41	38	59	36	26	40	41	37	41	37	40	37	40	40
62	71	49	64	65	53	59	64	66	66	60	61	66	66	73
85	89	82	88	89	81	83	85	89	86	85	89	85	86	93
50	60	37	49	53	47	47	47	60	47	53	48	41	55	47
53	59	45	75	47	38	36	57	65	39	48	60	51	53	51
na	na	na	na	na	na	na	na	na	na	na	na	na	na	na
39	47	30	55	40	27	31	41	51	32	41	46	30	38	45
46	52	41	60	46	41	42	44	54	39	49	53	47	47	47
36	63	10	36	42	22	31	36	47	31	43	39	33	39	39
64	70	58	79	60	54	21	62	71	58	69	66	58	68	76
na	na	na	na	na	na	na	na	na	na	na	na	na	na	na
28	32	24	41	31	14	13	31	35	17	20	37	19	31	39
na	na	na	na	na	na	na	na	na	na	na	na	na	na	na
59	66	51	65	63	46	41	65	75	45	61	74	55	62	71
24	26	21	42	19	11	8	27	31	18	14	33	22	25	24
45	56	35	54	42	36	35	54	64	40	46	56	44	47	48
50	52	48	60	54	37	36	52	60	45	46	59	45	55	57
65	74	55	82	72	46	44	75	85	58	67	76	59	71	66
50	63	37	50	53	41	49	51	64	50	60	50	45	57	43
45	45	45	67	45	29	33	45	55	46	43	49	35	47	na
na	na	na	na	na	na	na	na	na	na	na	na	na	na	na
86	90	82	85	88	79	84	85	91	86	87	85	85	86	90
35	37	33	54	39	22	26	39	48	25	29	47	23	41	35
na	na	na	na	na	na	na	na	na	na	na	na	na	na	na
31	56	4	25	31	44	38	24	23	36	35	18	36	25	27
64	74	54	66	63	59	59	60	72	59	66	70	54	65	71
57	70	44	53	63	52	57	56	59	55	56	60	54	59	60
na	na	na	na	na	na	na	na	na	na	na	na	na	na	na
53	na	40	76	55	36	43	71	73	20	54	71	43	60	67
39	48	34	51	45	30	22	36	43	35	40	42	31	42	37
51	59	39	72	45	32	58	49	53	48	54	50	52	50	56
37	45	30	56	41	18	20	37	44	30	35	43	33	42	44
62	70	55	77	70	48	47	67	75	49	67	72	57	68	69
51	58	44	53	54	36	35	56	70	37	51	61	45	54	43
na	na	na	na	na	na	na	na	na	na	na	na	na	na	na
50	61	40	71	54	29	32	57	53	42	47	57	37	51	61
46	55	37	42	57	28	44	48	63	40	49	56	40	50	55
47	56	37	67	52	28	35	57	63	33	50	57	39	51	65
54	56	51	66	50	51	44	56	56	59	54	50	39	51	na
na	na	na	na	na	na	na	na	na	na	na	na	na	na	na
na	na	na	na	na	na	na	na	na	na	na	na	na	na	na
77	79	73	71	80	79	73	76	90	72	81	89	72	78	88
52	73	27	55	55	39	43	62	80	47	54	64	49	54	60
61	75	48	56	70	48	55	62	75	76	67	73	57	62	66
44	54	35	61	51	25	20	44	53	32	43	59	38	48	50
54	59	49	66	52	46	56	52	54	49	59	54	50	54	56
na	na	na	na	na	na	na	na	na	na	na	na	na	na	na
51	58	43	58	50	37	39	49	67	49	51	54	47	51	70
72	76	69	78	78	59	67	78	78	68	72	76	61	77	54
52	60	45	46	59	53	49	56	100	57	54	58	51	53	52
51	**59**	**43**	**59**	**54**	**37**	**44**	**53**	**58**	**47**	**52**	**55**	**49**	**52**	**52**

RANKING

Country	2000
Nigeria	86
Indonesia	85
Tanzania	77
China	73
Vietnam	72
Egypt	70
Montenegro	65
Peru	64
Korea, South	64
Serbia	62
India	62
Bangladesh	62
Uganda	61
Macedonia	59
Bulgaria	57
Philippines	57
Albania	57
Belarus	56
Greece	56
United States	54
Sweden	54
Algeria	54
Portugal	53
Croatia	53
Ireland	53
Turkey	52
Zimbabwe	52
Romania	51
Singapore	51
Bosnia and Herz.	51
Venezuela	51
Morocco	50
Slovenia	50
Moldova	50
Iran	50
Finland	47
Spain	47
Japan	46
South Africa	46
Netherlands	45
Mexico	45
Ukraine	44
Great Britain	43
Estonia	42
Canada	42
Czech Republic	41
Iceland	40
Puerto Rico	39
Italy	39
Germany	38
Argentina	37
Denmark	37
Russian Fed.	37
Austria	36
Jordan	36
Northern Ireland	35
Belgium	35
Chile	34
France	31
Pakistan	31
Lithuania	28
Malta	24
Total	51

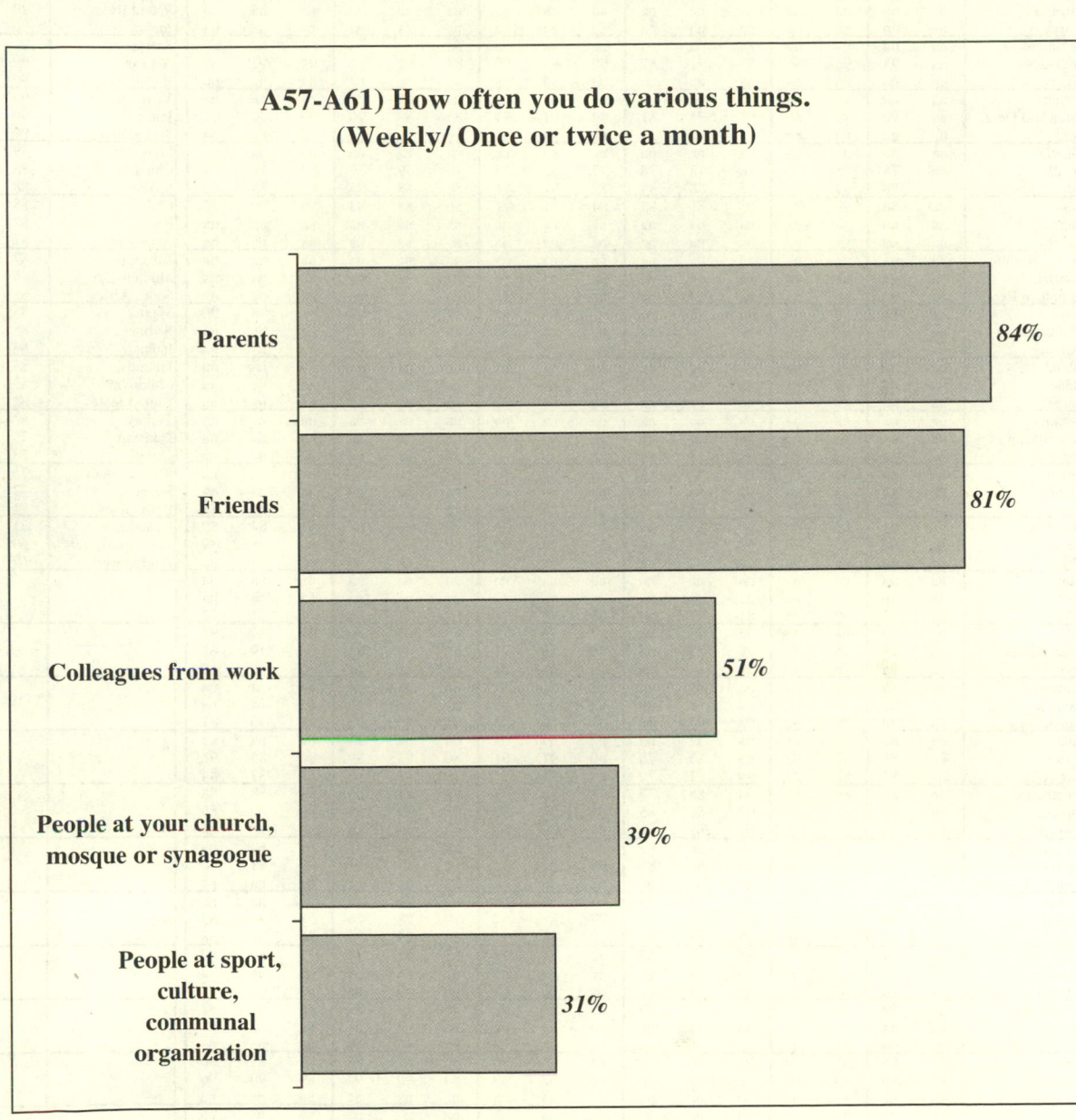

A57-A61) How often you do various things.
(Weekly/ Once or twice a month)

- Parents — 84%
- Friends — 81%
- Colleagues from work — 51%
- People at your church, mosque or synagogue — 39%
- People at sport, culture, communal organization — 31%

A057) SPEND TIME WITH THE PARENTS

I'm going to ask how of often you do various things? Spend time with parents or other relatives.

Weekly / Once or twice a month (%) (WVS: V27)

Country	Wave 1990	Wave 2000	Gender Male	Gender Female	Age 16-29	Age 30-49	Age 50+	Edu Lower	Edu Middle	Edu Upper	Inc Lower	Inc Middle	Inc Upper	Val Mat	Val Mixed	Val Postm.
Albania	na	87	87	87	95	88	78	88	86	86	88	87	86	87	88	82
Algeria	na	90	90	89	94	88	84	86	90	92	90	87	91	90	89	93
Argentina	na	87	86	88	92	86	84	85	90	91	86	87	88	86	87	87
Armenia	na	na	na	na	na	na	na	na	na	na	na	na	na	na	na	na
Australia	na	na	na	na	na	na	na	na	na	na	na	na	na	na	na	na
Austria	na	na	na	na	na	na	na	na	na	na	na	na	na	na	na	na
Azerbaijan	na	na	na	na	na	na	na	na	na	na	na	na	na	na	na	na
Bangladesh	na	91	95	86	93	91	87	90	94	90	87	95	91	91	92	95
Belarus	na	na	na	na	na	na	na	na	na	na	na	na	na	na	na	na
Belgium	na	na	na	na	na	na	na	na	na	na	na	na	na	na	na	na
Bosnia and Herz.	na	90	91	88	97	91	81	84	91	90	85	89	96	90	90	91
Brazil	na	na	na	na	na	na	na	na	na	na	na	na	na	na	na	na
Bulgaria	na	na	na	na	na	na	na	na	na	na	na	na	na	na	na	na
Canada	na	78	75	81	86	75	78	77	82	73	78	79	79	87	79	74
Chile	na	88	87	89	95	88	81	82	91	94	86	88	94	85	88	92
China	na	88	88	89	95	88	83	84	91	91	86	88	92	89	89	97
Colombia	na	na	na	na	na	na	na	na	na	na	na	na	na	na	na	na
Croatia	na	na	na	na	na	na	na	na	na	na	na	na	na	na	na	na
Czech Republic	na	na	na	na	na	na	na	na	na	na	na	na	na	na	na	na
Denmark	na	na	na	na	na	na	na	na	na	na	na	na	na	na	na	na
Dominican Rep.	na	na	na	na	na	na	na	na	na	na	na	na	na	na	na	na
Egypt	na	98	98	98	99	98	96	97	99	99	97	98	99	98	98	99
El Salvador	na	na	na	na	na	na	na	na	na	na	na	na	na	na	na	na
Estonia	na	na	na	na	na	na	na	na	na	na	na	na	na	na	na	na
Finland	na	na	na	na	na	na	na	na	na	na	na	na	na	na	na	na
France	na	na	na	na	na	na	na	na	na	na	na	na	na	na	na	na
Georgia	na	na	na	na	na	na	na	na	na	na	na	na	na	na	na	na
Germany	na	na	na	na	na	na	na	na	na	na	na	na	na	na	na	na
Great Britain	na	na	na	na	na	na	na	na	na	na	na	na	na	na	na	na
Greece	na	na	na	na	na	na	na	na	na	na	na	na	na	na	na	na
Hungary	na	na	na	na	na	na	na	na	na	na	na	na	na	na	na	na
Iceland	na	na	na	na	na	na	na	na	na	na	na	na	na	na	na	na
India	na	83	86	79	88	86	74	81	85	86	79	84	85	82	85	84
Indonesia	na	83	83	84	90	84	80	81	83	86	78	87	87	81	84	89
Iran	na	90	90	90	92	89	84	87	90	90	89	90	91	89	91	89
Ireland	na	na	na	na	na	na	na	na	na	na	na	na	na	na	na	na
Israel	na	na	na	na	na	na	na	na	na	na	na	na	na	na	na	na
Italy	na	na	na	na	na	na	na	na	na	na	na	na	na	na	na	na
Japan	na	72	69	75	81	77	64	66	72	74	69	74	71	74	71	72
Jordan	na	90	94	86	95	90	80	87	90	95	87	92	90	91	89	92
Korea, South	na	75	75	74	79	75	68	50	75	77	65	80	81	70	79	81
Latvia	na	na	na	na	na	na	na	na	na	na	na	na	na	na	na	na
Lithuania	na	na	na	na	na	na	na	na	na	na	na	na	na	na	na	na
Luxembourg	na	na	na	na	na	na	na	na	na	na	na	na	na	na	na	na
Macedonia	na	90	90	90	96	91	83	87	90	94	84	93	93	91	90	81
Malta	na	na	na	na	na	na	na	na	na	na	na	na	na	na	na	na
Mexico	na	85	87	83	93	83	76	80	91	91	80	83	89	84	85	91
Moldova	na	83	82	83	89	81	79	83	85	77	79	82	85	82	83	84
Montenegro	na	85	89	82	94	88	77	78	90	93	92	84	85	83	88	88
Morocco	na	89	88	89	92	88	85	87	94	92	82	89	86	88	90	89
Netherlands	na	na	na	na	na	na	na	na	na	na	na	na	na	na	na	na
New Zealand	na	na	na	na	na	na	na	na	na	na	na	na	na	na	na	na
Nigeria	na	92	93	91	94	90	88	91	92	93	91	93	91	93	91	90
Northern Ireland	na	na	na	na	na	na	na	na	na	na	na	na	na	na	na	na
Norway	na	na	na	na	na	na	na	na	na	na	na	na	na	na	na	na
Pakistan	na	79	83	74	89	78	59	77	81	77	79	78	76	78	80	83
Peru	na	87	89	86	91	85	85	85	80	88	83	89	94	86	87	88
Philippines	na	71	71	71	85	70	53	63	72	78	65	72	74	73	69	69
Poland	na	na	na	na	na	na	na	na	na	na	na	na	na	na	na	na
Portugal	na	na	na	na	na	na	na	na	na	na	na	na	na	na	na	na
Puerto Rico	na	90	88	92	95	90	89	87	87	93	86	92	92	86	92	87
Romania	na	na	na	na	na	na	na	na	na	na	na	na	na	na	na	na
Russian Fed.	na	85	85	84	96	86	78	81	84	90	80	85	88	85	85	86
Serbia	na	90	90	90	97	87	76	86	92	89	84	90	94	89	90	96
Singapore	na	na	na	na	na	na	na	na	na	na	na	na	na	na	na	na
Slovakia	na	na	na	na	na	na	na	na	na	na	na	na	na	na	na	na
Slovenia	na	na	na	na	na	na	na	na	na	na	na	na	na	na	na	na
South Africa	na	85	84	86	92	82	75	83	88	86	82	87	87	83	85	87
Spain	na	88	88	88	95	89	82	86	90	93	81	88	92	88	87	91
Sweden	na	na	na	na	na	na	na	na	na	na	na	na	na	na	na	na
Switzerland	na	na	na	na	na	na	na	na	na	na	na	na	na	na	na	na
Taiwan	na	na	na	na	na	na	na	na	na	na	na	na	na	na	na	na
Tanzania	na	69	68	71	76	64	70	72	71	54	73	66	62	70	68	71
Turkey	na	82	81	83	87	81	73	83	81	81	79	83	81	83	81	81
Uganda	na	71	79	63	81	63	50	56	76	80	64	78	71	71	69	77
Ukraine	na	na	na	na	na	na	na	na	na	na	na	na	na	na	na	na
United States	na	82	81	84	90	79	82	86	85	79	81	81	84	85	82	81
Uruguay	na	na	na	na	na	na	na	na	na	na	na	na	na	na	na	na
Venezuela	na	93	92	94	95	92	92	91	95	91	93	94	94	95	93	93
Vietnam	na	90	89	92	95	91	83	88	92	87	87	89	91	84	91	93*
Zimbabwe	na	67	75	61	78	57	62	63	75	40	67	70	67	66	70	66
Total	na	84	85	84	91	83	78	82	86	86	82	85	87	84	85	85

RANKING

Country	2000
Egypt	98
Venezuela	93
Nigeria	92
Bangladesh	91
Puerto Rico	90
Jordan	90
Singapore	90
Algeria	90
Bosnia and Herz.	90
Vietnam	90
Iran	90
Macedonia	90
Morocco	89
China	88
Spain	88
Chile	88
Peru	87
Argentina	87
Albania	87
Montenegro	85
South Africa	85
Mexico	85
Serbia	85
India	83
Indonesia	83
Moldova	83
United States	82
Turkey	82
Pakistan	79
Canada	78
Korea, South	75
Japan	72
Philippines	71
Uganda	71
Tanzania	69
Zimbabwe	67
Total	**84**

A058) SPEND TIME WITH FRIENDS

I'm going to ask how of often you do various things? Spend time with friends

Weekly / Once or twice a month (%)

Country	Wave 1990	Wave 2000	Gender Male	Gender Female	Age 16-29	Age 30-49	Age 50+	Edu Lower	Edu Middle	Edu Upper	Inc Lower
Albania	na	69	79	59	76	66	66	63	70	80	65
Algeria	na	81	90	72	88	78	73	68	83	88	79
Argentina	na	75	80	72	87	74	66	69	83	86	68
Armenia	na	na	na	na	na	na	na	83	93	93	82
Australia	na	na	na	na	na	na	na	na	na	na	na
Austria	na	88	90	86	99	90	81	na	na	na	na
Azerbaijan	na	na	na	na	na	na	na	na	na	na	na
Bangladesh	na	84	92	74	84	84	84	81	86	90	81
Belarus	na	81	84	78	91	81	72	75	82	84	78
Belgium	na	81	82	80	95	84	72	69	83	87	75
Bosnia and Herz.	na	97	98	96	98	98	95	94	98	97	96
Brazil	na	na	na	na	na	na	na	na	na	na	na
Bulgaria	na	83	84	81	95	87	73	78	84	89	75
Canada	na	90	89	91	96	89	88	84	91	93	89
Chile	na	59	65	53	78	58	41	45	64	75	54
China	na	61	58	65	70	63	49	58	64	64	53
Colombia	na	na	na	na	na	na	na	na	na	na	na
Croatia	na	90	95	86	98	92	84	88	92	94	89
Czech Republic	na	81	81	81	95	85	70	80	82	81	74
Denmark	na	91	90	92	100	93	84	88	98	92	88
Dominican Rep.	na	na	na	na	na	na	na	na	na	na	na
Egypt	na	86	92	80	92	85	80	82	91	92	86
El Salvador	na	na	na	na	na	na	na	na	na	na	na
Estonia	na	77	75	80	96	81	63	71	80	81	74
Finland	na	88	87	89	98	89	82	88	90	90	na
France	na	87	87	87	98	86	82	83	89	93	85
Georgia	na	na	na	na	na	na	na	na	na	na	na
Germany	na	86	85	87	94	86	82	82	90	89	80
Great Britain	na	93	93	93	98	92	90	89	94	97	90
Greece	na	92	92	92	99	90	79	80	90	95	89
Hungary	na	66	71	62	88	69	52	61	77	77	60
Iceland	na	89	87	92	99	91	80	88	90	94	88
India	na	72	79	62	77	73	64	67	71	83	76
Indonesia	na	97	98	97	99	98	97	97	97	99	98
Iran	na	74	77	70	81	70	62	66	77	78	70
Ireland	na	93	93	94	99	91	92	91	95	94	91
Israel	na	na	na	na	na	na	na	na	na	na	na
Italy	na	82	87	77	95	85	72	73	88	na	na
Japan	na	66	62	70	80	63	63	65	66	67	63
Jordan	na	78	88	68	80	76	77	78	78	77	63
Korea, South	na	78	81	75	93	74	71	63	78	81	74
Latvia	na	72	76	68	91	74	62	63	73	79	69
Lithuania	na	72	75	69	94	73	54	47	80	77	67
Luxembourg	na	88	89	87	94	89	81	85	90	88	87
Macedonia	na	91	93	89	96	91	88	87	93	96	na
Malta	na	61	66	56	77	57	34	30	64	75	55
Mexico	na	64	72	57	72	63	55	57	72	80	59
Moldova	na	75	79	71	88	72	67	71	76	75	67
Montenegro	na	92	93	90	96	94	87	87	94	97	92
Morocco	na	80	85	75	86	79	66	77	89	95	71
Netherlands	na	92	91	93	99	95	85	86	94	95	90
New Zealand	na	na	na	na	na	na	na	na	na	na	na
Nigeria	na	96	98	94	97	95	90	94	97	97	na
Northern Ireland	na	93	93	93	99	93	90	95	96	90	na
Norway	na	na	na	na	na	na	na	na	na	na	na
Pakistan	na	69	73	65	74	65	73	65	73	na	na
Peru	na	79	85	74	88	75	70	70	77	88	72
Philippines	na	79	84	75	85	78	74	78	78	83	76
Poland	na	67	70	65	89	70	51	62	73	75	59
Portugal	na	78	82	75	89	74	75	73	89	84	63
Puerto Rico	na	70	77	66	81	71	64	58	68	73	63
Romania	na	61	68	53	91	60	44	54	67	70	49
Russian Fed.	na	66	71	62	88	70	48	48	67	75	60
Serbia	na	92	94	90	97	93	88	89	93	96	89
Singapore	na	82	87	78	95	71	67	77	86	82	77
Slovakia	na	80	81	78	90	78	74	78	80	82	77
Slovenia	na	83	87	80	95	84	74	75	86	88	79
South Africa	na	82	84	80	87	80	73	77	86	89	81
Spain	na	86	91	82	96	89	78	80	93	92	87
Sweden	na	95	94	96	98	95	92	92	96	95	95
Switzerland	na	na	na	na	na	na	na	na	na	na	na
Taiwan	na	na	na	na	na	na	na	na	na	na	na
Tanzania	na	85	87	82	91	83	80	81	88	91	83
Turkey	na	92	93	91	93	92	88	91	91	96	92
Uganda	na	96	98	94	98	95	94	93	97	100	96
Ukraine	na	72	77	67	91	73	59	61	71	79	66
United States	na	92	92	91	96	91	91	91	94	89	94
Uruguay	na	na	na	na	na	na	na	na	na	na	na
Venezuela	na	77	82	73	83	76	71	71	77	85	74
Vietnam	na	72	77	67	80	71	66	66	79	74	80
Zimbabwe	na	87	90	85	88	86	85	84	87	100	89
Total	na	81	84	78	90	81	73	76	83	87	77

A059) SPEND TIME

I'm going to ask how

Weekly / Once or twice

Country	Wave 1990
Albania	na
Algeria	na
Argentina	na
Armenia	na
Australia	na
Austria	na
Azerbaijan	na
Bangladesh	na
Belarus	na
Belgium	na
Bosnia and Herz.	na
Brazil	na
Bulgaria	na
Canada	na
Chile	na
China	na
Colombia	na
Croatia	na
Czech Republic	na
Denmark	na
Dominican Rep.	na
Egypt	na
El Salvador	na
Estonia	na
Finland	na
France	na
Georgia	na
Germany	na
Great Britain	na
Greece	na
Hungary	na
Iceland	na
India	na
Indonesia	na
Iran	na
Ireland	na
Israel	na
Italy	na
Japan	na
Jordan	na
Korea, South	na
Latvia	na
Lithuania	na
Luxembourg	na
Macedonia	na
Malta	na
Mexico	na
Moldova	na
Montenegro	na
Morocco	na
Netherlands	na
New Zealand	na
Nigeria	na
Northern Ireland	na
Norway	na
Pakistan	na
Peru	na
Philippines	na
Poland	na
Portugal	na
Puerto Rico	na
Romania	na
Russian Fed.	na
Serbia	na
Singapore	na
Slovakia	na
Slovenia	na
South Africa	na
Spain	na
Sweden	na
Switzerland	na
Taiwan	na
Tanzania	na
Turkey	na
Uganda	na
Ukraine	na
United States	na
Uruguay	na
Venezuela	na
Vietnam	na
Zimbabwe	na
Total	na

A060) SPEND TIME WITH PEOPLE AT YOUR CHURCH, MOSQUE OR SYNAGOGUE

I'm going to ask how of often you do various things? Spend time with people at your church, mosque or synagogue

Weekly / Once or twice a month (%)

(WVS: V30; EVS: V50)

Country	Wave 1990	Wave 2000	Gender Male	Gender Female	Age 16-29	Age 30-49	Age 50+	Education Lower	Education Middle	Education Upper	Income Lower	Income Middle	Income Upper	Values Mat	Values Mixed	Values Postm.	RANKING Country	2000
Albania	na	28	24	31	22	25	37	32	25	22	31	27	25	26	28	20	Nigeria	92
Algeria	na	40	57	21	36	36	55	44	38	37	40	39	42	36	43	38	Indonesia	90
Argentina	na	32	22	40	22	35	39	35	27	30	37	32	27	31	34	27	Tanzania	83
Armenia	na	na	na	na	na	na	na	na	na	na	na	na	na	na	na	na	Zimbabwe	82
Australia	na	na	na	na	na	na	na	na	na	na	na	na	na	na	na	na	Uganda	77
Austria	na	26	26	26	19	29	27	25	24	33	23	28	27	19	27	27	South Africa	66
Azerbaijan	na	na	na	na	na	na	na	na	na	na	na	na	na	na	na	na	Puerto Rico	65
Bangladesh	na	61	90	24	49	67	81	54	66	74	49	65	68	57	65	60	Philippines	64
Belarus	na	32	23	39	29	25	44	46	29	20	40	31	20	33	33	21	Bangladesh	61
Belgium	na	21	20	22	20	17	26	22	20	23	29	24	15	18	22	20	India	61
Bosnia and Herz.	na	33	31	34	35	32	32	40	31	31	34	32	31	29	34	30	Malta	60
Brazil	na	na	na	na	na	na	na	na	na	na	na	na	na	na	na	na	Peru	58
Bulgaria	na	13	13	13	9	11	16	19	9	12	17	15	6	13	13	14	Egypt	57
Canada	na	29	25	33	16	27	39	35	24	31	31	32	22	28	32	23	Mexico	56
Chile	na	33	28	38	25	31	44	36	31	31	40	30	28	31	37	25	Pakistan	55
China	na	43	46	40	50	46	30	30	53	49	32	49	51	43	49	56	Croatia	52
Colombia	na	na	na	na	na	na	na	na	na	na	na	na	na	na	na	na	United States	52
Croatia	na	52	43	61	47	53	55	61	48	50	60	53	49	61	52	47	Iran	49
Czech Republic	na	12	10	14	11	7	16	14	9	12	16	11	7	14	11	14	Portugal	46
Denmark	na	9	7	11	5	8	12	8	5	12	12	6	8	5	9	5	Jordan	46
Dominican Rep.	na	na	na	na	na	na	na	na	na	na	na	na	na	na	na	na	Ireland	44
Egypt	na	57	78	35	51	57	67	53	58	68	54	56	63	54	60	63	China	43
El Salvador	na	na	na	na	na	na	na	na	na	na	na	na	na	na	na	na	Algeria	40
Estonia	na	24	22	26	20	16	32	30	19	24	31	23	26	28	23	na	Northern Ireland	39
Finland	na	23	19	27	16	21	30	25	21	24	28	23	19	18	25	28	Venezuela	37
France	na	9	7	10	6	7	11	9	8	9	10	9	8	9	9	6	Singapore	36
Georgia	na	na	na	na	na	na	na	na	na	na	na	na	na	na	na	na	Moldova	36
Germany	na	30	25	33	24	23	39	33	26	34	31	32	28	21	32	37	Morocco	35
Great Britain	na	20	17	23	12	17	27	16	19	26	17	20	25	na	na	na	Korea, South	33
Greece	na	23	22	24	18	22	36	38	26	19	27	22	22	22	25	18	Chile	33
Hungary	na	na	na	na	na	na	na	na	na	na	na	na	na	na	na	na	Bosnia and Herz.	33
Iceland	na	11	10	11	8	11	12	13	8	11	12	11	8	13	10	8	Belarus	32
India	na	61	60	62	57	62	63	61	61	62	55	59	65	60	62	67	Argentina	32
Indonesia	na	90	94	86	86	91	91	91	91	89	89	92	89	90	90	89	Romania	30
Iran	na	49	53	45	46	48	62	59	46	43	50	56	44	48	50	37	Germany	30
Ireland	na	44	39	48	25	40	61	54	37	40	59	38	37	42	44	39	Spain	29
Israel	na	na	na	na	na	na	na	na	na	na	na	na	na	na	na	na	Canada	29
Italy	na	24	18	31	18	22	30	28	21	22	29	21	22	33	24	21	Albania	28
Japan	na	9	7	11	3	9	11	10	11	5	10	9	9	8	9	10	Austria	26
Jordan	na	46	79	13	37	44	66	48	44	42	43	53	41	46	47	38	Estonia	24
Korea, South	na	33	28	38	26	35	36	32	35	30	29	34	37	33	33	39	Italy	24
Latvia	na	na	na	na	na	na	na	na	na	na	na	na	na	na	na	na	Macedonia	24
Lithuania	na	15	8	21	11	6	25	26	11	10	20	16	9	15	13	23	Slovenia	24
Luxembourg	na	na	na	na	na	na	na	na	na	na	na	na	na	na	na	na	Finland	23
Macedonia	na	24	29	19	22	25	24	33	20	20	25	25	21	22	25	29	Greece	23
Malta	na	60	53	66	45	59	71	75	54	54	64	60	58	67	57	55	Belgium	21
Mexico	na	56	53	58	51	57	61	61	49	50	62	56	52	58	58	49	Sweden	21
Moldova	na	36	26	45	25	30	52	53	32	28	43	38	30	40	30	37	Serbia	21
Montenegro	na	16	17	16	14	17	17	17	15	19	19	14	14	16	16	20	Netherlands	20
Morocco	na	35	53	19	26	37	57	38	25	24	39	39	33	35	36	37	Great Britain	20
Netherlands	na	20	19	21	15	12	32	25	18	18	23	21	14	28	20	17	Vietnam	18
New Zealand	na	na	na	na	na	na	na	na	na	na	na	na	na	na	na	na	Ukraine	16
Nigeria	na	92	94	90	92	92	89	88	95	93	91	93	92	90	94	92	Montenegro	16
Northern Ireland	na	39	38	39	31	28	52	42	32	43	35	38	42	42	41	33	Lithuania	15
Norway	na	na	na	na	na	na	na	na	na	na	na	na	na	na	na	na	Bulgaria	13
Pakistan	na	55	83	18	57	51	64	51	58	64	50	63	49	60	51	42	Czech Republic	12
Peru	na	58	51	65	50	64	65	64	62	48	62	59	50	59	58	57	Iceland	11
Philippines	na	64	61	67	61	65	65	60	64	68	62	66	63	60	66	69	Japan	9
Poland	na	na	na	na	na	na	na	na	na	na	na	na	na	na	na	na	Denmark	9
Portugal	na	46	40	51	36	43	54	50	37	37	58	45	41	51	44	34	France	9
Puerto Rico	na	65	60	67	53	56	77	81	64	62	69	67	59	60	67	61	Russian Fed.	8
Romania	na	30	24	36	18	23	42	47	23	15	38	32	21	35	24	22		
Russian Fed.	na	8	4	12	6	5	13	16	7	9	12	7	6	9	7	9		
Serbia	na	21	17	25	22	18	22	25	16	23	25	19	21	20	22	19		
Singapore	na	36	34	39	35	38	37	35	37	39	39	35	38	38	37	27		
Slovakia	na	na	na	na	na	na	na	na	na	na	na	na	na	na	na	na		
Slovenia	na	24	23	24	20	20	30	31	23	12	29	24	15	27	23	21		
South Africa	na	66	57	76	62	66	76	68	63	64	71	66	59	69	64	64		
Spain	na	29	20	38	15	23	43	36	22	23	38	27	25	40	28	16		
Sweden	na	21	18	23	17	20	24	24	20	20	23	20	17	31	20	21		
Switzerland	na	na	na	na	na	na	na	na	na	na	na	na	na	na	na	na		
Taiwan	na	na	na	na	na	na	na	na	na	na	na	na	na	na	na	na		
Tanzania	na	83	83	84	83	83	84	84	84	81	83	86	79	85	83	88		
Turkey	na	na	na	na	na	na	na	na	na	na	na	na	na	na	na	na		
Uganda	na	77	86	70	77	77	83	72	79	84	81	78	82	76	78	82		
Ukraine	na	16	8	23	13	13	22	38	14	8	16	16	16	17	13	22		
United States	na	52	45	59	42	52	61	53	51	53	52	53	50	62	52	48		
Uruguay	na	na	na	na	na	na	na	na	na	na	na	na	na	na	na	na		
Venezuela	na	37	32	42	31	39	37	42	34	37	43	39	33	40	36	34		
Vietnam	na	18	14	21	17	16	21	21	13	15	19	14	20	12	19	19		
Zimbabwe	na	82	70	92	82	84	77	83	80	52	76	87	84	80	82	92		
Total	na	39	39	38	38	38	41	42	36	38	41	40	36	42	39	34	Total	39

A061) SPEND TIME WITH PEOPLE AT SPORT, CULTURE, COMMUNAL ORGANIZATION

I'm going to ask how of often you do various things?

Spend time socially with people at sports clubs or voluntary or service organization

Weekly / Once or twice a month (%)

(WVS: V31; EVS: V51)

Country	Wave 1990	Wave 2000	Gender Male	Gender Female	Age 16-29	Age 30-49	Age 50+	Education Lower	Education Middle	Education Upper	Income Lower	Income Middle	Income Upper	Values Mat	Values Mixed	Values Postm.	RANKING Country	RANKING 2000
Albania	na	20	28	13	29	19	14	17	21	28	20	25	17	18	22	26	Denmark	59
Algeria	na	24	32	15	29	22	15	14	25	30	22	19	29	18	29	18	Germany	57
Argentina	na	24	29	19	24	26	21	20	28	33	21	21	30	21	23	27	Indonesia	57
Armenia	na	na	na	na	na	na	na	na	na	na	na	na	na	na	na	na	Netherlands	57
Australia	na	na	na	na	na	na	na	na	na	na	na	na	na	na	na	na	Uganda	56
Austria	na	42	50	34	48	45	36	34	49	51	36	43	45	31	43	44	Nigeria	53
Azerbaijan	na	na	na	na	na	na	na	na	na	na	na	na	na	na	na	na	Belgium	50
Bangladesh	na	31	45	15	27	34	38	24	37	44	21	30	45	31	33	25	Ireland	50
Belarus	na	18	24	14	33	15	8	6	21	24	11	20	25	15	20	33	Tanzania	49
Belgium	na	50	55	45	56	51	47	41	51	55	37	49	57	45	51	55	United States	48
Bosnia and Herz.	na	20	28	14	30	20	11	8	19	35	13	21	23	14	22	35	Malta	46
Brazil	na	na	na	na	na	na	na	na	na	na	na	na	na	na	na	na	Sweden	46
Bulgaria	na	24	29	18	39	29	13	10	25	38	13	29	29	19	29	22	Austria	42
Canada	na	39	40	38	39	41	37	32	40	44	35	38	43	42	38	40	Croatia	40
Chile	na	25	28	22	29	24	22	21	27	26	25	25	24	23	27	23	Canada	39
China	na	5	4	6	6	5	3	3	6	7	2	7	6	5	6	6	Peru	39
Colombia	na	na	na	na	na	na	na	na	na	na	na	na	na	na	na	na	Great Britain	39
Croatia	na	40	52	26	52	39	32	30	42	53	31	41	40	30	39	54	South Africa	38
Czech Republic	na	30	38	23	45	30	23	28	30	40	25	29	36	28	30	43	Finland	36
Denmark	na	59	61	56	61	60	55	55	64	62	54	59	64	54	60	57	Iceland	36
Dominican Rep.	na	na	na	na	na	na	na	na	na	na	na	na	na	na	na	na	Northern Ireland	34
Egypt	na	18	24	10	20	18	14	8	23	33	11	14	24	12	22	29	Estonia	34
El Salvador	na	na	na	na	na	na	na	na	na	na	na	na	na	na	na	na	Slovenia	34
Estonia	na	34	36	32	58	29	23	28	34	42	24	32	40	26	38	50	France	34
Finland	na	36	38	35	42	41	28	32	44	36	33	40	38	36	36	39	Philippines	33
France	na	34	36	32	41	30	33	30	30	45	32	36	37	30	34	40	Bangladesh	31
Georgia	na	na	na	na	na	na	na	na	na	na	na	na	na	na	na	na	Zimbabwe	31
Germany	na	57	61	55	63	59	53	50	63	68	42	61	68	51	59	62	Italy	31
Great Britain	na	39	42	36	39	38	41	35	41	44	34	33	47	na	na	na	Venezuela	31
Greece	na	30	33	27	30	30	28	19	31	30	27	29	34	32	29	28	Czech Republic	30
Hungary	na	na	na	na	na	na	na	na	na	na	na	na	na	na	na	na	Vietnam	30
Iceland	na	36	38	33	38	36	33	33	39	36	26	43	39	32	37	35	Greece	30
India	na	25	30	17	31	23	21	20	22	35	26	20	28	21	29	25	Portugal	28
Indonesia	na	57	67	48	59	61	53	48	60	62	58	59	59	57	58	75	Mexico	27
Iran	na	18	20	16	19	17	17	15	18	21	15	20	19	14	19	16	Montenegro	26
Ireland	na	50	54	45	58	46	48	41	52	60	45	49	57	51	48	54	Japan	25
Israel	na	na	na	na	na	na	na	na	na	na	na	na	na	na	na	na	Singapore	25
Italy	na	31	38	25	43	31	24	22	36	42	23	34	39	25	30	36	Serbia	25
Japan	na	25	25	26	14	20	35	26	25	26	24	27	27	28	24	31	Chile	25
Jordan	na	8	13	3	13	5	4	3	10	14	5	7	13	6	8	17	India	25
Korea, South	na	20	20	19	16	20	23	14	20	20	17	21	21	17	22	23	Spain	25
Latvia	na	na	na	na	na	na	na	na	na	na	na	na	na	na	na	na	Bulgaria	24
Lithuania	na	15	16	14	31	13	4	4	17	23	9	13	17	15	14	20	Algeria	24
Luxembourg	na	na	na	na	na	na	na	na	na	na	na	na	na	na	na	na	Argentina	24
Macedonia	na	17	24	11	24	20	8	11	19	25	14	20	18	18	16	31	Puerto Rico	22
Malta	na	46	52	40	40	45	40	11	17	45	41	53	56	45	47	45	Albania	20
Mexico	na	27	32	23	30	28	22	23	31	40	25	27	37	26	27	39	Bosnia and Herz.	20
Moldova	na	15	18	12	23	14	9	8	15	21	12	14	19	11	18	19	Pakistan	20
Montenegro	na	26	36	16	50	26	10	11	33	41	17	22	31	17	33	41	Korea, South	20
Morocco	na	14	18	10	20	12	4	9	30	36	8	21	15	11	16	23	Belarus	18
Netherlands	na	57	60	54	63	54	57	50	59	60	58	60	53	51	57	60	Iran	18
New Zealand	na	na	na	na	na	na	na	na	na	na	na	na	na	na	na	na	Egypt	18
Nigeria	na	53	62	43	57	50	32	45	55	62	50	51	59	48	55	56	Macedonia	17
Northern Ireland	na	34	41	28	39	29	37	29	36	46	30	34	41	34	35	37	Moldova	15
Norway	na	na	na	na	na	na	na	na	na	na	na	na	na	na	na	na	Lithuania	15
Pakistan	na	20	23	16	15	22	21	22	16	22	21	19	20	22	18	8	Turkey	15
Peru	na	39	48	30	41	40	31	28	39	46	34	40	46	29	41	44	Morocco	14
Philippines	na	33	42	23	35	31	32	25	31	44	29	30	41	33	34	23	Ukraine	14
Poland	na	na	na	na	na	na	na	na	na	na	na	na	na	na	na	na	Russian Fed.	13
Portugal	na	28	41	16	34	28	25	22	38	45	15	28	40	21	34	33	Romania	11
Puerto Rico	na	22	29	18	27	21	21	20	19	24	21	22	23	24	20	27	Jordan	8
Romania	na	11	14	8	21	7	8	5	10	17	5	4	17	7	13	14	China	5
Russian Fed.	na	13	16	10	29	10	5	6	12	19	10	11	15	10	15	20		
Serbia	na	25	39	12	41	28	15	11	30	37	16	27	32	19	30	41		
Singapore	na	25	31	19	34	19	10	18	27	37	18	23	31	18	27	30		
Slovakia	na	na	na	na	na	na	na	na	na	na	na	na	na	na	na	na		
Slovenia	na	34	44	25	51	32	23	17	39	42	21	34	46	28	34	39		
South Africa	na	38	43	32	43	37	29	34	42	50	34	41	42	32	41	56		
Spain	na	25	30	19	32	25	19	16	33	36	21	23	33	21	25	32		
Sweden	na	46	47	44	57	49	37	42	50	43	41	50	48	43	46	47		
Switzerland	na	na	na	na	na	na	na	na	na	na	na	na	na	na	na	na		
Taiwan	na	na	na	na	na	na	na	na	na	na	na	na	na	na	na	na		
Tanzania	na	49	52	45	52	47	49	47	51	50	48	49	46	45	51	50		
Turkey	na	15	20	8	17	13	11	7	23	29	6	19	24	12	15	20		
Uganda	na	56	73	40	61	54	36	43	60	70	56	60	67	52	55	67		
Ukraine	na	14	18	11	29	13	6	6	12	23	8	15	20	9	17	35		
United States	na	48	51	45	51	48	46	50	44	49	44	46	53	47	47	50		
Uruguay	na	na	na	na	na	na	na	na	na	na	na	na	na	na	na	na		
Venezuela	na	31	44	18	39	29	18	22	33	38	30	30	35	28	31	41		
Vietnam	na	30	37	23	39	27	29	28	31	39	25	27	37	29	30	36		
Zimbabwe	na	31	37	27	34	32	24	26	38	32	27	31	42	30	34	24		
Total	na	31	37	25	36	30	27	25	33	38	27	31	35	25	33	39	Total	31

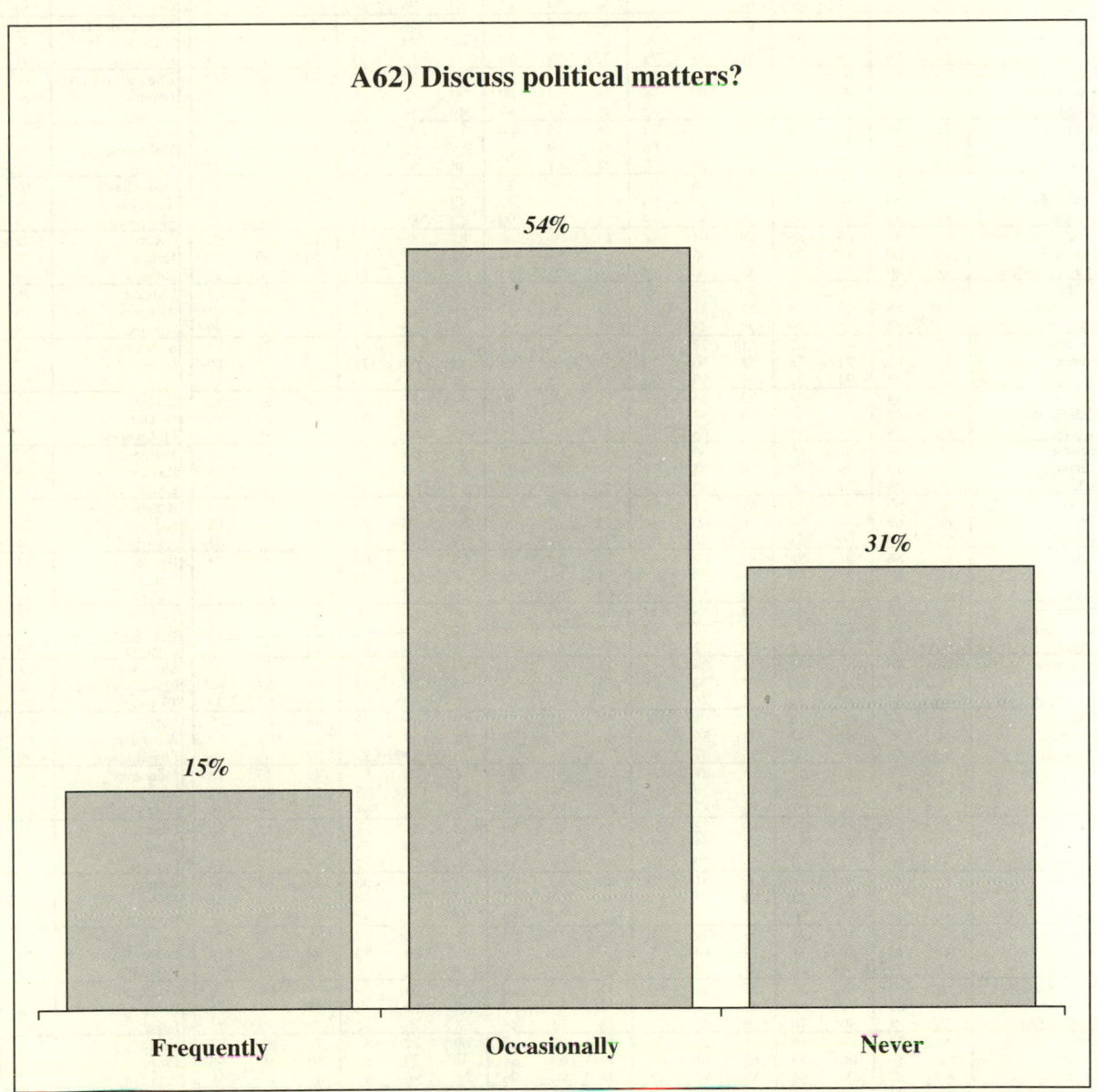

A62) Discuss political matters?

15%   54%   31%

Frequently   Occasionally   Never

A062) HOW OFTEN DISCUSSES POLITICAL MATTERS

When you get together with your friends, would you say you discuss political matters frequently, occasionally or never?

Frequently / Occasionally (%) (WVS: V32; EVS: V7)

Country	Wave 1990	Wave 2000	Gender Male	Gender Female	Age 16-29	Age 30-49	Age 50+	Educ. Lower	Educ. Middle	Educ. Upper	Income Lower	Income Middle	Income Upper	Values Mat	Values Mixed	Values Postm.
Albania	na	78	89	66	71	81	79	72	82	84	72	82	80	74	81	80
Algeria	na	74	80	68	74	77	68	57	75	84	68	80	81	66	79	86
Argentina	67	51	56	47	46	55	52	41	62	74	40	49	66	35	52	62
Armenia	na	78	83	73	72	82	79	69	77	84	78	78	79	76	80	67
Australia	na	69	72	67	56	75	75	57	65	84	64	69	83	64	67	75
Austria	69	74	79	70	63	80	74	66	79	91	66	76	80	54	73	82
Azerbaijan	na	53	61	44	51	54	50	47	47	64	47	56	59	46	63	77
Bangladesh	na	74	89	55	72	75	72	67	78	87	66	74	82	71	77	72
Belarus	91	80	86	75	78	83	78	72	82	89	74	83	83	78	83	93
Belgium	53	63	69	57	53	71	60	43	61	81	53	61	73	48	63	79
Bosnia and Herz.	na	73	80	66	61	80	76	68	72	79	70	72	79	68	75	71
Brazil	55	58	63	53	57	58	62	46	64	82	49	56	70	43	61	84
Bulgaria	88	74	79	69	64	82	72	68	75	80	71	75	78	73	77	66
Canada	75	64	70	58	58	65	66	51	60	81	54	62	75	57	62	70
Chile	60	57	62	52	58	60	52	44	61	72	48	60	68	49	57	72
China	89	70	80	60	82	68	65	55	80	88	63	71	79	74	75	87
Colombia	na	54	60	47	46	58	56	40	46	73	42	49	68	45	51	63
Croatia	na	80	85	75	76	83	78	71	84	90	72	80	84	77	80	82
Czech Republic	90	87	89	86	79	91	88	83	91	96	81	89	90	83	88	92
Denmark	79	80	82	78	77	85	77	72	87	94	72	83	94	66	79	94
Dominican Rep.	na	80	83	79	81	80	100	56	76	84	78	84	81	73	80	91
Egypt	na	57	56	59	60	55	59	58	57	57	58	58	57	57	58	62
El Salvador	na	38	49	28	42	35	37	23	45	72	19	44	64	na	na	na
Estonia	95	82	85	79	70	88	83	72	85	91	75	82	87	81	84	89
Finland	82	74	76	72	61	77	77	73	73	78	65	74	81	70	76	74
France	65	65	72	58	52	66	70	56	69	83	55	67	78	52	66	79
Georgia	na	73	74	71	58	79	80	67	72	77	74	75	70	70	74	77
Germany	94	84	92	78	82	86	83	75	90	96	74	87	90	80	86	86
Great Britain	66	49	57	40	40	52	51	39	50	74	42	48	58	na	na	na
Greece	na	79	84	75	71	86	83	69	74	85	71	82	82	75	79	82
Hungary	76	54	61	48	45	65	49	47	62	79	44	57	58	48	60	65
Iceland	78	78	79	77	66	85	79	70	81	92	70	79	86	75	78	88
India	73	58	74	36	60	57	56	42	66	81	52	51	67	58	68	69
Indonesia	na	68	78	59	81	71	60	44	69	86	63	72	73	64	73	100
Iran	na	69	74	64	76	69	51	52	70	86	65	70	74	62	75	82
Ireland	58	60	66	53	56	61	62	52	57	78	49	59	73	58	58	67
Israel	na	86	87	85	83	89	86	73	88	91	79	87	94	89	88	79
Italy	58	68	77	59	65	75	62	54	75	85	56	71	76	53	66	77
Japan	66	65	73	57	45	57	79	63	63	71	65	64	68	65	66	75
Jordan	na	50	57	44	54	53	38	36	60	69	38	56	59	41	57	65
Korea, South	88	75	82	67	70	74	80	57	75	76	72	77	75	70	79	77
Latvia	96	77	77	78	69	82	77	58	81	91	72	76	85	75	79	87
Lithuania	94	85	88	83	81	89	85	73	89	92	80	88	89	80	89	97
Luxembourg	na	69	72	66	54	74	73	53	76	82	56	72	83	65	68	81
Macedonia	na	80	89	71	72	86	78	73	82	89	76	80	88	79	82	77
Malta	na	62	69	56	60	64	65	57	62	71	57	67	72	58	65	65
Mexico	74	55	64	47	57	56	51	46	63	79	51	58	67	55	59	60
Moldova	na	81	85	78	76	87	80	72	83	87	80	82	82	78	85	86
Montenegro	na	79	90	67	75	81	79	72	81	89	86	78	82	79	80	78
Morocco	na	32	41	23	40	29	17	24	58	76	31	38	35	20	40	64
Netherlands	74	80	82	77	78	83	77	65	83	90	75	82	87	72	79	85
New Zealand	na	83	86	81	68	82	89	80	80	89	83	81	87	72	85	86
Nigeria	63	74	85	75	75	75	69	68	76	83	71	76	78	72	75	79
Northern Ireland	56	66	73	60	56	70	69	64	66	74	56	71	77	65	67	73
Norway	89	86	88	84	83	91	83	80	86	92	na	na	na	76	87	94
Pakistan	na	57	68	44	54	57	61	56	56	63	57	57	59	55	60	58
Peru	na	77	84	70	77	79	72	64	75	88	71	78	88	74	77	85
Philippines	na	76	79	74	73	79	74	74	73	84	76	76	77	75	77	79
Poland	83	76	83	71	72	84	70	68	83	95	70	80	80	68	82	79
Portugal	53	51	63	40	61	57	40	42	66	79	26	50	69	41	56	61
Puerto Rico	na	60	68	56	56	61	61	49	52	66	47	63	70	62	60	62
Romania	66	62	74	51	61	71	55	42	69	87	45	62	78	58	67	81
Russian Fed.	83	75	80	70	70	80	72	58	74	88	68	76	82	73	79	71
Serbia	na	77	84	70	73	79	76	65	80	87	69	79	86	71	82	84
Singapore	na	59	66	53	63	61	43	44	63	84	46	59	69	56	60	66
Slovakia	na	87	90	84	81	91	85	78	90	96	82	86	92	83	89	98
Slovenia	82	72	78	67	64	79	71	58	76	86	68	80	80	68	73	78
South Africa	70	62	71	51	55	69	59	58	66	79	61	63	65	53	67	75
Spain	50	55	64	46	57	63	47	44	61	78	45	58	65	47	56	71
Sweden	79	80	80	80	77	80	82	72	77	91	78	79	85	65	79	90
Switzerland	86	78	83	72	69	80	80	66	79	93	69	79	83	62	81	80
Taiwan	na	70	78	62	83	76	45	46	72	91	56	70	88	66	79	76
Tanzania	na	79	82	74	78	79	83	73	84	88	70	82	89	75	81	91
Turkey	56	54	67	41	55	54	51	43	65	83	43	59	72	47	55	66
Uganda	na	78	84	73	73	84	78	71	79	91	80	87	84	80	77	79
Ukraine	na	78	81	75	73	84	75	63	77	88	76	79	81	75	82	89
United States	72	75	78	71	65	76	80	61	70	83	66	77	82	73	74	77
Uruguay	na	53	61	47	55	58	48	42	65	77	45	51	65	45	55	57
Venezuela	na	56	62	50	54	59	55	41	57	71	44	55	69	54	55	64
Vietnam	na	75	82	68	76	76	74	69	83	83	66	75	81	70	80	76
Zimbabwe	na	48	60	37	44	54	47	47	48	100	49	47	57	43	52	50
Total	75	69	75	63	65	72	69	57	72	82	63	70	76	64	72	77

RANKING

Country	2000
Czech Republic	87
Slovakia	87
Israel	86
Norway	86
Lithuania	85
Germany	84
New Zealand	83
Estonia	82
Moldova	81
Dominican Rep.	80
Denmark	80
Sweden	80
Belarus	80
Macedonia	80
Croatia	80
Netherlands	80
Tanzania	79
Montenegro	79
Greece	79
Iceland	78
Uganda	78
Ukraine	78
Armenia	78
Albania	78
Switzerland	78
Latvia	77
Peru	77
Serbia	77
Poland	76
Philippines	76
Vietnam	75
Russian Fed.	75
United States	75
Korea, South	75
Nigeria	74
Austria	74
Bangladesh	74
Bulgaria	74
Algeria	74
Finland	74
Bosnia and Herz.	73
Georgia	73
Slovenia	72
China	70
Taiwan	70
Iran	69
Australia	69
Luxembourg	69
Indonesia	68
Italy	68
Northern Ireland	66
France	65
Japan	65
Canada	64
Belgium	63
Malta	62
Romania	62
South Africa	62
Puerto Rico	60
Ireland	60
Singapore	59
Brazil	58
India	58
Egypt	57
Chile	57
Pakistan	57
Venezuela	56
Spain	55
Mexico	55
Colombia	54
Hungary	54
Turkey	54
Uruguay	53
Azerbaijan	53
Argentina	51
Portugal	51
Jordan	50
Great Britain	49
Zimbabwe	48
El Salvador	38
Morocco	32
Total	69

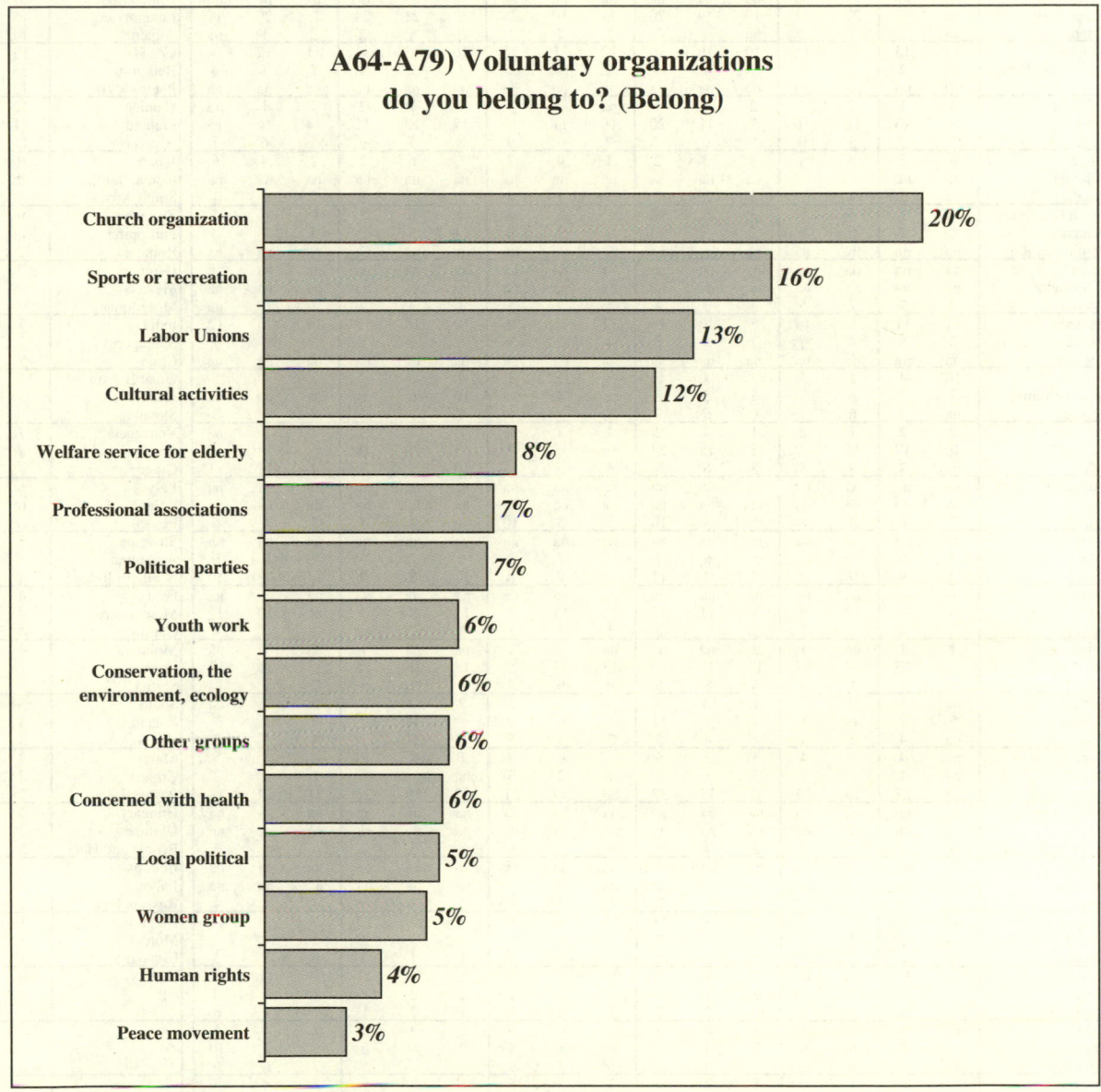

**A64-A79) Voluntary organizations
do you belong to? (Belong)**

Organization	Percentage
Church organization	20%
Sports or recreation	16%
Labor Unions	13%
Cultural activities	12%
Welfare service for elderly	8%
Professional associations	7%
Political parties	7%
Youth work	6%
Conservation, the environment, ecology	6%
Other groups	6%
Concerned with health	6%
Local political	5%
Women group	5%
Human rights	4%
Peace movement	3%

A064) BELONG SOCIAL WELFARE SERVICE FOR ELDERLY

Please look carefully at the following list of voluntary organizations and activities and say...which, if any, do you belong to?
Social welfare services for elderly, handicapped or deprived people

Belong (%)   (WVS: V39; EVS: V12)

Country	Wave		Gender		Age			Education			Income			Values		
	1990	2000	Male	Female	16-29	30-49	50+	Lower	Middle	Upper	Lower	Middle	Upper	Mat	Mixed	Postm.
Albania	na	14	14	14	9	13	18	11	14	19	14	11	16	12	17	5
Algeria	na	11	11	10	12	12	7	7	10	15	9	11	13	9	12	15
Argentina	2	5	4	5	2	4	9	5	5	4	5	5	5	5	5	4
Armenia	na	na	na	na	na	na	na	na	na	na	na	na	na	na	na	na
Australia	na	na	na	na	na	na	na	na	na	na	na	na	na	na	na	na
Austria	6	7	4	9	2	6	9	8	6	6	7	8	5	3	7	6
Azerbaijan	na	na	na	na	na	na	na	na	na	na	na	na	na	na	na	na
Bangladesh	na	17	22	11	15	19	20	14	19	25	5	21	24	15	20	11
Belarus	na	2	1	2	na	1	2	1	2	1	2	1	2	2	1	na
Belgium	12	13	10	15	10	10	16	12	11	15	16	13	11	11	12	14
Bosnia and Herz.	na	2	1	2	1	1	3	2	1	2	1	2	1	2	1	4
Brazil	10	na	na	na	na	na	na	na	na	na	na	na	na	na	na	na
Bulgaria	4	1	2	1	2	1	1	na	2	3	1	1	2	1	1	na
Canada	8	13	10	16	7	11	20	16	11	15	17	13	11	14	14	13
Chile	5	7	5	9	5	6	10	7	6	9	8	5	7	7	6	7
China	4	3	3	3	3	3	2	1	4	7	1	6	2	2	4	6
Colombia	na	na	na	na	na	na	na	na	na	na	na	na	na	na	na	na
Croatia	na	2	3	2	1	3	2	3	1	4	1	3	2	2	2	1
Czech Republic	na	7	5	8	3	5	10	7	6	7	9	6	5	9	6	5
Denmark	6	7	5	8	2	3	13	7	3	6	11	5	2	5	7	4
Dominican Rep.	na	na	na	na	na	na	na	na	na	na	na	na	na	na	na	na
Egypt	na	na	na	na	na	na	na	na	na	na	na	na	na	na	na	na
El Salvador	na	na	na	na	na	na	na	na	na	na	na	na	na	na	na	na
Estonia	2	3	2	5	3	3	4	4	2	5	4	3	4	3	3	na
Finland	11	11	8	14	5	10	16	11	11	16	10	15	12	10	13	12
France	7	6	4	7	2	5	8	4	5	9	6	6	7	5	6	7
Georgia	na	na	na	na	na	na	na	na	na	na	na	na	na	na	na	na
Germany	10	4	2	5	2	4	5	3	5	1	4	3	4	3	4	5
Great Britain	7	7	6	7	3	5	8	5	4	13	10	6	6	na	na	na
Greece	na	7	6	7	6	6	9	9	7	6	4	7	7	8	6	5
Hungary	2	2	1	2	1	3	2	1	2	6	1	2	3	1	3	na
Iceland	16	17	16	19	5	18	27	16	18	19	13	20	18	17	18	17
India	na	7	9	5	8	6	8	6	6	12	10	5	8	4	11	11
Indonesia	na	na	na	na	na	na	na	na	na	na	na	na	na	na	na	na
Iran	na	na	na	na	na	na	na	na	na	na	na	na	na	na	na	na
Ireland	7	6	4	8	5	3	10	5	5	10	8	4	7	7	6	6
Israel	na	na	na	na	na	na	na	na	na	na	na	na	na	na	na	na
Italy	4	6	5	7	5	6	7	6	7	8	5	7	7	7	6	6
Japan	2	9	9	10	2	4	17	18	9	8	12	8	9	14	8	10
Jordan	na	na	na	na	na	na	na	na	na	na	na	na	na	na	na	na
Korea, South	6	9	10	9	5	11	12	14	11	7	11	8	9	9	10	12
Latvia	2	2	2	1	2	2	2	1	1	3	2	2	na	1	2	4
Lithuania	1	1	na	1	2	na	na	1	1	na	na	na	1	na	1	na
Luxembourg	na	15	12	17	10	14	19	13	13	22	15	15	15	13	15	17
Macedonia	na	7	7	8	6	8	6	9	6	9	4	10	8	7	7	14
Malta	na	3	2	4	1	2	4	3	2	3	2	2	3	3	3	na
Mexico	5	7	6	8	4	7	11	8	6	9	7	9	7	9	7	7
Moldova	na	4	3	4	4	4	3	3	3	5	2	5	4	4	5	2
Montenegro	na	4	4	4	5	5	3	1	6	8	1	5	7	4	5	5
Morocco	na	1	1	1	1	1	2	1	2	3	na	1	6	1	2	2
Netherlands	15	21	19	24	8	17	32	23	19	21	22	19	22	21	22	18
New Zealand	na	na	na	na	na	na	na	na	na	na	na	na	na	na	na	na
Nigeria	na	na	na	na	na	na	na	na	na	na	na	na	na	na	na	na
Northern Ireland	9	4	3	5	2	4	6	4	3	8	3	5	7	4	5	3
Norway	11	na	na	na	na	na	na	na	na	na	na	na	na	na	na	na
Pakistan	na	na	na	na	na	na	na	na	na	na	na	na	na	na	na	na
Peru	na	4	3	5	2	4	8	4	3	6	3	4	6	4	4	4
Philippines	na	8	8	8	5	8	13	11	6	8	7	7	10	7	8	11
Poland	na	3	2	4	4	1	4	2	5	6	3	3	3	2	4	2
Portugal	5	2	2	3	3	2	2	1	3	10	1	3	2	2	2	2
Puerto Rico	na	12	10	13	8	9	17	11	8	15	13	13	11	24	11	11
Romania	2	2	2	2	2	1	2	1	2	2	1	2	2	1	2	0
Russian Fed.	2	2	1	2	na	2	1	2	2	1	1	2	1	1	1	6
Serbia	na	3	4	3	3	4	3	2	4	6	2	3	5	2	4	6
Singapore	na	7	6	8	8	6	7	6	8	8	7	8	6	5	7	10
Slovakia	na	7	5	8	4	6	10	6	7	9	8	7	5	7	6	6
Slovenia	1	5	4	6	4	3	9	7	5	5	8	5	5	8	4	5
South Africa	na	9	8	9	5	9	16	4	13	19	4	10	12	9	9	6
Spain	3	3	3	3	2	3	4	3	3	5	4	3	2	4	3	4
Sweden	8	21	16	25	12	21	26	18	19	26	21	15	27	14	19	28
Switzerland	9	na	na	na	na	na	na	na	na	na	na	na	na	na	na	na
Taiwan	na	na	na	na	na	na	na	na	na	na	na	na	na	na	na	na
Tanzania	na	27	27	27	27	26	28	28	24	28	28	28	22	24	29	25
Turkey	na	0	na	na	na	na	na	na	na	2	na	na	1	1	na	na
Uganda	na	12	15	10	11	12	19	15	11	14	19	14	12	10	13	13
Ukraine	na	2	2	2	1	3	2	2	2	3	2	2	2	2	2	na
United States	9	17	14	20	14	14	23	15	16	18	18	16	16	19	16	20
Uruguay	na	na	na	na	na	na	na	na	na	na	na	na	na	na	na	na
Venezuela	na	7	7	6	4	9	8	6	6	8	8	6	6	7	6	8
Vietnam	na	26	27	25	14	25	38	28	24	30	22	22	33	25	29	20
Zimbabwe	na	9	7	10	6	9	14	9	8	na	7	7	12	9	9	8
Total	6	8	7	8	6	7	10	7	7	10	8	8	8	6	8	9

RANKING

Country	2000
Tanzania	27
Vietnam	26
Netherlands	21
Sweden	21
Iceland	17
Bangladesh	17
United States	17
Luxembourg	15
Albania	14
Canada	13
Belgium	13
Puerto Rico	12
Uganda	12
Finland	11
Algeria	11
Japan	9
Korea, South	9
South Africa	9
Zimbabwe	9
Philippines	8
Romania	2
Denmark	7
Mexico	7
Macedonia	7
India	7
Singapore	7
Chile	7
Great Britain	7
Austria	7
Slovakia	7
Venezuela	7
Czech Republic	7
Greece	7
Italy	6
Ireland	6
France	6
Slovenia	5
Argentina	5
Northern Ireland	4
Peru	4
Montenegro	4
Germany	4
Moldova	4
Estonia	3
Serbia	3
Spain	3
Poland	3
China	3
Malta	2
Croatia	2
Portugal	2
Hungary	2
Ukraine	2
Bosnia and Herz.	2
Belarus	2
Latvia	2
Russian Fed.	2
Bulgaria	1
Morocco	1
Lithuania	1
Turkey	0
Total	8

A065) BELONG CHURCH ORGANIZATION

Please look carefully at the following list of voluntary organizations and activities and say...which, if any, do you belong to?.
Religious or church organizations.

Belong (%) (WVS: V40; EVS: V13)

Country	Wave 1990	Wave 2000	Gender Male	Gender Female	Age 16-29	Age 30-49	Age 50+	Education Lower	Education Middle	Education Upper	Income Lower	Income Middle	Income Upper	Values Mat	Values Mixed	Values Postm.
Albania	na	20	16	24	19	18	25	24	18	17	22	22	18	21	20	18
Algeria	na	7	9	5	8	5	9	7	6	9	5	8	8	6	8	12
Argentina	7	16	9	21	10	16	21	17	14	13	18	16	12	14	16	14
Armenia	na	na	na	na	na	na	na	na	na	na	na	na	na	na	na	na
Australia	na	na	na	na	na	na	na	na	na	na	na	na	na	na	na	na
Austria	16	26	27	24	23	28	25	20	29	38	20	25	32	21	25	29
Azerbaijan	na	na	na	na	na	na	na	na	na	na	na	na	na	na	na	na
Bangladesh	na	43	60	23	35	47	59	38	52	45	33	47	47	43	45	36
Belarus	na	2	1	4	1	2	4	4	2	2	3	2	1	3	2	2
Belgium	12	12	10	14	6	11	16	12	9	16	14	14	11	11	12	12
Bosnia and Herz.	na	8	7	9	6	7	12	16	6	6	13	6	8	8	8	8
Brazil	22	na	na	na	na	na	na	na	na	na	na	na	na	na	na	na
Bulgaria	2	2	1	3	2	1	3	4	1	1	4	1	1	2	2	2
Canada	25	30	26	33	20	26	39	31	26	35	29	30	26	27	33	22
Chile	18	21	16	25	16	20	27	23	19	21	25	19	17	22	21	16
China	1	4	3	5	3	4	3	2	5	5	3	3	5	3	4	na
Colombia	na	na	na	na	na	na	na	na	na	na	na	na	na	na	na	na
Croatia	na	13	15	12	11	10	18	14	12	14	7	16	13	11	14	11
Czech Republic	na	7	6	7	6	4	9	7	5	10	8	7	4	8	6	9
Denmark	7	12	9	14	10	14	11	10	12	14	10	12	14	8	14	7
Dominican Rep.	na	na	na	na	na	na	na	na	na	na	na	na	na	na	na	na
Egypt	na	na	na	na	na	na	na	na	na	na	na	na	na	na	na	na
El Salvador	na	na	na	na	na	na	na	na	na	na	na	na	na	na	na	na
Estonia	4	7	5	9	4	6	11	9	6	8	10	8	6	7	7	na
Finland	18	51	46	55	46	49	55	51	47	63	54	52	45	43	55	52
France	6	4	4	5	2	5	5	3	5	7	4	6	5	5	4	5
Georgia	na	na	na	na	na	na	na	na	na	na	na	na	na	na	na	na
Germany	20	14	11	16	13	12	16	14	14	13	11	17	17	11	14	16
Great Britain	16	5	5	5	3	3	7	4	3	10	8	4	4	na	na	na
Greece	na	7	6	7	5	7	10	17	6	5	9	6	5	10	6	4
Hungary	11	12	12	13	9	14	13	13	9	15	11	13	13	13	10	17
Iceland	50	71	74	68	66	68	79	73	72	67	73	71	70	71	73	58
India	na	18	20	15	14	19	19	16	19	20	18	15	21	14	23	18
Indonesia	na	na	na	na	na	na	na	na	na	na	na	na	na	na	na	na
Iran	na	na	na	na	na	na	na	na	na	na	na	na	na	na	na	na
Ireland	14	16	14	18	8	13	26	19	12	20	20	12	18	14	17	16
Israel	na	na	na	na	na	na	na	na	na	na	na	na	na	na	na	na
Italy	8	10	7	13	9	9	12	9	11	12	10	12	10	11	10	10
Japan	7	11	10	11	4	11	13	7	13	8	12	10	10	8	11	12
Jordan	na	na	na	na	na	na	na	na	na	na	na	na	na	na	na	na
Korea, South	39	42	35	50	38	44	43	45	46	37	39	40	48	41	42	47
Latvia	3	5	3	7	7	4	6	8	4	6	7	5	3	4	6	6
Lithuania	3	6	4	7	4	3	9	12	4	2	6	8	3	3	6	9
Luxembourg	na	10	10	10	4	7	17	7	10	14	10	9	11	7	10	14
Macedonia	na	11	12	10	12	12	8	16	8	8	9	12	8	12	10	15
Malta	na	14	12	17	9	10	22	17	12	21	16	16	12	13	15	19
Mexico	14	23	19	27	18	23	30	25	19	28	24	27	23	26	24	20
Moldova	na	14	9	19	13	11	19	16	14	13	12	14	15	18	12	9
Montenegro	na	3	4	2	3	3	4	3	4	4	3	3	3	3	4	3
Morocco	na	1	1	1	na	1	1	1	na	3	na	1	2	na	1	1
Netherlands	33	35	34	36	25	27	47	35	37	32	32	37	32	50	34	30
New Zealand	na	na	na	na	na	na	na	na	na	na	na	na	na	na	na	na
Nigeria	na	na	na	na	na	na	na	na	na	na	na	na	na	na	na	na
Northern Ireland	25	24	20	27	18	19	30	25	19	32	19	24	31	25	26	14
Norway	11	na	na	na	na	na	na	na	na	na	na	na	na	na	na	na
Pakistan	na	na	na	na	na	na	na	na	na	na	na	na	na	na	na	na
Peru	na	25	20	31	24	25	32	28	27	22	24	26	28	25	25	26
Philippines	na	31	29	33	26	31	36	29	27	39	31	31	30	30	33	20
Poland	na	6	6	6	9	4	6	5	7	6	7	5	6	6	5	8
Portugal	11	6	4	7	5	8	5	6	4	9	7	6	5	5	6	7
Puerto Rico	na	42	38	43	31	35	51	56	39	41	52	41	35	58	41	36
Romania	5	4	4	5	4	3	6	4	5	3	7	3	4	4	5	7
Russian Fed.	1	2	1	4	1	2	4	3	2	2	3	2	1	2	3	2
Serbia	na	3	4	2	1	3	3	3	3	3	2	3	4	2	3	6
Singapore	na	20	20	20	19	22	17	14	21	32	16	18	26	19	20	18
Slovakia	na	17	12	21	10	13	26	25	13	11	23	16	14	18	16	13
Slovenia	3	7	7	6	9	5	7	8	7	5	7	10	5	5	7	9
South Africa	na	54	46	65	49	54	70	55	54	51	52	62	50	57	54	41
Spain	4	7	5	8	4	6	9	7	5	9	7	7	8	7	6	7
Sweden	10	72	68	75	72	70	73	74	70	73	70	71	74	62	73	69
Switzerland	11	na	na	na	na	na	na	na	na	na	na	na	na	na	na	na
Taiwan	na	na	na	na	na	na	na	na	na	na	na	na	na	na	na	na
Tanzania	na	57	55	60	55	59	59	57	58	59	57	65	55	58	56	71
Turkey	na	1	1	na	1	na	1	na	1	2	na	1	1	na	1	na
Uganda	na	42	52	32	39	47	37	39	43	40	47	39	45	46	41	32
Ukraine	na	4	3	5	3	4	5	7	4	3	5	3	5	3	5	5
United States	49	57	52	63	42	61	65	47	57	62	50	60	65	67	59	51
Uruguay	na	na	na	na	na	na	na	na	na	na	na	na	na	na	na	na
Venezuela	na	23	22	24	16	25	34	29	19	26	24	26	21	29	22	16
Vietnam	na	11	8	13	9	10	12	13	7	6	7	9	13	6	13	5
Zimbabwe	na	76	63	87	78	77	70	75	78	60	70	79	81	72	78	88
Total	14	20	19	22	19	20	22	21	19	23	21	21	20	19	22	21

RANKING

Country	2000
Zimbabwe	76
Sweden	72
Iceland	71
United States	57
Tanzania	57
South Africa	54
Finland	51
Bangladesh	43
Korea, South	42
Uganda	42
Puerto Rico	42
Netherlands	35
Philippines	31
Canada	30
Austria	26
Peru	25
Northern Ireland	24
Mexico	23
Venezuela	23
Chile	21
Albania	20
Singapore	20
Romania	4
India	18
Slovakia	17
Ireland	16
Argentina	16
Malta	14
Moldova	14
Denmark	12
Germany	14
Croatia	13
Hungary	12
Belgium	12
Macedonia	11
Japan	11
Vietnam	11
Italy	10
Luxembourg	10
Bosnia and Herz.	8
Estonia	7
Algeria	7
Greece	7
Czech Republic	7
Slovenia	7
Spain	7
Poland	6
Portugal	6
Lithuania	6
Latvia	5
Great Britain	5
France	4
Ukraine	4
China	4
Montenegro	3
Serbia	3
Belarus	2
Russian Fed.	2
Bulgaria	2
Morocco	1
Turkey	1
Total	20

A066) BELONG CULTURAL ACTIVITIES

**Please look carefully at the following list of voluntary organizations and activities and say...which, if any, do you belong to?.
Education, arts, music or cultural activities.**

Belong (%)

(WVS: V41; EVS: V14)

Country	Wave		Gender		Age			Education			Income			Values				RANKING Country	2000
	1990	2000	Male	Female	16-29	30-49	50+	Lower	Middle	Upper	Lower	Middle	Upper	Mat	Mixed	Postm.			
Albania	na	14	16	12	24	12	7	8	16	21	13	15	13	11	16	26		Netherlands	45
Algeria	na	12	13	10	14	11	10	5	11	18	12	10	15	8	13	17		United States	37
Argentina	6	9	7	11	14	10	4	3	13	33	5	9	14	3	8	17		Bangladesh	30
Armenia	na	na	na	na	na	na	na	na	na	na	na	na	na	na	na	na		Tanzania	28
Australia	na	na	na	na	na	na	na	na	na	na	na	na	na	na	na	na		Sweden	26
Austria	8	14	15	12	12	14	14	8	15	29	9	13	18	7	12	18		Canada	21
Azerbaijan	na	na	na	na	na	na	na	na	na	na	na	na	na	na	na	na		Uganda	21
Bangladesh	na	30	36	21	32	28	27	19	41	44	20	33	33	30	30	22		Greece	21
Belarus	na	3	2	3	4	2	2	na	3	6	3	2	5	2	3	2		Belgium	21
Belgium	17	21	23	19	23	22	19	6	20	34	15	18	30	14	20	31		Denmark	17
Bosnia and Herz.	na	4	4	5	7	2	4	1	3	12	2	4	6	5	4	8		Korea, South	19
Brazil	5	na	na	na	na	na	na	na	na	na	na	na	na	na	na	na		Venezuela	18
Bulgaria	4	4	4	4	7	6	1	1	3	12	2	5	5	2	5	10		Luxembourg	18
Canada	18	21	18	24	25	24	17	9	19	38	15	20	29	20	21	24		Vietnam	17
Chile	9	9	8	10	14	7	8	3	8	24	4	9	17	8	9	11		South Africa	17
China	7	2	2	3	4	2	2	na	3	19	1	2	4	1	2	19		Finland	16
Colombia	na	na	na	na	na	na	na	na	na	na	na	na	na	na	na	na		Iceland	16
Croatia	na	6	6	6	13	5	2	3	5	17	3	6	7	1	7	7		India	15
Czech Republic	na	10	11	9	17	10	7	7	10	24	6	10	13	6	11	18		Singapore	14
Denmark	13	17	16	17	17	16	17	10	22	28	13	17	23	9	17	23		Albania	14
Dominican Rep.	na	na	na	na	na	na	na	na	na	na	na	na	na	na	na	na		Austria	14
Egypt	na	na	na	na	na	na	na	na	na	na	na	na	na	na	na	na		Puerto Rico	13
El Salvador	na	na	na	na	na	na	na	na	na	na	na	na	na	na	na	na		Peru	13
Estonia	11	8	7	8	11	7	6	4	8	14	3	7	11	4	11	15		Moldova	12
Finland	20	16	12	18	21	14	15	8	21	33	19	13	15	13	15	26		Algeria	12
France	9	8	7	8	8	9	7	4	8	18	6	9	11	6	7	14		Romania	12
Georgia	na	na	na	na	na	na	na	na	na	na	na	na	na	na	na	na		Macedonia	12
Germany	9	8	8	8	6	9	8	5	9	18	5	7	11	7	7	12		Japan	11
Great Britain	10	10	8	11	12	11	7	2	10	28	8	6	17	na	na	na		Czech Republic	10
Greece	na	21	19	22	22	21	16	6	19	25	14	23	25	23	19	23		Ireland	10
Hungary	3	3	3	4	3	4	4	1	4	17	2	4	4	1	5	16		Italy	10
Iceland	14	16	12	19	10	19	16	11	12	31	11	16	19	11	16	22		Great Britain	10
India	na	15	17	11	18	15	12	10	15	26	14	11	19	9	24	31		Slovenia	9
Indonesia	na	na	na	na	na	na	na	na	na	na	na	na	na	na	na	na		Argentina	9
Iran	na	na	na	na	na	na	na	na	na	na	na	na	na	na	na	na		Montenegro	9
Ireland	10	10	10	11	10	11	9	6	9	21	6	10	16	8	10	17		Chile	9
Israel	na	na	na	na	na	na	na	na	na	na	na	na	na	na	na	na		Germany	8
Italy	4	10	10	10	14	10	8	4	12	23	7	10	14	6	9	14		France	8
Japan	6	11	12	10	6	9	15	15	9	15	10	9	15	13	11	14		Estonia	8
Jordan	na	na	na	na	na	na	na	na	na	na	na	na	na	na	na	na		Mexico	8
Korea, South	11	19	18	20	32	16	11	4	15	27	15	20	23	16	19	43		Northern Ireland	8
Latvia	7	4	3	4	6	4	3	1	4	6	3	4	4	2	5	2		Zimbabwe	7
Lithuania	7	2	2	2	3	3	1	1	2	7	1	2	3	1	2	3		Slovakia	7
Luxembourg	na	18	17	18	15	19	18	12	18	28	13	12	23	14	17	21		Spain	7
Macedonia	na	12	13	11	19	12	6	6	13	20	7	12	17	9	12	26		Croatia	6
Malta	na	5	6	3	4	4	6	3	5	6	3	6	6	5	5	5		Philippines	5
Mexico	12	8	8	8	9	7	6	4	8	25	4	8	14	6	8	13		Malta	5
Moldova	na	12	10	14	18	13	8	2	10	26	7	12	18	10	13	25		Bosnia and Herz.	4
Montenegro	na	9	10	8	23	7	3	2	13	19	5	10	14	6	14	8		Bulgaria	4
Morocco	na	3	4	3	3	5	1	1	8	20	1	3	15	2	5	6		Latvia	4
Netherlands	36	45	41	50	45	48	43	29	43	64	42	45	48	24	45	56		Hungary	3
New Zealand	na	na	na	na	na	na	na	na	na	na	na	na	na	na	na	na		Morocco	3
Nigeria	na	na	na	na	na	na	na	na	na	na	na	na	na	na	na	na		Portugal	3
Northern Ireland	11	8	9	7	9	8	7	4	8	18	6	5	15	7	10	4		Ukraine	3
Norway	14	na	na	na	na	na	na	na	na	na	na	na	na	na	na	na		Serbia	3
Pakistan	na	na	na	na	na	na	na	na	na	na	na	na	na	na	na	na		Belarus	3
Peru	na	13	15	11	14	13	9	9	10	21	9	14	19	9	13	18		China	2
Philippines	na	5	5	6	7	4	7	2	4	12	3	4	9	4	7	7		Poland	2
Poland	na	2	4	1	5	2	1	1	3	7	1	3	5	1	3	1		Lithuania	2
Portugal	8	3	4	2	5	4	2	2	4	14	na	2	4	2	4	3		Russian Fed.	1
Puerto Rico	na	13	17	11	17	14	11	4	7	18	9	12	20	18	11	19		Turkey	1
Romania	2	3	3	2	5	3	1	0	3	5	0	2	5	2	3	4			
Russian Fed.	5	1	1	2	2	1	1	na	1	2	1	2	2	1	1	6			
Serbia	na	3	3	3	6	3	1	1	4	3	2	3	3	3	3	3			
Singapore	na	14	12	16	24	6	4	13	13	21	8	12	18	9	15	19			
Slovakia	na	7	6	8	10	6	6	3	8	14	5	7	9	5	9	10			
Slovenia	3	9	10	9	14	9	6	5	8	23	3	12	16	4	10	13			
South Africa	na	17	18	16	23	15	9	12	22	45	10	24	21	23	15	7			
Spain	6	7	7	7	10	8	4	4	6	17	5	7	12	6	5	14			
Sweden	13	26	24	29	32	21	28	16	21	43	27	22	30	16	23	39			
Switzerland	7	na	na	na	na	na	na	na	na	na	na	na	na	na	na	na			
Taiwan	na	na	na	na	na	na	na	na	na	na	na	na	na	na	na	na			
Tanzania	na	28	26	30	34	27	20	23	34	38	27	32	27	22	32	29			
Turkey	na	1	2	1	1	1	na	na	1	6	na	1	4	na	2	1			
Uganda	na	21	29	15	33	11	7	11	27	8	19	22	23	19	24	17			
Ukraine	na	3	2	4	5	4	2	1	2	8	3	2	5	3	4	2			
United States	20	37	38	37	48	35	32	23	29	48	29	37	49	30	35	45			
Uruguay	na	na	na	na	na	na	na	na	na	na	na	na	na	na	na	na			
Venezuela	na	18	18	17	21	17	12	10	15	34	14	17	23	17	18	20			
Vietnam	na	17	17	18	21	19	13	14	21	27	13	14	24	16	20	14			
Zimbabwe	na	7	10	5	9	6	3	3	12	39	3	6	18	6	8	8			
Total	10	12	12	12	16	12	9	7	12	24	9	12	16	8	13	19		Total	12

A067) BELONG LABOR UNIONS

Please look carefully at the following list of voluntary organizations and activities and say...which, if any, do you belong to?

Labor unions.

Belong (%) (WVS: V42; EVS: V15)

Country	Wave		Gender		Age			Education			Income			Values			RANKING Country	2000
	1990	2000	Male	Female	16-29	30-49	50+	Lower	Middle	Upper	Lower	Middle	Upper	Mat	Mixed	Postm.		
Albania	na	9	12	7	7	12	8	6	10	17	9	9	11	9	9	26	Denmark	54
Algeria	na	na	na	na	na	na	na	na	na	na	na	na	na	na	na	na	Sweden	64
Argentina	1	3	4	1	2	2	3	2	2	6	2	3	3	2	2	3	Iceland	60
Armenia	na	na	na	na	na	na	na	na	na	na	na	na	na	na	na	na	Belarus	44
Australia	na	na	na	na	na	na	na	na	na	na	na	na	na	na	na	na	Romania	9
Austria	19	20	25	16	16	24	18	20	19	24	14	23	25	16	21	20	Finland	35
Azerbaijan	na	na	na	na	na	na	na	na	na	na	na	na	na	na	na	na	Tanzania	29
Bangladesh	na	15	22	6	11	18	17	12	21	14	12	17	15	13	17	12	Russian Fed.	24
Belarus	na	44	45	42	48	57	24	25	49	53	41	47	40	39	48	45	Netherlands	22
Belgium	16	18	23	13	16	25	13	15	18	19	11	22	23	20	19	16	Ukraine	21
Bosnia and Herz.	na	7	8	6	3	11	5	4	7	8	3	8	10	6	7	8	Austria	20
Brazil	6	na	na	na	na	na	na	na	na	na	na	na	na	na	na	na	Belgium	18
Bulgaria	19	7	7	6	3	13	3	2	7	13	3	10	9	3	11	8	Slovenia	17
Canada	12	14	19	10	11	18	13	10	15	17	7	16	21	19	13	17	Slovakia	16
Chile	6	3	5	1	1	4	3	3	3	3	2	3	5	1	4	2	Montenegro	16
China	2	7	9	5	3	9	6	1	11	21	1	8	15	10	6	9	Bangladesh	15
Colombia	na	na	na	na	na	na	na	na	na	na	na	na	na	na	na	na	Moldova	15
Croatia	na	11	15	7	6	17	7	5	15	14	5	13	11	12	11	10	Canada	14
Czech Republic	na	11	12	9	6	13	11	11	10	13	7	12	13	12	11	8	United States	14
Denmark	49	54	57	52	47	69	43	53	57	59	34	72	64	49	55	62	Serbia	14
Dominican Rep.	na	na	na	na	na	na	na	na	na	na	na	na	na	na	na	na	Luxembourg	12
Egypt	na	na	na	na	na	na	na	na	na	na	na	na	na	na	na	na	Latvia	11
El Salvador	na	na	na	na	na	na	na	na	na	na	na	na	na	na	na	na	Vietnam	11
Estonia	59	5	6	4	3	7	4	2	5	9	2	6	6	4	5	8	Croatia	11
Finland	36	35	36	34	25	51	27	32	34	49	22	38	47	37	35	31	Czech Republic	11
France	5	4	5	3	na	5	5	3	3	8	1	6	7	1	4	8	Poland	10
Georgia	na	na	na	na	na	na	na	na	na	na	na	na	na	na	na	na	Ireland	10
Germany	56	7	10	5	4	9	7	6	8	8	4	9	13	6	8	7	South Africa	10
Great Britain	14	8	9	7	4	11	8	7	9	12	7	8	16	na	na	na	Albania	9
Greece	na	8	10	7	5	11	10	6	8	10	5	10	12	9	8	10	Malta	9
Hungary	32	7	8	6	3	9	8	5	8	14	6	7	8	6	8	5	Greece	8
Iceland	60	60	61	58	68	55	59	65	61	47	61	62	58	59	62	50	Great Britain	8
India	na	8	11	5	7	10	7	8	9	8	11	8	7	6	10	18	India	8
Indonesia	na	na	na	na	na	na	na	na	na	na	na	na	na	na	na	na	Germany	7
Iran	na	na	na	na	na	na	na	na	na	na	na	na	na	na	na	na	Hungary	7
Ireland	9	10	15	6	9	12	9	7	8	20	4	12	16	8	10	12	China	7
Israel	na	na	na	na	na	na	na	na	na	na	na	na	na	na	na	na	Bosnia and Herz.	7
Italy	6	6	8	5	3	8	6	5	6	9	3	6	10	4	7	6	Uganda	7
Japan	7	7	10	4	6	9	4	4	6	9	3	8	10	7	8	4	Bulgaria	7
Jordan	na	na	na	na	na	na	na	na	na	na	na	na	na	na	na	na	Japan	7
Korea, South	7	6	8	3	5	6	6	2	6	6	6	7	4	5	7	7	Northern Ireland	7
Latvia	52	11	9	13	9	18	7	3	11	23	6	12	20	13	12	2	Italy	6
Lithuania	43	2	3	1	2	3	1	1	2	3	1	1	4	1	2	3	Macedonia	6
Luxembourg	na	12	16	9	5	15	14	11	14	13	10	13	15	10	14	13	Mexico	6
Macedonia	na	6	8	4	2	10	4	3	8	7	6	7	5	6	6	6	Korea, South	6
Malta	na	9	14	4	12	10	6	2	12	12	3	9	19	7	10	9	Estonia	5
Mexico	4	6	9	3	3	8	6	4	6	15	4	7	8	6	6	7	Peru	5
Moldova	na	15	14	15	14	16	13	4	12	29	12	17	17	12	18	22	Puerto Rico	4
Montenegro	na	16	20	11	10	26	10	4	23	27	9	16	24	13	19	21	Singapore	4
Morocco	na	1	1	1	na	1	1	na	2	6	na	1	4	na	1	3	France	4
Netherlands	17	22	28	17	15	24	25	24	20	24	20	27	22	22	20	30	Philippines	4
New Zealand	na	na	na	na	na	na	na	na	na	na	na	na	na	na	na	na	Spain	4
Nigeria	na	na	na	na	na	na	na	na	na	na	na	na	na	na	na	na	Zimbabwe	3
Northern Ireland	12	7	9	4	6	7	6	5	7	11	3	11	10	5	8	4	Chile	3
Norway	42	na	na	na	na	na	na	na	na	na	na	na	na	na	na	na	Venezuela	3
Pakistan	na	na	na	na	na	na	na	na	na	na	na	na	na	na	na	na	Argentina	3
Peru	na	5	6	3	3	6	5	3	6	4	4	6	3	4	5	6	Lithuania	2
Philippines	na	4	6	2	3	5	5	4	4	5	5	4	4	5	4	5	Portugal	2
Poland	na	10	12	8	5	15	8	7	14	17	6	13	12	8	11	17	Turkey	2
Portugal	5	2	2	1	na	4	1	1	2	5	na	2	3	1	2	3	Morocco	1
Puerto Rico	na	4	6	4	3	6	4	3	3	6	1	5	8	2	3	9		
Romania	20	9	11	7	8	16	4	1	11	22	1	7	18	8	10	19		
Russian Fed.	62	24	25	23	20	35	13	9	24	32	17	27	29	24	25	18		
Serbia	na	14	16	11	4	24	9	5	17	20	8	15	20	12	16	18		
Singapore	na	4	5	3	2	6	6	4	4	8	5	3	6	6	4	2		
Slovakia	na	16	17	15	10	22	13	9	18	24	9	18	21	14	17	25		
Slovenia	19	17	17	17	12	30	7	13	18	21	17	24	24	20	17	13		
South Africa	na	10	13	6	4	16	5	9	11	4	4	15	14	10	10	8		
Spain	4	4	6	2	3	6	3	2	4	7	2	4	8	2	4	8		
Sweden	59	64	60	68	52	75	61	58	61	73	58	68	70	59	63	69		
Switzerland	6	na	na	na	na	na	na	na	na	na	na	na	na	na	na	na		
Taiwan	na	na	na	na	na	na	na	na	na	na	na	na	na	na	na	na		
Tanzania	na	29	27	30	21	37	23	22	30	51	20	39	37	28	28	46		
Turkey	na	2	3	1	2	2	1	1	2	4	na	2	3	1	2	3		
Uganda	na	7	11	3	7	7	8	9	6	4	9	4	7	8	6	11		
Ukraine	na	21	22	20	19	28	16	5	20	33	15	24	26	23	22	20		
United States	9	14	19	8	12	15	14	15	14	13	10	17	17	17	13	14		
Uruguay	na	na	na	na	na	na	na	na	na	na	na	na	na	na	na	na		
Venezuela	na	3	4	2	2	4	4	2	3	4	4	3	3	3	3	3		
Vietnam	na	11	12	11	8	15	9	6	15	31	8	11	13	10	13	12		
Zimbabwe	na	3	5	2	4	4	na	3	4	na	2	4	5	3	4	4		
Total	23	13	16	11	10	17	11	10	14	18	10	16	17	11	14	15	Total	13

A068) BELONG POLITICAL PARTIES

Please look carefully at the following list of voluntary organizations and activities and say...which, if any, do you belong to?
Political parties or groups.

Belong (%)

(WVS: V43; EVS: V16)

Country	Wave		Gender		Age			Education			Income			Values				Country	2000
	1990	2000	Male	Female	16-29	30-49	50+	Lower	Middle	Upper	Lower	Middle	Upper	Mat	Mixed	Postm.			
Albania	na	15	22	7	10	15	17	12	16	17	17	13	14	13	17	8		Vietnam	29
Algeria	na	6	8	3	3	6	10	6	3	8	5	4	7	5	6	8		Tanzania	26
Argentina	2	5	5	4	4	5	4	3	7	8	4	4	7	1	5	7		Bangladesh	24
Armenia	na	na	na	na	na	na	na	na	na	na	na	na	na	na	na	na		Montenegro	20
Australia	na	na	na	na	na	na	na	na	na	na	na	na	na	na	na	na		United States	19
Austria	12	12	15	8	7	13	13	13	8	19	9	13	15	5	12	11		Iceland	19
Azerbaijan	na	na	na	na	na	na	na	na	na	na	na	na	na	na	na	na		Albania	15
Bangladesh	na	24	36	9	22	24	29	17	29	34	24	21	26	22	25	25		South Africa	12
Belarus	na	1	2	na	na	1	na	na	1	2	1	1	na	na	1	na		Austria	12
Belgium	6	7	9	5	5	6	9	4	7	10	5	7	8	3	7	10		Macedonia	12
Bosnia and Herz.	na	7	11	4	7	7	7	4	6	12	6	6	11	6	8	4		India	11
Brazil	5	na	na	na	na	na	na	na	na	na	na	na	na	na	na	na		Sweden	11
Bulgaria	11	4	6	3	4	4	4	2	4	9	3	5	5	2	5	5		Romania	10
Canada	7	6	9	4	4	6	8	4	4	13	5	4	10	2	5	9		Netherlands	9
Chile	5	2	4	1	2	4	1	1	3	4	2	2	5	1	2	5		Uganda	9
China	35	8	12	5	9	7	11	4	8	49	4	8	16	9	9	25		China	8
Colombia	na	na	na	na	na	na	na	na	na	na	na	na	na	na	na	na		Denmark	7
Croatia	na	4	6	2	2	4	4	1	5	11	3	3	6	3	4	6		Greece	8
Czech Republic	na	4	5	2	2	2	6	4	3	7	4	4	3	3	4	3		Belgium	7
Denmark	7	7	8	5	5	7	8	6	7	8	5	6	9	8	6	11		Bosnia and Herz.	7
Dominican Rep.	na	na	na	na	na	na	na	na	na	na	na	na	na	na	na	na		Finland	7
Egypt	na	na	na	na	na	na	na	na	na	na	na	na	na	na	na	na		Zimbabwe	7
El Salvador	na	na	na	na	na	na	na	na	na	na	na	na	na	na	na	na		Slovakia	7
Estonia	8	2	3	1	1	1	3	1	1	3	na	1	3	1	2	na		Canada	6
Finland	14	7	10	5	3	5	11	6	10	8	4	8	11	5	8	6		Puerto Rico	6
France	3	2	2	2	1	2	2	1	2	5	1	2	3	na	1	6		Luxembourg	6
Georgia	na	na	na	na	na	na	na	na	na	na	na	na	na	na	na	na		Malta	6
Germany	11	3	4	2	1	3	4	2	3	10	2	3	4	1	3	4		Serbia	6
Great Britain	6	3	3	2	2	2	3	1	2	5	2	3	3	na	na	na		Algeria	6
Greece	na	8	11	6	6	9	11	6	9	8	4	11	11	8	8	10		Moldova	5
Hungary	2	2	2	1	1	1	3	1	2	6	1	2	3	1	3	na		Peru	5
Iceland	15	19	22	17	14	17	26	17	21	19	18	17	23	21	19	18		Argentina	5
India	na	11	16	5	11	12	10	9	14	14	10	11	13	13	13	13		Ireland	4
Indonesia	na	na	na	na	na	na	na	na	na	na	na	na	na	na	na	na		Italy	4
Iran	na	na	na	na	na	na	na	na	na	na	na	na	na	na	na	na		Philippines	4
Ireland	4	4	7	2	4	3	6	5	3	6	5	4	6	3	5	3		Bulgaria	4
Israel	na	na	na	na	na	na	na	na	na	na	na	na	na	na	na	na		Mexico	4
Italy	5	4	6	2	2	5	5	3	4	8	3	5	5	2	3	7		Venezuela	4
Japan	2	4	5	2	na	3	5	5	3	4	3	2	6	4	3	6		Croatia	4
Jordan	na	na	na	na	na	na	na	na	na	na	na	na	na	na	na	na		Czech Republic	4
Korea, South	5	3	4	2	2	3	3	na	2	4	3	3	2	3	2	4		Japan	4
Latvia	18	2	2	2	1	1	3	1	2	2	3	1	1	2	2	4		Turkey	4
Lithuania	7	1	2	1	1	1	1	na	1	6	1	1	2	na	2	4		Slovenia	3
Luxembourg	na	6	8	5	2	6	9	4	8	7	5	6	8	7	6	10		Germany	3
Macedonia	na	12	15	8	12	14	8	9	12	17	9	15	10	11	12	17		Korea, South	3
Malta	na	6	9	3	3	6	8	6	6	5	7	5	7	5	6	5		Great Britain	3
Mexico	5	4	6	2	3	4	4	3	3	10	4	4	5	3	4	5		Chile	2
Moldova	na	5	7	4	4	6	5	2	4	11	3	6	6	5	6	9		Northern Ireland	2
Montenegro	na	20	28	11	18	24	17	9	26	30	17	22	25	17	23	31		Ukraine	2
Morocco	na	1	2	1	1	1	1	1	1	6	1	2	4	1	1	2		France	2
Netherlands	8	9	11	8	3	7	15	8	7	14	8	6	14	8	8	14		Latvia	2
New Zealand	na	na	na	na	na	na	na	na	na	na	na	na	na	na	na	na		Hungary	2
Nigeria	na	na	na	na	na	na	na	na	na	na	na	na	na	na	na	na		Spain	2
Northern Ireland	2	2	3	2	2	3	3	2	1	6	1	5	3	1	3	3		Estonia	2
Norway	14	na	na	na	na	na	na	na	na	na	na	na	na	na	na	na		Lithuania	1
Pakistan	na	na	na	na	na	na	na	na	na	na	na	na	na	na	na	na		Morocco	1
Peru	na	5	7	3	4	5	6	2	4	8	3	5	8	4	5	7		Portugal	1
Philippines	na	4	6	2	1	5	5	4	3	7	3	4	6	3	5	4		Belarus	1
Poland	na	1	1	na	na	na	2	na	1	2	1	1	na	na	1	1		Poland	1
Portugal	5	1	1	1	na	1	1	1	1	2	na	1	2	na	1	2		Russian Fed.	1
Puerto Rico	na	6	8	6	6	8	5	1	2	9	3	6	11	5	5	11		Singapore	0
Romania	3	2	4	1	2	3	1	0	2	6	1	2	3	2	3	5			
Russian Fed.	11	1	1	1	1	1	1	na	1	2	na	1	1	1	1	3			
Serbia	na	6	9	3	6	8	4	2	7	10	5	6	8	4	8	13			
Singapore	na	0	na	na	na	na	1	na	na	2	na	na	1	1	na	na			
Slovakia	na	7	9	4	3	7	9	1	9	12	4	7	8	4	9	15			
Slovenia	3	3	4	2	2	3	4	3	4	1	2	5	5	3	3	3			
South Africa	na	12	17	6	9	16	9	13	10	14	13	13	13	12	12	12			
Spain	2	2	3	1	1	2	1	1	2	4	1	1	3	1	1	4			
Sweden	10	11	12	10	5	8	16	12	9	12	8	15	8	11	9	14			
Switzerland	9	na	na	na	na	na	na	na	na	na	na	na	na	na	na	na			
Taiwan	na	na	na	na	na	na	na	na	na	na	na	na	na	na	na	na			
Tanzania	na	26	27	25	21	24	42	31	20	22	32	22	26	26	26	33			
Turkey	na	4	6	2	3	5	2	3	4	6	3	4	4	2	3	7			
Uganda	na	9	14	5	8	9	17	5	10	18	11	12	12	10	10	7			
Ukraine	na	2	4	1	1	4	2	1	2	4	2	3	3	1	4	na			
United States	14	19	22	17	13	17	27	8	15	26	13	24	23	23	17	24			
Uruguay	na	na	na	na	na	na	na	na	na	na	na	na	na	na	na	na			
Venezuela	na	4	6	2	4	5	3	1	4	7	3	4	5	5	4	4			
Vietnam	na	29	34	24	28	28	30	22	35	52	23	25	36	19	35	24			
Zimbabwe	na	7	10	5	5	8	10	7	7	na	8	8	6	8	5	15			
Total	8	7	9	5	6	7	8	6	6	10	6	7	9	6	7	9		Total	7

A069) BELONG LOCAL COMMUNITY ACTIONS

Please look carefully at the following list of voluntary organizations and activities and say...which, if any, do you belong to?

Local community action on issues like poverty, employment, housing, racial equality

Belong (%)

(WVS: V44; EVS: V17)

Country	Wave 1990	Wave 2000	Gender Male	Gender Female	Age 16-29	Age 30-49	Age 50+	Education Lower	Education Middle	Education Upper	Income Lower	Income Middle	Income Upper	Values Mat	Values Mixed	Values Postm.
Albania	na	12	13	10	11	11	12	9	12	15	12	8	15	12	12	8
Algeria	na	6	8	4	6	4	7	5	5	8	4	6	7	5	6	5
Argentina	1	3	2	5	4	2	4	2	5	5	3	3	5	3	4	3
Armenia	na	na	na	na	na	na	na	na	na	na	na	na	na	na	na	na
Australia	na	na	na	na	na	na	na	na	na	na	na	na	na	na	na	na
Austria	2	3	2	3	na	4	3	2	2	6	3	2	4	2	3	3
Azerbaijan	na	na	na	na	na	na	na	na	na	na	na	na	na	na	na	na
Bangladesh	na	26	32	19	22	28	30	22	30	34	14	30	32	25	27	22
Belarus	na	0	na	na	na	na	na	na	na	na	na	na	na	na	na	na
Belgium	5	5	5	5	4	5	6	2	4	8	6	5	6	2	4	8
Bosnia and Herz.	na	1	1	1	1	1	1	na	1	2	na	1	1	1	1	2
Brazil	8	na	na	na	na	na	na	na	na	na	na	na	na	na	na	na
Bulgaria	2	1	1	1	3	1	na	1	2	2	1	2	1	1	2	2
Canada	5	8	8	8	5	8	10	6	7	13	7	7	9	5	8	9
Chile	4	5	4	5	4	4	6	5	4	5	4	4	6	5	4	8
China	1	2	2	1	3	1	1	1	2	5	1	2	2	1	3	3
Colombia	na	na	na	na	na	na	na	na	na	na	na	na	na	na	na	na
Croatia	na	2	3	1	2	1	2	1	3	2	na	2	3	2	1	3
Czech Republic	na	3	3	3	4	4	3	4	3	4	4	3	4	4	3	5
Denmark	5	6	7	5	3	7	7	5	6	9	8	5	6	4	6	8
Dominican Rep.	na	na	na	na	na	na	na	na	na	na	na	na	na	na	na	na
Egypt	na	na	na	na	na	na	na	na	na	na	na	na	na	na	na	na
El Salvador	na	na	na	na	na	na	na	na	na	na	na	na	na	na	na	na
Estonia	5	2	2	2	na	2	3	3	2	1	2	2	2	2	2	na
Finland	3	3	2	3	1	4	3	2	4	3	5	2	2	4	2	3
France	3	2	2	3	na	2	4	2	1	5	1	2	5	2	2	5
Georgia	na	na	na	na	na	na	na	na	na	na	na	na	na	na	na	na
Germany	3	1	1	na	na	1	1	1	1	1	1	1	1	na	1	2
Great Britain	4	4	4	4	4	4	3	4	3	5	4	5	5	na	na	na
Greece	na	4	4	5	3	4	6	5	5	4	3	5	4	3	4	7
Hungary	1	1	1	1	na	1	2	1	1	2	1	1	2	na	2	6
Iceland	2	3	3	2	2	2	4	2	2	4	3	3	2	2	2	6
India	na	6	7	5	6	6	6	5	6	9	6	5	7	4	9	4
Indonesia	na	na	na	na	na	na	na	na	na	na	na	na	na	na	na	na
Iran	na	na	na	na	na	na	na	na	na	na	na	na	na	na	na	na
Ireland	3	6	6	6	3	6	8	5	5	8	6	7	6	5	5	7
Israel	na	na	na	na	na	na	na	na	na	na	na	na	na	na	na	na
Italy	2	2	2	3	2	3	2	1	3	5	1	1	2	1	1	3
Japan	0	1	2	1	na	1	2	1	1	2	1	1	2	1	1	3
Jordan	na	na	na	na	na	na	na	na	na	na	na	na	na	na	na	na
Korea, South	13	7	10	4	5	6	11	7	8	6	8	5	7	5	9	6
Latvia	5	1	1	1	na	1	1	na	1	2	1	1	1	na	1	na
Lithuania	2	1	1	1	1	1	1	na	1	1	1	1	1	na	1	1
Luxembourg	na	6	6	5	5	5	8	4	5	10	4	6	9	4	6	6
Macedonia	na	6	5	6	5	7	5	6	5	6	4	7	6	4	6	12
Malta	na	3	4	2	1	3	4	1	3	3	2	3	4	?	3	3
Mexico	4	5	5	5	3	5	7	5	4	6	4	8	5	6	5	4
Moldova	na	3	2	3	2	3	2	1	3	3	1	2	3	2	3	4
Montenegro	na	1	1	na	na	na	1	1	1	1	na	1	1	1	1	na
Morocco	na	1	1	1	1	1	na	1	1	2	na	1	3	na	2	1
Netherlands	5	7	6	8	5	8	7	6	6	9	5	8	8	5	7	8
New Zealand	na	na	na	na	na	na	na	na	na	na	na	na	na	na	na	na
Nigeria	na	na	na	na	na	na	na	na	na	na	na	na	na	na	na	na
Northern Ireland	2	3	3	4	2	4	3	4	2	4	4	3	5	2	4	4
Norway	3	na	na	na	na	na	na	na	na	na	na	na	na	na	na	na
Pakistan	na	na	na	na	na	na	na	na	na	na	na	na	na	na	na	na
Peru	na	7	7	7	3	9	9	5	7	6	5	8	7	6	7	7
Philippines	na	7	9	5	6	6	9	6	5	9	6	6	9	5	8	7
Poland	na	2	3	1	1	2	2	1	2	5	2	2	2	na	2	6
Portugal	2	1	1	1	2	1	1	na	1	8	na	na	1	1	1	2
Puerto Rico	na	9	10	8	5	10	10	6	5	12	8	6	14	5	9	12
Romania	1	1	1	1	2	0	1	0	1	1	0	1	1	0	2	0
Russian Fed.	3	1	1	1	1	1	1	1	1	2	1	1	1	1	1	na
Serbia	na	1	1	na	1	na	1	1	1	na	1	1	na	1	na	1
Singapore	na	2	2	3	1	3	4	3	2	2	2	3	2	3	2	4
Slovakia	na	8	10	6	6	8	10	6	8	13	8	7	9	7	10	8
Slovenia	6	9	10	9	4	8	16	10	9	10	9	15	7	10	10	7
South Africa	na	9	10	7	5	9	16	9	7	19	8	9	10	12	7	8
Spain	1	2	2	2	2	2	2	1	2	5	2	2	4	1	1	6
Sweden	2	9	10	9	7	9	11	10	8	12	13	8	8	11	8	15
Switzerland	3	na	na	na	na	na	na	na	na	na	na	na	na	na	na	na
Taiwan	na	na	na	na	na	na	na	na	na	na	na	na	na	na	na	na
Tanzania	na	24	23	24	22	24	23	22	25	27	21	25	29	20	25	25
Turkey	na	0	na	na	na	na	na	na	na	1	na	na	1	na	na	na
Uganda	na	10	17	3	10	10	7	8	10	17	12	8	13	11	9	11
Ukraine	na	2	2	2	1	2	2	1	1	4	1	2	3	1	3	3
United States	5	13	12	14	12	11	16	10	12	15	10	14	15	15	10	19
Uruguay	na	na	na	na	na	na	na	na	na	na	na	na	na	na	na	na
Venezuela	na	10	12	8	8	11	12	10	10	11	10	11	13	8	11	10
Vietnam	na	26	29	24	17	29	29	26	26	27	21	23	33	24	30	26
Zimbabwe	na	5	5	4	5	3	6	4	5	na	4	4	8	4	5	1
Total	3	5	6	5	5	6	5	5	5	7	5	6	7	4	6	7

RANKING

Country	2000
Vietnam	26
Bangladesh	26
Tanzania	24
United States	13
Albania	12
Venezuela	10
Uganda	10
Sweden	9
Slovenia	9
Puerto Rico	9
South Africa	9
Canada	8
Slovakia	8
Denmark	6
Korea, South	7
Netherlands	7
Philippines	7
Peru	7
India	6
Algeria	6
Luxembourg	6
Ireland	6
Macedonia	6
Belgium	5
Mexico	5
Chile	5
Zimbabwe	5
Greece	4
Romania	1
Great Britain	4
Argentina	3
Northern Ireland	3
Czech Republic	3
Finland	3
Austria	3
Malta	3
Moldova	3
Iceland	3
Italy	2
Singapore	2
France	2
Spain	2
Estonia	2
Ukraine	2
Poland	2
Croatia	2
China	2
Bulgaria	1
Japan	1
Bosnia and Herz.	1
Hungary	1
Portugal	1
Morocco	1
Germany	1
Russian Fed.	1
Latvia	1
Montenegro	1
Lithuania	1
Serbia	1
Turkey	0
Belarus	0
Total	5

A070) BELONG THIRD WORLD DEVELOPMENT / HUMAN RIGHTS

Please look carefully at the following list of voluntary organizations and activities and say...which, if any, do you belong to? Third world development / human rights.

Belong (%)

(WVS: V45; EVS: V18)

Country	Wave		Gender		Age			Education			Income			Values			RANKING Country	2000
	1990	2000	Male	Female	16-29	30-49	50+	Lower	Middle	Upper	Lower	Middle	Upper	Mat	Mixed	Postm.		
Albania	na	6	6	7	7	7	5	4	7	10	6	5	8	6	8	5	Netherlands	24
Algeria	na	3	4	3	4	3	2	1	3	5	3	4	3	2	4	3	Tanzania	19
Argentina	0	1	1	1	1	na	1	na	1	1	1	na	1	na	1	1	Sweden	15
Armenia	na	na	na	na	na	na	na	na	na	na	na	na	na	na	na	na	Luxembourg	12
Australia	na	na	na	na	na	na	na	na	na	na	na	na	na	na	na	na	Bangladesh	11
Austria	2	3	3	4	4	2	4	2	3	9	2	3	4	na	3	6	Belgium	10
Azerbaijan	na	na	na	na	na	na	na	na	na	na	na	na	na	na	na	na	Venezuela	9
Bangladesh	na	11	16	5	8	12	16	8	12	18	6	11	16	9	13	5	Iceland	8
Belarus	na	1	1	1	na	1	1	na	1	1	na	1	1	na	1	2	Albania	6
Belgium	7	10	9	10	8	10	10	3	7	18	10	7	11	5	7	17	Finland	6
Bosnia and Herz.	na	0	na	na	na	na	1	na	na	na	na	na	na	na	na	na	United States	6
Brazil	1	na	na	na	na	na	na	na	na	na	na	na	na	na	na	na	Canada	5
Bulgaria	2	0	na	1	na	1	na	1	na	1	1	1	na	na	na	na	Greece	5
Canada	5	5	5	5	3	5	6	3	4	9	4	6	6	2	6	5	Uganda	5
Chile	1	2	2	2	2	2	2	1	3	2	1	2	4	2	2	2	Denmark	4
China	1	0	na	na	1	na	na	na	1	na	na	1	na	na	1	3	Philippines	5
Colombia	na	na	na	na	na	na	na	na	na	na	na	na	na	na	na	na	Puerto Rico	5
Croatia	na	1	1	na	na	1	na	na	1	1	na	1	1	na	1	1	South Africa	4
Czech Republic	na	1	1	1	1	1	1	1	1	2	1	1	1	1	1	2	Austria	3
Denmark	3	4	3	5	5	4	4	1	7	9	4	3	7	3	3	11	Macedonia	3
Dominican Rep.	na	na	na	na	na	na	na	na	na	na	na	na	na	na	na	na	Algeria	3
Egypt	na	na	na	na	na	na	na	na	na	na	na	na	na	na	na	na	Italy	3
El Salvador	na	na	na	na	na	na	na	na	na	na	na	na	na	na	na	na	India	3
Estonia	1	0	na	na	na	na	na	na	na	na	na	na	na	na	na	na	Romania	1
Finland	6	6	5	8	5	7	7	5	5	15	7	4	9	4	7	8	Great Britain	3
France	3	1	1	2	1	1	2	na	1	5	1	2	3	na	1	4	Spain	3
Georgia	na	na	na	na	na	na	na	na	na	na	na	na	na	na	na	na	Mexico	3
Germany	1	1	1	1	na	1	1	na	1	2	na	1	1	na	na	2	Ireland	2
Great Britain	2	3	2	3	3	2	2	1	4	3	2	2	4	na	na	na	Moldova	2
Greece	na	5	4	6	7	4	3	1	5	6	4	6	5	5	5	6	Peru	2
Hungary	0	0	1	na	na	na	1	na	na	1	1	1	na	na	1	1	Korea, South	2
Iceland	3	8	6	9	5	9	9	5	7	15	5	11	7	4	8	15	Northern Ireland	2
India	na	3	3	2	3	3	3	3	2	4	5	2	3	3	4	4	Chile	2
Indonesia	na	na	na	na	na	na	na	na	na	na	na	na	na	na	na	na	Japan	2
Iran	na	na	na	na	na	na	na	na	na	na	na	na	na	na	na	na	Zimbabwe	2
Ireland	2	2	2	3	na	3	4	1	2	6	2	3	3	1	2	7	Vietnam	2
Israel	na	na	na	na	na	na	na	na	na	na	na	na	na	na	na	na	France	1
Italy	1	3	3	3	4	2	3	2	3	5	3	3	3	2	3	4	Montenegro	1
Japan	0	2	2	2	1	1	3	1	1	3	2	1	2	2	2	3	Portugal	1
Jordan	na	na	na	na	na	na	na	na	na	na	na	na	na	na	na	na	Slovenia	1
Korea, South	2	2	3	2	3	1	4	2	2	3	4	2	1	2	2	7	Croatia	1
Latvia	1	1	1	1	1	1	na	na	1	1	na	1	1	na	1	na	Czech Republic	1
Lithuania	1	0	na	na	na	na	na	na	na	na	na	na	na	na	na	na	Ukraine	1
Luxembourg	na	12	9	14	6	15	12	8	10	22	10	9	18	8	10	18	Belarus	1
Macedonia	na	3	3	4	3	5	2	4	1	7	1	5	4	3	4	10	Germany	1
Malta	na	0	1	na	1	na	na	na	1	1	na	1	na	na	na	na	Latvia	1
Mexico	1	3	3	2	5	3	2	2	3	3	2	2	3	3	2	2	Argentina	1
Moldova	na	2	3	2	4	2	1	1	2	4	1	2	4	2	3	5	Singapore	1
Montenegro	na	1	1	1	na	2	1	na	2	2	1	1	2	na	2	3	Serbia	1
Morocco	na	0	na	na	na	na	na	na	na	2	na	na	1	na	na	na	Bulgaria	0
Netherlands	14	24	20	27	14	27	26	14	23	33	15	25	33	7	25	28	China	0
New Zealand	na	na	na	na	na	na	na	na	na	na	na	na	na	na	na	na	Poland	0
Nigeria	na	na	na	na	na	na	na	na	na	na	na	na	na	na	na	na	Bosnia and Herz.	0
Northern Ireland	3	2	2	3	na	4	2	1	1	7	2	2	4	2	3	1	Hungary	0
Norway	5	na	na	na	na	na	na	na	na	na	na	na	na	na	na	na	Malta	0
Pakistan	na	na	na	na	na	na	na	na	na	na	na	na	na	na	na	na	Lithuania	0
Peru	na	2	2	3	1	3	4	3	1	4	2	2	3	1	2	4	Turkey	0
Philippines	na	5	7	2	4	5	6	5	3	6	3	4	7	3	6	2	Estonia	0
Poland	na	0	1	na	1	na	na	na	1	1	na	na	2	na	1	1	Morocco	0
Portugal	1	1	1	1	1	1	1	na	1	5	na	na	1	na	1	1	Russian Fed.	0
Puerto Rico	na	5	4	5	6	5	4	4	3	6	4	3	7	1	4	6	Slovakia	0
Romania	0	1	1	0	0	0	1	0	0	2	0	0	1	0	1	1		
Russian Fed.	0	0	na	na	na	na	na	na	na	na	na	na	na	na	na	na		
Serbia	na	1	1	1	1	1	na	na	1	1	na	1	1	1	na	1		
Singapore	na	1	na	1	na	1	na	1	na	1	na	1	1	na	1	2		
Slovakia	na	0	na	na	na	na	na	na	na	na	na	na	na	na	na	na		
Slovenia	0	1	1	na	na	1	1	1	1	1	1	1	1	1	1	1		
South Africa	na	4	5	2	3	5	2	4	4	2	2	7	4	4	3	7		
Spain	1	3	2	3	3	3	2	2	2	8	2	3	4	2	2	5		
Sweden	9	15	12	18	13	17	15	7	12	27	13	12	22	8	12	26		
Switzerland	na	na	na	na	na	na	na	na	na	na	na	na	na	na	na	na		
Taiwan	na	na	na	na	na	na	na	na	na	na	na	na	na	na	na	na		
Tanzania	na	19	18	20	22	17	14	17	21	19	18	20	19	16	20	21		
Turkey	na	0	na	na	na	na	na	na	1	na	na	na	na	na	na	na		
Uganda	na	5	10	1	8	3	1	6	4	10	5	6	10	5	5	5		
Ukraine	na	1	1	1	2	na	na	na	1	1	1	1	na	na	1	3		
United States	2	6	5	6	6	4	7	4	6	6	3	5	8	6	5	7		
Uruguay	na	na	na	na	na	na	na	na	na	na	na	na	na	na	na	na		
Venezuela	na	9	11	7	8	10	10	6	8	14	9	8	9	8	9	10		
Vietnam	na	2	2	1	na	2	2	1	2	na	1	2	2	1	2	1		
Zimbabwe	na	2	2	2	2	1	na	1	3	na	1	1	4	2	2	2		
Total	2	4	4	4	3	4	3	3	3	7	3	4	5	2	4	6	Total	4

A071) BELONG CONSERVATION, THE ENVIRONMENT, ECOLOGY, ANIMAL RIGHTS

Please look carefully at the following list of voluntary organizations and activities and say...which, if any, do you belong to?
Conservation, environment, animal rights groups.

Belong (%)

(WVS: V46; EVS: V19)

Country	Wave 1990	Wave 2000	Male	Female	Age 16-29	Age 30-49	Age 50+	Educ. Lower	Educ. Middle	Educ. Upper	Income Lower	Income Middle	Income Upper	Mat	Mixed	Postm.	RANKING Country	RANKING 2000
Albania	na	10	11	10	9	10	12	9	10	17	11	7	14	9	12	8	Netherlands	44
Algeria	na	4	5	4	4	6	2	2	5	6	4	4	5	4	5	5	Bangladesh	20
Argentina	0	2	3	2	3	2	2	2	3	4	1	3	3	1	2	3	Tanzania	20
Armenia	na	na	na	na	na	na	na	na	na	na	na	na	na	na	na	na	United States	16
Australia	na	na	na	na	na	na	na	na	na	na	na	na	na	na	na	na	Denmark	13
Austria	3	9	8	10	10	9	9	6	11	15	7	9	12	2	10	10	Venezuela	12
Azerbaijan	na	na	na	na	na	na	na	na	na	na	na	na	na	na	na	na	Belgium	12
Bangladesh	na	20	24	16	19	20	25	15	27	27	9	22	29	18	22	22	Sweden	11
Belarus	na	1	2	1	2	1	na	na	2	1	na	1	2	1	1	2	Greece	11
Belgium	8	12	12	12	13	11	12	5	13	15	10	10	14	9	11	15	Luxembourg	11
Bosnia and Herz.	na	2	2	2	2	2	1	1	2	5	1	2	4	1	2	4	Albania	10
Brazil	3	na	na	na	na	na	na	na	na	na	na	na	na	na	na	na	Uganda	10
Bulgaria	4	1	1	2	3	2	na	1	1	3	1	2	2	1	2	2	Austria	9
Canada	8	9	11	8	8	8	11	5	8	14	6	11	11	5	8	12	Canada	9
Chile	2	3	3	3	3	3	3	1	3	6	1	4	6	2	3	4	Philippines	8
China	1	1	2	1	2	1	na	1	2	5	1	1	2	1	1	3	Vietnam	8
Colombia	na	na	na	na	na	na	na	na	na	na	na	na	na	na	na	na	India	7
Croatia	na	2	4	1	4	2	1	na	3	7	na	1	5	na	3	2	Czech Republic	7
Czech Republic	na	7	7	6	7	6	7	6	8	8	7	7	6	7	7	6	Korea, South	6
Denmark	13	13	10	16	9	12	17	10	16	18	10	13	19	4	13	20	Macedonia	5
Dominican Rep.	na	na	na	na	na	na	na	na	na	na	na	na	na	na	na	na	Finland	5
Egypt	na	na	na	na	na	na	na	na	na	na	na	na	na	na	na	na	Romania	1
El Salvador	na	na	na	na	na	na	na	na	na	na	na	na	na	na	na	na	Iceland	5
Estonia	3	2	2	2	1	2	2	2	1	3	1	1	3	2	2	8	Moldova	5
Finland	5	5	4	6	5	7	3	3	6	10	3	3	9	3	6	7	Mexico	5
France	2	2	2	3	1	2	3	2	2	3	2	2	2	1	3	3	Algeria	4
Georgia	na	na	na	na	na	na	na	na	na	na	na	na	na	na	na	na	Montenegro	4
Germany	4	3	3	3	2	4	2	2	3	7	1	2	7	2	3	4	South Africa	4
Great Britain	6	2	1	2	2	1	1	1	2	1	2	1	2	na	na	na	Italy	4
Greece	na	11	10	12	15	8	8	4	9	14	11	9	14	10	11	10	Puerto Rico	4
Hungary	1	2	1	2	2	1	2	1	2	4	1	2	2	1	2	9	Slovenia	3
Iceland	5	5	6	3	1	7	5	4	2	11	3	6	4	2	5	11	Japan	3
India	na	7	9	5	8	7	7	5	6	12	8	5	8	4	11	22	Peru	3
Indonesia	na	na	na	na	na	na	na	na	na	na	na	na	na	na	na	na	Chile	3
Iran	na	na	na	na	na	na	na	na	na	na	na	na	na	na	na	na	Ireland	3
Ireland	2	3	3	3	4	2	3	na	2	8	2	2	4	2	2	6	Germany	3
Israel	na	na	na	na	na	na	na	na	na	na	na	na	na	na	na	na	Slovakia	3
Italy	3	4	3	4	5	4	3	1	5	7	4	3	4	2	3	6	Zimbabwe	2
Japan	1	3	4	3	1	3	5	3	3	3	3	3	4	2	3	6	France	2
Jordan	na	na	na	na	na	na	na	na	na	na	na	na	na	na	na	na	Argentina	2
Korea, South	2	6	8	4	4	7	8	4	7	5	8	6	4	3	8	10	Croatia	2
Latvia	4	1	1	1	1	na	1	na	1	2	na	1	1	na	1	na	Spain	2
Lithuania	2	1	1	1	2	1	na	na	1	1	na	na	1	na	1	2	Malta	2
Luxembourg	na	11	8	15	10	13	10	8	11	18	9	6	16	9	11	15	Bosnia and Herz.	2
Macedonia	na	5	5	5	5	6	3	4	4	9	3	5	7	4	5	9	Estonia	2
Malta	na	2	2	2	3	2	2	1	2	5	na	3	3	2	2	6	Hungary	2
Mexico	3	5	5	4	4	5	5	4	5	6	5	4	7	5	4	6	Great Britain	2
Moldova	na	5	4	5	5	5	4	3	5	7	3	5	6	6	3	6	Bulgaria	1
Montenegro	na	4	6	3	4	5	3	1	5	12	3	5	6	4	5	2	China	1
Morocco	na	1	1	na	na	na	1	na	1	4	na	1	1	na	1	1	Poland	1
Netherlands	24	44	40	47	28	47	49	38	41	53	35	48	50	35	43	49	Northern Ireland	1
New Zealand	na	na	na	na	na	na	na	na	na	na	na	na	na	na	na	na	Belarus	1
Nigeria	na	na	na	na	na	na	na	na	na	na	na	na	na	na	na	na	Singapore	1
Northern Ireland	2	1	2	1	na	2	1	1	1	3	1	na	3	na	2	1	Serbia	1
Norway	4	na	na	na	na	na	na	na	na	na	na	na	na	na	na	na	Latvia	1
Pakistan	na	na	na	na	na	na	na	na	na	na	na	na	na	na	na	na	Lithuania	1
Peru	na	3	4	2	3	3	5	3	3	4	3	3	4	2	3	5	Russian Fed.	1
Philippines	na	8	10	7	6	8	11	10	8	7	5	5	15	6	10	9	Ukraine	1
Poland	na	1	2	1	1	1	1	1	2	2	1	1	3	na	2	na	Morocco	1
Portugal	1	1	1	1	na	1	1	na	1	3	na	na	1	na	na	3	Portugal	1
Puerto Rico	na	4	3	4	6	5	2	3	1	6	3	3	5	4	4	3	Turkey	0
Romania	1	1	2	0	1	1	1	0	1	3	0	1	2	0	2	1		
Russian Fed.	2	1	1	1	1	1	1	na	na	2	na	1	1	1	1	3		
Serbia	na	1	1	na	1	1	1	1	1	na	1	na	1	1	1	na		
Singapore	na	1	na	2	1	1	na	1	1	na	2	1	1	1	1	na		
Slovakia	na	3	3	2	3	2	3	2	2	5	2	3	3	2	3	na		
Slovenia	2	3	6	1	3	4	3	3	3	5	2	6	5	3	4	2		
South Africa	na	4	4	4	3	5	3	3	5	10	2	6	4	3	4	9		
Spain	1	2	2	2	4	2	1	1	2	7	1	2	3	1	1	6		
Sweden	11	11	11	12	11	13	10	7	10	17	8	13	14	7	11	15		
Switzerland	11	na	na	na	na	na	na	na	na	na	na	na	na	na	na	na		
Taiwan	na	na	na	na	na	na	na	na	na	na	na	na	na	na	na	na		
Tanzania	na	20	20	20	24	19	14	15	26	26	17	25	21	16	22	25		
Turkey	na	0	na	na	na	na	na	na	na	na	na	na	na	na	na	na		
Uganda	na	10	19	2	13	7	11	10	11	5	14	16	17	7	13	6		
Ukraine	na	1	1	na	1	1	1	1	na	1	1	na	2	1	1	na		
United States	9	16	14	17	13	15	19	13	12	19	9	20	18	15	14	21		
Uruguay	na	na	na	na	na	na	na	na	na	na	na	na	na	na	na	na		
Venezuela	na	12	15	9	13	13	9	8	9	24	8	11	15	11	12	15		
Vietnam	na	8	9	6	8	9	6	7	7	13	6	8	9	6	9	11		
Zimbabwe	na	2	4	1	3	1	4	1	4	na	1	2	6	2	3	1		
Total	5	6	6	5	6	6	5	4	5	10	5	6	7	4	7	9	**Total**	6

A072) BELONG PROFESSIONAL ASSOCIATIONS

Please look carefully at the following list of voluntary organizations and activities and say...which, if any, do you belong to?
Professional associations.

Belong (%)

(WVS: V47; EVS: V20)

Country	Wave 1990	Wave 2000	Male	Female	16-29	30-49	50+	Edu Lower	Edu Middle	Edu Upper	Inc Lower	Inc Middle	Inc Upper	Mat	Mixed	Postm.
Albania	na	11	15	7	8	14	8	6	12	22	9	13	11	10	11	13
Algeria	na	9	10	8	8	9	9	4	11	10	9	9	9	10	8	8
Argentina	3	2	2	1	1	2	2	na	1	13	1	1	4	na	2	4
Armenia	na	na	na	na	na	na	na	na	na	na	na	na	na	na	na	na
Australia	na	na	na	na	na	na	na	na	na	na	na	na	na	na	na	na
Austria	6	7	10	5	4	9	7	5	6	21	5	6	12	5	8	8
Azerbaijan	na	na	na	na	na	na	na	na	na	na	na	na	na	na	na	na
Bangladesh	na	21	28	11	17	24	19	15	24	32	17	20	24	21	21	18
Belarus	na	1	1	na	na	1	na	na	1	na	na	1	1	1	1	na
Belgium	7	9	11	7	7	12	8	4	8	15	5	8	13	4	10	11
Bosnia and Herz.	na	2	3	2	2	3	2	na	2	6	1	2	6	3	2	4
Brazil	5	na	na	na	na	na	na	na	na	na	na	na	na	na	na	na
Bulgaria	5	3	4	2	1	6	1	na	2	8	1	3	5	2	4	na
Canada	16	18	22	14	13	22	16	4	11	41	7	14	33	14	15	25
Chile	3	4	4	3	2	5	2	na	2	13	na	3	10	2	4	6
China	26	1	2	1	3	1	na	na	2	7	na	1	3	1	2	na
Colombia	na	na	na	na	na	na	na	na	na	na	na	na	na	na	na	na
Croatia	na	3	4	3	2	4	3	2	2	10	na	3	6	2	4	2
Czech Republic	na	6	7	5	4	7	6	3	7	18	3	4	12	4	6	13
Denmark	12	11	13	9	4	12	13	7	10	19	6	14	16	5	10	20
Dominican Rep.	na	na	na	na	na	na	na	na	na	na	na	na	na	na	na	na
Egypt	na	na	na	na	na	na	na	na	na	na	na	na	na	na	na	na
El Salvador	na	na	na	na	na	na	na	na	na	na	na	na	na	na	na	na
Estonia	4	4	3	4	2	7	2	2	2	10	1	2	8	3	4	7
Finland	15	6	9	4	6	8	5	3	7	15	6	4	9	3	7	7
France	5	3	4	2	1	6	2	2	3	7	1	4	5	1	3	7
Georgia	na	na	na	na	na	na	na	na	na	na	na	na	na	na	na	na
Germany	6	4	7	3	4	6	3	2	5	12	1	4	6	1	6	6
Great Britain	11	2	2	2	na	3	1	na	2	5	1	na	5	na	na	na
Greece	na	14	18	12	8	20	17	5	12	18	8	16	22	15	15	13
Hungary	6	4	4	4	2	6	2	2	3	17	2	4	5	3	5	8
Iceland	15	19	20	18	9	25	20	7	16	50	9	19	30	12	21	24
India	na	9	11	7	8	11	8	6	12	15	7	6	13	7	14	4
Indonesia	na	na	na	na	na	na	na	na	na	na	na	na	na	na	na	na
Iran	na	na	na	na	na	na	na	na	na	na	na	na	na	na	na	na
Ireland	5	8	10	5	11	9	4	1	3	31	2	4	18	7	8	6
Israel	na	na	na	na	na	na	na	na	na	na	na	na	na	na	na	na
Italy	4	7	10	4	5	9	7	4	5	23	4	5	13	3	8	9
Japan	4	5	7	3	2	3	8	6	5	6	4	4	8	5	5	9
Jordan	na	na	na	na	na	na	na	na	na	na	na	na	na	na	na	na
Korea, South	13	9	13	5	11	8	8	2	5	16	7	8	11	6	11	12
Latvia	6	1	na	2	na	2	1	na	1	5	1	2	2	2	1	2
Lithuania	3	1	1	na	1	1	1	na	na	2	na	na	1	1	1	3
Luxembourg	na	6	8	5	5	7	6	3	7	11	3	4	10	8	5	9
Macedonia	na	7	8	6	5	9	5	3	6	14	5	8	9	7	6	9
Malta	na	3	3	2	1	4	2	na	2	18	na	1	8	1	4	9
Mexico	3	3	4	2	3	3	2	1	1	16	1	2	6	3	3	6
Moldova	na	7	7	8	7	9	6	4	7	12	3	8	10	8	7	8
Montenegro	na	6	7	5	4	6	6	2	6	14	2	7	8	3	8	8
Morocco	na	3	3	2	2	4	2	2	1	10	1	4	8	1	4	7
Netherlands	12	16	21	12	13	20	15	4	15	30	10	15	28	5	16	23
New Zealand	na	na	na	na	na	na	na	na	na	na	na	na	na	na	na	na
Nigeria	na	na	na	na	na	na	na	na	na	na	na	na	na	na	na	na
Northern Ireland	7	4	6	3	3	5	5	2	2	15	3	2	12	3	6	2
Norway	16	na	na	na	na	na	na	na	na	na	na	na	na	na	na	na
Pakistan	na	na	na	na	na	na	na	na	na	na	na	na	na	na	na	na
Peru	na	6	8	4	5	6	8	2	3	13	3	6	10	5	6	6
Philippines	na	4	4	4	3	4	6	1	1	12	2	4	7	3	5	3
Poland	na	4	5	4	3	5	4	2	6	14	3	5	7	3	5	7
Portugal	4	1	2	1	2	2	1	na	2	7	na	1	1	1	1	na
Puerto Rico	na	11	12	10	9	14	9	3	4	15	4	11	17	7	11	11
Romania	2	2	2	2	2	2	2	0	1	7	0	0	4	0	3	7
Russian Fed.	2	1	1	1	2	1	1	na	1	2	1	1	1	1	1	na
Serbia	na	3	3	2	2	3	3	na	2	7	1	3	3	2	3	6
Singapore	na	4	6	3	3	6	3	na	2	25	na	2	11	6	4	6
Slovakia	na	5	6	4	4	6	4	1	4	26	3	3	8	3	6	10
Slovenia	6	7	9	5	2	11	5	2	5	21	3	9	13	4	7	7
South Africa	na	6	8	2	2	8	6	1	9	35	na	6	13	6	6	2
Spain	2	2	3	2	1	4	2	1	1	9	1	2	5	1	2	4
Sweden	12	15	14	15	8	17	16	9	8	30	10	14	21	12	13	18
Switzerland	14	na	na	na	na	na	na	na	na	na	na	na	na	na	na	na
Taiwan	na	na	na	na	na	na	na	na	na	na	na	na	na	na	na	na
Tanzania	na	23	23	23	22	24	21	14	26	49	15	30	31	18	26	38
Turkey	na	1	2	na	1	1	2	1	1	7	na	1	4	na	2	1
Uganda	na	9	14	5	8	11	6	4	12	10	7	12	18	8	10	10
Ukraine	na	2	2	2	3	1	3	1	1	5	1	2	3	1	2	3
United States	15	28	33	23	23	30	30	10	19	40	15	30	44	26	28	30
Uruguay	na	na	na	na	na	na	na	na	na	na	na	na	na	na	na	na
Venezuela	na	9	11	7	8	12	7	3	7	22	5	9	13	9	9	9
Vietnam	na	13	16	11	9	16	12	11	16	15	11	13	16	11	15	12
Zimbabwe	na	4	7	2	3	5	5	2	6	78	1	3	15	4	5	3
Total	8	7	9	5	6	9	6	4	6	17	4	7	12	5	8	10

RANKING

Country	2000
United States	28
Tanzania	23
Bangladesh	21
Iceland	19
Canada	18
Netherlands	16
Sweden	15
Greece	14
Vietnam	13
Denmark	11
Albania	11
Puerto Rico	11
Venezuela	9
India	9
Belgium	9
Uganda	9
Korea, South	9
Algeria	9
Romania	2
Ireland	8
Austria	7
Moldova	7
Italy	7
Slovenia	7
Macedonia	7
Luxembourg	6
Finland	6
Czech Republic	6
Peru	6
Montenegro	6
South Africa	6
Slovakia	5
Japan	5
Germany	4
Singapore	4
Poland	4
Northern Ireland	4
Zimbabwe	4
Philippines	4
Estonia	4
Hungary	4
Chile	4
Croatia	3
France	3
Malta	3
Mexico	3
Morocco	3
Bulgaria	3
Serbia	3
Bosnia and Herz.	2
Spain	2
Ukraine	2
Argentina	2
Great Britain	2
Latvia	1
China	1
Portugal	1
Turkey	1
Russian Fed.	1
Belarus	1
Lithuania	1
Total	7

A073) BELONG YOUTH WORK

Please look carefully at the following list of voluntary organizations and activities and say...which, if any, do you belong to?
Youth work (e.g. scouts, guides, youth clubs etc.).

Belong (%) (WVS: V48; EVS: V21)

Country	Wave 1990	2000	Gender Male	Female	Age 16-29	30-49	50+	Education Lower	Middle	Upper	Income Lower	Middle	Upper	Values Mat	Mixed	Postm.
Albania	na	12	15	9	33	6	3	10	12	18	13	12	11	10	14	18
Algeria	na	10	13	7	15	7	4	2	10	15	11	8	11	4	13	9
Argentina	2	3	2	3	5	2	2	2	4	5	2	2	5	1	4	2
Armenia	na	na	na	na	na	na	na	na	na	na	na	na	na	na	na	na
Australia	na	na	na	na	na	na	na	na	na	na	na	na	na	na	na	na
Austria	3	3	2	4	5	4	2	2	4	8	2	3	3	2	3	6
Azerbaijan	na	na	na	na	na	na	na	na	na	na	na	na	na	na	na	na
Bangladesh	na	12	17	6	14	11	10	6	17	23	11	11	15	11	13	13
Belarus	na	1	1	na	2	na	1	na	1	2	na	1	1	na	1	na
Belgium	8	8	9	7	18	9	3	3	9	10	4	6	12	6	8	12
Bosnia and Herz.	na	2	3	2	6	1	na	1	2	4	1	3	2	2	2	4
Brazil	4	na	na	na	na	na	na	na	na	na	na	na	na	na	na	na
Bulgaria	2	1	2	1	3	2	na	1	1	4	1	1	2	1	2	na
Canada	10	11	10	12	12	14	7	6	11	15	7	12	14	4	12	10
Chile	6	5	6	4	10	4	1	1	6	8	4	5	5	4	5	7
China	9	1	1	1	5	na	na	na	2	7	1	1	1	1	2	3
Colombia	na	na	na	na	na	na	na	na	na	na	na	na	na	na	na	na
Croatia	na	2	2	3	7	1	na	1	2	5	1	1	5	na	3	3
Czech Republic	na	7	7	7	9	9	4	6	7	14	5	7	8	5	7	10
Denmark	5	7	8	5	8	8	5	5	10	9	5	7	10	4	7	9
Dominican Rep.	na	na	na	na	na	na	na	na	na	na	na	na	na	na	na	na
Egypt	na	na	na	na	na	na	na	na	na	na	na	na	na	na	na	na
El Salvador	na	na	na	na	na	na	na	na	na	na	na	na	na	na	na	na
Estonia	3	2	3	2	5	1	2	1	2	5	1	1	4	1	3	4
Finland	5	7	7	8	11	9	4	3	12	13	5	7	10	8	7	7
France	3	2	2	2	3	2	1	2	1	5	2	3	1	2	2	2
Georgia	na	na	na	na	na	na	na	na	na	na	na	na	na	na	na	na
Germany	3	2	1	3	2	3	1	1	3	2	1	2	2	na	2	4
Great Britain	4	6	4	7	5	8	4	6	5	7	5	6	9	na	na	na
Greece	na	6	7	4	6	5	5	2	4	7	4	6	6	10	4	4
Hungary	2	1	1	1	1	na	1	na	na	4	1	1	1	na	2	na
Iceland	8	7	7	7	7	9	5	6	9	5	6	9	7	6	8	3
India	na	6	8	4	10	6	3	5	4	11	8	4	7	3	10	9
Indonesia	na	na	na	na	na	na	na	na	na	na	na	na	na	na	na	na
Iran	na	na	na	na	na	na	na	na	na	na	na	na	na	na	na	na
Ireland	6	7	8	7	10	8	4	3	9	10	5	7	10	5	8	8
Israel	na	na	na	na	na	na	na	na	na	na	na	na	na	na	na	na
Italy	3	4	4	5	7	5	3	2	7	6	3	5	4	2	4	6
Japan	1	2	3	2	1	2	2	na	2	3	1	2	4	2	2	2
Jordan	na	na	na	na	na	na	na	na	na	na	na	na	na	na	na	na
Korea, South	7	4	6	3	5	4	5	2	4	6	3	4	6	3	6	6
Latvia	2	1	1	1	3	na	na	na	1	na	na	1	1	na	1	na
Lithuania	5	2	1	3	6	na	na	1	2	2	1	1	2	1	2	1
Luxembourg	na	9	10	8	17	6	6	6	8	13	5	10	11	8	8	15
Macedonia	na	5	6	4	13	4	1	3	6	7	3	4	9	4	6	10
Malta	na	2	3	2	4	2	2	1	3	5	1	3	3	1	3	1
Mexico	4	4	5	4	6	4	2	3	5	10	3	3	7	4	5	6
Moldova	na	6	5	6	13	3	2	2	6	9	2	4	10	4	5	15
Montenegro	na	3	3	2	9	2	na	1	4	4	3	5	1	1	4	5
Morocco	na	1	1	1	2	1	1	1	4	3	1	1	4	1	1	3
Netherlands	7	7	6	7	14	7	2	3	9	7	7	6	5	3	8	4
New Zealand	na	na	na	na	na	na	na	na	na	na	na	na	na	na	na	na
Nigeria	na	na	na	na	na	na	na	na	na	na	na	na	na	na	na	na
Northern Ireland	11	6	6	6	10	7	3	4	7	10	3	6	9	4	7	7
Norway	6	na	na	na	na	na	na	na	na	na	na	na	na	na	na	na
Pakistan	na	na	na	na	na	na	na	na	na	na	na	na	na	na	na	na
Peru	na	6	7	5	10	3	3	6	5	7	4	7	6	4	6	7
Philippines	na	8	9	6	11	6	4	4	8	12	6	5	13	5	9	7
Poland	na	2	2	1	2	1	2	1	2	3	2	1	3	1	2	3
Portugal	3	1	2	1	2	1	1	1	3	1	1	1	3	1	2	2
Puerto Rico	na	9	12	8	10	12	8	4	6	12	7	11	11	6	9	13
Romania	1	1	1	1	2	0	0	0	1	1	0	1	1	1	0	3
Russian Fed.	3	1	1	1	3	na	na	na	1	1	na	1	1	1	1	na
Serbia	na	1	1	1	5	1	na	1	1	3	1	na	2	1	2	1
Singapore	na	8	8	8	15	2	1	11	7	8	7	9	8	5	9	12
Slovakia	na	7	6	7	11	6	5	4	7	12	3	7	8	5	8	11
Slovenia	2	5	6	3	8	4	2	1	5	8	4	5	9	3	5	6
South Africa	na	10	10	11	17	6	6	7	14	17	6	14	13	12	10	7
Spain	2	2	2	2	4	2	1	1	3	5	2	1	4	1	1	5
Sweden	9	7	8	6	10	9	3	6	8	6	6	5	11	4	7	9
Switzerland	4	na	na	na	na	na	na	na	na	na	na	na	na	na	na	na
Taiwan	na	na	na	na	na	na	na	na	na	na	na	na	na	na	na	na
Tanzania	na	18	18	18	26	17	10	17	22	16	20	20	14	15	21	13
Turkey	na	1	1	na	1	na	na	na	1	4	na	na	2	na	1	1
Uganda	na	21	27	16	35	8	7	14	25	13	21	25	21	19	21	26
Ukraine	na	1	2	1	3	1	na	na	1	4	1	1	2	na	2	na
United States	13	26	24	28	26	33	18	19	28	28	19	27	37	30	26	24
Uruguay	na	na	na	na	na	na	na	na	na	na	na	na	na	na	na	na
Venezuela	na	8	11	5	11	8	5	3	9	13	8	8	10	9	8	10
Vietnam	na	16	19	12	37	12	5	11	21	24	13	17	16	14	17	14
Zimbabwe	na	6	8	3	8	2	4	2	11	na	4	6	9	4	6	7
Total	5	6	7	5	11	5	3	4	6	9	5	6	7	4	7	8

RANKING

Country	2000
United States	26
Uganda	21
Tanzania	18
Vietnam	16
Albania	12
Bangladesh	12
Canada	11
South Africa	10
Algeria	10
Puerto Rico	9
Luxembourg	9
Venezuela	8
Singapore	8
Belgium	8
Denmark	7
Philippines	8
Finland	7
Ireland	7
Czech Republic	7
Iceland	7
Sweden	7
Slovakia	7
Netherlands	7
India	6
Northern Ireland	6
Peru	6
Great Britain	6
Moldova	6
Greece	6
Zimbabwe	6
Macedonia	5
Chile	5
Slovenia	5
Korea, South	4
Italy	4
Mexico	4
Austria	3
Romania	3
Argentina	3
Montenegro	3
Estonia	2
Malta	2
Croatia	2
Bosnia and Herz.	2
Japan	2
France	2
Spain	2
Germany	2
Lithuania	2
Poland	2
Bulgaria	1
Morocco	1
Ukraine	1
Serbia	1
Portugal	1
China	1
Hungary	1
Belarus	1
Latvia	1
Russian Fed.	1
Turkey	1
Total	6

A074) BELONG SPORTS OR RECREATION
Please look carefully at the following list of voluntary organizations and activities and say...which, if any, do you belong to?
Sports or recreation.
Belong (%)

(WVS: V49; EVS: V22)

Country	Wave		Gender		Age			Education			Income			Values		
	1990	2000	Male	Female	16-29	30-49	50+	Lower	Middle	Upper	Lower	Middle	Upper	Mat	Mixed	Postm.
Albania	na	11	18	4	24	8	3	7	12	16	7	12	12	7	14	15
Algeria	na	14	20	9	22	11	5	4	18	17	14	14	18	13	16	11
Argentina	5	8	11	5	9	9	5	6	10	11	4	7	11	6	8	9
Armenia	na	na	na	na	na	na	na	na	na	na	na	na	na	na	na	na
Australia	na	na	na	na	na	na	na	na	na	na	na	na	na	na	na	na
Austria	17	23	30	16	30	25	17	17	31	23	16	23	28	14	24	24
Azerbaijan	na	na	na	na	na	na	na	na	na	na	na	na	na	na	na	na
Bangladesh	na	25	33	15	29	23	22	12	36	45	20	27	27	23	27	22
Belarus	na	2	3	1	5	1	1	na	3	3	1	2	4	2	2	na
Belgium	20	26	31	21	40	31	14	13	27	34	18	21	37	22	28	28
Bosnia and Herz.	na	11	19	5	23	10	3	4	11	19	5	10	16	8	12	17
Brazil	8	na	na	na	na	na	na	na	na	na	na	na	na	na	na	na
Bulgaria	4	5	8	2	11	5	2	1	6	9	2	7	5	3	7	2
Canada	23	28	32	23	34	32	19	16	28	37	17	27	36	22	28	28
Chile	12	15	23	8	25	14	7	9	17	21	10	18	20	12	16	18
China	4	3	3	4	6	3	na	1	5	7	2	2	6	4	4	3
Colombia	na	na	na	na	na	na	na	na	na	na	na	na	na	na	na	na
Croatia	na	12	21	4	22	12	5	5	16	19	5	10	18	11	10	21
Czech Republic	na	23	30	16	35	25	14	20	24	30	14	24	28	19	25	27
Denmark	34	33	37	29	40	38	24	29	45	37	22	39	41	28	34	35
Dominican Rep.	na	na	na	na	na	na	na	na	na	na	na	na	na	na	na	na
Egypt	na	na	na	na	na	na	na	na	na	na	na	na	na	na	na	na
El Salvador	na	na	na	na	na	na	na	na	na	na	na	na	na	na	na	na
Estonia	14	9	12	6	22	7	4	8	10	9	3	7	12	6	12	7
Finland	23	26	33	20	29	33	17	20	36	27	16	28	35	25	27	23
France	16	17	20	13	21	18	12	12	19	26	11	18	23	12	16	24
Georgia	na	na	na	na	na	na	na	na	na	na	na	na	na	na	na	na
Germany	21	28	32	26	41	33	18	18	37	32	15	28	42	26	28	35
Great Britain	18	3	3	3	2	5	1	2	3	5	2	3	5	na	na	na
Greece	na	15	22	10	20	13	9	7	18	15	14	16	18	15	14	18
Hungary	4	4	5	3	9	3	2	2	6	12	1	4	6	2	5	5
Iceland	30	34	39	29	38	38	25	29	38	39	25	36	43	26	38	32
India	na	11	15	7	14	11	8	8	10	18	13	9	12	7	17	24
Indonesia	na	na	na	na	na	na	na	na	na	na	na	na	na	na	na	na
Iran	na	na	na	na	na	na	na	na	na	na	na	na	na	na	na	na
Ireland	24	28	37	19	41	28	18	17	28	45	12	30	41	32	27	31
Israel	na	na	na	na	na	na	na	na	na	na	na	na	na	na	na	na
Italy	10	12	16	8	16	14	6	7	14	18	8	10	18	10	12	11
Japan	9	14	16	13	9	15	16	13	15	13	13	17	14	18	13	18
Jordan	na	na	na	na	na	na	na	na	na	na	na	na	na	na	na	na
Korea, South	17	25	29	21	26	26	20	2	21	33	22	23	28	21	28	31
Latvia	9	7	10	4	18	7	3	4	6	13	4	4	12	5	8	13
Lithuania	8	4	4	3	10	2	na	na	5	5	1	3	4	4	4	2
Luxembourg	na	26	30	22	35	30	16	18	30	30	15	28	33	24	27	27
Macedonia	na	13	19	7	19	15	6	6	15	20	9	13	19	11	14	26
Malta	na	9	17	2	14	10	5	4	11	16	4	10	20	7	10	16
Mexico	8	9	13	5	15	7	4	4	13	24	5	9	17	7	10	14
Moldova	na	6	7	4	14	3	2	1	5	9	3	5	9	5	6	7
Montenegro	na	11	18	5	24	12	3	4	16	18	9	9	16	7	16	16
Morocco	na	5	7	3	9	3	1	4	12	11	3	5	9	4	6	7
Netherlands	43	51	54	49	63	54	42	41	55	57	40	54	60	41	53	53
New Zealand	na	na	na	na	na	na	na	na	na	na	na	na	na	na	na	na
Nigeria	na	na	na	na	na	na	na	na	na	na	na	na	na	na	na	na
Northern Ireland	17	14	19	10	23	13	11	7	16	29	11	14	22	9	16	18
Norway	33	na	na	na	na	na	na	na	na	na	na	na	na	na	na	na
Pakistan	na	na	na	na	na	na	na	na	na	na	na	na	na	na	na	na
Peru	na	11	18	6	15	10	7	7	11	16	9	12	14	8	12	15
Philippines	na	12	19	6	19	10	8	7	12	19	8	10	20	10	15	10
Poland	na	3	5	1	5	3	2	2	4	8	2	2	7	2	4	4
Portugal	14	9	16	3	13	12	6	6	14	16	1	9	19	6	10	12
Puerto Rico	na	8	13	6	15	8	5	4	5	11	6	7	13	7	8	9
Romania	3	2	3	1	5	2	1	0	2	4	0	1	4	1	3	4
Russian Fed.	5	4	6	3	11	3	1	na	4	8	3	3	6	2	6	8
Serbia	na	8	14	3	13	9	5	4	10	12	5	8	11	7	10	11
Singapore	na	15	22	9	21	12	5	9	17	24	8	14	22	10	16	26
Slovakia	na	18	30	7	23	20	11	12	20	18	13	18	20	15	20	21
Slovenia	8	17	25	10	25	19	9	6	20	28	7	17	31	16	17	16
South Africa	na	24	33	14	34	21	8	19	29	47	16	27	32	20	24	44
Spain	6	8	11	5	14	8	4	4	12	11	4	7	14	5	8	12
Sweden	32	37	40	34	42	44	27	29	40	39	27	39	49	33	36	44
Switzerland	na	na	na	na	na	na	na	na	na	na	na	na	na	na	na	na
Taiwan	na	na	na	na	na	na	na	na	na	na	na	na	na	na	na	na
Tanzania	na	29	32	26	36	28	19	23	38	33	25	34	28	27	30	42
Turkey	na	1	1	1	na	1	na	na	1	2	na	1	1	na	1	1
Uganda	na	24	39	10	32	18	9	15	28	22	24	30	29	20	25	31
Ukraine	na	2	3	1	3	3	na	na	2	4	1	2	5	2	2	2
United States	20	36	45	27	43	41	24	28	39	38	25	38	51	33	37	35
Uruguay	na	na	na	na	na	na	na	na	na	na	na	na	na	na	na	na
Venezuela	na	21	32	10	28	18	11	10	22	32	15	20	30	20	21	28
Vietnam	na	19	26	12	24	19	15	14	23	36	18	14	25	13	23	18
Zimbabwe	na	8	16	1	13	5	2	4	15	10	5	7	18	7	9	8
Total	16	16	21	11	22	16	10	11	17	22	11	16	21	11	18	22

RANKING

Country	2000
Netherlands	51
Denmark	33
Sweden	37
United States	36
Iceland	34
Tanzania	29
Germany	28
Ireland	28
Canada	28
Luxembourg	26
Belgium	26
Finland	26
Bangladesh	25
Korea, South	25
Uganda	24
South Africa	24
Czech Republic	23
Austria	23
Venezuela	21
Vietnam	19
Slovakia	18
Slovenia	17
France	17
Greece	15
Singapore	15
Chile	15
Algeria	14
Northern Ireland	14
Japan	14
Macedonia	13
Philippines	12
Croatia	12
Italy	12
Peru	11
Bosnia and Herz.	11
Montenegro	11
India	11
Albania	11
Malta	9
Romania	2
Estonia	9
Portugal	9
Mexico	9
Zimbabwe	8
Puerto Rico	8
Serbia	8
Spain	8
Argentina	8
Latvia	7
Moldova	6
Morocco	5
Bulgaria	5
Russian Fed.	4
Hungary	4
Lithuania	4
China	3
Poland	3
Great Britain	3
Belarus	2
Ukraine	2
Turkey	1
Total	16

A075) BELONG WOMEN'S GROUP

Please look carefully at the following list of voluntary organizations and activities and say...which, if any, do you belong to?
Women's groups.

Belong (%)   (WVS: V50; EVS: V23)

Country	Wave 1990	Wave 2000	Gender Male	Gender Female	Age 16-29	Age 30-49	Age 50+	Education Lower	Education Middle	Education Upper	Income Lower	Income Middle	Income Upper	Values Mat	Values Mixed	Values Postm.
Albania	na	14	2	25	10	16	14	14	14	12	14	16	12	12	15	10
Algeria	na	4	1	8	4	5	4	3	5	4	4	4	7	4	5	3
Argentina	1	1	na	1	1	1	1	na	2	1	1	1	1	1	1	1
Armenia	na	na	na	na	na	na	na	na	na	na	na	na	na	na	na	na
Australia	na	na	na	na	na	na	na	na	na	na	na	na	na	na	na	na
Austria	4	4	na	8	2	4	5	5	3	5	4	4	4	2	4	5
Azerbaijan	na	na	na	na	na	na	na	na	na	na	na	na	na	na	na	na
Bangladesh	na	14	11	19	14	15	14	15	13	15	11	17	13	15	15	9
Belarus	na	0	na	1	na	1	na	na	1	1	na	1	1	na	1	na
Belgium	9	10	2	16	2	8	15	13	7	9	13	9	8	13	9	7
Bosnia and Herz.	na	3	1	5	2	4	2	2	3	2	1	3	4	2	3	8
Brazil	2	na	na	na	na	na	na	na	na	na	na	na	na	na	na	na
Bulgaria	2	1	na	2	1	2	1	na	2	1	1	2	1	1	1	na
Canada	7	8	2	14	5	7	11	7	8	10	8	7	9	8	8	9
Chile	3	5	na	10	4	6	7	6	5	5	6	5	5	7	5	5
China	3	3	1	6	3	4	2	1	5	5	1	4	6	3	4	3
Colombia	na	na	na	na	na	na	na	na	na	na	na	na	na	na	na	na
Croatia	na	2	1	4	na	5	na	5	1	1	2	2	3	3	2	2
Czech Republic	na	3	1	4	1	2	3	3	3	1	4	2	2	5	2	4
Denmark	2	2	0	4	0	3	3	2	2	3	3	2	1	1	2	3
Dominican Rep.	na	na	na	na	na	na	na	na	na	na	na	na	na	na	na	na
Egypt	na	na	na	na	na	na	na	na	na	na	na	na	na	na	na	na
El Salvador	na	na	na	na	na	na	na	na	na	na	na	na	na	na	na	na
Estonia	2	2	na	4	1	4	2	2	2	4	3	3	1	1	3	na
Finland	3	4	na	8	1	4	7	6	4	2	6	4	5	4	5	3
France	1	0	na	1	1	na	na	na	na	1	1	na	1	1	na	1
Georgia	na	na	na	na	na	na	na	na	na	na	na	na	na	na	na	na
Germany	7	4	na	6	na	5	4	3	4	5	3	4	5	5	3	5
Great Britain	5	2	1	3	2	1	3	2	1	2	2	2	1	na	na	na
Greece	na	4	2	6	1	5	8	2	6	3	1	7	4	5	3	6
Hungary	1	0	na	na	1	1	na	na	na	2	na	na	1	na	na	na
Iceland	7	6	1	11	2	4	11	6	4	10	6	6	6	6	6	5
India	na	6	4	9	7	6	5	6	5	7	6	5	7	4	8	7
Indonesia	na	na	na	na	na	na	na	na	na	na	na	na	na	na	na	na
Iran	na	na	na	na	na	na	na	na	na	na	na	na	na	na	na	na
Ireland	5	4	1	8	3	3	7	5	4	5	5	6	4	4	4	6
Israel	na	na	na	na	na	na	na	na	na	na	na	na	na	na	na	na
Italy	0	0	na	1	na	na	na	na	1	na	1	1	na	1	na	na
Japan	3	4	1	7	na	2	7	5	5	1	4	4	4	3	4	4
Jordan	na	na	na	na	na	na	na	na	na	na	na	na	na	na	na	na
Korea, South	3	4	1	7	3	4	3	na	4	4	3	5	3	4	3	4
Latvia	1	0	na	1	na	na	1	na	1	na	1	na	na	na	na	2
Lithuania	3	0	na	1	na	1	na	na	na	1	na	na	1	na	na	na
Luxembourg	na	6	5	7	4	7	6	6	6	6	7	5	5	4	6	7
Macedonia	na	6	2	10	5	8	5	6	5	10	3	7	9	6	6	2
Malta	na	1	na	2	na	na	3	3	1	na	1	na	1	1	1	2
Mexico	2	3	1	5	3	4	3	3	3	4	4	3	3	3	3	4
Moldova	na	3	1	4	3	3	2	1	3	4	na	3	4	2	3	na
Montenegro	na	3	na	6	2	6	2	1	5	7	2	3	5	4	4	na
Morocco	na	2	na	3	2	2	1	1	1	6	1	3	3	1	2	1
Netherlands	8	5	1	8	2	3	8	5	4	5	4	4	5	7	4	6
New Zealand	na	na	na	na	na	na	na	na	na	na	na	na	na	na	na	na
Nigeria	na	na	na	na	na	na	na	na	na	na	na	na	na	na	na	na
Northern Ireland	5	4	1	7	1	3	5	5	3	4	4	3	6	4	4	4
Norway	3	na	na	na	na	na	na	na	na	na	na	na	na	na	na	na
Pakistan	na	na	na	na	na	na	na	na	na	na	na	na	na	na	na	na
Peru	na	6	1	11	4	8	5	9	6	4	8	6	4	5	7	4
Philippines	na	10	2	19	7	12	11	11	10	10	9	10	12	9	11	16
Poland	na	1	1	2	1	2	1	1	1	2	2	na	2	1	2	na
Portugal	0	na	na	na	na	na	na	na	na	na	na	na	na	na	na	na
Puerto Rico	na	3	4	2	4	2	3	1	1	4	3	1	5	2	2	5
Romania	1	0	0	1	1	0	0	0	0	1	1	0	1	0	1	1
Russian Fed.	2	1	na	1	na	1	na	na	1	na	1	na	na	1	na	na
Serbia	na	0	na	1	na	1	na	na	na	1	na	1	1	na	na	1
Singapore	na	1	na	2	1	2	2	1	1	2	1	1	2	2	1	2
Slovakia	na	7	1	12	2	7	11	8	7	3	9	6	7	7	8	2
Slovenia	0	2	2	2	1	1	3	3	2	2	2	3	2	1	2	1
South Africa	na	9	1	19	3	12	15	8	11	10	7	15	7	9	9	11
Spain	1	2	1	3	1	2	2	2	2	3	2	2	3	2	2	4
Sweden	3	4	na	7	na	3	6	3	2	6	3	2	5	5	2	5
Switzerland	na	na	na	na	na	na	na	na	na	na	na	na	na	na	na	na
Taiwan	na	na	na	na	na	na	na	na	na	na	na	na	na	na	na	na
Tanzania	na	24	10	41	22	28	18	24	20	30	24	25	22	23	23	33
Turkey	na	0	na	1	na	na	na	na	na	2	na	na	1	na	na	1
Uganda	na	16	1	29	10	23	15	25	13	4	17	14	16	19	14	12
Ukraine	na	1	na	2	1	2	na	na	1	2	na	1	2	na	1	2
United States	8	14	3	26	8	14	20	12	14	15	14	12	15	21	14	12
Uruguay	na	na	na	na	na	na	na	na	na	na	na	na	na	na	na	na
Venezuela	na	5	4	7	5	5	5	6	4	7	6	5	6	7	4	5
Vietnam	na	29	9	51	22	36	22	30	29	18	27	28	31	30	30	30
Zimbabwe	na	10	1	19	6	13	17	12	8	na	7	9	12	11	10	9
Total	3	5	1	8	4	6	5	5	5	5	5	5	5	5	5	5

RANKING

Country	2000
Vietnam	29
Tanzania	24
Uganda	16
Bangladesh	14
United States	14
Albania	14
Philippines	10
Zimbabwe	10
Belgium	10
South Africa	9
Canada	8
Slovakia	7
Peru	6
Macedonia	6
Luxembourg	6
Iceland	6
India	6
Chile	5
Venezuela	5
Netherlands	5
Algeria	4
Finland	4
Ireland	4
Austria	4
Greece	4
Northern Ireland	4
Japan	4
Germany	4
Korea, South	4
Sweden	4
China	3
Montenegro	3
Mexico	3
Puerto Rico	3
Bosnia and Herz.	3
Moldova	3
Czech Republic	3
Denmark	2
Croatia	2
Estonia	2
Spain	2
Romania	0
Slovenia	2
Great Britain	2
Morocco	2
Poland	1
Singapore	1
Malta	1
Bulgaria	1
Argentina	1
Ukraine	1
Russian Fed.	1
Belarus	0
France	0
Italy	0
Serbia	0
Hungary	0
Latvia	0
Lithuania	0
Turkey	0
Total	5

A076) BELONG PEACE MOVEMENT

Please look carefully at the following list of voluntary organizations and activities and say...which, if any, do you belong to?

Peace movement.

Belong (%)

(WVS: V51; EVS: V24)

Country	Wave		Gender		Age			Education			Income			Values			RANKING Country	2000
	1990	2000	Male	Female	16-29	30-49	50+	Lower	Middle	Upper	Lower	Middle	Upper	Mat	Mixed	Postm.		
Albania	na	7	8	7	7	7	8	4	9	12	8	6	8	6	9	8	Bangladesh	23
Algeria	na	na	na	na	na	na	na	na	na	na	na	na	na	na	na	na	Philippines	11
Argentina	0	na	na	na	na	na	na	na	na	na	na	na	na	na	na	na	Uganda	10
Armenia	na	na	na	na	na	na	na	na	na	na	na	na	na	na	na	na	Vietnam	9
Australia	na	na	na	na	na	na	na	na	na	na	na	na	na	na	na	na	Albania	7
Austria	1	1	1	1	1	1	1	1	1	1	2	1	1	2	1	1	South Africa	6
Azerbaijan	na	na	na	na	na	na	na	na	na	na	na	na	na	na	na	na	Venezuela	6
Bangladesh	na	23	30	15	22	22	35	20	27	28	12	26	29	21	25	21	Macedonia	5
Belarus	na	0	na	na	na	na	na	na	na	na	na	na	na	na	na	na	Tanzania	5
Belgium	2	2	2	2	2	3	2	2	2	2	1	2	2	1	2	2	India	5
Bosnia and Herz.	na	0	na	na	na	na	na	1	na	na	na	na	na	na	na	na	United States	5
Brazil	2	na	na	na	na	na	na	na	na	na	na	na	na	na	na	na	Greece	4
Bulgaria	1	1	na	1	na	2	na	1	na	2	1	1	na	na	1	2	Zimbabwe	3
Canada	2	2	2	2	na	3	3	3	2	3	2	2	3	2	2	2	Mexico	3
Chile	1	2	2	2	1	2	2	1	2	3	1	2	2	2	2	na	Netherlands	3
China	1	1	1	1	1	1	1	na	1	5	1	1	1	1	1	3	Luxembourg	2
Colombia	na	na	na	na	na	na	na	na	na	na	na	na	na	na	na	na	Moldova	2
Croatia	na	1	1	1	1	1	2	1	1	1	1	2	1	na	1	1	Northern Ireland	2
Czech Republic	na	1	1	2	1	1	2	1	2	na	2	1	1	1	1	3	Canada	2
Denmark	2	1	1	1	0	1	1	1	1	1	1	1	0	0	1	2	Belgium	2
Dominican Rep.	na	na	na	na	na	na	na	na	na	na	na	na	na	na	na	na	Japan	2
Egypt	na	na	na	na	na	na	na	na	na	na	na	na	na	na	na	na	Korea, South	2
El Salvador	na	na	na	na	na	na	na	na	na	na	na	na	na	na	na	na	Ireland	2
Estonia	1	0	na	na	na	na	na	na	na	na	na	na	1	na	na	na	Chile	2
Finland	2	1	2	1	2	1	2	1	1	2	1	2	2	na	1	5	Sweden	2
France	1	1	na	1	na	na	1	na	na	1	1	na	na	1	1	na	Finland	1
Georgia	na	na	na	na	na	na	na	na	na	na	na	na	na	na	na	na	Italy	1
Germany	2	0	na	na	na	na	na	na	na	na	na	na	na	na	na	na	Czech Republic	1
Great Britain	1	1	1	na	1	1	na	1	na	1	1	1	1	na	na	na	Puerto Rico	1
Greece	na	4	5	4	4	4	4	4	5	3	4	5	3	5	4	5	Croatia	1
Hungary	1	0	1	na	1	na	na	na	na	1	na	na	na	na	na	na	Iceland	1
Iceland	1	1	1	2	na	1	2	1	1	2	2	1	1	na	1	4	Spain	1
India	na	5	6	4	5	5	3	5	4	6	8	4	4	2	8	9	Austria	1
Indonesia	na	na	na	na	na	na	na	na	na	na	na	na	na	na	na	na	China	1
Iran	na	na	na	na	na	na	na	na	na	na	na	na	na	na	na	na	Denmark	1
Ireland	1	2	2	2	2	1	3	2	2	2	2	2	1	1	2	4	Peru	1
Israel	na	na	na	na	na	na	na	na	na	na	na	na	na	na	na	na	Singapore	1
Italy	1	1	1	2	1	2	1	1	2	2	1	2	1	1	1	2	Slovenia	1
Japan	1	2	2	2	na	1	3	4	2	2	3	1	2	2	1	4	Montenegro	1
Jordan	na	na	na	na	na	na	na	na	na	na	na	na	na	na	na	na	Bulgaria	1
Korea, South	2	2	2	1	2	2	3	na	2	1	2	3	1	1	3	na	Poland	1
Latvia	1	0	na	na	na	na	na	na	na	na	na	na	na	na	na	na	Portugal	1
Lithuania	1	0	na	na	na	na	na	na	na	na	na	na	na	na	na	na	Great Britain	1
Luxembourg	na	2	3	2	2	2	3	1	2	5	1	na	4	2	3	2	France	1
Macedonia	na	5	5	6	7	6	3	5	5	8	3	6	8	4	6	9	Morocco	0
Malta	na	0	na	na	na	na	na	na	na	na	1	na	na	na	na	na	Romania	0
Mexico	1	3	4	3	2	3	4	4	3	2	4	3	3	3	3	4	Bosnia and Herz.	0
Moldova	na	2	2	2	3	2	2	1	3	3	1	3	3	2	3	na	Hungary	0
Montenegro	na	1	1	na	na	na	2	1	1	1	2	1	na	1	na	na	Slovakia	0
Morocco	na	0	na	na	na	1	na	na	1	3	na	na	2	na	1	na	Estonia	0
Netherlands	3	3	2	4	1	na	6	2	3	3	3	2	4	1	2	6	Germany	0
New Zealand	na	na	na	na	na	na	na	na	na	na	na	na	na	na	na	na	Latvia	0
Nigeria	na	na	na	na	na	na	na	na	na	na	na	na	na	na	na	na	Lithuania	0
Northern Ireland	1	2	2	3	3	4	1	2	2	5	1	3	5	1	2	5	Malta	0
Norway	2	na	na	na	na	na	na	na	na	na	na	na	na	na	na	na	Belarus	0
Pakistan	na	na	na	na	na	na	na	na	na	na	na	na	na	na	na	na	Russian Fed.	0
Peru	na	1	1	1	1	1	1	2	1	1	1	1	1	na	1	1	Turkey	0
Philippines	na	11	16	7	7	13	14	12	10	13	9	11	14	11	12	8	Ukraine	0
Poland	na	1	1	na	1	na	1	na	1	na	1	na	2	na	1	na		
Portugal	1	1	1	na	na	1	1	na	1	1	na	1	1	na	na	1		
Puerto Rico	na	1	2	1	3	na	1	1	na	2	2	na	2	na	1	3		
Romania	0	0	0	0	0	0	0	0	0	0	0	0	0	0	0	0		
Russian Fed.	1	0	na	na	na	na	na	na	na	na	na	na	na	na	na	na		
Serbia	na	na	na	na	na	na	na	na	na	na	na	na	na	na	na	na		
Singapore	na	1	1	1	1	1	na	1	1	na	3	na	na	1	1	na		
Slovakia	na	0	1	na	1	1	na	na	1	2	1	1	na	na	na	2		
Slovenia	0	1	1	1	1	na	1	2	1	na	1	1	1	2	na	1		
South Africa	na	6	5	8	7	5	8	6	6	3	6	9	3	8	5	8		
Spain	1	1	1	1	1	2	1	na	1	4	1	1	2	1	1	3		
Sweden	3	2	1	2	1	2	1	2	1	3	1	1	2	3	1	3		
Switzerland	na	na	na	na	na	na	na	na	na	na	na	na	na	na	na	na		
Taiwan	na	na	na	na	na	na	na	na	na	na	na	na	na	na	na	na		
Tanzania	na	5	5	6	5	5	4	5	5	7	6	4	5	4	5	8		
Turkey	na	0	na	na	na	na	na	na	na	na	na	na	na	na	na	na		
Uganda	na	10	16	4	10	10	8	11	8	20	15	9	13	9	10	12		
Ukraine	na	0	na	na	na	na	na	na	na	na	na	na	na	na	na	na		
United States	2	5	5	4	6	3	6	4	4	5	4	4	5	5	4	4		
Uruguay	na	na	na	na	na	na	na	na	na	na	na	na	na	na	na	na		
Venezuela	na	6	8	4	5	7	5	4	6	7	7	5	5	6	6	5		
Vietnam	na	9	9	10	9	10	9	8	10	15	8	10	9	9	10	13		
Zimbabwe	na	3	3	3	4	2	3	2	4	14	1	4	8	2	5	2		
Total	1	3	3	2	3	3	2	2	2	3	2	3	3	2	3	3	Total	3

A077) BELONG GROUPS CONCERNED WITH HEALTH

Please look carefully at the following list of voluntary organizations and activities and say...which, if any, do you belong to?
Voluntary organizations concerned with health.

Belong (%)

(WVS: V52; EVS: V25)

Country	Wave 1990	Wave 2000	Male	Female	16-29	30-49	50+	Lower	Middle	Upper	Lower	Middle	Upper	Mat	Mixed	Postm.
Albania	na	13	12	14	10	14	14	11	14	15	14	12	13	14	13	5
Algeria	na	na	na	na	na	na	na	na	na	na	na	na	na	na	na	na
Argentina	2	2	1	4	2	3	2	1	4	6	4	1	3	na	3	3
Armenia	na	na	na	na	na	na	na	na	na	na	na	na	na	na	na	na
Australia	na	na	na	na	na	na	na	na	na	na	na	na	na	na	na	na
Austria	3	9	9	8	8	8	9	7	10	12	8	9	9	10	9	9
Azerbaijan	na	na	na	na	na	na	na	na	na	na	na	na	na	na	na	na
Bangladesh	na	22	26	17	21	22	25	16	28	30	10	25	29	20	24	18
Belarus	na	1	1	1	1	1	1	na	1	1	na	1	1	1	1	na
Belgium	4	6	5	6	6	4	6	4	5	7	5	7	6	5	5	7
Bosnia and Herz.	na	3	3	2	3	3	2	1	2	5	2	2	5	2	3	na
Brazil	3	na	na	na	na	na	na	na	na	na	na	na	na	na	na	na
Bulgaria	2	1	1	1	2	1	1	1	1	3	1	1	1	1	1	na
Canada	9	11	10	12	7	11	14	9	11	14	9	11	13	9	10	14
Chile	3	3	2	4	3	3	4	2	3	6	2	3	7	4	3	3
China	2	3	2	3	4	2	2	1	4	7	2	3	5	4	2	6
Colombia	na	na	na	na	na	na	na	na	na	na	na	na	na	na	na	na
Croatia	na	3	4	2	2	5	2	2	4	6	1	3	5	4	2	4
Czech Republic	na	6	4	8	4	6	7	5	6	8	8	6	5	7	6	4
Denmark	6	4	4	4	2	4	5	2	8	6	4	3	5	4	4	3
Dominican Rep.	na	na	na	na	na	na	na	na	na	na	na	na	na	na	na	na
Egypt	na	na	na	na	na	na	na	na	na	na	na	na	na	na	na	na
El Salvador	na	na	na	na	na	na	na	na	na	na	na	na	na	na	na	na
Estonia	2	1	1	na	1	1	1	1	1	1	1	na	2	1	1	na
Finland	7	10	8	12	4	7	16	9	11	14	10	9	11	11	10	8
France	3	3	2	3	3	2	3	3	2	2	4	3	2	2	3	3
Georgia	na	na	na	na	na	na	na	na	na	na	na	na	na	na	na	na
Germany	5	3	3	2	2	2	4	2	3	3	2	2	4	2	3	3
Great Britain	4	3	2	4	3	1	5	2	3	5	4	2	4	na	na	na
Greece	na	5	4	5	5	4	6	3	5	5	3	4	6	5	4	7
Hungary	4	2	1	3	1	4	1	2	1	5	3	2	2	2	2	9
Iceland	5	3	3	3	2	3	5	3	2	5	3	2	3	1	4	2
India	na	8	8	7	8	8	7	5	9	12	7	6	10	6	11	16
Indonesia	na	na	na	na	na	na	na	na	na	na	na	na	na	na	na	na
Iran	na	na	na	na	na	na	na	na	na	na	na	na	na	na	na	na
Ireland	3	4	3	5	2	6	4	2	3	9	5	3	6	3	4	3
Israel	na	na	na	na	na	na	na	na	na	na	na	na	na	na	na	na
Italy	3	5	4	6	5	6	4	3	5	8	4	6	6	4	4	6
Japan	1	3	2	4	na	1	6	5	3	3	3	3	4	3	3	7
Jordan	na	na	na	na	na	na	na	na	na	na	na	na	na	na	na	na
Korea, South	15	10	12	8	7	10	12	na	12	9	9	8	11	9	11	4
Latvia	2	1	na	2	1	1	1	na	1	1	1	1	1	1	1	na
Lithuania	1	2	1	3	4	2	1	1	2	4	2	2	2	2	2	3
Luxembourg	na	8	7	9	6	7	10	7	8	9	8	6	7	5	8	10
Macedonia	na	8	7	9	6	10	6	6	8	12	6	9	8	5	9	17
Malta	na	1	1	1	2	1	1	1	1	2	na	1	2	1	1	3
Mexico	2	6	5	7	5	7	6	6	7	8	6	6	8	7	7	5
Moldova	na	3	2	3	3	3	2	1	2	6	1	3	3	2	3	6
Montenegro	na	3	3	2	2	3	2	1	3	4	1	2	3	2	2	2
Morocco	na	1	1	1	1	1	na	1	2	4	na	1	3	na	1	1
Netherlands	20	9	7	11	4	6	14	10	7	9	8	7	11	7	10	6
New Zealand	na	na	na	na	na	na	na	na	na	na	na	na	na	na	na	na
Nigeria	na	na	na	na	na	na	na	na	na	na	na	na	na	na	na	na
Northern Ireland	3	4	3	5	3	3	6	3	3	11	4	3	7	6	5	na
Norway	12	na	na	na	na	na	na	na	na	na	na	na	na	na	na	na
Pakistan	na	na	na	na	na	na	na	na	na	na	na	na	na	na	na	na
Peru	na	5	4	6	5	5	5	3	5	5	4	5	6	3	5	7
Philippines	na	9	11	8	8	9	11	10	6	13	8	8	12	7	11	10
Poland	na	1	2	1	na	1	2	na	2	5	2	1	1	1	2	3
Portugal	3	2	3	2	1	4	2	3	1	2	na	5	2	2	2	2
Puerto Rico	na	5	4	6	3	7	4	6	2	6	5	4	7	5	5	5
Romania	1	1	0	2	2	1	0	0	1	3	0	1	2	0	1	3
Russian Fed.	1	1	na	1	1	1	na	na	1	2	1	na	1	1	1	na
Serbia	na	1	2	1	1	2	1	1	2	2	1	2	1	2	1	1
Singapore	na	4	3	4	4	4	1	4	3	5	3	3	4	2	4	1
Slovakia	na	4	4	5	4	5	5	3	4	11	4	4	5	4	5	8
Slovenia	1	3	3	3	3	2	4	3	2	6	2	3	5	1	3	4
South Africa	na	6	3	9	7	5	7	4	9	3	3	11	4	7	5	2
Spain	1	2	3	2	2	3	3	1	3	5	3	2	4	2	3	2
Sweden	2	7	5	8	3	6	9	6	6	8	8	4	9	11	5	8
Switzerland	na	na	na	na	na	na	na	na	na	na	na	na	na	na	na	na
Taiwan	na	na	na	na	na	na	na	na	na	na	na	na	na	na	na	na
Tanzania	na	19	16	24	20	19	16	17	20	25	19	22	17	16	21	13
Turkey	na	0	na	na	1	1	1	na	na	2	na	na	1	1	na	na
Uganda	na	12	15	9	12	13	8	7	14	18	10	15	18	12	12	12
Ukraine	na	1	1	1	1	2	1	2	1	3	1	1	2	1	2	na
United States	8	17	14	19	13	17	20	13	15	19	15	17	18	22	16	16
Uruguay	na	na	na	na	na	na	na	na	na	na	na	na	na	na	na	na
Venezuela	na	10	11	9	8	12	9	6	9	16	9	10	12	6	11	10
Vietnam	na	15	16	14	11	15	18	13	17	22	13	14	17	15	17	14
Zimbabwe	na	5	5	4	5	4	6	3	7	14	3	5	10	3	6	7
Total	4	6	5	6	5	6	6	4	5	8	5	6	7	5	6	6

RANKING

Country	2000
Bangladesh	22
Tanzania	19
United States	17
Vietnam	15
Albania	13
Uganda	12
Canada	11
Finland	10
Korea, South	10
Venezuela	10
Philippines	9
Netherlands	9
Austria	9
Macedonia	8
Luxembourg	8
India	8
Sweden	7
Mexico	6
Czech Republic	6
South Africa	6
Belgium	6
Puerto Rico	5
Peru	5
Zimbabwe	5
Denmark	4
Greece	5
Italy	5
Slovakia	4
Romania	1
Northern Ireland	4
Ireland	4
Singapore	4
Chile	3
Croatia	3
Japan	3
Iceland	3
Great Britain	3
Slovenia	3
Moldova	3
China	3
Bosnia and Herz.	3
France	3
Germany	3
Montenegro	3
Argentina	2
Spain	2
Portugal	2
Hungary	2
Lithuania	2
Poland	1
Ukraine	1
Serbia	1
Bulgaria	1
Malta	1
Latvia	1
Belarus	1
Estonia	1
Russian Fed.	1
Morocco	1
Turkey	0
Total	6

A079) BELONG OTHER GROUPS

Please look carefully at the following list of voluntary organizations and activities and say...which, if any, do you belong to? Other groups.

Belong (%)

(WVS: V53; EVS: V26)

Country	Wave		Gender		Age			Education			Income			Values				RANKING	
	1990	2000	Male	Female	16-29	30-49	50+	Lower	Middle	Upper	Lower	Middle	Upper	Mat	Mixed	Postm.		Country	2000
Albania	na	5	5	6	7	4	5	4	7	4	7	5	5	4	6	10		Sweden	25
Algeria	na	na	na	na	na	na	na	na	na	na	na	na	na	na	na	na		United States	22
Argentina	3	4	4	4	4	3	5	3	5	4	4	3	6	2	4	7		Tanzania	18
Armenia	na	na	na	na	na	na	na	na	na	na	na	na	na	na	na	na		Denmark	14
Australia	na	na	na	na	na	na	na	na	na	na	na	na	na	na	na	na		Finland	13
Austria	6	9	10	8	6	9	11	9	9	10	9	7	11	13	9	8		Canada	11
Azerbaijan	na	na	na	na	na	na	na	na	na	na	na	na	na	na	na	na		Belgium	11
Bangladesh	na	2	2	1	2	2	1	1	1	5	1	2	2	1	2	1		Slovenia	10
Belarus	na	1	2	na	2	na	1	na	1	1	na	1	1	1	1	na		South Africa	9
Belgium	5	11	12	9	7	10	13	11	10	12	10	10	13	11	11	12		Romania	2
Bosnia and Herz.	na	3	5	2	1	3	5	2	3	6	3	3	4	2	4	2		Austria	9
Brazil	0	na	na	na	na	na	na	na	na	na	na	na	na	na	na	na		Netherlands	9
Bulgaria	3	2	2	2	3	2	1	1	2	2	2	1	1	1	2	na		Czech Republic	9
Canada	13	11	12	10	8	12	11	8	13	11	11	10	13	8	10	13		Slovakia	8
Chile	4	1	2	1	1	1	3	1	1	2	1	1	2	1	2	1		Macedonia	8
China	2	na	na	na	na	na	na	na	na	na	na	na	na	na	na	na		France	7
Colombia	na	na	na	na	na	na	na	na	na	na	na	na	na	na	na	na		Japan	7
Croatia	na	5	9	1	4	5	4	2	6	5	3	5	4	2	5	3		Northern Ireland	7
Czech Republic	na	9	12	6	6	8	11	9	8	13	10	9	8	8	9	4		Greece	7
Denmark	11	14	15	14	11	12	19	13	11	17	17	12	15	15	15	10		India	7
Dominican Rep.	na	na	na	na	na	na	na	na	na	na	na	na	na	na	na	na		Uganda	7
Egypt	na	na	na	na	na	na	na	na	na	na	na	na	na	na	na	na		Ireland	5
El Salvador	na	na	na	na	na	na	na	na	na	na	na	na	na	na	na	na		Albania	5
Estonia	4	5	6	4	3	6	5	3	6	5	3	4	7	4	5	12		Latvia	5
Finland	9	13	12	14	6	11	18	11	14	19	13	13	14	12	14	8		Great Britain	5
France	5	7	8	6	5	6	9	6	6	9	6	8	9	6	7	8		Puerto Rico	5
Georgia	na	na	na	na	na	na	na	na	na	na	na	na	na	na	na	na		Estonia	5
Germany	8	4	5	3	3	3	5	4	4	4	6	3	3	3	4	5		Croatia	5
Great Britain	8	5	5	5	2	5	6	4	5	7	4	4	8	na	na	na		Luxembourg	4
Greece	na	7	7	6	8	4	8	7	7	7	6	8	7	4	7	10		Montenegro	4
Hungary	2	3	3	3	3	1	4	3	2	3	3	3	1	3	2	na		Philippines	4
Iceland	10	3	1	5	1	3	4	2	2	6	2	3	3	3	3	2		Argentina	4
India	na	7	8	5	6	7	7	5	8	9	4	6	9	4	10	13		Germany	4
Indonesia	na	na	na	na	na	na	na	na	na	na	na	na	na	na	na	na		Singapore	4
Iran	na	na	na	na	na	na	na	na	na	na	na	na	na	na	na	na		Vietnam	4
Ireland	2	5	7	4	5	6	6	4	6	8	7	5	4	5	6	6		Serbia	4
Israel	na	na	na	na	na	na	na	na	na	na	na	na	na	na	na	na		Malta	3
Italy	2	3	3	2	2	3	2	2	3	3	3	2	4	2	3	3		Portugal	3
Japan	5	7	8	6	2	5	11	9	7	6	7	8	7	6	6	16		Bosnia and Herz.	3
Jordan	na	na	na	na	na	na	na	na	na	na	na	na	na	na	na	na		Iceland	3
Korea, South	4	na	na	na	na	na	na	na	na	na	na	na	na	na	na	na		Moldova	3
Latvia	4	5	6	4	8	4	5	4	5	8	5	5	5	4	5	13		Poland	3
Lithuania	2	2	2	2	2	4	1	na	2	6	2	2	3	1	3	4		Hungary	3
Luxembourg	na	4	5	4	6	3	4	5	4	4	6	4	5	6	5	2		Italy	3
Macedonia	na	8	9	7	12	7	5	9	8	6	6	10	6	6	9	10		Lithuania	2
Malta	na	3	4	2	3	4	3	3	3	4	4	4	3	3	4	1		Spain	2
Mexico	2	1	2	1	1	1	1	1	1	1	1	2	1	2	1	2		Ukraine	2
Moldova	na	3	3	2	4	3	2	na	4	4	2	3	4	3	3	4		Bulgaria	2
Montenegro	na	4	5	4	5	4	5	3	5	6	5	5	4	4	5	5		Bangladesh	2
Morocco	na	1	1	1	1	1	na	na	1	3	1	na	2	na	1	1		Turkey	2
Netherlands	9	9	11	8	7	8	11	8	9	11	8	11	9	14	8	11		Chile	1
New Zealand	na	na	na	na	na	na	na	na	na	na	na	na	na	na	na	na		Zimbabwe	1
Nigeria	na	na	na	na	na	na	na	na	na	na	na	na	na	na	na	na		Russian Fed.	1
Northern Ireland	7	7	6	7	6	7	7	7	8	6	5	10	4	9	6	7		Mexico	1
Norway	19	na	na	na	na	na	na	na	na	na	na	na	na	na	na	na		Belarus	1
Pakistan	na	na	na	na	na	na	na	na	na	na	na	na	na	na	na	na		Venezuela	1
Peru	na	0	na	na	na	na	na	na	na	na	na	na	1	na	na	na		Morocco	1
Philippines	na	4	5	4	4	4	5	4	4	4	3	5	5	4	5	2		Peru	0
Poland	na	3	4	2	2	3	3	2	3	4	4	2	2	2	3	4			
Portugal	3	3	4	2	3	3	4	3	4	4	3	3	3	1	4	7			
Puerto Rico	na	5	8	4	7	3	5	3	4	6	4	5	6	8	4	6			
Romania	2	2	2	2	3	2	2	1	2	5	1	1	4	1	3	7			
Russian Fed.	2	1	2	1	2	1	1	na	1	2	1	1	1	1	1	na			
Serbia	na	4	5	3	4	4	3	3	3	5	2	4	5	4	3	1			
Singapore	na	4	4	3	3	4	5	4	3	5	5	3	4	5	3	4			
Slovakia	na	8	9	6	6	7	10	8	8	8	10	8	7	7	7	13			
Slovenia	5	10	15	6	11	7	12	10	10	11	9	9	7	11	9	12			
South Africa	na	9	11	8	11	8	10	9	10	6	10	10	10	10	10	5			
Spain	4	2	2	2	2	2	2	2	2	4	3	1	3	2	2	3			
Sweden	19	25	28	22	21	24	29	25	21	31	24	25	27	27	25	25			
Switzerland	na	na	na	na	na	na	na	na	na	na	na	na	na	na	na	na			
Taiwan	na	na	na	na	na	na	na	na	na	na	na	na	na	na	na	na			
Tanzania	na	18	17	19	19	18	17	14	20	24	15	20	19	16	19	29			
Turkey	na	2	2	1	2	1	3	na	3	4	na	2	4	2	2	2			
Uganda	na	7	9	4	7	6	6	6	7	9	5	5	5	7	7	2			
Ukraine	na	2	3	1	2	2	2	na	2	4	2	2	3	1	3	3			
United States	10	22	26	17	22	19	26	17	20	25	20	20	28	16	23	21			
Uruguay	na	na	na	na	na	na	na	na	na	na	na	na	na	na	na	na			
Venezuela	na	1	1	na	1	1	1	1	1	1	1	na	1	1	1	1			
Vietnam	na	4	5	2	2	3	6	3	5	2	4	3	4	4	4	4			
Zimbabwe	na	1	2	1	1	2	3	1	2	na	2	1	3	2	1	3			
Total	6	6	7	5	5	5	7	5	5	8	6	6	6	4	6	7		Total	6

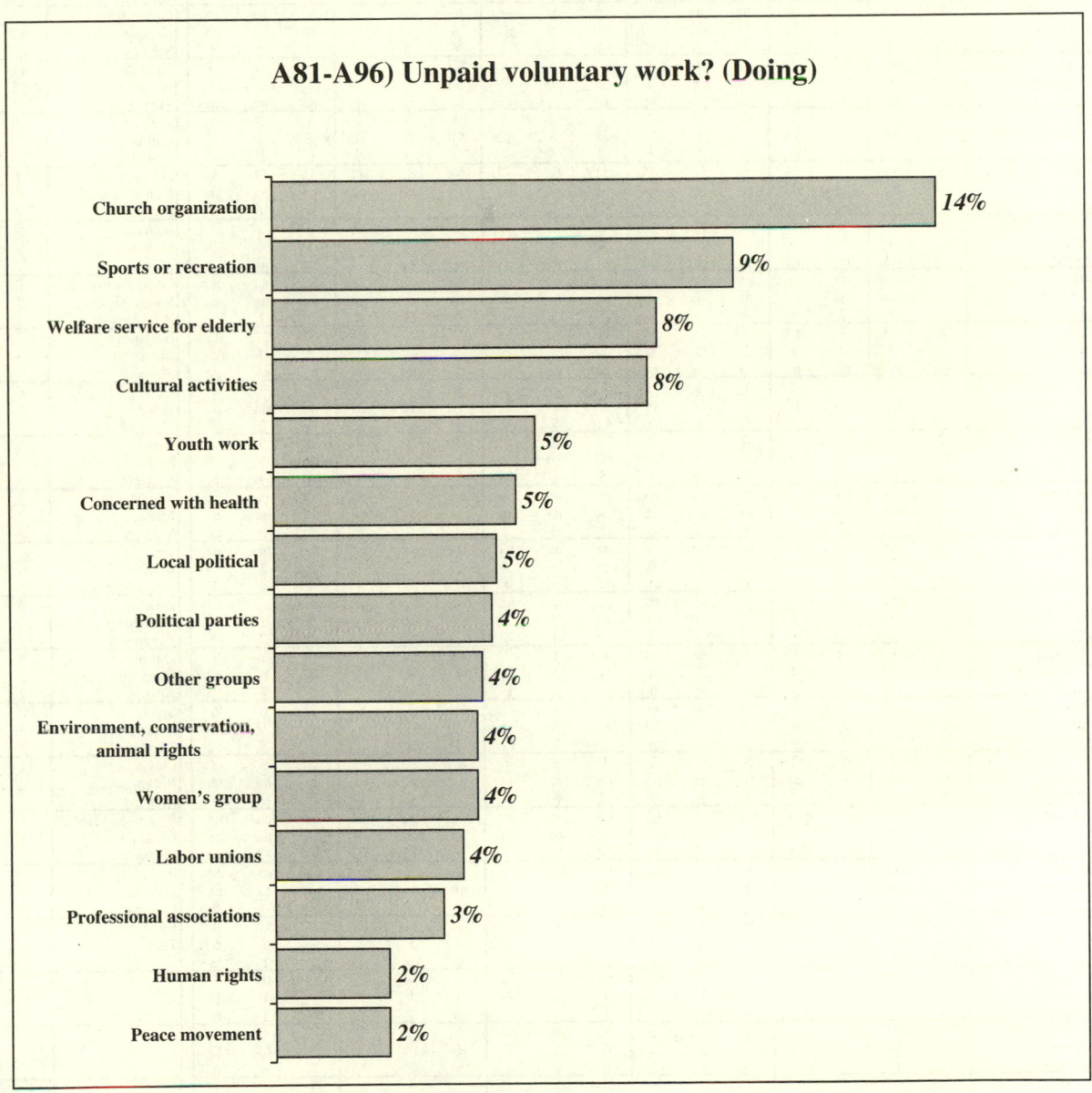

A81-A96) Unpaid voluntary work? (Doing)

Church organization	14%
Sports or recreation	9%
Welfare service for elderly	8%
Cultural activities	8%
Youth work	5%
Concerned with health	5%
Local political	5%
Political parties	4%
Other groups	4%
Environment, conservation, animal rights	4%
Women's group	4%
Labor unions	4%
Professional associations	3%
Human rights	2%
Peace movement	2%

A081) UNPAID WORK SOCIAL WELFARE SERVICE FOR ELDERLY

And for which, if any, are you currently doing unpaid voluntary work? Social welfare services for elderly, handicapped or deprived people.

Belong (%)

(WVS: V54; EVS: V30)

Country	Wave		Gender		Age			Education			Income			Values			RANKING Country	2000
	1990	2000	Male	Female	16-29	30-49	50+	Lower	Middle	Upper	Lower	Middle	Upper	Mat	Mixed	Postm.		
Albania	na	11	10	11	7	12	12	9	11	13	12	11	10	11	12	3	China	56
Algeria	na	19	21	17	21	20	13	12	20	23	15	21	21	16	20	28	Vietnam	28
Argentina	2	3	2	3	2	3	4	2	4	2	2	3	3	1	3	3	Tanzania	25
Armenia	na	na	na	na	na	na	na	na	na	na	na	na	na	na	na	na	Bangladesh	19
Australia	na	na	na	na	na	na	na	na	na	na	na	na	na	na	na	na	Algeria	19
Austria	3	2	1	3	1	2	4	3	2	2	4	2	1	3	3	2	United States	14
Azerbaijan	na	na	na	na	na	na	na	na	na	na	na	na	na	na	na	na	Great Britain	13
Bangladesh	na	19	25	12	18	20	19	15	21	31	8	23	25	15	23	15	Northern Ireland	12
Belarus	na	4	3	5	3	6	3	4	5	1	4	4	5	4	5	5	Singapore	12
Belgium	6	6	5	8	5	5	8	8	5	8	7	8	5	5	6	7	Uganda	11
Bosnia and Herz.	na	1	na	2	1	1	1	2	1	2	na	1	1	1	1	4	Albania	11
Brazil	6	na	na	na	na	na	na	na	na	na	na	na	na	na	na	na	Puerto Rico	11
Bulgaria	2	2	1	2	2	2	1	1	2	3	1	1	2	1	2	5	Finland	10
Canada	6	10	9	11	3	9	14	9	8	12	10	9	10	6	10	11	Philippines	10
Chile	4	6	4	7	4	5	9	7	5	7	7	4	6	6	5	6	Canada	10
China	16	56	58	54	64	58	45	51	62	37	58	63	44	55	61	69	Netherlands	9
Colombia	na	na	na	na	na	na	na	na	na	na	na	na	na	na	na	na	Korea, South	9
Croatia	na	1	na	2	1	1	2	2	na	2	1	1	1	2	1	1	Sweden	9
Czech Republic	na	3	2	5	3	4	3	3	3	6	5	3	3	5	3	1	Iceland	9
Denmark	2	4	3	5	1	2	8	4	1	6	7	3	1	1	4	3	Greece	8
Dominican Rep.	na	na	na	na	na	na	na	na	na	na	na	na	na	na	na	na	Moldova	7
Egypt	na	na	na	na	na	na	na	na	na	na	na	na	na	na	na	na	Luxembourg	7
El Salvador	na	na	na	na	na	na	na	na	na	na	na	na	na	na	na	na	South Africa	7
Estonia	1	3	2	3	3	4	2	2	3	4	2	3	4	3	2	9	Zimbabwe	7
Finland	8	10	7	13	4	10	14	8	11	18	9	17	8	7	12	13	Belgium	6
France	5	4	3	6	2	3	6	4	3	6	5	4	5	3	5	5	India	6
Georgia	na	na	na	na	na	na	na	na	na	na	na	na	na	na	na	na	Slovakia	6
Germany	4	2	1	2	1	2	3	1	3	1	2	2	1	1	3	2	Chile	6
Great Britain	5	13	10	17	8	14	17	9	14	22	12	12	22	na	na	na	Japan	5
Greece	na	8	5	10	8	8	7	11	7	8	6	10	9	9	8	9	Mexico	5
Hungary	2	3	2	3	4	3	2	2	2	7	3	2	3	2	3	1	Italy	5
Iceland	10	9	8	9	2	9	15	8	10	9	6	11	11	8	9	7	Malta	5
India	na	6	8	4	5	6	8	5	6	10	7	4	8	4	9	11	Slovenia	5
Indonesia	na	na	na	na	na	na	na	na	na	na	na	na	na	na	na	na	Macedonia	5
Iran	na	na	na	na	na	na	na	na	na	na	na	na	na	na	na	na	France	4
Ireland	7	4	3	5	4	2	6	3	3	8	4	2	6	4	3	6	Belarus	4
Israel	na	na	na	na	na	na	na	na	na	na	na	na	na	na	na	na	Denmark	4
Italy	3	5	4	6	3	5	6	5	5	7	5	7	4	5	5	6	Ireland	4
Japan	2	5	5	6	2	2	10	11	5	4	7	4	5	9	4	7	Czech Republic	3
Jordan	na	na	na	na	na	na	na	na	na	na	na	na	na	na	na	na	Peru	3
Korea, South	7	9	9	9	7	9	12	13	10	7	10	7	10	9	10	9	Montenegro	3
Latvia	4	2	1	2	1	3	2	2	1	4	2	2	2	1	2	2	Argentina	3
Lithuania	1	1	na	1	1	na	na	na	1	1	na	na	1	1	1	1	Estonia	3
Luxembourg	na	7	5	9	6	7	8	5	6	14	8	8	10	8	6	12	Hungary	3
Macedonia	na	5	4	6	5	6	4	6	4	6	3	6	6	5	4	12	Austria	2
Malta	na	5	4	6	4	4	6	4	4	11	4	3	8	3	6	6	Spain	2
Mexico	3	5	5	6	2	5	10	6	3	7	6	6	3	8	5	1	Poland	2
Moldova	na	7	5	9	8	8	6	5	7	11	4	10	8	6	8	12	Germany	2
Montenegro	na	3	5	2	5	3	2	1	3	7	na	3	6	2	5	3	Latvia	2
Morocco	na	na	na	na	na	na	na	na	na	na	na	na	na	na	na	na	Bulgaria	2
Netherlands	9	9	8	11	4	6	16	11	8	9	9	9	9	8	10	8	Serbia	1
New Zealand	na	na	na	na	na	na	na	na	na	na	na	na	na	na	na	na	Bosnia and Herz.	1
Nigeria	na	na	na	na	na	na	na	na	na	na	na	na	na	na	na	na	Croatia	1
Northern Ireland	5	12	7	18	6	12	16	12	10	17	5	14	16	15	12	10	Romania	1
Norway	4	na	na	na	na	na	na	na	na	na	na	na	na	na	na	na	Portugal	1
Pakistan	na	na	na	na	na	na	na	na	na	na	na	na	na	na	na	na	Lithuania	1
Peru	na	3	2	4	2	4	6	3	2	5	2	4	5	3	4	2	Ukraine	1
Philippines	na	10	10	10	9	9	14	9	9	13	7	11	12	8	12	4	Russian Fed.	1
Poland	na	2	2	2	4	1	3	1	2	7	1	3	2	1	3	5	Turkey	0
Portugal	3	1	1	1	1	1	1	na	2	4	na	na	1	1	na	na		
Puerto Rico	na	11	8	12	9	6	15	10	9	12	9	14	8	19	10	7		
Romania	2	1	1	1	1	1	1	1	1	1	0	1	2	1	1	0		
Russian Fed.	1	1	1	1	na	1	1	1	1	1	na	1	1	na	1	6		
Serbia	na	1	2	1	na	2	2	1	1	2	1	na	2	2	1	1		
Singapore	na	12	11	12	18	5	7	12	12	7	10	14	11	7	13	17		
Slovakia	na	6	4	8	4	5	9	6	6	8	6	7	5	7	6	6		
Slovenia	1	5	4	6	4	3	8	5	5	4	7	4	3	5	4	7		
South Africa	na	7	5	9	5	7	12	4	11	7	3	10	9	9	7	1		
Spain	4	2	3	2	2	2	3	2	2	5	3	3	2	2	2	3		
Sweden	3	9	7	12	4	7	14	9	9	10	8	6	13	10	8	12		
Switzerland	na	na	na	na	na	na	na	na	na	na	na	na	na	na	na	na		
Taiwan	na	na	na	na	na	na	na	na	na	na	na	na	na	na	na	na		
Tanzania	na	25	24	25	25	24	24	25	21	31	27	24	24	19	27	33		
Turkey	na	0	1	na	na	1	na	na	1	2	na	na	1	1	na	1		
Uganda	na	11	13	10	11	12	15	14	10	10	18	11	12	9	13	12		
Ukraine	na	1	1	1	na	1	1	na	1	1	1	1	1	na	1	na		
United States	6	14	11	17	11	11	20	9	14	16	14	13	15	16	13	16		
Uruguay	na	na	na	na	na	na	na	na	na	na	na	na	na	na	na	na		
Venezuela	na	na	na	na	na	na	na	na	na	na	na	na	na	na	na	na		
Vietnam	na	28	29	28	20	26	39	30	26	33	25	26	34	28	31	21		
Zimbabwe	na	7	6	7	4	9	9	7	6	na	6	6	11	6	7	4		
Total	4	8	7	8	7	8	8	7	8	9	8	8	8	7	8	7	Total	8

A082) UNPAID WORK CHURCH ORGANIZATION

And for which, if any, are you currently doing unpaid voluntary work? Religious or church organizations.

Belong (%) (WVS: V55; EVS: V31)

Country	Wave		Gender		Age			Education			Income			Values		
	1990	2000	Male	Female	16-29	30-49	50+	Lower	Middle	Upper	Lower	Middle	Upper	Mat	Mixed	Postm.
Albania	na	15	12	18	14	13	19	18	13	10	18	15	11	15	14	10
Algeria	na	14	18	9	18	11	11	10	13	17	14	15	11	10	15	19
Argentina	5	9	6	12	5	9	13	9	9	11	10	9	9	6	10	10
Armenia	na	na	na	na	na	na	na	na	na	na	na	na	na	na	na	na
Australia	na	na	na	na	na	na	na	na	na	na	na	na	na	na	na	na
Austria	6	7	7	7	5	8	7	4	11	9	7	7	8	2	7	10
Azerbaijan	na	na	na	na	na	na	na	na	na	na	na	na	na	na	na	na
Bangladesh	na	40	57	20	34	43	54	35	48	45	32	44	44	38	44	30
Belarus	na	7	4	9	7	7	6	8	7	5	6	7	7	6	8	na
Belgium	7	6	5	7	3	5	8	5	4	10	7	6	6	5	6	5
Bosnia and Herz.	na	5	4	5	3	5	5	7	4	3	8	3	4	4	5	6
Brazil	13	na	na	na	na	na	na	na	na	na	na	na	na	na	na	na
Bulgaria	2	2	2	2	1	1	3	3	1	2	3	1	2	2	2	9
Canada	16	18	16	21	9	19	24	16	16	24	17	22	16	16	21	13
Chile	12	17	13	20	13	15	22	20	14	16	21	14	15	18	17	12
China	2	4	4	5	4	5	3	3	5	5	4	4	5	4	4	6
Colombia	na	na	na	na	na	na	na	na	na	na	na	na	na	na	na	na
Croatia	na	5	5	6	4	5	7	4	6	7	3	6	7	6	5	6
Czech Republic	na	3	3	2	3	2	4	3	3	5	3	3	2	3	2	4
Denmark	2	3	2	4	1	4	4	3	2	5	4	2	5	1	3	3
Dominican Rep.	na	na	na	na	na	na	na	na	na	na	na	na	na	na	na	na
Egypt	na	na	na	na	na	na	na	na	na	na	na	na	na	na	na	na
El Salvador	na	na	na	na	na	na	na	na	na	na	na	na	na	na	na	na
Estonia	1	3	3	3	3	1	4	4	3	2	4	3	3	2	3	4
Finland	7	11	8	14	8	8	17	11	11	16	11	14	9	9	12	11
France	5	3	3	4	2	4	3	2	4	5	3	4	3	3	3	4
Georgia	na	na	na	na	na	na	na	na	na	na	na	na	na	na	na	na
Germany	9	6	4	7	5	5	7	5	6	9	3	8	9	4	6	7
Great Britain	6	6	6	7	2	7	8	5	6	12	5	4	12	na	na	na
Greece	na	6	6	7	4	7	10	14	6	5	8	7	5	8	6	4
Hungary	3	6	6	5	4	6	6	6	5	7	7	7	4	6	6	8
Iceland	4	5	5	5	1	6	6	4	4	7	5	5	3	5	5	4
India	na	14	17	11	10	15	17	13	17	14	14	11	17	10	19	9
Indonesia	na	na	na	na	na	na	na	na	na	na	na	na	na	na	na	na
Iran	na	na	na	na	na	na	na	na	na	na	na	na	na	na	na	na
Ireland	7	8	6	10	5	5	12	7	6	14	8	6	9	7	8	10
Israel	na	na	na	na	na	na	na	na	na	na	na	na	na	na	na	na
Italy	6	7	6	8	6	7	7	5	8	8	5	8	8	6	7	7
Japan	3	3	3	3	1	2	5	4	4	2	4	4	3	2	3	3
Jordan	na	na	na	na	na	na	na	na	na	na	na	na	na	na	na	na
Korea, South	7	27	23	31	24	28	27	27	30	23	25	24	31	25	28	29
Latvia	3	4	2	5	4	3	5	4	3	7	5	4	2	4	4	na
Lithuania	3	5	3	6	4	2	7	10	3	2	4	7	3	2	5	9
Luxembourg	na	6	6	7	4	5	10	5	6	10	6	6	9	4	6	9
Macedonia	na	9	9	8	10	10	5	13	6	7	7	9	8	10	7	12
Malta	na	13	10	15	7	9	20	14	11	20	13	14	12	9	15	16
Mexico	10	20	17	23	15	20	26	21	17	19	21	23	19	21	21	17
Moldova	na	16	11	20	15	13	20	17	16	14	10	16	18	20	13	11
Montenegro	na	2	2	2	1	2	2	1	3	2	2	3	1	1	3	2
Morocco	na	na	na	na	na	na	na	na	na	na	na	na	na	na	na	na
Netherlands	10	11	11	11	4	9	18	13	10	11	11	12	11	12	11	11
New Zealand	na	na	na	na	na	na	na	na	na	na	na	na	na	na	na	na
Nigeria	na	na	na	na	na	na	na	na	na	na	na	na	na	na	na	na
Northern Ireland	10	43	44	42	30	32	55	50	30	49	50	36	43	50	48	18
Norway	6	na	na	na	na	na	na	na	na	na	na	na	na	na	na	na
Pakistan	na	na	na	na	na	na	na	na	na	na	na	na	na	na	na	na
Peru	na	20	16	24	19	20	26	20	22	17	19	20	24	20	21	19
Philippines	na	30	28	32	24	29	39	29	26	36	30	30	29	29	31	25
Poland	na	4	4	4	7	2	4	3	4	6	3	4	5	3	3	8
Portugal	6	3	3	4	2	3	2	2	3	8	1	3	3	2	3	1
Puerto Rico	na	31	26	33	23	24	40	42	29	30	37	32	24	42	29	31
Romania	4	4	3	4	2	3	5	4	4	2	6	2	3	3	4	5
Russian Fed.	1	1	na	1	1	1	na	1	na	1	na	1	na	na	1	na
Serbia	na	1	1	1	1	1	2	1	1	1	1	1	1	1	1	na
Singapore	na	12	12	12	13	12	10	8	12	23	10	12	16	12	12	8
Slovakia	na	13	9	17	7	10	22	22	9	9	19	13	10	15	12	9
Slovenia	2	5	5	4	4	3	6	5	4	3	7	4	3	4	5	5
South Africa	na	37	30	47	31	38	51	36	38	48	36	44	33	39	38	24
Spain	7	4	3	5	2	4	6	4	4	5	4	5	5	4	4	5
Sweden	3	23	20	27	26	20	26	24	21	27	24	20	25	16	24	23
Switzerland	na	na	na	na	na	na	na	na	na	na	na	na	na	na	na	na
Taiwan	na	na	na	na	na	na	na	na	na	na	na	na	na	na	na	na
Tanzania	na	62	60	65	58	65	64	64	56	67	66	71	53	62	63	67
Turkey	na	1	1	na	1	1	1	na	1	2	na	1	1	na	1	na
Uganda	na	39	48	31	36	43	37	36	40	34	43	37	41	43	38	31
Ukraine	na	2	2	3	3	2	3	3	2	2	2	2	3	2	2	7
United States	29	38	34	42	29	43	39	27	36	43	29	39	50	47	40	30
Uruguay	na	na	na	na	na	na	na	na	na	na	na	na	na	na	na	na
Venezuela	na	na	na	na	na	na	na	na	na	na	na	na	na	na	na	na
Vietnam	na	10	9	11	8	10	9	12	6	5	7	8	12	5	12	5
Zimbabwe	na	54	42	65	52	58	50	54	55	52	49	55	66	51	56	59
Total	7	14	13	14	13	14	14	14	12	15	14	14	13	13	14	13

RANKING

Country	2000
Tanzania	62
Zimbabwe	54
Northern Ireland	43
Bangladesh	40
Uganda	39
United States	38
South Africa	37
Puerto Rico	31
Philippines	30
Korea, South	27
Sweden	23
Peru	20
Mexico	20
Canada	18
Chile	17
Moldova	16
Albania	15
India	14
Algeria	14
Slovakia	13
Malta	13
Singapore	12
Netherlands	11
Finland	11
Vietnam	10
Argentina	9
Macedonia	9
Ireland	8
Austria	7
Belarus	7
Italy	7
Luxembourg	6
Great Britain	6
Greece	6
Belgium	6
Germany	6
Hungary	6
Croatia	5
Iceland	5
Bosnia and Herz.	5
Lithuania	5
Slovenia	5
China	4
Spain	4
Romania	4
Latvia	4
Poland	4
Japan	3
France	3
Denmark	3
Estonia	3
Czech Republic	3
Portugal	3
Ukraine	2
Bulgaria	2
Montenegro	2
Serbia	1
Turkey	1
Russian Fed.	1
Total	14

A083) UNPAID WORK CULTURAL ACTIVITIES

And for which, if any, are you currently doing unpaid voluntary work? Education, arts, music or cultural activities.

Belong (%)

(WVS: V56; EVS: V32)

Country	Wave		Gender		Age			Education			Income			Values		
	1990	2000	Male	Female	16-29	30-49	50+	Lower	Middle	Upper	Lower	Middle	Upper	Mat	Mixed	Postm.
Albania	na	10	11	9	16	10	5	5	13	14	11	11	7	10	11	13
Algeria	na	12	13	10	14	10	11	6	12	17	13	11	13	10	12	16
Argentina	4	4	3	4	5	4	2	2	5	14	1	4	6	2	3	7
Armenia	na	na	na	na	na	na	na	na	na	na	na	na	na	na	na	na
Australia	na	na	na	na	na	na	na	na	na	na	na	na	na	na	na	na
Austria	4	7	9	5	7	7	6	4	8	15	4	7	9	4	6	10
Azerbaijan	na	na	na	na	na	na	na	na	na	na	na	na	na	na	na	na
Bangladesh	na	29	37	18	30	29	24	18	39	44	19	31	34	27	31	24
Belarus	na	3	3	3	6	3	2	na	4	7	4	3	4	1	5	3
Belgium	7	10	11	10	10	12	8	3	9	18	7	9	15	6	10	14
Bosnia and Herz.	na	3	2	3	4	2	3	na	2	7	1	3	3	4	2	4
Brazil	3	na	na	na	na	na	na	na	na	na	na	na	na	na	na	na
Bulgaria	3	3	4	2	4	4	1	na	1	11	1	4	3	1	4	7
Canada	9	11	10	13	8	13	11	4	10	19	7	10	15	11	11	12
Chile	6	7	6	8	12	4	7	3	7	16	3	8	12	5	8	7
China	8	16	16	16	20	16	14	12	18	40	15	17	19	14	20	38
Colombia	na	na	na	na	na	na	na	na	na	na	na	na	na	na	na	na
Croatia	na	3	3	3	7	3	na	1	2	9	2	2	4	na	3	3
Czech Republic	na	6	7	5	10	6	4	4	6	15	3	6	8	4	6	8
Denmark	5	5	6	5	5	6	5	3	8	10	4	5	7	0	5	11
Dominican Rep.	na	na	na	na	na	na	na	na	na	na	na	na	na	na	na	na
Egypt	na	na	na	na	na	na	na	na	na	na	na	na	na	na	na	na
El Salvador	na	na	na	na	na	na	na	na	na	na	na	na	na	na	na	na
Estonia	7	6	6	6	10	5	4	4	6	9	3	4	9	3	7	13
Finland	9	7	6	8	8	7	6	4	9	15	9	4	8	6	6	15
France	5	5	5	5	6	6	4	3	5	10	4	5	7	3	5	9
Georgia	na	na	na	na	na	na	na	na	na	na	na	na	na	na	na	na
Germany	4	3	3	2	1	3	3	2	3	5	2	3	3	2	3	4
Great Britain	3	3	2	4	5	3	1	1	3	7	3	2	4	na	na	na
Greece	na	14	13	15	14	16	10	7	12	17	10	16	16	19	12	18
Hungary	2	3	3	3	3	4	3	1	3	16	1	3	4	2	5	11
Iceland	5	6	5	7	5	8	4	4	4	15	2	8	6	3	6	7
India	na	12	14	8	13	12	10	7	11	22	12	8	15	8	18	27
Indonesia	na	na	na	na	na	na	na	na	na	na	na	na	na	na	na	na
Iran	na	na	na	na	na	na	na	na	na	na	na	na	na	na	na	na
Ireland	4	5	5	5	4	5	5	2	5	8	2	6	7	4	4	9
Israel	na	na	na	na	na	na	na	na	na	na	na	na	na	na	na	na
Italy	3	6	7	6	10	6	4	3	7	14	4	7	8	3	5	10
Japan	3	4	5	3	3	4	5	6	3	5	4	4	6	5	4	3
Jordan	na	na	na	na	na	na	na	na	na	na	na	na	na	na	na	na
Korea, South	3	9	8	9	13	7	7	4	7	11	8	9	9	7	10	12
Latvia	5	5	4	5	5	6	4	2	4	9	4	4	5	3	6	2
Lithuania	6	2	1	2	2	3	1	1	1	7	na	2	2	1	2	3
Luxembourg	na	9	8	10	10	7	9	5	9	13	4	7	14	8	9	12
Macedonia	na	7	7	8	13	7	3	4	8	13	3	7	12	5	9	8
Malta	na	4	6	2	4	2	5	2	4	7	3	4	5	2	4	7
Mexico	5	5	5	5	7	3	1	3	6	14	3	6	9	5	5	10
Moldova	na	9	8	10	12	10	6	2	8	17	6	9	12	7	9	26
Montenegro	na	3	2	3	5	2	2	1	3	5	1	4	4	1	4	5
Morocco	na	na	na	na	na	na	na	na	na	na	na	na	na	na	na	na
Netherlands	11	16	15	17	13	21	12	9	13	26	13	16	18	9	15	22
New Zealand	na	na	na	na	na	na	na	na	na	na	na	na	na	na	na	na
Nigeria	na	na	na	na	na	na	na	na	na	na	na	na	na	na	na	na
Northern Ireland	3	10	9	11	10	16	6	3	12	15	3	7	15	8	11	7
Norway	5	na	na	na	na	na	na	na	na	na	na	na	na	na	na	na
Pakistan	na	na	na	na	na	na	na	na	na	na	na	na	na	na	na	na
Peru	na	10	11	9	10	10	8	7	8	14	6	10	15	7	10	12
Philippines	na	4	4	4	4	3	5	2	2	10	2	4	6	2	5	2
Poland	na	2	2	2	3	2	1	1	1	8	na	3	3	1	2	1
Portugal	4	2	4	1	3	1	1	2	3	9	na	2	2	2	3	3
Puerto Rico	na	8	9	7	9	10	6	3	4	11	4	9	11	9	6	12
Romania	2	2	2	1	4	2	0	0	3	2	0	2	3	1	2	4
Russian Fed.	3	0	na	1	1	na	na	na	na	1	na	na	1	na	na	na
Serbia	na	1	1	1	2	1	na	na	1	1	na	1	1	1	na	3
Singapore	na	6	5	8	11	3	3	4	7	12	3	6	8	4	7	13
Slovakia	na	6	5	6	8	5	5	3	6	10	4	6	7	4	7	6
Slovenia	3	7	8	6	9	6	5	4	6	15	3	8	13	3	8	8
South Africa	na	7	9	5	9	7	4	5	9	26	5	8	10	8	7	4
Spain	4	3	3	3	5	3	2	1	3	9	2	2	7	2	2	8
Sweden	3	11	11	11	19	7	12	7	9	18	11	11	12	6	10	18
Switzerland	na	na	na	na	na	na	na	na	na	na	na	na	na	na	na	na
Taiwan	na	na	na	na	na	na	na	na	na	na	na	na	na	na	na	na
Tanzania	na	26	25	26	29	26	18	22	28	34	23	28	29	21	28	29
Turkey	na	1	2	1	1	1	1	na	2	6	na	1	4	na	2	2
Uganda	na	16	22	11	26	7	5	8	21	7	15	17	14	14	17	17
Ukraine	na	2	1	2	3	2	2	1	1	4	1	2	3	1	3	2
United States	10	20	18	22	23	18	19	9	19	25	14	19	27	20	19	22
Uruguay	na	na	na	na	na	na	na	na	na	na	na	na	na	na	na	na
Venezuela	na	na	na	na	na	na	na	na	na	na	na	na	na	na	na	na
Vietnam	na	16	15	16	26	16	11	14	18	22	12	13	21	15	18	16
Zimbabwe	na	4	6	2	5	4	2	2	7	9	1	4	10	4	4	6
Total	5	8	8	7	10	8	5	5	7	14	6	8	10	6	8	11

RANKING

Country	2000
Bangladesh	29
Tanzania	26
United States	20
China	16
Uganda	16
Netherlands	16
Vietnam	16
Greece	14
Algeria	12
India	12
Sweden	11
Canada	11
Belgium	10
Albania	10
Peru	10
Northern Ireland	10
Moldova	9
Luxembourg	9
Korea, South	9
Puerto Rico	8
South Africa	7
Macedonia	7
Chile	7
Finland	7
Austria	7
Slovenia	7
Singapore	6
Italy	6
Czech Republic	6
Iceland	6
Estonia	6
Slovakia	6
Mexico	5
Denmark	5
France	5
Ireland	5
Latvia	5
Zimbabwe	4
Philippines	4
Japan	4
Argentina	4
Malta	4
Belarus	3
Hungary	3
Spain	3
Croatia	3
Germany	3
Great Britain	3
Bosnia and Herz.	3
Bulgaria	3
Montenegro	3
Portugal	2
Romania	2
Poland	2
Ukraine	2
Lithuania	2
Turkey	1
Serbia	1
Russian Fed.	0
Total	8

A084) UNPAID WORK LABOR UNIONS

And for which, if any, are you currently doing unpaid voluntary work? Labor unions / Trade unions.

Belong (%) (WVS: V57; EVS: V33)

Country	Wave		Gender		Age			Education			Income			Values			RANKING Country	2000
	1990	2000	Male	Female	16-29	30-49	50+	Lower	Middle	Upper	Lower	Middle	Upper	Mat	Mixed	Postm.		
Albania	na	4	6	3	2	5	5	4	4	5	6	4	4	5	5	3	Tanzania	21
Algeria	na	na	na	na	na	na	na	na	na	na	na	na	na	na	na	na	Bangladesh	14
Argentina	1	1	2	na	na	1	1	1	na	2	na	1	1	1	1	1	Sweden	10
Armenia	na	na	na	na	na	na	na	na	na	na	na	na	na	na	na	na	Vietnam	10
Australia	na	na	na	na	na	na	na	na	na	na	na	na	na	na	na	na	Belarus	9
Austria	2	2	4	1	2	3	1	3	1	3	1	3	3	1	2	2	Moldova	8
Azerbaijan	na	na	na	na	na	na	na	na	na	na	na	na	na	na	na	na	China	7
Bangladesh	na	14	21	6	10	17	17	12	18	15	11	16	14	11	17	12	India	7
Belarus	na	9	9	9	10	12	5	3	11	11	7	10	9	6	10	23	Romania	6
Belgium	2	3	4	2	1	3	3	2	2	4	1	2	4	2	3	3	Finland	6
Bosnia and Herz.	na	2	2	2	1	3	2	2	2	3	2	2	3	2	2	4	Slovakia	6
Brazil	2	na	na	na	na	na	na	na	na	na	na	na	na	na	na	na	Northern Ireland	6
Bulgaria	5	3	4	3	1	6	2	1	3	9	1	4	5	2	6	na	South Africa	5
Canada	4	3	5	2	2	4	3	na	4	6	2	3	7	6	3	5	Greece	5
Chile	2	2	4	1	1	3	2	2	3	2	2	2	5	1	4	1	Albania	4
China	1	7	10	5	6	7	9	3	10	14	3	10	11	8	8	9	Denmark	4
Colombia	na	na	na	na	na	na	na	na	na	na	na	na	na	na	na	na	Uganda	4
Croatia	na	4	5	2	2	6	3	1	5	5	2	3	5	6	4	2	Ukraine	4
Czech Republic	na	3	3	3	1	3	4	2	4	3	2	4	4	3	3	2	Croatia	4
Denmark	3	4	4	3	1	7	3	3	5	4	1	5	7	3	3	7	Russian Fed.	4
Dominican Rep.	na	na	na	na	na	na	na	na	na	na	na	na	na	na	na	na	Bulgaria	3
Egypt	na	na	na	na	na	na	na	na	na	na	na	na	na	na	na	na	Canada	3
El Salvador	na	na	na	na	na	na	na	na	na	na	na	na	na	na	na	na	Philippines	3
Estonia	11	1	1	na	1	1	na	1	1	1	na	1	1	1	na	na	Slovenia	3
Finland	8	6	6	5	2	10	4	6	5	9	2	7	9	5	6	7	United States	3
France	2	1	2	1	na	2	2	1	1	2	na	2	2	1	2	1	Iceland	3
Georgia	na	na	na	na	na	na	na	na	na	na	na	na	na	na	na	na	Luxembourg	3
Germany	10	0	1	na	1	na	na	1	na	2	na	1	1	1	na	na	Czech Republic	3
Great Britain	1	2	2	2	na	3	3	2	2	5	3	3	2	na	na	na	Peru	3
Greece	na	5	6	3	3	6	4	5	4	5	3	6	5	5	4	4	Belgium	3
Hungary	5	1	2	1	1	1	2	1	1	5	1	2	1	1	2	na	Chile	2
Iceland	3	3	4	2	2	5	2	3	2	6	2	4	4	2	3	7	Korea, South	2
India	na	7	8	4	5	8	6	7	7	6	11	6	6	5	9	13	Latvia	2
Indonesia	na	na	na	na	na	na	na	na	na	na	na	na	na	na	na	na	Mexico	2
Iran	na	na	na	na	na	na	na	na	na	na	na	na	na	na	na	na	Great Britain	2
Ireland	1	2	3	1	1	2	1	1	1	5	1	1	3	1	2	1	Italy	2
Israel	na	na	na	na	na	na	na	na	na	na	na	na	na	na	na	na	Poland	2
Italy	3	2	3	2	1	3	2	2	2	3	1	2	3	2	3	2	Netherlands	2
Japan	1	1	1	na	na	na	na	1	1	na	na	1	1	1	1	1	Puerto Rico	2
Jordan	na	na	na	na	na	na	na	na	na	na	na	na	na	na	na	na	Austria	2
Korea, South	1	2	4	1	1	2	6	4	3	2	2	4	2	1	3	3	Malta	2
Latvia	9	2	2	3	3	3	1	na	1	9	1	3	4	2	3	na	Bosnia and Herz.	2
Lithuania	9	1	1	1	2	2	na	na	2	2	1	1	2	1	2	1	Serbia	2
Luxembourg	na	3	4	2	3	3	3	3	3	3	3	4	4	2	3	2	Ireland	2
Macedonia	na	2	3	1	na	3	2	na	3	na	1	2	1	2	2	na	Macedonia	2
Malta	na	2	3	1	3	1	2	na	2	4	na	2	5	1	3	5	France	1
Mexico	2	2	3	1	2	2	3	2	3	5	2	3	3	3	2	2	Hungary	1
Moldova	na	8	8	8	9	8	7	1	7	16	6	9	9	8	7	21	Lithuania	1
Montenegro	na	1	2	1	na	2	1	1	1	3	1	1	2	na	2	3	Spain	1
Morocco	na	na	na	na	na	na	na	na	na	na	na	na	na	na	na	na	Montenegro	1
Netherlands	1	2	3	1	1	2	3	2	1	3	2	3	3	2	2	2	Singapore	1
New Zealand	na	na	na	na	na	na	na	na	na	na	na	na	na	na	na	na	Zimbabwe	1
Nigeria	na	na	na	na	na	na	na	na	na	na	na	na	na	na	na	na	Turkey	1
Northern Ireland	2	6	6	5	11	4	5	5	6	6	9	9	5	7	7	2	Argentina	1
Norway	6	na	na	na	na	na	na	na	na	na	na	na	na	na	na	na	Japan	1
Pakistan	na	na	na	na	na	na	na	na	na	na	na	na	na	na	na	na	Estonia	1
Peru	na	3	4	2	1	4	4	1	4	2	2	4	2	3	3	3	Germany	0
Philippines	na	3	5	2	2	4	4	5	3	3	4	2	4	3	4	1	Portugal	0
Poland	na	2	3	2	1	4	2	2	3	3	1	2	4	2	2	3		
Portugal	1	0	1	na	na	1	na	na	1	1	na	1	1	na	1	na		
Puerto Rico	na	2	3	2	2	2	2	3	1	3	1	3	2	1	2	3		
Romania	14	6	8	4	5	11	2	1	7	14	1	4	11	4	7	13		
Russian Fed.	9	4	4	3	4	5	2	na	3	7	2	4	5	4	4	7		
Serbia	na	2	2	1	na	4	1	1	2	4	1	1	1	3	1	1		
Singapore	na	1	1	1	na	2	na	1	1	1	1	1	1	1	1	1		
Slovakia	na	6	6	6	5	9	3	2	7	8	4	6	8	6	5	10		
Slovenia	2	3	4	3	2	5	2	3	3	7	4	3	5	4	3	4		
South Africa	na	5	7	3	2	8	2	4	6	na	1	8	8	5	5	7		
Spain	1	1	2	1	na	2	1	1	1	3	1	1	4	na	1	3		
Sweden	6	10	11	10	8	11	11	8	10	12	9	10	13	10	9	13		
Switzerland	na	na	na	na	na	na	na	na	na	na	na	na	na	na	na	na		
Taiwan	na	na	na	na	na	na	na	na	na	na	na	na	na	na	na	na		
Tanzania	na	21	21	20	14	27	16	15	22	39	14	29	27	19	21	33		
Turkey	na	1	2	na	1	1	1	na	1	3	na	1	2	1	1	2		
Uganda	na	4	6	2	5	4	1	5	4	2	4	3	4	5	3	5		
Ukraine	na	4	4	4	4	5	4	1	4	7	2	5	5	3	5	5		
United States	2	3	5	2	3	3	4	2	3	4	2	4	4	1	4	3		
Uruguay	na	na	na	na	na	na	na	na	na	na	na	na	na	na	na	na		
Venezuela	na	na	na	na	na	na	na	na	na	na	na	na	na	na	na	na		
Vietnam	na	10	10	10	8	13	6	6	13	24	8	11	10	9	11	10		
Zimbabwe	na	1	2	na	1	1	1	1	2	na	1	1	2	na	2	na		
Total	4	4	5	3	3	5	3	3	4	5	3	4	5	4	4	4	Total	4

A085) UNPAID WORK POLITICAL PARTIES

And for which, if any, are you currently doing unpaid voluntary work? Political parties or groups.

Belong (%)
(WVS: V58; EVS: V34)

Country	Wave 1990	Wave 2000	Male	Female	16-29	30-49	50+	Education Lower	Middle	Upper	Income Lower	Middle	Upper	Mat	Mixed	Postm.
Albania	na	11	18	5	6	13	13	9	13	13	15	10	9	12	12	5
Algeria	na	6	8	4	4	7	9	5	4	8	6	4	7	4	7	8
Argentina	1	3	4	2	2	4	3	2	4	5	3	3	4	1	3	5
Armenia	na	na	na	na	na	na	na	na	na	na	na	na	na	na	na	na
Australia	na	na	na	na	na	na	na	na	na	na	na	na	na	na	na	na
Austria	3	3	5	2	2	4	3	4	2	5	1	5	4	na	3	5
Azerbaijan	na	na	na	na	na	na	na	na	na	na	na	na	na	na	na	na
Bangladesh	na	23	34	9	21	24	25	16	30	32	24	21	24	20	25	26
Belarus	na	1	2	1	1	3	na	na	2	4	1	2	na	1	2	3
Belgium	2	3	4	2	3	3	2	2	2	5	2	2	4	1	3	5
Bosnia and Herz.	na	3	5	1	4	4	2	1	3	5	3	3	5	3	3	2
Brazil	2	na	na	na	na	na	na	na	na	na	na	na	na	na	na	na
Bulgaria	5	3	5	2	2	3	4	2	3	7	2	4	3	2	4	8
Canada	4	3	4	2	2	2	4	1	2	6	2	2	4	3	2	3
Chile	2	2	3	1	2	2	1	1	2	3	2	1	3	1	2	4
China	26	10	12	8	12	9	10	7	11	28	8	10	13	9	12	25
Colombia	na	na	na	na	na	na	na	na	na	na	na	na	na	na	na	na
Croatia	na	2	3	1	2	1	3	na	2	4	1	1	3	na	1	4
Czech Republic	na	2	3	1	1	2	3	2	1	6	2	3	1	2	2	3
Denmark	2	3	3	2	3	2	3	2	2	3	1	2	3	0	3	5
Dominican Rep.	na	na	na	na	na	na	na	na	na	na	na	na	na	na	na	na
Egypt	na	na	na	na	na	na	na	na	na	na	na	na	na	na	na	na
El Salvador	na	na	na	na	na	na	na	na	na	na	na	na	na	na	na	na
Estonia	4	2	2	1	2	1	2	1	2	2	na	1	2	1	2	4
Finland	7	4	7	1	1	3	6	4	3	7	2	4	7	2	4	5
France	2	1	1	1	1	1	1	1	1	2	1	na	1	na	na	4
Georgia	na	na	na	na	na	na	na	na	na	na	na	na	na	na	na	na
Germany	6	1	1	1	na	1	1	na	1	4	1	1	1	na	1	2
Great Britain	2	1	2	1	1	2	1	1	1	2	1	2	2	na	na	na
Greece	na	5	7	4	4	6	6	2	6	6	4	7	7	4	5	8
Hungary	1	1	2	1	2	1	1	1	1	4	1	1	1	2	1	na
Iceland	4	3	4	3	3	4	3	2	4	5	3	4	4	3	3	7
India	na	8	12	3	9	9	7	6	12	9	9	8	8	10	9	13
Indonesia	na	na	na	na	na	na	na	na	na	na	na	na	na	na	na	na
Iran	na	na	na	na	na	na	na	na	na	na	na	na	na	na	na	na
Ireland	2	2	3	1	1	1	3	1	1	3	1	1	3	1	2	1
Israel	na	na	na	na	na	na	na	na	na	na	na	na	na	na	na	na
Italy	4	2	4	1	2	2	3	2	2	5	1	3	3	1	2	4
Japan	1	1	2	1	na	1	2	3	1	1	1	1	3	1	1	2
Jordan	na	na	na	na	na	na	na	na	na	na	na	na	na	na	na	na
Korea, South	2	2	3	1	1	2	3	2	2	2	3	2	1	3	2	4
Latvia	6	1	1	1	1	1	1	na	1	1	1	1	1	1	1	4
Lithuania	4	1	2	1	2	1	1	na	1	6	1	1	2	na	1	4
Luxembourg	na	3	3	3	2	3	3	2	3	4	3	3	4	3	3	4
Macedonia	na	8	11	5	9	10	5	7	8	10	6	10	8	8	8	13
Malta	na	4	6	3	3	4	6	4	4	4	3	4	6	3	5	5
Mexico	3	4	5	2	3	3	4	3	3	8	5	4	4	3	4	4
Moldova	na	5	6	4	4	6	5	2	4	9	5	5	5	5	6	9
Montenegro	na	3	4	2	3	3	2	1	4	5	na	3	5	1	4	10
Morocco	na	na	na	na	na	na	na	na	na	na	na	na	na	na	na	na
Netherlands	2	3	3	2	2	2	4	2	2	4	2	2	4	3	3	3
New Zealand	na	na	na	na	na	na	na	na	na	na	na	na	na	na	na	na
Nigeria	na	na	na	na	na	na	na	na	na	na	na	na	na	na	na	na
Northern Ireland	1	4	6	3	4	5	4	7	2	4	1	9	3	na	5	6
Norway	4	na	na	na	na	na	na	na	na	na	na	na	na	na	na	na
Pakistan	na	na	na	na	na	na	na	na	na	na	na	na	na	na	na	na
Peru	na	3	5	2	3	4	5	1	3	6	2	4	6	4	3	6
Philippines	na	4	5	3	3	5	4	4	3	6	4	4	3	1	6	3
Poland	na	1	1	na	na	na	1	na	1	2	1	1	na	na	1	1
Portugal	3	1	1	na	na	1	1	na	1	2	na	na	2	na	1	1
Puerto Rico	na	4	6	3	4	5	3	4	2	6	2	5	6	4	4	7
Romania	2	2	3	1	1	3	1	0	1	6	1	2	2	1	2	5
Russian Fed.	5	0	1	na	na	na	na	na	na	1	na	na	1	na	na	3
Serbia	na	1	2	1	1	2	1	1	1	3	1	1	2	1	2	3
Singapore	na	0	na	na	na	na	1	na	na	1	na	na	1	1	na	na
Slovakia	na	5	6	3	3	4	7	1	7	5	3	6	5	3	6	11
Slovenia	1	1	2	1	2	1	1	1	1	1	na	2	3	na	1	2
South Africa	na	6	9	3	4	8	4	6	6	7	8	6	5	6	7	5
Spain	1	1	2	na	1	2	1	1	2	3	1	1	2	1	1	4
Sweden	4	4	6	3	1	4	7	6	3	4	3	6	3	7	4	6
Switzerland	na	na	na	na	na	na	na	na	na	na	na	na	na	na	na	na
Taiwan	na	na	na	na	na	na	na	na	na	na	na	na	na	na	na	na
Tanzania	na	21	22	20	18	22	28	27	15	14	27	20	15	20	22	29
Turkey	na	3	5	1	3	3	2	2	3	6	2	3	4	2	2	6
Uganda	na	6	9	4	8	5	3	4	6	12	8	8	7	5	7	5
Ukraine	na	1	2	1	na	3	1	1	1	3	1	1	2	1	2	na
United States	5	7	9	5	8	4	11	3	6	9	6	7	9	8	6	10
Uruguay	na	na	na	na	na	na	na	na	na	na	na	na	na	na	na	na
Venezuela	na	na	na	na	na	na	na	na	na	na	na	na	na	na	na	na
Vietnam	na	24	29	19	23	23	27	19	30	36	21	19	31	14	29	20
Zimbabwe	na	5	7	3	3	7	4	5	4	na	6	5	3	5	4	10
Total	4	4	6	3	4	5	4	4	4	6	4	5	5	4	5	5

RANKING

Country	2000
Vietnam	24
Bangladesh	23
Tanzania	21
Albania	11
China	10
India	8
Macedonia	8
United States	7
South Africa	6
Uganda	6
Algeria	6
Greece	5
Moldova	5
Slovakia	5
Zimbabwe	5
Sweden	4
Malta	4
Northern Ireland	4
Puerto Rico	4
Philippines	4
Finland	4
Mexico	4
Iceland	3
Austria	3
Peru	3
Argentina	3
Bosnia and Herz.	3
Bulgaria	3
Denmark	3
Turkey	3
Montenegro	3
Belgium	3
Luxembourg	3
Canada	3
Netherlands	3
Italy	2
Korea, South	2
Czech Republic	2
Romania	2
Chile	2
Ireland	2
Croatia	2
Estonia	2
Great Britain	1
Belarus	1
Lithuania	1
Slovenia	1
Spain	1
Ukraine	1
Serbia	1
Hungary	1
Japan	1
Germany	1
Latvia	1
France	1
Poland	1
Portugal	1
Russian Fed.	0
Singapore	0
Total	4

A086) UNPAID WORK LOCAL POLITICAL

And for which, if any, are you currently doing unpaid voluntary work? Local community action on issues like poverty, employment, housing, racial equality.

Belong (%)　　　　　　　　　　　　　　　　　　　　　　　　　　　　　　　　　(WVS: V59; EVS: V35)

Country	Wave 1990	Wave 2000	Gender Male	Gender Female	Age 16-29	Age 30-49	Age 50+	Education Lower	Education Middle	Education Upper	Income Lower	Income Middle	Income Upper	Values Mat	Values Mixed	Values Postm.
Albania	na	8	9	7	7	9	7	9	7	6	11	6	6	9	7	3
Algeria	na	7	9	5	8	6	8	5	7	9	7	8	6	7	7	11
Argentina	1	3	2	3	3	2	3	2	4	4	2	2	5	2	3	3
Armenia	na	na	na	na	na	na	na	na	na	na	na	na	na	na	na	na
Australia	na	na	na	na	na	na	na	na	na	na	na	na	na	na	na	na
Austria	1	1	1	1	na	2	1	1	1	2	1	1	2	na	1	1
Azerbaijan	na	na	na	na	na	na	na	na	na	na	na	na	na	na	na	na
Bangladesh	na	24	31	17	21	25	30	21	27	31	14	28	30	23	26	22
Belarus	na	2	2	1	1	2	2	1	2	1	1	2	na	1	2	5
Belgium	3	3	3	2	2	2	3	1	2	5	4	2	3	2	2	3
Bosnia and Herz.	na	1	1	1	1	2	1	1	1	2	na	2	1	2	1	2
Brazil	4	na	na	na	na	na	na	na	na	na	na	na	na	na	na	na
Bulgaria	2	1	1	1	2	1	na	na	1	2	1	1	2	1	1	na
Canada	4	5	5	5	3	5	6	4	4	8	4	4	7	3	5	6
Chile	3	4	3	4	4	3	4	5	3	4	4	3	4	3	3	7
China	5	14	15	13	12	16	11	12	15	16	13	17	14	12	18	28
Colombia	na	na	na	na	na	na	na	na	na	na	na	na	na	na	na	na
Croatia	na	1	1	1	1	na	2	1	1	1	na	1	2	2	1	2
Czech Republic	na	2	2	2	2	2	2	2	3	2	3	2	2	3	2	3
Denmark	2	3	4	3	1	4	3	2	2	5	4	2	4	0	3	5
Dominican Rep.	na	na	na	na	na	na	na	na	na	na	na	na	na	na	na	na
Egypt	na	na	na	na	na	na	na	na	na	na	na	na	na	na	na	na
El Salvador	na	na	na	na	na	na	na	na	na	na	na	na	na	na	na	na
Estonia	4	2	2	2	2	2	2	2	2	2	1	2	2	2	1	4
Finland	3	2	2	3	1	3	2	3	3	1	4	2	2	3	3	1
France	3	2	2	2	na	1	2	2	1	2	1	1	3	1	2	3
Georgia	na	na	na	na	na	na	na	na	na	na	na	na	na	na	na	na
Germany	1	0	1	na	na	na	1	na	1	na	1	na	1	na	1	1
Great Britain	1	2	2	2	1	3	1	1	2	2	2	2	3	na	na	na
Greece	na	7	6	7	7	7	7	7	7	6	7	7	6	5	7	10
Hungary	2	1	2	1	na	2	1	1	na	4	1	1	3	na	3	na
Iceland	1	1	na	1	na	1	1	1	na	1	na	1	1	1	1	1
India	na	5	7	4	5	5	5	4	5	8	6	4	6	5	7	2
Indonesia	na	na	na	na	na	na	na	na	na	na	na	na	na	na	na	na
Iran	na	na	na	na	na	na	na	na	na	na	na	na	na	na	na	na
Ireland	3	4	3	4	2	3	5	4	3	4	2	8	3	3	3	8
Israel	na	na	na	na	na	na	na	na	na	na	na	na	na	na	na	na
Italy	1	2	2	2	2	2	2	1	2	5	2	2	3	2	2	2
Japan	1	0	1	na	na	na	1	1	na	1	na	na	1	na	na	2
Jordan	na	na	na	na	na	na	na	na	na	na	na	na	na	na	na	na
Korea, South	3	7	9	5	6	6	11	5	8	6	7	8	7	6	8	7
Latvia	8	2	1	2	2	2	2	na	2	4	2	2	2	2	2	2
Lithuania	2	1	1	1	1	1	na	na	1	1	na	1	1	na	1	1
Luxembourg	na	3	4	3	3	2	4	2	3	4	5	1	3	3	3	6
Macedonia	na	3	3	4	3	4	3	4	3	4	2	4	4	2	4	6
Malta	na	4	5	3	3	3	5	2	4	6	3	3	6	2	4	7
Mexico	3	4	5	4	3	4	6	5	3	5	4	7	4	5	4	4
Moldova	na	3	3	3	4	3	2	1	4	3	1	3	4	3	3	4
Montenegro	na	0	na	na	1	na	na	na	na	1	na	na	na	na	na	na
Morocco	na	na	na	na	na	na	na	na	na	na	na	na	na	na	na	na
Netherlands	3	4	4	4	3	4	4	2	4	6	2	5	5	2	4	6
New Zealand	na	na	na	na	na	na	na	na	na	na	na	na	na	na	na	na
Nigeria	na	na	na	na	na	na	na	na	na	na	na	na	na	na	na	na
Northern Ireland	2	5	3	7	na	8	4	9	3	2	13	5	3	4	4	11
Norway	1	na	na	na	na	na	na	na	na	na	na	na	na	na	na	na
Pakistan	na	na	na	na	na	na	na	na	na	na	na	na	na	na	na	na
Peru	na	4	4	4	2	5	7	4	5	4	4	5	4	5	4	5
Philippines	na	7	8	5	6	5	9	6	5	9	5	8	7	4	8	6
Poland	na	1	2	1	1	1	1	na	2	5	1	2	1	na	1	7
Portugal	1	1	1	1	1	na	1	1	na	3	na	1	1	na	1	2
Puerto Rico	na	4	5	4	3	4	4	3	2	6	3	4	6	2	5	4
Romania	1	1	1	1	1	0	0	0	1	0	0	1	1	0	1	0
Russian Fed.	2	1	na	1	1	1	1	na	na	1	1	1	na	na	1	na
Serbia	na	0	1	na	1	na	na	na	1	na	na	1	na	na	1	na
Singapore	na	2	2	2	1	3	5	3	2	2	1	3	2	2	2	na
Slovakia	na	7	10	4	6	7	7	6	7	9	6	8	7	6	8	6
Slovenia	3	6	5	7	4	5	8	7	5	6	8	8	5	8	6	3
South Africa	na	5	6	4	3	5	9	5	5	6	4	4	8	7	4	4
Spain	1	2	2	2	2	2	2	1	2	4	1	2	3	1	1	5
Sweden	1	6	6	5	2	5	8	6	4	8	6	5	5	3	5	9
Switzerland	na	na	na	na	na	na	na	na	na	na	na	na	na	na	na	na
Taiwan	na	na	na	na	na	na	na	na	na	na	na	na	na	na	na	na
Tanzania	na	23	22	25	21	25	23	23	22	28	21	25	27	19	26	25
Turkey	na	0	na	na	na	na	na	na	na	1	na	na	1	na	na	na
Uganda	na	6	11	2	7	7	1	6	6	7	10	6	5	7	6	5
Ukraine	na	1	1	1	1	1	1	1	1	2	1	1	2	na	2	3
United States	3	7	7	7	6	8	8	4	7	9	6	7	9	6	6	11
Uruguay	na	na	na	na	na	na	na	na	na	na	na	na	na	na	na	na
Venezuela	na	na	na	na	na	na	na	na	na	na	na	na	na	na	na	na
Vietnam	na	26	27	25	20	28	27	26	27	25	20	24	31	22	30	24
Zimbabwe	na	2	3	1	1	2	2	2	3	na	1	1	5	2	2	na
Total	2	5	5	4	4	5	4	4	4	6	4	5	5	4	5	5

RANKING

Country	2000
Vietnam	26
Bangladesh	24
Tanzania	23
China	14
Albania	8
United States	7
Algeria	7
Korea, South	7
Greece	7
Slovakia	7
Philippines	7
Uganda	6
Slovenia	6
Sweden	6
India	5
Canada	5
South Africa	5
Northern Ireland	5
Puerto Rico	4
Mexico	4
Peru	4
Netherlands	4
Chile	4
Ireland	4
Malta	4
Macedonia	3
Denmark	3
Luxembourg	3
Moldova	3
Argentina	3
Belgium	3
Finland	2
Czech Republic	2
Singapore	2
Estonia	2
Zimbabwe	2
Italy	2
Latvia	2
Spain	2
Great Britain	2
Belarus	2
France	2
Bosnia and Herz.	1
Hungary	1
Poland	1
Austria	1
Romania	1
Croatia	1
Ukraine	1
Bulgaria	1
Iceland	1
Lithuania	1
Portugal	1
Russian Fed.	1
Germany	0
Japan	0
Serbia	0
Montenegro	0
Turkey	0
Total	5

A087) UNPAID WORK HUMAN RIGHTS

And for which, if any, are you currently doing unpaid voluntary work? Third world development or human rights.

Belong (%)

(WVS: V60; EVS: V36)

Country	Wave 1990	Wave 2000	Gender Male	Gender Female	Age 16-29	Age 30-49	Age 50+	Educ Lower	Educ Middle	Educ Upper	Income Lower	Income Middle	Income Upper	Values Mat	Values Mixed	Values Postm.
Albania	na	2	2	3	4	2	2	2	3	2	4	2	1	2	2	5
Algeria	na	6	6	6	8	4	3	3	5	8	5	5	6	5	7	4
Argentina	0	0	1	na	na	na	1	na	na	1	na	na	na	na	na	1
Armenia	na	na	na	na	na	na	na	na	na	na	na	na	na	na	na	na
Australia	na	na	na	na	na	na	na	na	na	na	na	na	na	na	na	na
Austria	1	1	1	1	na	1	1	na	1	3	na	1	1	na	1	1
Azerbaijan	na	na	na	na	na	na	na	na	na	na	na	na	na	na	na	na
Bangladesh	na	11	16	5	7	13	17	8	10	21	5	11	15	8	13	9
Belarus	na	1	2	na	1	1	1	2	1	1	1	1	3	1	2	na
Belgium	3	4	4	4	4	5	5	2	3	8	5	3	4	2	4	6
Bosnia and Herz.	na	0	1	na	na	na	1	na	na	na	na	na	na	na	na	na
Brazil	1	na	na	na	na	na	na	na	na	na	na	na	na	na	na	na
Bulgaria	1	0	na	na	na	na	na	na	na	1	na	1	na	na	na	2
Canada	3	3	2	3	1	3	3	2	2	4	3	4	1	1	3	3
Chile	1	2	2	2	1	2	2	1	3	1	1	2	3	1	2	1
China	0	5	4	5	8	4	4	3	6	5	3	6	6	4	5	16
Colombia	na	na	na	na	na	na	na	na	na	na	na	na	na	na	na	na
Croatia	na	0	na	na	1	na	na	1	na	2	na	na	1	na	na	na
Czech Republic	na	0	na	na	na	na	na	na	na	1	na	1	na	1	na	na
Denmark	1	1	1	2	1	1	2	1	2	2	1	0	3	0	1	3
Dominican Rep.	na	na	na	na	na	na	na	na	na	na	na	na	na	na	na	na
Egypt	na	na	na	na	na	na	na	na	na	na	na	na	na	na	na	na
El Salvador	na	na	na	na	na	na	na	na	na	na	na	na	na	na	na	na
Estonia	1	0	1	na	1	na	na	na	1	na	na	na	1	na	na	na
Finland	2	5	3	6	5	6	3	5	3	7	7	3	4	4	5	2
France	1	1	na	1	na	1	1	na	na	3	na	1	1	na	1	2
Georgia	na	na	na	na	na	na	na	na	na	na	na	na	na	na	na	na
Germany	0	0	na	na	na	na	na	na	na	1	na	na	na	na	na	na
Great Britain	1	4	4	5	5	5	4	1	5	9	3	2	7	na	na	na
Greece	na	6	4	7	8	5	3	4	5	7	6	6	5	4	6	8
Hungary	0	0	1	na	1	na	na	na	na	1	na	1	na	na	na	na
Iceland	0	1	1	2	1	1	2	1	1	2	1	2	na	2	1	1
India	na	2	3	1	2	2	3	2	1	4	3	2	3	1	4	4
Indonesia	na	na	na	na	na	na	na	na	na	na	na	na	na	na	na	na
Iran	na	na	na	na	na	na	na	na	na	na	na	na	na	na	na	na
Ireland	1	2	2	2	1	1	4	2	2	3	1	3	2	2	1	5
Israel	na	na	na	na	na	na	na	na	na	na	na	na	na	na	na	na
Italy	1	2	2	2	3	2	2	2	2	2	2	2	2	1	2	2
Japan	0	0	na	na	na	na	1	na	na	1	na	na	1	1	na	na
Jordan	na	na	na	na	na	na	na	na	na	na	na	na	na	na	na	na
Korea, South	2	1	2	1	2	1	3	2	1	2	2	2	1	1	2	3
Latvia	4	0	na	na	na	1	na	na	na	1	na	1	na	na	na	na
Lithuania	1	0	na	na	na	na	na	na	na	na	na	na	na	na	na	na
Luxembourg	na	5	5	6	4	5	7	5	4	10	8	5	7	6	5	10
Macedonia	na	2	2	2	2	3	1	3	1	4	1	2	3	1	3	2
Malta	na	2	1	2	2	2	1	1	2	3	na	2	3	1	2	4
Mexico	1	1	1	2	2	1	2	1	2	1	2	1	1	2	1	1
Moldova	na	2	2	3	3	2	2	na	3	2	na	2	4	2	3	2
Montenegro	na	0	1	na	1	na	na	na	na	2	na	na	1	na	1	na
Morocco	na	na	na	na	na	na	na	na	na	na	na	na	na	na	na	na
Netherlands	3	4	3	5	3	4	6	4	3	6	3	5	4	1	4	4
New Zealand	na	na	na	na	na	na	na	na	na	na	na	na	na	na	na	na
Nigeria	na	na	na	na	na	na	na	na	na	na	na	na	na	na	na	na
Northern Ireland	0	5	5	5	na	9	3	2	2	13	3	7	6	6	6	2
Norway	1	na	na	na	na	na	na	na	na	na	na	na	na	na	na	na
Pakistan	na	na	na	na	na	na	na	na	na	na	na	na	na	na	na	na
Peru	na	2	1	2	1	2	3	2	1	3	2	1	3	1	2	3
Philippines	na	5	7	4	3	6	7	8	3	6	4	4	8	4	6	7
Poland	na	0	na	na	na	na	na	na	na	1	na	na	na	na	na	1
Portugal	1	1	1	1	na	1	1	1	1	2	na	na	1	na	na	2
Puerto Rico	na	2	1	2	2	2	1	3	na	2	1	2	2	1	1	3
Romania	0	0	1	0	0	0	1	0	0	1	0	0	1	0	1	1
Russian Fed.	0	na	na	na	na	na	na	na	na	na	na	na	na	na	na	na
Serbia	na	0	na	na	na	na	na	na	na	na	na	na	na	na	na	na
Singapore	na	1	na	1	1	1	na	1	1	1	na	1	1	1	1	na
Slovakia	na	0	na	na	na	na	na	na	na	1	na	na	na	na	na	na
Slovenia	1	0	1	na	na	na	1	1	na	1	1	na	1	na	na	1
South Africa	na	1	2	1	2	1	1	1	2	1	1	2	1	1	1	2
Spain	1	1	1	2	2	1	na	1	1	5	1	1	2	1	1	3
Sweden	3	5	4	5	3	4	5	1	4	7	4	3	7	3	3	11
Switzerland	na	na	na	na	na	na	na	na	na	na	na	na	na	na	na	na
Taiwan	na	na	na	na	na	na	na	na	na	na	na	na	na	na	na	na
Tanzania	na	20	19	20	24	19	12	19	21	19	20	22	16	14	23	17
Turkey	na	0	na	na	na	na	na	na	1	na	na	na	na	na	na	na
Uganda	na	3	6	na	5	1	1	6	2	3	5	5	1	4	3	2
Ukraine	na	0	na	na	na	1	na	na	1	na	na	na	na	na	na	na
United States	1	3	3	3	4	2	3	1	4	3	2	3	4	4	3	3
Uruguay	na	na	na	na	na	na	na	na	na	na	na	na	na	na	na	na
Venezuela	na	na	na	na	na	na	na	na	na	na	na	na	na	na	na	na
Vietnam	na	1	1	1	1	2	1	1	2	5	1	1	1	2	1	2
Zimbabwe	na	1	1	na	1	1	na	na	1	na	1	na	na	1	na	na
Total	1	2	3	2	3	2	2	2	2	4	2	2	2	2	2	3

RANKING

Country	2000
Tanzania	20
Bangladesh	11
Greece	6
Algeria	6
Luxembourg	5
Philippines	5
Northern Ireland	5
China	5
Finland	5
Sweden	5
Belgium	4
Great Britain	4
Netherlands	4
Uganda	3
United States	3
Canada	3
Albania	2
India	2
Moldova	2
Macedonia	2
Italy	2
Ireland	2
Chile	2
Peru	2
Malta	2
Puerto Rico	2
Mexico	1
Spain	1
Iceland	1
Korea, South	1
Vietnam	1
South Africa	1
Belarus	1
Denmark	1
Austria	1
France	1
Portugal	1
Singapore	1
Zimbabwe	1
Croatia	0
Czech Republic	0
Slovenia	0
Montenegro	0
Argentina	0
Bosnia and Herz.	0
Estonia	0
Japan	0
Latvia	0
Bulgaria	0
Germany	0
Hungary	0
Turkey	0
Ukraine	0
Serbia	0
Lithuania	0
Poland	0
Slovakia	0
Romania	0
Total	2

A088) UNPAID WORK ENVIRONMENT, CONSERVATION, ANIMAL RIGHTS

And for which, if any, are you currently doing unpaid voluntary work? Conservation, environmental, animal rights groups.

Belong (%)

(WVS: V61; EVS: V37)

Country	Wave 1990	Wave 2000	Gender Male	Gender Female	Age 16-29	Age 30-49	Age 50+	Education Lower	Education Middle	Education Upper	Income Lower	Income Middle	Income Upper	Values Mat	Values Mixed	Values Postm.
Albania	na	7	8	6	5	8	7	5	7	12	6	6	9	6	8	5
Algeria	na	6	7	5	8	6	3	3	6	8	7	5	5	6	7	5
Argentina	0	1	2	1	2	1	1	1	2	3	1	2	2	1	1	2
Armenia	na	na	na	na	na	na	na	na	na	na	na	na	na	na	na	na
Australia	na	na	na	na	na	na	na	na	na	na	na	na	na	na	na	na
Austria	1	2	3	2	2	2	2	2	3	4	2	2	3	1	2	1
Azerbaijan	na	na	na	na	na	na	na	na	na	na	na	na	na	na	na	na
Bangladesh	na	19	25	12	18	19	25	14	25	27	8	20	30	15	22	24
Belarus	na	4	4	3	4	4	3	4	3	5	4	4	2	3	4	3
Belgium	3	4	5	3	6	3	4	2	4	5	2	4	4	3	3	4
Bosnia and Herz.	na	2	2	1	1	2	1	na	1	4	1	1	3	1	2	4
Brazil	1	na	na	na	na	na	na	na	na	na	na	na	na	na	na	na
Bulgaria	3	1	1	2	3	1	1	na	1	4	na	2	2	1	2	2
Canada	4	4	6	3	4	5	5	3	4	7	4	4	6	2	5	5
Chile	1	2	2	2	2	2	2	1	2	4	1	3	4	1	2	3
China	2	28	29	27	31	28	24	21	32	40	24	29	32	29	31	47
Colombia	na	na	na	na	na	na	na	na	na	na	na	na	na	na	na	na
Croatia	na	2	3	na	1	2	1	na	2	4	na	1	3	na	2	2
Czech Republic	na	3	4	2	5	3	3	3	4	5	3	3	5	5	2	4
Denmark	1	2	3	1	2	2	3	1	3	3	1	3	1	0	2	6
Dominican Rep.	na	na	na	na	na	na	na	na	na	na	na	na	na	na	na	na
Egypt	na	na	na	na	na	na	na	na	na	na	na	na	na	na	na	na
El Salvador	na	na	na	na	na	na	na	na	na	na	na	na	na	na	na	na
Estonia	2	1	2	na	2	1	2	1	1	3	1	na	3	1	1	9
Finland	3	3	2	3	5	5	na	2	3	4	3	2	4	2	3	6
France	2	1	1	1	na	1	1	1	1	1	1	1	1	na	2	1
Georgia	na	na	na	na	na	na	na	na	na	na	na	na	na	na	na	na
Germany	2	1	1	1	1	1	1	1	2	1	1	1	2	1	2	1
Great Britain	2	8	10	6	4	12	7	1	7	28	2	3	20	na	na	na
Greece	na	10	9	10	13	8	5	5	8	12	11	9	11	10	9	14
Hungary	1	2	2	2	1	2	2	1	2	6	1	2	2	1	3	4
Iceland	2	1	1	1	na	3	1	1	1	3	1	1	2	1	1	4
India	na	5	7	4	6	5	6	3	5	10	5	3	7	2	9	18
Indonesia	na	na	na	na	na	na	na	na	na	na	na	na	na	na	na	na
Iran	na	na	na	na	na	na	na	na	na	na	na	na	na	na	na	na
Ireland	1	1	1	1	na	1	2	na	1	3	1	1	1	1	1	2
Israel	na	na	na	na	na	na	na	na	na	na	na	na	na	na	na	na
Italy	1	2	2	2	3	2	1	1	3	2	2	1	2	1	2	2
Japan	1	1	2	1	na	1	2	1	1	1	2	1	2	1	2	na
Jordan	na	na	na	na	na	na	na	na	na	na	na	na	na	na	na	na
Korea, South	2	5	6	3	4	4	7	4	5	4	5	4	4	3	6	6
Latvia	5	1	na	1	na	1	1	na	na	2	na	2	na	1	na	na
Lithuania	2	1	na	1	1	na	na	na	1	1	na	na	na	na	1	2
Luxembourg	na	5	4	5	5	4	4	3	4	8	5	4	8	5	5	6
Macedonia	na	3	3	3	4	3	2	3	2	6	2	2	5	1	4	8
Malta	na	2	2	2	2	1	2	1	2	4	na	2	3	1	2	7
Mexico	2	3	3	3	3	3	3	2	3	6	3	2	4	4	3	5
Moldova	na	4	4	4	6	4	3	1	5	7	3	5	5	5	4	1
Montenegro	na	3	3	2	3	3	2	2	2	6	na	1	5	3	3	na
Morocco	na	na	na	na	na	na	na	na	na	na	na	na	na	na	na	na
Netherlands	3	2	3	2	2	3	3	2	2	4	2	2	4	1	2	4
New Zealand	na	na	na	na	na	na	na	na	na	na	na	na	na	na	na	na
Nigeria	na	na	na	na	na	na	na	na	na	na	na	na	na	na	na	na
Northern Ireland	1	3	2	3	na	4	3	3	1	5	5	2	3	2	3	2
Norway	1	na	na	na	na	na	na	na	na	na	na	na	na	na	na	na
Pakistan	na	na	na	na	na	na	na	na	na	na	na	na	na	na	na	na
Peru	na	2	3	1	1	2	4	2	2	3	2	2	4	1	2	4
Philippines	na	9	12	6	6	9	12	10	7	10	7	6	15	6	11	9
Poland	na	1	1	na	na	1	na	na	na	2	na	1	na	na	1	na
Portugal	1	0	1	na	na	na	1	na	na	2	na	na	1	na	na	2
Puerto Rico	na	3	2	3	6	3	1	1	1	4	1	3	4	2	3	2
Romania	1	1	1	0	0	1	1	0	1	1	0	0	1	0	1	0
Russian Fed.	1	0	na	1	na	na	1	na	na	1	na	1	1	na	na	na
Serbia	na	0	1	na	na	na	na	na	na	na	1	na	na	na	na	na
Singapore	na	1	1	2	2	1	na	1	1	na	2	1	1	1	1	2
Slovakia	na	2	3	1	3	2	2	1	2	3	2	3	2	1	3	na
Slovenia	1	3	5	1	2	3	3	3	3	4	na	5	5	1	4	1
South Africa	na	2	2	1	2	1	2	1	2	5	1	na	2	1	1	5
Spain	1	1	1	1	2	1	1	1	1	3	1	1	2	1	1	3
Sweden	3	4	3	4	3	3	5	4	3	5	3	5	4	3	4	5
Switzerland	na	na	na	na	na	na	na	na	na	na	na	na	na	na	na	na
Taiwan	na	na	na	na	na	na	na	na	na	na	na	na	na	na	na	na
Tanzania	na	21	21	22	26	20	16	17	24	28	20	24	22	17	23	25
Turkey	na	0	na	na	na	na	na	na	na	na	na	na	na	na	na	na
Uganda	na	8	16	1	10	5	9	8	8	6	11	14	12	6	10	3
Ukraine	na	na	na	na	na	na	na	1	na	na	1	na	na	na	1	na
United States	4	9	7	10	8	7	11	7	6	11	6	10	10	7	8	10
Uruguay	na	na	na	na	na	na	na	na	na	na	na	na	na	na	na	na
Venezuela	na	na	na	na	na	na	na	na	na	na	na	na	na	na	na	na
Vietnam	na	8	10	6	10	8	6	6	9	15	7	9	8	4	10	11
Zimbabwe	na	1	2	na	1	1	2	1	2	na	1	1	3	1	1	1
Total	2	4	5	3	5	4	3	3	4	6	3	4	5	3	4	4

RANKING

Country	2000
China	28
Tanzania	21
Bangladesh	19
Greece	10
Philippines	9
United States	9
Uganda	8
Vietnam	8
Great Britain	8
Albania	7
Algeria	6
India	5
Korea, South	5
Luxembourg	5
Canada	4
Moldova	4
Belgium	4
Sweden	4
Belarus	4
Czech Republic	3
Macedonia	3
Mexico	3
Slovenia	3
Finland	3
Northern Ireland	3
Puerto Rico	3
Montenegro	3
Netherlands	2
Peru	2
Austria	2
Denmark	2
Chile	2
Slovakia	2
Hungary	2
Italy	2
Malta	2
Bosnia and Herz.	2
Croatia	2
South Africa	2
Argentina	1
Bulgaria	1
Iceland	1
Estonia	1
Japan	1
Singapore	1
Zimbabwe	1
Germany	1
Spain	1
Romania	1
France	1
Ireland	1
Latvia	1
Lithuania	1
Poland	1
Portugal	0
Russian Fed.	0
Ukraine	0
Serbia	0
Turkey	0
Total	4

A089) UNPAID WORK PROFESSIONAL ASSOCIATIONS

And for which, if any, are you currently doing unpaid voluntary work?. Professional associations.

Belong (%)

(WVS: V62; EVS: V38)

Country	Wave		Gender		Age			Education			Income			Values			RANKING Country	2000
	1990	2000	Male	Female	16-29	30-49	50+	Lower	Middle	Upper	Lower	Middle	Upper	Mat	Mixed	Postm.		
Albania	na	7	9	5	5	10	5	5	7	14	6	10	6	7	8	na	Tanzania	20
Algeria	na	9	9	8	9	9	8	4	11	11	9	11	8	9	8	13	United States	11
Argentina	1	1	1	1	na	2	1	na	1	7	na	1	2	na	1	3	Vietnam	11
Armenia	na	na	na	na	na	na	na	na	na	na	na	na	na	na	na	na	Algeria	9
Australia	na	na	na	na	na	na	na	na	na	na	na	na	na	na	na	na	Great Britain	8
Austria	1	2	3	1	na	2	2	2	1	3	1	1	2	3	2	1	Albania	7
Azerbaijan	na	na	na	na	na	na	na	na	na	na	na	na	na	na	na	na	Canada	6
Bangladesh	na	na	na	na	na	na	na	na	na	na	na	na	na	na	na	na	Puerto Rico	6
Belarus	na	1	2	na	2	1	na	na	2	na	1	1	2	na	2	na	Greece	6
Belgium	2	3	4	2	3	4	2	2	2	5	2	2	5	2	3	3	India	6
Bosnia and Herz.	na	1	1	1	1	1	1	1	na	4	na	1	3	1	1	2	Uganda	5
Brazil	2	na	2	na	na	na	na	na	na	na	na	na	na	na	na	na	Sweden	4
Bulgaria	2	2	2	1	na	4	1	na	1	6	1	2	2	1	3	na	Korea, South	4
Canada	5	6	7	5	4	8	6	1	4	14	3	4	12	3	5	10	Denmark	4
Chile	1	2	3	2	2	4	1	na	2	7	na	4	4	2	2	3	Moldova	4
China	17	4	4	3	4	4	3	3	4	12	4	4	4	4	4	6	China	4
Colombia	na	na	na	na	na	na	na	na	na	na	na	na	na	na	na	na	Netherlands	3
Croatia	na	2	3	2	1	3	2	1	2	6	na	2	5	na	3	1	Italy	3
Czech Republic	na	2	3	2	2	3	2	1	2	8	2	1	4	2	2	3	Peru	3
Denmark	3	4	5	2	1	5	4	3	3	4	3	4	6	1	3	7	Ireland	3
Dominican Rep.	na	na	na	na	na	na	na	na	na	na	na	na	na	na	na	na	Iceland	3
Egypt	na	na	na	na	na	na	na	na	na	na	na	na	na	na	na	na	Slovakia	3
El Salvador	na	na	na	na	na	na	na	na	na	na	na	na	na	na	na	na	Belgium	3
Estonia	2	2	2	1	2	3	na	na	1	5	na	na	4	1	2	na	Finland	3
Finland	7	3	5	1	2	4	3	2	4	5	3	3	4	2	3	2	Macedonia	3
France	3	1	2	1	na	2	1	1	2	2	na	2	3	1	1	2	Slovenia	3
Georgia	na	na	na	na	na	na	na	na	na	na	na	na	na	na	na	na	Czech Republic	2
Germany	3	1	1	na	1	1	na	na	1	1	na	na	1	na	1	na	Philippines	2
Great Britain	2	8	6	9	6	11	5	7	7	13	8	6	14	na	na	na	Northern Ireland	2
Greece	na	6	8	4	4	7	7	2	5	7	4	6	8	6	5	7	Chile	2
Hungary	2	2	2	2	1	3	2	1	1	11	2	2	2	1	3	6	Croatia	2
Iceland	3	3	3	3	1	5	3	2	2	8	na	3	6	2	3	7	Zimbabwe	2
India	na	6	6	5	6	6	5	4	6	9	4	5	7	5	8	4	Hungary	2
Indonesia	na	na	na	na	na	na	na	na	na	na	na	na	na	na	na	na	South Africa	2
Iran	na	na	na	na	na	na	na	na	na	na	na	na	na	na	na	na	Bulgaria	2
Ireland	1	3	4	2	4	4	1	1	1	13	na	2	8	3	4	2	Malta	2
Israel	na	na	na	na	na	na	na	na	na	na	na	na	na	na	na	na	Montenegro	2
Italy	1	3	5	2	1	4	4	2	2	10	2	3	6	1	3	5	Estonia	2
Japan	1	1	2	na	na	1	2	1	1	2	1	2	2	2	1	1	Austria	2
Jordan	na	na	na	na	na	na	na	na	na	na	na	na	na	na	na	na	Luxembourg	2
Korea, South	2	4	6	2	4	4	5	2	2	7	4	4	5	3	5	6	Mexico	2
Latvia	3	1	na	1	1	1	na	na	1	2	na	2	1	1	na	2	France	1
Lithuania	1	0	1	na	na	na	na	na	na	1	na	na	1	na	na	2	Japan	1
Luxembourg	na	2	2	1	1	2	2	2	1	2	2	1	4	1	2	1	Poland	1
Macedonia	na	3	3	3	2	4	2	1	3	4	3	2	4	3	3	na	Bosnia and Herz.	1
Malta	na	1	0	1	2	1	2	na	1	9	na	1	4	na	2	8	Romania	1
Mexico	1	2	2	1	2	1	2	1	1	7	na	2	3	1	2	3	Argentina	1
Moldova	na	4	5	3	4	4	3	1	4	7	1	6	3	3	5	11	Belarus	1
Montenegro	na	2	2	2	2	2	1	na	2	4	na	2	2	na	3	5	Singapore	1
Morocco	na	na	na	na	na	na	na	na	na	na	na	na	na	na	na	na	Spain	1
Netherlands	2	3	5	2	1	6	2	2	3	6	2	3	6	1	3	5	Serbia	1
New Zealand	na	na	na	na	na	na	na	na	na	na	na	na	na	na	na	na	Turkey	1
Nigeria	na	na	na	na	na	na	na	na	na	na	na	na	na	na	na	na	Germany	1
Northern Ireland	1	2	3	2	na	4	2	na	2	6	3	na	5	1	3	2	Portugal	1
Norway	3	na	na	na	na	na	na	na	na	na	na	na	na	na	na	na	Ukraine	1
Pakistan	na	na	na	na	na	na	na	na	na	na	na	na	na	na	na	na	Latvia	1
Peru	na	3	5	2	2	4	4	1	2	7	2	4	5	3	3	4	Russian Fed.	0
Philippines	na	2	3	2	2	2	5	1	1	7	2	2	4	1	3	2	Lithuania	0
Poland	na	1	2	1	1	2	1	1	2	2	1	1	3	1	2	na		
Portugal	1	1	1	na	na	1	1	na	1	4	na	1	na	1	1	na		
Puerto Rico	na	6	6	5	3	8	5	1	2	8	2	6	9	4	7	3		
Romania	2	1	1	1	2	1	1	0	0	4	0	0	2	0	1	5		
Russian Fed.	1	0	na	na	na	na	na	na	na	1	na	1	na	na	na	na		
Serbia	na	1	1	1	2	na	na	na	1	2	na	1	1	1	1	3		
Singapore	na	1	1	na	1	1	na	na	1	3	na	na	2	1	1	1		
Slovakia	na	3	4	2	3	4	2	1	2	16	1	1	6	2	4	8		
Slovenia	2	3	3	2	1	4	3	2	2	9	2	3	7	1	3	3		
South Africa	na	2	3	1	1	3	2	na	3	10	na	3	3	1	2	2		
Spain	1	1	1	na	1	1	1	1	1	2	na	1	1	1	1	1		
Sweden	3	4	4	4	2	5	5	2	2	10	2	5	6	2	4	6		
Switzerland	na	na	na	na	na	na	na	na	na	na	na	na	na	na	na	na		
Taiwan	na	na	na	na	na	na	na	na	na	na	na	na	na	na	na	na		
Tanzania	na	20	20	21	22	21	16	13	22	43	14	26	28	17	23	29		
Turkey	na	1	1	na	1	1	1	na	1	5	na	1	2	na	1	1		
Uganda	na	5	7	3	5	5	4	4	5	5	5	5	6	5	4	7		
Ukraine	na	1	1	1	1	na	1	1	na	2	na	na	1	na	1	3		
United States	5	11	13	9	9	11	12	3	7	16	7	11	17	9	12	9		
Uruguay	na	na	na	na	na	na	na	na	na	na	na	na	na	na	na	na		
Venezuela	na	na	na	na	na	na	na	na	na	na	na	na	na	na	na	na		
Vietnam	na	11	13	8	8	13	9	9	12	13	8	11	11	9	11	10		
Zimbabwe	na	2	4	1	2	2	2	1	4	18	1	1	8	2	2	6		
Total	3	3	4	3	3	4	3	2	3	7	2	3	5	2	4	4	Total	3

A090) UNPAID WORK YOUTH WORK

And for which, if any, are you currently doing unpaid voluntary work? Youth work (scouts, guides, youth clubs, etc.).

Belong (%)

(WVS: V63; EVS: V39)

Country	Wave 1990	Wave 2000	Gender Male	Gender Female	Age 16-29	Age 30-49	Age 50+	Education Lower	Education Middle	Education Upper	Income Lower	Income Middle	Income Upper	Values Mat	Values Mixed	Values Postm.	RANKING Country	2000
Albania	na	9	11	7	24	4	2	8	9	11	10	9	8	9	9	10	United States	22
Algeria	na	10	13	7	14	9	4	2	11	15	11	9	10	6	13	11	Tanzania	20
Argentina	2	2	2	2	4	2	1	1	3	3	1	2	3	2	3	2	Uganda	18
Armenia	na	na	na	na	na	na	na	na	na	na	na	na	na	na	na	na	Great Britain	15
Australia	na	na	na	na	na	na	na	na	na	na	na	na	na	na	na	na	Northern Ireland	15
Austria	2	2	1	3	3	3	1	1	3	5	1	2	2	na	2	4	Vietnam	14
Azerbaijan	na	na	na	na	na	na	na	na	na	na	na	na	na	na	na	na	Bangladesh	14
Bangladesh	na	14	20	6	15	13	11	7	17	27	13	12	15	12	15	17	Algeria	10
Belarus	na	2	1	2	4	1	na	na	2	2	1	3	na	1	2	3	China	10
Belgium	5	5	7	4	14	5	1	2	6	7	2	5	7	4	5	5	Albania	9
Bosnia and Herz.	na	2	1	2	5	na	na	1	1	3	na	2	na	1	2	4	Canada	8
Brazil	2	na	na	na	na	na	na	na	na	na	na	na	na	na	na	na	Singapore	8
Bulgaria	1	2	2	1	4	1	1	na	1	4	1	2	2	1	2	2	South Africa	7
Canada	7	8	7	9	8	12	5	5	8	11	6	9	10	4	10	7	Finland	6
Chile	4	4	5	3	9	3	1	1	5	8	3	4	5	3	4	5	Philippines	6
China	10	10	9	11	11	10	9	9	10	16	9	11	9	8	12	9	Luxembourg	6
Colombia	na	na	na	na	na	na	na	na	na	na	na	na	na	na	na	na	Czech Republic	6
Croatia	na	2	2	2	4	1	na	1	1	3	1	1	4	na	2	1	Slovakia	6
Czech Republic	na	6	7	5	9	7	3	4	7	12	2	6	8	5	6	10	India	5
Denmark	3	5	6	4	6	6	4	4	8	7	3	6	8	3	5	8	Sweden	5
Dominican Rep.	na	na	na	na	na	na	na	na	na	na	na	na	na	na	na	na	Denmark	5
Egypt	na	na	na	na	na	na	na	na	na	na	na	na	na	na	na	na	Belgium	5
El Salvador	na	na	na	na	na	na	na	na	na	na	na	na	na	na	na	na	Ireland	5
Estonia	2	2	2	2	5	2	1	1	2	3	1	1	4	1	2	4	Peru	5
Finland	5	6	6	7	9	9	3	2	10	12	5	6	8	6	6	10	Greece	5
France	3	2	1	2	2	2	1	1	1	3	1	2	1	2	2	1	Netherlands	5
Georgia	na	na	na	na	na	na	na	na	na	na	na	na	na	na	na	na	Puerto Rico	4
Germany	2	2	na	3	3	3	na	1	2	1	1	2	2	na	2	3	Chile	4
Great Britain	3	15	21	10	17	17	10	10	15	31	10	14	23	na	na	na	Zimbabwe	4
Greece	na	5	5	5	6	4	4	4	3	6	4	5	5	8	4	4	Mexico	4
Hungary	1	1	1	1	na	2	1	na	na	10	na	1	2	na	2	na	Moldova	4
Iceland	5	3	4	3	3	5	2	2	3	7	2	4	5	3	4	2	Slovenia	4
India	na	5	7	3	7	5	3	3	5	9	8	3	6	4	7	16	Iceland	3
Indonesia	na	na	na	na	na	na	na	na	na	na	na	na	na	na	na	na	Korea, South	3
Iran	na	na	na	na	na	na	na	na	na	na	na	na	na	na	na	na	Macedonia	3
Ireland	5	5	5	5	5	6	2	3	6	6	3	5	7	4	5	9	Malta	3
Israel	na	na	na	na	na	na	na	na	na	na	na	na	na	na	na	na	Italy	3
Italy	3	3	2	4	5	3	2	1	5	3	2	3	4	1	3	3	Austria	2
Japan	1	1	1	1	na	1	1	na	1	2	na	1	2	1	1	na	Argentina	2
Jordan	na	na	na	na	na	na	na	na	na	na	na	na	na	na	na	na	Estonia	2
Korea, South	3	3	5	2	5	3	3	4	3	4	4	2	4	2	5	3	Germany	2
Latvia	3	1	1	1	3	na	1	na	1	1	na	2	na	1	na	na	Bulgaria	2
Lithuania	4	1	na	2	4	na	na	na	2	1	na	na	1	1	2	na	Croatia	2
Luxembourg	na	6	6	6	10	4	5	5	7	7	4	6	9	6	5	11	Bosnia and Herz.	2
Macedonia	na	3	4	3	9	2	1	2	4	4	2	3	6	2	4	6	Belarus	2
Malta	na	3	3	3	6	3	2	na	3	9	1	4	6	1	5	4	France	2
Mexico	2	4	4	4	6	3	2	2	5	9	3	3	6	3	5	4	Hungary	1
Moldova	na	4	4	4	9	2	2	1	4	6	1	3	7	3	4	9	Lithuania	1
Montenegro	na	1	1	1	2	1	na	na	1	2	na	1	1	na	2	2	Spain	1
Morocco	na	na	na	na	na	na	na	na	na	na	na	na	na	na	na	na	Romania	1
Netherlands	5	5	4	5	10	5	2	2	8	4	5	4	4	3	5	3	Japan	1
New Zealand	na	na	na	na	na	na	na	na	na	na	na	na	na	na	na	na	Portugal	1
Nigeria	na	na	na	na	na	na	na	na	na	na	na	na	na	na	na	na	Ukraine	1
Northern Ireland	8	15	15	14	34	13	8	12	16	15	18	15	14	11	17	10	Montenegro	1
Norway	4	na	na	na	na	na	na	na	na	na	na	na	na	na	na	na	Latvia	1
Pakistan	na	na	na	na	na	na	na	na	na	na	na	na	na	na	na	na	Poland	1
Peru	na	5	6	4	9	2	2	4	4	6	3	6	6	4	5	6	Turkey	1
Philippines	na	6	8	5	9	5	6	4	5	12	4	5	11	5	8	9	Russian Fed.	0
Poland	na	1	1	1	3	na	na	na	1	2	1	na	2	1	1	na	Serbia	0
Portugal	2	1	1	1	1	1	1	1	2	1	1	1	3	na	1	1		
Puerto Rico	na	4	5	4	4	6	3	3	1	7	3	6	4	2	5	3		
Romania	1	1	1	1	2	0	0	0	1	1	0	1	1	0	0	3		
Russian Fed.	3	0	na	na	1	na	na	na	na	na	na	na	na	na	na	na		
Serbia	na	0	na	na	1	na	na	1	na	1	na	na	na	na	1	na		
Singapore	na	8	9	7	14	1	2	9	7	7	5	8	8	5	8	12		
Slovakia	na	6	4	7	9	5	4	4	6	9	3	6	7	5	6	9		
Slovenia	1	4	4	3	7	3	2	1	4	5	2	4	5	2	3	7		
South Africa	na	7	7	7	11	4	6	6	8	7	5	9	6	8	6	8		
Spain	1	1	1	1	3	1	na	na	2	3	1	1	2	1	1	3		
Sweden	7	5	7	3	7	7	2	6	6	4	4	4	8	2	5	6		
Switzerland	na	na	na	na	na	na	na	na	na	na	na	na	na	na	na	na		
Taiwan	na	na	na	na	na	na	na	na	na	na	na	na	na	na	na	na		
Tanzania	na	20	19	20	26	18	12	19	21	20	20	19	20	16	22	21		
Turkey	na	1	1	na	1	na	na	na	1	4	na	na	2	na	1	1		
Uganda	na	18	22	14	30	6	3	9	21	15	14	21	19	15	19	21		
Ukraine	na	1	1	1	2	1	na	na	1	3	na	1	2	na	2	na		
United States	10	22	20	24	19	28	16	13	23	25	14	22	31	27	22	21		
Uruguay	na	na	na	na	na	na	na	na	na	na	na	na	na	na	na	na		
Venezuela	na	na	na	na	na	na	na	na	na	na	na	na	na	na	na	na		
Vietnam	na	14	17	11	35	10	5	10	18	25	12	16	14	14	15	17		
Zimbabwe	na	4	7	1	6	1	2	2	7	na	3	4	8	2	5	7		
Total	4	5	6	5	9	5	3	4	6	8	4	5	6	4	6	6	Total	5

A091) UNPAID WORK SPORTS OR RECREATION

And for which, if any, are you currently doing unpaid voluntary work? Sports or recreation.

Belong (%) (WVS: V64; EVS: V40)

Country	Wave 1990	Wave 2000	Male	Female	16-29	30-49	50+	Edu Lower	Edu Middle	Edu Upper	Inc Lower	Inc Middle	Inc Upper	Mat	Mixed	Postm.
Albania	na	8	14	2	19	6	2	6	9	12	6	10	8	6	9	13
Algeria	na	15	20	9	22	11	6	6	17	18	15	16	17	13	16	16
Argentina	2	3	4	1	3	3	2	3	2	6	1	2	4	2	3	3
Armenia	na	na	na	na	na	na	na	na	na	na	na	na	na	na	na	na
Australia	na	na	na	na	na	na	na	na	na	na	na	na	na	na	na	na
Austria	7	9	13	5	11	10	6	6	13	8	6	10	10	7	8	11
Azerbaijan	na	na	na	na	na	na	na	na	na	na	na	na	na	na	na	na
Bangladesh	na	25	33	15	28	24	20	13	35	44	21	26	27	21	28	28
Belarus	na	2	3	1	4	2	1	na	3	1	1	2	2	1	3	3
Belgium	6	9	13	4	10	12	5	3	9	11	3	7	13	7	10	7
Bosnia and Herz.	na	7	12	3	16	5	1	2	7	13	3	6	11	4	8	13
Brazil	4	na	na	na	na	na	na	na	na	na	na	na	na	na	na	na
Bulgaria	4	4	6	2	9	4	2	na	6	6	2	6	5	3	6	2
Canada	12	13	14	12	15	16	8	7	14	16	8	13	17	11	13	13
Chile	7	12	18	7	19	12	6	7	15	15	10	13	15	10	13	13
China	6	13	12	13	18	13	9	9	15	19	10	14	14	13	14	16
Colombia	na	na	na	na	na	na	na	na	na	na	na	na	na	na	na	na
Croatia	na	7	12	2	11	8	3	4	9	11	5	6	10	7	7	8
Czech Republic	na	11	16	6	16	11	7	9	12	15	7	11	13	10	11	13
Denmark	11	14	17	12	15	19	9	14	18	12	7	19	17	15	14	17
Dominican Rep.	na	na	na	na	na	na	na	na	na	na	na	na	na	na	na	na
Egypt	na	na	na	na	na	na	na	na	na	na	na	na	na	na	na	na
El Salvador	na	na	na	na	na	na	na	na	na	na	na	na	na	na	na	na
Estonia	8	4	5	2	8	3	2	2	5	4	1	3	6	3	4	4
Finland	16	17	23	12	17	23	11	14	23	16	9	18	25	17	17	17
France	6	9	12	6	7	11	8	8	7	12	4	10	12	7	9	11
Georgia	na	na	na	na	na	na	na	na	na	na	na	na	na	na	na	na
Germany	11	7	9	6	5	9	5	4	9	9	3	9	10	8	6	8
Great Britain	na	4	na	7	2	6	4	2	4	4	4	3	3	na	na	na
Greece	na	9	12	7	11	7	6	4	10	9	6	10	13	12	8	12
Hungary	2	3	4	2	6	3	1	2	4	9	2	2	4	2	3	na
Iceland	14	11	17	6	10	14	9	8	14	14	10	10	15	10	12	10
India	na	9	12	4	10	9	7	6	9	14	12	7	9	6	14	20
Indonesia	na	na	na	na	na	na	na	na	na	na	na	na	na	na	na	na
Iran	na	na	na	na	na	na	na	na	na	na	na	na	na	na	na	na
Ireland	7	14	19	8	20	14	9	7	15	23	4	15	20	16	12	19
Israel	na	na	na	na	na	na	na	na	na	na	na	na	na	na	na	na
Italy	6	6	10	3	9	8	3	4	9	6	6	5	10	5	7	6
Japan	3	3	5	2	1	3	5	4	3	3	4	4	3	4	3	4
Jordan	na	na	na	na	na	na	na	na	na	na	na	na	na	na	na	na
Korea, South	3	12	14	10	14	11	12	4	11	14	13	11	12	12	12	12
Latvia	9	6	9	4	16	7	2	4	6	11	4	3	11	5	8	7
Lithuania	7	2	4	1	6	2	na	na	3	6	1	2	3	3	2	na
Luxembourg	na	9	10	8	13	8	8	7	11	9	6	10	13	10	9	10
Macedonia	na	9	12	5	14	9	4	3	11	13	6	7	14	7	9	17
Malta	na	6	11	1	8	6	3	1	6	12	1	6	13	5	6	9
Mexico	5	7	10	4	12	6	4	3	11	15	4	8	12	6	7	12
Moldova	na	4	6	3	10	2	1	1	4	7	2	4	6	3	5	5
Montenegro	na	5	9	2	10	5	3	2	7	10	1	6	10	4	7	8
Morocco	na	na	na	na	na	na	na	na	na	na	na	na	na	na	na	na
Netherlands	8	17	22	13	27	15	15	11	21	20	12	18	21	12	19	17
New Zealand	na	na	na	na	na	na	na	na	na	na	na	na	na	na	na	na
Nigeria	na	na	na	na	na	na	na	na	na	na	na	na	na	na	na	na
Northern Ireland	6	18	19	17	36	18	13	13	18	24	5	17	20	14	18	19
Norway	14	na	na	na	na	na	na	na	na	na	na	na	na	na	na	na
Pakistan	na	na	na	na	na	na	na	na	na	na	na	na	na	na	na	na
Peru	na	8	13	4	11	7	4	5	9	10	7	9	10	6	8	11
Philippines	na	12	18	7	18	10	8	7	13	17	8	11	17	11	14	7
Poland	na	2	4	1	3	2	1	1	3	7	2	2	4	2	2	3
Portugal	6	4	9	1	5	6	2	2	9	7	1	2	11	3	5	6
Puerto Rico	na	5	9	3	9	5	3	4	3	7	5	5	7	7	5	6
Romania	3	1	2	0	3	1	1	0	1	3	0	0	2	0	2	4
Russian Fed.	3	1	1	1	4	1	1	na	1	3	1	1	2	1	2	5
Serbia	na	3	6	1	4	4	3	3	4	4	2	4	4	4	4	na
Singapore	na	6	8	4	9	5	1	4	7	10	5	5	8	4	6	14
Slovakia	na	13	23	5	17	16	8	9	15	14	10	14	15	12	15	15
Slovenia	3	9	13	5	12	10	4	3	10	13	4	11	11	9	8	9
South Africa	na	15	22	8	22	14	5	12	18	41	12	14	21	11	17	32
Spain	4	3	5	1	5	3	2	2	5	4	2	3	6	3	3	4
Sweden	17	18	20	15	18	24	12	16	19	16	11	20	24	17	17	20
Switzerland	na	na	na	na	na	na	na	na	na	na	na	na	na	na	na	na
Taiwan	na	na	na	na	na	na	na	na	na	na	na	na	na	na	na	na
Tanzania	na	31	33	27	40	28	23	28	35	30	29	35	27	26	33	42
Turkey	na	1	1	na	na	1	na	na	1	2	na	1	1	na	1	1
Uganda	na	20	34	9	28	15	6	13	24	19	21	26	25	16	22	26
Ukraine	na	1	2	na	2	1	na	na	1	1	na	na	2	1	1	na
United States	8	19	24	14	23	23	10	15	23	18	14	17	30	16	20	16
Uruguay	na	na	na	na	na	na	na	na	na	na	na	na	na	na	na	na
Venezuela	na	na	na	na	na	na	na	na	na	na	na	na	na	na	na	na
Vietnam	na	18	25	11	23	17	15	14	22	31	18	13	23	10	21	24
Zimbabwe	na	4	7	1	5	3	2	2	6	10	3	1	11	4	4	3
Total	7	9	13	6	14	10	5	7	10	12	7	10	12	8	10	11

RANKING

Country	2000
Tanzania	31
Bangladesh	25
Uganda	20
United States	19
Northern Ireland	18
Vietnam	18
Sweden	18
Netherlands	17
Finland	17
South Africa	15
Algeria	15
Denmark	14
Ireland	14
Slovakia	13
Canada	13
China	13
Philippines	12
Chile	12
Korea, South	12
Iceland	11
Czech Republic	11
Luxembourg	9
Greece	9
India	9
Austria	9
France	9
Macedonia	9
Belgium	9
Slovenia	9
Albania	8
Peru	8
Bosnia and Herz.	7
Mexico	7
Croatia	7
Germany	7
Italy	6
Latvia	6
Singapore	6
Malta	6
Montenegro	5
Puerto Rico	5
Portugal	4
Bulgaria	4
Moldova	4
Great Britain	4
Zimbabwe	4
Estonia	4
Serbia	3
Japan	3
Spain	3
Hungary	3
Argentina	3
Lithuania	2
Poland	2
Belarus	2
Russian Fed.	1
Romania	1
Ukraine	1
Turkey	1
Total	9

A092) UNPAID WORK WOMEN'S GROUP

And for which, if any, are you currently doing unpaid voluntary work? Women's groups.

Belong (%)

(WVS: V65; EVS: V41)

Country	Wave 1990	Wave 2000	Gender Male	Gender Female	Age 16-29	Age 30-49	Age 50+	Edu Lower	Edu Middle	Edu Upper	Inc Lower	Inc Middle	Inc Upper	Val Mat	Val Mixed	Val Postm.
Albania	na	9	2	17	5	11	11	10	10	6	12	9	7	9	9	8
Algeria	na	6	2	9	6	6	4	2	7	6	5	6	6	6	6	7
Argentina	0	1	1	1	1	1	na	na	1	1	1	1	1	na	1	1
Armenia	na	na	na	na	na	na	na	na	na	na	na	na	na	na	na	na
Australia	na	na	na	na	na	na	na	na	na	na	na	na	na	na	na	na
Austria	2	2	na	5	1	2	3	3	3	1	2	2	2	1	2	3
Azerbaijan	na	na	na	na	na	na	na	na	na	na	na	na	na	na	na	na
Bangladesh	na	13	10	17	14	13	13	14	13	13	10	17	13	14	14	9
Belarus	na	1	na	2	na	2	na	na	1	4	na	2	na	na	1	5
Belgium	3	3	1	5	1	3	5	5	3	2	4	3	3	3	4	2
Bosnia and Herz.	na	2	1	3	2	3	1	1	2	1	na	2	3	2	2	6
Brazil	1	na	na	na	na	na	na	na	na	na	na	na	na	na	na	na
Bulgaria	1	1	na	2	1	2	na	na	1	1	1	2	1	1	1	na
Canada	5	5	1	8	1	5	6	4	4	6	5	3	5	3	5	5
Chile	2	5	na	8	2	5	6	6	4	2	6	4	4	5	5	4
China	3	15	6	24	12	16	14	15	15	14	12	18	14	15	15	19
Colombia	na	na	na	na	na	na	na	5	1	1	na	na	na	3	3	2
Croatia	na	2	1	4	na	5	na	5	1	1	2	2	3	3	3	2
Czech Republic	na	1	1	2	1	1	1	1	2	1	1	1	1	2	1	na
Denmark	1	1	0	1	0	1	1	1	1	1	1	0	0	1	1	1
Dominican Rep.	na	na	na	na	na	na	na	na	na	na	na	na	na	na	na	na
Egypt	na	na	na	na	na	na	na	na	na	na	na	na	na	na	na	na
El Salvador	na	na	na	na	na	na	na	na	na	na	na	na	na	na	na	na
Estonia	2	2	1	2	2	2	1	na	2	2	2	2	1	1	2	na
Finland	3	3	na	5	na	3	4	3	4	1	3	4	3	2	3	1
France	1	0	na	na	na	na	na	na	na	na	na	na	na	na	na	na
Georgia	na	na	na	na	na	na	na	na	na	na	na	na	na	na	na	na
Germany	3	2	na	3	na	2	2	1	3	2	1	1	4	2	1	4
Great Britain	na	1	1	1	2	1	1	1	2	2	1	2	1	na	na	na
Greece	na	3	2	4	2	3	5	2	3	3	2	3	4	3	3	3
Hungary	1	0	na	na	na	1	na	na	na	2	na	na	na	na	1	na
Iceland	3	2	na	4	na	1	5	3	2	1	2	2	2	3	2	1
India	na	6	4	8	6	6	5	6	4	7	6	5	6	4	8	4
Indonesia	na	na	na	na	na	na	na	na	na	na	na	na	na	na	na	na
Iran	na	na	na	na	na	na	na	na	na	na	na	na	na	na	na	na
Ireland	2	3	1	4	2	2	4	4	1	4	3	4	2	1	2	7
Israel	na	na	na	na	na	na	na	na	na	na	na	na	na	na	na	na
Italy	0	0	na	1	1	na	na	1	na	na	1	na	na	na	1	na
Japan	2	1	1	2	na	na	3	1	2	na	1	1	2	3	1	2
Jordan	na	na	na	na	na	na	na	na	na	na	na	na	na	na	na	na
Korea, South	2	4	2	6	3	5	4	4	5	3	3	5	4	4	4	4
Latvia	2	0	na	1	1	na	na	na	1	na	1	na	na	1	na	2
Lithuania	2	0	na	na	na	1	na	na	na	na	na	na	1	na	na	na
Luxembourg	na	2	2	3	2	3	2	3	2	2	4	1	2	4	3	1
Macedonia	na	4	1	7	3	5	3	4	3	6	3	4	5	3	4	2
Malta	na	2	1	2	1	1	3	2	1	3	1	1	2	1	1	4
Mexico	1	3	2	5	2	4	4	3	4	2	4	3	3	3	4	4
Moldova	na	3	2	4	3	3	2	1	2	4	1	3	3	3	3	na
Montenegro	na	1	na	2	1	2	na	na	1	4	na	2	1	na	2	na
Morocco	na	na	na	na	na	na	na	na	na	na	na	na	na	na	na	na
Netherlands	3	2	na	4	1	2	4	2	2	3	2	3	1	3	2	3
New Zealand	na	na	na	na	na	na	na	na	na	na	na	na	na	na	na	na
Nigeria	na	na	na	na	na	na	na	na	na	na	na	na	na	na	na	na
Northern Ireland	2	5	2	8	na	4	6	9	2	2	8	3	5	2	6	7
Norway	1	na	na	na	na	na	na	na	na	na	na	na	na	na	na	na
Pakistan	na	na	na	na	na	na	na	na	na	na	na	na	na	na	na	na
Peru	na	5	1	9	4	6	5	7	5	3	6	5	3	5	5	3
Philippines	na	9	3	15	6	9	13	12	7	9	8	8	11	7	10	15
Poland	na	1	na	1	1	na	1	na	na	2	1	na	1	na	1	na
Portugal	0	0	na	na	na	na	na	na	na	na	na	na	na	na	na	na
Puerto Rico	na	2	2	1	2	2	1	1	1	2	1	na	4	na	1	3
Romania	0	0	0	1	0	1	0	0	0	0	1	0	0	0	0	1
Russian Fed.	1	0	na	1	na	1	na	na	na	na	1	na	na	na	na	na
Serbia	na	0	na	1	na	1	na	na	na	1	na	1	1	na	na	1
Singapore	na	1	na	1	1	na	1	na	1	na	na	1	1	na	na	2
Slovakia	na	5	1	8	2	4	7	5	5	2	6	4	5	5	5	2
Slovenia	0	1	1	2	na	1	2	1	1	1	2	2	1	1	1	1
South Africa	na	8	1	15	2	10	13	8	8	6	7	11	6	9	7	9
Spain	0	1	na	1	1	1	1	1	1	1	1	1	1	1	1	2
Sweden	2	2	na	4	na	2	4	2	1	4	1	2	4	2	2	3
Switzerland	na	na	na	na	na	na	na	na	na	na	na	na	na	na	na	na
Taiwan	na	na	na	na	na	na	na	na	na	na	na	na	na	na	na	na
Tanzania	na	23	8	42	20	28	17	24	21	25	23	25	20	24	23	17
Turkey	na	0	na	1	na	na	2	na	na	2	na	na	1	na	na	1
Uganda	na	12	2	22	9	20	3	19	11	4	17	13	12	12	13	12
Ukraine	na	0	na	1	na	1	na	na	1	na	na	1	na	na	1	na
United States	5	8	2	15	5	9	11	7	8	9	9	7	8	13	8	6
Uruguay	na	na	na	na	na	na	na	na	na	na	na	na	na	na	na	na
Venezuela	na	na	na	na	na	na	na	na	na	na	na	na	na	na	na	na
Vietnam	na	27	4	49	23	32	22	29	28	13	24	29	27	31	28	21
Zimbabwe	na	7	1	11	3	8	12	7	6	14	4	5	9	6	7	5
Total	2	4	1	7	3	5	3	5	4	4	4	5	4	4	4	4

RANKING

Country	2000
Vietnam	27
Tanzania	23
China	15
Bangladesh	13
Uganda	12
Albania	9
Philippines	9
United States	8
South Africa	8
Zimbabwe	7
Algeria	6
India	6
Peru	5
Northern Ireland	5
Slovakia	5
Canada	5
Chile	5
Korea, South	4
Macedonia	4
Mexico	3
Belgium	3
Greece	3
Finland	3
Ireland	3
Moldova	3
Austria	2
Luxembourg	2
Iceland	2
Netherlands	2
Croatia	2
Sweden	2
Bosnia and Herz.	2
Germany	2
Estonia	2
Malta	2
Puerto Rico	2
Slovenia	1
Great Britain	1
Japan	1
Montenegro	1
Czech Republic	1
Denmark	1
Bulgaria	1
Belarus	1
Spain	1
Argentina	1
Poland	1
Singapore	1
Italy	0
Serbia	0
Latvia	0
Russian Fed.	0
Ukraine	0
Hungary	0
Lithuania	0
Turkey	0
France	0
Portugal	0
Romania	0
Total	4

A093) UNPAID WORK PEACE MOVEMENT

And for which, if any, are you currently doing unpaid voluntary work? Peace movement.

Belong (%)

(WVS: V66; EVS: V42)

Country	Wave 1990	Wave 2000	Gender Male	Gender Female	Age 16-29	Age 30-49	Age 50+	Education Lower	Education Middle	Education Upper	Income Lower	Income Middle	Income Upper	Values Mat	Values Mixed	Values Postm.
Albania	na	3	4	3	4	3	3	2	3	7	4	2	3	3	3	10
Algeria	na	na	na	na	na	na	na	na	na	na	na	na	na	na	na	na
Argentina	0	0	1	na	na	1	na	na	na	na	na	na	na	na	na	1
Armenia	na	na	na	na	na	na	na	na	na	na	na	na	na	na	na	na
Australia	na	na	na	na	na	na	na	na	na	na	na	na	na	na	na	na
Austria	0	0	na	na	na	na	na	na	na	1	na	na	na	na	na	na
Azerbaijan	na	na	na	na	na	na	na	na	na	na	na	na	na	na	na	na
Bangladesh	na	27	34	18	25	27	35	23	29	37	18	29	33	25	29	26
Belarus	na	1	1	1	1	2	na	1	1	1	1	1	na	1	1	na
Belgium	1	1	1	1	1	1	1	1	1	2	1	2	1	na	1	1
Bosnia and Herz.	na	0	na	na	na	na	na	na	na	na	na	na	na	na	na	na
Brazil	1	na	na	na	na	na	na	na	na	na	na	na	na	na	na	na
Bulgaria	1	0	na	1	na	1	na	na	na	2	1	1	na	na	1	3
Canada	2	1	1	1	na	1	1	1	1	1	1	1	1	1	1	2
Chile	1	2	2	2	2	3	2	1	2	4	1	3	4	1	3	2
China	0	16	18	14	17	17	12	11	20	26	12	18	19	15	19	41
Colombia	na	na	na	na	na	na	na	na	na	na	na	na	na	na	na	na
Croatia	na	1	1	na	1	na	na	na	1	1	na	1	1	na	1	na
Czech Republic	na	0	na	na	na	na	na	na	na	na	na	1	na	na	na	na
Denmark	0	0	0	0	0	0	1	1	0	0	1	0	0	0	0	1
Dominican Rep.	na	na	na	na	na	na	na	na	na	na	na	na	na	na	na	na
Egypt	na	na	na	na	na	na	na	na	na	na	na	na	na	na	na	na
El Salvador	na	na	na	na	na	na	na	na	na	na	na	na	na	na	na	na
Estonia	1	0	1	na	1	na	na	na	na	na	na	na	1	na	na	na
Finland	1	1	1	1	1	2	1	1	1	3	na	2	1	na	1	4
France	1	0	na	na	na	na	na	na	na	1	na	na	1	na	na	na
Georgia	na	na	na	na	na	na	na	na	na	na	na	na	na	na	na	na
Germany	1	0	na	na	na	na	na	na	na	na	na	na	na	na	na	na
Great Britain	na	4	3	6	4	2	6	2	4	6	5	2	6	na	na	na
Greece	na	5	5	6	7	4	4	5	6	5	6	6	5	5	5	10
Hungary	0	0	1	ña	na	1	na	na	na	2	na	na	1	na	1	na
Iceland	0	0	na	na	na	na	na	na	na	na	na	na	na	na	na	na
India	na	4	5	3	4	5	3	4	3	5	7	4	3	2	7	4
Indonesia	na	na	na	na	na	na	na	na	na	na	na	na	na	na	na	na
Iran	na	na	na	na	na	na	na	na	na	na	na	na	na	na	na	na
Ireland	0	1	1	1	na	na	2	1	na	2	2	na	1	1	na	3
Israel	na	na	na	na	na	na	na	na	na	na	na	na	na	na	na	na
Italy	1	1	1	1	1	1	1	1	1	1	1	2	1	na	1	1
Japan	1	1	1	1	na	1	1	1	1	na	1	na	1	na	1	1
Jordan	na	na	na	na	na	na	na	na	na	na	na	na	na	na	na	na
Korea, South	2	2	2	2	2	2	3	2	2	2	2	1	2	1	2	na
Latvia	1	0	na	na	na	na	na	na	na	na	na	na	na	na	na	na
Lithuania	1	0	na	na	na	na	na	na	na	na	na	1	na	na	na	na
Luxembourg	na	1	2	1	2	1	2	1	1	3	1	1	2	2	1	2
Macedonia	na	3	3	3	3	4	2	4	2	3	2	4	3	1	3	6
Malta	na	1	na	na	1	na	na	na	na	2	na	na	1	na	1	2
Mexico	1	3	3	3	3	3	3	3	3	3	3	4	2	4	5	1
Moldova	na	2	2	2	2	2	2	1	3	2	1	3	2	1	3	2
Montenegro	na	1	na	1	1	1	1	na	1	1	na	na	1	na	1	na
Morocco	na	na	na	na	na	na	na	na	na	na	na	na	na	na	na	na
Netherlands	1	1	na	1	1	na	1	1	1	1	1	1	na	na	1	1
New Zealand	na	na	na	na	na	na	na	na	na	na	na	na	na	na	na	na
Nigeria	na	na	na	na	na	na	na	na	na	na	na	na	na	na	na	na
Northern Ireland	0	5	2	9	9	9	2	7	4	5	5	na	12	na	6	8
Norway	0	na	na	na	na	na	na	na	na	na	na	na	na	na	na	na
Pakistan	na	na	na	na	na	na	na	na	na	na	na	na	na	na	na	na
Peru	na	0	na	na	1	1	na	1	na	na	1	na	na	na	na	1
Philippines	na	11	15	6	8	11	14	11	8	14	8	10	13	10	11	7
Poland	na	na	na	na	na	na	na	na	na	na	na	na	na	na	na	na
Portugal	0	0	na	na	na	na	na	na	na	1	na	na	1	na	na	na
Puerto Rico	na	1	1	1	1	1	1	1	na	1	1	1	2	1	1	1
Romania	0	0	0	0	0	0	0	0	0	0	0	0	0	0	0	0
Russian Fed.	1	na	na	na	na	na	na	na	na	na	na	na	na	na	na	na
Serbia	na	na	na	na	na	na	na	na	na	na	na	na	na	na	na	na
Singapore	na	1	1	1	1	na	na	1	1	na	1	1	1	1	1	na
Slovakia	na	0	na	na	na	na	na	na	na	na	na	na	na	na	na	na
Slovenia	0	1	1	1	1	na	1	1	na	na	na	1	1	1	na	1
South Africa	na	4	3	5	3	5	2	4	4	2	4	4	3	3	4	4
Spain	1	1	na	1	1	na	1	na	na	2	1	na	na	na	na	2
Sweden	2	0	1	na	1	na	1	1	na	1	na	1	na	na	na	1
Switzerland	na	na	na	na	na	na	na	na	na	na	na	na	na	na	na	na
Taiwan	na	na	na	na	na	na	na	na	na	na	na	na	na	na	na	na
Tanzania	na	4	4	5	5	4	4	4	5	6	5	5	3	2	5	4
Turkey	na	0	na	na	na	na	na	na	na	na	na	na	na	na	na	na
Uganda	na	6	11	2	6	6	3	7	5	12	9	7	6	6	6	8
Ukraine	na	na	na	na	na	na	na	na	na	na	na	na	na	na	na	na
United States	1	2	2	2	3	1	3	1	2	3	2	2	2	1	2	2
Uruguay	na	na	na	na	na	na	na	na	na	na	na	na	na	na	na	na
Venezuela	na	na	na	na	na	na	na	na	na	na	na	na	na	na	na	na
Vietnam	na	7	8	6	8	7	6	6	7	12	6	8	6	6	7	14
Zimbabwe	na	1	2	na	1	1	2	na	2	14	1	1	4	1	2	na
Total	1	2	3	2	3	3	2	2	2	3	2	3	3	2	2	2

RANKING

Country	2000
Bangladesh	27
China	16
Philippines	11
Vietnam	7
Uganda	6
Greece	5
Northern Ireland	5
Great Britain	4
Tanzania	4
India	4
South Africa	4
Albania	3
Mexico	3
Macedonia	3
Chile	2
Moldova	2
United States	2
Korea, South	2
Luxembourg	1
Finland	1
Belgium	1
Zimbabwe	1
Belarus	1
Canada	1
Puerto Rico	1
Italy	1
Ireland	1
Japan	1
Singapore	1
Croatia	1
Netherlands	1
Slovenia	1
Montenegro	1
Malta	1
Spain	1
Bulgaria	0
Estonia	0
Hungary	0
Peru	0
Sweden	0
Argentina	0
France	0
Bosnia and Herz.	0
Czech Republic	0
Austria	0
Germany	0
Iceland	0
Latvia	0
Lithuania	0
Portugal	0
Slovakia	0
Turkey	0
Denmark	0
Total	2

A094) UNPAID WORK CONCERNED WITH HEALTH

And for which, if any, are you currently doing unpaid voluntary work? Voluntary organizations concerned with health.

Belong (%)

(WVS: V67; EVS: V43)

Country	Wave 1990	Wave 2000	Gender Male	Gender Female	Age 16-29	Age 30-49	Age 50+	Education Lower	Education Middle	Education Upper	Income Lower	Income Middle	Income Upper	Values Mat	Values Mixed	Values Postm.
Albania	na	8	7	9	7	8	11	9	9	6	9	10	6	10	8	3
Algeria	na	na	na	na	na	na	na	na	na	na	na	na	na	na	na	na
Argentina	2	2	1	3	1	3	2	1	3	6	3	2	2	1	2	3
Armenia	na	na	na	na	na	na	na	na	na	na	na	na	na	na	na	na
Australia	na	na	na	na	na	na	na	na	na	na	na	na	na	na	na	na
Austria	2	3	2	3	3	2	3	2	3	2	3	3	1	1	3	3
Azerbaijan	na	na	na	na	na	na	na	na	na	na	na	na	na	na	na	na
Bangladesh	na	22	27	16	22	22	20	16	25	33	11	25	27	19	24	22
Belarus	na	3	3	2	5	3	2	1	4	2	2	3	2	1	5	3
Belgium	2	5	5	6	4	4	6	4	4	7	4	6	5	5	5	5
Bosnia and Herz.	na	2	2	1	2	2	1	1	1	4	2	1	4	1	2	na
Brazil	2	na	na	na	na	na	na	na	na	na	na	na	na	na	na	na
Bulgaria	2	1	1	1	1	1	na	na	na	3	na	1	1	1	1	na
Canada	7	8	7	9	5	8	12	7	8	10	7	9	9	8	8	11
Chile	2	3	2	3	2	2	4	4	2	3	3	1	5	3	3	3
China	2	24	23	25	28	25	19	21	27	16	19	26	30	24	25	38
Colombia	na	na	na	na	na	na	na	na	na	na	na	na	na	na	na	na
Croatia	na	2	2	2	1	2	2	2	1	4	1	1	3	2	1	2
Czech Republic	na	3	2	4	2	4	3	3	3	5	3	3	3	4	3	4
Denmark	1	1	1	1	1	1	1	0	2	1	1	1	1	3	1	1
Dominican Rep.	na	na	na	na	na	na	na	na	na	na	na	na	na	na	na	na
Egypt	na	na	na	na	na	na	na	na	na	na	na	na	na	na	na	na
El Salvador	na	na	na	na	na	na	na	na	na	na	na	na	na	na	na	na
Estonia	1	1	na	1	1	1	na	na	1	2	na	na	1	1	na	na
Finland	4	6	5	7	3	5	9	5	7	8	6	6	6	7	6	3
France	2	2	2	2	2	1	2	2	1	1	2	2	1	1	2	1
Georgia	na	na	na	na	na	na	na	na	na	na	na	na	na	na	na	na
Germany	2	1	2	1	3	na	2	1	2	na	1	1	1	1	1	1
Great Britain	na	10	9	11	5	10	13	9	9	13	8	5	14	na	na	na
Greece	na	6	4	7	6	6	4	7	5	6	5	7	7	7	5	8
Hungary	2	1	1	1	na	3	1	1	1	4	1	2	1	1	1	4
Iceland	4	2	1	2	na	2	3	3	na	4	2	1	2	2	2	1
India	na	7	8	6	8	7	7	5	8	11	5	6	9	6	10	11
Indonesia	na	na	na	na	na	na	na	na	na	na	na	na	na	na	na	na
Iran	na	na	na	na	na	na	na	na	na	na	na	na	na	na	na	na
Ireland	2	3	2	4	1	3	4	3	2	5	3	3	4	1	3	6
Israel	na	na	na	na	na	na	na	na	na	na	na	na	na	na	na	na
Italy	2	3	3	3	3	3	3	2	3	5	3	4	4	2	3	4
Japan	1	2	1	2	na	na	3	3	2	1	1	2	2	2	1	5
Jordan	na	na	na	na	na	na	na	na	na	na	na	na	na	na	na	na
Korea, South	3	na	na	na	na	na	na	na	na	na	na	na	na	na	na	na
Latvia	2	1	na	1	na	1	1	na	na	2	1	1	na	1	1	na
Lithuania	1	1	na	1	na	1	na	na	1	1	na	1	1	na	na	3
Luxembourg	na	3	2	4	2	2	5	3	3	4	2	3	3	3	3	3
Macedonia	na	5	4	5	4	6	3	4	5	7	4	7	3	2	6	8
Malta	na	2	2	2	3	1	2	1	2	5	na	2	3	1	2	5
Mexico	1	5	4	6	4	7	4	5	5	7	4	7	7	6	6	3
Moldova	na	4	3	4	4	3	4	2	4	6	3	5	4	3	4	6
Montenegro	na	3	3	2	4	3	2	1	3	3	1	3	4	2	2	2
Morocco	na	na	na	na	na	na	na	na	na	na	na	na	na	na	na	na
Netherlands	3	7	5	9	3	5	11	9	6	7	7	6	8	7	8	5
New Zealand	na	na	na	na	na	na	na	na	na	na	na	na	na	na	na	na
Nigeria	na	na	na	na	na	na	na	na	na	na	na	na	na	na	na	na
Northern Ireland	2	15	11	19	13	11	19	15	10	24	20	11	21	25	18	na
Norway	3	na	na	na	na	na	na	na	na	na	na	na	na	na	na	na
Pakistan	na	na	na	na	na	na	na	na	na	na	na	na	na	na	na	na
Peru	na	4	3	4	4	4	4	2	5	4	3	4	4	2	4	6
Philippines	na	9	10	8	8	10	9	7	8	13	9	8	12	8	10	9
Poland	na	1	1	1	na	1	1	na	1	3	1	1	na	na	1	2
Portugal	2	1	1	1	na	2	1	1	1	1	na	2	na	na	1	2
Puerto Rico	na	3	3	4	na	5	3	9	na	4	3	3	5	5	3	3
Romania	0	1	0	1	1	1	0	0	1	1	0	1	1	0	1	1
Russian Fed.	1	0	na	1	na	na	na	na	na	1	na	na	na	na	na	na
Serbia	na	0	1	na	na	na	na	na	na	1	na	1	1	1	na	na
Singapore	na	4	3	6	5	4	1	4	5	2	3	4	5	2	6	1
Slovakia	na	4	3	4	4	4	3	1	4	9	3	3	4	3	4	9
Slovenia	1	2	2	2	1	2	3	2	1	6	1	2	4	1	2	3
South Africa	na	5	4	7	7	3	6	4	7	5	4	9	3	7	4	4
Spain	1	2	1	2	2	1	1	1	2	3	2	1	3	1	2	2
Sweden	1	3	3	3	2	3	3	3	2	3	3	na	4	3	2	6
Switzerland	na	na	na	na	na	na	na	na	na	na	na	na	na	na	na	na
Taiwan	na	na	na	na	na	na	na	na	na	na	na	na	na	na	na	na
Tanzania	na	21	20	23	24	20	20	19	22	29	19	23	25	16	24	25
Turkey	na	0	na	na	na	1	1	na	na	2	na	na	1	1	na	na
Uganda	na	10	12	8	10	10	6	6	10	16	8	12	14	9	9	11
Ukraine	na	1	1	1	na	1	1	1	na	1	1	1	1	1	1	na
United States	5	11	8	14	10	11	13	8	10	13	10	12	12	14	11	11
Uruguay	na	na	na	na	na	na	na	na	na	na	na	na	na	na	na	na
Venezuela	na	na	na	na	na	na	na	na	na	na	na	na	na	na	na	na
Vietnam	na	15	17	14	12	15	18	13	17	25	19	14	15	17	17	13
Zimbabwe	na	3	3	2	2	2	6	2	3	na	3	2	4	2	3	7
Total	2	5	5	5	5	5	5	4	5	6	4	5	6	4	5	5

RANKING

Country	2000
China	24
Bangladesh	22
Tanzania	21
Vietnam	15
Northern Ireland	15
United States	11
Great Britain	10
Uganda	10
Philippines	9
Canada	8
Albania	8
India	7
Netherlands	7
Finland	6
Greece	6
Mexico	5
Belgium	5
South Africa	5
Macedonia	5
Singapore	4
Moldova	4
Peru	4
Slovakia	4
Puerto Rico	3
Czech Republic	3
Luxembourg	3
Chile	3
Italy	3
Belarus	3
Ireland	3
Zimbabwe	3
Sweden	3
Austria	3
Montenegro	3
Argentina	2
Slovenia	2
Iceland	2
Bosnia and Herz.	2
Croatia	2
France	2
Malta	2
Japan	2
Spain	2
Germany	1
Hungary	1
Denmark	1
Romania	1
Portugal	1
Bulgaria	1
Estonia	1
Poland	1
Ukraine	1
Latvia	1
Lithuania	1
Serbia	0
Russian Fed.	0
Turkey	0
Total	5

A096_1) UNPAID WORK OTHER GROUPS

And for which, if any, are you currently doing unpaid voluntary work? Other social groups.

Belong (%) (WVS: V67B; EVS: V44)

Country	Wave 1990	Wave 2000	Male	Female	16-29	30-49	50+	Education Lower	Middle	Upper	Income Lower	Middle	Upper	Mat	Mixed	Postm.
Albania	na	na	na	na	na	na	na	na	na	na	na	na	na	na	na	na
Algeria	na	na	na	na	na	na	na	na	na	na	na	na	na	na	na	na
Argentina	2	2	2	2	2	2	2	1	3	2	1	2	3	1	1	4
Armenia	na	na	na	na	na	na	na	na	na	na	na	na	na	na	na	na
Australia	na	na	na	na	na	na	na	na	na	na	na	na	na	na	na	na
Austria	3	4	6	2	2	5	4	4	5	3	3	5	4	2	5	4
Azerbaijan	na	na	na	na	na	na	na	na	na	na	na	na	na	na	na	na
Bangladesh	na	2	2	2	2	2	2	1	2	4	1	2	2	2	2	3
Belarus	na	2	4	1	3	2	1	na	3	2	1	3	2	1	3	na
Belgium	3	8	9	6	5	9	8	5	7	11	5	7	11	7	8	9
Bosnia and Herz.	na	na	na	na	na	na	na	na	na	na	na	na	na	na	na	na
Brazil	0	na	na	na	na	na	na	na	na	na	na	na	na	na	na	na
Bulgaria	2	2	2	2	1	2	2	1	1	4	2	1	1	1	2	na
Canada	9	8	8	8	4	9	9	6	9	8	8	7	10	7	8	10
Chile	3	na	na	na	na	na	na	na	na	na	na	na	na	na	na	na
China	2	2	1	2	1	1	3	2	1	2	2	1	1	1	1	na
Colombia	na	na	na	na	na	na	na	na	na	na	na	na	na	na	na	na
Croatia	na	3	6	1	1	3	5	1	5	4	3	4	2	2	4	3
Czech Republic	na	4	7	3	4	3	6	4	4	8	4	4	5	4	5	2
Denmark	4	7	8	5	5	8	6	5	7	10	6	5	10	6	7	5
Dominican Rep.	na	na	na	na	na	na	na	na	na	na	na	na	na	na	na	na
Egypt	na	na	na	na	na	na	na	na	na	na	na	na	na	na	na	na
El Salvador	na	na	na	na	na	na	na	na	na	na	na	na	na	na	na	na
Estonia	2	3	4	2	3	4	2	2	3	4	2	3	4	3	3	na
Finland	7	8	8	8	4	8	10	8	6	11	6	10	7	9	8	4
France	4	6	6	6	5	5	8	6	5	7	4	7	7	6	6	5
Georgia	na	na	na	na	na	na	na	na	na	na	na	na	na	na	na	na
Germany	4	3	3	2	2	2	3	3	2	3	3	3	2	2	3	3
Great Britain	na	na	na	na	na	na	na	na	na	na	na	na	na	na	na	na
Greece	na	5	5	4	4	4	4	2	5	5	4	4	6	5	4	7
Hungary	1	2	3	1	2	2	2	2	1	3	2	3	1	2	2	na
Iceland	4	2	1	2	na	2	3	1	1	3	2	1	2	2	2	1
India	na	5	7	4	5	5	6	3	8	8	4	4	8	4	8	13
Indonesia	na	na	na	na	na	na	na	na	na	na	na	na	na	na	na	na
Iran	na	na	na	na	na	na	na	na	na	na	na	na	na	na	na	na
Ireland	2	4	4	4	4	3	5	3	4	6	5	4	4	5	5	3
Israel	na	na	na	na	na	na	na	na	na	na	na	na	na	na	na	na
Italy	2	2	2	1	1	2	1	1	2	3	2	2	2	1	2	2
Japan	4	na	na	na	na	na	na	na	na	na	na	na	na	na	na	na
Jordan	na	na	na	na	na	na	na	na	na	na	na	na	na	na	na	na
Korea, South	3	na	na	na	na	na	na	na	na	na	na	na	na	na	na	na
Latvia	2	5	7	3	7	4	5	4	4	8	5	6	4	3	6	11
Lithuania	2	2	2	2	2	4	1	na	3	5	2	2	3	1	3	3
Luxembourg	na	2	3	1	2	1	2	1	3	3	1	2	3	2	2	2
Macedonia	na	na	na	na	na	na	na	na	na	na	na	na	na	na	na	na
Malta	na	2	2	2	3	2	2	na	2	4	3	1	3	1	2	5
Mexico	1	na	na	na	na	na	na	na	na	na	na	na	na	na	na	na
Moldova	na	na	na	na	na	na	na	na	na	na	na	na	na	na	na	na
Montenegro	na	na	na	na	na	na	na	na	na	na	na	na	na	na	na	na
Morocco	na	na	na	na	na	na	na	na	na	na	na	na	na	na	na	na
Netherlands	5	6	8	5	5	5	9	6	6	7	5	8	6	11	5	9
New Zealand	na	na	na	na	na	na	na	na	na	na	na	na	na	na	na	na
Nigeria	na	na	na	na	na	na	na	na	na	na	na	na	na	na	na	na
Northern Ireland	2	20	16	23	20	25	16	23	22	13	21	23	10	26	17	22
Norway	7	na	na	na	na	na	na	na	na	na	na	na	na	na	na	na
Pakistan	na	na	na	na	na	na	na	na	na	na	na	na	na	na	na	na
Peru	na	0	na	na	na	na	na	na	na	na	na	na	1	na	na	na
Philippines	na	na	na	na	na	na	na	na	na	na	na	na	na	na	na	na
Poland	na	2	3	2	2	2	3	2	2	4	3	1	1	2	2	na
Portugal	2	3	3	2	2	2	3	3	2	3	3	3	3	1	3	4
Puerto Rico	na	3	4	3	4	2	3	na	2	4	2	3	4	5	2	5
Romania	2	1	2	1	2	1	1	1	1	4	1	1	3	1	2	5
Russian Fed.	2	1	1	1	1	1	na	na	1	2	1	1	1	1	1	na
Serbia	na	na	na	na	na	na	na	na	na	na	na	na	na	na	na	na
Singapore	na	na	na	na	na	na	na	na	na	na	na	na	na	na	na	na
Slovakia	na	6	8	4	6	6	6	3	8	6	7	7	6	6	6	7
Slovenia	3	6	9	3	7	5	6	7	6	4	4	6	4	8	5	8
South Africa	na	na	na	na	na	na	na	na	na	na	na	na	na	na	na	na
Spain	1	2	2	3	3	3	1	2	2	5	3	2	4	2	2	5
Sweden	9	10	12	8	10	11	10	10	9	12	9	10	12	8	10	11
Switzerland	na	na	na	na	na	na	na	na	na	na	na	na	na	na	na	na
Taiwan	na	na	na	na	na	na	na	na	na	na	na	na	na	na	na	na
Tanzania	na	na	na	na	na	na	na	na	na	na	na	na	na	na	na	na
Turkey	na	1	2	1	1	na	3	na	2	4	na	1	3	1	1	2
Uganda	na	na	na	na	na	na	na	na	na	na	na	na	na	na	na	na
Ukraine	na	1	2	1	na	1	1	na	1	1	1	1	1	na	2	3
United States	6	15	19	11	14	14	17	11	13	18	12	14	19	9	16	16
Uruguay	na	na	na	na	na	na	na	na	na	na	na	na	na	na	na	na
Venezuela	na	na	na	na	na	na	na	na	na	na	na	na	na	na	na	na
Vietnam	na	na	na	na	na	na	na	na	na	na	na	na	na	na	na	na
Zimbabwe	na	na	na	na	na	na	na	na	na	na	na	na	na	na	na	na
Total	3	4	5	3	4	4	5	3	4	6	4	4	5	3	5	6

RANKING

Country	2000
Northern Ireland	20
United States	15
Sweden	10
Canada	8
Finland	8
Belgium	8
Denmark	7
Netherlands	6
France	6
Slovakia	6
Slovenia	6
India	5
Latvia	5
Greece	5
Czech Republic	4
Ireland	4
Austria	4
Croatia	3
Estonia	3
Puerto Rico	3
Germany	3
Portugal	3
Spain	2
Lithuania	2
Bangladesh	2
Poland	2
Argentina	2
Belarus	2
Luxembourg	2
Malta	2
Hungary	2
Bulgaria	2
Iceland	2
China	2
Italy	2
Turkey	1
Romania	1
Ukraine	1
Russian Fed.	1
Peru	0
Total	4

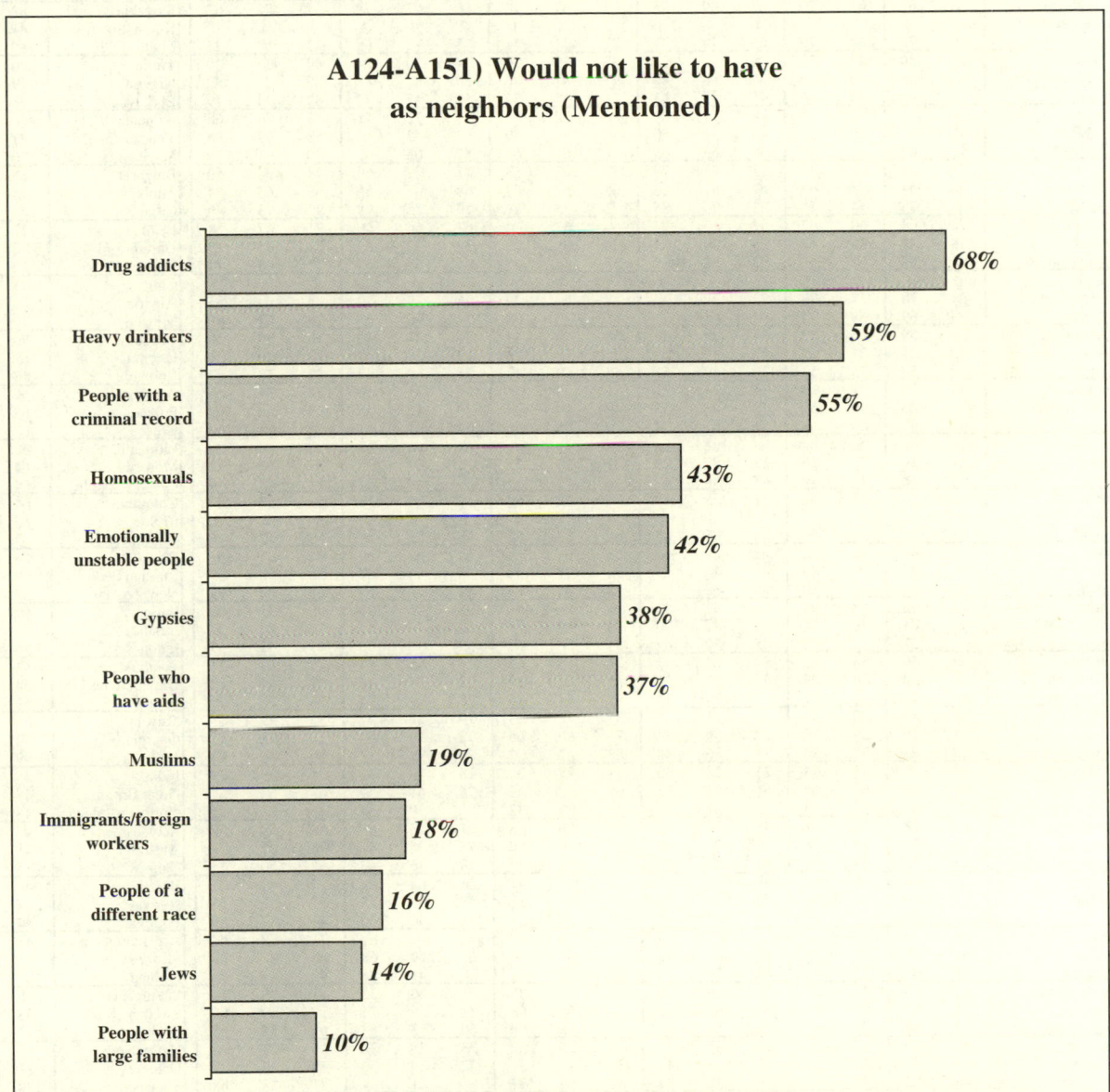

A124-A151) Would not like to have as neighbors (Mentioned)

Category	Percentage
Drug addicts	68%
Heavy drinkers	59%
People with a criminal record	55%
Homosexuals	43%
Emotionally unstable people	42%
Gypsies	38%
People who have aids	37%
Muslims	19%
Immigrants/foreign workers	18%
People of a different race	16%
Jews	14%
People with large families	10%

A124) NEIGHBORS: PEOPLE WITH A CRIMINAL RECORD

On this list are various groups of people. Could you please sort out any that you would not like to have as neighbors?

People with a criminal record (%)   (WVS: V68; EVS: V52)

Country	Wave 1990	Wave 2000	Gender Male	Female	Age 16-29	30-49	50+	Education Lower	Middle	Upper	Income Lower	Middle	Upper	Values Mat	Mixed	Postm.
Albania	na	97	97	97	97	97	98	98	97	96	98	96	97	98	96	97
Algeria	na	70	69	71	65	72	77	75	71	66	70	71	70	73	70	64
Argentina	41	43	43	44	35	42	53	46	39	43	44	42	44	49	44	38
Armenia	na	78	73	83	75	78	83	77	78	77	78	77	82	78	78	79
Australia	na	45	45	45	41	45	50	48	45	43	48	44	43	58	48	39
Austria	32	27	25	29	21	23	33	30	23	24	29	25	25	44	28	19
Azerbaijan	na	69	67	70	65	69	75	77	67	70	60	67	77	67	72	62
Bangladesh	na	4	3	5	4	4	3	4	2	6	2	4	4	3	4	4
Belarus	72	72	68	76	65	74	77	77	71	71	75	72	68	77	68	75
Belgium	28	30	27	33	28	26	35	37	29	26	34	30	24	40	28	20
Bosnia and Herz.	na	88	86	90	86	88	89	91	87	88	89	87	88	85	89	89
Brazil	52	45	44	46	45	45	45	41	45	56	42	47	48	45	44	49
Bulgaria	70	75	72	77	70	71	81	80	72	71	77	72	75	73	76	68
Canada	42	45	39	51	45	41	50	50	41	49	42	42	46	58	47	38
Chile	46	63	59	65	58	63	65	61	64	61	57	65	67	70	61	55
China	41	71	67	75	57	73	79	77	67	63	72	72	69	74	66	59
Colombia	na	64	61	66	69	61	60	68	67	57	68	67	56	66	65	64
Croatia	na	74	74	75	62	73	85	72	75	77	70	75	78	90	73	70
Czech Republic	72	64	60	67	52	62	72	66	62	60	67	64	60	71	62	58
Denmark	28	31	29	32	25	29	35	36	28	23	32	27	35	34	35	15
Dominican Rep.	na	62	62	63	63	62	64	56	58	65	64	65	69	51	63	74
Egypt	na	3	3	3	3	2	4	3	3	3	3	3	2	2	3	5
El Salvador	na	78	77	79	79	79	78	77	80	79	76	79	79	na	na	na
Estonia	63	69	63	74	62	68	74	68	70	68	72	76	63	73	67	69
Finland	34	39	36	42	34	39	43	38	40	44	36	41	40	50	39	20
France	20	21	21	21	17	17	27	25	18	13	22	22	19	32	20	9
Georgia	na	50	45	53	39	49	61	53	50	47	51	49	48	52	48	47
Germany	35	25	21	28	16	23	31	31	22	15	31	25	19	34	24	15
Great Britain	41	48	46	51	38	48	53	49	50	38	49	45	48	na	na	na
Greece	na	67	66	68	61	67	78	70	65	68	64	71	67	73	67	62
Hungary	77	na	na	na	na	na	na	na	na	na	na	na	na	na	na	na
Iceland	24	26	26	26	29	22	28	27	25	25	25	24	26	33	26	12
India	93	48	47	49	48	48	47	40	55	59	30	49	57	51	48	44
Indonesia	na	56	55	57	51	55	58	59	52	60	49	60	58	57	55	57
Iran	na	1	1	2	1	2	1	1	2	2	1	1	2	na	2	1
Ireland	52	56	53	59	43	56	65	61	53	52	58	55	55	58	57	48
Israel	na	na	na	na	na	na	na	na	na	na	na	na	na	na	na	na
Italy	48	47	46	49	41	46	52	53	43	46	49	46	47	58	50	39
Japan	50	na	na	na	na	na	na	na	na	na	na	na	na	na	na	na
Jordan	na	96	98	94	96	97	94	97	96	96	96	97	95	96	97	92
Korea, South	31	81	79	84	75	81	90	89	83	78	80	79	84	82	82	72
Latvia	63	57	51	62	45	50	67	51	56	67	58	56	55	61	55	57
Lithuania	69	66	56	75	59	64	73	71	65	63	74	65	67	75	64	51
Luxembourg	na	30	30	29	27	27	34	35	26	27	33	31	24	28	31	22
Macedonia	na	76	76	77	74	79	74	82	73	75	78	77	74	76	76	79
Malta	na	80	80	80	78	75	86	85	77	83	79	82	77	83	79	79
Mexico	69	70	69	70	67	69	74	73	66	66	72	70	67	72	72	57
Moldova	na	83	78	88	79	86	84	87	82	82	86	86	82	86	80	85
Montenegro	na	29	25	33	23	28	35	31	28	30	18	29	34	31	29	29
Morocco	na	64	60	68	61	64	73	66	58	52	75	61	59	68	63	55
Netherlands	28	32	31	33	26	31	36	36	29	32	31	30	33	43	33	25
New Zealand	na	58	53	61	47	54	64	56	59	58	57	53	61	58	58	50
Nigeria	80	79	79	78	78	79	79	77	80	80	78	78	81	75	81	79
Northern Ireland	46	48	44	51	46	44	52	47	50	44	49	46	43	52	50	35
Norway	37	44	40	48	38	41	52	51	40	41	na	na	na	55	45	27
Pakistan	na	58	59	56	58	58	58	57	59	58	58	58	55	57	59	58
Peru	na	53	53	53	50	52	63	54	55	50	58	46	54	47	54	59
Philippines	na	72	70	74	71	70	76	76	71	68	74	72	69	71	72	67
Poland	na	68	68	68	61	68	73	67	69	70	66	69	68	68	67	73
Portugal	59	44	43	44	40	39	51	48	39	22	58	41	35	42	44	41
Puerto Rico	na	36	37	37	34	36	38	44	37	35	38	36	35	41	36	34
Romania	67	69	67	71	65	68	72	71	68	68	71	65	71	70	69	65
Russian Fed.	63	58	52	62	49	56	65	61	56	60	60	58	55	61	54	55
Serbia	na	29	26	32	22	27	35	35	25	30	33	28	30	30	29	24
Singapore	na	30	26	35	23	35	44	35	27	31	32	29	30	39	28	23
Slovakia	na	82	79	84	79	82	84	82	82	81	81	81	84	81	83	68
Slovenia	37	41	42	39	33	42	44	49	38	33	47	39	27	49	39	38
South Africa	na	54	53	55	57	52	50	54	56	40	55	57	49	56	53	52
Spain	36	32	31	34	23	30	40	37	28	26	33	32	33	41	32	22
Sweden	35	33	34	32	28	35	35	35	34	31	34	33	31	50	35	23
Switzerland	7	20	18	22	23	17	22	23	19	24	24	15	23	24	21	17
Taiwan	na	51	49	54	37	50	64	57	45	51	53	47	54	57	48	43
Tanzania	na	89	88	91	91	86	93	89	90	88	87	92	89	89	89	88
Turkey	81	80	77	83	77	81	85	84	77	68	84	77	77	85	80	74
Uganda	na	88	92	84	87	87	99	88	87	94	93	89	83	86	89	92
Ukraine	na	72	66	77	69	69	76	69	73	72	76	66	76	76	72	60
United States	50	54	47	61	48	54	59	53	51	56	48	54	62	60	56	46
Uruguay	na	70	67	72	61	68	75	72	66	66	72	67	70	72	73	64
Venezuela	na	77	77	77	78	76	78	78	78	76	79	72	75	77	77	77
Vietnam	na	49	48	49	51	46	50	52	47	37	55	47	48	63	45	39
Zimbabwe	na	75	74	75	76	75	72	71	80	70	71	74	73	75	76	68
Total	49	55	53	58	53	55	59	56	56	54	57	56	55	61	55	44

RANKING

Country	2000
Albania	97
Jordan	96
Tanzania	89
Uganda	88
Bosnia and Herz.	88
Moldova	83
Slovakia	82
Korea, South	81
Malta	80
Turkey	80
Nigeria	79
El Salvador	78
Armenia	78
Venezuela	77
Macedonia	76
Bulgaria	75
Zimbabwe	75
Croatia	74
Belarus	72
Ukraine	72
Philippines	72
China	71
Algeria	70
Mexico	70
Uruguay	70
Estonia	69
Romania	69
Azerbaijan	69
Poland	68
Greece	67
Lithuania	66
Morocco	64
Czech Republic	64
Colombia	64
Chile	63
Dominican Rep.	62
Pakistan	58
Russian Fed.	58
New Zealand	58
Latvia	57
Ireland	56
Indonesia	56
South Africa	54
United States	54
Peru	53
Taiwan	51
Georgia	50
Vietnam	49
India	48
Great Britain	48
Northern Ireland	48
Italy	47
Australia	45
Canada	45
Brazil	45
Norway	44
Portugal	44
Argentina	43
Slovenia	41
Finland	39
Puerto Rico	36
Sweden	33
Spain	32
Netherlands	32
Denmark	31
Singapore	30
Belgium	30
Luxembourg	30
Serbia	29
Montenegro	29
Austria	27
Iceland	26
Germany	25
France	21
Switzerland	20
Bangladesh	4
Egypt	3
Iran	1
Total	55

A125) NEIGHBORS: PEOPLE OF A DIFFERENT RACE

On this list are various groups of people. Could you please sort out any that you would not like to have as neighbors?

People of a different race (%) (WVS: V69; EVS: V53)

Country	Wave		Gender		Age			Education			Income			Values				RANKING Country	2000
	1990	2000	Male	Female	16-29	30-49	50+	Lower	Middle	Upper	Lower	Middle	Upper	Mat	Mixed	Postm.			
Albania	na	30	26	35	22	35	32	33	32	18	31	34	27	27	30	51		Bangladesh	72
Algeria	na	28	29	27	28	26	32	35	28	24	36	22	23	28	28	29		Egypt	66
Argentina	3	5	5	4	3	3	8	6	3	na	7	4	2	9	4	2		India	42
Armenia	na	19	16	22	17	20	23	24	20	14	15	19	27	22	18	10		Indonesia	35
Australia	na	5	7	3	4	4	7	7	5	3	6	5	4	6	5	5		Korea, South	35
Austria	8	7	7	6	4	6	9	9	4	6	8	8	5	19	7	2		Vietnam	32
Azerbaijan	na	12	12	13	11	12	17	18	12	12	11	14	8	13	11	12		Turkey	32
Bangladesh	na	72	72	71	72	71	75	69	73	77	69	72	74	74	72	79		Albania	30
Belarus	17	17	13	19	9	15	24	26	14	11	19	16	12	20	14	5		Nigeria	30
Belgium	17	17	18	16	13	13	22	25	16	10	22	15	14	22	15	10		Bulgaria	28
Bosnia and Herz.	na	13	13	13	10	15	14	15	13	12	13	15	11	14	14	6		Algeria	28
Brazil	5	3	2	3	1	4	4	5	2	na	5	2	2	2	4	na		Iran	24
Bulgaria	39	28	30	27	28	29	28	32	27	23	31	31	22	34	25	12		Romania	24
Canada	5	3	4	3	2	4	5	6	2	3	5	4	2	5	4	2		South Africa	24
Chile	11	9	9	9	8	9	9	8	9	11	9	9	8	8	9	8		Philippines	21
China	12	15	13	16	8	14	21	18	12	9	15	14	14	12	14	16		Jordan	20
Colombia	na	2	2	2	3	2	2	4	2	1	3	2	1	3	3	1		Zimbabwe	20
Croatia	na	20	18	21	16	22	19	20	21	14	18	20	20	23	21	11		Croatia	20
Czech Republic	31	10	11	9	7	10	12	12	9	4	12	10	8	14	9	7		Armenia	19
Denmark	7	7	9	6	4	5	11	11	5	3	9	7	4	13	9	na		Montenegro	19
Dominican Rep.	na	19	14	22	19	17	27	28	23	16	20	13	15	22	18	15		Macedonia	19
Egypt	na	66	67	65	66	66	66	65	62	74	62	66	69	63	68	70		Malta	19
El Salvador	na	na	na	na	na	na	na	na	na	na	na	na	na	na	na	na		Dominican Rep.	19
Estonia	19	15	16	15	12	15	17	22	13	11	20	17	10	15	16	4		Uganda	18
Finland	25	12	16	9	14	12	12	14	11	7	13	14	12	20	11	3		Poland	17
France	9	9	10	8	7	7	12	12	6	3	12	9	7	15	8	2		Taiwan	17
Georgia	na	10	12	7	11	8	10	10	9	9	9	9	11	8	10	15		Slovakia	17
Germany	12	5	4	5	2	4	7	8	3	2	7	6	3	8	3	3		Tanzania	17
Great Britain	9	9	9	9	7	7	10	11	7	6	7	9	7	na	na	na		Belgium	17
Greece	na	14	16	13	14	10	24	23	17	11	14	14	13	14	16	8		Belarus	17
Hungary	23	na	na	na	na	na	na	na	na	na	na	na	na	na	na	na		Italy	16
Iceland	8	3	4	2	2	3	5	4	3	1	5	2	3	3	3	3		Venezuela	16
India	35	42	42	41	42	41	43	47	41	33	51	42	37	44	38	29		Estonia	15
Indonesia	na	35	34	36	31	35	37	43	38	26	39	33	29	40	33	25		Mexico	15
Iran	na	24	24	25	25	26	20	19	25	29	20	28	28	22	23	28		China	15
Ireland	6	12	11	13	6	8	19	20	8	8	22	11	5	10	13	9		Greece	14
Israel	na	na	na	na	na	na	na	na	na	na	na	na	na	na	na	na		Bosnia and Herz.	13
Italy	13	16	16	15	14	10	22	21	13	7	23	11	8	24	16	10		Finland	12
Japan	11	na	na	na	na	na	na	na	na	na	na	na	na	na	na	na		Azerbaijan	12
Jordan	na	20	20	20	20	19	22	25	15	16	20	22	20	23	19	13		Ireland	12
Korea, South	58	35	35	34	18	34	56	61	41	23	37	33	33	39	33	15		Slovenia	12
Latvia	13	5	5	5	2	2	8	6	4	6	7	3	3	4	5	6		Morocco	11
Lithuania	20	10	8	11	10	6	13	14	9	6	10	9	10	11	9	10		Peru	11
Luxembourg	na	6	5	7	5	5	9	9	5	4	11	5	2	10	6	3		Northern Ireland	11
Macedonia	na	19	21	17	16	20	21	21	20	13	24	17	15	19	20	12		Moldova	11
Malta	na	19	16	21	11	15	27	28	16	11	23	16	14	23	16	15		Spain	11
Mexico	17	15	13	17	9	16	21	21	8	9	20	13	11	16	14	12		Ukraine	11
Moldova	na	11	11	11	12	11	10	13	12	8	13	11	10	10	9	18		Czech Republic	10
Montenegro	na	19	16	22	13	18	24	26	14	14	14	18	17	18	21	18		Lithuania	10
Morocco	na	11	10	13	10	13	13	12	9	4	25	7	11	12	11	7		Georgia	10
Netherlands	6	5	5	5	1	2	10	9	3	4	6	4	4	16	4	2		Chile	9
New Zealand	na	3	5	2	4	3	2	5	2	2	4	2	3	5	2	2		France	9
Nigeria	31	30	30	30	30	31	29	32	31	27	31	34	27	32	28	38		Switzerland	9
Northern Ireland	7	11	12	11	11	10	9	12	12	9	11	6	5	10	10	17		Great Britain	9
Norway	12	8	10	7	5	6	13	12	7	5	na	na	na	15	8	2		Norway	8
Pakistan	na	7	7	7	6	7	7	6	7	7	5	7	7	7	6	na		Russian Fed.	8
Peru	na	11	12	11	13	9	12	15	10	10	13	11	9	14	12	5		United States	8
Philippines	na	21	21	22	17	23	25	27	20	17	27	17	21	22	21	20		Portugal	8
Poland	na	17	16	18	7	15	26	22	13	7	20	15	17	21	16	15		Denmark	7
Portugal	16	8	9	7	9	6	8	8	8	3	13	11	4	7	6	11		Uruguay	7
Puerto Rico	na	4	5	4	3	5	4	3	7	4	5	4	5	5	3	5		Austria	7
Romania	28	24	22	26	14	21	33	39	19	9	37	24	14	28	20	11		Pakistan	7
Russian Fed.	11	8	8	8	8	8	9	10	9	6	9	9	7	7	9	10		Luxembourg	6
Serbia	na	6	5	7	4	4	10	12	3	3	8	5	5	8	4	na		Serbia	6
Singapore	na	5	5	5	4	4	8	4	5	3	6	4	5	4	5	4		Netherlands	5
Slovakia	na	17	19	16	17	15	19	18	17	16	20	15	15	17	17	10		Australia	5
Slovenia	40	12	12	12	6	11	18	22	9	6	14	11	5	19	10	11		Germany	5
South Africa	na	24	24	23	17	28	29	24	24	21	25	23	21	24	23	23		Latvia	5
Spain	12	11	10	12	5	10	16	15	7	7	12	10	12	15	11	6		Singapore	5
Sweden	7	3	4	1	2	1	4	2	3	2	3	2	2	4	3	1		Argentina	5
Switzerland	2	9	10	8	7	6	13	13	8	8	11	7	8	8	11	4		Puerto Rico	4
Taiwan	na	17	16	18	7	15	29	25	18	9	24	16	10	20	14	19		Canada	3
Tanzania	na	17	15	19	17	14	22	21	13	11	24	13	11	18	15	25		Iceland	3
Turkey	34	32	30	33	29	31	40	43	21	5	45	24	14	38	31	21		New Zealand	3
Uganda	na	18	19	18	17	17	27	19	18	14	20	12	11	17	17	27		Brazil	3
Ukraine	na	11	11	10	9	11	11	12	11	8	12	9	8	10	11	na		Sweden	3
United States	9	8	8	8	10	7	9	10	9	7	8	7	8	10	7	8		Colombia	2
Uruguay	na	7	6	8	3	8	8	8	4	8	7	7	6	4	7	8			
Venezuela	na	16	15	16	14	16	19	18	16	11	16	17	16	19	15	11			
Vietnam	na	32	30	34	33	34	30	32	32	36	40	31	30	41	32	35			
Zimbabwe	na	20	20	20	21	18	20	23	15	30	20	25	19	21	19	22			
Total	16	16	16	16	15	15	17	20	14	12	18	16	14	19	15	10		Total	16

A126) NEIGHBORS: HEAVY DRINKERS

On this list are various groups of people. Could you please sort out any that you would not like to have as neighbors?

Heavy drinkers (%)

(WVS: V70; EVS: V55)

Country	Wave 1990	Wave 2000	Gender Male	Gender Female	Age 16-29	Age 30-49	Age 50+	Education Lower	Education Middle	Education Upper	Income Lower	Income Middle	Income Upper	Values Mat	Values Mixed	Values Postm.	RANKING Country	2000
Albania	na	81	76	85	81	78	83	83	81	73	85	76	80	81	79	80	Jordan	94
Algeria	na	69	65	73	68	72	68	71	68	70	68	70	68	75	66	67	El Salvador	90
Argentina	45	37	32	41	27	33	50	40	32	32	39	36	35	42	38	29	Turkey	87
Armenia	na	86	82	91	81	90	90	89	87	84	86	85	92	88	85	82	Morocco	87
Australia	na	60	54	65	54	59	66	62	59	59	64	57	57	66	61	57	Armenia	86
Austria	60	53	49	56	43	54	57	52	52	60	50	53	56	51	56	49	Azerbaijan	85
Azerbaijan	na	85	84	87	86	84	87	84	85	87	88	86	82	86	86	79	Moldova	85
Bangladesh	na	4	5	4	5	4	3	5	3	6	4	5	4	3	5	7	Estonia	84
Belarus	82	83	76	89	88	79	83	78	84	89	83	85	79	80	86	88	Belarus	83
Belgium	50	45	42	47	42	41	49	50	43	43	47	47	40	49	46	38	Lithuania	82
Bosnia and Herz.	na	77	72	83	76	79	77	80	78	75	79	77	77	79	77	83	Taiwan	81
Brazil	41	46	42	51	48	45	46	48	44	48	44	46	50	50	45	42	Albania	81
Bulgaria	73	76	73	78	70	74	80	77	75	74	72	76	79	75	78	82	Slovakia	80
Canada	55	51	45	57	52	50	52	51	50	53	54	50	49	52	51	50	Tanzania	79
Chile	52	51	46	55	51	53	47	47	51	59	46	53	57	55	48	53	Ukraine	79
China	58	74	70	78	73	73	77	71	76	77	72	72	80	73	76	75	Poland	78
Colombia	na	33	29	38	31	36	31	31	32	36	33	34	33	29	30	42	Bosnia and Herz.	77
Croatia	na	63	58	67	51	63	70	62	63	63	61	63	65	74	64	53	Romania	77
Czech Republic	74	76	69	81	72	75	77	72	79	82	76	76	76	78	75	69	Bulgaria	76
Denmark	34	36	36	36	33	38	36	37	39	36	38	31	42	38	38	27	Korea, South	76
Dominican Rep.	na	55	51	58	54	58	46	53	54	56	59	59	48	49	56	62	Czech Republic	76
Egypt	na	1	2	1	1	1	2	1	1	2	1	1	1	1	1	1	Latvia	75
El Salvador	na	90	90	90	91	91	88	88	92	93	87	91	92	na	na	na	China	74
Estonia	90	84	79	89	84	84	84	80	86	86	83	85	84	85	84	84	Malta	74
Finland	54	51	49	53	55	51	49	48	54	61	48	50	54	55	50	46	Russian Fed.	73
France	50	47	45	49	39	44	54	52	40	41	55	46	43	58	46	32	Uganda	70
Georgia	na	70	60	77	63	71	75	73	69	69	70	73	68	72	68	52	Georgia	70
Germany	72	56	51	60	56	55	58	56	55	63	53	54	57	55	58	56	Algeria	69
Great Britain	48	51	47	55	36	47	64	54	50	47	55	48	51	na	na	na	Slovenia	69
Greece	na	37	37	38	32	38	50	54	36	35	33	43	39	42	37	34	New Zealand	66
Hungary	82	na	na	na	na	na	na	na	na	na	na	na	na	na	na	na	Nigeria	65
Iceland	61	62	62	61	67	61	59	61	64	60	63	61	65	67	62	53	Singapore	64
India	91	46	44	47	45	46	44	37	52	56	31	46	53	47	47	53	Macedonia	64
Indonesia	na	58	57	59	58	59	57	56	55	65	50	62	67	57	58	68	Montenegro	63
Iran	na	2	2	1	2	1	1	1	2	2	2	1	2	na	2	2	Croatia	63
Ireland	34	36	33	39	23	38	44	44	34	29	46	32	38	41	37	32	Iceland	62
Israel	na	na	na	na	na	na	na	na	na	na	na	na	na	na	na	na	Australia	60
Italy	51	40	39	42	36	37	46	48	34	37	46	38	37	52	41	34	Uruguay	59
Japan	58	na	na	na	na	na	na	na	na	na	na	na	na	na	na	na	Netherlands	59
Jordan	na	94	93	94	94	94	95	95	94	91	96	95	91	95	95	81	Indonesia	58
Korea, South	17	76	68	83	68	77	81	86	81	67	77	71	78	80	73	62	Venezuela	57
Latvia	85	75	67	81	72	71	79	73	74	82	70	75	80	78	75	68	Germany	56
Lithuania	92	82	76	87	80	84	82	80	82	87	84	78	87	84	82	85	Zimbabwe	56
Luxembourg	na	32	32	32	35	26	37	39	29	27	35	29	24	36	31	30	Serbia	56
Macedonia	na	64	62	66	63	68	59	73	60	58	67	64	57	62	63	69	Mexico	56
Malta	na	74	70	70	64	73	81	81	70	75	73	77	72	77	72	77	Philippines	56
Mexico	56	56	52	59	55	52	63	58	53	54	58	59	55	57	56	52	United States	56
Moldova	na	85	78	91	86	82	87	88	81	88	87	86	86	87	83	85	Dominican Rep.	55
Montenegro	na	63	52	74	60	62	66	66	61	61	61	60	68	67	60	65	Austria	53
Morocco	na	87	82	91	85	87	88	87	87	83	90	86	85	88	86	82	Peru	52
Netherlands	60	59	56	61	51	59	62	60	60	55	57	58	60	62	61	50	Northern Ireland	51
New Zealand	na	66	63	69	56	66	69	58	69	71	66	64	64	64	64	73	Great Britain	51
Nigeria	72	65	61	70	64	66	68	66	66	63	65	65	67	62	68	62	Canada	51
Northern Ireland	43	51	48	54	47	52	53	53	54	41	49	56	48	54	48	56	Finland	51
Norway	32	32	33	31	32	29	36	40	29	28	na	na	na	48	31	21	Chile	51
Pakistan	na	1	1	1	1	1	1	1	2	1	1	1	1	1	2	na	South Africa	50
Peru	na	52	50	53	48	53	55	56	50	50	54	49	50	49	51	56	Switzerland	47
Philippines	na	56	51	61	56	52	64	57	55	56	62	58	47	59	54	53	France	47
Poland	na	78	75	80	74	77	80	76	78	86	75	80	79	74	80	72	Brazil	46
Portugal	51	38	32	44	30	41	41	41	35	29	44	42	32	42	37	35	India	46
Puerto Rico	na	41	41	41	37	39	44	45	37	43	41	41	43	39	41	42	Belgium	45
Romania	79	77	75	78	75	76	78	78	75	79	77	69	82	76	79	77	Vietnam	44
Russian Fed.	82	73	65	80	72	70	77	70	72	80	70	73	77	74	73	63	Puerto Rico	41
Serbia	na	56	49	63	52	54	60	61	51	60	55	58	57	57	55	48	Italy	40
Singapore	na	64	57	70	64	63	68	66	63	62	64	64	63	68	63	51	Spain	39
Slovakia	na	80	76	84	83	79	79	77	82	81	77	80	84	82	79	78	Portugal	38
Slovenia	45	69	66	72	66	68	73	72	69	66	71	73	63	74	69	68	Greece	37
South Africa	na	50	50	49	51	49	50	46	56	30	47	50	52	55	48	37	Argentina	37
Spain	40	39	39	40	32	38	45	44	34	35	41	39	42	48	38	35	Ireland	36
Sweden	45	33	33	34	38	32	32	30	33	36	34	35	30	32	35	30	Denmark	36
Switzerland	23	47	44	51	44	43	54	48	48	46	52	45	50	55	47	47	Colombia	33
Taiwan	na	81	77	84	82	81	80	76	80	86	78	78	87	82	82	78	Sweden	33
Tanzania	na	79	78	81	82	77	83	79	80	78	77	80	79	81	79	79	Luxembourg	32
Turkey	87	87	83	91	86	88	89	91	83	76	91	86	80	90	88	81	Norway	32
Uganda	na	70	64	75	73	66	71	72	69	76	62	67	65	69	69	76	Bangladesh	4
Ukraine	na	79	73	84	75	78	82	76	78	83	82	76	77	79	82	78	Iran	2
United States	60	56	52	60	50	58	58	61	58	53	57	54	56	57	58	50	Pakistan	1
Uruguay	na	59	56	61	52	56	64	60	56	58	62	54	59	69	59	56	Egypt	1
Venezuela	na	57	56	59	53	58	64	58	55	62	55	53	60	54	57	63		
Vietnam	na	44	43	45	44	42	47	44	46	37	50	42	44	62	41	42		
Zimbabwe	na	56	50	62	57	56	56	56	57	40	53	58	56	57	56	58		
Total	59	59	55	62	56	58	62	58	60	58	60	59	59	63	58	51	Total	59

A127) NEIGHBORS: EMOTIONALLY UNSTABLE PEOPLE

On this list are various groups of people. Could you please sort out any that you would not like to have as neighbors?

Emotionally unstable people (%) (WVS: V71; EVS: V58)

Country	Wave 1990	Wave 2000	Gender Male	Gender Female	Age 16-29	Age 30-49	Age 50+	Education Lower	Education Middle	Education Upper	Income Lower	Income Middle	Income Upper	Values Mat	Values Mixed	Values Postm.
Albania	na	61	56	65	60	61	57	61	61	57	59	62	61	64	56	80
Algeria	na	44	44	44	47	44	39	39	47	45	48	41	40	50	40	46
Argentina	22	22	23	22	18	19	30	20	24	32	21	23	23	21	24	20
Armenia	na	75	74	77	74	77	75	74	75	76	79	67	81	76	74	82
Australia	na	39	42	37	32	40	45	39	39	40	42	38	40	50	39	37
Austria	20	18	19	18	28	17	15	20	17	18	19	18	19	30	19	15
Azerbaijan	na	75	73	77	78	73	73	72	74	77	76	79	68	77	72	74
Bangladesh	na	28	31	25	28	29	27	29	26	31	24	34	25	26	29	40
Belarus	63	60	58	61	58	64	56	54	61	63	60	60	57	59	61	54
Belgium	21	22	23	22	21	20	26	28	20	22	27	21	20	25	22	17
Bosnia and Herz.	na	58	57	59	55	59	60	60	58	55	59	58	58	59	59	59
Brazil	16	18	19	16	13	20	23	16	18	23	17	16	21	14	20	19
Bulgaria	53	44	42	46	49	45	41	41	45	48	38	46	46	44	46	37
Canada	30	33	33	32	29	36	32	33	32	34	33	29	33	37	35	27
Chile	28	25	24	26	21	28	24	25	24	30	23	25	30	27	24	27
China	46	64	60	67	60	65	64	62	66	65	55	68	73	63	65	56
Colombia	na	17	19	16	14	20	15	12	14	25	12	16	22	11	18	17
Croatia	na	41	43	40	42	39	43	38	44	39	44	43	39	42	41	45
Czech Republic	33	19	19	19	17	16	22	19	18	19	19	19	20	21	19	14
Denmark	11	14	14	15	15	14	14	14	15	13	18	12	14	16	14	9
Dominican Rep.	na	52	60	47	49	59	64	66	55	51	55	52	52	44	52	64
Egypt	na	28	31	25	25	29	30	31	24	26	28	30	27	27	28	27
El Salvador	na	82	84	80	82	81	82	81	84	79	79	85	81	na	na	na
Estonia	37	54	49	58	50	53	57	52	55	52	52	56	54	55	54	67
Finland	24	29	34	26	26	32	29	28	31	33	26	32	31	32	30	20
France	17	22	23	22	22	21	24	25	21	17	25	21	21	25	24	14
Georgia	na	55	53	56	49	56	59	61	53	56	54	58	54	61	50	49
Germany	20	22	21	23	19	24	22	26	21	12	24	24	25	29	20	14
Great Britain	28	39	41	38	27	42	44	42	37	38	33	41	42	na	na	na
Greece	na	62	63	61	65	58	62	60	62	62	64	63	61	67	63	53
Hungary	23	na	na	na	na	na	na	na	na	na	na	na	na	na	na	na
Iceland	33	31	36	26	40	31	23	30	34	26	31	29	33	38	31	20
India	69	39	38	39	39	38	39	33	41	49	30	37	45	41	39	44
Indonesia	na	49	46	53	53	48	49	47	46	57	46	50	53	46	53	39
Iran	na	2	1	2	2	2	1	1	2	2	2	na	2	1	2	2
Ireland	30	25	27	23	20	26	27	24	25	25	27	22	27	29	23	26
Israel	na	na	na	na	na	na	na	na	na	na	na	na	na	na	na	na
Italy	34	38	37	39	35	36	42	40	36	37	40	38	37	45	39	34
Japan	62	na	na	na	na	na	na	na	na	na	na	na	na	na	na	na
Jordan	na	66	67	64	63	67	68	68	66	60	62	68	70	70	65	50
Korea, South	17	89	88	90	84	89	93	89	89	88	89	86	91	90	89	78
Latvia	54	35	32	37	37	34	35	27	35	43	33	30	40	34	36	28
Lithuania	48	61	55	66	58	62	63	59	61	66	59	63	64	67	60	49
Luxembourg	na	19	19	19	21	17	20	19	19	21	20	20	19	24	19	16
Macedonia	na	47	49	46	44	48	49	44	48	53	47	49	49	49	48	46
Malta	na	30	26	34	28	29	32	33	28	29	25	32	27	33	29	26
Mexico	38	34	34	33	29	34	38	34	30	40	33	33	37	35	34	31
Moldova	na	68	67	70	71	69	66	68	69	68	73	68	66	68	69	73
Montenegro	na	77	75	80	73	78	80	79	75	78	79	77	78	83	73	69
Morocco	na	69	67	71	68	70	68	69	71	59	70	67	65	70	67	64
Netherlands	15	25	29	21	24	24	25	27	23	24	25	27	23	21	27	21
New Zealand	na	60	62	58	50	61	63	62	62	56	59	60	63	61	61	57
Nigeria	57	52	54	51	51	54	52	49	54	56	49	55	55	50	55	47
Northern Ireland	23	35	34	35	27	37	35	33	36	37	30	32	36	33	37	30
Norway	22	37	38	36	33	36	41	40	36	35	na	na	na	47	37	27
Pakistan	na	40	38	42	38	41	39	44	35	33	44	37	36	41	38	25
Peru	na	38	39	38	36	40	40	41	36	40	39	36	41	34	39	41
Philippines	na	26	24	27	24	23	32	26	26	25	32	25	20	23	27	22
Poland	na	59	57	60	61	60	55	57	59	61	57	60	61	57	60	60
Portugal	47	28	25	30	25	29	28	26	28	37	25	28	29	29	24	30
Puerto Rico	na	34	35	33	29	36	34	31	30	35	30	32	36	32	32	37
Romania	64	53	53	53	55	54	51	55	50	55	54	50	54	56	52	55
Russian Fed.	51	54	52	56	57	56	50	48	54	58	53	52	57	55	53	56
Serbia	na	57	55	60	61	57	56	58	55	59	58	62	53	57	58	51
Singapore	na	58	57	58	53	61	66	55	57	69	50	54	66	60	58	49
Slovakia	na	22	21	23	24	20	23	21	21	28	21	22	22	20	23	24
Slovenia	36	30	34	28	28	30	33	36	29	27	32	32	21	38	27	35
South Africa	na	39	36	42	39	38	40	37	42	41	36	41	43	39	40	33
Spain	25	25	25	25	21	25	27	27	22	24	24	28	28	27	26	22
Sweden	17	17	18	15	20	17	14	16	18	14	18	17	14	24	18	13
Switzerland	4	17	20	15	17	14	21	19	17	18	16	19	16	18	17	16
Taiwan	na	73	73	72	73	72	76	72	71	75	73	68	77	73	74	73
Tanzania	na	5	4	7	5	6	2	5	5	7	5	5	4	5	5	8
Turkey	72	76	73	79	78	75	73	77	75	72	79	72	74	76	76	72
Uganda	na	46	47	46	50	42	43	43	49	35	36	45	41	46	46	49
Ukraine	na	63	61	64	67	61	62	59	62	66	60	60	65	65	65	49
United States	43	52	54	49	45	53	56	49	51	53	47	52	59	51	55	46
Uruguay	na	33	33	33	30	31	36	33	33	32	33	31	33	37	31	36
Venezuela	na	46	46	46	44	46	52	44	45	52	44	43	46	48	45	49
Vietnam	na	39	38	39	37	36	44	40	37	36	40	36	42	55	36	39
Zimbabwe	na	42	44	41	45	40	40	38	48	32	38	39	53	37	46	51
Total	35	42	42	43	42	43	42	40	43	45	42	43	43	47	41	35

RANKING

Country	2000
Korea, South	89
El Salvador	82
Montenegro	77
Turkey	76
Armenia	75
Azerbaijan	75
Taiwan	73
Morocco	69
Moldova	68
Jordan	66
China	64
Ukraine	63
Greece	62
Lithuania	61
Albania	61
New Zealand	60
Belarus	60
Poland	59
Bosnia and Herz.	58
Singapore	58
Serbia	57
Georgia	55
Russian Fed.	54
Estonia	54
Romania	53
Nigeria	52
Dominican Rep.	52
United States	52
Indonesia	49
Macedonia	47
Uganda	46
Venezuela	46
Algeria	44
Bulgaria	44
Zimbabwe	42
Croatia	41
Pakistan	40
Great Britain	39
Australia	39
South Africa	39
India	39
Vietnam	39
Peru	38
Italy	38
Norway	37
Northern Ireland	35
Latvia	35
Mexico	34
Puerto Rico	34
Uruguay	33
Canada	33
Iceland	31
Slovenia	30
Malta	30
Finland	29
Bangladesh	28
Egypt	28
Portugal	28
Philippines	26
Chile	25
Ireland	25
Spain	25
Netherlands	25
Belgium	22
France	22
Argentina	22
Slovakia	22
Germany	22
Luxembourg	19
Czech Republic	19
Austria	18
Brazil	18
Colombia	17
Switzerland	17
Sweden	17
Denmark	14
Tanzania	5
Iran	2
Total	42

A128) NEIGHBORS: MUSLIMS

On this list are various groups of people. Could you please sort out any that you would not like to have as neighbors?
Minority group (1).

Muslims (%)

(WVS: V72; EVS: V59)

Country	Wave 1990	Wave 2000	Gender Male	Gender Female	Age 16-29	Age 30-49	Age 50+	Education Lower	Education Middle	Education Upper	Income Lower	Income Middle	Income Upper	Values Mat	Values Mixed	Values Postm.
Albania	na	30	28	33	27	33	30	31	33	22	27	32	31	25	32	39
Algeria	na	na	na	na	na	na	na	na	na	na	na	na	na	na	na	na
Argentina	6	6	8	5	4	4	11	8	5	2	10	5	4	9	6	4
Armenia	na	na	na	na	na	na	na	na	na	na	na	na	na	na	na	na
Australia	na	na	na	na	na	na	na	na	na	na	na	na	na	na	na	na
Austria	14	15	16	15	11	12	21	19	12	13	20	16	12	28	17	10
Azerbaijan	na	na	na	na	na	na	na	na	na	na	na	na	na	na	na	na
Bangladesh	na	na	na	na	na	na	na	na	na	na	na	na	na	na	na	na
Belarus	24	27	26	27	20	25	33	36	23	23	30	25	23	29	25	14
Belgium	26	22	22	22	17	18	28	31	22	14	27	21	20	30	20	14
Bosnia and Herz.	na	13	14	12	9	15	14	14	13	11	12	15	11	13	13	6
Brazil	na	na	na	na	na	na	na	na	na	na	na	na	na	na	na	na
Bulgaria	41	21	22	20	22	22	21	18	24	21	19	26	19	23	20	16
Canada	10	7	8	5	5	6	9	9	6	6	9	7	5	7	7	5
Chile	12	7	6	9	6	8	9	7	8	7	8	9	5	10	7	4
China	12	na	na	na	na	na	na	na	na	na	na	na	na	na	na	na
Colombia	na	na	na	na	na	na	na	na	na	na	na	na	na	na	na	na
Croatia	na	27	30	23	27	26	27	28	27	22	25	26	28	27	27	26
Czech Republic	49	15	17	13	15	13	17	17	15	10	17	16	14	22	14	11
Denmark	15	16	19	14	12	13	23	23	12	5	20	15	13	20	19	6
Dominican Rep.	na	na	na	na	na	na	na	na	na	na	na	na	na	na	na	na
Egypt	na	na	na	na	na	na	na	na	na	na	na	na	na	na	na	na
El Salvador	na	na	na	na	na	na	na	na	na	na	na	na	na	na	na	na
Estonia	21	22	22	23	18	21	26	25	21	20	23	23	21	22	23	12
Finland	10	19	23	16	18	18	21	21	19	12	18	24	16	29	17	7
France	18	16	17	15	9	15	21	20	16	6	21	15	14	25	15	7
Georgia	na	na	na	na	na	na	na	na	na	na	na	na	na	na	na	na
Germany	20	11	12	10	8	10	14	15	8	9	16	11	9	13	11	8
Great Britain	17	14	14	13	9	13	17	16	13	9	9	13	11	na	na	na
Greece	na	21	22	21	20	17	30	35	24	16	23	19	19	21	22	19
Hungary	18	na	na	na	na	na	na	na	na	na	na	na	na	na	na	na
Iceland	12	12	14	9	10	11	14	13	13	6	15	8	12	12	13	2
India	29	na	na	na	na	na	na	na	na	na	na	na	na	na	na	na
Indonesia	na	na	na	na	na	na	na	na	na	na	na	na	na	na	na	na
Iran	na	na	na	na	na	na	na	na	na	na	na	na	na	na	na	na
Ireland	13	14	15	12	9	11	20	18	12	10	23	11	8	13	14	9
Israel	na	na	na	na	na	na	na	na	na	na	na	na	na	na	na	na
Italy	15	17	17	18	14	12	24	23	14	12	25	12	11	25	18	11
Japan	29	na	na	na	na	na	na	na	na	na	na	na	na	na	na	na
Jordan	na	na	na	na	na	na	na	na	na	na	na	na	na	na	na	na
Korea, South	21	57	57	58	45	59	69	68	64	46	58	57	57	61	55	43
Latvia	26	15	15	15	9	12	19	11	15	18	16	12	16	14	15	17
Lithuania	34	33	31	35	27	33	38	42	31	25	39	33	31	42	29	31
Luxembourg	na	14	16	13	15	13	16	18	13	9	20	11	10	19	14	10
Macedonia	na	26	27	26	23	26	29	31	26	18	30	23	24	26	27	14
Malta	na	28	23	32	21	31	36	38	25	15	31	31	18	35	24	21
Mexico	19	17	16	18	14	17	21	22	11	9	19	18	12	18	17	11
Moldova	na	44	41	47	42	44	47	45	49	37	39	48	47	46	42	46
Montenegro	na	20	19	21	14	20	24	27	18	11	36	20	13	24	17	13
Morocco	na	na	na	na	na	na	na	na	na	na	na	na	na	na	na	na
Netherlands	12	12	14	10	7	9	18	18	12	6	11	12	10	22	13	4
New Zealand	na	na	na	na	na	na	na	na	na	na	na	na	na	na	na	na
Nigeria	24	na	na	na	na	na	na	na	na	na	na	na	na	na	na	na
Northern Ireland	15	16	16	15	16	14	14	17	17	10	15	11	13	19	14	19
Norway	21	19	23	16	10	17	29	29	16	14	na	na	na	28	20	6
Pakistan	na	na	na	na	na	na	na	na	na	na	na	na	na	na	na	na
Peru	na	14	13	14	13	13	15	17	15	10	16	13	11	18	14	7
Philippines	na	26	24	28	24	26	30	34	24	20	29	26	24	24	29	18
Poland	na	24	22	25	11	25	30	29	21	11	25	23	24	27	23	20
Portugal	18	8	9	7	4	8	10	9	8	2	11	10	5	8	8	10
Puerto Rico	na	na	na	na	na	na	na	na	na	na	na	na	na	na	na	na
Romania	35	31	31	32	25	28	38	41	29	18	41	29	25	36	29	17
Russian Fed.	16	14	14	13	14	14	13	14	15	10	15	14	12	14	13	16
Serbia	na	14	12	15	14	13	14	20	11	9	18	11	10	16	12	6
Singapore	na	na	na	na	na	na	na	na	na	na	na	na	na	na	na	na
Slovakia	na	25	27	23	25	25	26	27	24	21	27	27	19	26	24	20
Slovenia	38	23	22	23	18	21	28	33	21	12	30	21	12	33	20	23
South Africa	na	24	26	21	24	23	27	23	25	36	23	21	26	24	24	23
Spain	14	13	11	15	9	12	17	16	11	9	14	12	18	17	14	7
Sweden	17	9	12	7	8	6	12	12	10	4	10	10	6	13	11	3
Switzerland	na	19	22	15	18	17	22	19	19	18	15	20	19	26	19	12
Taiwan	na	19	19	19	8	18	28	25	22	12	28	16	13	18	21	16
Tanzania	na	13	12	13	15	12	8	12	14	12	15	13	9	11	13	13
Turkey	55	na	na	na	na	na	na	na	na	na	na	na	na	na	na	na
Uganda	na	14	13	16	15	14	10	13	16	5	4	10	12	18	14	6
Ukraine	na	24	23	25	26	22	25	23	25	21	21	24	28	25	26	10
United States	14	11	10	11	12	10	11	15	10	10	12	9	9	16	10	10
Uruguay	na	na	na	na	na	na	na	na	na	na	na	na	na	na	na	na
Venezuela	na	na	na	na	na	na	na	na	na	na	na	na	na	na	na	na
Vietnam	na	27	27	28	30	26	28	29	25	28	31	29	24	37	26	33
Zimbabwe	na	18	18	18	20	16	16	16	20	18	14	22	19	15	18	35
Total	21	19	20	19	17	18	22	21	20	15	21	19	18	24	19	12

RANKING Country	2000
Korea, South	57
Moldova	44
Lithuania	33
Romania	31
Albania	30
Malta	28
Vietnam	27
Belarus	27
Croatia	27
Philippines	26
Macedonia	26
Slovakia	25
Ukraine	24
South Africa	24
Poland	24
Slovenia	23
Estonia	22
Belgium	22
Bulgaria	21
Greece	21
Montenegro	20
Finland	19
Norway	19
Taiwan	19
Switzerland	19
Zimbabwe	18
Italy	17
Mexico	17
Denmark	16
France	16
Northern Ireland	16
Austria	15
Czech Republic	15
Latvia	15
Luxembourg	14
Uganda	14
Russian Fed.	14
Ireland	14
Great Britain	14
Serbia	14
Peru	14
Spain	13
Bosnia and Herz.	13
Tanzania	13
Netherlands	12
Iceland	12
Germany	11
United States	11
Sweden	9
Portugal	8
Chile	7
Canada	7
Argentina	6
Total	19

A129) NEIGHBORS: IMMIGRANTS / FOREIGN WORKERS

On this list are various groups of people. Could you please sort out any that you would not like to have as neighbors?

Immigrants / Foreign workers (%) (WVS: V73; EVS: V60)

Country	Wave 1990	Wave 2000	Gender Male	Gender Female	Age 16-29	Age 30-49	Age 50+	Education Lower	Education Middle	Education Upper	Income Lower	Income Middle	Income Upper	Values Mat	Values Mixed	Values Postm.
Albania	na	17	15	18	12	19	17	17	17	14	17	18	14	12	18	31
Algeria	na	24	25	22	24	21	28	30	24	19	31	22	16	23	23	24
Argentina	2	6	8	4	6	5	8	7	5	2	8	6	4	13	5	2
Armenia	na	22	23	21	23	20	22	20	22	22	18	20	29	22	21	24
Australia	na	5	6	3	4	4	6	6	5	3	6	4	3	3	5	4
Austria	20	12	13	12	11	9	16	16	9	5	18	10	9	32	13	6
Azerbaijan	na	20	17	23	20	19	24	30	20	18	23	23	14	21	18	15
Bangladesh	na	67	67	67	69	66	66	65	68	73	64	66	71	68	68	78
Belarus	17	17	15	19	11	17	22	25	14	14	19	17	14	17	18	9
Belgium	21	18	19	18	14	13	25	29	18	11	26	17	14	27	16	10
Bosnia and Herz.	na	25	26	24	19	27	28	25	26	21	23	28	24	25	25	21
Brazil	4	4	4	4	3	5	2	5	3	na	5	3	2	3	4	1
Bulgaria	34	25	28	22	23	23	27	28	24	21	26	27	20	29	22	17
Canada	6	4	4	4	3	4	6	7	4	3	6	5	3	7	4	3
Chile	12	11	11	11	11	10	11	12	10	12	12	11	9	12	11	8
China	13	16	14	18	8	16	22	22	12	7	20	14	12	13	16	19
Colombia	na	na	na	na	na	na	na	na	na	na	na	na	na	na	na	na
Croatia	na	22	25	19	24	21	21	23	22	16	21	21	23	24	23	17
Czech Republic	34	19	21	18	17	19	22	23	17	12	23	18	16	27	18	12
Denmark	12	11	10	11	7	9	14	15	6	4	13	10	7	18	12	4
Dominican Rep.	na	18	12	22	17	18	18	44	20	14	19	13	18	22	18	9
Egypt	na	42	47	38	43	40	45	40	38	55	38	41	46	37	46	48
El Salvador	na	na	na	na	na	na	na	na	na	na	na	na	na	na	na	na
Estonia	17	21	22	21	17	20	24	25	19	18	23	24	20	20	23	13
Finland	5	13	15	11	13	12	13	16	10	9	13	14	12	24	11	3
France	13	12	13	11	8	12	14	15	10	6	13	12	11	19	11	5
Georgia	na	11	14	9	10	10	13	11	12	8	12	14	8	11	10	21
Germany	19	9	10	8	8	9	9	9	8	7	12	7	7	8	10	6
Great Britain	12	16	17	14	11	17	18	21	13	11	14	13	17	na	na	na
Greece	na	14	16	12	14	10	19	19	16	11	12	15	11	14	14	11
Hungary	22	na	na	na	na	na	na	na	na	na	na	na	na	na	na	na
Iceland	8	3	4	2	2	2	5	4	3	1	4	2	3	4	3	3
India	37	38	40	36	40	38	37	42	35	33	45	39	35	40	35	29
Indonesia	na	40	41	40	41	38	42	46	43	34	44	37	41	46	39	25
Iran	na	10	10	10	11	9	7	7	11	12	8	12	11	10	10	15
Ireland	5	12	12	13	7	11	17	16	10	11	18	11	8	9	13	11
Israel	na	na	na	na	na	na	na	na	na	na	na	na	na	na	na	na
Italy	15	17	18	16	17	12	21	21	15	10	21	12	10	25	16	11
Japan	17	na	na	na	na	na	na	na	na	na	na	na	na	na	na	na
Jordan	na	40	46	34	41	41	37	40	41	39	38	41	40	43	38	38
Korea, South	53	47	46	48	37	46	60	63	52	37	49	48	44	52	44	32
Latvia	31	10	12	8	5	9	12	10	9	13	10	8	11	10	10	11
Lithuania	15	24	20	26	20	20	30	35	19	23	29	21	21	29	21	18
Luxembourg	na	8	8	9	9	7	10	11	8	4	13	8	4	7	9	5
Macedonia	na	19	19	18	16	19	20	20	19	14	21	19	16	16	21	8
Malta	na	15	14	16	8	14	21	23	14	7	18	14	10	21	13	8
Mexico	18	14	14	15	12	15	15	18	10	9	20	14	9	14	14	13
Moldova	na	19	16	21	18	20	18	16	22	16	20	18	21	14	19	33
Montenegro	na	20	19	21	15	20	24	26	17	15	21	17	22	26	17	10
Morocco	na	18	18	19	15	18	26	21	10	8	25	11	16	22	14	13
Netherlands	7	5	5	5	1	3	9	8	5	2	5	5	4	12	5	2
New Zealand	na	5	6	5	6	6	5	10	3	2	7	5	4	5	5	3
Nigeria	26	28	29	27	27	30	27	30	27	26	30	29	25	32	26	24
Northern Ireland	7	18	19	18	16	19	15	20	18	14	18	15	15	22	17	17
Norway	16	10	12	8	7	7	15	15	9	6	na	na	na	17	9	5
Pakistan	na	29	35	23	29	28	31	26	34	30	26	28	33	31	26	42
Peru	na	11	10	12	11	10	11	13	12	8	13	11	7	16	11	4
Philippines	na	15	17	14	13	15	18	20	13	14	19	13	15	15	16	14
Poland	na	24	23	24	14	23	29	27	20	18	25	22	26	28	22	21
Portugal	10	3	4	2	2	2	3	3	2	3	5	2	3	2	2	6
Puerto Rico	na	6	4	7	3	6	6	7	9	4	6	6	5	4	6	4
Romania	30	21	21	21	14	21	25	30	19	10	31	20	15	24	20	5
Russian Fed.	12	11	12	11	8	10	14	13	12	9	12	12	9	11	11	15
Serbia	na	8	7	9	4	7	10	12	6	4	11	7	5	9	7	3
Singapore	na	26	23	29	25	27	25	24	26	32	28	22	31	24	27	18
Slovakia	na	23	23	23	21	24	23	22	23	23	25	19	23	23	22	8
Slovenia	40	16	18	14	13	14	20	24	15	8	19	14	9	23	15	13
South Africa	na	31	32	29	30	33	27	31	32	22	33	34	23	30	33	22
Spain	11	10	8	12	5	10	14	13	7	6	12	9	12	12	11	5
Sweden	9	3	4	1	3	1	4	3	4	1	2	4	3	6	3	1
Switzerland	2	10	11	9	10	8	13	15	9	7	14	11	7	11	12	5
Taiwan	na	27	27	27	21	25	39	35	28	20	37	23	22	27	29	24
Tanzania	na	18	16	19	17	16	19	20	17	12	25	13	13	14	19	8
Turkey	28	39	37	41	38	39	41	49	30	18	49	35	26	42	40	29
Uganda	na	13	14	12	12	12	22	13	14	5	7	5	11	18	11	12
Ukraine	na	15	15	15	11	15	18	16	16	13	15	14	16	14	16	9
United States	10	10	10	10	11	10	10	13	11	8	10	10	8	13	9	10
Uruguay	na	7	8	7	6	7	8	9	6	3	8	9	5	6	8	5
Venezuela	na	18	20	16	17	16	24	21	18	14	22	17	19	20	18	15
Vietnam	na	33	31	35	30	33	35	34	30	37	40	31	31	36	35	33
Zimbabwe	na	21	21	20	21	20	20	23	17	40	20	26	20	20	20	32
Total	17	18	19	17	17	18	19	21	17	14	20	18	17	22	17	11

RANKING

Country	2000
Bangladesh	67
Korea, South	47
Egypt	42
Indonesia	40
Jordan	40
Turkey	39
India	38
Vietnam	33
South Africa	31
Pakistan	29
Nigeria	28
Taiwan	27
Singapore	26
Bosnia and Herz.	25
Bulgaria	25
Lithuania	24
Algeria	24
Poland	24
Slovakia	23
Armenia	22
Croatia	22
Romania	21
Estonia	21
Zimbabwe	21
Montenegro	20
Azerbaijan	20
Czech Republic	19
Moldova	19
Macedonia	19
Belgium	18
Morocco	18
Northern Ireland	18
Venezuela	18
Dominican Rep.	18
Tanzania	18
Belarus	17
Albania	17
Italy	17
China	16
Slovenia	16
Great Britain	16
Malta	15
Philippines	15
Ukraine	15
Mexico	14
Greece	14
Finland	13
Uganda	13
Ireland	12
Austria	12
France	12
Russian Fed.	11
Georgia	11
Peru	11
Chile	11
Denmark	11
Spain	10
United States	10
Switzerland	10
Latvia	10
Norway	10
Iran	10
Germany	9
Luxembourg	8
Serbia	8
Uruguay	7
Argentina	6
Puerto Rico	6
New Zealand	5
Netherlands	5
Australia	5
Canada	4
Brazil	4
Iceland	3
Sweden	3
Portugal	3
Total	18

A130) NEIGHBORS: PEOPLE WHO HAVE AIDS

On this list are various groups of people. Could you please sort out any that you would not like to have as neighbors?

People who have AIDS (%)   (WVS: V74; EVS: V61)

Country	Wave		Gender		Age			Education			Income			Values			RANKING Country	2000
	1990	2000	Male	Female	16-29	30-49	50+	Lower	Middle	Upper	Lower	Middle	Upper	Mat	Mixed	Postm.		
Albania	na	70	69	71	64	71	75	77	68	56	76	69	64	73	66	80	Jordan	96
Algeria	na	68	68	69	65	71	70	73	69	64	69	72	62	71	68	65	Korea, South	89
Argentina	32	12	14	10	5	10	20	16	6	3	18	11	6	19	11	6	Azerbaijan	89
Armenia	na	85	84	87	78	89	90	85	87	79	82	87	92	91	81	82	Armenia	85
Australia	na	15	20	11	8	13	24	22	15	10	21	14	9	19	16	12	Turkey	83
Austria	32	17	20	15	13	14	23	21	14	16	22	19	14	38	16	14	Morocco	81
Azerbaijan	na	89	90	88	88	90	90	90	90	88	96	92	81	90	89	82	China	79
Bangladesh	na	6	5	6	8	4	4	6	5	7	5	6	6	4	7	8	Montenegro	76
Belarus	73	58	53	61	53	55	64	63	58	48	59	58	53	61	59	32	Taiwan	72
Belgium	24	13	12	15	11	9	19	23	12	9	20	13	10	19	11	8	Georgia	71
Bosnia and Herz.	na	60	60	59	55	62	62	66	63	45	67	61	51	64	58	57	Albania	70
Brazil	24	14	14	14	12	13	20	20	11	4	19	12	10	20	12	8	Algeria	68
Bulgaria	63	52	52	52	55	42	59	61	51	39	60	50	45	55	53	49	Nigeria	68
Canada	21	12	13	12	7	11	17	21	10	10	17	10	9	21	13	8	El Salvador	67
Chile	41	24	23	25	18	24	29	28	22	21	22	26	22	31	22	15	Moldova	66
China	76	79	79	79	77	82	76	75	83	77	75	82	84	81	80	84	Philippines	62
Colombia	na	8	8	9	10	8	9	12	10	4	11	9	6	11	11	7	Bosnia and Herz.	60
Croatia	na	51	51	51	41	52	56	55	50	42	48	54	48	56	51	50	Ukraine	59
Czech Republic	64	21	22	19	13	17	28	25	17	14	23	22	17	32	18	12	Belarus	58
Denmark	9	6	6	5	3	4	10	8	3	4	9	4	4	9	7	1	Lithuania	55
Dominican Rep.	na	30	29	30	27	36	18	44	37	26	31	22	32	33	30	21	Bulgaria	52
Egypt	na	2	1	2	2	1	2	2	1	3	2	2	1	1	2	2	Russian Fed.	52
El Salvador	na	67	68	67	64	66	74	79	63	40	81	65	49	na	na	na	Macedonia	52
Estonia	63	42	39	44	32	40	50	50	40	36	49	47	36	45	40	44	Indonesia	52
Finland	24	21	25	17	15	19	26	23	21	12	20	24	19	29	20	12	Serbia	51
France	15	9	9	8	5	6	13	11	6	4	14	8	6	15	8	2	Croatia	51
Georgia	na	71	71	71	67	73	74	75	73	63	74	73	66	74	70	57	Romania	47
Germany	20	11	11	11	5	10	15	16	8	5	14	13	9	17	10	6	Slovakia	45
Great Britain	23	25	26	24	19	21	31	31	22	17	28	22	20	na	na	na	Poland	44
Greece	na	27	28	26	23	25	39	46	28	23	30	26	24	36	28	15	Venezuela	44
Hungary	66	na	na	na	na	na	na	na	na	na	na	na	na	na	na	na	Estonia	42
Iceland	18	7	8	6	4	5	13	7	8	4	10	6	4	8	7	5	India	39
India	93	39	38	41	42	39	38	30	50	50	23	40	47	41	43	40	Malta	38
Indonesia	na	52	52	53	53	51	53	53	48	58	48	54	58	49	55	57	Singapore	35
Iran	na	1	1	na	1	1	na	na	1	1	1	na	1	na	1	2	Mexico	34
Ireland	35	23	22	23	11	20	34	34	18	14	33	21	16	26	22	17	Vietnam	33
Israel	na	na	na	na	na	na	na	na	na	na	na	na	na	na	na	na	Slovenia	33
Italy	44	31	32	30	25	22	43	42	23	19	41	27	22	47	31	24	Tanzania	33
Japan	77	na	na	na	na	na	na	na	na	na	na	na	na	na	na	na	Italy	31
Jordan	na	96	96	96	95	97	95	96	96	95	97	95	95	97	96	91	Northern Ireland	31
Korea, South	4	89	89	90	84	90	93	95	91	86	89	89	90	92	89	71	Zimbabwe	30
Latvia	65	29	28	30	19	22	39	34	26	32	34	28	23	34	27	28	Dominican Rep.	30
Lithuania	78	55	52	58	47	52	63	65	52	50	67	54	50	64	52	41	Latvia	29
Luxembourg	na	12	12	12	8	13	15	18	9	8	15	10	6	12	13	8	Peru	29
Macedonia	na	52	52	52	51	52	53	62	51	38	58	52	43	45	56	53	Portugal	27
Malta	na	38	35	41	29	34	49	53	34	28	47	35	28	47	34	28	Greece	27
Mexico	57	34	34	33	28	35	40	42	25	17	43	32	24	39	34	21	South Africa	27
Moldova	na	66	66	66	69	65	65	65	69	61	61	62	72	69	65	58	Great Britain	25
Montenegro	na	76	76	76	72	75	80	79	77	68	83	81	75	82	72	60	Chile	24
Morocco	na	81	80	83	79	82	86	86	68	48	85	74	82	86	80	56	Ireland	23
Netherlands	13	8	10	6	2	6	13	13	7	4	11	7	5	13	9	3	Finland	21
New Zealand	na	17	22	12	7	14	23	21	19	10	18	16	15	18	17	11	Spain	21
Nigeria	79	68	66	69	66	70	65	67	68	68	69	69	64	64	70	71	Czech Republic	21
Northern Ireland	28	31	32	30	23	28	35	36	29	20	35	27	21	30	31	31	Uruguay	19
Norway	25	14	16	12	6	11	24	23	12	8	na	na	na	29	13	5	Austria	17
Pakistan	na	7	10	3	8	7	5	4	11	9	4	7	11	7	7	8	Uganda	17
Peru	na	29	27	30	27	28	35	33	32	20	36	25	20	35	27	26	United States	17
Philippines	na	62	60	64	57	61	72	70	61	54	69	62	57	63	62	60	New Zealand	17
Poland	na	44	46	41	23	41	59	54	32	28	48	41	39	47	41	44	Australia	15
Portugal	44	27	27	27	20	30	29	31	21	11	32	29	19	31	26	11	Norway	14
Puerto Rico	na	12	16	11	9	11	15	25	14	10	16	12	10	17	12	10	Brazil	14
Romania	66	47	48	46	37	41	57	64	43	23	61	50	35	58	40	25	Belgium	13
Russian Fed.	68	52	50	54	42	53	58	60	53	45	55	54	48	57	48	40	Canada	12
Serbia	na	51	48	54	37	52	57	60	51	38	58	49	47	59	46	27	Puerto Rico	12
Singapore	na	35	35	35	31	36	50	43	34	22	38	32	32	44	32	30	Luxembourg	12
Slovakia	na	45	45	44	40	45	49	49	43	42	46	48	43	48	44	32	Switzerland	12
Slovenia	41	33	38	29	17	33	45	49	29	22	51	33	18	42	33	23	Argentina	12
South Africa	na	27	28	25	22	28	33	28	24	32	29	25	23	26	28	19	Germany	11
Spain	33	21	20	21	13	17	28	27	15	12	26	20	20	26	22	10	France	9
Sweden	18	7	10	4	4	7	9	10	7	3	6	9	5	12	7	5	Colombia	8
Switzerland	na	12	13	11	9	9	18	18	11	10	13	11	14	13	13	11	Netherlands	8
Taiwan	na	72	71	73	62	71	81	79	76	64	78	71	68	76	72	70	Iceland	7
Tanzania	na	33	30	36	34	31	33	32	32	37	39	27	36	30	32	42	Pakistan	7
Turkey	89	83	83	83	79	85	88	90	80	55	90	81	70	90	83	73	Sweden	7
Uganda	na	17	15	19	17	16	20	18	17	11	11	13	10	24	12	19	Denmark	6
Ukraine	na	59	55	63	52	54	69	62	62	52	67	55	55	63	59	37	Bangladesh	6
United States	28	17	20	14	12	15	23	18	21	14	15	17	16	25	16	14	Egypt	2
Uruguay	na	19	22	17	16	15	24	24	13	8	26	17	13	29	21	12	Iran	1
Venezuela	na	44	47	40	42	43	49	52	45	29	53	39	37	50	42	38		
Vietnam	na	33	31	36	31	33	35	33	33	18	34	35	32	46	31	25		
Zimbabwe	na	30	29	31	34	28	26	34	26	40	33	33	28	30	30	41		
Total	44	37	38	37	34	37	41	40	38	31	42	38	34	48	35	23	Total	37

A131) NEIGHBORS: DRUG ADDICTS

On this list are various groups of people. Could you please sort out any that you would not like to have as neighbors?

Drug addicts (%)

(WVS: V75; EVS: V62)

Country	Wave		Gender		Age			Education			Income			Values			RANKING Country	2000
	1990	2000	Male	Female	16-29	30-49	50+	Lower	Middle	Upper	Lower	Middle	Upper	Mat	Mixed	Postm.		
Albania	na	85	83	86	80	84	89	89	84	74	84	85	86	87	82	87	Jordan	99
Algeria	na	77	74	80	74	80	78	79	74	78	73	80	78	79	77	75	Azerbaijan	97
Argentina	50	32	35	29	25	29	42	35	28	26	35	31	30	41	31	25	Turkey	94
Armenia	na	93	90	95	89	95	95	94	93	90	93	92	96	93	92	94	Korea, South	93
Australia	na	74	73	74	67	74	79	76	74	72	75	72	75	80	76	69	Armenia	93
Austria	60	53	54	52	49	51	56	55	51	48	48	56	56	68	56	41	Morocco	92
Azerbaijan	na	97	96	98	95	98	98	100	97	97	99	97	95	97	97	99	Moldova	91
Bangladesh	na	2	2	2	2	2	1	2	2	3	1	2	2	1	2	3	China	90
Belarus	82	87	84	89	86	85	89	89	86	86	90	87	81	86	88	82	Estonia	90
Belgium	53	51	50	52	50	47	56	60	51	46	56	55	45	59	53	41	El Salvador	89
Bosnia and Herz.	na	82	80	83	80	82	83	84	82	78	81	84	77	84	81	77	Taiwan	89
Brazil	58	57	55	58	52	58	62	59	54	59	54	61	57	63	56	45	Ukraine	88
Bulgaria	69	72	71	72	71	67	76	76	70	68	73	70	70	71	75	70	Belarus	87
Canada	63	64	62	66	61	62	68	64	65	63	61	60	69	73	65	61	Uganda	87
Chile	55	53	51	55	49	54	55	53	53	51	52	49	58	57	53	45	Lithuania	86
China	76	90	90	91	90	91	89	90	91	86	89	91	91	91	91	94	Montenegro	86
Colombia	na	30	31	30	28	29	38	38	31	24	36	31	26	33	28	27	Albania	85
Croatia	na	69	67	71	54	70	79	71	69	65	67	74	66	76	69	64	Russian Fed.	84
Czech Republic	81	73	72	75	71	73	75	74	72	73	74	76	71	79	73	60	Philippines	82
Denmark	54	60	58	61	70	61	53	60	66	59	59	57	64	63	63	49	Bosnia and Herz.	82
Dominican Rep.	na	71	74	69	69	76	73	56	68	74	79	73	72	66	72	71	Tanzania	81
Egypt	na	1	1	1	1	na	1	1	1	2	1	1	1	na	1	1	Georgia	81
El Salvador	na	89	89	89	89	89	88	90	89	85	90	90	85	na	na	na	Slovakia	79
Estonia	87	90	87	92	87	91	90	90	91	87	88	93	90	91	89	90	New Zealand	79
Finland	68	75	74	77	74	80	72	74	76	77	71	76	78	80	75	71	Northern Ireland	78
France	44	48	50	46	44	43	55	54	42	37	54	46	42	59	48	33	Algeria	77
Georgia	na	81	78	84	70	84	88	87	81	75	83	82	77	83	80	71	Iceland	76
Germany	59	59	59	58	44	60	63	66	52	55	57	65	59	69	58	45	Finland	75
Great Britain	62	72	74	65	74	75	73	75	63	68	73	76	na	na	na	Latvia	75
Greece	na	45	49	43	39	46	57	60	44	44	43	50	44	52	46	36	Nigeria	74
Hungary	84	na	na	na	na	na	na	na	na	na	na	na	na	na	na	na	United States	74
Iceland	74	76	75	77	83	77	70	73	78	79	72	78	79	79	77	68	Australia	74
India	93	44	44	45	42	45	44	36	52	53	31	46	50	46	46	49	Romania	74
Indonesia	na	60	60	60	62	61	57	53	56	70	53	65	67	56	62	68	Czech Republic	73
Iran	na	1	1	1	2	1	na	na	2	2	1	1	2	1	2	1	Netherlands	73
Ireland	64	66	65	68	57	67	71	71	64	62	67	66	70	68	67	63	Macedonia	73
Israel	na	na	na	na	na	na	na	na	na	na	na	na	na	na	na	na	Venezuela	73
Italy	60	55	55	54	46	51	63	61	49	51	55	55	56	69	55	48	Singapore	73
Japan	91	na	na	na	na	na	na	na	na	na	na	na	na	na	na	na	Great Britain	72
Jordan	na	99	99	99	99	99	98	98	100	99	100	99	99	99	99	96	Bulgaria	72
Korea, South	4	93	92	95	89	95	96	93	94	92	92	94	95	95	93	85	Malta	71
Latvia	89	75	71	78	71	76	75	68	76	77	75	77	75	79	75	62	Dominican Rep.	71
Lithuania	89	86	85	87	83	88	87	84	87	88	89	87	86	89	85	88	Serbia	70
Luxembourg	na	43	43	44	46	38	46	48	42	36	45	42	33	48	44	32	Croatia	69
Macedonia	na	73	72	74	71	76	71	77	71	71	77	73	66	74	72	83	Poland	69
Malta	na	71	70	73	61	72	78	78	70	65	70	78	67	76	70	66	Mexico	68
Mexico	69	68	68	68	69	65	72	70	66	60	71	67	67	68	71	57	Peru	66
Moldova	na	91	89	92	87	93	92	92	91	90	92	92	88	94	91	85	Ireland	66
Montenegro	na	86	85	87	80	87	89	86	87	86	86	89	88	92	83	69	Norway	66
Morocco	na	92	90	95	91	93	94	92	93	89	94	93	90	94	91	85	Slovenia	65
Netherlands	73	73	74	72	71	73	75	78	72	70	75	70	76	78	76	65	Canada	64
New Zealand	na	79	79	79	69	80	82	77	81	80	76	79	84	78	80	80	Zimbabwe	64
Nigeria	77	74	73	75	74	76	70	74	74	75	74	74	75	85	78	76	South Africa	62
Northern Ireland	59	78	78	79	72	80	81	81	78	71	80	81	81	85	78	69	Sweden	60
Norway	55	66	67	65	68	63	67	64	63	71	na	na	na	70	67	54	Denmark	60
Pakistan	na	59	61	57	58	58	63	56	62	64	55	60	61	55	65	67	Indonesia	60
Peru	na	66	65	67	63	70	65	68	67	65	68	65	67	67	66	69	Pakistan	59
Philippines	na	82	80	84	81	80	88	84	82	80	83	85	76	85	80	79	Germany	59
Poland	na	69	73	65	62	68	74	73	61	69	68	70	70	69	68	73	Brazil	57
Portugal	61	48	48	48	40	48	53	53	40	35	54	48	51	55	46	32	Italy	55
Puerto Rico	na	47	53	43	46	50	45	47	46	48	45	47	49	55	44	47	Vietnam	54
Romania	76	74	75	73	66	76	76	75	75	69	73	73	75	77	74	64	Austria	53
Russian Fed.	86	84	82	86	80	84	86	84	84	85	83	86	84	87	82	72	Chile	53
Serbia	na	70	68	72	63	72	72	73	69	68	71	72	72	77	66	51	Spain	53
Singapore	na	73	70	75	70	74	79	72	72	76	69	72	75	77	71	67	Belgium	51
Slovakia	na	79	78	81	79	81	79	74	81	85	77	80	83	80	80	73	Switzerland	49
Slovenia	47	65	69	62	58	65	70	69	65	60	70	66	59	69	65	63	Portugal	48
South Africa	na	62	62	63	64	62	60	63	62	54	62	67	58	60	64	62	France	48
Spain	54	53	53	53	43	50	60	59	46	48	56	56	51	63	52	41	Puerto Rico	47
Sweden	65	60	62	59	68	62	55	54	62	62	60	63	59	59	63	50	Greece	45
Switzerland	32	49	48	50	43	45	58	52	49	45	53	47	50	61	52	36	Uruguay	44
Taiwan	na	89	88	89	81	90	89	87	89	90	88	89	91	90	89	95	India	44
Tanzania	na	81	80	84	84	79	85	84	79	78	82	85	75	84	81	83	Luxembourg	43
Turkey	92	94	94	95	93	95	96	96	94	90	96	94	91	97	95	90	Argentina	32
Uganda	na	87	87	87	86	87	89	88	85	97	85	91	83	83	89	89	Colombia	30
Ukraine	na	88	89	87	89	87	90	88	88	89	89	86	90	90	88	78	Bangladesh	2
United States	79	74	72	76	62	77	79	70	75	74	71	75	79	72	76	70	Iran	1
Uruguay	na	44	45	44	31	40	54	49	39	37	48	43	42	49	47	37	Egypt	1
Venezuela	na	73	73	73	72	73	73	74	74	68	74	72	68	75	72	73		
Vietnam	na	54	55	53	52	55	54	55	53	45	56	48	60	68	52	50		
Zimbabwe	na	64	60	68	62	63	69	63	66	22	62	62	58	61	67	59		
Total	67	68	67	69	65	68	70	67	69	67	69	69	67	73	68	58	Total	68

A132) NEIGHBORS: HOMOSEXUALS

On this list are various groups of people. Could you please sort out any that you would not like to have as neighbors?

Homosexuals (%)

(WVS: V76; EVS: V63)

Country	Wave 1990	Wave 2000	Gender Male	Gender Female	Age 16-29	Age 30-49	Age 50+	Education Lower	Education Middle	Education Upper	Income Lower	Income Middle	Income Upper	Values Mat	Values Mixed	Values Postm.	RANKING Country	RANKING 2000
Albania	na	83	83	83	79	84	84	87	81	76	81	83	83	85	81	82	Jordan	98
Algeria	na	81	80	81	78	83	83	83	79	81	77	82	83	82	81	81	Morocco	93
Argentina	39	22	26	19	16	18	32	28	13	18	30	22	15	34	22	13	Azerbaijan	91
Armenia	na	83	83	83	74	89	90	89	84	80	77	87	89	87	80	88	Turkey	90
Australia	na	25	33	16	21	20	34	39	23	15	32	26	14	35	26	20	Armenia	83
Austria	43	25	31	21	12	22	36	33	20	12	31	29	19	48	26	17	Albania	83
Azerbaijan	na	91	93	88	89	91	93	92	91	89	96	93	83	91	90	87	Korea, South	82
Bangladesh	na	5	5	5	5	5	4	5	4	6	4	7	3	1	7	1	Algeria	81
Belarus	79	63	65	62	54	63	71	71	62	57	64	66	55	66	64	43	El Salvador	78
Belgium	24	17	20	15	16	12	23	26	17	11	24	19	12	23	15	12	Moldova	77
Bosnia and Herz.	na	64	65	64	60	65	67	73	65	54	70	66	56	65	64	64	Georgia	77
Brazil	30	26	31	22	25	25	32	30	25	18	27	26	26	31	25	19	Uganda	76
Bulgaria	68	54	57	51	50	47	62	63	51	45	61	51	47	56	54	57	Tanzania	74
Canada	30	17	19	15	14	14	22	27	15	11	24	15	13	26	18	11	Montenegro	74
Chile	58	33	36	30	29	34	35	33	33	32	29	37	32	38	34	21	Nigeria	74
China	72	73	77	70	71	76	67	64	80	72	65	76	83	74	76	81	China	73
Colombia	na	15	18	11	16	14	15	17	16	12	15	16	13	18	15	17	Taiwan	73
Croatia	na	53	59	48	40	55	59	55	55	39	53	57	47	55	56	44	Lithuania	68
Czech Republic	59	20	22	18	12	16	27	25	14	12	25	20	14	27	18	12	Zimbabwe	67
Denmark	12	8	11	5	5	3	15	12	3	3	13	6	3	10	9	2	Ukraine	66
Dominican Rep.	na	49	52	47	44	57	55	50	54	48	52	50	47	44	50	50	Romania	65
Egypt	na	0	na	na	1	na	na	na	na	1	na	na	na	na	1	na	Bosnia and Herz.	64
El Salvador	na	78	83	74	77	76	83	86	75	63	84	80	64	na	na	na	Belarus	63
Estonia	73	46	47	46	38	43	54	49	47	39	50	51	41	51	44	38	Russian Fed.	58
Finland	25	21	29	15	17	19	25	26	17	11	22	28	14	30	19	15	Venezuela	57
France	24	16	20	12	9	14	21	20	10	9	19	16	15	26	14	6	Poland	55
Georgia	na	77	80	75	74	78	79	80	77	76	80	82	70	78	78	68	Indonesia	55
Germany	34	13	15	11	4	10	21	20	8	9	19	13	10	18	14	4	Bulgaria	54
Great Britain	31	24	26	23	18	17	34	33	19	15	24	25	21	na	na	na	Macedonia	54
Greece	na	27	32	23	18	26	49	52	29	21	33	24	25	28	28	21	Croatia	53
Hungary	75	na	na	na	na	na	na	na	na	na	na	na	na	na	na	na	Peru	49
Iceland	20	8	11	5	3	5	17	12	6	2	13	5	5	11	7	5	Serbia	49
India	91	29	30	28	27	30	28	20	36	40	18	25	39	22	41	49	Dominican Rep.	49
Indonesia	na	55	54	56	60	55	52	49	52	63	52	56	63	53	56	68	Estonia	46
Iran	na	1	1	1	1	1	na	1	1	1	1	1	1	1	1	na	South Africa	46
Ireland	33	27	29	25	16	23	40	42	21	14	36	29	19	34	27	18	Singapore	46
Israel	na	na	na	na	na	na	na	na	na	na	na	na	na	na	na	na	Latvia	46
Italy	39	29	31	27	24	21	39	40	22	17	36	24	23	38	31	19	Mexico	45
Japan	69	na	na	na	na	na	na	na	na	na	na	na	na	na	na	na	Slovenia	44
Jordan	na	98	99	98	98	99	97	98	99	99	98	99	99	99	98	98	Slovakia	44
Korea, South	4	82	86	79	69	87	88	86	86	77	82	83	83	85	82	66	Malta	40
Latvia	78	46	49	43	35	45	51	46	44	49	50	46	39	50	44	45	Vietnam	39
Lithuania	87	68	70	65	56	69	74	72	68	57	77	67	66	69	68	65	Northern Ireland	35
Luxembourg	na	19	20	17	16	15	25	27	14	16	22	17	11	20	22	8	Chile	33
Macedonia	na	54	56	52	54	55	51	61	51	47	61	53	45	52	55	58	Uruguay	32
Malta	na	40	50	30	27	36	57	51	37	25	47	43	31	47	37	25	India	29
Mexico	60	45	50	40	37	44	56	53	36	30	50	44	40	49	45	33	Italy	29
Moldova	na	77	78	77	73	80	79	76	80	75	82	82	71	78	78	73	Ireland	27
Montenegro	na	74	73	74	68	71	80	77	74	65	81	82	73	83	68	53	Greece	27
Morocco	na	93	93	94	92	94	96	95	91	82	97	91	94	95	92	83	Brazil	26
Netherlands	9	6	9	4	6	3	9	11	6	2	9	5	3	13	6	3	Austria	25
New Zealand	na	22	33	14	19	17	29	28	27	13	27	21	17	29	23	15	Portugal	25
Nigeria	76	74	73	74	74	74	70	72	74	75	73	74	74	71	76	71	Australia	25
Northern Ireland	48	35	37	34	31	33	38	38	36	26	35	32	29	42	34	33	Great Britain	24
Norway	20	14	20	9	6	11	25	23	12	8	na	na	na	24	14	5	Philippines	24
Pakistan	na	na	na	na	na	na	na	na	na	na	na	na	na	na	na	na	United States	23
Peru	na	49	51	48	46	51	54	55	51	42	55	47	41	51	49	47	New Zealand	22
Philippines	na	24	25	23	23	21	31	26	22	24	27	22	22	24	25	18	Argentina	22
Poland	na	55	60	51	41	54	65	62	50	39	58	54	53	54	56	60	Puerto Rico	22
Portugal	50	25	27	23	14	27	31	28	22	11	35	24	20	29	25	16	Finland	21
Puerto Rico	na	22	28	19	15	21	26	30	26	19	25	23	18	26	21	19	Czech Republic	20
Romania	75	65	68	62	58	65	70	70	65	57	70	64	63	68	65	55	Luxembourg	19
Russian Fed.	81	58	59	57	55	59	59	56	59	56	57	61	56	60	57	52	Switzerland	19
Serbia	na	49	50	48	41	45	57	56	49	38	54	52	45	54	47	31	Belgium	17
Singapore	na	46	48	44	41	48	55	47	46	41	46	46	44	50	43	46	Canada	17
Slovakia	na	44	45	43	41	42	48	46	44	37	49	47	39	46	44	35	France	16
Slovenia	43	44	52	38	31	41	58	58	43	25	58	47	29	60	42	38	Spain	16
South Africa	na	46	47	46	45	46	48	49	42	53	52	49	35	44	47	58	Colombia	15
Spain	27	16	16	15	9	12	23	20	12	10	21	13	16	23	15	7	Norway	14
Sweden	18	6	9	3	3	5	9	12	6	2	7	7	4	14	6	4	Germany	13
Switzerland	na	19	22	15	12	15	27	24	17	20	20	22	16	25	20	10	Denmark	8
Taiwan	na	73	75	71	58	73	81	81	74	65	80	73	67	74	72	78	Iceland	8
Tanzania	na	74	73	76	82	69	76	77	75	63	75	80	58	77	73	83	Netherlands	6
Turkey	92	90	91	89	88	91	94	95	90	71	95	90	80	95	91	82	Sweden	6
Uganda	na	76	81	72	79	73	73	76	76	76	71	82	69	76	77	72	Bangladesh	5
Ukraine	na	66	67	65	56	67	70	67	67	62	66	67	65	68	66	43	Iran	1
United States	39	23	27	19	24	22	25	29	29	18	24	21	24	40	22	21	Egypt	0
Uruguay	na	32	35	30	25	27	39	38	26	15	36	30	28	32	34	27		
Venezuela	na	57	59	56	56	57	62	65	59	45	65	56	51	63	56	53		
Vietnam	na	39	40	37	39	37	42	40	37	36	38	40	39	59	35	41		
Zimbabwe	na	67	66	67	66	68	65	64	71	52	62	66	67	63	70	65		
Total	49	43	46	41	42	43	46	46	45	37	48	44	40	52	42	29	Total	43

A133) NEIGHBORS: JEWS
On this list are various groups of people. Could you please sort out any that you would not like to have as neighbors?

Jews (%)

(WVS: V77; EVS: V64)

Country	Wave 1990	Wave 2000	Gender Male	Gender Female	Age 16-29	Age 30-49	Age 50+	Education Lower	Education Middle	Education Upper	Income Lower	Income Middle	Income Upper	Values Mat	Values Mixed	Values Postm.
Albania	na	17	14	20	14	17	20	19	17	12	19	18	14	15	17	31
Algeria	na	na	na	na	na	na	na	na	na	na	na	na	na	na	na	na
Argentina	6	6	9	4	5	5	10	8	4	na	10	7	3	12	7	2
Armenia	na	na	na	na	na	na	na	na	na	na	na	na	na	na	na	na
Australia	na	na	na	na	na	na	na	na	na	na	na	na	na	na	na	na
Austria	11	8	9	8	7	6	11	11	6	4	13	9	6	23	8	5
Azerbaijan	na	na	na	na	na	na	na	na	na	na	na	na	na	na	na	na
Bangladesh	na	20	22	19	25	16	22	18	24	25	17	21	24	22	20	24
Belarus	21	15	16	14	16	13	17	18	14	10	15	14	15	15	15	7
Belgium	13	13	13	13	13	10	16	21	12	9	20	11	11	20	11	8
Bosnia and Herz.	na	28	26	30	26	28	30	30	29	22	29	29	26	28	28	23
Brazil	na	na	na	na	na	na	na	na	na	na	na	na	na	na	na	na
Bulgaria	30	18	18	18	21	18	17	20	19	13	21	22	13	18	19	13
Canada	6	4	4	4	3	3	5	8	3	1	6	3	2	7	4	3
Chile	16	9	8	9	8	9	10	9	9	10	9	9	8	9	9	6
China	na	na	na	na	na	na	na	na	na	na	na	na	na	na	na	na
Colombia	na	na	na	na	na	na	na	na	na	na	na	na	na	na	na	na
Croatia	na	18	21	16	19	17	19	18	20	11	16	20	18	19	19	16
Czech Republic	23	4	6	3	4	4	5	6	3	1	7	4	2	7	4	2
Denmark	3	3	3	2	2	2	4	4	1	1	2	3	1	4	3	1
Dominican Rep.	na	na	na	na	na	na	na	na	na	na	na	na	na	na	na	na
Egypt	na	17	17	16	18	18	12	16	21	11	17	18	13	12	20	21
El Salvador	na	na	na	na	na	na	na	na	na	na	na	na	na	na	na	na
Estonia	13	11	13	10	13	10	12	13	10	11	13	13	9	10	11	19
Finland	5	9	11	6	7	9	9	10	7	6	10	10	6	14	8	1
France	7	6	6	6	5	5	7	8	4	3	8	5	5	9	6	na
Georgia	na	na	na	na	na	na	na	na	na	na	na	na	na	na	na	na
Germany	8	5	7	4	2	5	7	7	4	3	7	5	5	6	6	3
Great Britain	7	6	6	6	3	5	9	8	5	6	5	3	6	na	na	na
Greece	na	19	21	17	17	17	24	35	20	15	20	17	18	21	19	16
Hungary	10	na	na	na	na	na	na	na	na	na	na	na	na	na	na	na
Iceland	7	4	5	3	2	3	8	5	4	1	6	2	3	7	4	1
India	53	na	na	na	na	na	na	na	na	na	na	na	na	na	na	na
Indonesia	na	na	na	na	na	na	na	na	na	na	na	na	na	na	na	na
Iran	na	na	na	na	na	na	na	na	na	na	na	na	na	na	na	na
Ireland	6	11	10	12	6	10	15	16	8	7	18	10	6	11	11	8
Israel	na	na	na	na	na	na	na	na	na	na	na	na	na	na	na	na
Italy	13	13	14	12	12	10	16	17	11	7	18	8	8	19	13	8
Japan	28	na	na	na	na	na	na	na	na	na	na	na	na	na	na	na
Jordan	na	na	na	na	na	na	na	na	na	na	na	na	na	na	na	na
Korea, South	na	41	44	38	24	42	58	63	48	29	46	39	37	44	40	27
Latvia	9	5	5	5	6	4	6	6	6	4	6	4	4	4	6	4
Lithuania	18	23	23	23	19	23	26	26	23	18	30	23	19	26	22	15
Luxembourg	na	8	8	9	9	7	9	11	7	6	11	8	5	9	8	7
Macedonia	na	20	19	21	21	19	21	27	17	15	23	18	17	19	21	11
Malta	na	21	18	23	15	20	26	28	19	10	25	18	16	26	19	13
Mexico	19	na	na	na	na	na	na	na	na	na	na	na	na	na	na	na
Moldova	na	25	24	26	26	25	24	25	30	16	26	21	28	26	23	33
Montenegro	na	na	na	na	na	na	na	na	na	na	na	na	na	na	na	na
Morocco	na	na	na	na	na	na	na	na	na	na	na	na	na	na	na	na
Netherlands	3	2	2	1	1	1	2	3	1	1	1	2	1	3	2	na
New Zealand	na	na	na	na	na	na	na	na	na	na	na	na	na	na	na	na
Nigeria	35	na	na	na	na	na	na	na	na	na	na	na	na	na	na	na
Northern Ireland	6	12	12	12	12	10	11	13	11	9	8	8	9	9	12	16
Norway	9	na	na	na	na	na	na	na	na	na	na	na	na	na	na	na
Pakistan	na	na	na	na	na	na	na	na	na	na	na	na	na	na	na	na
Peru	na	na	na	na	na	na	na	na	na	na	na	na	na	na	na	na
Philippines	na	na	na	na	na	na	na	na	na	na	na	na	na	na	na	na
Poland	na	25	27	24	13	25	33	31	20	11	28	23	25	27	24	29
Portugal	19	11	10	12	4	13	13	12	9	5	21	9	7	12	10	11
Puerto Rico	na	na	na	na	na	na	na	na	na	na	na	na	na	na	na	na
Romania	28	23	23	23	20	22	26	32	22	10	33	20	17	30	18	13
Russian Fed.	13	11	12	11	10	10	13	14	12	7	13	12	9	12	10	15
Serbia	na	na	na	na	na	na	na	na	na	na	na	na	na	na	na	na
Singapore	na	na	na	na	na	na	na	na	na	na	na	na	na	na	na	na
Slovakia	na	10	10	10	11	9	10	11	10	6	13	8	8	12	9	9
Slovenia	37	17	16	18	11	15	22	30	13	5	26	17	7	24	16	14
South Africa	na	24	25	24	25	24	24	25	23	32	26	27	20	22	26	31
Spain	12	22	21	22	21	21	23	23	18	27	16	28	24	26	22	18
Sweden	6	2	3	2	1	1	4	4	2	1	2	2	2	5	2	1
Switzerland	na	na	na	na	na	na	na	na	na	na	na	na	na	na	na	na
Taiwan	na	na	na	na	na	na	na	na	na	na	na	na	na	na	na	na
Tanzania	na	na	na	na	na	na	na	na	na	na	na	na	na	na	na	na
Turkey	59	62	58	65	61	61	68	76	49	23	78	61	33	64	65	48
Uganda	na	22	24	21	23	23	16	25	22	12	14	12	19	24	23	15
Ukraine	na	10	11	10	9	9	12	17	10	7	10	11	10	12	9	5
United States	5	9	9	9	11	8	8	12	9	8	10	8	9	13	8	9
Uruguay	na	10	9	11	8	10	12	12	7	9	11	11	9	10	11	8
Venezuela	na	na	na	na	na	na	na	na	na	na	na	na	na	na	na	na
Vietnam	na	na	na	na	na	na	na	na	na	na	na	na	na	na	na	na
Zimbabwe	na	19	18	21	22	17	17	20	19	na	19	23	21	15	20	39
Total	**16**	**14**	**14**	**14**	**14**	**13**	**15**	**16**	**14**	**10**	**16**	**14**	**12**	**17**	**13**	**10**

RANKING

Country	2000
Turkey	62
Korea, South	41
Bosnia and Herz.	28
Poland	25
Moldova	25
South Africa	24
Romania	23
Lithuania	23
Uganda	22
Spain	22
Malta	21
Bangladesh	20
Macedonia	20
Zimbabwe	19
Greece	19
Croatia	18
Bulgaria	18
Albania	17
Slovenia	17
Egypt	17
Belarus	15
Belgium	13
Italy	13
Northern Ireland	12
Russian Fed.	11
Estonia	11
Ireland	11
Portugal	11
Ukraine	10
Uruguay	10
Slovakia	10
United States	9
Chile	9
Finland	9
Austria	8
Luxembourg	8
Argentina	6
Great Britain	6
France	6
Germany	5
Latvia	5
Czech Republic	4
Iceland	4
Canada	4
Denmark	3
Sweden	2
Netherlands	2
Total	**14**

A140_1) NEIGHBORS: GYPSIES

On this list are various groups of people. Could you please sort out any that you would not like to have as neighbors?

Gypsies (%) (WVS: V77H; EVS: V65)

Country	Wave 1990	Wave 2000	Gender Male	Female	Age 16-29	30-49	50+	Education Lower	Middle	Upper	Income Lower	Middle	Upper	Values Mat	Mixed	Postm.
Albania	na	na	na	na	na	na	na	na	na	na	na	na	na	na	na	na
Algeria	na	na	na	na	na	na	na	na	na	na	na	na	na	na	na	na
Argentina	na	na	na	na	na	na	na	na	na	na	na	na	na	na	na	na
Armenia	na	na	na	na	na	na	na	na	na	na	na	na	na	na	na	na
Australia	na	na	na	na	na	na	na	na	na	na	na	na	na	na	na	na
Austria	na	25	24	26	18	22	32	27	24	18	29	23	23	39	27	16
Azerbaijan	na	na	na	na	na	na	na	na	na	na	na	na	na	na	na	na
Bangladesh	na	na	na	na	na	na	na	na	na	na	na	na	na	na	na	na
Belarus	na	51	46	55	53	49	52	52	51	50	50	49	56	53	51	46
Belgium	na	35	33	37	33	32	39	43	36	28	41	32	34	47	35	21
Bosnia and Herz.	na	na	na	na	na	na	na	na	na	na	na	na	na	na	na	na
Brazil	na	na	na	na	na	na	na	na	na	na	na	na	na	na	na	na
Bulgaria	na	54	54	53	53	49	58	57	53	50	53	52	58	59	52	40
Canada	na	na	na	na	na	na	na	na	na	na	na	na	na	na	na	na
Chile	na	na	na	na	na	na	na	na	na	na	na	na	na	na	na	na
China	na	na	na	na	na	na	na	na	na	na	na	na	na	na	na	na
Colombia	na	na	na	na	na	na	na	na	na	na	na	na	na	na	na	na
Croatia	na	39	44	34	33	33	49	43	38	28	34	40	39	40	40	34
Czech Republic	na	40	39	41	38	45	36	41	39	34	40	41	38	52	37	27
Denmark	na	15	15	15	7	15	21	20	10	10	13	15	17	20	16	9
Dominican Rep.	na	na	na	na	na	na	na	na	na	na	na	na	na	na	na	na
Egypt	na	na	na	na	na	na	na	na	na	na	na	na	na	na	na	na
El Salvador	na	na	na	na	na	na	na	na	na	na	na	na	na	na	na	na
Estonia	na	50	47	52	49	49	51	53	51	41	51	55	46	51	48	54
Finland	na	44	48	41	46	45	44	47	41	42	41	48	45	53	44	28
France	na	40	40	39	38	34	46	44	36	32	45	38	41	50	40	23
Georgia	na	na	na	na	na	na	na	na	na	na	na	na	na	na	na	na
Germany	na	32	32	33	16	35	37	39	28	23	38	35	31	40	31	24
Great Britain	na	37	35	29	37	42	39	39	30	27	36	43	na	na	na	
Greece	na	33	31	34	34	31	34	47	33	30	30	34	35	34	34	27
Hungary	na	na	na	na	na	na	na	na	na	na	na	na	na	na	na	na
Iceland	na	9	12	7	9	8	12	10	11	4	10	7	11	14	9	4
India	na	na	na	na	na	na	na	na	na	na	na	na	na	na	na	na
Indonesia	na	na	na	na	na	na	na	na	na	na	na	na	na	na	na	na
Iran	na	na	na	na	na	na	na	na	na	na	na	na	na	na	na	na
Ireland	na	25	26	23	16	26	31	30	23	20	29	26	25	25	27	16
Israel	na	na	na	na	na	na	na	na	na	na	na	na	na	na	na	na
Italy	na	56	53	58	53	49	63	61	50	54	55	54	55	69	56	50
Japan	na	na	na	na	na	na	na	na	na	na	na	na	na	na	na	na
Jordan	na	na	na	na	na	na	na	na	na	na	na	na	na	na	na	na
Korea, South	na	na	na	na	na	na	na	na	na	na	na	na	na	na	na	na
Latvia	na	27	26	28	40	26	23	24	25	37	24	26	30	25	28	34
Lithuania	na	63	57	69	60	61	68	66	63	60	71	60	63	75	58	57
Luxembourg	na	25	25	25	22	25	28	30	24	20	26	23	15	27	26	17
Macedonia	na	na	na	na	na	na	na	na	na	na	na	na	na	na	na	na
Malta	na	30	20	22	27	30	33	37	28	26	29	32	28	34	28	28
Mexico	na	na	na	na	na	na	na	na	na	na	na	na	na	na	na	na
Moldova	na	na	na	na	na	na	na	na	na	na	na	na	na	na	na	na
Montenegro	na	24	21	26	19	22	28	31	20	15	31	24	20	28	18	15
Morocco	na	na	na	na	na	na	na	na	na	na	na	na	na	na	na	na
Netherlands	na	19	19	20	14	17	25	24	19	16	14	19	23	23	22	11
New Zealand	na	na	na	na	na	na	na	na	na	na	na	na	na	na	na	na
Nigeria	na	na	na	na	na	na	na	na	na	na	na	na	na	na	na	na
Northern Ireland	na	58	57	60	54	57	62	59	58	58	57	61	63	65	61	39
Norway	na	na	na	na	na	na	na	na	na	na	na	na	na	na	na	na
Pakistan	na	na	na	na	na	na	na	na	na	na	na	na	na	na	na	na
Peru	na	na	na	na	na	na	na	na	na	na	na	na	na	na	na	na
Philippines	na	na	na	na	na	na	na	na	na	na	na	na	na	na	na	na
Poland	na	39	39	38	33	39	42	43	34	34	40	36	46	43	37	37
Portugal	na	37	34	39	30	36	41	41	28	25	46	37	34	44	34	28
Puerto Rico	na	na	na	na	na	na	na	na	na	na	na	na	na	na	na	na
Romania	na	52	49	54	48	49	55	57	50	43	56	48	51	53	49	49
Russian Fed.	na	46	39	51	53	43	43	42	46	48	43	45	48	46	44	40
Serbia	na	12	11	14	11	13	13	20	9	8	14	11	11	14	12	3
Singapore	na	na	na	na	na	na	na	na	na	na	na	na	na	na	na	na
Slovakia	na	77	76	78	83	76	74	75	79	77	75	76	80	77	80	61
Slovenia	na	37	38	36	33	34	42	42	35	33	42	34	29	46	35	31
South Africa	na	na	na	na	na	na	na	na	na	na	na	na	na	na	na	na
Spain	na	28	26	30	20	28	33	33	26	20	27	30	28	35	28	17
Sweden	na	20	21	19	13	21	23	22	21	16	18	20	21	27	22	12
Switzerland	na	na	na	na	na	na	na	na	na	na	na	na	na	na	na	na
Taiwan	na	na	na	na	na	na	na	na	na	na	na	na	na	na	na	na
Tanzania	na	na	na	na	na	na	na	na	na	na	na	na	na	na	na	na
Turkey	na	72	71	73	73	69	76	78	68	47	80	72	56	74	75	62
Uganda	na	na	na	na	na	na	na	na	na	na	na	na	na	na	na	na
Ukraine	na	53	52	54	60	51	51	54	52	55	50	52	57	56	52	36
United States	na	na	na	na	na	na	na	na	na	na	na	na	na	na	na	na
Uruguay	na	na	na	na	na	na	na	na	na	na	na	na	na	na	na	na
Venezuela	na	na	na	na	na	na	na	na	na	na	na	na	na	na	na	na
Vietnam	na	na	na	na	na	na	na	na	na	na	na	na	na	na	na	na
Zimbabwe	na	na	na	na	na	na	na	na	na	na	na	na	na	na	na	na
Total	na	38	37	39	36	36	41	41	38	32	38	37	39	45	36	26

RANKING

Country	2000
Slovakia	77
Turkey	72
Lithuania	63
Northern Ireland	58
Italy	56
Bulgaria	54
Ukraine	53
Romania	52
Belarus	51
Estonia	50
Russian Fed.	46
Finland	44
Czech Republic	40
France	40
Croatia	39
Poland	39
Great Britain	37
Slovenia	37
Portugal	37
Belgium	35
Greece	33
Germany	32
Malta	30
Spain	28
Latvia	27
Luxembourg	25
Austria	25
Ireland	25
Montenegro	24
Sweden	20
Netherlands	19
Denmark	15
Serbia	12
Iceland	9
Total	38

A151_1) NEIGHBORS: PEOPLE WITH LARGE FAMILIES

On this list are various groups of people. Could you please sort out any that you would not like to have as neighbors?.

(EVS: V57)

People with large families (%)

Country	Wave 1990	Wave 2000	Gender Male	Gender Female	Age 16-29	Age 30-49	Age 50+	Education Lower	Education Middle	Education Upper	Income Lower	Income Middle	Income Upper	Values Mat	Values Mixed	Values Postm.
Albania	na	na	na	na	na	na	na	na	na	na	na	na	na	na	na	na
Algeria	na	na	na	na	na	na	na	na	na	na	na	na	na	na	na	na
Argentina	5	na	na	na	na	na	na	na	na	na	na	na	na	na	na	na
Armenia	na	na	na	na	na	na	na	na	na	na	na	na	na	na	na	na
Australia	na	na	na	na	na	na	na	na	na	na	na	na	na	na	na	na
Austria	5	4	5	3	4	4	5	4	5	3	7	4	2	6	5	2
Azerbaijan	na	na	na	na	na	na	na	na	na	na	na	na	na	na	na	na
Bangladesh	na	na	na	na	na	na	na	na	na	na	na	na	na	na	na	na
Belarus	16	10	10	11	8	13	10	9	10	13	9	11	12	11	9	14
Belgium	8	9	10	9	10	8	10	10	9	8	10	9	9	11	8	5
Bosnia and Herz.	na	na	na	na	na	na	na	na	na	na	na	na	na	na	na	na
Brazil	6	na	na	na	na	na	na	na	na	na	na	na	na	na	na	na
Bulgaria	24	12	12	12	14	13	10	11	11	15	13	13	9	12	13	4
Canada	6	na	na	na	na	na	na	na	na	na	na	na	na	na	na	na
Chile	14	na	na	na	na	na	na	na	na	na	na	na	na	na	na	na
China	19	na	na	na	na	na	na	na	na	na	na	na	na	na	na	na
Colombia	na	na	na	na	na	na	na	na	na	na	na	na	na	na	na	na
Croatia	na	15	17	13	18	13	15	14	17	13	16	13	18	6	16	14
Czech Republic	15	9	10	8	7	8	10	9	9	5	11	9	8	10	8	7
Denmark	3	4	4	5	6	3	5	5	3	4	7	2	3	8	5	3
Dominican Rep.	na	na	na	na	na	na	na	na	na	na	na	na	na	na	na	na
Egypt	na	na	na	na	na	na	na	na	na	na	na	na	na	na	na	na
El Salvador	na	na	na	na	na	na	na	na	na	na	na	na	na	na	na	na
Estonia	11	14	13	15	9	14	17	16	14	12	18	13	14	15	14	8
Finland	4	8	7	8	9	6	8	8	7	6	8	7	7	9	7	6
France	8	10	10	9	8	8	12	10	11	8	12	9	8	12	10	5
Georgia	na	na	na	na	na	na	na	na	na	na	na	na	na	na	na	na
Germany	7	6	7	5	5	6	7	8	5	5	7	6	7	5	7	5
Great Britain	11	14	15	14	8	12	21	18	10	19	14	12	13	9	12	8
Greece	na	11	12	10	10	9	12	10	12	10	8	10	12	na	na	na
Hungary	7	na	na	na	na	na	na	na	na	na	na	na	na	na	na	na
Iceland	2	3	3	2	4	2	3	3	3	1	4	3	1	4	2	2
India	35	na	na	na	na	na	na	na	na	na	na	na	na	na	na	na
Indonesia	na	na	na	na	na	na	na	na	na	na	na	na	na	na	na	na
Iran	na	na	na	na	na	na	na	na	na	na	na	na	na	na	na	na
Ireland	3	9	10	8	7	8	13	13	8	5	12	8	6	8	10	6
Israel	na	na	na	na	na	na	na	na	na	na	na	na	na	na	na	na
Italy	12	14	15	13	13	12	16	16	12	12	18	11	8	18	14	11
Japan	6	na	na	na	na	na	na	na	na	na	na	na	na	na	na	na
Jordan	na	na	na	na	na	na	na	na	na	na	na	na	na	na	na	na
Korea, South	79	na	na	na	na	na	na	na	na	na	na	na	na	na	na	na
Latvia	12	5	5	5	3	4	6	3	5	6	5	4	4	7	3	2
Lithuania	17	12	11	12	11	9	13	13	11	11	20	7	11	10	11	15
Luxembourg	na	8	9	8	8	8	8	8	7	10	11	8	6	6	10	5
Macedonia	na	na	na	na	na	na	na	na	na	na	na	na	na	na	na	na
Malta	na	15	17	14	14	15	17	14	16	14	15	22	13	17	15	12
Mexico	23	na	na	na	na	na	na	na	na	na	na	na	na	na	na	na
Moldova	na	na	na	na	na	na	na	na	na	na	na	na	na	na	na	na
Montenegro	na	na	na	na	na	na	na	na	na	na	na	na	na	na	na	na
Morocco	na	na	na	na	na	na	na	na	na	na	na	na	na	na	na	na
Netherlands	6	8	9	7	8	5	11	8	8	8	7	9	7	8	8	6
New Zealand	na	na	na	na	na	na	na	na	na	na	na	na	na	na	na	na
Nigeria	33	na	na	na	na	na	na	na	na	na	na	na	na	na	na	na
Northern Ireland	9	14	15	14	10	16	12	13	15	15	15	13	13	14	13	19
Norway	6	na	na	na	na	na	na	na	na	na	na	na	na	na	na	na
Pakistan	na	na	na	na	na	na	na	na	na	na	na	na	na	na	na	na
Peru	na	na	na	na	na	na	na	na	na	na	na	na	na	na	na	na
Philippines	na	na	na	na	na	na	na	na	na	na	na	na	na	na	na	na
Poland	na	11	11	11	10	10	13	13	10	8	10	11	13	11	11	18
Portugal	15	5	7	3	4	6	5	5	7	1	4	6	6	4	5	12
Puerto Rico	na	na	na	na	na	na	na	na	na	na	na	na	na	na	na	na
Romania	22	14	12	16	13	14	14	15	14	11	15	15	14	14	14	9
Russian Fed.	12	6	6	6	6	6	7	7	6	7	6	7	6	7	6	13
Serbia	na	na	na	na	na	na	na	na	na	na	na	na	na	na	na	na
Singapore	na	na	na	na	na	na	na	na	na	na	na	na	na	na	na	na
Slovakia	na	10	11	10	10	9	12	9	10	15	12	8	10	11	9	6
Slovenia	40	9	11	7	5	9	12	13	8	5	15	9	6	11	9	9
South Africa	na	na	na	na	na	na	na	na	na	na	na	na	na	na	na	na
Spain	10	6	5	7	4	7	6	6	5	8	5	10	6	7	7	2
Sweden	5	4	5	3	6	2	5	5	4	3	5	4	3	4	5	2
Switzerland	1	na	na	na	na	na	na	na	na	na	na	na	na	na	na	na
Taiwan	na	na	na	na	na	na	na	na	na	na	na	na	na	na	na	na
Tanzania	na	na	na	na	na	na	na	na	na	na	na	na	na	na	na	na
Turkey	41	41	39	42	38	41	48	44	37	34	43	41	34	36	41	43
Uganda	na	na	na	na	na	na	na	na	na	na	na	na	na	na	na	na
Ukraine	na	9	7	11	13	8	9	8	10	8	8	10	9	8	11	4
United States	8	na	na	na	na	na	na	na	na	na	na	na	na	na	na	na
Uruguay	na	na	na	na	na	na	na	na	na	na	na	na	na	na	na	na
Venezuela	na	na	na	na	na	na	na	na	na	na	na	na	na	na	na	na
Vietnam	na	na	na	na	na	na	na	na	na	na	na	na	na	na	na	na
Zimbabwe	na	na	na	na	na	na	na	na	na	na	na	na	na	na	na	na
Total	14	10	10	9	9	9	11	10	10	9	11	9	9	10	9	8

RANKING

Country	2000
Turkey	41
Malta	15
Croatia	15
Northern Ireland	14
Great Britain	14
Estonia	14
Romania	14
Italy	14
Bulgaria	12
Lithuania	12
Poland	11
Greece	11
Belarus	10
Slovakia	10
France	10
Ireland	9
Ukraine	9
Slovenia	9
Belgium	9
Czech Republic	9
Luxembourg	8
Netherlands	8
Finland	8
Russian Fed.	6
Germany	6
Spain	6
Portugal	5
Latvia	5
Denmark	4
Austria	4
Sweden	4
Iceland	3
Total	10

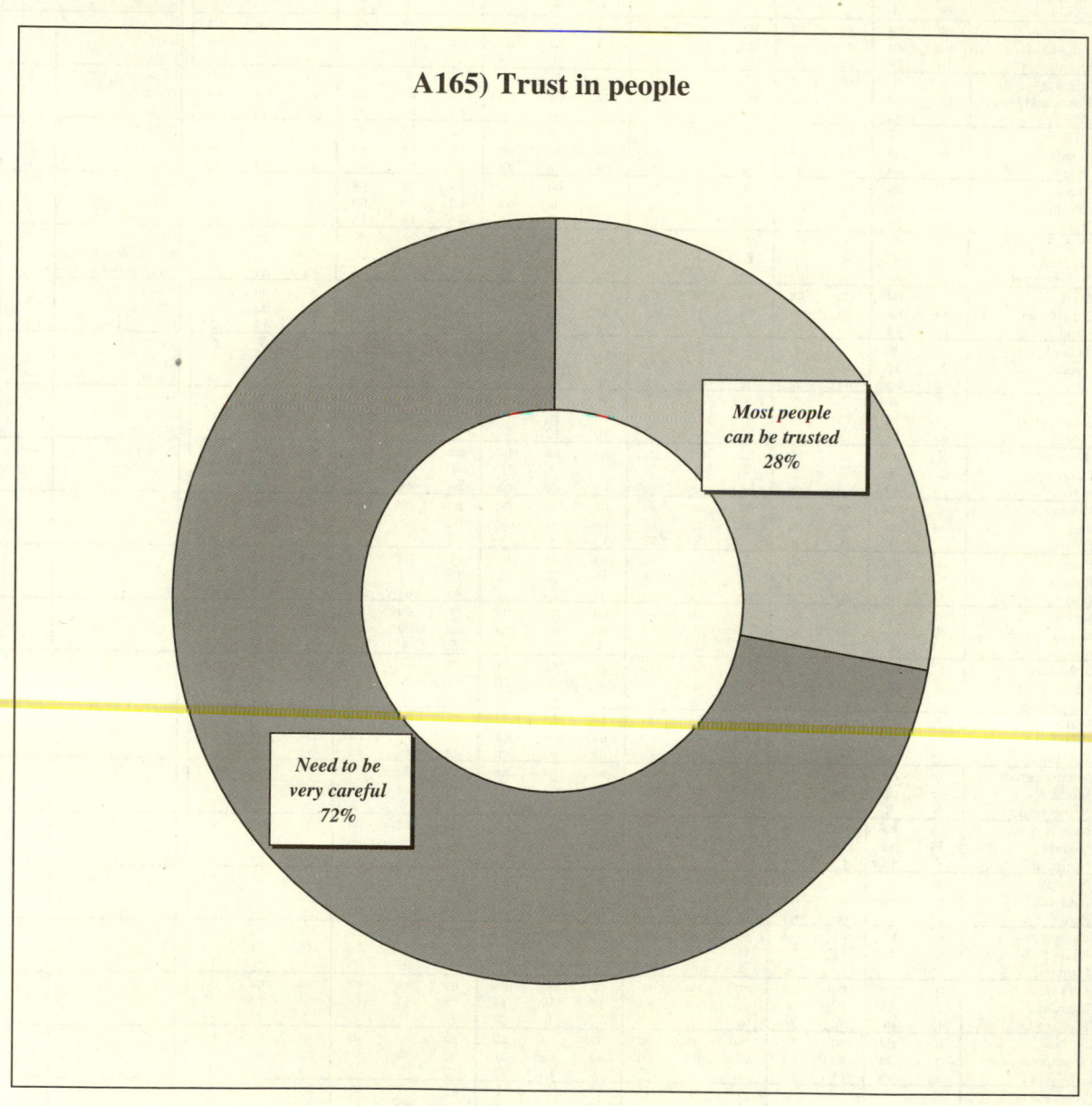

A165) Trust in people

Most people
can be trusted
28%

Need to be
very careful
72%

A165) MOST PEOPLE CAN BE TRUSTED

Generally speaking, would you say that most people can be trusted or that you need to be very careful in dealing with people?

Most people can be trusted (%) (WVS: V25; EVS: V66)

Country	Wave		Gender		Age			Education			Income			Values		
	1990	2000	Male	Female	16-29	30-49	50+	Lower	Middle	Upper	Lower	Middle	Upper	Mat	Mixed	Postm.
Albania	na	24	24	25	25	25	24	27	23	24	24	27	22	22	24	42
Algeria	na	11	11	11	8	12	16	16	10	10	12	10	13	12	11	10
Argentina	23	15	16	15	10	18	18	14	17	21	15	14	18	15	15	17
Armenia	na	25	24	25	26	26	22	26	24	28	26	24	22	23	26	31
Australia	na	40	41	39	32	45	41	31	38	50	35	44	47	28	39	45
Austria	32	34	37	31	31	40	30	24	38	58	25	33	44	20	30	44
Azerbaijan	na	21	21	20	21	19	24	21	19	24	20	19	24	19	23	33
Bangladesh	na	24	24	23	22	23	31	30	17	15	23	26	21	21	25	29
Belarus	26	42	41	43	37	43	44	38	43	44	39	43	46	39	44	46
Belgium	33	31	34	28	29	34	28	18	27	47	22	28	41	21	31	46
Bosnia and Herz.	na	16	16	15	15	15	17	19	15	16	21	13	20	16	16	11
Brazil	7	3	3	2	2	4	1	2	3	5	3	2	3	2	3	6
Bulgaria	30	27	29	25	27	26	27	23	26	34	25	23	30	24	31	24
Canada	52	39	41	37	36	40	39	30	34	54	28	37	51	36	37	43
Chile	23	23	22	24	20	22	26	20	24	26	19	24	29	24	22	23
China	60	55	53	56	48	56	55	50	57	74	52	56	58	53	55	69
Colombia	na	11	13	9	9	12	10	9	8	17	9	9	16	10	11	11
Croatia	na	18	21	16	17	23	14	14	19	30	17	16	23	16	18	19
Czech Republic	28	24	23	25	21	24	25	20	25	40	22	23	27	16	24	39
Denmark	58	67	68	66	68	75	57	56	79	83	58	70	83	58	65	82
Dominican Rep.	na	26	25	28	26	26	55	19	17	32	22	31	25	16	29	26
Egypt	na	38	37	39	34	37	46	45	34	26	41	41	35	40	38	24
El Salvador	na	15	16	14	15	15	13	15	13	15	15	15	15	na	na	na
Estonia	28	23	23	22	29	18	24	19	22	33	23	17	29	19	25	27
Finland	63	58	56	60	61	55	59	53	63	70	53	56	62	49	60	69
France	23	22	22	23	23	24	21	14	27	41	18	20	35	14	20	41
Georgia	na	19	17	20	19	18	19	16	19	21	18	17	22	16	21	26
Germany	26	35	37	33	44	32	34	28	41	46	31	33	40	35	33	40
Great Britain	44	30	31	29	25	32	32	21	31	50	24	36	38	na	na	na
Greece	na	24	25	23	20	29	20	13	20	30	19	21	31	21	23	33
Hungary	25	22	23	21	24	21	22	16	31	35	19	18	28	19	25	18
Iceland	44	41	40	42	33	44	44	32	38	67	35	44	43	34	40	64
India	35	41	42	40	40	40	43	45	36	37	41	45	38	46	34	33
Indonesia	na	51	53	50	49	51	54	56	49	52	43	56	62	52	50	52
Iran	na	65	66	65	63	68	66	65	63	68	66	67	64	64	65	68
Ireland	47	35	41	30	30	39	36	33	33	45	25	36	45	28	38	34
Israel	na	23	22	25	24	23	22	11	21	36	18	18	33	23	24	19
Italy	34	33	34	31	33	36	29	21	37	55	25	33	45	15	31	44
Japan	42	43	42	44	45	46	40	30	42	54	36	48	47	45	42	60
Jordan	na	28	30	26	27	28	29	28	23	33	28	31	24	28	27	20
Korea, South	34	27	27	28	27	27	29	23	26	29	22	32	30	27	28	28
Latvia	19	17	17	17	18	18	16	13	17	23	18	14	19	14	19	16
Lithuania	31	25	29	21	30	26	20	21	25	33	20	23	28	22	26	24
Luxembourg	na	26	27	25	21	28	27	20	28	35	16	29	35	23	25	34
Macedonia	na	14	16	11	16	13	12	14	12	18	13	15	15	14	12	24
Malta	na	21	21	20	20	20	22	18	20	31	15	21	28	21	20	29
Mexico	34	21	23	20	22	20	23	22	18	28	23	22	21	25	19	25
Moldova	na	15	15	14	14	13	17	16	14	14	12	17	14	15	16	9
Montenegro	na	34	33	34	37	36	30	29	36	39	31	32	34	28	37	61
Morocco	na	24	21	26	23	22	29	25	18	23	26	17	25	24	24	23
Netherlands	56	60	62	58	67	63	53	38	62	79	50	58	76	43	56	78
New Zealand	na	48	49	48	38	51	49	43	41	61	43	50	54	53	48	53
Nigeria	23	26	26	25	25	26	28	28	24	24	27	25	24	24	26	35
Northern Ireland	44	40	42	37	30	42	44	40	38	43	38	41	42	36	38	54
Norway	65	65	64	67	69	74	52	46	65	84	na	na	na	49	66	80
Pakistan	na	31	33	29	35	32	21	31	32	27	30	28	38	28	35	55
Peru	na	11	11	10	10	12	9	8	9	15	9	10	15	8	11	13
Philippines	na	8	9	8	8	9	9	8	9	8	9	7	10	9	8	10
Poland	35	19	17	21	17	18	21	16	20	26	16	20	25	17	19	25
Portugal	21	10	12	9	9	11	10	9	12	14	7	13	12	10	10	13
Puerto Rico	na	23	25	21	15	21	27	13	18	27	15	25	28	24	22	24
Romania	16	10	11	10	11	9	10	10	9	13	9	9	12	7	13	13
Russian Fed.	38	24	23	24	22	24	25	21	24	25	24	23	25	22	26	25
Serbia	na	19	19	19	17	20	18	21	18	18	17	19	22	16	21	25
Singapore	na	17	19	14	20	15	10	11	18	29	11	14	23	16	17	23
Slovakia	na	16	16	15	16	18	13	12	17	17	11	15	19	13	17	29
Slovenia	17	22	23	21	21	23	21	7	23	46	13	24	34	19	22	28
South Africa	28	12	13	11	11	12	13	12	12	12	16	7	12	13	10	15
Spain	32	36	36	36	38	39	33	33	37	45	33	35	39	33	37	39
Sweden	66	66	66	67	67	68	65	53	63	82	63	60	80	57	62	81
Switzerland	43	41	40	42	35	40	45	32	41	57	37	39	47	33	39	54
Taiwan	na	38	39	38	56	38	29	27	40	48	33	33	48	37	38	47
Tanzania	na	8	9	7	6	10	7	9	5	9	11	7	7	9	6	21
Turkey	10	16	18	14	15	15	18	15	14	25	16	15	16	16	15	18
Uganda	na	8	9	7	9	6	8	7	8	9	9	11	3	7	8	8
Ukraine	na	27	29	26	27	28	27	24	27	29	24	31	27	27	26	27
United States	52	36	34	38	24	35	47	24	33	42	28	41	40	37	35	40
Uruguay	na	22	23	21	20	24	22	19	25	32	21	23	23	25	21	25
Venezuela	na	16	18	14	16	16	15	11	16	22	18	16	16	14	17	15
Vietnam	na	41	43	40	41	39	46	42	39	48	39	45	40	32	42	42
Zimbabwe	na	12	11	13	10	12	17	14	10	na	18	11	6	13	11	12
Total	35	28	29	27	25	29	29	24	27	36	25	27	31	24	28	37

RANKING

Country	2000
Denmark	67
Sweden	66
Iran	65
Norway	65
Netherlands	60
Finland	58
China	55
Indonesia	51
New Zealand	48
Japan	43
Belarus	42
Vietnam	41
Iceland	41
India	41
Switzerland	41
Australia	40
Northern Ireland	40
Canada	39
Taiwan	38
Egypt	38
Spain	36
United States	36
Ireland	35
Germany	35
Austria	34
Montenegro	34
Italy	33
Pakistan	31
Belgium	31
Great Britain	30
Jordan	28
Korea, South	27
Ukraine	27
Bulgaria	27
Dominican Rep.	26
Luxembourg	26
Nigeria	26
Lithuania	25
Armenia	25
Albania	24
Czech Republic	24
Greece	24
Russian Fed.	24
Bangladesh	24
Morocco	24
Israel	23
Chile	23
Estonia	23
Puerto Rico	23
France	22
Uruguay	22
Hungary	22
Slovenia	22
Mexico	21
Malta	21
Azerbaijan	21
Poland	19
Serbia	19
Georgia	19
Croatia	18
Latvia	17
Singapore	17
Venezuela	16
Bosnia and Herz.	16
Slovakia	16
Turkey	16
Argentina	15
Moldova	15
El Salvador	15
Macedonia	14
Zimbabwe	12
South Africa	12
Algeria	11
Colombia	11
Peru	11
Romania	10
Portugal	10
Philippines	8
Tanzania	8
Uganda	8
Brazil	3
Total	28

A168) MOST PEOPLE TRY TO BE FAIR

Do you think most people would try to take advantage of you
if they got a chance, or would they try to be fair?

Try to be fair (%)

(WVS: V26)

Country	Wave		Gender		Age			Education			Income			Values				Country	2000
	1990	2000	Male	Female	16-29	30-49	50+	Lower	Middle	Upper	Lower	Middle	Upper	Mat	Mixed	Postm.		**RANKING**	
Albania	na	**43**	41	44	41	43	43	44	43	39	48	41	38	43	41	51		Sweden	87
Algeria	na	**34**	34	34	33	33	35	32	34	35	32	30	35	33	33	32		China	80
Argentina	na	**39**	38	41	39	38	41	35	44	55	38	37	45	37	38	43		Vietnam	72
Armenia	na	**na**	na	na	na	na	na	na	na	na	na	na	na	na	na	na		Philippines	72
Australia	na	**na**	na	na	na	na	na	na	na	na	na	na	na	na	na	na		Indonesia	67
Austria	na	**na**	na	na	na	na	na	na	na	na	na	na	na	na	na	na		Canada	67
Azerbaijan	na	**na**	na	na	na	na	na	na	na	na	na	na	na	na	na	na		Iran	66
Bangladesh	na	**38**	34	44	38	39	40	48	31	26	56	32	30	48	33	19		United States	62
Belarus	na	**na**	na	na	na	na	na	na	na	na	na	na	na	na	na	na		Spain	50
Belgium	na	**na**	na	na	na	na	na	na	na	na	na	na	na	na	na	na		Egypt	49
Bosnia and Herz.	na	**29**	29	29	27	27	35	33	25	40	33	28	33	25	32	28		Singapore	49
Brazil	na	**na**	na	na	na	na	na	na	na	na	na	na	na	na	na	na		Serbia	48
Bulgaria	na	**na**	na	na	na	na	na	na	na	na	na	na	na	na	na	na		Tanzania	47
Canada	na	**67**	64	70	66	68	66	59	65	77	55	67	75	61	66	71		Korea, South	46
Chile	na	**29**	27	31	32	26	30	27	30	30	25	29	36	29	28	32		Montenegro	45
China	na	**80**	75	85	79	81	77	78	81	78	77	83	79	80	79	81		Albania	43
Colombia	na	**na**	na	na	na	na	na	na	na	na	na	na	na	na	na	na		India	41
Croatia	na	**na**	na	na	na	na	na	na	na	na	na	na	na	na	na	na		Argentina	39
Czech Republic	na	**na**	na	na	na	na	na	na	na	na	na	na	na	na	na	na		Jordan	39
Denmark	na	**na**	na	na	na	na	na	na	na	na	na	na	na	na	na	na		Bangladesh	38
Dominican Rep.	na	**na**	na	na	na	na	na	na	na	na	na	na	na	na	na	na		Puerto Rico	38
Egypt	na	**49**	47	52	48	47	55	53	48	40	52	49	48	48	51	42		Pakistan	34
El Salvador	na	**na**	na	na	na	na	na	na	na	na	na	na	na	na	na	na		Algeria	34
Estonia	na	**na**	na	na	na	na	na	na	na	na	na	na	na	na	na	na		Japan	34
Finland	na	**na**	na	na	na	na	na	na	na	na	na	na	na	na	na	na		Zimbabwe	33
France	na	**na**	na	na	na	na	na	na	na	na	na	na	na	na	na	na		South Africa	33
Georgia	na	**na**	na	na	na	na	na	na	na	na	na	na	na	na	na	na		Venezuela	33
Germany	na	**na**	na	na	na	na	na	na	na	na	na	na	na	na	na	na		Macedonia	31
Great Britain	na	**na**	na	na	na	na	na	na	na	na	na	na	na	na	na	na		Mexico	30
Greece	na	**na**	na	na	na	na	na	na	na	na	na	na	na	na	na	na		Bosnia and Herz.	29
Hungary	na	**na**	na	na	na	na	na	na	na	na	na	na	na	na	na	na		Nigeria	29
Iceland	na	**na**	na	na	na	na	na	na	na	na	na	na	na	na	na	na		Chile	29
India	na	**41**	39	43	44	38	41	41	39	42	42	41	39	43	40	41		Morocco	28
Indonesia	na	**67**	70	66	64	71	66	72	66	67	75	63	69	67	69	50		Peru	27
Iran	na	**66**	67	65	64	68	66	66	66	68	66	66	66	62	66	72		Uganda	23
Ireland	na	**na**	na	na	na	na	na	na	na	na	na	na	na	na	na	na		Turkey	18
Israel	na	**na**	na	na	na	na	na	na	na	na	na	na	na	na	na	na		Moldova	17
Italy	na	**na**	na	na	na	na	na	na	na	na	na	na	na	na	na	na			
Japan	na	**34**	32	36	16	28	46	41	33	30	33	36	34	37	32	32			
Jordan	na	**39**	32	45	41	38	35	37	40	42	41	35	41	40	39	28			
Korea, South	na	**46**	39	53	41	48	45	52	48	41	44	49	45	42	47	57			
Latvia	na	**na**	na	na	na	na	na	na	na	na	na	na	na	na	na	na			
Lithuania	na	**na**	na	na	na	na	na	na	na	na	na	na	na	na	na	na			
Luxembourg	na	**na**	na	na	na	na	na	na	na	na	na	na	na	na	na	na			
Macedonia	na	**31**	29	33	33	32	27	28	28	40	27	31	35	27	33	30			
Malta	na	**na**	na	na	na	na	na	na	na	na	na	na	na	na	na	na			
Mexico	na	**30**	30	31	31	30	30	29	32	31	29	30	30	33	27	38			
Moldova	na	**17**	16	17	15	16	20	19	16	16	16	16	16	14	19	18			
Montenegro	na	**45**	45	45	51	45	42	38	47	55	42	44	46	39	49	67			
Morocco	na	**28**	25	32	29	28	29	29	26	31	14	27	39	26	30	25			
Netherlands	na	**na**	na	na	na	na	na	na	na	na	na	na	na	na	na	na			
New Zealand	na	**na**	na	na	na	na	na	na	na	na	na	na	na	na	na	na			
Nigeria	na	**29**	28	31	30	28	25	30	29	29	26	28	35	27	29	42			
Northern Ireland	na	**na**	na	na	na	na	na	na	na	na	na	na	na	na	na	na			
Norway	na	**na**	na	na	na	na	na	na	na	na	na	na	na	na	na	na			
Pakistan	na	**34**	36	33	39	35	22	34	36	30	33	32	39	32	37	50			
Peru	na	**27**	27	27	25	29	27	26	28	26	27	26	28	32	26	26			
Philippines	na	**72**	71	73	73	71	72	75	73	67	70	73	72	68	75	62			
Poland	na	**na**	na	na	na	na	na	na	na	na	na	na	na	na	na	na			
Portugal	na	**na**	na	na	na	na	na	na	na	na	na	na	na	na	na	na			
Puerto Rico	na	**38**	34	40	35	36	40	28	34	41	22	38	51	29	39	40			
Romania	na	**na**	na	na	na	na	na	na	na	na	na	na	na	na	na	na			
Russian Fed.	na	**na**	na	na	na	na	na	na	na	na	na	na	na	na	na	na			
Serbia	na	**48**	43	53	51	52	44	45	46	57	44	47	57	43	51	62			
Singapore	na	**49**	50	48	53	46	43	46	49	58	47	49	50	47	50	46			
Slovakia	na	**na**	na	na	na	na	na	na	na	na	na	na	na	na	na	na			
Slovenia	na	**na**	na	na	na	na	na	na	na	na	na	na	na	na	na	na			
South Africa	na	**33**	34	31	33	30	40	34	32	29	31	32	35	34	32	28			
Spain	na	**50**	49	50	51	51	47	45	52	60	45	50	48	53	45	61			
Sweden	na	**87**	87	88	84	89	88	84	85	94	85	88	90	84	87	89			
Switzerland	na	**na**	na	na	na	na	na	na	na	na	na	na	na	na	na	na			
Taiwan	na	**na**	na	na	na	na	na	na	na	na	na	na	na	na	na	na			
Tanzania	na	**47**	45	50	50	46	45	53	44	34	54	47	37	48	46	70			
Turkey	na	**18**	17	19	19	19	17	17	17	28	16	18	25	17	17	23			
Uganda	na	**23**	20	26	24	21	26	27	22	14	24	15	21	28	21	21			
Ukraine	na	**na**	na	na	na	na	na	na	na	na	na	na	na	na	na	na			
United States	na	**62**	61	63	44	64	74	50	59	68	53	62	74	59	60	67			
Uruguay	na	**na**	na	na	na	na	na	na	na	na	na	na	na	na	na	na			
Venezuela	na	**33**	30	35	37	28	33	32	30	40	29	35	32	29	32	39			
Vietnam	na	**72**	70	75	71	75	70	74	71	72	71	74	72	70	74	64			
Zimbabwe	na	**33**	33	33	33	33	30	36	29	na	33	34	32	36	31	30			
Total	na	**43**	42	45	41	44	46	42	43	47	42	43	46	41	44	48		Total	43

A169) GOOD HUMAN RELATIONSHIPS

To build good human relationships, what is most important: to try to understand others' preferences or to express one's own preferences clearly?

Understand other's preferences (%)

(WVS: V38)

Country	Wave 1990	Wave 2000	Gender Male	Gender Female	Age 16-29	Age 30-49	Age 50+	Education Lower	Education Middle	Education Upper	Income Lower	Income Middle	Income Upper	Values Mat	Values Mixed	Values Postm.
Albania	na	51	51	52	56	51	48	46	52	61	41	56	58	50	52	49
Algeria	na	54	54	55	51	53	64	62	53	52	55	57	51	54	53	60
Argentina	na	57	54	60	54	57	60	52	67	59	57	53	63	48	57	63
Armenia	na	63	61	65	64	63	61	61	62	66	66	65	57	65	63	52
Australia	na	72	68	75	69	74	71	64	72	77	71	72	73	70	73	69
Austria	na	na	na	na	na	na	na	na	na	na	na	na	na	na	na	na
Azerbaijan	na	54	51	57	55	54	51	57	53	56	51	46	66	54	54	49
Bangladesh	na	54	55	53	53	56	50	51	56	61	56	54	52	55	54	54
Belarus	na	na	na	na	na	na	na	na	na	na	na	na	na	na	na	na
Belgium	na	na	na	na	na	na	na	na	na	na	na	na	na	na	na	na
Bosnia and Herz.	na	82	82	82	82	81	82	82	81	83	82	81	80	83	83	78
Brazil	na	44	45	42	41	44	49	40	47	47	46	43	44	42	44	49
Bulgaria	na	na	na	na	na	na	na	na	na	na	na	na	na	na	na	na
Canada	na	67	66	67	62	66	70	60	65	74	58	64	75	59	65	70
Chile	na	55	53	56	53	54	56	55	51	62	52	56	58	55	57	45
China	na	73	71	75	68	75	74	72	74	79	72	71	79	76	71	79
Colombia	na	na	na	na	na	na	na	na	na	na	na	na	na	na	na	na
Croatia	na	na	na	na	na	na	na	na	na	na	na	na	na	na	na	na
Czech Republic	na	na	na	na	na	na	na	na	na	na	na	na	na	na	na	na
Denmark	na	na	na	na	na	na	na	na	na	na	na	na	na	na	na	na
Dominican Rep.	na	72	70	73	70	75	78	72	68	73	72	76	63	68	72	77
Egypt	na	76	77	75	78	76	74	75	77	78	76	74	77	76	76	72
El Salvador	na	52	53	51	48	53	55	46	56	61	44	55	60	na	na	na
Estonia	na	na	na	na	na	na	na	na	na	na	na	na	na	na	na	na
Finland	na	na	na	na				na	na	na	na	na	na	na	na	na
France	na	na	na	na				na	na	na	na	na	na	na	na	na
Georgia	na	54	53	55	49	56	57	51	53	60	52	56	57	55	54	47
Germany	na	na	na	na	na	na	na	na	na	na	na	na	na	na	na	na
Great Britain	na	na	na	na	na	na	na	na	na	na	na	na	na	na	na	na
Greece	na	na	na	na	na	na	na	na	na	na	na	na	na	na	na	na
Hungary	na	na	na	na	na	na	na	na	na	na	na	na	na	na	na	na
Iceland	na	na	na	na	na	na	na	na	na	na	na	na	na	na	na	na
India	na	64	64	64	64	64	65	66	61	65	67	67	61	69	60	67
Indonesia	na	79	79	80	80	84	74	72	83	80	78	82	79	79	80	78
Iran	na	63	62	64	61	66	63	63	64	61	62	64	60	61	62	61
Ireland	na	na	na	na	na	na	na	na	na	na	na	na	na	na	na	na
Israel	na	na	na	na	na	na	na	na	na	na	na	na	na	na	na	na
Italy	na	na	na	na	na	na	na	na	na	na	na	na	na	na	na	na
Japan	na	81	81	81	78	85	79	72	82	83	80	81	83	86	81	81
Jordan	na	na	na	na	na	na	na	na	na	na	na	na	na	na	na	na
Korea, South	na	79	81	77	77	80	79	67	80	78	79	79	79	78	80	74
Latvia	na	na	na	na	na	na	na	na	na	na	na	na	na	na	na	na
Lithuania	na	na	na	na	na	na	na	na	na	na	na	na	na	na	na	na
Luxembourg	na	na	na	na	na	na	na	na	na	na	na	na	na	na	na	na
Macedonia	na	57	57	57	53	56	62	55	59	55	60	57	55	57	56	68
Malta	na	na	na	na	na	na	na	na	na	na	na	na	na	na	na	na
Mexico	na	46	48	45	48	44	50	43	48	55	43	45	49	46	47	45
Moldova	na	59	59	58	61	56	60	58	56	64	54	59	61	58	60	53
Montenegro	na	46	47	46	44	43	51	51	41	49	52	51	42	48	46	34
Morocco	na	83	82	85	82	84	89	84	83	73	85	81	80	87	81	75
Netherlands	na	na	na	na	na	na	na	na	na	na	na	na	na	na	na	na
New Zealand	na	81	80	82	81	81	81	76	82	86	79	83	82	77	84	84
Nigeria	na	65	65	64	64	66	65	65	65	65	63	65	65	63	67	60
Northern Ireland	na	na	na	na	na	na	na	na	na	na	na	na	na	na	na	na
Norway	na	83	83	84	80	86	82	80	84	87	na	na	na	75	85	85
Pakistan	na	80	83	77	79	80	83	76	83	88	79	79	84	80	81	78
Peru	na	61	61	61	59	63	63	51	61	69	58	62	66	58	62	66
Philippines	1990	55	56	54	55	53	59	55	52	60	53	57	56	57	54	55
Poland	na	na	na	na	na	na	na	na	na	na	na	na	na	na	na	na
Portugal	na	na	na	na	na	na	na	na	na	na	na	na	na	na	na	na
Puerto Rico	na	72	73	71	62	72	76	70	72	72	76	72	69	73	71	71
Romania	na	na	na	na	na	na	na	na	na	na	na	na	na	na	na	na
Russian Fed.	na	na	na	na	na	na	na	na	na	na	na	na	na	na	na	na
Serbia	na	41	39	43	41	36	45	41	43	38	39	42	43	40	43	33
Singapore	na	na	na	na	na	na	na	na	na	na	na	na	na	na	na	na
Slovakia	na	na	na	na	na	na	na	na	na	na	na	na	na	na	na	na
Slovenia	na	na	na	na	na	na	na	na	na	na	na	na	na	na	na	na
South Africa	na	65	65	65	65	66	64	62	68	80	65	65	69	65	65	66
Spain	na	72	69	75	70	72	72	71	72	73	72	70	75	73	70	78
Sweden	na	68	71	64	64	71	68	66	67	70	62	71	71	61	68	68
Switzerland	na	na	na	na	na	na	na	na	na	na	na	na	na	na	na	na
Taiwan	na	74	74	74	78	74	69	69	73	78	70	75	76	74	77	62
Tanzania	na	65	66	63	61	68	65	63	66	73	66	62	69	65	66	59
Turkey	na	53	57	50	54	52	56	52	53	60	54	52	53	54	52	52
Uganda	na	66	64	67	66	63	78	65	66	63	62	66	57	68	66	60
Ukraine	na	na	na	na	na	na	na	na	na	na	na	na	na	na	na	na
United States	na	74	71	76	65	74	81	61	71	80	69	77	76	70	75	74
Uruguay	na	55	59	52	54	54	56	50	61	63	50	49	63	53	54	60
Venezuela	na	39	42	36	35	42	41	37	40	39	38	35	44	42	39	35
Vietnam	na	87	88	86	88	88	84	86	85	96	84	88	87	93	86	69
Zimbabwe	na	65	62	67	65	67	62	69	60	27	74	68	58	68	64	57
Total	na	64	64	64	62	65	66	61	64	69	62	64	65	63	65	64

RANKING

Country	2000
Vietnam	87
Morocco	83
Norway	83
Bosnia and Herz.	82
Japan	81
New Zealand	81
Pakistan	80
Indonesia	79
Korea, South	79
Egypt	76
United States	74
Taiwan	74
China	73
Dominican Rep.	72
Spain	72
Australia	72
Puerto Rico	72
Sweden	68
Canada	67
Uganda	66
South Africa	65
Zimbabwe	65
Tanzania	65
Nigeria	65
India	64
Armenia	63
Iran	63
Peru	61
Moldova	59
Argentina	57
Macedonia	57
Philippines	55
Uruguay	55
Chile	55
Algeria	54
Bangladesh	54
Georgia	54
Azerbaijan	54
Turkey	53
El Salvador	52
Albania	51
Mexico	46
Montenegro	46
Brazil	44
Serbia	41
Venezuela	39
Total	64

A170) LIFE SATISFACTION

All things considered, how satisfied are you with your life as a whole these days?

% Satisfied (7-10) (WVS: V81; EVS: V68)

Country	Wave 1990	Wave 2000	Gender Male	Gender Female	Age 16-29	Age 30-49	Age 50+	Education Lower	Education Middle	Education Upper	Income Lower	Income Middle	Income Upper	Values Mat	Values Mixed	Values Postm.
Albania	na	30	33	26	32	31	26	21	35	39	19	25	46	29	31	39
Algeria	na	44	39	49	42	45	44	40	45	45	37	42	55	44	43	47
Argentina	69	69	69	69	73	68	66	67	71	77	61	69	77	65	69	71
Armenia	na	19	21	18	25	17	15	26	18	21	28	14	10	16	23	16
Australia	na	77	76	79	75	78	79	72	79	79	70	78	86	77	77	78
Austria	64	83	85	81	87	84	80	79	84	91	76	81	88	73	81	89
Azerbaijan	na	32	34	30	39	27	30	34	30	35	22	27	46	33	30	32
Bangladesh	na	32	32	34	36	29	36	28	40	33	17	28	55	37	30	35
Belarus	33	24	25	24	34	20	22	18	26	27	16	24	40	19	27	53
Belgium	79	79	78	79	84	77	78	70	78	86	64	78	88	76	79	80
Bosnia and Herz.	na	38	38	38	46	38	30	28	37	52	25	33	61	34	40	36
Brazil	68	63	68	57	62	62	67	65	61	61	60	64	64	66	60	66
Bulgaria	25	36	39	33	51	40	25	21	40	53	21	35	49	32	40	46
Canada	84	81	81	81	82	79	82	79	79	87	71	82	88	78	80	83
Chile	70	63	62	64	65	62	63	57	62	79	56	62	76	58	66	64
China	68	53	52	55	54	51	58	55	53	51	46	56	61	51	54	63
Colombia	na	85	86	84	85	86	82	82	84	91	79	86	90	84	84	83
Croatia	na	54	53	55	67	54	45	49	53	69	50	53	57	46	54	57
Czech Republic	50	67	67	67	70	68	64	61	71	81	57	66	76	60	68	73
Denmark	86	86	84	88	88	88	82	83	90	88	77	89	94	86	86	91
Dominican Rep.	na	68	72	65	67	68	70	66	60	71	61	68	84	68	67	66
Egypt	na	44	43	44	44	44	43	43	44	45	44	43	43	43	45	40
El Salvador	na	71	73	69	76	67	69	65	76	79	63	68	84	na	na	na
Estonia	45	44	44	44	54	41	40	39	42	56	31	41	52	36	49	54
Finland	79	84	84	85	86	84	84	79	91	90	75	88	92	85	84	88
France	59	66	68	64	71	66	63	63	67	71	51	67	77	66	66	65
Georgia	na	25	26	24	31	24	20	26	24	26	17	26	35	23	27	27
Germany	59	79	78	79	84	78	77	76	81	79	70	81	83	82	78	78
Great Britain	74	73	77	69	78	74	71	75	72	76	66	73	80	na	na	na
Greece	na	61	62	60	57	64	63	54	58	65	52	60	69	61	61	59
Hungary	44	37	37	37	47	35	33	31	45	58	20	29	55	35	41	30
Iceland	85	87	86	88	87	91	82	82	88	96	77	90	94	89	87	82
India	53	28	31	24	28	28	28	22	33	35	22	21	37	28	32	33
Indonesia	na	62	62	62	59	66	59	53	64	68	45	69	84	59	64	71
Iran	na	52	48	57	53	53	49	46	52	58	41	48	63	49	54	57
Ireland	80	85	87	84	83	87	85	83	87	87	80	87	91	88	84	86
Israel	na	65	64	67	75	64	56	53	65	75	48	59	80	69	65	70
Italy	71	70	72	67	68	72	68	65	73	75	63	68	79	65	70	72
Japan	53	53	52	54	51	50	57	44	52	61	46	51	65	51	54	54
Jordan	na	37	33	42	39	37	35	33	33	51	28	37	50	35	39	48
Korea, South	61	47	46	49	44	48	49	34	47	49	36	45	61	46	48	48
Latvia	40	33	32	34	48	29	30	26	34	40	27	32	43	30	34	36
Lithuania	44	33	35	31	52	24	26	25	34	42	23	23	40	30	31	47
Luxembourg	na	82	83	81	81	81	84	76	85	86	76	84	89	82	80	90
Macedonia	na	31	30	32	38	31	25	19	35	41	16	32	53	29	33	28
Malta	na	86	86	86	88	87	84	82	89	86	82	88	89	84	87	88
Mexico	72	80	80	79	81	78	81	78	81	86	75	80	82	80	80	78
Moldova	na	19	19	19	26	19	14	12	19	26	8	16	29	17	21	27
Montenegro	na	41	40	43	43	42	39	32	45	52	24	38	54	32	51	44
Morocco	na	38	37	40	38	39	38	36	45	53	22	40	37	42	36	36
Netherlands	85	90	91	89	93	92	86	82	94	92	80	93	95	86	90	91
New Zealand	na	77	77	77	76	74	80	73	75	82	68	76	85	72	77	82
Nigeria	54	64	63	65	68	59	60	57	65	72	54	63	80	65	65	54
Northern Ireland	83	85	84	85	87	83	88	83	87	86	77	86	92	85	85	85
Norway	78	79	82	76	82	82	73	75	79	83	na	na	na	75	80	79
Pakistan	na	10	10	9	12	10	5	5	13	20	2	10	18	8	12	17
Peru	na	50	49	51	51	48	54	48	46	56	44	53	57	47	51	54
Philippines	na	53	53	54	57	49	57	53	49	61	40	49	72	55	53	50
Poland	57	51	51	50	61	48	47	46	56	59	38	54	66	47	51	62
Portugal	63	62	64	61	80	64	51	56	74	82	35	59	78	58	65	67
Puerto Rico	na	85	87	85	88	83	86	82	82	88	79	88	89	80	85	90
Romania	44	38	37	39	45	36	36	34	36	51	36	29	44	35	38	38
Russian Fed.	32	27	31	24	42	26	19	20	25	37	20	24	35	25	28	46
Serbia	na	40	41	39	50	40	35	30	43	48	30	41	50	34	45	51
Singapore	na	71	70	71	71	70	71	66	73	74	60	67	83	71	71	68
Slovakia	na	47	47	46	51	48	42	38	49	62	36	42	57	46	49	52
Slovenia	47	67	68	67	78	66	60	55	71	77	59	69	78	64	68	69
South Africa	51	42	45	38	37	45	46	35	50	62	21	47	66	42	44	31
Spain	66	65	65	65	68	66	63	61	69	71	56	69	70	63	66	70
Sweden	84	80	81	78	79	80	80	79	78	83	71	83	87	77	79	81
Switzerland	86	85	88	82	85	84	86	81	85	92	75	85	91	81	85	85
Taiwan	na	50	47	52	52	53	40	41	46	60	36	51	63	52	49	54
Tanzania	na	21	19	24	23	19	24	21	20	22	20	22	19	20	22	30
Turkey	48	39	33	45	41	36	41	39	36	38	34	39	50	41	38	35
Uganda	na	36	30	41	38	32	42	36	35	43	38	36	39	40	33	41
Ukraine	na	25	26	23	36	25	17	13	23	34	12	22	44	21	26	36
United States	81	79	79	78	79	76	83	74	77	82	72	79	90	75	79	80
Uruguay	na	63	62	63	63	60	65	60	64	72	53	65	70	56	65	63
Venezuela	na	70	73	68	71	70	69	65	69	78	59	69	77	67	71	71
Vietnam	na	44	45	44	41	46	45	40	50	55	29	36	62	46	48	49
Zimbabwe	na	18	16	20	22	16	12	16	21	39	15	18	29	19	18	16
Total	62	56	56	56	57	55	56	51	55	65	45	54	65	46	58	68

RANKING

Country	2000
Netherlands	90
Iceland	87
Malta	86
Denmark	86
Ireland	85
Puerto Rico	85
Colombia	85
Switzerland	85
Northern Ireland	85
Finland	84
Austria	83
Luxembourg	82
Canada	81
Sweden	80
Mexico	80
Norway	79
United States	79
Germany	79
Belgium	79
Australia	77
New Zealand	77
Great Britain	73
El Salvador	71
Singapore	71
Venezuela	70
Italy	70
Argentina	69
Dominican Rep.	68
Slovenia	67
Czech Republic	67
France	66
Israel	65
Spain	65
Nigeria	64
Chile	63
Brazil	63
Uruguay	63
Portugal	62
Indonesia	62
Greece	61
Croatia	54
China	53
Philippines	53
Japan	53
Iran	52
Poland	51
Peru	50
Taiwan	50
Korea, South	47
Slovakia	47
Vietnam	44
Estonia	44
Algeria	44
Egypt	44
South Africa	42
Montenegro	41
Serbia	40
Turkey	39
Morocco	38
Bosnia and Herz.	38
Romania	38
Jordan	37
Hungary	37
Uganda	36
Bulgaria	36
Latvia	33
Lithuania	33
Bangladesh	32
Azerbaijan	32
Macedonia	31
Albania	30
India	28
Russian Fed.	27
Georgia	25
Ukraine	25
Belarus	24
Tanzania	21
Armenia	19
Moldova	19
Zimbabwe	18
Pakistan	10
Total	56

A173) FREEDOM FEELING

Some people feel they have completely free choice and control over their lives; while other people feel that what they do, has no real effect on what happens to them.

% Great deal (7-10)

(WVS: V82; EVS: V67)

Country	Wave 1990	Wave 2000	Male	Female	Age 16-29	30-49	50+	Education Lower	Middle	Upper	Income Lower	Middle	Upper	Mat	Mixed	Postm.
Albania	na	46	47	44	50	49	37	42	47	53	41	45	51	45	49	44
Algeria	na	56	55	58	50	63	58	53	56	59	49	59	61	53	58	61
Argentina	68	68	68	69	72	68	65	67	71	66	64	67	73	59	70	72
Armenia	na	36	42	31	43	34	29	34	36	37	43	31	30	33	39	35
Australia	na	76	76	76	74	76	78	71	76	80	72	78	80	68	77	76
Austria	57	70	72	68	79	64	70	68	71	72	67	67	75	62	70	71
Azerbaijan	na	41	48	34	39	38	50	45	38	44	28	37	53	41	38	41
Bangladesh	na	33	34	30	30	32	45	31	33	37	28	25	47	42	27	22
Belarus	40	37	42	32	48	40	24	19	42	46	28	37	50	32	41	64
Belgium	57	59	60	58	66	58	56	46	61	66	49	57	70	55	58	66
Bosnia and Herz.	na	47	48	47	54	47	41	42	46	58	41	43	61	44	50	53
Brazil	63	66	73	58	69	62	68	65	68	63	66	66	65	68	64	66
Bulgaria	28	46	52	41	58	49	39	35	50	57	37	45	57	46	47	49
Canada	77	77	75	78	82	76	76	72	76	82	71	77	82	75	75	82
Chile	61	65	66	64	64	64	66	60	62	81	57	67	75	59	66	71
China	63	64	67	61	61	65	65	67	63	56	61	67	68	61	65	71
Colombia	na	78	82	74	79	78	75	72	76	85	69	78	84	80	77	70
Croatia	na	60	63	57	61	62	57	57	59	73	56	55	68	55	61	57
Czech Republic	42	59	63	56	65	63	54	53	64	74	51	56	69	56	59	71
Denmark	64	72	73	71	80	76	63	63	81	85	62	72	90	60	72	83
Dominican Rep.	na	70	72	69	71	70	55	53	58	75	69	70	80	65	69	70
Egypt	na	43	42	44	44	43	40	40	45	45	40	43	46	43	41	49
El Salvador	na	70	76	64	71	66	75	65	75	81	61	70	84	na	na	na
Estonia	50	43	42	43	53	43	36	38	41	56	33	37	47	37	47	49
Finland	79	78	80	76	85	83	71	70	86	92	70	79	85	76	77	85
France	45	51	53	49	51	50	52	50	50	53	44	51	56	50	51	52
Georgia	na	49	58	42	53	52	41	46	49	51	41	52	59	47	52	50
Germany	53	73	76	71	70	70	77	71	75	69	71	68	77	82	72	67
Great Britain	65	67	67	68	71	67	65	67	66	72	66	60	75	na	na	na
Greece	na	65	69	62	66	64	65	60	63	67	62	61	69	58	66	69
Hungary	50	44	48	41	54	46	37	38	56	57	32	42	54	41	49	43
Iceland	70	81	81	81	90	85	67	73	86	89	71	81	92	80	83	77
India	50	22	26	16	26	22	17	17	25	29	20	18	27	24	23	21
Indonesia	na	67	65	69	66	69	65	65	66	72	52	76	85	66	69	70
Iran	na	55	54	55	55	55	52	50	56	58	48	55	59	57	54	57
Ireland	65	70	70	69	77	70	63	60	72	81	57	67	82	63	70	76
Israel	na	na	na	na	na	na	na	na	na	na	na	na	na	na	na	na
Italy	52	51	56	46	68	51	41	36	60	69	41	51	62	41	50	58
Japan	29	39	39	39	54	40	32	30	38	48	35	38	41	34	40	47
Jordan	na	65	76	55	62	66	70	63	62	72	60	68	75	64	67	70
Korea, South	73	64	61	66	73	63	54	43	62	68	58	60	73	59	66	83
Latvia	48	42	45	39	52	45	34	30	45	46	38	40	46	41	40	53
Lithuania	55	50	50	49	61	50	41	41	51	57	45	48	54	47	48	70
Luxembourg	na	64	67	61	68	62	64	59	66	70	64	65	72	68	63	71
Macedonia	na	42	40	44	48	42	36	30	44	55	31	43	57	41	43	51
Malta	na	75	77	73	78	78	71	72	77	76	68	77	78	72	78	73
Mexico	70	79	81	78	79	79	80	77	80	87	76	81	82	79	81	80
Moldova	na	46	48	43	49	48	39	40	43	54	34	49	52	42	50	43
Montenegro	na	45	51	38	51	48	37	32	49	59	30	45	59	36	54	54
Morocco	na	46	51	42	46	46	47	45	54	51	38	49	44	46	48	35
Netherlands	52	65	70	60	75	71	53	50	68	75	58	66	75	54	66	69
New Zealand	na	77	76	78	81	78	74	73	79	80	67	78	84	77	77	80
Nigeria	57	67	68	66	68	66	66	61	69	73	62	64	79	72	65	59
Northern Ireland	75	74	77	72	72	75	76	73	75	70	74	75	78	79	76	65
Norway	67	71	69	72	79	73	61	62	71	79	na	na	na	60	71	77
Pakistan	na	11	13	9	7	12	15	9	14	12	7	11	15	12	10	10
Peru	na	64	67	61	63	64	69	65	62	68	61	66	67	61	65	71
Philippines	na	55	53	57	56	53	55	49	53	63	46	57	60	51	58	56
Poland	52	48	51	45	58	47	42	44	52	52	36	52	64	41	50	66
Portugal	52	55	59	50	61	54	52	49	65	70	44	53	62	49	57	70
Puerto Rico	na	83	80	85	83	80	84	80	78	85	80	81	85	77	85	83
Romania	49	58	61	54	63	61	51	46	61	67	54	56	62	57	57	60
Russian Fed.	47	38	45	32	49	39	29	25	36	52	27	37	49	34	41	45
Serbia	na	44	49	39	55	43	40	33	47	54	36	44	52	37	50	59
Singapore	na	69	68	69	70	67	67	66	69	75	65	64	74	63	70	75
Slovakia	na	50	53	48	54	51	45	42	52	65	41	48	58	44	54	64
Slovenia	44	64	65	63	75	66	53	48	67	80	52	67	81	55	65	68
South Africa	57	55	57	52	51	57	59	49	61	81	41	56	73	53	57	53
Spain	56	58	58	58	62	59	55	54	62	64	53	58	61	53	60	61
Sweden	74	74	74	74	83	77	66	63	74	82	67	75	83	62	74	77
Switzerland	66	70	69	72	79	69	67	68	71	72	64	63	80	70	69	70
Taiwan	na	68	68	69	71	70	62	63	71	71	59	68	77	66	74	65
Tanzania	na	41	44	37	42	38	47	45	37	35	48	43	32	41	41	42
Turkey	31	39	45	34	42	39	33	31	49	57	30	42	54	34	38	52
Uganda	na	51	52	49	50	51	56	49	52	45	44	57	48	49	52	49
Ukraine	na	34	38	31	47	36	25	17	34	42	24	31	50	30	39	39
United States	77	82	83	81	85	80	82	78	79	85	76	84	89	75	82	85
Uruguay	na	60	63	58	61	57	62	59	61	70	51	64	67	56	57	70
Venezuela	na	82	85	78	85	80	78	75	84	84	74	81	88	75	84	85
Vietnam	na	66	71	61	59	70	64	67	65	70	50	64	77	74	67	60
Zimbabwe	na	44	45	43	43	45	42	45	41	44	38	47	50	42	46	35
Total	57	58	60	56	61	58	55	53	58	66	51	57	65	51	60	67

RANKING

Country	2000
Puerto Rico	83
United States	82
Venezuela	82
Iceland	81
Mexico	79
Colombia	78
Finland	78
Canada	77
New Zealand	77
Australia	76
Malta	75
Northern Ireland	74
Sweden	74
Germany	73
Denmark	72
Norway	71
Switzerland	70
El Salvador	70
Dominican Rep.	70
Austria	70
Ireland	70
Singapore	69
Argentina	68
Taiwan	68
Great Britain	67
Nigeria	67
Indonesia	67
Brazil	66
Vietnam	66
Jordan	65
Netherlands	65
Greece	65
Chile	65
China	64
Peru	64
Luxembourg	64
Korea, South	64
Slovenia	64
Uruguay	60
Croatia	60
Czech Republic	59
Belgium	59
Spain	58
Romania	58
Algeria	56
South Africa	55
Philippines	55
Portugal	55
Iran	55
France	51
Italy	51
Uganda	51
Slovakia	50
Lithuania	50
Georgia	49
Poland	48
Bosnia and Herz.	47
Bulgaria	46
Morocco	46
Albania	46
Moldova	46
Montenegro	45
Hungary	44
Serbia	44
Zimbabwe	44
Estonia	43
Egypt	43
Macedonia	42
Latvia	42
Tanzania	41
Azerbaijan	41
Turkey	39
Japan	39
Russian Fed.	38
Belarus	37
Armenia	36
Ukraine	34
Bangladesh	33
India	22
Pakistan	11
Total	58

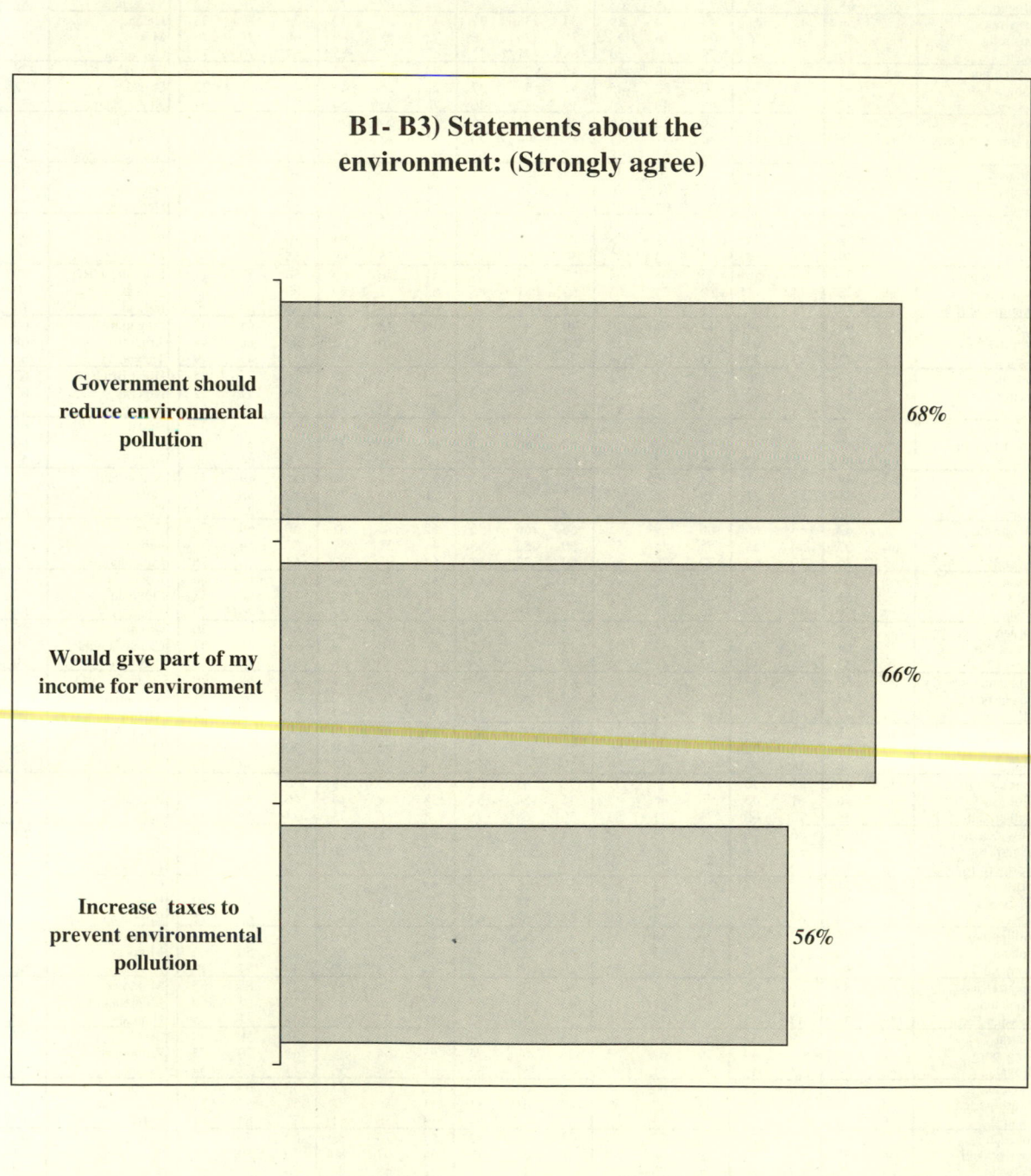

B1- B3) Statements about the environment: (Strongly agree)

Government should reduce environmental pollution — 68%

Would give part of my income for environment — 66%

Increase taxes to prevent environmental pollution — 56%

B001) ENVIRONMENT: INCOME

I would give part of my income if I were certain that the money would be used to prevent environmental pollution

Strongly agree / Agree (%)

(WVS: V33; EVS: V8)

Country	Wave 1990	Wave 2000	Gender Male	Gender Female	Age 16-29	Age 30-49	Age 50+	Education Lower	Education Middle	Education Upper	Income Lower	Income Middle	Income Upper	Values Mat	Values Mixed	Values Postm.	RANKING Country	RANKING 2000
Albania	na	70	71	69	74	68	69	62	71	85	61	73	78	69	73	59	Vietnam	96
Algeria	na	na	na	na	na	na	na	na	na	na	na	na	na	na	na	na	Tanzania	84
Argentina	62	67	67	68	74	65	64	65	71	70	65	66	71	57	68	74	Korea, South	84
Armenia	na	na	na	na	na	na	na	na	na	na	na	na	na	na	na	na	Greece	82
Australia	na	na	na	na	na	na	na	na	na	na	na	na	na	na	na	na	China	82
Austria	60	49	50	47	52	55	41	41	54	63	38	48	58	32	46	59	Slovenia	82
Azerbaijan	na	na	na	na	na	na	na	na	na	na	na	na	na	na	na	na	Puerto Rico	82
Bangladesh	na	80	82	77	81	80	73	76	83	84	72	80	85	81	79	70	Peru	81
Belarus	80	58	57	58	62	60	51	48	59	70	49	63	61	54	60	71	Serbia	81
Belgium	56	58	58	58	62	63	52	41	58	71	49	56	68	44	59	73	Bangladesh	80
Bosnia and Herz.	na	76	77	74	80	73	75	69	75	84	76	74	79	64	80	89	Croatia	79
Brazil	72	na	na	na	na	na	na	na	na	na	na	na	na	na	na	na	Denmark	79
Bulgaria	83	58	56	59	66	69	43	34	65	78	38	61	72	44	69	74	Sweden	79
Canada	74	70	68	71	79	68	67	62	71	75	66	73	72	64	69	74	Macedonia	79
Chile	84	70	70	70	72	69	69	62	74	75	66	73	73	67	69	77	Mexico	78
China	78	82	82	82	88	81	80	74	87	88	79	82	85	82	85	90	Czech Republic	78
Colombia	na	na	na	na	na	na	na	na	na	na	na	na	na	na	na	na	Turkey	77
Croatia	na	79	77	81	83	81	74	73	81	88	79	78	78	77	78	84	Bosnia and Herz.	76
Czech Republic	79	78	74	81	80	79	76	75	80	80	76	78	79	68	80	90	Netherlands	75
Denmark	84	79	75	83	81	81	75	75	78	86	78	80	82	71	78	91	Philippines	73
Dominican Rep.	na	na	na	na	na	na	na	na	na	na	na	na	na	na	na	na	Latvia	71
Egypt	na	na	na	na	na	na	na	na	na	na	na	na	na	na	na	na	Japan	70
El Salvador	na	na	na	na	na	na	na	na	na	na	na	na	na	na	na	na	Albania	70
Estonia	77	48	44	51	50	49	46	40	49	57	41	43	57	42	53	51	Chile	70
Finland	67	53	50	57	52	56	50	49	59	62	54	55	57	49	54	56	Canada	70
France	61	46	48	45	51	46	44	41	47	59	50	43	52	40	45	60	United States	69
Georgia	na	na	na	na	na	na	na	na	na	na	na	na	na	na	na	na	Zimbabwe	69
Germany	63	33	33	33	40	34	29	22	39	61	24	30	42	22	35	46	Moldova	68
Great Britain	68	49	46	51	53	46	49	40	53	64	46	46	55	na	na	na	Argentina	67
Greece	na	82	78	86	84	82	79	81	78	86	82	83	81	78	84	82	India	67
Hungary	60	51	55	49	57	57	43	43	61	82	38	50	62	47	56	47	Italy	65
Iceland	78	64	55	72	62	62	67	66	59	67	65	61	65	62	63	70	Luxembourg	64
India	81	67	69	63	70	69	60	57	70	79	60	62	74	62	73	81	Iceland	64
Indonesia	na	na	na	na	na	na	na	na	na	na	na	na	na	na	na	na	Russian Fed.	63
Iran	na	na	na	na	na	na	na	na	na	na	na	na	na	na	na	na	Poland	63
Ireland	69	55	59	51	59	58	48	40	58	74	39	55	71	48	54	63	Ukraine	62
Israel	na	na	na	na	na	na	na	na	na	na	na	na	na	na	na	na	Malta	61
Italy	68	65	63	67	67	68	61	61	67	70	61	67	72	53	66	69	Montenegro	61
Japan	68	70	74	67	62	66	77	75	68	74	67	67	76	70	70	78	Singapore	60
Jordan	na	na	na	na	na	na	na	na	na	na	na	na	na	na	na	na	Spain	59
Korea, South	84	84	83	84	83	85	81	62	84	86	83	86	83	79	87	90	Belgium	58
Latvia	78	71	72	69	75	74	66	62	72	77	67	69	77	65	73	81	Belarus	58
Lithuania	75	27	30	24	31	30	21	16	29	38	15	27	34	17	28	46	Bulgaria	58
Luxembourg	na	64	65	63	65	63	64	56	67	70	56	65	71	69	61	71	Portugal	57
Macedonia	na	79	80	78	79	82	75	70	83	83	74	78	86	79	78	89	Slovakia	57
Malta	na	61	60	61	68	60	56	44	64	82	47	61	73	51	65	68	South Africa	55
Mexico	81	78	78	78	82	77	75	73	83	86	73	82	85	70	83	88	Ireland	55
Moldova	na	68	69	67	70	74	58	55	70	75	68	68	68	63	72	72	Finland	53
Montenegro	na	61	63	58	67	63	54	48	64	80	64	58	68	57	64	74	Romania	52
Morocco	na	na	na	na	na	na	na	na	na	na	na	na	na	na	na	na	Hungary	51
Netherlands	83	75	74	75	78	78	69	65	79	79	68	76	82	58	73	88	Great Britain	49
New Zealand	na	na	na	na	na	na	na	na	na	na	na	na	na	na	na	na	Austria	49
Nigeria	78	na	na	na	na	na	na	na	na	na	na	na	na	na	na	na	Estonia	48
Northern Ireland	75	46	46	45	44	50	44	42	44	56	42	40	60	44	43	59	France	46
Norway	80	na	na	na	na	na	na	na	na	na	na	na	na	na	na	na	Uganda	46
Pakistan	na	na	na	na	na	na	na	na	na	na	na	na	na	na	na	na	Northern Ireland	46
Peru	na	81	82	80	82	82	76	79	82	80	80	83	80	77	82	84	Germany	33
Philippines	na	73	74	72	80	68	72	67	73	79	69	75	73	68	76	71	Lithuania	27
Poland	na	63	67	59	70	65	55	57	67	78	49	72	69	57	64	75		
Portugal	84	57	56	58	63	66	46	51	69	73	36	58	59	49	60	84		
Puerto Rico	na	82	80	83	83	82	81	89	80	82	79	78	87	72	83	83		
Romania	na	52	54	51	66	53	42	39	53	68	45	49	59	48	55	60		
Russian Fed.	78	63	63	64	72	66	55	44	64	72	55	66	70	60	68	62		
Serbia	na	81	81	80	81	81	80	68	83	93	74	82	87	75	84	94		
Singapore	na	60	62	58	74	49	38	51	63	70	49	62	66	47	63	70		
Slovakia	na	57	56	57	61	59	50	45	60	71	48	56	65	51	61	64		
Slovenia	89	82	83	81	80	83	83	80	82	84	81	87	85	80	83	85		
South Africa	na	55	54	57	54	58	51	55	54	70	55	54	54	50	57	68		
Spain	72	59	59	58	65	61	52	52	64	69	51	61	64	54	59	71		
Sweden	82	79	77	81	83	78	78	79	79	79	79	78	79	72	78	84		
Switzerland	na	na	na	na	na	na	na	na	na	na	na	na	na	na	na	na		
Taiwan	na	na	na	na	na	na	na	na	na	na	na	na	na	na	na	na		
Tanzania	na	84	85	84	83	84	89	83	87	86	82	85	89	83	86	88		
Turkey	87	77	74	79	80	74	73	73	81	81	72	76	85	79	76	79		
Uganda	na	46	59	34	46	44	52	42	46	58	52	60	57	37	48	60		
Ukraine	na	62	61	64	68	68	53	39	63	71	57	65	67	56	68	65		
United States	74	69	69	70	67	68	74	69	67	71	69	71	68	67	69	72		
Uruguay	na	na	na	na	na	na	na	na	na	na	na	na	na	na	na	na		
Venezuela	na	na	na	na	na	na	na	na	na	na	na	na	na	na	na	na		
Vietnam	na	96	96	97	98	95	97	95	97	97	95	99	94	97	96	98		
Zimbabwe	na	69	71	67	71	70	60	64	75	62	65	66	79	63	72	71		
Total	75	66	66	65	70	67	61	58	67	75	62	67	71	60	68	74	Total	66

B002) ENVIRONMENT: TAXES

I would agree to an increase in taxes if the extra
money were used to prevent environmental pollution

Strongly agree / Agree (%)

(WVS: V34; EVS: V9)

Country	Wave		Gender		Age			Education			Income			Values				RANKING Country	2000
	1990	2000	Male	Female	16-29	30-49	50+	Lower	Middle	Upper	Lower	Middle	Upper	Mat	Mixed	Postm.			
Albania	na	63	65	61	68	63	57	53	65	79	55	63	71	60	65	64		Vietnam	91
Algeria	na	na	na	na	na	na	na	na	na	na	na	na	na	na	na	na		Dominican Rep.	86
Argentina	50	41	42	41	44	42	38	40	43	46	36	42	46	34	43	45		Taiwan	86
Armenia	na	57	58	56	64	54	50	58	56	59	65	51	50	56	58	68		El Salvador	84
Australia	na	69	67	72	72	70	66	62	69	75	66	70	72	62	67	75		Sweden	77
Austria	52	39	41	37	39	44	33	31	44	52	33	40	44	25	37	48		Bangladesh	76
Azerbaijan	na	55	54	56	66	49	48	48	50	65	52	51	68	51	61	68		Norway	75
Bangladesh	na	76	79	71	76	76	73	72	79	81	74	78	74	77	75	70		Tanzania	75
Belarus	67	46	45	47	51	48	41	33	50	51	38	52	46	43	49	58		China	74
Belgium	41	44	45	42	40	47	41	31	42	56	35	46	51	31	43	60		Serbia	74
Bosnia and Herz.	na	70	70	71	74	66	73	62	70	80	69	71	71	62	73	75		Brazil	73
Brazil	71	73	71	75	75	71	73	76	74	59	77	76	68	75	74	65		Puerto Rico	71
Bulgaria	70	45	44	45	53	55	31	25	52	58	28	49	56	34	53	61		Bosnia and Herz.	70
Canada	64	58	55	61	65	56	56	55	56	64	57	61	61	61	55	66		Australia	69
Chile	76	62	62	63	62	64	60	57	65	68	57	67	66	58	62	72		Georgia	69
China	82	74	74	75	74	75	74	68	78	76	72	79	70	75	76	87		Colombia	67
Colombia	na	67	68	67	76	66	54	59	69	71	60	68	71	62	65	76		Czech Republic	65
Croatia	na	55	53	56	55	54	55	50	55	67	49	55	58	52	53	61		Denmark	65
Czech Republic	67	65	61	69	64	69	62	61	69	73	64	64	70	57	67	75		Greece	65
Denmark	70	65	62	69	62	67	65	61	62	76	64	66	70	55	64	76		Macedonia	65
Dominican Rep.	na	86	83	88	88	83	82	78	87	88	83	86	93	82	86	88		Philippines	64
Egypt	na	na	na	na	na	na	na	na	na	na	na	na	na	na	na	na		Albania	63
El Salvador	na	84	88	81	89	83	77	79	89	91	80	85	93	na	na	na		Chile	62
Estonia	59	33	33	34	30	34	35	27	32	48	26	30	43	28	38	35		Japan	62
Finland	56	50	47	53	51	53	46	43	59	62	48	52	55	44	53	53		Slovenia	62
France	54	37	37	36	41	37	34	33	33	49	35	37	43	30	36	50		United States	61
Georgia	na	69	68	70	72	69	65	59	69	76	66	72	72	67	71	73		Montenegro	61
Germany	65	29	28	29	36	32	23	19	35	46	21	25	39	18	30	42		Uruguay	58
Great Britain	70	50	46	54	51	49	50	43	53	65	47	55	52	na	na	na		Canada	58
Greece	na	65	65	64	63	66	65	66	61	68	59	69	67	60	65	69		Iceland	57
Hungary	35	33	35	32	43	34	27	30	39	38	27	31	39	31	36	48		Mexico	57
Iceland	60	57	55	59	50	58	62	55	53	71	56	57	60	46	60	62		Armenia	57
India	66	53	55	49	53	55	49	47	55	61	55	49	56	45	60	66		Korea, South	57
Indonesia	na	na	na	na	na	na	na	na	na	na	na	na	na	na	na	na		Peru	56
Iran	na	na	na	na	na	na	na	na	na	na	na	na	na	na	na	na		Luxembourg	56
Ireland	51	39	45	33	35	43	38	33	38	51	32	38	50	34	38	50		Turkey	56
Israel	na	na	na	na	na	na	na	na	na	na	na	na	na	na	na	na		Azerbaijan	55
Italy	54	44	44	43	39	47	44	40	43	55	39	45	50	37	43	48		Netherlands	55
Japan	51	62	66	58	50	60	69	66	58	71	59	58	73	63	62	71		Croatia	55
Jordan	na	na	na	na	na	na	na	na	na	na	na	na	na	na	na	na		Russian Fed.	54
Korea, South	76	57	59	55	53	57	61	42	56	60	50	59	62	50	63	59		New Zealand	53
Latvia	64	45	44	47	49	43	46	46	46	42	46	43	47	42	48	50		India	53
Lithuania	66	20	21	19	23	21	16	11	20	34	12	19	27	13	23	27		Poland	51
Luxembourg	na	56	57	55	54	56	58	50	58	62	50	59	68	59	52	69		Finland	50
Macedonia	na	64	64	65	64	68	60	61	66	65	62	63	70	64	64	72		Great Britain	50
Malta	na	48	48	48	50	47	47	34	52	61	38	50	58	42	51	52		Ukraine	50
Mexico	67	57	55	59	59	56	55	54	60	62	50	63	63	50	61	67		Spain	49
Moldova	na	38	42	35	41	41	32	28	39	47	35	39	41	30	45	45		Malta	48
Montenegro	na	61	62	60	68	63	54	46	66	80	60	57	72	57	64	75		Romania	46
Morocco	na	na	na	na	na	na	na	na	na	na	na	na	na	na	na	na		Belarus	46
Netherlands	69	55	57	53	53	59	52	46	52	67	48	59	63	36	52	74		Latvia	45
New Zealand	na	53	53	53	50	52	56	47	52	62	55	54	51	47	53	62		Zimbabwe	45
Nigeria	59	na	na	na	na	na	na	na	na	na	na	na	na	na	na	na		Singapore	45
Northern Ireland	65	44	45	43	36	49	45	42	43	51	45	43	57	40	41	59		South Africa	45
Norway	73	75	72	79	82	73	73	71	73	83	na	na	na	70	75	87		Bulgaria	45
Pakistan	na	na	na	na	na	na	na	na	na	na	na	na	na	na	na	na		Uganda	44
Peru	na	56	57	56	55	59	54	54	58	56	52	61	56	49	57	65		Northern Ireland	44
Philippines	na	64	63	66	71	62	60	56	67	69	61	63	68	62	66	66		Belgium	44
Poland	na	51	55	48	58	54	44	45	58	62	39	57	64	47	52	66		Italy	44
Portugal	65	43	43	43	47	46	37	39	52	44	37	45	42	36	45	55		Switzerland	43
Puerto Rico	na	71	73	70	76	70	71	69	70	73	69	71	73	67	72	73		Portugal	43
Romania	na	46	47	46	57	49	37	33	46	66	37	42	56	42	49	58		Argentina	41
Russian Fed.	66	54	51	57	60	56	48	39	54	61	47	56	59	50	59	54		Slovakia	40
Serbia	na	74	74	74	73	76	72	62	77	85	63	77	82	67	79	90		Ireland	39
Singapore	na	45	46	44	56	35	33	43	46	44	40	47	47	34	49	47		Austria	39
Slovakia	na	40	38	41	43	40	37	33	40	55	36	39	43	34	43	50		Moldova	38
Slovenia	69	62	63	60	64	65	57	65	58	68	63	61	69	59	61	68		France	37
South Africa	na	45	42	48	41	49	43	45	45	46	46	41	46	40	45	68		Estonia	33
Spain	60	49	48	50	55	52	43	42	54	61	39	51	58	45	50	56		Hungary	33
Sweden	77	77	75	80	83	76	76	77	78	77	77	76	80	66	77	84		Germany	29
Switzerland	na	43	40	46	52	38	43	31	43	62	47	39	45	26	41	57		Lithuania	20
Taiwan	na	86	85	87	85	88	81	83	84	89	81	86	90	85	87	89			
Tanzania	na	75	75	74	72	76	79	73	76	77	72	77	80	74	76	75			
Turkey	72	56	54	58	58	53	55	52	59	64	49	56	67	51	55	63			
Uganda	na	44	55	35	45	43	47	39	45	57	45	61	56	37	47	56			
Ukraine	na	50	47	52	51	52	46	29	50	58	44	51	56	44	57	42			
United States	64	61	60	62	57	58	68	61	58	62	62	62	59	54	61	64			
Uruguay	na	58	56	60	62	59	56	55	62	66	51	57	69	44	61	66			
Venezuela	na	na	na	na	na	na	na	na	na	na	na	na	na	na	na	na			
Vietnam	na	91	92	89	91	91	89	90	91	91	88	89	93	90	92	88			
Zimbabwe	na	45	44	46	51	43	34	42	50	22	41	46	52	37	50	52			
Total	63	56	56	56	59	57	52	50	56	66	53	57	60	50	57	64		Total	56

B003) ENVIRONMENT: NO COST

Government should reduce environmental pollution,

but it should not cost me any money

Strongly agree / Agree (%)

(WVS: V35; EVS: V10)

Country	Wave		Gender		Age			Education			Income			Values			RANKING	
	1990	2000	Male	Female	16-29	30-49	50+	Lower	Middle	Upper	Lower	Middle	Upper	Mat	Mixed	Postm.	Country	2000
Albania	na	63	63	63	57	64	67	71	61	46	67	68	54	68	56	71	Bangladesh	96
Algeria	na	na	na	na	na	na	na	na	na	na	na	na	na	na	na	na	Lithuania	89
Argentina	72	86	87	86	84	87	87	91	84	69	91	90	78	90	86	83	Spain	88
Armenia	na	na	na	na	na	na	na	na	na	na	na	na	na	na	na	na	Estonia	88
Australia	na	na	na	na	na	na	na	na	na	na	na	na	na	na	na	na	Latvia	87
Austria	61	63	62	65	56	56	75	73	56	48	74	62	59	73	66	55	Argentina	86
Azerbaijan	na	na	na	na	na	na	na	na	na	na	na	na	na	na	na	na	Hungary	86
Bangladesh	na	96	96	97	96	97	97	97	96	95	98	96	96	98	95	99	France	84
Belarus	72	75	73	77	65	74	85	86	73	66	79	74	71	78	76	46	Bulgaria	83
Belgium	62	63	61	64	57	58	69	80	63	48	75	65	49	74	63	49	Macedonia	83
Bosnia and Herz.	na	63	62	64	63	65	60	67	65	52	62	67	53	67	59	67	Croatia	82
Brazil	65	na	na	na	na	na	na	na	na	na	na	na	na	na	na	na	Italy	81
Bulgaria	74	83	83	83	80	77	89	93	82	68	92	77	79	91	76	50	Ukraine	81
Canada	52	63	62	64	59	61	67	72	65	51	67	63	55	68	67	53	Russian Fed.	80
Chile	58	74	73	75	71	73	77	81	72	64	84	66	67	76	77	59	Slovakia	79
China	46	36	35	37	21	39	42	42	32	26	41	33	34	34	35	29	Montenegro	78
Colombia	na	na	na	na	na	na	na	na	na	na	na	na	na	na	na	na	Great Britain	77
Croatia	na	82	85	80	80	84	82	90	81	69	81	85	80	87	81	83	Romania	76
Czech Republic	46	55	57	54	50	53	60	66	46	35	65	56	45	73	52	35	South Africa	76
Denmark	29	30	31	29	29	23	38	33	32	21	34	28	22	45	32	13	Belarus	75
Dominican Rep.	na	na	na	na	na	na	na	na	na	na	na	na	na	na	na	na	Portugal	75
Egypt	na	na	na	na	na	na	na	na	na	na	na	na	na	na	na	na	Turkey	75
El Salvador	na	na	na	na	na	na	na	na	na	na	na	na	na	na	na	na	Chile	74
Estonia	72	88	87	89	80	89	91	88	89	84	92	90	82	89	87	82	Singapore	73
Finland	51	64	65	63	59	60	70	70	60	43	63	70	57	72	64	50	Mexico	73
France	74	84	83	85	80	83	87	90	77	74	88	84	75	91	84	73	Poland	72
Georgia	na	na	na	na	na	na	na	na	na	na	na	na	na	na	na	na	Philippines	72
Germany	48	68	68	68	65	63	74	75	64	50	78	70	62	85	64	53	Peru	72
Great Britain	56	77	78	76	79	76	77	88	71	57	84	77	64	na	na	na	Zimbabwe	71
Greece	na	71	72	70	67	72	76	78	75	65	76	69	63	77	69	68	Northern Ireland	71
Hungary	75	86	86	86	84	86	87	88	83	81	84	87	85	87	85	77	Greece	71
Iceland	28	32	35	29	32	32	33	40	31	20	37	33	28	45	30	23	Ireland	70
India	52	55	53	58	56	54	57	54	54	54	58	55	54	61	52	29	Moldova	68
Indonesia	na	na	na	na	na	na	na	na	na	na	na	na	na	na	na	na	Germany	68
Iran	na	na	na	na	na	na	na	na	na	na	na	na	na	na	na	na	Korea, South	67
Ireland	60	70	65	74	64	69	74	76	72	51	80	71	58	70	71	62	Tanzania	66
Israel	na	na	na	na	na	na	na	na	na	na	na	na	na	na	na	na	Malta	66
Italy	80	81	79	84	75	82	84	88	78	71	86	79	76	90	83	73	Puerto Rico	66
Japan	56	56	52	59	59	56	54	60	62	39	63	59	45	59	54	49	Finland	64
Jordan	na	na	na	na	na	na	na	na	na	na	na	na	na	na	na	na	Austria	63
Korea, South	50	67	63	71	66	68	65	80	69	62	70	69	61	71	63	57	Slovenia	63
Latvia	71	87	86	88	75	87	92	87	87	86	88	91	81	89	86	82	Albania	63
Lithuania	69	89	89	88	86	90	89	89	90	84	90	92	88	90	89	86	Bosnia and Herz.	63
Luxembourg	na	61	61	61	67	60	58	72	56	51	76	53	43	67	61	49	Canada	63
Macedonia	na	83	82	84	80	83	84	85	83	78	85	82	81	84	82	79	Belgium	63
Malta	na	66	66	65	61	66	69	79	64	40	74	64	51	72	63	53	Luxembourg	61
Mexico	40	73	73	73	71	74	75	79	69	58	77	74	65	75	73	66	Uganda	60
Moldova	na	68	69	68	61	69	74	78	68	61	69	70	64	76	62	50	United States	57
Montenegro	na	78	77	78	75	77	80	83	76	70	72	78	75	77	79	73	Japan	56
Morocco	na	na	na	na	na	na	na	na	na	na	na	na	na	na	na	na	Czech Republic	55
Netherlands	17	23	21	25	17	18	32	37	22	12	32	21	15	45	24	11	India	55
New Zealand	na	na	na	na	na	na	na	na	na	na	na	na	na	na	na	na	Serbia	55
Nigeria	61	na	na	na	na	na	na	na	na	na	na	na	na	na	na	na	Sweden	43
Northern Ireland	63	71	68	74	72	69	73	75	72	57	71	75	64	77	73	54	Vietnam	38
Norway	44	na	na	na	na	na	na	na	na	na	na	na	na	na	na	na	China	36
Pakistan	na	na	na	na	na	na	na	na	na	na	na	na	na	na	na	na	Iceland	32
Peru	na	72	73	71	69	73	76	75	72	69	74	71	69	81	70	68	Denmark	30
Philippines	na	72	73	71	71	71	76	77	72	68	75	72	69	73	72	69	Netherlands	23
Poland	na	72	71	74	73	68	77	78	71	54	80	68	66	76	74	49		
Portugal	92	75	74	76	78	69	79	77	70	75	77	73	70	80	74	63		
Puerto Rico	na	66	63	67	64	68	65	79	66	63	66	70	62	71	66	65		
Romania	na	76	75	77	76	76	77	81	79	64	78	83	72	83	74	58		
Russian Fed.	49	80	79	80	72	79	85	90	81	72	83	81	74	83	77	60		
Serbia	na	55	54	55	59	53	56	64	55	43	61	56	43	60	51	44		
Singapore	na	73	72	75	63	81	85	79	71	66	81	71	70	84	69	73		
Slovakia	na	79	78	80	76	77	84	84	78	65	84	79	76	83	76	69		
Slovenia	56	63	65	61	54	62	71	79	62	37	71	60	46	74	61	58		
South Africa	na	76	76	76	74	76	81	79	75	47	74	80	78	81	73	70		
Spain	76	88	88	89	87	87	90	92	86	81	91	91	83	90	90	80		
Sweden	36	43	46	40	29	45	49	55	43	32	42	49	39	50	45	33		
Switzerland	na	na	na	na	na	na	na	na	na	na	na	na	na	na	na	na		
Taiwan	na	na	na	na	na	na	na	na	na	na	na	na	na	na	na	na		
Tanzania	na	66	68	65	60	70	66	69	62	66	70	64	70	63	67	50		
Turkey	56	75	75	76	75	74	77	77	76	59	78	78	67	80	75	71		
Uganda	na	60	47	72	60	62	55	66	59	44	60	44	46	65	59	51		
Ukraine	na	81	80	81	74	77	88	92	81	73	83	80	77	85	78	81		
United States	53	57	56	58	58	61	50	63	67	49	59	57	53	73	57	51		
Uruguay	na	na	na	na	na	na	na	na	na	na	na	na	na	na	na	na		
Venezuela	na	na	na	na	na	na	na	na	na	na	na	na	na	na	na	na		
Vietnam	na	38	34	42	37	36	41	38	38	29	48	42	27	49	35	37		
Zimbabwe	na	71	69	73	67	73	78	77	64	48	71	73	62	77	66	69		
Total	58	68	67	69	66	67	72	75	68	58	72	68	62	76	66	57	Total	68

B008) ENVIRONMENTAL PROTECTION VS. ECONOMIC GROWTH

Which statement comes closer to your own point of view: protecting the environment should be given priority or economic growth and creating jobs?

Protecting the environment (%)

(WVS: V36)

Country	Wave 1990	Wave 2000	Gender Male	Gender Female	Age 16-29	Age 30-49	Age 50+	Education Lower	Education Middle	Education Upper	Income Lower	Income Middle	Income Upper	Values Mat	Values Mixed	Values Postm.
Albania	na	48	50	45	54	46	45	39	49	65	41	47	55	41	54	50
Algeria	na	34	32	35	31	38	33	29	36	34	38	32	34	28	35	44
Argentina	na	45	46	44	49	47	39	41	51	51	44	43	50	37	45	50
Armenia	na	44	41	47	50	42	37	38	44	45	54	36	40	38	47	64
Australia	na	63	65	60	68	67	51	54	62	70	53	67	67	52	60	69
Austria	na	na	na	na	na	na	na	na	na	na	na	na	na	na	na	na
Azerbaijan	na	50	49	51	56	46	48	50	48	55	45	48	62	52	48	52
Bangladesh	na	55	55	55	54	53	70	59	50	51	45	53	66	60	52	47
Belarus	na	na	na	na	na	na	na	na	na	na	na	na	na	na	na	na
Belgium	na	na	na	na	na	na	na	na	na	na	na	na	na	na	na	na
Bosnia and Herz.	na	42	43	42	45	42	39	32	43	48	35	42	49	47	41	40
Brazil	na	49	52	46	53	48	43	47	51	50	47	52	50	51	47	55
Bulgaria	na	na	na	na	na	na	na	na	na	na	na	na	na	na	na	na
Canada	na	64	66	62	67	66	59	53	65	70	56	64	71	61	62	68
Chile	na	50	52	49	55	48	49	47	49	61	50	48	54	46	51	56
China	na	61	63	59	62	62	56	53	65	63	58	61	67	61	62	63
Colombia	na	na	na	na	na	na	na	na	na	na	na	na	na	na	na	na
Croatia	na	na	na	na	na	na	na	na	na	na	na	na	na	na	na	na
Czech Republic	na	na	na	na	na	na	na	na	na	na	na	na	na	na	na	na
Denmark	na	na	na	na	na	na	na	na	na	na	na	na	na	na	na	na
Dominican Rep.	na	72	67	75	70	73	90	73	74	71	80	69	64	69	71	77
Egypt	na	52	51	52	53	52	48	50	55	49	54	48	50	48	54	60
El Salvador	na	85	85	84	86	85	82	80	89	91	81	85	90	na	na	na
Estonia	na	na	na	na	na	na	na	na	na	na	na	na	na	na	na	na
Finland	na	na	na	na	na	na	na	na	na	na	na	na	na	na	na	na
France	na	na	na	na	na	na	na	na	na	na	na	na	na	na	na	na
Georgia	na	64	63	65	63	67	61	61	64	67	64	64	65	64	65	65
Germany	na	na	na	na	na	na	na	na	na	na	na	na	na	na	na	na
Great Britain	na	na	na	na	na	na	na	na	na	na	na	na	na	na	na	na
Greece	na	na	na	na	na	na	na	na	na	na	na	na	na	na	na	na
Hungary	na	na	na	na	na	na	na	na	na	na	na	na	na	na	na	na
Iceland	na	na	na	na	na	na	na	na	na	na	na	na	na	na	na	na
India	na	48	50	45	49	49	44	42	49	55	45	44	52	45	51	52
Indonesia	na	35	36	35	33	38	33	33	36	36	34	39	33	31	37	39
Iran	na	46	48	43	42	48	52	51	43	42	47	42	46	40	48	39
Ireland	na	na	na	na	na	na	na	na	na	na	na	na	na	na	na	na
Israel	na	32	33	31	37	32	25	26	32	34	30	27	33	32	30	51
Italy	na	na	na	na	na	na	na	na	na	na	na	na	na	na	na	na
Japan	na	49	51	47	48	47	51	47	48	53	44	49	57	44	50	61
Jordan	na	54	42	65	53	56	50	53	51	59	55	50	56	55	52	54
Korea, South	na	53	52	53	48	57	47	51	49	57	53	48	55	49	55	57
Latvia	na	na	na	na	na	na	na	na	na	na	na	na	na	na	na	na
Lithuania	na	na	na	na	na	na	na	na	na	na	na	na	na	na	na	na
Luxembourg	na	na	na	na	na	na	na	na	na	na	na	na	na	na	na	na
Macedonia	na	48	50	46	50	48	46	45	50	48	50	44	49	48	48	48
Malta	na	na	na	na	na	na	na	na	na	na	na	na	na	na	na	na
Mexico	na	55	54	56	59	53	54	53	55	64	58	58	52	53	55	54
Moldova	na	58	60	56	54	60	59	61	56	58	64	58	55	53	62	60
Montenegro	na	35	40	31	36	36	35	29	37	46	43	38	34	31	39	62
Morocco	na	55	51	60	54	54	63	57	49	44	47	46	60	53	57	52
Netherlands	na	na	na	na	na	na	na	na	na	na	na	na	na	na	na	na
New Zealand	na	49	49	49	60	62	36	34	44	70	39	51	59	43	47	67
Nigeria	na	46	46	47	46	46	51	50	45	42	48	45	47	45	46	50
Northern Ireland	na	na	na	na	na	na	na	na	na	na	na	na	na	na	na	na
Norway	na	63	63	63	66	66	57	56	64	68	na	na	na	54	62	79
Pakistan	na	7	8	7	8	8	4	1	11	22	na	4	23	2	14	70
Peru	na	61	63	59	63	61	56	56	59	67	57	63	65	53	64	60
Philippines	na	63	63	63	68	59	64	56	62	73	61	63	65	66	61	62
Poland	na	na	na	na	na	na	na	na	na	na	na	na	na	na	na	na
Portugal	na	na	na	na	na	na	na	na	na	na	na	na	na	na	na	na
Puerto Rico	na	65	70	63	67	68	62	46	67	67	63	67	67	59	64	72
Romania	na	na	na	na	na	na	na	na	na	na	na	na	na	na	na	na
Russian Fed.	na	na	na	na	na	na	na	na	na	na	na	na	na	na	na	na
Serbia	na	45	43	47	40	44	48	42	45	48	41	45	52	42	47	58
Singapore	na	35	36	34	43	28	27	32	37	38	31	36	39	22	39	42
Slovakia	na	na	na	na	na	na	na	na	na	na	na	na	na	na	na	na
Slovenia	na	na	na	na	na	na	na	na	na	na	na	na	na	na	na	na
South Africa	na	36	37	36	32	40	36	36	38	25	38	33	36	36	35	46
Spain	na	54	51	57	61	55	48	48	61	61	46	53	65	48	54	63
Sweden	na	73	70	76	76	74	70	68	74	75	72	73	75	59	71	83
Switzerland	na	47	45	49	50	48	44	38	49	51	47	46	50	33	46	58
Taiwan	na	64	60	68	74	63	61	59	61	70	60	66	68	63	64	78
Tanzania	na	62	60	64	60	63	60	65	59	61	61	64	62	64	61	61
Turkey	na	67	63	71	67	67	67	67	66	69	67	66	67	61	68	69
Uganda	na	39	42	35	35	38	58	39	37	48	42	31	40	37	38	48
Ukraine	na	na	na	na	na	na	na	na	na	na	na	na	na	na	na	na
United States	na	61	62	60	56	63	63	53	60	65	59	64	62	50	61	66
Uruguay	na	61	57	65	62	64	59	57	67	65	55	63	64	61	59	66
Venezuela	na	70	72	68	69	71	71	71	68	74	70	70	70	68	72	66
Vietnam	na	61	63	59	60	59	65	62	61	61	60	58	65	56	63	49
Zimbabwe	na	34	33	36	38	32	30	30	40	62	28	33	45	29	38	42
Total	na	52	52	53	53	53	50	48	52	59	51	52	55	46	52	61

RANKING

Country	2000
El Salvador	85
Sweden	73
Dominican Rep.	72
Venezuela	70
Turkey	67
Puerto Rico	65
Taiwan	64
Georgia	64
Canada	64
Philippines	63
Norway	63
Australia	63
Tanzania	62
Uruguay	61
Vietnam	61
United States	61
Peru	61
China	61
Moldova	58
Morocco	55
Mexico	55
Bangladesh	55
Jordan	54
Spain	54
Korea, South	53
Egypt	52
Azerbaijan	50
Chile	50
Japan	49
New Zealand	49
Brazil	49
India	48
Macedonia	48
Albania	48
Switzerland	47
Nigeria	46
Iran	46
Argentina	45
Serbia	45
Armenia	44
Bosnia and Herz.	42
Uganda	39
South Africa	36
Indonesia	35
Montenegro	35
Singapore	35
Zimbabwe	34
Algeria	34
Israel	32
Pakistan	7
Total	52

B009) HUMAN & NATURE

Which statement comes closest to your own views: human beings should master nature or humans should coexist with nature?

Coexist with nature (%) (WVS: V37)

Country	Wave		Gender		Age			Education			Income			Values			RANKING	
	1990	2000	Male	Female	16-29	30-49	50+	Lower	Middle	Upper	Lower	Middle	Upper	Mat	Mixed	Postm.	Country	2000
Albania	na	66	64	68	64	66	67	64	67	67	68	66	64	68	65	63	Japan	99
Algeria	na	na	na	na	na	na	na	na	na	na	na	na	na	na	na	na	Korea, South	95
Argentina	na	92	91	92	92	92	91	89	96	94	90	90	96	85	92	95	Sweden	95
Armenia	na	78	78	78	75	81	76	78	76	84	83	73	73	74	80	86	Brazil	95
Australia	na	93	93	93	92	93	93	91	94	94	92	93	95	94	92	94	Dominican Rep.	94
Austria	na	na	na	na	na	na	na	na	na	na	na	na	na	na	na	na	Puerto Rico	94
Azerbaijan	na	66	63	70	65	66	71	69	63	71	58	66	73	68	64	57	Serbia	94
Bangladesh	na	85	83	86	86	83	88	85	85	82	87	81	86	87	83	84	Norway	93
Belarus	na	na	na	na	na	na	na	na	na	na	na	na	na	na	na	na	Australia	93
Belgium	na	na	na	na	na	na	na	na	na	na	na	na	na	na	na	na	Canada	92
Bosnia and Herz.	na	85	84	86	88	83	85	84	84	89	85	84	85	85	85	91	Spain	92
Brazil	na	95	96	94	97	95	91	92	98	98	93	95	97	92	96	96	Chile	92
Bulgaria	na	na	na	na	na	na	na	na	na	na	na	na	na	na	na	na	Argentina	92
Canada	na	92	91	93	93	93	92	90	93	94	90	92	95	92	91	94	Uruguay	90
Chile	na	92	91	93	91	92	92	92	91	92	92	93	89	90	92	94	Taiwan	90
China	na	68	63	73	81	68	50	64	69	71	69	62	72	65	71	65	Peru	90
Colombia	na	na	na	na	na	na	na	na	na	na	na	na	na	na	na	na	New Zealand	89
Croatia	na	na	na	na	na	na	na	na	na	na	na	na	na	na	na	na	Macedonia	88
Czech Republic	na	na	na	na	na	na	na	na	na	na	na	na	na	na	na	na	Montenegro	88
Denmark	na	na	na	na	na	na	na	na	na	na	na	na	na	na	na	na	Mexico	87
Dominican Rep.	na	94	95	93	96	90	100	91	91	95	93	94	93	88	94	98	United States	85
Egypt	na	na	na	na	na	na	na	na	na	na	na	na	na	na	na	na	Georgia	85
El Salvador	na	84	86	83	89	80	83	80	87	95	79	86	88	na	na	na	Bosnia and Herz.	85
Estonia	na	na	na	na	na	na	na	na	na	na	na	na	na	na	na	na	Bangladesh	85
Finland	na	na	na	na	na	na	na	na	na	na	na	na	na	na	na	na	El Salvador	84
France	na	na	na	na	na	na	na	na	na	na	na	na	na	na	na	na	India	83
Georgia	na	85	83	87	84	87	84	83	84	89	84	87	85	86	85	81	Armenia	78
Germany	na	na	na	na	na	na	na	na	na	na	na	na	na	na	na	na	Uganda	74
Great Britain	na	na	na	na	na	na	na	na	na	na	na	na	na	na	na	na	Moldova	71
Greece	na	na	na	na	na	na	na	na	na	na	na	na	na	na	na	na	China	68
Hungary	na	na	na	na	na	na	na	na	na	na	na	na	na	na	na	na	Azerbaijan	66
Iceland	na	na	na	na	na	na	na	na	na	na	na	na	na	na	na	na	Albania	66
India	na	83	82	85	83	82	86	82	83	85	78	84	85	84	82	89	South Africa	62
Indonesia	na	na	na	na	na	na	na	na	na	na	na	na	na	na	na	na	Zimbabwe	61
Iran	na	na	na	na	na	na	na	na	na	na	na	na	na	na	na	na	Jordan	57
Ireland	na	na	na	na	na	na	na	na	na	na	na	na	na	na	na	na	Tanzania	53
Israel	na	na	na	na	na	na	na	na	na	na	na	na	na	na	na	na	Vietnam	53
Italy	na	na	na	na	na	na	na	na	na	na	na	na	na	na	na	na	Philippines	50
Japan	na	99	98	99	98	100	98	99	99	97	98	100	98	98	99	99		
Jordan	na	57	61	53	61	55	52	57	59	54	57	60	54	51	62	56		
Korea, South	na	95	95	96	97	95	94	87	95	98	93	96	97	94	96	99		
Latvia	na	na	na	na	na	na	na	na	na	na	na	na	na	na	na	na		
Lithuania	na	na	na	na	na	na	na	na	na	na	na	na	na	na	na	na		
Luxembourg	na	na	na	na	na	na	na	na	na	na	na	na	na	na	na	na		
Macedonia	na	88	86	90	83	90	91	85	89	92	87	89	89	90	87	94		
Malta	na	na	na	na	na	na	na	na	na	na	na	na	na	na	na	na		
Mexico	na	87	85	88	88	88	83	86	87	89	82	86	90	89	84	91		
Moldova	na	71	74	69	74	74	66	66	68	81	66	71	71	70	72	76		
Montenegro	na	88	86	90	84	90	88	88	88	88	91	89	83	87	89	85		
Morocco	na	na	na	na	na	na	na	na	na	na	na	na	na	na	na	na		
Netherlands	na	na	na	na	na	na	na	na	na	na	na	na	na	na	na	na		
New Zealand	na	89	89	90	92	91	87	85	92	94	85	92	93	80	91	95		
Nigeria	na	na	na	na	na	na	na	na	na	na	na	na	na	na	na	na		
Northern Ireland	na	na	na	na	na	na	na	na	na	na	na	na	na	na	na	na		
Norway	na	93	93	94	91	95	94	92	93	95	na	na	na	92	93	96		
Pakistan	na	na	na	na	na	na	na	na	na	na	na	na	na	na	na	na		
Peru	na	90	90	90	91	88	91	89	89	91	89	89	92	87	90	92		
Philippines	na	50	49	50	49	49	54	57	47	45	52	47	52	49	51	43		
Poland	na	na	na	na	na	na	na	na	na	na	na	na	na	na	na	na		
Portugal	na	na	na	na	na	na	na	na	na	na	na	na	na	na	na	na		
Puerto Rico	na	94	93	94	95	94	93	92	94	94	96	93	93	94	94	93		
Romania	na	na	na	na	na	na	na	na	na	na	na	na	na	na	na	na		
Russian Fed.	na	na	na	na	na	na	na	na	na	na	na	na	na	na	na	na		
Serbia	na	94	93	94	92	96	92	90	94	97	93	92	95	91	95	97		
Singapore	na	na	na	na	na	na	na	na	na	na	na	na	na	na	na	na		
Slovakia	na	na	na	na	na	na	na	na	na	na	na	na	na	na	na	na		
Slovenia	na	na	na	na	na	na	na	na	na	na	na	na	na	na	na	na		
South Africa	na	62	61	64	62	62	67	58	70	52	55	66	68	62	65	49		
Spain	na	92	92	93	92	92	93	92	94	90	95	93	88	92	91	96		
Sweden	na	95	94	97	96	95	95	94	95	96	94	96	96	96	95	95		
Switzerland	na	na	na	na	na	na	na	na	na	na	na	na	na	na	na	na		
Taiwan	na	90	90	89	96	90	84	86	92	91	88	92	90	90	89	86		
Tanzania	na	53	51	56	56	52	51	47	59	65	49	52	58	54	53	42		
Turkey	na	na	na	na	na	na	na	na	na	na	na	na	na	na	na	na		
Uganda	na	74	82	68	74	74	76	71	75	79	70	78	73	77	73	72		
Ukraine	na	na	na	na	na	na	na	na	na	na	na	na	na	na	na	na		
United States	na	85	85	86	82	86	88	81	84	88	85	86	85	81	85	89		
Uruguay	na	90	89	90	93	88	89	87	93	89	88	91	91	82	91	94		
Venezuela	na	na	na	na	na	na	na	na	na	na	na	na	na	na	na	na		
Vietnam	na	53	50	56	59	51	50	55	49	62	54	54	50	62	50	42		
Zimbabwe	na	61	61	61	60	61	63	61	61	100	58	61	63	58	63	65		
Total	na	82	81	83	81	81	83	78	82	87	80	81	83	78	82	88	Total	82

C1-C2) Do you agree or disagree with the following statements? (Agree)

Employers should give priority to (nation) people than immigrants — 72%

When jobs are scarce men should have more right to a job than women — 34%

C001) MEN MORE RIGHT TO A JOB

Do you agree or disagree with the following statements?

"When jobs are scarce, men should have more right to a job than women."

Agree (%)

(WVS: V78; EVS: V99)

Country	Wave		Gender		Age			Education			Income			Values			Country	2000
	1990	2000	Male	Female	16-29	30-49	50+	Lower	Middle	Upper	Lower	Middle	Upper	Mat	Mixed	Postm.		
Albania	na	47	55	38	34	48	56	56	44	30	51	46	43	48	47	31	Egypt	90
Algeria	na	68	80	54	69	65	69	76	67	62	68	64	67	71	66	64	Morocco	83
Argentina	24	26	30	22	22	22	33	34	17	8	35	28	14	35	26	16	Jordan	80
Armenia	na	60	71	50	54	64	63	63	61	54	54	61	69	68	56	38	Iran	73
Australia	na	26	27	24	12	20	44	35	27	16	35	24	16	37	27	20	Philippines	69
Austria	50	27	28	26	16	22	37	35	21	14	37	28	19	35	29	18	Bangladesh	68
Azerbaijan	na	64	70	57	66	63	61	67	64	63	67	63	63	65	62	64	Algeria	68
Bangladesh	na	68	76	58	61	72	76	72	64	63	82	61	65	71	67	57	Pakistan	67
Belarus	38	25	31	20	21	23	31	33	24	15	26	24	25	27	23	17	Georgia	65
Belgium	38	25	22	28	10	21	36	46	25	10	41	27	14	37	24	13	Azerbaijan	64
Bosnia and Herz.	na	27	31	23	23	25	32	33	27	18	34	27	20	31	24	25	Turkey	60
Brazil	38	36	41	31	30	38	44	50	27	16	49	30	25	48	32	22	Nigeria	60
Bulgaria	46	39	45	33	33	37	44	47	40	24	48	33	34	42	36	43	Armenia	60
Canada	19	15	14	15	8	11	22	28	11	9	23	14	7	25	16	9	India	57
Chile	37	25	31	20	22	24	30	32	23	17	29	24	22	28	24	26	Taiwan	57
China	41	45	47	43	27	50	48	51	43	23	45	48	42	45	43	40	Indonesia	52
Colombia	na	29	30	28	28	28	36	46	31	15	44	32	18	41	34	34	Vietnam	48
Croatia	na	29	32	27	13	34	34	38	27	11	52	28	18	27	33	16	Malta	47
Czech Republic	55	18	17	20	14	14	25	24	14	8	25	17	14	25	17	9	Albania	47
Denmark	11	6	7	5	4	2	11	9	1	2	12	5	na	14	6	1	China	45
Dominican Rep.	na	15	22	10	13	19	20	29	23	11	23	14	6	17	15	14	Moldova	45
Egypt	na	90	93	86	86	91	92	92	87	89	90	89	91	92	88	82	Macedonia	43
El Salvador	na	27	28	26	26	27	29	36	23	8	44	22	12	na	na	na	Uganda	41
Estonia	45	14	18	10	14	12	15	16	13	11	19	13	12	13	13	14	Zimbabwe	40
Finland	15	10	13	7	5	9	13	14	5	4	8	13	8	14	9	4	Bulgaria	39
France	33	22	21	22	13	18	30	30	12	9	26	23	18	31	22	8	Korea, South	39
Georgia	na	65	74	56	64	63	67	63	67	57	67	66	60	66	63	63	Romania	38
Germany	31	27	33	22	17	22	37	38	18	17	36	30	19	35	28	13	Russian Fed.	36
Great Britain	34	23	25	21	14	17	34	35	16	8	25	21	17	na	na	na	Brazil	36
Greece	na	20	28	14	13	21	35	44	25	12	27	18	19	22	21	13	Poland	35
Hungary	42	25	25	25	18	25	28	32	11	11	26	27	22	27	21	13	Mexico	34
Iceland	6	4	4	3	4	3	4	6	2	1	5	2	4	7	3	1	Japan	32
India	49	57	61	52	53	59	58	62	59	46	68	61	49	65	50	41	South Africa	32
Indonesia	na	52	61	43	53	52	52	62	52	47	54	49	57	54	50	57	Venezuela	31
Iran	na	73	80	65	69	75	80	80	69	68	76	74	68	81	70	62	Serbia	31
Ireland	36	15	14	16	4	12	28	29	9	6	28	14	7	22	16	7	Ukraine	31
Israel	na	na	na	na	na	na	na	na	na	na	na	na	na	na	na	na	Singapore	30
Italy	43	27	27	27	13	20	41	42	18	9	40	26	15	43	28	17	Montenegro	30
Japan	34	32	33	31	20	25	43	56	30	24	37	32	28	37	31	21	Portugal	30
Jordan	na	80	87	74	78	82	84	85	82	70	84	81	77	87	78	66	Colombia	29
Korea, South	42	39	44	33	14	42	60	62	43	30	41	37	38	45	35	19	Croatia	29
Latvia	34	20	20	19	18	16	24	27	19	15	22	16	16	19	21	11	Uruguay	28
Lithuania	66	24	30	20	22	19	32	33	23	15	30	27	24	27	23	16	Switzerland	27
Luxembourg	na	26	30	22	18	22	36	37	23	16	34	31	17	34	28	14	El Salvador	27
Macedonia	na	43	46	40	40	43	45	55	41	26	51	42	33	44	40	42	Tanzania	27
Malta	na	47	49	46	28	46	62	68	44	14	60	53	30	52	47	30	Italy	27
Mexico	23	34	37	31	29	34	40	43	25	15	42	32	23	40	31	26	Germany	27
Moldova	na	45	46	44	43	38	55	55	46	35	56	43	37	45	42	42	Austria	27
Montenegro	na	30	43	16	22	26	39	40	26	15	35	22	28	31	28	22	Bosnia and Herz.	27
Morocco	na	83	88	78	81	83	88	86	76	55	90	84	79	85	82	74	Luxembourg	26
Netherlands	22	12	11	13	4	8	21	26	10	3	19	9	6	28	13	4	Argentina	26
New Zealand	na	13	12	13	2	9	20	17	12	8	17	10	10	14	13	8	Australia	26
Nigeria	48	60	73	47	60	60	60	61	61	58	64	59	58	57	61	68	Chile	25
Northern Ireland	34	16	17	15	7	11	25	22	10	12	17	16	7	18	16	11	Belgium	25
Norway	16	14	15	14	8	11	24	22	15	7	na	na	na	24	14	5	Belarus	25
Pakistan	na	67	71	63	65	65	80	74	64	50	74	69	56	70	65	64	Hungary	25
Peru	na	15	18	13	13	17	17	21	16	9	20	10	13	19	14	13	Lithuania	24
Philippines	na	69	72	66	61	72	75	75	71	58	74	68	66	70	69	63	Slovakia	24
Poland	55	35	36	34	17	32	48	47	21	18	37	34	33	41	32	28	Great Britain	23
Portugal	34	30	32	28	15	29	39	35	20	13	42	37	20	34	27	30	France	22
Puerto Rico	na	21	22	20	17	17	25	30	26	16	28	20	14	28	21	14	Puerto Rico	21
Romania	42	38	38	38	34	32	45	58	31	17	57	42	20	45	33	15	Greece	20
Russian Fed.	40	36	43	31	37	36	36	40	39	27	36	39	34	37	35	38	Latvia	20
Serbia	na	31	37	27	22	29	37	46	29	15	39	29	27	37	28	17	Spain	19
Singapore	na	30	33	27	21	37	43	41	27	15	41	31	23	37	29	18	Czech Republic	18
Slovakia	na	24	29	20	17	22	32	33	21	12	29	25	20	29	22	14	Slovenia	18
Slovenia	29	18	18	18	8	16	27	34	14	5	25	18	8	28	16	15	Northern Ireland	16
South Africa	45	32	43	18	30	32	38	39	23	17	38	28	27	28	34	35	Ireland	15
Spain	31	19	19	19	10	14	29	27	13	9	29	17	14	28	17	8	Dominican Rep.	15
Sweden	8	2	3	2	1	1	4	4	3	1	4	2	1	3	3	na	Peru	15
Switzerland	na	27	29	26	17	22	41	43	25	15	34	32	17	37	30	14	Canada	15
Taiwan	na	57	56	58	41	57	67	70	57	45	64	67	44	62	53	53	Norway	14
Tanzania	na	27	33	20	28	24	34	30	25	21	36	22	25	28	26	41	Estonia	14
Turkey	51	60	67	54	55	62	67	71	50	34	72	56	41	69	60	47	New Zealand	13
Uganda	na	41	58	25	42	39	42	47	36	59	51	50	29	35	44	42	Netherlands	12
Ukraine	na	31	35	27	25	30	34	43	33	19	33	30	30	35	25	35	Finland	10
United States	24	10	11	9	7	8	14	12	10	9	12	11	6	11	12	5	United States	10
Uruguay	na	28	33	24	27	17	37	37	15	14	37	30	16	44	28	14	Denmark	6
Venezuela	na	31	36	27	30	30	36	38	33	18	38	30	29	39	31	22	Iceland	4
Vietnam	na	48	54	43	45	49	50	53	45	32	56	42	51	54	48	43	Sweden	2
Zimbabwe	na	40	51	31	42	35	46	43	36	30	49	41	27	42	39	42		
Total	35	34	39	30	32	34	38	44	32	24	42	34	29	44	32	21	Total	34

C002) JOBS PREFERENCE TO OWN NATIONALITY

Do you agree or disagree with the following statements:

"When jobs are scarce, employers should give priority to own nationality immigrants?"

Agree (%)

(WVS: V79; EVS: V98)

Country	Wave		Gender		Age			Education			Income			Values		
	1990	2000	Male	Female	16-29	30-49	50+	Lower	Middle	Upper	Lower	Middle	Upper	Mat	Mixed	Postm.
Albania	na	80	83	77	78	80	80	81	81	73	79	82	78	82	79	56
Algeria	na	87	88	87	87	87	91	92	87	85	90	90	80	88	88	81
Argentina	60	74	75	73	77	72	73	75	75	62	77	76	68	80	75	69
Armenia	na	66	68	65	66	68	64	70	67	63	62	74	67	72	64	42
Australia	na	45	44	46	48	42	46	55	51	30	50	45	37	47	48	40
Austria	77	72	73	72	58	70	82	81	66	55	80	73	68	78	78	60
Azerbaijan	na	86	86	86	88	83	88	95	86	83	92	85	76	86	86	86
Bangladesh	na	92	92	92	92	93	91	92	94	92	98	91	89	92	92	97
Belarus	56	85	85	85	83	82	91	91	85	76	87	84	85	88	83	80
Belgium	66	56	51	60	48	51	64	72	60	37	62	58	48	72	58	28
Bosnia and Herz.	na	9	8	11	11	8	10	15	8	9	12	8	8	9	10	8
Brazil	82	89	90	87	88	88	91	90	88	83	92	87	85	90	89	84
Bulgaria	87	88	88	88	85	86	92	91	87	86	93	87	85	92	85	81
Canada	53	47	45	50	38	48	52	62	47	34	56	50	39	60	49	40
Chile	83	83	82	84	84	81	85	83	84	80	85	82	82	86	81	83
China	65	73	73	72	52	76	82	80	68	61	77	72	69	74	70	53
Colombia	na	na	na	na	na	na	na	na	na	na	na	na	na	na	na	na
Croatia	na	91	92	90	87	89	95	95	88	86	93	91	88	96	91	84
Czech Republic	88	84	83	85	83	84	85	87	84	68	87	84	80	88	84	72
Denmark	53	34	34	35	28	28	45	46	24	16	40	35	19	51	37	10
Dominican Rep.	na	46	47	46	44	48	78	48	40	49	45	46	53	42	48	48
Egypt	na	99	99	98	98	99	99	99	98	98	98	99	99	99	99	96
El Salvador	na	na	na	na	na	na	na	na	na	na	na	na	na	na	na	na
Estonia	82	47	50	45	48	42	52	54	47	38	55	48	43	47	49	28
Finland	71	65	68	63	61	62	70	76	55	42	65	72	61	79	63	44
France	63	54	53	55	46	48	64	67	43	31	63	54	42	74	53	30
Georgia	na	83	84	81	84	83	81	82	83	81	84	83	80	83	82	85
Germany	69	59	62	56	47	55	68	68	54	34	70	60	52	71	59	38
Great Britain	51	58	58	58	58	55	60	70	56	36	65	55	51	na	na	na
Greece	na	78	78	79	72	83	85	89	87	70	81	78	80	85	81	62
Hungary	87	90	89	91	87	91	90	92	88	84	90	91	89	94	86	83
Iceland	87	70	71	68	65	68	77	78	72	50	78	70	62	77	72	45
India	84	85	85	85	85	85	86	85	87	83	81	86	85	88	83	78
Indonesia	na	87	90	85	90	89	85	89	88	88	86	89	89	88	88	89
Iran	na	94	94	94	94	94	93	93	94	94	94	94	94	94	94	93
Ireland	69	73	70	76	67	71	80	83	70	61	82	74	61	82	74	53
Israel	na	na	na	na	na	na	na	na	na	na	na	na	na	na	na	na
Italy	74	61	60	63	58	54	70	73	56	43	69	61	51	77	64	47
Japan	65	61	64	58	44	54	73	69	60	57	65	60	58	67	61	42
Jordan	na	93	97	89	92	93	96	93	92	93	92	96	90	94	93	86
Korea, South	72	84	84	83	72	85	94	91	86	80	84	83	85	89	81	68
Latvia	80	74	73	76	65	72	80	81	73	71	78	71	72	75	75	64
Lithuania	92	94	94	95	92	96	94	95	95	90	97	96	92	97	95	87
Luxembourg	na	48	46	50	40	41	60	51	52	35	57	50	37	58	48	36
Macedonia	na	78	77	79	75	80	79	81	78	75	78	78	79	80	77	86
Malta	na	94	92	95	93	94	91	97	94	84	93	93	93	95	93	94
Mexico	83	80	79	81	80	79	82	82	76	81	84	74	79	80	80	77
Moldova	na	65	65	66	63	64	69	70	64	63	70	67	66	67	62	59
Montenegro	na	85	85	85	80	84	89	91	83	76	90	83	81	89	82	80
Morocco	na	95	95	94	95	95	95	95	95	88	97	93	91	96	93	91
Netherlands	30	28	25	31	33	23	31	43	26	17	32	30	21	46	31	12
New Zealand	na	49	45	53	53	46	51	59	52	36	55	50	43	54	52	40
Nigeria	80	81	82	79	80	80	86	80	80	83	83	81	79	78	83	79
Northern Ireland	62	75	75	75	70	76	78	84	71	59	75	75	64	83	72	72
Norway	59	41	42	41	35	38	50	56	44	25	na	na	na	60	41	20
Pakistan	na	57	58	55	46	62	60	68	43	45	71	56	38	60	51	50
Peru	na	73	74	72	73	72	75	70	75	71	74	73	71	70	74	75
Philippines	na	86	86	86	84	88	86	84	88	86	89	84	86	89	84	81
Poland	67	91	90	92	87	88	96	95	86	82	94	90	85	94	89	91
Portugal	88	63	59	68	57	63	68	65	62	59	71	58	60	63	63	69
Puerto Rico	na	76	76	77	69	79	78	76	77	77	78	78	74	86	76	74
Romania	75	74	72	76	64	71	83	82	74	62	79	77	69	79	72	55
Russian Fed.	63	73	72	74	70	72	77	78	74	69	74	75	72	75	71	74
Serbia	na	80	80	81	78	80	82	86	78	76	86	81	76	85	78	62
Singapore	na	82	81	83	76	85	94	86	82	71	88	83	81	86	81	76
Slovakia	na	88	88	89	86	88	90	91	88	77	91	90	85	90	88	76
Slovenia	79	76	74	77	72	74	81	83	76	62	78	77	67	82	78	66
South Africa	74	79	81	78	76	82	80	79	79	86	82	71	80	82	79	78
Spain	75	60	59	61	53	55	70	69	53	46	64	60	57	72	60	43
Sweden	35	11	15	8	10	8	16	18	12	5	12	14	8	26	12	5
Switzerland	na	60	60	60	54	59	65	73	58	48	66	60	55	67	62	48
Taiwan	na	91	90	91	89	92	87	91	87	92	91	92	92	94	90	87
Tanzania	na	71	74	68	73	72	67	65	79	75	63	73	79	73	72	77
Turkey	75	66	66	66	63	68	68	69	62	60	68	65	63	72	66	55
Uganda	na	92	94	91	91	93	94	92	92	97	92	96	90	92	93	89
Ukraine	na	70	71	69	67	70	72	79	72	60	68	74	68	75	65	60
United States	51	49	45	54	45	52	48	60	50	45	57	44	46	56	52	40
Uruguay	na	83	81	85	82	85	82	84	81	80	80	85	83	88	83	82
Venezuela	na	82	80	83	82	80	84	81	84	76	81	83	82	85	80	81
Vietnam	na	79	80	79	74	81	79	78	80	81	80	78	79	82	81	77
Zimbabwe	na	79	81	77	80	78	77	79	78	70	83	81	68	78	77	89
Total	70	72	72	72	71	71	74	78	72	63	76	72	70	80	71	58

RANKING

Country	2000
Egypt	99
Morocco	95
Lithuania	94
Iran	94
Malta	94
Jordan	93
Bangladesh	92
Uganda	92
Croatia	91
Poland	91
Taiwan	91
Hungary	90
Brazil	89
Bulgaria	88
Slovakia	88
Algeria	87
Indonesia	87
Philippines	86
Azerbaijan	86
Belarus	85
Montenegro	85
India	85
Czech Republic	84
Korea, South	84
Chile	83
Uruguay	83
Georgia	83
Singapore	82
Venezuela	82
Nigeria	81
Serbia	80
Mexico	80
Albania	80
South Africa	79
Vietnam	79
Zimbabwe	79
Greece	78
Macedonia	78
Puerto Rico	76
Slovenia	76
Northern Ireland	75
Latvia	74
Romania	74
Argentina	74
Russian Fed.	73
Ireland	73
Peru	73
China	73
Austria	72
Tanzania	71
Ukraine	70
Iceland	70
Armenia	66
Turkey	66
Finland	65
Moldova	65
Portugal	63
Italy	61
Japan	61
Spain	60
Switzerland	60
Germany	59
Great Britain	58
Pakistan	57
Belgium	56
France	54
United States	49
New Zealand	49
Luxembourg	48
Estonia	47
Canada	47
Dominican Rep.	46
Australia	45
Norway	41
Denmark	34
Netherlands	28
Sweden	11
Bosnia and Herz.	9
Total	72

C006) FINANCIAL SATISFACTION

How satisfied are you with the financial situation of your household?
("1" = completely dissatisfied / "10" = completely satisfied)
% Satisfied (7-10)

(WVS: V80)

Country	Wave 1990	Wave 2000	Gender Male	Gender Female	Age 16-29	Age 30-49	Age 50+	Education Lower	Education Middle	Education Upper	Income Lower	Income Middle	Income Upper	Values Mat	Values Mixed	Values Postm.	RANKING Country	RANKING 2000
Albania	na	22	25	19	27	21	19	14	24	37	10	18	39	20	25	23	Colombia	81
Algeria	na	45	40	51	45	49	40	38	45	50	36	44	61	40	48	52	Switzerland	72
Argentina	36	37	39	35	46	31	35	36	38	44	26	36	49	35	37	39	Puerto Rico	69
Armenia	na	13	14	12	18	11	8	11	13	12	21	7	6	8	17	8	Canada	64
Australia	na	53	56	50	52	49	60	52	51	57	40	51	72	49	54	54	Norway	60
Austria	61	na	na	na	na	na	na	na	na	na	na	na	na	na	na	na	Mexico	58
Azerbaijan	na	19	21	17	24	16	15	17	17	22	10	14	35	19	18	12	United States	58
Bangladesh	na	29	28	31	34	25	31	24	36	33	14	25	51	34	26	24	Singapore	55
Belarus	27	na	na	na	na	na	na	na	na	na	na	na	na	na	na	na	Uruguay	55
Belgium	70	na	na	na	na	na	na	na	na	na	na	na	na	na	na	na	Nigeria	54
Bosnia and Herz.	na	25	27	24	32	26	18	17	23	39	8	20	54	18	29	34	Australia	53
Brazil	37	36	41	31	35	32	46	39	31	41	30	36	40	39	34	35	New Zealand	53
Bulgaria	17	na	na	na	na	na	na	na	na	na	na	na	na	na	na	na	Indonesia	52
Canada	68	64	64	63	60	59	71	62	60	72	46	65	74	63	63	65	El Salvador	50
Chile	41	36	32	40	41	33	35	27	37	53	25	34	59	34	37	36	Spain	48
China	47	39	35	43	43	37	42	41	38	35	32	40	49	37	38	56	Venezuela	47
Colombia	na	81	83	79	81	81	82	80	79	84	74	79	88	77	80	81	Dominican Rep.	47
Croatia	na	na	na	na	na	na	na	na	na	na	na	na	na	na	na	na	Japan	46
Czech Republic	30	na	na	na	na	na	na	na	na	na	na	na	na	na	na	na	Algeria	45
Denmark	66	na	na	na	na	na	na	na	na	na	na	na	na	na	na	na	Egypt	40
Dominican Rep.	na	47	51	45	52	38	55	27	32	55	31	49	69	45	48	47	Korea, South	40
Egypt	na	40	37	42	41	39	39	38	44	38	36	40	42	38	42	39	China	39
El Salvador	na	50	51	50	56	44	51	44	53	65	39	47	73	na	na	na	Philippines	39
Estonia	31	na	na	na	na	na	na	na	na	na	na	na	na	na	na	na	Taiwan	39
Finland	59	na	na	na	na	na	na	na	na	na	na	na	na	na	na	na	Iran	37
France	42	na	na	na	na	na	na	na	na	na	na	na	na	na	na	na	Argentina	37
Georgia	na	9	10	8	14	8	6	8	9	10	5	7	16	8	9	10	Chile	36
Germany	43	na	na	na	na	na	na	na	na	na	na	na	na	na	na	na	Brazil	36
Great Britain	56	na	na	na	na	na	na	na	na	na	na	na	na	na	na	na	Vietnam	34
Greece	na	na	na	na	na	na	na	na	na	na	na	na	na	na	na	na	Peru	31
Hungary	30	na	na	na	na	na	na	na	na	na	na	na	na	na	na	na	Bangladesh	29
Iceland	53	na	na	na	na	na	na	na	na	na	na	na	na	na	na	na	Uganda	28
India	47	26	28	23	26	26	26	20	28	36	19	18	36	24	32	29	Morocco	27
Indonesia	na	52	53	51	45	56	51	42	52	61	31	62	80	48	55	63	Jordan	27
Iran	na	37	34	41	42	34	32	31	39	42	27	31	47	32	40	39	India	26
Ireland	59	na	na	na	na	na	na	na	na	na	na	na	na	na	na	na	Bosnia and Herz.	25
Israel	na	na	na	na	na	na	na	na	na	na	na	na	na	na	na	na	South Africa	25
Italy	67	na	na	na	na	na	na	na	na	na	na	na	na	na	na	na	Albania	22
Japan	41	46	43	49	46	42	50	43	46	48	37	44	61	46	47	46	Macedonia	21
Jordan	na	27	23	30	30	23	27	21	24	42	17	25	44	26	28	31	Montenegro	20
Korea, South	40	40	41	38	40	40	39	18	38	45	22	34	62	38	40	52	Azerbaijan	19
Latvia	21	na	na	na	na	na	na	na	na	na	na	na	na	na	na	na	Turkey	16
Lithuania	na	na	na	na	na	na	na	na	na	na	na	na	na	na	na	na	Tanzania	16
Luxembourg	na	na	na	na	na	na	na	na	na	na	na	na	na	na	na	na	Serbia	15
Macedonia	na	21	20	22	26	19	18	14	20	33	7	19	45	18	23	21	Moldova	14
Malta	na	na	na	na	na	na	na	na	na	na	na	na	na	na	na	na	Zimbabwe	13
Mexico	51	58	60	57	65	56	53	53	63	70	54	56	70	55	60	63	Armenia	13
Moldova	na	14	13	15	22	14	8	8	15	18	4	10	25	12	14	26	Georgia	9
Montenegro	na	20	20	20	17	23	17	15	23	24	8	12	34	19	22	15	Pakistan	5
Morocco	na	27	23	31	29	27	20	22	40	55	15	34	26	26	26	35		
Netherlands	75	na	na	na	na	na	na	na	na	na	na	na	na	na	na	na		
New Zealand	na	53	54	52	43	51	59	49	56	56	35	51	72	54	53	57		
Nigeria	38	54	54	55	58	51	41	50	54	62	45	52	72	54	55	49		
Northern Ireland	58	na	na	na	na	na	na	na	na	na	na	na	na	na	na	na		
Norway	56	60	62	57	58	56	65	52	59	68	na	na	na	48	62	56		
Pakistan	na	5	6	5	4	7	4	1	7	16	na	2	17	4	8	18		
Peru	na	31	31	31	33	27	32	27	27	39	23	34	40	33	31	29		
Philippines	na	39	38	40	43	35	43	37	37	45	27	33	59	37	40	44		
Poland	30	na	na	na	na	na	na	na	na	na	na	na	na	na	na	na		
Portugal	43	na	na	na	na	na	na	na	na	na	na	na	na	na	na	na		
Puerto Rico	na	69	75	66	73	62	73	70	65	71	64	70	75	61	71	69		
Romania	29	na	na	na	na	na	na	na	na	na	na	na	na	na	na	na		
Russian Fed.	27	na	na	na	na	na	na	na	na	na	na	na	na	na	na	na		
Serbia	na	15	15	14	20	15	13	11	14	22	10	12	23	13	16	21		
Singapore	na	55	54	57	58	52	56	52	55	65	41	50	69	50	59	48		
Slovakia	na	na	na	na	na	na	na	na	na	na	na	na	na	na	na	na		
Slovenia	23	na	na	na	na	na	na	na	na	na	na	na	na	na	na	na		
South Africa	34	25	25	25	19	28	33	20	31	36	10	28	37	25	24	30		
Spain	48	48	49	47	54	48	44	43	52	59	33	51	57	41	50	51		
Sweden	63	na	na	na	na	na	na	na	na	na	na	na	na	na	na	na		
Switzerland	83	72	73	72	71	68	78	69	71	87	55	69	86	63	71	80		
Taiwan	na	39	37	40	39	42	30	29	31	52	26	32	55	38	39	51		
Tanzania	na	16	13	20	17	16	16	17	15	16	13	20	16	16	17	26		
Turkey	21	16	15	18	23	13	13	14	20	19	8	18	38	13	17	20		
Uganda	na	28	22	33	27	27	37	23	30	38	16	33	32	31	25	34		
Ukraine	na	na	na	na	na	na	na	na	na	na	na	na	na	na	na	na		
United States	62	58	63	53	54	52	70	52	57	61	43	59	78	60	58	57		
Uruguay	na	55	53	56	56	51	58	53	58	61	44	56	67	49	58	53		
Venezuela	na	47	49	46	46	48	49	43	44	60	35	46	57	39	51	50		
Vietnam	na	34	35	33	29	36	36	30	38	46	20	25	53	30	40	33		
Zimbabwe	na	13	12	13	19	8	7	8	20	9	10	10	24	10	15	16		
Total	46	37	37	38	39	35	39	31	37	48	26	35	51	30	39	46	Total	37

C11-C25) Aspects of a job that people
say are important (Mentioned)

Good pay	82%
Pleasant people to work with	71%
Good job security	71%
A job that meets one's abilities	64%
A job that is interesting	64%
You can achieve something	62%
Good hours	53%
A job respected	52%
An opportunity to use initiative	50%
A responsible job	50%
Meeting people	49%
A useful job for society	42%
Not too much pressure	42%
Good chances for promotion	40%
Generous holidays	32%

C011) IMPORTANT IN A JOB: GOOD PAY

Here are some more aspects of a job that people say are important.

Please tell me which ones you personally think are important in a job?

Good pay (%)

(WVS: V86; EVS: V71)

Country	Wave 1990	Wave 2000	Gender Male	Gender Female	Age 16-29	Age 30-49	Age 50+	Education Lower	Education Middle	Education Upper	Income Lower	Income Middle	Income Upper	Values Mat	Values Mixed	Values Postm.	RANKING Country	RANKING 2000
Albania	na	95	96	95	95	96	95	96	95	93	94	96	95	97	94	87	Morocco	98
Algeria	na	90	90	89	91	88	92	88	92	88	91	92	90	93	89	87	Jordan	98
Argentina	84	75	80	71	79	73	75	78	73	67	78	73	75	82	76	68	Nigeria	97
Armenia	na	94	95	93	92	97	90	89	94	94	92	94	96	96	91	92	Turkey	97
Australia	na	61	66	55	68	63	51	60	60	62	57	61	66	62	61	60	Indonesia	97
Austria	60	66	71	62	78	68	58	67	66	61	63	70	68	76	68	60	Korea, South	96
Azerbaijan	na	95	97	94	95	96	93	90	95	96	96	97	95	96	96	94	Albania	95
Bangladesh	na	92	92	92	88	95	98	95	88	91	95	89	95	95	92	78	Azerbaijan	95
Belarus	87	88	92	85	93	94	78	77	92	93	87	88	91	87	90	91	Armenia	94
Belgium	71	73	77	69	81	72	69	76	76	66	69	72	73	81	75	57	Poland	93
Bosnia and Herz.	na	91	90	92	92	93	88	95	91	88	90	92	90	94	90	91	Lithuania	93
Brazil	82	56	55	56	58	54	54	57	55	50	58	57	53	60	55	46	Georgia	93
Bulgaria	90	91	92	90	91	92	90	85	94	95	88	89	95	90	94	88	Uganda	93
Canada	76	76	78	74	83	77	69	72	77	76	72	75	79	87	75	74	Bangladesh	92
Chile	77	85	87	84	84	87	84	86	86	81	86	86	83	89	86	80	India	92
China	68	65	66	64	63	70	54	63	67	63	66	66	64	69	69	53	Bosnia and Herz.	91
Colombia	na	66	65	66	66	65	68	79	67	54	76	67	57	75	71	49	Slovakia	91
Croatia	na	86	91	82	91	84	86	87	87	82	77	86	91	94	85	86	Bulgaria	91
Czech Republic	83	74	77	71	84	78	65	78	72	65	67	76	77	80	72	70	South Africa	91
Denmark	55	54	60	48	60	58	46	54	55	55	48	56	61	55	53	56	Romania	91
Dominican Rep.	na	85	84	85	85	83	91	78	83	87	79	87	94	84	86	85	Uruguay	90
Egypt	na	85	85	85	82	86	89	88	81	83	86	86	83	89	81	81	Algeria	90
El Salvador	na	na	na	na	na	na	na	na	na	na	na	na	na	na	na	na	Russian Fed.	90
Estonia	86	89	90	87	90	93	84	86	90	88	85	89	89	91	88	80	Hungary	90
Finland	66	65	69	61	73	73	52	64	65	66	64	67	65	75	61	60	Greece	90
France	54	68	70	67	72	70	65	69	70	65	70	67	69	71	68	63	Malta	89
Georgia	na	93	94	92	90	93	95	96	92	93	92	94	93	95	91	92	Macedonia	89
Germany	71	75	81	71	76	78	72	77	75	65	78	78	74	84	74	62	Ireland	89
Great Britain	69	81	85	77	84	87	74	83	80	82	80	83	84	na	na	na	United States	89
Greece	na	90	88	91	94	87	84	85	89	91	89	91	89	93	90	88	Northern Ireland	89
Hungary	85	90	92	88	97	96	80	87	95	95	82	90	94	89	92	88	Tanzania	89
Iceland	86	86	87	85	89	88	82	84	89	85	85	88	89	89	87	78	Estonia	89
India	87	92	92	92	94	93	89	91	93	93	90	92	93	94	93	93	Ukraine	89
Indonesia	na	97	96	98	98	97	96	94	97	99	98	98	99	96	98	96	Zimbabwe	88
Iran	na	80	82	78	78	83	83	84	79	77	82	78	81	82	80	76	Belarus	88
Ireland	73	89	89	89	91	87	89	90	89	86	89	90	87	90	91	79	Slovenia	87
Israel	na	na	na	na	na	na	na	na	na	na	na	na	na	na	na	na	Croatia	86
Italy	72	85	86	84	88	85	82	85	85	84	85	86	85	88	85	83	Iceland	86
Japan	78	83	82	84	87	91	75	70	85	85	83	84	83	85	84	79	Moldova	86
Jordan	na	98	98	98	97	100	96	98	98	98	99	99	97	98	98	99	Chile	85
Korea, South	18	96	94	97	98	95	94	91	95	97	94	96	97	96	95	94	Dominican Rep.	85
Latvia	69	75	76	75	82	77	71	75	76	73	75	72	78	78	75	75	Egypt	85
Lithuania	79	93	93	92	95	95	89	90	94	93	94	87	95	96	92	81	Italy	85
Luxembourg	na	66	67	64	74	64	62	68	65	63	70	66	70	75	67	55	Spain	84
Macedonia	na	89	89	90	92	91	86	92	90	84	91	91	85	94	88	77	Japan	83
Malta	na	89	91	88	91	90	88	91	89	90	87	89	88	87	90	91	Great Britain	81
Mexico	89	79	80	78	79	79	79	80	77	78	81	78	77	84	80	62	Montenegro	81
Moldova	na	86	85	87	84	87	87	89	82	90	85	90	87	88	83	80	Iran	80
Montenegro	na	81	81	81	86	80	78	79	81	82	86	79	81	84	78	66	Portugal	80
Morocco	na	98	98	98	98	99	95	98	98	96	99	98	99	98	98	100	Mexico	79
Netherlands	69	72	78	67	82	77	62	70	74	72	68	74	77	77	73	68	New Zealand	79
New Zealand	na	79	83	76	88	85	70	76	80	82	74	79	88	79	81	79	Singapore	79
Nigeria	93	97	98	97	98	97	95	98	97	97	97	98	98	97	98	97	Philippines	78
Northern Ireland	74	89	91	87	91	90	87	89	89	85	85	91	85	90	89	87	Puerto Rico	77
Norway	60	58	66	52	60	64	51	57	57	63	na	na	na	57	60	53	Vietnam	76
Pakistan	na	na	na	na	na	na	na	na	na	na	na	na	na	na	na	na	Canada	76
Peru	na	73	71	76	75	73	71	75	75	70	72	78	68	78	73	73	Latvia	75
Philippines	na	78	80	76	75	79	80	81	75	79	75	79	80	79	78	73	Argentina	75
Poland	na	93	94	92	95	94	90	96	92	84	94	91	96	96	92	85	Germany	75
Portugal	79	80	81	79	82	79	80	82	80	67	83	82	78	78	82	71	Czech Republic	74
Puerto Rico	na	77	78	76	80	81	72	78	79	76	77	75	78	81	79	66	Peru	73
Romania	76	91	93	89	92	91	90	91	91	88	90	93	90	91	92	85	Belgium	73
Russian Fed.	83	90	91	89	92	93	85	86	91	89	89	91	90	91	89	89	Netherlands	72
Serbia	na	72	70	74	72	74	70	79	71	66	74	73	68	76	69	61	Serbia	72
Singapore	na	79	80	77	77	79	82	78	80	74	83	80	76	81	79	68	France	68
Slovakia	na	91	92	90	91	93	88	89	92	91	87	93	93	91	92	86	Austria	66
Slovenia	82	87	89	85	91	88	83	89	88	80	90	85	84	88	88	86	Colombia	66
South Africa	84	91	93	89	89	93	91	95	87	75	94	89	89	91	92	85	Luxembourg	66
Spain	75	84	86	83	84	84	84	86	82	81	86	84	81	88	85	77	China	65
Sweden	73	58	63	54	64	65	48	53	60	60	51	59	66	59	60	53	Switzerland	65
Switzerland	na	65	71	59	67	68	60	64	65	64	65	63	65	77	64	64	Finland	65
Taiwan	na	56	52	59	63	55	54	56	56	55	58	59	52	59	55	35	Australia	61
Tanzania	na	89	88	90	90	90	84	88	91	90	89	90	92	92	88	100	Norway	58
Turkey	90	97	97	98	97	98	97	99	96	95	98	98	95	98	98	95	Sweden	58
Uganda	na	93	94	91	94	92	90	88	94	94	87	94	95	96	93	81	Taiwan	56
Ukraine	na	89	90	87	92	94	82	71	91	92	84	90	93	89	89	81	Brazil	56
United States	86	89	90	88	93	92	81	90	91	87	89	88	89	92	91	83	Denmark	54
Uruguay	na	90	91	90	90	89	91	92	88	83	91	90	89	91	92	86		
Venezuela	na	na	na	na	na	na	na	na	na	na	na	na	na	na	na	na		
Vietnam	na	76	75	76	81	75	73	76	78	72	74	71	81	91	76	81		
Zimbabwe	na	88	88	89	90	85	90	89	87	70	90	88	83	92	87	76		
Total	75	82	84	81	85	84	78	82	83	81	82	83	83	87	82	74	Total	82

C012) IMPORTANT IN A JOB: NOT TOO MUCH PRESSURE

Here are some more aspects of a job that people say are important.

Please tell me which ones you personally think are important in a job?

Not too much pressure (%)

(WVS: V87; EVS: V73)

Country	Wave 1990	Wave 2000	Gender Male	Gender Female	Age 16-29	Age 30-49	Age 50+	Education Lower	Education Middle	Education Upper	Income Lower	Income Middle	Income Upper	Values Mat	Values Mixed	Values Postm.
Albania	na	46	46	45	47	44	47	42	46	54	45	44	47	46	45	56
Algeria	na	60	62	57	66	57	50	53	60	64	67	54	53	59	60	67
Argentina	41	33	33	33	37	31	31	35	29	30	33	34	31	33	35	26
Armenia	na	53	44	61	53	50	59	59	54	48	52	55	55	55	50	62
Australia	na	24	22	25	22	22	27	26	24	21	27	22	19	24	24	23
Austria	17	18	21	15	19	17	18	26	16	13	17	20	16	39	18	12
Azerbaijan	na	56	55	57	54	57	57	51	58	52	63	64	42	57	56	50
Bangladesh	na	39	38	41	37	42	37	45	34	30	42	36	41	39	39	40
Belarus	60	20	22	19	25	22	15	20	21	18	20	20	22	19	22	14
Belgium	26	32	31	33	28	31	34	33	33	28	32	33	31	34	32	26
Bosnia and Herz.	na	52	50	53	54	52	49	50	50	59	53	51	53	50	53	49
Brazil	40	33	31	35	32	34	33	32	33	38	34	33	31	35	32	34
Bulgaria	35	40	38	41	44	43	35	37	44	35	37	38	44	38	42	51
Canada	28	28	27	29	26	26	30	35	27	22	32	28	23	34	29	23
Chile	46	41	40	42	40	44	38	38	43	44	41	43	40	40	40	48
China	30	27	27	28	28	31	19	21	33	30	24	28	32	28	30	25
Colombia	na	24	24	25	24	25	23	22	26	24	23	25	24	23	27	30
Croatia	na	63	63	64	67	66	59	65	64	55	70	61	65	63	64	61
Czech Republic	58	36	35	36	41	36	33	37	35	35	32	37	38	38	35	30
Denmark	16	14	12	16	13	16	13	14	7	17	14	16	11	19	14	13
Dominican Rep.	na	27	28	27	29	23	36	63	32	21	29	24	19	35	26	20
Egypt	na	66	66	67	69	64	66	63	68	72	66	66	69	65	68	61
El Salvador	na	na	na	na	na	na	na	na	na	na	na	na	na	na	na	na
Estonia	32	24	21	26	30	22	23	26	25	20	25	26	20	24	24	19
Finland	20	31	31	31	36	34	24	33	27	28	35	29	24	31	30	28
France	8	12	13	10	15	12	10	12	10	11	13	9	11	11	11	13
Georgia	na	30	27	33	30	29	31	33	32	23	31	28	31	29	31	33
Germany	19	24	23	24	30	25	20	25	25	10	27	25	26	31	21	21
Great Britain	19	28	30	26	31	34	21	25	30	30	26	31	32	na	na	na
Greece	na	54	53	54	55	52	53	47	52	56	49	53	59	49	53	57
Hungary	46	57	57	57	67	59	49	60	57	42	52	59	59	56	59	77
Iceland	35	32	34	31	39	30	31	38	29	28	33	36	26	37	33	24
India	48	54	53	55	55	54	53	53	57	53	47	58	54	57	55	47
Indonesia	na	85	83	88	88	87	83	83	86	86	80	91	87	87	86	89
Iran	na	53	54	52	55	52	47	52	53	51	54	49	53	59	51	55
Ireland	26	44	42	45	39	42	48	49	40	42	49	47	36	49	42	42
Israel	na	na	na	na	na	na	na	na	na	na	na	na	na	na	na	na
Italy	31	60	58	62	65	62	57	62	61	51	64	65	55	64	60	61
Japan	42	69	63	75	71	73	65	59	74	63	68	71	67	72	69	69
Jordan	na	81	82	80	80	84	74	80	81	83	80	85	78	81	81	77
Korea, South	8	89	86	93	91	91	84	82	90	89	88	88	92	90	89	88
Latvia	19	8	11	6	12	9	6	9	9	8	5	11	12	11	7	11
Lithuania	40	34	33	35	37	31	35	32	35	36	36	31	35	35	35	23
Luxembourg	na	36	38	34	45	34	32	39	36	30	40	36	28	36	36	38
Macedonia	na	32	30	34	34	37	24	31	34	30	31	32	34	31	32	30
Malta	na	68	65	70	67	65	71	75	66	56	67	67	55	65	70	58
Mexico	47	30	30	30	27	31	31	33	27	21	34	23	20	31	31	27
Moldova	na	49	49	49	51	46	51	57	51	38	47	50	51	51	46	42
Montenegro	na	36	36	36	35	34	39	43	35	24	43	35	35	42	30	24
Morocco	na	94	93	94	94	94	92	94	94	87	96	94	90	93	95	91
Netherlands	44	33	28	37	31	34	33	33	36	30	37	33	28	38	33	32
New Zealand	na	35	35	36	32	33	40	42	32	31	37	38	30	40	34	34
Nigeria	64	64	64	63	64	64	58	64	62	66	65	67	59	63	65	59
Northern Ireland	20	40	35	45	43	45	33	39	41	41	36	39	31	37	40	43
Norway	23	24	23	24	25	23	24	31	22	20	na	na	na	28	23	22
Pakistan	na	na	na	na	na	na	na	na	na	na	na	na	na	na	na	na
Peru	na	17	16	17	14	20	17	20	17	14	21	14	12	19	17	14
Philippines	na	36	33	39	34	35	43	48	36	23	40	33	36	39	35	30
Poland	na	63	61	66	65	60	67	64	63	63	67	61	63	63	63	65
Portugal	41	24	23	26	26	28	21	23	29	24	12	27	26	23	23	30
Puerto Rico	na	21	17	23	21	18	23	38	22	18	22	23	19	31	21	15
Romania	37	34	33	34	32	33	35	43	33	15	42	34	27	38	32	19
Russian Fed.	19	17	16	18	19	16	18	22	18	12	19	18	15	18	17	11
Serbia	na	23	26	21	26	25	20	26	23	17	24	24	19	25	23	10
Singapore	na	47	44	50	43	47	63	55	47	24	56	45	42	52	46	40
Slovakia	na	19	20	17	21	18	17	21	18	13	22	18	15	22	16	21
Slovenia	48	71	70	73	73	73	69	76	72	62	75	74	60	69	72	72
South Africa	29	50	52	49	56	49	41	50	51	44	50	52	49	49	51	56
Spain	38	39	40	39	46	41	34	37	42	42	40	40	37	37	42	39
Sweden	48	35	32	38	38	38	31	37	36	31	39	36	29	40	35	32
Switzerland	na	31	29	33	35	29	30	34	31	23	30	28	29	35	28	37
Taiwan	na	62	60	65	67	61	62	62	66	61	67	64	58	63	65	57
Tanzania	na	55	52	58	53	54	58	52	57	63	53	58	61	51	58	46
Turkey	78	91	91	92	92	92	89	92	90	93	91	92	91	93	91	93
Uganda	na	60	64	56	63	57	56	60	61	45	51	53	62	67	58	49
Ukraine	na	29	23	35	33	28	28	31	30	26	29	31	29	29	31	23
United States	33	38	35	41	37	35	42	41	45	33	42	37	33	40	38	36
Uruguay	na	57	56	58	58	58	56	55	60	59	54	56	62	52	61	55
Venezuela	na	na	na	na	na	na	na	na	na	na	na	na	na	na	na	na
Vietnam	na	54	56	52	52	53	59	55	54	63	59	48	60	62	57	61
Zimbabwe	na	27	28	27	30	25	23	26	29	18	23	26	38	30	26	23
Total	35	42	42	43	45	43	39	44	42	39	43	43	41	45	42	38

RANKING

Country	2000
Morocco	94
Turkey	91
Korea, South	89
Indonesia	85
Jordan	81
Slovenia	71
Japan	69
Malta	68
Egypt	66
Nigeria	64
Croatia	63
Poland	63
Taiwan	62
Italy	60
Uganda	60
Algeria	60
Uruguay	57
Hungary	57
Azerbaijan	56
Tanzania	55
Vietnam	54
India	54
Greece	54
Armenia	53
Iran	53
Bosnia and Herz.	52
South Africa	50
Moldova	49
Singapore	47
Albania	46
Ireland	44
Chile	41
Northern Ireland	40
Bulgaria	40
Spain	39
Bangladesh	39
United States	38
Philippines	36
Luxembourg	36
Montenegro	36
Czech Republic	36
New Zealand	35
Sweden	35
Lithuania	34
Romania	34
Brazil	33
Netherlands	33
Argentina	33
Iceland	32
Macedonia	32
Belgium	32
Finland	31
Switzerland	31
Georgia	30
Mexico	30
Ukraine	29
Great Britain	28
Canada	28
China	27
Dominican Rep.	27
Zimbabwe	27
Portugal	24
Colombia	24
Estonia	24
Norway	24
Germany	24
Australia	24
Serbia	23
Puerto Rico	21
Belarus	20
Slovakia	19
Austria	18
Russian Fed.	17
Peru	17
Denmark	14
France	12
Latvia	8
Total	42

C013) IMPORTANT IN A JOB: SECURITY

Here are some more aspects of a job that people say are important.

Please tell me which ones you personally think are important in a job?

Job security (%) (WVS: V88; EVS: V74)

Country	Wave 1990	Wave 2000	Gender Male	Gender Female	Age 16-29	Age 30-49	Age 50+	Educ. Lower	Educ. Middle	Educ. Upper	Income Lower	Income Middle	Income Upper	Values Mat	Values Mixed	Values Postm.
Albania	na	81	81	82	77	83	82	81	81	83	83	80	80	84	79	77
Algeria	na	86	86	87	88	86	85	82	87	88	88	86	85	89	85	87
Argentina	63	70	71	68	70	68	71	75	63	59	75	71	63	76	71	60
Armenia	na	77	76	78	70	82	82	77	78	75	78	79	76	81	76	60
Australia	na	59	58	59	56	59	61	62	65	48	64	59	54	65	59	56
Austria	65	75	77	74	73	74	78	83	72	57	76	77	75	81	80	66
Azerbaijan	na	74	77	72	70	76	80	72	74	76	73	77	71	74	77	72
Bangladesh	na	97	97	98	97	98	97	98	97	96	98	96	98	98	97	97
Belarus	37	30	31	28	32	30	28	24	31	35	30	29	31	28	31	21
Belgium	39	47	49	46	46	44	51	58	49	36	49	51	44	57	47	35
Bosnia and Herz.	na	90	89	91	90	91	89	91	91	88	91	92	86	93	89	89
Brazil	71	55	52	58	51	58	55	52	58	56	53	60	54	54	58	48
Bulgaria	57	81	81	81	79	77	85	81	83	75	83	80	80	83	80	68
Canada	67	65	64	66	63	66	65	69	69	55	68	68	61	78	68	57
Chile	69	74	77	71	72	77	71	75	73	73	77	73	71	79	72	71
China	44	68	72	64	72	62	62	62	74	40	66	75	62	75	71	53
Colombia	na	37	36	39	39	35	42	45	41	27	40	40	31	46	40	35
Croatia	na	81	80	82	78	81	83	84	81	72	83	83	78	81	83	77
Czech Republic	71	52	49	55	50	53	53	58	49	38	54	57	47	65	50	34
Denmark	52	50	49	50	43	50	54	55	46	45	50	53	48	60	52	42
Dominican Rep.	na	66	61	68	64	68	82	75	69	63	69	64	66	70	64	67
Egypt	na	81	82	79	81	80	81	79	85	79	82	80	83	82	81	77
El Salvador	na	na	na	na	na	na	na	na	na	na	na	na	na	na	na	na
Estonia	40	51	53	49	54	50	50	60	50	39	50	55	48	53	50	43
Finland	53	68	70	67	66	69	70	73	62	63	69	72	62	74	67	59
France	35	46	45	48	49	46	45	50	46	37	48	50	38	55	46	34
Georgia	na	65	67	63	59	68	68	67	65	63	65	64	66	71	61	45
Germany	72	79	82	77	79	80	78	83	79	62	79	85	80	85	79	72
Great Britain	57	65	70	60	61	69	63	66	64	65	61	68	65	na	na	na
Greece	na	65	62	68	67	63	66	68	67	63	70	62	65	62	65	71
Hungary	72	89	91	87	97	95	79	87	95	89	83	90	92	88	92	89
Iceland	57	58	59	57	63	57	56	62	60	45	58	63	53	63	60	40
India	74	91	92	88	94	91	87	88	93	94	89	90	92	96	93	96
Indonesia	na	96	96	96	96	97	96	94	97	97	98	97	99	98	97	96
Iran	na	77	78	76	79	78	70	72	81	77	78	72	79	80	77	81
Ireland	61	68	69	67	66	66	71	68	70	62	69	68	68	64	70	63
Israel	na	na	na	na	na	na	na	na	na	na	na	na	na	na	na	na
Italy	61	76	74	78	79	72	78	81	76	62	80	77	69	86	76	74
Japan	58	80	78	83	82	82	78	73	83	78	80	81	81	86	81	73
Jordan	na	97	98	95	97	97	94	96	97	98	95	98	98	97	97	95
Korea, South	35	97	97	97	96	97	98	100	98	96	96	96	99	99	96	93
Latvia	22	38	37	39	36	36	40	35	39	38	37	40	39	40	38	36
Lithuania	38	75	74	75	78	78	69	65	79	73	74	75	77	83	74	62
Luxembourg	na	59	60	58	66	57	57	67	57	51	64	61	53	62	62	52
Macedonia	na	85	88	83	81	88	86	86	87	81	88	85	81	87	86	75
Malta	na	72	70	73	71	70	74	80	69	65	75	65	66	74	72	56
Mexico	63	65	64	65	67	66	61	65	66	63	69	63	63	64	68	56
Moldova	na	86	87	86	86	87	86	90	85	85	86	85	88	86	86	82
Montenegro	na	48	51	45	38	48	55	55	48	33	60	40	45	59	39	40
Morocco	na	98	98	96	99	99	97	99	99	95	98	98	98	98	98	98
Netherlands	40	29	26	31	32	26	29	36	29	21	30	32	22	31	30	25
New Zealand	na	72	75	70	74	69	75	78	79	61	76	76	66	86	74	60
Nigeria	88	82	83	82	83	83	77	80	83	86	79	85	83	82	83	83
Northern Ireland	62	76	80	73	79	77	75	74	78	79	71	77	76	78	78	76
Norway	78	69	70	69	69	68	71	79	73	56	na	na	na	76	70	57
Pakistan	na	na	na	na	na	na	na	na	na	na	na	na	na	na	na	na
Peru	na	47	48	46	45	50	43	49	47	45	48	48	42	47	47	49
Philippines	na	76	76	76	73	77	77	74	75	79	77	78	71	78	74	70
Poland	na	80	80	80	73	79	84	83	77	73	86	79	68	79	81	77
Portugal	73	64	63	66	66	61	66	64	66	59	58	60	67	69	63	65
Puerto Rico	na	69	70	69	71	66	72	73	74	67	71	71	65	81	69	65
Romania	43	87	86	88	84	88	87	86	91	78	86	92	86	93	87	65
Russian Fed.	38	69	67	71	64	73	68	63	71	67	71	70	66	71	69	62
Serbia	na	39	43	34	33	39	41	41	43	26	43	40	36	39	41	18
Singapore	na	66	67	64	61	70	69	68	66	58	67	70	60	76	62	60
Slovakia	na	72	70	74	71	75	70	68	75	64	72	73	74	74	73	61
Slovenia	73	88	88	89	86	90	88	90	91	76	92	88	82	89	89	87
South Africa	68	84	84	84	85	85	80	84	86	72	82	92	81	87	84	80
Spain	67	75	76	74	74	75	76	79	71	71	78	76	71	79	77	68
Sweden	65	51	51	51	46	48	56	61	54	39	55	53	43	57	53	44
Switzerland	na	64	70	59	64	63	67	68	65	55	64	69	61	75	67	54
Taiwan	na	75	71	79	67	74	81	79	73	72	79	76	70	78	72	73
Tanzania	na	79	80	80	82	81	72	75	83	87	75	84	84	84	80	58
Turkey	83	98	98	98	98	98	98	98	98	94	98	99	96	98	98	97
Uganda	na	81	84	78	82	79	82	75	84	75	73	84	82	87	81	66
Ukraine	na	72	73	72	69	78	69	60	76	70	72	74	71	73	74	65
United States	72	72	72	72	73	74	68	72	79	68	73	73	70	80	74	63
Uruguay	na	77	78	75	79	79	74	78	76	67	79	73	75	79	79	73
Venezuela	na	na	na	na	na	na	na	na	na	na	na	na	na	na	na	na
Vietnam	na	82	83	81	80	84	81	78	88	91	83	78	87	87	88	87
Zimbabwe	na	81	82	81	79	83	84	81	82	91	79	83	83	82	81	79
Total	58	71	72	71	72	72	70	74	72	66	72	72	69	76	71	63

RANKING

Country	2000
Morocco	98
Turkey	98
Bangladesh	97
Korea, South	97
Jordan	97
Indonesia	96
India	91
Bosnia and Herz.	90
Hungary	89
Slovenia	88
Romania	87
Algeria	86
Moldova	86
Macedonia	85
South Africa	84
Nigeria	82
Vietnam	82
Zimbabwe	81
Albania	81
Croatia	81
Uganda	81
Bulgaria	81
Egypt	81
Japan	80
Poland	80
Germany	79
Tanzania	79
Armenia	77
Iran	77
Uruguay	77
Northern Ireland	76
Italy	76
Philippines	76
Austria	75
Taiwan	75
Spain	75
Lithuania	75
Azerbaijan	74
Chile	74
Ukraine	72
New Zealand	72
Slovakia	72
United States	72
Malta	72
Argentina	70
Norway	69
Puerto Rico	69
Russian Fed.	69
Finland	68
Ireland	68
China	68
Singapore	66
Dominican Rep.	66
Greece	65
Great Britain	65
Georgia	65
Canada	65
Mexico	65
Portugal	64
Switzerland	64
Luxembourg	59
Australia	59
Iceland	58
Brazil	55
Czech Republic	52
Sweden	51
Estonia	51
Denmark	50
Montenegro	48
Belgium	47
Peru	47
France	46
Serbia	39
Latvia	38
Colombia	37
Belarus	30
Netherlands	29
Total	71

C014) IMPORTANT IN A JOB: A JOB RESPECTED

Here are some more aspects of a job that people say are important.
Please tell me which ones you personally think are important in a job?

A job respected by people in general (%)

(WVS: V89; EVS: V76)

Country	Wave		Gender		Age			Education			Income			Values				RANKING Country	2000
	1990	2000	Male	Female	16-29	30-49	50+	Lower	Middle	Upper	Lower	Middle	Upper	Mat	Mixed	Postm.		
Albania	na	65	64	65	67	63	65	61	68	67	65	66	63	68	65	67	Turkey	94
Algeria	na	72	69	75	75	71	68	68	74	72	74	73	69	71	72	72	Jordan	94
Argentina	43	32	33	32	28	32	36	33	29	34	34	33	30	36	33	26	Morocco	92
Armenia	na	70	68	71	68	72	69	60	70	72	71	64	78	70	69	79	Bangladesh	91
Australia	na	27	29	26	27	26	29	29	26	27	30	24	28	27	28	28	Indonesia	87
Austria	35	36	37	35	32	34	40	37	33	41	40	35	34	44	37	32	Egypt	85
Azerbaijan	na	65	69	61	67	64	64	63	65	66	61	71	65	63	69	79	Hungary	84
Bangladesh	na	91	90	93	90	91	94	90	93	92	92	89	93	93	90	92	India	77
Belarus	42	30	32	29	45	30	19	16	35	39	25	32	37	25	36	38	Slovenia	75
Belgium	40	46	44	48	39	48	48	49	44	47	47	45	46	49	47	42	Malta	74
Bosnia and Herz.	na	54	53	55	55	54	55	50	54	58	54	53	57	49	56	59	Greece	73
Brazil	58	54	50	58	51	54	59	59	51	45	60	55	47	55	56	45	Algeria	72
Bulgaria	58	52	53	51	55	54	49	43	53	65	43	52	60	45	60	54	Nigeria	71
Canada	36	36	36	36	32	37	36	37	34	37	31	37	38	37	37	34	Moldova	70
Chile	60	55	53	57	52	56	56	51	56	60	53	55	59	53	53	62	Armenia	70
China	47	58	59	57	57	61	53	51	63	67	53	61	63	60	64	59	Taiwan	70
Colombia	na	29	29	30	30	30	28	35	29	26	30	32	26	36	27	37	Romania	69
Croatia	na	51	52	50	46	53	53	53	52	43	60	49	52	43	53	51	Korea, South	68
Czech Republic	33	35	35	35	33	35	36	34	35	43	37	34	36	36	35	32	Vietnam	67
Denmark	13	11	14	8	10	9	14	10	10	13	11	9	13	11	11	9	Poland	67
Dominican Rep.	na	46	44	47	44	50	55	59	48	44	42	43	52	46	47	39	Azerbaijan	65
Egypt	na	85	83	86	87	83	84	84	85	84	86	84	86	85	84	85	Albania	65
El Salvador	na	na	na	na	na	na	na	na	na	na	na	na	na	na	na	na	Tanzania	64
Estonia	38	32	26	36	31	26	38	28	31	38	32	33	31	31	32	32	Italy	61
Finland	24	30	31	29	33	31	27	28	32	34	32	27	30	30	29	32	Iran	61
France	17	26	28	24	25	25	28	27	24	25	29	24	27	27	27	21	Puerto Rico	60
Georgia	na	44	43	45	43	45	44	41	43	49	43	46	42	44	45	40	Peru	59
Germany	51	43	44	42	36	43	46	40	43	56	40	42	53	49	41	42	China	58
Great Britain	27	25	22	28	28	24	23	21	27	29	18	24	26	na	na	na	Uruguay	56
Greece	na	73	68	76	75	69	75	75	72	73	70	71	74	71	72	78	Chile	55
Hungary	16	84	84	83	90	90	74	80	90	91	73	85	89	80	90	97	Philippines	55
Iceland	45	51	50	52	46	49	59	53	50	51	49	47	55	56	51	35	Bosnia and Herz.	54
India	59	77	79	75	79	78	73	72	81	86	71	75	83	81	83	71	Brazil	54
Indonesia	na	87	86	89	90	87	87	82	90	89	87	89	91	89	87	82	Uganda	54
Iran	na	61	62	59	62	62	58	59	61	61	61	55	63	60	63	63	Ukraine	53
Ireland	29	44	43	45	33	44	52	49	39	45	49	43	44	47	44	37	Bulgaria	52
Israel	na	na	na	na	na	na	na	na	na	na	na	na	na	na	na	na	Croatia	51
Italy	40	61	60	63	57	58	67	69	57	51	68	63	55	66	63	59	Iceland	51
Japan	26	37	40	35	30	30	46	45	34	40	35	34	40	40	35	38	Mexico	51
Jordan	na	94	94	94	93	95	92	94	96	91	93	95	93	94	94	90	Netherlands	50
Korea, South	7	68	66	70	56	69	77	80	68	65	64	65	73	70	65	72	Portugal	50
Latvia	31	33	33	33	24	28	41	41	29	36	33	35	32	37	31	32	Spain	48
Lithuania	28	21	22	21	28	19	19	14	23	28	18	17	23	21	22	23	South Africa	48
Luxembourg	na	37	40	35	44	34	36	42	35	32	40	39	34	44	40	21	Montenegro	48
Macedonia	na	43	42	43	44	44	41	41	44	43	40	45	45	39	45	61	Russian Fed.	47
Malta	na	74	71	77	71	73	77	83	70	72	72	70	71	76	74	65	Dominican Rep.	46
Mexico	54	51	51	52	52	51	51	53	49	48	51	49	51	51	54	47	Belgium	46
Moldova	na	70	71	70	73	68	70	68	70	73	68	70	76	70	69	69	United States	46
Montenegro	na	48	48	48	46	49	48	41	50	59	42	48	50	46	51	52	Switzerland	44
Morocco	na	92	92	91	93	92	87	92	91	86	85	86	95	94	93	86	Ireland	44
Netherlands	55	50	51	49	47	52	50	50	47	53	45	51	56	46	51	51	Georgia	44
New Zealand	na	36	37	36	30	36	39	35	37	39	35	36	37	36	37	33	Northern Ireland	44
Nigeria	74	71	70	72	72	71	63	71	70	72	70	73	69	71	72	64	Germany	43
Northern Ireland	20	44	42	45	48	39	44	41	43	51	42	35	45	41	45	47	Macedonia	43
Norway	30	23	19	28	17	23	29	28	23	20	na	na	na	32	22	21	Singapore	40
Pakistan	na	na	na	na	na	na	na	na	na	na	na	na	na	na	na	na	Zimbabwe	39
Peru	na	59	58	60	58	58	64	65	59	54	59	61	56	59	59	61	Luxembourg	37
Philippines	na	55	55	55	56	53	56	56	52	57	54	52	58	52	57	49	Japan	37
Poland	na	67	70	63	67	62	72	70	65	59	69	65	65	67	68	65	New Zealand	36
Portugal	59	50	46	53	46	50	52	50	49	45	52	50	44	49	50	50	Austria	36
Puerto Rico	na	60	57	63	63	60	59	65	59	60	60	63	57	69	60	58	Canada	36
Romania	55	69	66	71	68	70	68	68	70	68	69	72	69	71	70	57	Czech Republic	35
Russian Fed.	40	47	45	48	45	45	50	44	45	52	45	52	45	45	48	57	Latvia	33
Serbia	na	32	31	33	32	30	35	32	32	34	32	33	32	34	32	32	Serbia	32
Singapore	na	40	36	44	42	40	33	37	41	43	36	39	43	38	41	35	Argentina	32
Slovakia	na	22	20	23	22	21	24	19	22	31	20	21	25	20	23	28	Estonia	32
Slovenia	59	75	73	76	67	76	79	85	74	59	80	76	63	75	76	73	Belarus	30
South Africa	22	48	47	49	54	45	42	46	52	32	43	52	48	46	51	47	Finland	30
Spain	37	48	48	48	46	48	50	52	43	49	46	55	50	54	50	41	Colombia	29
Sweden	43	29	29	28	24	30	31	28	27	32	27	29	27	27	30	27	Sweden	29
Switzerland	na	44	44	45	31	43	55	47	44	43	45	45	42	39	48	42	Australia	27
Taiwan	na	70	67	72	78	69	66	63	71	75	65	66	76	73	67	65	France	26
Tanzania	na	64	60	70	63	67	61	63	64	72	63	66	74	63	66	58	Great Britain	25
Turkey	87	94	93	95	94	94	95	95	93	91	94	95	92	94	96	91	Norway	23
Uganda	na	54	58	50	59	49	49	55	54	44	46	53	54	59	54	42	Slovakia	22
Ukraine	na	53	50	55	49	56	52	41	53	59	52	50	57	51	57	51	Lithuania	21
United States	44	46	44	47	48	46	44	45	46	45	40	47	51	47	46	43	Denmark	11
Uruguay	na	56	54	58	49	56	60	58	56	48	57	58	54	59	58	53		
Venezuela	na	na	na	na	na	na	na	na	na	na	na	na	na	na	na	na		
Vietnam	na	67	69	66	65	67	70	65	70	81	69	65	70	72	72	73		
Zimbabwe	na	39	33	43	41	37	36	41	36	22	34	39	38	42	36	37		
Total	40	52	52	53	54	53	51	53	51	54	52	53	54	56	53	47	Total	52

C015) IMPORTANT IN A JOB: GOOD HOURS

Here are some more aspects of a job that people say are important.
Please tell me which ones you personally think are important in a job?

Good hours (%)

(WVS: V90; EVS: V77)

Country	Wave 1990	Wave 2000	Gender Male	Gender Female	Age 16-29	Age 30-49	Age 50+	Education Lower	Education Middle	Education Upper	Income Lower	Income Middle	Income Upper	Values Mat	Values Mixed	Values Postm.	Ranking Country	Ranking 2000
Albania	na	55	53	57	64	55	48	52	59	52	54	59	52	56	56	46	Turkey	93
Algeria	na	51	49	54	57	48	45	46	51	55	57	51	44	52	51	49	Jordan	92
Argentina	44	42	44	41	48	41	39	45	38	40	44	45	38	44	45	33	Morocco	92
Armenia	na	49	39	57	46	54	44	49	50	45	48	53	47	54	45	35	Indonesia	87
Australia	na	35	32	38	40	36	29	38	36	31	37	33	33	42	34	36	Korea, South	83
Austria	35	43	38	47	50	46	35	43	43	40	40	47	41	50	41	43	Malta	79
Azerbaijan	na	55	48	62	55	55	51	38	54	59	55	57	52	55	56	56	Hungary	79
Bangladesh	na	37	37	37	38	37	30	38	37	37	34	39	39	35	38	42	Taiwan	72
Belarus	59	54	54	55	57	62	43	42	58	63	51	52	67	51	56	61	Japan	72
Belgium	40	45	42	47	47	45	44	49	45	41	42	43	46	50	44	39	Northern Ireland	70
Bosnia and Herz.	na	59	60	59	63	60	55	62	60	54	63	57	59	54	61	60	Egypt	69
Brazil	46	36	33	38	39	34	32	40	34	24	44	34	28	43	34	26	Croatia	69
Bulgaria	55	62	60	64	65	64	59	54	68	62	56	62	68	62	66	62	South Africa	68
Canada	52	47	45	50	55	50	40	51	48	43	50	47	45	52	50	41	Nigeria	67
Chile	48	52	51	52	48	53	53	49	55	46	51	54	50	51	51	55	United States	66
China	37	33	33	33	37	34	27	26	38	33	27	36	39	32	40	38	India	66
Colombia	na	11	10	13	13	9	13	14	14	5	16	12	7	17	12	8	Italy	64
Croatia	na	69	69	68	67	69	69	77	66	58	67	69	73	67	71	65	Dominican Rep.	63
Czech Republic	59	31	30	32	37	34	25	34	28	27	33	33	29	36	30	23	Ireland	63
Denmark	32	32	30	34	31	37	28	33	32	32	30	35	35	31	32	34	Vietnam	63
Dominican Rep.	na	63	57	68	64	60	82	75	63	62	67	59	60	66	66	58	Bulgaria	62
Egypt	na	69	66	73	73	68	68	65	74	73	69	68	71	68	71	70	Tanzania	61
El Salvador	na	na	na	na	na	na	na	na	na	na	na	na	na	na	na	na	Iceland	60
Estonia	58	56	53	59	55	62	52	56	60	48	57	61	53	59	56	29	Bosnia and Herz.	59
Finland	37	48	48	49	56	54	39	50	45	47	52	48	43	57	44	44	Romania	59
France	26	36	35	37	41	42	28	37	34	37	36	38	34	39	35	35	Moldova	57
Georgia	na	26	19	31	24	29	23	22	26	28	23	30	26	25	26	23	Spain	57
Germany	40	39	34	43	41	42	34	39	41	23	39	44	47	46	36	35	Puerto Rico	57
Great Britain	37	55	53	57	62	59	45	56	57	48	53	58	53	na	na	na	Uganda	57
Greece	na	52	48	54	57	48	45	52	50	53	48	49	55	54	51	51	Estonia	56
Hungary	60	79	79	79	88	87	67	75	88	84	69	79	86	75	85	89	New Zealand	56
Iceland	64	60	58	62	65	61	56	63	62	51	59	66	56	64	62	44	Albania	55
India	55	66	65	66	71	65	61	62	68	71	66	64	67	73	65	69	Great Britain	55
Indonesia	na	87	87	87	88	87	87	82	87	90	87	89	93	88	89	82	Azerbaijan	55
Iran	na	55	53	56	60	52	44	51	54	58	54	51	56	59	53	52	Iran	55
Ireland	46	63	61	64	59	62	65	67	63	55	67	68	55	67	62	61	Belarus	54
Israel	na	na	na	na	na	na	na	na	na	na	na	na	na	na	na	na	Lithuania	54
Italy	39	64	59	68	68	64	62	66	65	57	68	65	61	64	65	64	Zimbabwe	54
Japan	55	72	62	80	77	74	67	59	75	69	71	73	72	74	72	69	Luxembourg	52
Jordan	na	92	92	92	92	92	91	90	94	93	88	93	95	91	93	93	Greece	52
Korea, South	11	83	80	86	88	83	76	77	83	84	83	84	84	82	84	85	Chile	52
Latvia	34	19	18	19	26	18	16	18	19	18	18	17	21	20	19	21	Algeria	51
Lithuania	54	54	53	55	56	54	52	47	59	43	53	55	55	63	52	46	Poland	50
Luxembourg	na	52	51	53	62	53	45	56	50	51	52	53	53	57	52	53	Ukraine	50
Macedonia	na	48	47	49	55	49	39	49	50	38	48	47	48	45	50	50	Uruguay	49
Malta	na	79	77	81	79	78	80	83	78	75	77	81	75	78	81	69	Armenia	49
Mexico	56	43	39	47	43	43	43	46	40	34	44	40	41	47	45	31	Finland	48
Moldova	na	57	56	59	62	56	55	57	59	55	54	60	57	62	53	43	Macedonia	48
Montenegro	na	46	40	52	47	49	43	47	49	36	49	44	46	48	44	45	Canada	47
Morocco	na	92	91	92	94	92	86	92	93	86	87	91	92	92	93	86	Singapore	47
Netherlands	47	37	31	42	39	37	35	41	37	32	42	34	32	41	36	36	Philippines	46
New Zealand	na	56	51	59	60	60	51	56	61	53	55	61	53	59	56	52	Montenegro	46
Nigeria	80	67	67	67	66	70	63	67	65	70	66	69	67	68	67	65	Belgium	45
Northern Ireland	42	70	69	71	74	71	61	73	72	61	69	70	63	73	71	66	Sweden	44
Norway	32	41	37	45	35	46	40	45	41	38	na	na	na	47	41	42	Portugal	44
Pakistan	na	na	na	na	na	na	na	na	na	na	na	na	na	na	na	na	Slovakia	43
Peru	na	36	33	39	38	37	32	41	40	28	40	36	30	44	35	31	Mexico	43
Philippines	na	46	47	45	47	46	45	46	47	44	50	40	49	46	46	40	Austria	43
Poland	na	50	52	48	54	49	48	54	48	37	54	49	45	54	48	47	Argentina	42
Portugal	62	44	38	49	44	48	41	46	44	27	34	46	40	45	41	50	Norway	41
Puerto Rico	na	57	53	59	60	56	56	63	58	56	52	57	60	65	57	54	Slovenia	41
Romania	36	59	57	60	65	62	53	59	64	45	59	62	58	64	58	37	Russian Fed.	40
Russian Fed.	46	40	33	46	41	43	35	36	43	33	40	42	39	40	40	45	Switzerland	40
Serbia	na	35	32	39	40	40	29	35	37	34	31	39	37	39	35	20	Germany	39
Singapore	na	47	43	50	42	49	56	50	49	29	55	47	43	53	45	34	Bangladesh	37
Slovakia	na	43	39	48	46	46	38	44	45	32	42	45	43	44	44	42	Netherlands	37
Slovenia	39	41	38	43	24	43	50	54	38	27	54	44	25	50	41	31	Peru	36
South Africa	na	68	69	67	72	69	56	70	66	54	73	69	60	70	67	78	France	36
Spain	43	57	56	58	62	60	52	54	59	62	59	56	59	56	59	56	Brazil	36
Sweden	64	44	44	45	40	50	42	48	46	38	49	46	41	48	46	39	Serbia	35
Switzerland	na	40	37	43	45	43	33	45	38	41	41	44	38	47	37	44	Australia	35
Taiwan	na	72	69	74	65	74	70	68	77	72	75	71	71	74	71	76	China	33
Tanzania	na	61	58	65	62	61	57	58	64	67	58	62	67	60	63	63	Denmark	32
Turkey	88	93	91	94	93	93	91	93	93	90	92	93	91	94	93	92	Czech Republic	31
Uganda	na	57	60	54	59	54	60	52	60	41	51	60	61	58	58	50	Georgia	26
Ukraine	na	50	43	55	54	51	46	44	52	48	48	48	53	50	52	37	Latvia	19
United States	55	66	61	71	72	67	64	75	65	64	73	63	62	70	66	64	Colombia	11
Uruguay	na	49	48	50	56	49	46	50	51	41	53	47	48	46	54	45		
Venezuela	na	na	na	na	na	na	na	na	na	na	na	na	na	na	na	na		
Vietnam	na	63	61	65	58	63	65	63	64	67	64	58	68	71	67	62		
Zimbabwe	na	54	52	55	59	54	41	50	59	18	47	62	55	55	53	56		
Total	48	53	51	56	57	55	49	55	54	51	54	54	53	57	54	49	Total	53

C016) IMPORTANT IN A JOB: USE INITIATIVE

Here are some more aspects of a job that people say are important.

Please tell me which ones you personally think are important in a job?

An opportunity to use initiative (%)

(WVS: V91; EVS: V78)

Country	Wave 1990	Wave 2000	Male	Female	16-29	30-49	50+	Lower	Middle	Upper	Lower	Middle	Upper	Mat	Mixed	Postm.	RANKING Country	2000
Albania	na	40	45	35	42	42	34	29	44	57	34	37	49	37	44	44	Turkey	91
Algeria	na	44	48	39	50	43	31	31	44	53	49	41	37	35	49	50	Morocco	89
Argentina	55	41	42	39	35	43	44	33	45	71	35	35	54	32	38	52	Jordan	88
Armenia	na	46	52	40	47	50	36	35	44	57	50	45	40	40	50	54	Bangladesh	84
Australia	na	52	56	49	51	59	46	36	51	67	46	53	64	47	51	57	Indonesia	84
Austria	42	49	52	45	52	54	42	38	55	71	38	45	61	36	45	60	Korea, South	81
Azerbaijan	na	35	38	33	42	31	32	29	32	42	32	37	38	30	42	60	Slovenia	78
Bangladesh	na	84	85	83	82	84	91	85	82	83	86	81	86	88	81	80	New Zealand	73
Belarus	40	25	28	23	33	28	16	9	28	42	24	23	34	17	33	34	Malta	69
Belgium	41	49	52	47	51	49	49	36	47	62	41	45	58	41	49	57	Italy	65
Bosnia and Herz.	na	46	49	44	47	47	44	40	44	58	47	47	44	39	49	59	India	64
Brazil	51	45	51	39	44	45	46	39	46	62	42	40	51	36	46	59	Iceland	63
Bulgaria	47	50	57	44	60	55	42	32	57	68	37	51	61	42	58	72	Dominican Rep.	63
Canada	54	50	52	48	40	57	48	38	49	62	40	52	58	37	48	60	Netherlands	62
Chile	55	48	48	48	47	51	45	40	50	61	44	48	55	46	44	63	Taiwan	62
China	52	34	38	29	39	34	28	20	44	40	25	37	43	31	44	34	United States	62
Colombia	na	25	29	21	24	28	19	14	23	36	18	22	34	13	26	32	Hungary	61
Croatia	na	56	62	50	60	57	52	45	61	69	54	51	65	42	59	55	Switzerland	61
Czech Republic	55	30	33	27	35	31	26	25	33	42	26	31	32	22	31	41	Tanzania	61
Denmark	44	50	48	51	57	55	40	40	63	62	44	47	70	40	51	58	Romania	59
Dominican Rep.	na	63	63	62	60	67	73	56	54	67	55	67	68	55	63	74	Ireland	59
Egypt	na	45	49	41	48	43	46	39	50	55	44	44	50	41	50	54	Vietnam	58
El Salvador	na	na	na	na	na	na	na	na	na	na	na	na	na	na	na	na	Greece	56
Estonia	30	35	36	34	41	35	31	21	37	53	25	33	39	24	42	49	Poland	56
Finland	45	48	50	47	50	54	41	41	55	62	45	50	50	44	49	51	Croatia	56
France	38	43	43	42	46	48	36	37	47	55	37	43	51	33	45	51	Puerto Rico	53
Georgia	na	20	22	19	21	18	22	19	19	24	18	20	24	18	22	25	Germany	53
Germany	58	53	58	48	59	53	49	43	57	74	41	48	63	45	52	65	Australia	52
Great Britain	46	39	41	38	42	42	35	28	47	54	28	40	49	na	na	na	Sweden	52
Greece	na	56	56	57	64	53	43	40	53	62	50	58	61	45	59	65	Northern Ireland	52
Hungary	37	61	65	59	73	68	48	54	74	81	47	62	70	54	70	79	South Africa	51
Iceland	55	63	64	62	66	67	56	56	67	73	58	61	71	59	65	61	Bulgaria	50
India	54	64	65	61	67	64	59	57	65	76	54	61	70	64	72	76	Canada	50
Indonesia	na	84	81	87	87	86	80	72	86	90	82	89	88	85	86	86	Iran	50
Iran	na	50	54	45	54	48	41	41	49	60	49	47	53	45	51	57	Japan	50
Ireland	50	59	62	55	63	58	56	49	59	75	51	61	67	55	61	55	Denmark	50
Israel	na	na	na	na	na	na	na	na	na	na	na	na	na	na	na	na	Norway	50
Italy	45	65	69	60	71	65	60	57	67	77	60	62	73	51	67	70	Belgium	49
Japan	34	50	58	43	53	48	50	44	46	64	48	46	55	44	52	60	Luxembourg	49
Jordan	na	88	90	86	89	88	85	84	90	92	83	92	89	85	90	86	Austria	49
Korea, South	15	81	82	80	81	82	78	75	79	85	78	83	83	78	83	88	Finland	48
Latvia	17	14	15	13	17	13	14	11	13	23	11	13	19	13	15	23	Chile	48
Lithuania	29	32	34	30	47	32	21	11	37	49	20	32	37	31	31	50	Uruguay	48
Luxembourg	na	49	49	49	52	51	44	42	50	60	45	49	51	46	49	59	Moldova	48
Macedonia	na	29	30	28	27	33	25	20	30	44	23	29	40	25	33	28	Bosnia and Herz.	46
Malta	na	69	71	67	72	70	67	60	60	79	59	66	74	64	72	74	Armenia	46
Mexico	60	42	47	38	45	44	37	34	50	64	33	45	53	38	41	66	Egypt	45
Moldova	na	48	50	46	49	46	47	43	47	53	48	51	51	42	51	61	Brazil	45
Montenegro	na	26	31	22	36	26	21	13	31	47	18	22	35	23	32	23	Singapore	44
Morocco	na	89	90	88	91	90	82	87	96	94	80	87	91	88	92	90	Algeria	44
Netherlands	64	62	63	61	72	68	51	47	69	69	53	66	71	44	64	67	Uganda	44
New Zealand	na	73	79	68	75	76	70	66	74	79	69	74	78	66	73	80	France	43
Nigeria	82	na	na	na	na	na	na	na	na	na	na	na	na	na	na	na	Mexico	42
Northern Ireland	38	52	55	49	59	53	45	43	53	74	42	40	57	41	55	60	Ukraine	42
Norway	45	50	52	48	53	56	39	40	51	59	na	na	na	32	51	63	Argentina	41
Pakistan	na	na	na	na	na	na	na	na	na	na	na	na	na	na	na	na	Peru	40
Peru	na	40	41	40	39	42	40	36	39	46	34	43	48	36	42	41	Albania	40
Philippines	na	31	32	30	30	30	35	32	31	30	31	31	31	29	33	25	Great Britain	39
Poland	na	56	60	53	55	56	56	53	58	67	53	59	55	51	59	64	Spain	39
Portugal	55	35	35	36	44	37	29	31	40	58	26	31	36	28	40	41	Portugal	35
Puerto Rico	na	53	59	50	51	55	53	54	48	56	46	53	59	55	53	54	Azerbaijan	35
Romania	38	59	65	54	68	62	52	48	61	78	50	56	71	55	63	77	Estonia	35
Russian Fed.	29	31	34	28	37	31	26	20	29	43	25	32	35	27	34	46	Zimbabwe	34
Serbia	na	24	27	20	29	29	17	10	22	48	15	21	31	15	30	51	China	34
Singapore	na	44	48	41	45	49	30	31	50	59	34	45	51	39	46	45	Lithuania	32
Slovakia	na	31	31	31	33	35	25	22	33	46	28	29	36	26	33	46	Philippines	31
Slovenia	55	78	79	78	83	82	71	69	82	83	77	78	83	75	79	86	Slovakia	31
South Africa	28	51	51	50	55	47	49	42	60	76	40	55	59	52	50	48	Russian Fed.	31
Spain	37	39	41	38	45	43	33	34	40	54	37	39	51	35	40	46	Czech Republic	30
Sweden	71	52	53	51	52	54	50	38	55	59	46	53	58	42	50	61	Macedonia	29
Switzerland	na	61	66	57	71	60	57	53	62	76	58	53	69	47	62	71	Montenegro	26
Taiwan	na	62	66	58	64	64	56	57	66	64	62	59	67	63	63	62	Colombia	25
Tanzania	na	61	61	61	57	64	61	56	63	74	55	66	73	60	62	63	Belarus	25
Turkey	81	91	91	91	91	92	88	89	92	96	89	91	94	89	92	93	Serbia	24
Uganda	na	44	48	44	49	37	43	41	45	33	37	43	32	50	42	34	Georgia	20
Ukraine	na	42	43	42	52	43	36	25	43	52	36	41	52	37	49	62	Latvia	14
United States	52	62	65	58	55	60	71	45	61	68	53	65	68	59	61	63		
Uruguay	na	48	51	46	50	56	41	43	55	55	43	48	54	38	52	52		
Venezuela	na	na	na	na	na	na	na	na	na	na	na	na	na	na	na	na		
Vietnam	na	58	61	54	59	56	60	54	61	78	61	51	65	55	64	70		
Zimbabwe	na	34	33	35	39	31	28	33	34	91	27	35	45	33	35	40		
Total	47	50	53	47	53	52	44	44	50	61	44	50	56	44	53	59	Total	50

C017) IMPORTANT IN A JOB: GENEROUS HOLIDAYS

Here are some more aspects of a job that people say are important.

Please tell me which ones you personally think are important in a job?

Generous holidays (%)

(WVS: V92; EVS: V80)

Country	Wave 1990	Wave 2000	Gender Male	Gender Female	Age 16-29	Age 30-49	Age 50+	Education Lower	Education Middle	Education Upper	Income Lower	Income Middle	Income Upper	Values Mat	Values Mixed	Values Postm.
Albania	na	48	48	49	55	49	41	44	52	51	46	50	49	46	52	33
Algeria	na	21	21	20	23	21	15	20	22	20	25	21	17	17	22	24
Argentina	30	21	26	17	25	18	20	24	15	19	22	22	19	20	23	16
Armenia	na	31	26	35	30	34	26	32	30	31	33	30	31	32	31	22
Australia	na	14	15	12	15	14	13	15	13	13	13	15	13	14	12	16
Austria	16	20	22	19	28	21	16	21	20	20	19	21	21	31	19	20
Azerbaijan	na	38	34	42	39	38	40	38	38	40	46	42	31	39	39	31
Bangladesh	na	28	29	27	29	29	23	29	30	25	23	34	27	23	32	36
Belarus	53	36	37	35	39	41	28	26	41	37	34	36	41	36	36	36
Belgium	30	34	34	34	34	35	33	39	34	29	33	34	34	39	34	27
Bosnia and Herz.	na	42	42	42	47	44	35	43	42	40	40	42	42	39	44	43
Brazil	18	13	12	14	12	13	17	20	8	8	21	12	8	19	11	8
Bulgaria	33	34	36	32	37	37	30	30	38	33	32	30	37	33	35	40
Canada	26	26	28	25	25	30	24	26	26	28	23	26	28	28	27	25
Chile	23	32	33	31	30	34	31	30	34	30	35	34	25	33	33	28
China	15	11	10	12	12	12	9	9	13	12	9	11	14	9	15	6
Colombia	na	5	5	6	6	5	6	12	5	1	11	6	2	9	7	6
Croatia	na	48	52	44	55	47	44	50	46	47	38	50	52	47	49	46
Czech Republic	38	17	19	15	23	20	11	18	16	13	14	18	20	22	15	12
Denmark	17	16	18	14	13	18	16	17	13	17	16	16	18	20	16	12
Dominican Rep.	na	24	22	24	25	22	18	34	27	21	22	19	27	21	24	26
Egypt	na	13	12	14	15	12	12	13	13	12	14	13	11	14	12	13
El Salvador	na	na	na	na	na	na	na	na	na	na	na	na	na	na	na	na
Estonia	32	20	19	22	24	22	17	18	21	22	20	21	17	25	17	19
Finland	20	21	26	16	26	25	14	22	18	20	22	23	18	26	19	15
France	15	20	22	18	28	22	14	19	20	23	18	17	22	20	19	22
Georgia	na	14	13	15	16	14	11	14	14	12	12	17	13	13	13	27
Germany	29	24	24	24	29	24	22	25	24	20	24	28	30	32	20	22
Great Britain	25	39	42	37	42	39	36	42	37	36	34	43	39	na	na	na
Greece	na	32	38	29	40	29	23	22	30	36	28	33	37	31	33	32
Hungary	37	54	55	53	59	56	49	55	52	50	47	55	59	53	56	63
Iceland	17	18	22	13	16	20	16	18	19	13	16	18	17	17	19	11
India	28	56	55	57	57	56	55	57	56	53	61	54	55	63	52	49
Indonesia	na	30	25	35	32	28	31	30	27	32	28	30	40	32	28	39
Iran	na	38	38	37	41	36	31	36	38	35	35	33	40	41	35	37
Ireland	29	44	45	43	39	42	50	50	42	38	48	46	42	44	44	43
Israel	na	na	na	na	na	na	na	na	na	na	na	na	na	na	na	na
Italy	19	35	35	34	37	35	33	37	33	33	35	36	34	36	36	34
Japan	52	71	66	75	81	78	60	54	73	73	66	73	72	69	72	70
Jordan	na	35	34	36	37	32	37	36	34	34	34	35	35	36	32	36
Korea, South	8	85	82	88	91	84	80	73	85	87	84	88	85	84	86	94
Latvia	31	10	10	9	12	9	10	8	9	16	7	11	13	11	9	15
Lithuania	40	30	29	30	32	28	30	26	32	28	30	28	31	36	29	14
Luxembourg	na	37	39	35	51	38	27	40	35	34	43	34	27	38	39	31
Macedonia	na	16	17	14	18	16	13	17	17	10	16	19	12	14	17	19
Malta	na	36	34	37	40	35	33	39	35	30	31	32	31	35	38	19
Mexico	33	14	15	13	14	13	17	18	10	10	16	13	12	12	13	8
Moldova	na	39	36	41	45	35	38	41	36	41	37	40	41	37	42	35
Montenegro	na	31	29	33	31	30	30	30	35	21	36	29	31	34	27	15
Morocco	na	78	75	80	79	78	73	79	76	69	65	79	80	79	79	76
Netherlands	35	28	26	29	31	26	27	30	26	28	32	25	24	25	28	28
New Zealand	na	32	34	30	37	34	29	30	33	36	32	34	33	36	32	31
Nigeria	51	49	47	51	51	47	42	50	49	47	50	49	48	50	49	45
Northern Ireland	27	56	56	55	57	56	53	57	57	52	50	53	50	52	58	58
Norway	9	11	12	10	10	12	10	12	9	12	na	na	na	13	10	13
Pakistan	na	na	na	na	na	na	na	na	na	na	na	na	na	na	na	na
Peru	na	12	12	11	11	12	14	19	10	9	14	12	7	12	12	8
Philippines	na	11	12	11	11	12	11	13	10	11	8	9	17	10	12	12
Poland	na	31	33	28	37	26	31	35	27	20	33	31	26	29	33	27
Portugal	47	37	38	37	38	40	35	38	38	31	33	39	35	35	39	36
Puerto Rico	na	27	27	27	26	27	27	37	30	24	23	27	28	34	28	19
Romania	35	41	39	42	47	41	37	44	42	29	43	40	37	46	37	31
Russian Fed.	43	29	27	30	26	30	29	29	30	27	30	30	28	30	28	30
Serbia	na	18	18	19	24	20	15	21	17	16	20	17	12	21	16	11
Singapore	na	27	24	30	25	28	32	31	27	15	31	28	24	32	26	18
Slovakia	na	19	19	18	22	19	15	19	19	12	18	18	20	20	18	17
Slovenia	29	46	45	47	55	48	36	52	46	35	49	46	40	43	45	53
South Africa	8	37	38	35	38	38	30	40	33	30	35	43	33	37	37	38
Spain	32	37	40	35	42	38	34	39	33	40	36	40	39	38	39	33
Sweden	35	30	19	20	18	20	20	19	20	18	18	24	16	21	20	16
Switzerland	na	26	26	26	38	26	19	25	26	29	22	26	28	25	24	32
Taiwan	na	39	36	42	43	39	36	35	38	43	39	42	37	42	36	32
Tanzania	na	51	47	56	54	50	44	47	53	60	48	51	60	49	52	54
Turkey	44	57	54	60	59	55	55	61	51	44	62	54	49	58	57	51
Uganda	na	46	49	44	49	42	50	43	47	44	39	51	37	50	45	40
Ukraine	na	43	40	45	44	43	42	37	44	42	43	42	45	43	45	34
United States	31	37	36	37	43	38	29	39	35	37	36	35	40	43	37	33
Uruguay	na	38	40	36	42	36	38	42	36	20	44	38	33	35	41	34
Venezuela	na	na	na	na	na	na	na	na	na	na	na	na	na	na	na	na
Vietnam	na	42	40	44	40	39	48	39	46	48	49	38	43	54	43	45
Zimbabwe	na	39	40	38	43	37	33	37	42	38	33	45	41	40	36	50
Total	30	32	33	32	35	33	29	34	32	31	32	33	32	34	32	29

RANKING

Country	2000
Korea, South	85
Morocco	78
Japan	71
Turkey	57
India	56
Northern Ireland	56
Hungary	54
Tanzania	51
Nigeria	49
Albania	48
Croatia	48
Uganda	46
Slovenia	46
Ireland	44
Ukraine	43
Vietnam	42
Bosnia and Herz.	42
Romania	41
Great Britain	39
Zimbabwe	39
Taiwan	39
Moldova	39
Azerbaijan	38
Uruguay	38
Iran	38
Portugal	37
Spain	37
South Africa	37
Luxembourg	37
United States	37
Belarus	36
Malta	36
Jordan	35
Italy	35
Bulgaria	34
Belgium	34
Greece	32
New Zealand	32
Chile	32
Armenia	31
Poland	31
Montenegro	31
Indonesia	30
Lithuania	30
Russian Fed.	29
Bangladesh	28
Netherlands	28
Singapore	27
Puerto Rico	27
Canada	26
Switzerland	26
Germany	24
Dominican Rep.	24
Argentina	21
Finland	21
Algeria	21
Estonia	20
Austria	20
France	20
Sweden	20
Slovakia	19
Serbia	18
Iceland	18
Czech Republic	17
Denmark	16
Macedonia	16
Mexico	14
Australia	14
Georgia	14
Brazil	13
Egypt	13
Peru	12
Philippines	11
China	11
Norway	11
Latvia	10
Colombia	5
Total	32

C018) IMPORTANT IN A JOB: ACHIEVING

Here are some more aspects of a job that people say are important.

Please tell me which ones you personally think are important in a job?

A job in which you feel you can achieve something (%) (WVS: V93; EVS: V82)

Country	Wave 1990	Wave 2000	Gender Male	Gender Female	Age 16-29	Age 30-49	Age 50+	Education Lower	Education Middle	Education Upper	Income Lower	Income Middle	Income Upper	Values Mat	Values Mixed	Values Postm.	RANKING Country	RANKING 2000
Albania	na	51	55	47	55	52	47	45	52	64	46	51	58	49	56	54	Turkey	94
Algeria	na	60	57	63	66	59	50	50	59	69	66	58	58	56	62	71	Jordan	94
Argentina	50	48	49	46	53	49	41	45	52	47	45	48	51	48	48	48	Morocco	93
Armenia	na	66	68	63	69	67	58	56	65	70	71	62	69	63	68	68	Korea, South	92
Australia	na	72	69	74	71	74	70	63	70	81	68	72	78	67	70	76	Slovenia	90
Austria	49	57	59	55	63	57	52	51	62	64	51	55	63	56	55	61	Bangladesh	88
Azerbaijan	na	49	53	46	57	45	42	39	48	53	42	51	57	47	53	63	Indonesia	88
Bangladesh	na	88	88	88	88	88	90	89	87	89	90	85	90	90	87	84	United States	84
Belarus	42	31	35	28	47	29	21	14	34	51	24	34	39	22	41	36	New Zealand	83
Belgium	40	47	49	44	52	47	44	39	48	50	46	43	50	40	47	50	Nigeria	82
Bosnia and Herz.	na	66	66	67	74	64	61	55	66	75	65	66	66	62	68	77	Iceland	81
Brazil	53	50	49	50	45	53	54	50	47	59	52	42	55	49	49	55	Hungary	77
Bulgaria	42	65	67	62	72	68	58	50	71	78	55	64	73	60	70	82	Italy	75
Canada	74	73	70	76	72	74	72	64	72	81	66	72	77	66	72	77	South Africa	75
Chile	58	63	63	64	63	67	59	59	65	69	61	63	69	60	62	75	Norway	74
China	38	31	35	27	40	29	27	24	35	44	27	33	35	27	40	47	Romania	74
Colombia	na	44	45	43	43	47	40	30	40	60	32	39	58	33	42	50	Canada	73
Croatia	na	66	69	62	73	66	61	60	70	67	68	63	68	53	68	70	Sweden	72
Czech Republic	48	38	42	35	52	38	31	35	40	47	37	38	40	37	39	44	Australia	72
Denmark	55	55	52	59	57	58	52	50	55	67	49	56	70	55	54	64	Ireland	71
Dominican Rep.	na	67	65	68	68	67	55	75	65	66	65	68	65	78	65	70	Egypt	71
Egypt	na	71	76	65	73	70	69	65	76	79	71	66	76	67	73	82	Japan	70
El Salvador	na	na	na	na	na	na	na	na	na	na	na	na	na	na	na	na	Malta	69
Estonia	43	45	45	44	54	49	36	34	47	57	34	41	51	33	52	55	India	69
Finland	54	56	56	56	62	57	52	50	65	67	53	51	60	54	57	52	Taiwan	69
France	42	50	51	50	51	55	46	47	53	56	50	48	54	48	51	52	Vietnam	68
Georgia	na	45	48	43	51	45	39	42	44	51	39	47	52	44	46	49	Tanzania	68
Germany	68	52	54	50	59	52	48	45	55	70	46	51	60	50	51	55	Dominican Rep.	67
Great Britain	66	58	58	58	62	60	55	51	62	68	52	54	66	na	na	na	Northern Ireland	67
Greece	na	60	63	58	66	56	54	50	59	63	55	60	67	61	61	62	Poland	67
Hungary	58	77	79	76	87	81	68	72	87	91	66	79	83	73	83	84	Bosnia and Herz.	66
Iceland	83	81	80	81	79	82	80	80	81	82	76	84	82	81	82	73	Armenia	66
India	61	69	71	67	73	69	64	62	72	82	61	64	77	69	77	78	Croatia	66
Indonesia	na	88	86	90	91	89	86	81	88	93	89	90	89	86	90	96	Bulgaria	65
Iran	na	53	56	48	57	51	43	43	52	63	49	48	56	51	52	60	Moldova	65
Ireland	60	71	71	71	71	74	68	66	71	81	69	72	75	66	72	76	Chile	63
Israel	na	na	na	na	na	na	na	na	na	na	na	na	na	na	na	na	Singapore	61
Italy	51	75	74	76	83	76	70	70	79	81	70	78	80	70	75	82	Zimbabwe	61
Japan	48	70	74	66	78	69	67	61	67	81	66	67	75	72	70	77	Uganda	61
Jordan	na	94	93	94	94	95	88	92	93	97	90	96	95	93	94	97	Algeria	60
Korea, South	24	92	91	92	94	92	88	88	89	96	89	94	93	90	93	97	Greece	60
Latvia	27	32	30	34	41	32	29	28	33	38	30	31	35	29	34	43	Uruguay	60
Lithuania	44	42	41	43	59	40	33	30	44	58	35	40	47	46	42	41	Great Britain	58
Luxembourg	na	55	56	54	57	55	53	53	53	64	50	56	59	51	59	61	Austria	57
Macedonia	na	50	51	49	55	53	42	34	56	64	41	53	60	44	58	47	Switzerland	56
Malta	na	69	73	66	76	67	67	61	70	83	56	68	74	63	72	75	Finland	56
Mexico	66	53	55	51	55	53	50	46	61	67	45	56	64	47	57	57	Denmark	55
Moldova	na	65	66	64	68	65	62	61	61	74	67	66	66	62	67	68	Luxembourg	55
Montenegro	na	53	58	48	61	52	49	42	56	72	52	52	55	51	58	50	Philippines	54
Morocco	na	93	94	93	94	94	89	92	97	96	87	91	94	93	96	94	Puerto Rico	53
Netherlands	45	40	44	36	57	39	32	37	42	41	41	39	41	40	42	35	Mexico	53
New Zealand	na	83	84	82	83	85	80	77	85	88	82	85	84	81	85	86	Montenegro	53
Nigeria	91	82	82	82	82	82	80	81	81	82	83	82	78	82	82	76	Iran	53
Northern Ireland	62	67	65	69	71	66	65	63	66	80	59	59	69	59	72	68	Germany	52
Norway	69	74	69	80	72	74	76	71	74	80	na	na	na	71	75	79	Albania	51
Pakistan	na	na	na	na	na	na	na	na	na	na	na	na	na	na	na	na	Ukraine	51
Peru	na	47	49	44	46	49	45	47	49	43	48	49	41	50	46	49	Serbia	50
Philippines	na	54	52	55	57	54	50	50	53	60	54	52	56	52	55	51	France	50
Poland	na	67	69	64	67	65	68	66	67	70	64	68	72	60	71	73	Macedonia	50
Portugal	68	48	48	48	56	52	40	44	55	57	38	44	52	40	55	46	Brazil	50
Puerto Rico	na	53	53	54	61	53	50	49	58	52	50	57	51	60	53	50	Azerbaijan	49
Romania	63	74	76	72	81	77	67	65	78	81	67	77	80	72	78	77	Spain	48
Russian Fed.	28	39	43	35	55	39	28	26	37	51	31	40	44	34	43	54	Portugal	48
Serbia	na	50	53	48	60	52	45	39	50	68	40	46	66	45	55	66	Argentina	48
Singapore	na	61	65	58	72	57	37	47	67	75	50	58	72	58	62	67	Belgium	47
Slovakia	na	36	37	35	39	38	32	30	37	55	30	35	42	34	38	54	Peru	47
Slovenia	71	90	89	91	92	92	87	89	91	91	91	93	89	88	91	93	Georgia	45
South Africa	na	75	74	76	77	75	71	70	82	81	65	76	85	74	77	70	Estonia	45
Spain	39	48	50	47	55	51	42	44	51	58	45	47	55	47	49	52	Colombia	44
Sweden	85	72	72	72	73	73	71	66	73	77	73	69	75	65	72	76	Lithuania	42
Switzerland	na	56	56	57	57	54	58	60	55	60	53	54	56	53	57	58	Netherlands	40
Taiwan	na	69	70	67	72	71	60	64	74	70	66	68	73	71	72	54	Russian Fed.	39
Tanzania	na	68	68	68	71	68	64	63	72	77	63	71	77	66	70	58	Czech Republic	38
Turkey	86	94	94	94	94	94	93	93	95	94	93	94	96	92	95	94	Slovakia	36
Uganda	na	61	61	60	64	54	67	64	60	46	48	63	57	65	60	49	Latvia	32
Ukraine	na	51	53	49	68	51	42	30	51	63	43	53	60	44	60	68	Belarus	31
United States	71	84	81	86	80	85	85	81	82	86	81	85	89	82	83	84	China	31
Uruguay	na	60	59	60	63	62	57	58	61	65	59	62	60	53	65	56		
Venezuela	na	na	na	na	na	na	na	na	na	na	na	na	na	na	na	na		
Vietnam	na	68	72	64	68	67	71	64	73	87	74	65	70	73	73	77		
Zimbabwe	na	61	62	60	65	58	57	57	67	57	55	63	67	56	64	74		
Total	56	62	63	61	67	62	56	57	61	69	58	61	66	58	64	66	Total	62

C019) IMPORTANT IN A JOB: A RESPONSIBLE JOB

Here are some more aspects of a job that people say are important.

Please tell me which ones you personally think are important in a job?

A responsible job (%)

(WVS: V94; EVS: V83)

Country	Wave 1990	Wave 2000	Gender Male	Gender Female	Age 16-29	Age 30-49	Age 50+	Education Lower	Education Middle	Education Upper	Income Lower	Income Middle	Income Upper	Values Mat	Values Mixed	Values Postm.	RANKING Country	RANKING 2000
Albania	na	25	27	24	28	24	25	19	29	33	19	26	31	22	30	18	Indonesia	95
Algeria	na	46	47	46	49	46	42	40	44	55	49	45	44	38	51	55	Jordan	92
Argentina	58	41	42	40	36	43	43	41	40	41	44	41	38	47	42	37	Korea, South	91
Armenia	na	43	48	38	46	44	35	32	44	45	49	39	43	43	41	55	Turkey	90
Australia	na	38	41	35	34	38	42	35	35	42	38	36	41	38	36	41	Bangladesh	88
Austria	45	49	54	45	49	51	47	45	51	59	40	50	53	48	48	52	Morocco	84
Azerbaijan	na	45	50	40	49	44	38	43	44	46	49	47	40	43	48	53	Nigeria	84
Bangladesh	na	88	89	87	89	87	90	86	90	91	87	86	91	89	87	88	Hungary	78
Belarus	27	14	15	13	15	15	13	9	15	20	12	14	19	11	19	11	India	73
Belgium	38	41	46	37	43	40	42	35	38	50	39	38	44	37	42	45	Egypt	73
Bosnia and Herz.	na	46	48	44	46	46	46	42	45	53	45	47	43	43	47	43	Slovenia	73
Brazil	59	42	46	39	40	42	47	47	38	38	46	40	40	44	42	40	Taiwan	70
Bulgaria	28	40	43	38	47	46	33	29	46	50	32	44	43	34	46	48	Japan	67
Canada	56	43	44	42	36	42	48	42	43	43	39	44	45	41	43	44	South Africa	67
Chile	52	44	43	44	43	45	43	38	46	49	39	45	48	43	43	46	Vietnam	67
China	22	22	24	21	26	22	20	20	26	5	22	24	20	19	29	25	Switzerland	62
Colombia	na	20	22	18	19	20	22	16	19	24	18	19	22	16	17	17	Malta	60
Croatia	na	44	47	42	45	44	45	41	46	49	49	40	50	36	45	49	Dominican Rep.	59
Czech Republic	48	29	31	28	26	31	29	27	30	37	26	30	32	29	29	30	Iran	58
Denmark	42	48	50	45	56	50	41	40	54	58	41	49	57	44	48	48	Romania	57
Dominican Rep.	na	59	57	61	57	62	64	69	60	57	62	51	57	64	59	55	Philippines	57
Egypt	na	73	76	70	75	73	72	71	77	74	74	73	74	71	75	77	Uganda	56
El Salvador	na	na	na	na	na	na	na	na	na	na	na	na	na	na	na	na	Germany	55
Estonia	17	17	19	16	22	17	16	15	17	23	16	17	18	14	20	18	Luxembourg	55
Finland	30	40	42	39	42	41	39	37	43	50	32	44	42	37	42	33	United States	55
France	53	49	51	47	55	49	45	48	48	53	49	47	51	48	50	50	Sweden	55
Georgia	na	28	32	24	25	28	32	28	25	36	26	28	30	28	29	28	Tanzania	55
Germany	49	55	61	51	59	53	55	49	56	75	48	51	66	54	55	57	Puerto Rico	54
Great Britain	42	37	42	32	38	39	33	31	41	44	31	33	40	na	na	na	Ireland	54
Greece	na	51	51	51	50	49	58	54	50	51	46	52	55	49	53	49	Poland	53
Hungary	51	78	81	75	84	82	70	75	83	86	67	80	83	75	83	84	Italy	53
Iceland	36	39	40	37	39	40	37	35	40	44	33	36	47	38	41	27	Mexico	53
India	65	73	75	71	76	75	69	66	78	86	61	70	83	75	81	84	Greece	51
Indonesia	na	95	95	96	96	97	95	90	98	97	96	96	99	96	97	93	New Zealand	51
Iran	na	58	61	54	59	58	54	54	59	57	58	53	60	60	57	62	Uruguay	50
Ireland	41	54	55	52	54	49	58	52	54	55	55	54	53	55	56	44	Northern Ireland	49
Israel	na	na	na	na	na	na	na	na	na	na	na	na	na	na	na	na	Austria	49
Italy	32	53	59	47	56	51	52	52	53	53	52	52	57	48	53	56	France	49
Japan	48	67	72	63	65	65	69	63	65	74	67	65	71	71	68	66	Peru	48
Jordan	na	92	94	90	92	93	89	91	93	93	88	94	95	90	93	95	Denmark	48
Korea, South	23	91	90	92	85	94	93	95	93	89	90	93	91	92	92	87	Singapore	48
Latvia	12	15	16	14	20	13	15	14	14	20	12	14	20	17	14	17	Algeria	46
Lithuania	24	18	21	16	26	16	15	13	19	24	18	12	19	18	18	21	Bosnia and Herz.	46
Luxembourg	na	55	56	54	59	55	52	50	57	60	48	58	64	61	57	58	Azerbaijan	45
Macedonia	na	38	41	35	35	40	40	35	39	41	39	36	41	38	39	40	Croatia	44
Malta	na	60	62	58	64	58	60	57	58	78	57	53	63	56	62	68	Chile	44
Mexico	57	53	57	49	54	51	52	48	58	58	47	54	58	54	55	52	Canada	43
Moldova	na	43	45	40	40	42	45	45	39	47	48	44	44	38	46	58	Armenia	43
Montenegro	na	25	25	25	23	28	24	19	26	39	13	23	33	24	27	24	Moldova	43
Morocco	na	84	86	82	84	85	81	82	90	90	73	82	87	83	86	86	Portugal	42
Netherlands	43	42	49	34	48	40	40	34	46	44	43	37	49	33	43	42	Brazil	42
New Zealand	na	51	56	47	49	51	52	47	53	55	47	53	53	51	52	50	Norway	42
Nigeria	84	84	82	85	83	85	81	84	83	85	84	85	81	85	84	76	Netherlands	42
Northern Ireland	35	49	52	47	55	51	45	44	50	60	42	40	46	41	54	54	Belgium	41
Norway	43	42	41	43	46	41	41	38	40	48	na	na	na	36	43	44	Zimbabwe	41
Pakistan	na	na	na	na	na	na	na	na	na	na	na	na	na	na	na	.na	Argentina	41
Peru	na	48	49	47	46	51	47	53	47	48	51	46	48	48	49	44	Bulgaria	40
Philippines	na	57	58	55	55	55	61	59	53	59	55	53	62	57	56	58	Finland	40
Poland	na	53	61	46	48	50	60	57	50	49	53	54	56	50	54	58	Iceland	39
Portugal	54	42	40	44	44	40	40	42	44	44	37	47	36	43	42	40	Spain	39
Puerto Rico	na	54	55	55	50	52	59	63	58	52	58	53	51	64	55	50	Macedonia	38
Romania	28	57	58	56	56	60	54	53	56	64	52	57	63	57	59	53	Australia	38
Russian Fed.	21	26	28	24	26	25	27	23	25	32	23	29	28	26	27	41	Great Britain	37
Serbia	na	18	19	17	16	16	21	15	20	22	16	19	20	17	18	27	Ukraine	35
Singapore	na	48	51	44	45	51	47	45	49	49	50	46	48	48	48	42	Czech Republic	29
Slovakia	na	21	23	20	23	21	20	15	24	28	21	19	26	19	23	28	Georgia	28
Slovenia	53	73	74	72	69	74	74	76	72	68	79	73	68	74	74	70	Russian Fed.	26
South Africa	25	67	66	67	67	67	66	67	68	54	65	68	68	65	69	69	Albania	25
Spain	32	39	42	36	41	39	37	38	38	43	37	39	43	38	40	37	Montenegro	25
Sweden	72	55	53	56	52	56	55	51	54	59	51	56	59	57	54	55	China	22
Switzerland	na	62	68	56	62	64	60	55	63	69	56	58	68	51	65	62	Slovakia	21
Taiwan	na	70	72	69	73	69	72	70	73	69	75	68	67	72	70	76	Colombia	20
Tanzania	na	55	54	56	48	59	57	51	53	72	48	58	72	50	59	67	Lithuania	18
Turkey	78	90	90	90	90	91	89	89	91	94	89	90	93	91	90	91	Serbia	18
Uganda	na	56	58	54	62	48	61	60	56	46	46	52	45	62	55	46	Estonia	17
Ukraine	na	35	36	34	31	38	35	25	36	39	31	35	41	33	39	41	Latvia	15
United States	56	55	57	52	54	52	60	55	55	54	51	54	59	47	56	55	Belarus	14
Uruguay	na	50	52	48	50	52	48	47	54	53	50	47	55	42	53	51		
Venezuela	na	na	na	na	na	na	na	na	na	na	na	na	na	na	na	na		
Vietnam	na	67	70	64	63	65	72	64	68	85	72	61	72	74	70	76		
Zimbabwe	na	41	41	41	44	44	29	37	47	18	31	44	47	42	41	45		
Total	43	50	52	48	52	51	47	49	48	55	48	49	52	48	52	51	Total	50

C020) IMPORTANT IN A JOB: A JOB THAT IS INTERESTING

Here are some more aspects of a job that people say are important.

Please tell me which ones you personally think are important in a job?

A job that is interesting (%)

(WVS: V95; EVS: V84)

Country	Wave 1990	Wave 2000	Gender Male	Gender Female	Age 16-29	Age 30-49	Age 50+	Education Lower	Education Middle	Education Upper	Income Lower	Income Middle	Income Upper	Values Mat	Values Mixed	Values Postm.
Albania	na	41	45	37	51	41	33	34	42	57	37	39	48	43	42	41
Algeria	na	57	55	58	61	59	43	44	59	64	59	53	55	53	60	56
Argentina	51	39	43	37	44	40	35	38	38	57	35	37	47	37	39	41
Armenia	na	77	78	77	76	83	71	63	78	83	80	74	80	75	79	83
Australia	na	74	74	74	75	77	70	67	74	81	71	75	78	66	74	78
Austria	56	57	62	53	66	61	49	47	65	72	43	56	69	49	55	63
Azerbaijan	na	81	83	80	84	81	77	68	80	86	78	81	85	81	83	85
Bangladesh	na	87	88	85	88	86	89	88	85	89	91	87	84	86	88	86
Belarus	73	58	59	57	68	64	44	32	65	78	49	61	69	51	65	77
Belgium	47	56	58	54	65	55	53	49	53	66	50	55	61	51	55	63
Bosnia and Herz.	na	71	71	71	74	72	67	67	71	76	71	70	73	73	70	74
Brazil	46	28	26	29	29	26	28	28	26	32	29	22	30	31	24	34
Bulgaria	51	64	65	62	75	68	54	47	70	80	52	61	75	54	73	85
Canada	72	70	73	68	74	72	67	61	72	76	61	73	75	59	70	74
Chile	50	58	58	57	61	62	49	49	60	70	50	59	67	56	56	66
China	34	18	16	19	19	18	17	17	19	16	19	15	20	15	24	9
Colombia	na	12	12	13	13	12	10	8	10	18	11	9	18	8	11	17
Croatia	na	77	82	71	85	79	68	72	79	80	75	75	80	66	78	84
Czech Republic	69	57	56	57	66	58	51	51	61	71	51	56	63	51	59	65
Denmark	63	65	67	63	78	70	53	56	82	75	61	66	79	56	66	70
Dominican Rep.	na	57	54	59	56	58	64	63	48	60	52	56	68	51	58	58
Egypt	na	47	49	44	51	46	42	42	52	49	48	46	48	43	50	52
El Salvador	na	na	na	na	na	na	na	na	na	na	na	na	na	na	na	na
Estonia	68	65	62	68	74	67	59	57	68	73	65	63	69	65	66	57
Finland	65	76	76	76	86	81	68	69	85	86	74	75	79	77	76	74
France	59	66	66	66	72	68	60	60	70	78	62	66	68	58	67	75
Georgia	na	65	62	67	65	67	62	61	62	75	62	67	68	66	64	65
Germany	65	70	73	68	76	74	63	67	72	76	64	66	70	73	70	66
Great Britain	72	68	67	69	66	69	68	61	71	80	63	67	69	na	na	na
Greece	na	69	65	71	79	63	58	59	64	74	62	70	72	67	69	73
Hungary	51	77	79	75	86	83	66	72	85	89	67	78	82	74	81	94
Iceland	76	76	76	76	86	76	67	70	80	81	71	78	81	76	78	73
India	64	75	76	72	77	74	73	68	78	85	68	71	81	75	81	84
Indonesia	na	82	78	86	86	81	81	77	80	87	80	85	87	83	82	79
Iran	na	57	60	53	63	53	45	49	57	62	57	50	61	60	56	62
Ireland	70	72	72	72	75	72	69	65	72	83	67	74	75	71	72	71
Israel	na	na	na	na	na	na	na	na	na	na	na	na	na	na	na	na
Italy	56	76	76	75	84	74	73	71	79	79	72	77	79	69	77	79
Japan	36	64	65	62	81	70	51	49	64	72	60	62	66	59	64	75
Jordan	na	88	89	88	89	90	86	88	88	90	86	92	89	89	89	89
Korea, South	7	79	77	81	85	80	70	73	76	84	77	80	80	76	82	84
Latvia	60	48	51	46	56	50	43	37	48	61	42	51	55	48	50	43
Lithuania	64	63	63	64	77	70	48	44	69	76	52	63	72	60	64	77
Luxembourg	na	64	63	65	73	65	58	58	63	80	58	65	72	58	66	75
Macedonia	na	52	51	53	57	54	45	42	56	59	43	53	62	55	53	42
Malta	na	85	84	86	85	85	86	66	84	88	84	87	80	80	87	90
Mexico	60	42	44	40	44	38	46	39	43	55	40	38	49	41	43	59
Moldova	na	75	76	74	83	74	69	72	74	79	72	75	77	75	75	79
Montenegro	na	58	57	58	67	62	48	42	66	74	52	52	66	56	59	71
Morocco	na	94	94	94	95	95	89	94	95	94	89	89	97	95	96	92
Netherlands	60	56	60	51	68	63	42	36	62	68	46	58	66	35	57	65
New Zealand	na	84	84	84	89	84	83	80	84	89	80	85	89	89	84	88
Nigeria	83	82	81	82	83	80	78	83	82	80	84	81	79	84	81	78
Northern Ireland	69	75	76	75	79	76	72	71	77	84	68	71	76	70	79	77
Norway	64	70	70	70	78	77	56	59	70	81	na	na	na	55	71	82
Pakistan	na	na	na	na	na	na	na	na	na	na	na	na	na	na	na	na
Peru	na	33	34	32	35	34	26	32	32	35	31	36	33	32	33	38
Philippines	na	45	46	43	43	42	51	50	38	48	42	43	49	45	45	34
Poland	na	74	78*	71	80	70	76	74	75	77	73	76	77	72	77	66
Portugal	53	45	39	51	49	46	42	43	50	46	41	42	43	44	43	51
Puerto Rico	na	55	58	53	60	53	54	49	50	59	47	56	60	58	53	60
Romania	43	66	67	65	74	69	60	60	71	68	62	68	70	67	67	71
Russian Fed.	67	69	70	69	79	69	63	56	69	78	62	72	74	67	71	80
Serbia	na	45	45	46	56	49	37	36	44	61	38	43	52	39	50	63
Singapore	na	60	62	59	66	58	46	53	66	55	53	63	65	55	62	63
Slovakia	na	49	49	50	56	51	43	42	52	57	44	49	54	47	52	62
Slovenia	76	92	93	91	95	92	88	88	94	91	92	89	94	92	91	93
South Africa	na	65	67	63	68	66	55	61	71	65	60	67	68	62	67	71
Spain	47	55	56	55	60	58	50	51	56	68	55	57	58	52	57	60
Sweden	80	70	71	69	79	73	61	54	74	76	60	68	74	60	69	76
Switzerland	na	72	74	70	82	71	68	68	73	77	72	67	76	67	72	76
Taiwan	na	77	79	75	83	79	69	72	79	81	78	75	78	78	80	81
Tanzania	na	49	48	50	46	51	48	47	47	58	46	52	57	44	52	50
Turkey	49	49	48	50	51	47	49	49	48	54	50	47	54	48	48	53
Uganda	na	54	53	54	60	44	59	54	54	45	49	41	42	54	55	47
Ukraine	na	70	70	70	79	73	63	48	71	82	67	70	77	67	77	72
United States	69	82	84	79	83	80	83	78	78	85	78	80	90	76	82	83
Uruguay	na	50	51	49	59	50	46	45	56	60	46	50	56	37	55	52
Venezuela	na	na	na	na	na	na	na	na	na	na	na	na	na	na	na	na
Vietnam	na	59	60	59	57	59	62	56	63	70	59	55	64	66	63	67
Zimbabwe	na	57	56	58	60	53	56	56	59	32	50	59	55	58	56	62
Total	60	64	64	63	68	64	58	57	65	72	59	63	67	61	65	68

RANKING

Country	2000
Morocco	94
Slovenia	92
Jordan	88
Bangladesh	87
Malta	85
New Zealand	84
Indonesia	82
Nigeria	82
United States	82
Azerbaijan	81
Korea, South	79
Armenia	77
Taiwan	77
Hungary	77
Croatia	77
Iceland	76
Finland	76
Italy	76
Northern Ireland	75
Moldova	75
India	75
Poland	74
Australia	74
Switzerland	72
Ireland	72
Bosnia and Herz.	71
Canada	70
Ukraine	70
Germany	70
Norway	70
Sweden	70
Russian Fed.	69
Greece	69
Great Britain	68
Romania	66
France	66
Estonia	65
Denmark	65
South Africa	65
Georgia	65
Luxembourg	64
Japan	64
Bulgaria	64
Lithuania	63
Singapore	60
Vietnam	59
Belarus	58
Chile	58
Montenegro	58
Austria	57
Dominican Rep.	57
Zimbabwe	57
Czech Republic	57
Algeria	57
Iran	57
Belgium	56
Netherlands	56
Spain	55
Puerto Rico	55
Uganda	54
Macedonia	52
Uruguay	50
Slovakia	49
Turkey	49
Tanzania	49
Latvia	48
Egypt	47
Serbia	45
Portugal	45
Philippines	45
Mexico	42
Albania	41
Argentina	39
Peru	33
Brazil	28
China	18
Colombia	12
Total	64

C021) IMPORTANT IN A JOB: THAT MEETS ONE'S ABILITIES

Here are some more aspects of a job that people say are important.

Please tell me which ones you personally think are important in a job?

A job that meets one's abilities (%)

(WVS: V96; EVS: V85)

Country	Wave 1990	Wave 2000	Gender Male	Gender Female	Age 16-29	Age 30-49	Age 50+	Education Lower	Education Middle	Education Upper	Income Lower	Income Middle	Income Upper	Values Mat	Values Mixed	Values Postm.
Albania	na	29	36	23	31	30	28	24	30	43	24	28	36	24	33	36
Algeria	na	70	73	68	74	69	65	65	71	73	74	64	71	70	70	76
Argentina	59	51	49	53	46	51	56	50	53	53	49	52	52	47	51	55
Armenia	na	66	64	68	66	68	63	67	67	62	64	74	66	70	62	73
Australia	na	45	43	47	37	49	49	43	42	51	48	46	46	50	44	46
Austria	58	59	61	58	61	61	56	54	62	71	51	57	64	49	58	65
Azerbaijan	na	73	76	71	73	72	78	69	75	71	78	76	71	73	74	82
Bangladesh	na	91	92	89	89	92	94	90	91	91	91	91	90	93	89	91
Belarus	50	39	40	38	42	41	34	29	41	51	39	37	46	32	47	43
Belgium	49	56	57	55	63	58	52	44	54	68	50	51	63	45	57	64
Bosnia and Herz.	na	74	76	73	74	73	76	73	74	76	76	73	75	74	74	77
Brazil	66	48	46	50	43	48	56	46	49	50	50	47	48	45	51	46
Bulgaria	52	78	79	78	82	81	75	67	83	88	72	74	87	75	82	84
Canada	56	52	52	52	47	50	57	49	53	55	50	53	52	46	53	52
Chile	59	66	65	67	66	67	65	68	65	65	66	66	66	70	64	67
China	66	59	63	54	68	59	50	47	67	72	52	63	67	62	67	56
Colombia	na	24	23	26	23	23	28	24	23	25	24	26	21	22	20	19
Croatia	na	74	75	74	77	75	72	71	76	76	74	73	78	68	75	77
Czech Republic	81	56	59	53	62	57	52	51	59	72	52	56	60	53	56	67
Denmark	56	54	52	56	53	55	55	53	51	57	52	56	56	59	54	52
Dominican Rep.	na	79	77	81	77	82	91	94	81	77	85	80	72	82	79	80
Egypt	na	85	86	84	86	85	85	82	88	90	83	84	89	82	88	90
El Salvador	na	na	na	na	na	na	na	na	na	na	na	na	na	na	na	na
Estonia	55	55	55	54	52	54	57	57	54	54	53	60	51	56	55	35
Finland	45	54	53	56	58	60	47	50	58	64	56	53	53	60	52	51
France	43	50	50	50	57	51	46	46	51	60	52	48	50	44	51	58
Georgia	na	47	48	45	44	48	48	47	45	51	47	51	44	47	46	51
Germany	65	54	57	52	57	54	54	50	56	67	50	52	54	55	53	58
Great Britain	42	39	41	37	45	40	34	32	44	46	31	39	42	na	na	na
Greece	na	56	53	58	58	55	54	61	56	55	56	55	59	53	57	59
Hungary	66	86	88	85	93	93	76	83	93	93	78	87	92	85	90	97
Iceland	72	65	65	66	64	69	61	61	66	73	64	67	67	65	66	68
India	67	77	79	74	79	77	73	70	80	90	69	73	84	78	84	89
Indonesia	na	93	92	96	96	94	93	90	95	95	94	95	98	94	95	96
Iran	na	67	69	64	69	66	62	64	65	70	66	61	70	69	67	71
Ireland	50	60	60	61	48	63	67	63	58	61	64	63	57	66	60	51
Israel	na	na	na	na	na	na	na	na	na	na	na	na	na	na	na	na
Italy	54	75	76	75	76	74	76	77	74	76	78	79	73	76	76	76
Japan	71	90	89	91	92	91	87	85	92	89	89	89	90	94	89	91
Jordan	na	96	98	94	97	96	93	94	97	98	93	99	97	94	97	99
Korea, South	31	96	94	97	97	96	94	95	96	96	96	95	97	95	97	94
Latvia	44	42	42	42	38	42	43	42	42	43	43	39	43	39	44	51
Lithuania	56	52	53	51	52	54	49	42	54	62	47	53	53	55	53	40
Luxembourg	na	57	58	56	59	60	52	51	56	73	50	59	60	51	60	61
Macedonia	na	42	44	40	39	44	43	38	45	42	41	44	42	41	44	46
Malta	na	93	92	93	95	92	92	93	92	94	91	92	93	90	94	90
Mexico	65	49	49	48	44	50	54	49	49	46	48	51	47	50	51	40
Moldova	na	79	78	80	81	81	75	74	79	85	79	80	79	77	80	78
Montenegro	na	53	57	49	56	53	50	46	53	69	46	53	58	55	52	53
Morocco	na	96	96	96	97	96	94	95	99	97	92	96	95	96	97	94
Netherlands	74	69	73	65	79	70	63	52	77	76	64	68	80	51	70	77
New Zealand	na	61	60	62	62	57	65	60	62	60	67	60	55	64	59	59
Nigeria	86	79	78	80	79	79	79	76	80	83	78	82	77	79	79	78
Northern Ireland	41	61	61	61	58	64	59	58	59	72	51	55	59	53	65	64
Norway	43	47	41	53	48	43	52	52	46	44	na	na	na	52	46	48
Pakistan	na	na	na	na	na	na	na	na	na	na	na	na	na	na	na	na
Peru	na	61	63	60	60	60	67	61	56	68	59	63	64	58	62	64
Philippines	na	58	57	58	58	56	59	59	52	63	58	55	60	58	58	49
Poland	na	66	70	63	70	63	67	65	65	72	67	66	67	63	69	62
Portugal	57	47	47	46	59	46	40	42	54	61	32	40	52	38	51	52
Puerto Rico	na	73	69	75	73	74	72	73	68	76	70	72	79	66	75	74
Romania	52	79	82	77	82	84	73	72	84	85	74	83	84	83	80	76
Russian Fed.	54	54	54	54	56	57	50	46	54	60	52	57	53	53	56	61
Serbia	na	40	41	40	44	39	39	34	40	49	33	38	50	36	44	48
Singapore	na	54	57	51	57	56	40	43	58	68	49	56	59	55	54	48
Slovakia	na	55	57	54	61	55	51	44	59	70	48	54	63	49	62	79
Slovenia	61	86	85	88	86	88	85	87	88	80	87	90	82	84	88	88
South Africa	32	63	63	64	65	61	65	58	70	69	56	75	61	66	63	50
Spain	46	60	61	60	62	61	59	59	59	69	58	65	65	62	61	61
Sweden	53	41	41	41	38	40	44	43	39	43	43	39	39	39	41	40
Switzerland	na	62	60	65	55	62	67	59	63	67	59	65	62	66	61	68
Taiwan	na	84	84	83	91	84	77	77	89	87	80	85	88	86	85	70
Tanzania	na	65	65	66	64	68	61	63	67	75	63	65	74	62	69	67
Turkey	90	96	96	96	96	96	96	96	96	98	95	96	98	95	97	96
Uganda	na	59	57	60	63	54	57	60	59	45	49	57	50	61	61	39
Ukraine	na	61	64	59	67	61	58	46	62	67	59	62	66	57	67	64
United States	57	62	61	63	60	59	66	58	63	63	58	64	65	56	62	63
Uruguay	na	59	58	59	60	59	58	61	56	55	64	60	55	64	62	52
Venezuela	na	na	na	na	na	na	na	na	na	na	na	na	na	na	na	na
Vietnam	na	82	85	80	83	83	81	79	87	96	76	83	87	92	86	80
Zimbabwe	na	55	55	55	55	57	53	52	59	70	48	55	64	53	58	47
Total	57	64	64	63	66	65	61	61	64	69	62	65	66	64	65	63

RANKING

Country	2000
Turkey	96
Korea, South	96
Jordan	96
Morocco	96
Indonesia	93
Malta	93
Bangladesh	91
Japan	90
Slovenia	86
Hungary	86
Egypt	85
Taiwan	84
Vietnam	82
Dominican Rep.	79
Romania	79
Moldova	79
Nigeria	79
Bulgaria	78
India	77
Italy	75
Bosnia and Herz.	74
Croatia	74
Azerbaijan	73
Puerto Rico	73
Algeria	70
Netherlands	69
Iran	67
Armenia	66
Chile	66
Poland	66
Iceland	65
Tanzania	65
South Africa	63
Switzerland	62
United States	62
Peru	61
Ukraine	61
New Zealand	61
Northern Ireland	61
Ireland	60
Spain	60
Austria	59
Uruguay	59
China	59
Uganda	59
Philippines	58
Luxembourg	57
Czech Republic	56
Greece	56
Belgium	56
Slovakia	55
Zimbabwe	55
Estonia	55
Germany	54
Denmark	54
Finland	54
Russian Fed.	54
Singapore	54
Montenegro	53
Canada	52
Lithuania	52
Argentina	51
France	50
Mexico	49
Brazil	48
Norway	47
Georgia	47
Portugal	47
Australia	45
Macedonia	42
Latvia	42
Sweden	41
Serbia	40
Belarus	39
Great Britain	39
Albania	29
Colombia	24
Total	64

C022_1) IMPORTANT IN A JOB: PLEASANT PEOPLE TO WORK WITH

Here are some more aspects of a job that people say are important.

Please tell me which ones you personally think are important in a job?

Pleasant people to work with (%)

(EVS: V72)

Country	Wave 1990	Wave 2000	Gender Male	Gender Female	Age 16-29	Age 30-49	Age 50+	Education Lower	Education Middle	Education Upper	Income Lower	Income Middle	Income Upper	Values Mat	Values Mixed	Values Postm.
Albania	na	na	na	na	na	na	na	na	na	na	na	na	na	na	na	na
Algeria	na	na	na	na	na	na	na	na	na	na	na	na	na	na	na	na
Argentina	61	na	na	na	na	na	na	na	na	na	na	na	na	na	na	na
Armenia	na	na	na	na	na	na	na	na	na	na	na	na	na	na	na	na
Australia	na	na	na	na	na	na	na	na	na	na	na	na	na	na	na	na
Austria	62	68	67	69	81	74	55	66	70	66	58	69	73	77	65	71
Azerbaijan	na	na	na	na	na	na	na	na	na	na	na	na	na	na	na	na
Bangladesh	na	na	na	na	na	na	na	na	na	na	na	na	na	na	na	na
Belarus	82	69	66	72	76	72	61	51	73	85	66	69	74	66	71	73
Belgium	68	75	75	74	83	75	71	67	75	80	70	72	80	74	75	73
Bosnia and Herz.	na	na	na	na	na	na	na	na	na	na	na	na	na	na	na	na
Brazil	58	na	na	na	na	na	na	na	na	na	na	na	na	na	na	na
Bulgaria	63	64	68	61	74	67	57	50	72	74	55	63	72	58	70	80
Canada	73	na	na	na	na	na	na	na	na	na	na	na	na	na	na	na
Chile	57	na	na	na	na	na	na	na	na	na	na	na	na	na	na	na
China	55	na	na	na	na	na	na	na	na	na	na	na	na	na	na	na
Colombia	na	na	na	na	na	na	na	na	na	na	na	na	na	na	na	na
Croatia	na	76	77	75	82	78	71	75	76	80	74	76	79	71	77	80
Czech Republic	83	64	61	67	70	68	58	63	64	68	55	68	67	62	65	61
Denmark	77	78	74	82	87	79	72	76	81	80	77	77	81	75	79	80
Dominican Rep.	na	na	na	na	na	na	na	na	na	na	na	na	na	na	na	na
Egypt	na	na	na	na	na	na	na	na	na	na	na	na	na	na	na	na
El Salvador	na	na	na	na	na	na	na	na	na	na	na	na	na	na	na	na
Estonia	77	71	65	76	76	71	68	64	75	73	68	73	72	70	73	62
Finland	64	74	71	77	88	75	66	74	76	70	77	78	69	79	72	66
France	53	65	63	67	72	70	57	65	65	65	64	68	64	60	65	74
Georgia	na	na	na	na	na	na	na	na	na	na	na	na	na	na	na	na
Germany	72	65	60	69	68	66	63	64	66	65	61	70	67	59	66	69
Great Britain	65	73	69	76	75	71	72	68	74	77	70	68	78	na	na	na
Greece	na	76	75	77	85	72	66	68	75	79	71	76	81	74	77	78
Hungary	65	85	86	84	94	89	76	80	95	94	73	86	93	82	90	92
Iceland	89	83	81	85	87	83	80	83	85	78	82	85	81	86	83	72
India	69	na	na	na	na	na	na	na	na	na	na	na	na	na	na	na
Indonesia	na	na	na	na	na	na	na	na	na	na	na	na	na	na	na	na
Iran	na	na	na	na	na	na	na	na	na	na	na	na	na	na	na	na
Ireland	64	77	73	80	81	75	76	73	77	82	74	78	79	76	78	73
Israel	na	na	na	na	na	na	na	na	na	na	na	na	na	na	na	na
Italy	50	72	70	73	76	73	68	71	74	69	74	75	69	68	74	74
Japan	78	na	na	na	na	na	na	na	na	na	na	na	na	na	na	na
Jordan	na	na	na	na	na	na	na	na	na	na	na	na	na	na	na	na
Korea, South	14	na	na	na	na	na	na	na	na	na	na	na	na	na	na	na
Latvia	55	32	32	32	41	32	29	31	30	40	28	35	39	32	34	34
Lithuania	73	60	59	61	72	65	46	41	64	75	53	54	62	56	60	63
Luxembourg	na	74	73	76	83	76	66	73	76	70	73	77	73	73	76	75
Macedonia	na	na	na	na	na	na	na	na	na	na	na	na	na	na	na	na
Malta	na	83	83	83	85	84	82	84	83	85	79	79	85	78	86	86
Mexico	69	na	na	na	na	na	na	na	na	na	na	na	na	na	na	na
Moldova	na	na	na	na	na	na	na	na	na	na	na	na	na	na	na	na
Montenegro	na	na	na	na	na	na	na	na	na	na	na	na	na	na	na	na
Morocco	na	na	na	na	na	na	na	na	na	na	na	na	na	na	na	na
Netherlands	93	89	89	89	95	92	83	86	91	89	89	90	89	85	90	90
New Zealand	na	na	na	na	na	na	na	na	na	na	na	na	na	na	na	na
Nigeria	85	na	na	na	na	na	na	na	na	na	na	na	na	na	na	na
Northern Ireland	68	71	64	77	78	71	67	66	75	77	67	70	65	70	72	71
Norway	80	na	na	na	na	na	na	na	na	na	na	na	na	na	na	na
Pakistan	na	na	na	na	na	na	na	na	na	na	na	na	na	na	na	na
Peru	na	na	na	na	na	na	na	na	na	na	na	na	na	na	na	na
Philippines	na	na	na	na	na	na	na	na	na	na	na	na	na	na	na	na
Poland	na	74	75	74	78	73	74	74	76	76	75	73	77	76	73	81
Portugal	80	67	63	70	74	65	64	62	76	75	53	67	70	66	65	80
Puerto Rico	na	na	na	na	na	na	na	na	na	na	na	na	na	na	na	na
Romania	56	75	74	77	80	77	72	72	80	71	72	80	76	78	77	59
Russian Fed.	71	55	53	57	59	55	53	48	55	58	53	58	55	57	54	71
Serbia	na	na	na	na	na	na	na	na	na	na	na	na	na	na	na	na
Singapore	na	na	na	na	na	na	na	na	na	na	na	na	na	na	na	na
Slovakia	na	51	47	55	58	51	46	43	54	58	46	53	55	45	55	66
Slovenia	82	90	89	91	93	90	87	89	91	87	91	94	90	85	91	91
South Africa	40	na	na	na	na	na	na	na	na	na	na	na	na	na	na	na
Spain	62	66	67	65	74	66	62	63	67	76	64	72	75	62	69	67
Sweden	91	84	80	88	92	88	76	82	88	80	86	82	84	87	84	84
Switzerland	na	na	na	na	na	na	na	na	na	na	na	na	na	na	na	na
Taiwan	na	na	na	na	na	na	na	na	na	na	na	na	na	na	na	na
Tanzania	na	na	na	na	na	na	na	na	na	na	na	na	na	na	na	na
Turkey	86	97	97	98	98	98	94	98	97	95	97	98	96	97	98	96
Uganda	na	na	na	na	na	na	na	na	na	na	na	na	na	na	na	na
Ukraine	na	66	63	68	69	66	64	61	68	64	67	64	68	65	70	55
United States	74	na	na	na	na	na	na	na	na	na	na	na	na	na	na	na
Uruguay	na	na	na	na	na	na	na	na	na	na	na	na	na	na	na	na
Venezuela	na	na	na	na	na	na	na	na	na	na	na	na	na	na	na	na
Vietnam	na	na	na	na	na	na	na	na	na	na	na	na	na	na	na	na
Zimbabwe	na	na	na	na	na	na	na	na	na	na	na	na	na	na	na	na
Total	69	71	70	73	78	73	66	69	72	75	68	73	73	67	73	75

RANKING

Country	2000
Turkey	97
Slovenia	90
Netherlands	89
Hungary	85
Sweden	84
Malta	83
Iceland	83
Denmark	78
Ireland	77
Greece	76
Croatia	76
Romania	75
Belgium	75
Poland	74
Finland	74
Luxembourg	74
Great Britain	73
Italy	72
Northern Ireland	71
Estonia	71
Belarus	69
Austria	68
Portugal	67
Spain	66
Ukraine	66
Germany	65
France	65
Bulgaria	64
Czech Republic	64
Lithuania	60
Russian Fed.	55
Slovakia	51
Latvia	32
Total	71

C023_1) IMPORTANT IN A JOB: CHANCES FOR PROMOTION

Here are some more aspects of a job that people say are important.

Please tell me which ones you personally think are important in a job?

Good chances for promotion (%)

(EVS: V75)

Country	Wave 1990	Wave 2000	Gender Male	Gender Female	Age 16-29	Age 30-49	Age 50+	Education Lower	Education Middle	Education Upper	Income Lower	Income Middle	Income Upper	Values Mat	Values Mixed	Values Postm.	RANKING Country	RANKING 2000
Albania	na	na	na	na	na	na	na	na	na	na	na	na	na	na	na	na	Slovenia	74
Algeria	na	na	na	na	na	na	na	na	na	na	na	na	na	na	na	na	Turkey	73
Argentina	45	na	na	na	na	na	na	na	na	na	na	na	na	na	na	na	Greece	68
Armenia	na	na	na	na	na	na	na	na	na	na	na	na	na	na	na	na	Hungary	67
Australia	na	na	na	na	na	na	na	na	na	na	na	na	na	na	na	na	Malta	62
Austria	33	36	39	33	50	31	34	35	38	34	35	36	37	45	36	35	Romania	61
Azerbaijan	na	na	na	na	na	na	na	na	na	na	na	na	na	na	na	na	Croatia	60
Bangladesh	na	na	na	na	na	na	na	na	na	na	na	na	na	na	na	na	Ireland	51
Belarus	22	26	27	25	42	24	15	12	30	35	20	25	38	20	29	38	Poland	50
Belgium	31	33	35	31	44	26	33	36	33	30	28	34	33	34	33	28	Northern Ireland	49
Bosnia and Herz.	na	na	na	na	na	na	na	na	na	na	na	na	na	na	na	na	Italy	48
Brazil	53	na	na	na	na	na	na	na	na	na	na	na	na	na	na	na	Bulgaria	45
Bulgaria	36	45	48	41	54	50	36	34	48	56	36	43	53	39	51	53	Iceland	44
Canada	49	na	na	na	na	na	na	na	na	na	na	na	na	na	na	na	Spain	44
Chile	49	na	na	na	na	na	na	na	na	na	na	na	na	na	na	na	Ukraine	39
China	27	na	na	na	na	na	na	na	na	na	na	na	na	na	na	na	Germany	37
Colombia	na	na	na	na	na	na	na	na	na	na	na	na	na	na	na	na	Lithuania	37
Croatia	na	60	63	57	70	60	53	56	63	59	59	56	65	53	61	61	Austria	36
Czech Republic	30	24	24	24	32	24	21	21	27	30	21	27	27	23	24	30	Great Britain	36
Denmark	16	17	18	16	31	18	9	12	27	23	15	16	23	18	17	17	Luxembourg	35
Dominican Rep.	na	na	na	na	na	na	na	na	na	na	na	na	na	na	na	na	Belgium	33
Egypt	na	na	na	na	na	na	na	na	na	na	na	na	na	na	na	na	Portugal	32
El Salvador	na	na	na	na	na	na	na	na	na	na	na	na	na	na	na	na	Netherlands	32
Estonia	12	27	29	25	45	23	20	21	27	36	20	25	30	22	30	40	France	30
Finland	30	20	23	16	31	18	15	17	23	25	19	18	21	19	20	18	Sweden	30
France	25	30	32	28	30	32	29	32	30	26	29	34	27	31	31	26	Russian Fed.	29
Georgia	na	na	na	na	na	na	na	na	na	na	na	na	na	na	na	na	Estonia	27
Germany	28	37	44	32	55	35	32	34	39	43	30	39	45	36	38	37	Belarus	26
Great Britain	35	36	37	34	45	34	31	27	42	40	26	34	40	na	na	na	Slovakia	25
Greece	na	68	68	68	76	61	61	50	64	74	59	69	74	64	68	73	Czech Republic	24
Hungary	42	67	68	67	81	69	57	65	76	66	53	68	76	66	71	86	Latvia	20
Iceland	37	44	45	43	58	45	31	44	47	39	39	42	50	49	45	29	Finland	20
India	72	na	na	na	na	na	na	na	na	na	na	na	na	na	na	na	Denmark	17
Indonesia	na	na	na	na	na	na	na	na	na	na	na	na	na	na	na	na		
Iran	na	na	na	na	na	na	na	na	na	na	na	na	na	na	na	na		
Ireland	38	51	52	50	58	45	51	49	51	54	49	50	55	55	52	44		
Israel	na	na	na	na	na	na	na	na	na	na	na	na	na	na	na	na		
Italy	28	48	51	45	51	43	50	49	48	43	47	46	48	53	48	46		
Japan	23	na	na	na	na	na	na	na	na	na	na	na	na	na	na	na		
Jordan	na	na	na	na	na	na	na	na	na	na	na	na	na	na	na	na		
Korea, South	2	na	na	na	na	na	na	na	na	na	na	na	na	na	na	na		
Latvia	9	20	20	20	37	17	16	15	20	26	16	22	24	21	20	32		
Lithuania	16	37	39	36	55	36	26	25	40	49	31	30	44	37	38	33		
Luxembourg	na	35	38	32	42	33	34	40	32	33	36	37	31	34	39	30		
Macedonia	na	na	na	na	na	na	na	na	na	na	na	na	na	na	na	na		
Malta	na	62	66	57	72	57	59	57	62	72	51	57	68	53	66	66		
Mexico	61	na	na	na	na	na	na	na	na	na	na	na	na	na	na	na		
Moldova	na	na	na	na	na	na	na	na	na	na	na	na	na	na	na	na		
Montenegro	na	na	na	na	na	na	na	na	na	na	na	na	na	na	na	na		
Morocco	na	na	na	na	na	na	na	na	na	na	na	na	na	na	na	na		
Netherlands	35	32	36	28	48	28	27	28	38	29	28	34	32	32	35	24		
New Zealand	na	na	na	na	na	na	na	na	na	na	na	na	na	na	na	na		
Nigeria	89	na	na	na	na	na	na	na	na	na	na	na	na	na	na	na		
Northern Ireland	41	49	48	50	62	45	45	43	50	61	39	44	46	47	49	54		
Norway	19	na	na	na	na	na	na	na	na	na	na	na	na	na	na	na		
Pakistan	na	na	na	na	na	na	na	na	na	na	na	na	na	na	na	na		
Peru	na	na	na	na	na	na	na	na	na	na	na	na	na	na	na	na		
Philippines	na	na	na	na	na	na	na	na	na	na	na	na	na	na	na	na		
Poland	na	50	52	48	58	46	50	50	51	46	52	49	48	51	50	51		
Portugal	57	32	30	34	34	36	27	30	38	30	21	31	36	31	33	32		
Puerto Rico	na	na	na	na	na	na	na	na	na	na	na	na	na	na	na	na		
Romania	30	61	62	60	69	65	54	52	66	67	54	65	66	60	64	68		
Russian Fed.	17	29	33	26	45	28	22	21	28	38	24	30	34	25	33	42		
Serbia	na	na	na	na	na	na	na	na	na	na	na	na	na	na	na	na		
Singapore	na	na	na	na	na	na	na	na	na	na	na	na	na	na	na	na		
Slovakia	na	25	26	24	34	24	18	17	27	35	18	23	30	22	27	41		
Slovenia	62	74	75	72	80	71	71	76	74	69	75	73	67	71	74	74		
South Africa	38	na	na	na	na	na	na	na	na	na	na	na	na	na	na	na		
Spain	33	44	48	40	54	41	40	40	44	53	43	44	55	41	44	48		
Sweden	41	30	33	27	39	30	25	20	37	27	31	29	28	33	30	28		
Switzerland	na	na	na	na	na	na	na	na	na	na	na	na	na	na	na	na		
Taiwan	na	na	na	na	na	na	na	na	na	na	na	na	na	na	na	na		
Tanzania	na	na	na	na	na	na	na	na	na	na	na	na	na	na	na	na		
Turkey	61	73	67	79	74	72	73	77	70	61	80	71	65	79	74	65		
Uganda	na	na	na	na	na	na	na	na	na	na	na	na	na	na	na	na		
Ukraine	na	39	39	39	46	39	35	28	40	44	35	38	48	37	44	46		
United States	58	na	na	na	na	na	na	na	na	na	na	na	na	na	na	na		
Uruguay	na	na	na	na	na	na	na	na	na	na	na	na	na	na	na	na		
Venezuela	na	na	na	na	na	na	na	na	na	na	na	na	na	na	na	na		
Vietnam	na	na	na	na	na	na	na	na	na	na	na	na	na	na	na	na		
Zimbabwe	na	na	na	na	na	na	na	na	na	na	na	na	na	na	na	na		
Total	36	40	42	39	52	39	35	36	43	44	36	39	44	39	42	41	Total	40

C024_1) IMPORTANT IN A JOB: A USEFUL FOR SOCIETY

Here are some more aspects of a job that people say are important.

Please tell me which ones you personally think are important in a job?

A useful job for society (%)

(EVS: V79)

Country	Wave 1990	Wave 2000	Gender Male	Gender Female	Age 16-29	Age 30-49	Age 50+	Education Lower	Education Middle	Education Upper	Income Lower	Income Middle	Income Upper	Values Mat	Values Mixed	Values Postm.
Albania	na	na	na	na	na	na	na	na	na	na	na	na	na	na	na	na
Algeria	na	na	na	na	na	na	na	na	na	na	na	na	na	na	na	na
Argentina	43	na	na	na	na	na	na	na	na	na	na	na	na	na	na	na
Armenia	na	na	na	na	na	na	na	na	na	na	na	na	na	na	na	na
Australia	na	na	na	na	na	na	na	na	na	na	na	na	na	na	na	na
Austria	35	36	34	38	31	35	40	34	35	43	36	35	39	26	36	38
Azerbaijan	na	na	na	na	na	na	na	na	na	na	na	na	na	na	na	na
Bangladesh	na	na	na	na	na	na	na	na	na	na	na	na	na	na	na	na
Belarus	42	26	26	26	29	24	26	19	27	35	28	25	26	22	30	34
Belgium	40	41	41	41	37	39	45	40	39	45	42	42	40	40	39	45
Bosnia and Herz.	na	na	na	na	na	na	na	na	na	na	na	na	na	na	na	na
Brazil	58	na	na	na	na	na	na	na	na	na	na	na	na	na	na	na
Bulgaria	58	57	56	58	55	60	55	52	57	69	51	58	62	50	65	60
Canada	36	na	na	na	na	na	na	na	na	na	na	na	na	na	na	na
Chile	60	na	na	na	na	na	na	na	na	na	na	na	na	na	na	na
China	47	na	na	na	na	na	na	na	na	na	na	na	na	na	na	na
Colombia	na	na	na	na	na	na	na	na	na	na	na	na	na	na	na	na
Croatia	na	59	61	57	56	62	57	61	58	56	62	62	56	55	60	58
Czech Republic	33	32	30	35	32	29	35	29	35	42	35	31	32	34	31	36
Denmark	13	26	26	26	24	24	29	23	21	33	29	24	26	26	26	30
Dominican Rep.	na	na	na	na	na	na	na	na	na	na	na	na	na	na	na	na
Egypt	na	na	na	na	na	na	na	na	na	na	na	na	na	na	na	na
El Salvador	na	na	na	na	na	na	na	na	na	na	na	na	na	na	na	na
Estonia	38	27	22	31	25	26	30	26	26	32	22	33	26	25	28	38
Finland	24	31	30	31	28	30	32	29	29	41	34	28	30	23	33	30
France	17	30	31	30	30	31	30	28	30	35	32	30	30	26	31	35
Georgia	na	na	na	na	na	na	na	na	na	na	na	na	na	na	na	na
Germany	51	33	31	35	33	32	35	29	36	43	31	32	40	34	33	36
Great Britain	27	27	27	28	29	25	25	21	31	36	24	26	30	na	na	na
Greece	na	53	50	54	52	49	62	67	49	52	47	55	52	47	53	57
Hungary	16	74	72	75	81	77	67	72	77	82	67	75	78	69	81	77
Iceland	45	47	47	46	38	42	60	46	45	53	50	44	44	46	47	44
India	59	na	na	na	na	na	na	na	na	na	na	na	na	na	na	na
Indonesia	na	na	na	na	na	na	na	na	na	na	na	na	na	na	na	na
Iran	na	na	na	na	na	na	na	na	na	na	na	na	na	na	na	na
Ireland	29	41	41	41	35	37	50	42	38	46	46	38	41	43	40	44
Israel	na	na	na	na	na	na	na	na	na	na	na	na	na	na	na	na
Italy	40	66	65	66	66	65	66	66	65	65	67	67	64	64	66	66
Japan	26	na	na	na	na	na	na	na	na	na	na	na	na	na	na	na
Jordan	na	na	na	na	na	na	na	na	na	na	na	na	na	na	na	na
Korea, South	7	na	na	na	na	na	na	na	na	na	na	na	na	na	na	na
Latvia	31	29	30	29	24	21	38	31	26	38	31	29	29	31	29	32
Lithuania	28	29	28	30	30	27	30	22	30	35	29	29	28	30	28	28
Luxembourg	na	44	46	42	41	43	47	47	42	45	48	44	48	48	45	42
Macedonia	na	na	na	na	na	na	na	na	na	na	na	na	na	na	na	na
Malta	na	72	71	73	71	71	76	78	68	78	71	73	69	69	74	71
Mexico	54	na	na	na	na	na	na	na	na	na	na	na	na	na	na	na
Moldova	na	na	na	na	na	na	na	na	na	na	na	na	na	na	na	na
Montenegro	na	na	na	na	na	na	na	na	na	na	na	na	na	na	na	na
Morocco	na	na	na	na	na	na	na	na	na	na	na	na	na	na	na	na
Netherlands	55	39	39	39	33	33	48	41	32	45	42	35	43	38	37	45
New Zealand	na	na	na	na	na	na	na	na	na	na	na	na	na	na	na	na
Nigeria	74	na	na	na	na	na	na	na	na	na	na	na	na	na	na	na
Northern Ireland	20	40	42	39	41	38	42	38	36	57	36	32	42	32	44	44
Norway	30	na	na	na	na	na	na	na	na	na	na	na	na	na	na	na
Pakistan	na	na	na	na	na	na	na	na	na	na	na	na	na	na	na	na
Peru	na	na	na	na	na	na	na	na	na	na	na	na	na	na	na	na
Philippines	na	na	na	na	na	na	na	na	na	na	na	na	na	na	na	na
Poland	na	48	48	48	42	43	57	51	44	50	53	46	45	51	46	46
Portugal	59	52	47	55	50	47	56	50	52	62	49	47	44	49	53	57
Puerto Rico	na	na	na	na	na	na	na	na	na	na	na	na	na	na	na	na
Romania	55	65	64	66	67	66	63	61	69	64	64	70	65	68	66	59
Russian Fed.	40	22	21	23	23	22	22	17	23	23	20	23	23	21	23	32
Serbia	na	na	na	na	na	na	na	na	na	na	na	na	na	na	na	na
Singapore	na	na	na	na	na	na	na	na	na	na	na	na	na	na	na	na
Slovakia	na	24	22	26	24	22	28	21	25	27	28	21	25	23	25	40
Slovenia	59	73	71	75	62	77	77	78	73	64	77	74	69	76	74	70
South Africa	22	na	na	na	na	na	na	na	na	na	na	na	na	na	na	na
Spain	37	44	44	44	43	45	44	43	42	49	50	45	50	43	42	53
Sweden	43	25	23	27	28	22	26	21	25	28	28	24	21	25	22	32
Switzerland	na	na	na	na	na	na	na	na	na	na	na	na	na	na	na	na
Taiwan	na	na	na	na	na	na	na	na	na	na	na	na	na	na	na	na
Tanzania	na	na	na	na	na	na	na	na	na	na	na	na	na	na	na	na
Turkey	87	98	98	98	98	98	97	98	98	97	98	99	96	98	99	98
Uganda	na	na	na	na	na	na	na	na	na	na	na	na	na	na	na	na
Ukraine	na	31	30	32	28	28	35	28	30	35	29	29	37	27	37	38
United States	44	na	na	na	na	na	na	na	na	na	na	na	na	na	na	na
Uruguay	na	na	na	na	na	na	na	na	na	na	na	na	na	na	na	na
Venezuela	na	na	na	na	na	na	na	na	na	na	na	na	na	na	na	na
Vietnam	na	na	na	na	na	na	na	na	na	na	na	na	na	na	na	na
Zimbabwe	na	na	na	na	na	na	na	na	na	na	na	na	na	na	na	na
Total	40	42	42	43	42	41	44	42	41	46	42	42	43	41	44	47

RANKING

Country	2000
Turkey	98
Hungary	74
Slovenia	73
Malta	72
Italy	66
Romania	65
Croatia	59
Bulgaria	57
Greece	53
Portugal	52
Poland	48
Iceland	47
Luxembourg	44
Spain	44
Ireland	41
Belgium	41
Northern Ireland	40
Netherlands	39
Austria	36
Germany	33
Czech Republic	32
Ukraine	31
Finland	31
France	30
Latvia	29
Lithuania	29
Great Britain	27
Estonia	27
Belarus	26
Denmark	26
Sweden	25
Slovakia	24
Russian Fed.	22
Total	42

C025_1) IMPORTANT IN A JOB: MEETING PEOPLE

Here are some more aspects of a job that people say are important.

Please tell me which ones you personally think are important in a job?

(EVS: V81)

Meeting people (%)

Country	Wave 1990	Wave 2000	Gender Male	Gender Female	Age 16-29	Age 30-49	Age 50+	Education Lower	Education Middle	Education Upper	Income Lower	Income Middle	Income Upper	Values Mat	Values Mixed	Values Postm.
Albania	na	na	na	na	na	na	na	na	na	na	na	na	na	na	na	na
Algeria	na	na	na	na	na	na	na	na	na	na	na	na	na	na	na	na
Argentina	50	na	na	na	na	na	na	na	na	na	na	na	na	na	na	na
Armenia	na	na	na	na	na	na	na	na	na	na	na	na	na	na	na	na
Australia	na	na	na	na	na	na	na	na	na	na	na	na	na	na	na	na
Austria	39	47	43	51	50	47	46	43	49	56	40	45	54	39	46	52
Azerbaijan	na	na	na	na	na	na	na	na	na	na	na	na	na	na	na	na
Bangladesh	na	na	na	na	na	na	na	na	na	na	na	na	na	na	na	na
Belarus	53	37	35	38	35	42	32	28	38	48	37	36	37	33	41	32
Belgium	45	53	49	57	58	55	49	45	50	62	48	51	57	51	52	57
Bosnia and Herz.	na	na	na	na	na	na	na	na	na	na	na	na	na	na	na	na
Brazil	42	na	na	na	na	na	na	na	na	na	na	na	na	na	na	na
Bulgaria	44	56	59	54	70	58	48	43	62	69	44	53	70	47	65	86
Canada	42	na	na	na	na	na	na	na	na	na	na	na	na	na	na	na
Chile	39	na	na	na	na	na	na	na	na	na	na	na	na	na	na	na
China	26	na	na	na	na	na	na	na	na	na	na	na	na	na	na	na
Colombia	na	na	na	na	na	na	na	na	na	na	na	na	na	na	na	na
Croatia	na	62	66	59	70	64	55	59	66	57	65	64	59	51	62	73
Czech Republic	54	34	28	39	40	33	32	35	32	37	33	35	34	34	35	32
Denmark	43	46	42	50	48	46	45	46	47	49	45	44	56	58	45	44
Dominican Rep.	na	na	na	na	na	na	na	na	na	na	na	na	na	na	na	na
Egypt	na	na	na	na	na	na	na	na	na	na	na	na	na	na	na	na
El Salvador	na	na	na	na	na	na	na	na	na	na	na	na	na	na	na	na
Estonia	57	44	37	50	47	43	44	40	48	41	42	45	44	40	48	47
Finland	30	41	38	43	48	43	34	37	45	46	39	46	36	43	38	42
France	39	44	36	50	54	46	36	41	46	47	42	41	48	40	42	52
Georgia	na	na	na	na	na	na	na	na	na	na	na	na	na	na	na	na
Germany	50	52	48	55	59	52	49	47	56	57	49	51	60	52	50	61
Great Britain	43	42	37	47	48	39	43	43	45	36	41	43	40	na	na	na
Greece	na	53	50	55	60	48	50	44	55	54	49	53	55	54	53	56
Hungary	40	69	69	70	77	75	60	66	77	72	65	68	75	66	74	74
Iceland	59	54	51	57	60	50	53	54	57	45	55	53	53	59	54	40
India	45	na	na	na	na	na	na	na	na	na	na	na	na	na	na	na
Indonesia	na	na	na	na	na	na	na	na	na	na	na	na	na	na	na	na
Iran	na	na	na	na	na	na	na	na	na	na	na	na	na	na	na	na
Ireland	35	52	50	54	53	49	55	52	52	53	55	55	51	56	52	47
Israel	na	na	na	na	na	na	na	na	na	na	na	na	na	na	na	na
Italy	43	66	64	67	71	68	61	64	67	67	67	66	67	62	65	71
Japan	48	na	na	na	na	na	na	na	na	na	na	na	na	na	na	na
Jordan	na	na	na	na	na	na	na	na	na	na	na	na	na	na	na	na
Korea, South	24	na	na	na	na	na	na	na	na	na	na	na	na	na	na	na
Latvia	39	43	36	48	37	43	45	43	41	50	44	39	45	46	43	38
Lithuania	59	40	33	47	47	42	34	31	43	48	36	36	45	42	40	46
Luxembourg	na	48	46	49	62	48	38	54	45	43	47	51	41	48	51	45
Macedonia	na	na	na	na	na	na	na	na	na	na	na	na	na	na	na	na
Malta	na	59	57	61	64	55	60	60	60	53	54	51	57	53	63	62
Mexico	47	na	na	na	na	na	na	na	na	na	na	na	na	na	na	na
Moldova	na	na	na	na	na	na	na	na	na	na	na	na	na	na	na	na
Montenegro	na	na	na	na	na	na	na	na	na	na	na	na	na	na	na	na
Morocco	na	na	na	na	na	na	na	na	na	na	na	na	na	na	na	na
Netherlands	71	61	56	66	67	63	56	53	62	68	56	63	66	51	62	65
New Zealand	na	na	na	na	na	na	na	na	na	na	na	na	na	na	na	na
Nigeria	68	na	na	na	na	na	na	na	na	na	na	na	na	na	na	na
Northern Ireland	16	59	56	61	62	60	56	58	59	59	52	53	52	56	60	62
Norway	41	na	na	na	na	na	na	na	na	na	na	na	na	na	na	na
Pakistan	na	na	na	na	na	na	na	na	na	na	na	na	na	na	na	na
Peru	na	na	na	na	na	na	na	na	na	na	na	na	na	na	na	na
Philippines	na	na	na	na	na	na	na	na	na	na	na	na	na	na	na	na
Poland	na	52	52	52	59	48	53	54	53	42	51	55	50	48	53	58
Portugal	53	36	31	40	41	38	31	34	42	36	19	39	36	33	37	38
Puerto Rico	na	na	na	na	na	na	na	na	na	na	na	na	na	na	na	na
Romania	27	55	55	55	61	58	50	53	60	48	53	58	57	60	54	49
Russian Fed.	27	34	30	37	34	34	34	33	34	36	34	36	34	35	35	27
Serbia	na	na	na	na	na	na	na	na	na	na	na	na	na	na	na	na
Singapore	na	na	na	na	na	na	na	na	na	na	na	na	na	na	na	na
Slovakia	na	23	20	27	33	20	19	16	26	31	20	23	26	19	27	35
Slovenia	56	69	67	72	73	70	66	71	71	62	73	68	67	68	69	72
South Africa	na	na	na	na	na	na	na	na	na	na	na	na	na	na	na	na
Spain	35	38	37	39	44	39	33	34	39	48	40	40	44	35	37	44
Sweden	64	46	44	48	55	44	42	40	50	43	47	44	46	42	46	47
Switzerland	na	na	na	na	na	na	na	na	na	na	na	na	na	na	na	na
Taiwan	na	na	na	na	na	na	na	na	na	na	na	na	na	na	na	na
Tanzania	na	na	na	na	na	na	na	na	na	na	na	na	na	na	na	na
Turkey	68	88	88	88	89	87	86	87	92	79	86	89	89	84	89	90
Uganda	na	na	na	na	na	na	na	na	na	na	na	na	na	na	na	na
Ukraine	na	42	38	45	43	43	40	32	42	47	40	40	46	41	46	42
United States	38	na	na	na	na	na	na	na	na	na	na	na	na	na	na	na
Uruguay	na	na	na	na	na	na	na	na	na	na	na	na	na	na	na	na
Venezuela	na	na	na	na	na	na	na	na	na	na	na	na	na	na	na	na
Vietnam	na	na	na	na	na	na	na	na	na	na	na	na	na	na	na	na
Zimbabwe	na	na	na	na	na	na	na	na	na	na	na	na	na	na	na	na
Total	45	49	46	52	55	49	46	47	50	51	47	49	51	46	51	55

RANKING

Country	2000
Turkey	88
Hungary	69
Slovenia	69
Italy	66
Croatia	62
Netherlands	61
Malta	59
Northern Ireland	59
Bulgaria	56
Romania	55
Iceland	54
Greece	53
Belgium	53
Germany	52
Ireland	52
Poland	52
Luxembourg	48
Austria	47
Denmark	46
Sweden	46
Estonia	44
France	44
Latvia	43
Great Britain	42
Ukraine	42
Finland	41
Lithuania	40
Spain	38
Belarus	37
Portugal	36
Russian Fed.	34
Czech Republic	34
Slovakia	23
Total	49

C036) WORK: NEED A JOB TO DEVELOP TALENTS

Do you agree or disagree with the following statements: "To fully develop your talents, you need to have a job?"

Strongly agree / Agree (%)

(WVS: V97; EVS: V90)

Country	Wave 1990	Wave 2000	Gender Male	Gender Female	Age 16-29	Age 30-49	Age 50+	Education Lower	Education Middle	Education Upper	Income Lower	Income Middle	Income Upper	Values Mat	Values Mixed	Values Postm.
Albania	na	80	82	78	81	82	77	78	81	85	83	77	80	79	81	90
Algeria	na	na	na	na	na	na	na	na	na	na	na	na	na	na	na	na
Argentina	na	89	89	89	85	86	94	92	85	78	93	87	86	93	88	86
Armenia	na	na	na	na	na	na	na	na	na	na	na	na	na	na	na	na
Australia	na	na	na	na	na	na	na	na	na	na	na	na	na	na	na	na
Austria	na	na	na	na	na	na	na	na	na	na	na	na	na	na	na	na
Azerbaijan	na	na	na	na	na	na	na	na	na	na	na	na	na	na	na	na
Bangladesh	na	78	76	80	76	79	76	84	69	73	74	79	78	78	78	70
Belarus	na	75	76	73	71	77	76	72	74	81	76	73	75	75	75	71
Belgium	na	51	54	48	43	46	58	57	50	47	56	57	43	50	51	51
Bosnia and Herz.	na	85	85	85	88	85	83	85	85	86	85	85	84	86	86	85
Brazil	na	na	na	na	na	na	na	na	na	na	na	na	na	na	na	na
Bulgaria	na	87	86	88	79	89	90	89	87	84	92	87	82	89	85	83
Canada	na	54	62	47	49	52	61	63	55	46	61	58	48	59	57	47
Chile	na	73	78	68	69	74	74	75	74	66	78	67	74	74	73	71
China	na	83	83	83	81	83	84	81	84	83	82	83	83	81	84	87
Colombia	na	na	na	na	na	na	na	na	na	na	na	na	na	na	na	na
Croatia	na	63	65	62	53	61	73	60	66	61	73	59	64	70	64	56
Czech Republic	na	80	82	78	67	77	89	81	78	79	82	78	78	79	80	79
Denmark	na	73	76	71	73	67	80	78	70	65	79	69	75	80	76	63
Dominican Rep.	na	na	na	na	na	na	na	na	na	na	na	na	na	na	na	na
Egypt	na	na	na	na	na	na	na	na	na	na	na	na	na	na	na	na
El Salvador	na	na	na	na	na	na	na	na	na	na	na	na	na	na	na	na
Estonia	na	80	81	79	75	85	77	74	81	86	80	78	82	79	81	81
Finland	na	59	60	58	48	55	69	65	52	54	60	58	59	65	60	47
France	na	78	82	74	75	72	84	80	71	76	81	77	77	81	79	68
Georgia	na	na	na	na	na	na	na	na	na	na	na	na	na	na	na	na
Germany	na	83	89	78	87	78	86	82	84	81	81	82	80	83	85	78
Great Britain	na	54	64	44	55	51	56	57	51	54	54	57	51	na	na	na
Greece	na	68	70	66	59	72	79	74	65	69	72	69	66	70	71	58
Hungary	na	82	84	81	85	78	84	80	87	86	76	82	86	81	84	81
Iceland	na	36	40	32	30	31	48	41	34	27	45	33	31	38	35	36
India	na	79	79	80	80	80	76	79	80	78	82	80	78	78	84	77
Indonesia	na	na	na	na	na	na	na	na	na	na	na	na	na	na	na	na
Iran	na	na	na	na	na	na	na	na	na	na	na	na	na	na	na	na
Ireland	na	60	74	48	58	57	67	67	56	59	62	62	58	65	60	54
Israel	na	87	89	86	85	87	91	90	88	85	85	90	85	90	88	91
Italy	na	73	77	70	70	69	79	75	71	75	74	73	74	73	73	74
Japan	na	64	69	60	58	62	69	75	64	60	66	64	64	71	62	60
Jordan	na	na	na	na	na	na	na	na	na	na	na	na	na	na	na	na
Korea, South	na	89	90	89	90	89	89	84	88	92	86	91	92	87	92	88
Latvia	na	85	81	89	85	80	90	87	85	83	85	85	86	85	85	85
Lithuania	na	71	74	69	76	71	68	61	73	82	68	68	75	71	71	84
Luxembourg	na	69	75	64	68	64	76	74	70	62	76	74	64	71	72	60
Macedonia	na	68	70	66	68	69	67	75	66	61	73	67	62	69	65	82
Malta	na	50	63	37	34	47	60	46	51	53	47	52	52	50	49	54
Mexico	na	69	73	66	65	69	75	74	65	61	73	67	63	73	60	64
Moldova	na	80	80	79	76	83	78	81	79	80	85	80	77	78	83	72
Montenegro	na	78	82	75	73	80	81	78	79	79	84	85	75	81	78	72
Morocco	na	97	98	97	97	97	99	98	95	90	99	98	89	98	97	96
Netherlands	na	38	46	31	41	33	42	48	34	34	46	35	35	51	40	29
New Zealand	na	na	na	na	na	na	na	na	na	na	na	na	na	na	na	na
Nigeria	na	na	na	na	na	na	na	na	na	na	na	na	na	na	na	na
Northern Ireland	na	58	67	49	56	53	61	60	54	61	61	56	46	61	55	65
Norway	na	na	na	na	na	na	na	na	na	na	na	na	na	na	na	na
Pakistan	na	na	na	na	na	na	na	na	na	na	na	na	na	na	na	na
Peru	na	61	60	62	59	61	67	68	62	56	65	62	54	69	61	54
Philippines	na	92	94	91	91	93	93	93	92	92	93	91	94	92	93	91
Poland	na	92	93	91	89	90	96	93	89	96	93	93	87	91	92	92
Portugal	na	90	90	90	89	88	91	91	89	85	92	84	87	89	89	94
Puerto Rico	na	50	53	49	38	47	59	63	61	43	62	50	40	64	52	38
Romania	na	79	80	78	74	81	79	75	80	83	78	80	80	78	81	71
Russian Fed.	na	81	82	79	79	82	80	76	79	88	78	80	84	79	83	82
Serbia	na	65	66	65	60	64	70	67	67	61	67	68	67	66	66	55
Singapore	na	72	73	71	70	74	73	74	73	64	76	71	68	73	72	68
Slovakia	na	67	66	68	61	68	71	66	67	68	68	68	69	70	67	59
Slovenia	na	72	72	72	56	71	84	82	69	62	80	78	61	78	73	65
South Africa	na	70	72	68	72	68	72	75	64	62	79	69	58	68	71	72
Spain	na	69	71	68	66	65	75	73	66	67	77	67	69	72	70	66
Sweden	na	50	54	46	36	46	62	68	46	43	52	50	49	56	52	42
Switzerland	na	na	na	na	na	na	na	na	na	na	na	na	na	na	na	na
Taiwan	na	na	na	na	na	na	na	na	na	na	na	na	na	na	na	na
Tanzania	na	96	95	96	94	95	98	97	95	94	96	95	95	96	95	96
Turkey	na	88	91	85	86	88	97	91	84	88	93	87	83	87	89	87
Uganda	na	67	59	75	69	67	56	77	64	61	68	72	62	66	68	63
Ukraine	na	80	79	82	80	82	80	71	78	90	79	78	86	76	85	87
United States	na	48	55	41	53	43	50	59	46	45	50	47	46	46	48	49
Uruguay	na	na	na	na	na	na	na	na	na	na	na	na	na	na	na	na
Venezuela	na	na	na	na	na	na	na	na	na	na	na	na	na	na	na	na
Vietnam	na	95	95	94	95	95	93	94	95	96	93	93	96	95	97	95
Zimbabwe	na	72	68	75	74	68	75	74	70	40	74	75	66	71	71	89
Total	na	72	75	70	70	71	75	76	71	67	75	73	70	76	72	64

RANKING

Country	2000
Morocco	97
Tanzania	96
Vietnam	95
Philippines	92
Poland	92
Portugal	90
Korea, South	89
Argentina	89
Turkey	88
Israel	87
Bulgaria	87
Bosnia and Herz.	85
Latvia	85
China	83
Germany	83
Hungary	82
Russian Fed.	81
Ukraine	80
Albania	80
Estonia	80
Czech Republic	80
Moldova	80
India	79
Romania	79
Montenegro	78
France	78
Bangladesh	78
Belarus	75
Italy	73
Denmark	73
Chile	73
Zimbabwe	72
Singapore	72
Slovenia	72
Lithuania	71
South Africa	70
Spain	69
Luxembourg	69
Mexico	69
Macedonia	68
Greece	68
Slovakia	67
Uganda	67
Serbia	65
Japan	64
Croatia	63
Peru	61
Ireland	60
Finland	59
Northern Ireland	58
Canada	54
Great Britain	54
Belgium	51
Puerto Rico	50
Sweden	50
Malta	50
United States	48
Netherlands	38
Iceland	36
Total	72

C037) WORK: HUMILIATING TO RECEIVE MONEY WITHOUT WORKING FOR IT

Do you agree or disagree with the following statement: "It is humiliating to receive money without having to work for it?"

Strongly agree / Agree (%)

(WVS: V98; EVS: V91)

Country	Wave 1990	Wave 2000	Gender Male	Gender Female	Age 16-29	Age 30-49	Age 50+	Education Lower	Education Middle	Education Upper	Income Lower	Income Middle	Income Upper	Values Mat	Values Mixed	Values Postm	RANKING Country	2000
Albania	na	76	73	79	73	74	81	77	74	81	76	78	75	79	76	67	Bangladesh	96
Algeria	na	na	na	na	na	na	na	na	na	na	na	na	na	na	na	na	Morocco	94
Argentina	na	69	65	72	61	71	74	71	67	61	73	67	67	66	69	69	Turkey	88
Armenia	na	na	na	na	na	na	na	na	na	na	na	na	na	na	na	na	India	81
Australia	na	na	na	na	na	na	na	na	na	na	na	na	na	na	na	na	Philippines	78
Austria	na	na	na	na	na	na	na	na	na	na	na	na	na	na	na	na	Albania	76
Azerbaijan	na	na	na	na	na	na	na	na	na	na	na	na	na	na	na	na	Montenegro	74
Bangladesh	na	96	95	97	95	97	93	96	97	94	95	96	95	97	95	93	China	73
Belarus	na	54	54	54	45	48	68	58	51	59	58	53	49	57	53	53	Macedonia	73
Belgium	na	42	43	42	33	38	51	44	45	36	47	43	38	43	43	40	Vietnam	72
Bosnia and Herz.	na	60	59	60	54	63	61	58	59	64	59	61	57	60	60	54	Serbia	72
Brazil	na	na	na	na	na	na	na	na	na	na	na	na	na	na	na	na	Bulgaria	72
Bulgaria	na	72	70	73	52	72	81	76	71	67	76	68	70	73	71	79	Lithuania	70
Canada	na	48	50	46	40	45	56	57	48	41	54	48	44	54	48	45	Argentina	69
Chile	na	61	65	57	54	63	64	63	62	53	61	59	63	65	61	52	Italy	67
China	na	73	71	75	64	74	80	74	73	71	69	75	75	75	71	78	Croatia	67
Colombia	na	na	na	na	na	na	na	na	na	na	na	na	na	na	na	na	Korea, South	67
Croatia	na	67	63	70	50	67	77	65	67	71	72	64	69	75	65	68	Tanzania	66
Czech Republic	na	47	44	49	37	41	57	47	48	44	51	47	46	41	48	55	Romania	65
Denmark	na	37	39	36	41	29	45	45	35	23	43	39	28	46	40	23	Peru	65
Dominican Rep.	na	na	na	na	na	na	na	na	na	na	na	na	na	na	na	na	Zimbabwe	64
Egypt	na	na	na	na	na	na	na	na	na	na	na	na	na	na	na	na	Malta	64
El Salvador	na	na	na	na	na	na	na	na	na	na	na	na	na	na	na	na	Russian Fed.	64
Estonia	na	53	50	55	40	50	63	53	52	56	55	57	50	47	57	52	Poland	64
Finland	na	43	41	45	31	38	54	48	37	35	45	40	44	46	44	33	Ukraine	63
France	na	44	44	44	35	37	56	48	38	40	53	42	40	45	46	37	Latvia	63
Georgia	na	na	na	na	na	na	na	na	na	na	na	na	na	na	na	na	Puerto Rico	62
Germany	na	38	39	37	30	37	43	39	36	44	41	35	45	45	38	31	Chile	61
Great Britain	na	39	42	35	33	39	42	44	35	35	41	38	37	na	na	na	Israel	60
Greece	na	54	52	56	42	61	69	79	54	50	60	55	51	59	54	50	Bosnia and Herz.	60
Hungary	na	51	50	52	37	47	63	52	49	53	56	50	50	54	48	52	Singapore	58
Iceland	na	42	43	40	33	36	57	51	36	32	47	40	38	42	43	34	Moldova	57
India	na	81	81	82	81	82	80	81	81	81	78	83	82	85	80	82	Portugal	57
Indonesia	na	na	na	na	na	na	na	na	na	na	na	na	na	na	na	na	Mexico	56
Iran	na	na	na	na	na	na	na	na	na	na	na	na	na	na	na	na	Luxembourg	55
Ireland	na	47	54	40	41	47	51	46	47	50	42	49	52	44	46	56	Uganda	54
Israel	na	60	61	59	50	64	67	68	59	55	58	58	59	68	59	67	Greece	54
Italy	na	67	67	68	55	67	75	73	63	63	76	66	63	71	68	66	Belarus	54
Japan	na	43	44	41	35	36	51	53	43	36	46	39	43	46	42	38	Slovakia	54
Jordan	na	na	na	na	na	na	na	na	na	na	na	na	na	na	na	na	Slovenia	53
Korea, South	na	67	70	63	52	69	78	76	69	62	67	69	64	65	69	58	Estonia	53
Latvia	na	63	62	63	44	57	74	65	60	67	65	64	59	64	63	49	South Africa	53
Lithuania	na	70	66	73	60	68	79	76	68	67	76	75	67	68	71	78	Hungary	51
Luxembourg	na	55	55	56	48	53	63	59	54	51	56	58	52	58	56	51	Canada	48
Macedonia	na	73	74	72	71	73	75	81	68	70	77	71	69	77	70	78	Ireland	47
Malta	na	64	65	63	57	60	72	71	62	57	64	66	62	67	65	47	Czech Republic	47
Mexico	na	56	58	55	49	57	64	59	50	59	54	55	57	56	54	61	Spain	44
Moldova	na	57	53	61	48	60	61	61	57	54	63	54	53	62	58	35	France	44
Montenegro	na	74	76	71	65	70	83	76	69	80	83	72	68	78	73	65	Finland	43
Morocco	na	94	95	93	93	94	97	95	91	84	97	93	92	95	94	91	Japan	43
Netherlands	na	27	28	25	26	19	35	35	26	20	32	25	20	40	26	20	Belgium	42
New Zealand	na	na	na	na	na	na	na	na	na	na	na	na	na	na	na	na	Iceland	42
Nigeria	na	na	na	na	na	na	na	na	na	na	na	na	na	na	na	na	Sweden	40
Northern Ireland	na	36	36	36	31	34	41	40	35	28	36	38	34	41	36	34	Great Britain	39
Norway	na	na	na	na	na	na	na	na	na	na	na	na	na	na	na	na	Germany	38
Pakistan	na	na	na	na	na	na	na	na	na	na	na	na	na	na	na	na	Denmark	37
Peru	na	65	63	66	61	67	67	62	66	65	63	68	62	66	64	·70	United States	37
Philippines	na	78	78	79	75	80	80	79	76	81	82	80	73	80	77	73	Northern Ireland	36
Poland	na	64	64	63	45	65	73	65	64	58	67	65	56	61	64	72	Netherlands	27
Portugal	na	57	59	55	49	55	62	59	51	56	60	52	58	59	57	52		
Puerto Rico	na	62	59	64	50	59	70	70	62	60	63	59	62	64	61	65		
Romania	na	65	63	67	54	64	72	67	62	68	62	67	66	64	67	54		
Russian Fed.	na	64	61	67	47	63	76	72	61	69	66	65	63	66	62	82		
Serbia	na	72	69	76	60	70	79	71	74	71	73	73	74	77	68	73		
Singapore	na	58	58	58	55	60	62	58	59	57	57	60	59	57	58	60		
Slovakia	na	54	52	55	46	52	62	55	53	54	56	51	56	54	55	47		
Slovenia	na	53	50	56	37	49	68	64	49	49	58	54	47	64	52	47		
South Africa	na	53	49	57	49	53	62	52	54	55	50	57	55	56	50	59		
Spain	na	44	44	44	39	40	51	48	40	43	47	49	37	50	43	38		
Sweden	na	40	39	41	39	33	47	49	39	33	42	41	34	41	43	30		
Switzerland	na	na	na	na	na	na	na	na	na	na	na	na	na	na	na	na		
Taiwan	na	na	na	na	na	na	na	na	na	na	na	na	na	na	na	na		
Tanzania	na	66	65	68	65	65	72	63	71	70	67	64	67	69	67	57		
Turkey	na	88	89	87	87	90	84	88	88	84	88	90	85	88	87	89		
Uganda	na	54	57	52	48	61	57	59	51	65	64	69	59	48	57	61		
Ukraine	na	63	61	66	45	63	75	67	62	65	67	65	60	61	64	67		
United States	na	37	37	36	33	35	43	45	39	33	37	39	33	31	37	40		
Uruguay	na	na	na	na	na	na	na	na	na	na	na	na	na	na	na	na		
Venezuela	na	na	na	na	na	na	na	na	na	na	na	na	na	na	na	na		
Vietnam	na	72	75	70	71	74	71	71	73	74	66	76	71	79	71	61		
Zimbabwe	na	64	59	69	58	71	69	68	58	100	66	61	66	61	67	66		
Total	na	58	58	58	52	58	64	62	57	54	61	59	57	63	58	52	Total	58

C038) WORK: PEOPLE WHO DON'T WORK TURN LAZY

Do you agree or disagree with the following statements: "People who don't work turn lazy?"

Strongly agree / Agree (%)

(WVS: V99; EVS: V92)

Country	Wave 1990	Wave 2000	Gender Male	Gender Female	Age 16-29	Age 30-49	Age 50+	Education Lower	Education Middle	Education Upper	Income Lower	Income Middle	Income Upper	Values Mat	Values Mixed	Values Postm.	RANKING Country	RANKING 2000
Albania	na	80	80	80	77	78	87	81	79	83	80	81	81	82	79	82	Turkey	90
Algeria	na	na	na	na	na	na	na	na	na	na	na	na	na	na	na	na	Morocco	89
Argentina	na	78	77	78	76	77	80	83	74	56	84	78	71	85	80	66	Vietnam	88
Armenia	na	na	na	na	na	na	na	na	na	na	na	na	na	na	na	na	Tanzania	88
Australia	na	na	na	na	na	na	na	na	na	na	na	na	na	na	na	na	China	86
Austria	na	na	na	na	na	na	na	na	na	na	na	na	na	na	na	na	Slovenia	86
Azerbaijan	na	na	na	na	na	na	na	na	na	na	na	na	na	na	na	na	Korea, South	85
Bangladesh	na	85	84	86	84	85	91	84	88	85	87	82	86	89	82	81	India	85
Belarus	na	66	63	69	58	65	75	72	64	66	69	66	62	71	63	61	Bangladesh	85
Belgium	na	50	53	48	47	44	57	58	53	40	54	49	50	57	53	36	Romania	80
Bosnia and Herz.	na	68	68	68	70	69	65	69	69	65	73	67	65	68	69	70	Albania	80
Brazil	na	na	na	na	na	na	na	na	na	na	na	na	na	na	na	na	Peru	80
Bulgaria	na	68	68	67	56	61	79	73	66	62	74	66	61	67	72	60	Mexico	80
Canada	na	53	58	49	48	52	59	69	53	40	60	57	45	64	56	45	Czech Republic	79
Chile	na	67	68	66	66	67	69	68	66	67	67	67	68	73	65	61	Slovakia	79
China	na	86	85	87	81	86	90	85	86	93	85	87	87	88	86	68	Poland	78
Colombia	na	na	na	na	na	na	na	na	na	na	na	na	na	na	na	na	Puerto Rico	78
Croatia	na	68	68	67	62	66	73	69	68	62	73	64	71	68	69	63	Macedonia	78
Czech Republic	na	79	77	81	68	78	86	77	82	78	78	81	77	77	81	70	Argentina	78
Denmark	na	65	69	62	75	59	67	75	59	50	70	65	61	74	69	46	Singapore	77
Dominican Rep.	na	na	na	na	na	na	na	na	na	na	na	na	na	na	na	na	Serbia	77
Egypt	na	na	na	na	na	na	na	na	na	na	na	na	na	na	na	na	Montenegro	77
El Salvador	na	na	na	na	na	na	na	na	na	na	na	na	na	na	na	na	Italy	76
Estonia	na	65	65	64	64	62	67	67	62	68	60	66	68	60	69	66	Uganda	75
Finland	na	55	60	51	48	56	58	59	54	43	57	57	54	63	55	39	Israel	75
France	na	55	59	50	46	48	65	61	49	42	59	55	50	62	57	38	Latvia	75
Georgia	na	na	na	na	na	na	na	na	na	na	na	na	na	na	na	na	Hungary	74
Germany	na	50	56	46	43	48	55	52	48	48	48	55	47	43	56	43	Malta	74
Great Britain	na	43	49	38	41	40	49	47	45	34	48	44	39	na	na	na	Russian Fed.	74
Greece	na	56	58	55	49	58	72	71	59	51	56	55	59	61	57	46	Japan	72
Hungary	na	74	73	74	71	70	78	74	72	72	68	75	74	75	74	73	Portugal	70
Iceland	na	17	21	14	14	13	27	23	16	7	25	13	15	18	19	6	Zimbabwe	69
India	na	85	84	86	84	86	86	85	87	84	81	86	87	85	85	84	Bosnia and Herz.	68
Indonesia	na	na	na	na	na	na	na	na	na	na	na	na	na	na	na	na	Croatia	68
Iran	na	na	na	na	na	na	na	na	na	na	na	na	na	na	na	na	Bulgaria	68
Ireland	na	57	62	51	51	57	62	59	58	51	58	62	58	62	57	48	Chile	67
Israel	na	75	78	73	70	75	81	85	77	66	76	75	71	75	75	76	Ukraine	66
Italy	na	76	77	74	71	70	84	82	72	66	81	76	71	80	78	70	Belarus	66
Japan	na	72	75	70	71	68	76	76	71	74	73	71	73	75	73	65	Denmark	65
Jordan	na	na	na	na	na	na	na	na	na	na	na	na	na	na	na	na	Philippines	65
Korea, South	na	85	87	84	78	86	93	89	87	82	87	86	83	87	84	79	Estonia	65
Latvia	na	75	74	75	63	71	83	78	74	73	76	80	72	74	75	80	Spain	63
Lithuania	na	55	51	57	43	55	63	64	51	54	58	57	53	55	53	66	Luxembourg	61
Luxembourg	na	61	65	57	63	55	65	67	62	45	66	62	50	66	63	46	Ireland	57
Macedonia	na	78	78	77	72	78	82	85	74	74	81	78	74	77	76	86	Greece	56
Malta	na	74	78	69	77	70	76	71	75	73	69	75	78	73	73	80	Finland	55
Mexico	na	80	80	80	79	78	85	82	78	78	80	79	81	79	81	76	France	55
Moldova	na	20	20	20	17	18	26	23	23	13	17	22	17	21	22	22	Lithuania	55
Montenegro	na	77	79	74	69	75	83	82	72	75	88	76	75	84	71	66	South Africa	55
Morocco	na	89	90	88	88	90	90	90	87	79	91	89	81	88	90	87	Canada	53
Netherlands	na	35	37	32	30	27	45	53	30	22	41	28	33	59	35	22	United States	53
New Zealand	na	na	na	na	na	na	na	na	na	na	na	na	na	na	na	na	Belgium	50
Nigeria	na	na	na	na	na	na	na	na	na	na	na	na	na	na	na	na	Germany	50
Northern Ireland	na	48	48	48	50	42	52	52	46	41	54	49	39	52	48	41	Northern Ireland	48
Norway	na	na	na	na	na	na	na	na	na	na	na	na	na	na	na	na	Great Britain	43
Pakistan	na	na	na	na	na	na	na	na	na	na	na	na	na	na	na	na	Sweden	37
Peru	na	80	78	82	78	81	84	78	81	80	80	81	80	80	81	81	Netherlands	35
Philippines	na	65	65	65	63	64	69	64	64	66	67	63	65	64	65	68	Moldova	20
Poland	na	78	81	75	72	77	83	79	76	77	76	81	78	74	80	79	Iceland	17
Portugal	na	70	70	70	64	69	74	72	69	58	78	66	69	76	67	63		
Puerto Rico	na	78	79	78	70	75	84	83	80	76	79	78	75	82	78	76		
Romania	na	80	81	80	68	82	85	85	78	77	83	83	77	83	78	72		
Russian Fed.	na	74	73	74	67	72	80	76	72	78	73	73	75	75	72	77		
Serbia	na	77	77	77	68	76	81	77	78	74	79	78	77	79	77	63		
Singapore	na	77	78	76	75	81	76	77	80	66	77	79	75	80	77	68		
Slovakia	na	79	77	81	72	77	86	81	78	79	80	76	83	79	80	80		
Slovenia	na	86	85	87	76	85	94	90	85	79	92	89	79	93	86	80		
South Africa	na	55	55	54	51	56	59	57	52	51	48	58	62	59	51	55		
Spain	na	63	63	63	61	54	71	69	60	48	66	66	57	70	62	53		
Sweden	na	37	42	31	39	36	36	39	43	25	38	41	29	44	40	23		
Switzerland	na	na	na	na	na	na	na	na	na	na	na	na	na	na	na	na		
Taiwan	na	na	na	na	na	na	na	na	na	na	na	na	na	na	na	na		
Tanzania	na	88	89	86	88	86	92	89	90	78	88	89	83	91	87	83		
Turkey	na	90	92	88	87	92	94	92	87	87	92	89	89	93	89	89		
Uganda	na	75	74	77	74	77	74	79	72	88	81	88	77	71	78	77		
Ukraine	na	66	65	68	60	62	74	76	63	71	67	66	68	66	68	80		
United States	na	53	61	44	59	50	51	65	57	46	56	56	45	59	52	52		
Uruguay	na	na	na	na	na	na	na	na	na	na	na	na	na	na	na	na		
Venezuela	na	na	na	na	na	na	na	na	na	na	na	na	na	na	na	na		
Vietnam	na	88	89	87	91	88	86	87	90	90	85	89	88	93	87	83		
Zimbabwe	na	69	64	73	62	73	77	71	65	70	73	65	66	69	68	79		
Total	na	67	69	66	64	66	71	72	67	60	70	68	66	72	68	57	Total	67

C039) WORK: IS A DUTY TOWARDS SOCIETY

Do you agree or disagree with the following statement: "Work is a duty towards society?"

Strongly agree / Agree (%)   (WVS: V100; EVS: V93)

Country	Wave 1990	Wave 2000	Gender Male	Gender Female	Age 16-29	Age 30-49	Age 50+	Education Lower	Education Middle	Education Upper	Income Lower	Income Middle	Income Upper	Values Mat	Values Mixed	Values Postm.
Albania	na	64	66	61	61	61	71	63	61	70	63	60	67	65	65	55
Algeria	na	na	na	na	na	na	na	na	na	na	na	na	na	na	na	na
Argentina	na	79	78	79	69	79	88	86	68	69	87	79	71	86	80	71
Armenia	na	na	na	na	na	na	na	na	na	na	na	na	na	na	na	na
Australia	na	na	na	na	na	na	na	na	na	na	na	na	na	na	na	na
Austria	na	na	na	na	na	na	na	na	na	na	na	na	na	na	na	na
Azerbaijan	na	na	na	na	na	na	na	na	na	na	na	na	na	na	na	na
Bangladesh	na	97	96	97	98	96	96	96	97	99	97	96	97	98	96	95
Belarus	na	63	60	66	46	59	81	77	59	55	66	63	57	68	62	40
Belgium	na	62	65	59	55	53	73	69	63	56	65	65	60	64	64	56
Bosnia and Herz.	na	49	45	52	44	49	54	55	47	51	53	49	46	45	52	49
Brazil	na	na	na	na	na	na	na	na	na	na	na	na	na	na	na	na
Bulgaria	na	75	72	79	54	73	87	86	70	69	81	78	70	75	76	73
Canada	na	65	68	63	54	62	76	75	65	59	70	68	58	74	69	56
Chile	na	68	70	67	67	68	71	71	68	64	68	72	66	71	68	68
China	na	86	87	84	75	87	92	85	86	90	85	88	84	84	87	81
Colombia	na	na	na	na	na	na	na	na	na	na	na	na	na	na	na	na
Croatia	na	61	55	67	52	65	64	63	60	63	73	57	59	68	59	63
Czech Republic	na	63	59	67	52	53	77	66	60	57	70	65	56	67	64	54
Denmark	na	70	76	64	70	62	78	77	71	56	76	66	66	82	73	52
Dominican Rep.	na	na	na	na	na	na	na	na	na	na	na	na	na	na	na	na
Egypt	na	na	na	na	na	na	na	na	na	na	na	na	na	na	na	na
El Salvador	na	na	na	na	na	na	na	na	na	na	na	na	na	na	na	na
Estonia	na	60	58	62	45	54	74	65	59	54	60	69	53	62	60	43
Finland	na	62	59	64	53	50	76	66	59	52	65	60	60	63	62	53
France	na	56	61	52	47	45	71	62	48	48	61	57	51	64	58	43
Georgia	na	na	na	na	na	na	na	na	na	na	na	na	na	na	na	na
Germany	na	64	67	61	55	61	70	64	63	68	63	63	67	65	65	61
Great Britain	na	49	50	48	46	44	58	51	51	45	56	44	44	na	na	na
Greece	na	49	46	51	35	54	73	77	49	44	57	50	40	54	49	46
Hungary	na	70	68	71	67	62	79	72	67	60	63	69	74	72	68	84
Iceland	na	59	65	52	43	55	77	64	59	45	67	59	50	65	59	37
India	na	82	83	80	81	83	80	78	84	85	72	82	85	80	85	91
Indonesia	na	na	na	na	na	na	na	na	na	na	na	na	na	na	na	na
Iran	na	na	na	na	na	na	na	na	na	na	na	na	na	na	na	na
Ireland	na	60	64	56	49	59	72	67	57	57	66	65	55	62	60	54
Israel	na	70	72	68	65	70	75	78	70	65	72	73	63	74	70	76
Italy	na	68	69	66	54	64	79	74	62	64	72	68	66	69	69	65
Japan	na	61	66	56	41	52	77	74	58	61	61	62	63	69	60	59
Jordan	na	na	na	na	na	na	na	na	na	na	na	na	na	na	na	na
Korea, South	na	61	66	56	48	61	75	71	63	56	63	56	61	62	61	49
Latvia	na	67	65	69	49	62	79	72	68	60	71	73	60	71	66	64
Lithuania	na	45	41	49	34	46	52	47	46	38	43	57	40	47	44	52
Luxembourg	na	69	71	67	65	62	79	75	69	58	68	72	70	72	68	65
Macedonia	na	67	67	67	62	67	72	74	63	64	75	61	64	73	63	74
Malta	na	88	86	90	84	84	93	90	87	85	87	89	83	85	90	84
Mexico	na	78	78	78	75	78	83	81	76	72	79	79	77	80	78	76
Moldova	na	53	49	55	42	48	67	64	52	44	61	58	45	55	50	44
Montenegro	na	54	58	51	39	53	64	61	46	57	52	53	56	54	55	54
Morocco	na	96	96	96	95	96	98	96	94	94	96	93	96	98	96	89
Netherlands	na	59	62	56	60	46	71	74	56	48	65	60	48	73	60	48
New Zealand	na	na	na	na	na	na	na	na	na	na	na	na	na	na	na	na
Nigeria	na	na	na	na	na	na	na	na	na	na	na	na	na	na	na	na
Northern Ireland	na	50	48	53	47	44	58	56	46	46	53	48	47	57	50	43
Norway	na	na	na	na	na	na	na	na	na	na	na	na	na	na	na	na
Pakistan	na	na	na	na	na	na	na	na	na	na	na	na	na	na	na	na
Peru	na	84	84	85	83	85	87	86	87	80	88	85	76	86	83	89
Philippines	na	76	74	79	76	77	77	76	76	78	76	77	76	75	77	78
Poland	na	73	74	73	59	70	85	79	66	65	76	73	66	72	73	72
Portugal	na	86	83	89	78	87	90	90	77	80	91	82	83	88	84	90
Puerto Rico	na	85	86	85	74	84	92	91	88	83	88	87	80	87	87	80
Romania	na	79	79	80	67	75	90	88	75	75	86	80	74	82	79	63
Russian Fed.	na	56	53	58	36	52	72	71	53	55	60	58	51	60	52	43
Serbia	na	65	62	67	52	62	73	68	65	60	70	67	65	66	64	55
Singapore	na	75	76	74	75	75	76	77	77	59	78	80	69	76	76	64
Slovakia	na	63	58	68	54	61	72	66	62	61	68	61	64	64	64	61
Slovenia	na	76	75	77	60	74	90	86	76	61	83	83	63	85	77	70
South Africa	na	77	78	75	74	79	76	78	76	72	79	78	75	77	76	79
Spain	na	63	63	63	53	57	75	71	56	55	71	66	56	71	63	53
Sweden	na	58	62	55	53	53	67	71	55	53	63	56	53	67	63	41
Switzerland	na	na	na	na	na	na	na	na	na	na	na	na	na	na	na	na
Taiwan	na	na	na	na	na	na	na	na	na	na	na	na	na	na	na	na
Tanzania	na	97	97	97	97	98	98	97	98	98	97	98	99	98	98	100
Turkey	na	89	91	87	86	91	93	91	87	81	91	90	83	93	90	83
Uganda	na	80	83	78	81	80	82	78	82	79	82	86	84	75	84	80
Ukraine	na	53	47	58	27	51	70	73	50	49	58	51	49	53	55	46
United States	na	58	60	56	61	53	62	71	59	53	63	58	50	60	58	57
Uruguay	na	na	na	na	na	na	na	na	na	na	na	na	na	na	na	na
Venezuela	na	na	na	na	na	na	na	na	na	na	na	na	na	na	na	na
Vietnam	na	95	96	94	93	96	95	94	97	100	95	95	96	96	97	94
Zimbabwe	na	85	86	85	83	85	92	84	87	100	81	89	90	87	84	89
Total	na	69	69	68	63	66	76	75	66	62	72	70	65	71	69	62

RANKING

Country	2000
Tanzania	97
Bangladesh	97
Morocco	96
Vietnam	95
Turkey	89
Malta	88
Portugal	86
China	86
Zimbabwe	85
Puerto Rico	85
Peru	84
India	82
Uganda	80
Romania	79
Argentina	79
Mexico	78
South Africa	77
Philippines	76
Slovenia	76
Bulgaria	75
Singapore	75
Poland	73
Denmark	70
Hungary	70
Israel	70
Luxembourg	69
Chile	68
Italy	68
Latvia	67
Macedonia	67
Canada	65
Serbia	65
Germany	64
Albania	64
Spain	63
Belarus	63
Slovakia	63
Czech Republic	63
Belgium	62
Finland	62
Croatia	61
Korea, South	61
Japan	61
Ireland	60
Estonia	60
Netherlands	59
Iceland	59
Sweden	58
United States	58
France	56
Russian Fed.	56
Montenegro	54
Ukraine	53
Moldova	53
Northern Ireland	50
Great Britain	49
Greece	49
Bosnia and Herz.	49
Lithuania	45
Total	69

C040) WORK: PEOPLE SHOULD NOT HAVE TO WORK

Do you agree or disagree with the following statement: "People should not have to work if they don't want to?"

Strongly agree / Agree (%)

(WVS: V101; EVS: V94)

Country	Wave 1990	Wave 2000	Gender Male	Gender Female	Age 16-29	Age 30-49	Age 50+	Education Lower	Education Middle	Education Upper	Income Lower	Income Middle	Income Upper	Values Mat	Values Mixed	Values Postm.
Albania	na	44	46	43	37	44	51	48	43	37	45	45	42	47	42	30
Algeria	na	na	na	na	na	na	na	na	na	na	na	na	na	na	na	na
Argentina	na	20	20	20	26	20	14	20	19	21	21	21	17	14	21	21
Armenia	na	na	na	na	na	na	na	na	na	na	na	na	na	na	na	na
Australia	na	na	na	na	na	na	na	na	na	na	na	na	na	na	na	na
Austria	na	na	na	na	na	na	na	na	na	na	na	na	na	na	na	na
Azerbaijan	na	na	na	na	na	na	na	na	na	na	na	na	na	na	na	na
Bangladesh	na	38	37	40	39	41	24	41	38	34	37	42	35	35	41	44
Belarus	na	54	57	51	61	55	45	55	55	46	51	51	62	57	49	61
Belgium	na	30	29	32	35	35	24	24	32	33	24	28	36	25	30	37
Bosnia and Herz.	na	36	34	38	38	37	34	35	37	35	42	36	32	35	37	40
Brazil	na	na	na	na	na	na	na	na	na	na	na	na	na	na	na	na
Bulgaria	na	33	36	31	50	36	23	19	39	45	27	28	44	30	36	43
Canada	na	14	14	15	21	16	9	10	14	17	12	14	16	11	12	18
Chile	na	32	31	32	31	33	30	33	31	29	34	31	27	31	32	29
China	na	31	31	31	30	35	23	26	33	46	30	28	36	32	30	45
Colombia	na	na	na	na	na	na	na	na	na	na	na	na	na	na	na	na
Croatia	na	22	25	19	30	16	24	18	24	27	28	21	20	17	24	18
Czech Republic	na	32	37	27	41	36	23	30	32	41	21	34	40	24	32	45
Denmark	na	9	10	9	11	11	7	8	15	10	7	12	10	6	8	16
Dominican Rep.	na	na	na	na	na	na	na	na	na	na	na	na	na	na	na	na
Egypt	na	na	na	na	na	na	na	na	na	na	na	na	na	na	na	na
El Salvador	na	na	na	na	na	na	na	na	na	na	na	na	na	na	na	na
Estonia	na	33	36	31	41	36	26	31	34	35	36	28	36	33	32	45
Finland	na	27	31	22	34	28	20	28	25	22	28	30	23	30	25	28
France	na	33	30	37	39	38	26	29	38	39	32	32	37	31	32	41
Georgia	na	na	na	na	na	na	na	na	na	na	na	na	na	na	na	na
Germany	na	20	18	21	27	19	18	22	20	8	24	20	18	22	20	18
Great Britain	na	19	17	21	22	18	19	21	19	17	24	15	20	na	na	na
Greece	na	29	30	28	32	29	22	24	28	30	27	29	33	26	29	33
Hungary	na	26	28	24	34	26	20	26	25	25	29	24	25	23	29	26
Iceland	na	42	46	37	50	39	37	40	42	43	41	41	41	41	42	44
India	na	41	40	42	40	42	41	44	38	38	39	46	38	41	40	36
Indonesia	na	na	na	na	na	na	na	na	na	na	na	na	na	na	na	na
Iran	na	na	na	na	na	na	na	na	na	na	na	na	na	na	na	na
Ireland	na	28	25	32	34	28	23	28	29	28	30	27	30	31	26	34
Israel	na	42	44	40	51	39	35	41	43	42	44	39	39	52	39	40
Italy	na	24	21	27	25	28	20	24	25	25	24	22	25	23	23	26
Japan	na	21	23	18	41	23	10	12	18	32	17	19	22	20	20	30
Jordan	na	na	na	na	na	na	na	na	na	na	na	na	na	na	na	na
Korea, South	na	34	28	40	41	33	27	40	32	36	33	33	36	32	36	38
Latvia	na	34	36	32	50	40	23	26	35	41	32	30	40	32	36	34
Lithuania	na	38	41	37	45	42	30	30	41	40	34	42	41	37	38	45
Luxembourg	na	30	35	24	36	31	25	24	29	45	30	26	39	25	29	38
Macedonia	na	31	33	29	42	29	23	34	31	24	35	28	27	26	33	33
Malta	na	47	42	52	51	51	40	44	49	44	49	46	45	49	46	48
Mexico	na	31	31	31	35	28	30	32	31	25	36	30	24	27	33	32
Moldova	na	40	45	36	49	38	36	43	41	36	42	37	45	36	48	38
Montenegro	na	39	39	40	50	38	35	36	43	39	42	41	39	40	39	38
Morocco	na	48	45	50	50	45	52	49	47	34	48	49	46	52	43	54
Netherlands	na	20	23	18	20	24	16	14	21	26	18	19	25	11	18	33
New Zealand	na	na	na	na	na	na	na	na	na	na	na	na	na	na	na	na
Nigeria	na	na	na	na	na	na	na	na	na	na	na	na	na	na	na	na
Northern Ireland	na	24	25	24	26	26	22	23	25	24	27	19	21	30	24	17
Norway	na	na	na	na	na	na	na	na	na	na	na	na	na	na	na	na
Pakistan	na	na	na	na	na	na	na	na	na	na	na	na	na	na	na	na
Peru	na	24	25	24	26	23	24	27	25	21	24	27	21	26	25	20
Philippines	na	39	39	40	35	40	44	43	39	34	38	38	41	38	39	38
Poland	na	67	72	61	77	66	60	67	67	64	64	68	68	59	72	68
Portugal	na	16	17	15	16	19	15	16	16	21	17	20	14	18	15	20
Puerto Rico	na	28	30	26	32	32	22	30	31	25	32	26	27	26	29	25
Romania	na	56	57	54	58	54	56	62	56	42	62	59	46	61	51	53
Russian Fed.	na	36	40	32	49	38	23	30	35	39	32	33	40	33	38	39
Serbia	na	39	41	37	54	42	30	34	39	46	35	41	41	33	44	52
Singapore	na	26	27	26	25	28	26	25	26	32	22	23	29	23	28	27
Slovakia	na	22	24	20	29	23	15	17	23	29	17	21	24	20	23	38
Slovenia	na	17	21	13	25	15	12	15	19	9	15	15	20	11	17	21
South Africa	na	32	31	33	33	35	22	34	29	34	33	33	27	26	34	50
Spain	na	26	27	24	31	27	21	23	27	32	21	28	31	22	28	28
Sweden	na	12	11	12	14	12	10	10	12	12	12	12	11	7	12	12
Switzerland	na	na	na	na	na	na	na	na	na	na	na	na	na	na	na	na
Taiwan	na	na	na	na	na	na	na	na	na	na	na	na	na	na	na	na
Tanzania	na	24	23	26	21	26	25	27	20	22	30	22	20	25	25	24
Turkey	na	42	41	44	44	41	39	46	37	37	50	40	32	31	44	47
Uganda	na	32	28	36	31	35	29	29	34	33	31	30	42	34	32	29
Ukraine	na	39	42	36	50	43	28	29	39	42	31	43	43	33	43	65
United States	na	22	24	19	31	19	18	23	22	21	21	22	23	20	22	21
Uruguay	na	na	na	na	na	na	na	na	na	na	na	na	na	na	na	na
Venezuela	na	na	na	na	na	na	na	na	na	na	na	na	na	na	na	na
Vietnam	na	62	63	62	60	63	63	62	62	71	59	64	62	69	64	53
Zimbabwe	na	36	37	36	41	34	27	36	37	na	39	37	24	42	30	56
Total	na	32	33	31	37	33	26	31	33	31	32	32	33	33	32	31

RANKING

Country	2000
Poland	67
Vietnam	62
Romania	56
Belarus	54
Morocco	48
Malta	47
Albania	44
Turkey	42
Israel	42
Iceland	42
India	41
Moldova	40
Montenegro	39
Philippines	39
Serbia	39
Ukraine	39
Bangladesh	38
Lithuania	38
Bosnia and Herz.	36
Zimbabwe	36
Russian Fed.	36
Korea, South	34
Latvia	34
Bulgaria	33
France	33
Estonia	33
Uganda	32
South Africa	32
Czech Republic	32
Chile	32
China	31
Mexico	31
Macedonia	31
Belgium	30
Luxembourg	30
Greece	29
Ireland	28
Puerto Rico	28
Finland	27
Singapore	26
Spain	26
Hungary	26
Northern Ireland	24
Italy	24
Peru	24
Tanzania	24
Croatia	22
United States	22
Slovakia	22
Japan	21
Netherlands	20
Germany	20
Argentina	20
Great Britain	19
Slovenia	17
Portugal	16
Canada	14
Sweden	12
Denmark	9
Total	32

C041) WORK: SHOULD ALWAYS COME FIRST

Do you agree or disagree with the following statement: "Work should always come first, even if it means less spare time?"

Strongly agree / Agree (%) (WVS: V102; EVS: V95)

Country	Wave		Gender		Age			Education			Income			Values			RANKING Country	2000
	1990	2000	Male	Female	16-29	30-49	50+	Lower	Middle	Upper	Lower	Middle	Upper	Mat	Mixed	Postm.		
Albania	na	88	89	87	84	87	94	90	88	84	89	87	89	92	87	78	Morocco	94
Algeria	na	na	na	na	na	na	na	na	na	na	na	na	na	na	na	na	Bangladesh	93
Argentina	na	77	78	76	69	78	84	85	68	61	82	80	69	82	79	71	Albania	88
Armenia	na	na	na	na	na	na	na	na	na	na	na	na	na	na	na	na	Tanzania	87
Australia	na	na	na	na	na	na	na	na	na	na	na	na	na	na	na	na	Zimbabwe	86
Austria	na	na	na	na	na	na	na	na	na	na	na	na	na	na	na	na	China	84
Azerbaijan	na	na	na	na	na	na	na	na	na	na	na	na	na	na	na	na	Philippines	83
Bangladesh	na	93	91	94	92	93	94	92	95	92	92	90	98	93	92	90	Uganda	81
Belarus	na	36	35	36	22	32	50	46	33	27	39	35	29	42	31	20	Romania	80
Belgium	na	33	33	34	19	24	48	48	33	23	45	39	24	37	35	26	Macedonia	79
Bosnia and Herz.	na	67	69	66	63	67	71	71	69	60	73	66	66	72	66	62	Vietnam	79
Brazil	na	na	na	na	na	na	na	na	na	na	na	na	na	na	na	na	Hungary	78
Bulgaria	na	53	53	53	46	48	60	52	53	55	56	52	53	49	57	56	Argentina	77
Canada	na	45	47	43	37	36	59	63	42	33	54	43	33	54	48	36	Peru	75
Chile	na	53	59	47	47	51	60	61	51	39	58	53	43	54	55	44	South Africa	73
China	na	84	82	85	72	85	90	88	82	67	87	84	78	84	82	71	India	72
Colombia	na	na	na	na	na	na	na	na	na	na	na	na	na	na	na	na	Turkey	72
Croatia	na	54	55	53	32	55	67	61	51	43	77	49	45	58	56	44	Mexico	70
Czech Republic	na	56	55	57	40	51	68	57	55	52	64	56	49	62	54	51	Montenegro	69
Denmark	na	49	54	45	33	36	72	57	41	38	60	46	41	55	53	30	Bosnia and Herz.	67
Dominican Rep.	na	na	na	na	na	na	na	na	na	na	na	na	na	na	na	na	Israel	67
Egypt	na	na	na	na	na	na	na	na	na	na	na	na	na	na	na	na	Serbia	66
El Salvador	na	na	na	na	na	na	na	na	na	na	na	na	na	na	na	na	Moldova	65
Estonia	na	48	48	47	34	41	61	54	44	48	50	50	46	46	50	37	Poland	62
Finland	na	39	37	40	21	28	59	47	29	28	45	36	35	44	39	29	Slovakia	61
France	na	34	38	31	21	23	51	43	27	18	45	34	27	45	35	16	Czech Republic	56
Georgia	na	na	na	na	na	na	na	na	na	na	na	na	na	na	na	na	Slovenia	56
Germany	na	47	52	44	39	45	54	49	46	49	51	51	50	47	49	47	Lithuania	55
Great Britain	na	26	27	26	24	18	37	36	19	18	35	25	15	na	na	na	Singapore	54
Greece	na	38	40	37	24	42	64	63	44	29	44	38	36	45	38	30	Croatia	54
Hungary	na	78	75	80	69	73	87	78	77	76	78	77	77	80	77	78	Bulgaria	53
Iceland	na	34	36	32	19	26	57	44	30	18	41	33	25	39	34	18	Chile	53
India	na	72	72	72	70	74	72	71	71	75	66	74	73	74	71	72	Puerto Rico	52
Indonesia	na	na	na	na	na	na	na	na	na	na	na	na	na	na	na	na	Russian Fed.	50
Iran	na	na	na	na	na	na	na	na	na	na	na	na	na	na	na	na	Latvia	50
Ireland	na	35	38	33	25	30	50	49	30	22	50	38	26	33	36	34	Italy	50
Israel	na	67	68	67	60	66	78	84	66	58	71	71	61	69	68	65	Spain	50
Italy	na	50	53	46	35	40	66	64	41	31	65	47	39	64	50	43	Denmark	49
Japan	na	19	22	17	5	10	33	44	17	13	26	17	17	23	18	10	Estonia	48
Jordan	na	na	na	na	na	na	na	na	na	na	na	na	na	na	na	na	Germany	47
Korea, South	na	39	43	34	22	39	57	60	42	31	44	36	35	42	38	23	Ukraine	47
Latvia	na	50	49	51	28	42	66	62	48	41	56	54	39	54	50	30	Portugal	46
Lithuania	na	55	56	54	40	55	67	65	53	51	64	62	49	52	57	51	Malta	45
Luxembourg	na	40	45	36	29	34	55	49	37	33	51	42	32	49	43	26	Canada	45
Macedonia	na	79	79	79	72	80	84	88	77	69	86	76	74	83	77	74	Luxembourg	40
Malta	na	45	50	40	30	40	61	61	41	30	58	41	36	45	48	30	Finland	39
Mexico	na	70	71	68	63	70	79	78	64	49	78	68	62	75	69	56	Korea, South	39
Moldova	na	65	64	65	54	63	75	75	61	61	74	69	59	62	68	48	Greece	38
Montenegro	na	69	69	70	58	69	77	79	64	60	84	71	71	77	64	53	United States	36
Morocco	na	94	95	93	93	94	96	96	88	85	96	95	91	97	92	89	Belarus	36
Netherlands	na	23	25	21	13	14	38	37	18	14	31	18	19	37	23	15	Ireland	35
New Zealand	na	na	na	na	na	na	na	na	na	na	na	na	na	na	na	na	France	34
Nigeria	na	na	na	na	na	na	na	na	na	na	na	na	na	na	na	na	Iceland	34
Northern Ireland	na	31	33	29	20	24	41	38	26	22	37	34	22	37	29	27	Belgium	33
Norway	na	na	na	na	na	na	na	na	na	na	na	na	na	na	na	na	Northern Ireland	31
Pakistan	na	na	na	na	na	na	na	na	na	na	na	na	na	na	na	na	Sweden	29
Peru	na	75	74	75	71	77	76	80	76	68	78	75	67	80	73	78	Great Britain	26
Philippines	na	83	83	83	80	85	84	84	84	80	88	82	80	84	82	81	Netherlands	23
Poland	na	62	66	59	41	61	76	71	50	52	70	60	52	64	61	57	Japan	19
Portugal	na	46	47	46	36	46	53	53	36	24	58	50	50	43	49	40		
Puerto Rico	na	52	58	48	39	42	66	77	63	43	68	49	44	57	56	40		
Romania	na	80	79	81	62	80	90	86	77	78	83	83	77	85	79	63		
Russian Fed.	na	50	53	48	36	48	62	62	50	46	53	53	45	54	48	53		
Serbia	na	66	66	66	48	63	77	71	65	60	74	67	64	68	64	63		
Singapore	na	54	58	50	48	54	74	59	54	39	61	56	49	55	54	53		
Slovakia	na	61	58	64	48	60	73	66	60	50	65	61	60	65	61	47		
Slovenia	na	56	56	55	30	52	77	71	53	37	67	56	45	70	55	48		
South Africa	na	73	73	74	78	69	75	76	71	54	78	80	61	76	72	75		
Spain	na	50	49	50	40	41	63	60	42	32	63	46	44	56	51	33		
Sweden	na	29	34	24	16	23	42	46	27	18	34	29	21	45	31	18		
Switzerland	na	na	na	na	na	na	na	na	na	na	na	na	na	na	na	na		
Taiwan	na	na	na	na	na	na	na	na	na	na	na	na	na	na	na	na		
Tanzania	na	87	88	86	85	87	91	87	87	85	88	84	90	86	87	96		
Turkey	na	72	71	73	65	76	83	81	62	51	81	70	58	76	73	64		
Uganda	na	81	86	76	77	83	89	78	81	91	80	87	84	81	80	84		
Ukraine	na	47	48	47	27	46	60	56	47	43	52	40	49	49	47	53		
United States	na	36	40	32	36	33	39	51	37	28	42	35	27	36	37	32		
Uruguay	na	na	na	na	na	na	na	na	na	na	na	na	na	na	na	na		
Venezuela	na	na	na	na	na	na	na	na	na	na	na	na	na	na	na	na		
Vietnam	na	79	80	78	78	78	81	77	81	90	83	80	77	84	81	84		
Zimbabwe	na	86	86	87	84	87	90	89	83	62	87	89	84	84	87	96		
Total	na	56	58	55	50	54	65	66	54	45	63	57	52	63	56	43	Total	56

C059) WORK: EFFICIENCY IS PAID MORE

Imagine two secretaries, of the same age, doing practically the same job. One finds out that the other earns considerably more than she does. The better paid secretary, however, is quicker, more efficient and more reliable at her job. In your opinion, is it fair or not fair that one secretary is paid more than the other? (% "fair")   (WVS: V103; EVS: V96)

Country	Wave 1990	Wave 2000	Gender Male	Gender Female	Age 16-29	Age 30-49	Age 50+	Education Lower	Education Middle	Education Upper	Income Lower	Income Middle	Income Upper	Values Mat	Values Mixed	Values Postm.	RANKING Country	RANKING 2000
Albania	na	83	83	82	86	81	83	83	81	86	82	83	85	84	84	74	Egypt	97
Algeria	na	82	81	83	81	82	84	81	81	84	82	87	81	77	85	83	Czech Republic	96
Argentina	83	60	60	60	54	60	66	53	71	69	53	58	69	54	60	66	Morocco	95
Armenia	na	94	94	94	94	96	92	88	94	97	97	94	88	94	95	92	Armenia	94
Australia	na	82	83	81	80	82	84	75	82	88	79	84	85	83	81	84	Vietnam	94
Austria	90	89	90	88	88	88	91	87	90	93	86	89	89	82	90	88	Russian Fed.	93
Azerbaijan	na	93	93	93	94	91	95	94	93	93	92	94	94	92	94	93	Singapore	93
Bangladesh	na	82	80	84	83	81	80	78	86	87	86	80	82	83	81	83	Azerbaijan	93
Belarus	93	85	85	85	87	87	82	81	86	90	82	87	88	85	85	89	China	93
Belgium	72	70	74	65	68	69	71	61	69	77	66	69	75	61	72	77	Taiwan	92
Bosnia and Herz.	na	89	90	87	90	88	88	85	88	94	86	87	94	87	90	83	Georgia	92
Brazil	78	77	79	74	74	76	82	74	77	84	73	75	82	73	77	84	Ukraine	92
Bulgaria	86	89	91	88	85	93	88	87	89	94	87	89	93	91	89	98	Slovakia	91
Canada	82	84	87	80	84	82	85	79	82	91	76	84	89	78	84	83	United States	91
Chile	62	67	69	66	69	66	68	61	68	79	62	69	73	70	66	66	Dominican Rep.	91
China	97	93	95	91	90	92	97	93	93	95	91	93	96	96	90	87	New Zealand	90
Colombia	na	82	83	81	82	82	83	77	81	87	76	82	86	76	82	79	Bulgaria	89
Croatia	na	88	92	84	85	90	88	80	92	95	81	89	92	87	87	93	Romania	89
Czech Republic	44	96	96	97	96	97	97	95	98	97	95	97	97	96	97	97	Slovenia	89
Denmark	76	82	87	78	83	83	81	79	93	83	77	82	91	74	83	79	Austria	89
Dominican Rep.	na	91	89	91	88	95	91	88	87	92	89	90	95	86	90	95	Bosnia and Herz.	89
Egypt	na	97	96	98	97	97	96	96	98	98	97	97	97	97	97	98	Croatia	88
El Salvador	na	70	72	68	66	73	72	67	66	83	61	73	82	na	na	na	Poland	88
Estonia	95	85	86	83	83	85	85	80	85	91	78	83	91	85	84	87	Greece	88
Finland	74	76	82	71	79	77	73	71	82	83	71	78	79	75	76	74	Serbia	88
France	79	77	82	72	73	77	78	76	75	81	72	77	81	72	79	77	Japan	88
Georgia	na	92	91	93	92	91	93	92	91	95	91	92	94	93	90	96	Korea, South	87
Germany	96	87	89	85	86	87	87	86	87	93	84	84	92	86	87	89	Germany	87
Great Britain	79	73	75	71	67	72	77	66	76	85	67	69	81	na	na	na	Moldova	87
Greece	na	88	87	88	87	89	88	82	87	90	88	88	88	88	88	86	Iceland	86
Hungary	90	83	87	80	86	85	80	78	92	97	77	81	90	79	89	75	Indonesia	86
Iceland	75	86	90	82	89	87	83	81	92	89	85	84	90	86	87	81	Belarus	85
India	78	63	64	61	62	63	63	58	62	71	68	60	63	65	66	56	Switzerland	85
Indonesia	na	86	87	86	93	87	84	80	86	92	87	87	85	88	87	61	Estonia	85
Iran	na	79	81	77	79	80	81	80	80	83	81	82	77	84	80	75	Canada	84
Ireland	73	65	70	60	71	63	62	53	67	80	53	62	77	53	66	76	Hungary	83
Israel	na	na	na	na	na	na	na	na	na	na	na	na	na	na	na	na	Montenegro	83
Italy	79	78	83	73	78	84	72	69	82	90	75	76	85	75	77	82	Albania	83
Japan	59	88	89	86	86	90	86	76	87	94	86	87	90	84	89	92	Luxembourg	83
Jordan	na	82	81	82	81	81	85	79	84	84	81	85	83	80	83	82	Colombia	82
Korea, South	73	87	87	87	82	86	94	91	89	83	86	90	87	89	86	75	Denmark	82
Latvia	95	81	82	80	80	82	81	71	81	91	78	79	86	78	83	83	Lithuania	82
Lithuania	94	82	83	81	84	79	83	76	82	89	84	78	84	78	84	79	Bangladesh	82
Luxembourg	na	83	84	81	81	82	84	76	85	89	83	82	86	83	82	88	Algeria	82
Macedonia	na	72	72	72	76	73	67	61	74	83	67	72	78	74	72	56	Australia	82
Malta	na	77	80	75	74	76	80	77	76	82	78	78	86	78	75	86	Jordan	82
Mexico	85	78	78	78	81	75	78	75	81	80	72	79	80	78	77	80	Latvia	81
Moldova	na	87	90	84	90	85	86	88	87	86	88	86	90	84	91	85	Iran	79
Montenegro	na	83	82	85	86	85	80	82	84	86	90	86	84	87	81	75	Turkey	78
Morocco	na	95	95	95	95	95	95	95	95	97	92	95	96	98	93	93	Mexico	78
Netherlands	68	76	80	72	72	76	78	69	77	80	67	75	86	68	79	69	Italy	78
New Zealand	na	90	93	88	90	90	90	87	91	94	87	91	95	89	91	94	Nigeria	77
Nigeria	80	77	77	78	77	78	77	74	79	79	78	78	78	80	76	75	Malta	77
Northern Ireland	71	71	72	70	68	71	73	67	72	75	65	69	71	75	71	67	Brazil	77
Norway	54	54	62	48	51	55	56	47	54	62	na	na	na	50	55	57	France	77
Pakistan	na	na	na	na	na	na	na	na	na	na	na	na	na	na	na	na	Puerto Rico	77
Peru	na	76	76	75	76	75	76	73	76	76	73	79	75	79	73	81	Finland	76
Philippines	na	68	70	67	71	65	71	68	68	69	68	66	72	71	67	66	Tanzania	76
Poland	na	88	90	86	91	88	87	85	90	94	86	91	85	85	90	87	Uganda	76
Portugal	74	73	73	73	75	75	70	72	75	83	68	71	72	75	71	73	Netherlands	76
Puerto Rico	na	77	82	74	76	76	78	76	72	79	67	80	81	76	76	80	Peru	76
Romania	88	89	89	90	92	87	90	88	89	93	87	87	93	86	93	93	Sweden	74
Russian Fed.	94	93	94	93	93	94	93	89	93	96	91	93	96	93	93	94	Portugal	73
Serbia	na	88	90	86	88	89	87	80	91	93	85	85	92	85	91	91	Great Britain	73
Singapore	na	93	93	93	92	93	97	92	94	95	88	95	95	96	93	88	Uruguay	72
Slovakia	na	91	92	91	95	90	90	87	92	97	86	91	96	90	93	92	Macedonia	72
Slovenia	91	89	92	87	92	87	90	77	93	97	85	90	97	85	90	92	Northern Ireland	71
South Africa	na	60	59	60	60	61	56	56	61	88	51	61	67	56	61	71	El Salvador	70
Spain	75	66	67	64	65	65	67	63	66	74	63	62	68	66	64	65	Belgium	70
Sweden	62	74	75	74	76	73	75	62	72	89	68	74	83	74	76	71	Philippines	68
Switzerland	69	85	88	82	79	85	88	81	86	87	77	85	90	80	85	89	Chile	67
Taiwan	na	92	92	92	93	94	87	89	91	95	90	91	95	93	93	83	Spain	66
Tanzania	na	76	78	73	76	73	84	75	78	73	71	79	77	75	77	79	Ireland	65
Turkey	72	78	77	79	79	77	79	76	77	86	76	80	81	77	79	78	India	63
Uganda	na	76	71	80	72	79	79	70	79	74	69	80	70	76	76	77	Argentina	60
Ukraine	na	92	94	90	94	93	90	79	94	93	90	93	92	90	93	97	South Africa	60
United States	86	91	92	91	88	92	93	87	90	94	89	90	96	88	92	91	Zimbabwe	59
Uruguay	na	72	74	71	70	70	75	68	79	75	70	71	75	69	73	72	Norway	54
Venezuela	na	na	na	na	na	na	na	na	na	na	na	na	na	na	na	na		
Vietnam	na	94	94	93	94	94	93	93	94	96	94	94	93	96	93	92		
Zimbabwe	na	59	60	59	59	59	61	57	61	100	53	60	69	55	63	59		
Total	79	81	83	80	81	82	82	77	83	86	79	82	85	82	82	81	Total	81

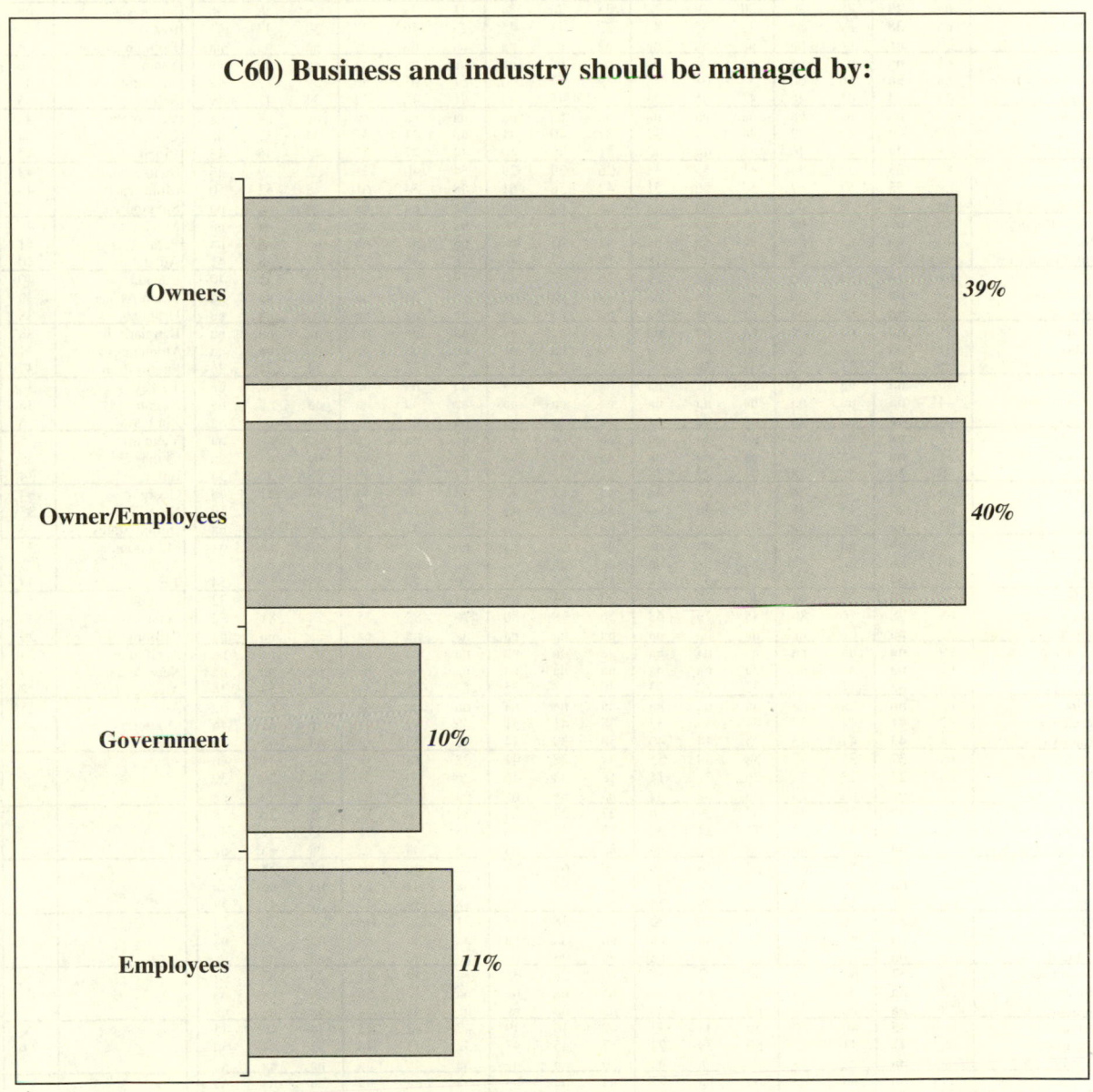

C60) Business and industry should be managed by:

Owners — 39%

Owner/Employees — 40%

Government — 10%

Employees — 11%

C060) BUSINESS MANAGEMENT: OWNERS AND EMPLOYEES

There is a lot of discussion about how business and industry should be managed.
Which of these four statements comes closest to your opinion?

Owners & employees participate (%) (WVS: V104)

Country	Wave 1990	Wave 2000	Gender Male	Gender Female	Age 16-29	Age 30-49	Age 50+	Education Lower	Education Middle	Education Upper	Income Lower	Income Middle	Income Upper	Values Mat	Values Mixed	Values Postm.
Albania	na	25	26	23	28	25	22	23	24	32	22	28	25	21	29	19
Algeria	na	27	26	28	29	25	25	25	27	27	27	27	23	25	26	31
Argentina	47	45	45	45	44	48	43	47	43	45	49	44	44	40	44	50
Armenia	na	31	28	34	36	29	28	26	33	28	31	32	30	31	29	56
Australia	na	40	39	41	44	44	32	34	36	50	37	43	44	36	37	47
Austria	42	na	na	na	na	na	na	na	na	na	na	na	na	na	na	na
Azerbaijan	na	29	28	30	30	29	24	25	26	34	21	34	32	28	28	36
Bangladesh	na	38	39	35	41	35	40	33	41	45	23	46	38	30	43	41
Belarus	23	na	na	na	na	na	na	na	na	na	na	na	na	na	na	na
Belgium	44	na	na	na	na	na	na	na	na	na	na	na	na	na	na	na
Bosnia and Herz.	na	58	56	60	54	61	58	59	57	60	51	61	56	59	57	52
Brazil	43	44	41	46	47	45	34	41	45	48	41	48	42	34	47	49
Bulgaria	23	na	na	na	na	na	na	na	na	na	na	na	na	na	na	na
Canada	37	40	37	42	44	44	32	37	40	41	43	41	37	33	37	48
Chile	47	44	43	46	47	44	42	41	48	40	44	47	45	42	45	45
China	40	35	35	34	41	33	33	26	39	29	34	40	31	32	39	36
Colombia	na	55	54	57	57	56	51	47	56	61	48	54	61	48	52	50
Croatia	na	na	na	na	na	na	na	na	na	na	na	na	na	na	na	na
Czech Republic	43	na	na	na	na	na	na	na	na	na	na	na	na	na	na	na
Denmark	46	na	na	na	na	na	na	na	na	na	na	na	na	na	na	na
Dominican Rep.	na	46	34	54	51	39	18	19	47	48	48	48	37	45	48	41
Egypt	na	34	32	36	38	32	29	26	37	48	29	31	39	32	35	40
El Salvador	na	na	na	na	na	na	na	na	na	na	na	na	na	na	na	na
Estonia	26	na	na	na	na	na	na	na	na	na	na	na	na	na	na	na
Finland	51	na	na	na	na	na	na	na	na	na	na	na	na	na	na	na
France	61	na	na	na	na	na	na	na	na	na	na	na	na	na	na	na
Georgia	na	34	31	36	33	39	28	34	32	37	34	33	35	34	34	26
Germany	46	na	na	na	na	na	na	na	na	na	na	na	na	na	na	na
Great Britain	44	na	na	na	na	na	na	na	na	na	na	na	na	na	na	na
Greece	na	na	na	na	na	na	na	na	na	na	na	na	na	na	na	na
Hungary	47	na	na	na	na	na	na	na	na	na	na	na	na	na	na	na
Iceland	37	na	na	na	na	na	na	na	na	na	na	na	na	na	na	na
India	48	30	31	28	31	29	28	22	33	39	27	23	38	23	36	34
Indonesia	na	48	48	48	47	53	43	43	47	52	53	46	44	44	51	48
Iran	na	46	45	48	47	46	44	38	48	49	44	50	49	39	49	59
Ireland	42	na	na	na	na	na	na	na	na	na	na	na	na	na	na	na
Israel	na	na	na	na	na	na	na	na	na	na	na	na	na	na	na	na
Italy	46	na	na	na	na	na	na	na	na	na	na	na	na	na	na	na
Japan	47	54	51	57	57	52	54	55	53	54	56	49	56	52	55	54
Jordan	na	36	28	44	40	38	24	30	41	41	35	38	35	34	38	32
Korea, South	68	78	76	80	85	79	68	56	78	80	76	83	75	74	81	82
Latvia	31	na	na	na	na	na	na	na	na	na	na	na	na	na	na	na
Lithuania	19	na	na	na	na	na	na	na	na	na	na	na	na	na	na	na
Luxembourg	na	na	na	na	na	na	na	na	na	na	na	na	na	na	na	na
Macedonia	na	33	31	34	33	32	33	30	33	35	29	35	34	29	34	38
Malta	na	na	na	na	na	na	na	na	na	na	na	na	na	na	na	na
Mexico	42	41	44	37	44	39	37	38	41	51	35	41	42	38	41	46
Moldova	na	43	41	45	45	44	40	50	39	44	42	43	43	44	45	35
Montenegro	na	37	35	39	38	39	35	34	38	41	32	38	39	33	41	46
Morocco	na	22	23	21	26	21	14	18	33	46	26	30	23	18	23	39
Netherlands	57	na	na	na	na	na	na	na	na	na	na	na	na	na	na	na
New Zealand	na	29	26	31	37	29	26	27	27	33	32	28	27	31	26	38
Nigeria	31	33	34	32	33	34	30	32	31	38	35	32	31	33	33	32
Northern Ireland	36	na	na	na	na	na	na	na	na	na	na	na	na	na	na	na
Norway	62	59	57	62	62	58	59	59	61	58	na	na	na	61	58	66
Pakistan	na	na	na	na	na	na	na	na	na	na	na	na	na	na	na	na
Peru	na	41	41	41	43	39	38	35	40	45	38	39	47	37	41	44
Philippines	na	29	30	29	31	28	30	29	28	33	31	26	33	29	30	24
Poland	42	na	na	na	na	na	na	na	na	na	na	na	na	na	na	na
Portugal	36	na	na	na	na	na	na	na	na	na	na	na	na	na	na	na
Puerto Rico	na	37	34	38	40	37	35	40	34	38	34	39	37	24	35	47
Romania	33	na	na	na	na	na	na	na	na	na	na	na	na	na	na	na
Russian Fed.	18	na	na	na	na	na	na	na	na	na	na	na	na	na	na	na
Serbia	na	45	40	50	49	43	45	40	46	49	42	48	45	44	46	45
Singapore	na	42	41	43	50	39	24	37	45	47	37	43	46	37	44	50
Slovakia	na	na	na	na	na	na	na	na	na	na	na	na	na	na	na	na
Slovenia	37	na	na	na	na	na	na	na	na	na	na	na	na	na	na	na
South Africa	45	39	34	45	37	42	35	42	37	24	42	38	36	44	34	48
Spain	53	46	46	46	47	44	43	44	44	54	46	50	41	49	44	50
Sweden	65	na	na	na	na	na	na	na	na	na	na	na	na	na	na	na
Switzerland	43	43	40	47	48	43	41	43	43	46	43	51	39	39	43	51
Taiwan	na	55	54	56	63	56	46	48	55	61	54	56	59	54	55	71
Tanzania	na	31	30	31	36	31	20	26	38	33	22	35	31	28	32	38
Turkey	38	36	34	39	41	34	33	33	39	43	34	37	42	33	37	41
Uganda	na	30	33	27	33	27	24	26	32	27	31	24	38	29	30	34
Ukraine	na	na	na	na	na	na	na	na	na	na	na	na	na	na	na	na
United States	35	33	32	34	30	36	31	29	31	35	33	33	31	23	32	40
Uruguay	na	38	35	40	42	39	35	36	43	37	41	34	40	26	40	45
Venezuela	na	44	43	46	45	46	40	37	44	53	40	47	50	35	47	52
Vietnam	na	35	37	34	38	34	35	30	42	35	40	34	34	29	39	31
Zimbabwe	na	36	39	33	36	35	38	35	38	44	30	38	45	33	39	33
Total	42	40	38	41	42	40	37	35	41	45	38	41	40	36	41	45

RANKING

Country	2000
Korea, South	78
Norway	59
Bosnia and Herz.	58
Colombia	55
Taiwan	55
Japan	54
Indonesia	48
Iran	46
Dominican Rep.	46
Spain	46
Argentina	45
Serbia	45
Venezuela	44
Chile	44
Brazil	44
Switzerland	43
Moldova	43
Singapore	42
Mexico	41
Peru	41
Australia	40
Canada	40
South Africa	39
Uruguay	38
Bangladesh	38
Montenegro	37
Puerto Rico	37
Turkey	36
Jordan	36
Zimbabwe	36
Vietnam	35
China	35
Egypt	34
Georgia	34
Nigeria	33
United States	33
Macedonia	33
Armenia	31
Tanzania	31
Uganda	30
India	30
Philippines	29
Azerbaijan	29
New Zealand	29
Algeria	27
Albania	25
Morocco	22
Total	40

C060B) BUSINESS MANAGEMENT: OWNERS ALONE

There is a lot of discussion about how business and industry should be managed.

Which of these four statements comes closest to your opinion?

Owners should run their business or appoint the managers (%)

(WVS: V104)

Country	Wave 1990	Wave 2000	Gender Male	Gender Female	Age 16-29	Age 30-49	Age 50+	Education Lower	Education Middle	Education Upper	Income Lower	Income Middle	Income Upper	Values Mat	Values Mixed	Values Postm.
Albania	na	53	52	55	55	53	52	52	54	54	51	51	58	59	50	56
Algeria	na	37	39	36	39	38	32	31	36	43	33	37	45	37	38	38
Argentina	31	29	28	31	26	28	35	25	35	36	24	26	38	35	29	29
Armenia	na	26	32	19	30	27	16	20	23	37	32	20	21	22	29	22
Australia	na	51	52	49	45	48	58	52	56	43	52	47	52	54	54	44
Austria	50	na	na	na	na	na	na	na	na	na	na	na	na	na	na	na
Azerbaijan	na	30	33	27	35	29	19	19	32	27	26	26	36	28	33	33
Bangladesh	na	43	39	48	44	43	39	41	48	42	49	34	51	47	41	35
Belarus	9	na	na	na	na	na	na	na	na	na	na	na	na	na	na	na
Belgium	46	na	na	na	na	na	na	na	na	na	na	na	na	na	na	na
Bosnia and Herz.	na	20	21	18	22	20	17	17	18	25	14	18	28	20	19	23
Brazil	32	35	36	35	33	34	44	35	36	36	35	32	40	40	34	32
Bulgaria	38	na	na	na	na	na	na	na	na	na	na	na	na	na	na	na
Canada	53	52	53	50	47	47	59	52	50	53	43	51	56	59	54	42
Chile	24	41	42	40	40	41	42	40	40	46	40	39	43	47	40	33
China	22	30	32	29	22	34	31	37	28	21	33	25	34	39	25	4
Colombia	na	42	44	41	42	41	47	52	43	34	50	44	35	51	47	49
Croatia	na	na	na	na	na	na	na	na	na	na	na	na	na	na	na	na
Czech Republic	34	na	na	na	na	na	na	na	na	na	na	na	na	na	na	na
Denmark	47	na	na	na	na	na	na	na	na	na	na	na	na	na	na	na
Dominican Rep.	na	44	57	36	40	51	55	65	39	44	38	44	57	45	45	41
Egypt	na	33	35	30	31	33	33	34	31	32	33	32	32	34	32	27
El Salvador	na	na	na	na	na	na	na	na	na	na	na	na	na	na	na	na
Estonia	42	na	na	na	na	na	na	na	na	na	na	na	na	na	na	na
Finland	42	na	na	na	na	na	na	na	na	na	na	na	na	na	na	na
France	24	na	na	na	na	na	na	na	na	na	na	na	na	na	na	na
Georgia	na	33	39	28	41	30	28	32	33	34	29	31	39	34	31	38
Germany	32	na	na	na	na	na	na	na	na	na	na	na	na	na	na	na
Great Britain	44	na	na	na	na	na	na	na	na	na	na	na	na	na	na	na
Greece	na	na	na	na	na	na	na	na	na	na	na	na	na	na	na	na
Hungary	24	na	na	na	na	na	na	na	na	na	na	na	na	na	na	na
Iceland	48	na	na	na	na	na	na	na	na	na	na	na	na	na	na	na
India	22	26	26	26	24	27	27	26	23	27	25	26	26	28	25	18
Indonesia	na	43	43	44	50	37	47	42	44	44	38	44	52	43	44	37
Iran	na	22	23	20	21	22	22	24	22	21	19	18	22	24	20	12
Ireland	43	na	na	na	na	na	na	na	na	na	na	na	na	na	na	na
Israel	na	na	na	na	na	na	na	na	na	na	na	na	na	na	na	na
Italy	43	na	na	na	na	na	na	na	na	na	na	na	na	na	na	na
Japan	44	39	43	35	28	40	43	37	40	38	38	43	38	44	38	35
Jordan	na	36	42	29	32	35	45	41	30	32	38	29	39	39	35	25
Korea, South	23	14	16	12	9	13	21	20	13	15	13	12	17	16	13	4
Latvia	31	na	na	na	na	na	na	na	na	na	na	na	na	na	na	na
Lithuania	38	na	na	na	na	na	na	na	na	na	na	na	na	na	na	na
Luxembourg	na	na	na	na	na	na	na	na	na	na	na	na	na	na	na	na
Macedonia	na	41	43	40	45	45	32	46	38	42	37	43	42	43	40	50
Malta	na	na	na	na	na	na	na	na	na	na	na	na	na	na	na	na
Mexico	47	45	44	46	43	45	50	45	46	40	47	42	47	49	44	40
Moldova	na	21	23	20	23	25	16	13	23	26	18	16	28	20	23	27
Montenegro	na	30	31	30	43	31	21	20	34	41	24	30	38	28	33	24
Morocco	na	49	46	52	45	51	50	51	40	40	42	44	49	53	46	35
Netherlands	33	na	na	na	na	na	na	na	na	na	na	na	na	na	na	na
New Zealand	na	62	67	59	55	63	65	64	65	60	55	63	70	62	68	55
Nigeria	53	48	48	48	49	47	51	43	54	47	43	50	53	48	49	44
Northern Ireland	55	na	na	na	na	na	na	na	na	na	na	na	na	na	na	na
Norway	32	34	36	32	29	38	34	33	33	38	na	na	na	31	36	27
Pakistan	na	na	na	na	na	na	na	na	na	na	na	na	na	na	na	na
Peru	na	35	37	33	32	36	38	31	35	38	33	36	37	34	36	32
Philippines	na	56	55	57	54	60	54	55	59	54	54	60	54	59	54	56
Poland	15	na	na	na	na	na	na	na	na	na	na	na	na	na	na	na
Portugal	48	na	na	na	na	na	na	na	na	na	na	na	na	na	na	na
Puerto Rico	na	48	52	47	47	48	49	46	49	48	52	46	50	57	51	39
Romania	35	na	na	na	na	na	na	na	na	na	na	na	na	na	na	na
Russian Fed.	11	na	na	na	na	na	na	na	na	na	na	na	na	na	na	na
Serbia	na	26	32	19	28	31	20	18	27	35	20	25	29	20	28	45
Singapore	na	49	50	48	41	55	64	51	47	50	53	48	48	58	47	36
Slovakia	na	na	na	na	na	na	na	na	na	na	na	na	na	na	na	na
Slovenia	26	na	na	na	na	na	na	na	na	na	na	na	na	na	na	na
South Africa	40	47	51	43	50	43	53	42	51	71	38	48	57	44	51	28
Spain	31	38	36	40	34	34	44	40	38	32	40	35	42	43	39	24
Sweden	30	na	na	na	na	na	na	na	na	na	na	na	na	na	na	na
Switzerland	51	46	52	39	38	43	53	43	46	49	41	38	54	52	48	32
Taiwan	na	30	29	31	23	30	36	36	31	25	29	31	28	35	25	15
Tanzania	na	26	28	23	21	26	34	20	27	42	20	24	42	28	25	17
Turkey	27	32	35	30	30	33	36	35	29	29	32	34	35	37	32	27
Uganda	na	64	64	65	62	68	61	65	63	71	62	67	59	66	65	56
Ukraine	na	na	na	na	na	na	na	na	na	na	na	na	na	na	na	na
United States	57	59	59	59	58	56	64	59	60	58	60	57	62	70	62	49
Uruguay	na	47	48	46	41	45	51	50	43	43	44	47	48	64	46	32
Venezuela	na	47	49	45	47	46	50	51	47	43	48	44	44	57	46	33
Vietnam	na	23	20	26	30	23	18	24	21	27	20	22	25	25	23	26
Zimbabwe	na	51	49	53	50	50	55	53	48	57	55	47	47	56	47	48
Total	36	39	41	38	39	39	41	40	39	40	37	37	42	39	40	36

RANKING

Country	2000
Uganda	64
New Zealand	62
United States	59
Philippines	56
Albania	53
Canada	52
Zimbabwe	51
Australia	51
Singapore	49
Morocco	49
Nigeria	48
Puerto Rico	48
Venezuela	47
South Africa	47
Uruguay	47
Switzerland	46
Mexico	45
Dominican Rep.	44
Bangladesh	43
Indonesia	43
Colombia	42
Macedonia	41
Chile	41
Japan	39
Spain	38
Algeria	37
Jordan	36
Brazil	35
Peru	35
Norway	34
Georgia	33
Egypt	33
Turkey	32
China	30
Montenegro	30
Taiwan	30
Azerbaijan	30
Argentina	29
Serbia	26
India	26
Armenia	26
Tanzania	26
Vietnam	23
Iran	22
Moldova	21
Bosnia and Herz.	20
Korea, South	14
Total	39

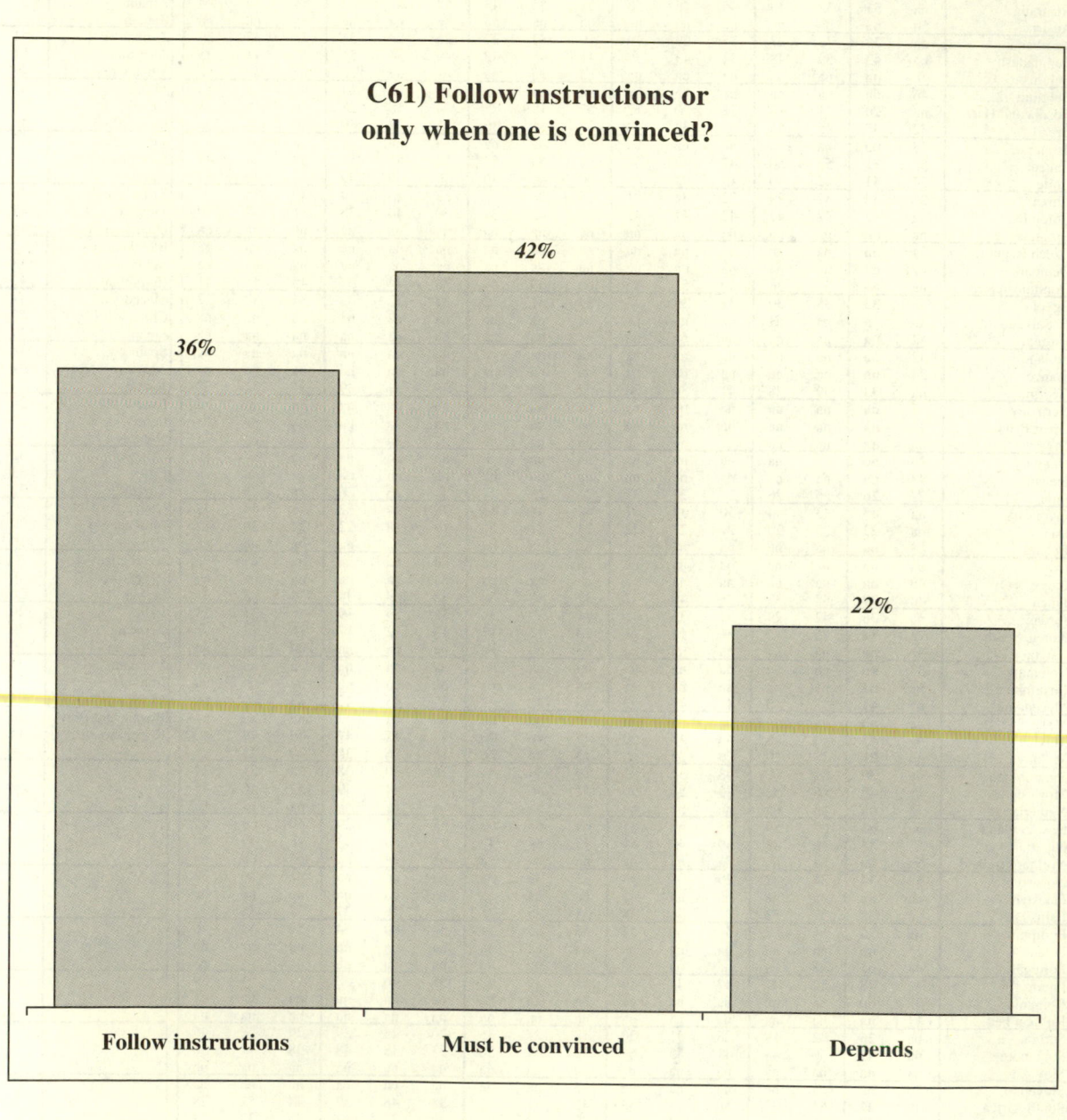

**C61) Follow instructions or
only when one is convinced?**

42%

36%

22%

Follow instructions   Must be convinced   Depends

C061) FOLLOWING INSTRUCTIONS: MUST BE CONVINCED

Some say that one should follow one's superior's instructions even when one does not fully agree with them. Others say that one should follow one's superior's instructions only when one is convinced that they are right.

Must be convinced first (%)

(WVS: V105; EVS: V97)

Country	Wave 1990	Wave 2000	Gender Male	Gender Female	Age 16-29	Age 30-49	Age 50+	Education Lower	Education Middle	Education Upper	Income Lower	Income Middle	Income Upper	Values Mat	Values Mixed	Values Postm.
Albania	na	30	27	33	26	31	31	30	29	31	33	28	28	31	29	28
Algeria	na	45	45	46	52	41	39	36	46	51	46	48	39	42	47	51
Argentina	50	47	47	48	54	47	41	45	47	60	43	47	51	39	48	52
Armenia	na	62	59	65	65	66	52	39	64	65	64	60	66	57	66	72
Australia	na	41	42	39	40	41	41	40	36	46	40	41	41	33	39	46
Austria	38	40	42	38	39	43	37	38	42	41	36	45	36	34	40	43
Azerbaijan	na	46	46	47	49	46	40	43	46	49	56	47	40	46	47	57
Bangladesh	na	54	56	52	60	49	60	55	53	55	57	50	58	62	50	55
Belarus	55	38	36	39	37	38	38	35	38	40	32	38	45	39	38	44
Belgium	43	44	44	44	45	46	41	42	40	51	40	44	46	42	43	50
Bosnia and Herz.	na	38	38	38	34	37	43	34	39	38	37	39	38	36	39	49
Brazil	78	78	77	78	79	78	74	70	84	85	72	84	80	72	79	86
Bulgaria	65	46	47	44	54	53	35	25	56	55	37	49	50	43	49	66
Canada	29	31	32	30	33	31	29	24	32	35	30	28	35	25	30	35
Chile	49	35	35	34	42	35	27	27	36	49	32	33	41	27	38	39
China	34	67	68	66	63	66	72	71	64	63	67	71	63	63	71	56
Colombia	na	na	na	na	na	na	na	na	na	na	na	na	na	na	na	na
Croatia	na	51	47	55	54	54	46	43	56	57	49	51	53	46	51	58
Czech Republic	51	34	33	35	31	33	37	36	33	29	39	33	31	37	33	36
Denmark	54	26	28	25	28	25	28	26	29	27	26	26	27	24	26	32
Dominican Rep.	na	53	47	57	55	48	55	50	52	54	59	44	57	51	53	58
Egypt	na	43	44	42	53	41	31	36	51	48	41	39	44	34	48	58
El Salvador	na	32	33	32	37	30	29	30	35	34	33	28	34	na	na	na
Estonia	44	31	35	27	27	29	34	30	27	41	27	35	30	24	34	36
Finland	45	59	59	59	60	63	56	60	59	58	61	60	61	55	60	68
France	48	40	43	38	36	45	38	38	42	45	36	43	46	35	41	46
Georgia	na	11	10	12	13	11	10	13	10	14	9	10	15	11	11	8
Germany	36	28	28	28	37	29	23	22	32	34	22	29	34	21	29	38
Great Britain	43	33	33	33	39	29	34	31	36	33	36	27	32	25	34	37
Greece	na	32	31	33	28	34	38	32	31	33	31	32	32	29	33	52
Hungary	59	34	33	35	33	36	33	33	34	37	31	34	35	29	39	48
Iceland	33	33	30	35	34	33	31	32	34	34	36	31	31	29	33	36
India	55	39	40	37	37	40	37	34	39	46	38	33	43	33	44	52
Indonesia	na	51	49	53	48	53	50	48	49	56	49	52	56	49	53	65
Iran	na	59	59	61	62	59	53	56	61	59	59	61	61	57	61	71
Ireland	41	38	37	39	37	36	42	40	38	34	36	37	39	31	39	45
Israel	na	na	na	na	na	na	na	na	na	na	na	na	na	na	na	na
Italy	46	33	33	33	33	32	34	31	34	37	31	34	35	25	35	33
Japan	11	10	12	7	9	9	10	16	9	9	9	10	10	10	10	7
Jordan	na	72	69	76	75	71	69	70	78	71	73	74	73	69	74	78
Korea, South	48	51	50	52	49	53	47	52	50	51	52	52	48	47	53	59
Latvia	45	46	43	50	45	44	49	42	48	49	45	50	47	46	48	45
Lithuania	33	47	46	48	44	56	39	32	49	58	45	43	49	38	51	49
Luxembourg	na	32	32	33	33	34	30	30	33	34	29	29	37	22	31	45
Macedonia	na	44	44	43	41	45	44	38	46	46	42	44	45	41	46	40
Malta	na	51	48	53	53	55	45	44	52	57	41	50	56	48	50	69
Mexico	38	41	41	41	46	43	30	34	47	54	37	44	49	38	42	50
Moldova	na	54	55	53	58	55	50	50	53	60	56	53	55	51	57	59
Montenegro	na	40	39	40	40	39	40	38	38	46	32	44	46	38	43	38
Morocco	na	51	52	50	55	49	43	46	68	70	62	60	42	44	55	66
Netherlands	48	31	29	32	25	32	32	32	30	30	33	30	30	38	27	38
New Zealand	na	23	25	22	16	21	28	21	24	23	23	22	25	23	22	28
Nigeria	49	43	46	40	42	43	49	41	45	42	42	46	39	44	43	38
Northern Ireland	38	36	40	33	41	36	34	33	39	39	32	39	44	36	34	49
Norway	34	33	31	35	37	34	29	36	35	29	na	na	na	41	31	38
Pakistan	na	na	na	na	na	na	na	na	na	na	na	na	na	na	na	na
Peru	na	54	56	52	55	57	47	48	56	56	55	55	53	50	55	59
Philippines	na	49	49	49	55	49	43	47	49	53	46	52	50	44	50	70
Poland	na	50	50	49	43	49	54	48	48	60	51	48	51	46	53	45
Portugal	39	44	43	45	50	44	41	42	51	45	39	46	48	41	40	61
Puerto Rico	na	43	39	45	49	46	37	34	43	45	45	38	46	42	41	45
Romania	75	29	30	28	29	27	31	24	32	33	26	30	30	31	30	25
Russian Fed.	56	47	50	44	50	50	41	31	48	50	43	47	50	43	52	31
Serbia	na	43	43	44	48	44	40	33	48	50	40	43	50	38	48	51
Singapore	na	55	55	55	62	53	35	49	58	58	51	54	59	49	56	66
Slovakia	na	32	33	31	31	34	30	28	33	36	29	31	33	27	35	44
Slovenia	58	48	48	48	40	45	57	51	48	42	54	54	43	50	47	50
South Africa	na	44	46	42	47	44	37	42	47	41	43	43	48	41	45	53
Spain	52	42	43	41	47	46	35	38	48	41	37	40	41	38	43	50
Sweden	41	33	31	35	36	30	35	33	35	30	40	30	30	29	31	42
Switzerland	na	41	42	40	44	40	40	36	41	48	43	40	43	30	41	49
Taiwan	na	56	59	54	61	57	52	51	57	61	51	61	57	52	59	73
Tanzania	na	28	28	27	25	27	33	28	27	29	29	27	30	30	27	46
Turkey	54	55	52	59	56	57	51	53	59	62	52	57	62	50	56	64
Uganda	na	47	52	42	48	49	36	48	47	40	52	53	47	49	48	39
Ukraine	na	42	43	42	48	47	35	30	42	50	38	42	51	41	45	60
United States	23	20	18	22	25	18	19	18	19	22	20	20	20	15	21	21
Uruguay	na	15	16	15	21	14	14	14	15	23	14	16	15	9	16	16
Venezuela	na	57	54	59	57	58	52	54	58	56	55	60	58	50	58	64
Vietnam	na	40	40	40	41	41	38	35	45	44	46	36	40	32	44	39
Zimbabwe	na	47	48	46	50	43	48	48	46	31	45	50	42	45	48	53
Total	45	42	42	42	45	43	38	39	43	44	41	42	43	41	43	46

RANKING

Country	2000
Brazil	78
Jordan	72
China	67
Armenia	62
Iran	59
Finland	59
Venezuela	57
Taiwan	56
Turkey	55
Singapore	55
Bangladesh	54
Peru	54
Moldova	54
Dominican Rep.	53
Croatia	51
Morocco	51
Korea, South	51
Malta	51
Indonesia	51
Poland	50
Philippines	49
Slovenia	48
Argentina	47
Zimbabwe	47
Uganda	47
Lithuania	47
Russian Fed.	47
Azerbaijan	46
Latvia	46
Bulgaria	46
Algeria	45
Portugal	44
South Africa	44
Belgium	44
Macedonia	44
Serbia	43
Egypt	43
Nigeria	43
Puerto Rico	43
Ukraine	42
Spain	42
Mexico	41
Switzerland	41
Australia	41
France	40
Vietnam	40
Austria	40
Montenegro	40
India	39
Bosnia and Herz.	38
Ireland	38
Belarus	38
Northern Ireland	36
Chile	35
Czech Republic	34
Hungary	34
Sweden	33
Italy	33
Norway	33
Great Britain	33
Iceland	33
El Salvador	32
Luxembourg	32
Greece	32
Slovakia	32
Netherlands	31
Canada	31
Estonia	31
Albania	30
Romania	29
Germany	28
Tanzania	28
Denmark	26
New Zealand	23
United States	20
Uruguay	15
Georgia	11
Japan	10
Total	42

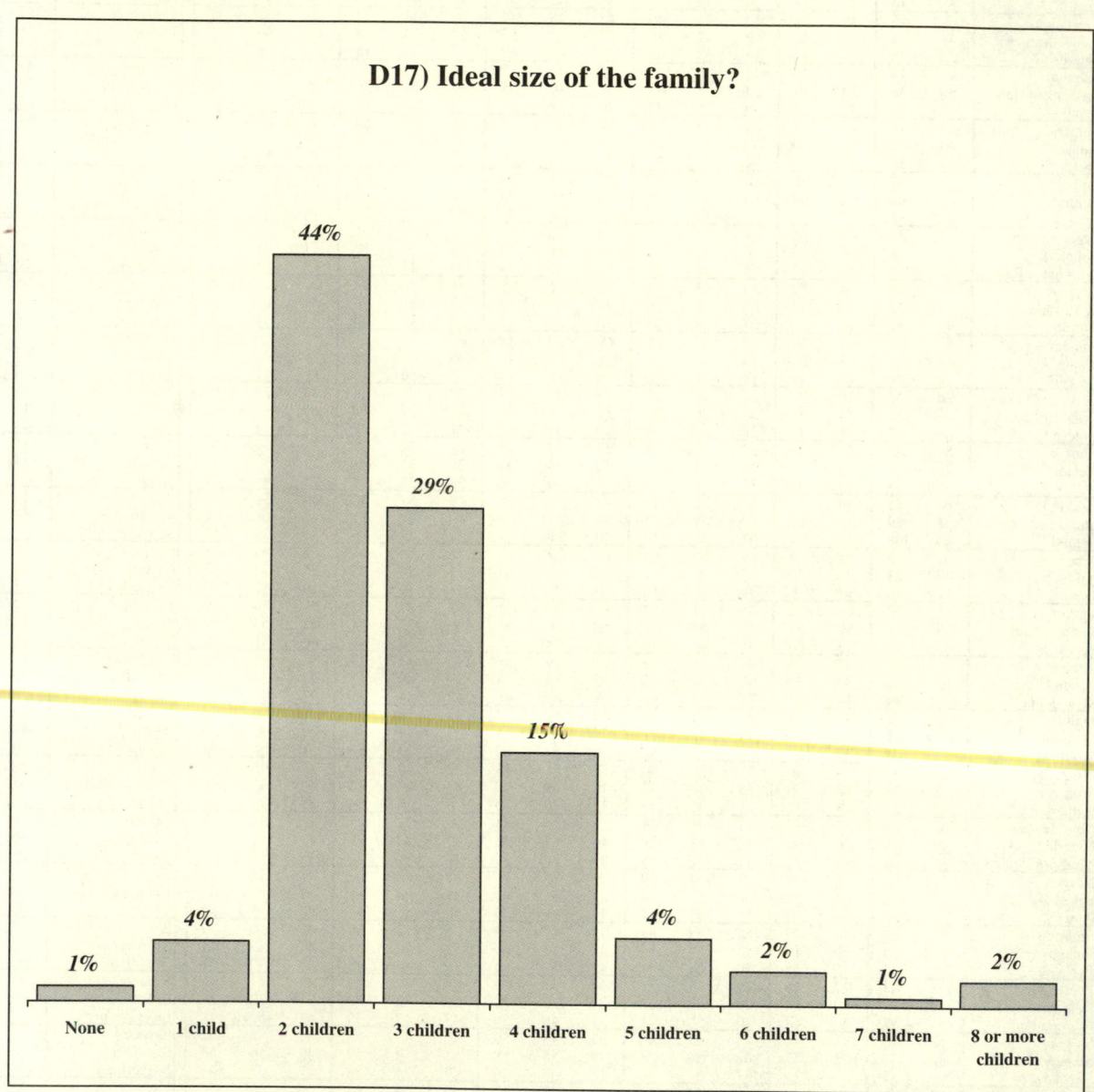

D17) Ideal size of the family?

1%	4%	44%	29%	15%	4%	2%	1%	2%
None	1 child	2 children	3 children	4 children	5 children	6 children	7 children	8 or more children

D017) IDEAL NUMBER OF CHILDREN

What do you think is the ideal size of the family? How many children, if any?

% two or fewer - codes 0 to 2

(WVS: V108)

Country	Wave 1990	Wave 2000	Gender Male	Gender Female	Age 16-29	Age 30-49	Age 50+	Education Lower	Education Middle	Education Upper	Income Lower	Income Middle	Income Upper	Values Mat	Values Mixed	Values Postm.
Albania	na	48	51	45	65	49	30	41	52	54	41	49	49	46	50	33
Algeria	na	32	31	34	36	30	28	23	34	36	31	34	47	29	34	31
Argentina	44	49	51	46	55	47	44	47	51	49	45	48	52	39	48	54
Armenia	na	42	39	44	57	37	26	32	44	40	42	42	39	40	42	59
Australia	na	52	54	50	53	61	42	44	56	54	46	51	59	51	52	54
Austria	66	na	na	na	na	na	na	na	na	na	na	na	na	na	na	na
Azerbaijan	na	58	57	59	69	57	38	38	60	59	61	58	47	59	58	53
Bangladesh	na	91	90	91	92	90	85	91	91	89	92	89	91	92	90	92
Belarus	56	na	na	na	na	na	na	na	na	na	na	na	na	na	na	na
Belgium	61	na	na	na	na	na	na	na	na	na	na	na	na	na	na	na
Bosnia and Herz.	na	52	54	51	58	55	43	50	53	52	48	56	44	51	53	48
Brazil	54	60	58	62	71	56	49	57	62	65	60	62	64	56	61	67
Bulgaria	68	na	na	na	na	na	na	na	na	na	na	na	na	na	na	na
Canada	49	56	57	55	62	58	49	50	57	60	50	55	63	60	53	61
Chile	36	51	52	51	57	54	42	47	56	49	51	52	52	53	51	52
China	93	na	na	na	na	na	na	na	na	na	na	na	na	na	na	na
Colombia	na	56	55	56	68	51	46	49	58	57	51	57	55	56	54	51
Croatia	na	na	na	na	na	na	na	na	na	na	na	na	na	na	na	na
Czech Republic	70	na	na	na	na	na	na	na	na	na	na	na	na	na	na	na
Denmark	57	na	na	na	na	na	na	na	na	na	na	na	na	na	na	na
Dominican Rep.	na	32	36	30	38	23	18	14	31	34	29	35	35	27	33	37
Egypt	na	40	35	45	46	37	37	39	40	44	38	39	42	41	40	37
El Salvador	na	51	53	49	57	48	46	39	59	71	34	50	66	0	0	0
Estonia	43	na	na	na	na	na	na	na	na	na	na	na	na	na	na	na
Finland	50	na	na	na	na	na	na	na	na	na	na	na	na	na	na	na
France	49	na	na	na	na	na	na	na	na	na	na	na	na	na	na	na
Georgia	na	21	19	23	30	19	14	16	22	21	21	21	32	19	22	21
Germany	83	na	na	na	na	na	na	na	na	na	na	na	na	na	na	na
Great Britain	64	na	na	na	na	na	na	na	na	na	na	na	na	na	na	na
Greece	na	na	na	na	na	na	na	na	na	na	na	na	na	na	na	na
Hungary	67	na	na	na	na	na	na	na	na	na	na	na	na	na	na	na
Iceland	24	na	na	na	na	na	na	na	na	na	na	na	na	na	na	na
India	72	73	75	70	84	71	64	62	79	87	67	83	59	72	77	90
Indonesia	na	35	39	31	43	38	29	25	39	36	42	38	31	32	38	32
Iran	na	78	80	75	85	73	67	68	81	86	81	76	83	75	79	83
Ireland	24	na	na	na	na	na	na	na	na	na	na	na	na	na	na	na
Israel	na	na	na	na	na	na	na	na	na	na	na	na	na	na	na	na
Italy	61	na	na	na	na	na	na	na	na	na	na	na	na	na	na	na
Japan	38	39	38	40	64	42	26	22	39	46	37	41	36	34	41	34
Jordan	na	11	12	10	11	12	7	8	15	11	11	10	15	9	12	14
Korea, South	78	61	61	61	70	62	47	35	59	67	61	62	58	58	64	63
Latvia	40	na	na	na	na	na	na	na	na	na	na	na	na	na	na	na
Lithuania	36	na	na	na	na	na	na	na	na	na	na	na	na	na	na	na
Luxembourg	na	na	na	na	na	na	na	na	na	na	na	na	na	na	na	na
Macedonia	na	51	50	53	57	52	45	43	55	56	49	53	53	51	52	38
Malta	na	na	na	na	na	na	na	na	na	na	na	na	na	na	na	na
Mexico	50	46	47	46	58	41	39	39	54	59	41	49	52	45	48	50
Moldova	na	50	47	53	66	46	40	44	50	55	45	51	65	44	54	65
Montenegro	na	25	26	25	38	25	17	16	33	25	21	27	25	22	29	33
Morocco	na	55	54	56	62	51	42	52	68	61	50	56	55	55	54	64
Netherlands	55	na	na	na	na	na	na	na	na	na	na	na	na	na	na	na
New Zealand	na	44	42	46	40	46	44	46	46	42	41	44	48	55	46	40
Nigeria	6	6	6	6	7	5	4	7	7	5	7	6	6	6	6	9
Northern Ireland	42	na	na	na	na	na	na	na	na	na	na	na	na	na	na	na
Norway	55	46	53	38	53	47	39	41	51	43	0	0	0	47	46	40
Pakistan	na	42	37	48	51	45	16	36	52	45	40	42	45	43	42	64
Peru	na	70	68	72	80	65	61	72	69	71	71	70	68	70	69	76
Philippines	na	29	29	30	36	27	25	26	29	34	28	30	31	29	30	29
Poland	58	na	na	na	na	na	na	na	na	na	na	na	na	na	na	na
Portugal	68	na	na	na	na	na	na	na	na	na	na	na	na	na	na	na
Puerto Rico	na	55	55	55	70	63	42	38	55	57	52	61	62	56	54	56
Romania	70	na	na	na	na	na	na	na	na	na	na	na	na	na	na	na
Russian Fed.	49	na	na	na	na	na	na	na	na	na	na	na	na	na	na	na
Serbia	na	47	46	47	57	46	42	45	49	43	44	47	45	51	43	47
Singapore	na	55	57	53	62	54	32	49	59	52	54	57	54	49	56	65
Slovakia	na	na	na	na	na	na	na	na	na	na	na	na	na	na	na	na
Slovenia	65	na	na	na	na	na	na	na	na	na	na	na	na	na	na	na
South Africa	35	54	51	56	63	51	36	44	66	56	41	56	71	52	52	71
Spain	65	69	73	65	75	74	61	67	74	71	64	70	67	70	69	72
Sweden	58	54	58	50	55	56	51	52	56	53	51	50	58	48	55	53
Switzerland	55	68	70	66	74	71	60	64	70	59	62	69	72	64	70	65
Taiwan	na	58	55	61	79	59	42	48	60	67	57	52	64	57	59	68
Tanzania	na	18	18	19	23	17	10	14	23	23	14	22	26	15	19	25
Turkey	71	63	61	64	66	62	57	54	75	76	56	77	77	65	64	63
Uganda	na	19	17	22	28	12	2	15	21	13	13	19	0	20	20	13
Ukraine	na	na	na	na	na	na	na	na	na	na	na	na	na	na	na	na
United States	55	56	57	55	56	60	50	53	58	56	51	59	55	44	56	61
Uruguay	na	63	67	60	71	64	59	63	66	56	64	65	59	67	64	64
Venezuela	na	48	47	48	56	45	35	37	51	53	39	47	50	48	47	51
Vietnam	na	86	87	84	92	85	81	83	91	84	84	88	77	90	84	94
Zimbabwe	na	15	16	15	21	11	8	7	26	26	11	13	39	14	17	8
Total	55	48	49	48	54	48	41	44	51	51	44	52	51	45	49	53

RANKING

Country	2000
Bangladesh	91
Vietnam	86
Iran	78
India	73
Peru	70
Spain	69
Switzerland	68
Turkey	63
Uruguay	63
Korea, South	61
Brazil	60
Azerbaijan	58
Taiwan	58
Canada	56
Colombia	56
United States	56
Morocco	55
Puerto Rico	55
Singapore	55
South Africa	54
Sweden	54
Australia	52
Bosnia and Herz.	52
Chile	51
El Salvador	51
Macedonia	51
Moldova	50
Argentina	49
Albania	48
Venezuela	48
Serbia	47
Mexico	46
Norway	46
New Zealand	44
Armenia	42
Pakistan	42
Egypt	40
Japan	39
Indonesia	35
Algeria	32
Dominican Rep.	32
Philippines	29
Montenegro	25
Georgia	21
Uganda	19
Tanzania	18
Zimbabwe	15
Jordan	11
Nigeria	6
Total	48

D18) A child needs a home with both a father and a mother to grow up happily?

Tend to disagree
11%

Tend to agree
89%

D018) CHILD NEEDS PARENTS

If someone says a child needs a home with both a father and a mother to grow up happily, would you tend to agree or disagree?

Tend to agree (%) (WVS: V109; EVS: V148)

Country	Wave		Gender		Age			Education			Income			Values			RANKING Country	2000
	1990	2000	Male	Female	16-29	30-49	50+	Lower	Middle	Upper	Lower	Middle	Upper	Mat	Mixed	Postm.		
Albania	na	99	99	99	98	100	98	99	99	99	99	99	99	99	98	100	Bangladesh	99
Algeria	na	98	97	98	97	98	98	100	98	96	98	99	96	98	98	98	Albania	99
Argentina	95	91	94	89	89	90	95	94	87	88	93	90	92	94	92	89	Egypt	99
Armenia	na	98	99	97	98	98	97	98	98	99	97	99	97	99	97	100	Zimbabwe	98
Australia	na	71	80	62	60	69	82	75	69	69	72	71	71	86	72	65	Morocco	98
Austria	94	88	92	84	80	87	93	92	84	84	90	87	89	95	89	83	Pakistan	98
Azerbaijan	na	92	91	92	95	91	86	89	92	91	88	91	92	91	94	93	Georgia	98
Bangladesh	na	99	99	99	98	100	99	99	100	99	99	98	100	99	99	100	Jordan	98
Belarus	na	95	95	94	94	94	96	94	95	96	94	95	94	96	92	96	Armenia	98
Belgium	92	81	83	79	77	75	89	90	81	74	84	83	78	84	81	78	Taiwan	98
Bosnia and Herz.	na	95	97	93	93	95	95	95	95	94	96	94	94	95	94	94	Algeria	98
Brazil	88	87	93	82	85	89	87	90	85	83	89	87	86	90	86	85	Vietnam	98
Bulgaria	95	97	96	98	95	97	99	98	96	98	98	96	97	98	96	100	Bulgaria	97
Canada	78	72	79	64	63	69	79	81	71	65	76	74	64	79	75	64	Ukraine	97
Chile	93	83	85	81	81	81	89	87	83	76	87	80	79	87	85	72	Korea, South	97
China	98	95	94	97	92	96	97	97	94	91	96	95	95	96	95	91	Macedonia	97
Colombia	na	86	88	85	86	85	91	92	87	82	90	87	84	90	87	81	Poland	97
Croatia	na	89	92	87	83	92	90	93	88	81	89	88	90	95	89	84	Moldova	97
Czech Republic	99	86	89	83	79	83	92	86	84	91	87	85	85	87	86	86	Tanzania	97
Denmark	73	67	74	60	57	62	77	76	56	52	66	70	63	84	68	45	Montenegro	97
Dominican Rep.	na	85	88	83	83	89	91	91	88	84	91	87	76	88	87	80	Nigeria	97
Egypt	na	99	98	99	98	99	99	99	98	98	99	99	99	99	98	98	Philippines	97
El Salvador	na	94	96	93	92	95	96	97	93	88	97	95	88	na	na	na	Turkey	96
Estonia	99	96	97	95	95	95	97	97	95	96	95	95	96	96	95	100	Uganda	96
Finland	86	60	69	52	51	52	73	65	56	53	58	61	63	62	61	58	Greece	96
France	94	86	91	82	80	83	92	87	83	87	82	86	89	90	86	80	Estonia	96
Georgia	na	98	98	98	97	98	99	98	97	100	98	97	98	98	98	99	India	96
Germany	97	90	92	89	80	90	95	94	87	90	90	92	90	97	89	82	China	95
Great Britain	74	67	74	60	55	61	78	72	62	66	62	65	68	na	na	na	Hungary	95
Greece	na	96	95	97	95	96	99	95	97	96	94	97	97	96	97	94	Slovakia	95
Hungary	99	95	96	95	94	94	98	95	95	97	97	94	96	96	95	91	Russian Fed.	95
Iceland	79	71	77	65	61	68	84	74	72	62	71	72	66	74	72	60	Bosnia and Herz.	95
India	97	96	96	95	96	96	95	96	95	96	94	95	96	98	93	98	Romania	95
Indonesia	na	89	88	89	89	93	85	87	88	91	86	91	88	88	89	86	Belarus	95
Iran	na	86	86	86	84	86	90	89	85	85	89	88	85	87	86	80	El Salvador	94
Ireland	83	66	75	58	55	60	82	77	60	64	71	68	65	72	66	56	Singapore	94
Israel	na	na	na	na	na	na	na	na	na	na	na	na	na	na	na	na	Peru	94
Italy	97	92	92	93	89	91	96	95	91	89	93	93	92	94	93	89	Latvia	93
Japan	95	90	92	88	83	88	95	96	90	89	88	90	93	95	89	87	Malta	93
Jordan	na	98	97	99	97	98	99	98	98	98	98	97	99	98	98	100	Italy	92
Korea, South	na	97	97	97	93	98	99	100	97	96	98	96	97	98	97	87	Azerbaijan	92
Latvia	99	93	96	91	89	93	94	97	91	95	93	95	93	93	93	89	Argentina	91
Lithuania	94	80	81	78	70	78	88	86	76	82	86	77	80	82	80	62	Germany	90
Luxembourg	na	85	86	85	79	83	92	89	84	85	87	87	81	89	85	85	Japan	90
Macedonia	na	97	97	97	98	98	95	97	97	97	96	98	97	96	98	98	Uruguay	90
Malta	na	93	94	92	89	92	96	96	93	88	94	96	90	95	93	82	South Africa	90
Mexico	88	87	88	87	86	88	89	90	86	79	86	90	86	88	88	78	Serbia	89
Moldova	na	97	97	97	96	97	98	98	96	97	98	98	96	97	97	92	Croatia	89
Montenegro	na	97	98	95	94	98	97	98	96	94	97	97	98	98	96	90	Venezuela	89
Morocco	na	98	99	98	98	98	99	98	97	98	98	98	98	99	98	100	Indonesia	89
Netherlands	74	66	75	58	54	61	79	75	64	61	69	63	66	74	67	61	Switzerland	89
New Zealand	na	76	84	70	66	70	85	78	80	72	77	75	75	78	78	65	Slovenia	88
Nigeria	97	97	96	97	97	96	97	98	97	95	96	97	96	98	96	94	Austria	88
Northern Ireland	81	70	75	65	52	66	80	76	65	64	71	66	71	75	71	61	Mexico	87
Norway	86	85	92	79	82	83	90	87	87	82	na	na	na	89	85	79	Brazil	87
Pakistan	na	98	98	98	97	98	99	99	98	98	99	98	97	98	98	100	Spain	87
Peru	na	94	95	92	93	93	96	95	94	93	96	92	92	94	94	93	Colombia	86
Philippines	na	97	97	97	97	97	95	97	96	97	97	97	96	97	96	95	France	86
Poland	98	97	98	96	94	98	98	98	96	94	97	97	96	97	96	98	Czech Republic	86
Portugal	93	73	77	71	64	72	80	78	65	60	86	73	70	74	75	65	Iran	86
Puerto Rico	na	76	83	72	67	70	84	87	82	71	78	78	73	85	75	72	Luxembourg	85
Romania	97	95	95	95	90	94	97	97	95	91	96	96	92	95	96	84	Dominican Rep.	85
Russian Fed.	97	95	96	94	91	95	97	94	95	94	95	96	94	95	95	97	Norway	85
Serbia	na	89	92	87	84	90	91	93	90	84	92	90	88	92	86	90	Chile	83
Singapore	na	94	96	92	92	96	96	95	94	90	95	93	93	95	94	85	Belgium	81
Slovakia	na	95	96	95	94	95	96	95	96	93	94	95	97	97	95	89	Lithuania	80
Slovenia	94	88	92	84	81	88	94	93	86	87	89	86	86	90	88	88	New Zealand	76
South Africa	92	90	92	86	84	93	93	92	87	83	92	87	89	88	91	85	Puerto Rico	76
Spain	91	87	87	86	78	84	95	93	82	75	91	86	81	93	87	75	Portugal	73
Sweden	85	60	73	47	51	58	68	75	55	56	64	64	61	82	61	50	Canada	72
Switzerland	na	89	91	86	86	88	91	91	87	92	90	88	88	92	90	84	Iceland	71
Taiwan	na	98	98	97	98	98	97	98	97	98	97	98	99	97	98	100	Australia	71
Tanzania	na	97	97	96	99	96	96	97	97	95	97	97	96	97	97	100	Northern Ireland	70
Turkey	96	96	96	96	96	96	97	98	95	93	98	96	94	96	96	95	Denmark	67
Uganda	na	96	97	96	96	95	99	98	95	98	96	96	92	98	96	94	Great Britain	67
Ukraine	na	97	97	98	95	97	99	100	97	97	98	98	96	98	97	96	Ireland	66
United States	73	64	72	57	61	62	71	65	62	65	63	61	70	65	65	63	Netherlands	66
Uruguay	na	90	91	89	88	87	93	91	87	91	90	89	91	95	91	86	United States	64
Venezuela	na	89	91	86	87	90	91	91	88	87	90	86	90	93	87	88	Finland	60
Vietnam	na	98	97	98	96	98	98	98	97	94	97	97	99	96	98	98	Sweden	60
Zimbabwe	na	98	98	98	98	98	99	99	98	100	99	97	99	99	98	98		
Total	91	89	91	87	87	88	91	91	88	85	90	89	88	93	88	80	Total	89

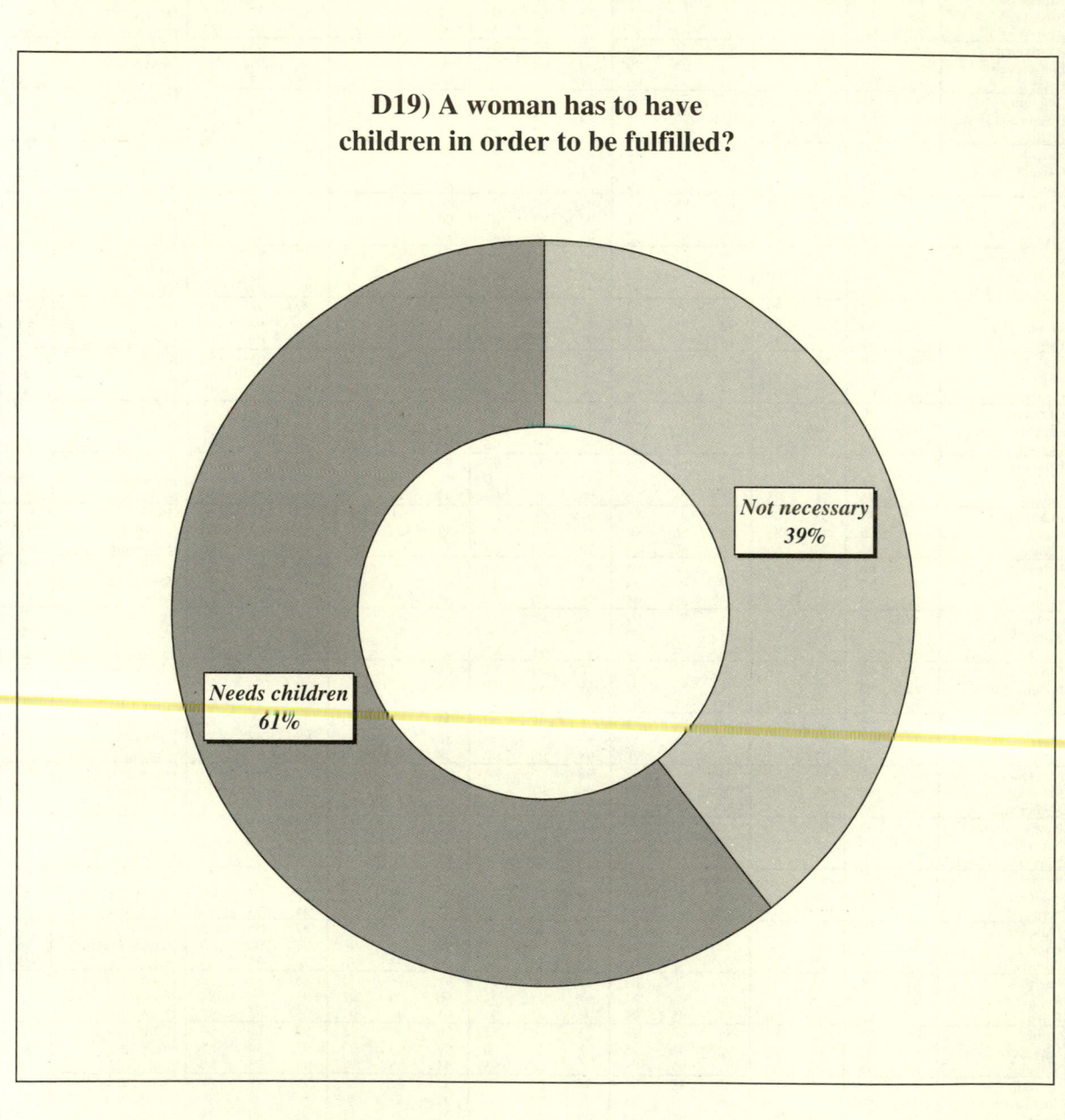

**D19) A woman has to have
children in order to be fulfilled?**

Not necessary
39%

Needs children
61%

D019) WOMAN NEEDS CHILD

Do you think that a woman has to have children in order to be fulfilled or is this not necessary?

Needs children (%) (WVS: V110; EVS: V149)

Country	Wave 1990	Wave 2000	Gender Male	Gender Female	Age 16-29	Age 30-49	Age 50+	Education Lower	Education Middle	Education Upper	Income Lower	Income Middle	Income Upper	Values Mat	Values Mixed	Values Postm.
Albania	na	92	92	93	91	92	94	93	92	90	92	91	94	93	92	85
Algeria	na	81	84	78	79	82	83	85	82	77	79	84	83	84	81	78
Argentina	60	56	56	56	49	58	61	61	50	44	59	55	54	61	59	45
Armenia	na	83	83	83	78	85	88	86	83	83	83	86	78	88	81	62
Australia	na	20	25	15	12	19	27	24	17	18	24	19	16	28	22	14
Austria	51	34	36	33	21	32	42	41	29	21	41	37	31	45	36	26
Azerbaijan	na	61	63	59	55	64	68	78	64	53	67	56	58	65	56	51
Bangladesh	na	98	98	98	97	99	99	99	99	96	99	98	98	99	98	96
Belarus	97	77	77	76	66	80	82	83	75	71	81	76	70	80	73	73
Belgium	46	33	36	31	28	27	42	42	32	29	42	35	27	32	33	34
Bosnia and Herz.	na	87	86	88	85	88	87	92	87	82	90	86	87	86	87	81
Brazil	56	53	57	50	48	55	61	57	52	44	58	51	52	56	52	53
Bulgaria	92	76	74	77	63	73	84	88	70	67	86	74	68	80	72	71
Canada	24	19	20	17	14	18	22	27	18	13	27	19	11	25	20	13
Chile	64	65	63	67	60	61	76	70	65	56	66	67	64	70	66	56
China	46	37	30	43	27	39	40	48	29	36	39	35	36	34	34	33
Colombia	na	56	54	59	51	57	65	70	56	47	66	58	48	61	65	54
Croatia	na	59	55	62	46	59	67	64	56	54	64	55	62	78	60	41
Czech Republic	87	44	42	46	32	40	54	47	40	42	50	44	39	49	44	38
Denmark	82	80	84	76	75	77	85	79	75	82	81	80	80	76	80	83
Dominican Rep.	na	65	66	64	62	69	82	81	71	60	74	60	59	60	67	62
Egypt	na	88	89	88	86	89	91	91	85	88	92	89	86	90	88	85
El Salvador	na	69	69	69	59	74	76	80	61	52	80	68	56	na	na	na
Estonia	91	75	71	78	61	74	83	74	75	78	77	77	74	78	73	73
Finland	20	12	12	12	8	9	18	17	7	6	13	12	10	16	10	15
France	75	67	69	66	61	63	73	70	62	64	67	68	65	74	67	55
Georgia	na	81	79	83	77	83	84	87	82	'76	84	81	77	84	79	77
Germany	66	54	56	53	36	52	64	62	48	44	59	58	57	79	50	30
Great Britain	21	21	22	20	15	18	27	26	19	14	23	24	18	76	na	na
Greece	na	75	72	77	73	74	82	82	76	73	77	77	72	76	78	67
Hungary	96	94	92	96	89	94	97	94	94	93	94	94	95	94	95	97
Iceland	42	35	40	31	26	31	50	41	33	27	41	34	32	40	35	22
India	89	85	83	88	83	87	86	89	85	78	90	89	80	87	81	86
Indonesia	na	93	93	94	83	94	96	98	97	85	95	93	91	95	92	86
Iran	na	49	49	49	43	51	62	61	46	39	54	49	44	56	44	35
Ireland	26	15	19	12	6	14	25	26	9	12	28	14	11	19	15	11
Israel	na	na	na	na	na	na	na	na	na	na	na	na	na	na	na	na
Italy	67	56	55	58	46	51	67	65	51	47	61	55	52	71	57	46
Japan	76	66	70	62	40	58	79	83	66	54	71	58	70	74	62	60
Jordan	na	91	92	90	88	93	93	94	87	90	96	90	90	91	92	92
Korea, South	76	92	95	89	86	93	98	94	95	88	92	95	90	94	92	75
Latvia	96	91	90	91	77	93	94	88	91	93	92	93	88	92	90	86
Lithuania	89	68	65	71	56	69	75	76	66	67	71	68	68	73	68	50
Luxembourg	na	38	41	35	32	35	45	43	37	33	40	39	27	43	38	26
Macedonia	na	70	71	69	70	70	70	83	65	58	74	69	64	70	68	79
Malta	na	44	52	37	30	45	52	54	41	36	53	47	39	45	44	37
Mexico	52	45	45	46	33	48	59	56	33	31	55	40	37	53	41	31
Moldova	na	79	75	82	75	80	81	78	80	77	79	79	76	77	83	63
Montenegro	na	78	79	77	61	78	86	87	73	67	85	75	75	84	71	64
Morocco	na	88	88	87	85	89	90	91	75	76	93	82	89	90	86	84
Netherlands	9	7	7	7	3	3	13	12	4	5	11	5	5	14	5	8
New Zealand	na	17	19	16	9	16	21	20	15	16	23	13	15	22	16	11
Nigeria	87	92	91	92	92	93	89	90	93	91	91	92	93	93	91	93
Northern Ireland	32	18	21	16	9	19	23	22	17	11	24	17	17	18	20	11
Norway	23	19	22	17	20	16	23	22	21	15	na	na	na	27	19	8
Pakistan	na	98	99	98	98	98	99	99	98	96	99	98	97	99	98	100
Peru	na	40	39	40	32	41	54	48	39	36	44	39	32	47	38	34
Philippines	na	87	83	91	88	88	84	89	88	82	88	87	86	88	86	91
Poland	79	70	73	67	57	66	82	75	65	59	74	69	62	72	67	75
Portugal	61	68	64	71	51	66	79	75	57	42	78	69	56	75	65	54
Puerto Rico	na	34	34	34	26	29	42	43	32	34	46	31	29	48	34	29
Romania	85	83	81	86	71	82	90	92	80	77	90	82	81	87	81	70
Russian Fed.	92	83	81	86	75	83	89	88	83	83	85	84	82	86	82	72
Serbia	na	67	66	68	54	67	73	75	69	53	71	70	60	73	62	53
Singapore	na	56	55	57	45	61	83	70	49	50	64	55	51	68	53	39
Slovakia	na	46	44	47	37	46	52	50	44	39	53	44	43	50	44	34
Slovenia	58	38	37	39	25	31	55	50	34	32	46	40	33	46	37	37
South Africa	70	45	44	46	38	47	54	57	30	21	63	32	31	46	45	39
Spain	46	48	47	49	33	41	63	59	38	33	59	49	42	62	47	28
Sweden	21	25	29	21	22	26	26	26	27	21	24	28	24	41	25	21
Switzerland	31	35	41	30	27	33	43	47	33	33	37	39	34	55	34	26
Taiwan	na	55	51	58	40	54	66	68	52	44	59	56	48	59	49	50
Tanzania	na	85	85	84	80	85	93	87	83	78	85	85	81	87	84	96
Turkey	72	75	73	77	67	77	87	84	65	58	82	73	60	81	75	64
Uganda	na	63	57	69	56	69	75	67	61	68	56	67	65	66	63	58
Ukraine	na	86	82	89	73	87	91	89	85	86	86	87	85	88	83	83
United States	20	15	18	13	16	15	14	20	17	12	20	12	13	22	15	12
Uruguay	na	59	62	58	56	59	61	60	62	48	58	64	56	66	62	52
Venezuela	na	54	54	54	49	52	68	63	53	45	55	53	52	62	51	50
Vietnam	na	86	83	89	82	87	88	87	86	75	87	86	85	88	86	80
Zimbabwe	na	77	73	80	74	76	86	85	67	30	85	74	65	81	75	70
Total	61	61	61	60	56	61	65	67	58	53	66	62	58	72	58	43

RANKING

Country	2000
Pakistan	98
Bangladesh	98
Hungary	94
Indonesia	93
Albania	92
Korea, South	92
Nigeria	92
Jordan	91
Latvia	91
Egypt	88
Morocco	88
Bosnia and Herz.	87
Philippines	87
Vietnam	86
Ukraine	86
India	85
Tanzania	85
Russian Fed.	83
Romania	83
Armenia	83
Algeria	81
Georgia	81
Denmark	80
Moldova	79
Montenegro	78
Zimbabwe	77
Belarus	77
Bulgaria	76
Greece	75
Turkey	75
Estonia	75
Macedonia	70
Poland	70
El Salvador	69
Lithuania	68
Portugal	68
Serbia	67
France	67
Japan	66
Chile	65
Dominican Rep.	65
Uganda	63
Azerbaijan	61
Uruguay	59
Croatia	59
Italy	56
Colombia	56
Singapore	56
Argentina	56
Taiwan	55
Germany	54
Venezuela	54
Brazil	53
Iran	49
Spain	48
Slovakia	46
Mexico	45
South Africa	45
Czech Republic	44
Malta	44
Peru	40
Slovenia	38
Luxembourg	38
China	37
Switzerland	35
Iceland	35
Puerto Rico	34
Austria	34
Belgium	33
Sweden	25
Great Britain	21
Australia	20
Norway	19
Canada	19
Northern Ireland	18
New Zealand	17
Ireland	15
United States	15
Finland	12
Netherlands	7
Total	61

D020_1) MAN NEEDS CHILDREN

Do you agree or disagree with the following statement: "A man has to have children in order to be fulfilled?"

Agree strongly / Agree (%)　　　　　　　　　　　　　　　　　　　　　(EVS: V152)

Country	Wave		Gender		Age			Education			Income			Values			RANKING Country	2000
	1990	2000	Male	Female	16-29	30-49	50+	Lower	Middle	Upper	Lower	Middle	Upper	Mat	Mixed	Postm.		
Albania	na	na	na	na	na	na	na	na	na	na	na	na	na	na	na	na	Latvia	90
Algeria	na	na	na	na	na	na	na	na	na	na	na	na	na	na	na	na	Belarus	77
Argentina	na	na	na	na	na	na	na	na	na	na	na	na	na	na	na	na	Croatia	77
Armenia	na	na	na	na	na	na	na	na	na	na	na	na	na	na	na	na	Hungary	76
Australia	na	na	na	na	na	na	na	na	na	na	na	na	na	na	na	na	Romania	75
Austria	na	26	32	21	21	21	35	31	24	17	33	26	25	33	28	22	Ukraine	73
Azerbaijan	na	na	na	na	na	na	na	na	na	na	na	na	na	na	na	na	Russian Fed.	71
Bangladesh	na	na	na	na	na	na	na	na	na	na	na	na	na	na	na	na	Estonia	67
Belarus	na	77	75	79	62	79	87	86	74	73	84	73	72	81	73	66	Denmark	65
Belgium	na	25	29	22	23	22	30	27	27	23	33	28	20	23	25	29	Turkey	63
Bosnia and Herz.	na	na	na	na	na	na	na	na	na	na	na	na	na	na	na	na	Czech Republic	60
Brazil	na	na	na	na	na	na	na	na	na	na	na	na	na	na	na	na	Bulgaria	54
Bulgaria	na	54	54	55	33	50	68	73	46	42	75	49	40	58	49	65	Poland	54
Canada	na	na	na	na	na	na	na	na	na	na	na	na	na	na	na	na	France	53
Chile	na	na	na	na	na	na	na	na	na	na	na	na	na	na	na	na	Portugal	50
China	na	na	na	na	na	na	na	na	na	na	na	na	na	na	na	na	Greece	48
Colombia	na	na	na	na	na	na	na	na	na	na	na	na	na	na	na	na	Lithuania	48
Croatia	na	77	73	80	65	79	83	84	74	67	90	74	72	85	79	65	Italy	45
Czech Republic	na	60	60	60	48	56	71	65	56	51	67	58	56	66	61	43	Germany	39
Denmark	na	65	68	61	63	62	68	62	67	67	63	63	68	61	64	72	Slovakia	39
Dominican Rep.	na	na	na	na	na	na	na	na	na	na	na	na	na	na	na	na	Slovenia	37
Egypt	na	na	na	na	na	na	na	na	na	na	na	na	na	na	na	na	Spain	36
El Salvador	na	na	na	na	na	na	na	na	na	na	na	na	na	na	na	na	Malta	34
Estonia	na	67	63	70	51	65	77	68	65	71	69	70	63	70	66	53	Luxembourg	30
Finland	na	28	29	27	26	24	32	32	24	17	30	26	27	32	27	28	Iceland	29
France	na	53	56	51	48	52	56	55	46	54	53	56	55	57	54	45	Finland	28
Georgia	na	na	na	na	na	na	na	na	na	na	na	na	na	na	na	na	Austria	26
Germany	na	39	44	35	22	37	49	46	34	30	42	47	36	58	34	27	Belgium	25
Great Britain	na	11	14	9	6	9	17	13	10	8	14	16	11	na	na	na	Northern Ireland	16
Greece	na	48	49	47	47	44	58	61	43	49	47	50	45	45	50	45	Ireland	15
Hungary	na	76	79	73	60	76	85	79	68	75	78	76	75	82	72	51	Great Britain	11
Iceland	na	29	37	21	23	26	38	32	28	24	33	28	27	31	31	17	Netherlands	5
India	na	na	na	na	na	na	na	na	na	na	na	na	na	na	na	na		
Indonesia	na	na	na	na	na	na	na	na	na	na	na	na	na	na	na	na		
Iran	na	na	na	na	na	na	na	na	na	na	na	na	na	na	na	na		
Ireland	na	15	18	13	6	16	22	23	11	11	22	15	11	17	15	17		
Israel	na	na	na	na	na	na	na	na	na	na	na	na	na	na	na	na		
Italy	na	45	47	42	36	39	54	52	40	36	52	45	39	56	45	37		
Japan	na	na	na	na	na	na	na	na	na	na	na	na	na	na	na	na		
Jordan	na	na	na	na	na	na	na	na	na	na	na	na	na	na	na	na		
Korea, South	na	na	na	na	na	na	na	na	na	na	na	na	na	na	na	na		
Latvia	na	90	89	90	79	91	93	93	87	94	90	90	88	89	91	82		
Lithuania	na	48	48	47	32	45	61	57	45	43	60	41	47	51	49	38		
Luxembourg	na	30	35	25	30	27	33	34	29	25	41	31	18	33	29	23		
Macedonia	na	na	na	na	na	na	na	na	na	na	na	na	na	na	na	na		
Malta	na	34	37	30	21	30	16	44	30	26	44	33	30	37	32	30		
Mexico	na	na	na	na	na	na	na	na	na	na	na	na	na	na	na	na		
Moldova	na	na	na	na	na	na	na	na	na	na	na	na	na	na	na	na		
Montenegro	na	na	na	na	na	na	na	na	na	na	na	na	na	na	na	na		
Morocco	na	na	na	na	na	na	na	na	na	na	na	na	na	na	na	na		
Netherlands	na	5	6	4	4	3	7	8	3	4	8	3	5	11	4	4		
New Zealand	na	na	na	na	na	na	na	na	na	na	na	na	na	na	na	na		
Nigeria	na	na	na	na	na	na	na	na	na	na	na	na	na	na	na	na		
Northern Ireland	na	16	18	15	6	17	21	21	13	11	21	12	13	17	17	10		
Norway	na	na	na	na	na	na	na	na	na	na	na	na	na	na	na	na		
Pakistan	na	na	na	na	na	na	na	na	na	na	na	na	na	na	na	na		
Peru	na	na	na	na	na	na	na	na	na	na	na	na	na	na	na	na		
Philippines	na	na	na	na	na	na	na	na	na	na	na	na	na	na	na	na		
Poland	na	54	56	53	39	51	67	61	51	34	57	56	43	59	51	54		
Portugal	na	50	46	53	34	47	62	58	36	22	64	49	44	59	45	41		
Puerto Rico	na	na	na	na	na	na	na	na	na	na	na	na	na	na	na	na		
Romania	na	75	77	72	60	73	84	86	71	62	83	77	71	79	72	53		
Russian Fed.	na	71	72	70	61	70	79	77	72	65	76	70	68	73	69	63		
Serbia	na	na	na	na	na	na	na	na	na	na	na	na	na	na	na	na		
Singapore	na	na	na	na	na	na	na	na	na	na	na	na	na	na	na	na		
Slovakia	na	39	39	39	34	40	42	41	39	31	46	36	39	42	38	31		
Slovenia	na	37	42	33	26	31	52	47	35	32	43	40	33	45	35	44		
South Africa	na	na	na	na	na	na	na	na	na	na	na	na	na	na	na	na		
Spain	na	36	36	36	27	28	47	48	27	28	42	35	28	52	33	21		
Sweden	na	na	na	na	na	na	na	na	na	na	na	na	na	na	na	na		
Switzerland	na	na	na	na	na	na	na	na	na	na	na	na	na	na	na	na		
Taiwan	na	na	na	na	na	na	na	na	na	na	na	na	na	na	na	na		
Tanzania	na	na	na	na	na	na	na	na	na	na	na	na	na	na	na	na		
Turkey	na	63	62	64	58	65	69	71	54	46	74	63	42	70	64	53		
Uganda	na	na	na	na	na	na	na	na	na	na	na	na	na	na	na	na		
Ukraine	na	73	71	75	55	75	82	84	71	73	79	70	71	75	72	69		
United States	na	na	na	na	na	na	na	na	na	na	na	na	na	na	na	na		
Uruguay	na	na	na	na	na	na	na	na	na	na	na	na	na	na	na	na		
Venezuela	na	na	na	na	na	na	na	na	na	na	na	na	na	na	na	na		
Vietnam	na	na	na	na	na	na	na	na	na	na	na	na	na	na	na	na		
Zimbabwe	na	na	na	na	na	na	na	na	na	na	na	na	na	na	na	na		
Total	na	47	48	46	38	45	55	52	45	42	55	49	45	58	46	36	Total	47

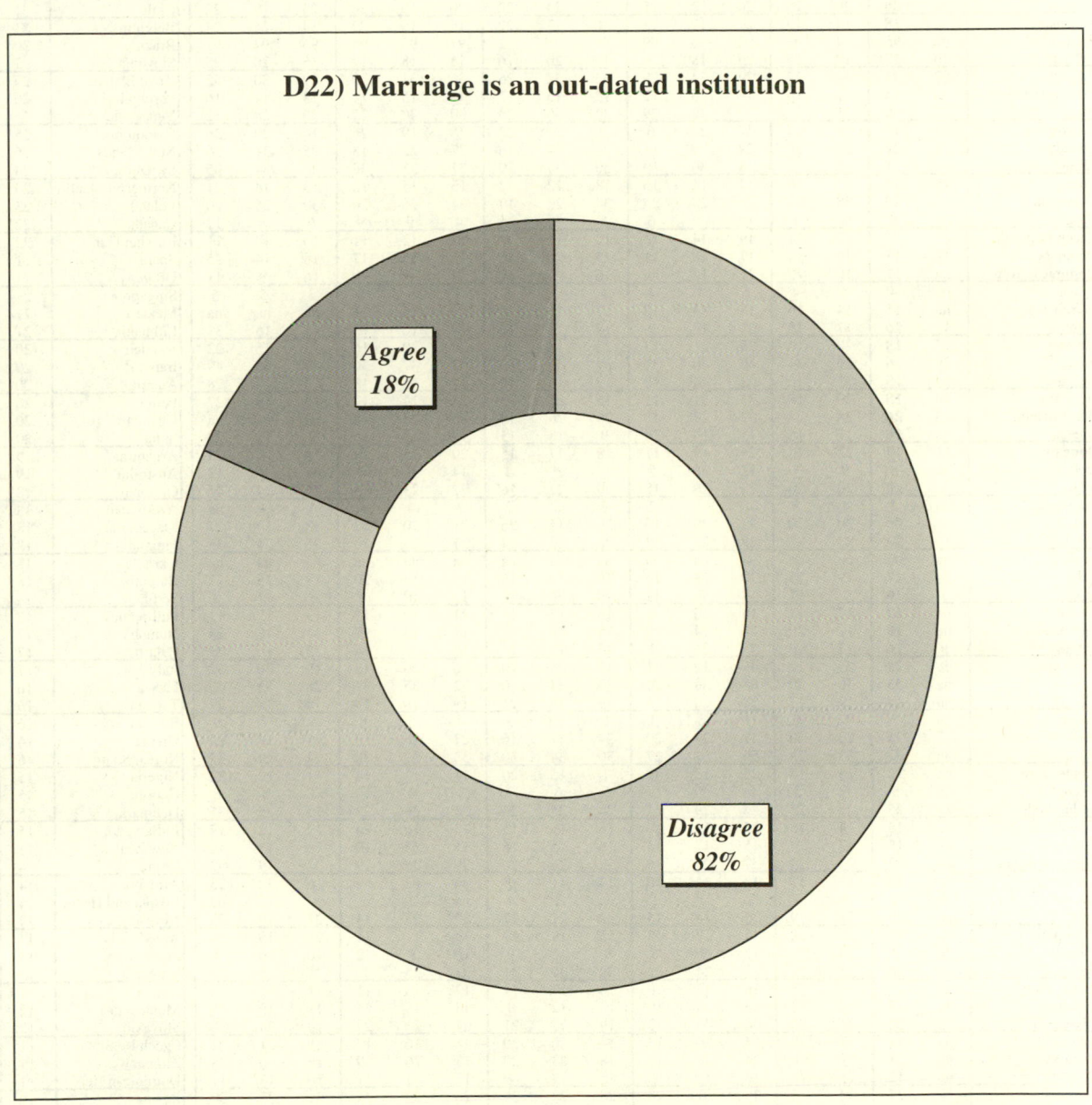

D22) Marriage is an out-dated institution

Agree
18%

Disagree
82%

D022) MARRIAGE IS AN OUT-DATED INSTITUTION

Do you agree or disagree with the following statement: "Marriage is an out-dated institution?"

Agree (%)   (WVS: V111; EVS: V150)

Country	Wave		Gender		Age			Education			Income			Values		
	1990	2000	Male	Female	16-29	30-49	50+	Lower	Middle	Upper	Lower	Middle	Upper	Mat	Mixed	Postm.
Albania	na	9	12	6	16	7	5	8	8	12	6	13	7	6	10	18
Algeria	na	13	13	13	16	10	12	13	12	13	13	12	15	13	12	13
Argentina	9	19	20	19	26	19	13	18	22	20	20	19	19	18	19	22
Armenia	na	14	15	13	17	16	8	12	15	13	14	11	18	11	17	19
Australia	na	19	19	18	25	18	13	19	20	16	22	16	16	18	16	23
Austria	12	20	20	20	26	22	15	17	24	22	20	19	20	23	19	22
Azerbaijan	na	18	17	19	20	19	13	10	17	22	16	19	22	14	25	24
Bangladesh	na	95	94	96	92	96	99	96	95	91	97	93	95	96	94	97
Belarus	16	17	19	15	26	18	8	10	20	16	16	18	17	15	20	25
Belgium	22	31	34	27	29	34	29	33	32	26	36	31	30	29	30	35
Bosnia and Herz.	na	14	11	16	14	16	12	12	15	12	14	15	11	13	14	16
Brazil	27	30	28	32	27	32	29	34	26	26	30	30	27	30	28	32
Bulgaria	11	18	19	17	37	22	6	9	23	22	9	19	26	14	20	26
Canada	13	22	25	20	29	24	16	25	24	16	27	22	18	25	21	26
Chile	15	31	31	32	38	36	19	30	34	29	31	33	30	25	34	35
China	15	14	13	16	14	14	16	18	12	12	15	15	12	13	14	21
Colombia	na	25	28	23	26	25	25	34	26	19	34	26	20	30	26	20
Croatia	na	8	8	8	15	7	6	5	9	16	4	9	9	6	8	12
Czech Republic	10	11	12	11	19	14	6	12	11	6	13	12	11	10	13	11
Denmark	18	15	16	14	17	18	11	13	20	15	15	15	17	18	14	25
Dominican Rep.	na	11	10	12	11	12	na	16	8	11	14	9	8	16	9	11
Egypt	na	4	4	4	4	4	4	4	3	7	3	4	5	3	5	5
El Salvador	na	15	14	16	18	13	12	17	15	9	22	15	11	na	na	na
Estonia	11	16	17	15	27	17	9	14	18	13	19	12	15	15	16	31
Finland	13	18	20	16	23	21	13	22	15	9	20	20	16	23	15	22
France	29	36	39	34	40	40	31	37	39	33	37	37	36	29	36	49
Georgia	na	15	15	16	22	14	10	12	16	15	14	15	18	13	17	28
Germany	14	18	20	18	32	21	11	16	22	15	23	14	17	12	19	27
Great Britain	18	26	28	24	37	27	18	28	26	19	35	25	18	na	na	na
Greece	na	16	17	15	15	19	10	9	18	15	18	13	16	9	15	26
Hungary	11	17	22	13	24	19	11	18	17	15	20	15	19	15	20	35
Iceland	6	8	9	7	12	8	5	9	9	4	14	6	7	8	8	13
India	5	20	20	20	20	20	18	20	22	16	22	23	15	16	24	20
Indonesia	na	3	4	3	4	4	2	2	5	2	3	4	1	4	3	na
Iran	na	20	20	20	22	20	17	20	15	26	21	20	22	18	19	27
Ireland	10	23	23	23	29	25	17	28	22	14	31	23	16	25	21	25
Israel	na	na	na	na	na	na	na	na	na	na	na	na	na	na	na	na
Italy	14	17	19	15	20	18	14	16	19	16	19	14	20	17	15	22
Japan	7	10	9	12	15	8	11	18	9	10	13	10	8	8	11	8
Jordan	na	12	12	13	16	10	9	13	13	11	11	10	15	13	12	11
Korea, South	na	16	12	20	24	14	10	18	14	17	17	13	17	14	16	24
Latvia	9	16	17	16	25	21	9	13	19	11	18	16	14	15	16	22
Lithuania	9	21	25	17	36	19	11	12	24	20	16	20	18	19	20	32
Luxembourg	na	33	36	30	35	38	26	33	34	30	32	35	33	28	33	43
Macedonia	na	18	19	17	22	20	13	19	17	21	19	18	19	18	18	27
Malta	na	7	8	5	11	6	4	6	8	3	4	5	8	6	7	9
Mexico	17	21	22	20	17	23	20	24	17	16	27	18	18	21	19	22
Moldova	na	32	35	28	36	32	27	30	34	30	35	27	36	34	29	32
Montenegro	na	12	13	11	25	12	6	7	15	20	11	11	14	11	12	22
Morocco	na	5	6	5	6	5	3	5	6	3	3	4	10	4	6	6
Netherlands	20	25	25	25	23	29	22	24	25	26	25	26	23	15	25	31
New Zealand	na	15	14	15	25	16	10	16	13	15	13	16	14	12	12	17
Nigeria	13	15	17	14	15	17	13	16	15	16	15	15	19	13	17	19
Northern Ireland	14	23	23	23	37	22	16	22	26	20	29	22	19	24	19	33
Norway	10	14	17	11	18	14	10	14	11	15	na	na	na	16	12	23
Pakistan	na	1	1	2	2	2	1	na	2	4	na	2	3	1	2	na
Peru	na	20	21	19	25	18	15	22	21	17	22	22	14	21	19	23
Philippines	na	17	17	18	18	19	13	15	19	17	14	17	21	21	15	15
Poland	8	9	10	9	12	9	8	9	10	9	10	8	12	10	10	4
Portugal	23	26	27	24	33	24	22	22	32	31	31	25	30	21	26	35
Puerto Rico	na	13	12	13	16	15	10	10	17	11	12	14	11	11	12	16
Romania	9	13	13	12	15	14	10	15	12	9	14	13	11	11	13	17
Russian Fed.	15	22	24	20	34	23	13	19	23	21	21	21	22	19	24	20
Serbia	na	18	17	19	25	20	13	14	20	20	18	16	17	15	21	22
Singapore	na	21	21	20	24	20	13	18	23	20	17	26	19	18	20	38
Slovakia	na	12	15	9	16	12	8	10	13	7	12	11	11	10	13	11
Slovenia	18	27	30	25	33	31	20	28	28	25	28	24	31	31	27	30
South Africa	13	34	31	38	33	37	27	38	29	17	41	37	22	32	34	45
Spain	17	21	24	19	33	23	13	17	25	29	18	21	23	15	21	31
Sweden	14	20	23	18	17	28	16	19	23	18	26	20	14	10	21	25
Switzerland	13	24	25	24	30	26	18	21	26	16	32	21	24	27	22	29
Taiwan	na	16	13	19	15	16	18	20	16	13	22	15	13	14	19	17
Tanzania	na	8	8	9	9	8	8	9	9	4	12	7	6	7	8	4
Turkey	11	8	8	8	9	8	6	6	10	9	7	7	12	7	8	10
Uganda	na	20	15	25	27	14	7	18	22	8	14	22	16	17	23	14
Ukraine	na	18	21	15	27	18	13	14	18	19	16	16	23	16	21	23
United States	8	10	12	9	16	9	6	15	12	7	12	10	7	12	8	14
Uruguay	na	21	18	23	30	24	15	19	22	28	17	24	19	17	18	27
Venezuela	na	25	27	23	28	24	24	25	27	22	30	30	20	23	27	22
Vietnam	na	8	9	8	10	8	9	11	5	9	10	7	9	6	9	11
Zimbabwe	na	11	9	12	13	10	9	11	11	8	13	12	10	11	11	13
Total	14	18	19	18	22	19	13	18	19	17	19	18	18	16	18	23

RANKING

Country	2000
Bangladesh	95
France	36
South Africa	34
Luxembourg	33
Moldova	32
Chile	31
Belgium	31
Brazil	30
Slovenia	27
Great Britain	26
Portugal	26
Venezuela	25
Colombia	25
Netherlands	25
Switzerland	24
Northern Ireland	23
Ireland	23
Canada	22
Russian Fed.	22
Spain	21
Uruguay	21
Singapore	21
Mexico	21
Lithuania	21
Sweden	20
Iran	20
Austria	20
Peru	20
Uganda	20
India	20
Argentina	19
Australia	19
Germany	18
Azerbaijan	18
Macedonia	18
Finland	18
Ukraine	18
Bulgaria	18
Serbia	18
Philippines	17
Hungary	17
Belarus	17
Italy	17
Latvia	16
Taiwan	16
Estonia	16
Greece	16
Korea, South	16
Nigeria	15
Georgia	15
Denmark	15
El Salvador	15
New Zealand	15
China	14
Armenia	14
Bosnia and Herz.	14
Norway	14
Algeria	13
Puerto Rico	13
Romania	13
Jordan	12
Montenegro	12
Slovakia	12
Czech Republic	11
Zimbabwe	11
Dominican Rep.	11
Japan	10
United States	10
Poland	9
Albania	9
Vietnam	8
Croatia	8
Iceland	8
Tanzania	8
Turkey	8
Malta	7
Morocco	5
Egypt	4
Indonesia	3
Pakistan	1
Total	18

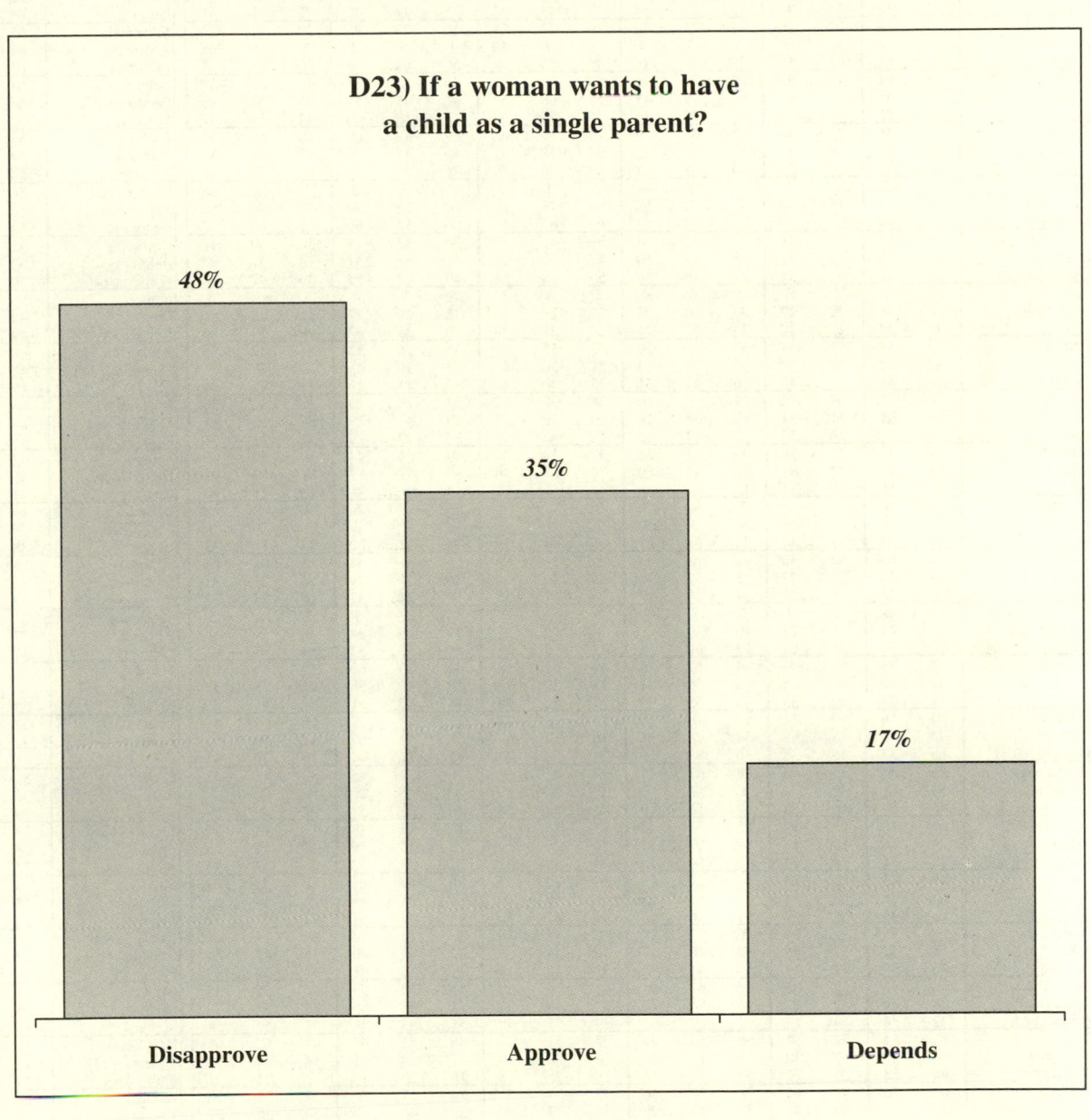

D23) If a woman wants to have a child as a single parent?

48%

35%

17%

Disapprove   Approve   Depends

D023) WOMAN AS A SINGLE PARENT

If a woman wants to have a child as a single parent, but she doesn't want to have a stable relationship with a man, do you approve or disapprove?

Approve (%)

(WVS: V112; EVS: V151)

Country	Wave		Gender		Age			Education			Income			Values		
	1990	2000	Male	Female	16-29	30-49	50+	Lower	Middle	Upper	Lower	Middle	Upper	Mat	Mixed	Postm.
Albania	na	12	12	12	18	10	8	7	14	16	7	16	12	7	13	24
Algeria	na	6	6	7	7	4	9	8	6	6	6	4	9	5	8	5
Argentina	58	61	58	65	64	65	55	60	64	64	59	64	61	65	61	60
Armenia	na	37	36	38	35	43	30	26	36	46	40	41	26	31	43	33
Australia	na	36	36	37	51	36	22	29	38	41	31	37	43	27	33	44
Austria	39	38	42	35	42	41	34	33	43	43	35	42	40	27	38	43
Azerbaijan	na	24	22	26	25	25	20	16	23	28	16	23	35	20	31	37
Bangladesh	na	4	4	3	5	3	4	2	2	10	1	5	4	3	4	na
Belarus	47	61	63	59	72	65	47	49	64	69	56	63	64	55	68	67
Belgium	32	52	48	56	54	58	44	43	56	52	46	53	55	48	52	53
Bosnia and Herz.	na	48	46	49	51	49	43	35	48	57	44	47	51	44	50	48
Brazil	51	52	43	61	64	49	36	43	57	67	46	48	60	44	53	71
Bulgaria	47	46	45	48	57	61	29	25	55	65	29	49	60	38	55	50
Canada	38	45	46	45	52	54	31	34	48	51	40	41	56	42	41	55
Chile	60	73	71	75	79	78	61	68	76	76	71	74	76	67	74	85
China	6	2	3	1	3	1	1	3	1	5	2	2	2	1	2	na
Colombia	na	76	76	76	76	78	68	66	78	80	68	76	80	75	76	86
Croatia	na	66	63	69	70	67	63	66	67	65	66	67	66	61	65	78
Czech Republic	23	39	37	41	47	41	34	39	41	37	34	42	41	36	40	47
Denmark	67	52	52	52	53	54	50	47	57	59	53	51	57	44	51	69
Dominican Rep.	na	48	42	51	49	46	36	50	48	48	49	42	55	39	47	52
Egypt	na	5	5	5	4	6	4	5	5	5	5	5	4	5	5	3
El Salvador	na	28	28	29	30	30	23	23	27	46	25	29	37	na	na	na
Estonia	32	29	22	34	33	32	24	24	31	29	30	25	32	26	29	39
Finland	56	54	53	54	57	55	50	52	56	53	55	56	52	51	52	65
France	39	50	49	50	56	52	44	51	50	46	52	50	48	46	49	57
Georgia	na	41	37	45	50	41	31	36	40	48	37	41	49	39	42	54
Germany	34	31	29	32	44	36	19	24	36	37	27	29	29	22	33	39
Great Britain	36	31	31	31	42	36	18	30	29	37	39	31	29	na	na	na
Greece	na	31	28	33	33	34	20	22	32	31	34	29	29	27	31	38
Hungary	39	38	39	38	45	41	32	37	39	45	40	34	44	39	39	46
Iceland	84	82	82	81	78	84	82	79	83	86	80	81	87	81	80	94
India	3	10	10	11	12	9	9	9	7	14	14	9	9	10	11	na
Indonesia	na	4	4	5	7	4	3	2	4	6	3	4	5	4	5	na
Iran	na	3	4	3	4	3	3	3	3	4	4	2	3	3	3	4
Ireland	23	33	33	34	44	38	21	35	34	29	33	32	32	28	35	33
Israel	na	na	na	na	na	na	na	na	na	na	na	na	na	na	na	na
Italy	39	28	28	27	26	31	26	26	29	29	26	31	29	24	27	31
Japan	15	23	23	23	37	29	12	14	21	35	17	24	27	16	24	33
Jordan	na	2	2	3	2	2	2	2	2	3	2	2	3	2	2	5
Korea, South	na	22	19	25	40	19	7	4	20	27	21	20	24	17	24	46
Latvia	26	55	47	62	57	60	51	47	58	58	56	55	54	52	57	64
Lithuania	55	61	59	63	74	67	46	49	65	63	52	60	68	59	63	53
Luxembourg	na	46	45	46	44	51	42	43	50	43	43	41	56	42	46	53
Macedonia	na	53	50	55	58	59	39	47	50	68	44	53	61	49	55	65
Malta	na	16	17	14	20	10	10	11	17	19	11	14	17	16	15	21
Mexico	43	47	46	48	54	48	34	36	59	67	38	48	61	11	50	59
Moldova	na	37	36	38	50	38	26	28	38	44	33	33	44	36	37	47
Montenegro	na	37	33	41	58	41	20	19	45	60	26	39	45	32	42	53
Morocco	na	3	2	3	3	2	1	2	4	5	1	2	5	1	4	2
Netherlands	44	50	46	54	57	56	40	42	53	54	45	53	54	37	49	60
New Zealand	na	15	13	17	25	18	10	13	15	18	14	15	18	11	14	21
Nigeria	9	18	18	18	19	17	17	15	21	19	18	16	19	16	18	28
Northern Ireland	25	31	28	34	49	34	20	28	35	32	32	25	32	27	29	44
Norway	27	23	22	24	26	24	20	22	22	27	na	na	na	22	23	29
Pakistan	na	0	na	na	na	na	na	na	na	na	na	na	na	na	na	na
Peru	na	49	47	51	51	50	43	44	47	56	43	48	61	42	51	52
Philippines	na	15	15	14	16	14	14	13	14	18	13	13	18	14	14	17
Poland	18	42	37	46	42	46	37	40	46	39	42	42	40	38	42	54
Portugal	40	37	39	34	50	41	25	31	48	48	21	35	41	34	39	39
Puerto Rico	na	56	53	58	68	67	43	41	54	60	51	53	63	45	60	55
Romania	38	49	51	47	56	54	40	33	54	66	41	46	58	38	57	70
Russian Fed.	42	54	49	58	62	57	44	39	55	58	51	53	56	51	56	58
Serbia	na	54	51	57	60	59	47	37	57	73	46	55	65	45	63	61
Singapore	na	18	17	20	23	15	12	14	20	25	17	18	21	14	19	30
Slovakia	na	23	25	22	29	25	18	18	25	28	18	23	27	22	25	37
Slovenia	60	56	51	60	58	54	56	49	59	57	54	57	59	52	57	56
South Africa	19	36	30	44	37	41	20	32	42	39	29	46	38	34	38	37
Spain	65	72	72	73	84	81	58	66	79	81	65	77	79	63	75	84
Sweden	25	32	27	36	25	32	36	28	34	31	37	27	30	23	29	39
Switzerland	38	37	38	36	41	40	32	32	39	34	35	40	39	27	39	43
Taiwan	na	11	11	12	18	12	4	9	10	14	12	12	10	8	16	8
Tanzania	na	15	14	16	16	16	10	12	14	29	15	11	25	13	13	13
Turkey	7	6	7	6	8	6	3	2	9	20	2	6	17	3	6	13
Uganda	na	19	14	23	26	14	3	17	21	9	13	21	17	16	22	12
Ukraine	na	40	37	42	47	46	31	28	42	42	39	42	41	37	45	42
United States	38	42	41	42	43	45	37	52	43	37	46	43	37	47	37	52
Uruguay	na	66	62	68	73	70	59	61	73	68	59	70	69	57	65	76
Venezuela	na	65	61	68	63	69	62	58	65	71	56	67	67	67	63	71
Vietnam	na	16	17	15	17	18	12	18	13	20	11	19	15	10	16	12
Zimbabwe	na	7	6	8	9	8	3	5	10	8	7	4	14	7	8	5
Total	37	35	33	37	38	37	31	29	38	40	32	36	39	29	37	46

RANKING

Country	2000
Iceland	82
Colombia	76
Chile	73
Spain	72
Croatia	66
Uruguay	66
Venezuela	65
Argentina	61
Lithuania	61
Belarus	61
Puerto Rico	56
Slovenia	56
Latvia	55
Serbia	54
Finland	54
Russian Fed.	54
Macedonia	53
Denmark	52
Brazil	52
Belgium	52
Netherlands	50
France	50
Peru	49
Romania	49
Bosnia and Herz.	48
Dominican Rep.	48
Mexico	47
Bulgaria	46
Luxembourg	46
Canada	45
Poland	42
United States	42
Georgia	41
Ukraine	40
Czech Republic	39
Hungary	38
Austria	38
Moldova	37
Switzerland	37
Montenegro	37
Armenia	37
Portugal	37
South Africa	36
Australia	36
Ireland	33
Sweden	32
Northern Ireland	31
Great Britain	31
Greece	31
Germany	31
Estonia	29
El Salvador	28
Italy	28
Azerbaijan	24
Slovakia	23
Norway	23
Japan	23
Korea, South	22
Uganda	19
Singapore	18
Nigeria	16
Vietnam	16
Malta	16
New Zealand	15
Tanzania	15
Philippines	15
Albania	12
Taiwan	11
India	10
Zimbabwe	7
Turkey	6
Algeria	6
Egypt	5
Indonesia	4
Bangladesh	4
Iran	3
Morocco	3
Jordan	2
China	2
Pakistan	0
Total	35

D026_1) MARRIAGE HAPPINESS: LONG-TERM RELATIONSHIP

How would you feel about the following statements: "A marriage or a long-term stable relationship is necessary to be happy?"

Agree strongly / Agree (%)

(EVS: V153)

Country	Wave 1990	Wave 2000	Gender Male	Gender Female	Age 16-29	Age 30-49	Age 50+	Education Lower	Education Middle	Education Upper	Income Lower	Income Middle	Income Upper	Values Mat	Values Mixed	Values Postm.
Albania	na	na	na	na	na	na	na	na	na	na	na	na	na	na	na	na
Algeria	na	na	na	na	na	na	na	na	na	na	na	na	na	na	na	na
Argentina	na	na	na	na	na	na	na	na	na	na	na	na	na	na	na	na
Armenia	na	na	na	na	na	na	na	na	na	na	na	na	na	na	na	na
Australia	na	na	na	na	na	na	na	na	na	na	na	na	na	na	na	na
Austria	na	55	59	51	45	47	68	62	49	46	60	56	53	68	57	48
Azerbaijan	na	na	na	na	na	na	na	na	na	na	na	na	na	na	na	na
Bangladesh	na	na	na	na	na	na	na	na	na	na	na	na	na	na	na	na
Belarus	na	73	73	73	65	72	80	80	70	70	74	72	73	77	70	64
Belgium	na	55	57	53	53	49	61	64	56	47	61	58	49	52	57	52
Bosnia and Herz.	na	na	na	na	na	na	na	na	na	na	na	na	na	na	na	na
Brazil	na	na	na	na	na	na	na	na	na	na	na	na	na	na	na	na
Bulgaria	na	81	79	82	65	81	89	94	74	73	90	79	75	85	78	76
Canada	na	na	na	na	na	na	na	na	na	na	na	na	na	na	na	na
Chile	na	na	na	na	na	na	na	na	na	na	na	na	na	na	na	na
China	na	na	na	na	na	na	na	na	na	na	na	na	na	na	na	na
Colombia	na	na	na	na	na	na	na	na	na	na	na	na	na	na	na	na
Croatia	na	69	64	73	58	69	76	77	64	65	77	69	65	72	69	66
Czech Republic	na	69	72	67	60	67	77	71	68	65	73	70	66	75	68	67
Denmark	na	36	39	32	34	28	44	42	32	24	42	35	27	51	36	24
Dominican Rep.	na	na	na	na	na	na	na	na	na	na	na	na	na	na	na	na
Egypt	na	na	na	na	na	na	na	na	na	na	na	na	na	na	na	na
El Salvador	na	na	na	na	na	na	na	na	na	na	na	na	na	na	na	na
Estonia	na	75	75	76	68	72	83	78	74	75	74	77	75	78	75	59
Finland	na	36	39	33	29	30	46	42	30	25	37	35	35	42	36	30
France	na	65	66	65	61	61	72	68	60	64	67	66	67	72	65	55
Georgia	na	na	na	na	na	na	na	na	na	na	na	na	na	na	na	na
Germany	na	63	66	61	45	60	74	70	58	55	65	68	67	81	61	48
Great Britain	na	37	42	33	28	28	51	42	32	31	40	39	26	na	na	na
Greece	na	85	84	85	87	82	84	92	81	86	87	82	86	84	84	88
Hungary	na	90	89	90	84	89	94	90	88	95	91	90	90	91	89	83
Iceland	na	36	44	27	30	32	45	41	34	26	40	33	33	41	35	28
India	na	na	na	na	na	na	na	na	na	na	na	na	na	na	na	na
Indonesia	na	na	na	na	na	na	na	na	na	na	na	na	na	na	na	na
Iran	na	na	na	na	na	na	na	na	na	na	na	na	na	na	na	na
Ireland	na	37	43	32	29	31	49	48	35	24	45	41	31	42	37	33
Israel	na	na	na	na	na	na	na	na	na	na	na	na	na	na	na	na
Italy	na	63	63	63	53	60	72	68	62	52	67	63	59	73	64	56
Japan	na	na	na	na	na	na	na	na	na	na	na	na	na	na	na	na
Jordan	na	na	na	na	na	na	na	na	na	na	na	na	na	na	na	na
Korea, South	na	na	na	na	na	na	na	na	na	na	na	na	na	na	na	na
Latvia	na	82	83	80	66	79	90	87	79	84	82	83	81	83	80	80
Lithuania	na	71	68	73	62	73	75	74	69	73	75	69	71	72	71	66
Luxembourg	na	60	59	60	58	56	64	62	60	55	59	60	48	64	58	57
Macedonia	na	na	na	na	na	na	na	na	na	na	na	na	na	na	na	na
Malta	na	65	67	62	58	64	70	72	63	57	65	64	68	73	61	54
Mexico	na	na	na	na	na	na	na	na	na	na	na	na	na	na	na	na
Moldova	na	na	na	na	na	na	na	na	na	na	na	na	na	na	na	na
Montenegro	na	na	na	na	na	na	na	na	na	na	na	na	na	na	na	na
Morocco	na	na	na	na	na	na	na	na	na	na	na	na	na	na	na	na
Netherlands	na	21	26	16	20	15	27	25	19	20	23	19	22	32	20	18
New Zealand	na	na	na	na	na	na	na	na	na	na	na	na	na	na	na	na
Nigeria	na	na	na	na	na	na	na	na	na	na	na	na	na	na	na	na
Northern Ireland	na	34	35	33	24	31	41	40	30	25	41	31	22	42	34	22
Norway	na	na	na	na	na	na	na	na	na	na	na	na	na	na	na	na
Pakistan	na	na	na	na	na	na	na	na	na	na	na	na	na	na	na	na
Peru	na	na	na	na	na	na	na	na	na	na	na	na	na	na	na	na
Philippines	na	na	na	na	na	na	na	na	na	na	na	na	na	na	na	na
Poland	na	72	75	69	62	69	82	76	70	60	74	73	66	72	72	63
Portugal	na	70	67	73	55	71	79	75	62	48	75	68	67	72	69	60
Puerto Rico	na	na	na	na	na	na	na	na	na	na	na	na	na	na	na	na
Romania	na	84	85	84	75	81	92	93	79	80	90	84	80	89	81	70
Russian Fed.	na	74	72	76	64	72	82	81	74	68	74	74	73	77	72	63
Serbia	na	na	na	na	na	na	na	na	na	na	na	na	na	na	na	na
Singapore	na	na	na	na	na	na	na	na	na	na	na	na	na	na	na	na
Slovakia	na	77	74	80	75	77	80	78	77	72	74	79	81	78	78	69
Slovenia	na	82	78	86	80	80	86	88	81	77	86	85	78	84	83	78
South Africa	na	na	na	na	na	na	na	na	na	na	na	na	na	na	na	na
Spain	na	54	52	55	45	48	64	66	46	41	61	56	49	65	55	40
Sweden	na	42	51	32	42	36	47	55	41	33	41	44	40	40	44	36
Switzerland	na	na	na	na	na	na	na	na	na	na	na	na	na	na	na	na
Taiwan	na	na	na	na	na	na	na	na	na	na	na	na	na	na	na	na
Tanzania	na	na	na	na	na	na	na	na	na	na	na	na	na	na	na	na
Turkey	na	77	77	76	74	78	80	80	75	58	83	75	69	80	75	74
Uganda	na	na	na	na	na	na	na	na	na	na	na	na	na	na	na	na
Ukraine	na	78	75	80	66	78	84	84	77	76	82	76	75	79	77	75
United States	na	na	na	na	na	na	na	na	na	na	na	na	na	na	na	na
Uruguay	na	na	na	na	na	na	na	na	na	na	na	na	na	na	na	na
Venezuela	na	na	na	na	na	na	na	na	na	na	na	na	na	na	na	na
Vietnam	na	na	na	na	na	na	na	na	na	na	na	na	na	na	na	na
Zimbabwe	na	na	na	na	na	na	na	na	na	na	na	na	na	na	na	na
Total	na	62	63	62	56	59	70	66	62	56	66	63	61	73	61	51

RANKING

Country	2000
Hungary	90
Greece	85
Romania	84
Slovenia	82
Latvia	82
Bulgaria	81
Ukraine	78
Slovakia	77
Turkey	77
Estonia	75
Russian Fed.	74
Belarus	73
Poland	72
Lithuania	71
Portugal	70
Czech Republic	69
Croatia	69
France	65
Malta	65
Germany	63
Italy	63
Luxembourg	60
Belgium	55
Austria	55
Spain	54
Sweden	42
Ireland	37
Great Britain	37
Finland	36
Denmark	36
Iceland	36
Northern Ireland	34
Netherlands	21
Total	62

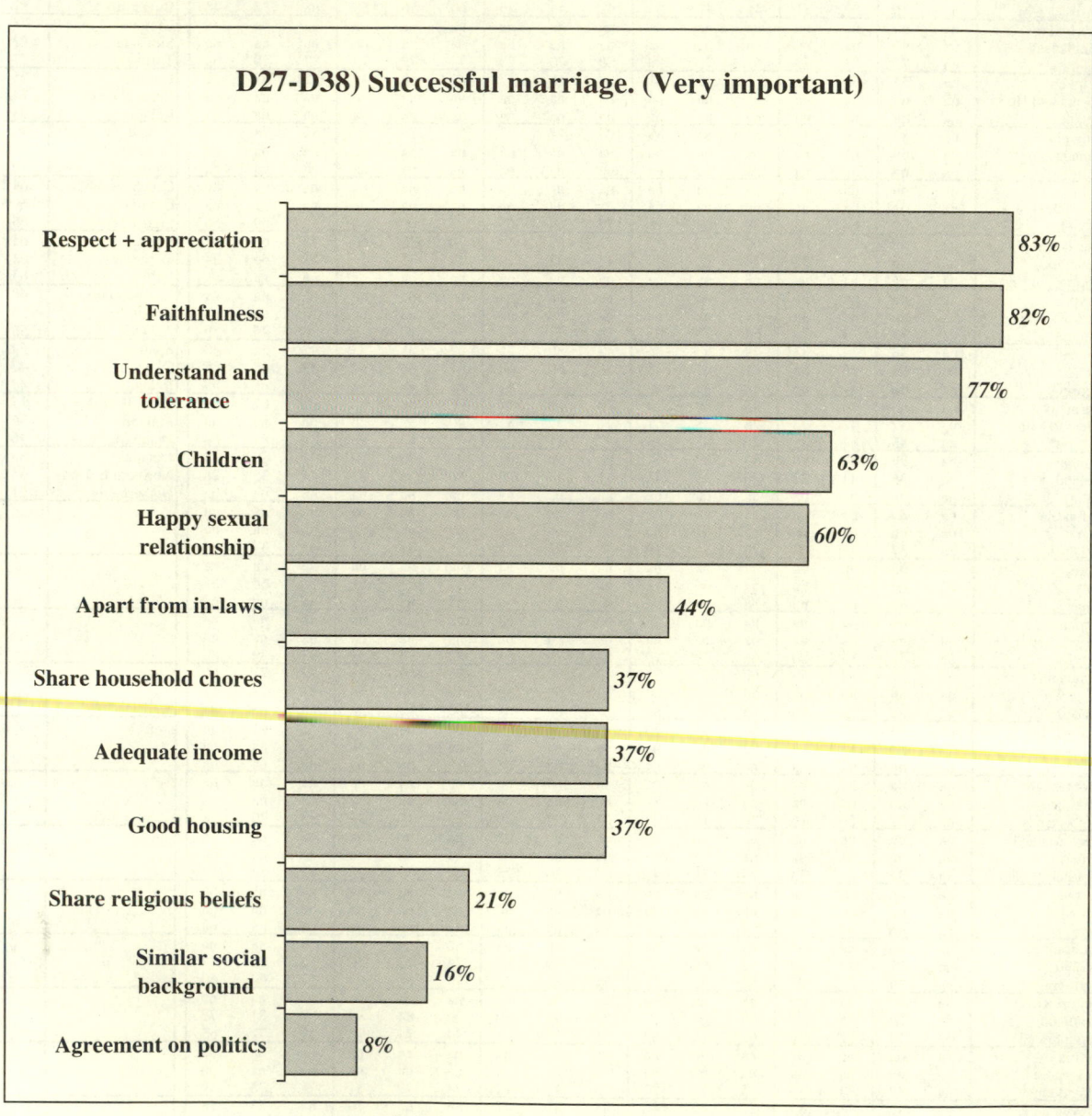

D27-D38) Successful marriage. (Very important)

Category	Percentage
Respect + appreciation	83%
Faithfulness	82%
Understand and tolerance	77%
Children	63%
Happy sexual relationship	60%
Apart from in-laws	44%
Share household chores	37%
Adequate income	37%
Good housing	37%
Share religious beliefs	21%
Similar social background	16%
Agreement on politics	8%

D027_1) MARRIAGE SUCCESS: FAITHFULNESS

Here is a list of things which some people think make for a successful marriage. Please tell me, for each one, whether you think it is...

Very important (%)

(EVS: V133)

Country	Wave		Gender		Age			Education			Income			Values			RANKING Country	2000
	1990	2000	Male	Female	16-29	30-49	50+	Lower	Middle	Upper	Lower	Middle	Upper	Mat	Mixed	Postm.		
Albania	na	na	na	na	na	na	na	na	na	na	na	na	na	na	na	na	Malta	97
Algeria	na	na	na	na	na	na	na	na	na	na	na	na	na	na	na	na	Iceland	96
Argentina	85	na	na	na	na	na	na	na	na	na	na	na	na	na	na	na	Turkey	96
Armenia	na	na	na	na	na	na	na	na	na	na	na	na	na	na	na	na	Ireland	95
Australia	na	na	na	na	na	na	na	na	na	na	na	na	na	na	na	na	Northern Ireland	94
Austria	83	86	84	88	88	84	88	92	84	73	87	90	83	91	88	81	Great Britain	90
Azerbaijan	na	na	na	na	na	na	na	na	na	na	na	na	na	na	na	na	Belgium	89
Bangladesh	na	na	na	na	na	na	na	na	na	na	na	na	na	na	na	na	Sweden	89
Belarus	79	70	63	75	67	69	73	70	70	69	73	68	65	72	67	58	Luxembourg	88
Belgium	85	89	88	91	93	87	89	91	90	87	87	91	88	94	88	86	Netherlands	87
Bosnia and Herz.	na	na	na	na	na	na	na	na	na	na	na	na	na	na	na	na	Poland	87
Brazil	76	na	na	na	na	na	na	na	na	na	na	na	na	na	na	na	Greece	87
Bulgaria	63	74	70	77	63	71	81	83	72	60	81	72	67	80	68	65	Austria	86
Canada	91	na	na	na	na	na	na	na	na	na	na	na	na	na	na	na	Hungary	85
Chile	92	na	na	na	na	na	na	na	na	na	na	na	na	na	na	na	Germany	85
China	90	na	na	na	na	na	na	na	na	na	na	na	na	na	na	na	Denmark	84
Colombia	na	na	na	na	na	na	na	na	na	na	na	na	na	na	na	na	Italy	84
Croatia	na	72	67	77	73	72	71	72	72	72	74	68	77	72	74	70	Romania	83
Czech Republic	na	73	71	76	78	70	73	79	68	64	76	76	68	82	72	65	Finland	82
Denmark	81	84	82	86	91	83	83	89	83	74	85	85	78	89	86	72	Slovenia	81
Dominican Rep.	na	na	na	na	na	na	na	na	na	na	na	na	na	na	na	na	Slovakia	81
Egypt	na	na	na	na	na	na	na	na	na	na	na	na	na	na	na	na	France	80
El Salvador	na	na	na	na	na	na	na	na	na	na	na	na	na	na	na	na	Spain	80
Estonia	61	61	57	65	57	58	67	63	61	60	64	66	58	64	59	66	Ukraine	79
Finland	75	82	78	85	86	81	81	82	82	79	87	79	79	80	84	76	Latvia	78
France	74	80	77	83	83	78	81	85	77	72	83	80	79	88	81	70	Portugal	74
Georgia	na	na	na	na	na	na	na	na	na	na	na	na	na	na	na	na	Bulgaria	74
Germany	78	85	80	88	78	83	89	87	82	83	85	84	83	91	84	77	Czech Republic	73
Great Britain	90	90	87	93	86	89	92	92	88	88	92	88	91	na	na	na	Croatia	72
Greece	na	87	85	88	90	82	91	94	86	86	86	85	89	88	86	86	Russian Fed.	72
Hungary	84	85	80	90	85	80	90	86	85	81	80	86	88	88	84	79	Belarus	70
Iceland	90	96	94	98	98	97	93	97	96	95	96	97	96	96	97	88	Lithuania	65
India	94	na	na	na	na	na	na	na	na	na	na	na	na	na	na	na	Estonia	61
Indonesia	na	na	na	na	na	na	na	na	na	na	na	na	na	na	na	na		
Iran	na	na	na	na	na	na	na	na	na	na	na	na	na	na	na	na		
Ireland	93	95	95	96	94	95	97	97	94	96	95	97	95	97	96	91		
Israel	na	na	na	na	na	na	na	na	na	na	na	na	na	na	na	na		
Italy	85	84	80	88	85	84	84	87	85	74	85	84	80	91	84	81		
Japan	73	na	na	na	na	na	na	na	na	na	na	na	na	na	na	na		
Jordan	na	na	na	na	na	na	na	na	na	na	na	na	na	na	na	na		
Korea, South	90	na	na	na	na	na	na	na	na	na	na	na	na	na	na	na		
Latvia	74	78	72	84	75	77	81	80	79	72	80	79	76	79	78	72		
Lithuania	70	65	55	73	62	61	70	67	64	64	74	66	62	68	64	60		
Luxembourg	na	88	85	90	88	85	90	92	84	89	89	84	86	88	88	82		
Macedonia	na	na	na	na	na	na	na	na	na	na	na	na	na	na	na	na		
Malta	na	97	95	99	98	95	99	98	97	94	98	96	96	97	97	99		
Mexico	81	na	na	na	na	na	na	na	na	na	na	na	na	na	na	na		
Moldova	na	na	na	na	na	na	na	na	na	na	na	na	na	na	na	na		
Montenegro	na	na	na	na	na	na	na	na	na	na	na	na	na	na	na	na		
Morocco	na	na	na	na	na	na	na	na	na	na	na	na	na	na	na	na		
Netherlands	88	87	87	88	90	83	90	89	90	83	84	88	89	90	88	84		
New Zealand	na	na	na	na	na	na	na	na	na	na	na	na	na	na	na	na		
Nigeria	99	na	na	na	na	na	na	na	na	na	na	na	na	na	na	na		
Northern Ireland	94	94	94	94	96	91	97	94	94	93	96	95	95	97	94	87		
Norway	91	na	na	na	na	na	na	na	na	na	na	na	na	na	na	na		
Pakistan	na	na	na	na	na	na	na	na	na	na	na	na	na	na	na	na		
Peru	na	na	na	na	na	na	na	na	na	na	na	na	na	na	na	na		
Philippines	na	na	na	na	na	na	na	na	na	na	na	na	na	na	na	na		
Poland	na	87	85	89	91	86	86	88	88	78	88	88	86	89	85	86		
Portugal	77	74	72	76	80	71	73	73	75	78	68	73	85	71	78	75		
Puerto Rico	na	na	na	na	na	na	na	na	na	na	na	na	na	na	na	na		
Romania	77	83	82	83	81	82	85	81	85	81	79	86	85	86	81	80		
Russian Fed.	77	72	68	75	63	71	78	79	73	65	75	75	65	75	70	58		
Serbia	na	na	na	na	na	na	na	na	na	na	na	na	na	na	na	na		
Singapore	na	na	na	na	na	na	na	na	na	na	na	na	na	na	na	na		
Slovakia	na	81	75	86	80	81	82	81	82	71	83	81	82	83	80	71		
Slovenia	80	81	79	83	83	79	82	85	81	71	82	87	73	81	82	80		
South Africa	na	na	na	na	na	na	na	na	na	na	na	na	na	na	na	na		
Spain	79	80	76	83	72	76	87	85	76	75	82	82	76	86	79	71		
Sweden	89	89	88	89	91	87	89	93	88	86	91	88	87	91	91	82		
Switzerland	81	na	na	na	na	na	na	na	na	na	na	na	na	na	na	na		
Taiwan	na	na	na	na	na	na	na	na	na	na	na	na	na	na	na	na		
Tanzania	na	na	na	na	na	na	na	na	na	na	na	na	na	na	na	na		
Turkey	87	96	96	96	96	95	97	95	97	95	95	97	96	96	96	97		
Uganda	na	na	na	na	na	na	na	na	na	na	na	na	na	na	na	na		
Ukraine	na	79	74	84	71	79	85	87	81	73	86	78	74	79	79	82		
United States	94	na	na	na	na	na	na	na	na	na	na	na	na	na	na	na		
Uruguay	na	na	na	na	na	na	na	na	na	na	na	na	na	na	na	na		
Venezuela	na	na	na	na	na	na	na	na	na	na	na	na	na	na	na	na		
Vietnam	na	na	na	na	na	na	na	na	na	na	na	na	na	na	na	na		
Zimbabwe	na	na	na	na	na	na	na	na	na	na	na	na	na	na	na	na		
Total	82	82	79	85	82	80	84	85	81	79	84	82	80	83	82	79	Total	82

D028_1) MARRIAGE SUCCESS: ADEQUATE INCOME

Here is a list of things which some people think make for a successful marriage. Please tell me, for each one, whether you think it is...

Very important (%)

(EVS: V134)

Country	Wave		Gender		Age			Education			Income			Values				RANKING Country	2000
	1990	2000	Male	Female	16-29	30-49	50+	Lower	Middle	Upper	Lower	Middle	Upper	Mat	Mixed	Postm.			
Albania	na	na	na	na	na	na	na	na	na	na	na	na	na	na	na	na		Turkey	84
Algeria	na	na	na	na	na	na	na	na	na	na	na	na	na	na	na	na		Ukraine	66
Argentina	44	na	na	na	na	na	na	na	na	na	na	na	na	na	na	na		Hungary	58
Armenia	na	na	na	na	na	na	na	na	na	na	na	na	na	na	na	na		Romania	54
Australia	na	na	na	na	na	na	na	na	na	na	na	na	na	na	na	na		Greece	54
Austria	30	28	29	27	25	20	37	34	24	16	32	30	22	44	31	17		Russian Fed.	54
Azerbaijan	na	na	na	na	na	na	na	na	na	na	na	na	na	na	na	na		Bulgaria	51
Bangladesh	na	na	na	na	na	na	na	na	na	na	na	na	na	na	na	na		Slovakia	47
Belarus	66	38	41	36	35	43	36	40	38	38	42	37	35	41	35	40		Ireland	45
Belgium	45	40	42	38	32	32	51	53	39	31	48	42	30	50	40	26		Poland	45
Bosnia and Herz.	na	na	na	na	na	na	na	na	na	na	na	na	na	na	na	na		Lithuania	42
Brazil	55	na	na	na	na	na	na	na	na	na	na	na	na	na	na	na		Belgium	40
Bulgaria	45	51	53	50	53	52	50	50	56	45	55	47	50	56	47	53		Malta	40
Canada	40	na	na	na	na	na	na	na	na	na	na	na	na	na	na	na		Belarus	38
Chile	67	na	na	na	na	na	na	na	na	na	na	na	na	na	na	na		Latvia	36
China	31	na	na	na	na	na	na	na	na	na	na	na	na	na	na	na		Czech Republic	36
Colombia	na	na	na	na	na	na	na	na	na	na	na	na	na	na	na	na		France	36
Croatia	na	23	26	19	20	21	27	26	22	15	27	22	22	25	22	25		Portugal	36
Czech Republic	na	36	35	38	32	35	39	42	33	18	39	35	34	46	34	25		Great Britain	35
Denmark	11	5	6	4	4	3	7	6	3	4	6	4	3	10	4	4		Northern Ireland	34
Dominican Rep.	na	na	na	na	na	na	na	na	na	na	na	na	na	na	na	na		Spain	34
Egypt	na	na	na	na	na	na	na	na	na	na	na	na	na	na	na	na		Iceland	31
El Salvador	na	na	na	na	na	na	na	na	na	na	na	na	na	na	na	na		Slovenia	30
Estonia	30	29	31	27	33	31	24	28	30	25	31	26	28	29	30	23		Italy	29
Finland	32	17	17	16	13	14	21	22	9	13	22	16	12	25	14	14		Estonia	29
France	38	36	38	34	32	32	42	42	32	23	40	37	32	45	36	23		Austria	28
Georgia	na	na	na	na	na	na	na	na	na	na	na	na	na	na	na	na		Germany	26
Germany	28	26	29	24	23	26	29	29	25	21	29	29	26	36	26	15		Luxembourg	26
Great Britain	35	35	36	33	33	33	35	37	33	30	38	39	32	na	na	na		Croatia	23
Greece	na	54	55	54	48	59	60	73	58	47	61	53	49	57	55	53		Netherlands	23
Hungary	52	58	58	59	57	58	59	61	55	46	68	56	55	61	57	42		Sweden	19
Iceland	40	31	33	30	16	33	41	38	26	26	33	30	31	37	29	29		Finland	17
India	59	na	na	na	na	na	na	na	na	na	na	na	na	na	na	na		Denmark	5
Indonesia	na	na	na	na	na	na	na	na	na	na	na	na	na	na	na	na			
Iran	na	na	na	na	na	na	na	na	na	na	na	na	na	na	na	na			
Ireland	52	45	47	44	33	41	59	55	44	33	55	44	37	48	45	39			
Israel	na	na	na	na	na	na	na	na	na	na	na	na	na	na	na	na			
Italy	32	29	30	28	25	28	33	35	26	21	34	31	22	37	30	24			
Japan	55	na	na	na	na	na	na	na	na	na	na	na	na	na	na	na			
Jordan	na	na	na	na	na	na	na	na	na	na	na	na	na	na	na	na			
Korea, South	34	na	na	na	na	na	na	na	na	na	na	na	na	na	na	na			
Latvia	35	36	37	35	42	37	33	39	38	26	40	36	29	39	34	24			
Lithuania	36	42	45	40	43	43	41	40	45	35	41	47	42	45	41	35			
Luxembourg	na	26	29	22	21	22	33	34	22	19	29	29	19	31	26	16			
Macedonia	na	na	na	na	na	na	na	na	na	na	na	na	na	na	na	na			
Malta	na	40	44	36	37	41	40	42	40	21	40	39	38	39	40	36			
Mexico	55	na	na	na	na	na	na	na	na	na	na	na	na	na	na	na			
Moldova	na	na	na	na	na	na	na	na	na	na	na	na	na	na	na	na			
Montenegro	na	na	na	na	na	na	na	na	na	na	na	na	na	na	na	na			
Morocco	na	na	na	na	na	na	na	na	na	na	na	na	na	na	na	na			
Netherlands	24	23	21	24	14	19	30	36	18	15	29	21	18	43	22	15			
New Zealand	na	na	na	na	na	na	na	na	na	na	na	na	na	na	na	na			
Nigeria	75	na	na	na	na	na	na	na	na	na	na	na	na	na	na	na			
Northern Ireland	40	34	38	31	26	33	39	40	26	37	42	33	26	34	35	30			
Norway	21	na	na	na	na	na	na	na	na	na	na	na	na	na	na	na			
Pakistan	na	na	na	na	na	na	na	na	na	na	na	na	na	na	na	na			
Peru	na	na	na	na	na	na	na	na	na	na	na	na	na	na	na	na			
Philippines	na	na	na	na	na	na	na	na	na	na	na	na	na	na	na	na			
Poland	na	45	45	45	37	43	52	51	40	33	54	41	37	47	46	34			
Portugal	49	36	34	38	38	35	34	39	34	15	39	35	37	32	37	34			
Puerto Rico	na	na	na	na	na	na	na	na	na	na	na	na	na	na	na	na			
Romania	45	54	56	53	52	54	56	54	55	54	52	58	54	52	57	57			
Russian Fed.	54	54	55	53	53	57	51	55	56	46	54	55	51	55	53	52			
Serbia	na	na	na	na	na	na	na	na	na	na	na	na	na	na	na	na			
Singapore	na	na	na	na	na	na	na	na	na	na	na	na	na	na	na	na			
Slovakia	na	47	49	45	45	50	45	50	47	37	48	51	43	52	46	31			
Slovenia	40	30	30	30	18	32	37	41	29	13	39	30	19	37	29	28			
South Africa	na	na	na	na	na	na	na	na	na	na	na	na	na	na	na	na			
Spain	46	34	36	32	27	33	38	39	32	25	37	35	33	48	31	26			
Sweden	23	19	21	17	12	18	24	28	17	14	18	20	18	44	20	9			
Switzerland	35	na	na	na	na	na	na	na	na	na	na	na	na	na	na	na			
Taiwan	na	na	na	na	na	na	na	na	na	na	na	na	na	na	na	na			
Tanzania	na	na	na	na	na	na	na	na	na	na	na	na	na	na	na	na			
Turkey	58	84	86	82	81	86	90	85	84	75	84	85	83	82	85	87			
Uganda	na	na	na	na	na	na	na	na	na	na	na	na	na	na	na	na			
Ukraine	na	66	69	64	61	70	65	70	67	60	71	63	64	69	66	42			
United States	46	na	na	na	na	na	na	na	na	na	na	na	na	na	na	na			
Uruguay	na	na	na	na	na	na	na	na	na	na	na	na	na	na	na	na			
Venezuela	na	na	na	na	na	na	na	na	na	na	na	na	na	na	na	na			
Vietnam	na	na	na	na	na	na	na	na	na	na	na	na	na	na	na	na			
Zimbabwe	na	na	na	na	na	na	na	na	na	na	na	na	na	na	na	na			
Total	42	37	38	36	34	36	39	40	37	31	41	37	34	45	35	26		Total	37

D029_1) MARRIAGE SUCCESS: SAME SOCIAL BACKGROUND

Here is a list of things which some people think make for a successful marriage. Please tell me, for each one, whether you think it is...

Very important (%)

(EVS: V135)

Country	Wave		Gender		Age			Education			Income			Values		
	1990	2000	Male	Female	16-29	30-49	50+	Lower	Middle	Upper	Lower	Middle	Upper	Mat	Mixed	Postm.
Albania	na	na	na	na	na	na	na	na	na	na	na	na	na	na	na	na
Algeria	na	na	na	na	na	na	na	na	na	na	na	na	na	na	na	na
Argentina	26	na	na	na	na	na	na	na	na	na	na	na	na	na	na	na
Armenia	na	na	na	na	na	na	na	na	na	na	na	na	na	na	na	na
Australia	na	na	na	na	na	na	na	na	na	na	na	na	na	na	na	na
Austria	15	13	13	13	10	10	18	16	11	7	19	12	9	27	13	9
Azerbaijan	na	na	na	na	na	na	na	na	na	na	na	na	na	na	na	na
Bangladesh	na	na	na	na	na	na	na	na	na	na	na	na	na	na	na	na
Belarus	16	11	11	11	10	11	12	10	11	13	14	10	11	10	10	22
Belgium	22	21	18	23	9	14	32	25	20	18	26	21	15	18	23	14
Bosnia and Herz.	na	na	na	na	na	na	na	na	na	na	na	na	na	na	na	na
Brazil	28	na	na	na	na	na	na	na	na	na	na	na	na	na	na	na
Bulgaria	18	30	32	28	32	34	26	27	32	29	30	27	30	29	31	29
Canada	20	na	na	na	na	na	na	na	na	na	na	na	na	na	na	na
Chile	34	na	na	na	na	na	na	na	na	na	na	na	na	na	na	na
China	13	na	na	na	na	na	na	na	na	na	na	na	na	na	na	na
Colombia	na	na	na	na	na	na	na	na	na	na	na	na	na	na	na	na
Croatia	na	7	10	4	5	5	10	6	8	6	4	7	8	5	8	4
Czech Republic	na	7	5	9	4	5	11	9	5	4	11	5	5	10	6	7
Denmark	12	6	7	6	3	3	11	8	2	6	9	6	4	8	7	3
Dominican Rep.	na	na	na	na	na	na	na	na	na	na	na	na	na	na	na	na
Egypt	na	na	na	na	na	na	na	na	na	na	na	na	na	na	na	na
El Salvador	na	na	na	na	na	na	na	na	na	na	na	na	na	na	na	na
Estonia	8	8	8	9	5	10	9	9	8	10	8	10	7	7	9	13
Finland	8	9	6	12	6	7	13	11	4	12	11	9	8	11	8	9
France	21	16	17	16	11	12	23	17	18	12	18	15	14	19	17	9
Georgia	na	na	na	na	na	na	na	na	na	na	na	na	na	na	na	na
Germany	7	14	13	15	11	14	16	17	13	9	18	14	16	19	14	9
Great Britain	21	18	19	17	12	15	24	20	17	13	19	16	17	na	na	na
Greece	na	21	17	24	14	21	37	34	22	18	20	20	22	25	22	13
Hungary	16	15	13	16	11	11	21	17	11	12	16	18	12	17	13	25
Iceland	14	7	6	8	5	6	9	6	7	8	8	6	8	9	6	6
India	47	na	na	na	na	na	na	na	na	na	na	na	na	na	na	na
Indonesia	na	na	na	na	na	na	na	na	na	na	na	na	na	na	na	na
Iran	na	na	na	na	na	na	na	na	na	na	na	na	na	na	na	na
Ireland	25	27	25	29	11	25	41	37	24	16	37	24	21	32	26	21
Israel	na	na	na	na	na	na	na	na	na	na	na	na	na	na	na	na
Italy	17	13	11	14	7	10	18	17	9	9	17	12	8	19	13	7
Japan	23	na	na	na	na	na	na	na	na	na	na	na	na	na	na	na
Jordan	na	na	na	na	na	na	na	na	na	na	na	na	na	na	na	na
Korea, South	22	na	na	na	na	na	na	na	na	na	na	na	na	na	na	na
Latvia	12	15	15	15	15	12	18	18	15	11	17	16	12	17	14	9
Lithuania	8	12	12	12	13	12	11	11	12	13	11	9	13	8	12	18
Luxembourg	na	15	15	15	12	14	18	17	14	12	20	13	14	16	16	13
Macedonia	na	na	na	na	na	na	na	na	na	na	na	na	na	na	na	na
Malta	na	51	49	53	43	52	56	59	50	38	55	52	44	51	52	43
Mexico	30	na	na	na	na	na	na	na	na	na	na	na	na	na	na	na
Moldova	na	na	na	na	na	na	na	na	na	na	na	na	na	na	na	na
Montenegro	na	na	na	na	na	na	na	na	na	na	na	na	na	na	na	na
Morocco	na	na	na	na	na	na	na	na	na	na	na	na	na	na	na	na
Netherlands	21	15	13	16	7	10	23	18	12	14	16	13	15	21	15	10
New Zealand	na	na	na	na	na	na	na	na	na	na	na	na	na	na	na	na
Nigeria	49	na	na	na	na	na	na	na	na	na	na	na	na	na	na	na
Northern Ireland	21	23	22	24	14	21	28	26	19	20	23	18	13	27	23	18
Norway	14	na	na	na	na	na	na	na	na	na	na	na	na	na	na	na
Pakistan	na	na	na	na	na	na	na	na	na	na	na	na	na	na	na	na
Peru	na	na	na	na	na	na	na	na	na	na	na	na	na	na	na	na
Philippines	na	na	na	na	na	na	na	na	na	na	na	na	na	na	na	na
Poland	na	17	18	17	10	13	28	22	12	9	19	18	12	19	17	16
Portugal	26	14	15	13	13	18	11	14	16	7	16	16	13	8	18	7
Puerto Rico	na	na	na	na	na	na	na	na	na	na	na	na	na	na	na	na
Romania	25	28	28	29	19	26	36	33	27	24	29	31	26	32	28	12
Russian Fed.	9	10	9	10	8	9	11	14	10	7	12	10	7	10	9	11
Serbia	na	na	na	na	na	na	na	na	na	na	na	na	na	na	na	na
Singapore	na	na	na	na	na	na	na	na	na	na	na	na	na	na	na	na
Slovakia	na	16	15	16	12	15	20	20	14	15	22	13	14	17	15	10
Slovenia	24	15	13	17	7	14	20	25	11	11	20	15	9	14	15	16
South Africa	na	na	na	na	na	na	na	na	na	na	na	na	na	na	na	na
Spain	25	17	17	18	10	15	24	23	12	15	18	20	18	26	16	12
Sweden	12	8	6	9	2	5	13	6	7	9	8	7	8	12	7	8
Switzerland	16	na	na	na	na	na	na	na	na	na	na	na	na	na	na	na
Taiwan	na	na	na	na	na	na	na	na	na	na	na	na	na	na	na	na
Tanzania	na	na	na	na	na	na	na	na	na	na	na	na	na	na	na	na
Turkey	47	65	63	67	62	67	68	69	60	60	68	64	61	64	67	63
Uganda	na	na	na	na	na	na	na	na	na	na	na	na	na	na	na	na
Ukraine	na	16	14	16	8	16	19	23	13	18	16	14	17	15	15	23
United States	29	na	na	na	na	na	na	na	na	na	na	na	na	na	na	na
Uruguay	na	na	na	na	na	na	na	na	na	na	na	na	na	na	na	na
Venezuela	na	na	na	na	na	na	na	na	na	na	na	na	na	na	na	na
Vietnam	na	na	na	na	na	na	na	na	na	na	na	na	na	na	na	na
Zimbabwe	na	na	na	na	na	na	na	na	na	na	na	na	na	na	na	na
Total	21	16	16	17	12	15	21	18	16	15	19	15	14	18	16	12

RANKING

Country	2000
Turkey	65
Malta	51
Bulgaria	30
Romania	28
Ireland	27
Northern Ireland	23
Greece	21
Belgium	21
Great Britain	18
Poland	17
Spain	17
France	16
Slovakia	16
Ukraine	16
Luxembourg	15
Latvia	15
Hungary	15
Slovenia	15
Netherlands	15
Germany	14
Portugal	14
Austria	13
Italy	13
Lithuania	12
Belarus	11
Russian Fed.	10
Finland	9
Estonia	8
Sweden	8
Croatia	7
Czech Republic	7
Iceland	7
Denmark	6
Total	16

D030_1) MARRIAGE SUCCESS: RESPECT + APPRECIATION

Here is a list of things which some people think make for a successful marriage. Please tell me, for each one, whether you think it is...

Very important (%)

(EVS: V136)

Country	Wave		Gender		Age			Education			Income			Values			RANKING Country	2000
	1990	2000	Male	Female	16-29	30-49	50+	Lower	Middle	Upper	Lower	Middle	Upper	Mat	Mixed	Postm.		
Albania	na	na	na	na	na	na	na	na	na	na	na	na	na	na	na	na	Malta	97
Algeria	na	na	na	na	na	na	na	na	na	na	na	na	na	na	na	na	Iceland	97
Argentina	90	na	na	na	na	na	na	na	na	na	na	na	na	na	na	na	Turkey	95
Armenia	na	na	na	na	na	na	na	na	na	na	na	na	na	na	na	na	Netherlands	95
Australia	na	na	na	na	na	na	na	na	na	na	na	na	na	na	na	na	Greece	94
Austria	82	89	87	91	88	91	88	89	88	94	84	90	92	86	91	87	Sweden	94
Azerbaijan	na	na	na	na	na	na	na	na	na	na	na	na	na	na	na	na	Belgium	91
Bangladesh	na	na	na	na	na	na	na	na	na	na	na	na	na	na	na	na	Italy	90
Belarus	85	76	68	83	81	75	73	69	78	82	78	73	80	75	77	80	France	89
Belgium	87	91	90	92	93	90	90	86	91	93	90	88	93	88	91	94	Slovenia	89
Bosnia and Herz.	na	na	na	na	na	na	na	na	na	na	na	na	na	na	na	na	Austria	89
Brazil	73	na	na	na	na	na	na	na	na	na	na	na	na	na	na	na	Poland	88
Bulgaria	68	81	79	82	76	80	84	83	79	80	83	78	79	81	80	87	Czech Republic	87
Canada	92	na	na	na	na	na	na	na	na	na	na	na	na	na	na	na	Ireland	87
Chile	96	na	na	na	na	na	na	na	na	na	na	na	na	na	na	na	Hungary	87
China	82	na	na	na	na	na	na	na	na	na	na	na	na	na	na	na	Finland	86
Colombia	na	na	na	na	na	na	na	na	na	na	na	na	na	na	na	na	Denmark	85
Croatia	na	74	69	79	77	76	71	75	74	75	76	71	80	69	74	80	Ukraine	84
Czech Republic	na	87	84	91	85	87	89	84	90	94	84	88	90	85	88	93	Luxembourg	84
Denmark	83	85	80	89	91	87	79	81	89	90	81	84	92	75	85	91	Northern Ireland	84
Dominican Rep.	na	na	na	na	na	na	na	na	na	na	na	na	na	na	na	na	Slovakia	81
Egypt	na	na	na	na	na	na	na	na	na	na	na	na	na	na	na	na	Bulgaria	81
El Salvador	na	na	na	na	na	na	na	na	na	na	na	na	na	na	na	na	Germany	81
Estonia	74	71	64	77	67	73	72	65	72	77	68	73	71	72	72	61	Great Britain	81
Finland	83	86	83	88	86	88	82	82	89	94	85	88	85	83	87	88	Spain	79
France	84	89	88	91	90	89	90	88	91	91	91	89	86	89	89	90	Romania	76
Georgia	na	na	na	na	na	na	na	na	na	na	na	na	na	na	na	na	Belarus	76
Germany	78	81	78	83	76	84	79	75	84	90	75	80	87	81	80	82	Latvia	75
Great Britain	84	81	83	79	81	79	83	79	83	82	80	79	81	na	na	na	Croatia	74
Greece	na	94	92	96	95	92	95	93	93	95	95	92	96	94	95	92	Estonia	71
Hungary	90	87	83	90	85	87	88	83	93	93	79	90	89	86	89	76	Russian Fed.	68
Iceland	96	97	95	98	97	97	95	97	96	97	96	97	97	98	96	94	Portugal	66
India	80	na	na	na	na	na	na	na	na	na	na	na	na	na	na	na	Lithuania	53
Indonesia	na	na	na	na	na	na	na	na	na	na	na	na	na	na	na	na		
Iran	na	na	na	na	na	na	na	na	na	na	na	na	na	na	na	na		
Ireland	83	87	84	90	80	90	89	85	86	94	88	84	89	87	87	88		
Israel	na	na	na	na	na	na	na	na	na	na	na	na	na	na	na	na		
Italy	90	90	88	92	94	90	89	88	93	92	87	89	93	87	91	92		
Japan	74	na	na	na	na	na	na	na	na	na	na	na	na	na	na	na		
Jordan	na	na	na	na	na	na	na	na	na	na	na	na	na	na	na	na		
Korea, South	68	na	na	na	na	na	na	na	na	na	na	na	na	na	na	na		
Latvia	74	75	74	77	79	75	74	71	77	76	73	77	77	73	77	67		
Lithuania	65	53	48	56	52	51	54	47	52	67	50	52	59	47	54	57		
Luxembourg	na	84	83	85	81	83	87	81	83	91	75	88	89	79	84	88		
Macedonia	na	na	na	na	na	na	na	na	na	na	na	na	na	na	na	na		
Malta	na	97	97	97	97	97	97	93	97	100	95	99	99	94	98	99		
Mexico	88	na	na	na	na	na	na	na	na	na	na	na	na	na	na	na		
Moldova	na	na	na	na	na	na	na	na	na	na	na	na	na	na	na	na		
Montenegro	na	na	na	na	na	na	na	na	na	na	na	na	na	na	na	na		
Morocco	na	na	na	na	na	na	na	na	na	na	na	na	na	na	na	na		
Netherlands	93	95	94	95	96	97	92	93	95	96	95	93	97	96	95	93		
New Zealand	na	na	na	na	na	na	na	na	na	na	na	na	na	na	na	na		
Nigeria	97	na	na	na	na	na	na	na	na	na	na	na	na	na	na	na		
Northern Ireland	83	84	84	84	79	83	88	85	84	80	87	80	84	88	84	82		
Norway	93	na	na	na	na	na	na	na	na	na	na	na	na	na	na	na		
Pakistan	na	na	na	na	na	na	na	na	na	na	na	na	na	na	na	na		
Peru	na	na	na	na	na	na	na	na	na	na	na	na	na	na	na	na		
Philippines	na	na	na	na	na	na	na	na	na	na	na	na	na	na	na	na		
Poland	na	88	84	90	89	86	88	85	91	89	87	88	88	88	88	89		
Portugal	83	66	66	67	80	60	62	63	70	80	61	64	75	61	71	64		
Puerto Rico	na	na	na	na	na	na	na	na	na	na	na	na	na	na	na	na		
Romania	82	76	78	75	81	75	75	69	80	82	65	80	82	75	79	83		
Russian Fed.	78	68	65	71	67	71	66	65	68	72	66	68	70	67	70	64		
Serbia	na	na	na	na	na	na	na	na	na	na	na	na	na	na	na	na		
Singapore	na	na	na	na	na	na	na	na	na	na	na	na	na	na	na	na		
Slovakia	na	81	76	86	81	79	84	80	81	89	81	80	84	82	81	79		
Slovenia	87	89	87	91	89	90	89	88	89	91	89	90	91	88	89	91		
South Africa	na	na	na	na	na	na	na	na	na	na	na	na	na	na	na	na		
Spain	78	79	77	81	83	79	77	76	80	85	77	85	80	79	78	85		
Sweden	91	94	92	96	96	94	93	89	94	97	93	93	95	94	93	97		
Switzerland	90	na	na	na	na	na	na	na	na	na	na	na	na	na	na	na		
Taiwan	na	na	na	na	na	na	na	na	na	na	na	na	na	na	na	na		
Tanzania	na	na	na	na	na	na	na	na	na	na	na	na	na	na	na	na		
Turkey	89	95	96	95	96	95	96	93	99	96	93	97	97	96	96	98		
Uganda	na	na	na	na	na	na	na	na	na	na	na	na	na	na	na	na		
Ukraine	na	84	82	86	83	82	87	83	84	85	89	81	81	82	87	84		
United States	92	na	na	na	na	na	na	na	na	na	na	na	na	na	na	na		
Uruguay	na	na	na	na	na	na	na	na	na	na	na	na	na	na	na	na		
Venezuela	na	na	na	na	na	na	na	na	na	na	na	na	na	na	na	na		
Vietnam	na	na	na	na	na	na	na	na	na	na	na	na	na	na	na	na		
Zimbabwe	na	na	na	na	na	na	na	na	na	na	na	na	na	na	na	na		
Total	84	83	81	85	84	83	83	81	83	88	82	83	85	80	85	88	Total	83

D031_1) MARRIAGE SUCCESS: SHARE RELIGIOUS BELIEFS
Here is a list of things which some people think make for a successful marriage. Please tell me, for each one, whether you think it is...

Very important (%)

(EVS: V137)

Country	Wave 1990	Wave 2000	Gender Male	Gender Female	Age 16-29	Age 30-49	Age 50+	Education Lower	Education Middle	Education Upper	Income Lower	Income Middle	Income Upper	Values Mat	Values Mixed	Values Postm.
Albania	na	na	na	na	na	na	na	na	na	na	na	na	na	na	na	na
Algeria	na	na	na	na	na	na	na	na	na	na	na	na	na	na	na	na
Argentina	28	na	na	na	na	na	na	na	na	na	na	na	na	na	na	na
Armenia	na	na	na	na	na	na	na	na	na	na	na	na	na	na	na	na
Australia	na	na	na	na	na	na	na	na	na	na	na	na	na	na	na	na
Austria	23	19	16	22	12	16	26	24	15	12	27	19	13	33	20	13
Azerbaijan	na	na	na	na	na	na	na	na	na	na	na	na	na	na	na	na
Bangladesh	na	na	na	na	na	na	na	na	na	na	na	na	na	na	na	na
Belarus	14	14	8	19	8	11	22	22	12	8	18	13	9	16	12	4
Belgium	22	18	17	20	14	13	26	28	16	14	27	19	12	21	18	15
Bosnia and Herz.	na	na	na	na	na	na	na	na	na	na	na	na	na	na	na	na
Brazil	35	na	na	na	na	na	na	na	na	na	na	na	na	na	na	na
Bulgaria	14	27	25	28	21	24	32	37	22	17	36	21	21	29	24	22
Canada	28	na	na	na	na	na	na	na	na	na	na	na	na	na	na	na
Chile	52	na	na	na	na	na	na	na	na	na	na	na	na	na	na	na
China	6	na	na	na	na	na	na	na	na	na	na	na	na	na	na	na
Colombia	na	na	na	na	na	na	na	na	na	na	na	na	na	na	na	na
Croatia	na	28	28	28	19	26	36	32	26	24	36	30	22	39	29	13
Czech Republic	na	9	6	10	4	7	12	11	6	8	12	6	7	10	8	9
Denmark	16	13	14	12	10	10	18	16	10	8	13	12	12	19	13	11
Dominican Rep.	na	na	na	na	na	na	na	na	na	na	na	na	na	na	na	na
Egypt	na	na	na	na	na	na	na	na	na	na	na	na	na	na	na	na
El Salvador	na	na	na	na	na	na	na	na	na	na	na	na	na	na	na	na
Estonia	8	11	10	12	13	9	13	14	10	9	12	12	10	10	11	8
Finland	13	15	12	18	9	13	20	18	11	14	18	18	10	16	15	15
France	17	13	11	14	9	11	17	15	8	12	14	14	11	14	15	8
Georgia	na	na	na	na	na	na	na	na	na	na	na	na	na	na	na	na
Germany	16	15	13	17	10	12	20	19	11	10	18	15	17	17	15	11
Great Britain	19	14	14	13	10	13	16	13	15	14	16	13	13	na	na	na
Greece	na	33	26	38	24	31	55	57	39	23	36	29	32	36	33	25
Hungary	22	15	10	20	4	11	25	18	9	13	22	16	10	18	13	na
Iceland	18	10	9	11	4	7	19	14	8	8	13	10	8	11	10	6
India	40	na	na	na	na	na	na	na	na	na	na	na	na	na	na	na
Indonesia	na	na	na	na	na	na	na	na	na	na	na	na	na	na	na	na
Iran	na	na	na	na	na	na	na	na	na	na	na	na	na	na	na	na
Ireland	33	26	24	28	8	22	44	43	20	11	44	25	15	33	25	24
Israel	na	na	na	na	na	na	na	na	na	na	na	na	na	na	na	na
Italy	26	23	20	26	16	18	33	34	17	12	32	20	16	38	24	14
Japan	18	na	na	na	na	na	na	na	na	na	na	na	na	na	na	na
Jordan	na	na	na	na	na	na	na	na	na	na	na	na	na	na	na	na
Korea, South	21	na	na	na	na	na	na	na	na	na	na	na	na	na	na	na
Latvia	9	11	9	13	8	7	15	18	9	10	15	9	7	10	11	7
Lithuania	14	16	15	16	11	11	24	25	12	14	27	13	11	20	14	9
Luxembourg	na	15	16	14	11	12	21	22	12	11	20	11	13	19	16	7
Macedonia	na	na	na	na	na	na	na	na	na	na	na	na	na	na	na	na
Malta	na	56	50	62	39	54	70	73	53	31	66	56	49	58	57	37
Mexico	50	na	na	na	na	na	na	na	na	na	na	na	na	na	na	na
Moldova	na	na	na	na	na	na	na	na	na	na	na	na	na	na	na	na
Montenegro	na	na	na	na	na	na	na	na	na	na	na	na	na	na	na	na
Morocco	na	na	na	na	na	na	na	na	na	na	na	na	na	na	na	na
Netherlands	16	11	10	12	7	5	20	18	10	7	17	7	10	19	11	6
New Zealand	na	na	na	na	na	na	na	na	na	na	na	na	na	na	na	na
Nigeria	83	na	na	na	na	na	na	na	na	na	na	na	na	na	na	na
Northern Ireland	37	33	33	32	24	25	44	41	24	31	37	28	20	42	32	26
Norway	24	na	na	na	na	na	na	na	na	na	na	na	na	na	na	na
Pakistan	na	na	na	na	na	na	na	na	na	na	na	na	na	na	na	na
Peru	na	na	na	na	na	na	na	na	na	na	na	na	na	na	na	na
Philippines	na	na	na	na	na	na	na	na	na	na	na	na	na	Mat	na	na
Poland	na	40	38	41	31	33	52	47	33	25	45	39	29	44	38	33
Portugal	34	20	20	19	11	21	24	23	15	7	29	23	16	14	25	7
Puerto Rico	na	na	na	na	na	na	na	na	na	na	na	na	na	na	na	na
Romania	31	41	38	43	29	36	52	51	37	30	46	43	37	45	40	19
Russian Fed.	11	12	9	14	7	12	14	18	11	10	15	11	9	12	11	5
Serbia	na	na	na	na	na	na	na	na	na	na	na	na	na	na	na	na
Singapore	na	na	na	na	na	na	na	na	na	na	na	na	na	na	na	na
Slovakia	na	26	19	32	17	21	39	36	21	20	36	23	21	30	22	14
Slovenia	34	20	18	22	9	20	29	37	16	7	31	17	11	27	19	20
South Africa	na	na	na	na	na	na	na	na	na	na	na	na	na	na	na	na
Spain	29	21	17	24	8	17	31	31	13	13	25	18	12	35	18	9
Sweden	18	13	9	17	8	11	18	17	10	14	15	13	11	19	14	7
Switzerland	21	na	na	na	na	na	na	na	na	na	na	na	na	na	na	na
Taiwan	na	na	na	na	na	na	na	na	na	na	na	na	na	na	na	na
Tanzania	na	na	na	na	na	na	na	na	na	na	na	na	na	na	na	na
Turkey	68	74	70	77	70	74	84	84	63	44	83	74	54	79	76	63
Uganda	na	na	na	na	na	na	na	na	na	na	na	na	na	na	na	na
Ukraine	na	24	20	28	18	22	30	37	23	20	29	21	21	23	23	42
United States	44	na	na	na	na	na	na	na	na	na	na	na	na	na	na	na
Uruguay	na	na	na	na	na	na	na	na	na	na	na	na	na	na	na	na
Venezuela	na	na	na	na	na	na	na	na	na	na	na	na	na	na	na	na
Vietnam	na	na	na	na	na	na	na	na	na	na	na	na	na	na	na	na
Zimbabwe	na	na	na	na	na	na	na	na	na	na	na	na	na	na	na	na
Total	26	21	19	23	15	18	28	27	19	17	27	20	16	25	21	15

RANKING

Country	2000
Turkey	74
Malta	56
Romania	41
Poland	40
Northern Ireland	33
Greece	33
Croatia	28
Bulgaria	27
Ireland	26
Slovakia	26
Ukraine	24
Italy	23
Spain	21
Slovenia	20
Portugal	20
Austria	19
Belgium	18
Lithuania	16
Finland	15
Hungary	15
Luxembourg	15
Germany	15
Belarus	14
Great Britain	14
France	13
Sweden	13
Denmark	13
Russian Fed.	12
Netherlands	11
Estonia	11
Latvia	11
Iceland	10
Czech Republic	9
Total	21

D032_1) MARRIAGE SUCCESS: GOOD HOUSING

Here is a list of things which some people think make for a successful marriage. Please tell me, for each one, whether you think it is...

Very important (%)   (EVS: V138)

Country	Wave 1990	Wave 2000	Gender Male	Gender Female	Age 16-29	Age 30-49	Age 50+	Education Lower	Education Middle	Education Upper	Income Lower	Income Middle	Income Upper	Values Mat	Values Mixed	Values Postm.
Albania	na	na	na	na	na	na	na	na	na	na	na	na	na	na	na	na
Algeria	na	na	na	na	na	na	na	na	na	na	na	na	na	na	na	na
Argentina	40	na	na	na	na	na	na	na	na	na	na	na	na	na	na	na
Armenia	na	na	na	na	na	na	na	na	na	na	na	na	na	na	na	na
Australia	na	na	na	na	na	na	na	na	na	na	na	na	na	na	na	na
Austria	40	33	31	35	31	28	40	39	30	19	35	35	30	54	34	27
Azerbaijan	na	na	na	na	na	na	na	na	na	na	na	na	na	na	na	na
Bangladesh	na	na	na	na	na	na	na	na	na	na	na	na	na	na	na	na
Belarus	61	48	45	50	46	56	39	37	51	54	48	46	50	47	48	53
Belgium	39	41	41	41	41	32	49	58	39	32	51	45	30	51	41	29
Bosnia and Herz.	na	na	na	na	na	na	na	na	na	na	na	na	na	na	na	na
Brazil	47	na	na	na	na	na	na	na	na	na	na	na	na	na	na	na
Bulgaria	43	45	43	46	44	45	45	42	50	38	47	43	45	46	45	60
Canada	33	na	na	na	na	na	na	na	na	na	na	na	na	na	na	na
Chile	61	na	na	na	na	na	na	na	na	na	na	na	na	na	na	na
China	25	na	na	na	na	na	na	na	na	na	na	na	na	na	na	na
Colombia	na	na	na	na	na	na	na	na	na	na	na	na	na	na	na	na
Croatia	na	18	20	17	15	17	21	18	20	13	23	19	14	22	17	16
Czech Republic	na	41	41	40	35	39	44	49	32	26	45	40	37	50	39	26
Denmark	30	18	18	19	12	11	29	24	8	12	24	16	12	25	20	11
Dominican Rep.	na	na	na	na	na	na	na	na	na	na	na	na	na	na	na	na
Egypt	na	na	na	na	na	na	na	na	na	na	na	na	na	na	na	na
El Salvador	na	na	na	na	na	na	na	na	na	na	na	na	na	na	na	na
Estonia	35	26	25	26	29	23	26	29	27	18	26	25	24	26	27	23
Finland	22	18	16	20	12	13	26	23	10	13	26	17	10	26	16	15
France	37	36	37	36	34	36	37	41	34	25	37	38	32	43	36	27
Georgia	na	na	na	na	na	na	na	na	na	na	na	na	na	na	na	na
Germany	41	26	25	27	17	26	30	30	23	19	31	28	23	32	27	16
Great Britain	37	39	41	36	38	36	41	45	37	24	44	45	36	na	na	na
Greece	na	60	53	64	57	59	70	72	63	54	63	54	60	63	60	54
Hungary	51	60	61	59	57	57	64	62	60	48	65	58	59	59	63	62
Iceland	33	26	27	24	18	21	38	34	21	15	30	24	22	28	25	19
India	41	na	na	na	na	na	na	na	na	na	na	na	na	na	na	na
Indonesia	na	na	na	na	na	na	na	na	na	na	na	na	na	na	na	na
Iran	na	na	na	na	na	na	na	na	na	na	na	na	na	na	na	na
Ireland	46	47	47	47	31	44	62	64	43	26	58	49	36	50	47	39
Israel	na	na	na	na	na	na	na	na	na	na	na	na	na	na	na	na
Italy	25	20	18	22	17	15	27	28	16	11	28	16	13	29	22	12
Japan	35	na	na	na	na	na	na	na	na	na	na	na	na	na	na	na
Jordan	na	na	na	na	na	na	na	na	na	na	na	na	na	na	na	na
Korea, South	7	na	na	na	na	na	na	na	na	na	na	na	na	na	na	na
Latvia	45	30	29	30	33	26	31	33	30	24	34	31	23	31	29	31
Lithuania	33	27	28	26	31	22	29	27	28	21	30	26	27	29	26	26
Luxembourg	na	28	30	27	26	25	34	35	26	24	34	32	20	29	30	20
Macedonia	na	na	na	na	na	na	na	na	na	na	na	na	na	na	na	na
Malta	na	38	39	38	34	38	41	45	50	27	41	41	37	39	39	32
Mexico	44	na	na	na	na	na	na	na	na	na	na	na	na	na	na	na
Moldova	na	na	na	na	na	na	na	na	na	na	na	na	na	na	na	na
Montenegro	na	na	na	na	na	na	na	na	na	na	na	na	na	na	na	na
Morocco	na	na	na	na	na	na	na	na	na	na	na	na	na	na	na	na
Netherlands	33	26	26	26	17	19	37	44	19	16	36	24	14	44	25	21
New Zealand	na	na	na	na	na	na	na	na	na	na	na	na	na	na	na	na
Nigeria	74	na	na	na	na	na	na	na	na	na	na	na	na	na	na	na
Northern Ireland	36	36	38	34	28	31	44	44	28	31	44	34	24	41	34	36
Norway	23	na	na	na	na	na	na	na	na	na	na	na	na	na	na	na
Pakistan	na	na	na	na	na	na	na	na	na	na	na	na	na	na	na	na
Peru	na	na	na	na	na	na	na	na	na	na	na	na	na	na	na	na
Philippines	na	na	na	na	na	na	na	na	na	na	na	na	na	na	na	na
Poland	na	52	52	53	42	50	61	57	47	45	57	50	46	53	53	46
Portugal	52	35	35	34	39	31	35	36	35	23	41	36	32	28	39	31
Puerto Rico	na	na	na	na	na	na	na	na	na	na	na	na	na	na	na	na
Romania	51	51	54	48	50	49	53	50	52	50	47	53	53	52	52	40
Russian Fed.	51	45	44	45	44	46	44	46	48	35	46	44	42	45	45	33
Serbia	na	na	na	na	na	na	na	na	na	na	na	na	na	na	na	na
Singapore	na	na	na	na	na	na	na	na	na	na	na	na	na	na	na	na
Slovakia	na	49	49	48	49	49	48	50	49	38	47	49	48	52	47	39
Slovenia	39	30	29	31	20	29	39	42	28	19	40	29	18	38	29	28
South Africa	na	na	na	na	na	na	na	na	na	na	na	na	na	na	na	na
Spain	40	31	32	30	28	28	35	36	28	22	34	30	33	37	31	22
Sweden	39	29	31	27	18	25	39	42	25	24	30	31	24	49	30	20
Switzerland	34	na	na	na	na	na	na	na	na	na	na	na	na	na	na	na
Taiwan	na	na	na	na	na	na	na	na	na	na	na	na	na	na	na	na
Tanzania	na	na	na	na	na	na	na	na	na	na	na	na	na	na	na	na
Turkey	50	62	62	61	56	67	68	69	56	40	69	62	50	61	63	61
Uganda	na	na	na	na	na	na	na	na	na	na	na	na	na	na	na	na
Ukraine	na	62	62	62	57	63	63	68	64	55	68	57	62	65	63	48
United States	40	na	na	na	na	na	na	na	na	na	na	na	na	na	na	na
Uruguay	na	na	na	na	na	na	na	na	na	na	na	na	na	na	na	na
Venezuela	na	na	na	na	na	na	na	na	na	na	na	na	na	na	na	na
Vietnam	na	na	na	na	na	na	na	na	na	na	na	na	na	na	na	na
Zimbabwe	na	na	na	na	na	na	na	na	na	na	na	na	na	na	na	na
Total	40	37	37	37	34	34	41	40	36	32	42	37	33	43	36	27

RANKING

Country	2000
Ukraine	62
Turkey	62
Hungary	60
Greece	60
Poland	52
Romania	51
Slovakia	49
Belarus	48
Ireland	47
Bulgaria	45
Russian Fed.	45
Belgium	41
Czech Republic	41
Great Britain	39
Malta	38
France	36
Northern Ireland	36
Portugal	35
Austria	33
Spain	31
Slovenia	30
Latvia	30
Sweden	29
Luxembourg	28
Lithuania	27
Germany	26
Estonia	26
Netherlands	26
Iceland	26
Italy	20
Denmark	18
Croatia	18
Finland	18
Total	37

D033_1) MARRIAGE SUCCESS: AGREEMENT IN POLITICS

Here is a list of things which some people think make for a successful marriage. Please tell me, for each one, whether you think it is...

Very important (%)

(EVS: V139)

Country	Wave		Gender		Age			Education			Income			Values				RANKING Country	2000
	1990	2000	Male	Female	16-29	30-49	50+	Lower	Middle	Upper	Lower	Middle	Upper	Mat	Mixed	Postm.			
Albania	na	na	na	na	na	na	na	na	na	na	na	na	na	na	na	na		Turkey	49
Algeria	na	na	na	na	na	na	na	na	na	na	na	na	na	na	na	na		Malta	24
Argentina	8	na	na	na	na	na	na	na	na	na	na	na	na	na	na	na		Romania	15
Armenia	na	na	na	na	na	na	na	na	na	na	na	na	na	na	na	na		Bulgaria	15
Australia	na	na	na	na	na	na	na	na	na	na	na	na	na	na	na	na		Greece	14
Austria	8	6	5	6	4	4	8	5	6	8	8	6	4	9	6	5		Poland	13
Azerbaijan	na	na	na	na	na	na	na	na	na	na	na	na	na	na	na	na		Northern Ireland	13
Bangladesh	na	na	na	na	na	na	na	na	na	na	na	na	na	na	na	na		Spain	10
Belarus	9	5	4	6	3	5	7	8	4	7	6	4	6	6	5	6		Germany	10
Belgium	9	7	6	7	4	4	10	11	6	4	10	6	4	7	7	5		Ukraine	10
Bosnia and Herz.	na	na	na	na	na	na	na	na	na	na	na	na	na	na	na	na		Portugal	9
Brazil	13	na	na	na	na	na	na	na	na	na	na	na	na	na	na	na		Slovakia	8
Bulgaria	15	15	13	17	9	16	18	19	13	14	19	13	12	14	16	5		France	8
Canada	6	na	na	na	na	na	na	na	na	na	na	na	na	na	na	na		Lithuania	8
Chile	18	na	na	na	na	na	na	na	na	na	na	na	na	na	na	na		Luxembourg	8
China	24	na	na	na	na	na	na	na	na	na	na	na	na	na	na	na		Hungary	7
Colombia	na	na	na	na	na	na	na	na	na	na	na	na	na	na	na	na		Italy	7
Croatia	na	4	6	2	2	2	7	4	4	3	4	3	5	4	3	5		Ireland	7
Czech Republic	na	6	5	7	3	2	10	7	4	4	7	6	4	5	6	7		Belgium	7
Denmark	4	2	2	1	1	1	3	3	na	1	1	2	1	na	2	1		Great Britain	7
Dominican Rep.	na	na	na	na	na	na	na	na	na	na	na	na	na	na	na	na		Latvia	7
Egypt	na	na	na	na	na	na	na	na	na	na	na	na	na	na	na	na		Slovenia	6
El Salvador	na	na	na	na	na	na	na	na	na	na	na	na	na	na	na	na		Sweden	6
Estonia	6	5	5	5	3	4	7	5	4	7	5	6	3	5	4	8		Czech Republic	6
Finland	5	4	3	5	2	2	7	6	1	4	6	4	4	5	4	2		Austria	6
France	8	8	7	8	8	6	9	7	9	8	7	7	9	8	7	9		Belarus	5
Georgia	na	na	na	na	na	na	na	na	na	na	na	na	na	na	na	na		Estonia	5
Germany	12	10	10	10	8	8	13	11	9	11	12	9	12	12	11	7		Finland	4
Great Britain	7	7	8	6	4	6	8	8	5	4	11	5	4	na	na	na		Netherlands	4
Greece	na	14	13	15	9	11	30	29	13	12	13	14	16	15	13	13		Croatia	4
Hungary	11	7	6	9	5	6	10	8	6	10	8	8	7	7	8	5		Russian Fed.	3
Iceland	5	2	2	2	2	1	4	3	1	1	3	1	1	3	2	1		Iceland	2
India	12	na	na	na	na	na	na	na	na	na	na	na	na	na	na	na		Denmark	2
Indonesia	na	na	na	na	na	na	na	na	na	na	na	na	na	na	na	na			
Iran	na	na	na	na	na	na	na	na	na	na	na	na	na	na	na	na			
Ireland	4	7	5	8	4	6	11	11	5	3	10	8	3	9	7	3			
Israel	na	na	na	na	na	na	na	na	na	na	na	na	na	na	na	na			
Italy	10	7	7	7	6	5	10	10	6	5	9	8	5	9	7	5			
Japan	8	na	na	na	na	na	na	na	na	na	na	na	na	na	na	na			
Jordan	na	na	na	na	na	na	na	na	na	na	na	na	na	na	na	na			
Korea, South	10	na	na	na	na	na	na	na	na	na	na	na	na	na	na	na			
Latvia	13	7	8	6	2	6	9	8	5	8	9	5	5	6	6	9			
Lithuania	8	8	8	7	7	6	9	10	7	6	13	6	6	7	7	6			
Luxembourg	na	8	8	7	8	6	9	9	7	7	9	7	5	8	8	6			
Macedonia	na	na	na	na	na	na	na	na	na	na	na	na	na	na	na	na			
Malta	na	24	21	27	16	21	32	33	21	15	30	23	15	26	24	11			
Mexico	18	na	na	na	na	na	na	na	na	na	na	na	na	na	na	na			
Moldova	na	na	na	na	na	na	na	na	na	na	na	na	na	na	na	na			
Montenegro	na	na	na	na	na	na	na	na	na	na	na	na	na	na	na	na			
Morocco	na	na	na	na	na	na	na	na	na	na	na	na	na	na	na	na			
Netherlands	7	4	3	5	1	2	7	5	4	3	5	3	3	4	4	3			
New Zealand	na	na	na	na	na	na	na	na	na	na	na	na	na	na	na	na			
Nigeria	20	na	na	na	na	na	na	na	na	na	na	na	na	na	na	na			
Northern Ireland	10	13	14	11	13	10	14	15	9	12	13	9	7	14	12	7			
Norway	7	na	na	na	na	na	na	na	na	na	na	na	na	na	na	na			
Pakistan	na	na	na	na	na	na	na	na	na	na	na	na	na	na	na	na			
Peru	na	na	na	na	na	na	na	na	na	na	na	na	na	na	na	na			
Philippines	na	na	na	na	na	na	na	na	na	na	na	na	na	na	na	na			
Poland	na	13	14	12	10	9	20	15	12	7	16	13	8	15	13	9			
Portugal	15	9	9	10	10	8	9	9	11	6	10	9	13	7	12	4			
Puerto Rico	na	na	na	na	na	na	na	na	na	na	na	na	na	na	na	na			
Romania	7	15	16	15	11	14	20	18	15	11	14	21	13	17	14	10			
Russian Fed.	8	3	3	3	1	4	3	2	3	3	3	2	3	2	4	6			
Serbia	na	na	na	na	na	na	na	na	na	na	na	na	na	na	na	na			
Singapore	na	na	na	na	na	na	na	na	na	na	na	na	na	na	na	na			
Slovakia	na	8	7	9	6	8	11	8	9	8	9	8	9	8	9	8			
Slovenia	14	6	5	7	2	7	9	12	4	3	8	5	3	5	6	8			
South Africa	na	na	na	na	na	na	na	na	na	na	na	na	na	na	na	na			
Spain	15	10	10	10	6	9	14	15	7	6	12	10	11	15	9	8			
Sweden	10	6	4	8	2	6	8	9	5	4	7	6	5	9	6	6			
Switzerland	9	na	na	na	na	na	na	na	na	na	na	na	na	na	na	na			
Taiwan	na	na	na	na	na	na	na	na	na	na	na	na	na	na	na	na			
Tanzania	na	na	na	na	na	na	na	na	na	na	na	na	na	na	na	na			
Turkey	35	49	49	48	45	51	54	53	42	42	54	48	42	38	51	53			
Uganda	na	na	na	na	na	na	na	na	na	na	na	na	na	na	na	na			
Ukraine	na	10	10	9	4	9	13	13	10	7	11	9	9	9	9	17			
United States	12	na	na	na	na	na	na	na	na	na	na	na	na	na	na	na			
Uruguay	na	na	na	na	na	na	na	na	na	na	na	na	na	na	na	na			
Venezuela	na	na	na	na	na	na	na	na	na	na	na	na	na	na	na	na			
Vietnam	na	na	na	na	na	na	na	na	na	na	na	na	na	na	na	na			
Zimbabwe	na	na	na	na	na	na	na	na	na	na	na	na	na	na	na	na			
Total	11	8	8	9	6	7	11	10	8	7	10	8	7	9	8	7		Total	8

D034_1) MARRIAGE SUCCESS: E10698UNDERSTAND AND TOLERANCE

Here is a list of things which some people think make for a successful marriage. Please tell me, for each one, whether you think it is...

Very important (%)

(EVS: V140)

Country	Wave 1990	Wave 2000	Gender Male	Gender Female	Age 16-29	Age 30-49	Age 50+	Education Lower	Education Middle	Education Upper	Income Lower	Income Middle	Income Upper	Values Mat	Values Mixed	Values Postm.
Albania	na	na	na	na	na	na	na	na	na	na	na	na	na	na	na	na
Algeria	na	na	na	na	na	na	na	na	na	na	na	na	na	na	na	na
Argentina	89	na	na	na	na	na	na	na	na	na	na	na	na	na	na	na
Armenia	na	na	na	na	na	na	na	na	na	na	na	na	na	na	na	na
Australia	na	na	na	na	na	na	na	na	na	na	na	na	na	na	na	na
Austria	83	84	83	85	86	86	81	81	85	93	77	84	87	83	84	87
Azerbaijan	na	na	na	na	na	na	na	na	na	na	na	na	na	na	na	na
Bangladesh	na	na	na	na	na	na	na	na	na	na	na	na	na	na	na	na
Belarus	69	74	70	77	77	75	70	65	77	76	74	72	76	73	74	82
Belgium	78	83	80	85	80	84	83	81	81	86	85	81	83	81	81	85
Bosnia and Herz.	na	na	na	na	na	na	na	na	na	na	na	na	na	na	na	na
Brazil	70	na	na	na	na	na	na	na	na	na	na	na	na	na	na	na
Bulgaria	63	75	73	76	74	73	76	73	75	77	75	72	74	75	74	80
Canada	84	na	na	na	na	na	na	na	na	na	na	na	na	na	na	na
Chile	90	na	na	na	na	na	na	na	na	na	na	na	na	na	na	na
China	70	na	na	na	na	na	na	na	na	na	na	na	na	na	na	na
Colombia	na	na	na	na	na	na	na	na	na	na	na	na	na	na	na	na
Croatia	na	68	65	71	69	70	65	65	70	68	64	68	71	61	68	74
Czech Republic	na	86	84	87	89	83	86	84	87	90	85	86	86	83	86	89
Denmark	80	79	72	86	83	80	76	77	80	85	79	77	83	75	80	82
Dominican Rep.	na	na	na	na	na	na	na	na	na	na	na	na	na	na	na	na
Egypt	na	na	na	na	na	na	na	na	na	na	na	na	na	na	na	na
El Salvador	na	na	na	na	na	na	na	na	na	na	na	na	na	na	na	na
Estonia	57	61	56	65	60	61	61	56	62	65	58	64	59	61	60	71
Finland	70	69	65	73	72	71	66	67	68	77	75	67	65	70	68	77
France	74	79	75	83	78	80	79	77	79	84	82	77	78	76	79	85
Georgia	na	na	na	na	na	na	na	na	na	na	na	na	na	na	na	na
Germany	74	81	79	83	79	85	79	74	87	89	77	82	89	80	81	86
Great Britain	86	81	78	84	78	79	86	80	83	80	81	79	81	na	na	na
Greece	na	90	86	92	93	88	87	91	87	91	92	87	90	88	91	87
Hungary	76	80	75	85	79	81	81	75	90	89	75	81	83	80	81	80
Iceland	86	88	87	88	90	87	87	84	90	90	86	88	90	85	89	89
India	81	na	na	na	na	na	na	na	na	na	na	na	na	na	na	na
Indonesia	na	na	na	na	na	na	na	na	na	na	na	na	na	na	na	na
Iran	na	na	na	na	na	na	na	na	na	na	na	na	na	na	na	na
Ireland	81	86	85	86	86	87	84	84	86	89	87	83	85	86	85	89
Israel	na	na	na	na	na	na	na	na	na	na	na	na	na	na	na	na
Italy	80	81	78	85	81	82	81	79	84	83	79	82	84	78	81	85
Japan	77	na	na	na	na	na	na	na	na	na	na	na	na	na	na	na
Jordan	na	na	na	na	na	na	na	na	na	na	na	na	na	na	na	na
Korea, South	73	na	na	na	na	na	na	na	na	na	na	na	na	na	na	na
Latvia	62	66	63	69	68	65	67	60	66	75	65	66	69	64	67	63
Lithuania	33	42	37	47	46	43	39	34	42	57	39	42	47	42	42	43
Luxembourg	na	80	78	83	83	79	80	77	80	89	72	79	85	71	82	86
Macedonia	na	na	na	na	na	na	na	na	na	na	na	na	na	na	na	na
Malta	na	94	93	95	93	92	95	93	94	98	91	94	96	92	95	96
Mexico	82	na	na	na	na	na	na	na	na	na	na	na	na	na	na	na
Moldova	na	na	na	na	na	na	na	na	na	na	na	na	na	na	na	na
Montenegro	na	na	na	na	na	na	na	na	na	na	na	na	na	na	na	na
Morocco	na	na	na	na	na	na	na	na	na	na	na	na	na	na	na	na
Netherlands	87	87	85	89	89	87	86	84	90	87	84	86	90	83	87	88
New Zealand	na	na	na	na	na	na	na	na	na	na	na	na	na	na	na	na
Nigeria	99	na	na	na	na	na	na	na	na	na	na	na	na	na	na	na
Northern Ireland	81	82	83	82	78	81	88	82	84	81	84	82	82	88	83	78
Norway	84	na	na	na	na	na	na	na	na	na	na	na	na	na	na	na
Pakistan	na	na	na	na	na	na	na	na	na	na	na	na	na	na	na	na
Peru	na	na	na	na	na	na	na	na	na	na	na	na	na	na	na	na
Philippines	na	na	na	na	na	na	na	na	na	na	na	na	na	na	na	na
Poland	na	78	75	80	77	76	80	76	81	74	78	76	81	79	77	77
Portugal	76	59	58	60	69	53	58	55	66	72	48	60	68	53	63	59
Puerto Rico	na	na	na	na	na	na	na	na	na	na	na	na	na	na	na	na
Romania	72	73	72	73	72	74	71	68	75	77	64	75	78	71	75	75
Russian Fed.	67	62	57	66	58	64	62	61	61	64	60	64	63	61	63	48
Serbia	na	na	na	na	na	na	na	na	na	na	na	na	na	na	na	na
Singapore	na	na	na	na	na	na	na	na	na	na	na	na	na	na	na	na
Slovakia	na	79	74	83	75	80	81	77	79	82	75	82	81	79	80	84
Slovenia	78	83	80	86	84	84	81	82	82	88	83	82	84	84	83	86
South Africa	na	na	na	na	na	na	na	na	na	na	na	na	na	na	na	na
Spain	73	76	74	78	80	78	73	73	79	79	76	78	80	77	75	85
Sweden	89	87	82	92	92	88	84	82	87	91	87	85	89	88	86	91
Switzerland	86	na	na	na	na	na	na	na	na	na	na	na	na	na	na	na
Taiwan	na	na	na	na	na	na	na	na	na	na	na	na	na	na	na	na
Tanzania	na	na	na	na	na	na	na	na	na	na	na	na	na	na	na	na
Turkey	80	92	93	91	92	92	92	90	96	97	91	92	96	93	92	95
Uganda	na	na	na	na	na	na	na	na	na	na	na	na	na	na	na	na
Ukraine	na	81	78	84	82	82	81	81	82	80	86	78	79	80	82	76
United States	83	na	na	na	na	na	na	na	na	na	na	na	na	na	na	na
Uruguay	na	na	na	na	na	na	na	na	na	na	na	na	na	na	na	na
Venezuela	na	na	na	na	na	na	na	na	na	na	na	na	na	na	na	na
Vietnam	na	na	na	na	na	na	na	na	na	na	na	na	na	na	na	na
Zimbabwe	na	na	na	na	na	na	na	na	na	na	na	na	na	na	na	na
Total	77	77	75	80	79	78	77	75	78	82	77	77	79	74	78	83

RANKING

Country	2000
Malta	94
Turkey	92
Greece	90
Iceland	88
Sweden	87
Netherlands	87
Ireland	86
Czech Republic	86
Austria	84
Slovenia	83
Belgium	83
Northern Ireland	82
Italy	81
Germany	81
Ukraine	81
Great Britain	81
Hungary	80
Luxembourg	80
Denmark	79
France	79
Slovakia	79
Poland	78
Spain	76
Bulgaria	75
Belarus	74
Romania	73
Finland	69
Croatia	68
Latvia	66
Russian Fed.	62
Estonia	61
Portugal	59
Lithuania	42
Total	77

D035_1) MARRIAGE SUCCESS: LIVING APART FROM YOUR IN-LAWS

Here is a list of things which some people think make for a successful marriage. Please tell me, for each one, whether you think it is...

Very important (%)

(EVS: V141)

Country	Wave 1990	Wave 2000	Gender Male	Gender Female	Age 16-29	Age 30-49	Age 50+	Education Lower	Education Middle	Education Upper	Income Lower	Income Middle	Income Upper	Values Mat	Values Mixed	Values Postm.
Albania	na	na	na	na	na	na	na	na	na	na	na	na	na	na	na	na
Algeria	na	na	na	na	na	na	na	na	na	na	na	na	na	na	na	na
Argentina	41	na	na	na	na	na	na	na	na	na	na	na	na	na	na	na
Armenia	na	na	na	na	na	na	na	na	na	na	na	na	na	na	na	na
Australia	na	na	na	na	na	na	na	na	na	na	na	na	na	na	na	na
Austria	36	44	40	47	40	43	47	43	43	46	46	44	41	36	44	46
Azerbaijan	na	na	na	na	na	na	na	na	na	na	na	na	na	na	na	na
Bangladesh	na	na	na	na	na	na	na	na	na	na	na	na	na	na	na	na
Belarus	50	46	43	48	51	50	36	36	48	53	43	46	48	47	43	53
Belgium	57	60	58	62	50	61	65	64	60	58	68	62	54	60	61	63
Bosnia and Herz.	na	na	na	na	na	na	na	na	na	na	na	na	na	na	na	na
Brazil	48	na	na	na	na	na	na	na	na	na	na	na	na	na	na	na
Bulgaria	43	58	58	57	60	62	53	47	63	64	53	58	63	56	62	62
Canada	51	na	na	na	na	na	na	na	na	na	na	na	na	na	na	na
Chile	53	na	na	na	na	na	na	na	na	na	na	na	na	na	na	na
China	8	na	na	na	na	na	na	na	na	na	na	na	na	na	na	na
Colombia	na	na	na	na	na	na	na	na	na	na	na	na	na	na	na	na
Croatia	na	26	23	29	34	23	24	19	31	29	29	24	28	17	29	24
Czech Republic	na	40	38	42	42	41	38	40	39	41	41	38	44	42	40	35
Denmark	54	55	54	56	58	55	53	56	57	51	61	55	53	53	57	51
Dominican Rep.	na	na	na	na	na	na	na	na	na	na	na	na	na	na	na	na
Egypt	na	na	na	na	na	na	na	na	na	na	na	na	na	na	na	na
El Salvador	na	na	na	na	na	na	na	na	na	na	na	na	na	na	na	na
Estonia	42	39	34	43	47	44	30	38	42	33	32	39	40	40	39	45
Finland	24	24	22	26	27	28	20	21	29	24	26	27	23	29	23	20
France	64	69	67	71	62	69	73	70	70	68	70	69	67	72	68	70
Georgia	na	na	na	na	na	na	na	na	na	na	na	na	na	na	na	na
Germany	44	31	33	30	27	37	27	32	30	32	31	38	29	27	34	30
Great Britain	54	51	50	51	47	54	49	51	51	44	54	51	54	na	na	na
Greece	na	51	47	54	53	50	50	53	55	47	52	53	48	52	51	52
Hungary	48	49	46	52	53	53	43	46	57	49	52	50	48	47	53	56
Iceland	43	40	37	42	32	48	35	45	36	38	37	40	43	44	38	39
India	20	na	na	na	na	na	na	na	na	na	na	na	na	na	na	na
Indonesia	na	na	na	na	na	na	na	na	na	na	na	na	na	na	na	na
Iran	na	na	na	na	na	na	na	na	na	na	na	na	na	na	na	na
Ireland	46	45	44	45	40	47	46	50	44	38	48	45	42	39	47	40
Israel	na	na	na	na	na	na	na	na	na	na	na	na	na	na	na	na
Italy	46	47	45	49	51	52	40	42	51	51	43	46	48	40	47	50
Japan	7	na	na	na	na	na	na	na	na	na	na	na	na	na	na	na
Jordan	na	na	na	na	na	na	na	na	na	na	na	na	na	na	na	na
Korea, South	5	na	na	na	na	na	na	na	na	na	na	na	na	na	na	na
Latvia	42	32	32	33	37	38	26	23	35	35	29	35	37	33	31	31
Lithuania	35	34	31	37	44	36	26	20	39	41	28	33	40	33	34	43
Luxembourg	na	54	52	57	54	58	51	55	53	57	50	59	52	54	54	58
Macedonia	na	na	na	na	na	na	na	na	na	na	na	na	na	na	na	na
Malta	na	57	55	58	58	59	54	55	59	50	54	57	60	55	56	72
Mexico	40	na	na	na	na	na	na	na	na	na	na	na	na	na	na	na
Moldova	na	na	na	na	na	na	na	na	na	na	na	na	na	na	na	na
Montenegro	na	na	na	na	na	na	na	na	na	na	na	na	na	na	na	na
Morocco	na	na	na	na	na	na	na	na	na	na	na	na	na	na	na	na
Netherlands	59	56	53	60	51	54	61	53	57	59	58	54	58	48	57	60
New Zealand	na	na	na	na	na	na	na	na	na	na	na	na	na	na	na	na
Nigeria	57	na	na	na	na	na	na	na	na	na	na	na	na	na	na	na
Northern Ireland	54	47	48	46	47	50	44	44	47	52	51	47	39	52	47	37
Norway	42	na	na	na	na	na	na	na	na	na	na	na	na	na	na	na
Pakistan	na	na	na	na	na	na	na	na	na	na	na	na	na	na	na	na
Peru	na	na	na	na	na	na	na	na	na	na	na	na	na	na	na	na
Philippines	na	na	na	na	na	na	na	na	na	na	na	na	na	Mat	na	na
Poland	na	61	56	65	55	65	61	61	61	62	65	59	61	58	64	54
Portugal	54	31	32	31	43	32	24	30	36	29	22	34	48	26	35	26
Puerto Rico	na	na	na	na	na	na	na	na	na	na	na	na	na	na	na	na
Romania	40	38	37	39	47	43	30	28	43	47	27	39	47	37	39	47
Russian Fed.	36	37	37	37	45	40	27	26	38	37	31	35	42	35	39	37
Serbia	na	na	na	na	na	na	na	na	na	na	na	na	na	na	na	na
Singapore	na	na	na	na	na	na	na	na	na	na	na	na	na	na	na	na
Slovakia	na	18	20	17	22	21	13	17	19	20	15	21	19	18	20	16
Slovenia	31	30	26	34	25	33	30	26	31	33	32	34	28	31	30	31
South Africa	na	na	na	na	na	na	na	na	na	na	na	na	na	na	na	na
Spain	36	33	34	31	33	36	30	29	36	34	32	35	43	34	32	36
Sweden	54	42	37	46	38	41	44	42	42	42	41	41	46	46	43	40
Switzerland	59	na	na	na	na	na	na	na	na	na	na	na	na	na	na	na
Taiwan	na	na	na	na	na	na	na	na	na	na	na	na	na	na	na	na
Tanzania	na	na	na	na	na	na	na	na	na	na	na	na	na	na	na	na
Turkey	42	60	61	59	58	61	63	58	63	62	57	57	71	57	58	70
Uganda	na	na	na	na	na	na	na	na	na	na	na	na	na	na	na	na
Ukraine	na	52	51	53	65	53	44	38	54	55	49	51	59	52	54	63
United States	47	na	na	na	na	na	na	na	na	na	na	na	na	na	na	na
Uruguay	na	na	na	na	na	na	na	na	na	na	na	na	na	na	na	na
Venezuela	na	na	na	na	na	na	na	na	na	na	na	na	na	na	na	na
Vietnam	na	na	na	na	na	na	na	na	na	na	na	na	na	na	na	na
Zimbabwe	na	na	na	na	na	na	na	na	na	na	na	na	na	na	na	na
Total	42	44	42	46	45	46	41	42	45	47	43	45	45	42	44	46

RANKING

Country	2000
France	69
Poland	61
Belgium	60
Turkey	60
Bulgaria	58
Malta	57
Netherlands	56
Denmark	55
Luxembourg	54
Ukraine	52
Greece	51
Great Britain	51
Hungary	49
Italy	47
Northern Ireland	47
Belarus	46
Ireland	45
Austria	44
Sweden	42
Czech Republic	40
Iceland	40
Estonia	39
Romania	38
Russian Fed.	37
Lithuania	34
Spain	33
Latvia	32
Germany	31
Portugal	31
Slovenia	30
Croatia	26
Finland	24
Slovakia	18
Total	44

D036_1) MARRIAGE SUCCESS: HAPPY SEXUAL RELATIONSHIP

Here is a list of things which some people think make for a successful marriage. Please tell me, for each one, whether you think it is...

Very important (%)

(EVS: V142)

Country	Wave		Gender		Age			Education			Income			Values		
	1990	2000	Male	Female	16-29	30-49	50+	Lower	Middle	Upper	Lower	Middle	Upper	Mat	Mixed	Postm.
Albania	na	na	na	na	na	na	na	na	na	na	na	na	na	na	na	na
Algeria	na	na	na	na	na	na	na	na	na	na	na	na	na	na	na	na
Argentina	81	na	na	na	na	na	na	na	na	na	na	na	na	na	na	na
Armenia	na	na	na	na	na	na	na	na	na	na	na	na	na	na	na	na
Australia	na	na	na	na	na	na	na	na	na	na	na	na	na	na	na	na
Austria	57	64	65	62	71	65	59	63	65	62	57	64	66	59	64	64
Azerbaijan	na	na	na	na	na	na	na	na	na	na	na	na	na	na	na	na
Bangladesh	na	na	na	na	na	na	na	na	na	na	na	na	na	na	na	na
Belarus	58	54	57	52	66	56	41	39	59	60	51	53	63	51	57	64
Belgium	65	67	69	64	67	67	66	65	68	66	72	67	64	65	67	67
Bosnia and Herz.	na	na	na	na	na	na	na	na	na	na	na	na	na	na	na	na
Brazil	72	na	na	na	na	na	na	na	na	na	na	na	na	na	na	na
Bulgaria	48	61	65	58	76	62	53	48	70	63	53	61	68	59	66	68
Canada	72	na	na	na	na	na	na	na	na	na	na	na	na	na	na	na
Chile	74	na	na	na	na	na	na	na	na	na	na	na	na	na	na	na
China	37	na	na	na	na	na	na	na	na	na	na	na	na	na	na	na
Colombia	na	na	na	na	na	na	na	na	na	na	na	na	na	na	na	na
Croatia	na	37	41	34	45	37	31	30	39	50	40	30	44	27	37	45
Czech Republic	na	56	59	53	63	56	52	59	54	43	53	56	59	58	54	55
Denmark	65	56	55	57	64	53	55	56	58	56	60	52	57	61	56	60
Dominican Rep.	na	na	na	na	na	na	na	na	na	na	na	na	na	na	na	na
Egypt	na	na	na	na	na	na	na	na	na	na	na	na	na	na	na	na
El Salvador	na	na	na	na	na	na	na	na	na	na	na	na	na	na	na	na
Estonia	53	52	53	51	63	57	41	49	53	53	48	52	51	53	51	55
Finland	61	52	55	49	64	57	40	48	58	49	56	49	51	53	51	53
France	68	73	73	72	73	74	71	73	74	71	71	73	69	73	72	72
Georgia	na	na	na	na	na	na	na	na	na	na	na	na	na	na	na	na
Germany	54	48	49	46	62	58	30	37	59	49	43	51	51	45	50	46
Great Britain	66	65	70	59	76	67	57	62	69	64	63	69	67	na	na	na
Greece	na	82	81	84	87	83	70	76	84	82	80	82	83	83	84	78
Hungary	69	70	75	65	82	73	60	65	79	81	65	66	77	66	74	80
Iceland	73	71	72	71	73	72	68	74	71	66	67	69	78	76	71	62
India	78	na	na	na	na	na	na	na	na	na	na	na	na	na	na	na
Indonesia	na	na	na	na	na	na	na	na	na	na	na	na	na	na	na	na
Iran	na	na	na	na	na	na	na	na	na	na	na	na	na	na	na	na
Ireland	68	72	72	72	76	72	70	71	73	72	74	74	70	68	73	72
Israel	na	na	na	na	na	na	na	na	na	na	na	na	na	na	na	na
Italy	67	67	72	63	79	71	57	62	73	69	65	65	65	59	69	68
Japan	28	na	na	na	na	na	na	na	na	na	na	na	na	na	na	na
Jordan	na	na	na	na	na	na	na	na	na	na	na	na	na	na	na	na
Korea, South	na	na	na	na	na	na	na	na	na	na	na	na	na	na	na	na
Latvia	59	53	56	51	64	57	46	48	56	52	49	53	57	55	52	50
Lithuania	37	37	40	34	51	40	21	17	43	43	29	34	46	35	36	44
Luxembourg	na	61	63	59	66	61	57	61	59	66	51	61	68	58	62	65
Macedonia	na	na	na	na	na	na	na	na	na	na	na	na	na	na	na	na
Malta	na	82	83	81	89	81	79	76	84	85	78	83	88	77	86	82
Mexico	77	na	na	na	na	na	na	na	na	na	na	na	na	na	na	na
Moldova	na	na	na	na	na	na	na	na	na	na	na	na	na	na	na	na
Montenegro	na	na	na	na	na	na	na	na	na	na	na	na	na	na	na	na
Morocco	na	na	na	na	na	na	na	na	na	na	na	na	na	na	na	na
Netherlands	62	51	55	48	56	48	52	52	54	47	56	49	50	47	52	51
New Zealand	na	na	na	na	na	na	na	na	na	na	na	na	na	na	na	na
Nigeria	91	na	na	na	na	na	na	na	na	na	na	na	na	na	na	na
Northern Ireland	69	67	68	66	67	71	64	63	70	68	70	72	68	69	68	63
Norway	62	na	na	na	na	na	na	na	na	na	na	na	na	na	na	na
Pakistan	na	na	na	na	na	na	na	na	na	na	na	na	na	na	na	na
Peru	na	na	na	na	na	na	na	na	na	na	na	na	na	na	na	na
Philippines	na	na	na	na	na	na	na	na	na	na	na	na	na	na	na	na
Poland	na	66	69	64	67	67	64	64	71	66	65	65	75	58	71	71
Portugal	69	41	47	35	58	37	33	36	52	48	29	39	60	33	47	41
Puerto Rico	na	na	na	na	na	na	na	na	na	na	na	na	na	na	na	na
Romania	59	49	54	45	62	55	37	37	54	60	37	51	59	46	53	55
Russian Fed.	46	50	55	46	58	58	35	35	51	55	46	46	56	47	53	61
Serbia	na	na	na	na	na	na	na	na	na	na	na	na	na	na	na	na
Singapore	na	na	na	na	na	na	na	na	na	na	na	na	na	na	na	na
Slovakia	na	59	59	58	64	65	47	53	60	69	51	60	63	56	61	63
Slovenia	61	64	65	63	70	67	57	62	66	58	68	62	65	65	64	69
South Africa	na	na	na	na	na	na	na	na	na	na	na	na	na	na	na	na
Spain	63	60	62	57	72	61	51	51	66	63	55	67	69	59	60	64
Sweden	67	60	59	61	60	62	58	57	60	61	58	63	61	64	61	57
Switzerland	68	na	na	na	na	na	na	na	na	na	na	na	na	na	na	na
Taiwan	na	na	na	na	na	na	na	na	na	na	na	na	na	na	na	na
Tanzania	na	na	na	na	na	na	na	na	na	na	na	na	na	na	na	na
Turkey	73	84	85	84	87	83	79	81	89	90	79	86	91	85	84	90
Uganda	na	na	na	na	na	na	na	na	na	na	na	na	na	na	na	na
Ukraine	na	67	71	63	76	67	62	56	67	72	67	63	73	65	67	84
United States	71	na	na	na	na	na	na	na	na	na	na	na	na	na	na	na
Uruguay	na	na	na	na	na	na	na	na	na	na	na	na	na	na	na	na
Venezuela	na	na	na	na	na	na	na	na	na	na	na	na	na	na	na	na
Vietnam	na	na	na	na	na	na	na	na	na	na	na	na	na	na	na	na
Zimbabwe	na	na	na	na	na	na	na	na	na	na	na	na	na	na	na	na
Total	63	60	62	58	69	62	53	55	63	63	58	59	63	57	61	62

RANKING

Country	2000
Turkey	84
Greece	82
Malta	82
France	73
Ireland	72
Iceland	71
Hungary	70
Italy	67
Ukraine	67
Northern Ireland	67
Belgium	67
Poland	66
Great Britain	65
Slovenia	64
Austria	64
Bulgaria	61
Luxembourg	61
Sweden	60
Spain	60
Slovakia	59
Denmark	56
Czech Republic	56
Belarus	54
Latvia	53
Estonia	52
Finland	52
Netherlands	51
Russian Fed.	50
Romania	49
Germany	48
Portugal	41
Croatia	37
Lithuania	37
Total	60

D037_1) MARRIAGE SUCCESS: SHARING HOUSEHOLD CHORES

Here is a list of things which some people think make for a successful marriage. Please tell me, for each one, whether you think it is...

Very important (%)

(EVS: V143)

Country	Wave		Gender		Age			Education			Income			Values				RANKING Country	2000
	1990	2000	Male	Female	16-29	30-49	50+	Lower	Middle	Upper	Lower	Middle	Upper	Mat	Mixed	Postm.			
Albania	na	na	na	na	na	na	na	na	na	na	na	na	na	na	na	na		Turkey	60
Algeria	na	na	na	na	na	na	na	na	na	na	na	na	na	na	na	na		Malta	55
Argentina	53	na	na	na	na	na	na	na	na	na	na	na	na	na	na	na		Poland	55
Armenia	na	na	na	na	na	na	na	na	na	na	na	na	na	na	na	na		Ireland	54
Australia	na	na	na	na	na	na	na	na	na	na	na	na	na	na	na	na		Sweden	52
Austria	29	30	30	29	39	28	26	30	29	30	34	26	27	32	29	31		Great Britain	50
Azerbaijan	na	na	na	na	na	na	na	na	na	na	na	na	na	na	na	na		Northern Ireland	47
Bangladesh	na	na	na	na	na	na	na	na	na	na	na	na	na	na	na	na		Ukraine	45
Belarus	29	45	38	50	44	43	47	49	43	43	48	42	44	44	45	46		Belarus	45
Belgium	38	42	45	40	40	43	43	43	42	42	46	44	40	46	39	46		Iceland	45
Bosnia and Herz.	na	na	na	na	na	na	na	na	na	na	na	na	na	na	na	na		Greece	44
Brazil	37	na	na	na	na	na	na	na	na	na	na	na	na	na	na	na		Romania	43
Bulgaria	42	34	30	38	38	37	31	29	40	30	35	35	34	30	37	39		Belgium	42
Canada	53	na	na	na	na	na	na	na	na	na	na	na	na	na	na	na		Hungary	41
Chile	62	na	na	na	na	na	na	na	na	na	na	na	na	na	na	na		Denmark	41
China	35	na	na	na	na	na	na	na	na	na	na	na	na	na	na	na		France	40
Colombia	na	na	na	na	na	na	na	na	na	na	na	na	na	na	na	na		Luxembourg	37
Croatia	na	23	24	21	25	20	24	20	25	23	24	23	22	21	22	24		Spain	36
Czech Republic	na	24	21	27	23	21	27	26	23	19	26	23	23	25	24	21		Slovenia	36
Denmark	48	41	40	42	47	41	37	42	39	39	42	41	43	48	40	42		Bulgaria	34
Dominican Rep.	na	na	na	na	na	na	na	na	na	na	na	na	na	na	na	na		Netherlands	33
Egypt	na	na	na	na	na	na	na	na	na	na	na	na	na	na	na	na		Slovakia	31
El Salvador	na	na	na	na	na	na	na	na	na	na	na	na	na	na	na	na		Austria	30
Estonia	19	18	16	19	18	18	17	16	18	19	14	21	17	17	19	16		Italy	29
Finland	25	29	27	30	36	30	23	28	33	24	33	30	26	30	27	34		Finland	29
France	35	40	36	43	45	43	35	41	37	38	43	41	37	41	40	40		Russian Fed.	28
Georgia	na	na	na	na	na	na	na	na	na	na	na	na	na	na	na	na		Latvia	26
Germany	30	20	18	22	22	24	16	17	24	19	23	20	19	18	21	23		Lithuania	26
Great Britain	44	50	51	49	49	48	53	51	50	46	62	44	49	na	na	na		Czech Republic	24
Greece	na	44	34	51	51	39	35	42	41	46	45	39	42	41	43	49		Portugal	23
Hungary	40	41	42	41	36	41	45	42	38	44	38	41	44	40	42	41		Croatia	23
Iceland	42	45	44	45	52	44	38	48	42	42	52	41	44	45	45	41		Germany	20
India	58	na	na	na	na	na	na	na	na	na	na	na	na	na	na	na		Estonia	18
Indonesia	na	na	na	na	na	na	na	na	na	na	na	na	na	na	na	na			
Iran	na	na	na	na	na	na	na	na	na	na	na	na	na	na	na	na			
Ireland	38	54	54	53	55	54	53	56	54	48	53	58	50	58	53	55			
Israel	na	na	na	na	na	na	na	na	na	na	na	na	na	na	na	na			
Italy	30	29	28	30	35	29	26	28	31	27	27	28	27	24	30	28			
Japan	10	na	na	na	na	na	na	na	na	na	na	na	na	na	na	na			
Jordan	na	na	na	na	na	na	na	na	na	na	na	na	na	na	na	na			
Korea, South	na	na	na	na	na	na	na	na	na	na	na	na	na	na	na	na			
Latvia	31	26	24	28	23	24	29	29	25	27	29	25	25	27	26	22			
Lithuania	25	26	21	30	27	26	25	24	25	33	28	26	28	27	26	20			
Luxembourg	na	37	33	40	43	37	32	39	33	41	36	38	35	32	38	44			
Macedonia	na	na	na	na	na	na	na	na	na	na	na	na	na	na	na	na			
Malta	na	55	55	55	58	52	56	55	53	66	60	58	57	48	57	68			
Mexico	47	na	na	na	na	na	na	na	na	na	na	na	na	na	na	na			
Moldova	na	na	na	na	na	na	na	na	na	na	na	na	na	na	na	na			
Montenegro	na	na	na	na	na	na	na	na	na	na	na	na	na	na	na	na			
Morocco	na	na	na	na	na	na	na	na	na	na	na	na	na	na	na	na			
Netherlands	34	33	34	31	44	31	28	30	35	32	37	31	30	36	31	36			
New Zealand	na	na	na	na	na	na	na	na	na	na	na	na	na	na	na	na			
Nigeria	67	na	na	na	na	na	na	na	na	na	na	na	na	na	na	na			
Northern Ireland	45	47	46	47	52	47	45	43	49	53	49	45	49	53	44	47			
Norway	34	na	na	na	na	na	na	na	na	na	na	na	na	na	na	na			
Pakistan	na	na	na	na	na	na	na	na	na	na	na	na	na	na	na	na			
Peru	na	na	na	na	na	na	na	na	na	na	na	na	na	na	na	na			
Philippines	na	na	na	na	na	na	na	na	na	na	na	na	na	na	na	na			
Poland	na	55	51	58	55	54	55	55	55	54	56	53	55	53	56	51			
Portugal	50	23	20	26	29	23	20	21	27	33	23	22	31	19	26	27			
Puerto Rico	na	na	na	na	na	na	na	na	na	na	na	na	na	na	na	na			
Romania	42	43	40	46	46	39	45	44	44	41	42	44	45	43	42	49			
Russian Fed.	38	28	24	31	22	31	28	28	30	23	32	28	24	29	28	11			
Serbia	na	na	na	na	na	na	na	na	na	na	na	na	na	na	na	na			
Singapore	na	na	na	na	na	na	na	na	na	na	na	na	na	na	na	na			
Slovakia	na	31	25	36	32	28	32	30	31	30	28	32	30	31	31	23			
Slovenia	35	36	30	41	37	36	35	41	35	27	44	34	26	38	33	45			
South Africa	na	na	na	na	na	na	na	na	na	na	na	na	na	na	na	na			
Spain	40	36	33	39	43	40	29	30	40	42	34	41	38	31	35	44			
Sweden	48	52	48	56	61	53	46	42	55	57	52	50	54	48	51	57			
Switzerland	33	na	na	na	na	na	na	na	na	na	na	na	na	na	na	na			
Taiwan	na	na	na	na	na	na	na	na	na	na	na	na	na	na	na	na			
Tanzania	na	na	na	na	na	na	na	na	na	na	na	na	na	na	na	na			
Turkey	31	60	58	62	58	60	63	61	57	62	60	58	62	53	61	66			
Uganda	na	na	na	na	na	na	na	na	na	na	na	na	na	na	na	na			
Ukraine	na	45	40	50	38	43	51	52	45	40	54	37	43	46	46	44			
United States	47	na	na	na	na	na	na	na	na	na	na	na	na	na	na	na			
Uruguay	na	na	na	na	na	na	na	na	na	na	na	na	na	na	na	na			
Venezuela	na	na	na	na	na	na	na	na	na	na	na	na	na	na	na	na			
Vietnam	na	na	na	na	na	na	na	na	na	na	na	na	na	na	na	na			
Zimbabwe	na	na	na	na	na	na	na	na	na	na	na	na	na	na	na	na			
Total	38	37	35	39	40	37	35	36	37	39	40	36	36	36	37	39		Total	37

D038_1) MARRIAGE SUCCESS: CHILDREN

Here is a list of things which some people think make for a successful marriage. Please tell me, for each one, whether you think it is...

Very important (%)

(EVS: V144)

Country	Wave		Gender		Age			Education			Income			Values				RANKING	
	1990	2000	Male	Female	16-29	30-49	50+	Lower	Middle	Upper	Lower	Middle	Upper	Mat	Mixed	Postm.		Country	2000
Albania	na	na	na	na	na	na	na	na	na	na	na	na	na	na	na	na		Ukraine	84
Algeria	na	na	na	na	na	na	na	na	na	na	na	na	na	na	na	na		Hungary	83
Argentina	88	na	na	na	na	na	na	na	na	na	na	na	na	na	na	na		Bulgaria	79
Armenia	na	na	na	na	na	na	na	na	na	na	na	na	na	na	na	na		Turkey	78
Australia	na	na	na	na	na	na	na	na	na	na	na	na	na	na	na	na		Czech Republic	78
Austria	63	60	56	64	51	61	64	65	58	51	62	66	55	65	63	56		Belarus	76
Azerbaijan	na	na	na	na	na	na	na	na	na	na	na	na	na	na	na	na		Russian Fed.	74
Bangladesh	na	na	na	na	na	na	na	na	na	na	na	na	na	na	na	na		Poland	73
Belarus	81	76	72	80	75	74	80	79	76	74	81	74	74	81	73	70		Latvia	73
Belgium	55	59	58	59	55	57	61	61	62	50	55	63	56	60	59	55		Greece	72
Bosnia and Herz.	na	na	na	na	na	na	na	na	na	na	na	na	na	na	na	na		Slovenia	71
Brazil	60	na	na	na	na	na	na	na	na	na	na	na	na	na	na	na		Romania	70
Bulgaria	84	79	77	80	69	80	82	81	78	75	84	74	76	82	75	70		Malta	70
Canada	66	na	na	na	na	na	na	na	na	na	na	na	na	na	na	na		Slovakia	70
Chile	92	na	na	na	na	na	na	na	na	na	na	na	na	na	na	na		Spain	66
China	55	na	na	na	na	na	na	na	na	na	na	na	na	na	na	na		Estonia	64
Colombia	na	na	na	na	na	na	na	na	na	na	na	na	na	na	na	na		Croatia	63
Croatia	na	63	59	66	55	67	64	65	62	59	68	63	61	59	64	63		France	63
Czech Republic	na	78	73	81	71	77	81	79	76	76	77	80	76	79	78	73		Austria	60
Denmark	42	36	36	36	24	32	47	42	23	33	45	33	31	41	37	32		Ireland	59
Dominican Rep.	na	na	na	na	na	na	na	na	na	na	na	na	na	na	na	na		Sweden	59
Egypt	na	na	na	na	na	na	na	na	na	na	na	na	na	na	na	na		Belgium	59
El Salvador	na	na	na	na	na	na	na	na	na	na	na	na	na	na	na	na		Italy	58
Estonia	74	64	55	71	51	68	68	58	67	65	65	69	61	64	65	64		Northern Ireland	55
Finland	60	55	52	58	38	57	62	58	52	49	56	58	54	56	55	55		Finland	55
France	65	63	59	66	59	60	66	68	55	55	64	64	59	70	63	53		Lithuania	51
Georgia	na	na	na	na	na	na	na	na	na	na	na	na	na	na	na	na		Iceland	51
Germany	65	48	43	52	39	50	50	49	48	47	48	54	44	53	46	51		Germany	48
Great Britain	58	48	45	51	39	48	53	52	49	38	48	53	46	na	na	na		Great Britain	48
Greece	na	72	72	71	66	72	84	85	72	69	74	70	72	74	73	67		Netherlands	47
Hungary	85	83	79	86	77	84	85	81	86	86	81	82	85	84	82	77		Portugal	43
Iceland	66	51	52	50	31	51	66	54	49	47	51	50	50	57	49	46		Luxembourg	43
India	79	na	na	na	na	na	na	na	na	na	na	na	na	na	na	na		Denmark	36
Indonesia	na	na	na	na	na	na	na	na	na	na	na	na	na	na	na	na			
Iran	na	na	na	na	na	na	na	na	na	na	na	na	na	na	na	na			
Ireland	62	59	58	60	46	61	67	72	56	45	66	63	51	57	60	58			
Israel	na	na	na	na	na	na	na	na	na	na	na	na	na	na	na	na			
Italy	65	58	57	59	51	54	66	66	54	46	64	57	53	67	60	51			
Japan	52	na	na	na	na	na	na	na	na	na	na	na	na	na	na	na			
Jordan	na	na	na	na	na	na	na	na	na	na	na	na	na	na	na	na			
Korea, South	na	na	na	na	na	na	na	na	na	na	na	na	na	na	na	na			
Latvia	78	73	66	79	70	74	74	74	73	74	74	74	72	74	74	70			
Lithuania	66	51	46	55	49	49	54	54	50	51	57	52	53	54	49	57			
Luxembourg	na	43	44	43	37	41	49	53	38	39	47	44	36	46	44	34			
Macedonia	na	na	na	na	na	na	na	na	na	na	na	na	na	na	na	na			
Malta	na	70	73	68	66	72	72	73	72	57	76	73	70	72	71	60			
Mexico	75	na	na	na	na	na	na	na	na	na	na	na	na	na	na	na			
Moldova	na	na	na	na	na	na	na	na	na	na	na	na	na	na	na	na			
Montenegro	na	na	na	na	na	na	na	na	na	na	na	na	na	na	na	na			
Morocco	na	na	na	na	na	na	na	na	na	na	na	na	na	na	na	na			
Netherlands	56	47	40	53	31	45	57	61	48	32	50	47	38	58	47	41			
New Zealand	na	na	na	na	na	na	na	na	na	na	na	na	na	na	na	na			
Nigeria	94	na	na	na	na	na	na	na	na	na	na	na	na	na	na	na			
Northern Ireland	69	55	55	55	50	56	58	61	53	45	59	60	50	55	58	48			
Norway	61	na	na	na	na	na	na	na	na	na	na	na	na	na	na	na			
Pakistan	na	na	na	na	na	na	na	na	na	na	na	na	na	na	na	na			
Peru	na	na	na	na	na	na	na	na	na	na	na	na	na	na	na	na			
Philippines	na	na	na	na	na	na	na	na	na	na	na	na	na	na	na	na			
Poland	na	73	73	74	64	77	74	76	73	64	77	72	71	71	74	78			
Portugal	65	43	41	46	48	39	44	45	43	32	43	50	45	39	46	37			
Puerto Rico	na	na	na	na	na	na	na	na	na	na	na	na	na	na	na	na			
Romania	68	70	71	70	59	73	74	73	69	69	67	75	71	73	69	67			
Russian Fed.	80	74	70	78	64	76	78	75	74	73	76	75	73	76	72	68			
Serbia	na	na	na	na	na	na	na	na	na	na	na	na	na	na	na	na			
Singapore	na	na	na	na	na	na	na	na	na	na	na	na	na	na	na	na			
Slovakia	na	70	66	73	61	72	74	71	69	74	70	70	72	71	71	62			
Slovenia	73	71	69	73	69	73	71	75	70	67	72	72	67	74	72	70			
South Africa	na	na	na	na	na	na	na	na	na	na	na	na	na	na	na	na			
Spain	68	66	63	68	63	63	69	68	64	63	67	69	65	69	64	67			
Sweden	61	59	57	61	46	61	65	65	57	57	55	60	64	60	60	56			
Switzerland	54	na	na	na	na	na	na	na	na	na	na	na	na	na	na	na			
Taiwan	na	na	na	na	na	na	na	na	na	na	na	na	na	na	na	na			
Tanzania	na	na	na	na	na	na	na	na	na	na	na	na	na	na	na	na			
Turkey	69	78	78	78	74	80	88	83	72	69	82	79	69	81	79	76			
Uganda	na	na	na	na	na	na	na	na	na	na	na	na	na	na	na	na			
Ukraine	na	84	80	88	75	86	88	89	84	83	87	84	82	84	85	78			
United States	65	na	na	na	na	na	na	na	na	na	na	na	na	na	na	na			
Uruguay	na	na	na	na	na	na	na	na	na	na	na	na	na	na	na	na			
Venezuela	na	na	na	na	na	na	na	na	na	na	na	na	na	na	na	na			
Vietnam	na	na	na	na	na	na	na	na	na	na	na	na	na	na	na	na			
Zimbabwe	na	na	na	na	na	na	na	na	na	na	na	na	na	na	na	na			
Total	68	63	60	65	56	63	67	64	63	59	66	64	61	68	63	55		Total	63

D039_1) MARRIAGE SUCCESS: WILLING TO DISCUSS PROBLEMS

Here is a list of things which some people think make for a successful marriage. Please tell me, for each one, whether you think it is...

Very important (%)

(EVS: V145)

Country	Wave 1990	Wave 2000	Gender Male	Gender Female	Age 16-29	Age 30-49	Age 50+	Education Lower	Education Middle	Education Upper	Income Lower	Income Middle	Income Upper	Values Mat	Values Mixed	Values Postm.
Albania	na	na	na	na	na	na	na	na	na	na	na	na	na	na	na	na
Algeria	na	na	na	na	na	na	na	na	na	na	na	na	na	na	na	na
Argentina	na	na	na	na	na	na	na	na	na	na	na	na	na	na	na	na
Armenia	na	na	na	na	na	na	na	na	na	na	na	na	na	na	na	na
Australia	na	na	na	na	na	na	na	na	na	na	na	na	na	na	na	na
Austria	na	75	74	76	77	80	69	71	77	83	72	76	76	66	76	78
Azerbaijan	na	na	na	na	na	na	na	na	na	na	na	na	na	na	na	na
Bangladesh	na	na	na	na	na	na	na	na	na	na	na	na	na	na	na	na
Belarus	na	53	47	58	64	50	48	44	54	63	53	51	58	54	52	62
Belgium	na	83	81	85	86	84	80	79	84	84	83	78	85	81	82	87
Bosnia and Herz.	na	na	na	na	na	na	na	na	na	na	na	na	na	na	na	na
Brazil	na	na	na	na	na	na	na	na	na	na	na	na	na	na	na	na
Bulgaria	na	58	54	62	65	57	55	48	62	65	56	55	60	54	63	62
Canada	na	na	na	na	na	na	na	na	na	na	na	na	na	na	na	na
Chile	na	na	na	na	na	na	na	na	na	na	na	na	na	na	na	na
China	na	na	na	na	na	na	na	na	na	na	na	na	na	na	na	na
Colombia	na	na	na	na	na	na	na	na	na	na	na	na	na	na	na	na
Croatia	na	56	52	58	63	56	50	51	57	65	52	56	57	47	54	64
Czech Republic	na	73	70	76	82	74	67	70	76	77	67	74	77	68	73	83
Denmark	na	76	72	81	84	77	72	74	79	82	75	74	82	72	78	79
Dominican Rep.	na	na	na	na	na	na	na	na	na	na	na	na	na	na	na	na
Egypt	na	na	na	na	na	na	na	na	na	na	na	na	na	na	na	na
El Salvador	na	na	na	na	na	na	na	na	na	na	na	na	na	na	na	na
Estonia	na	51	43	57	55	54	45	47	53	49	45	52	53	47	53	65
Finland	na	64	59	69	78	68	54	58	72	74	69	62	63	59	66	65
France	na	77	71	82	79	78	74	77	74	78	79	76	72	79	76	75
Georgia	na	na	na	na	na	na	na	na	na	na	na	na	na	na	na	na
Germany	na	60	57	63	60	65	56	49	71	68	53	61	69	59	61	63
Great Britain	na	84	82	87	83	87	83	82	84	91	85	83	88	na	na	na
Greece	na	91	86	95	94	89	88	93	91	91	93	92	89	89	92	91
Hungary	na	78	75	82	82	79	77	74	86	87	69	79	85	76	83	67
Iceland	na	89	85	93	92	91	84	88	89	92	87	89	92	90	89	89
India	na	na	na	na	na	na	na	na	na	na	na	na	na	na	na	na
Indonesia	na	na	na	na	na	na	na	na	na	na	na	na	na	na	na	na
Iran	na	na	na	na	na	na	na	na	na	na	na	na	na	na	na	na
Ireland	na	90	89	90	93	90	87	87	90	92	87	90	90	83	91	94
Israel	na	na	na	na	na	na	na	na	na	na	na	na	na	na	na	na
Italy	na	81	79	82	87	84	74	75	85	86	76	81	83	76	81	84
Japan	na	na	na	na	na	na	na	na	na	na	na	na	na	na	na	na
Jordan	na	na	na	na	na	na	na	na	na	na	na	na	na	na	na	na
Korea, South	na	na	na	na	na	na	na	na	na	na	na	na	na	na	na	na
Latvia	na	42	37	47	53	41	39	42	43	42	41	38	46	41	42	42
Lithuania	na	33	28	38	37	35	30	30	33	40	34	28	39	33	33	39
Luxembourg	na	73	70	76	73	74	72	76	70	78	66	77	72	69	74	76
Macedonia	na	na	na	na	na	na	na	na	na	na	na	na	na	na	na	na
Malta	na	96	94	97	96	95	96	95	95	99	95	96	97	92	98	96
Mexico	na	na	na	na	na	na	na	na	na	na	na	na	na	na	na	na
Moldova	na	na	na	na	na	na	na	na	na	na	na	na	na	na	na	na
Montenegro	na	na	na	na	na	na	na	na	na	na	na	na	na	na	na	na
Morocco	na	na	na	na	na	na	na	na	na	na	na	na	na	na	na	na
Netherlands	na	87	83	91	93	88	83	85	88	88	84	88	89	86	88	87
New Zealand	na	na	na	na	na	na	na	na	na	na	na	na	na	na	na	na
Nigeria	na	na	na	na	na	na	na	na	na	na	na	na	na	na	na	na
Northern Ireland	na	82	81	84	83	84	82	81	83	85	80	81	84	83	84	78
Norway	na	na	na	na	na	na	na	na	na	na	na	na	na	na	na	na
Pakistan	na	na	na	na	na	na	na	na	na	na	na	na	na	na	na	na
Peru	na	na	na	na	na	na	na	na	na	na	na	na	na	na	na	na
Philippines	na	na	na	na	na	na	na	na	na	na	na	na	na	na	na	na
Poland	na	74	72	76	84	74	69	69	83	73	72	76	76	72	76	78
Portugal	na	56	56	56	69	50	53	53	60	64	49	53	69	46	62	54
Puerto Rico	na	na	na	na	na	na	na	na	na	na	na	na	na	na	na	na
Romania	na	66	69	64	76	68	60	55	70	80	54	66	76	62	70	79
Russian Fed.	na	43	41	45	45	45	39	40	43	45	41	45	43	42	43	34
Serbia	na	na	na	na	na	na	na	na	na	na	na	na	na	na	na	na
Singapore	na	na	na	na	na	na	na	na	na	na	na	na	na	na	na	na
Slovakia	na	66	61	70	71	65	63	61	67	76	61	64	72	64	68	74
Slovenia	na	80	75	85	84	81	76	77	80	84	77	79	82	81	81	82
South Africa	na	na	na	na	na	na	na	na	na	na	na	na	na	na	na	na
Spain	na	63	62	65	74	63	57	57	67	70	61	68	67	62	62	74
Sweden	na	82	75	88	86	84	77	73	83	87	82	79	85	85	80	87
Switzerland	na	na	na	na	na	na	na	na	na	na	na	na	na	na	na	na
Taiwan	na	na	na	na	na	na	na	na	na	na	na	na	na	na	na	na
Tanzania	na	na	na	na	na	na	na	na	na	na	na	na	na	na	na	na
Turkey	na	89	88	89	90	88	88	86	92	96	86	88	95	88	89	95
Uganda	na	na	na	na	na	na	na	na	na	na	na	na	na	na	na	na
Ukraine	na	64	61	66	68	63	63	60	62	69	68	56	67	58	70	79
United States	na	na	na	na	na	na	na	na	na	na	na	na	na	na	na	na
Uruguay	na	na	na	na	na	na	na	na	na	na	na	na	na	na	na	na
Venezuela	na	na	na	na	na	na	na	na	na	na	na	na	na	na	na	na
Vietnam	na	na	na	na	na	na	na	na	na	na	na	na	na	na	na	na
Zimbabwe	na	na	na	na	na	na	na	na	na	na	na	na	na	na	na	na
Total	na	71	67	73	76	71	66	67	70	77	68	70	73	64	72	78

RANKING

Country	2000
Malta	96
Greece	91
Ireland	90
Iceland	89
Turkey	89
Netherlands	87
Great Britain	84
Belgium	83
Northern Ireland	82
Sweden	82
Italy	81
Slovenia	80
Hungary	78
France	77
Denmark	76
Austria	75
Poland	74
Luxembourg	73
Czech Republic	73
Romania	66
Slovakia	66
Finland	64
Ukraine	64
Spain	63
Germany	60
Bulgaria	58
Portugal	56
Croatia	56
Belarus	53
Estonia	51
Russian Fed.	43
Latvia	42
Lithuania	33
Total	71

D040_1) MARRIAGE SUCCESS: SPENDING TIME TOGETHER

Here is a list of things which some people think make for a successful marriage. Please tell me, for each one, whether you think it is...

Very important (%)

(EVS: V146)

Country	Wave 1990	Wave 2000	Male	Female	16-29	30-49	50+	Lower	Middle	Upper	Lower	Middle	Upper	Mat	Mixed	Postm.
Albania	na	na	na	na	na	na	na	na	na	na	na	na	na	na	na	na
Algeria	na	na	na	na	na	na	na	na	na	na	na	na	na	na	na	na
Argentina	na	na	na	na	na	na	na	na	na	na	na	na	na	na	na	na
Armenia	na	na	na	na	na	na	na	na	na	na	na	na	na	na	na	na
Australia	na	na	na	na	na	na	na	na	na	na	na	na	na	na	na	na
Austria	na	49	48	50	45	49	52	58	44	31	50	54	46	50	53	43
Azerbaijan	na	na	na	na	na	na	na	na	na	na	na	na	na	na	na	na
Bangladesh	na	na	na	na	na	na	na	na	na	na	na	na	na	na	na	na
Belarus	na	36	33	38	41	34	33	31	39	33	40	34	34	38	36	35
Belgium	na	50	50	50	48	48	53	60	51	40	58	51	44	56	50	41
Bosnia and Herz.	na	na	na	na	na	na	na	na	na	na	na	na	na	na	na	na
Brazil	na	na	na	na	na	na	na	na	na	na	na	na	na	na	na	na
Bulgaria	na	41	38	43	49	40	37	36	46	38	40	41	40	41	42	24
Canada	na	na	na	na	na	na	na	na	na	na	na	na	na	na	na	na
Chile	na	na	na	na	na	na	na	na	na	na	na	na	na	na	na	na
China	na	na	na	na	na	na	na	na	na	na	na	na	na	na	na	na
Colombia	na	na	na	na	na	na	na	na	na	na	na	na	na	na	na	na
Croatia	na	43	44	43	50	42	40	43	44	44	41	42	48	39	44	46
Czech Republic	na	33	31	34	40	28	33	37	30	21	38	35	27	33	33	30
Denmark	na	39	37	41	41	33	45	46	29	32	45	38	31	49	41	32
Dominican Rep.	na	na	na	na	na	na	na	na	na	na	na	na	na	na	na	na
Egypt	na	na	na	na	na	na	na	na	na	na	na	na	na	na	na	na
El Salvador	na	na	na	na	na	na	na	na	na	na	na	na	na	na	na	na
Estonia	na	27	25	29	34	25	25	29	28	20	26	30	25	26	26	47
Finland	na	38	39	38	49	38	32	39	36	43	45	37	35	41	36	45
France	na	54	51	57	53	52	56	61	49	42	57	56	48	63	55	40
Georgia	na	na	na	na	na	na	na	na	na	na	na	na	na	na	na	na
Germany	na	39	38	40	37	41	39	37	42	37	38	39	44	41	41	32
Great Britain	na	53	50	55	46	51	58	59	50	46	62	53	50	na	na	na
Greece	na	61	58	64	62	58	66	71	65	57	61	63	58	63	59	62
Hungary	na	58	55	62	63	55	59	58	62	51	55	60	61	56	61	64
Iceland	na	48	45	50	43	47	54	51	45	46	47	49	45	53	48	34
India	na	na	na	na	na	na	na	na	na	na	na	na	na	na	na	na
Indonesia	na	na	na	na	na	na	na	na	na	na	na	na	na	na	na	na
Iran	na	na	na	na	na	na	na	na	na	na	na	na	na	na	na	na
Ireland	na	58	56	59	47	61	61	62	58	50	65	65	49	55	58	57
Israel	na	na	na	na	na	na	na	na	na	na	na	na	na	na	na	na
Italy	na	51	49	52	49	50	51	54	50	42	51	51	45	55	53	47
Japan	na	na	na	na	na	na	na	na	na	na	na	na	na	na	na	na
Jordan	na	na	na	na	na	na	na	na	na	na	na	na	na	na	na	na
Korea, South	na	na	na	na	na	na	na	na	na	na	na	na	na	na	na	na
Latvia	na	36	33	39	46	32	35	42	36	28	38	34	35	38	34	33
Lithuania	na	22	19	24	25	25	16	12	24	27	22	17	25	18	22	27
Luxembourg	na	48	47	49	44	42	56	55	47	37	49	48	41	46	48	41
Macedonia	na	na	na	na	na	na	na	na	na	na	na	na	na	na	na	na
Malta	na	87	86	88	84	85	91	90	88	86	92	86	83	81	90	94
Mexico	na	na	na	na	na	na	na	na	na	na	na	na	na	na	na	na
Moldova	na	na	na	na	na	na	na	na	na	na	na	na	na	na	na	na
Montenegro	na	na	na	na	na	na	na	na	na	na	na	na	na	na	na	na
Morocco	na	na	na	na	na	na	na	na	na	na	na	na	na	na	na	na
Netherlands	na	31	29	32	31	23	39	49	28	16	34	33	21	43	31	23
New Zealand	na	na	na	na	na	na	na	na	na	na	na	na	na	na	na	na
Nigeria	na	na	na	na	na	na	na	na	na	na	na	na	na	na	na	na
Northern Ireland	na	56	57	55	55	54	59	57	54	55	59	52	49	53	58	56
Norway	na	na	na	na	na	na	na	na	na	na	na	na	na	na	na	na
Pakistan	na	na	na	na	na	na	na	na	na	na	na	na	na	na	na	na
Peru	na	na	na	na	na	na	na	na	na	na	na	na	na	na	na	na
Philippines	na	na	na	na	na	na	na	na	na	na	na	na	na	na	na	na
Poland	na	61	59	62	71	56	60	60	63	59	65	58	58	59	62	64
Portugal	na	34	36	32	32	31	37	35	33	26	32	36	41	27	38	32
Puerto Rico	na	na	na	na	na	na	na	na	na	na	na	na	na	na	na	na
Romania	na	58	57	58	65	58	53	53	60	59	50	58	62	57	58	64
Russian Fed.	na	30	27	32	28	30	30	34	30	26	31	33	25	29	30	20
Serbia	na	na	na	na	na	na	na	na	na	na	na	na	na	na	na	na
Singapore	na	na	na	na	na	na	na	na	na	na	na	na	na	na	na	na
Slovakia	na	43	39	47	47	41	43	42	45	38	46	41	45	43	42	52
Slovenia	na	52	51	53	48	51	57	57	53	40	59	51	42	54	52	52
South Africa	na	na	na	na	na	na	na	na	na	na	na	na	na	na	na	na
Spain	na	46	45	48	46	46	47	49	45	43	49	50	44	54	46	41
Sweden	na	37	39	36	35	36	40	42	36	36	33	39	42	44	39	31
Switzerland	na	na	na	na	na	na	na	na	na	na	na	na	na	na	na	na
Taiwan	na	na	na	na	na	na	na	na	na	na	na	na	na	na	na	na
Tanzania	na	na	na	na	na	na	na	na	na	na	na	na	na	na	na	na
Turkey	na	78	79	77	76	79	80	78	77	78	78	77	80	75	79	83
Uganda	na	na	na	na	na	na	na	na	na	na	na	na	na	na	na	na
Ukraine	na	47	43	50	42	46	50	51	47	44	50	39	51	44	51	53
United States	na	na	na	na	na	na	na	na	na	na	na	na	na	na	na	na
Uruguay	na	na	na	na	na	na	na	na	na	na	na	na	na	na	na	na
Venezuela	na	na	na	na	na	na	na	na	na	na	na	na	na	na	na	na
Vietnam	na	na	na	na	na	na	na	na	na	na	na	na	na	na	na	na
Zimbabwe	na	na	na	na	na	na	na	na	na	na	na	na	na	na	na	na
Total	na	46	45	47	48	44	47	49	46	41	48	46	44	46	47	44

RANKING

Country	2000
Malta	87
Turkey	78
Greece	61
Poland	61
Hungary	58
Ireland	58
Romania	58
Northern Ireland	56
France	54
Great Britain	53
Slovenia	52
Italy	51
Belgium	50
Austria	49
Luxembourg	48
Iceland	48
Ukraine	47
Spain	46
Croatia	43
Slovakia	43
Bulgaria	41
Germany	39
Denmark	39
Finland	38
Sweden	37
Belarus	36
Latvia	36
Portugal	34
Czech Republic	33
Netherlands	31
Russian Fed.	30
Estonia	27
Lithuania	22
Total	46

D041_1) MARRIAGE SUCCESS: TALKING A LOT
Here is a list of things which some people think make for a successful marriage. Please tell me, for each one, whether you think it is...

Very important (%)

(EVS: V147)

Country	Wave 1990	Wave 2000	Gender Male	Gender Female	Age 16-29	Age 30-49	Age 50+	Education Lower	Education Middle	Education Upper	Income Lower	Income Middle	Income Upper	Values Mat	Values Mixed	Values Postm.
Albania	na	na	na	na	na	na	na	na	na	na	na	na	na	na	na	na
Algeria	na	na	na	na	na	na	na	na	na	na	na	na	na	na	na	na
Argentina	na	na	na	na	na	na	na	na	na	na	na	na	na	na	na	na
Armenia	na	na	na	na	na	na	na	na	na	na	na	na	na	na	na	na
Australia	na	na	na	na	na	na	na	na	na	na	na	na	na	na	na	na
Austria	na	53	50	56	56	51	54	55	53	46	52	53	53	47	55	52
Azerbaijan	na	na	na	na	na	na	na	na	na	na	na	na	na	na	na	na
Bangladesh	na	na	na	na	na	na	na	na	na	na	na	na	na	na	na	na
Belarus	na	34	31	37	34	32	37	33	34	37	34	35	33	33	34	46
Belgium	na	50	49	51	46	50	52	52	50	48	55	51	47	53	48	51
Bosnia and Herz.	na	na	na	na	na	na	na	na	na	na	na	na	na	na	na	na
Brazil	na	na	na	na	na	na	na	na	na	na	na	na	na	na	na	na
Bulgaria	na	45	42	48	53	46	40	36	52	42	44	44	45	43	47	46
Canada	na	na	na	na	na	na	na	na	na	na	na	na	na	na	na	na
Chile	na	na	na	na	na	na	na	na	na	na	na	na	na	na	na	na
China	na	na	na	na	na	na	na	na	na	na	na	na	na	na	na	na
Colombia	na	na	na	na	na	na	na	na	na	na	na	na	na	na	na	na
Croatia	na	46	44	47	51	47	40	41	48	49	40	46	51	39	45	53
Czech Republic	na	28	26	29	29	24	31	29	26	26	31	26	26	26	28	32
Denmark	na	38	36	40	35	33	45	39	36	38	42	34	39	31	40	34
Dominican Rep.	na	na	na	na	na	na	na	na	na	na	na	na	na	na	na	na
Egypt	na	na	na	na	na	na	na	na	na	na	na	na	na	na	na	na
El Salvador	na	na	na	na	na	na	na	na	na	na	na	na	na	na	na	na
Estonia	na	21	19	22	22	20	21	22	22	16	21	22	20	21	21	29
Finland	na	41	36	45	47	39	39	40	41	45	48	39	37	42	39	49
France	na	49	46	53	43	51	51	52	47	46	50	48	49	51	51	44
Georgia	na	na	na	na	na	na	na	na	na	na	na	na	na	na	na	na
Germany	na	49	47	50	46	51	48	44	54	43	48	50	51	57	49	39
Great Britain	na	48	45	50	41	45	54	50	48	37	55	45	51	na	na	na
Greece	na	62	55	67	58	63	68	74	61	60	63	60	64	63	62	61
Hungary	na	54	50	57	52	52	56	52	56	56	51	55	55	52	55	64
Iceland	na	33	30	35	27	30	41	37	28	32	35	30	31	37	30	37
India	na	na	na	na	na	na	na	na	na	na	na	na	na	na	na	na
Indonesia	na	na	na	na	na	na	na	na	na	na	na	na	na	na	na	na
Iran	na	na	na	na	na	na	na	na	na	na	na	na	na	na	na	na
Ireland	na	50	51	49	44	47	57	55	49	45	56	52	41	53	51	42
Israel	na	na	na	na	na	na	na	na	na	na	na	na	na	na	na	na
Italy	na	64	60	67	67	64	61	63	66	60	63	64	62	61	64	65
Japan	na	na	na	na	na	na	na	na	na	na	na	na	na	na	na	na
Jordan	na	na	na	na	na	na	na	na	na	na	na	na	na	na	na	na
Korea, South	na	na	na	na	na	na	na	na	na	na	na	na	na	na	na	na
Latvia	na	31	26	35	30	29	34	32	32	27	33	31	28	34	29	26
Lithuania	na	20	19	21	24	22	15	14	22	22	20	15	25	19	19	24
Luxembourg	na	54	52	55	50	50	60	59	52	47	53	53	45	52	55	54
Macedonia	na	na	na	na	na	na	na	na	na	na	na	na	na	na	na	na
Malta	na	83	82	83	76	84	86	85	82	79	86	82	81	76	86	85
Mexico	na	na	na	na	na	na	na	na	na	na	na	na	na	na	na	na
Moldova	na	na	na	na	na	na	na	na	na	na	na	na	na	na	na	na
Montenegro	na	na	na	na	na	na	na	na	na	na	na	na	na	na	na	na
Morocco	na	na	na	na	na	na	na	na	na	na	na	na	na	na	na	na
Netherlands	na	34	29	39	35	26	41	43	33	27	42	31	26	41	33	34
New Zealand	na	na	na	na	na	na	na	na	na	na	na	na	na	na	na	na
Nigeria	na	na	na	na	na	na	na	na	na	na	na	na	na	na	na	na
Northern Ireland	na	54	53	55	53	49	60	56	52	53	57	50	46	51	53	59
Norway	na	na	na	na	na	na	na	na	na	na	na	na	na	na	na	na
Pakistan	na	na	na	na	na	na	na	na	na	na	na	na	na	na	na	na
Peru	na	na	na	na	na	na	na	na	na	na	na	na	na	na	na	na
Philippines	na	na	na	na	na	na	na	na	na	na	na	na	na	na	na	na
Poland	na	54	54	54	58	48	58	53	56	49	54	52	56	50	57	54
Portugal	na	47	47	47	52	44	45	45	48	54	45	45	58	35	55	42
Puerto Rico	na	na	na	na	na	na	na	na	na	na	na	na	na	na	na	na
Romania	na	56	57	56	61	59	52	49	59	63	45	58	64	53	59	68
Russian Fed.	na	29	25	32	29	30	27	29	30	26	30	32	26	27	31	25
Serbia	na	na	na	na	na	na	na	na	na	na	na	na	na	na	na	na
Singapore	na	na	na	na	na	na	na	na	na	na	na	na	na	na	na	na
Slovakia	na	44	40	48	46	43	45	46	43	45	45	44	45	44	44	53
Slovenia	na	60	56	63	59	58	61	66	59	51	63	59	49	61	61	57
South Africa	na	na	na	na	na	na	na	na	na	na	na	na	na	na	na	na
Spain	na	50	47	52	56	48	48	47	51	56	49	57	51	52	49	54
Sweden	na	43	42	44	37	42	47	44	41	45	42	40	48	46	42	44
Switzerland	na	na	na	na	na	na	na	na	na	na	na	na	na	na	na	na
Taiwan	na	na	na	na	na	na	na	na	na	na	na	na	na	na	na	na
Tanzania	na	na	na	na	na	na	na	na	na	na	na	na	na	na	na	na
Turkey	na	71	71	71	69	72	75	73	69	62	72	70	69	78	70	73
Uganda	na	na	na	na	na	na	na	na	na	na	na	na	na	na	na	na
Ukraine	na	50	48	50	47	48	52	53	49	50	55	42	50	44	56	60
United States	na	na	na	na	na	na	na	na	na	na	na	na	na	na	na	na
Uruguay	na	na	na	na	na	na	na	na	na	na	na	na	na	na	na	na
Venezuela	na	na	na	na	na	na	na	na	na	na	na	na	na	na	na	na
Vietnam	na	na	na	na	na	na	na	na	na	na	na	na	na	na	na	na
Zimbabwe	na	na	na	na	na	na	na	na	na	na	na	na	na	na	na	na
Total	na	46	44	48	46	45	48	47	46	45	47	44	45	44	47	49

RANKING

Country	2000
Malta	83
Turkey	71
Italy	64
Greece	62
Slovenia	60
Romania	56
Northern Ireland	54
Poland	54
Luxembourg	54
Hungary	54
Austria	53
Ireland	50
Belgium	50
Spain	50
Ukraine	50
France	49
Germany	49
Great Britain	48
Portugal	47
Croatia	46
Bulgaria	45
Slovakia	44
Sweden	43
Finland	41
Denmark	38
Belarus	34
Netherlands	34
Iceland	33
Latvia	31
Russian Fed.	29
Czech Republic	28
Estonia	21
Lithuania	20
Total	46

D054) MAKE MY PARENTS PROUD

For each of the following statements I read out, can you tell me how much you agree with each. Do you agree strongly, agree, disagree, or disagree strongly? "One of my main goals in life has been to make my parents proud"

Agree strongly / Agree (%)

(WVS: V113)

Country	Wave 1990	Wave 2000	Gender Male	Gender Female	Age 16-29	Age 30-49	Age 50+	Education Lower	Education Middle	Education Upper	Income Lower	Income Middle	Income Upper	Values Mat	Values Mixed	Values Postm.
Albania	na	94	93	94	95	94	92	92	94	96	94	92	95	93	94	97
Algeria	na	92	90	94	94	90	93	93	92	92	95	94	92	90	93	94
Argentina	na	85	87	84	85	84	87	89	82	70	90	88	77	92	87	76
Armenia	na	84	84	85	84	87	81	79	85	83	84	84	84	85	85	78
Australia	na	69	67	70	72	63	72	76	70	61	72	68	64	79	71	63
Austria	na	na	na	na	na	na	na	na	na	na	na	na	na	na	na	na
Azerbaijan	na	86	86	87	91	86	76	87	87	85	93	86	82	87	86	87
Bangladesh	na	96	96	96	97	95	96	95	98	95	94	94	100	96	96	92
Belarus	na	na	na	na	na	na	na	na	na	na	na	na	na	na	na	na
Belgium	na	na	na	na	na	na	na	na	na	na	na	na	na	na	na	na
Bosnia and Herz.	na	88	88	89	92	88	86	90	87	89	91	88	86	87	89	83
Brazil	na	88	89	86	89	87	88	91	88	77	90	88	85	93	86	85
Bulgaria	na	na	na	na	na	na	na	na	na	na	na	na	na	na	na	na
Canada	na	81	79	82	84	78	82	83	83	76	84	83	77	83	83	76
Chile	na	84	85	84	91	84	78	78	88	86	81	86	87	85	84	82
China	na	61	59	64	52	64	64	66	60	43	65	61	56	62	57	63
Colombia	na	93	93	94	95	92	95	96	96	89	95	95	90	93	95	92
Croatia	na	na	na	na	na	na	na	na	na	na	na	na	na	na	na	na
Czech Republic	na	na	na	na	na	na	na	na	na	na	na	na	na	na	na	na
Denmark	na	na	na	na	na	na	na	na	na	na	na	na	na	na	na	na
Dominican Rep.	na	89	87	91	90	88	80	90	89	89	90	86	93	90	90	84
Egypt	na	99	98	99	98	98	99	99	99	98	99	98	99	99	99	97
El Salvador	na	96	97	96	96	96	98	96	98	94	96	97	94	na	na	na
Estonia	na	na	na	na	na	na	na	na	na	na	na	na	na	na	na	na
Finland	na	na	na	na	na	na	na	na	na	na	na	na	na	na	na	na
France	na	na	na	na	na	na	na	na	na	na	na	na	na	na	na	na
Georgia	na	85	85	85	86	87	80	85	85	84	85	86	84	85	85	85
Germany	na	na	na	na	na	na	na	na	na	na	na	na	na	na	na	na
Great Britain	na	na	na	na	na	na	na	na	na	na	na	na	na	na	na	na
Greece	na	na	na	na	na	na	na	na	na	na	na	na	na	na	na	na
Hungary	na	na	na	na	na	na	na	na	na	na	na	na	na	na	na	na
Iceland	na	na	na	na	na	na	na	na	na	na	na	na	na	na	na	na
India	na	89	89	88	90	90	86	89	91	86	88	89	90	88	90	89
Indonesia	na	92	92	92	92	93	91	93	93	90	90	93	93	95	90	93
Iran	na	92	92	92	93	91	93	92	92	91	92	88	93	93	91	93
Ireland	na	na	na	na	na	na	na	na	na	na	na	na	na	na	na	na
Israel	na	na	na	na	na	na	na	na	na	na	na	na	na	na	na	na
Italy	na	na	na	na	na	na	na	na	na	na	na	na	na	na	na	na
Japan	na	73	75	70	70	67	79	80	72	71	76	71	71	80	72	63
Jordan	na	99	99	99	99	100	99	99	100	98	99	99	99	100	99	96
Korea, South	na	75	80	70	73	72	84	87	75	74	72	74	79	76	73	83
Latvia	na	na	na	na	na	na	na	na	na	na	na	na	na	na	na	na
Lithuania	na	na	na	na	na	na	na	na	na	na	na	na	na	na	na	na
Luxembourg	na	na	na	na	na	na	na	na	na	na	na	na	na	na	na	na
Macedonia	na	84	85	83	86	81	87	93	81	77	88	82	81	80	86	92
Malta	na	na	na	na	na	na	na	na	na	na	na	na	na	na	na	na
Mexico	na	93	93	94	94	93	93	93	94	94	94	92	95	94	93	93
Moldova	na	93	90	95	91	93	93	94	92	92	96	91	95	93	92	85
Montenegro	na	74	73	75	74	72	75	73	74	72	82	74	74	76	69	72
Morocco	na	97	98	97	98	97	97	98	98	96	99	99	93	97	98	98
Netherlands	na	na	na	na	na	na	na	na	na	na	na	na	na	na	na	na
New Zealand	na	55	55	54	66	45	59	59	55	50	59	53	53	64	53	46
Nigeria	na	98	98	98	98	99	96	99	98	98	98	99	98	98	99	99
Northern Ireland	na	na	na	na	na	na	na	na	na	na	na	na	na	na	na	na
Norway	na	54	55	54	63	46	59	65	56	42	na	na	na	59	55	45
Pakistan	na	97	97	97	96	97	98	97	97	97	97	97	98	97	97	92
Peru	na	96	96	96	96	96	96	95	96	96	96	96	95	96	96	97
Philippines	na	96	97	96	96	95	98	97	97	95	96	95	97	94	98	95
Poland	na	na	na	na	na	na	na	na	na	na	na	na	na	na	na	na
Portugal	na	na	na	na	na	na	na	na	na	na	na	na	na	na	na	na
Puerto Rico	na	95	97	95	93	95	98	97	97	94	97	93	96	95	95	96
Romania	na	na	na	na	na	na	na	na	na	na	na	na	na	na	na	na
Russian Fed.	na	na	na	na	na	na	na	na	na	na	na	na	na	na	na	na
Serbia	na	75	69	81	68	71	83	82	72	71	80	71	75	79	74	57
Singapore	na	91	91	91	94	86	92	93	92	83	90	93	90	92	91	85
Slovakia	na	na	na	na	na	na	na	na	na	na	na	na	na	na	na	na
Slovenia	na	na	na	na	na	na	na	na	na	na	na	na	na	na	na	na
South Africa	na	95	94	96	97	94	91	95	95	83	95	99	91	94	95	93
Spain	na	85	82	87	79	79	93	89	80	75	92	85	77	87	86	74
Sweden	na	38	42	34	43	29	43	50	37	30	43	38	31	55	40	28
Switzerland	na	45	45	44	45	39	51	56	42	45	50	51	38	58	46	29
Taiwan	na	65	62	67	57	64	71	72	68	56	66	65	63	66	66	53
Tanzania	na	88	89	86	91	85	88	88	88	85	90	84	89	87	88	88
Turkey	na	97	96	98	97	97	97	98	97	90	98	97	93	98	97	94
Uganda	na	94	93	94	97	92	86	93	96	75	96	90	95	94	94	91
Ukraine	na	na	na	na	na	na	na	na	na	na	na	na	na	na	na	na
United States	na	83	87	78	87	80	83	83	84	82	82	83	82	87	83	80
Uruguay	na	68	69	68	67	63	73	73	63	58	68	69	67	68	71	61
Venezuela	na	97	97	98	98	97	97	98	97	98	94	99	98	95	98	98
Vietnam	na	97	98	97	98	97	97	97	98	96	95	98	98	93	98	100
Zimbabwe	na	97	95	98	96	98	98	98	95	100	96	97	97	96	97	97
Total	na	85	85	85	88	83	83	88	84	81	86	86	84	88	84	77

RANKING

Country	2000
Jordan	99
Egypt	99
Nigeria	98
Morocco	97
Venezuela	97
Vietnam	97
Zimbabwe	97
Pakistan	97
Turkey	97
El Salvador	96
Philippines	96
Peru	96
Bangladesh	96
Puerto Rico	95
South Africa	95
Uganda	94
Albania	94
Colombia	93
Mexico	93
Moldova	93
Algeria	92
Iran	92
Indonesia	92
Singapore	91
Dominican Rep.	89
India	89
Bosnia and Herz.	88
Brazil	88
Tanzania	88
Azerbaijan	86
Argentina	85
Georgia	85
Spain	85
Macedonia	84
Armenia	84
Chile	84
United States	83
Canada	81
Serbia	75
Korea, South	75
Montenegro	74
Japan	73
Australia	69
Uruguay	68
Taiwan	65
China	61
New Zealand	55
Norway	54
Switzerland	45
Sweden	38
Total	85

D055) LIVE UP TO WHAT MY FRIENDS EXPECT

For each of the following statements I read out, can you tell me how much you agree with each. Do you agree strongly, agree, disagree, or disagree strongly? "I make a lot of effort to live up to what my friends expect"

Agree strongly / Agree (%) (WVS: V114)

Country	Wave 1990	Wave 2000	Gender Male	Gender Female	Age 16-29	Age 30-49	Age 50+	Education Lower	Education Middle	Education Upper	Income Lower	Income Middle	Income Upper	Values Mat	Values Mixed	Values Postm.	RANKING Country	2000
Albania	na	52	53	50	42	53	58	56	49	47	58	46	50	52	51	54	Georgia	89
Algeria	na	71	73	69	71	72	72	70	72	71	73	77	68	67	74	77	Jordan	87
Argentina	na	25	32	20	25	23	29	28	23	18	28	27	21	30	28	17	Uganda	80
Armenia	na	73	79	69	72	75	74	71	73	74	72	73	76	71	76	73	Vietnam	77
Australia	na	34	36	32	30	29	43	42	33	29	41	29	30	42	35	31	Nigeria	77
Austria	na	na	na	na	na	na	na	na	na	na	na	na	na	na	na	na	China	77
Azerbaijan	na	74	76	72	83	72	60	73	73	77	76	76	74	72	77	82	Brazil	75
Bangladesh	na	59	64	53	60	59	59	55	62	65	45	59	73	54	64	54	Azerbaijan	74
Belarus	na	na	na	na	na	na	na	na	na	na	na	na	na	na	na	na	Armenia	73
Belgium	na	na	na	na	na	na	na	na	na	na	na	na	na	na	na	na	Morocco	73
Bosnia and Herz.	na	31	33	30	30	32	33	38	32	25	32	34	27	26	32	38	Egypt	72
Brazil	na	75	75	76	70	75	87	85	70	60	81	78	67	81	75	62	Korea, South	72
Bulgaria	na	na	na	na	na	na	na	na	na	na	na	na	na	na	na	na	Algeria	71
Canada	na	44	48	40	47	38	51	53	45	36	52	46	37	48	46	39	Dominican Rep.	70
Chile	na	35	35	35	38	32	37	36	36	31	39	33	32	33	36	33	Moldova	70
China	na	77	75	78	74	77	77	77	77	66	80	75	71	72	80	77	Montenegro	69
Colombia	na	41	41	41	40	41	47	52	48	26	54	44	30	55	53	39	Japan	65
Croatia	na	na	na	na	na	na	na	na	na	na	na	na	na	na	na	na	Serbia	63
Czech Republic	na	na	na	na	na	na	na	na	na	na	na	na	na	na	na	na	Bangladesh	59
Denmark	na	na	na	na	na	na	na	na	na	na	na	na	na	na	na	na	Taiwan	59
Dominican Rep.	na	70	72	68	70	67	91	83	79	66	75	61	65	83	68	63	Indonesia	58
Egypt	na	72	74	70	76	71	69	67	77	77	73	72	74	71	74	74	Spain	58
El Salvador	na	na	na	na	na	na	na	na	na	na	na	na	na	na	na	na	Peru	57
Estonia	na	na	na	na	na	na	na	na	na	na	na	na	na	na	na	na	India	55
Finland	na	na	na	na	na	na	na	na	na	na	na	na	na	na	na	na	Philippines	55
France	na	na	na	na	na	na	na	na	na	na	na	na	na	na	na	na	Mexico	54
Georgia	na	89	89	89	91	90	85	89	89	90	88	89	91	89	89	91	Iran	53
Germany	na	na	na	na	na	na	na	na	na	na	na	na	na	na	na	na	Puerto Rico	52
Great Britain	na	na	na	na	na	na	na	na	na	na	na	na	na	na	na	na	Albania	52
Greece	na	na	na	na	na	na	na	na	na	na	na	na	na	na	na	na	Zimbabwe	50
Hungary	na	na	na	na	na	na	na	na	na	na	na	na	na	na	na	na	Pakistan	48
Iceland	na	na	na	na	na	na	na	na	na	na	na	na	na	na	na	na	Switzerland	47
India	na	55	58	51	58	55	53	55	53	57	59	54	54	56	58	44	Canada	44
Indonesia	na	58	62	55	48	65	56	61	60	54	62	60	56	56	60	64	Singapore	43
Iran	na	53	55	51	52	51	57	55	54	48	54	48	53	50	53	53	Colombia	41
Ireland	na	na	na	na	na	na	na	na	na	na	na	na	na	na	na	na	Tanzania	40
Israel	na	na	na	na	na	na	na	na	na	na	na	na	na	na	na	na	South Africa	38
Italy	na	na	na	na	na	na	na	na	na	na	na	na	na	na	na	na	Venezuela	37
Japan	na	65	70	60	69	61	67	65	63	68	64	67	63	72	62	65	Macedonia	35
Jordan	na	87	88	87	87	88	87	85	90	88	89	86	89	88	87	84	Chile	35
Korea, South	na	72	77	67	74	71	72	64	72	74	67	75	75	69	74	79	Australia	34
Latvia	na	na	na	na	na	na	na	na	na	na	na	na	na	na	na	na	United States	33
Lithuania	na	na	na	na	na	na	na	na	na	na	na	na	na	na	na	na	Bosnia and Herz.	31
Luxembourg	na	na	na	na	na	na	na	na	na	na	na	na	na	na	na	na	Uruguay	29
Macedonia	na	35	37	33	46	33	29	47	30	29	38	36	27	28	37	55	New Zealand	28
Malta	na	na	na	na	na	na	na	na	na	na	na	na	na	na	na	na	Argentina	25
Mexico	na	54	54	54	57	51	56	56	52	52	56	54	53	58	53	53	Norway	19
Moldova	na	70	67	72	71	68	70	74	70	65	77	69	69	72	65	63		
Montenegro	na	69	69	69	71	69	67	70	70	62	81	65	68	72	63	68		
Morocco	na	73	77	70	76	73	67	73	73	76	76	70	71	74	76	77		
Netherlands	na	na	na	na	na	na	na	na	na	na	na	na	na	na	na	na		
New Zealand	na	28	32	25	27	20	36	33	30	21	36	23	23	38	26	23		
Nigeria	na	77	80	73	78	76	67	75	79	76	76	76	79	77	76	81		
Northern Ireland	na	na	na	na	na	na	na	na	na	na	na	na	na	na	na	na		
Norway	na	19	19	19	22	14	23	23	19	16	na	na	na	29	17	21		
Pakistan	na	48	48	48	42	51	52	57	32	51	56	45	42	49	47	18		
Peru	na	57	60	54	58	57	54	58	58	54	59	58	52	55	57	62		
Philippines	na	55	53	56	56	53	56	55	56	52	56	52	56	55	54	56		
Poland	na	na	na	na	na	na	na	na	na	na	na	na	na	na	na	na		
Portugal	na	na	na	na	na	na	na	na	na	na	na	na	na	na	na	na		
Puerto Rico	na	52	54	51	51	48	56	62	55	50	63	51	46	49	56	45		
Romania	na	na	na	na	na	na	na	na	na	na	na	na	na	na	na	na		
Russian Fed.	na	na	na	na	na	na	na	na	na	na	na	na	na	na	na	na		
Serbia	na	63	61	64	61	60	66	64	63	62	62	62	64	62	64	56		
Singapore	na	43	48	38	51	36	34	44	44	35	41	47	43	36	46	42		
Slovakia	na	na	na	na	na	na	na	na	na	na	na	na	na	na	na	na		
Slovenia	na	na	na	na	na	na	na	na	na	na	na	na	na	na	na	na		
South Africa	na	38	41	33	38	40	28	39	37	31	40	38	35	32	40	49		
Spain	na	58	58	59	54	55	64	59	57	56	60	56	58	54	63	46		
Sweden	na	na	na	na	na	na	na	na	na	na	na	na	na	na	na	na		
Switzerland	na	47	49	45	47	43	53	53	47	37	50	52	42	55	50	35		
Taiwan	na	59	57	61	58	59	57	60	66	53	64	62	53	59	60	51		
Tanzania	na	40	43	36	36	43	38	39	40	42	40	40	47	39	39	46		
Turkey	na	na	na	na	na	na	na	na	na	na	na	na	na	na	na	na		
Uganda	na	80	87	73	83	77	77	78	80	87	85	87	81	75	83	79		
Ukraine	na	na	na	na	na	na	na	na	na	na	na	na	na	na	na	na		
United States	na	33	35	32	30	28	43	35	32	33	29	35	37	32	35	29		
Uruguay	na	29	33	26	27	24	34	35	22	17	29	35	23	30	32	20		
Venezuela	na	37	39	35	38	35	38	45	40	21	46	40	29	36	40	28		
Vietnam	na	77	78	76	77	78	75	78	75	77	72	76	80	72	80	76		
Zimbabwe	na	50	50	49	52	47	48	52	47	32	54	49	42	51	49	44		
Total	na	55	57	53	58	54	54	57	56	52	59	55	54	59	55	46	Total	55

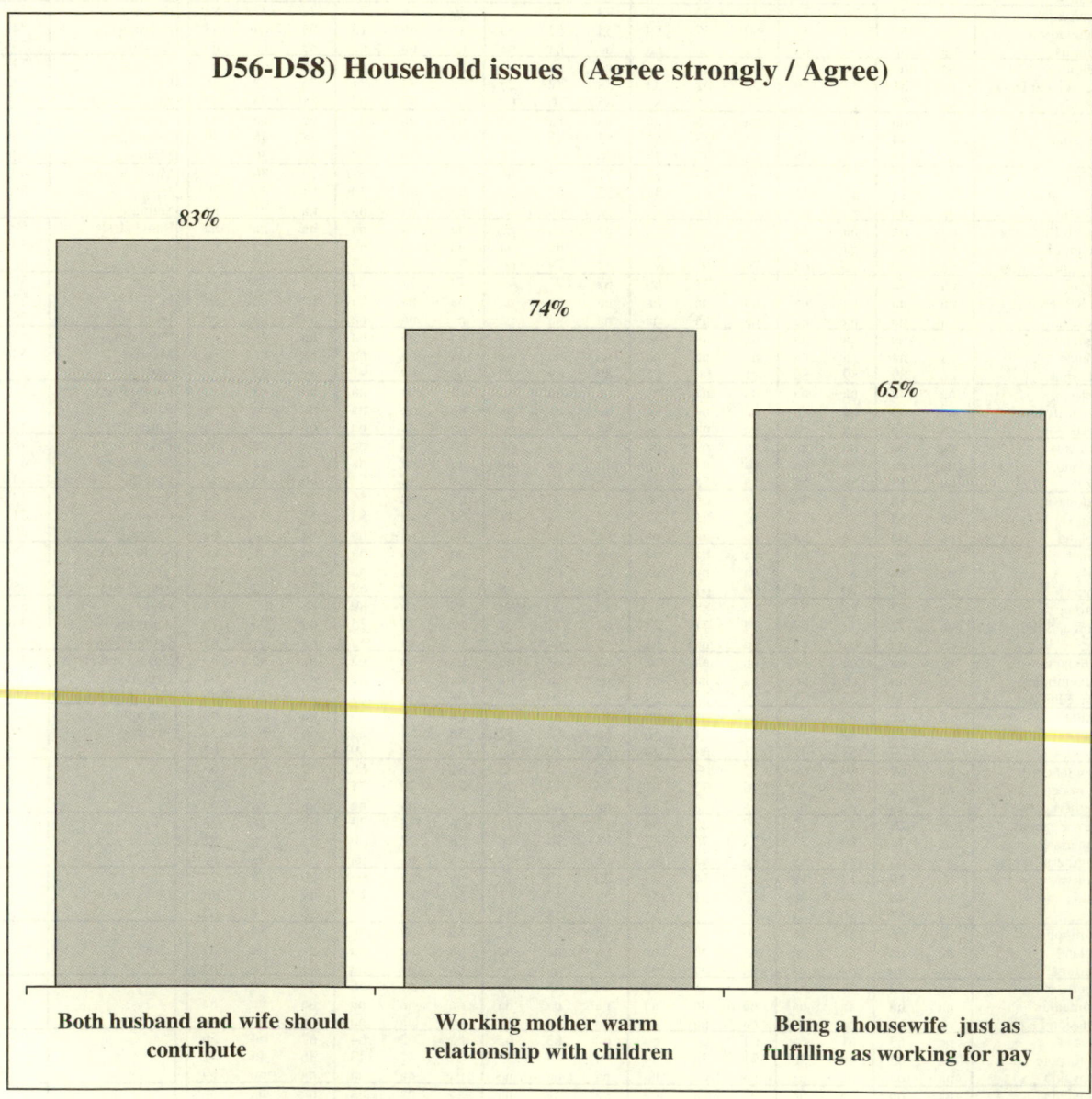

D56-D58) Household issues (Agree strongly / Agree)

- 83% — Both husband and wife should contribute
- 74% — Working mother warm relationship with children
- 65% — Being a housewife just as fulfilling as working for pay

D056) A WORKING MOTHER RELATIONSHIP

Do you agree strongly, agree, disagree, or disagree strongly? "A working mother can establish just as warm and secure a relationship with her children as a mother who does not work"

Agree strongly / Agree (%)　　　　　　　　　　　　　　　　　　　　　　　　　　(WVS: V115; EVS: V154)

Country	Wave 1990	Wave 2000	Gender Male	Gender Female	Age 16-29	Age 30-49	Age 50+	Education Lower	Education Middle	Education Upper	Income Lower	Income Middle	Income Upper	Values Mat	Values Mixed	Values Postm.	RANKING Country	RANKING 2000
Albania	na	76	75	77	78	75	76	73	76	82	70	78	80	75	76	74	Japan	95
Algeria	na	65	56	74	63	69	62	58	61	75	62	65	72	61	65	74	Finland	95
Argentina	74	76	70	81	77	76	74	72	80	84	75	75	77	76	75	78	China	94
Armenia	na	82	77	87	82	82	83	82	81	85	83	78	84	80	84	81	Taiwan	92
Australia	na	69	62	75	76	71	59	65	68	72	64	68	75	62	68	73	Denmark	86
Austria	53	na	na	na	na	na	na	na	na	na	na	na	na	na	na	na	Iceland	86
Azerbaijan	na	80	77	83	81	80	78	77	79	82	82	79	80	80	79	82	Moldova	86
Bangladesh	na	60	61	58	62	59	51	53	68	63	38	67	69	51	65	67	Sweden	84
Belarus	65	82	80	83	87	81	79	79	83	81	83	81	82	85	82	78	Vietnam	84
Belgium	74	79	75	82	80	80	77	68	79	85	72	79	84	70	80	83	Korea, South	83
Bosnia and Herz.	na	82	78	86	83	82	82	79	82	86	74	85	83	83	81	90	Ukraine	83
Brazil	64	68	64	73	75	64	65	61	71	84	62	69	74	61	70	79	Russian Fed.	83
Bulgaria	61	79	80	78	86	79	77	81	79	77	77	83	77	81	78	67	Romania	83
Canada	70	78	75	80	80	80	73	71	80	79	77	76	80	73	77	81	Slovenia	83
Chile	72	78	76	80	81	79	74	71	81	85	74	80	82	77	77	83	Bosnia and Herz.	82
China	91	94	94	94	88	95	96	94	95	88	94	95	94	95	92	97	Armenia	82
Colombia	na	61	60	63	61	62	58	53	57	72	54	58	70	55	61	67	Belarus	82
Croatia	na	66	65	67	77	70	54	54	71	85	49	69	71	67	65	70	Netherlands	81
Czech Republic	59	81	78	84	79	81	82	79	82	86	83	78	83	81	81	79	Slovakia	81
Denmark	83	86	85	88	87	88	85	83	91	91	84	90	89	81	86	93	Czech Republic	81
Dominican Rep.	na	62	54	67	63	60	27	34	48	69	54	64	72	57	61	63	South Africa	80
Egypt	na	46	37	55	50	43	45	42	50	48	45	43	48	45	46	45	Azerbaijan	80
El Salvador	na	47	46	48	50	46	44	41	47	63	40	45	58	na	na	na	Bulgaria	79
Estonia	82	71	63	77	72	73	68	67	71	77	70	74	69	67	74	72	Serbia	79
Finland	94	95	93	97	94	95	95	93	97	96	93	96	95	94	95	96	Georgia	79
France	73	77	74	81	78	82	73	72	83	86	72	79	81	74	76	88	Spain	79
Georgia	na	79	72	84	82	79	75	74	79	83	77	80	82	80	79	73	United States	79
Germany	57	67	62	71	78	68	62	61	71	79	65	64	69	60	67	77	Belgium	79
Great Britain	70	73	69	77	83	72	67	71	75	67	69	74	75	na	na	na	Chile	78
Greece	na	76	70	80	77	79	66	65	71	81	73	78	78	77	76	72	Puerto Rico	78
Hungary	70	78	77	79	80	72	81	79	73	82	69	79	81	82	74	69	Hungary	78
Iceland	82	86	80	92	80	92	82	85	85	92	83	85	91	85	86	92	Canada	78
India	58	62	59	67	65	61	59	61	58	66	63	59	64	55	68	51	France	77
Indonesia	na	64	64	65	60	66	65	67	64	63	59	70	66	63	66	61	Iran	77
Iran	na	77	80	74	74	79	84	85	81	68	81	78	72	83	74	74	Lithuania	77
Ireland	63	na	na	na	na	na	na	na	na	na	na	na	na	na	na	na	Montenegro	77
Israel	na	na	na	na	na	na	na	na	na	na	na	na	na	na	na	na	Albania	76
Italy	63	64	60	68	69	68	58	55	68	81	56	64	75	52	63	72	Luxembourg	76
Japan	89	95	94	97	95	95	96	93	96	94	96	96	93	96	95	96	Argentina	76
Jordan	na	47	37	57	50	44	49	47	45	50	49	44	46	48	46	53	Greece	76
Korea, South	43	83	81	86	89	82	80	59	84	85	82	85	84	79	87	88	Latvia	76
Latvia	47	76	71	79	71	81	74	73	74	82	74	80	74	78	74	69	Macedonia	74
Lithuania	42	77	75	78	83	75	73	68	79	83	74	74	77	67	80	89	Tanzania	74
Luxembourg	na	76	73	79	82	76	71	72	76	83	65	77	82	71	78	84	Nigeria	74
Macedonia	na	74	75	74	76	75	73	71	74	81	71	73	81	76	75	70	Singapore	74
Malta	na	61	57	64	73	62	51	52	62	77	47	57	72	56	64	57	Zimbabwe	73
Mexico	64	69	67	72	71	71	64	66	72	77	66	71	74	69	69	69	Great Britain	73
Moldova	na	86	86	85	81	88	87	86	85	86	89	81	87	84	90	87	Philippines	73
Montenegro	na	77	73	80	82	80	69	69	79	87	62	78	80	72	81	76	Venezuela	72
Morocco	na	60	50	69	61	60	57	59	63	71	57	66	60	62	58	65	Estonia	71
Netherlands	75	81	77	86	82	82	80	72	85	86	73	85	88	68	82	88	Norway	71
New Zealand	na	68	63	72	74	68	66	68	64	71	65	69	72	70	68	71	Peru	70
Nigeria	65	74	71	77	74	75	70	73	75	73	71	75	76	73	75	71	Turkey	70
Northern Ireland	71	na	na	na	na	na	na	na	na	na	na	na	na	na	na	na	Uruguay	70
Norway	69	71	64	76	66	73	71	62	68	81	na	na	na	66	69	83	Mexico	69
Pakistan	na	18	14	24	25	19	4	14	19	32	15	14	26	19	17	33	Australia	69
Peru	na	70	70	70	67	73	68	61	66	82	62	74	80	70	68	78	Brazil	68
Philippines	na	73	69	77	73	72	75	74	72	73	73	74	72	72	74	71	New Zealand	68
Poland	na	54	49	59	64	56	46	52	58	55	53	55	56	50	55	58	Germany	67
Portugal	76	67	66	68	78	66	62	64	73	80	67	60	71	62	68	78	Portugal	67
Puerto Rico	na	78	74	80	80	82	74	66	72	84	73	76	84	70	79	81	Croatia	66
Romania	84	83	83	83	81	87	81	78	84	90	79	84	87	83	83	90	Algeria	65
Russian Fed.	64	83	82	84	83	83	84	86	83	82	83	84	84	85	83	68	Indonesia	64
Serbia	na	79	74	85	90	82	72	71	81	88	73	81	86	76	83	81	Italy	64
Singapore	na	74	72	75	72	73	80	73	75	67	71	71	77	69	76	66	India	62
Slovakia	na	81	77	85	83	81	79	76	83	82	78	83	83	83	80	86	Dominican Rep.	62
Slovenia	74	83	82	83	89	84	77	76	84	87	79	80	89	77	83	86	Colombia	61
South Africa	na	80	77	84	80	82	73	79	83	64	79	82	78	78	82	81	Malta	61
Spain	67	79	78	80	85	83	71	74	83	85	72	82	81	72	81	86	Morocco	60
Sweden	73	84	78	90	85	84	83	79	86	86	82	84	87	80	83	87	Bangladesh	60
Switzerland	na	na	na	na	na	na	na	na	na	na	na	na	na	na	na	na	Uganda	58
Taiwan	na	92	92	91	97	90	92	90	92	93	89	92	93	89	94	89	Poland	54
Tanzania	na	74	73	76	74	75	74	76	73	70	79	75	76	74	74	83	Jordan	47
Turkey	57	70	68	72	70	71	68	67	73	81	67	71	78	64	72	73	El Salvador	47
Uganda	na	58	60	56	60	56	57	53	60	60	55	67	65	56	58	61	Egypt	46
Ukraine	na	83	83	83	80	81	87	83	84	81	85	82	82	82	84	73	Pakistan	18
United States	72	79	75	83	81	80	75	77	79	79	77	77	82	78	77	83		
Uruguay	na	70	67	72	74	75	64	65	78	69	70	69	70	61	73	68		
Venezuela	na	72	67	76	74	71	68	68	71	79	70	66	75	64	74	77		
Vietnam	na	84	81	86	83	87	81	84	84	83	81	85	83	84	83	85		
Zimbabwe	na	73	73	73	72	72	78	73	74	100	71	70	77	76	71	74		
Total	68	74	70	77	74	74	72	68	75	78	71	74	77	71	75	78	Total	74

D057) BEING A HOUSEWIFE FULFILLING

For each of the following statements I read out, can you tell me how much you agree with each. Do you agree strongly, agree, disagree, or disagree strongly? "Being a housewife is just as fulfilling as working for pay"

Agree strongly / Agree (%)

(WVS: V116; EVS: V157)

Country	Wave		Gender		Age			Education			Income			Values				RANKING Country	2000
	1990	2000	Male	Female	16-29	30-49	50+	Lower	Middle	Upper	Lower	Middle	Upper	Mat	Mixed	Postm.			
Albania	na	46	46	45	41	46	48	50	44	38	46	49	42	45	45	40		China	90
Algeria	na	66	63	70	62	69	72	67	67	66	68	69	64	65	65	74		Japan	89
Argentina	62	75	79	72	72	75	78	80	71	59	78	79	66	81	77	67		Korea, South	89
Armenia	na	75	81	70	72	78	78	77	78	68	72	77	79	76	75	77		Malta	87
Australia	na	70	71	68	68	67	75	76	70	64	73	69	65	72	71	67		Taiwan	86
Austria	63	na	na	na	na	na	na	na	na	na	na	na	na	na	na	na		Vietnam	86
Azerbaijan	na	73	76	70	74	72	74	81	75	67	83	74	62	74	70	82		Philippines	86
Bangladesh	na	29	29	29	30	28	30	31	25	29	20	31	35	27	30	23		Canada	82
Belarus	81	64	61	66	56	60	75	75	61	58	69	63	57	66	63	48		Puerto Rico	81
Belgium	67	64	68	60	60	58	71	76	64	55	71	67	58	70	64	57		Finland	81
Bosnia and Herz.	na	71	75	68	64	71	77	76	73	61	74	74	67	77	67	79		United States	80
Brazil	61	61	66	56	56	59	74	68	59	45	63	62	58	65	61	52		Georgia	79
Bulgaria	87	49	54	46	49	45	53	58	49	36	59	43	42	49	47	73		Lithuania	79
Canada	71	82	84	81	81	78	88	86	81	81	85	83	80	87	81	83		Turkey	78
Chile	74	69	71	67	66	65	77	71	68	67	67	73	66	73	69	62		Czech Republic	76
China	88	90	90	90	86	91	92	90	90	91	89	91	90	91	89	88		Pakistan	76
Colombia	na	66	67	64	64	65	70	71	68	59	69	67	62	70	70	61		Jordan	76
Croatia	na	56	55	56	45	59	64	62	57	34	63	58	51	63	55	52		Armenia	75
Czech Republic	39	76	83	71	74	76	78	77	75	80	82	76	73	78	76	79		Argentina	75
Denmark	55	54	56	53	51	51	60	54	52	54	58	52	49	51	56	47		Iran	75
Dominican Rep.	na	49	50	48	46	51	50	38	53	48	47	54	41	53	49	45		Egypt	74
Egypt	na	74	77	72	71	75	78	79	71	69	77	75	74	77	73	74		Mexico	73
El Salvador	na	70	68	72	66	71	75	76	66	60	75	70	59	na	na	na		Peru	73
Estonia	71	59	67	53	54	56	64	69	56	51	64	62	54	57	61	50		Azerbaijan	73
Finland	54	81	81	81	77	76	88	83	80	76	81	80	81	83	80	82		Moldova	72
France	60	62	66	59	56	60	68	66	59	56	67	64	55	66	64	53		Singapore	72
Georgia	na	79	80	78	78	79	81	86	80	72	81	80	76	80	78	78		Bosnia and Herz.	71
Germany	34	43	45	41	29	38	53	55	33	28	52	44	41	56	41	23		Slovakia	71
Great Britain	60	61	59	63	61	54	69	68	59	46	73	57	57	na	na	na		El Salvador	70
Greece	na	42	53	34	31	44	62	74	48	30	55	38	37	50	40	40		Australia	70
Hungary	76	61	64	59	58	56	69	69	47	45	61	63	59	64	59	49		Serbia	69
Iceland	71	65	65	64	58	62	74	65	64	64	66	63	64	66	65	56		Chile	69
India	46	64	64	65	63	63	66	64	59	70	59	63	67	61	65	69		Uruguay	69
Indonesia	na	23	20	25	23	24	21	20	24	24	22	22	29	19	24	32		Algeria	66
Iran	na	75	77	72	74	75	80	80	72	74	74	75	76	75	75	72		Zimbabwe	66
Ireland	72	na	na	na	na	na	na	na	na	na	na	na	na	na	na	na		Colombia	66
Israel	na	na	na	na	na	na	na	na	na	na	na	na	na	na	na	na		New Zealand	66
Italy	57	55	59	51	45	49	65	65	50	39	62	57	50	63	56	49		Morocco	65
Japan	83	89	91	87	82	88	92	91	90	86	91	87	86	88	89	89		Montenegro	65
Jordan	na	76	78	74	74	75	83	77	73	77	73	77	75	74	76	82		Venezuela	65
Korea, South	67	89	84	93	91	89	83	82	89	89	88	90	89	88	89	88		Iceland	65
Latvia	66	40	44	37	37	35	46	49	38	34	42	41	35	43	39	33		Luxembourg	65
Lithuania	85	79	79	78	76	75	84	85	79	67	81	79	76	77	78	85		India	64
Luxembourg	na	65	70	59	57	62	72	71	63	58	74	64	59	73	65	57		Belgium	64
Macedonia	na	52	52	51	53	50	52	61	48	45	52	52	48	53	51	58		Belarus	64
Malta	na	87	89	84	79	87	91	92	86	76	91	90	83	90	87	73		Russian Fed.	64
Mexico	68	73	74	73	67	76	75	76	71	68	71	71	73	00	71	67		France	62
Moldova	na	72	76	69	70	73	74	77	75	64	75	71	69	70	78	66		Hungary	61
Montenegro	na	65	71	60	58	62	72	71	63	59	53	64	66	65	65	58		Great Britain	61
Morocco	na	65	63	67	63	65	74	67	59	57	57	65	70	69	63	65		Brazil	61
Netherlands	53	52	55	48	46	46	59	65	47	43	60	49	43	60	51	49		Norway	61
New Zealand	na	66	63	68	68	61	70	68	71	59	71	67	60	61	64	68		Poland	61
Nigeria	49	44	44	44	43	47	44	50	40	42	45	42	45	44	45	42		Spain	60
Northern Ireland	70	na	na	na	na	na	na	na	na	na	na	na	na	na	na	na		Estonia	59
Norway	53	61	62	59	53	60	67	66	61	54	na	na	na	70	58	62		Ukraine	58
Pakistan	na	76	80	72	67	76	94	84	67	68	83	78	70	80	71	73		South Africa	56
Peru	na	73	72	74	68	76	78	74	72	73	72	76	70	75	72	75		Croatia	56
Philippines	na	86	84	87	84	86	88	89	85	82	88	85	84	84	88	78		Italy	55
Poland	na	61	66	56	58	55	69	68	53	48	65	57	58	61	61	58		Denmark	54
Portugal	49	51	54	48	41	45	61	55	45	37	61	54	47	56	46	47		Slovenia	54
Puerto Rico	na	81	82	81	72	79	87	77	85	80	82	82	81	81	81	85		Macedonia	52
Romania	48	48	49	48	46	49	49	53	47	40	50	52	44	52	44	54		Netherlands	52
Russian Fed.	86	64	69	59	60	62	67	77	64	55	68	65	59	64	63	55		Portugal	51
Serbia	na	69	75	64	72	68	69	72	72	61	70	74	65	71	69	61		Sweden	51
Singapore	na	72	74	71	68	74	82	72	70	81	74	67	77	73	72	71		Bulgaria	49
Slovakia	na	71	75	67	67	69	75	75	70	63	74	72	68	70	73	69		Dominican Rep.	49
Slovenia	63	54	60	49	49	48	65	69	54	28	69	53	36	63	53	51		Romania	48
South Africa	na	56	59	54	48	59	66	61	50	59	55	50	60	49	61	60		Albania	46
Spain	61	60	61	59	50	52	72	68	51	49	60	61	56	72	58	47		Nigeria	44
Sweden	62	51	52	49	44	49	56	61	49	44	52	50	47	53	53	42		Tanzania	43
Switzerland	na	na	na	na	na	na	na	na	na	na	na	na	na	na	na	na		Germany	43
Taiwan	na	86	86	86	88	86	87	85	86	88	87	87	86	86	87	89		Greece	42
Tanzania	na	43	49	35	33	45	52	47	34	46	47	39	49	42	41	58		Latvia	40
Turkey	79	78	81	75	76	79	82	83	76	62	83	77	65	78	80	72		Uganda	37
Uganda	na	37	42	32	35	36	48	40	35	45	49	35	32	39	36	35		Bangladesh	29
Ukraine	na	58	63	54	54	56	62	68	60	47	64	53	53	60	57	45		Indonesia	23
United States	76	80	81	79	75	78	87	79	77	82	77	81	82	83	80	79			
Uruguay	na	69	74	65	62	62	76	74	64	49	72	71	64	70	72	58			
Venezuela	na	65	66	63	60	65	73	68	64	63	64	62	67	56	67	70			
Vietnam	na	86	84	88	88	87	84	87	86	78	85	86	87	85	86	88			
Zimbabwe	na	66	62	70	62	67	75	73	56	52	74	62	56	72	63	57			
Total	65	65	67	63	60	64	70	69	64	60	67	65	63	67	64	62		Total	65

D058) HUSBAND AND WIFE SHOULD CONTRIBUTE

For each of the following statements I read out, can you tell me how much you agree with each. Do you agree strongly, agree, disagree, or disagree strongly? "Both the husband and wife should contribute to household income"

Agree strongly / Agree (%)

(WVS: V117; EVS: V159)

Country	Wave 1990	Wave 2000	Male	Female	Age 16-29	Age 30-49	Age 50+	Edu Lower	Edu Middle	Edu Upper	Inc Lower	Inc Middle	Inc Upper	Mat	Mixed	Postm.
Albania	na	96	96	97	98	96	95	95	96	99	97	96	96	96	96	97
Algeria	na	71	62	80	69	73	71	65	72	74	71	79	72	68	75	65
Argentina	77	91	86	94	92	91	88	90	92	91	90	91	90	86	91	93
Armenia	na	80	69	90	81	78	82	85	79	81	75	81	88	83	77	83
Australia	na	67	67	67	73	64	64	70	67	65	70	64	64	65	68	67
Austria	73	na	na	na	na	na	na	na	na	na	na	na	na	na	na	na
Azerbaijan	na	82	78	87	85	81	80	81	82	83	85	80	84	82	84	85
Bangladesh	na	87	82	93	91	85	78	85	89	90	88	86	87	88	86	87
Belarus	83	85	84	87	85	81	91	90	84	82	88	85	83	89	83	77
Belgium	67	70	64	76	75	67	72	74	67	73	75	71	68	68	71	69
Bosnia and Herz.	na	94	93	95	95	94	92	92	94	95	91	94	94	93	94	89
Brazil	93	96	94	98	95	97	96	95	97	97	95	98	97	96	96	98
Bulgaria	83	92	92	91	91	90	94	93	91	91	93	90	92	93	90	95
Canada	69	75	75	76	77	73	77	78	77	70	83	77	70	74	75	78
Chile	88	87	85	90	90	89	82	85	88	91	87	90	86	88	86	93
China	95	98	98	99	96	98	99	99	98	95	99	97	98	99	97	97
Colombia	na	95	93	96	95	95	94	93	94	97	94	94	96	95	96	93
Croatia	na	94	93	96	96	96	91	93	95	97	97	94	93	93	94	97
Czech Republic	88	93	91	95	87	92	96	95	91	86	93	93	91	96	93	85
Denmark	71	68	67	69	75	63	70	70	72	62	70	68	59	75	67	71
Dominican Rep.	na	92	88	95	94	88	90	90	94	92	94	91	92	88	92	99
Egypt	na	76	67	85	75	74	79	76	75	77	75	77	75	78	75	70
El Salvador	na	94	93	96	95	94	94	94	96	93	94	95	93	na	na	na
Estonia	81	82	80	84	75	84	85	83	83	81	87	83	80	83	83	79
Finland	78	71	71	72	75	69	72	74	72	58	75	74	65	75	71	71
France	80	81	81	82	86	76	85	82	81	79	84	80	77	82	82	79
Georgia	na	88	83	92	88	87	89	88	88	88	87	91	87	88	88	86
Germany	88	74	74	74	89	72	69	65	81	78	74	73	73	67	75	81
Great Britain	70	70	71	70	69	63	77	74	66	65	77	72	57	na	na	na
Greece	na	88	84	90	90	89	79	78	86	91	84	92	85	87	88	87
Hungary	83	89	87	92	90	87	91	92	86	83	93	89	88	91	88	75
Iceland	68	64	60	68	67	54	73	68	60	63	69	65	57	64	62	71
India	82	84	82	86	85	84	81	86	81	81	89	84	81	83	84	84
Indonesia	na	85	85	86	80	84	88	90	86	82	85	86	85	87	84	79
Iran	na	70	66	75	74	68	63	67	70	72	68	67	70	72	68	76
Ireland	70	na	na	na	na	na	na	na	na	na	na	na	na	na	na	na
Israel	na	na	na	na	na	na	na	na	na	na	na	na	na	na	na	na
Italy	80	81	78	84	82	80	81	79	83	80	79	78	82	75	82	82
Japan	46	57	54	59	63	53	57	62	55	55	65	55	47	56	56	57
Jordan	na	77	69	84	72	81	77	78	74	78	79	75	79	77	76	79
Korea, South	59	75	73	76	78	72	78	79	77	71	76	75	73	73	75	85
Latvia	77	89	89	88	83	88	91	92	87	89	89	94	87	90	88	93
Lithuania	75	90	90	89	89	89	90	87	91	87	92	88	89	92	89	95
Luxembourg	na	54	54	55	64	52	50	60	52	49	55	57	46	56	55	50
Macedonia	na	93	92	95	92	92	95	91	94	95	92	93	95	92	94	96
Malta	na	74	75	72	80	73	70	71	74	76	75	73	79	69	76	77
Mexico	82	89	87	90	90	90	85	87	91	91	88	87	89	86	90	90
Moldova	na	92	92	91	90	91	93	91	93	90	97	93	86	88	94	85
Montenegro	na	94	93	94	97	94	91	92	95	96	93	95	96	94	95	83
Morocco	na	74	68	81	75	74	74	73	80	84	59	79	81	78	72	79
Netherlands	32	38	34	42	42	35	38	41	38	35	42	35	36	36	37	44
New Zealand	na	60	61	59	73	53	62	64	55	59	65	57	57	61	60	57
Nigeria	94	90	91	88	90	89	90	87	91	93	87	92	91	91	90	85
Northern Ireland	83	na	na	na	na	na	na	na	na	na	na	na	na	na	na	na
Norway	74	80	79	81	84	76	83	81	80	78	na	na	na	80	80	81
Pakistan	na	70	65	76	76	70	61	73	66	67	78	70	58	70	70	58
Peru	na	94	93	95	93	96	92	94	94	94	93	95	95	92	95	96
Philippines	na	92	91	94	90	93	94	94	92	91	92	92	93	94	91	96
Poland	na	87	87	88	83	87	91	88	88	82	89	87	83	86	88	91
Portugal	98	88	85	91	95	88	85	87	90	95	90	82	91	88	86	91
Puerto Rico	na	94	94	95	97	95	93	92	96	95	95	94	95	95	95	96
Romania	91	85	84	87	81	85	88	89	83	83	88	84	82	86	86	76
Russian Fed.	80	83	80	85	76	83	86	86	83	81	86	85	80	86	81	72
Serbia	na	89	86	92	94	89	87	87	90	92	88	90	89	89	90	86
Singapore	na	81	79	83	84	79	77	77	84	76	81	83	79	85	79	83
Slovakia	na	89	87	90	90	90	87	87	90	85	87	90	89	89	88	92
Slovenia	93	91	89	93	92	89	92	94	91	84	91	92	87	93	91	91
South Africa	na	88	87	90	92	86	85	89	88	84	88	96	82	90	88	83
Spain	85	87	86	88	91	88	84	85	89	90	81	90	89	85	87	92
Sweden	87	89	88	91	90	85	92	91	89	87	90	89	88	92	90	87
Switzerland	na	na	na	na	na	na	na	na	na	na	na	na	na	na	na	na
Taiwan	na	89	87	91	88	90	87	87	90	90	88	89	89	90	87	97
Tanzania	na	89	90	89	89	89	93	88	90	93	86	92	91	89	90	96
Turkey	85	88	82	93	87	88	89	87	88	92	85	89	91	86	88	89
Uganda	na	92	96	88	93	93	84	90	92	98	92	93	92	88	94	96
Ukraine	na	86	83	88	83	84	89	90	86	83	87	86	84	87	85	82
United States	67	69	73	65	79	66	63	77	69	65	75	68	60	67	68	72
Uruguay	na	94	90	97	96	96	91	93	96	94	93	93	96	92	94	96
Venezuela	na	95	95	95	95	96	95	93	96	97	94	94	96	95	96	95
Vietnam	na	97	97	98	97	97	97	98	97	96	96	97	98	96	98	98
Zimbabwe	na	92	91	93	89	95	95	93	91	100	93	90	92	93	91	92
Total	78	83	81	85	85	83	83	84	84	82	84	84	82	85	83	82

RANKING

Country	2000
China	98
Vietnam	97
Albania	96
Brazil	96
Venezuela	95
Colombia	95
El Salvador	94
Puerto Rico	94
Croatia	94
Peru	94
Uruguay	94
Bosnia and Herz.	94
Montenegro	94
Macedonia	93
Czech Republic	93
Philippines	92
Dominican Rep.	92
Uganda	92
Bulgaria	92
Zimbabwe	92
Moldova	92
Slovenia	91
Argentina	91
Nigeria	90
Lithuania	90
Hungary	89
Tanzania	89
Sweden	89
Serbia	89
Mexico	89
Taiwan	89
Latvia	89
Slovakia	89
Portugal	88
South Africa	88
Georgia	88
Greece	88
Turkey	88
Chile	87
Poland	87
Spain	87
Bangladesh	87
Ukraine	86
Belarus	85
Romania	85
Indonesia	85
India	84
Russian Fed.	83
Estonia	82
Azerbaijan	82
France	81
Italy	81
Singapore	81
Armenia	80
Norway	80
Jordan	77
Egypt	76
Canada	75
Korea, South	75
Morocco	74
Germany	74
Malta	74
Finland	71
Algeria	71
Belgium	70
Great Britain	70
Pakistan	70
Iran	70
United States	69
Denmark	68
Australia	67
Iceland	64
New Zealand	60
Japan	57
Luxembourg	54
Netherlands	38
Total	83

D059) MEN MAKE BETTER POLITICAL LEADERS

For each of the following statements I read out, can you tell me how much you agree with each. Do you agree strongly, agree, disagree, or disagree strongly? "On the whole, men make better political leaders than women do"

Agree strongly / Agree (%)

(WVS: V118)

Country	Wave 1990	Wave 2000	Gender Male	Gender Female	Age 16-29	Age 30-49	Age 50+	Education Lower	Education Middle	Education Upper	Income Lower	Income Middle	Income Upper	Values Mat	Values Mixed	Values Postm.
Albania	na	52	65	39	43	52	59	60	47	42	53	50	51	52	50	46
Algeria	na	70	83	55	72	65	73	79	69	64	71	66	64	74	67	66
Argentina	na	32	39	26	35	28	35	35	32	21	42	32	24	40	32	27
Armenia	na	83	90	77	80	85	85	87	83	81	82	85	84	88	80	74
Australia	na	24	31	18	19	20	34	28	25	21	28	24	19	32	27	17
Austria	na	na	na	na	na	na	na	na	na	na	na	na	na	na	na	na
Azerbaijan	na	72	77	66	72	71	72	75	71	73	69	73	73	71	72	77
Bangladesh	na	67	70	65	66	69	66	69	66	64	83	63	59	69	65	72
Belarus	na	na	na	na	na	na	na	na	na	na	na	na	na	na	na	na
Belgium	na	na	na	na	na	na	na	na	na	na	na	na	na	na	na	na
Bosnia and Herz.	na	33	44	23	31	34	34	37	33	29	33	34	33	34	34	27
Brazil	na	47	56	39	43	48	54	55	44	32	55	40	44	54	47	34
Bulgaria	na	na	na	na	na	na	na	na	na	na	na	na	na	na	na	na
Canada	na	21	25	17	19	20	23	30	19	17	24	22	18	32	22	15
Chile	na	39	49	31	33	37	48	46	37	32	48	34	33	42	42	29
China	na	50	50	51	41	53	52	61	43	42	53	49	48	53	46	48
Colombia	na	33	39	27	32	32	37	46	32	24	42	34	26	44	39	25
Croatia	na	na	na	na	na	na	na	na	na	na	na	na	na	na	na	na
Czech Republic	na	na	na	na	na	na	na	na	na	na	na	na	na	na	na	na
Denmark	na	na	na	na	na	na	na	na	na	na	na	na	na	na	na	na
Dominican Rep.	na	41	53	33	42	40	36	63	54	33	39	46	37	51	41	23
Egypt	na	85	90	79	80	86	88	87	83	80	88	84	83	85	84	83
El Salvador	na	37	38	36	37	38	35	42	37	25	46	33	32	na	na	na
Estonia	na	na	na	na	na	na	na	na	na	na	na	na	na	na	na	na
Finland	na	na	na	na	na	na	na	na	na	na	na	na	na	na	na	na
France	na	na	na	na	na	na	na	na	na	na	na	na	na	na	na	na
Georgia	na	80	86	75	77	80	82	81	80	78	82	81	77	82	78	75
Germany	na	na	na	na	na	na	na	na	na	na	na	na	na	na	na	na
Great Britain	na	na	na	na	na	na	na	na	na	na	na	na	na	na	na	na
Greece	na	na	na	na	na	na	na	na	na	na	na	na	na	na	na	na
Hungary	na	na	na	na	na	na	na	na	na	na	na	na	na	na	na	na
Iceland	na	na	na	na	na	na	na	na	na	na	na	na	na	na	na	na
India	na	58	62	53	53	60	61	66	59	43	73	60	50	63	55	31
Indonesia	na	60	69	52	58	59	63	67	59	60	56	65	63	64	57	79
Iran	na	66	73	58	61	68	76	76	60	66	72	64	62	72	65	54
Ireland	na	na	na	na	na	na	na	na	na	na	na	na	na	na	na	na
Israel	na	na	na	na	na	na	na	na	na	na	na	na	na	na	na	na
Italy	na	na	na	na	na	na	na	na	na	na	na	na	na	na	na	na
Japan	na	43	48	40	25	34	58	59	43	34	45	42	45	50	41	33
Jordan	na	87	94	80	88	85	91	90	88	81	91	90	82	91	85	76
Korea, South	na	48	59	38	27	51	66	61	51	42	51	48	45	54	45	27
Latvia	na	na	na	na	na	na	na	na	na	na	na	na	na	na	na	na
Lithuania	na	na	na	na	na	na	na	na	na	na	na	na	na	na	na	na
Luxembourg	na	na	na	na	na	na	na	na	na	na	na	na	na	na	na	na
Macedonia	na	41	50	31	40	38	47	59	35	25	50	42	27	37	43	47
Malta	na	na	na	na	na	na	na	na	na	na	na	na	na	na	na	na
Mexico	na	42	45	39	37	41	47	51	32	27	49	37	36	48	50	34
Moldova	na	61	73	50	56	59	69	72	59	55	71	63	57	66	59	45
Montenegro	na	55	72	38	39	52	69	70	49	37	56	57	54	62	51	38
Morocco	na	73	81	65	69	76	80	78	59	49	82	70	73	75	73	68
Netherlands	na	na	na	na	na	na	na	na	na	na	na	na	na	na	na	na
New Zealand	na	17	23	13	13	12	23	22	19	11	23	16	11	25	17	14
Nigeria	na	80	87	72	80	80	77	81	81	77	82	78	80	76	82	78
Northern Ireland	na	na	na	na	na	na	na	na	na	na	na	na	na	na	na	na
Norway	na	16	16	16	14	12	22	21	16	11	na	na	na	28	15	7
Pakistan	na	49	53	46	44	48	63	49	50	46	50	47	53	47	52	25
Peru	na	24	31	17	21	24	29	30	24	19	27	23	20	33	22	15
Philippines	na	63	67	59	59	64	66	70	61	58	64	62	63	61	65	60
Poland	na	na	na	na	na	na	na	na	na	na	na	na	na	na	na	na
Portugal	na	na	na	na	na	na	na	na	na	na	na	na	na	na	na	na
Puerto Rico	na	19	23	17	15	14	25	37	28	11	31	19	8	20	21	10
Romania	na	na	na	na	na	na	na	na	na	na	na	na	na	na	na	na
Russian Fed.	na	na	na	na	na	na	na	na	na	na	na	na	na	na	na	na
Serbia	na	47	58	37	48	43	51	59	46	33	49	48	42	56	40	27
Singapore	na	50	51	50	43	56	62	54	48	49	50	53	51	58	50	30
Slovakia	na	na	na	na	na	na	na	na	na	na	na	na	na	na	na	na
Slovenia	na	na	na	na	na	na	na	na	na	na	na	na	na	na	na	na
South Africa	na	44	53	34	40	49	42	53	33	29	54	43	36	48	42	36
Spain	na	19	23	15	14	15	25	21	14	17	27	17	18	22	19	11
Sweden	na	19	20	18	17	13	26	27	19	13	25	17	13	26	21	11
Switzerland	na	na	na	na	na	na	na	na	na	na	na	na	na	na	na	na
Taiwan	na	49	46	52	41	48	54	53	45	46	52	46	49	50	45	62
Tanzania	na	44	51	34	48	39	49	46	43	37	48	38	43	41	44	63
Turkey	na	62	66	58	60	62	67	70	54	43	71	56	50	67	62	49
Uganda	na	68	76	61	69	66	75	75	64	79	69	77	59	70	67	69
Ukraine	na	na	na	na	na	na	na	na	na	na	na	na	na	na	na	na
United States	na	23	28	19	23	19	30	31	24	20	24	22	21	28	23	20
Uruguay	na	38	43	33	34	31	45	45	26	36	42	36	33	49	36	31
Venezuela	na	40	48	32	38	42	42	46	43	27	43	43	38	53	37	32
Vietnam	na	56	58	54	53	54	61	59	53	52	67	57	50	71	55	38
Zimbabwe	na	52	60	46	54	48	56	56	48	77	58	53	38	55	50	55
Total	na	49	56	43	49	48	51	56	48	40	54	48	46	59	47	33

RANKING

Country	2000
Jordan	87
Egypt	85
Armenia	83
Georgia	80
Nigeria	80
Morocco	73
Azerbaijan	72
Algeria	70
Uganda	68
Bangladesh	67
Iran	66
Philippines	63
Turkey	62
Moldova	61
Indonesia	60
India	58
Vietnam	56
Montenegro	55
Zimbabwe	52
Albania	52
Singapore	50
China	50
Pakistan	49
Taiwan	49
Korea, South	48
Brazil	47
Serbia	47
South Africa	44
Tanzania	44
Japan	43
Mexico	42
Dominican Rep.	41
Macedonia	41
Venezuela	40
Chile	39
Uruguay	38
El Salvador	37
Bosnia and Herz.	33
Colombia	33
Argentina	32
Australia	24
Peru	24
United States	23
Canada	21
Sweden	19
Puerto Rico	19
Spain	19
New Zealand	17
Norway	16
Total	49

D060) UNIVERSITY IS MORE IMPORTANT FOR A BOY

For each of the following statements I read out, can you tell me how much you agree with each. Do you agree strongly, agree, disagree, or disagree strongly? "A university education is more important for a boy than for a girl"

Agree strongly / Agree (%)

(WVS: V119)

Country	Wave 1990	Wave 2000	Gender Male	Gender Female	Age 16-29	Age 30-49	Age 50+	Education Lower	Education Middle	Education Upper	Income Lower	Income Middle	Income Upper	Values Mat	Values Mixed	Values Postm.
Albania	na	15	21	10	12	14	20	21	13	9	14	16	15	15	14	11
Algeria	na	29	42	15	28	28	30	37	28	23	34	26	20	30	28	22
Argentina	na	15	19	12	12	12	22	19	10	9	20	16	10	22	16	10
Armenia	na	42	51	35	43	42	43	38	43	40	43	41	41	45	42	25
Australia	na	11	15	7	5	8	19	19	7	8	18	6	8	17	12	8
Austria	na	na	na	na	na	na	na	na	na	na	na	na	na	na	na	na
Azerbaijan	na	37	42	33	37	39	35	37	36	39	37	37	42	37	40	35
Bangladesh	na	63	65	59	58	66	64	71	58	48	72	60	58	66	60	54
Belarus	na	na	na	na	na	na	na	na	na	na	na	na	na	na	na	na
Belgium	na	na	na	na	na	na	na	na	na	na	na	na	na	na	na	na
Bosnia and Herz.	na	18	22	14	15	17	21	26	17	12	19	18	17	19	18	12
Brazil	na	24	32	16	22	23	31	33	20	9	29	25	18	33	23	10
Bulgaria	na	na	na	na	na	na	na	na	na	na	na	na	na	na	na	na
Canada	na	5	6	4	2	2	9	10	3	3	7	4	2	7	5	3
Chile	na	30	37	24	22	32	35	35	28	26	38	27	25	36	31	18
China	na	9	10	9	8	9	13	11	8	10	11	8	8	8	11	6
Colombia	na	11	13	9	11	11	14	19	12	6	16	12	8	16	16	11
Croatia	na	na	na	na	na	na	na	na	na	na	na	na	na	na	na	na
Czech Republic	na	na	na	na	na	na	na	na	na	na	na	na	na	na	na	na
Denmark	na	na	na	na	na	na	na	na	na	na	na	na	na	na	na	na
Dominican Rep.	na	20	24	17	20	22	10	26	26	17	23	18	13	23	21	8
Egypt	na	31	39	22	26	34	33	36	28	22	36	33	25	31	31	26
El Salvador	na	14	12	16	15	13	15	16	12	11	20	11	14	na	na	na
Estonia	na	na	na	na	na	na	na	na	na	na	na	na	na	na	na	na
Finland	na	na	na	na	na	na	na	na	na	na	na	na	na	na	na	na
France	na	na	na	na	na	na	na	na	na	na	na	na	na	na	na	na
Georgia	na	34	40	29	35	33	34	34	35	29	38	31	29	32	35	32
Germany	na	na	na	na	na	na	na	na	na	na	na	na	na	na	na	na
Great Britain	na	na	na	na	na	na	na	na	na	na	na	na	na	na	na	na
Greece	na	na	na	na	na	na	na	na	na	na	na	na	na	na	na	na
Hungary	na	na	na	na	na	na	na	na	na	na	na	na	na	na	na	na
Iceland	na	na	na	na	na	na	na	na	na	na	na	na	na	na	na	na
India	na	42	42	41	35	43	47	55	38	22	57	48	30	47	38	19
Indonesia	na	17	20	14	10	17	20	29	14	12	19	13	17	21	14	11
Iran	na	38	43	33	33	39	50	51	33	30	42	36	34	42	37	28
Ireland	na	na	na	na	na	na	na	na	na	na	na	na	na	na	na	na
Israel	na	na	na	na	na	na	na	na	na	na	na	na	na	na	na	na
Italy	na	na	na	na	na	na	na	na	na	na	na	na	na	na	na	na
Japan	na	23	26	20	13	17	32	45	22	14	29	23	18	33	21	7
Jordan	na	39	51	27	41	33	47	46	32	32	40	43	35	40	38	35
Korea, South	na	24	29	19	12	25	36	40	26	18	29	19	23	29	20	18
Latvia	na	na	na	na	na	na	na	na	na	na	na	na	na	na	na	na
Lithuania	na	na	na	na	na	na	na	na	na	na	na	na	na	na	na	na
Luxembourg	na	na	na	na	na	na	na	na	na	na	na	na	na	na	na	na
Macedonia	na	12	15	10	9	12	15	21	10	3	18	11	7	10	13	15
Malta	na	na	na	na	na	na	na	na	na	na	na	na	na	na	na	na
Mexico	na	33	33	33	30	33	38	41	26	19	42	31	28	42	30	27
Moldova	na	24	28	20	19	25	27	26	26	17	29	22	24	21	23	29
Montenegro	na	24	30	18	14	18	36	36	18	11	25	22	23	27	22	13
Morocco	na	42	50	34	37	43	54	47	27	19	67	37	35	41	43	35
Netherlands	na	na	na	na	na	na	na	na	na	na	na	na	na	na	na	na
New Zealand	na	8	11	6	3	4	14	12	9	4	11	7	4	11	9	4
Nigeria	na	44	51	36	45	42	45	53	41	33	48	40	42	42	46	38
Northern Ireland	na	na	na	na	na	na	na	na	na	na	na	na	na	na	na	na
Norway	na	11	11	11	10	8	16	14	11	8	na	na	na	16	11	3
Pakistan	na	23	29	16	15	22	38	30	16	8	31	21	16	24	20	na
Peru	na	21	25	17	20	20	23	25	22	15	24	20	16	28	19	15
Philippines	na	37	39	36	39	36	39	45	37	30	38	37	37	34	41	33
Poland	na	na	na	na	na	na	na	na	na	na	na	na	na	na	na	na
Portugal	na	na	na	na	na	na	na	na	na	na	na	na	na	na	na	na
Puerto Rico	na	11	16	9	7	9	15	17	15	8	11	13	8	11	11	11
Romania	na	na	na	na	na	na	na	na	na	na	na	na	na	na	na	na
Russian Fed.	na	na	na	na	na	na	na	na	na	na	na	na	na	na	na	na
Serbia	na	21	27	15	21	15	27	31	19	9	25	20	14	26	16	9
Singapore	na	15	17	14	15	15	17	17	15	11	18	15	15	16	15	11
Slovakia	na	na	na	na	na	na	na	na	na	na	na	na	na	na	na	na
Slovenia	na	na	na	na	na	na	na	na	na	na	na	na	na	na	na	na
South Africa	na	19	22	16	17	20	25	26	12	4	24	22	13	17	20	25
Spain	na	12	14	10	9	9	16	14	8	9	22	13	10	15	11	8
Sweden	na	7	8	6	7	6	7	11	6	5	10	6	3	8	6	7
Switzerland	na	na	na	na	na	na	na	na	na	na	na	na	na	na	na	na
Taiwan	na	24	23	25	20	23	30	31	20	20	26	22	25	23	25	22
Tanzania	na	16	18	14	15	14	21	20	12	8	23	12	11	12	17	21
Turkey	na	29	35	24	27	28	36	37	22	11	40	21	18	36	27	21
Uganda	na	23	35	13	21	25	27	32	17	45	35	31	20	21	21	40
Ukraine	na	na	na	na	na	na	na	na	na	na	na	na	na	na	na	na
United States	na	7	7	8	6	6	11	13	6	6	8	7	7	15	8	5
Uruguay	na	13	15	12	12	8	17	17	7	9	19	11	7	17	12	6
Venezuela	na	15	17	14	16	15	15	22	14	10	23	14	11	20	15	8
Vietnam	na	24	22	26	19	22	30	28	20	15	27	26	21	42	19	24
Zimbabwe	na	18	22	15	17	15	26	24	11	na	25	19	5	21	16	16
Total	na	23	27	19	22	22	25	30	21	16	28	22	20	28	22	14

RANKING

Country	2000
Bangladesh	63
Nigeria	44
Armenia	42
Morocco	42
India	42
Jordan	39
Iran	38
Azerbaijan	37
Philippines	37
Georgia	34
Mexico	33
Egypt	31
Chile	30
Turkey	29
Algeria	29
Brazil	24
Taiwan	24
Vietnam	24
Montenegro	24
Korea, South	24
Moldova	24
Uganda	23
Japan	23
Pakistan	23
Serbia	21
Peru	21
Dominican Rep.	20
South Africa	19
Zimbabwe	18
Bosnia and Herz.	18
Indonesia	17
Tanzania	16
Albania	15
Argentina	15
Singapore	15
Venezuela	15
El Salvador	14
Uruguay	13
Macedonia	12
Spain	12
Colombia	11
Puerto Rico	11
Norway	11
Australia	11
China	9
New Zealand	8
United States	7
Sweden	7
Canada	5
Total	23

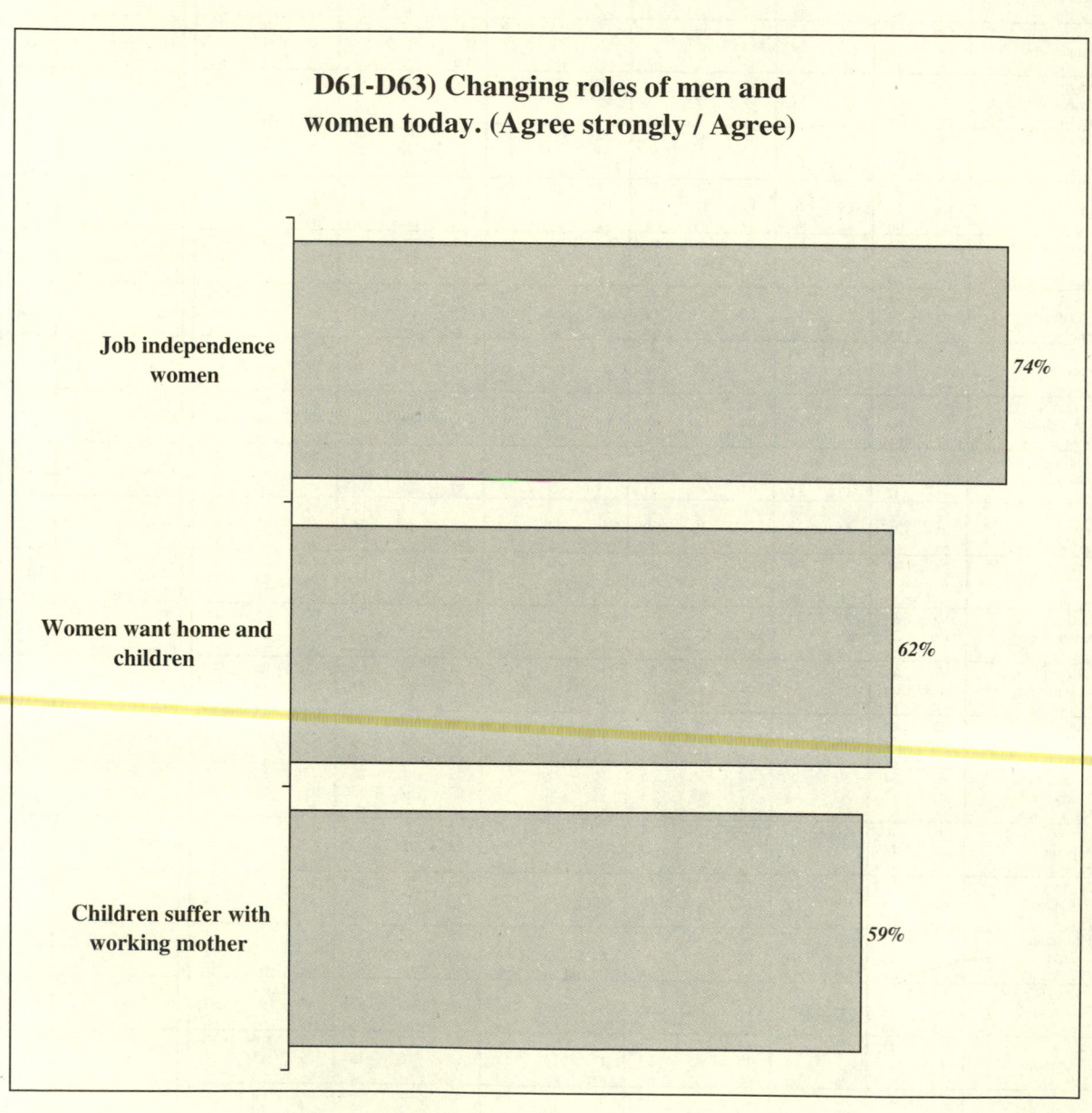

D61-D63) Changing roles of men and women today. (Agree strongly / Agree)

Job independence women — 74%

Women want home and children — 62%

Children suffer with working mother — 59%

D061_1) CHILDREN SUFFER WITH WORKING MOTHER

For each of the following statements I read out, can you tell me how much you agree with each. "A pre-school child is likely to suffer if his or her mother works"

Agree strongly / Agree (%)

(EVS: V155)

Country	Wave		Gender		Age			Education			Income			Values		
	1990	2000	Male	Female	16-29	30-49	50+	Lower	Middle	Upper	Lower	Middle	Upper	Mat	Mixed	Postm.
Albania	na	na	na	na	na	na	na	na	na	na	na	na	na	na	na	na
Algeria	na	na	na	na	na	na	na	na	na	na	na	na	na	na	na	na
Argentina	78	na	na	na	na	na	na	na	na	na	na	na	na	na	na	na
Armenia	na	na	na	na	na	na	na	na	na	na	na	na	na	na	na	na
Australia	na	na	na	na	na	na	na	na	na	na	na	na	na	na	na	na
Austria	83	na	na	na	na	na	na	na	na	na	na	na	na	na	na	na
Azerbaijan	na	na	na	na	na	na	na	na	na	na	na	na	na	na	na	na
Bangladesh	na	na	na	na	na	na	na	na	na	na	na	na	na	na	na	na
Belarus	81	60	58	63	51	63	65	61	58	67	66	59	55	60	59	57
Belgium	61	51	56	47	45	46	59	64	53	40	66	53	40	58	53	38
Bosnia and Herz.	na	na	na	na	na	na	na	na	na	na	na	na	na	na	na	na
Brazil	75	na	na	na	na	na	na	na	na	na	na	na	na	na	na	na
Bulgaria	76	61	60	62	49	62	65	67	58	57	60	56	63	59	63	65
Canada	53	na	na	na	na	na	na	na	na	na	na	na	na	na	na	na
Chile	82	na	na	na	na	na	na	na	na	na	na	na	na	na	na	na
China	61	na	na	na	na	na	na	na	na	na	na	na	na	na	na	na
Colombia	na	na	na	na	na	na	na	na	na	na	na	na	na	na	na	na
Croatia	na	64	66	63	56	64	70	70	64	49	73	68	55	67	63	67
Czech Republic	78	47	53	42	36	43	57	51	43	46	54	46	41	51	47	42
Denmark	32	18	24	13	9	10	31	24	8	9	23	17	7	18	20	6
Dominican Rep.	na	na	na	na	na	na	na	na	na	na	na	na	na	na	na	na
Egypt	na	na	na	na	na	na	na	na	na	na	na	na	na	na	na	na
El Salvador	na	na	na	na	na	na	na	na	na	na	na	na	na	na	na	na
Estonia	91	65	66	65	58	67	67	66	66	61	66	64	63	67	65	48
Finland	52	41	47	36	30	31	55	48	33	27	43	40	38	41	41	40
France	65	56	60	53	53	48	66	63	51	44	61	55	49	68	56	37
Georgia	na	na	na	na	na	na	na	na	na	na	na	na	na	na	na	na
Germany	79	66	74	61	53	62	76	76	58	64	69	69	67	73	65	62
Great Britain	55	46	54	39	40	41	55	46	46	51	49	42	46	na	na	na
Greece	na	78	81	76	76	76	89	84	82	73	81	77	78	79	78	73
Hungary	70	63	61	65	50	63	71	67	56	54	65	64	62	66	61	58
Iceland	52	33	41	25	25	26	50	40	33	16	40	32	25	35	34	21
India	92	na	na	na	na	na	na	na	na	na	na	na	na	na	na	na
Indonesia	na	na	na	na	na	na	na	na	na	na	na	na	na	na	na	na
Iran	na	na	na	na	na	na	na	na	na	na	na	na	na	na	na	na
Ireland	53	na	na	na	na	na	na	na	na	na	na	na	na	na	na	na
Israel	na	na	na	na	na	na	na	na	na	na	na	na	na	na	na	na
Italy	78	81	83	80	79	77	86	87	80	71	88	85	72	86	83	76
Japan	70	na	na	na	na	na	na	na	na	na	na	na	na	na	na	na
Jordan	na	na	na	na	na	na	na	na	na	na	na	na	na	na	na	na
Korea, South	72	na	na	na	na	na	na	na	na	na	na	na	na	na	na	na
Latvia	92	75	76	75	69	77	76	78	73	79	74	77	76	79	74	65
Lithuania	90	71	69	74	62	72	77	77	70	69	79	67	72	76	70	61
Luxembourg	na	68	73	63	65	62	77	74	66	58	78	72	59	66	69	63
Macedonia	na	na	na	na	na	na	na	na	na	na	na	na	na	na	na	na
Malta	na	87	89	86	82	87	92	93	86	83	94	91	82	90	87	78
Mexico	78	na	na	na	na	na	na	na	na	na	na	na	na	na	na	na
Moldova	na	na	na	na	na	na	na	na	na	na	na	na	na	na	na	na
Montenegro	na	na	na	na	na	na	na	na	na	na	na	na	na	na	na	na
Morocco	na	na	na	na	na	na	na	na	na	na	na	na	na	na	na	na
Netherlands	56	46	56	36	47	40	52	59	42	37	53	43	37	58	47	34
New Zealand	na	na	na	na	na	na	na	na	na	na	na	na	na	na	na	na
Nigeria	54	na	na	na	na	na	na	na	na	na	na	na	na	na	na	na
Northern Ireland	44	na	na	na	na	na	na	na	na	na	na	na	na	na	na	na
Norway	46	na	na	na	na	na	na	na	na	na	na	na	na	na	na	na
Pakistan	na	na	na	na	na	na	na	na	na	na	na	na	na	na	na	na
Peru	na	na	na	na	na	na	na	na	na	na	na	na	na	na	na	na
Philippines	na	na	na	na	na	na	na	na	na	na	na	na	na	na	na	na
Poland	na	77	79	74	68	75	84	81	74	67	79	78	68	80	75	73
Portugal	84	72	75	69	71	71	74	74	71	58	81	73	77	71	72	77
Puerto Rico	na	na	na	na	na	na	na	na	na	na	na	na	na	na	na	na
Romania	58	47	48	46	42	44	53	58	42	42	56	44	43	50	45	39
Russian Fed.	70	73	75	72	65	74	78	74	74	71	75	73	71	73	74	67
Serbia	na	na	na	na	na	na	na	na	na	na	na	na	na	na	na	na
Singapore	na	na	na	na	na	na	na	na	na	na	na	na	na	na	na	na
Slovakia	na	63	64	62	55	62	71	70	61	56	69	61	60	63	65	52
Slovenia	67	47	51	43	34	40	62	64	43	30	58	48	29	55	45	44
South Africa	na	na	na	na	na	na	na	na	na	na	na	na	na	na	na	na
Spain	56	46	46	46	30	37	62	58	40	27	55	45	34	59	44	30
Sweden	74	38	46	30	26	35	48	59	35	26	40	40	31	50	40	26
Switzerland	na	na	na	na	na	na	na	na	na	na	na	na	na	na	na	na
Taiwan	na	na	na	na	na	na	na	na	na	na	na	na	na	na	na	na
Tanzania	na	na	na	na	na	na	na	na	na	na	na	na	na	na	na	na
Turkey	85	na	na	na	na	na	na	na	na	na	na	na	na	na	na	na
Uganda	na	na	na	na	na	na	na	na	na	na	na	na	na	na	na	na
Ukraine	na	73	75	72	62	74	78	74	75	68	79	72	67	75	70	76
United States	52	na	na	na	na	na	na	na	na	na	na	na	na	na	na	na
Uruguay	na	na	na	na	na	na	na	na	na	na	na	na	na	na	na	na
Venezuela	na	na	na	na	na	na	na	na	na	na	na	na	na	na	na	na
Vietnam	na	na	na	na	na	na	na	na	na	na	na	na	na	na	na	na
Zimbabwe	na	na	na	na	na	na	na	na	na	na	na	na	na	na	na	na
Total	69	59	62	57	52	56	67	64	59	51	64	59	55	66	59	50

RANKING

Country	2000
Malta	87
Italy	81
Greece	78
Poland	77
Latvia	75
Russian Fed.	73
Ukraine	73
Portugal	72
Lithuania	71
Luxembourg	68
Germany	66
Estonia	65
Croatia	64
Slovakia	63
Hungary	63
Bulgaria	61
Belarus	60
France	56
Belgium	51
Czech Republic	47
Romania	47
Slovenia	47
Great Britain	46
Spain	46
Netherlands	46
Finland	41
Sweden	38
Iceland	33
Denmark	18
Total	59

D062_1) WOMEN WANT HOME AND CHILDREN

For each of the following statements I read out, can you tell me how much you agree with each. "A job is alright but what most women really want is a home and children"

Agree strongly / Agree (%)

(EVS: V156)

Country	Wave 1990	Wave 2000	Gender Male	Gender Female	Age 16-29	Age 30-49	Age 50+	Education Lower	Education Middle	Education Upper	Income Lower	Income Middle	Income Upper	Values Mat	Values Mixed	Values Postm.
Albania	na	na	na	na	na	na	na	na	na	na	na	na	na	na	na	na
Algeria	na	na	na	na	na	na	na	na	na	na	na	na	na	na	na	na
Argentina	73	na	na	na	na	na	na	na	na	na	na	na	na	na	na	na
Armenia	na	na	na	na	na	na	na	na	na	na	na	na	na	na	na	na
Australia	na	na	na	na	na	na	na	na	na	na	na	na	na	na	na	na
Austria	62	na	na	na	na	na	na	na	na	na	na	na	na	na	na	na
Azerbaijan	na	na	na	na	na	na	na	na	na	na	na	na	na	na	na	na
Bangladesh	na	na	na	na	na	na	na	na	na	na	na	na	na	na	na	na
Belarus	81	68	70	67	59	69	74	74	68	59	75	68	57	73	66	54
Belgium	61	54	55	53	45	46	66	71	54	41	66	59	45	65	53	42
Bosnia and Herz.	na	na	na	na	na	na	na	na	na	na	na	na	na	na	na	na
Brazil	72	na	na	na	na	na	na	na	na	na	na	na	na	na	na	na
Bulgaria	90	76	75	76	75	74	78	80	78	64	80	70	75	77	73	95
Canada	43	na	na	na	na	na	na	na	na	na	na	na	na	na	na	na
Chile	77	na	na	na	na	na	na	na	na	na	na	na	na	na	na	na
China	78	na	na	na	na	na	na	na	na	na	na	na	na	na	na	na
Colombia	na	na	na	na	na	na	na	na	na	na	na	na	na	na	na	na
Croatia	na	66	66	67	52	71	70	77	63	47	77	66	61	77	66	58
Czech Republic	93	72	73	71	64	70	78	79	64	67	76	75	65	77	72	60
Denmark	25	18	19	18	17	16	22	23	12	12	22	18	13	24	19	10
Dominican Rep.	na	na	na	na	na	na	na	na	na	na	na	na	na	na	na	na
Egypt	na	na	na	na	na	na	na	na	na	na	na	na	na	na	na	na
El Salvador	na	na	na	na	na	na	na	na	na	na	na	na	na	na	na	na
Estonia	85	68	69	66	64	64	73	73	66	64	71	70	61	73	64	55
Finland	42	50	54	46	43	38	64	59	40	29	54	53	39	58	48	41
France	68	65	66	64	61	57	75	72	60	51	69	65	60	75	67	46
Georgia	na	na	na	na	na	na	na	na	na	na	na	na	na	na	na	na
Germany	50	44	47	42	32	39	55	55	36	28	51	44	46	62	41	24
Great Britain	45	44	52	38	37	35	58	53	40	37	52	44	33	na	na	na
Greece	na	65	72	60	55	69	79	88	72	55	70	62	64	69	66	59
Hungary	76	70	68	72	63	67	78	76	64	47	73	72	66	74	67	68
Iceland	71	62	65	59	53	55	79	73	61	40	62	66	56	73	61	41
India	91	na	na	na	na	na	na	na	na	na	na	na	na	na	na	na
Indonesia	na	na	na	na	na	na	na	na	na	na	na	na	na	na	na	na
Iran	na	na	na	na	na	na	na	na	na	na	na	na	na	na	na	na
Ireland	59	na	na	na	na	na	na	na	na	na	na	na	na	na	na	na
Israel	na	na	na	na	na	na	na	na	na	na	na	na	na	na	na	na
Italy	72	68	69	66	59	58	81	77	63	52	73	69	62	85	69	56
Japan	81	na	na	na	na	na	na	na	na	na	na	na	na	na	na	na
Jordan	na	na	na	na	na	na	na	na	na	na	na	na	na	na	na	na
Korea, South	70	na	na	na	na	na	na	na	na	na	na	na	na	na	na	na
Latvia	90	67	72	63	66	65	69	72	66	63	68	69	66	69	66	58
Lithuania	97	94	94	94	92	93	96	95	94	91	98	91	93	93	93	96
Luxembourg	na	56	60	52	46	50	69	71	52	34	64	59	41	66	58	32
Macedonia	na	na	na	na	na	na	na	na	na	na	na	na	na	na	na	na
Malta	na	70	71	69	58	70	77	78	69	55	75	71	61	74	69	54
Mexico	61	na	na	na	na	na	na	na	na	na	na	na	na	na	na	na
Moldova	na	na	na	na	na	na	na	na	na	na	na	na	na	na	na	na
Montenegro	na	na	na	na	na	na	na	na	na	na	na	na	na	na	na	na
Morocco	na	na	na	na	na	na	na	na	na	na	na	na	na	na	na	na
Netherlands	37	34	36	33	25	23	52	55	30	20	42	29	28	53	36	22
New Zealand	na	na	na	na	na	na	na	na	na	na	na	na	na	na	na	na
Nigeria	87	na	na	na	na	na	na	na	na	na	na	na	na	na	na	na
Northern Ireland	53	na	na	na	na	na	na	na	na	na	na	na	na	na	na	na
Norway	51	na	na	na	na	na	na	na	na	na	na	na	na	na	na	na
Pakistan	na	na	na	na	na	na	na	na	na	na	na	na	na	na	na	na
Peru	na	na	na	na	na	na	na	na	na	na	na	na	na	na	na	na
Philippines	na	na	na	na	na	na	na	na	na	na	na	na	na	na	na	na
Poland	na	74	79	70	64	74	81	82	68	54	79	71	72	76	74	71
Portugal	62	53	56	50	42	50	61	57	47	36	59	57	48	57	49	47
Puerto Rico	na	na	na	na	na	na	na	na	na	na	na	na	na	na	na	na
Romania	82	85	87	83	76	81	93	93	82	79	88	85	83	90	81	78
Russian Fed.	91	86	88	84	83	85	88	90	87	81	87	87	83	87	85	77
Serbia	na	na	na	na	na	na	na	na	na	na	na	na	na	na	na	na
Singapore	na	na	na	na	na	na	na	na	na	na	na	na	na	na	na	na
Slovakia	na	61	63	60	58	56	69	68	60	45	69	58	57	62	60	61
Slovenia	77	65	69	62	55	59	78	85	62	37	79	66	42	77	64	55
South Africa	na	na	na	na	na	na	na	na	na	na	na	na	na	na	na	na
Spain	57	47	46	47	30	37	65	64	38	26	59	47	30	62	47	23
Sweden	na	40	44	37	36	36	48	61	39	27	43	46	29	43	45	24
Switzerland	na	na	na	na	na	na	na	na	na	na	na	na	na	na	na	na
Taiwan	na	na	na	na	na	na	na	na	na	na	na	na	na	na	na	na
Tanzania	na	na	na	na	na	na	na	na	na	na	na	na	na	na	na	na
Turkey	88	na	na	na	na	na	na	na	na	na	na	na	na	na	na	na
Uganda	na	na	na	na	na	na	na	na	na	na	na	na	na	na	na	na
Ukraine	na	80	84	78	77	80	82	84	81	75	82	79	80	82	79	76
United States	56	na	na	na	na	na	na	na	na	na	na	na	na	na	na	na
Uruguay	na	na	na	na	na	na	na	na	na	na	na	na	na	na	na	na
Venezuela	na	na	na	na	na	na	na	na	na	na	na	na	na	na	na	na
Vietnam	na	na	na	na	na	na	na	na	na	na	na	na	na	na	na	na
Zimbabwe	na	na	na	na	na	na	na	na	na	na	na	na	na	na	na	na
Total	69	62	65	61	56	58	71	70	63	48	68	63	58	73	61	45

RANKING Country	2000
Lithuania	94
Russian Fed.	86
Romania	85
Ukraine	80
Bulgaria	76
Poland	74
Czech Republic	72
Hungary	70
Malta	70
Belarus	68
Estonia	68
Italy	68
Latvia	67
Croatia	66
France	65
Greece	65
Slovenia	65
Iceland	62
Slovakia	61
Luxembourg	56
Belgium	54
Portugal	53
Finland	50
Spain	47
Great Britain	44
Germany	44
Sweden	40
Netherlands	34
Denmark	18
Total	62

D063_1) JOB INDEPENDENCE WOMEN

For each of the following statements I read out, can you tell me how much you agree with each. "Having a job is the best way for a woman to be an independent person"

Agree strongly / Agree (%)

(EVS: V158)

Country	Wave 1990	Wave 2000	Gender Male	Gender Female	Age 16-29	Age 30-49	Age 50+	Education Lower	Education Middle	Education Upper	Income Lower	Income Middle	Income Upper	Values Mat	Values Mixed	Values Postm.
Albania	na	na	na	na	na	na	na	na	na	na	na	na	na	na	na	na
Algeria	na	na	na	na	na	na	na	na	na	na	na	na	na	na	na	na
Argentina	63	na	na	na	na	na	na	na	na	na	na	na	na	na	na	na
Armenia	na	na	na	na	na	na	na	na	na	na	na	na	na	na	na	na
Australia	na	na	na	na	na	na	na	na	na	na	na	na	na	na	na	na
Austria	74	na	na	na	na	na	na	na	na	na	na	na	na	na	na	na
Azerbaijan	na	na	na	na	na	na	na	na	na	na	na	na	na	na	na	na
Bangladesh	na	na	na	na	na	na	na	na	na	na	na	na	na	na	na	na
Belarus	62	58	50	65	57	59	57	52	59	62	60	56	58	56	60	51
Belgium	70	77	74	80	72	75	81	80	75	78	77	74	78	78	76	79
Bosnia and Herz.	na	na	na	na	na	na	na	na	na	na	na	na	na	na	na	na
Brazil	74	na	na	na	na	na	na	na	na	na	na	na	na	na	na	na
Bulgaria	63	79	73	85	78	76	83	81	77	81	83	79	78	82	76	81
Canada	55	na	na	na	na	na	na	na	na	na	na	na	na	na	na	na
Chile	72	na	na	na	na	na	na	na	na	na	na	na	na	na	na	na
China	75	na	na	na	na	na	na	na	na	na	na	na	na	na	na	na
Colombia	na	na	na	na	na	na	na	na	na	na	na	na	na	na	na	na
Croatia	na	79	72	86	77	80	80	87	74	80	90	77	76	77	79	83
Czech Republic	55	76	72	79	74	76	77	77	76	69	75	78	75	78	75	76
Denmark	81	85	84	85	75	84	90	85	83	85	83	86	88	78	85	86
Dominican Rep.	na	na	na	na	na	na	na	na	na	na	na	na	na	na	na	na
Egypt	na	na	na	na	na	na	na	na	na	na	na	na	na	na	na	na
El Salvador	na	na	na	na	na	na	na	na	na	na	na	na	na	na	na	na
Estonia	56	79	74	82	78	79	79	77	79	80	74	81	80	79	78	77
Finland	77	63	60	66	58	59	70	66	56	65	67	60	62	66	63	64
France	79	84	81	86	85	82	85	83	83	86	86	81	85	84	83	88
Georgia	na	na	na	na	na	na	na	na	na	na	na	na	na	na	na	na
Germany	75	81	79	83	86	82	78	77	84	89	78	81	84	77	81	89
Great Britain	68	65	64	66	63	59	70	65	63	63	72	66	59	na	na	na
Greece	na	82	75	88	83	84	81	75	83	83	80	82	83	85	82	82
Hungary	48	72	71	74	69	70	77	70	76	74	73	71	74	71	74	62
Iceland	43	46	43	49	42	42	54	46	40	56	51	39	50	41	46	53
India	58	na	na	na	na	na	na	na	na	na	na	na	na	na	na	na
Indonesia	na	na	na	na	na	na	na	na	na	na	na	na	na	na	na	na
Iran	na	na	na	na	na	na	na	na	na	na	na	na	na	na	na	na
Ireland	61	na	na	na	na	na	na	na	na	na	na	na	na	na	na	na
Israel	na	na	na	na	na	na	na	na	na	na	na	na	na	na	na	na
Italy	74	77	73	81	75	80	75	73	79	82	73	74	82	70	79	78
Japan	78	na	na	na	na	na	na	na	na	na	na	na	na	na	na	na
Jordan	na	na	na	na	na	na	na	na	na	na	na	na	na	na	na	na
Korea, South	34	na	na	na	na	na	na	na	na	na	na	na	na	na	na	na
Latvia	62	85	82	88	83	86	85	84	86	84	85	81	89	85	86	77
Lithuania	41	77	73	80	77	74	80	75	76	80	81	79	75	74	80	63
Luxembourg	na	84	82	85	86	84	82	83	84	86	84	84	86	81	83	90
Macedonia	na	na	na	na	na	na	na	na	na	na	na	na	na	na	na	na
Malta	na	45	45	44	52	41	42	42	43	57	48	39	47	36	48	55
Mexico	62	na	na	na	na	na	na	na	na	na	na	na	na	na	na	na
Moldova	na	na	na	na	na	na	na	na	na	na	na	na	na	na	na	na
Montenegro	na	na	na	na	na	na	na	na	na	na	na	na	na	na	na	na
Morocco	na	na	na	na	na	na	na	na	na	na	na	na	na	na	na	na
Netherlands	56	61	60	61	53	60	65	59	56	67	60	59	64	54	62	61
New Zealand	na	na	na	na	na	na	na	na	na	na	na	na	na	na	na	na
Nigeria	62	na	na	na	na	na	na	na	na	na	na	na	na	na	na	na
Northern Ireland	70	na	na	na	na	na	na	na	na	na	na	na	na	na	na	na
Norway	75	na	na	na	na	na	na	na	na	na	na	na	na	na	na	na
Pakistan	na	na	na	na	na	na	na	na	na	na	na	na	na	na	na	na
Peru	na	na	na	na	na	na	na	na	na	na	na	na	na	na	na	na
Philippines	na	na	na	na	na	na	na	na	na	na	na	na	Mat	na	na	na
Poland	na	76	74	78	79	73	78	73	77	84	75	77	75	74	78	74
Portugal	80	79	73	84	84	74	80	78	80	79	80	71	80	76	81	77
Puerto Rico	na	na	na	na	na	na	na	na	na	na	na	na	na	na	na	na
Romania	68	82	78	85	77	80	85	83	80	84	80	84	81	80	81	87
Russian Fed.	58	70	62	77	68	71	71	66	71	71	71	69	71	70	71	68
Serbia	na	na	na	na	na	na	na	na	na	na	na	na	na	na	na	na
Singapore	na	na	na	na	na	na	na	na	na	na	na	na	na	na	na	na
Slovakia	na	75	73	76	75	76	73	71	77	72	71	78	74	74	76	74
Slovenia	73	79	77	81	74	77	86	83	78	82	80	77	79	84	79	79
South Africa	na	na	na	na	na	na	na	na	na	na	na	na	na	na	na	na
Spain	79	81	82	80	85	83	77	75	86	85	77	84	84	78	81	86
Sweden	74	84	84	83	76	80	91	87	80	86	84	83	84	77	85	82
Switzerland	na	na	na	na	na	na	na	na	na	na	na	na	na	na	na	na
Taiwan	na	na	na	na	na	na	na	na	na	na	na	na	na	na	na	na
Tanzania	na	na	na	na	na	na	na	na	na	na	na	na	na	na	na	na
Turkey	45	na	na	na	na	na	na	na	na	na	na	na	na	na	na	na
Uganda	na	na	na	na	na	na	na	na	na	na	na	na	na	na	na	na
Ukraine	na	73	68	78	73	75	72	67	73	76	72	70	77	75	71	88
United States	60	na	na	na	na	na	na	na	na	na	na	na	na	na	na	na
Uruguay	na	na	na	na	na	na	na	na	na	na	na	na	na	na	na	na
Venezuela	na	na	na	na	na	na	na	na	na	na	na	na	na	na	na	na
Vietnam	na	na	na	na	na	na	na	na	na	na	na	na	na	na	na	na
Zimbabwe	na	na	na	na	na	na	na	na	na	na	na	na	na	na	na	na
Total	65	74	71	77	72	73	76	74	73	77	75	73	75	73	75	77

RANKING

Country	2000
Latvia	85
Denmark	85
Luxembourg	84
France	84
Sweden	84
Greece	82
Romania	82
Germany	81
Spain	81
Croatia	79
Slovenia	79
Bulgaria	79
Portugal	79
Estonia	79
Italy	77
Belgium	77
Lithuania	77
Poland	76
Czech Republic	76
Slovakia	75
Ukraine	73
Hungary	72
Russian Fed.	70
Great Britain	65
Finland	63
Netherlands	61
Belarus	58
Iceland	46
Malta	45
Total	74

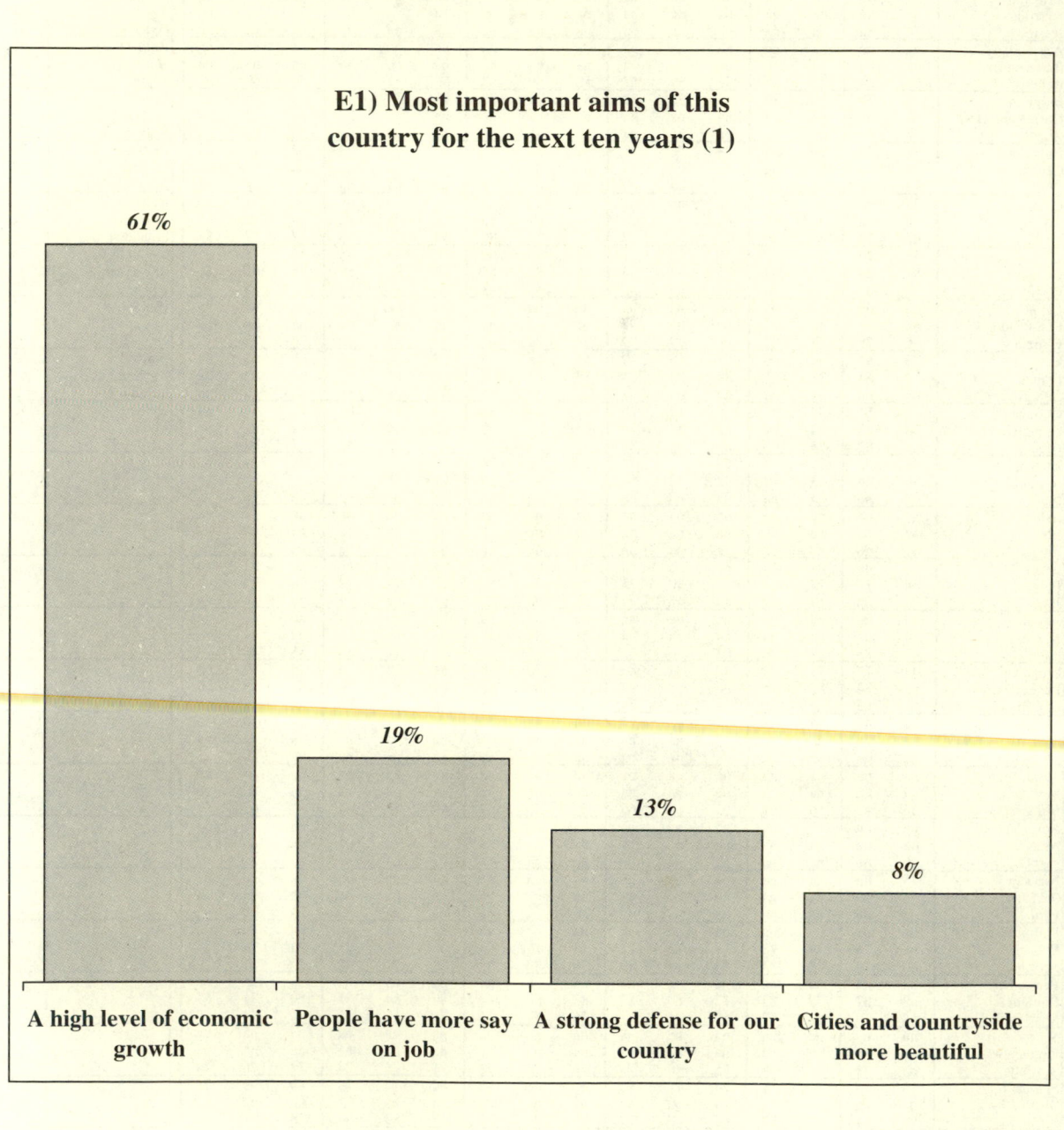

E1) Most important aims of this country for the next ten years (1)

- A high level of economic growth — 61%
- People have more say on job — 19%
- A strong defense for our country — 13%
- Cities and countryside more beautiful — 8%

E001A) AIMS OF COUNTRY / 1 - MORE SAY ON THE JOB

People sometimes talk about what the aims of this country should be for the next ten years. Would you please say which one of these you, yourself, consider the most important?

Seeing that people have more say about how things are done at their jobs and in their communities (%)

(WVS: V120)

Country	Wave 1990	Wave 2000	Gender Male	Gender Female	Age 16-29	Age 30-49	Age 50+	Education Lower	Education Middle	Education Upper	Income Lower	Income Middle	Income Upper	Values Mat	Values Mixed	Values Postm.		RANKING Country	2000
Albania	na	3	4	2	4	3	2	1	4	5	1	3	5	1	5	10		Norway	49
Algeria	na	13	14	11	13	14	9	8	13	16	14	9	17	5	14	37		Switzerland	42
Argentina	25	31	29	33	31	35	28	26	38	44	30	27	38	18	27	52		Australia	41
Armenia	na	11	7	14	13	9	10	11	11	9	10	11	11	6	13	25		Canada	40
Australia	na	41	39	43	47	42	34	34	39	50	39	44	43	16	37	53		Japan	36
Austria	29	na	na	na	na	na	na	na	na	na	na	na	na	na	na	na		Spain	35
Azerbaijan	na	8	6	9	10	6	5	4	7	9	8	9	7	6	10	13		Sweden	34
Bangladesh	na	11	10	12	10	11	10	12	10	9	11	8	14	11	10	15		Puerto Rico	32
Belarus	17	na	na	na	na	na	na	na	na	na	na	na	na	na	na	na		Argentina	31
Belgium	38	na	na	na	na	na	na	na	na	na	na	na	na	na	na	na		United States	31
Bosnia and Herz.	na	6	6	7	9	6	5	5	7	6	4	6	9	3	7	17		Dominican Rep.	29
Brazil	26	29	30	28	29	30	27	24	31	40	26	30	32	18	30	52		Brazil	29
Bulgaria	16	na	na	na	na	na	na	na	na	na	na	na	na	na	na	na		Peru	28
Canada	34	40	35	45	42	39	40	39	39	42	42	44	36	22	37	51		Mexico	27
Chile	25	26	24	28	30	23	27	25	24	33	27	23	31	16	28	39		Chile	26
China	2	5	4	7	9	4	4	3	7	5	5	7	4	2	7	19		Uruguay	23
Colombia	na	na	na	na	na	na	na	na	na	na	na	na	na	na	na	na		Korea, South	23
Croatia	na	na	na	na	na	na	na	na	na	na	na	na	na	na	na	na		El Salvador	23
Czech Republic	25	na	na	na	na	na	na	na	na	na	na	na	na	na	na	na		Philippines	22
Denmark	40	na	na	na	na	na	na	na	na	na	na	na	na	na	na	na		New Zealand	22
Dominican Rep.	na	29	28	30	31	27	27	24	28	30	35	30	26	23	25	44		South Africa	22
Egypt	na	10	10	11	10	11	9	10	11	9	10	12	11	9	11	18		Venezuela	22
El Salvador	na	23	20	25	29	21	14	16	29	30	16	23	28	na	na	na		Iran	20
Estonia	12	na	na	na	na	na	na	na	na	na	na	na	na	na	na	na		Singapore	17
Finland	54	na	na	na	na	na	na	na	na	na	na	na	na	na	na	na		Zimbabwe	17
France	36	na	na	na	na	na	na	na	na	na	na	na	na	na	na	na		Nigeria	14
Georgia	na	9	9	10	9	9	10	9	9	9	11	9	8	6	12	20		Algeria	13
Germany	19	na	na	na	na	na	na	na	na	na	na	na	na	na	na	na		Turkey	12
Great Britain	40	na	na	na	na	na	na	na	na	na	na	na	na	na	na	na		Vietnam	11
Greece	na	na	na	na	na	na	na	na	na	na	na	na	na	na	na	na		Morocco	11
Hungary	22	na	na	na	na	na	na	na	na	na	na	na	na	na	na	na		Moldova	11
Iceland	39	na	na	na	na	na	na	na	na	na	na	na	na	na	na	na		Armenia	11
India	9	10	9	11	10	10	10	10	9	10	12	8	10	8	11	28		Bangladesh	11
Indonesia	na	3	2	3	6	2	2	1	2	6	3	3	3	2	4	7		Israel	10
Iran	na	20	21	19	20	22	18	18	20	23	21	24	17	10	26	32		Egypt	10
Ireland	35	na	na	na	na	na	na	na	na	na	na	na	na	na	na	na		India	10
Israel	na	10	11	10	12	11	8	15	10	7	12	14	6	22	8	9		Serbia	9
Italy	38	na	na	na	na	na	na	na	na	na	na	na	na	na	na	na		Georgia	9
Japan	31	36	33	39	46	37	32	33	37	39	38	34	36	22	38	60		Uganda	9
Jordan	na	8	6	10	9	7	7	7	9	9	7	9	7	5	9	18		Jordan	8
Korea, South	25	23	22	24	34	20	15	9	20	28	21	19	27	17	27	41		Azerbaijan	8
Latvia	8	na	na	na	na	na	na	na	na	na	na	na	na	na	na	na		Montenegro	8
Lithuania	13	na	na	na	na	na	na	na	na	na	na	na	na	na	na	na		Macedonia	7
Luxembourg	na	na	na	na	na	na	na	na	na	na	na	na	na	na	na	na		Bosnia and Herz.	6
Macedonia	na	7	6	7	10	6	5	9	6	5	7	4	8	4	7	26		Taiwan	6
Malta	na	na	na	na	na	na	na	na	na	na	na	na	na	na	na	na		China	5
Mexico	25	27	27	27	28	30	23	25	29	35	25	29	32	27	25	38		Pakistan	5
Moldova	na	11	12	10	13	10	10	9	11	12	7	11	12	10	12	15		Tanzania	5
Montenegro	na	8	7	8	12	5	8	6	9	9	10	8	5	3	9	26		Albania	3
Morocco	na	11	12	10	12	12	7	10	15	21	8	19	10	5	15	18		Indonesia	3
Netherlands	52	na	na	na	na	na	na	na	na	na	na	na	na	na	na	na			
New Zealand	na	22	20	23	30	23	19	16	23	29	20	25	23	11	21	42			
Nigeria	17	14	13	15	14	15	14	14	15	13	12	16	13	11	15	21			
Northern Ireland	31	na	na	na	na	na	na	na	na	na	na	na	na	na	na	na			
Norway	43	49	46	52	49	50	48	46	49	52	na	na	na	41	48	70			
Pakistan	na	5	5	4	5	4	5	2	6	13	na	3	13	3	7	33			
Peru	na	28	27	30	27	29	30	23	28	32	27	27	35	16	30	38			
Philippines	na	22	20	24	23	25	16	22	26	18	27	22	17	17	26	26			
Poland	17	na	na	na	na	na	na	na	na	na	na	na	na	na	na	na			
Portugal	15	na	na	na	na	na	na	na	na	na	na	na	na	na	na	na			
Puerto Rico	na	32	27	35	38	30	31	17	28	37	24	35	35	20	30	44			
Romania	na	na	na	na	na	na	na	na	na	na	na	na	na	na	na	na			
Russian Fed.	15	na	na	na	na	na	na	na	na	na	na	na	na	na	na	na			
Serbia	na	9	9	10	12	8	9	10	9	10	7	9	11	6	11	28			
Singapore	na	17	16	19	22	14	7	11	20	21	14	16	21	8	17	58			
Slovakia	na	na	na	na	na	na	na	na	na	na	na	na	na	na	na	na			
Slovenia	29	na	na	na	na	na	na	na	na	na	na	na	na	na	na	na			
South Africa	26	22	22	22	22	22	20	22	22	19	22	28	14	15	25	29			
Spain	39	35	37	34	40	39	29	32	39	38	30	34	35	21	35	60			
Sweden	33	34	30	39	40	32	33	35	36	32	38	34	30	18	30	54			
Switzerland	42	42	39	44	49	39	40	44	42	37	45	48	36	28	37	64			
Taiwan	na	6	6	6	11	6	3	5	6	7	5	9	5	4	8	11			
Tanzania	na	5	5	4	4	5	4	5	5	2	6	3	4	4	5	4			
Turkey	12	12	10	13	15	10	7	9	13	18	12	10	14	5	11	21			
Uganda	na	9	8	9	7	9	14	12	7	12	6	8	11	5	9	18			
Ukraine	na	na	na	na	na	na	na	na	na	na	na	na	na	na	na	na			
United States	26	31	30	33	42	31	23	30	32	31	36	30	28	18	28	44			
Uruguay	na	23	22	23	29	26	18	19	27	35	21	23	25	16	21	31			
Venezuela	na	22	19	24	22	22	20	21	23	21	22	22	21	17	23	28			
Vietnam	na	11	12	11	13	11	11	11	12	16	14	8	14	3	13	29			
Zimbabwe	na	17	16	17	16	14	22	18	15	na	15	17	17	14	18	23			
Total	27	19	17	20	20	18	18	16	19	22	18	18	19	10	20	39		Total	19

E001B) AIMS OF COUNTRY / 1 - HIGHER ECONOMIC GROWTH

People sometimes talk about what the aims of this country should be for the next ten years. Would you please say which one of these you, yourself, consider the most important?

A high level of economic growth (%)

(WVS: V120)

Country	Wave 1990	Wave 2000	Gender Male	Gender Female	Age 16-29	Age 30-49	Age 50+	Education Lower	Education Middle	Education Upper	Income Lower	Income Middle	Income Upper	Values Mat	Values Mixed	Values Postm.	RANKING Country	RANKING 2000
Albania	na	88	87	89	87	90	87	90	86	89	86	91	88	91	86	80	Albania	88
Algeria	na	68	66	71	69	67	70	64	68	71	65	72	67	70	69	54	Indonesia	84
Argentina	66	53	57	50	52	52	55	54	52	51	51	56	51	64	56	38	Bosnia and Herz.	84
Armenia	na	46	49	43	44	49	45	44	44	54	47	45	44	44	48	41	Tanzania	82
Australia	na	44	45	43	38	47	48	42	49	41	41	44	47	65	48	33	Serbia	80
Austria	52	na	na	na	na	na	na	na	na	na	na	na	na	na	na	na	Montenegro	78
Azerbaijan	na	59	60	59	61	59	58	53	57	65	52	56	68	59	58	68	Moldova	77
Bangladesh	na	76	79	72	76	76	76	73	78	79	71	81	73	74	78	65	Macedonia	77
Belarus	73	na	na	na	na	na	na	na	na	na	na	na	na	na	na	na	Pakistan	76
Belgium	42	na	na	na	na	na	na	na	na	na	na	na	na	na	na	na	Bangladesh	76
Bosnia and Herz.	na	84	86	82	82	85	83	82	82	90	83	84	82	82	85	70	Nigeria	71
Brazil	51	46	47	45	48	44	47	41	50	49	43	46	49	47	47	35	Algeria	68
Bulgaria	76	na	na	na	na	na	na	na	na	na	na	na	na	na	na	na	Zimbabwe	67
Canada	56	51	55	47	45	54	50	45	53	53	47	49	55	63	54	40	Chile	66
Chile	66	66	69	63	62	70	65	65	70	60	64	71	62	76	65	53	Jordan	66
China	66	40	39	41	41	40	40	38	40	50	41	37	41	44	37	29	Uruguay	66
Colombia	na	na	na	na	na	na	na	na	na	na	na	na	na	na	na	na	Turkey	65
Croatia	na	na	na	na	na	na	na	na	na	na	na	na	na	na	na	na	Uganda	65
Czech Republic	66	na	na	na	na	na	na	na	na	na	na	na	na	na	na	na	Dominican Rep.	65
Denmark	47	na	na	na	na	na	na	na	na	na	na	na	na	na	na	na	Vietnam	64
Dominican Rep.	na	65	63	65	62	69	55	55	64	66	58	63	73	69	68	53	Venezuela	64
Egypt	na	55	56	54	52	56	57	54	54	58	52	55	58	58	54	44	Georgia	63
El Salvador	na	51	56	47	46	51	60	48	51	61	45	54	59	na	na	na	Peru	63
Estonia	80	na	na	na	na	na	na	na	na	na	na	na	na	na	na	na	New Zealand	61
Finland	34	na	na	na	na	na	na	na	na	na	na	na	na	na	na	na	South Africa	61
France	52	na	na	na	na	na	na	na	na	na	na	na	na	na	na	na	Azerbaijan	59
Georgia	na	63	60	65	61	64	62	61	63	63	60	64	65	66	60	53	Singapore	59
Germany	73	na	na	na	na	na	na	na	na	na	na	na	na	na	na	na	Morocco	58
Great Britain	43	na	na	na	na	na	na	na	na	na	na	na	na	na	na	na	Sweden	57
Greece	na	na	na	na	na	na	na	na	na	na	na	na	na	na	na	na	Philippines	57
Hungary	63	na	na	na	na	na	na	na	na	na	na	na	na	na	na	na	Puerto Rico	56
Iceland	53	na	na	na	na	na	na	na	na	na	na	na	na	na	na	na	Iran	56
India	54	54	57	51	58	55	47	44	56	70	42	53	62	56	57	58	Egypt	55
Indonesia	na	84	84	85	84	86	84	83	86	84	83	86	84	86	84	75	India	54
Iran	na	56	55	57	56	55	56	59	56	52	55	55	57	67	51	39	Mexico	53
Ireland	55	na	na	na	na	na	na	na	na	na	na	na	na	na	na	na	Argentina	53
Israel	na	51	50	52	51	49	53	45	51	54	50	50	49	36	55	49	El Salvador	51
Italy	43	na	na	na	na	na	na	na	na	na	na	na	na	na	na	na	Israel	51
Japan	43	42	41	43	29	41	49	46	44	37	43	44	41	58	40	26	Canada	51
Jordan	na	66	67	64	62	67	71	63	65	73	63	65	70	66	66	63	Korea, South	51
Korea, South	52	51	49	52	49	50	54	54	53	46	49	54	49	57	46	32	Spain	50
Latvia	83	na	na	na	na	na	na	na	na	na	na	na	na	na	na	na	United States	49
Lithuania	76	na	na	na	na	na	na	na	na	na	na	na	na	na	na	na	Brazil	46
Luxembourg	na	na	na	na	na	na	na	na	na	na	na	na	na	na	na	na	Armenia	46
Macedonia	na	77	77	77	76	78	78	70	80	83	76	80	79	81	77	55	Australia	44
Malta	na	na	na	na	na	na	na	na	na	na	na	na	na	na	na	na	Switzerland	44
Mexico	62	53	57	49	53	53	54	50	57	53	52	50	54	57	56	45	Japan	42
Moldova	na	77	76	79	74	78	79	81	74	80	79	77	79	80	74	73	Taiwan	41
Montenegro	na	78	81	74	78	83	74	73	81	81	74	79	83	79	80	58	China	40
Morocco	na	58	61	54	60	56	58	56	64	68	58	59	66	60	56	65	Norway	40
Netherlands	41	na	na	na	na	na	na	na	na	na	na	na	na	na	na	na		
New Zealand	na	61	62	61	54	64	62	61	61	64	56	62	68	80	73	53		
Nigeria	67	71	72	69	71	70	69	70	70	74	71	67	75	74	70	62		
Northern Ireland	53	na	na	na	na	na	na	na	na	na	na	na	na	na	na	na		
Norway	48	40	42	37	40	43	35	39	40	40	na	na	na	43	41	25		
Pakistan	na	76	77	76	79	76	73	81	74	66	83	79	62	79	73	33		
Peru	na	63	64	61	64	63	61	62	63	62	61	66	61	70	63	55		
Philippines	na	57	62	52	58	53	62	51	55	67	53	54	64	63	53	57		
Poland	74	na	na	na	na	na	na	na	na	na	na	na	na	na	na	na		
Portugal	71	na	na	na	na	na	na	na	na	na	na	na	na	na	na	na		
Puerto Rico	na	56	63	53	53	61	54	63	60	53	63	53	56	67	58	46		
Romania	na	na	na	na	na	na	na	na	na	na	na	na	na	na	na	na		
Russian Fed.	72	na	na	na	na	na	na	na	na	na	na	na	na	na	na	na		
Serbia	na	80	81	80	80	83	78	76	81	84	78	84	84	80	82	69		
Singapore	na	59	61	57	49	66	71	64	55	62	60	58	57	71	57	30		
Slovakia	na	na	na	na	na	na	na	na	na	na	na	na	na	na	na	na		
Slovenia	64	na	na	na	na	na	na	na	na	na	na	na	na	na	na	na		
South Africa	54	61	63	58	60	60	63	56	65	77	57	55	71	64	61	40		
Spain	46	50	50	50	47	48	53	51	46	50	55	55	44	60	52	27		
Sweden	51	57	61	53	51	59	59	57	57	58	53	59	63	75	61	40		
Switzerland	28	44	48	39	37	48	42	38	44	51	39	39	50	54	48	26		
Taiwan	na	41	41	41	33	42	41	43	40	39	40	37	44	44	38	31		
Tanzania	na	82	83	80	78	85	82	75	89	92	72	88	90	81	82	67		
Turkey	59	65	69	61	61	68	68	61	71	74	62	68	68	68	66	61		
Uganda	na	65	69	62	66	65	59	62	67	53	64	69	57	68	65	57		
Ukraine	na	na	na	na	na	na	na	na	na	na	na	na	na	na	na	na		
United States	54	49	48	49	44	51	49	46	48	51	41	50	58	70	50	36		
Uruguay	na	66	68	64	64	62	69	67	65	60	64	64	68	76	66	59		
Venezuela	na	64	67	60	63	65	62	58	63	73	58	64	70	66	63	61		
Vietnam	na	64	67	61	60	64	67	65	62	69	55	68	64	85	58	57		
Zimbabwe	na	67	71	63	67	68	64	64	71	100	64	65	73	73	64	52		
Total	58	61	63	59	60	62	61	60	61	62	59	62	63	67	61	47	Total	61

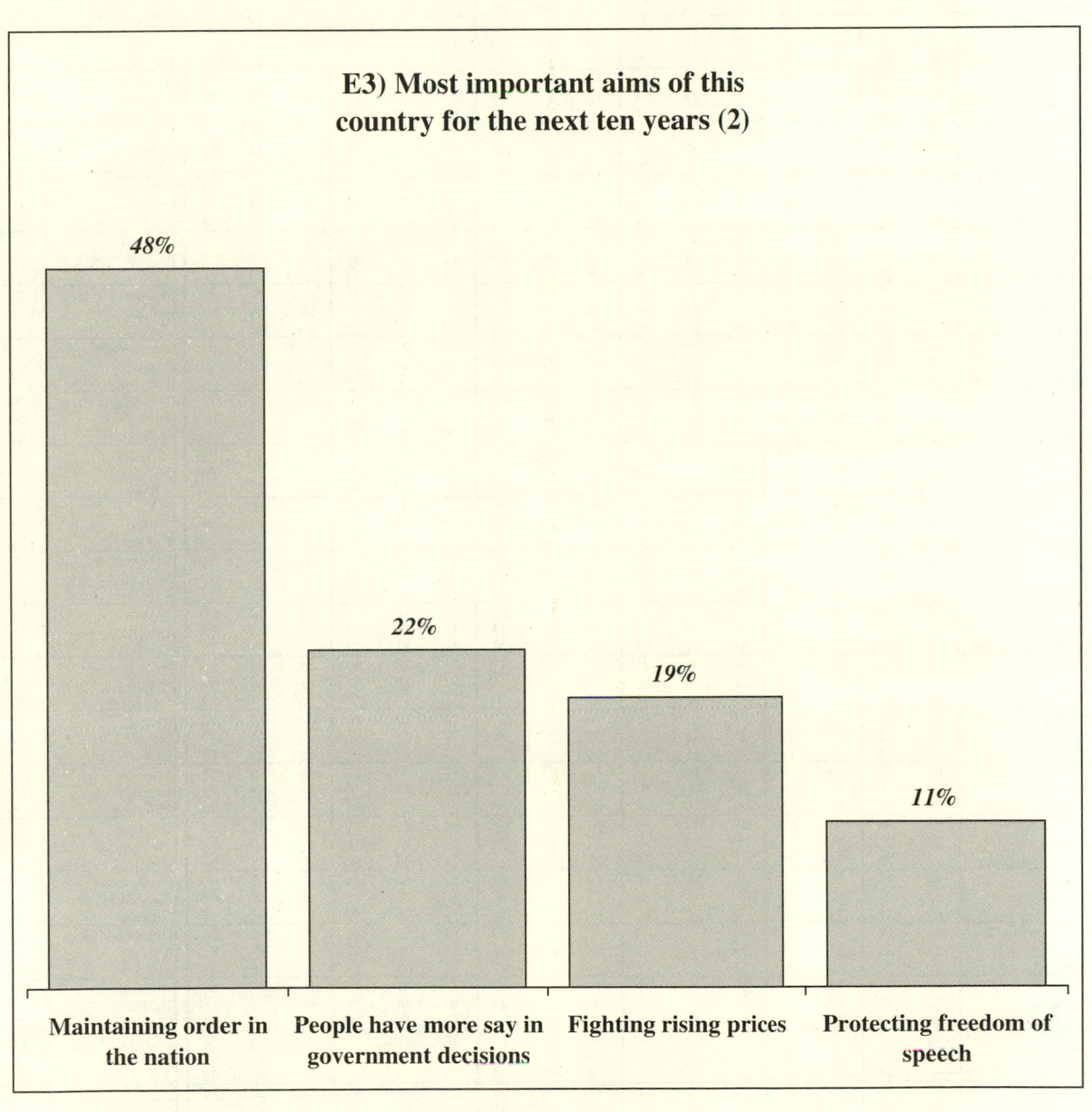

E3) Most important aims of this country for the next ten years (2)

48%

22%

19%

11%

Maintaining order in the nation

People have more say in government decisions

Fighting rising prices

Protecting freedom of speech

E003A) AIMS OF COUNTRY / 2 - MORE SAY IN GOVERNMENT DECISIONS

If you had to choose, which one of the things on this card would you say is most important?

Give people more say in government decisions (%)

(WVS: V122; EVS: V190)

Country	Wave 1990	Wave 2000	Gender Male	Gender Female	Age 16-29	Age 30-49	Age 50+	Education Lower	Education Middle	Education Upper	Income Lower	Income Middle	Income Upper	Values Mat	Values Mixed	Values Postm.	RANKING Country	2000
Albania	na	11	14	9	11	12	11	7	13	19	9	11	13	na	15	90	Japan	45
Algeria	na	12	14	11	14	12	10	8	11	18	13	10	13	na	14	56	Croatia	45
Argentina	32	30	31	30	29	34	27	23	38	47	22	28	42	na	22	70	Israel	43
Armenia	na	13	14	12	15	14	10	15	11	20	15	12	11	na	21	52	Australia	40
Australia	na	40	38	42	44	43	33	39	41	40	39	39	44	na	34	60	Canada	40
Austria	26	33	32	34	32	38	29	30	36	35	30	39	31	na	24	60	Italy	39
Azerbaijan	na	9	10	9	9	11	6	3	9	11	10	11	9	na	19	82	New Zealand	38
Bangladesh	na	19	20	18	22	18	13	19	19	18	15	25	14	na	26	86	Uruguay	37
Belarus	35	13	16	11	17	16	7	7	14	21	9	14	21	na	22	61	Slovenia	36
Belgium	18	25	27	23	22	28	23	13	24	34	19	28	30	na	23	58	Ireland	36
Bosnia and Herz.	na	15	16	14	16	15	14	12	17	13	14	14	18	na	19	79	Greece	36
Brazil	22	32	35	28	36	33	21	22	37	47	24	31	42	na	40	75	Lithuania	33
Bulgaria	29	5	5	5	8	6	4	4	5	8	6	5	5	na	9	32	Austria	33
Canada	43	40	37	42	40	39	41	40	39	42	40	41	38	na	36	60	Germany	32
Chile	31	28	30	26	31	31	20	19	30	40	23	29	34	na	31	63	United States	32
China	14	12	13	10	16	12	6	6	15	7	8	16	10	na	20	59	Sweden	32
Colombia	na	23	24	22	25	23	19	17	25	35	19	23	29	na	25	69	Brazil	32
Croatia	na	45	48	42	52	47	39	42	49	41	45	44	47	na	47	78	Peru	31
Czech Republic	27	26	26	27	29	29	23	26	26	30	27	26	25	na	32	61	Argentina	30
Denmark	16	17	16	18	17	21	12	13	20	21	12	18	22	na	12	52	Luxembourg	30
Dominican Rep.	na	26	29	25	26	27	18	16	23	29	22	31	23	na	23	68	Vietnam	29
Egypt	na	8	10	6	12	6	6	6	9	12	6	8	9	na	9	59	Northern Ireland	28
El Salvador	na	22	25	20	25	22	19	14	27	37	12	23	39	na	na	na	Poland	28
Estonia	21	21	22	19	25	22	17	20	21	22	18	22	22	na	34	77	Chile	28
Finland	59	24	23	26	27	26	22	23	25	33	26	24	25	na	27	65	Puerto Rico	27
France	21	24	25	23	24	26	21	17	27	37	20	23	30	na	22	66	Turkey	27
Georgia	na	11	14	9	11	12	11	9	11	14	12	10	11	na	18	60	Czech Republic	26
Germany	35	32	34	32	40	35	26	27	35	46	27	32	36	na	37	73	Dominican Rep.	26
Great Britain	29	na	na	na	na	na	na	na	na	na	na	na	na	na	na	na	Portugal	26
Greece	na	36	38	35	39	36	31	40	32	38	39	36	34	na	38	68	Iceland	25
Hungary	18	17	17	17	22	16	14	14	22	21	19	16	18	na	32	80	Belgium	25
Iceland	26	25	24	26	28	28	20	20	29	30	23	25	28	na	28	64	Spain	25
India	18	12	13	11	12	13	10	7	14	18	6	10	16	na	22	51	Latvia	24
Indonesia	na	6	8	5	4	7	7	5	5	8	3	6	10	na	8	57	Finland	24
Iran	na	20	20	19	22	19	16	13	24	20	17	19	23	na	23	59	France	24
Ireland	32	36	35	37	40	37	32	31	40	34	33	33	39	na	38	78	Colombia	23
Israel	na	43	38	48	41	42	46	53	43	37	47	43	43	na	50	84	El Salvador	22
Italy	29	39	39	39	48	42	32	32	44	48	33	42	45	na	35	69	Mexico	22
Japan	29	45	43	48	55	48	39	39	48	44	44	43	47	na	53	77	Ukraine	22
Jordan	na	10	9	10	12	9	6	8	12	11	9	10	9	na	12	56	Nigeria	21
Korea, South	15	18	21	16	26	17	12	9	15	24	17	19	19	na	31	65	Estonia	21
Latvia	26	24	31	19	31	28	19	18	25	30	18	31	30	na	35	72	South Africa	21
Lithuania	32	33	36	31	36	39	26	17	37	47	27	33	38	na	46	66	Venezuela	20
Luxembourg	na	30	27	33	28	34	26	23	32	35	25	31	37	na	30	69	Malta	20
Macedonia	na	11	12	10	14	10	9	14	9	10	11	12	9	na	13	71	Singapore	20
Malta	na	20	23	17	25	21	10	10	21	37	14	22	22	na	25	73	Iran	20
Mexico	23	22	25	19	25	23	16	15	27	38	17	26	27	na	24	62	Bangladesh	19
Moldova	na	14	14	14	15	15	11	14	13	17	14	11	16	na	23	77	Russian Fed.	19
Montenegro	na	12	13	10	17	13	6	8	13	17	11	13	12	na	16	69	Slovakia	18
Morocco	na	8	10	7	10	8	3	6	11	25	9	11	9	na	9	55	Korea, South	18
Netherlands	16	17	18	16	16	16	19	13	18	20	15	20	17	na	11	44	Philippines	18
New Zealand	na	38	35	40	41	40	35	39	37	38	38	42	34	na	42	72	Hungary	17
Nigeria	20	21	21	21	21	20	26	20	21	22	22	20	21	na	26	78	Netherlands	17
Northern Ireland	27	28	29	28	33	30	25	29	26	32	24	33	28	na	29	69	Denmark	17
Norway	14	14	15	14	16	15	11	11	14	18	na	na	na	na	12	46	Switzerland	16
Pakistan	na	4	4	3	3	4	3	1	5	10	na	2	11	na	8	83	Romania	15
Peru	na	31	34	29	32	30	33	23	28	41	29	29	38	na	32	74	Uganda	15
Philippines	na	18	20	17	19	17	18	18	17	20	14	21	18	Mat	26	66	Bosnia and Herz.	15
Poland	27	28	33	23	23	34	23	23	32	34	24	30	31	na	39	82	Norway	14
Portugal	22	26	26	25	34	31	17	20	35	47	12	25	33	na	36	59	Moldova	14
Puerto Rico	na	27	27	27	30	26	27	23	19	32	17	31	33	na	20	64	Armenia	13
Romania	12	15	19	12	19	17	12	8	17	25	10	14	20	na	25	56	Belarus	13
Russian Fed.	24	19	22	16	23	21	14	9	18	27	13	18	24	na	38	82	Zimbabwe	13
Serbia	na	11	13	8	12	12	9	7	10	19	8	11	13	na	15	68	Algeria	12
Singapore	na	20	20	20	23	19	12	15	23	24	19	19	21	na	23	63	India	12
Slovakia	na	18	20	17	21	20	15	12	20	29	13	17	24	na	31	76	Taiwan	12
Slovenia	28	36	36	37	40	38	32	33	39	34	38	40	36	na	36	77	China	12
South Africa	27	21	21	21	22	22	15	23	17	31	24	21	17	na	30	59	Montenegro	12
Spain	29	25	25	24	29	27	20	21	28	30	24	27	26	na	26	59	Albania	11
Sweden	28	32	29	35	34	34	29	20	35	36	31	31	34	na	26	61	Georgia	11
Switzerland	18	16	17	16	15	18	14	14	17	16	13	16	19	na	14	39	Tanzania	11
Taiwan	na	12	14	10	8	13	11	10	14	12	13	14	9	na	18	65	Macedonia	11
Tanzania	na	11	13	9	9	12	11	9	13	14	10	12	12	na	15	92	Serbia	11
Turkey	23	27	27	27	30	26	22	27	28	26	27	27	29	na	30	50	Jordan	10
Uganda	na	15	20	11	15	16	16	15	14	24	14	20	18	na	14	64	Azerbaijan	9
Ukraine	na	22	24	20	22	26	17	11	22	28	15	25	28	na	38	79	Morocco	8
United States	31	32	34	30	32	35	29	27	36	32	31	29	37	na	28	55	Egypt	8
Uruguay	na	37	38	36	46	41	29	30	46	48	30	38	45	na	34	72	Indonesia	6
Venezuela	na	20	23	17	18	23	20	17	19	27	19	18	23	na	19	61	Bulgaria	5
Vietnam	na	29	29	28	32	29	26	27	32	24	29	25	32	na	33	79	Pakistan	4
Zimbabwe	na	13	16	10	15	10	12	9	16	48	13	12	20	na	18	55		
Total	26	22	23	22	24	23	20	18	23	27	20	23	25	na	26	64	Total	22

E003B) AIMS OF COUNTRY / 2 - MAINTAINING ORDER

If you had to choose, which one of the things on this card would you say is most important?

Maintaining order in the nation (%)   (WVS: V122; EVS: V190)

Country	Wave 1990	Wave 2000	Gender Male	Gender Female	Age 16-29	Age 30-49	Age 50+	Education Lower	Education Middle	Education Upper	Income Lower	Income Middle	Income Upper	Values Mat	Values Mixed	Values Postm.
Albania	na	70	70	71	67	73	69	73	69	67	74	68	68	82	66	
Algeria	na	55	54	56	53	55	59	55	58	51	52	59	54	72	54	
Argentina	35	33	35	32	32	31	38	38	29	23	39	33	30	65	39	
Armenia	na	61	63	60	57	64	63	56	62	60	59	64	63	75	55	
Australia	na	23	25	21	19	21	28	23	24	20	22	24	22	63	32	
Austria	41	36	36	36	29	31	44	41	32	29	40	33	37	76	48	
Azerbaijan	na	74	75	73	74	73	78	81	74	73	75	74	72	83	66	
Bangladesh	na	64	64	63	60	65	67	64	64	62	61	60	70	80	58	
Belarus	44	56	55	57	52	54	62	59	57	48	57	56	54	66	53	
Belgium	21	38	36	41	34	36	43	48	39	31	42	38	36	61	43	
Bosnia and Herz.	na	71	69	73	72	71	70	72	71	71	71	73	65	85	68	
Brazil	31	29	28	30	25	27	39	31	26	30	30	27	28	44	26	
Bulgaria	51	76	76	76	76	78	74	75	76	79	71	78	79	82	75	
Canada	21	22	21	23	21	22	23	22	24	21	21	23	22	58	28	
Chile	39	35	36	33	31	33	41	37	37	24	35	37	32	61	32	
China	67	57	57	56	54	59	55	56	56	73	56	55	60	67	51	
Colombia	na	41	43	39	38	43	43	41	41	41	41	40	42	70	48	
Croatia	na	28	27	29	22	26	34	26	29	28	36	26	24	57	28	
Czech Republic	44	56	55	57	48	54	62	55	57	52	56	55	57	77	56	
Denmark	59	59	60	58	59	52	65	69	50	41	67	57	47	81	67	
Dominican Rep.	na	45	44	45	44	45	46	56	50	42	47	44	44	74	48	
Egypt	na	63	65	61	58	66	62	59	67	64	63	63	61	71	63	
El Salvador	na	26	25	26	21	27	31	29	22	23	27	24	23	na	na	
Estonia	59	57	59	56	52	57	60	54	57	64	55	56	60	70	51	
Finland	11	52	56	49	47	49	57	52	55	43	49	52	56	71	53	
France	28	43	42	45	39	39	49	50	38	28	49	42	36	69	44	
Georgia	na	65	65	66	68	64	64	69	65	65	64	69	65	77	59	
Germany	37	42	41	43	29	40	50	48	39	33	46	41	38	67	42	
Great Britain	25	na	na	na	na	na	na	na	na	na	na	na	na	na	na	na
Greece	na	40	37	41	35	41	46	37	43	37	37	40	41	67	42	
Hungary	37	53	55	51	50	52	55	50	55	65	44	57	52	62	45	
Iceland	49	57	54	59	54	54	62	64	55	45	56	61	52	75	59	
India	43	42	45	38	44	41	43	37	47	47	40	43	43	54	39	
Indonesia	na	77	76	78	75	77	78	73	79	76	78	79	74	79	79	
Iran	na	39	41	36	38	39	41	40	37	40	38	39	38	63	35	
Ireland	24	37	36	38	36	37	39	31	38	46	39	37	38	66	37	
Israel	na	41	46	37	39	43	41	35	43	43	35	42	45	65	39	
Italy	29	32	33	32	26	30	38	38	30	21	33	32	26	73	37	
Japan	35	34	39	29	23	30	42	37	32	34	35	34	34	68	30	
Jordan	na	63	67	59	61	62	69	65	59	63	60	65	65	74	61	
Korea, South	43	43	48	37	38	41	52	29	43	44	41	43	44	49	41	
Latvia	54	54	52	55	51	51	57	55	54	54	56	49	53	73	47	
Lithuania	29	24	25	24	21	24	27	31	21	25	22	19	25	45	17	
Luxembourg	na	45	49	42	44	40	51	51	45	36	47	41	38	78	47	
Macedonia	na	77	76	78	72	76	81	75	78	77	79	74	77	87	76	
Malta	na	33	35	30	33	30	35	31	34	33	32	35	35	41	32	
Mexico	28	32	33	31	29	32	38	36	29	23	34	35	30	53	31	
Moldova	na	63	62	63	59	61	68	69	64	55	69	65	55	71	58	
Montenegro	na	54	56	52	41	50	66	62	52	41	69	54	47	75	38	
Morocco	na	51	50	53	51	50	55	52	48	45	52	50	47	72	42	
Netherlands	27	41	40	41	36	39	45	48	38	37	41	42	37	67	49	
New Zealand	na	29	30	28	30	28	30	26	30	33	25	28	35	74	38	
Nigeria	43	48	48	48	49	48	43	49	45	52	44	52	50	69	42	
Northern Ireland	36	41	40	41	35	37	46	38	43	42	40	36	49	62	44	
Norway	64	66	67	65	58	64	75	73	70	56	na	na	na	86	73	
Pakistan	na	57	60	55	55	54	70	57	57	60	52	58	63	56	60	
Peru	na	43	43	44	42	46	41	47	44	39	43	47	39	70	45	
Philippines	na	51	49	52	51	53	45	47	50	56	48	45	60	64	47	
Poland	26	40	40	41	37	38	46	39	42	42	37	41	47	57	35	
Portugal	34	33	34	32	31	30	37	36	30	20	48	30	39	54	26	
Puerto Rico	na	46	49	44	37	48	48	52	53	41	53	43	44	79	57	
Romania	60	49	48	50	46	51	49	51	50	46	48	47	50	64	44	
Russian Fed.	59	56	57	56	49	58	59	56	56	58	57	57	56	68	45	
Serbia	na	49	50	49	47	46	53	46	52	49	49	51	52	57	48	
Singapore	na	68	70	66	65	70	73	71	66	71	65	69	70	84	69	
Slovakia	na	48	50	46	48	48	47	48	48	47	48	48	48	54	47	
Slovenia	27	42	43	40	35	39	50	46	39	45	41	38	39	66	45	
South Africa	38	41	39	43	34	43	49	35	48	42	36	40	48	56	36	
Spain	33	36	37	35	26	30	47	42	31	30	43	34	32	63	35	
Sweden	38	45	47	42	38	42	52	64	42	35	45	49	40	74	56	
Switzerland	32	32	32	32	21	28	43	44	30	19	38	36	24	57	36	
Taiwan	na	69	71	67	77	69	62	60	68	76	59	70	77	78	65	
Tanzania	20	83	81	84	86	82	78	84	83	78	82	83	80	90	81	
Turkey	20	26	27	25	21	26	35	28	24	18	28	25	21	48	25	
Uganda	na	51	55	46	50	50	54	45	54	37	47	48	46	73	48	
Ukraine	na	55	55	54	55	50	58	59	54	54	56	53	53	68	46	
United States	28	33	29	36	28	32	38	33	33	32	30	34	33	70	40	
Uruguay	na	26	27	25	19	21	34	31	20	17	33	22	22	68	24	
Venezuela	na	45	47	44	45	44	50	48	46	42	49	43	45	66	48	
Vietnam	na	57	58	55	50	58	59	58	55	60	53	62	53	69	58	
Zimbabwe	na	37	40	35	40	36	33	34	42	30	36	36	39	51	31	
Total	38	48	48	47	45	47	51	49	48	46	48	48	47	68	47	

RANKING

Country	2000
Tanzania	83
Macedonia	77
Indonesia	77
Bulgaria	76
Azerbaijan	74
Bosnia and Herz.	71
Albania	70
Taiwan	69
Singapore	68
Norway	66
Georgia	65
Bangladesh	64
Jordan	63
Moldova	63
Egypt	63
Armenia	61
Denmark	59
Pakistan	57
Estonia	57
China	57
Iceland	57
Vietnam	57
Russian Fed.	56
Belarus	56
Czech Republic	56
Algeria	55
Ukraine	55
Montenegro	54
Latvia	54
Hungary	53
Finland	52
Morocco	51
Philippines	51
Uganda	51
Serbia	49
Romania	49
Nigeria	48
Slovakia	48
Puerto Rico	46
Venezuela	45
Luxembourg	45
Sweden	45
Dominican Rep.	45
Peru	43
France	43
Korea, South	43
India	42
Germany	42
Slovenia	42
Israel	41
Colombia	41
Netherlands	41
South Africa	41
Northern Ireland	41
Poland	40
Greece	40
Iran	39
Belgium	38
Zimbabwe	37
Ireland	37
Spain	36
Austria	36
Chile	35
Japan	34
Argentina	33
Portugal	33
Malta	33
United States	33
Mexico	32
Italy	32
Switzerland	32
New Zealand	29
Brazil	29
Croatia	28
Uruguay	26
Turkey	26
El Salvador	26
Lithuania	24
Australia	23
Canada	22
Total	48

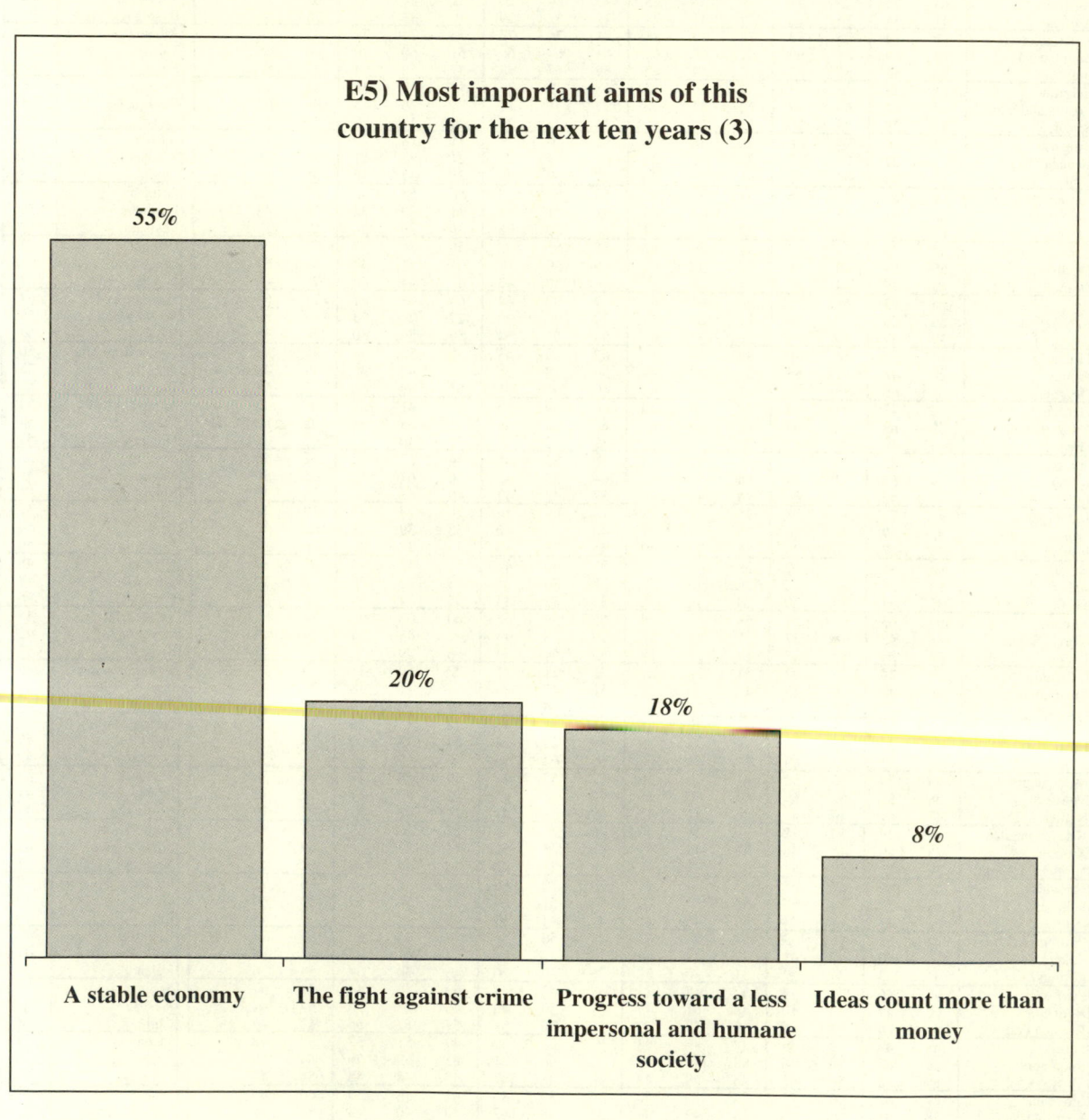

E5) **Most important aims of this country for the next ten years (3)**

55% — A stable economy

20% — The fight against crime

18% — Progress toward a less impersonal and humane society

8% — Ideas count more than money

E005A) AIMS OF COUNTRY / 3 - LESS IMPERSONAL SOCIETY

Here is another list. In your opinion, which one of these is most important?

Progress toward a less impersonal society (%) (WVS: V124)

Country	Wave 1990	Wave 2000	Gender Male	Gender Female	Age 16-29	Age 30-49	Age 50+	Educ. Lower	Educ. Middle	Educ. Upper	Income Lower	Income Middle	Income Upper	Mat	Mixed	Postm.
Albania	na	4	4	4	5	4	3	3	5	6	5	4	3	2	5	10
Algeria	na	16	15	18	20	14	12	11	16	20	20	15	17	12	18	24
Argentina	18	19	17	21	22	18	18	13	26	37	18	16	24	10	17	32
Armenia	na	15	15	15	19	12	13	11	15	18	20	10	13	7	21	25
Australia	na	23	21	25	25	26	18	15	20	34	18	25	28	10	20	30
Austria	20	na	na	na	na	na	na	na	na	na	na	na	na	na	na	na
Azerbaijan	na	21	19	23	22	21	18	15	20	24	21	23	21	18	27	24
Bangladesh	na	13	13	14	14	13	12	12	15	13	10	14	15	10	14	27
Belarus	11	na	na	na	na	na	na	na	na	na	na	na	na	na	na	na
Belgium	26	na	na	na	na	na	na	na	na	na	na	na	na	na	na	na
Bosnia and Herz.	na	6	7	6	7	6	6	7	5	10	5	6	8	4	7	8
Brazil	27	22	19	24	22	24	18	19	21	35	20	21	25	18	21	37
Bulgaria	9	na	na	na	na	na	na	na	na	na	na	na	na	na	na	na
Canada	22	20	17	22	24	21	16	13	19	27	17	19	22	8	18	27
Chile	22	20	18	22	20	22	18	18	20	26	19	17	27	9	21	36
China	6	7	6	9	10	8	4	5	9	7	6	8	9	5	9	22
Colombia	na	26	27	24	22	30	21	18	21	39	22	21	35	17	28	37
Croatia	na	na	na	na	na	na	na	na	na	na	na	na	na	na	na	na
Czech Republic	9	na	na	na	na	na	na	na	na	na	na	na	na	na	na	na
Denmark	21	na	na	na	na	na	na	na	na	na	na	na	na	na	na	na
Dominican Rep.	na	27	23	30	29	25	27	13	17	33	30	25	25	17	24	50
Egypt	na	22	22	23	25	21	21	23	22	23	24	24	19	19	24	32
El Salvador	na	11	13	10	11	11	14	8	12	21	6	11	18	na	na	na
Estonia	24	na	na	na	na	na	na	na	na	na	na	na	na	na	na	na
Finland	48	na	na	na	na	na	na	na	na	na	na	na	na	na	na	na
France	33	na	na	na	na	na	na	na	na	na	na	na	na	na	na	na
Georgia	na	17	17	17	17	18	16	15	16	23	18	16	16	12	21	31
Germany	17	na	na	na	na	na	na	na	na	na	na	na	na	na	na	na
Great Britain	21	na	na	na	na	na	na	na	na	na	na	na	na	na	na	na
Greece	na	na	na	na	na	na	na	na	na	na	na	na	na	na	na	na
Hungary	8	na	na	na	na	na	na	na	na	na	na	na	na	na	na	na
Iceland	25	na	na	na	na	na	na	na	na	na	na	na	na	na	na	na
India	20	16	16	16	14	16	17	14	20	16	17	17	15	12	20	23
Indonesia	na	8	9	8	10	9	7	7	9	9	6	9	12	6	10	18
Iran	na	16	15	18	17	15	15	13	17	19	14	17	20	12	18	26
Ireland	19	na	na	na	na	na	na	na	na	na	na	na	na	na	na	na
Israel	na	35	32	38	41	37	26	19	38	41	30	37	42	40	33	45
Italy	28	na	na	na	na	na	na	na	na	na	na	na	na	na	na	na
Japan	44	36	39	34	37	38	34	29	35	44	32	35	41	28	36	52
Jordan	na	14	13	16	16	12	17	14	17	11	16	16	11	13	14	22
Korea, South	36	29	29	28	37	29	17	18	23	39	26	29	31	21	34	47
Latvia	13	na	na	na	na	na	na	na	na	na	na	na	na	na	na	na
Lithuania	13	na	na	na	na	na	na	na	na	na	na	na	na	na	na	na
Luxembourg	na	na	na	na	na	na	na	na	na	na	na	na	na	na	na	na
Macedonia	na	6	6	7	8	6	4	7	6	6	4	8	7	5	7	11
Malta	na	na	na	na	na	na	na	na	na	na	na	na	na	na	na	na
Mexico	28	15	15	15	18	14	12	13	15	24	15	15	17	9	15	26
Moldova	na	15	15	16	18	12	16	13	17	15	10	16	14	11	18	31
Montenegro	na	7	6	8	12	6	5	6	8	9	6	5	8	3	8	29
Morocco	na	32	33	32	30	33	34	33	31	28	43	38	25	26	36	37
Netherlands	30	na	na	na	na	na	na	na	na	na	na	na	na	na	na	na
New Zealand	na	16	15	16	20	14	15	10	17	22	15	15	18	6	14	34
Nigeria	7	10	10	11	10	11	12	12	10	9	11	10	9	7	11	20
Northern Ireland	19	na	na	na	na	na	na	na	na	na	na	na	na	na	na	na
Norway	27	29	26	33	31	33	23	21	27	40	na	na	na	16	28	54
Pakistan	na	7	9	5	7	8	7	5	9	12	3	6	15	7	7	42
Peru	na	14	15	14	14	14	16	9	12	22	10	14	23	7	15	22
Philippines	na	14	13	14	14	13	15	17	13	12	14	15	13	8	17	24
Poland	9	na	na	na	na	na	na	na	na	na	na	na	na	na	na	na
Portugal	24	na	na	na	na	na	na	na	na	na	na	na	na	na	na	na
Puerto Rico	na	23	23	22	31	21	21	16	15	28	16	23	30	19	18	38
Romania	10	na	na	na	na	na	na	na	na	na	na	na	na	na	na	na
Russian Fed.	9	na	na	na	na	na	na	na	na	na	na	na	na	na	na	na
Serbia	na	9	8	10	10	9	9	7	9	13	8	8	10	7	9	23
Singapore	na	16	13	18	17	15	14	14	16	16	14	14	18	11	17	21
Slovakia	na	na	na	na	na	na	na	na	na	na	na	na	na	na	na	na
Slovenia	9	na	na	na	na	na	na	na	na	na	na	na	na	na	na	na
South Africa	17	6	7	6	6	7	5	7	5	8	7	5	7	4	8	10
Spain	27	27	27	27	33	28	23	23	30	36	25	30	25	16	30	37
Sweden	31	24	23	26	25	24	24	15	23	34	25	21	28	18	20	38
Switzerland	37	33	28	38	42	32	29	34	32	37	34	31	33	19	30	48
Taiwan	na	19	16	22	24	18	19	20	19	18	19	21	17	15	22	24
Tanzania	na	17	13	23	15	19	16	18	15	17	18	17	17	16	18	25
Turkey	27	24	21	28	25	24	22	25	20	29	25	23	25	20	24	32
Uganda	na	12	12	12	12	13	5	13	11	9	15	11	12	9	12	20
Ukraine	na	na	na	na	na	na	na	na	na	na	na	na	na	na	na	na
United States	16	19	16	22	19	22	16	12	20	22	20	19	19	20	16	28
Uruguay	na	26	26	26	30	30	21	20	33	42	19	25	34	10	24	42
Venezuela	na	12	13	11	11	12	12	12	10	16	13	9	12	5	12	20
Vietnam	na	21	18	25	20	22	22	19	25	18	26	20	20	13	25	25
Zimbabwe	na	7	6	8	9	5	5	8	6	na	7	8	7	4	9	17
Total	21	18	16	19	19	18	16	15	17	23	16	17	19	11	19	31

RANKING

Country	2000
Japan	36
Israel	35
Switzerland	33
Morocco	32
Norway	29
Korea, South	29
Dominican Rep.	27
Spain	27
Uruguay	26
Colombia	26
Sweden	24
Turkey	24
Australia	23
Puerto Rico	23
Egypt	22
Brazil	22
Vietnam	21
Azerbaijan	21
Chile	20
Canada	20
Argentina	19
Taiwan	19
United States	19
Georgia	17
Tanzania	17
Algeria	16
Iran	16
India	16
Singapore	16
New Zealand	16
Moldova	15
Armenia	15
Mexico	15
Jordan	14
Peru	14
Philippines	14
Bangladesh	13
Venezuela	12
Uganda	12
El Salvador	11
Nigeria	10
Serbia	9
Indonesia	8
China	7
Pakistan	7
Montenegro	7
Zimbabwe	7
South Africa	6
Macedonia	6
Bosnia and Herz.	6
Albania	4
Total	18

E005B) AIMS OF COUNTRY / 3 - STABLE ECONOMY

Here is another list. In your opinion, which one of these is most important?

A stable economy (%)

(WVS: V124)

Country	Wave 1990	Wave 2000	Male	Female	16-29	30-49	50+	Lower	Middle	Upper	Lower	Middle	Upper	Mat	Mixed	Postm.
Albania	na	69	70	68	69	68	70	71	67	67	68	69	69	73	64	74
Algeria	na	54	56	52	53	53	60	62	52	53	51	53	54	65	53	32
Argentina	64	52	54	51	46	58	52	54	51	45	50	56	50	64	55	38
Armenia	na	58	59	57	53	62	60	61	57	63	55	64	56	64	57	27
Australia	na	37	38	35	30	33	47	36	39	35	40	35	34	43	41	29
Austria	51	na	na	na	na	na	na	na	na	na	na	na	na	na	na	na
Azerbaijan	na	55	59	51	53	55	57	51	52	60	48	51	62	57	52	47
Bangladesh	na	67	71	61	64	68	73	65	66	75	69	66	66	68	68	45
Belarus	70	na	na	na	na	na	na	na	na	na	na	na	na	na	na	na
Belgium	32	na	na	na	na	na	na	na	na	na	na	na	na	na	na	na
Bosnia and Herz.	na	79	78	80	78	81	78	77	80	80	75	82	79	82	77	76
Brazil	30	17	18	15	16	15	20	15	16	24	15	11	21	13	18	17
Bulgaria	83	na	na	na	na	na	na	na	na	na	na	na	na	na	na	na
Canada	54	49	54	45	38	48	57	48	51	48	48	51	49	66	52	39
Chile	56	58	62	55	58	57	60	56	62	54	57	62	55	69	58	40
China	83	54	56	52	59	54	50	43	59	69	47	53	64	60	53	25
Colombia	na	33	34	32	34	32	34	31	36	31	30	36	31	46	36	18
Croatia	na	na	na	na	na	na	na	na	na	na	na	na	na	na	na	na
Czech Republic	63	na	na	na	na	na	na	na	na	na	na	na	na	na	na	na
Denmark	50	na	na	na	na	na	na	na	na	na	na	na	na	na	na	na
Dominican Rep.	na	44	52	38	42	48	36	47	49	41	38	43	52	57	44	32
Egypt	na	47	49	45	40	50	52	48	43	51	46	47	50	53	44	31
El Salvador	na	24	28	21	21	24	29	22	25	31	17	26	33	na	na	na
Estonia	60	na	na	na	na	na	na	na	na	na	na	na	na	na	na	na
Finland	40	na	na	na	na	na	na	na	na	na	na	na	na	na	na	na
France	26	na	na	na	na	na	na	na	na	na	na	na	na	na	na	na
Georgia	na	58	58	57	57	58	58	63	57	56	57	59	58	64	52	45
Germany	73	na	na	na	na	na	na	na	na	na	na	na	na	na	na	na
Great Britain	40	na	na	na	na	na	na	na	na	na	na	na	na	na	na	na
Greece	na	na	na	na	na	na	na	na	na	na	na	na	na	na	na	na
Hungary	67	na	na	na	na	na	na	na	na	na	na	na	na	na	na	na
Iceland	58	na	na	na	na	na	na	na	na	na	na	na	na	na	na	na
India	44	36	39	32	38	36	34	27	38	50	24	36	42	41	35	23
Indonesia	na	84	84	85	82	85	85	82	85	85	88	82	80	87	83	61
Iran	na	52	54	50	50	54	55	55	53	51	54	50	51	61	47	44
Ireland	49	na	na	na	na	na	na	na	na	na	na	na	na	na	na	na
Israel	na	39	43	35	33	39	44	42	38	38	36	37	38	36	41	29
Italy	30	na	na	na	na	na	na	na	na	na	na	na	na	na	na	na
Japan	44	44	43	45	36	41	50	47	44	40	49	41	42	53	44	33
Jordan	na	52	55	49	46	55	58	54	47	54	50	54	51	60	49	26
Korea, South	53	64	63	66	55	64	76	75	71	53	67	63	62	74	58	44
Latvia	77	na	na	na	na	na	na	na	na	na	na	na	na	na	na	na
Lithuania	61	na	na	na	na	na	na	na	na	na	na	na	na	na	na	na
Luxembourg	na	na	na	na	na	na	na	na	na	na	na	na	na	na	na	na
Macedonia	na	76	77	76	71	77	80	71	78	82	74	78	80	82	76	50
Malta	na	na	na	na	na	na	na	na	na	na	na	na	na	na	na	na
Mexico	53	55	60	50	52	57	54	53	58	52	53	56	56	58	57	46
Moldova	na	69	73	67	64	72	71	76	66	69	75	69	69	73	68	50
Montenegro	na	68	70	66	68	72	64	61	72	72	72	72	67	66	73	53
Morocco	na	38	39	37	42	35	32	37	38	45	30	33	48	48	33	25
Netherlands	32	na	na	na	na	na	na	na	na	na	na	na	na	na	na	na
New Zealand	na	57	57	57	45	59	59	59	57	57	54	61	60	80	65	50
Nigeria	61	65	66	64	68	63	59	64	66	66	63	66	68	69	64	56
Northern Ireland	51	na	na	na	na	na	na	na	na	na	na	na	na	na	na	na
Norway	46	39	45	33	30	40	43	41	40	35	na	na	na	43	39	27
Pakistan	na	69	70	68	68	68	72	73	67	60	77	70	55	69	70	33
Peru	na	65	66	64	62	67	65	65	66	63	67	67	58	72	65	57
Philippines	na	65	65	64	61	65	67	62	63	70	60	63	71	68	63	54
Poland	73	na	na	na	na	na	na	na	na	na	na	na	na	na	na	na
Portugal	47	na	na	na	na	na	na	na	na	na	na	na	na	na	na	na
Puerto Rico	na	39	44	37	30	38	45	38	45	37	46	39	36	51	43	25
Romania	67	na	na	na	na	na	na	na	na	na	na	na	na	na	na	na
Russian Fed.	65	na	na	na	na	na	na	na	na	na	na	na	na	na	na	na
Serbia	na	69	74	65	65	72	69	64	74	69	69	75	70	69	71	61
Singapore	na	73	77	70	68	79	78	74	72	76	74	75	72	80	73	54
Slovakia	na	na	na	na	na	na	na	na	na	na	na	na	na	na	na	na
Slovenia	81	na	na	na	na	na	na	na	na	na	na	na	na	na	na	na
South Africa	46	49	52	45	49	51	44	44	56	56	49	50	51	51	50	38
Spain	36	40	41	38	36	38	43	42	40	31	38	40	38	51	39	24
Sweden	39	44	46	41	35	45	48	49	45	37	41	46	45	56	47	31
Switzerland	26	43	49	38	33	47	44	37	46	36	40	43	48	54	48	25
Taiwan	na	50	52	47	45	52	48	49	53	49	53	50	50	53	49	46
Tanzania	na	72	76	67	68	74	73	69	75	79	69	74	77	75	70	58
Turkey	36	42	47	37	34	45	51	42	44	43	43	42	40	54	42	29
Uganda	na	63	69	58	66	60	61	59	67	53	52	58	65	73	61	45
Ukraine	na	na	na	na	na	na	na	na	na	na	na	na	na	na	na	na
United States	50	46	50	41	41	43	54	51	45	44	42	46	48	49	50	33
Uruguay	na	58	59	57	50	57	63	63	52	48	64	62	48	78	59	42
Venezuela	na	51	52	49	49	54	46	48	51	53	51	53	52	63	49	40
Vietnam	na	68	71	65	70	69	65	69	66	73	63	69	69	80	64	61
Zimbabwe	na	64	71	58	60	65	69	62	66	100	58	65	70	69	62	46
Total	53	55	57	52	51	56	57	54	57	53	54	56	55	63	55	38

RANKING

Country	2000
Indonesia	84
Bosnia and Herz.	79
Macedonia	76
Singapore	73
Tanzania	72
Serbia	69
Moldova	69
Pakistan	69
Albania	69
Vietnam	68
Montenegro	68
Bangladesh	67
Nigeria	65
Peru	65
Philippines	65
Korea, South	64
Zimbabwe	64
Uganda	63
Armenia	58
Chile	58
Uruguay	58
Georgia	58
New Zealand	57
Azerbaijan	55
Mexico	55
Algeria	54
China	54
Iran	52
Argentina	52
Jordan	52
Venezuela	51
Taiwan	50
Canada	49
South Africa	49
Egypt	47
United States	46
Dominican Rep.	44
Japan	44
Sweden	44
Switzerland	43
Turkey	42
Spain	40
Puerto Rico	39
Norway	39
Israel	39
Morocco	38
Australia	37
India	36
Colombia	33
El Salvador	24
Brazil	17
Total	55

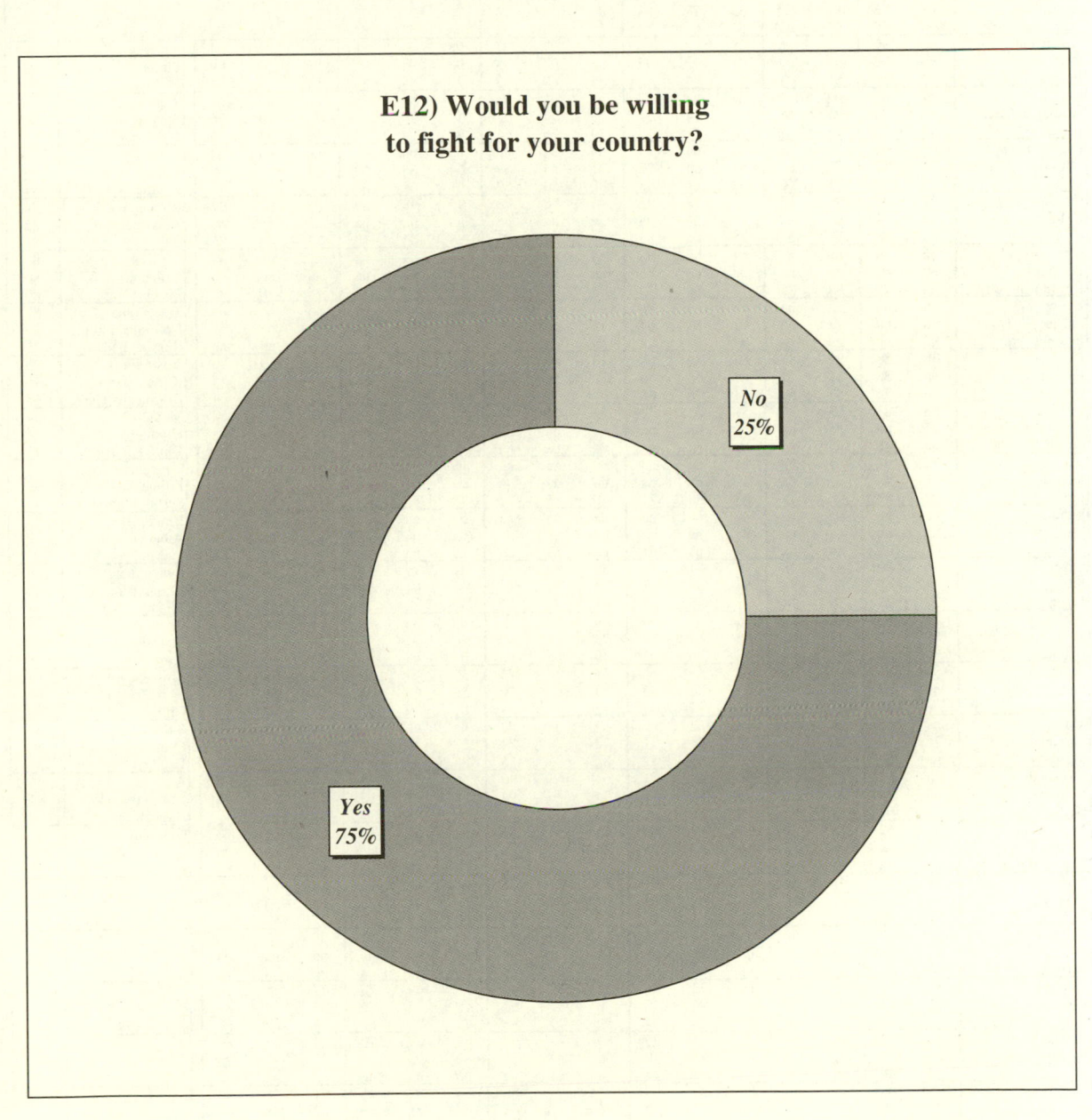

**E12) Would you be willing
to fight for your country?**

No
25%

Yes
75%

E012) BE WILLING TO FIGHT IN WAR FOR YOUR COUNTRY

Of course, we all hope that there will not be another war, but if it were to come to that, would you be willing to fight for your country?

Yes (%)

(WVS: V126; EVS: o24)

Country	Wave 1990	Wave 2000	Gender Male	Female	Age 16-29	30-49	50+	Education Lower	Middle	Upper	Income Lower	Middle	Upper	Values Mat	Mixed	Postm.
Albania	na	72	83	60	68	73	73	70	72	76	74	68	73	73	72	70
Algeria	na	na	na	na	na	na	na	na	na	na	na	na	na	na	na	na
Argentina	63	65	71	60	64	66	66	70	59	53	69	67	59	65	69	56
Armenia	na	80	88	73	80	83	77	78	80	82	80	81	78	75	85	84
Australia	na	75	80	70	63	78	82	79	74	74	76	77	75	72	77	72
Austria	66	55	63	47	57	60	49	57	54	53	48	53	63	58	56	54
Azerbaijan	na	97	98	96	98	97	96	96	97	97	98	96	98	98	97	94
Bangladesh	na	96	98	93	97	95	95	95	97	98	94	98	95	95	96	99
Belarus	92	84	88	81	88	90	75	75	89	83	79	88	85	82	89	84
Belgium	41	na	na	na	na	na	na	na	na	na	na	na	na	na	na	na
Bosnia and Herz.	na	74	81	68	79	74	71	73	77	67	74	76	71	75	74	76
Brazil	36	72	76	67	70	71	77	79	70	54	76	74	66	79	72	56
Bulgaria	91	na	na	na	na	na	na	na	na	na	na	na	na	na	na	na
Canada	68	67	72	61	63	64	72	71	64	68	64	68	69	64	66	68
Chile	83	60	71	50	62	61	58	65	60	50	67	58	55	58	64	51
China	97	97	98	95	97	98	94	94	98	98	95	98	99	97	97	97
Colombia	na	na	na	na	na	na	na	na	na	na	na	na	na	na	na	na
Croatia	na	85	87	82	85	86	83	83	87	81	83	89	78	87	84	85
Czech Republic	66	na	na	na	na	na	na	na	na	na	na	na	na	na	na	na
Denmark	89	na	na	na	na	na	na	na	na	na	na	na	na	na	na	na
Dominican Rep.	na	79	84	75	76	84	73	83	79	77	85	69	78	78	78	84
Egypt	na	na	na	na	na	na	na	na	na	na	na	na	na	na	na	na
El Salvador	na	69	72	66	70	71	64	75	66	56	77	72	55	na	na	na
Estonia	92	na	na	na	na	na	na	na	na	na	na	na	na	na	na	na
Finland	88	88	90	85	88	88	88	88	87	88	82	90	94	88	89	80
France	66	58	61	55	61	58	56	59	56	57	51	63	61	56	61	55
Georgia	na	73	87	60	74	76	66	67	73	76	70	74	76	72	74	74
Germany	53	47	63	33	51	53	39	42	51	50	37	49	54	40	50	50
Great Britain	75	na	na	na	na	na	na	na	na	na	na	na	na	na	na	na
Greece	na	na	na	na	na	na	na	na	na	na	na	na	na	na	na	na
Hungary	77	na	na	na	na	na	na	na	na	na	na	na	na	na	na	na
Iceland	77	na	na	na	na	na	na	na	na	na	na	na	na	na	na	na
India	92	82	90	71	88	84	71	76	85	91	78	83	84	84	87	96
Indonesia	na	na	na	na	na	na	na	na	na	na	na	na	na	na	na	na
Iran	na	na	na	na	na	na	na	na	na	na	na	na	na	na	na	na
Ireland	61	na	na	na	na	na	na	na	na	na	na	na	na	na	na	na
Israel	na	80	83	78	75	81	85	80	80	81	79	74	88	62	84	85
Italy	31	60	66	55	54	58	65	62	59	59	61	64	56	62	60	59
Japan	20	25	36	14	12	15	41	41	20	32	30	22	26	28	23	25
Jordan	na	na	na	na	na	na	na	na	na	na	na	na	na	na	na	na
Korea, South	87	75	82	67	65	77	82	73	78	70	78	74	71	75	75	66
Latvia	97	na	na	na	na	na	na	na	na	na	na	na	na	na	na	na
Lithuania	84	72	80	64	83	80	56	51	80	76	57	77	78	71	74	75
Luxembourg	na	54	59	48	55	54	53	55	54	52	56	65	54	58	59	39
Macedonia	na	80	87	72	79	82	77	73	82	84	81	79	78	78	82	68
Malta	na	na	na	na	na	na	na	na	na	na	na	na	na	na	na	na
Mexico	74	74	80	69	76	74	71	72	78	74	73	76	75	73	78	79
Moldova	na	85	87	82	85	88	82	83	86	85	86	83	83	85	89	80
Montenegro	na	65	71	59	53	67	71	64	67	66	66	71	66	68	62	75
Morocco	na	94	97	92	95	96	91	94	96	94	98	94	93	93	95	96
Netherlands	71	na	na	na	na	na	na	na	na	na	na	na	na	na	na	na
New Zealand	na	62	76	50	54	62	66	65	68	57	61	63	66	68	61	63
Nigeria	80	na	na	na	na	na	na	na	na	na	na	na	na	na	na	na
Northern Ireland	61	na	na	na	na	na	na	na	na	na	na	na	na	na	na	na
Norway	91	89	91	86	86	89	91	88	91	86	na	na	na	85	91	79
Pakistan	na	na	na	na	na	na	na	na	na	na	na	na	na	na	na	na
Peru	na	81	85	78	80	83	80	80	83	80	83	82	77	78	82	83
Philippines	na	87	92	82	85	90	84	85	90	85	89	84	91	88	87	86
Poland	92	na	na	na	na	na	na	na	na	na	na	na	na	na	na	na
Portugal	68	na	na	na	na	na	na	na	na	na	na	na	na	na	na	na
Puerto Rico	na	71	83	65	64	72	76	81	68	72	71	69	75	77	71	74
Romania	92	84	92	76	85	90	79	76	87	92	79	85	89	83	87	88
Russian Fed.	84	77	86	69	85	84	64	59	79	81	72	77	82	73	82	86
Serbia	na	72	78	67	63	74	75	69	77	68	73	76	70	72	73	67
Singapore	na	85	92	79	87	88	70	80	89	83	80	90	87	81	87	85
Slovakia	na	na	na	na	na	na	na	na	na	na	na	na	na	na	na	na
Slovenia	95	85	91	79	80	89	83	85	84	88	86	87	91	91	83	86
South Africa	70	68	74	60	70	72	52	66	71	68	68	71	63	63	73	62
Spain	62	43	48	38	38	43	47	45	42	36	46	44	43	44	43	42
Sweden	89	na	na	na	na	na	na	na	na	na	na	na	na	na	na	na
Switzerland	78	69	74	64	60	70	74	69	70	65	63	74	72	75	73	55
Taiwan	na	86	91	81	86	90	76	80	91	89	83	89	87	85	89	90
Tanzania	na	93	94	93	92	95	92	93	94	93	91	95	95	93	93	100
Turkey	93	na	na	na	na	na	na	na	na	na	na	na	na	na	na	na
Uganda	na	65	82	49	69	65	52	61	66	72	78	68	68	62	68	62
Ukraine	na	74	82	66	74	79	68	56	77	74	68	75	79	70	77	72
United States	80	73	82	63	60	74	82	72	70	75	71	74	74	72	72	76
Uruguay	na	57	60	55	53	56	60	64	49	42	62	60	50	58	60	49
Venezuela	na	82	87	77	83	85	75	79	85	80	82	81	84	76	83	90
Vietnam	na	98	99	96	99	99	95	97	99	100	97	98	98	97	99	99
Zimbabwe	na	54	64	45	61	49	42	53	55	32	56	56	48	50	56	56
Total	74	75	81	69	75	77	72	74	76	75	74	77	76	76	77	69

RANKING

Country	2000
Vietnam	98
Azerbaijan	97
China	97
Bangladesh	96
Morocco	94
Tanzania	93
Norway	89
Finland	88
Philippines	87
Taiwan	86
Singapore	85
Moldova	85
Slovenia	85
Croatia	85
Belarus	84
Romania	84
Venezuela	82
India	82
Peru	81
Armenia	80
Israel	80
Macedonia	80
Dominican Rep.	79
Russian Fed.	77
Australia	75
Korea, South	75
Bosnia and Herz.	74
Mexico	74
Ukraine	74
United States	73
Georgia	73
Lithuania	72
Serbia	72
Brazil	72
Albania	72
Puerto Rico	71
Switzerland	69
El Salvador	69
South Africa	68
Canada	67
Uganda	65
Argentina	65
Montenegro	65
New Zealand	62
Chile	60
Italy	60
France	58
Uruguay	57
Austria	55
Luxembourg	54
Zimbabwe	54
Germany	47
Spain	43
Japan	25
Total	75

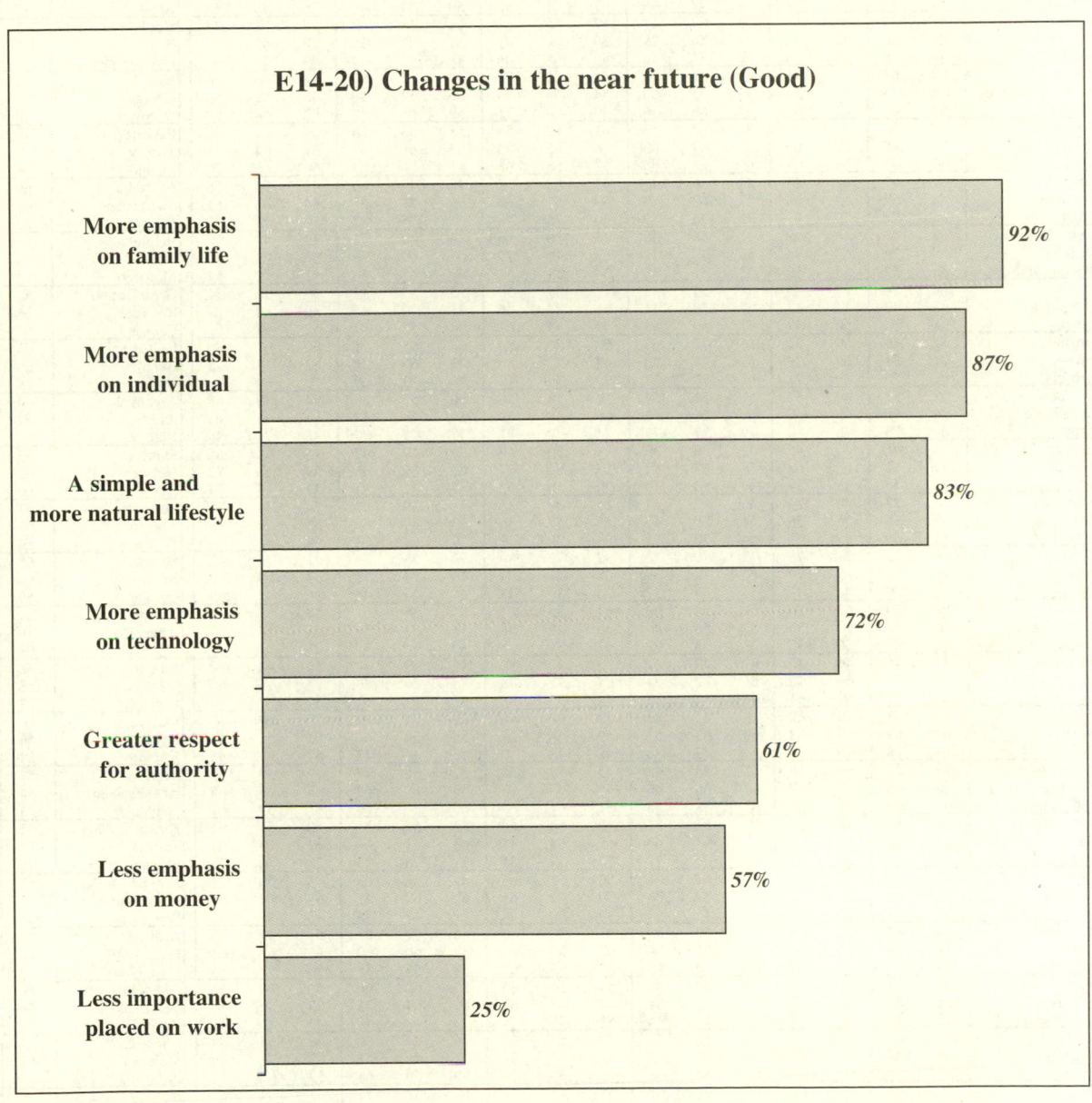

E14-20) Changes in the near future (Good)

More emphasis on family life — 92%

More emphasis on individual — 87%

A simple and more natural lifestyle — 83%

More emphasis on technology — 72%

Greater respect for authority — 61%

Less emphasis on money — 57%

Less importance placed on work — 25%

E014) LESS EMPHASIS ON MONEY

I'm going to read out a list of various changes in our way of life that might take place in the near future. If it were to happen, do you think it would be a good thing, a bad thing, or don't you mind?. Less emphasis on money

Good (%)

(WVS: V127; EVS: V192)

Country	Wave 1990	2000	Gender Male	Female	Age 16-29	30-49	50+	Education Lower	Middle	Upper	Income Lower	Middle	Upper	Values Mat	Mixed	Postm.	RANKING Country	2000
Albania	na	37	36	37	38	34	40	37	38	35	38	38	34	40	35	21	Malta	81
Algeria	na	40	40	40	36	43	42	37	41	40	39	37	40	44	37	48	Greece	78
Argentina	71	64	61	67	65	64	64	58	74	68	60	63	70	56	63	73	Croatia	77
Armenia	na	59	56	61	55	61	62	59	57	63	57	56	62	54	61	76	Spain	76
Australia	na	69	64	73	63	72	71	60	67	78	66	71	72	61	67	74	Uruguay	75
Austria	55	50	47	53	43	49	55	47	51	58	50	54	46	56	48	52	Israel	75
Azerbaijan	na	64	64	64	68	62	61	57	66	62	61	68	62	58	74	77	Northern Ireland	72
Bangladesh	na	36	40	32	39	36	29	30	44	43	31	42	35	27	42	42	France	71
Belarus	60	48	47	48	50	44	50	48	48	46	48	47	49	49	47	44	Luxembourg	71
Belgium	65	67	63	71	61	67	70	64	65	72	65	67	67	63	66	74	Italy	71
Bosnia and Herz.	na	54	52	56	49	53	60	54	54	55	60	52	50	47	57	55	Georgia	70
Brazil	62	65	62	67	67	66	56	59	68	71	59	66	70	62	66	68	Denmark	70
Bulgaria	61	58	55	61	52	62	57	61	55	59	58	56	56	60	58	56	Pakistan	70
Canada	62	65	62	69	65	69	62	58	65	73	63	66	68	57	64	71	Turkey	70
Chile	60	65	65	64	65	63	66	62	65	68	61	66	69	60	66	70	Ireland	69
China	67	47	48	45	46	48	48	43	48	64	48	49	45	44	50	56	Australia	69
Colombia	na	59	59	60	57	62	57	59	57	63	56	57	65	64	61	61	Switzerland	68
Croatia	na	77	73	81	79	75	79	80	75	78	76	75	82	77	76	82	Sweden	67
Czech Republic	52	49	48	49	55	46	48	46	50	56	49	48	48	49	48	60	Belgium	67
Denmark	78	70	65	75	65	71	71	63	76	79	67	69	76	56	70	80	Finland	66
Dominican Rep.	na	52	55	50	53	51	46	34	55	54	46	61	56	52	52	54	Morocco	66
Egypt	na	56	57	54	58	54	57	53	57	59	55	55	57	56	56	54	Great Britain	66
El Salvador	na	43	44	42	47	39	41	41	43	46	43	40	45	na	na	na	Romania	66
Estonia	na	54	50	58	57	56	51	49	54	62	54	52	57	52	55	51	Canada	65
Finland	71	66	60	72	66	74	59	60	71	82	64	65	71	60	67	75	United States	65
France	71	71	69	73	67	74	70	67	73	80	73	69	78	63	73	78	Brazil	65
Georgia	na	70	69	71	66	73	72	73	70	69	70	73	69	72	69	63	Chile	65
Germany	49	53	49	57	51	51	57	52	54	56	56	56	53	54	49	65	Argentina	64
Great Britain	64	66	63	68	68	66	66	66	68	59	59	68	68	na	na	na	Azerbaijan	64
Greece	na	78	76	80	79	77	78	71	77	81	77	77	77	78	77	85	Nigeria	63
Hungary	44	45	46	45	47	50	39	41	50	59	39	47	47	45	44	65	Slovenia	63
Iceland	59	62	55	68	58	63	62	53	62	77	63	59	65	52	63	72	Iceland	62
India	43	43	45	39	44	44	40	36	46	56	37	41	47	41	48	64	Puerto Rico	62
Indonesia	na	27	30	24	36	26	24	25	24	33	31	29	21	24	31	20	Slovakia	61
Iran	na	56	55	56	54	59	55	55	57	56	53	52	60	55	54	63	Norway	61
Ireland	73	69	67	71	64	70	71	67	70	71	70	64	71	68	68	76	Tanzania	60
Israel	na	75	71	78	72	79	72	73	72	80	72	75	79	77	75	67	Poland	60
Italy	72	71	69	72	67	74	69	68	71	77	70	75	71	63	69	78	Netherlands	60
Japan	41	39	42	37	33	45	37	26	39	43	34	44	42	36	41	49	Colombia	59
Jordan	na	59	62	56	59	58	60	61	55	61	61	58	58	58	58	66	Jordan	59
Korea, South	63	53	50	55	57	54	46	50	49	58	51	53	55	51	54	62	Armenia	59
Latvia	na	32	30	33	33	38	26	31	31	38	30	30	37	27	34	35	Mexico	58
Lithuania	33	46	46	45	49	42	47	53	42	50	42	43	44	56	42	32	Bulgaria	58
Luxembourg	na	71	66	76	65	72	74	67	71	78	73	74	73	67	70	86	Vietnam	58
Macedonia	na	52	52	51	46	52	55	44	55	58	47	51	61	57	52	40	Portugal	57
Malta	na	81	79	84	78	82	83	82	80	00	02	84	82	79	83	83	Iran	56
Mexico	68	58	59	58	60	55	63	59	56	65	58	58	63	56	57	66	Egypt	56
Moldova	na	46	46	46	44	47	46	48	43	50	46	46	47	51	43	45	Estonia	54
Montenegro	na	52	51	54	57	53	48	45	57	56	57	58	47	47	55	63	Bosnia and Herz.	54
Morocco	na	66	65	67	66	66	66	66	68	63	59	69	62	68	66	65	New Zealand	54
Netherlands	64	60	56	64	67	58	58	51	61	68	60	60	60	51	59	69	Germany	53
New Zealand	na	54	48	59	51	54	54	46	54	64	52	55	55	50	56	62	Korea, South	53
Nigeria	64	63	62	64	63	64	60	62	63	64	63	61	66	62	63	67	Taiwan	52
Northern Ireland	60	72	71	73	70	71	73	72	67	81	71	78	73	71	70	78	Montenegro	52
Norway	60	61	54	68	59	62	61	56	61	66	na	na	na	55	60	74	Dominican Rep.	52
Pakistan	na	70	70	70	68	69	78	70	72	65	67	69	75	69	71	67	Macedonia	52
Peru	na	49	46	52	49	47	54	49	50	48	51	48	48	47	49	53	Serbia	51
Philippines	na	49	49	50	47	50	50	51	50	46	46	47	53	51	47	53	Austria	50
Poland	59	60	58	62	62	61	58	62	55	65	59	60	60	60	61	61	Peru	49
Portugal	63	57	54	60	58	60	55	57	55	67	52	54	58	56	57	56	Philippines	49
Puerto Rico	na	62	65	60	63	62	61	54	56	66	55	62	66	61	60	66	Czech Republic	49
Romania	na	66	64	67	67	69	61	60	68	68	61	64	71	65	69	59	Venezuela	48
Russian Fed.	42	45	43	48	46	44	46	51	45	44	43	48	45	49	42	41	Belarus	48
Serbia	na	51	47	56	58	52	47	42	53	60	46	47	60	46	54	68	China	47
Singapore	na	38	36	40	39	38	37	32	39	51	31	41	41	39	38	39	Moldova	46
Slovakia	na	61	60	63	63	63	58	56	63	72	59	60	65	59	62	73	Lithuania	46
Slovenia	50	63	61	65	61	65	61	58	62	74	60	58	71	63	64	62	Russian Fed.	45
South Africa	45	35	37	34	33	37	38	33	38	29	28	38	47	36	34	41	Hungary	45
Spain	81	76	75	78	74	81	74	75	76	82	77	76	77	72	77	80	Ukraine	44
Sweden	66	67	61	74	66	68	68	61	65	77	70	66	66	60	65	79	India	43
Switzerland	82	68	62	74	72	64	72	67	69	65	78	70	66	59	68	77	El Salvador	43
Taiwan	na	52	51	54	59	54	44	42	53	62	49	53	56	53	53	70	Algeria	40
Tanzania	na	60	61	60	63	59	61	64	57	57	66	64	52	61	60	71	Japan	39
Turkey	56	70	70	70	73	69	66	67	72	80	69	70	73	71	68	75	Singapore	38
Uganda	na	25	29	21	19	31	29	26	22	49	35	29	28	19	27	32	Albania	37
Ukraine	na	44	47	42	44	41	48	51	43	44	45	43	44	50	41	35	Bangladesh	36
United States	71	65	59	71	58	70	65	57	63	70	64	66	66	66	64	69	South Africa	35
Uruguay	na	75	74	76	75	77	74	74	77	79	74	76	77	75	74	76	Latvia	32
Venezuela	na	48	48	49	46	48	55	50	49	45	50	44	49	46	49	48	Zimbabwe	28
Vietnam	na	58	58	57	58	59	56	57	61	57	59	55	61	69	62	50	Indonesia	27
Zimbabwe	na	28	29	27	28	27	30	26	31	14	17	31	36	29	29	13	Uganda	25
Total	60	57	55	58	56	57	58	54	57	62	55	57	59	54	58	66	Total	57

E015) LESS IMPORTANCE PLACED ON WORK

I'm going to read out a list of various changes in our way of life that might take place in the near future. If it were to happen, do you think it would be a good thing, a bad thing, or don't you mind? Less importance placed on work in our lives

(WVS: V128; EVS: V193)

Good (%)

Country	Wave 1990	Wave 2000	Gender Male	Gender Female	Age 16-29	Age 30-49	Age 50+	Education Lower	Education Middle	Education Upper	Income Lower	Income Middle	Income Upper	Values Mat	Values Mixed	Values Postm.
Albania	na	10	11	10	11	9	11	10	11	9	10	11	9	9	11	21
Algeria	na	9	9	9	10	9	9	10	9	9	9	11	8	8	9	8
Argentina	20	20	21	20	21	22	18	18	24	21	16	21	24	17	20	23
Armenia	na	22	22	22	25	19	21	26	22	19	18	20	25	24	21	10
Australia	na	32	32	32	36	36	24	28	31	36	28	33	37	25	30	37
Austria	23	30	29	32	33	29	30	28	32	37	30	29	31	32	29	32
Azerbaijan	na	30	31	29	34	28	27	29	30	30	24	34	29	27	37	27
Bangladesh	na	7	8	6	7	7	9	7	8	5	5	8	9	5	9	9
Belarus	28	20	21	19	22	22	15	18	22	14	21	21	16	18	20	25
Belgium	42	46	48	45	48	51	41	44	45	49	45	44	49	40	44	60
Bosnia and Herz.	na	14	13	14	11	13	18	15	13	15	14	14	16	12	15	13
Brazil	19	22	22	21	23	19	23	25	19	20	25	18	21	24	21	19
Bulgaria	41	36	35	37	42	40	30	34	37	39	35	34	39	35	37	44
Canada	31	33	34	32	35	38	26	25	32	40	25	30	44	34	31	35
Chile	18	35	34	35	38	36	28	29	37	40	31	37	35	30	38	30
China	8	17	22	13	17	18	17	16	18	19	19	19	16	20	16	16
Colombia	na	12	11	14	12	12	13	16	14	8	14	15	8	20	19	14
Croatia	na	33	30	35	33	36	29	31	34	33	31	32	36	32	32	34
Czech Republic	8	10	12	9	13	11	9	12	10	7	8	11	11	11	10	13
Denmark	27	34	32	35	37	42	23	27	41	46	27	36	41	22	30	48
Dominican Rep.	na	10	10	9	9	10	11	15	17	6	13	7	5	6	10	14
Egypt	na	2	3	2	2	2	3	3	1	3	3	1	2	3	2	1
El Salvador	na	18	18	17	17	19	18	21	15	15	24	13	14	na	na	na
Estonia	na	13	15	12	16	17	9	10	13	21	10	10	18	12	13	11
Finland	24	25	26	23	34	32	13	20	30	35	24	25	27	23	24	34
France	35	65	66	65	70	72	57	62	70	71	61	64	71	58	66	76
Georgia	na	38	37	38	36	38	38	44	39	30	37	42	35	40	35	38
Germany	15	40	39	41	41	46	34	37	44	35	37	37	40	44	35	48
Great Britain	33	53	54	53	63	57	47	52	56	56	48	59	59	na	na	na
Greece	na	30	32	28	32	30	25	31	30	28	34	28	26	28	28	37
Hungary	25	20	23	17	28	25	10	19	23	19	17	22	20	18	22	25
Iceland	33	43	42	44	46	52	30	31	49	57	34	47	49	33	45	54
India	7	15	14	15	16	13	16	16	14	11	9	13	18	14	16	11
Indonesia	na	5	6	4	3	5	5	6	4	4	6	4	5	4	6	na
Iran	na	16	17	16	18	14	16	16	15	16	17	15	15	14	17	17
Ireland	22	38	35	41	43	39	31	36	36	46	39	32	40	36	37	46
Israel	na	34	36	33	34	35	33	35	32	36	38	37	34	40	33	28
Italy	25	25	26	24	28	31	18	19	29	31	19	27	30	16	25	28
Japan	6	5	5	5	12	4	4	2	5	7	6	4	5	5	6	5
Jordan	na	27	26	28	26	28	30	31	25	23	26	28	28	29	25	27
Korea, South	16	12	11	12	8	15	8	13	13	9	14	11	10	11	12	13
Latvia	na	9	12	8	13	11	6	8	10	11	8	10	12	5	12	12
Lithuania	12	13	15	11	16	14	10	9	15	13	12	10	11	15	13	na
Luxembourg	na	47	49	46	54	49	41	45	47	51	44	43	54	51	44	61
Macedonia	na	24	22	26	22	21	31	23	27	21	26	23	25	25	25	23
Malta	na	31	30	32	30	35	27	26	33	30	30	31	37	31	30	39
Mexico	28	29	26	32	32	28	24	31	29	18	36	26	26	25	31	28
Moldova	na	24	25	24	26	26	21	25	25	24	26	22	27	23	27	24
Montenegro	na	20	20	21	32	20	13	17	24	21	21	21	17	17	22	22
Morocco	na	44	40	47	42	44	46	44	44	34	51	46	39	42	47	36
Netherlands	36	38	37	38	36	40	36	32	34	47	37	39	39	31	35	51
New Zealand	na	26	26	27	37	32	17	19	26	36	19	28	32	30	27	29
Nigeria	15	34	32	35	35	34	25	35	34	32	30	34	41	36	31	41
Northern Ireland	22	42	44	40	49	41	39	41	44	39	49	43	44	47	41	43
Norway	17	26	25	28	29	31	18	22	23	33	na	na	na	22	27	30
Pakistan	na	10	9	12	15	9	5	11	8	12	10	8	12	10	11	8
Peru	na	13	13	14	14	14	12	13	15	11	14	11	15	15	14	10
Philippines	na	33	33	33	30	36	32	34	34	30	32	34	32	33	34	25
Poland	30	16	16	16	21	17	13	18	14	13	14	15	22	16	17	16
Portugal	38	20	17	23	23	20	19	19	23	23	14	23	19	23	17	23
Puerto Rico	na	32	36	30	35	37	28	34	31	33	30	29	40	29	34	30
Romania	na	19	22	16	27	19	15	17	21	18	19	16	22	16	19	35
Russian Fed.	26	16	15	16	22	15	11	12	16	16	17	14	15	15	16	9
Serbia	na	14	13	14	19	13	12	16	13	12	13	15	12	13	14	15
Singapore	na	29	28	30	30	28	28	28	27	36	27	25	31	28	29	35
Slovakia	na	8	9	7	10	9	6	5	9	11	8	7	8	9	8	14
Slovenia	12	20	22	17	24	21	15	22	19	18	21	20	18	18	19	26
South Africa	14	21	22	21	21	22	21	26	16	9	27	19	18	19	22	28
Spain	50	45	47	43	53	49	37	40	49	55	42	51	46	39	46	54
Sweden	27	51	48	54	54	58	42	40	54	54	48	50	55	41	48	61
Switzerland	46	39	38	41	47	41	33	38	41	34	48	40	36	42	37	48
Taiwan	na	12	10	13	16	11	11	10	9	14	6	15	13	10	13	11
Tanzania	na	6	6	7	7	5	8	7	6	6	7	7	6	6	7	13
Turkey	16	26	27	26	26	28	22	28	23	25	30	23	24	27	26	26
Uganda	na	9	13	6	7	12	14	15	6	17	18	13	7	10	8	14
Ukraine	na	21	23	20	26	23	17	18	22	21	18	25	24	25	19	13
United States	23	32	31	34	31	35	30	35	29	34	32	31	37	28	32	36
Uruguay	na	15	16	14	20	13	14	16	12	15	13	15	16	11	16	13
Venezuela	na	21	22	20	22	19	24	20	21	22	21	24	21	23	20	18
Vietnam	na	28	28	29	29	28	28	30	26	31	29	30	26	41	28	29
Zimbabwe	na	11	14	8	11	11	11	8	15	10	5	14	14	11	11	5
Total	25	25	25	25	26	26	22	24	25	26	23	24	25	21	25	32

RANKING

Country	2000
France	65
Great Britain	53
Sweden	51
Luxembourg	47
Belgium	46
Spain	45
Morocco	44
Iceland	43
Northern Ireland	42
Germany	40
Switzerland	39
Ireland	38
Netherlands	38
Georgia	38
Bulgaria	36
Chile	35
Israel	34
Nigeria	34
Denmark	34
Philippines	33
Canada	33
Croatia	33
United States	32
Puerto Rico	32
Australia	32
Malta	31
Austria	30
Azerbaijan	30
Greece	30
Mexico	29
Singapore	29
Vietnam	28
Jordan	27
Turkey	26
New Zealand	26
Norway	26
Finland	25
Italy	25
Moldova	24
Macedonia	24
Armenia	22
Brazil	22
Ukraine	21
South Africa	21
Venezuela	21
Argentina	20
Montenegro	20
Portugal	20
Hungary	20
Belarus	20
Slovenia	20
Romania	19
El Salvador	18
China	17
Iran	16
Poland	16
Russian Fed.	16
Uruguay	15
India	15
Bosnia and Herz.	14
Serbia	14
Peru	13
Estonia	13
Lithuania	13
Colombia	12
Taiwan	12
Korea, South	12
Zimbabwe	11
Czech Republic	10
Albania	10
Pakistan	10
Dominican Rep.	10
Latvia	9
Uganda	9
Algeria	9
Slovakia	8
Bangladesh	7
Tanzania	6
Japan	5
Indonesia	5
Egypt	2
Total	25

E016) MORE EMPHASIS ON TECHNOLOGY

I'm going to read out a list of various changes in our way of life that might take place in the near future. If it were to happen, do you think it would be a good thing, a bad thing, or don't you mind?. More emphasis on the development of technology

Good (%)

(WVS: V129; EVS: V194)

Country	Wave 1990	Wave 2000	Gender Male	Gender Female	Age 16-29	Age 30-49	Age 50+	Education Lower	Education Middle	Education Upper	Income Lower	Income Middle	Income Upper	Values Mat	Values Mixed	Values Postm.	RANKING Country	RANKING 2000
Albania	na	61	62	60	65	61	58	56	64	67	55	65	65	61	60	64	China	97
Algeria	na	87	89	86	87	89	85	84	86	90	86	90	89	87	88	88	Jordan	95
Argentina	78	68	74	62	64	71	67	65	73	66	65	67	72	65	68	71	Taiwan	93
Armenia	na	83	85	81	81	85	85	84	82	86	85	86	75	80	87	77	Morocco	93
Australia	na	58	66	51	55	56	63	56	58	60	56	55	65	57	59	59	Tanzania	90
Austria	42	57	65	50	64	59	51	56	57	61	50	59	63	49	60	57	Turkey	90
Azerbaijan	na	77	79	76	82	74	77	78	74	84	75	80	85	76	79	90	Ukraine	90
Bangladesh	na	89	90	88	87	90	93	87	92	92	92	86	91	92	88	84	Egypt	89
Belarus	84	82	85	79	89	83	74	61	87	92	76	84	85	79	85	89	Bangladesh	89
Belgium	55	56	60	52	52	55	59	57	57	54	50	60	59	56	58	56	Russian Fed.	88
Bosnia and Herz.	na	70	71	68	71	69	69	62	71	71	71	69	71	71	69	74	Malta	88
Brazil	78	70	76	65	67	70	77	68	73	68	71	71	68	71	69	73	Algeria	87
Bulgaria	81	84	85	83	84	85	82	81	84	86	81	86	85	85	84	78	Venezuela	87
Canada	63	58	65	50	55	59	59	57	57	60	58	58	59	59	59	55	Latvia	87
Chile	73	56	59	53	56	56	57	54	55	63	57	52	61	53	56	61	Nigeria	86
China	95	97	98	96	96	97	96	96	97	100	97	96	97	98	96	97	Romania	85
Colombia	na	83	86	81	85	83	82	76	84	88	75	84	87	80	83	90	Iceland	85
Croatia	na	79	82	76	78	80	78	80	77	82	82	81	75	82	79	77	Bulgaria	84
Czech Republic	85	76	80	72	71	76	78	74	77	80	75	77	75	75	77	78	Colombia	83
Denmark	59	62	71	52	60	63	62	61	74	58	57	64	68	68	64	49	Armenia	83
Dominican Rep.	na	51	60	45	52	51	60	38	50	54	50	55	60	53	52	49	Georgia	82
Egypt	na	89	92	87	92	89	86	86	92	94	87	88	91	86	91	96	Belarus	82
El Salvador	na	72	74	70	75	72	68	69	73	78	72	72	76	na	na	na	Serbia	81
Estonia	84	75	78	73	75	79	72	70	76	81	73	75	76	69	78	92	Iran	80
Finland	68	55	66	44	61	54	52	54	59	53	55	52	57	53	56	55	Poland	79
France	76	58	65	52	58	57	60	57	58	63	57	56	62	57	58	61	Puerto Rico	79
Georgia	na	82	84	81	83	83	82	86	82	81	84	82	81	84	81	77	Slovenia	79
Germany	83	63	73	55	65	65	60	56	67	74	57	65	70	65	64	60	Lithuania	79
Great Britain	64	70	74	66	70	69	74	71	66	77	64	79	68	na	na	na	Croatia	79
Greece	na	52	56	49	46	53	63	68	56	45	52	55	52	53	52	52	Slovakia	79
Hungary	75	59	63	55	70	59	52	57	63	60	53	58	64	58	62	40	Vietnam	79
Iceland	69	85	89	80	82	84	88	84	85	84	81	84	89	86	85	80	Peru	78
India	85	57	61	51	65	57	49	44	62	80	44	53	67	59	68	75	Israel	78
Indonesia	na	63	59	67	66	67	58	62	61	68	65	65	59	65	63	63	Azerbaijan	77
Iran	na	80	81	79	81	83	71	72	82	87	79	80	80	80	82	84	Pakistan	77
Ireland	61	69	69	69	72	67	70	70	70	67	72	71	67	76	67	70	Moldova	77
Israel	na	78	81	75	73	79	81	78	79	76	76	78	79	82	79	72	Zimbabwe	77
Italy	60	65	66	63	67	63	64	63	66	67	60	64	70	65	64	66	Czech Republic	76
Japan	65	61	66	56	54	56	68	64	59	62	62	59	62	62	61	61	Montenegro	76
Jordan	na	95	95	94	95	95	92	93	95	97	95	94	94	95	94	93	Mexico	76
Korea, South	90	69	73	65	63	70	76	73	67	71	70	73	65	70	68	69	Estonia	75
Latvia	81	87	91	84	87	86	88	83	88	89	83	86	94	87	87	91	El Salvador	72
Lithuania	88	79	84	75	84	81	73	72	81	82	69	81	84	79	79	91	Portugal	71
Luxembourg	na	65	69	61	63	66	66	59	67	74	62	58	77	63	67	74	Brazil	70
Macedonia	na	65	66	65	68	64	64	53	72	71	62	63	72	64	70	56	Great Britain	70
Malta	na	88	92	84	91	87	87	83	89	83	85	90	91	85	89	90	Bosnia and Herz.	70
Mexico	78	76	75	76	75	77	72	73	78	80	72	76	78	68	79	79	Uganda	69
Moldova	na	77	80	75	79	76	76	73	78	80	74	81	78	79	77	70	Ireland	69
Montenegro	na	76	77	75	83	78	68	69	77	85	74	79	82	78	75	57	Korea, South	69
Morocco	na	93	93	93	93	94	92	93	94	91	90	92	90	92	94	90	Argentina	68
Netherlands	47	48	59	38	45	47	52	52	57	35	44	50	49	43	51	45	Philippines	68
New Zealand	na	35	44	29	38	35	35	29	37	42	28	35	44	39	35	37	Singapore	67
Nigeria	96	86	88	85	88	85	84	82	88	90	87	86	87	86	87	85	Luxembourg	65
Northern Ireland	60	62	68	56	72	58	62	58	63	71	65	58	73	63	59	66	Macedonia	65
Norway	47	46	56	37	46	47	45	44	47	48	na	na	na	48	46	44	Italy	65
Pakistan	na	77	76	79	74	77	84	75	80	79	75	77	79	77	77	75	Uruguay	63
Peru	na	78	80	76	77	80	76	77	79	78	75	83	77	70	80	83	Germany	63
Philippines	na	68	68	68	69	67	67	64	65	76	66	68	69	68	68	64	Indonesia	63
Poland	89	79	82	77	79	79	80	81	79	76	78	82	75	75	81	84	Denmark	62
Portugal	74	71	68	74	77	68	70	71	70	78	60	65	75	70	70	74	South Africa	62
Puerto Rico	na	79	84	77	73	80	82	83	80	79	87	77	78	93	81	70	Northern Ireland	62
Romania	na	85	87	84	88	88	81	76	88	94	79	87	87	83	88	89	Albania	61
Russian Fed.	84	88	90	86	88	88	88	88	88	90	86	89	90	88	89	83	Japan	61
Serbia	na	81	83	79	84	81	81	77	83	86	76	80	86	80	83	86	Spain	60
Singapore	na	67	71	64	66	67	70	69	66	68	71	70	65	64	69	62	Hungary	59
Slovakia	na	79	83	75	80	79	78	73	81	77	75	80	79	75	83	90	France	58
Slovenia	87	79	85	74	77	80	80	72	81	83	78	81	81	79	80	76	Australia	58
South Africa	82	62	61	63	65	61	58	58	67	59	57	62	66	60	64	59	Canada	58
Spain	66	60	63	57	63	60	58	58	61	63	56	62	61	54	62	63	Austria	57
Sweden	35	35	41	30	31	34	40	40	38	28	37	35	33	46	37	26	India	57
Switzerland	57	34	41	27	35	35	31	26	34	50	27	33	41	34	36	25	United States	57
Taiwan	na	93	93	93	99	94	86	88	96	96	94	95	94	94	94	95	Belgium	56
Tanzania	na	90	93	87	88	91	92	87	93	97	87	91	95	92	91	88	Chile	56
Turkey	90	90	91	88	89	90	90	89	90	91	88	91	90	90	90	90	Finland	55
Uganda	na	69	72	67	75	68	49	67	70	70	68	60	70	72	72	52	Greece	52
Ukraine	na	90	91	88	89	89	90	89	91	87	90	90	90	90	90	84	Dominican Rep.	51
United States	70	57	63	50	54	55	61	59	56	56	55	60	56	50	57	57	Netherlands	48
Uruguay	na	63	66	61	57	64	66	62	64	69	57	62	71	58	65	62	Norway	46
Venezuela	na	87	87	87	87	87	88	85	87	90	83	86	91	78	90	89	New Zealand	35
Vietnam	na	79	84	74	78	78	81	74	85	93	73	80	82	79	86	88	Sweden	35
Zimbabwe	na	77	79	75	77	77	74	75	78	83	78	77	81	77	76	85	Switzerland	34
Total	72	72	75	68	73	72	70	69	73	72	70	72	74	74	72	66	Total	72

E017_1) MORE EMPHASIS ON INDIVIDUAL

Here is a list of various changes in our way of life that might take place in the near future. If it were to happen do you think it would be a good thing, a bad thing, or don't you mind?. Greater emphasis on the development of the individual

Good (%)

(EVS: V195)

Country	Wave 1990	Wave 2000	Gender Male	Gender Female	Age 16-29	Age 30-49	Age 50+	Education Lower	Education Middle	Education Upper	Income Lower	Income Middle	Income Upper	Values Mat	Values Mixed	Values Postm.	RANKING Country	RANKING 2000
Albania	na	na	na	na	na	na	na	na	na	na	na	na	na	na	na	na	Malta	96
Algeria	na	na	na	na	na	na	na	na	na	na	na	na	na	na	na	na	Iceland	96
Argentina	95	na	na	na	na	na	na	na	na	na	na	na	na	na	na	na	Turkey	95
Armenia	na	na	na	na	na	na	na	na	na	na	na	na	na	na	na	na	Ukraine	94
Australia	na	na	na	na	na	na	na	na	na	na	na	na	na	na	na	na	Denmark	93
Austria	76	89	89	89	87	88	91	87	89	96	83	90	90	73	88	96	Greece	93
Azerbaijan	na	na	na	na	na	na	na	na	na	na	na	na	na	na	na	na	Italy	92
Bangladesh	na	na	na	na	na	na	na	na	na	na	na	na	na	na	na	na	Russian Fed.	92
Belarus	96	87	89	86	93	90	79	73	91	97	84	89	89	84	91	93	Bulgaria	92
Belgium	81	86	86	86	87	86	85	80	84	94	82	86	90	77	87	95	Ireland	92
Bosnia and Herz.	na	na	na	na	na	na	na	na	na	na	na	na	na	na	na	na	Latvia	90
Brazil	92	na	na	na	na	na	na	na	na	na	na	na	na	na	na	na	Romania	90
Bulgaria	87	92	92	92	91	95	89	91	91	95	89	93	94	93	92	91	Finland	90
Canada	85	na	na	na	na	na	na	na	na	na	na	na	na	na	na	na	Sweden	90
Chile	90	na	na	na	na	na	na	na	na	na	na	na	na	na	na	na	Germany	89
China	40	na	na	na	na	na	na	na	na	na	na	na	na	na	na	na	Austria	89
Colombia	na	na	na	na	na	na	na	na	na	na	na	na	na	na	na	na	Czech Republic	88
Croatia	na	75	77	72	75	73	77	67	78	82	74	73	78	63	75	82	Belarus	87
Czech Republic	94	88	87	88	88	88	87	85	89	94	86	87	89	83	89	89	Poland	87
Denmark	93	93	93	94	91	95	93	91	95	96	92	95	94	93	94	97	Lithuania	87
Dominican Rep.	na	na	na	na	na	na	na	na	na	na	na	na	na	na	na	na	France	87
Egypt	na	na	na	na	na	na	na	na	na	na	na	na	na	na	na	na	Slovakia	86
El Salvador	na	na	na	na	na	na	na	na	na	na	na	na	na	na	na	na	Netherlands	86
Estonia	85	83	81	86	81	85	83	77	86	87	82	83	85	82	85	85	Spain	86
Finland	93	90	88	91	93	90	87	87	93	91	89	89	91	86	91	93	Belgium	86
France	88	87	86	88	87	87	87	85	87	91	87	87	89	82	87	93	Northern Ireland	84
Georgia	na	na	na	na	na	na	na	na	na	na	na	na	na	na	na	na	Estonia	83
Germany	88	89	89	89	92	91	87	84	93	96	85	89	88	85	90	94	Portugal	79
Great Britain	78	75	74	76	72	74	80	71	77	80	70	80	75	na	na	na	Luxembourg	78
Greece	na	93	92	93	94	92	90	92	92	93	92	95	90	94	92	96	Great Britain	75
Hungary	72	71	69	73	79	70	65	65	79	82	68	67	76	68	75	67	Croatia	75
Iceland	94	96	94	98	91	97	98	94	97	97	95	96	97	92	97	97	Hungary	71
India	71	na	na	na	na	na	na	na	na	na	na	na	na	na	na	na		
Indonesia	na	na	na	na	na	na	na	na	na	na	na	na	na	na	na	na		
Iran	na	na	na	na	na	na	na	na	na	na	na	na	na	na	na	na		
Ireland	90	92	92	91	91	93	91	90	92	94	90	91	94	88	92	95		
Israel	na	na	na	na	na	na	na	na	na	na	na	na	na	na	na	na		
Italy	93	92	91	94	90	93	94	91	93	96	89	93	95	90	92	96		
Japan	70	na	na	na	na	na	na	na	na	na	na	na	na	na	na	na		
Jordan	na	na	na	na	na	na	na	na	na	na	na	na	na	na	na	na		
Korea, South	84	na	na	na	na	na	na	na	na	na	na	na	na	na	na	na		
Latvia	86	90	90	90	87	89	92	89	90	92	89	87	94	92	90	86		
Lithuania	91	87	85	88	93	88	82	85	86	94	78	89	91	86	87	94		
Luxembourg	na	78	78	78	75	79	79	77	77	84	75	84	84	71	81	85		
Macedonia	na	na	na	na	na	na	na	na	na	na	na	na	na	na	na	na		
Malta	na	96	97	96	96	96	97	96	96	100	96	98	96	97	97	95		
Mexico	88	na	na	na	na	na	na	na	na	na	na	na	na	na	na	na		
Moldova	na	na	na	na	na	na	na	na	na	na	na	na	na	na	na	na		
Montenegro	na	na	na	na	na	na	na	na	na	na	na	na	na	na	na	na		
Morocco	na	na	na	na	na	na	na	na	na	na	na	na	na	na	na	na		
Netherlands	84	86	86	86	88	87	85	80	90	88	84	87	89	77	85	93		
New Zealand	na	na	na	na	na	na	na	na	na	na	na	na	na	na	na	na		
Nigeria	93	na	na	na	na	na	na	na	na	na	na	na	na	na	na	na		
Northern Ireland	81	84	84	83	87	84	83	83	83	86	84	86	84	81	83	85		
Norway	88	na	na	na	na	na	na	na	na	na	na	na	na	na	na	na		
Pakistan	na	na	na	na	na	na	na	na	na	na	na	na	na	na	na	na		
Peru	na	na	na	na	na	na	na	na	na	na	na	na	na	na	na	na		
Philippines	na	na	na	na	na	na	na	na	na	na	na	na	na	na	na	na		
Poland	94	87	87	88	87	86	90	86	87	94	87	88	84	83	89	94		
Portugal	76	79	76	81	88	75	76	78	78	83	74	72	83	77	80	74		
Puerto Rico	na	na	na	na	na	na	na	na	na	na	na	na	na	na	na	na		
Romania	na	90	91	90	89	91	90	85	91	96	87	90	92	88	92	96		
Russian Fed.	89	92	91	93	93	93	91	90	92	95	90	93	94	92	93	79		
Serbia	na	na	na	na	na	na	na	na	na	na	na	na	na	na	na	na		
Singapore	na	na	na	na	na	na	na	na	na	na	na	na	na	na	na	na		
Slovakia	na	86	86	87	85	89	85	80	89	89	83	86	89	85	87	92		
Slovenia	81	na	na	na	na	na	na	na	na	na	na	na	na	na	na	na		
South Africa	90	na	na	na	na	na	na	na	na	na	na	na	na	na	na	na		
Spain	91	86	84	88	85	88	85	86	84	90	85	86	90	79	85	93		
Sweden	88	90	89	90	92	89	89	85	92	91	87	90	93	86	89	93		
Switzerland	91	na	na	na	na	na	na	na	na	na	na	na	na	na	na	na		
Taiwan	na	na	na	na	na	na	na	na	na	na	na	na	na	na	na	na		
Tanzania	na	na	na	na	na	na	na	na	na	na	na	na	na	na	na	na		
Turkey	93	95	94	96	95	95	96	93	97	99	94	95	97	90	96	98		
Uganda	na	na	na	na	na	na	na	na	na	na	na	na	na	na	na	na		
Ukraine	na	94	93	95	97	92	95	97	93	96	94	94	95	94	95	98		
United States	87	na	na	na	na	na	na	na	na	na	na	na	na	na	na	na		
Uruguay	na	na	na	na	na	na	na	na	na	na	na	na	na	na	na	na		
Venezuela	na	na	na	na	na	na	na	na	na	na	na	na	na	na	na	na		
Vietnam	na	na	na	na	na	na	na	na	na	na	na	na	na	na	na	na		
Zimbabwe	na	na	na	na	na	na	na	na	na	na	na	na	na	na	na	na		
Total	86	87	87	88	88	88	87	83	89	92	86	87	89	85	89	92	Total	87

E018) GREATER RESPECT FOR AUTHORITY

I'm going to read out a list of various changes in our way of life that might take place in the near future. If it were to happen, do you think it would be a good thing, a bad thing, or don't you mind?. Greater respect for authority

Good (%)

(WVS: V130; EVS: V196)

Country	Wave 1990	Wave 2000	Gender Male	Gender Female	Age 16-29	Age 30-49	Age 50+	Education Lower	Education Middle	Education Upper	Income Lower	Income Middle	Income Upper	Values Mat	Values Mixed	Values Postm.
Albania	na	34	35	34	30	33	41	34	33	38	35	33	35	37	35	23
Algeria	na	63	62	63	59	63	68	67	63	59	66	59	63	66	65	47
Argentina	69	72	72	73	66	73	77	80	62	58	81	74	60	82	76	58
Armenia	na	63	63	63	60	61	70	67	62	64	56	70	63	61	64	58
Australia	na	73	71	75	68	69	82	80	78	61	79	72	67	92	78	61
Austria	47	39	35	42	30	34	50	49	32	23	52	37	33	59	43	25
Azerbaijan	na	61	62	59	62	59	65	72	58	65	53	68	68	59	61	83
Bangladesh	na	92	92	91	91	92	91	89	95	92	92	90	94	93	91	93
Belarus	71	72	73	72	71	70	76	68	73	79	72	73	73	73	73	63
Belgium	50	63	60	67	55	56	73	76	65	52	70	67	56	79	65	41
Bosnia and Herz.	na	26	27	26	21	26	33	34	24	26	29	29	21	28	27	21
Brazil	81	83	84	82	78	85	89	88	82	72	87	85	77	90	82	70
Bulgaria	78	69	73	65	51	72	75	76	65	68	74	71	62	69	70	66
Canada	64	66	64	69	59	63	75	76	69	55	67	72	60	72	70	59
Chile	80	56	56	56	53	55	61	61	57	44	61	55	49	60	57	48
China	24	64	59	69	68	61	68	74	59	54	67	62	61	61	65	74
Colombia	na	89	89	88	86	90	88	90	87	90	88	87	91	89	87	89
Croatia	na	56	59	53	50	55	61	66	52	43	66	56	51	56	59	47
Czech Republic	65	52	54	51	45	46	62	55	50	46	58	57	44	57	53	44
Denmark	35	38	40	36	45	34	39	49	29	23	45	38	23	54	40	17
Dominican Rep.	na	56	58	54	56	54	90	57	56	57	53	61	65	57	59	51
Egypt	na	86	87	85	86	86	88	86	85	88	88	85	85	85	88	81
El Salvador	na	86	86	85	85	85	87	88	87	79	91	85	80	na	na	na
Estonia	na	44	45	43	35	40	53	45	43	46	46	48	41	44	44	38
Finland	26	39	39	40	40	35	44	42	37	35	43	40	38	38	41	31
France	59	69	66	71	61	64	77	76	61	57	72	67	66	82	70	46
Georgia	na	75	76	75	68	77	81	77	75	74	77	77	73	78	73	71
Germany	57	46	46	45	26	42	58	52	40	42	49	47	43	57	47	25
Great Britain	72	71	67	75	59	69	82	75	70	63	71	74	68	na	na	na
Greece	na	17	18	16	11	16	32	30	18	14	18	17	16	22	16	13
Hungary	61	69	68	69	72	61	74	73	65	52	66	70	68	72	68	57
Iceland	42	47	49	44	40	46	54	55	43	36	47	47	46	54	47	27
India	54	43	48	38	45	44	41	41	43	49	37	45	45	49	47	36
Indonesia	na	37	36	39	31	43	34	34	38	39	33	44	38	35	40	36
Iran	na	71	72	70	73	72	66	66	75	74	70	71	71	77	71	72
Ireland	83	76	75	77	66	73	86	87	73	65	84	75	69	84	75	69
Israel	na	58	57	60	55	57	64	68	59	52	67	58	55	44	61	65
Italy	49	51	53	50	42	47	61	57	47	46	55	51	49	65	53	40
Japan	6	4	3	5	4	3	5	7	4	2	6	5	3	4	4	2
Jordan	na	90	91	90	89	93	87	92	90	88	89	91	90	94	89	78
Korea, South	14	19	18	21	14	20	24	34	21	16	22	16	19	20	19	21
Latvia	na	49	50	48	42	44	56	52	46	55	50	46	52	50	49	41
Lithuania	53	44	46	43	46	41	46	51	40	47	40	40	45	48	42	55
Luxembourg	na	53	55	51	50	46	62	62	51	42	63	53	44	63	57	30
Macedonia	na	49	48	49	44	47	54	44	54	43	55	44	48	49	50	32
Malta	na	92	93	92	91	90	95	93	93	88	91	93	93	93	93	86
Mexico	65	76	74	77	71	78	80	79	72	74	77	75	76	77	77	60
Moldova	na	48	48	48	39	46	59	52	49	43	57	50	43	51	44	41
Montenegro	na	45	44	47	33	46	53	55	40	35	42	42	51	53	39	29
Morocco	na	89	87	91	85	91	95	92	80	74	89	82	86	93	87	72
Netherlands	51	67	66	68	58	64	74	82	66	53	71	68	59	89	72	41
New Zealand	na	50	48	52	37	44	60	55	53	41	51	47	51	57	55	35
Nigeria	91	83	83	83	82	83	84	82	82	85	83	82	84	85	82	77
Northern Ireland	82	77	75	78	70	71	86	80	73	76	85	77	76	85	78	59
Norway	32	32	30	33	30	29	36	34	30	30	na	na	na	50	30	22
Pakistan	na	62	63	61	51	64	77	71	52	52	71	64	49	66	57	67
Peru	na	80	79	82	78	83	79	83	81	78	80	80	82	78	82	82
Philippines	na	70	71	68	69	72	67	69	71	68	72	70	68	71	70	65
Poland	73	55	60	49	44	50	68	56	53	51	53	58	49	54	55	58
Portugal	74	78	75	80	70	74	85	83	72	51	88	75	74	83	76	66
Puerto Rico	na	93	92	95	90	92	97	94	94	93	97	93	92	99	94	94
Romania	na	85	83	86	78	83	89	87	82	88	85	85	84	84	87	74
Russian Fed.	68	56	54	58	49	55	62	59	54	62	55	55	59	58	55	55
Serbia	na	55	56	54	46	49	65	61	53	51	60	59	49	59	52	52
Singapore	na	52	53	51	52	52	52	55	52	47	57	51	48	51	54	45
Slovakia	na	68	65	71	63	67	74	68	69	64	72	67	68	72	67	56
Slovenia	66	43	40	46	28	38	60	56	41	30	54	43	39	51	44	33
South Africa	88	73	70	76	75	71	73	71	74	78	69	73	77	77	72	62
Spain	69	59	56	63	46	55	72	68	51	50	64	59	56	69	60	41
Sweden	22	22	24	21	26	21	21	29	25	12	23	25	17	27	24	15
Switzerland	46	31	32	29	20	28	41	37	30	20	36	34	26	44	32	17
Taiwan	na	45	42	47	43	46	44	48	46	42	51	45	40	43	49	38
Tanzania	na	82	82	83	82	81	87	86	80	75	86	83	76	84	83	79
Turkey	65	68	67	69	65	68	75	76	62	43	77	64	53	72	70	54
Uganda	na	73	77	70	72	73	82	77	72	69	76	70	69	76	74	66
Ukraine	na	64	62	66	56	62	70	70	64	62	66	62	63	67	62	62
United States	78	70	65	76	61	71	77	69	75	68	75	70	64	73	73	61
Uruguay	na	58	61	56	44	48	72	69	45	37	65	60	49	76	59	42
Venezuela	na	91	93	90	90	91	93	92	92	90	90	90	93	87	92	95
Vietnam	na	80	82	79	75	82	82	77	86	84	78	80	83	82	87	86
Zimbabwe	na	90	87	92	90	89	90	90	89	92	94	88	91	89	90	94
Total	58	61	61	61	59	59	65	68	58	55	64	62	59	65	61	50

RANKING

Country	2000
Puerto Rico	93
Malta	92
Bangladesh	92
Venezuela	91
Jordan	90
Zimbabwe	90
Morocco	89
Colombia	89
Egypt	86
El Salvador	86
Romania	85
Brazil	83
Nigeria	83
Tanzania	82
Peru	80
Vietnam	80
Portugal	78
Northern Ireland	77
Ireland	76
Mexico	76
Georgia	75
Uganda	73
Australia	73
South Africa	73
Belarus	72
Argentina	72
Iran	71
Great Britain	71
United States	70
Philippines	70
Bulgaria	69
France	69
Hungary	69
Slovakia	68
Turkey	68
Netherlands	67
Canada	66
Ukraine	64
China	64
Belgium	63
Armenia	63
Algeria	63
Pakistan	62
Azerbaijan	61
Spain	59
Israel	58
Uruguay	58
Russian Fed.	56
Chile	56
Dominican Rep.	56
Croatia	56
Serbia	55
Poland	55
Luxembourg	53
Czech Republic	52
Singapore	52
Italy	51
New Zealand	50
Latvia	49
Macedonia	49
Moldova	48
Iceland	47
Germany	46
Montenegro	45
Taiwan	45
Lithuania	44
Estonia	44
India	43
Slovenia	43
Finland	39
Austria	39
Denmark	38
Indonesia	37
Albania	34
Norway	32
Switzerland	31
Bosnia and Herz.	26
Sweden	22
Korea, South	19
Greece	17
Japan	4
Total	61

E019) MORE EMPHASIS ON FAMILY LIFE

I'm going to read out a list of various changes in our way of life that might take place in the near future. If it were to happen, do you think it would be a good thing, a bad thing, or don't you mind?. More emphasis on family life

Good (%)

(WVS: V131; EVS: V197)

Country	Wave		Gender		Age			Education			Income			Values			RANKING Country	2000
	1990	2000	Male	Female	16-29	30-49	50+	Lower	Middle	Upper	Lower	Middle	Upper	Mat	Mixed	Postm.		
Albania	na	96	94	98	93	97	98	95	96	97	97	92	98	97	95	97	Malta	99
Algeria	na	96	96	97	96	96	97	98	95	96	96	97	94	96	96	98	Egypt	99
Argentina	96	97	96	98	96	97	98	97	96	95	97	98	96	97	97	96	Morocco	99
Armenia	na	92	91	93	92	92	92	94	91	93	94	93	90	93	91	89	Colombia	99
Australia	na	95	94	96	92	94	98	96	95	93	96	94	94	94	97	92	Jordan	98
Austria	92	92	90	95	86	92	96	95	91	86	89	96	91	95	93	89	Brazil	98
Azerbaijan	na	95	95	94	94	95	96	97	96	92	95	96	94	95	94	99	Venezuela	98
Bangladesh	na	92	92	92	92	92	95	93	93	89	95	91	93	95	90	97	Argentina	97
Belarus	95	92	88	94	90	94	90	89	92	94	89	93	93	93	91	91	Turkey	97
Belgium	85	90	88	91	85	89	93	94	90	85	91	91	89	94	90	84	Lithuania	97
Bosnia and Herz.	na	82	79	84	82	82	81	83	81	84	82	79	86	85	81	81	Iceland	96
Brazil	98	98	97	99	98	98	97	98	98	97	98	98	97	99	98	95	Algeria	96
Bulgaria	90	95	93	97	91	97	96	97	94	95	97	95	92	96	94	94	Albania	96
Canada	94	94	91	97	91	95	95	95	95	91	94	96	93	94	95	92	Taiwan	96
Chile	98	92	90	93	92	92	91	91	93	92	92	93	90	93	91	92	Zimbabwe	96
China	74	92	90	95	89	94	91	94	92	88	94	92	91	95	90	88	Slovenia	96
Colombia	na	99	99	99	99	99	99	99	99	99	99	99	99	98	98	99	Romania	96
Croatia	na	93	93	93	91	92	95	96	92	87	95	93	92	96	94	91	Tanzania	96
Czech Republic	94	93	91	95	90	92	95	94	92	92	93	95	91	95	93	89	Denmark	95
Denmark	95	95	94	97	91	97	96	96	94	94	95	97	96	90	96	95	Montenegro	95
Dominican Rep.	na	75	76	74	74	73	100	75	79	74	71	77	82	75	75	76	Norway	95
Egypt	na	99	99	99	100	99	100	99	100	99	100	99	99	99	99	100	Bulgaria	95
El Salvador	na	95	95	94	94	95	96	93	97	96	94	95	96	na	na	na	Finland	95
Estonia	86	89	86	91	86	88	91	88	90	89	90	90	90	90	89	92	Serbia	95
Finland	96	95	94	96	93	96	95	95	95	95	94	96	95	96	94	95	El Salvador	95
France	90	91	89	93	88	90	94	95	87	86	92	93	90	95	92	82	Peru	95
Georgia	na	94	94	94	92	95	94	94	94	93	93	94	95	94	94	96	Poland	95
Germany	92	90	87	92	79	92	93	89	90	93	86	93	92	92	91	86	Slovakia	95
Great Britain	88	90	87	93	81	92	95	95	88	84	89	96	91	94	95	91	Azerbaijan	95
Greece	na	91	88	93	88	92	97	97	93	89	92	91	91	96	92	87	Australia	95
Hungary	94	92	92	92	94	90	93	91	94	91	87	93	94	94	90	84	Ireland	95
Iceland	96	96	94	99	92	97	99	96	96	97	97	97	96	97	96	95	Puerto Rico	95
India	75	75	78	72	77	76	71	69	77	87	66	75	81	82	80	89	Uruguay	95
Indonesia	na	83	82	85	93	83	80	77	83	90	78	87	86	86	82	81	Nigeria	94
Iran	na	91	90	92	91	93	89	89	92	92	89	94	90	93	92	90	Georgia	94
Ireland	94	95	92	97	90	96	96	96	95	92	95	97	92	94	95	93	United States	94
Israel	na	93	92	93	91	93	95	95	93	91	90	94	95	91	93	95	Canada	94
Italy	93	92	91	94	90	91	95	95	91	88	92	94	90	95	93	90	Russian Fed.	94
Japan	85	89	88	90	88	91	87	82	91	88	88	93	87	89	90	93	Croatia	93
Jordan	na	98	100	97	99	99	96	98	98	99	98	99	98	99	98	98	Korea, South	93
Korea, South	89	93	93	94	92	93	94	89	92	95	91	95	94	94	93	91	Singapore	93
Latvia	85	92	88	95	89	90	95	93	91	94	95	90	92	94	91	93	Czech Republic	93
Lithuania	96	97	96	97	98	97	95	96	97	97	96	98	96	96	98	97	Israel	93
Luxembourg	na	88	86	90	85	88	90	90	88	88	89	90	88	93	89	83	China	92
Macedonia	na	82	82	81	75	84	84	80	84	80	82	83	83	80	85	77	Austria	92
Malta	na	99	99	100	98	100	100	100	99	99	100	100	99	99	100	97	Italy	92
Mexico	91	91	92	91	92	92	90	91	92	93	91	91	93	90	93	88	Bangladesh	92
Moldova	na	87	86	88	86	86	88	89	85	88	90	85	84	90	85	84	Latvia	92
Montenegro	na	95	93	97	93	96	97	96	94	98	92	97	96	97	96	84	Armenia	92
Morocco	na	99	99	99	99	99	100	99	99	100	99	99	99	99	99	98	Hungary	92
Netherlands	66	68	66	71	70	62	74	80	70	55	67	71	64	83	72	51	Philippines	92
New Zealand	na	88	84	92	81	88	91	88	92	86	91	88	88	90	90	89	Chile	92
Nigeria	92	94	94	94	94	95	94	92	95	96	93	95	95	96	93	92	Belarus	92
Northern Ireland	92	91	89	92	84	89	96	92	89	93	93	94	91	91	93	87	Mexico	91
Norway	95	95	93	97	95	94	97	96	96	94	na	na	na	97	95	93	France	91
Pakistan	na	89	87	90	84	91	92	93	84	83	94	89	84	92	84	92	Greece	91
Peru	na	95	94	96	94	96	94	95	95	95	95	94	96	93	95	97	Portugal	91
Philippines	na	92	91	93	94	92	89	88	92	97	89	94	91	94	91	90	Iran	91
Poland	97	95	94	96	90	95	98	95	96	91	97	95	91	96	95	89	Northern Ireland	91
Portugal	95	91	90	93	94	86	93	91	90	93	94	81	94	92	90	92	Ukraine	91
Puerto Rico	na	95	95	95	95	94	95	94	95	95	97	94	94	97	94	98	Germany	90
Romania	na	96	95	96	91	97	97	95	96	96	95	96	96	96	96	93	Great Britain	90
Russian Fed.	95	94	91	96	89	94	95	94	94	93	94	94	93	95	92	94	Belgium	90
Serbia	na	95	94	96	89	96	97	94	95	96	95	96	96	95	95	93	Estonia	89
Singapore	na	93	92	94	93	92	97	94	94	89	91	94	94	96	93	93	Switzerland	89
Slovakia	na	95	94	96	92	96	95	94	96	93	95	96	96	95	95	94	Pakistan	89
Slovenia	91	96	95	96	96	95	96	96	97	90	98	96	93	98	95	97	Japan	89
South Africa	94	79	78	81	81	79	77	77	81	95	72	82	87	78	82	72	New Zealand	88
Spain	89	88	87	89	83	87	92	91	85	83	90	86	85	91	88	82	Vietnam	88
Sweden	85	78	77	79	75	77	81	85	78	73	73	81	79	84	80	70	Luxembourg	88
Switzerland	91	89	86	92	84	87	94	93	88	88	91	95	87	92	89	88	Spain	88
Taiwan	na	96	96	96	97	97	93	93	98	97	95	98	97	97	98	97	Moldova	87
Tanzania	na	96	95	96	95	95	98	96	95	95	96	97	92	97	95	100	Indonesia	83
Turkey	95	97	96	97	95	98	98	98	96	91	98	97	93	98	97	94	Bosnia and Herz.	82
Uganda	na	80	86	75	80	80	81	83	78	80	76	73	77	84	79	72	Macedonia	82
Ukraine	na	91	88	93	86	89	95	95	92	86	92	92	86	92	90	88	Uganda	80
United States	95	94	92	96	90	96	95	91	97	94	94	95	94	89	95	94	South Africa	79
Uruguay	na	95	95	94	93	92	97	94	96	90	96	94	94	96	96	92	Sweden	78
Venezuela	na	98	97	98	98	97	98	97	98	98	94	98	99	98	97	98	India	75
Vietnam	na	88	88	89	90	90	85	87	92	88	86	91	88	93	91	92	Dominican Rep.	75
Zimbabwe	na	96	96	96	95	97	95	97	94	100	95	97	96	96	96	99	Netherlands	68
Total	91	92	91	93	90	92	93	93	92	90	91	92	92	93	92	89	Total	92

E020_1) A SIMPLE AND MORE NATURAL LIFESTYLE

Here is a list of various changes in our way of life that might take place in the near future. If it were to happen do you think it would be a good thing, a bad thing, or don't you mind?. A simple and more natural lifestyle

Good (%)

(EVS: V198)

Country	Wave		Gender		Age			Education			Income			Values		
	1990	2000	Male	Female	16-29	30-49	50+	Lower	Middle	Upper	Lower	Middle	Upper	Mat	Mixed	Postm.
Albania	na	na	na	na	na	na	na	na	na	na	na	na	na	na	na	na
Algeria	na	na	na	na	na	na	na	na	na	na	na	na	na	na	na	na
Argentina	92	na	na	na	na	na	na	na	na	na	na	na	na	na	na	na
Armenia	na	na	na	na	na	na	na	na	na	na	na	na	na	na	na	na
Australia	na	na	na	na	na	na	na	na	na	na	na	na	na	na	na	na
Austria	85	82	76	87	67	83	88	86	79	75	87	83	75	83	81	83
Azerbaijan	na	na	na	na	na	na	na	na	na	na	na	na	na	na	na	na
Bangladesh	na	na	na	na	na	na	na	na	na	na	na	na	na	na	na	na
Belarus	90	80	76	83	75	82	82	78	80	80	77	83	79	80	82	68
Belgium	84	85	81	89	76	85	90	89	85	83	91	90	80	85	86	84
Bosnia and Herz.	na	na	na	na	na	na	na	na	na	na	na	na	na	na	na	na
Brazil	93	na	na	na	na	na	na	na	na	na	na	na	na	na	na	na
Bulgaria	82	79	76	83	71	80	83	82	77	82	81	82	76	80	79	94
Canada	84	na	na	na	na	na	na	na	na	na	na	na	na	na	na	na
Chile	93	na	na	na	na	na	na	na	na	na	na	na	na	na	na	na
China	51	na	na	na	na	na	na	na	na	na	na	na	na	na	na	na
Colombia	na	na	na	na	na	na	na	na	na	na	na	na	na	na	na	na
Croatia	na	97	97	98	93	98	99	98	98	95	100	98	96	99	98	96
Czech Republic	86	82	81	83	79	84	82	82	82	84	82	85	79	84	82	81
Denmark	85	81	75	87	72	82	86	83	75	81	81	82	83	74	82	85
Dominican Rep.	na	na	na	na	na	na	na	na	na	na	na	na	na	na	na	na
Egypt	na	na	na	na	na	na	na	na	na	na	na	na	na	na	na	na
El Salvador	na	na	na	na	na	na	na	na	na	na	na	na	na	na	na	na
Estonia	84	86	85	87	80	87	89	84	86	90	86	89	85	84	88	86
Finland	91	80	71	88	72	82	81	81	78	78	85	78	76	80	79	84
France	92	94	93	94	90	93	96	95	93	91	96	95	92	94	93	94
Georgia	na	na	na	na	na	na	na	na	na	na	na	na	na	na	na	na
Germany	66	71	66	75	59	72	75	70	72	72	72	72	75	74	68	75
Great Britain	80	75	72	78	74	72	80	79	77	60	78	78	73	na	na	na
Greece	na	94	93	94	94	94	95	94	95	93	95	95	93	94	94	96
Hungary	85	84	84	84	87	84	82	82	88	83	78	83	87	82	85	94
Iceland	79	78	76	80	67	79	86	79	76	78	77	81	74	73	79	82
India	80	na	na	na	na	na	na	na	na	na	na	na	na	na	na	na
Indonesia	na	na	na	na	na	na	na	na	na	na	na	na	na	na	na	na
Iran	na	na	na	na	na	na	na	na	na	na	na	na	na	na	na	na
Ireland	87	82	79	86	69	86	89	88	80	79	87	82	77	86	81	83
Israel	na	na	na	na	na	na	na	na	na	na	na	na	na	na	na	na
Italy	93	89	86	92	85	89	91	90	89	87	90	90	88	88	89	90
Japan	76	na	na	na	na	na	na	na	na	na	na	na	na	na	na	na
Jordan	na	na	na	na	na	na	na	na	na	na	na	na	na	na	na	na
Korea, South	66	na	na	na	na	na	na	na	na	na	na	na	na	na	na	na
Latvia	80	82	80	83	76	79	86	86	81	78	82	83	80	86	80	82
Lithuania	89	90	92	89	95	93	84	88	91	90	89	88	92	90	90	95
Luxembourg	na	85	83	87	83	84	88	85	86	85	81	89	87	83	85	91
Macedonia	na	na	na	na	na	na	na	na	na	na	na	na	na	na	na	na
Malta	na	96	95	96	91	96	99	90	96	88	97	98	94	96	96	94
Mexico	83	na	na	na	na	na	na	na	na	na	na	na	na	na	na	na
Moldova	na	na	na	na	na	na	na	na	na	na	na	na	na	na	na	na
Montenegro	na	na	na	na	na	na	na	na	na	na	na	na	na	na	na	na
Morocco	na	na	na	na	na	na	na	na	na	na	na	na	na	na	na	na
Netherlands	78	67	58	75	57	63	76	75	60	67	75	63	62	67	66	70
New Zealand	na	na	na	na	na	na	na	na	na	na	na	na	na	na	na	na
Nigeria	90	na	na	na	na	na	na	na	na	na	na	na	na	na	na	na
Northern Ireland	86	75	70	79	68	75	78	76	75	75	78	73	71	78	74	76
Norway	80	na	na	na	na	na	na	na	na	na	na	na	na	na	na	na
Pakistan	na	na	na	na	na	na	na	na	na	na	na	na	na	na	na	na
Peru	na	na	na	na	na	na	na	na	na	na	na	na	na	na	na	na
Philippines	na	na	na	na	na	na	na	na	na	na	na	na	na	na	na	na
Poland	89	86	87	85	77	87	90	90	83	77	88	86	81	87	86	84
Portugal	92	81	79	83	78	81	83	83	78	73	86	74	78	82	80	76
Puerto Rico	na	na	na	na	na	na	na	na	na	na	na	na	na	na	na	na
Romania	na	84	80	88	79	84	87	86	83	82	84	85	84	85	84	71
Russian Fed.	89	59	58	59	59	58	59	62	60	53	62	61	53	61	57	57
Serbia	na	na	na	na	na	na	na	na	na	na	na	na	na	na	na	na
Singapore	na	na	na	na	na	na	na	na	na	na	na	na	na	na	na	na
Slovakia	na	88	87	90	86	88	90	89	87	88	89	89	88	88	88	88
Slovenia	90	92	90	93	90	91	93	92	92	89	94	93	91	93	91	95
South Africa	86	na	na	na	na	na	na	na	na	na	na	na	na	na	na	na
Spain	93	90	89	91	87	90	92	93	87	90	91	92	86	88	90	90
Sweden	90	84	79	89	74	85	89	89	81	84	82	85	84	87	82	88
Switzerland	91	na	na	na	na	na	na	na	na	na	na	na	na	na	na	na
Taiwan	na	na	na	na	na	na	na	na	na	na	na	na	na	na	na	na
Tanzania	na	na	na	na	na	na	na	na	na	na	na	na	na	na	na	na
Turkey	53	67	64	70	63	70	75	74	58	58	77	62	58	71	66	65
Uganda	na	na	na	na	na	na	na	na	na	na	na	na	na	na	na	na
Ukraine	na	64	61	67	55	66	69	73	68	52	70	62	62	67	62	65
United States	85	na	na	na	na	na	na	na	na	na	na	na	na	na	na	na
Uruguay	na	na	na	na	na	na	na	na	na	na	na	na	na	na	na	na
Venezuela	na	na	na	na	na	na	na	na	na	na	na	na	na	na	na	na
Vietnam	na	na	na	na	na	na	na	na	na	na	na	na	na	na	na	na
Zimbabwe	na	na	na	na	na	na	na	na	na	na	na	na	na	na	na	na
Total	83	83	80	85	78	83	85	84	82	81	84	83	81	83	83	85

RANKING

Country	2000
Croatia	97
Malta	96
Greece	94
France	94
Slovenia	92
Lithuania	90
Spain	90
Italy	89
Slovakia	88
Estonia	86
Poland	86
Belgium	85
Luxembourg	85
Romania	84
Hungary	84
Sweden	84
Ireland	82
Czech Republic	82
Austria	82
Latvia	82
Denmark	81
Portugal	81
Finland	80
Belarus	80
Bulgaria	79
Iceland	78
Northern Ireland	75
Great Britain	75
Germany	71
Turkey	67
Netherlands	67
Ukraine	64
Russian Fed.	59
Total	83

E021_1) MORE POWER TO LOCAL AUTHORITIES

Here is a list of various changes in our way of life that might take place in the near future. If it were to happen do you think it would be a good thing, a bad thing, or don't you mind?. More power to local authorities.

Good (%)

(EVS: V199)

Country	Wave		Gender		Age			Education			Income			Values			RANKING Country	2000
	1990	2000	Male	Female	16-29	30-49	50+	Lower	Middle	Upper	Lower	Middle	Upper	Mat	Mixed	Postm.		
Albania	na	na	na	na	na	na	na	na	na	na	na	na	na	na	na	na	Slovakia	74
Algeria	na	na	na	na	na	na	na	na	na	na	na	na	na	na	na	na	Romania	71
Argentina	na	na	na	na	na	na	na	na	na	na	na	na	na	na	na	na	Czech Republic	70
Armenia	na	na	na	na	na	na	na	na	na	na	na	na	na	na	na	na	Malta	68
Australia	na	na	na	na	na	na	na	na	na	na	na	na	na	na	na	na	Turkey	59
Austria	na	38	39	37	34	40	39	40	37	36	37	44	36	46	41	34	Ukraine	57
Azerbaijan	na	na	na	na	na	na	na	na	na	na	na	na	na	na	na	na	Poland	55
Bangladesh	na	na	na	na	na	na	na	na	na	na	na	na	na	na	na	na	Russian Fed.	54
Belarus	na	32	34	31	29	29	39	32	32	35	33	33	31	32	34	33	France	52
Belgium	na	32	33	32	26	29	38	33	31	33	37	34	28	32	32	35	Estonia	52
Bosnia and Herz.	na	na	na	na	na	na	na	na	na	na	na	na	na	na	na	na	Bulgaria	51
Brazil	na	na	na	na	na	na	na	na	na	na	na	na	na	na	na	na	Greece	51
Bulgaria	na	51	57	46	38	52	58	50	50	56	56	54	46	46	55	61	Lithuania	50
Canada	na	na	na	na	na	na	na	na	na	na	na	na	na	na	na	na	Iceland	49
Chile	na	na	na	na	na	na	na	na	na	na	na	na	na	na	na	na	Northern Ireland	48
China	na	na	na	na	na	na	na	na	na	na	na	na	na	na	na	na	Ireland	47
Colombia	na	na	na	na	na	na	na	na	na	na	na	na	na	na	na	na	Finland	46
Croatia	na	46	50	43	41	46	49	52	42	48	55	46	42	45	45	50	Croatia	46
Czech Republic	na	70	71	69	57	71	76	68	70	79	71	72	68	69	70	79	Germany	46
Denmark	na	44	43	45	42	49	39	40	47	50	39	47	53	33	42	58	Denmark	44
Dominican Rep.	na	na	na	na	na	na	na	na	na	na	na	na	na	na	na	na	Italy	42
Egypt	na	na	na	na	na	na	na	na	na	na	na	na	na	na	na	na	Latvia	42
El Salvador	na	na	na	na	na	na	na	na	na	na	na	na	na	na	na	na	Slovenia	42
Estonia	na	52	57	48	42	52	57	50	51	56	54	58	45	45	56	51	Spain	40
Finland	na	46	42	50	39	50	48	44	50	51	42	50	44	38	49	49	Austria	38
France	na	52	51	54	42	54	56	55	46	50	56	54	47	52	53	51	Luxembourg	38
Georgia	na	na	na	na	na	na	na	na	na	na	na	na	na	na	na	na	Great Britain	38
Germany	na	46	48	44	39	45	50	45	47	48	43	46	52	49	43	53	Sweden	35
Great Britain	na	38	37	38	46	38	34	39	38	37	41	33	40	na	na	na	Belarus	32
Greece	na	51	52	50	44	53	62	55	47	54	51	52	48	47	51	54	Belgium	32
Hungary	na	25	25	24	31	25	20	28	17	20	20	26	27	23	26	11	Netherlands	26
Iceland	na	49	49	50	37	55	53	52	46	50	47	51	51	54	46	58	Hungary	25
India	na	na	na	na	na	na	na	na	na	na	na	na	na	na	na	na		
Indonesia	na	na	na	na	na	na	na	na	na	na	na	na	na	na	na	na		
Iran	na	na	na	na	na	na	na	na	na	na	na	na	na	na	na	na		
Ireland	na	47	48	46	34	46	59	53	45	42	58	44	41	49	48	40		
Israel	na	na	na	na	na	na	na	na	na	na	na	na	na	na	na	na		
Italy	na	42	43	41	38	41	45	41	42	46	42	42	46	43	42	44		
Japan	na	na	na	na	na	na	na	na	na	na	na	na	na	na	na	na		
Jordan	na	na	na	na	na	na	na	na	na	na	na	na	na	na	na	na		
Korea, South	na	na	na	na	na	na	na	na	na	na	na	na	na	na	na	na		
Latvia	na	42	41	43	23	38	53	46	38	49	43	43	41	40	44	34		
Lithuania	na	50	50	50	50	48	53	56	48	48	50	47	51	50	51	46		
Luxembourg	na	38	40	36	32	35	46	44	35	38	40	39	40	39	38	38		
Macedonia	na	na	na	na	na	na	na	na	na	na	na	na	na	na	na	na		
Malta	na	68	68	67	62	65	74	68	66	74	65	76	73	68	67	74		
Mexico	na	na	na	na	na	na	na	na	na	na	na	na	na	na	na	na		
Moldova	na	na	na	na	na	na	na	na	na	na	na	na	na	na	na	na		
Montenegro	na	na	na	na	na	na	na	na	na	na	na	na	na	na	na	na		
Morocco	na	na	na	na	na	na	na	na	na	na	na	na	na	na	na	na		
Netherlands	na	26	23	29	26	28	25	19	28	31	27	28	26	22	26	29		
New Zealand	na	na	na	na	na	na	na	na	na	na	na	na	na	na	na	na		
Nigeria	na	na	na	na	na	na	na	na	na	na	na	na	na	na	na	na		
Northern Ireland	na	48	47	49	49	47	51	52	45	48	60	46	46	50	48	46		
Norway	na	na	na	na	na	na	na	na	na	na	na	na	na	na	na	na		
Pakistan	na	na	na	na	na	na	na	na	na	na	na	na	na	na	na	na		
Peru	na	na	na	na	na	na	na	na	na	na	na	na	na	na	na	na		
Philippines	na	na	na	na	na	na	na	na	na	na	na	na	na	na	na	na		
Poland	na	55	58	51	44	55	61	51	56	66	53	55	56	47	59	56		
Portugal	na	57	58	57	46	56	66	61	54	36	62	56	52	59	55	62		
Puerto Rico	na	na	na	na	na	na	na	na	na	na	na	na	na	na	na	na		
Romania	na	71	67	75	60	71	76	74	68	72	70	73	69	72	71	58		
Russian Fed.	na	54	52	56	43	54	62	58	53	54	52	55	57	57	50	46		
Serbia	na	na	na	na	na	na	na	na	na	na	na	na	na	na	na	na		
Singapore	na	na	na	na	na	na	na	na	na	na	na	na	na	na	na	na		
Slovakia	na	74	75	73	69	74	77	68	75	83	74	71	76	71	77	77		
Slovenia	na	42	43	41	27	38	56	44	40	45	49	43	46	44	41	41		
South Africa	na	na	na	na	na	na	na	na	na	na	na	na	na	na	na	na		
Spain	na	40	41	39	29	34	52	51	34	30	44	40	38	49	38	35		
Sweden	na	35	33	37	37	34	35	27	37	39	39	35	32	36	34	42		
Switzerland	na	na	na	na	na	na	na	na	na	na	na	na	na	na	na	na		
Taiwan	na	na	na	na	na	na	na	na	na	na	na	na	na	na	na	na		
Tanzania	na	na	na	na	na	na	na	na	na	na	na	na	na	na	na	na		
Turkey	na	59	60	58	54	62	67	63	53	57	60	60	56	66	59	53		
Uganda	na	na	na	na	na	na	na	na	na	na	na	na	na	na	na	na		
Ukraine	na	57	57	57	49	54	66	69	53	61	58	55	60	59	55	67		
United States	na	na	na	na	na	na	na	na	na	na	na	na	na	na	na	na		
Uruguay	na	na	na	na	na	na	na	na	na	na	na	na	na	na	na	na		
Venezuela	na	na	na	na	na	na	na	na	na	na	na	na	na	na	na	na		
Vietnam	na	na	na	na	na	na	na	na	na	na	na	na	na	na	na	na		
Zimbabwe	na	na	na	na	na	na	na	na	na	na	na	na	na	na	na	na		
Total	na	47	48	47	41	47	52	48	47	49	49	48	47	49	48	47	Total	47

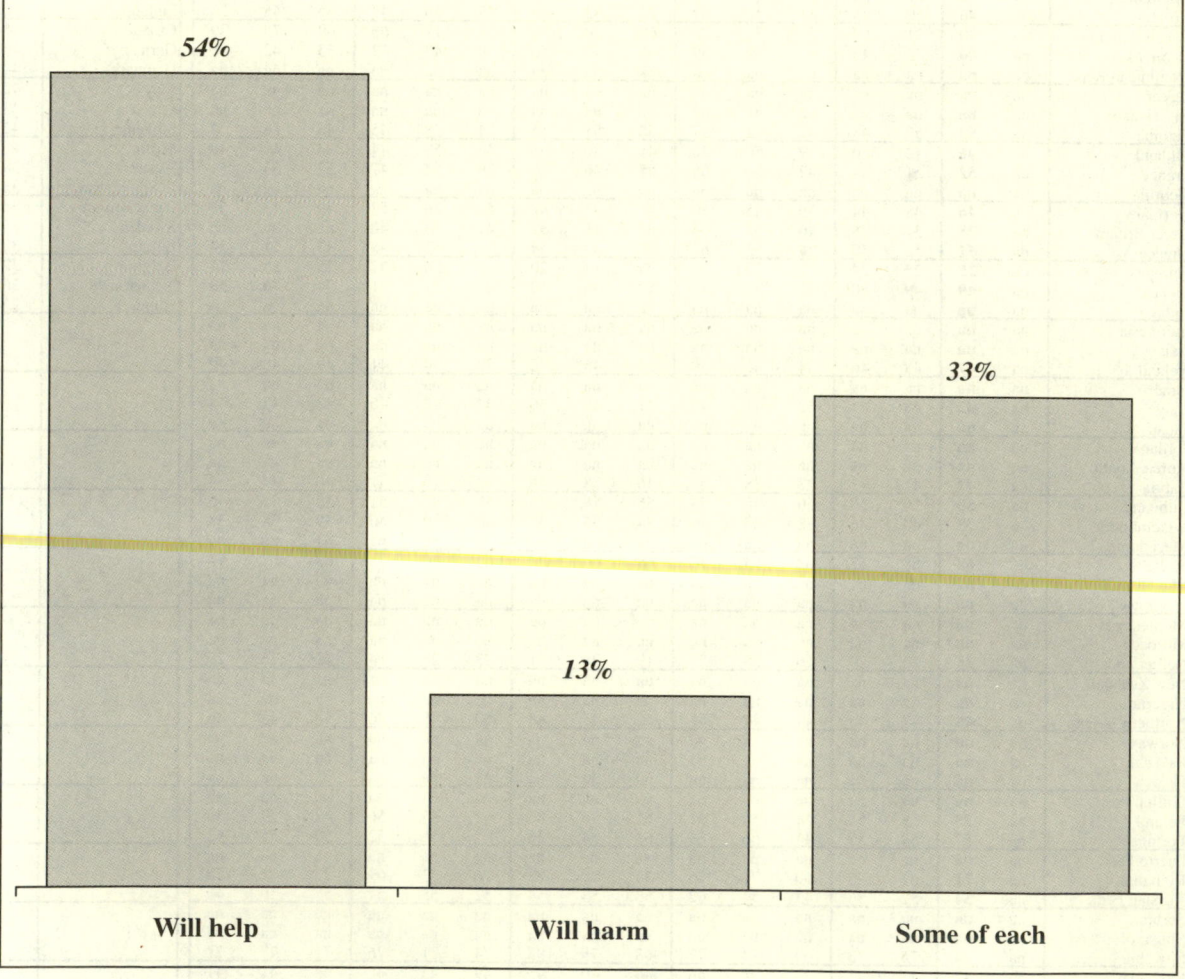

E22) In the long run, do you think the scientific advances we are making will help or harm mankind?

54%

33%

13%

Will help   Will harm   Some of each

E022) OPINION ABOUT SCIENTIFIC ADVANCE

In the long run, do you think the scientific advances we are making will help or harm mankind?

Will help (%) (WVS: V132; EVS: o25)

Country	Wave 1990	Wave 2000	Male	Female	16-29	30-49	50+	Education Lower	Middle	Upper	Income Lower	Middle	Upper	Mat	Mixed	Postm.	RANKING Country	2000
Albania	na	55	56	54	52	56	57	55	55	55	54	55	55	55	56	50	Nigeria	87
Algeria	na	55	55	55	53	53	63	67	59	42	61	57	51	59	55	44	Turkey	86
Argentina	47	51	52	50	53	52	48	50	50	61	49	50	55	52	49	53	Egypt	80
Armenia	na	74	76	73	78	71	72	69	76	68	75	72	75	76	72	77	China	80
Australia	na	57	62	52	52	60	57	50	54	66	51	59	65	55	57	58	Vietnam	78
Austria	31	35	39	32	41	37	31	29	41	42	33	32	39	26	37	37	Morocco	78
Azerbaijan	na	61	61	61	61	63	57	55	62	62	62	64	59	61	63	65	Armenia	74
Bangladesh	na	70	67	73	67	71	74	74	68	63	72	68	72	69	71	67	Iran	73
Belarus	38	56	58	54	51	60	55	51	58	55	54	55	60	56	58	54	Zimbabwe	72
Belgium	34	na	na	na	na	na	na	na	na	na	na	na	na	na	na	na	Georgia	70
Bosnia and Herz.	na	54	54	54	54	52	56	58	55	46	58	57	50	60	51	74	Bangladesh	70
Brazil	64	66	68	64	65	66	67	63	67	74	64	66	67	65	66	71	Jordan	68
Bulgaria	62	na	na	na	na	na	na	na	na	na	na	na	na	na	na	na	Philippines	68
Canada	55	52	60	44	52	52	52	49	50	58	49	52	56	55	52	51	Colombia	67
Chile	43	42	44	40	47	41	38	43	43	37	45	38	43	38	44	43	Iceland	66
China	58	80	79	81	64	81	89	91	74	51	82	81	75	78	77	75	Brazil	66
Colombia	na	67	67	67	70	66	65	67	67	68	68	65	70	68	67	69	Spain	66
Croatia	na	38	41	35	35	38	41	44	35	35	42	39	36	47	38	33	Macedonia	65
Czech Republic	30	na	na	na	na	na	na	na	na	na	na	na	na	na	na	na	Venezuela	63
Denmark	43	na	na	na	na	na	na	na	na	na	na	na	na	na	na	na	Lithuania	62
Dominican Rep.	na	44	54	37	40	50	64	53	50	40	47	48	46	51	44	32	Azerbaijan	61
Egypt	na	80	77	83	78	80	82	88	78	63	85	82	74	84	77	71	India	60
El Salvador	na	49	48	50	52	50	42	50	47	51	55	46	48	na	na	na	Uganda	58
Estonia	52	na	na	na	na	na	na	na	na	na	na	na	na	na	na	na	South Africa	57
Finland	42	na	na	na	na	na	na	na	na	na	na	na	na	na	na	na	Australia	57
France	42	na	na	na	na	na	na	na	na	na	na	na	na	na	na	na	United States	56
Georgia	na	70	70	70	72	69	70	78	71	63	75	71	64	70	70	73	Belarus	56
Germany	52	51	61	44	56	54	47	49	53	53	51	54	58	53	53	45	Moldova	56
Great Britain	48	40	44	36	42	43	35	39	38	46	34	47	42	na	na	na	Albania	55
Greece	na	na	na	na	na	na	na	na	na	na	na	na	na	na	na	na	Algeria	55
Hungary	55	na	na	na	na	na	na	na	na	na	na	na	na	na	na	na	Bosnia and Herz.	54
Iceland	54	66	75	58	66	69	64	62	68	73	60	69	70	67	66	70	Peru	54
India	51	60	62	56	65	60	52	57	64	59	58	62	59	59	59	50	Canada	52
Indonesia	na	49	53	47	39	54	50	59	47	46	51	51	48	57	45	46	Germany	51
Iran	na	73	73	74	70	74	82	81	74	62	74	73	72	75	71	73	Argentina	51
Ireland	40	41	41	41	43	38	42	38	42	44	41	35	47	42	40	45	Mexico	50
Israel	na	na	na	na	na	na	na	na	na	na	na	na	na	na	na	na	Indonesia	49
Italy	37	31	36	26	27	31	33	29	31	35	27	32	35	30	32	29	El Salvador	49
Japan	26	24	32	17	17	22	29	30	20	29	25	21	26	24	23	25	Korea, South	49
Jordan	na	68	71	66	63	70	76	75	64	60	70	71	69	72	67	58	Tanzania	49
Korea, South	40	49	54	44	49	46	55	61	47	51	49	50	48	49	50	40	Puerto Rico	46
Latvia	34	na	na	na	na	na	na	na	na	na	na	na	na	na	na	na	Serbia	45
Lithuania	61	62	68	57	63	67	56	56	63	67	64	63	63	53	64	73	Sweden	44
Luxembourg	na	na	na	na	na	na	na	na	na	na	na	na	na	na	na	na	Dominican Rep.	44
Macedonia	na	65	67	63	69	61	67	69	63	62	67	62	65	63	66	76	Montenegro	44
Malta	na	na	na	na	na	na	na	na	na	na	na	na	na	na	na	na	Chile	42
Mexico	44	50	52	49	55	48	46	47	53	55	49	48	57	47	49	60	Pakistan	41
Moldova	na	56	54	57	47	58	60	58	60	46	59	56	52	55	58	37	Ireland	41
Montenegro	na	44	47	41	46	46	41	45	42	45	29	43	54	50	41	19	Great Britain	40
Morocco	na	78	76	80	73	80	87	84	61	47	78	74	80	82	76	58	Uruguay	40
Netherlands	37	na	na	na	na	na	na	na	na	na	na	na	na	na	na	na	Singapore	39
New Zealand	na	26	34	20	19	25	30	24	21	32	20	23	34	28	26	29	Switzerland	39
Nigeria	79	87	88	87	89	87	84	87	88	87	86	90	88	90	86	91	Norway	39
Northern Ireland	46	38	40	36	41	37	37	35	39	42	38	33	37	37	37	43	Croatia	38
Norway	36	39	53	25	37	43	34	30	39	47	na	na	na	36	38	46	Northern Ireland	38
Pakistan	na	41	41	42	41	43	39	44	39	38	36	45	39	46	35	58	Taiwan	36
Peru	na	54	54	53	52	56	52	58	55	50	55	58	46	56	54	52	Austria	35
Philippines	na	68	69	68	70	69	65	70	65	71	63	72	69	65	71	70	Slovenia	35
Poland	70	na	na	na	na	na	na	na	na	na	na	na	na	na	na	na	Italy	31
Portugal	47	na	na	na	na	na	na	na	na	na	na	na	na	na	na	na	New Zealand	26
Puerto Rico	na	46	46	47	41	49	47	45	41	50	48	47	45	49	49	40	Japan	24
Romania	na	na	na	na	na	na	na	na	na	na	na	na	na	na	na	na		
Russian Fed.	60	na	na	na	na	na	na	na	na	na	na	na	na	na	na	na		
Serbia	na	45	43	46	40	43	48	46	45	41	45	46	48	45	46	43		
Singapore	na	39	42	37	38	39	44	43	37	37	38	39	39	36	40	46		
Slovakia	na	na	na	na	na	na	na	na	na	na	na	na	na	na	na	na		
Slovenia	41	35	40	30	25	34	42	39	32	36	35	38	36	36	35	32		
South Africa	57	57	57	57	54	60	56	60	53	57	57	61	54	53	60	51		
Spain	46	66	68	64	65	68	65	66	65	70	67	75	62	65	68	60		
Sweden	47	44	48	41	42	45	45	39	40	56	43	41	52	39	45	45		
Switzerland	na	39	43	34	39	38	39	42	38	44	37	40	43	33	41	39		
Taiwan	na	36	36	36	21	32	56	48	37	24	46	34	27	35	32	51		
Tanzania	na	49	48	49	47	49	53	56	41	41	55	45	51	50	49	41		
Turkey	72	86	88	85	84	88	87	88	85	84	87	87	83	89	86	84		
Uganda	na	58	62	55	70	50	33	54	60	54	56	58	55	57	60	56		
Ukraine	na	na	na	na	na	na	na	na	na	na	na	na	na	na	na	na		
United States	63	56	61	50	44	56	65	47	58	59	52	55	65	56	56	55		
Uruguay	na	40	42	38	33	41	42	37	42	48	42	36	43	50	39	36		
Venezuela	na	63	63	62	62	64	62	59	64	63	61	56	68	64	63	61		
Vietnam	na	78	74	83	69	79	85	82	77	60	79	82	74	82	77	76		
Zimbabwe	na	72	70	74	76	68	65	74	70	23	76	74	64	72	71	80		
Total	48	54	57	52	55	55	52	57	53	51	55	55	55	58	54	50	Total	54

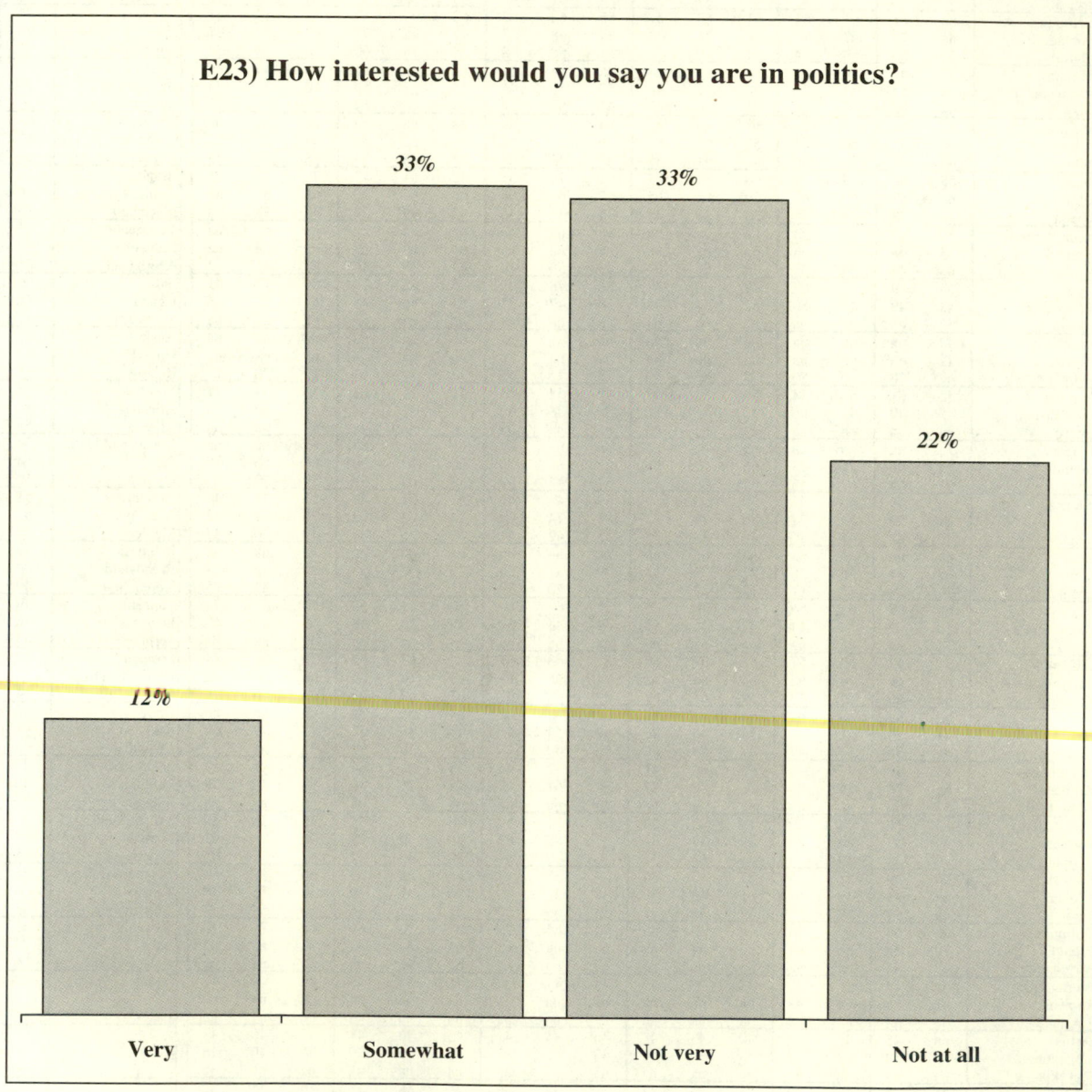

E23) How interested would you say you are in politics?

12%   33%   33%   22%

Very   Somewhat   Not very   Not at all

E023) INTERESTED IN POLITICS

How interested would you say you are in politics?

Very / Somewhat interested (%)

(WVS: V133; EVS: o17)

Country	Wave		Gender		Age			Education			Income			Values			Country	2000
	1990	2000	Male	Female	16-29	30-49	50+	Lower	Middle	Upper	Lower	Middle	Upper	Mat	Mixed	Postm.		
Albania	na	41	54	28	26	44	47	35	43	49	38	41	43	37	43	49	Vietnam	80
Algeria	na	24	29	20	21	29	23	17	21	33	21	22	27	19	26	36	Tanzania	72
Argentina	30	18	19	18	13	18	23	13	23	36	13	18	24	12	19	23	China	71
Armenia	na	52	61	44	43	57	57	45	49	64	51	53	53	48	57	37	Israel	70
Australia	na	56	59	53	40	60	65	44	51	71	51	57	66	45	55	60	Czech Republic	70
Austria	54	67	75	60	61	67	71	58	71	89	59	68	73	47	67	75	Norway	69
Azerbaijan	na	43	49	36	42	43	45	33	37	55	39	46	46	36	54	66	Austria	67
Bangladesh	na	41	55	23	40	40	46	30	48	60	30	39	53	37	44	41	Netherlands	67
Belarus	na	47	58	37	46	51	42	27	51	65	38	49	55	39	54	68	United States	66
Belgium	30	39	48	30	32	41	40	19	38	56	31	34	50	24	38	62	Japan	64
Bosnia and Herz.	na	39	50	29	29	39	49	34	37	48	37	39	41	32	41	51	Germany	61
Brazil	46	31	32	30	32	30	31	20	34	61	22	30	41	18	33	55	Denmark	61
Bulgaria	73	49	54	45	35	57	49	40	50	64	46	54	53	42	60	53	New Zealand	60
Canada	58	49	55	43	35	48	57	42	43	64	39	50	58	42	45	57	Iran	56
Chile	37	25	30	21	26	25	25	19	25	39	21	23	35	20	24	39	Australia	56
China	67	71	79	62	75	66	79	65	73	83	68	72	73	71	75	81	Nigeria	53
Colombia	na	29	31	27	25	33	28	22	23	42	22	26	39	27	27	36	Armenia	52
Croatia	na	na	na	na	na	na	na	na	na	na	na	na	na	na	na	na	South Africa	52
Czech Republic	na	70	72	67	57	70	77	63	75	86	68	70	72	62	72	82	Jordan	51
Denmark	54	61	67	55	55	59	65	49	66	80	55	60	74	34	61	76	Uganda	50
Dominican Rep.	na	46	45	47	43	50	64	34	43	48	47	47	45	38	47	50	Iceland	50
Egypt	na	43	54	30	40	42	48	36	46	55	42	43	47	37	48	51	Philippines	50
El Salvador	na	15	17	14	19	12	15	9	16	33	9	14	31	na	na	na	Korea, South	50
Estonia	60	na	na	na	na	na	na	na	na	na	na	na	na	na	na	na	Georgia	50
Finland	48	28	32	24	22	25	34	24	30	44	23	27	34	17	31	40	Bulgaria	49
France	38	37	45	28	27	36	42	29	38	56	28	36	50	25	37	53	Canada	49
Georgia	na	50	53	47	34	57	58	45	48	57	53	50	46	50	49	60	Moldova	48
Germany	85	61	71	52	57	61	62	50	66	87	51	60	64	50	63	75	Peru	48
Great Britain	49	37	47	28	31	36	43	27	37	67	25	33	51	40	41	49	Luxembourg	47
Greece	na	42	52	35	35	44	53	39	36	47	39	44	49	40	41	49	Belarus	47
Hungary	52	na	na	na	na	na	na	na	na	na	na	na	na	na	na	na	Macedonia	46
Iceland	47	50	57	44	37	53	57	39	51	72	41	48	62	41	49	74	Dominican Rep.	46
India	47	45	56	28	46	45	43	36	51	56	40	42	50	46	52	54	Lithuania	46
Indonesia	na	37	45	30	54	38	28	19	36	52	32	41	45	36	38	44	Montenegro	45
Iran	na	56	60	51	62	56	40	40	57	70	54	57	58	47	61	72	India	45
Ireland	37	43	50	37	40	42	47	35	42	63	29	43	56	38	42	61	Switzerland	44
Israel	na	70	77	65	65	72	74	57	69	80	61	75	77	74	72	58	Ireland	43
Italy	29	32	42	24	29	34	33	22	35	53	25	34	41	19	32	42	Azerbaijan	43
Japan	62	64	72	57	44	53	81	67	61	69	65	63	65	58	66	77	Egypt	43
Jordan	na	51	50	51	54	52	42	37	56	70	42	48	66	41	58	72	Ukraine	42
Korea, South	73	50	60	39	39	50	63	46	51	49	50	49	51	45	55	50	Slovenia	42
Latvia	79	na	na	na	na	na	na	na	na	na	na	na	na	na	na	na	Puerto Rico	42
Lithuania	74	46	52	40	34	49	51	38	44	69	42	44	53	36	51	50	Poland	42
Luxembourg	na	47	50	45	30	50	55	32	52	63	34	52	64	39	47	62	Greece	42
Macedonia	na	46	54	39	36	47	53	40	48	55	41	49	53	45	49	44	Bangladesh	41
Malta	na	na	na	na	na	na	na	na	na	na	na	na	na	na	na	na	Taiwan	41
Mexico	38	34	38	31	36	32	33	28	38	53	31	35	42	25	39	40	Albania	41
Moldova	na	48	53	43	36	54	50	33	51	57	45	49	49	42	54	60	Turkey	40
Montenegro	na	45	55	35	40	44	50	36	49	57	48	44	49	43	49	55	Northern Ireland	40
Morocco	na	20	26	13	25	18	12	14	36	56	18	23	22	11	25	41	Bosnia and Herz.	39
Netherlands	58	67	72	61	57	67	71	51	67	81	60	68	74	48	65	79	Russian Fed.	39
New Zealand	na	60	63	57	41	58	69	56	56	65	63	54	62	51	58	66	Belgium	39
Nigeria	35	53	61	44	55	50	47	51	52	57	50	51	57	49	54	60	Serbia	38
Northern Ireland	34	40	50	31	32	40	44	39	36	51	31	42	44	32	42	56	Great Britain	37
Norway	72	69	72	65	61	73	69	58	70	78	na	na	na	51	69	87	Uruguay	37
Pakistan	na	30	38	21	30	30	30	24	36	39	22	33	37	26	36	25	Indonesia	37
Peru	na	48	52	43	50	46	45	36	46	58	40	50	58	39	50	53	France	37
Philippines	na	50	51	48	50	52	45	48	49	53	50	45	57	50	50	50	Singapore	36
Poland	49	42	49	35	31	42	48	35	45	65	41	46	35	38	43	58	Mexico	34
Portugal	31	29	37	23	31	33	26	26	30	53	13	31	40	24	31	40	Italy	32
Puerto Rico	na	42	48	39	37	43	44	27	33	49	33	42	51	41	41	47	Zimbabwe	31
Romania	18	na	na	na	na	na	na	na	na	na	na	na	na	na	na	na	Brazil	31
Russian Fed.	53	39	49	31	29	40	45	31	36	54	34	41	43	37	42	56	Pakistan	30
Serbia	na	38	46	31	36	39	38	28	40	50	33	39	48	31	46	48	Colombia	29
Singapore	na	36	39	33	38	35	33	30	39	41	31	35	41	32	36	54	Portugal	29
Slovakia	na	na	na	na	na	na	na	na	na	na	na	na	na	na	na	na	Spain	28
Slovenia	58	42	50	35	33	38	53	32	43	58	38	43	52	44	42	43	Finland	28
South Africa	57	52	58	43	47	58	43	50	53	63	54	53	49	40	59	61	Chile	25
Spain	25	28	35	22	27	33	25	20	31	49	21	29	41	22	28	43	Venezuela	24
Sweden	47	na	na	na	na	na	na	na	na	na	na	na	na	na	na	na	Algeria	24
Switzerland	66	44	51	36	35	42	49	31	43	74	41	36	52	28	47	47	Morocco	20
Taiwan	na	41	44	38	32	46	33	30	50	46	38	41	46	35	48	54	Argentina	18
Tanzania	na	72	71	72	69	71	81	76	66	67	74	73	69	71	74	79	El Salvador	15
Turkey	48	40	49	32	40	41	38	32	47	74	32	44	58	31	42	55		
Uganda	na	50	60	41	46	57	48	48	50	65	59	62	56	51	50	54		
Ukraine	na	42	51	35	37	41	46	34	39	56	41	43	45	38	45	75		
United States	61	66	69	62	59	61	78	57	62	71	63	66	68	59	65	70		
Uruguay	na	37	42	34	36	42	34	25	51	64	24	36	53	31	37	45		
Venezuela	na	24	28	21	22	25	29	20	24	31	24	23	28	26	24	21		
Vietnam	na	80	88	72	77	81	80	76	86	82	72	80	84	76	86	82		
Zimbabwe	na	31	38	26	32	32	30	33	29	22	34	32	31	28	33	37		
Total	52	45	52	39	40	46	49	36	46	58	41	45	51	39	48	56	Total	45

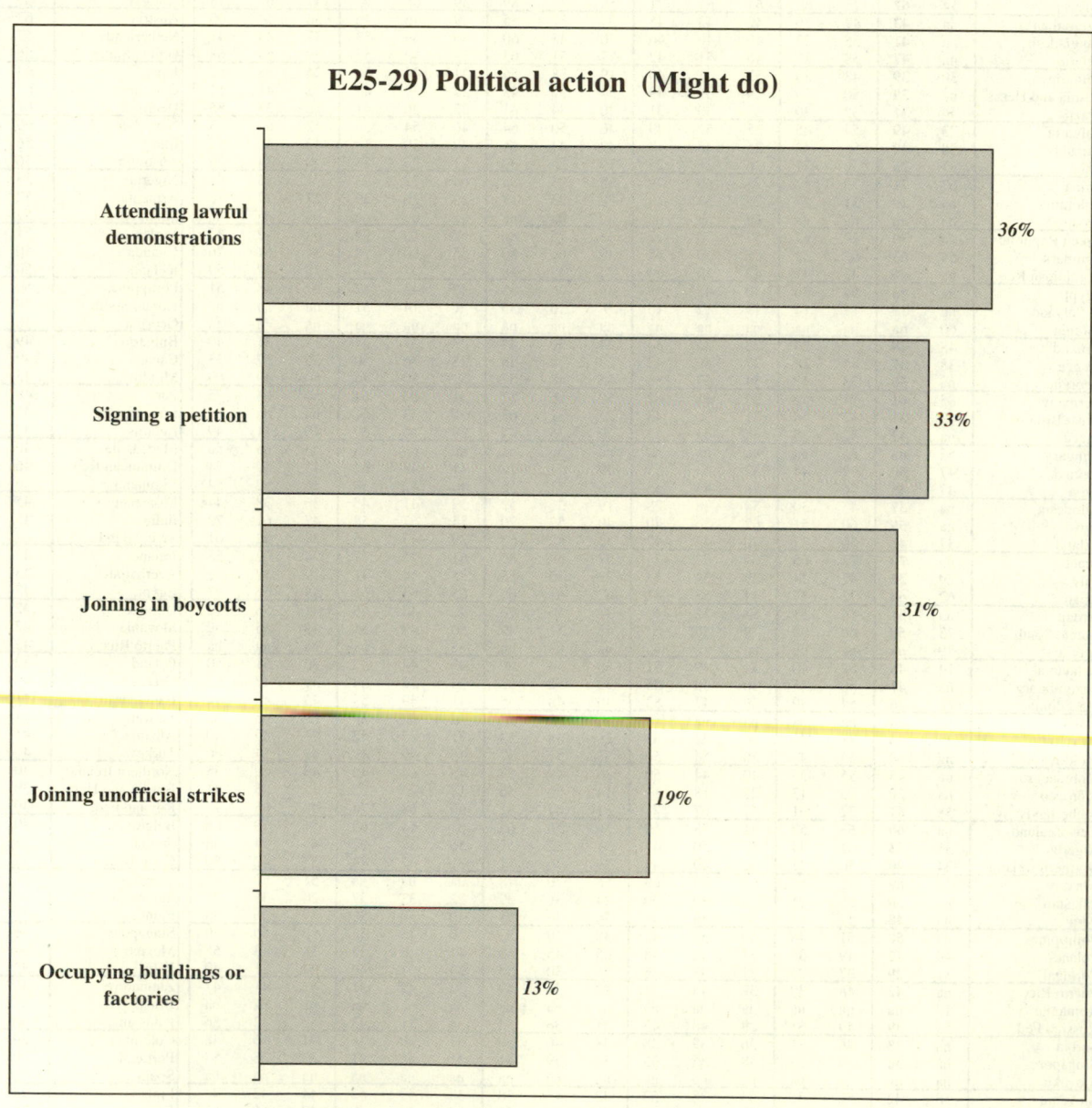

E25-29) Political action (Might do)

Attending lawful demonstrations — 36%

Signing a petition — 33%

Joining in boycotts — 31%

Joining unofficial strikes — 19%

Occupying buildings or factories — 13%

E025) POLITICAL ACTION: SIGNING A PETITION

I'd like you to tell me, for each one, whether you have actually done any of these things, whether you might do it or would never, under any circumstances, do it.

Might do (%) (WVS: V134; EVS: V179)

Country	Wave 1990	Wave 2000	Gender Male	Gender Female	Age 16-29	Age 30-49	Age 50+	Education Lower	Education Middle	Education Upper	Income Lower	Income Middle	Income Upper	Values Mat	Values Mixed	Values Postm.	RANKING Country	RANKING 2000
Albania	na	43	47	37	42	46	39	44	40	47	44	41	43	34	49	44	Venezuela	68
Algeria	na	29	33	25	33	27	22	17	28	38	27	35	26	27	31	29	Croatia	59
Argentina	33	31	31	32	35	34	26	31	35	23	30	33	31	30	33	31	Peru	59
Armenia	na	39	42	36	44	37	36	42	39	38	45	37	36	40	37	55	Dominican Rep.	59
Australia	na	16	18	15	23	14	12	18	20	10	16	17	13	21	17	14	Montenegro	51
Austria	30	24	24	24	29	23	22	29	22	12	28	24	21	31	23	23	Bosnia and Herz.	50
Azerbaijan	na	16	19	13	15	18	11	8	16	17	14	16	18	10	26	25	Colombia	49
Bangladesh	na	42	48	35	45	42	34	41	47	38	44	37	48	38	46	44	Tanzania	47
Belarus	52	28	34	23	34	32	18	10	32	45	19	31	35	21	33	52	Vietnam	47
Belgium	27	20	20	20	19	17	24	26	20	15	27	20	15	27	21	8	Puerto Rico	44
Bosnia and Herz.	na	50	51	48	52	50	47	46	49	53	47	50	50	47	50	53	Slovenia	44
Brazil	30	35	35	35	37	35	30	40	35	15	39	40	26	41	33	25	South Africa	43
Bulgaria	39	37	42	33	42	45	28	21	43	49	25	42	45	35	43	43	Uganda	43
Canada	15	19	19	18	24	17	18	26	20	11	21	20	15	22	20	16	Albania	43
Chile	34	27	29	25	32	27	23	23	27	38	25	26	33	22	29	32	Bangladesh	42
China	na	na	na	na	na	na	na	na	na	na	na	na	na	na	na	na	Turkey	42
Colombia	na	49	51	46	52	48	42	45	51	51	47	49	51	47	47	53	El Salvador	41
Croatia	na	59	61	58	56	59	62	61	60	54	54	64	55	65	61	50	Macedonia	40
Czech Republic	na	27	27	27	33	28	22	28	28	20	27	28	27	32	26	26	Singapore	40
Denmark	25	27	29	26	38	26	22	30	27	21	26	26	29	34	28	24	Armenia	39
Dominican Rep.	na	59	59	58	62	53	40	38	61	61	50	56	70	56	57	68	Portugal	39
Egypt	na	37	38	37	37	35	42	39	37	34	39	37	36	36	38	40	Lithuania	39
El Salvador	na	41	41	41	48	39	34	39	43	44	37	47	36	na	na	na	Greece	38
Estonia	39	33	36	30	37	34	29	31	33	35	27	33	37	26	38	22	Mexico	38
Finland	46	37	40	34	38	38	34	37	38	29	38	37	34	42	36	31	Egypt	37
France	29	22	24	21	32	20	20	24	23	17	23	21	21	26	23	18	Bulgaria	37
Georgia	na	15	15	15	15	16	13	11	16	14	15	15	15	13	16	19	Iceland	37
Germany	25	35	38	33	42	31	36	39	34	23	38	35	27	38	37	25	Korea, South	37
Great Britain	17	15	14	16	19	11	18	20	14	8	16	12	11	na	na	na	Spain	37
Greece	na	38	36	40	39	38	34	47	45	31	42	39	36	42	40	32	Finland	37
Hungary	30	32	35	30	40	35	25	28	42	34	25	34	35	31	33	54	Serbia	36
Iceland	37	37	36	38	40	32	42	43	37	25	38	38	33	45	36	25	Romania	36
India	45	29	29	27	32	30	22	26	30	32	24	32	27	27	33	39	Taiwan	36
Indonesia	na	21	26	16	38	19	16	9	20	31	16	23	25	17	24	43	Malta	36
Iran	na	na	na	na	na	na	na	na	na	na	na	na	na	na	na	na	Germany	35
Ireland	40	26	25	26	32	21	25	29	27	16	30	27	20	28	27	17	Ukraine	35
Israel	na	30	31	29	32	30	27	29	32	28	31	32	29	32	30	32	Brazil	35
Italy	35	30	29	32	38	27	30	35	29	21	34	34	26	35	31	28	Zimbabwe	34
Japan	25	30	33	26	46	28	25	29	28	32	31	26	28	28	32	23	Morocco	34
Jordan	na	9	10	8	9	10	6	6	10	14	7	12	10	6	11	10	Latvia	33
Korea, South	42	37	37	37	33	38	41	46	39	34	40	34	37	39	36	32	Estonia	33
Latvia	23	33	36	31	41	34	28	28	35	33	31	29	37	31	34	41	Luxembourg	32
Lithuania	29	39	41	37	46	37	36	36	40	38	32	37	39	41	37	45	Hungary	32
Luxembourg	na	32	34	31	34	33	30	36	33	25	33	32	31	31	36	22	Russian Fed.	32
Macedonia	na	40	41	39	40	44	35	35	41	45	35	42	43	38	42	29	Argentina	31
Malta	na	36	37	35	40	36	32	33	38	30	31	38	40	37	35	37	Italy	30
Mexico	44	38	42	35	48	34	31	32	45	45	33	44	42	32	41	48	Israel	30
Moldova	na	22	25	19	28	23	15	14	24	26	21	22	27	21	24	22	Netherlands	30
Montenegro	na	51	53	49	59	53	44	43	58	52	55	49	56	52	51	59	Japan	30
Morocco	na	34	36	31	39	30	27	32	42	39	42	36	31	24	40	42	Uruguay	30
Netherlands	33	30	28	31	40	25	29	34	33	22	25	29	31	26	32	25	Algeria	29
New Zealand	na	8	9	7	11	7	7	9	7	6	11	7	5	14	7	3	India	29
Nigeria	32	27	32	22	32	23	19	22	27	37	25	27	32	26	28	29	Poland	29
Northern Ireland	27	21	17	24	26	20	18	20	26	14	17	22	21	23	20	18	Belarus	28
Norway	28	26	27	25	25	23	30	30	26	22	na	na	na	30	26	18	Chile	27
Pakistan	na	24	35	13	26	22	30	23	26	26	24	29	20	24	25	25	Nigeria	27
Peru	na	59	59	58	64	58	46	57	61	55	60	59	57	56	59	63	Denmark	27
Philippines	na	23	24	22	25	24	18	18	24	28	20	23	27	19	23	43	Czech Republic	27
Poland	52	29	32	26	39	32	19	29	28	25	27	32	23	28	29	26	Norway	26
Portugal	46	39	43	36	46	47	28	35	52	29	24	39	52	37	43	33	Ireland	26
Puerto Rico	na	44	45	43	50	47	39	40	48	43	47	43	43	33	46	46	Pakistan	24
Romania	na	36	44	28	49	35	29	24	41	43	29	37	42	30	42	36	Austria	24
Russian Fed.	44	32	38	26	33	33	29	27	32	35	30	31	35	28	37	32	Philippines	23
Serbia	na	36	37	35	42	38	32	33	40	35	33	38	39	36	39	26	Slovakia	23
Singapore	na	40	40	40	53	31	17	26	46	51	32	40	50	27	42	68	France	22
Slovakia	na	23	24	21	31	21	18	22	24	18	20	27	21	21	25	17	Moldova	22
Slovenia	34	44	47	41	46	44	41	43	45	38	42	43	43	45	45	40	Northern Ireland	21
South Africa	47	43	44	43	54	40	26	43	46	19	48	43	41	37	45	64	Indonesia	21
Spain	36	37	42	33	44	37	33	34	42	38	33	40	39	35	39	36	Belgium	20
Sweden	24	10	12	9	10	8	13	14	9	9	12	10	8	11	11	7	Canada	19
Switzerland	17	18	19	17	25	16	16	26	17	5	22	15	11	14	19	15	Switzerland	18
Taiwan	na	36	39	33	45	39	22	23	36	47	31	37	42	31	41	41	Australia	16
Tanzania	na	47	50	42	52	45	44	39	55	59	36	48	63	45	49	42	Azerbaijan	16
Turkey	41	42	46	38	46	41	37	36	51	48	37	45	49	37	43	50	United States	16
Uganda	na	43	52	34	51	37	28	39	44	44	40	47	54	45	42	39	Great Britain	15
Ukraine	na	35	40	31	40	37	32	26	36	37	29	44	34	30	38	44	Georgia	15
United States	20	16	18	14	31	11	10	27	15	12	20	14	13	15	16	14	Sweden	10
Uruguay	na	30	30	29	39	28	27	31	31	18	29	35	26	20	32	28	Jordan	9
Venezuela	na	68	68	68	74	68	56	63	70	69	64	68	71	64	68	78	New Zealand	8
Vietnam	na	47	49	44	54	46	41	41	55	42	56	41	48	40	51	52		
Zimbabwe	na	34	37	32	38	36	21	30	39	88	28	39	39	30	37	44		
Total	34	33	35	31	39	32	28	31	35	32	31	34	33	31	34	31	Total	33

E026) POLITICAL ACTION: JOINING IN BOYCOTTS

I'd like you to tell me, for each one, whether you have actually done any of these things, whether you might do it or would never, under any circumstances, do it.

Might do (%) (WVS: V135; EVS: V180)

Country	Wave 1990	Wave 2000	Male	Female	Age 16-29	Age 30-49	Age 50+	Edu Lower	Edu Middle	Edu Upper	Inc Lower	Inc Middle	Inc Upper	Mat	Mixed	Postm.	RANKING Country	2000
Albania	na	23	31	15	29	21	21	19	25	27	22	21	27	16	27	41	Japan	64
Algeria	na	30	37	22	32	31	22	20	30	36	26	37	31	25	32	38	Korea, South	62
Argentina	9	7	9	6	11	8	3	7	8	10	3	7	11	4	8	8	Iceland	59
Armenia	na	22	26	18	27	20	16	18	21	25	28	17	17	19	22	40	Croatia	57
Australia	na	43	44	42	53	43	34	39	44	45	39	45	43	37	42	46	Montenegro	57
Austria	25	34	40	29	41	42	23	26	39	49	28	34	37	14	34	39	Norway	56
Azerbaijan	na	12	16	9	12	14	8	11	13	12	15	13	9	7	21	29	Sweden	55
Bangladesh	na	40	48	29	44	37	38	36	44	44	39	38	43	35	44	48	New Zealand	54
Belarus	38	21	27	16	31	23	10	9	23	33	16	23	25	15	23	47	Slovenia	54
Belgium	28	30	36	23	42	36	19	18	28	40	20	29	37	16	32	39	Finland	54
Bosnia and Herz.	na	45	49	42	49	49	37	39	46	49	34	50	45	41	47	49	United States	51
Brazil	36	29	31	27	29	32	23	23	32	40	23	31	35	19	30	48	Bosnia and Herz.	45
Bulgaria	33	27	35	20	38	35	16	14	30	41	17	30	33	20	36	38	Great Britain	44
Canada	43	42	43	41	52	45	33	34	46	42	37	50	43	45	41	45	Italy	44
Chile	11	13	15	11	14	15	10	11	14	17	13	13	14	12	14	14	France	43
China	na	na	na	na	na	na	na	na	na	na	na	na	na	na	na	na	Australia	43
Colombia	na	29	31	27	31	30	21	19	32	39	20	33	34	19	20	31	Canada	42
Croatia	na	57	65	49	64	57	52	52	59	66	49	59	60	49	55	71	Germany	42
Czech Republic	na	30	36	25	36	35	23	28	30	41	21	32	38	27	31	36	Peru	42
Denmark	32	37	38	36	48	42	26	32	45	44	30	39	43	34	37	37	Bangladesh	40
Dominican Rep.	na	26	29	24	25	28	27	21	25	27	17	35	23	17	26	37	Macedonia	40
Egypt	na	30	31	29	29	30	32	29	30	32	30	28	32	28	32	27	Luxembourg	40
El Salvador	na	na	na	na	na	na	na	na	na	na	na	na	na	na	na	na	Netherlands	39
Estonia	40	27	34	21	31	32	20	19	28	40	13	24	38	20	31	37	Lithuania	37
Finland	69	54	58	49	65	59	42	48	62	57	49	55	60	55	53	52	Uganda	37
France	40	43	48	38	54	47	33	38	47	53	37	40	51	34	44	54	Denmark	37
Georgia	na	10	11	8	10	10	9	8	9	12	10	10	9	9	10	16	Ireland	36
Germany	32	42	46	39	53	46	33	34	48	53	36	46	44	33	43	54	Switzerland	34
Great Britain	34	44	51	38	50	50	36	40	50	53	36	53	50	na	na	na	Austria	34
Greece	na	22	21	22	28	19	13	16	20	25	15	22	27	19	23	19	Portugal	33
Hungary	14	19	22	15	22	26	10	12	26	38	16	18	20	13	23	27	Taiwan	33
Iceland	53	59	61	58	61	61	56	55	65	57	61	60	58	59	62	49	Serbia	33
India	45	27	33	18	30	27	22	25	28	31	26	28	27	27	29	36	Israel	32
Indonesia	na	20	25	16	37	18	15	8	20	29	20	20	24	19	21	54	Czech Republic	30
Iran	na	na	na	na	na	na	na	na	na	na	na	na	na	na	na	na	Egypt	30
Ireland	33	36	38	34	52	35	24	22	43	45	25	45	39	32	38	34	Algeria	30
Israel	na	32	35	28	33	36	25	25	30	38	23	34	44	33	32	45	Belgium	30
Italy	46	44	45	42	53	49 -	33	34	49	56	31	47	54	29	44	52	South Africa	29
Japan	53	64	66	63	54	68	65	54	63	73	61	64	68	62	66	71	Brazil	29
Jordan	na	6	8	5	6	6	6	5	7	8	4	8	7	4	8	5	Slovakia	29
Korea, South	50	62	64	59	71	62	50	33	58	69	58	61	66	57	65	71	Colombia	29
Latvia	37	27	32	22	34	33	19	16	29	33	20	25	38	23	28	42	Zimbabwe	29
Lithuania	60	37	43	33	38	47	29	22	42	48	20	33	45	30	40	47	Turkey	29
Luxembourg	na	40	40	39	43	43	33	28	41	57	31	38	46	33	40	49	Malta	28
Macedonia	na	40	42	38	42	44	32	40	39	44	37	42	40	36	43	42	Morocco	28
Malta	na	28	32	25	37	30	21	20	30	41	22	30	41	25	29	41	India	27
Mexico	35	18	20	16	22	17	13	13	21	26	20	19	19	9	22	19	Bulgaria	27
Moldova	na	13	15	11	17	15	8	7	14	17	10	13	17	11	14	26	Estonia	27
Montenegro	na	57	58	55	68	59	47	45	67	56	57	56	61	56	58	62	Puerto Rico	27
Morocco	na	28	32	23	32	25	23	26	34	33	28	34	27	20	34	34	Latvia	27
Netherlands	36	39	43	34	49	44	27	32	42	41	35	41	40	27	41	37	Northern Ireland	26
New Zealand	na	54	58	51	62	59	48	49	56	60	51	59	58	55	56	60	Dominican Rep.	26
Nigeria	25	23	28	18	26	20	15	19	25	27	24	25	22	21	25	16	Ukraine	25
Northern Ireland	30	26	26	26	36	29	20	19	31	36	21	26	35	19	31	24	Poland	24
Norway	52	56	56	57	62	61	46	52	59	57	na	na	na	49	57	62	Spain	23
Pakistan	na	5	9	1	6	5	6	5	6	4	4	7	4	5	6	8	Albania	23
Peru	na	42	43	40	43	44	32	35	42	45	42	42	40	41	43	36	Nigeria	23
Philippines	na	12	15	10	15	12	10	7	13	18	9	12	16	11	13	18	Tanzania	23
Poland	35	24	30	19	30	28	15	22	28	24	23	23	27	19	28	22	Russian Fed.	22
Portugal	31	33	39	27	45	40	20	24	49	53	20	31	40	29	37	41	Armenia	22
Puerto Rico	na	27	32	24	35	27	23	15	26	30	20	30	31	18	25	37	Greece	22
Romania	na	17	22	12	22	17	13	9	18	23	11	15	22	11	21	25	Belarus	21
Russian Fed.	36	22	29	16	25	24	18	16	22	27	21	21	25	18	28	43	Indonesia	20
Serbia	na	33	37	28	41	39	23	22	38	38	28	32	37	27	38	36	Hungary	19
Singapore	na	18	20	16	24	13	8	11	19	33	10	19	24	12	18	37	Singapore	18
Slovakia	na	29	36	23	34	37	16	19	32	43	20	28	36	24	33	52	Uruguay	18
Slovenia	46	54	63	46	65	58	42	37	59	67	47	57	65	43	54	65	Mexico	18
South Africa	36	29	28	31	34	27	21	30	27	45	34	25	31	30	30	19	Romania	17
Spain	26	23	28	19	37	27	12	16	29	35	18	25	31	17	24	33	Vietnam	16
Sweden	62	55	57	53	59	53	54	59	59	45	54	56	54	64	58	43	Chile	13
Switzerland	na	34	37	32	41	41	22	22	37	36	30	33	37	27	33	44	Moldova	13
Taiwan	na	33	34	31	43	34	21	19	32	45	26	32	39	29	37	32	Azerbaijan	12
Tanzania	na	23	26	18	27	21	18	12	32	39	15	18	36	19	23	44	Philippines	12
Turkey	23	29	34	23	33	27	21	21	38	44	23	30	37	20	29	42	Georgia	10
Uganda	na	37	47	28	38	40	25	37	37	49	40	46	43	41	35	39	Argentina	7
Ukraine	na	25	34	17	31	28	18	16	27	24	19	32	25	19	30	18	Jordan	6
United States	45	51	52	50	60	52	43	48	50	53	49	53	54	53	54	44	Venezuela	6
Uruguay	na	18	21	16	25	22	12	13	23	34	11	17	24	9	19	22	Pakistan	5
Venezuela	na	6	7	5	7	6	6	6	6	6	8	4	6	7	5	8		
Vietnam	na	16	19	14	18	16	15	15	18	11	22	17	12	13	17	20		
Zimbabwe	na	29	30	28	33	30	18	28	29	46	28	30	30	25	32	33		
Total	37	31	35	28	35	33	25	25	33	37	27	32	35	24	34	39	Total	31

E027) POLITICAL ACTION: ATTENDING LAWFUL DEMONSTRATIONS

I'd like you to tell me, for each one, whether you have actually done any of these things, whether you might do it or would never, under any circumstances, do it.

Might do (%)   (WVS: V136; EVS: V181)

Country	Wave 1990	Wave 2000	Gender Male	Gender Female	Age 16-29	Age 30-49	Age 50+	Education Lower	Education Middle	Education Upper	Income Lower	Income Middle	Income Upper	Values Mat	Values Mixed	Values Postm.	RANKING Country	2000
Albania	na	52	50	54	54	52	51	54	53	46	57	53	46	57	50	40	Croatia	65
Algeria	na	30	34	27	36	31	17	22	31	36	32	33	29	28	32	34	Iceland	59
Argentina	21	23	24	22	32	23	14	19	30	24	22	23	24	16	24	27	Slovenia	58
Armenia	na	28	31	26	36	25	21	26	29	27	33	24	28	30	26	35	Tanzania	56
Australia	na	42	46	39	56	43	28	35	43	47	33	46	47	35	43	44	United States	54
Austria	33	36	38	34	48	40	26	33	40	35	24	43	37	23	36	41	Dominican Rep.	53
Azerbaijan	na	22	25	19	23	22	18	18	21	24	26	20	22	19	29	20	Sweden	53
Bangladesh	na	40	51	26	43	39	34	33	48	45	35	40	45	32	47	48	Norway	52
Belarus	55	30	36	24	39	33	18	18	32	41	26	29	36	21	35	59	Albania	52
Belgium	29	31	32	30	43	32	23	25	34	29	22	31	33	29	32	26	Peru	51
Bosnia and Herz.	na	49	52	45	53	52	40	43	50	49	42	51	50	47	49	51	New Zealand	50
Brazil	40	38	36	40	50	36	18	35	44	30	37	40	36	39	38	34	Bosnia and Herz.	49
Bulgaria	48	38	45	32	46	50	24	23	43	52	21	44	48	34	47	28	Lithuania	48
Canada	43	41	41	40	53	45	30	32	45	42	37	43	45	38	40	45	Montenegro	47
Chile	24	23	25	21	30	22	18	17	26	26	20	26	24	19	23	30	Ireland	45
China	na	na	na	na	na	na	na	na	na	na	na	na	na	na	na	na	Korea, South	45
Colombia	na	42	45	40	47	41	36	36	46	47	39	44	45	38	42	45	Finland	44
Croatia	na	65	71	59	75	66	56	61	65	73	53	67	68	53	63	78	Slovakia	43
Czech Republic	56	42	42	42	54	44	33	39	44	45	39	41	45	38	44	41	Macedonia	43
Denmark	32	39	39	40	50	43	30	39	45	38	33	44	38	37	41	35	Luxembourg	43
Dominican Rep.	na	53	47	57	60	40	40	26	54	56	52	50	56	46	56	57	Colombia	42
Egypt	na	15	15	16	15	15	16	16	15	14	18	15	13	15	15	15	Australia	42
El Salvador	na	14	17	12	18	13	11	11	19	18	14	15	13	na	na	na	Czech Republic	42
Estonia	42	31	35	28	36	34	26	25	31	39	22	32	37	22	35	49	Germany	42
Finland	53	44	49	40	60	52	28	39	52	48	41	44	49	41	45	45	Romania	41
France	32	34	33	35	44	37	26	34	38	29	32	35	30	33	37	28	Canada	41
Georgia	na	15	15	15	14	17	13	14	14	17	15	15	15	14	15	19	Bangladesh	40
Germany	34	42	43	41	48	46	34	37	46	41	36	42	39	29	46	49	Italy	39
Great Britain	35	39	46	32	49	45	28	32	45	47	30	44	46	na	na	na	Denmark	39
Greece	na	38	32	43	44	34	33	38	43	35	40	42	35	46	39	33	Portugal	39
Hungary	27	29	34	25	36	39	16	23	38	45	23	31	32	25	33	35	Great Britain	39
Iceland	53	59	63	56	65	60	54	58	65	51	58	63	56	59	62	44	Greece	38
India	43	29	35	21	36	30	20	25	32	35	27	30	30	33	27	43	Bulgaria	38
Indonesia	na	25	30	21	37	27	19	13	28	31	23	28	27	25	25	48	Puerto Rico	38
Iran	na	na	na	na	na	na	na	na	na	na	na	na	na	na	na	na	Brazil	38
Ireland	42	45	45	46	62	43	35	34	52	52	36	47	51	41	49	41	Vietnam	38
Israel	na	31	33	29	37	31	25	24	34	32	28	30	37	30	32	48	Spain	37
Italy	37	39	40	39	43	43	34	39	41	35	37	42	39	39	39	40	Latvia	37
Japan	25	37	40	34	39	38	35	29	35	45	30	41	41	27	40	44	Japan	37
Jordan	na	6	7	6	8	6	3	4	8	9	5	8	6	4	8	9	Netherlands	37
Korea, South	33	45	44	45	51	44	38	24	44	47	43	43	47	43	46	46	Zimbabwe	37
Latvia	42	37	39	35	47	41	30	28	40	38	30	39	44	32	40	52	Uganda	36
Lithuania	51	48	51	46	46	57	43	35	53	53	37	50	53	40	52	50	Austria	36
Luxembourg	na	43	43	42	51	44	36	39	43	48	40	47	38	46	43	40	Taiwan	36
Macedonia	na	43	46	40	47	46	35	36	45	48	36	44	48	42	44	34	Nigeria	35
Malta	na	22	24	21	32	24	14	11	27	27	13	24	31	24	21	25	Turkey	35
Mexico	43	10	14	7	14	9	7	8	11	19	9	11	12	8	12	11	Venezuela	34
Moldova	na	27	29	25	29	30	20	26	27	26	31	23	28	26	28	25	Ukraine	34
Montenegro	na	47	52	41	56	49	38	38	53	51	42	48	49	47	49	47	France	34
Morocco	na	29	33	24	34	26	20	26	41	38	25	34	30	22	34	38	Switzerland	33
Netherlands	41	37	43	31	56	37	27	32	45	33	36	33	40	28	40	33	Russian Fed.	33
New Zealand	na	50	52	49	60	52	47	46	53	54	47	55	51	54	51	55	South Africa	32
Nigeria	30	35	39	32	39	32	27	32	36	40	35	35	37	32	38	31	Serbia	32
Northern Ireland	31	30	31	30	39	34	24	25	35	36	22	33	42	28	31	31	Poland	31
Norway	56	52	52	52	58	53	49	53	58	45	na	na	na	52	54	42	Estonia	31
Pakistan	na	7	11	2	6	6	8	7	7	7	6	9	5	7	6	8	Israel	31
Peru	na	51	53	50	57	49	43	52	53	49	51	53	50	50	52	54	Belgium	31
Philippines	na	14	16	11	19	13	9	9	15	18	13	13	17	11	15	19	Algeria	30
Poland	51	31	35	28	36	37	21	28	36	34	32	32	29	25	36	30	Northern Ireland	30
Portugal	49	39	45	34	52	43	28	31	56	47	23	36	51	34	43	38	Belarus	30
Puerto Rico	na	38	45	34	46	41	33	24	37	42	37	37	43	31	38	45	Hungary	29
Romania	na	41	48	34	53	43	33	29	48	44	36	39	48	36	46	45	India	29
Russian Fed.	42	33	37	29	37	35	27	24	34	32	32	33	34	30	36	36	Morocco	29
Serbia	na	32	38	27	33	40	24	24	37	36	26	35	37	30	36	30	Armenia	28
Singapore	na	23	24	22	33	16	8	14	25	39	17	24	27	14	23	53	Moldova	27
Slovakia	na	43	49	38	51	49	31	33	48	46	34	45	44	41	45	60	Indonesia	25
Slovenia	50	58	63	54	72	59	47	49	61	63	55	61	60	54	58	63	Chile	23
South Africa	41	32	33	32	41	29	21	30	35	35	35	27	36	30	32	46	Argentina	23
Spain	34	37	42	33	47	38	30	36	39	38	31	43	38	31	41	34	Singapore	23
Sweden	59	53	54	52	55	55	49	53	57	45	49	58	53	52	57	40	Malta	22
Switzerland	21	33	34	32	48	39	17	25	34	44	28	30	37	29	34	35	Azerbaijan	22
Taiwan	na	36	35	37	51	37	22	24	35	47	33	34	41	30	43	38	Uruguay	16
Tanzania	na	56	58	53	60	56	59	50	65	59	51	54	67	53	58	67	Egypt	15
Turkey	32	35	41	28	39	34	27	25	46	52	29	36	47	26	36	45	Georgia	15
Uganda	na	36	45	28	37	38	24	40	34	45	40	41	43	33	36	41	El Salvador	14
Ukraine	na	34	37	31	38	40	27	24	36	35	28	39	37	29	40	20	Philippines	14
United States	44	54	54	55	60	58	44	50	57	54	56	55	52	59	55	51	Mexico	10
Uruguay	na	16	17	16	22	20	11	13	19	29	13	18	18	10	19	15	Pakistan	7
Venezuela	na	34	39	30	39	34	26	25	36	41	30	36	40	38	31	45	Jordan	6
Vietnam	na	38	38	38	46	38	33	33	44	38	34	44	49	23	44	49		
Zimbabwe	na	37	40	34	41	38	25	36	38	92	34	42	40	33	41	33		
Total	40	36	38	33	42	37	28	30	39	39	32	37	38	30	39	40	Total	36

E028) POLITICAL ACTION: JOINING UNOFFICIAL STRIKES

I'd like you to tell me, for each one, whether you have actually done any of these things, whether you might do it or would never, under any circumstances, do it.

Might do (%)

(WVS: V137; EVS: V182)

Country	Wave 1990	Wave 2000	Gender Male	Gender Female	Age 16-29	Age 30-49	Age 50+	Education Lower	Education Middle	Education Upper	Income Lower	Income Middle	Income Upper	Values Mat	Values Mixed	Values Postm.
Albania	na	5	7	3	4	6	3	5	4	5	5	4	5	5	4	11
Algeria	na	8	10	6	10	8	4	5	6	12	7	7	9	6	8	12
Argentina	11	10	10	10	15	10	5	8	14	12	7	11	12	5	11	14
Armenia	na	19	23	14	24	16	13	13	19	19	21	17	14	16	21	23
Australia	na	33	33	32	52	31	16	28	31	38	26	34	36	27	32	35
Austria	8	18	23	13	29	23	7	10	21	37	15	18	21	5	14	29
Azerbaijan	na	11	13	9	12	12	7	6	12	11	14	9	12	8	17	12
Bangladesh	na	24	30	15	26	23	17	20	27	27	15	30	22	19	27	28
Belarus	29	16	24	9	21	19	8	9	17	24	12	16	22	10	19	42
Belgium	18	19	23	15	28	25	9	12	18	26	14	16	24	12	16	33
Bosnia and Herz.	na	31	34	28	36	35	20	20	33	33	25	31	34	28	31	33
Brazil	19	15	16	14	21	14	5	13	16	18	17	10	17	13	16	17
Bulgaria	25	21	27	15	24	30	11	16	20	29	12	26	25	20	23	50
Canada	28	26	26	26	41	30	14	18	28	31	21	27	32	24	26	29
Chile	16	16	16	15	20	16	10	11	16	22	12	17	19	12	16	21
China	na	na	na	na	na	na	na	na	na	na	na	na	na	na	na	na
Colombia	na	18	21	16	22	18	12	12	19	28	14	20	22	15	17	19
Croatia	na	37	41	33	54	35	26	29	39	52	33	35	38	21	35	53
Czech Republic	na	29	34	24	45	31	18	26	31	34	22	30	35	27	30	31
Denmark	23	31	27	35	54	34	16	24	44	37	25	33	36	29	29	42
Dominican Rep.	na	12	14	10	12	13	na	7	12	12	9	13	9	7	14	14
Egypt	na	3	2	3	3	3	2	2	3	2	3	3	2	3	2	1
El Salvador	na	6	6	6	9	6	2	5	7	8	8	5	6	na	na	na
Estonia	19	12	15	9	18	15	6	9	11	18	4	12	18	8	13	23
Finland	35	25	29	21	41	31	11	21	31	28	27	26	24	19	25	37
France	25	32	36	29	47	38	19	25	38	45	27	31	39	19	34	45
Georgia	na	6	8	4	6	7	4	5	5	9	5	7	6	5	6	14
Germany	15	16	20	14	32	18	8	12	22	15	15	18	18	7	17	29
Great Britain	19	28	33	24	47	30	19	23	33	34	25	32	28	na	na	na
Greece	na	33	36	30	42	29	17	16	26	41	28	34	39	22	32	44
Hungary	27	10	12	8	13	14	3	8	14	13	9	11	9	7	10	28
Iceland	20	30	36	24	43	34	13	21	31	45	28	25	37	18	30	52
India	16	18	21	12	20	18	15	16	20	20	17	15	20	17	21	13
Indonesia	na	6	9	4	13	6	4	4	6	9	4	8	8	7	6	20
Iran	na	na	na	na	na	na	na	na	na	na	na	na	na	na	na	na
Ireland	23	31	34	28	46	33	17	15	37	47	20	38	34	27	32	37
Israel	na	24	25	23	37	22	13	12	25	32	20	24	31	25	24	42
Italy	18	16	19	13	24	21	7	7	20	27	10	20	19	10	14	22
Japan	13	19	22	17	24	24	14	15	20	22	14	21	23	11	20	35
Jordan	na	3	4	2	4	2	1	1	5	4	2	3	4	2	4	3
Korea, South	na	55	53	56	68	55	39	31	52	61	53	58	54	52	56	66
Latvia	30	15	19	10	23	16	10	8	16	17	12	11	21	9	17	30
Lithuania	50	24	31	18	32	28	16	11	28	31	11	20	32	16	26	36
Luxembourg	na	23	26	19	34	26	13	17	25	29	22	19	26	20	22	28
Macedonia	na	20	29	27	34	30	20	24	31	30	22	31	30	28	30	21
Malta	na	16	20	13	26	17	10	9	17	30	14	13	26	15	17	23
Mexico	36	12	15	9	18	10	7	8	14	22	11	15	12	8	13	16
Moldova	na	23	25	21	24	26	18	19	22	28	25	24	23	22	25	30
Montenegro	na	31	38	24	36	34	25	19	39	38	29	33	27	25	37	39
Morocco	na	2	4	1	4	1	1	2	5	2	2	3	4	1	3	7
Netherlands	22	28	32	24	35	36	16	19	28	38	29	27	31	11	27	39
New Zealand	na	33	33	33	55	41	19	22	34	47	30	39	34	26	31	52
Nigeria	14	19	19	18	21	16	18	17	19	20	20	17	19	16	20	22
Northern Ireland	17	20	25	16	27	23	15	17	25	20	19	21	24	14	20	31
Norway	58	28	29	27	43	32	12	18	32	33	na	na	na	13	29	42
Pakistan	na	1	2	na	2	1	2	2	1	1	1	2	1	1	2	na
Peru	na	15	16	14	17	14	12	17	13	16	18	15	10	14	14	17
Philippines	na	6	8	5	7	7	5	4	8	7	6	6	7	4	8	5
Poland	24	16	19	13	23	19	9	16	18	13	16	14	21	13	19	13
Portugal	19	21	26	15	34	23	11	13	34	38	11	22	24	17	24	20
Puerto Rico	na	11	14	9	21	11	6	3	6	14	4	12	15	7	10	15
Romania	na	8	11	5	16	7	5	6	10	8	7	9	9	7	10	12
Russian Fed.	30	16	22	12	20	18	11	9	17	18	15	16	17	11	22	33
Serbia	na	29	35	24	51	37	14	17	31	44	22	27	37	22	36	46
Singapore	na	na	na	na	na	na	na	na	na	na	na	na	na	na	na	na
Slovakia	na	21	27	15	29	25	11	13	24	31	13	22	25	17	24	35
Slovenia	8	33	37	29	47	35	19	23	34	47	27	33	38	25	33	42
South Africa	24	14	16	11	16	14	7	12	17	10	16	11	12	10	17	19
Spain	21	21	26	16	31	26	10	12	28	32	16	20	29	9	23	34
Sweden	41	48	50	45	62	57	31	33	54	49	48	46	49	34	46	56
Switzerland	22	16	20	13	25	20	7	9	17	26	15	17	19	7	14	29
Taiwan	na	12	14	10	25	11	5	7	12	16	9	13	13	8	15	15
Tanzania	na	7	9	5	6	9	7	3	8	18	5	4	19	6	8	9
Turkey	6	13	15	10	16	12	6	8	15	31	11	12	21	8	12	22
Uganda	na	22	29	17	21	24	21	24	20	36	33	28	14	26	19	27
Ukraine	na	16	25	9	22	20	10	9	17	18	13	17	19	12	20	20
United States	30	38	40	37	49	44	22	31	38	41	37	40	42	33	38	44
Uruguay	na	20	23	17	34	23	11	16	24	34	13	23	22	6	21	27
Venezuela	na	6	7	6	7	6	5	7	6	6	8	5	7	5	6	9
Vietnam	na	11	11	10	14	9	9	11	9	12	11	8	14	7	11	10
Zimbabwe	na	11	14	7	12	11	7	10	12	na	10	13	11	11	11	6
Total	23	19	22	16	25	21	12	13	21	25	16	19	22	13	20	29

RANKING

Country	2000
Korea, South	55
Sweden	48
United States	38
Croatia	37
New Zealand	33
Slovenia	33
Australia	33
Greece	33
France	32
Ireland	31
Montenegro	31
Bosnia and Herz.	31
Denmark	31
Iceland	30
Serbia	29
Czech Republic	29
Great Britain	28
Macedonia	28
Netherlands	28
Norway	28
Canada	26
Finland	25
Lithuania	24
Israel	24
Bangladesh	24
Luxembourg	23
Moldova	23
Uganda	22
Slovakia	21
Bulgaria	21
Spain	21
Portugal	21
Northern Ireland	20
Uruguay	20
Japan	19
Belgium	19
Nigeria	19
Armenia	19
Colombia	18
India	18
Austria	18
Germany	16
Malta	16
Russian Fed.	16
Switzerland	16
Ukraine	16
Poland	16
Belarus	16
Italy	16
Chile	16
Brazil	15
Peru	15
Latvia	15
South Africa	14
Turkey	13
Dominican Rep.	12
Estonia	12
Taiwan	12
Mexico	12
Azerbaijan	11
Puerto Rico	11
Vietnam	11
Zimbabwe	11
Argentina	10
Hungary	10
Romania	8
Algeria	8
Tanzania	7
Indonesia	6
Philippines	6
Venezuela	6
El Salvador	6
Georgia	6
Albania	5
Jordan	3
Egypt	3
Morocco	2
Pakistan	1
Total	19

E029) POLITICAL ACTION: OCCUPYING BUILDINGS OR FACTORIES

I'd like you to tell me, for each one, whether you have actually done any of these things, whether you might do it or would never, under any circumstances, do it.

Might do (%)

(WVS: V138; EVS: V183)

Country	Wave		Gender		Age			Education			Income			Values			RANKING Country	2000
	1990	2000	Male	Female	16-29	30-49	50+	Lower	Middle	Upper	Lower	Middle	Upper	Mat	Mixed	Postm.		
Albania	na	2	3	1	4	2	na	2	2	1	2	1	2	2	2	na	Uganda	45
Algeria	na	4	6	2	5	3	4	4	3	4	5	3	3	2	5	4	France	35
Argentina	8	9	11	8	13	10	5	8	11	14	8	9	11	5	10	11	Nigeria	33
Armenia	na	12	18	8	18	10	8	9	13	12	18	10	7	9	15	26	Dominican Rep.	28
Australia	na	17	19	16	28	18	8	14	16	22	15	18	19	13	16	21	Greece	27
Austria	6	10	12	7	15	12	5	5	13	18	9	7	14	4	7	16	Belgium	26
Azerbaijan	na	3	5	2	4	3	1	5	3	3	4	3	2	2	5	7	United States	25
Bangladesh	na	6	8	4	5	6	11	6	6	6	3	6	8	4	7	4	Slovenia	24
Belarus	12	4	8	1	7	4	2	2	5	8	2	5	7	2	5	16	Netherlands	23
Belgium	21	26	31	21	44	32	12	15	26	33	19	23	31	16	24	43	Vietnam	22
Bosnia and Herz.	na	12	15	9	14	15	7	8	15	8	10	13	12	15	10	19	Portugal	22
Brazil	12	16	15	17	19	19	6	15	17	16	20	14	15	15	16	22	South Africa	20
Bulgaria	14	14	18	10	17	19	8	10	16	17	9	13	20	11	18	27	Sweden	19
Canada	21	18	21	15	33	19	9	13	20	19	16	22	19	17	16	23	New Zealand	19
Chile	11	10	10	9	12	11	7	7	8	19	8	10	12	6	10	14	Luxembourg	19
China	na	na	na	na	na	na	na	na	na	na	na	na	na	na	na	na	Croatia	18
Colombia	na	11	11	11	15	10	6	8	12	14	9	12	11	10	10	15	Canada	18
Croatia	na	18	25	13	23	20	14	15	21	18	17	17	20	11	17	29	Italy	18
Czech Republic	na	10	15	6	16	11	7	10	10	13	8	11	12	9	10	15	Australia	17
Denmark	7	12	15	10	18	14	8	11	15	12	10	14	9	13	11	18	Uruguay	17
Dominican Rep.	na	28	27	28	29	27	18	25	31	26	27	28	22	34	26	27	Serbia	17
Egypt	na	2	2	3	3	2	2	3	3	2	3	2	2	2	3	1	Montenegro	16
El Salvador	na	5	6	5	7	5	2	4	5	6	6	4	5	na	na	na	Brazil	16
Estonia	7	5	8	3	9	6	2	3	5	10	3	5	6	3	5	27	Great Britain	16
Finland	20	15	18	13	25	18	7	13	17	16	17	14	16	13	14	22	Ireland	16
France	25	35	38	33	56	41	20	28	45	46	31	35	40	22	37	50	Poland	16
Georgia	na	2	3	1	3	2	1	2	2	3	2	2	3	1	3	7	Spain	16
Germany	14	14	16	13	27	14	7	11	17	14	15	15	16	7	15	24	Macedonia	16
Great Britain	10	16	20	12	26	19	9	13	20	18	14	22	18	na	na	na	Finland	15
Greece	na	27	25	27	27	31	17	15	27	28	21	33	29	20	29	27	Slovakia	15
Hungary	4	4	6	3	6	7	1	4	6	6	3	5	5	4	4	16	Bulgaria	14
Iceland	9	12	17	8	18	14	5	9	12	20	11	12	14	7	11	31	Germany	14
India	6	13	15	8	13	11	15	13	13	11	13	13	13	11	16	13	Malta	13
Indonesia	na	10	12	7	16	8	8	5	10	13	9	9	12	10	8	40	Switzerland	13
Iran	na	na	na	na	na	na	na	na	na	na	na	na	na	na	na	na	India	13
Ireland	19	16	19	13	21	17	10	7	20	22	10	25	16	13	15	26	Armenia	12
Israel	na	7	8	6	10	7	2	3	7	8	5	7	9	10	5	18	Peru	12
Italy	20	18	19	16	26	21	10	12	21	26	14	21	19	10	16	26	Iceland	12
Japan	7	8	10	6	9	8	7	8	6	11	7	8	9	5	6	19	Denmark	12
Jordan	na	1	1	1	na	1	1	1	na	na	1	na	1	1	1	na	Lithuania	12
Korea, South	37	na	na	na	na	na	na	na	na	na	na	na	na	na	na	na	Bosnia and Herz.	12
Latvia	5	4	7	2	6	4	3	3	5	2	3	2	6	2	5	12	Moldova	11
Lithuania	21	12	19	7	20	12	7	5	15	10	5	12	14	11	12	23	Colombia	11
Luxembourg	na	19	20	17	28	20	11	15	19	22	18	18	18	14	18	29	Norway	10
Macedonia	na	16	17	14	17	15	15	13	17	15	17	19	10	14	17	18	Northern Ireland	10
Malta	na	13	16	11	19	15	8	7	15	23	13	15	20	12	12	25	Czech Republic	10
Mexico	29	7	9	5	11	5	6	5	9	14	7	8	7	4	9	7	Chile	10
Moldova	na	11	14	8	12	12	10	8	12	12	10	11	15	12	11	15	Austria	10
Montenegro	na	16	23	10	20	16	15	12	20	18	12	14	17	12	19	30	Indonesia	10
Morocco	na	5	6	3	7	3	2	3	8	12	4	7	7	3	5	14	Argentina	9
Netherlands	22	23	26	21	31	27	16	17	22	31	25	23	25	7	22	36	Russian Fed.	8
New Zealand	na	19	21	16	35	24	8	11	20	27	17	21	20	8	19	30	Venezuela	8
Nigeria	11	33	36	29	35	32	18	28	35	37	26	37	33	33	34	29	Japan	8
Northern Ireland	8	10	14	7	16	13	5	8	14	8	9	9	13	6	9	20	Mexico	7
Norway	10	10	12	9	14	12	6	8	10	13	na	na	na	5	9	25	Puerto Rico	7
Pakistan	na	0	na	na	na	na	1	na	na	1	na	1	na	na	na	na	Israel	7
Peru	na	12	14	10	14	13	7	14	11	14	13	13	10	10	13	11	Philippines	7
Philippines	na	7	8	5	7	7	5	5	7	8	5	6	8	5	7	4	Bangladesh	6
Poland	19	16	19	13	27	17	7	14	21	11	15	16	20	14	18	13	Romania	6
Portugal	11	22	27	17	36	25	12	15	34	43	11	23	25	18	25	24	Taiwan	5
Puerto Rico	na	7	10	6	17	6	4	6	3	9	5	7	9	11	6	9	Ukraine	5
Romania	na	6	7	4	9	5	4	6	6	5	5	7	6	5	7	5	El Salvador	5
Russian Fed.	12	8	13	4	11	10	5	5	9	9	9	7	8	6	11	23	Estonia	5
Serbia	na	17	22	12	31	20	7	8	18	26	13	17	19	12	21	28	Morocco	5
Singapore	na	na	na	na	na	na	na	na	na	na	na	na	na	na	na	na	Turkey	5
Slovakia	na	15	21	9	16	19	9	11	15	26	10	14	16	11	17	27	Hungary	4
Slovenia	12	24	28	20	29	27	17	20	25	26	23	25	24	18	25	25	Tanzania	4
South Africa	24	20	24	16	24	20	11	22	18	8	28	14	16	18	21	25	Belarus	4
Spain	23	16	20	12	26	19	7	8	22	25	14	14	20	8	17	26	Zimbabwe	4
Sweden	19	19	19	19	24	23	12	12	22	21	21	19	18	14	16	30	Latvia	4
Switzerland	na	13	16	10	19	16	6	10	13	20	12	15	14	6	12	19	Algeria	4
Taiwan	na	5	4	6	10	5	2	3	8	5	5	4	6	4	5	14	Azerbaijan	3
Tanzania	na	4	5	3	4	5	3	2	7	8	5	4	6	3	4	8	Egypt	2
Turkey	3	5	6	3	6	5	2	3	6	9	5	4	6	3	4	9	Georgia	2
Uganda	na	45	66	34	53	41	32	42	45	66	51	48	51	47	42	55	Albania	2
Ukraine	na	5	8	3	8	6	3	4	5	5	5	6	5	4	7	7	Jordan	1
United States	17	25	29	21	38	27	13	24	26	25	29	25	21	18	24	29	Pakistan	0
Uruguay	na	17	19	15	28	18	10	12	22	26	10	19	20	5	18	22		
Venezuela	na	8	9	7	10	7	7	9	8	8	11	6	8	10	7	12		
Vietnam	na	22	21	24	25	19	25	23	21	19	26	18	25	23	23	16		
Zimbabwe	na	4	5	4	6	2	2	3	6	9	3	6	5	4	5	2		
Total	14	13	15	10	17	13	8	10	14	15	11	13	14	9	13	22	Total	13

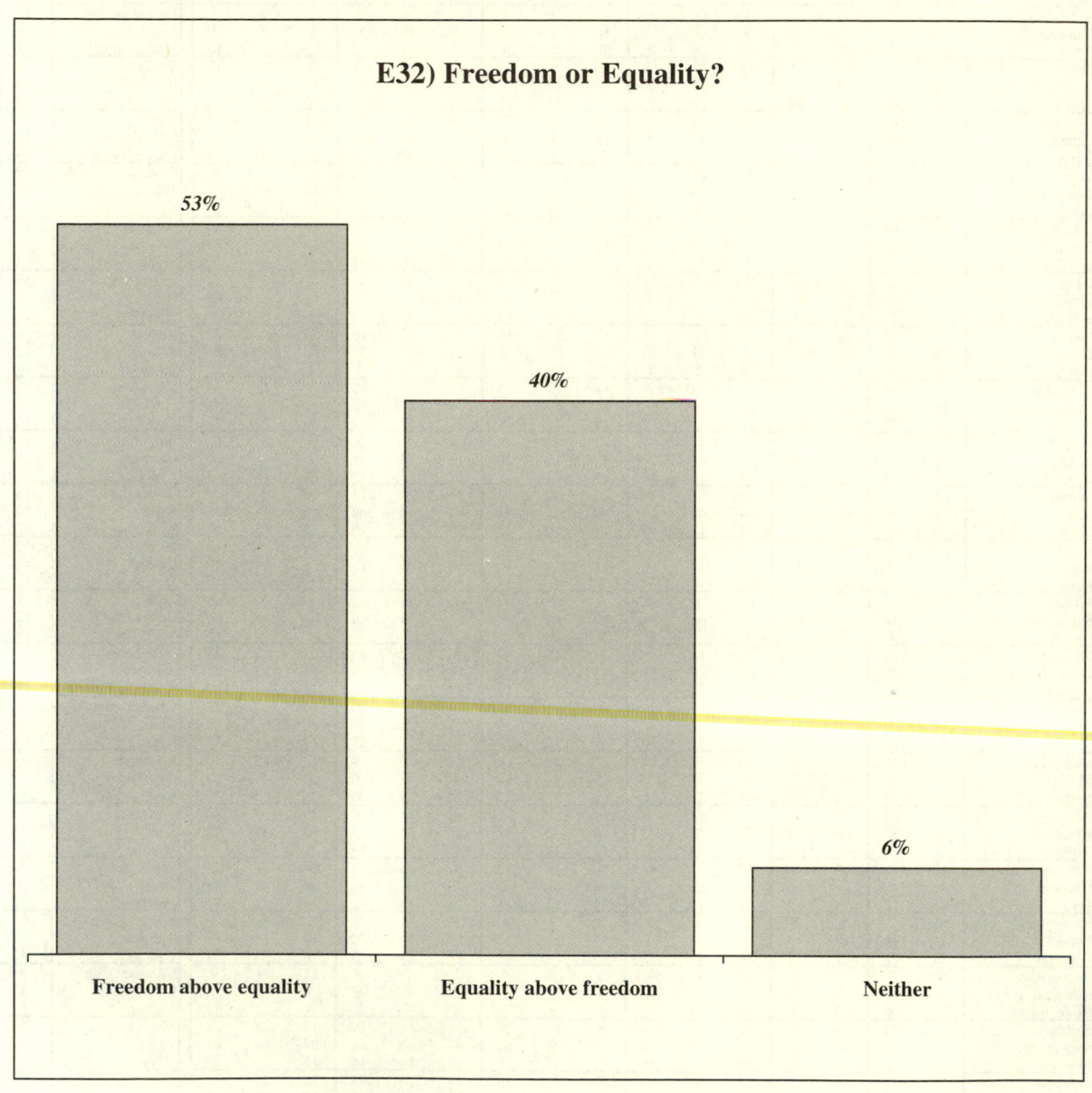

E32) Freedom or Equality?

53%

40%

6%

Freedom above equality   Equality above freedom   Neither

E032_1) FREEDOM OR EQUALITY?

Both freedom and equality are important, but if you were to choose one or the other, which of these two statements comes closest to your own opinion? A. personal freedom more important, or B equality more important

Freedom above equality (%)

(EVS: V184)

Country	Wave 1990	Wave 2000	Gender Male	Female	Age 16-29	30-49	50+	Education Lower	Middle	Upper	Income Lower	Middle	Upper	Values Mat	Mixed	Postm.
Albania	na	na	na	na	na	na	na	na	na	na	na	na	na	na	na	na
Algeria	na	na	na	na	na	na	na	na	na	na	na	na	na	na	na	na
Argentina	58	na	na	na	na	na	na	na	na	na	na	na	na	na	na	na
Armenia	na	na	na	na	na	na	na	na	na	na	na	na	na	na	na	na
Australia	na	na	na	na	na	na	na	na	na	na	na	na	na	na	na	na
Austria	64	56	61	51	62	56	54	52	59	65	50	52	61	55	55	58
Azerbaijan	na	na	na	na	na	na	na	na	na	na	na	na	na	na	na	na
Bangladesh	na	na	na	na	na	na	na	na	na	na	na	na	na	na	na	na
Belarus	41	62	65	59	75	63	47	44	66	71	54	65	67	58	63	83
Belgium	52	46	49	44	53	45	45	36	46	55	39	43	55	43	48	47
Bosnia and Herz.	na	na	na	na	na	na	na	na	na	na	na	na	na	na	na	na
Brazil	41	na	na	na	na	na	na	na	na	na	na	na	na	na	na	na
Bulgaria	48	60	60	60	70	65	50	43	64	77	47	59	72	54	64	78
Canada	61	na	na	na	na	na	na	na	na	na	na	na	na	na	na	na
Chile	53	na	na	na	na	na	na	na	na	na	na	na	na	na	na	na
China	21	na	na	na	na	na	na	na	na	na	na	na	na	na	na	na
Colombia	na	na	na	na	na	na	na	na	na	na	na	na	na	na	na	na
Croatia	na	42	47	38	49	42	38	37	44	52	36	34	55	38	42	45
Czech Republic	42	59	61	56	66	63	51	51	65	71	52	58	66	47	62	69
Denmark	62	69	74	65	76	72	63	69	72	69	65	72	70	65	74	57
Dominican Rep.	na	na	na	na	na	na	na	na	na	na	na	na	na	na	na	na
Egypt	na	na	na	na	na	na	na	na	na	na	na	na	na	na	na	na
El Salvador	na	na	na	na	na	na	na	na	na	na	na	na	na	na	na	na
Estonia	71	55	59	51	65	54	49	50	55	62	50	50	61	52	57	66
Finland	74	53	56	50	63	51	50	47	63	57	49	50	56	49	55	52
France	53	50	52	48	49	51	50	50	50	51	50	50	52	51	50	51
Georgia	na	na	na	na	na	na	na	na	na	na	na	na	na	na	na	na
Germany	50	62	66	58	60	61	63	63	61	61	59	65	65	62	61	67
Great Britain	65	60	62	57	57	57	63	58	62	57	62	58	58	na	na	na
Greece	na	na	na	na	na	na	na	na	na	na	na	na	na	na	na	na
Hungary	51	45	48	42	47	49	38	39	53	59	36	42	53	41	50	24
Iceland	45	46	48	44	52	48	37	39	51	49	38	46	52	44	46	47
India	45	na	na	na	na	na	na	na	na	na	na	na	na	na	na	na
Indonesia	na	na	na	na	na	na	na	na	na	na	na	na	na	na	na	na
Iran	na	na	na	na	na	na	na	na	na	na	na	na	na	na	na	na
Ireland	45	48	49	48	44	47	54	54	45	46	56	40	47	54	48	40
Israel	na	na	na	na	na	na	na	na	na	na	na	na	na	na	na	na
Italy	46	40	42	37	41	38	41	41	40	36	39	40	38	41	42	36
Japan	46	na	na	na	na	na	na	na	na	na	na	na	na	na	na	na
Jordan	na	na	na	na	na	na	na	na	na	na	na	na	na	na	na	na
Korea, South	51	na	na	na	na	na	na	na	na	na	na	na	na	na	na	na
Latvia	58	52	52	52	68	52	46	53	52	53	50	49	57	50	54	55
Lithuania	73	58	61	55	69	62	45	47	58	73	46	54	67	60	55	78
Luxembourg	na	49	52	47	51	46	52	51	48	53	49	52	51	52	50	47
Macedonia	na	na	na	na	na	na	na	na	na	na	na	na	na	na	na	na
Malta	na	58	61	55	65	54	56	54	58	68	59	57	63	62	54	66
Mexico	61	na	na	na	na	na	na	na	na	na	na	na	na	na	na	na
Moldova	na	na	na	na	na	na	na	na	na	na	na	na	na	na	na	na
Montenegro	na	na	na	na	na	na	na	na	na	na	na	na	na	na	na	na
Morocco	na	na	na	na	na	na	na	na	na	na	na	na	na	na	na	na
Netherlands	56	56	60	53	64	62	46	49	59	61	55	54	64	45	60	52
New Zealand	na	na	na	na	na	na	na	na	na	na	na	na	na	na	na	na
Nigeria	62	na	na	na	na	na	na	na	na	na	na	na	na	na	na	na
Northern Ireland	64	47	51	44	50	43	50	45	50	47	48	49	47	56	46	43
Norway	67	na	na	na	na	na	na	na	na	na	na	na	na	na	na	na
Pakistan	na	na	na	na	na	na	na	na	na	na	na	na	na	na	na	na
Peru	na	na	na	na	na	na	na	na	na	na	na	na	na	na	na	na
Philippines	na	na	na	na	na	na	na	na	na	na	na	na	na	na	na	na
Poland	55	55	58	52	57	57	50	51	55	68	49	60	57	48	56	69
Portugal	42	49	53	46	46	55	46	49	48	56	52	53	51	47	52	46
Puerto Rico	na	na	na	na	na	na	na	na	na	na	na	na	na	na	na	na
Romania	54	na	na	na	na	na	na	na	na	na	na	na	na	na	na	na
Russian Fed.	45	47	51	44	65	46	36	32	46	56	41	42	55	42	51	60
Serbia	na	na	na	na	na	na	na	na	na	na	na	na	na	na	na	na
Singapore	na	na	na	na	na	na	na	na	na	na	na	na	na	na	na	na
Slovakia	na	64	63	64	67	64	60	57	66	69	60	62	67	61	64	81
Slovenia	42	46	46	47	54	54	33	33	47	69	40	42	56	37	49	46
South Africa	48	na	na	na	na	na	na	na	na	na	na	na	na	na	na	na
Spain	43	49	52	46	54	46	49	48	51	47	49	51	51	49	50	46
Sweden	67	62	62	61	68	63	57	49	65	67	56	64	66	67	61	64
Switzerland	58	na	na	na	na	na	na	na	na	na	na	na	na	na	na	na
Taiwan	na	na	na	na	na	na	na	na	na	na	na	na	na	na	na	na
Tanzania	na	na	na	na	na	na	na	na	na	na	na	na	na	na	na	na
Turkey	58	42	47	36	41	39	53	45	37	39	50	37	36	44	41	41
Uganda	na	na	na	na	na	na	na	na	na	na	na	na	na	na	na	na
Ukraine	na	53	56	50	64	57	42	34	54	60	44	53	65	49	56	78
United States	71	na	na	na	na	na	na	na	na	na	na	na	na	na	na	na
Uruguay	na	na	na	na	na	na	na	na	na	na	na	na	na	na	na	na
Venezuela	na	na	na	na	na	na	na	na	na	na	na	na	na	na	na	na
Vietnam	na	na	na	na	na	na	na	na	na	na	na	na	na	na	na	na
Zimbabwe	na	na	na	na	na	na	na	na	na	na	na	na	na	na	na	na
Total	54	53	56	51	59	54	49	48	55	59	50	52	58	51	54	53

RANKING

Country	2000
Denmark	69
Slovakia	64
Belarus	62
Germany	62
Sweden	62
Bulgaria	60
Great Britain	60
Czech Republic	59
Lithuania	58
Malta	58
Austria	56
Netherlands	56
Poland	55
Estonia	55
Finland	53
Ukraine	53
Latvia	52
France	50
Luxembourg	49
Portugal	49
Spain	49
Ireland	48
Northern Ireland	47
Russian Fed.	47
Belgium	46
Slovenia	46
Iceland	46
Hungary	45
Croatia	42
Turkey	42
Italy	40
Total	53

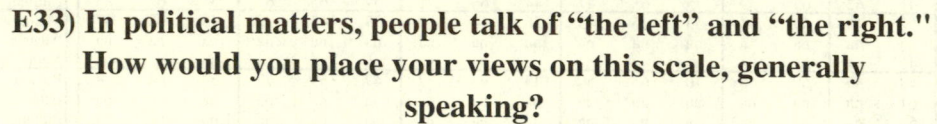

**E33) In political matters, people talk of "the left" and "the right."
How would you place your views on this scale, generally
speaking?**

44%

32%

25%

Left (1-4)   Center (5-6)   Right (7-10)

E033) SELF POSITIONING IN POLITICAL SCALE: RIGHT

In political matters, people talk of "the left" and "the right."
How would you place your views on this scale, generally speaking?
% Right (codes 7 to 10 on a 10-point scale)

(WVS: V139; EVS: V185)

Country	Wave 1990	Wave 2000	Gender Male	Gender Female	Age 16-29	Age 30-49	Age 50+	Education Lower	Education Middle	Education Upper	Income Lower	Income Middle	Income Upper	Values Mat	Values Mixed	Values Postm.	RANKING Country	RANKING 2000
Albania	na	36	40	33	37	37	35	32	39	41	32	36	41	35	38	33	Vietnam	92
Algeria	na	43	45	41	45	42	44	34	42	49	42	39	51	36	49	34	Bangladesh	66
Argentina	21	33	34	31	32	31	35	35	28	33	38	33	28	37	34	27	Tanzania	57
Armenia	na	27	27	27	34	24	22	25	28	27	33	21	24	27	26	32	Dominican Rep.	52
Australia	na	22	24	21	15	21	30	24	20	25	23	21	25	24	25	18	Mexico	51
Austria	41	19	19	20	14	18	23	21	17	20	22	18	21	23	18	20	Colombia	45
Azerbaijan	na	29	30	27	32	28	25	32	27	32	27	32	32	24	35	49	Algeria	43
Bangladesh	na	66	70	60	64	67	77	72	62	61	74	62	68	77	62	51	Taiwan	43
Belarus	10	28	31	25	33	29	20	24	26	37	19	29	36	18	29	64	Indonesia	43
Belgium	31	21	22	20	17	18	26	20	22	21	23	16	23	21	24	13	Uganda	43
Bosnia and Herz.	na	18	21	15	19	18	17	22	17	18	13	17	24	16	19	18	Puerto Rico	42
Brazil	31	41	43	38	36	39	54	49	36	29	45	39	36	46	40	31	El Salvador	41
Bulgaria	22	36	39	33	46	34	33	25	40	41	29	35	42	32	38	50	Philippines	41
Canada	26	25	30	20	20	26	27	25	23	29	22	23	30	19	24	28	Brazil	41
Chile	18	21	20	22	19	22	21	19	22	22	17	20	28	29	20	12	Venezuela	40
China	na	na	na	na	na	na	na	na	na	na	na	na	na	na	na	na	Nigeria	39
Colombia	na	45	45	45	42	45	51	57	46	36	53	44	41	55	50	45	Czech Republic	39
Croatia	na	16	16	16	18	17	14	19	16	13	13	16	15	18	18	10	Iceland	39
Czech Republic	30	39	39	39	44	40	35	34	43	48	29	38	48	27	41	56	Morocco	38
Denmark	35	32	38	26	36	29	33	32	46	26	27	31	36	34	35	16	Georgia	37
Dominican Rep.	na	52	47	57	57	46	46	65	53	51	54	46	57	54	53	48	Moldova	36
Egypt	na	na	na	na	na	na	na	na	na	na	na	na	na	na	na	na	Albania	36
El Salvador	na	41	37	46	39	42	44	48	35	34	46	40	35	na	na	na	Bulgaria	36
Estonia	na	31	34	28	37	27	32	32	29	35	26	24	39	24	34	30	Jordan	36
Finland	43	36	38	33	33	35	39	30	42	49	29	37	43	33	39	23	Finland	36
France	20	21	22	21	14	17	28	22	20	21	18	20	22	26	22	12	Pakistan	35
Georgia	na	37	36	38	35	38	39	38	38	33	40	36	35	36	38	43	Uruguay	33
Germany	18	23	26	21	12	23	28	26	20	19	25	24	26	28	23	15	South Africa	33
Great Britain	27	16	14	18	8	12	24	16	16	17	16	14	17	na	na	na	Turkey	33
Greece	na	22	23	22	17	25	28	37	23	19	26	18	24	34	21	15	Argentina	33
Hungary	18	14	15	12	10	13	16	13	14	16	16	11	15	15	13	na	Romania	32
Iceland	36	39	42	35	39	39	37	36	41	39	27	39	47	44	39	23	Sweden	32
India	29	32	31	32	33	30	34	32	31	31	29	35	30	36	29	26	Denmark	32
Indonesia	na	43	40	46	49	41	42	34	45	47	33	51	55	41	44	68	United States	32
Iran	na	22	18	27	20	24	24	24	23	16	18	21	25	25	21	12	India	32
Ireland	33	22	21	23	12	22	28	26	21	17	26	21	20	24	23	10	Latvia	31
Israel	na	30	32	28	33	29	28	22	28	39	18	34	36	56	26	23	New Zealand	31
Italy	18	28	31	25	30	25	29	27	31	23	28	24	30	33	30	23	Estonia	31
Japan	31	28	30	25	12	21	38	34	27	25	30	27	29	39	25	21	Peru	31
Jordan	na	36	32	41	40	37	22	34	37	36	37	29	40	40	33	35	Norway	30
Korea, South	50	30	31	29	20	29	45	48	33	25	32	26	32	37	25	18	Israel	30
Latvia	na	31	29	34	28	25	38	33	31	31	34	31	28	30	32	28	Korea, South	30
Lithuania	na	25	25	25	17	19	39	40	20	26	35	25	23	21	26	21	Serbia	30
Luxembourg	na	22	23	22	14	22	27	22	24	20	25	28	19	27	23	15	Ukraine	29
Macedonia	na	22	23	20	21	24	20	24	21	22	21	23	23	22	20	39	Azerbaijan	29
Malta	na	24	26	23	25	21	27	20	25	29	21	32	26	20	27	27	Belarus	28
Mexico	32	51	49	53	49	49	58	60	42	45	58	45	48	51	51	48	Italy	28
Moldova	na	36	37	36	41	38	31	31	32	47	36	38	37	32	39	49	Northern Ireland	28
Montenegro	na	25	28	20	31	27	17	20	27	26	22	23	24	21	27	30	Japan	28
Morocco	na	38	35	42	37	37	43	41	34	24	52	36	34	39	38	32	Armenia	27
Netherlands	30	23	28	18	21	23	25	22	25	23	20	20	32	29	25	15	Poland	27
New Zealand	na	31	31	32	20	34	32	27	33	37	24	23	44	40	34	24	Portugal	26
Nigeria	34	39	43	36	42	37	32	37	40	41	37	38	44	39	41	34	Canada	25
Northern Ireland	33	28	32	23	33	24	28	27	32	22	24	31	35	34	27	25	Lithuania	25
Norway	34	30	32	28	28	26	38	28	28	37	na	na	na	27	33	17	Montenegro	25
Pakistan	na	35	28	44	42	30	29	51	44	18	47	47	23	38	32	50	Malta	24
Peru	na	31	29	32	29	31	35	32	31	29	30	29	33	34	30	24	Switzerland	23
Philippines	na	41	41	41	40	38	50	45	39	40	40	36	50	40	44	33	Netherlands	23
Poland	30	27	25	29	21	23	35	26	27	29	24	25	37	29	26	27	Germany	23
Portugal	31	26	27	25	28	31	20	25	26	31	25	26	24	22	29	25	Luxembourg	22
Puerto Rico	na	42	44	42	27	36	54	51	51	37	53	36	41	42	44	40	Australia	22
Romania	29	32	35	29	40	31	29	39	31	30	40	29	30	32	30	42	Greece	22
Russian Fed.	11	19	20	17	24	17	17	18	18	21	14	19	23	16	20	17	Ireland	22
Serbia	na	30	32	27	42	32	21	21	32	34	29	29	29	27	33	29	Macedonia	22
Singapore	na	na	na	na	na	na	na	na	na	na	na	na	na	na	na	na	Iran	22
Slovakia	na	22	22	21	23	20	23	19	21	29	19	19	25	18	24	39	Slovakia	22
Slovenia	14	14	17	12	13	12	17	19	14	11	14	12	13	16	13	17	France	21
South Africa	29	33	35	31	37	32	29	37	31	11	38	40	22	30	35	32	Belgium	21
Spain	17	17	16	18	11	15	23	19	14	11	19	15	18	23	16	10	Chile	21
Sweden	35	32	34	31	33	31	34	18	35	40	25	33	40	32	35	24	Austria	19
Switzerland	30	23	27	19	21	20	28	29	22	24	22	23	25	30	26	13	Russian Fed.	19
Taiwan	na	43	38	48	25	44	52	52	41	36	42	45	43	47	37	44	Bosnia and Herz.	18
Tanzania	na	57	58	56	52	58	67	62	51	49	56	56	60	57	58	67	Spain	17
Turkey	25	33	34	32	30	33	40	37	29	23	34	35	26	42	34	23	Croatia	16
Uganda	na	43	42	43	43	38	61	48	39	51	41	56	33	46	41	43	Great Britain	16
Ukraine	na	29	33	25	32	36	22	17	28	37	21	30	38	24	29	48	Slovenia	14
United States	29	32	33	30	32	28	36	31	30	33	29	34	35	32	32	31	Hungary	14
Uruguay	na	33	32	35	18	25	46	43	21	19	40	31	28	48	32	18	Zimbabwe	11
Venezuela	na	40	39	40	40	38	44	42	40	36	43	42	35	44	37	44		
Vietnam	na	92	92	92	90	93	92	93	90	89	87	92	95	94	93	88		
Zimbabwe	na	11	12	10	10	12	13	12	11	na	9	12	13	13	10	18		
Total	27	32	33	31	32	31	33	33	30	32	31	31	34	33	32	26	Total	32

E033B) SELF POSITIONING IN POLITICAL SCALE: LEFT

In political matters, people talk of "the left" and "the right."

How would you place your views on this scale, generally speaking?

% Left (codes 1 to 4 on a 10-point scale)

(WVS: V139; EVS: V185)

Country	Wave 1990	Wave 2000	Gender Male	Gender Female	Age 16-29	Age 30-49	Age 50+	Education Lower	Education Middle	Education Upper	Income Lower	Income Middle	Income Upper	Values Mat	Values Mixed	Values Postm.
Albania	na	40	38	41	37	37	46	43	36	38	44	37	38	40	40	31
Algeria	na	20	18	22	16	22	26	29	20	14	17	19	14	20	19	20
Argentina	18	14	15	12	16	13	12	12	14	17	12	14	14	8	11	21
Armenia	na	29	29	28	21	29	40	35	28	29	22	30	40	32	28	19
Australia	na	23	23	24	24	26	20	18	20	31	22	23	26	21	18	32
Austria	11	20	21	19	19	21	20	16	21	28	21	20	21	11	17	28
Azerbaijan	na	25	24	26	21	27	26	24	27	21	23	23	26	27	21	21
Bangladesh	na	8	8	9	9	6	11	4	10	14	5	7	10	5	9	12
Belarus	60	15	16	14	8	16	23	19	14	17	17	16	12	20	13	4
Belgium	27	25	28	23	28	29	21	22	21	33	23	26	26	20	22	41
Bosnia and Herz.	na	24	24	25	21	24	27	23	24	27	28	23	24	22	25	25
Brazil	30	27	27	27	31	27	17	27	25	30	28	28	26	26	26	34
Bulgaria	31	25	27	23	16	21	34	40	19	21	38	23	18	32	20	3
Canada	16	21	21	21	28	21	18	17	17	30	22	17	25	22	19	26
Chile	30	31	37	25	34	29	31	30	29	36	31	31	31	22	31	44
China	na	na	na	na	na	na	na	na	na	na	na	na	na	na	na	na
Colombia	na	10	10	10	11	10	8	8	9	12	9	10	10	13	8	14
Croatia	na	19	17	20	23	17	18	16	17	32	20	16	22	13	16	32
Czech Republic	22	21	24	19	11	18	29	25	17	20	30	22	14	32	19	14
Denmark	24	26	24	29	27	33	20	20	20	41	23	26	32	16	22	54
Dominican Rep.	na	19	17	19	16	21	18	26	22	16	19	22	13	20	18	24
Egypt	na	na	na	na	na	na	na	na	na	na	na	na	na	na	na	na
El Salvador	na	17	18	16	19	16	15	14	21	20	15	17	20	na	na	na
Estonia	na	11	11	12	11	9	14	10	14	7	12	14	8	14	11	10
Finland	21	24	27	21	22	28	21	27	20	19	28	24	21	24	21	43
France	42	39	41	37	39	43	35	34	43	48	39	43	41	30	37	56
Georgia	na	20	22	18	18	20	21	20	20	20	21	20	18	19	21	25
Germany	36	29	28	29	39	30	23	21	33	40	27	32	28	25	29	34
Great Britain	24	26	27	25	31	29	21	24	24	36	27	30	24	na	na	24
Greece	na	35	37	33	32	38	33	24	31	39	32	35	33	19	32	54
Hungary	18	23	23	22	11	26	28	19	26	34	17	31	17	19	25	43
Iceland	30	28	26	29	27	27	30	26	25	37	38	26	23	18	26	57
India	30	22	23	21	20	23	23	23	22	21	30	21	20	21	22	19
Indonesia	na	9	13	5	9	8	11	14	9	7	13	6	4	11	9	na
Iran	na	39	42	35	43	38	27	32	41	46	39	36	39	38	42	49
Ireland	12	15	16	13	19	16	9	12	16	16	11	14	17	8	15	23
Israel	na	42	41	43	42	44	39	45	46	33	53	40	36	21	46	53
Italy	41	32	34	30	32	36	29	27	33	42	29	34	35	25	29	40
Japan	16	19	20	18	29	19	16	24	18	18	19	19	21	8	20	32
Jordan	na	17	18	17	20	15	17	17	18	17	18	17	17	18	15	26
Korea, South	14	32	34	31	44	32	18	25	25	43	31	32	34	22	39	56
Latvia	na	13	15	12	8	15	14	15	13	12	17	14	8	15	11	21
Lithuania	na	25	24	26	18	23	32	33	25	18	29	26	19	34	22	14
Luxembourg	na	26	27	25	24	28	26	26	26	28	29	30	27	22	23	41
Macedonia	na	27	26	29	22	28	31	29	27	26	31	25	25	25	29	31
Malta	na	13	14	12	12	15	11	14	13	9	19	10	16	15	12	10
Mexico	21	16	17	15	19	14	14	14	19	16	13	17	18	14	16	18
Moldova	na	31	32	29	19	28	44	44	31	20	36	36	23	39	24	27
Montenegro	na	46	44	49	41	42	55	50	44	45	64	45	43	48	45	47
Morocco	na	26	30	20	27	27	22	25	27	32	24	29	25	25	28	25
Netherlands	33	36	34	38	32	43	31	23	35	49	37	36	35	25	31	53
New Zealand	na	21	22	20	38	19	19	17	20	27	24	23	19	12	19	34
Nigeria	22	33	32	35	33	33	38	36	31	34	37	32	34	32	33	41
Northern Ireland	10	19	21	17	12	28	16	19	18	23	22	17	17	13	18	30
Norway	27	24	23	25	26	30	16	23	22	29	na	na	na	21	21	51
Pakistan	na	5	4	5	4	5	3	2	9	1	5	9	2	6	4	na
Peru	na	21	22	20	22	22	16	20	21	21	23	20	17	20	21	21
Philippines	na	10	11	10	12	10	9	9	10	13	14	9	9	9	10	16
Poland	20	27	26	27	23	26	30	24	28	29	31	27	20	28	27	22
Portugal	23	35	31	38	35	29	40	35	32	35	45	30	34	33	33	45
Puerto Rico	na	13	16	11	15	16	9	9	11	14	13	10	15	13	11	16
Romania	19	18	20	15	12	16	25	14	19	20	16	24	17	22	18	8
Russian Fed.	33	30	31	29	17	26	43	44	29	27	37	33	21	31	29	34
Serbia	na	25	25	24	11	22	33	31	23	21	28	21	26	29	21	19
Singapore	na	na	na	na	na	na	na	na	na	na	na	na	na	na	na	na
Slovakia	na	33	34	32	24	35	36	35	32	32	33	35	30	38	31	11
Slovenia	23	25	25	24	16	28	27	16	25	35	15	30	35	23	26	23
South Africa	39	26	25	27	24	26	32	23	29	38	24	27	27	29	24	25
Spain	50	40	44	36	48	44	31	36	42	49	40	40	44	31	38	61
Sweden	28	34	34	34	36	36	31	39	34	30	40	32	29	31	30	46
Switzerland	23	28	27	29	33	31	22	20	27	44	29	26	31	13	23	48
Taiwan	na	4	6	3	8	4	3	4	5	5	3	6	4	3	6	9
Tanzania	na	24	23	26	31	21	20	23	29	19	30	21	17	22	25	24
Turkey	25	20	21	19	23	20	15	15	24	36	17	19	33	13	19	34
Uganda	na	34	35	33	34	37	23	30	37	23	37	25	37	32	35	36
Ukraine	na	27	28	26	18	21	38	43	28	19	37	26	19	34	25	8
United States	17	18	20	15	24	17	15	16	15	20	19	17	19	10	16	25
Uruguay	na	28	27	28	39	34	18	18	37	50	23	26	37	17	26	45
Venezuela	na	17	18	16	16	18	17	19	17	16	21	15	18	20	18	11
Vietnam	na	2	3	2	3	2	3	2	2	2	7	2	na	1	2	5
Zimbabwe	na	59	57	61	62	57	56	59	61	40	63	53	62	56	61	66
Total	27	25	25	24	25	25	24	24	25	26	26	24	23	24	23	33

RANKING

Country	2000
Zimbabwe	59
Montenegro	46
Israel	42
Spain	40
Albania	40
Iran	39
France	39
Netherlands	36
Portugal	35
Greece	35
Uganda	34
Sweden	34
Nigeria	33
Slovakia	33
Korea, South	32
Italy	32
Chile	31
Moldova	31
Russian Fed.	30
Armenia	29
Germany	29
Switzerland	28
Uruguay	28
Iceland	28
Macedonia	27
Ukraine	27
Brazil	27
Poland	27
Denmark	26
Luxembourg	26
Morocco	26
South Africa	26
Great Britain	26
Belgium	25
Bulgaria	25
Lithuania	25
Azerbaijan	25
Slovenia	25
Serbia	25
Norway	24
Finland	24
Tanzania	24
Bosnia and Herz.	24
Australia	23
Hungary	23
India	22
Czech Republic	21
New Zealand	21
Canada	21
Peru	21
Turkey	20
Austria	20
Georgia	20
Algeria	20
Northern Ireland	19
Japan	19
Croatia	19
Dominican Rep.	19
Romania	18
United States	18
Jordan	17
Venezuela	17
El Salvador	17
Mexico	16
Belarus	15
Ireland	15
Argentina	14
Latvia	13
Malta	13
Puerto Rico	13
Estonia	11
Philippines	10
Colombia	10
Indonesia	9
Bangladesh	8
Pakistan	5
Taiwan	4
Vietnam	2
Total	25

E033C) SELF POSITIONING IN POLITICAL SCALE: CENTER

In political matters, people talk of "the left" and "the right."
How would you place your views on this scale, generally speaking?

(WVS: V139; EVS: V185)

% Center (codes 5 & 6 on a 10-point scale)

Country	Wave 1990	Wave 2000	Gender Male	Gender Female	Age 16-29	Age 30-49	Age 50+	Education Lower	Education Middle	Education Upper	Income Lower	Income Middle	Income Upper	Values Mat	Values Mixed	Values Postm.	RANKING Country	RANKING 2000
Albania	na	24	23	26	27	26	19	25	25	21	24	28	22	25	22	36	Croatia	65
Algeria	na	37	37	37	40	37	31	37	37	37	41	42	35	43	32	46	Hungary	64
Argentina	61	54	51	57	53	56	53	53	57	50	50	54	58	55	55	52	Ireland	64
Armenia	na	44	44	45	45	47	38	40	44	45	45	50	36	41	46	50	Malta	63
Australia	na	54	53	56	61	53	50	59	60	45	55	57	48	55	57	51	Slovenia	61
Austria	48	61	61	61	67	62	57	63	62	52	57	62	58	66	65	53	Austria	61
Azerbaijan	na	47	46	47	47	45	50	44	46	47	50	45	42	49	44	30	Pakistan	61
Bangladesh	na	26	22	32	27	27	13	24	28	25	21	31	22	18	29	37	Bosnia and Herz.	58
Belarus	30	57	53	61	59	55	57	58	60	47	63	55	52	62	58	31	Great Britain	58
Belgium	42	54	50	58	55	53	54	58	57	47	53	58	52	59	54	47	Estonia	58
Bosnia and Herz.	na	58	56	60	60	58	56	55	60	55	60	60	52	61	56	57	Belarus	57
Brazil	39	33	31	35	33	34	30	24	39	41	27	34	38	29	35	34	Latvia	56
Bulgaria	47	39	35	44	38	45	32	36	41	38	33	42	40	36	42	47	Australia	54
Canada	58	54	50	59	52	54	55	59	60	41	55	61	45	59	57	46	Argentina	54
Chile	52	48	43	54	48	50	48	51	49	42	52	49	41	50	49	44	Canada	54
China	na	na	na	na	na	na	na	na	na	na	na	na	na	na	na	na	Belgium	54
Colombia	na	46	46	45	47	46	41	35	46	52	38	46	49	31	42	41	Japan	54
Croatia	na	65	67	63	59	66	68	65	68	55	67	68	62	69	66	59	Northern Ireland	53
Czech Republic	49	40	38	42	45	42	35	41	40	33	41	40	38	42	40	30	Taiwan	53
Denmark	41	42	39	45	37	38	47	49	35	33	51	43	32	50	43	31	Russian Fed.	52
Dominican Rep.	na	29	36	24	27	33	36	10	25	33	27	32	30	26	29	29	Luxembourg	51
Egypt	na	na	na	na	na	na	na	na	na	na	na	na	na	na	na	na	Macedonia	51
El Salvador	na	42	45	39	42	42	41	38	44	46	39	43	45	na	na	na	United States	51
Estonia	na	58	56	60	52	64	54	58	57	58	62	62	52	62	56	61	Lithuania	50
Finland	36	40	35	45	45	36	40	44	38	32	44	39	36	43	40	34	Romania	49
France	38	40	38	42	47	40	37	45	37	31	43	38	37	44	41	32	Peru	49
Georgia	na	43	42	44	47	42	40	42	42	46	39	45	48	45	42	32	Switzerland	49
Germany	46	48	46	51	49	47	49	52	46	41	48	44	47	47	48	51	Philippines	49
Great Britain	50	58	59	58	61	60	55	61	61	48	58	55	59	na	na	na	Chile	48
Greece	na	43	41	45	52	37	39	39	46	42	42	47	43	48	47	31	Germany	48
Hungary	65	64	62	65	78	62	56	68	59	49	67	58	68	65	62	57	Indonesia	47
Iceland	34	34	32	36	34	34	34	38	34	24	35	36	30	38	35	20	Jordan	47
India	41	47	47	46	47	47	44	45	47	48	41	43	51	43	49	55	Poland	47
Indonesia	na	47	47	49	42	51	47	52	46	47	54	44	41	49	48	32	Azerbaijan	47
Iran	na	39	40	39	37	38	49	44	36	39	43	43	36	37	37	39	India	47
Ireland	55	64	63	64	70	62	62	62	63	67	63	65	63	69	62	67	Slovakia	46
Israel	na	28	27	28	24	27	33	32	26	28	29	26	27	24	29	25	Serbia	46
Italy	42	40	36	45	38	39	42	47	36	35	43	42	36	42	42	37	Colombia	46
Japan	54	54	50	58	59	61	46	42	55	57	52	54	51	54	54	47	Norway	45
Jordan	na	47	50	43	40	48	61	49	46	47	46	54	43	42	52	39	Puerto Rico	45
Korea, South	36	38	35	40	37	39	37	27	42	33	37	43	35	41	36	27	Armenia	44
Latvia	na	56	57	54	64	61	48	53	56	56	50	55	64	55	57	51	Ukraine	44
Lithuania	na	50	51	49	65	58	29	27	56	56	36	49	58	44	52	64	Greece	43
Luxembourg	na	51	50	53	62	50	47	53	50	52	46	43	54	51	53	45	Venezuela	43
Macedonia	na	51	51	50	56	49	50	47	52	52	49	52	52	54	50	30	Georgia	43
Malta	na	63	60	66	64	62	62	66	62	63	60	58	58	65	62	63	Spain	43
Mexico	48	33	34	33	32	36	28	27	39	38	29	38	34	35	33	34	Turkey	43
Moldova	na	33	31	35	40	34	26	25	37	33	29	26	40	30	37	24	New Zealand	42
Montenegro	na	29	28	31	28	31	28	29	28	30	15	32	33	31	28	23	Denmark	42
Morocco	na	36	35	38	37	36	35	34	39	44	25	35	41	36	35	43	El Salvador	42
Netherlands	37	41	38	44	47	35	45	56	41	29	43	44	34	46	44	32	Netherlands	41
New Zealand	na	42	43	41	39	43	42	48	42	33	46	49	33	43	42	41	South Africa	41
Nigeria	44	27	26	29	25	30	30	27	29	26	26	30	22	29	26	26	Finland	40
Northern Ireland	57	53	46	60	55	48	56	54	51	55	54	52	48	53	55	45	Italy	40
Norway	39	45	44	46	46	45	46	50	51	35	na	na	na	52	46	32	France	40
Pakistan	na	61	68	51	54	65	68	47	44	81	47	44	75	56	64	50	Czech Republic	40
Peru	na	49	50	48	50	48	50	49	48	50	46	51	51	46	49	55	Portugal	40
Philippines	na	49	48	49	49	52	42	47	51	47	47	55	41	51	46	51	Iran	39
Poland	50	47	49	44	57	51	35	50	45	42	45	48	43	43	47	51	Uruguay	39
Portugal	46	40	42	38	37	40	41	39	42	34	30	43	42	45	38	29	Bulgaria	39
Puerto Rico	na	45	40	48	58	48	37	40	38	50	34	54	43	45	45	45	Korea, South	38
Romania	53	49	45	56	47	53	46	47	50	51	45	47	53	46	52	50	Algeria	37
Russian Fed.	56	52	49	54	59	56	40	38	53	52	49	49	56	52	51	49	Morocco	36
Serbia	na	46	43	49	47	45	46	48	45	46	44	51	45	44	46	53	Sweden	34
Singapore	na	na	na	na	na	na	na	na	na	na	na	na	na	na	na	na	Iceland	34
Slovakia	na	46	44	48	53	46	41	46	47	39	48	46	45	44	46	50	Mexico	33
Slovenia	63	61	59	64	71	60	56	65	62	54	71	58	52	61	61	60	Moldova	33
South Africa	32	41	40	42	39	43	39	40	41	51	38	33	51	41	41	42	Brazil	33
Spain	33	43	41	45	41	41	46	45	44	34	41	45	38	46	46	30	Zimbabwe	29
Sweden	37	34	33	35	31	34	35	43	31	30	35	35	31	37	35	30	Montenegro	29
Switzerland	47	49	46	52	46	49	51	51	51	32	49	51	44	57	51	39	Dominican Rep.	29
Taiwan	na	53	57	49	67	52	44	44	55	60	54	49	53	50	58	47	Israel	28
Tanzania	na	19	19	18	17	22	13	15	20	32	14	24	23	21	17	10	Nigeria	27
Turkey	51	43	42	44	44	44	39	43	44	40	43	43	40	42	44	40	Bangladesh	26
Uganda	na	23	23	24	23	25	17	22	24	27	22	20	30	22	25	21	Albania	24
Ukraine	na	44	39	49	50	44	40	40	44	45	43	44	44	43	46	44	Uganda	23
United States	54	51	47	55	45	55	49	54	55	47	53	49	47	58	51	45	Tanzania	19
Uruguay	na	39	41	37	44	41	36	39	41	32	37	43	35	35	42	37	Vietnam	6
Venezuela	na	43	43	44	44	44	39	39	43	48	37	43	46	46	44	44		
Vietnam	na	6	6	6	7	6	6	4	7	9	7	6	5	5	6	7		
Zimbabwe	na	29	30	29	28	30	32	30	29	60	28	35	25	31	30	16		
Total	46	44	43	45	44	44	43	43	45	42	43	45	43	44	44	41	Total	44

E34) Society Changes

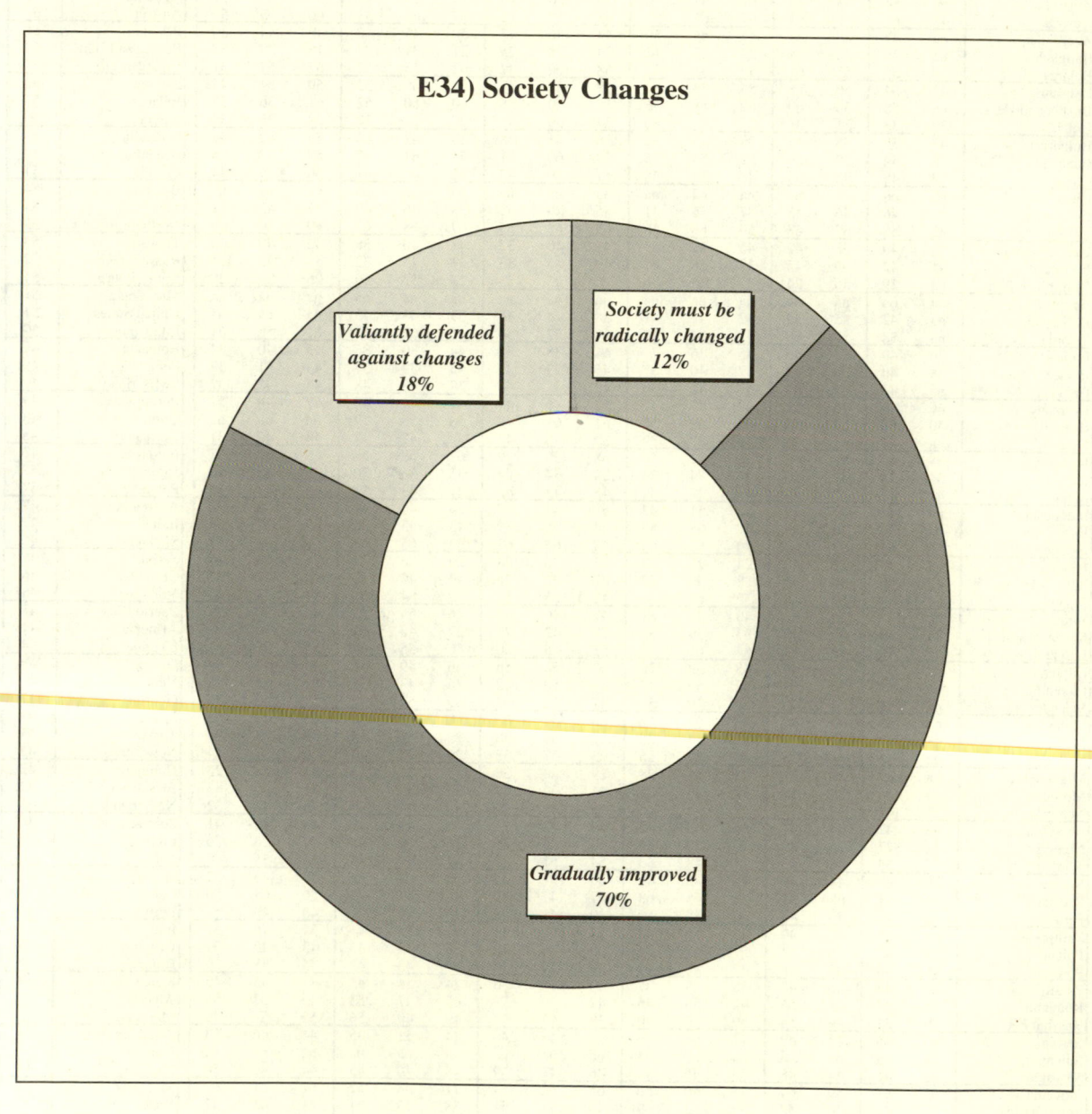

Society must be radically changed
12%

Valiantly defended against changes
18%

Gradually improved
70%

E034A) SOCIAL CHANGE: CONSERVATIVE

On this card are three basic kinds of attitudes concerning the society we live in.

Please choose the one which best describes your own opinion.

Our present society must be valiantly defended against all subversive forces (%)　　(WVS: V140; EVS: o23)

Country	Wave 1990	Wave 2000	Gender Male	Gender Female	Age 16-29	Age 30-49	Age 50+	Education Lower	Education Middle	Education Upper	Income Lower	Income Middle	Income Upper	Values Mat	Values Mixed	Values Postm.
Albania	na	20	18	22	21	19	21	26	19	9	22	17	20	18	22	22
Algeria	na	20	18	23	21	20	21	25	20	17	19	23	21	25	19	15
Argentina	11	15	14	15	14	14	16	18	11	5	18	14	11	20	14	10
Armenia	na	7	8	7	8	5	10	15	8	4	8	6	8	8	7	3
Australia	na	17	15	18	11	14	24	26	16	10	21	13	14	18	17	15
Austria	20	17	15	19	14	14	21	21	14	9	23	14	14	26	19	11
Azerbaijan	na	4	4	5	4	4	6	12	5	3	5	5	5	5	4	na
Bangladesh	na	44	43	47	42	47	44	51	38	35	41	40	54	48	43	41
Belarus	28	8	6	9	5	7	10	12	8	1	8	8	5	8	7	2
Belgium	21	na	na	na	na	na	na	na	na	na	na	na	na	na	na	na
Bosnia and Herz.	na	13	12	13	11	12	15	11	14	9	12	14	11	16	11	15
Brazil	10	21	22	21	19	22	24	24	20	15	22	26	17	22	23	14
Bulgaria	19	na	na	na	na	na	na	na	na	na	na	na	na	na	na	na
Canada	13	15	13	17	13	12	21	23	14	11	20	17	10	27	16	12
Chile	23	13	15	11	13	11	15	15	12	10	16	10	13	16	13	8
China	25	na	na	na	na	na	na	na	na	na	na	na	na	na	na	na
Colombia	na	19	16	22	26	15	17	22	24	10	25	22	12	18	20	23
Croatia	na	na	na	na	na	na	na	na	na	na	na	na	na	na	na	na
Czech Republic	15	19	19	19	28	16	16	21	17	18	22	18	18	22	17	18
Denmark	22	na	na	na	na	na	na	na	na	na	na	na	na	na	na	na
Dominican Rep.	na	16	19	15	16	16	18	28	24	12	16	17	11	30	14	9
Egypt	na	17	18	15	15	18	17	19	17	12	17	18	15	15	18	20
El Salvador	na	15	12	18	16	15	13	18	14	9	20	15	7	na	na	na
Estonia	17	na	na	na	na	na	na	na	na	na	na	na	na	na	na	na
Finland	9	na	na	na	na	na	na	na	na	na	na	na	na	na	na	na
France	21	na	na	na	na	na	na	na	na	na	na	na	na	na	na	na
Georgia	na	3	3	3	4	2	3	4	3	2	3	3	3	3	3	6
Germany	4	na	na	na	na	na	na	na	na	na	na	na	na	na	na	na
Great Britain	14	na	na	na	na	na	na	na	na	na	na	na	na	na	na	na
Greece	na	na	na	na	na	na	na	na	na	na	na	na	na	na	na	na
Hungary	17	na	na	na	na	na	na	na	na	na	na	na	na	na	na	na
Iceland	15	na	na	na	na	na	na	na	na	na	na	na	na	na	na	na
India	17	19	19	18	17	19	20	17	20	21	17	17	21	19	19	22
Indonesia	na	16	17	17	17	17	16	19	19	12	16	17	17	19	15	33
Iran	na	na	na	na	na	na	na	na	na	na	na	na	na	na	na	na
Ireland	20	na	na	na	na	na	na	na	na	na	na	na	na	na	na	na
Israel	na	na	na	na	na	na	na	na	na	na	12	11	6	14	9	6
Italy	10	9	8	10	8	7	12	13	8	3	12	11	6	14	9	6
Japan	21	14	17	12	5	14	18	22	15	11	17	10	17	27	12	11
Jordan	na	49	48	49	47	50	47	52	45	46	51	49	50	50	48	41
Korea, South	11	32	29	35	21	34	40	70	37	19	35	32	28	37	28	12
Latvia	11	na	na	na	na	na	na	na	na	na	na	na	na	na	na	na
Lithuania	10	10	8	12	11	11	8	8	11	9	8	11	8	13	8	22
Luxembourg	na	na	na	na	na	na	na	na	na	na	na	na	na	na	na	na
Macedonia	na	24	24	24	27	23	22	23	26	19	27	23	21	23	23	37
Malta	na	na	na	na	na	na	na	na	na	na	na	na	na	na	na	na
Mexico	13	26	22	30	25	26	27	29	25	15	27	27	25	29	24	25
Moldova	na	14	15	14	13	13	17	15	17	10	15	15	14	18	12	9
Montenegro	na	12	11	13	13	8	16	14	10	9	5	9	16	14	9	16
Morocco	na	9	9	9	8	10	6	8	7	16	2	10	11	7	9	13
Netherlands	23	na	na	na	na	na	na	na	na	na	na	na	na	na	na	na
New Zealand	na	10	10	10	7	7	15	16	7	6	13	10	8	8	11	7
Nigeria	13	13	14	12	15	12	9	12	14	14	12	14	14	13	13	15
Northern Ireland	21	na	na	na	na	na	na	na	na	na	na	na	na	na	na	na
Norway	31	30	29	32	23	24	44	43	31	18	na	na	na	46	30	15
Pakistan	na	17	16	18	14	20	13	17	16	18	19	16	18	14	21	20
Peru	na	20	17	22	21	19	18	25	20	17	22	19	17	23	20	16
Philippines	na	16	13	19	21	15	12	14	16	19	15	15	18	14	17	24
Poland	12	na	na	na	na	na	na	na	na	na	na	na	na	na	na	na
Portugal	11	na	na	na	na	na	na	na	na	na	na	na	na	na	na	na
Puerto Rico	na	17	17	17	22	10	20	19	19	15	19	17	13	15	17	16
Romania	na	na	na	na	na	na	na	na	na	na	na	na	na	na	na	na
Russian Fed.	34	6	5	6	5	5	7	11	6	2	7	6	4	6	6	na
Serbia	na	12	10	14	12	10	14	17	12	5	16	11	9	15	10	5
Singapore	na	na	na	na	na	na	na	na	na	na	na	na	na	na	na	na
Slovakia	na	na	na	na	na	na	na	na	na	na	na	na	na	na	na	na
Slovenia	12	11	10	12	12	10	13	17	11	2	14	5	8	16	10	9
South Africa	21	15	17	14	15	16	17	17	14	5	20	14	11	18	13	16
Spain	6	9	10	8	8	8	11	9	9	10	13	8	10	7	11	6
Sweden	8	na	na	na	na	na	na	na	na	na	na	na	na	na	na	na
Switzerland	na	17	16	19	12	15	23	31	16	5	20	20	10	26	19	8
Taiwan	na	24	23	25	21	27	19	27	22	23	27	24	19	27	23	14
Tanzania	na	41	37	48	43	38	49	49	36	28	46	44	30	42	42	38
Turkey	26	20	18	23	20	20	22	25	16	9	21	20	16	23	21	12
Uganda	na	15	22	9	17	14	14	15	15	25	17	16	19	11	17	21
Ukraine	na	4	4	4	6	2	4	5	4	3	4	3	4	5	2	3
United States	18	16	19	14	12	12	26	27	17	12	19	15	13	16	18	15
Uruguay	na	19	19	20	22	16	21	25	12	10	22	23	13	24	20	16
Venezuela	na	30	26	33	32	26	33	33	30	26	28	37	27	27	31	29
Vietnam	na	16	17	15	16	16	16	16	15	16	18	14	16	11	17	20
Zimbabwe	na	20	18	21	21	17	22	21	19	8	21	18	17	20	20	14
Total	17	18	17	18	18	17	18	22	16	13	19	17	16	19	18	14

RANKING

Country	2000
Jordan	49
Bangladesh	44
Tanzania	41
Korea, South	32
Norway	30
Venezuela	30
Mexico	26
Taiwan	24
Macedonia	24
Brazil	21
Algeria	20
Turkey	20
Albania	20
Peru	20
Zimbabwe	20
Uruguay	19
Colombia	19
Czech Republic	19
India	19
Switzerland	17
Egypt	17
Pakistan	17
Austria	17
Australia	17
Puerto Rico	17
Indonesia	16
United States	16
Dominican Rep.	16
Philippines	16
Vietnam	16
Uganda	15
Canada	15
South Africa	15
El Salvador	15
Argentina	15
Moldova	14
Japan	14
Nigeria	13
Chile	13
Bosnia and Herz.	13
Serbia	12
Montenegro	12
Slovenia	11
New Zealand	10
Lithuania	10
Spain	9
Italy	9
Morocco	9
Belarus	8
Armenia	7
Russian Fed.	6
Azerbaijan	4
Ukraine	4
Georgia	3
Total	18

E034B) SOCIAL CHANGE: RADICAL

On this card are three basic kinds of attitudes concerning the society we live in.
Please choose the one which best describes your own opinion.
Our society must be radically changed by revolutionary action (%)

(WVS: V140; EVS: o23)

Country	Wave 1990	Wave 2000	Gender Male	Gender Female	Age 16-29	Age 30-49	Age 50+	Education Lower	Education Middle	Education Upper	Income Lower	Income Middle	Income Upper	Values Mat	Values Mixed	Values Postm.
Albania	na	11	14	7	8	12	11	12	11	5	14	11	6	9	11	8
Algeria	na	7	9	5	9	6	7	9	7	7	8	7	6	6	8	7
Argentina	8	4	5	3	6	3	3	3	5	4	5	4	3	3	4	5
Armenia	na	16	19	13	17	15	16	17	16	14	13	15	22	15	18	12
Australia	na	6	6	7	11	5	3	8	7	3	8	5	4	9	5	7
Austria	2	2	2	2	4	2	1	2	3	2	3	2	2	4	2	2
Azerbaijan	na	24	22	25	23	26	20	23	25	22	29	25	19	22	26	31
Bangladesh	na	13	14	12	13	13	13	12	14	15	7	17	14	10	15	8
Belarus	26	5	7	4	7	5	4	4	5	8	6	4	7	5	5	8
Belgium	3	na	na	na	na	na	na	na	na	na	na	na	na	na	na	na
Bosnia and Herz.	na	12	12	12	11	13	12	11	12	14	13	12	13	13	12	15
Brazil	16	18	18	18	20	19	13	18	19	16	19	18	17	17	19	18
Bulgaria	22	14	na	na	na	na	na	na	na	na	na	na	na	na	na	na
Canada	5	7	6	8	17	5	3	8	9	4	10	9	4	9	7	8
Chile	5	8	9	7	9	9	6	9	8	7	9	7	7	4	8	14
China	5	na	na	na	na	na	na	na	na	na	na	na	na	na	na	na
Colombia	na	7	8	7	8	7	6	8	6	8	7	7	8	11	6	11
Croatia	na	na	na	na	na	na	na	na	na	na	na	na	na	na	na	na
Czech Republic	42	6	7	6	6	7	5	8	5	2	9	7	3	10	6	3
Denmark	2	na	na	na	na	na	na	na	na	na	na	na	na	na	na	na
Dominican Rep.	na	13	11	14	12	14	18	21	13	12	17	8	14	16	12	14
Egypt	na	5	5	5	5	5	5	5	5	6	5	6	6	7	4	5
El Salvador	na	6	6	6	7	6	5	7	6	6	6	6	6	na	na	na
Estonia	22	na	na	na	na	na	na	na	na	na	na	na	na	na	na	na
Finland	3	na	na	na	na	na	na	na	na	na	na	na	na	na	na	na
France	4	na	na	na	na	na	na	na	na	na	na	na	na	na	na	na
Georgia	na	10	11	9	10	9	11	9	10	10	11	9	8	9	10	16
Germany	13	na	na	na	na	na	na	na	na	na	na	na	na	na	na	na
Great Britain	5	na	na	na	na	na	na	na	na	na	na	na	na	na	na	na
Greece	na	na	na	na	na	na	na	na	na	na	na	na	na	na	na	na
Hungary	6	na	na	na	na	na	na	na	na	na	na	na	na	na	na	na
Iceland	3	na	na	na	na	na	na	na	na	na	na	na	na	na	na	na
India	14	14	17	10	19	12	12	13	15	16	14	16	12	15	14	10
Indonesia	na	5	6	4	4	3	8	8	5	4	9	3	4	8	3	4
Iran	na	na	na	na	na	na	na	na	na	na	na	na	na	na	na	na
Ireland	4	na	na	na	na	na	na	na	na	na	na	na	na	na	na	na
Israel	na	na	na	na	na	na	na	na	na	na	na	na	na	na	na	na
Italy	7	4	5	3	8	4	3	4	5	4	5	3	4	2	4	5
Japan	2	5	4	6	10	6	2	9	5	3	5	5	4	2	5	5
Jordan	na	10	10	9	12	8	7	6	11	13	8	6	10	10	9	15
Korea, South	7	10	11	8	10	11	6	4	10	10	13	8	8	7	10	25
Latvia	31	na	na	na	na	na	na	na	na	na	na	na	na	na	na	na
Lithuania	32	23	25	21	17	27	23	17	27	14	30	22	21	20	25	23
Luxembourg	na	na	na	na	na	na	na	na	na	na	na	na	na	na	na	na
Macedonia	na	15	16	15	16	14	16	20	14	12	19	14	14	14	17	5
Malta	na	na	na	na	na	na	na	na	na	na	na	na	na	na	na	na
Mexico	17	16	15	17	16	15	16	18	15	10	18	15	13	19	16	11
Moldova	na	28	28	27	32	26	27	28	26	30	28	26	28	23	29	28
Montenegro	na	11	12	9	11	9	11	10	11	11	12	9	7	8	13	11
Morocco	na	6	8	4	9	4	4	5	9	9	5	7	9	4	7	14
Netherlands	2	na	na	na	na	na	na	na	na	na	na	na	na	na	na	na
New Zealand	na	5	5	5	14	5	2	5	5	5	6	5	4	6	4	6
Nigeria	28	31	32	30	32	32	28	29	34	31	29	31	36	33	29	37
Northern Ireland	5	na	na	na	na	na	na	na	na	na	na	na	na	na	na	na
Norway	2	3	2	4	4	4	1	4	3	1	na	na	na	1	3	2
Pakistan	na	20	20	19	28	17	12	18	23	18	18	22	19	20	19	20
Peru	na	6	7	5	6	7	6	4	6	7	5	5	5	6	6	4
Philippines	na	21	21	20	23	19	22	25	21	16	19	19	25	19	22	22
Poland	23	na	na	na	na	na	na	na	na	na	na	na	na	na	na	na
Portugal	4	na	na	na	na	na	na	na	na	na	na	na	na	na	na	na
Puerto Rico	na	4	7	3	7	5	2	3	3	5	4	4	5	6	4	5
Romania	na	na	na	na	na	na	na	na	na	na	na	na	na	na	na	na
Russian Fed.	17	15	16	13	14	15	15	16	15	13	18	14	12	13	16	24
Serbia	na	9	11	7	8	8	9	10	9	5	10	7	7	8	9	12
Singapore	na	na	na	na	na	na	na	na	na	na	na	na	na	na	na	na
Slovakia	na	na	na	na	na	na	na	na	na	na	na	na	na	na	na	na
Slovenia	14	7	8	7	8	9	4	12	7	2	10	9	2	5	8	7
South Africa	19	20	20	20	19	20	18	23	15	25	20	26	12	16	21	25
Spain	4	6	6	5	7	7	4	6	6	6	2	5	9	4	6	7
Sweden	6	na	na	na	na	na	na	na	na	na	na	na	na	na	na	na
Switzerland	na	7	8	5	10	7	5	7	7	6	8	6	6	7	7	6
Taiwan	na	3	4	2	5	3	3	2	4	3	4	3	3	2	5	na
Tanzania	na	27	29	24	27	28	21	26	28	31	26	28	24	28	26	42
Turkey	14	22	22	23	25	22	17	20	26	25	23	21	27	15	22	33
Uganda	na	9	11	8	8	13	2	8	10	16	11	9	11	8	10	9
Ukraine	na	10	13	7	7	10	10	13	11	5	14	10	5	9	11	2
United States	7	9	9	9	16	8	4	16	9	5	12	7	5	9	7	12
Uruguay	na	9	10	8	8	13	6	6	12	13	8	9	9	6	10	7
Venezuela	na	13	14	11	11	15	12	11	13	14	13	9	14	15	12	9
Vietnam	na	54	55	54	58	54	51	59	50	43	57	54	53	55	53	48
Zimbabwe	na	13	14	12	12	16	10	13	12	30	15	11	14	13	13	10
Total	12	12	13	11	14	12	9	13	13	10	13	12	12	13	12	11

RANKING

Country	2000
Vietnam	54
Nigeria	31
Moldova	28
Tanzania	27
Azerbaijan	24
Lithuania	23
Turkey	22
Philippines	21
South Africa	20
Pakistan	20
Brazil	18
Armenia	16
Mexico	16
Macedonia	15
Russian Fed.	15
India	14
Bangladesh	13
Dominican Rep.	13
Zimbabwe	13
Venezuela	13
Bosnia and Herz.	12
Albania	11
Montenegro	11
Georgia	10
Ukraine	10
Jordan	10
Korea, South	10
Uganda	9
United States	9
Serbia	9
Uruguay	9
Chile	8
Algeria	7
Slovenia	7
Colombia	7
Canada	7
Switzerland	7
Czech Republic	6
El Salvador	6
Australia	6
Morocco	6
Peru	6
Spain	6
Belarus	5
Indonesia	5
Egypt	5
New Zealand	5
Japan	5
Puerto Rico	4
Italy	4
Argentina	4
Taiwan	3
Norway	3
Austria	2
Total	12

E034C) SOCIAL CHANGE: REFORMS

On this card are three basic kinds of attitudes concerning the society we live in.
Please choose the one which best describes your own opinion.

(WVS: V140; EVS: o23)

Our society must be gradually improved by reforms (%)

Country	Wave 1990	Wave 2000	Gender Male	Gender Female	Age 16-29	Age 30-49	Age 50+	Education Lower	Education Middle	Education Upper	Income Lower	Income Middle	Income Upper	Values Mat	Values Mixed	Values Postm.	RANKING Country	RANKING 2000
Albania	na	69	68	71	72	69	68	61	70	86	64	72	74	73	68	69	Georgia	87
Algeria	na	72	73	71	70	75	72	66	73	75	73	70	73	70	73	78	Belarus	87
Argentina	81	82	81	82	80	84	81	79	84	91	77	82	86	76	82	84	Italy	87
Armenia	na	77	74	80	76	80	74	68	76	82	79	79	70	77	75	85	Ukraine	87
Australia	na	77	79	76	78	81	73	67	77	87	72	82	82	73	78	78	Morocco	85
Austria	78	81	83	79	82	85	78	77	83	90	74	84	85	70	80	87	Spain	85
Azerbaijan	na	72	75	70	73	70	74	65	71	76	66	70	77	73	70	69	Argentina	82
Bangladesh	na	42	43	41	44	41	43	37	48	50	52	44	32	42	42	51	New Zealand	82
Belarus	46	87	87	87	88	88	85	85	87	91	86	88	87	86	89	90	Slovenia	82
Belgium	75	na	na	na	na	na	na	na	na	na	na	na	na	na	na	na	Austria	81
Bosnia and Herz.	na	75	76	75	77	75	73	78	74	77	74	74	76	71	78	71	Japan	81
Brazil	74	61	60	61	61	59	63	59	61	70	59	56	66	61	59	68	Russian Fed.	80
Bulgaria	59	na	na	na	na	na	na	na	na	na	na	na	na	na	na	na	Serbia	80
Canada	82	78	81	75	70	83	76	69	78	85	71	75	86	64	78	81	Chile	79
Chile	72	79	76	82	78	80	78	76	80	83	74	84	80	80	79	78	El Salvador	79
China	70	na	na	na	na	na	na	na	na	na	na	na	na	na	na	na	Puerto Rico	79
Colombia	na	74	76	71	66	78	77	70	70	82	68	71	81	71	74	66	Egypt	78
Croatia	na	na	na	na	na	na	na	na	na	na	na	na	na	na	na	na	Indonesia	78
Czech Republic	42	75	75	75	66	76	78	71	78	81	70	76	79	69	77	79	Montenegro	78
Denmark	77	na	na	na	na	na	na	na	na	na	na	na	na	na	na	na	Canada	78
Dominican Rep.	na	71	71	71	72	71	64	52	63	76	67	75	75	54	74	77	Australia	77
Egypt	na	78	77	80	80	77	78	76	78	81	78	76	80	78	78	76	Armenia	77
El Salvador	na	79	82	76	77	79	82	76	80	85	74	80	87	na	na	na	Switzerland	76
Estonia	61	na	na	na	na	na	na	na	na	na	na	na	na	na	na	na	Uganda	75
Finland	88	na	na	na	na	na	na	na	na	na	na	na	na	na	na	na	Bosnia and Herz.	75
France	75	na	na	na	na	na	na	na	na	na	na	na	na	na	na	na	United States	75
Georgia	na	87	86	88	86	88	87	87	87	89	86	88	89	88	87	78	Czech Republic	75
Germany	84	na	na	na	na	na	na	na	na	na	na	na	na	na	na	na	Peru	74
Great Britain	81	na	na	na	na	na	na	na	na	na	na	na	na	na	na	na	Colombia	74
Greece	na	na	na	na	na	na	na	na	na	na	na	na	na	na	na	na	Taiwan	73
Hungary	77	na	na	na	na	na	na	na	na	na	na	na	na	na	na	na	Algeria	72
Iceland	82	na	na	na	na	na	na	na	na	na	na	na	na	na	na	na	Azerbaijan	72
India	69	67	64	72	64	69	68	70	65	64	69	67	67	66	67	68	Uruguay	72
Indonesia	na	78	77	79	80	80	75	73	76	84	75	79	79	72	82	63	Dominican Rep.	71
Iran	na	na	na	na	na	na	na	na	na	na	na	na	na	na	na	na	Albania	69
Ireland	76	na	na	na	na	na	na	na	na	na	na	na	na	na	na	na	Zimbabwe	68
Israel	na	na	na	na	na	na	na	na	na	na	na	na	na	na	na	na	Lithuania	67
Italy	83	87	87	87	84	90	86	84	88	93	84	86	90	84	87	89	India	67
Japan	77	81	80	82	85	80	80	68	80	87	78	84	79	72	83	84	Norway	67
Jordan	na	42	42	42	41	41	46	41	44	41	41	44	40	40	43	44	South Africa	65
Korea, South	81	59	60	58	70	55	54	27	53	72	52	61	64	56	62	63	Pakistan	64
Latvia	59	na	na	na	na	na	na	na	na	na	na	na	na	na	na	na	Philippines	63
Lithuania	59	67	67	68	72	62	69	74	63	77	61	68	71	67	67	55	Macedonia	61
Luxembourg	na	na	na	na	na	na	na	na	na	na	na	na	na	na	na	na	Brazil	61
Macedonia	na	61	61	62	57	63	63	57	60	69	55	64	65	63	60	59	Korea, South	59
Malta	na	na	na	na	na	na	na	na	na	na	na	na	na	na	na	na	Mexico	59
Mexico	71	59	64	54	59	59	57	53	61	75	55	59	62	52	60	64	Moldova	58
Moldova	na	58	57	59	55	61	57	57	57	60	57	59	58	59	59	63	Venezuela	58
Montenegro	na	78	78	78	76	83	73	76	79	80	83	82	76	78	78	73	Nigeria	56
Morocco	na	85	84	87	83	86	90	87	84	75	93	84	80	89	85	74	Turkey	53
Netherlands	75	na	na	na	na	na	na	na	na	na	na	na	na	na	na	na	Bangladesh	42
New Zealand	na	82	82	81	78	84	81	76	85	87	79	83	86	84	83	85	Jordan	42
Nigeria	59	56	54	58	54	57	64	59	53	55	60	55	50	54	58	49	Tanzania	32
Northern Ireland	75	na	na	na	na	na	na	na	na	na	na	na	na	na	na	na	Vietnam	30
Norway	66	67	69	65	73	72	56	54	66	81	na	na	na	53	67	82		
Pakistan	na	64	64	64	59	63	75	65	61	64	63	63	63	66	60	60		
Peru	na	74	76	72	73	74	77	72	74	76	71	76	78	71	74	80		
Philippines	na	63	66	60	56	67	66	61	63	65	66	66	58	67	61	54		
Poland	65	na	na	na	na	na	na	na	na	na	na	na	na	na	na	na		
Portugal	85	na	na	na	na	na	na	na	na	na	na	na	na	na	na	na		
Puerto Rico	na	79	77	80	71	84	78	79	78	79	77	79	82	80	79	79		
Romania	na	na	na	na	na	na	na	na	na	na	na	na	na	na	na	na		
Russian Fed.	49	80	78	81	81	80	78	74	79	84	75	80	84	81	78	76		
Serbia	na	80	80	80	81	82	77	73	79	90	74	82	84	77	81	84		
Singapore	na	na	na	na	na	na	na	na	na	na	na	na	na	na	na	na		
Slovakia	na	na	na	na	na	na	na	na	na	na	na	na	na	na	na	na		
Slovenia	73	82	82	81	81	81	83	71	83	96	76	86	90	79	82	84		
South Africa	60	65	64	67	66	64	66	60	71	70	60	61	78	66	66	59		
Spain	91	85	84	86	85	86	85	85	85	85	84	87	82	89	83	87		
Sweden	86	na	na	na	na	na	na	na	na	na	na	na	na	na	na	na		
Switzerland	na	76	76	76	78	78	73	62	78	89	72	74	84	67	75	87		
Taiwan	na	73	73	72	74	71	78	71	74	74	69	73	78	72	72	86		
Tanzania	na	32	34	29	30	34	30	26	36	42	28	28	46	30	32	21		
Turkey	61	53	56	50	52	53	56	50	54	64	50	55	54	56	53	51		
Uganda	na	75	67	83	75	73	84	77	76	60	73	76	70	80	73	70		
Ukraine	na	87	83	90	87	88	85	82	86	92	82	87	92	86	86	95		
United States	75	75	73	78	73	81	70	57	74	83	69	77	82	75	76	74		
Uruguay	na	72	71	73	70	71	74	69	75	78	71	68	78	71	70	77		
Venezuela	na	58	60	56	57	59	56	56	57	61	59	54	59	58	57	63		
Vietnam	na	30	29	32	26	31	33	25	34	41	25	32	31	34	30	33		
Zimbabwe	na	68	68	68	68	67	68	67	69	62	64	71	69	68	67	76		
Total	71	70	70	71	69	71	72	65	71	77	68	71	73	69	70	75	Total	70

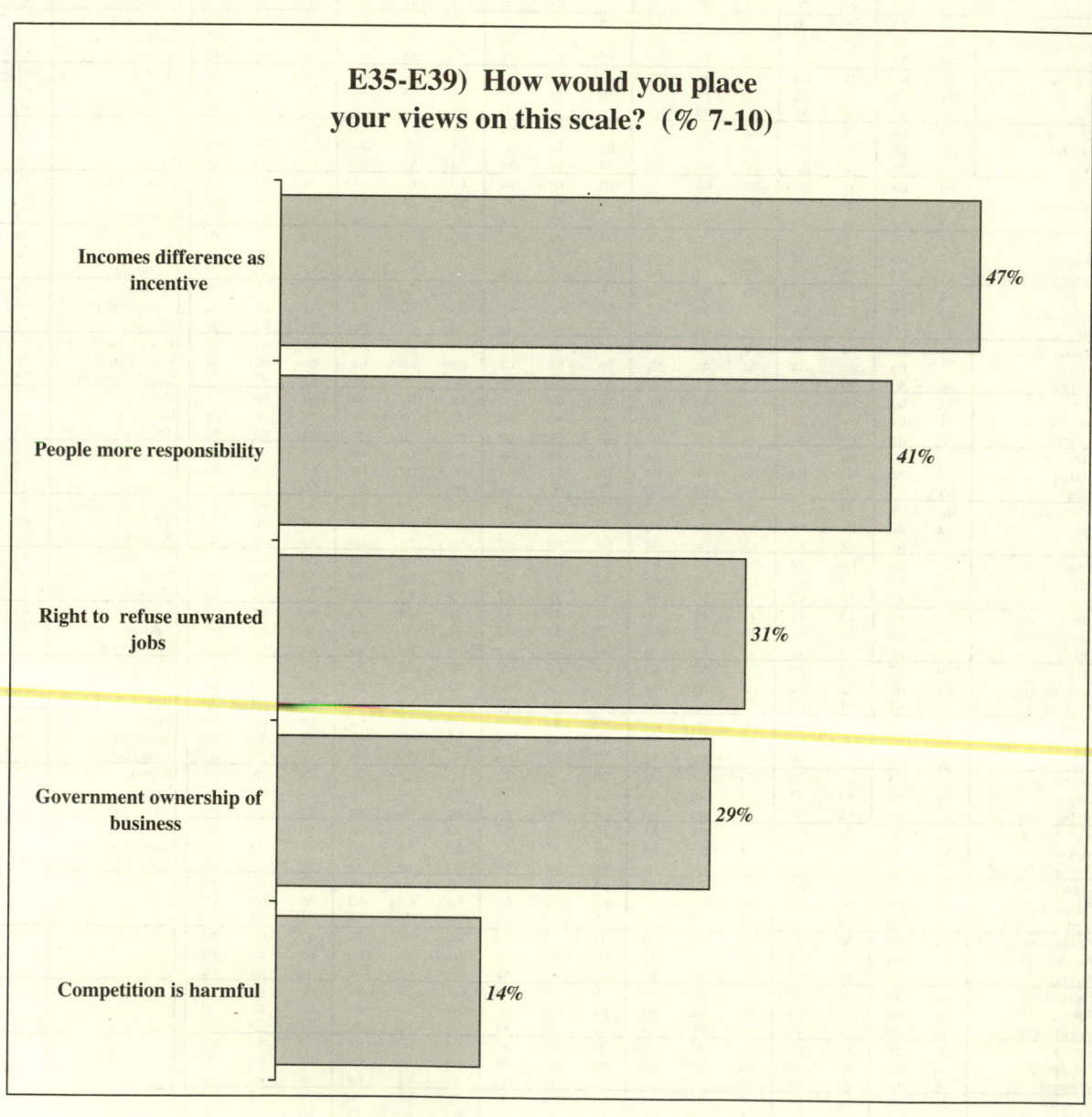

**E35-E39) How would you place
your views on this scale? (% 7-10)**

Incomes difference as incentive — 47%

People more responsibility — 41%

Right to refuse unwanted jobs — 31%

Government ownership of business — 29%

Competition is harmful — 14%

E035) INCOME: MORE EQUAL OR MORE UNEQUAL?

Now I'd like you to tell me your views on various issues. How would you place your views on this scale?

% "We need larger income differences as incentives for individual effort" (codes 7 to 10)   (WVS: V141; EVS: o18)

Country	Wave		Gender		Age			Education			Income			Values		
	1990	2000	Male	Female	16-29	30-49	50+	Lower	Middle	Upper	Lower	Middle	Upper	Mat	Mixed	Postm.
Albania	na	49	54	43	53	50	43	40	52	62	43	43	61	48	51	44
Algeria	na	77	76	78	78	80	69	66	78	84	76	82	77	68	81	85
Argentina	65	35	38	32	35	37	33	29	45	39	28	38	39	28	35	41
Armenia	na	53	57	49	54	58	45	47	52	61	62	46	47	51	56	52
Australia	na	41	43	39	38	43	41	38	42	43	35	44	45	51	43	36
Austria	42	26	32	20	31	26	23	18	29	44	16	23	38	20	27	26
Azerbaijan	na	43	44	43	39	47	44	38	39	52	36	36	60	38	52	50
Bangladesh	na	67	67	66	64	68	70	62	70	74	65	59	79	73	63	58
Belarus	71	36	42	31	49	35	26	21	37	57	30	35	49	27	40	80
Belgium	50	42	46	39	43	43	41	36	43	47	41	41	47	39	44	39
Bosnia and Herz.	na	46	49	43	49	44	44	34	44	60	40	44	54	50	43	51
Brazil	48	47	48	46	42	50	51	44	47	57	42	45	53	42	49	51
Bulgaria	61	48	52	44	61	56	33	23	56	72	28	49	64	37	59	70
Canada	63	40	43	37	36	43	39	38	39	44	36	38	46	43	42	36
Chile	47	22	22	22	23	24	18	21	22	25	21	23	23	21	21	24
China	80	56	59	53	55	56	58	58	54	60	62	53	55	54	58	61
Colombia	na	52	53	51	52	53	48	45	52	55	47	50	57	51	47	54
Croatia	na	22	23	22	27	21	21	19	22	35	20	21	27	12	23	27
Czech Republic	78	42	48	37	43	47	37	34	49	60	33	41	51	28	46	52
Denmark	57	na	na	na	na	na	na	na	na	na	na	na	na	na	na	na
Dominican Rep.	na	75	76	74	74	76	82	75	69	77	80	70	79	75	73	79
Egypt	na	87	87	87	87	87	86	85	88	91	87	88	89	88	87	88
El Salvador	na	63	64	61	62	62	66	58	65	70	55	64	71	na	na	na
Estonia	77	62	63	61	60	68	58	59	62	68	55	61	65	56	66	72
Finland	61	28	31	25	29	28	27	20	38	42	25	23	34	19	32	25
France	40	34	36	31	31	31	37	32	35	37	29	32	41	31	35	33
Georgia	na	72	73	72	73	75	68	75	70	75	70	74	74	72	72	75
Germany	74	na	na	na	na	na	na	na	na	na	na	na	na	na	na	na
Great Britain	58	39	43	35	33	43	39	34	43	47	29	37	56	na	na	na
Greece	na	na	na	na	na	na	na	na	na	na	na	na	na	na	na	na
Hungary	49	na	na	na	na	na	na	na	na	na	na	na	na	na	na	na
Iceland	47	44	46	43	52	44	39	41	51	40	42	39	53	48	46	29
India	47	31	33	27	32	32	25	24	35	36	23	31	34	32	31	48
Indonesia	na	65	65	66	68	69	61	55	68	71	58	72	79	66	68	64
Iran	na	33	32	34	33	34	32	39	32	28	37	29	32	35	32	34
Ireland	58	50	53	47	56	50	46	42	50	63	42	47	62	44	52	48
Israel	na	12	13	12	13	13	10	10	11	16	11	13	13	8	14	5
Italy	47	49	53	45	51	54	43	40	54	59	40	48	59	43	50	50
Japan	34	35	42	30	35	33	38	35	32	46	34	32	44	33	36	42
Jordan	na	72	76	69	71	72	77	65	80	77	67	74	78	72	72	77
Korea, South	39	60	60	60	60	60	61	59	59	62	55	61	65	57	62	63
Latvia	68	na	na	na	na	na	na	na	na	na	na	na	na	na	na	na
Lithuania	73	34	34	33	41	39	23	18	36	51	27	24	46	24	35	54
Luxembourg	na	62	62	62	64	63	61	55	64	68	60	61	68	58	65	61
Macedonia	na	35	35	36	35	36	34	29	35	47	31	34	42	36	36	27
Malta	na	na	na	na	na	na	na	na	na	na	na	na	na	na	na	na
Mexico	50	39	42	36	42	38	38	35	41	51	30	38	50	34	41	40
Moldova	na	58	57	59	60	59	54	53	55	67	64	57	54	51	61	75
Montenegro	na	40	44	36	55	42	29	26	45	61	42	29	53	38	44	42
Morocco	na	73	72	74	74	72	72	73	73	74	61	73	72	75	70	74
Netherlands	48	51	55	47	44	53	52	53	52	47	43	49	61	54	54	40
New Zealand	na	35	42	29	32	39	32	32	35	39	25	34	47	41	36	32
Nigeria	74	55	56	54	56	54	54	55	53	56	54	54	59	53	56	58
Northern Ireland	67	44	46	42	47	41	45	36	48	55	39	43	50	47	44	40
Norway	47	34	37	30	32	34	34	25	34	40	na	na	na	33	35	26
Pakistan	na	11	12	11	13	10	13	4	19	16	3	10	23	7	17	50
Peru	na	70	69	71	68	72	72	70	71	70	71	73	66	68	71	74
Philippines	na	51	52	49	51	50	51	46	49	57	48	50	54	50	51	49
Poland	79	51	53	49	52	55	46	42	59	73	41	58	60	44	54	68
Portugal	25	na	na	na	na	na	na	na	na	na	na	na	na	na	na	na
Puerto Rico	na	70	71	70	68	70	72	66	69	72	66	70	74	74	72	65
Romania	55	20	18	22	19	21	19	20	17	27	23	19	18	18	20	28
Russian Fed.	63	65	68	63	72	67	58	57	65	68	60	65	70	62	69	61
Serbia	na	47	50	44	52	51	42	35	48	62	35	46	59	40	53	63
Singapore	na	63	62	63	61	66	59	61	62	68	58	64	65	63	64	53
Slovakia	na	na	na	na	na	na	na	na	na	na	na	na	na	na	na	na
Slovenia	48	20	21	20	21	21	19	10	22	35	15	20	30	19	21	17
South Africa	37	39	43	34	45	36	33	33	45	59	31	38	50	37	40	48
Spain	32	35	36	35	39	33	35	34	34	42	34	37	35	36	37	29
Sweden	58	na	na	na	na	na	na	na	na	na	na	na	na	na	na	na
Switzerland	na	35	38	31	36	36	31	28	35	45	26	31	41	42	34	29
Taiwan	na	46	46	47	38	48	49	50	39	47	44	44	51	52	42	44
Tanzania	na	38	41	35	41	36	37	36	40	39	39	33	43	39	38	46
Turkey	31	25	25	25	26	25	25	25	25	28	23	26	27	25	26	25
Uganda	na	67	60	74	65	69	72	65	69	63	63	76	63	66	67	75
Ukraine	na	66	67	65	66	68	63	63	64	71	64	65	68	62	69	80
United States	62	44	45	42	39	43	48	43	42	45	42	40	55	39	46	38
Uruguay	na	36	36	36	36	34	38	34	38	38	31	31	46	28	37	39
Venezuela	na	44	44	43	45	44	39	34	44	55	34	41	53	41	44	47
Vietnam	na	50	55	46	54	54	41	45	55	61	46	45	58	32	57	52
Zimbabwe	na	63	63	62	59	64	70	63	62	70	66	59	67	57	68	52
Total	56	47	49	46	50	48	43	41	48	55	44	46	53	46	48	45

RANKING

Country	2000
Egypt	87
Algeria	77
Dominican Rep.	75
Morocco	73
Jordan	72
Georgia	72
Peru	70
Puerto Rico	70
Uganda	67
Bangladesh	67
Ukraine	66
Indonesia	65
Russian Fed.	65
El Salvador	63
Singapore	63
Zimbabwe	63
Luxembourg	62
Estonia	62
Korea, South	60
Moldova	58
China	56
Nigeria	55
Armenia	53
Colombia	52
Poland	51
Netherlands	51
Philippines	51
Vietnam	50
Ireland	50
Italy	49
Albania	49
Bulgaria	48
Serbia	47
Brazil	47
Taiwan	46
Bosnia and Herz.	46
Iceland	44
Northern Ireland	44
United States	44
Venezuela	44
Azerbaijan	43
Belgium	42
Czech Republic	42
Australia	41
Canada	40
Montenegro	40
Mexico	39
South Africa	39
Great Britain	39
Tanzania	38
Uruguay	36
Belarus	36
Japan	35
Macedonia	35
Spain	35
New Zealand	35
Argentina	35
Switzerland	35
Lithuania	34
France	34
Norway	34
Iran	33
India	31
Finland	28
Austria	26
Turkey	25
Croatia	22
Chile	22
Slovenia	20
Romania	20
Israel	12
Pakistan	11
Total	47

E036) OWNERSHIP OF BUSINESS: PRIVATE OR GOVERNMENT?

Now I'd like you to tell me your views on various issues. How would you place your views on this scale?

% Government ownership of business and industry should be increased (codes 7-10)　　(WVS: V142; EVS: o19)

Country	Wave 1990	Wave 2000	Gender Male	Gender Female	Age 16-29	Age 30-49	Age 50+	Education Lower	Education Middle	Education Upper	Income Lower	Income Middle	Income Upper	Values Mat	Values Mixed	Values Postm.	RANKING Country	RANKING 2000
Albania	na	16	16	16	12	15	21	17	16	13	20	16	12	16	14	36	China	61
Algeria	na	32	30	34	28	33	40	35	31	31	33	32	34	27	34	36	Colombia	58
Argentina	18	40	38	42	44	38	38	44	36	30	45	44	30	41	42	35	Egypt	57
Armenia	na	47	41	53	38	48	62	56	49	36	36	50	62	54	41	52	Moldova	52
Australia	na	12	14	11	12	14	11	13	13	11	13	13	12	12	12	12	El Salvador	52
Austria	8	7	7	8	6	8	8	10	5	2	10	6	6	16	8	4	India	51
Azerbaijan	na	38	34	41	38	34	46	51	36	38	44	38	31	38	37	31	Dominican Rep.	50
Bangladesh	na	34	32	37	34	34	33	39	31	24	39	28	37	45	26	26	Peru	49
Belarus	42	30	27	33	21	28	43	41	28	25	34	32	19	38	26	11	Philippines	48
Belgium	14	na	na	na	na	na	na	na	na	na	na	na	na	na	na	na	Armenia	47
Bosnia and Herz.	na	21	18	25	21	20	23	23	22	19	29	22	15	22	21	21	Russian Fed.	44
Brazil	37	35	30	40	39	32	34	41	34	20	42	35	28	42	34	25	Jordan	43
Bulgaria	20	na	na	na	na	na	na	na	na	na	na	na	na	na	na	na	Venezuela	41
Canada	10	11	10	12	12	13	9	13	12	10	16	12	8	16	12	10	Mexico	41
Chile	41	39	41	38	40	39	38	40	39	39	42	39	36	36	38	48	Argentina	40
China	61	61	62	60	51	62	69	69	58	40	66	63	54	64	56	63	Estonia	40
Colombia	na	58	54	62	58	56	61	71	61	44	69	62	44	67	56	58	Georgia	39
Croatia	na	28	21	34	22	28	31	35	26	13	47	30	15	33	30	18	Chile	39
Czech Republic	19	24	22	25	21	21	27	28	21	11	30	24	18	35	21	16	Poland	38
Denmark	11	na	na	na	na	na	na	na	na	na	na	na	na	na	na	na	Tanzania	38
Dominican Rep.	na	50	46	53	48	56	46	58	58	47	65	42	43	56	47	57	Azerbaijan	38
Egypt	na	57	56	59	54	59	58	63	58	41	61	64	50	62	53	50	Ukraine	37
El Salvador	na	52	47	57	53	53	49	54	53	48	56	52	51	na	na	na	Indonesia	37
Estonia	19	40	35	44	32	33	50	45	41	28	52	46	30	46	36	20	South Africa	36
Finland	6	15	13	16	11	14	17	19	9	9	17	16	12	12	15	19	Uruguay	36
France	18	12	11	13	12	13	11	14	10	9	12	15	9	10	11	17	Brazil	35
Georgia	na	39	35	43	33	36	52	43	42	29	48	36	30	42	37	33	Iran	35
Germany	9	12	13	12	13	14	11	11	14	9	14	12	11	10	14	13	Spain	34
Great Britain	22	21	22	19	20	21	21	23	22	13	22	26	22	na	na	na	Bangladesh	34
Greece	na	na	na	na	na	na	na	na	na	na	na	na	na	na	na	na	Turkey	33
Hungary	17	na	na	na	na	na	na	na	na	na	na	na	na	na	na	na	Algeria	32
Iceland	11	9	9	10	8	7	13	12	6	9	14	9	7	11	9	9	Morocco	32
India	31	51	48	55	50	51	49	59	52	38	57	59	42	58	46	37	Belarus	30
Indonesia	na	37	39	35	40	40	33	42	35	36	36	38	41	41	34	54	Vietnam	30
Iran	na	35	33	38	34	34	44	42	35	29	35	33	35	37	35	27	Croatia	28
Ireland	15	14	13	15	10	13	18	20	13	6	16	19	9	14	12	21	Serbia	28
Israel	na	na	na	na	na	na	na	na	na	na	na	na	na	na	na	na	Zimbabwe	27
Italy	18	13	11	15	10	13	15	17	10	9	17	11	10	19	13	9	Romania	27
Japan	17	9	7	12	11	8	10	16	9	7	10	9	9	9	9	8	Lithuania	27
Jordan	na	43	39	46	40	45	43	45	40	41	46	43	39	42	42	54	Montenegro	25
Korea, South	29	23	20	25	16	24	26	36	25	17	26	19	22	23	22	22	Czech Republic	24
Latvia	22	na	na	na	na	na	na	na	na	na	na	na	na	na	na	na	Korea, South	23
Lithuania	28	27	22	31	17	29	33	35	27	17	33	36	20	33	26	11	Puerto Rico	22
Luxembourg	na	na	na	na	na	na	na	na	na	na	na	na	na	na	na	na	Bosnia and Herz.	21
Macedonia	na	18	19	17	13	20	20	25	16	12	22	17	14	21	15	15	Taiwan	21
Malta	na	na	na	na	na	na	na	na	na	na	na	na	na	na	na	na	Uganda	21
Mexico	24	41	40	42	41	39	44	42	42	30	45	40	37	39	43	38	Great Britain	21
Moldova	na	52	49	55	46	49	63	57	53	47	58	54	44	55	50	40	Portugal	20
Montenegro	na	25	24	27	15	22	36	37	20	15	25	27	22	30	22	19	Singapore	19
Morocco	na	32	31	32	30	32	39	35	26	16	33	30	33	36	30	29	Macedonia	18
Netherlands	10	13	11	14	11	9	17	18	10	12	17	12	10	20	11	16	Northern Ireland	17
New Zealand	na	15	16	15	12	15	17	17	13	14	20	15	11	18	12	17	Pakistan	17
Nigeria	50	na	na	na	na	na	na	na	na	na	na	na	na	na	na	na	Albania	16
Northern Ireland	21	17	17	17	18	17	16	20	17	11	22	17	17	13	18	21	New Zealand	15
Norway	14	14	10	17	17	12	13	15	13	14	na	na	na	11	14	16	Finland	15
Pakistan	na	17	17	16	17	16	18	22	13	13	21	19	9	19	14	10	Ireland	14
Peru	na	49	44	53	50	50	42	59	54	34	60	49	30	54	48	45	Norway	14
Philippines	na	48	48	49	45	50	51	46	50	49	49	44	55	48	48	55	Italy	13
Poland	24	38	35	41	29	36	46	47	28	25	45	37	28	42	37	24	Netherlands	13
Portugal	18	20	19	22	23	21	17	21	18	18	18	21	17	19	21	19	Australia	12
Puerto Rico	na	22	19	23	18	19	26	35	29	16	34	18	17	29	23	15	Germany	12
Romania	31	27	21	34	23	22	34	45	22	9	39	30	16	35	22	8	France	12
Russian Fed.	40	44	41	46	26	42	59	62	44	35	52	47	36	49	39	40	Canada	11
Serbia	na	28	22	34	16	23	38	41	25	16	40	27	20	35	22	15	United States	10
Singapore	na	19	17	21	19	17	24	25	18	10	26	20	14	19	20	17	Japan	9
Slovakia	na	na	na	na	na	na	na	na	na	na	na	na	na	na	na	na	Iceland	9
Slovenia	17	na	na	na	na	na	na	na	na	na	na	na	na	na	na	na	Switzerland	8
South Africa	25	36	37	36	38	37	30	42	31	15	46	40	20	32	39	34	Austria	7
Spain	36	34	36	32	33	33	36	37	31	28	47	36	30	34	32	43		
Sweden	14	na	na	na	na	na	na	na	na	na	na	na	na	na	na	na		
Switzerland	na	8	8	9	11	8	8	17	7	5	13	7	6	13	9	6		
Taiwan	na	21	17	26	18	20	27	30	24	12	27	21	16	23	20	24		
Tanzania	na	38	33	44	44	35	33	44	31	30	47	37	22	38	38	21		
Turkey	42	33	31	36	34	33	33	38	29	19	38	32	25	33	33	34		
Uganda	na	21	10	30	19	21	27	31	17	7	15	29	15	18	21	26		
Ukraine	na	37	35	39	23	31	53	64	36	27	48	34	28	44	34	24		
United States	7	10	10	11	12	9	10	17	11	7	14	9	6	12	11	7		
Uruguay	na	36	40	33	42	36	34	36	36	40	40	36	33	37	38	33		
Venezuela	na	41	39	43	43	40	40	44	42	35	40	45	43	41	41	42		
Vietnam	na	30	30	29	24	29	36	27	32	38	32	31	28	22	32	31		
Zimbabwe	na	27	23	31	29	25	27	30	25	na	32	25	27	24	30	30		
Total	23	29	27	31	29	29	30	34	29	24	35	30	25	34	27	23	Total	29

E037) RESPONSIBILITY TO PROVIDE FOR PEOPLE

Now I'd like you to tell me your views on various issues. How would you place your views on this scale?

% "People should take more responsibility to provide for themselves" (codes 7 to 10)   (WVS: V143; EVS: V186)

Country	Wave		Gender		Age			Education			Income			Values		
	1990	2000	Male	Female	16-29	30-49	50+	Lower	Middle	Upper	Lower	Middle	Upper	Mat	Mixed	Postm.
Albania	na	50	47	54	48	49	54	56	49	40	53	54	44	52	47	54
Algeria	na	43	45	41	45	40	45	51	42	39	47	41	35	45	42	42
Argentina	33	53	52	54	52	52	54	53	54	50	56	55	46	60	52	50
Armenia	na	66	63	68	63	63	73	70	66	63	61	67	72	69	64	55
Australia	na	27	30	25	37	22	25	34	27	22	32	25	20	24	27	28
Austria	14	18	17	19	17	18	19	20	17	15	20	19	16	28	16	20
Azerbaijan	na	64	66	63	63	63	70	72	64	62	61	65	70	63	68	53
Bangladesh	na	36	32	41	36	36	36	42	31	29	45	33	31	50	28	19
Belarus	43	39	38	41	36	39	43	45	39	31	44	39	32	45	34	24
Belgium	29	33	31	34	30	34	33	43	32	26	40	37	27	39	31	29
Bosnia and Herz.	na	47	45	49	45	48	50	47	49	43	50	48	44	48	48	43
Brazil	41	39	34	43	40	38	38	42	36	40	43	38	35	42	40	28
Bulgaria	35	32	29	35	23	29	39	43	29	19	43	30	24	40	25	16
Canada	19	24	23	25	27	24	22	25	24	24	29	24	19	23	22	29
Chile	55	60	59	60	58	61	59	63	60	51	64	58	56	61	58	61
China	33	35	32	38	28	36	40	37	34	33	38	36	32	36	33	39
Colombia	na	45	45	45	44	46	42	49	42	46	50	45	43	46	44	42
Croatia	na	36	36	35	36	34	37	39	34	33	33	42	30	40	37	29
Czech Republic	40	28	29	28	28	25	31	34	24	15	35	32	19	42	25	22
Denmark	16	17	16	18	18	19	14	17	16	18	16	18	17	17	14	30
Dominican Rep.	na	41	36	44	41	41	27	38	38	42	41	43	38	44	37	52
Egypt	na	54	54	55	52	57	53	62	52	39	60	62	48	62	50	43
El Salvador	na	37	36	38	35	36	41	36	36	38	35	35	41	na	na	na
Estonia	35	43	42	43	39	41	47	49	44	29	58	46	32	51	37	40
Finland	20	26	24	27	21	27	28	31	20	13	33	24	20	31	23	30
France	19	16	14	18	18	16	15	18	12	14	22	17	10	20	15	14
Georgia	na	65	63	67	56	66	74	69	63	69	69	65	60	66	65	59
Germany	23	21	21	22	18	23	21	24	20	14	25	21	12	23	22	17
Great Britain	33	20	21	18	23	20	18	24	16	16	23	23	20	na	na	na
Greece	na	39	40	38	36	39	47	46	41	35	38	38	38	37	37	42
Hungary	50	48	48	48	45	48	50	52	45	28	57	49	41	49	47	56
Iceland	26	24	22	27	23	25	24	30	17	27	29	26	18	25	23	36
India	20	52	48	57	50	52	52	59	50	40	63	54	44	52	47	41
Indonesia	na	36	36	36	42	35	35	38	33	39	29	41	40	40	32	59
Iran	na	38	35	42	38	38	41	43	39	33	41	39	37	42	37	40
Ireland	30	24	22	25	18	24	29	34	19	17	38	19	20	19	25	24
Israel	na	79	78	80	78	79	79	84	78	76	82	81	73	80	78	83
Italy	39	37	34	41	34	36	41	44	35	25	44	40	27	42	38	34
Japan	55	51	44	57	54	54	47	50	53	47	52	55	45	45	51	53
Jordan	na	56	58	54	55	57	55	57	57	53	58	57	51	54	58	52
Korea, South	25	76	74	79	82	77	69	73	74	80	76	74	78	75	76	91
Latvia	55	54	54	54	53	51	57	63	53	46	60	53	47	53	56	43
Lithuania	44	34	28	39	29	27	45	40	34	23	48	39	26	32	37	26
Luxembourg	na	18	20	17	19	18	18	24	16	15	19	21	12	20	19	12
Macedonia	na	70	68	72	67	67	77	76	73	52	74	70	65	72	69	71
Malta	na	33	33	33	32	31	36	38	33	25	37	26	28	28	37	28
Mexico	35	45	46	44	43	45	47	52	38	35	47	41	42	52	41	44
Moldova	na	56	58	55	55	54	60	56	60	51	57	55	55	60	52	54
Montenegro	na	78	75	80	67	75	87	89	75	60	89	82	63	83	71	75
Morocco	na	50	52	49	49	51	54	53	42	34	51	41	56	52	51	44
Netherlands	23	23	21	25	17	21	28	29	23	17	27	24	18	31	20	26
New Zealand	na	26	26	26	36	27	23	25	26	28	31	29	21	30	25	28
Nigeria	54	68	66	69	67	69	64	68	69	66	69	66	70	70	68	62
Northern Ireland	36	25	27	23	21	26	25	28	22	19	28	24	21	20	26	24
Norway	21	30	29	31	40	30	23	28	31	30	na	na	na	29	30	34
Pakistan	na	57	55	58	55	59	53	68	46	42	73	58	36	63	48	33
Peru	na	34	35	33	37	33	30	38	34	32	34	38	28	28	35	36
Philippines	na	34	33	35	35	33	34	38	31	34	37	33	32	34	34	33
Poland	37	35	35	36	37	33	38	41	33	16	46	30	26	38	34	32
Portugal	28	26	25	27	26	27	26	27	27	18	27	24	24	25	28	14
Puerto Rico	na	20	22	19	15	21	22	27	22	18	25	15	21	20	21	17
Romania	37	33	29	38	28	31	38	43	32	18	46	31	24	37	31	22
Russian Fed.	32	40	37	42	30	39	47	48	41	31	49	42	29	44	35	40
Serbia	na	62	57	66	58	58	67	71	58	55	72	61	52	69	56	46
Singapore	na	40	38	43	42	37	44	45	39	30	41	42	35	44	38	46
Slovakia	na	50	49	51	46	49	54	59	47	39	57	52	45	57	48	34
Slovenia	44	50	47	53	47	51	52	65	47	33	57	48	42	58	49	48
South Africa	39	50	51	50	44	54	57	57	43	31	57	49	42	54	47	57
Spain	44	48	47	50	52	49	45	48	47	51	43	52	50	49	48	49
Sweden	11	17	17	17	20	16	17	21	16	16	20	16	14	20	16	22
Switzerland	na	13	12	15	18	14	10	20	13	5	18	13	8	22	12	15
Taiwan	na	32	33	31	33	30	36	34	29	32	37	30	30	30	33	43
Tanzania	na	65	66	64	63	62	74	74	58	50	75	70	50	66	65	63
Turkey	50	51	48	54	51	50	50	51	48	50	54	49	45	50	51	51
Uganda	na	45	45	46	43	47	50	64	37	45	58	49	40	45	46	40
Ukraine	na	47	43	50	37	44	55	66	45	41	58	43	39	52	45	33
United States	14	20	19	21	25	20	16	23	19	20	21	18	20	20	18	25
Uruguay	na	62	66	60	62	64	61	64	62	56	66	65	59	58	68	57
Venezuela	na	41	39	44	41	42	42	45	45	29	51	45	33	50	41	30
Vietnam	na	21	16	25	16	21	24	21	21	13	30	21	15	15	21	21
Zimbabwe	na	60	58	62	60	59	63	66	52	40	63	59	57	64	58	50
Total	33	41	40	42	42	41	41	45	41	36	47	41	36	48	39	35

RANKING

Country	2000
Israel	79
Montenegro	78
Korea, South	76
Macedonia	70
Nigeria	68
Armenia	66
Georgia	65
Tanzania	65
Azerbaijan	64
Uruguay	62
Serbia	62
Zimbabwe	60
Chile	60
Pakistan	57
Moldova	56
Jordan	56
Egypt	54
Latvia	54
Argentina	53
India	52
Japan	51
Turkey	51
Albania	50
South Africa	50
Morocco	50
Slovenia	50
Slovakia	50
Spain	48
Hungary	48
Bosnia and Herz.	47
Ukraine	47
Uganda	45
Colombia	45
Mexico	45
Algeria	43
Estonia	43
Venezuela	41
Dominican Rep.	41
Singapore	40
Russian Fed.	40
Belarus	39
Brazil	39
Greece	39
Iran	38
Italy	37
El Salvador	37
Bangladesh	36
Indonesia	36
Croatia	36
Poland	35
China	35
Lithuania	34
Peru	34
Philippines	34
Malta	33
Romania	33
Belgium	33
Taiwan	32
Bulgaria	32
Norway	30
Czech Republic	28
Australia	27
New Zealand	26
Portugal	26
Finland	26
Northern Ireland	25
Iceland	24
Canada	24
Ireland	24
Netherlands	23
Germany	21
Vietnam	21
Puerto Rico	20
United States	20
Great Britain	20
Luxembourg	18
Austria	18
Sweden	17
Denmark	17
France	16
Switzerland	13
Total	41

E038_7) RIGHT TO REFUSE UNWANTED JOBS

Now I'd like you to tell me your views on various issues. How would you place your views on this scale?

(%) Unemployed should have the right to refuse a job they do not want (codes 7 to 10)

(EVS: V187)

Country	Wave 1990	Wave 2000	Gender Male	Gender Female	Age 16-29	Age 30-49	Age 50+	Education Lower	Education Middle	Education Upper	Income Lower	Income Middle	Income Upper	Values Mat	Values Mixed	Values Postm.
Albania	na	na	na	na	na	na	na	na	na	na	na	na	na	na	na	na
Algeria	na	na	na	na	na	na	na	na	na	na	na	na	na	na	na	na
Argentina	23	na	na	na	na	na	na	na	na	na	na	na	na	na	na	na
Armenia	na	na	na	na	na	na	na	na	na	na	na	na	na	na	na	na
Australia	na	na	na	na	na	na	na	na	na	na	na	na	na	na	na	na
Austria	16	18	21	16	21	23	12	14	20	29	16	22	19	14	14	28
Azerbaijan	na	na	na	na	na	na	na	na	na	na	na	na	na	na	na	na
Bangladesh	na	na	na	na	na	na	na	na	na	na	na	na	na	na	na	na
Belarus	39	44	45	44	51	46	36	31	49	49	45	46	41	41	45	43
Belgium	29	32	32	31	34	36	27	27	32	36	32	34	30	25	31	39
Bosnia and Herz.	na	na	na	na	na	na	na	na	na	na	na	na	na	na	na	na
Brazil	38	na	na	na	na	na	na	na	na	na	na	na	na	na	na	na
Bulgaria	59	35	39	32	48	40	24	20	41	48	26	40	43	35	37	31
Canada	30	na	na	na	na	na	na	na	na	na	na	na	na	na	na	na
Chile	26	na	na	na	na	na	na	na	na	na	na	na	na	na	na	na
China	36	na	na	na	na	na	na	na	na	na	na	na	na	na	na	na
Colombia	na	na	na	na	na	na	na	na	na	na	na	na	na	na	na	na
Croatia	na	33	31	34	43	32	26	27	35	36	28	36	32	31	31	37
Czech Republic	41	28	28	27	36	30	21	29	26	27	27	28	28	25	28	34
Denmark	26	32	33	31	32	35	29	30	33	35	31	34	33	28	29	46
Dominican Rep.	na	na	na	na	na	na	na	na	na	na	na	na	na	na	na	na
Egypt	na	na	na	na	na	na	na	na	na	na	na	na	na	na	na	na
El Salvador	na	na	na	na	na	na	na	na	na	na	na	na	na	na	na	na
Estonia	57	52	51	52	55	55	47	50	52	52	52	52	49	57	47	65
Finland	12	33	32	33	39	38	25	37	24	32	37	36	27	39	29	41
France	25	28	27	29	32	34	20	24	29	36	31	27	26	22	25	45
Georgia	na	na	na	na	na	na	na	na	na	na	na	na	na	na	na	na
Germany	40	22	20	23	27	25	15	19	25	18	19	17	14	13	23	32
Great Britain	37	27	30	24	35	29	21	29	27	27	31	31	27	na	23	32
Greece	na	39	38	40	40	43	32	35	36	43	36	38	43	32	39	46
Hungary	39	25	27	22	24	33	18	22	29	29	31	26	20	20	29	38
Iceland	22	31	29	32	31	29	32	31	30	30	38	30	25	28	31	35
India	20	na	na	na	na	na	na	na	na	na	na	na	na	na	na	na
Indonesia	na	na	na	na	na	na	na	na	na	na	na	na	na	na	na	na
Iran	na	na	na	na	na	na	na	na	na	na	na	na	na	na	na	na
Ireland	37	39	38	40	39	39	38	43	38	33	49	41	32	34	37	53
Israel	na	na	na	na	na	na	na	na	na	na	na	na	na	na	na	na
Italy	16	13	12	14	17	16	8	10	16	14	11	16	14	8	13	16
Japan	24	na	na	na	na	na	na	na	na	na	na	na	na	na	na	na
Jordan	na	na	na	na	na	na	na	na	na	na	na	na	na	na	na	na
Korea, South	33	na	na	na	na	na	na	na	na	na	na	na	na	na	na	na
Latvia	68	45	47	43	55	54	32	36	45	54	40	45	53	37	47	64
Lithuania	45	40	41	40	47	50	26	27	45	43	40	38	42	38	44	34
Luxembourg	na	17	17	17	18	21	12	16	18	17	12	21	20	14	17	24
Macedonia	na	na	na	na	na	na	na	na	na	na	na	na	na	na	na	na
Malta	na	36	35	38	35	39	34	37	35	39	33	38	34	34	38	31
Mexico	31	na	na	na	na	na	na	na	na	na	na	na	na	na	na	na
Moldova	na	na	na	na	na	na	na	na	na	na	na	na	na	na	na	na
Montenegro	na	na	na	na	na	na	na	na	na	na	na	na	na	na	na	na
Morocco	na	na	na	na	na	na	na	na	na	na	na	na	na	na	na	na
Netherlands	28	32	33	31	28	35	30	25	32	39	33	33	29	18	27	51
New Zealand	na	na	na	na	na	na	na	na	na	na	na	na	na	na	na	na
Nigeria	29	na	na	na	na	na	na	na	na	na	na	na	na	na	na	na
Northern Ireland	39	31	32	30	34	33	28	33	31	23	36	30	23	25	31	40
Norway	12	na	na	na	na	na	na	na	na	na	na	na	na	na	na	na
Pakistan	na	na	na	na	na	na	na	na	na	na	na	na	na	na	na	na
Peru	na	na	na	na	na	na	na	na	na	na	na	na	na	na	na	na
Philippines	na	na	na	na	na	na	na	na	na	na	na	na	na	na	na	na
Poland	39	26	28	25	36	29	18	27	26	26	22	29	31	23	30	28
Portugal	27	25	26	24	33	26	19	22	32	26	11	22	31	22	26	33
Puerto Rico	na	na	na	na	na	na	na	na	na	na	na	na	na	na	na	na
Romania	42	39	38	40	50	43	28	27	45	45	31	33	48	32	43	53
Russian Fed.	41	50	52	48	56	52	43	38	52	50	48	52	50	46	54	57
Serbia	na	na	na	na	na	na	na	na	na	na	na	na	na	na	na	na
Singapore	na	na	na	na	na	na	na	na	na	na	na	na	na	na	na	na
Slovakia	na	27	29	26	35	30	19	23	30	26	27	28	25	24	31	32
Slovenia	11	16	17	15	23	15	11	14	16	16	13	16	17	13	16	20
South Africa	28	na	na	na	na	na	na	na	na	na	na	na	na	na	na	na
Spain	30	19	20	18	27	24	10	11	23	31	15	22	26	10	21	28
Sweden	19	15	16	15	15	18	13	17	17	11	18	16	12	10	15	18
Switzerland	na	na	na	na	na	na	na	na	na	na	na	na	na	na	na	na
Taiwan	na	na	na	na	na	na	na	na	na	na	na	na	na	na	na	na
Tanzania	na	na	na	na	na	na	na	na	na	na	na	na	na	na	na	na
Turkey	na	na	na	na	na	na	na	na	na	na	na	na	na	na	na	na
Uganda	na	na	na	na	na	na	na	na	na	na	na	na	na	na	na	na
Ukraine	na	53	52	54	55	56	49	45	53	57	51	52	57	56	51	69
United States	26	na	na	na	na	na	na	na	na	na	na	na	na	na	na	na
Uruguay	na	na	na	na	na	na	na	na	na	na	na	na	na	na	na	na
Venezuela	na	na	na	na	na	na	na	na	na	na	na	na	na	na	na	na
Vietnam	na	na	na	na	na	na	na	na	na	na	na	na	na	na	na	na
Zimbabwe	na	na	na	na	na	na	na	na	na	na	na	na	na	na	na	na
Total	32	31	32	31	36	35	25	26	34	36	31	33	32	31	31	35

RANKING

Country	2000
Ukraine	53
Estonia	52
Russian Fed.	50
Latvia	45
Belarus	44
Lithuania	40
Greece	39
Romania	39
Ireland	39
Malta	36
Bulgaria	35
Finland	33
Croatia	33
Denmark	32
Netherlands	32
Belgium	32
Iceland	31
Northern Ireland	31
Czech Republic	28
France	28
Slovakia	27
Great Britain	27
Poland	26
Portugal	25
Hungary	25
Germany	22
Spain	19
Austria	18
Luxembourg	17
Slovenia	16
Sweden	15
Italy	13
Total	31

E039A) COMPETITION IS GOOD

Now I'd like you to tell me your views on various issues. How would you place your views on this scale?

% Competition is good. It stimulates people to work hard and develop new ideas (codes 1 to 4)   (WVS: V144; EVS: V188)

Country	Wave 1990	Wave 2000	Gender Male	Gender Female	Age 16-29	Age 30-49	Age 50+	Education Lower	Education Middle	Education Upper	Income Lower	Income Middle	Income Upper	Values Mat	Values Mixed	Values Postm.
Albania	na	80	83	78	84	81	76	76	82	86	79	79	82	79	80	84
Algeria	na	na	na	na	na	na	na	na	na	na	na	na	na	na	na	na
Argentina	na	59	64	54	50	63	63	54	65	68	52	59	64	57	59	59
Armenia	na	56	58	54	50	63	54	52	53	64	55	56	55	52	59	57
Australia	na	76	76	75	71	77	78	74	74	80	72	79	79	75	76	75
Austria	na	74	78	71	74	75	74	73	74	79	73	72	79	65	76	74
Azerbaijan	na	64	67	60	63	65	62	59	64	64	64	62	71	59	73	60
Bangladesh	na	71	72	70	70	70	78	69	72	74	74	69	70	78	67	60
Belarus	na	65	69	61	75	64	56	51	68	72	60	63	76	62	65	93
Belgium	na	48	52	44	50	45	49	41	50	50	44	44	49	46	51	41
Bosnia and Herz.	na	74	75	73	75	74	71	65	74	79	70	73	80	77	73	79
Brazil	na	69	72	66	63	72	77	65	70	81	62	66	77	65	69	81
Bulgaria	na	66	70	61	72	70	59	52	69	77	58	65	72	62	70	84
Canada	na	70	75	66	68	70	71	68	69	73	63	72	75	72	70	70
Chile	na	46	48	45	49	44	48	42	48	50	42	50	48	43	49	46
China	na	80	82	78	79	78	88	83	79	83	81	79	84	76	85	77
Colombia	na	na	na	na	na	na	na	na	na	na	na	na	na	na	na	na
Croatia	na	75	79	71	69	79	74	76	73	78	68	75	76	71	77	71
Czech Republic	na	77	77	76	79	78	75	73	80	84	74	75	82	69	79	87
Denmark	na	61	68	55	71	62	55	60	76	55	54	61	70	54	65	52
Dominican Rep.	na	72	75	70	70	74	82	68	67	74	65	76	75	65	71	77
Egypt	na	na	na	na	na	na	na	na	na	na	na	na	na	na	na	na
El Salvador	na	66	68	64	66	64	68	63	68	72	62	65	76	na	na	na
Estonia	na	52	56	49	56	55	47	47	50	64	44	47	59	48	55	54
Finland	na	59	63	55	66	56	57	53	67	65	53	57	63	61	59	54
France	na	46	45	46	45	43	49	44	44	51	44	42	53	45	48	39
Georgia	na	73	76	71	75	75	68	71	73	76	70	72	78	71	75	78
Germany	na	66	69	64	65	64	69	65	66	73	69	74	66	71	66	59
Great Britain	na	59	61	57	53	58	63	57	56	68	55	58	64	na	na	na
Greece	na	55	56	55	49	58	62	58	60	51	57	56	55	61	57	45
Hungary	na	61	65	59	66	61	58	56	69	70	57	59	66	57	65	74
Iceland	na	84	87	81	88	87	75	80	88	83	75	86	88	87	85	71
India	na	64	65	63	62	65	64	64	64	63	64	64	64	64	64	61
Indonesia	na	na	na	na	na	na	na	na	na	na	na	na	na	na	na	na
Iran	na	na	na	na	na	na	na	na	na	na	na	na	na	na	na	na
Ireland	na	65	67	62	67	65	62	59	64	77	59	61	.74	62	68	61
Israel	na	na	na	na	na	na	na	na	na	na	na	na	na	na	na	na
Italy	na	57	62	53	58	55	58	54	60	61	55	57	61	59	57	58
Japan	na	56	62	51	54	55	58	54	53	64	56	52	64	57	56	62
Jordan	na	na	na	na	na	na	na	na	na	na	na	na	na	na	na	na
Korea, South	na	58	61	54	58	57	58	38	57	60	58	57	57	54	60	63
Latvia	na	68	71	65	69	67	69	57	71	71	69	64	68	63	71	63
Lithuania	na	60	62	57	68	59	54	41	63	69	43	58	68	53	62	69
Luxembourg	na	52	57	47	48	49	57	49	55	50	51	53	56	50	51	56
Macedonia	na	77	78	76	78	75	80	71	78	84	73	77	82	73	80	74
Malta	na	76	79	74	78	76	75	68	78	83	73	76	79	69	80	81
Mexico	na	60	66	54	59	62	55	55	61	75	54	62	68	56	61	67
Moldova	na	61	65	59	65	63	57	59	61	64	61	57	63	58	65	59
Montenegro	na	73	72	74	80	74	67	71	72	81	80	73	71	74	73	64
Morocco	na	83	86	81	82	85	81	83	84	90	74	82	86	82	84	92
Netherlands	na	50	58	43	50	51	49	53	45	53	44	50	57	51	52	44
New Zealand	na	69	72	66	70	69	69	67	67	73	62	68	78	70	72	65
Nigeria	na	na	na	na	na	na	na	na	na	na	na	na	na	na	na	na
Northern Ireland	na	64	64	64	63	63	68	62	66	67	64	64	66	67	66	55
Norway	na	70	78	63	69	73	68	65	71	75	na	na	na	67	72	61
Pakistan	na	na	na	na	na	na	na	na	na	na	na	na	na	na	na	na
Peru	na	67	67	67	65	69	69	64	65	72	64	69	69	59	68	73
Philippines	na	55	56	55	55	56	55	54	51	63	60	56	50	54	57	49
Poland	na	59	62	56	63	60	55	57	60	65	55	60	69	53	61	62
Portugal	na	49	49	50	47	49	51	48	49	60	44	44	47	55	47	41
Puerto Rico	na	73	78	70	61	74	78	71	70	75	72	73	74	63	76	71
Romania	na	79	82	76	83	77	78	72	79	89	75	76	84	78	81	80
Russian Fed.	na	58	63	53	65	58	52	46	55	72	51	53	69	54	62	57
Serbia	na	70	72	69	73	68	71	63	73	75	69	69	75	65	76	68
Singapore	na	75	79	71	78	75	66	72	75	87	67	75	82	70	77	75
Slovakia	na	68	70	66	71	69	65	62	69	82	64	68	72	64	70	80
Slovenia	na	73	74	72	75	73	70	72	70	83	71	73	79	70	74	71
South Africa	na	65	62	68	66	63	67	60	70	83	62	66	65	71	60	64
Spain	na	52	55	48	50	50	54	51	52	53	52	49	55	56	51	47
Sweden	na	74	79	68	75	72	75	69	75	74	69	73	82	80	75	66
Switzerland	na	75	79	72	71	75	79	70	76	79	67	74	80	76	77	67
Taiwan	na	60	66	54	56	63	56	55	60	64	55	60	66	58	62	62
Tanzania	na	75	80	69	67	78	84	75	75	78	75	80	81	76	76	57
Turkey	na	65	69	59	61	68	64	59	71	72	59	65	73	55	67	69
Uganda	na	78	85	72	81	77	67	73	79	90	83	71	78	78	76	85
Ukraine	na	62	72	54	73	68	50	36	63	72	53	65	69	56	66	66
United States	na	71	75	67	67	69	77	60	73	74	64	72	81	72	71	73
Uruguay	na	50	53	47	51	46	52	48	51	53	45	48	57	47	50	51
Venezuela	na	65	68	62	63	67	65	63	63	72	67	65	69	63	66	64
Vietnam	na	59	63	54	57	59	60	57	61	58	53	57	63	56	61	55
Zimbabwe	na	82	86	79	80	82	87	81	83	70	79	86	86	82	83	87
Total	na	66	69	62	66	66	64	62	67	69	62	65	70	64	67	64

RANKING

Country	2000
Iceland	84
Morocco	83
Zimbabwe	82
China	80
Albania	80
Romania	79
Uganda	78
Macedonia	77
Czech Republic	77
Malta	76
Australia	76
Switzerland	75
Singapore	75
Tanzania	75
Croatia	75
Austria	74
Bosnia and Herz.	74
Sweden	74
Georgia	73
Montenegro	73
Puerto Rico	73
Slovenia	73
Dominican Rep.	72
United States	71
Bangladesh	71
Serbia	70
Norway	70
Canada	70
Brazil	69
New Zealand	69
Slovakia	68
Latvia	68
Peru	67
Germany	66
El Salvador	66
Bulgaria	66
Venezuela	65
Belarus	65
Ireland	65
South Africa	65
Turkey	65
Northern Ireland	64
India	64
Azerbaijan	64
Ukraine	62
Hungary	61
Moldova	61
Denmark	61
Taiwan	60
Lithuania	60
Mexico	60
Great Britain	59
Poland	59
Finland	59
Argentina	59
Vietnam	59
Russian Fed.	58
Korea, South	58
Italy	57
Japan	56
Armenia	56
Philippines	55
Greece	55
Estonia	52
Luxembourg	52
Spain	52
Netherlands	50
Uruguay	50
Portugal	49
Belgium	48
Chile	46
France	46
Total	66

E039B) COMPETITION IS HARMFUL

Now I'd like you to tell me your views on various issues. How would you place your views on this scale?

% Competition is harmful. It brings out the worst in people (codes 7 to 10)   (WVS: V144; EVS: V188)

Country	Wave 1990	Wave 2000	Gender Male	Gender Female	Age 16-29	Age 30-49	Age 50+	Education Lower	Education Middle	Education Upper	Income Lower	Income Middle	Income Upper	Values Mat	Values Mixed	Values Postm.	RANKING Country	2000
Albania	na	7	7	6	5	6	9	8	6	5	7	6	7	8	6	8	Uruguay	27
Algeria	na	na	na	na	na	na	na	na	na	na	na	na	na	na	na	na	France	25
Argentina	11	23	19	27	31	22	17	27	19	12	25	26	18	25	23	22	Belgium	25
Armenia	na	15	13	16	15	11	20	24	15	10	14	15	17	15	15	11	Chile	25
Australia	na	8	8	8	9	8	6	10	8	7	11	6	6	8	7	9	Argentina	23
Austria	7	6	5	7	4	7	7	7	6	3	10	5	5	6	6	7	Mexico	23
Azerbaijan	na	13	13	13	13	12	14	16	12	13	10	16	11	14	11	16	El Salvador	23
Bangladesh	na	10	11	9	11	10	10	11	10	7	5	10	14	10	10	19	Turkey	21
Belarus	13	13	13	12	8	13	17	22	11	6	18	11	7	15	11	4	Luxembourg	21
Belgium	16	25	23	26	23	26	25	30	24	22	30	28	22	24	22	32	Ukraine	21
Bosnia and Herz.	na	6	6	7	7	5	9	7	6	7	8	7	5	8	5	8	Estonia	20
Brazil	18	16	14	19	20	15	13	21	14	8	23	16	10	19	17	6	Netherlands	20
Bulgaria	7	14	13	16	13	10	19	24	11	10	18	17	10	18	10	na	Greece	20
Canada	10	11	11	12	12	12	10	14	12	7	17	8	10	14	11	11	Portugal	20
Chile	21	25	24	26	23	29	20	30	22	21	31	20	21	25	23	30	Venezuela	19
China	5	8	7	9	9	8	6	8	8	7	8	9	5	9	7	10	Russian Fed.	19
Colombia	na	na	na	na	na	na	na	na	na	na	na	na	na	na	na	na	Poland	18
Croatia	na	10	8	11	15	10	7	8	11	10	13	11	7	11	9	13	Dominican Rep.	18
Czech Republic	5	10	10	9	10	9	10	11	9	7	11	10	9	14	9	7	Lithuania	17
Denmark	13	15	10	19	10	15	17	16	6	17	17	15	12	26	13	15	Italy	17
Dominican Rep.	na	18	15	19	19	15	18	26	21	16	25	15	14	27	17	9	Finland	17
Egypt	na	na	na	na	na	na	na	na	na	na	na	na	na	na	na	na	Moldova	17
El Salvador	na	23	22	23	23	23	23	25	22	16	23	26	13	na	na	na	Spain	16
Estonia	8	20	21	20	19	18	24	24	20	15	27	21	16	25	17	23	Brazil	16
Finland	8	17	14	19	11	17	20	19	13	18	19	20	14	15	16	21	Tanzania	15
France	16	25	25	25	27	27	22	26	26	21	28	26	24	27	22	31	Armenia	15
Georgia	na	10	9	11	9	9	13	10	11	9	12	12	7	11	10	12	Denmark	15
Germany	8	11	8	13	10	11	12	13	10	7	11	9	8	8	12	13	India	14
Great Britain	15	13	13	13	15	15	11	12	16	10	14	11	18	na	na	na	Peru	14
Greece	na	20	22	18	22	19	18	25	19	20	20	20	19	14	19	27	Bulgaria	14
Hungary	13	14	12	15	11	15	15	17	9	9	15	15	11	13	15	na	Philippines	14
Iceland	5	4	4	5	2	4	6	5	3	4	8	4	2	4	5	3	Hungary	14
India	7	14	14	16	15	14	14	17	15	11	17	15	13	15	14	11	Vietnam	14
Indonesia	na	na	na	na	na	na	na	na	na	na	na	na	na	na	na	na	Korea, South	13
Iran	na	na	na	na	na	na	na	na	na	na	na	na	na	na	na	na	South Africa	13
Ireland	13	13	15	11	11	13	14	15	12	11	17	13	8	12	13	12	Great Britain	13
Israel	na	na	na	na	na	na	na	na	na	na	na	na	na	na	na	na	Azerbaijan	13
Italy	18	17	14	20	15	19	16	18	17	15	18	17	16	15	17	18	Serbia	13
Japan	13	9	8	11	8	7	12	13	10	5	11	10	7	9	9	11	Montenegro	13
Jordan	na	na	na	na	na	na	na	na	na	na	na	na	na	na	na	na	Belarus	13
Korea, South	9	13	13	14	12	14	12	14	13	13	13	10	15	15	12	15	Ireland	13
Latvia	8	10	10	10	8	10	10	16	8	6	11	8	8	12	9	7	United States	12
Lithuania	10	17	15	19	12	18	20	22	16	13	25	18	11	18	17	12	Puerto Rico	12
Luxembourg	na	21	19	23	23	21	20	24	19	20	21	19	17	22	22	19	Canada	11
Macedonia	na	10	10	9	10	10	9	13	9	6	13	8	7	12	7	12	Germany	11
Malta	na	8	7	8	8	7	9	10	8	3	8	8	8	8	8	8	Taiwan	11
Mexico	16	23	18	27	23	21	26	28	20	10	25	21	17	28	21	17	Slovakia	11
Moldova	na	17	15	18	17	15	19	17	18	14	19	17	16	17	17	15	Georgia	10
Montenegro	na	13	14	12	9	11	17	17	12	11	13	13	11	11	14	20	Zimbabwe	10
Morocco	na	5	3	6	6	5	2	5	5	2	6	4	3	5	4	1	Bangladesh	10
Netherlands	14	20	17	23	14	20	24	24	20	18	25	20	15	28	18	22	Croatia	10
New Zealand	na	10	9	10	7	9	12	11	10	8	14	8	7	14	7	10	New Zealand	10
Nigeria	7	na	na	na	na	na	na	na	na	na	na	na	na	na	na	na	Czech Republic	10
Northern Ireland	16	9	9	10	9	10	8	11	8	8	10	10	9	6	9	na	Latvia	10
Norway	7	7	6	9	8	6	8	9	8	5	na	na	na	9	7	10	Slovenia	10
Pakistan	na	na	na	na	na	na	na	na	na	na	na	na	na	na	na	na	Macedonia	10
Peru	na	14	14	15	15	14	15	17	15	12	17	14	11	17	14	12	Japan	9
Philippines	na	14	13	15	12	15	15	14	15	12	12	11	19	16	12	18	Northern Ireland	9
Poland	12	18	18	18	18	18	17	25	15	13	20	18	12	20	17	18	Switzerland	9
Portugal	19	20	18	21	24	19	18	19	25	10	21	19	22	15	22	26	Romania	8
Puerto Rico	na	12	9	13	16	11	10	15	17	8	14	11	9	15	10	7	Australia	8
Romania	6	8	5	12	9	9	7	11	8	5	11	7	6	10	7	8	Sweden	8
Russian Fed.	12	19	16	21	15	19	20	24	20	12	23	20	14	21	17	21	Malta	8
Serbia	na	13	11	15	11	15	11	16	13	9	16	12	10	14	11	15	China	8
Singapore	na	6	5	7	5	6	11	9	6	3	8	7	4	7	6	7	Uganda	8
Slovakia	na	11	11	10	9	10	13	14	9	9	11	13	8	13	9	4	Norway	7
Slovenia	9	10	9	10	10	8	11	11	11	1	14	8	6	13	8	11	Albania	7
South Africa	14	13	14	12	12	14	13	16	11	3	15	11	15	11	14	16	Bosnia and Herz.	6
Spain	22	16	16	17	18	17	14	16	17	17	18	18	13	14	16	21	Singapore	6
Sweden	7	8	7	9	6	9	9	9	9	6	9	8	6	2	8	11	Austria	6
Switzerland	na	9	8	9	12	9	6	13	8	3	15	9	4	13	8	8	Morocco	5
Taiwan	na	11	8	13	8	9	17	15	10	7	14	11	6	12	8	16	Iceland	4
Tanzania	na	15	12	20	21	12	11	19	12	10	20	12	10	16	14	22		
Turkey	23	21	18	25	24	19	17	26	16	12	28	18	15	23	20	20		
Uganda	na	8	3	12	5	9	15	14	6	1	6	14	8	6	8	12		
Ukraine	na	21	15	26	12	17	31	42	20	13	27	18	17	24	19	18		
United States	10	12	11	13	14	11	11	21	12	8	17	10	6	13	12	9		
Uruguay	na	27	26	27	26	27	27	32	21	18	32	28	21	33	27	24		
Venezuela	na	19	16	22	21	16	21	21	21	13	17	21	16	19	19	19		
Vietnam	na	14	12	15	12	14	14	15	12	13	18	14	11	12	13	14		
Zimbabwe	na	10	8	13	12	9	8	14	6	na	14	7	3	11	10	10		
Total	12	14	12	15	14	13	14	17	13	11	16	14	11	15	13	15	Total	14

E042) FIRMS: CONTROL OR FREEDOM?

Now I'd like you to tell me your views on various issues. How would you place your views on this scale?.
The state should give more freedom to firms or the state should control firms more effectively.

% More control (codes 7 to 10)

(EVS: V189)

Country	Wave 1990	Wave 2000	Gender Male	Gender Female	Age 16-29	Age 30-49	Age 50+	Education Lower	Education Middle	Education Upper	Income Lower	Income Middle	Income Upper	Values Mat	Values Mixed	Values Postm.	RANKING Country	RANKING 2000
Albania	na	na	na	na	na	na	na	na	na	na	na	na	na	na	na	na	Latvia	67
Algeria	na	na	na	na	na	na	na	na	na	na	na	na	na	na	na	na	Slovakia	64
Argentina	na	na	na	na	na	na	na	na	na	na	na	na	na	na	na	na	Turkey	61
Armenia	na	na	na	na	na	na	na	na	na	na	na	na	na	na	na	na	Poland	56
Australia	na	na	na	na	na	na	na	na	na	na	na	na	na	na	na	na	Hungary	53
Austria	na	19	17	21	15	17	22	24	15	11	24	17	18	34	18	16	Romania	53
Azerbaijan	na	na	na	na	na	na	na	na	na	na	na	na	na	na	na	na	Luxembourg	50
Bangladesh	na	na	na	na	na	na	na	na	na	na	na	na	na	na	na	na	Estonia	48
Belarus	na	30	27	33	19	27	43	49	25	19	35	28	24	38	26	2	Russian Fed.	48
Belgium	na	42	42	42	35	40	46	55	41	32	49	49	33	46	37	46	Czech Republic	46
Bosnia and Herz.	na	na	na	na	na	na	na	na	na	na	na	na	na	na	na	na	Belgium	42
Brazil	na	na	na	na	na	na	na	na	na	na	na	na	na	na	na	na	Bulgaria	41
Bulgaria	na	41	37	45	31	40	48	53	39	30	50	48	32	48	38	13	Croatia	40
Canada	na	na	na	na	na	na	na	na	na	na	na	na	na	na	na	na	Slovenia	40
Chile	na	na	na	na	na	na	na	na	na	na	na	na	na	na	na	na	Greece	40
China	na	na	na	na	na	na	na	na	na	na	na	na	na	na	na	na	Ukraine	39
Colombia	na	na	na	na	na	na	na	na	na	na	na	na	na	na	na	na	Portugal	35
Croatia	na	40	39	41	35	39	46	50	37	28	59	41	30	41	43	28	Netherlands	35
Czech Republic	na	46	42	50	46	43	49	52	41	34	54	48	35	57	44	34	Malta	31
Denmark	na	21	18	24	23	22	18	23	11	23	25	19	18	23	19	31	Spain	31
Dominican Rep.	na	na	na	na	na	na	na	na	na	na	na	na	na	na	na	na	Belarus	30
Egypt	na	na	na	na	na	na	na	na	na	na	na	na	na	na	na	na	Italy	29
El Salvador	na	na	na	na	na	na	na	na	na	na	na	na	na	na	na	na	France	29
Estonia	na	48	45	50	38	46	55	52	50	36	56	54	41	53	45	46	Lithuania	26
Finland	na	23	22	24	17	24	26	26	19	16	26	24	22	25	22	27	Ireland	26
France	na	29	29	30	27	29	31	34	25	22	35	35	20	32	26	37	Germany	25
Georgia	na	na	na	na	na	na	na	na	na	na	na	na	na	na	na	na	Finland	23
Germany	na	25	26	24	25	24	25	25	23	27	27	25	16	16	28	30	Denmark	21
Great Britain	na	20	22	19	18	20	24	22	19	15	21	21	24	na	na	na	Great Britain	20
Greece	na	40	40	40	37	39	48	54	41	36	45	40	34	33	41	39	Northern Ireland	19
Hungary	na	53	53	54	47	51	59	58	48	38	55	58	48	57	52	39	Austria	19
Iceland	na	8	9	8	8	6	11	13	4	7	12	7	6	10	8	7	Sweden	11
India	na	na	na	na	na	na	na	na	na	na	na	na	na	na	na	na	Iceland	8
Indonesia	na	na	na	na	na	na	na	na	na	na	na	na	na	na	na	na		
Iran	na	na	na	na	na	na	na	na	na	na	na	na	na	na	na	na		
Ireland	na	26	30	22	21	28	27	32	23	23	30	28	25	25	25	31		
Israel	na	na	na	na	na	na	na	na	na	na	na	na	na	na	na	na		
Italy	na	29	28	31	25	28	33	35	27	23	32	31	23	42	29	26		
Japan	na	na	na	na	na	na	na	na	na	na	na	na	na	na	na	na		
Jordan	na	na	na	na	na	na	na	na	na	na	na	na	na	na	na	na		
Korea, South	na	na	na	na	na	na	na	na	na	na	na	na	na	na	na	na		
Latvia	na	67	66	68	53	66	74	74	66	63	74	69	55	71	65	57		
Lithuania	na	26	25	27	18	26	33	30	27	17	30	31	23	27	27	14		
Luxembourg	na	50	50	51	44	52	52	53	53	41	56	56	43	52	52	38		
Macedonia	na	na	na	na	na	na	na	na	na	na	na	na	na	na	na	na		
Malta	na	31	29	33	23	34	34	38	31	14	38	31	23	36	30	14		
Mexico	na	na	na	na	na	na	na	na	na	na	na	na	na	na	na	na		
Moldova	na	na	na	na	na	na	na	na	na	na	na	na	na	na	na	na		
Montenegro	na	na	na	na	na	na	na	na	na	na	na	na	na	na	na	na		
Morocco	na	na	na	na	na	na	na	na	na	na	na	na	na	na	na	na		
Netherlands	na	35	31	38	32	33	38	42	33	29	40	36	27	46	32	34		
New Zealand	na	na	na	na	na	na	na	na	na	na	na	na	na	na	na	na		
Nigeria	na	na	na	na	na	na	na	na	na	na	na	na	na	na	na	na		
Northern Ireland	na	19	21	18	25	19	16	19	22	16	19	25	19	14	21	26		
Norway	na	na	na	na	na	na	na	na	na	na	na	na	na	na	na	na		
Pakistan	na	na	na	na	na	na	na	na	na	na	na	na	na	na	na	na		
Peru	na	na	na	na	na	na	na	na	na	na	na	na	na	na	na	na		
Philippines	na	na	na	na	na	na	na	na	na	na	na	na	na	Mat	Mixed	Postm.		
Poland	na	56	56	56	46	57	60	59	55	45	64	52	46	62	52	52		
Portugal	na	35	35	35	39	33	34	36	33	28	22	34	38	31	36	40		
Puerto Rico	na	na	na	na	na	na	na	na	na	na	na	na	na	na	na	na		
Romania	na	53	46	61	47	48	63	69	51	33	66	59	39	61	48	29		
Russian Fed.	na	48	44	51	35	45	59	60	49	38	54	52	40	53	43	35		
Serbia	na	na	na	na	na	na	na	na	na	na	na	na	na	na	na	na		
Singapore	na	na	na	na	na	na	na	na	na	na	na	na	na	na	na	na		
Slovakia	na	64	58	69	59	65	66	72	62	50	70	66	61	69	63	34		
Slovenia	na	40	38	42	28	41	48	56	38	21	47	46	31	48	39	40		
South Africa	na	na	na	na	na	na	na	na	na	na	na	na	na	na	na	na		
Spain	na	31	33	28	29	32	31	32	29	33	35	35	24	33	28	41		
Sweden	na	11	11	11	8	11	13	18	10	7	16	9	7	18	10	15		
Switzerland	na	na	na	na	na	na	na	na	na	na	na	na	na	na	na	na		
Taiwan	na	na	na	na	na	na	na	na	na	na	na	na	na	na	na	na		
Tanzania	na	na	na	na	na	na	na	na	na	na	na	na	na	na	na	na		
Turkey	na	61	61	60	61	57	72	63	61	50	61	64	55	64	59	62		
Uganda	na	na	na	na	na	na	na	na	na	na	na	na	na	na	na	na		
Ukraine	na	39	36	42	25	32	55	66	39	28	52	35	30	47	38	12		
United States	na	na	na	na	na	na	na	na	na	na	na	na	na	na	na	na		
Uruguay	na	na	na	na	na	na	na	na	na	na	na	na	na	na	na	na		
Venezuela	na	na	na	na	na	na	na	na	na	na	na	na	na	na	na	na		
Vietnam	na	na	na	na	na	na	na	na	na	na	na	na	na	na	na	na		
Zimbabwe	na	na	na	na	na	na	na	na	na	na	na	na	na	na	na	na		
Total	na	36	35	38	31	35	40	41	36	28	42	38	31	44	34	30	Total	36

E042) FIRMS: CONTROL OR FREEDOM?

Now I'd like you to tell me your views on various issues. How would you place your views on this scale?.

The state should give more freedom to firms or the state should control firms more effectively.

% More freedom (codes 1 to 4)

(EVS: V189)

Country	Wave 1990	Wave 2000	Gender Male	Gender Female	Age 16-29	Age 30-49	Age 50+	Education Lower	Education Middle	Education Upper	Income Lower	Income Middle	Income Upper	Values Mat	Values Mixed	Values Postm.
Albania	na	na	na	na	na	na	na	na	na	na	na	na	na	na	na	na
Algeria	na	na	na	na	na	na	na	na	na	na	na	na	na	na	na	na
Argentina	na	na	na	na	na	na	na	na	na	na	na	na	na	na	na	na
Armenia	na	na	na	na	na	na	na	na	na	na	na	na	na	na	na	na
Australia	na	na	na	na	na	na	na	na	na	na	na	na	na	na	na	na
Austria	na	59	64	54	62	62	55	53	63	69	49	60	63	49	59	62
Azerbaijan	na	na	na	na	na	na	na	na	na	na	na	na	na	na	na	na
Bangladesh	na	na	na	na	na	na	na	na	na	na	na	na	na	na	na	na
Belarus	na	49	53	46	57	53	36	32	53	58	41	49	62	42	50	82
Belgium	na	32	36	28	33	34	29	25	31	38	27	28	38	26	36	30
Bosnia and Herz.	na	na	na	na	na	na	na	na	na	na	na	na	na	na	na	na
Brazil	na	na	na	na	na	na	na	na	na	na	na	na	na	na	na	na
Bulgaria	na	40	45	35	51	43	31	27	44	50	30	36	49	31	44	71
Canada	na	na	na	na	na	na	na	na	na	na	na	na	na	na	na	na
Chile	na	na	na	na	na	na	na	na	na	na	na	na	na	na	na	na
China	na	na	na	na	na	na	na	na	na	na	na	na	na	na	na	na
Colombia	na	na	na	na	na	na	na	na	na	na	na	na	na	na	na	na
Croatia	na	40	47	34	42	40	38	28	45	54	24	40	48	35	39	48
Czech Republic	na	30	34	26	30	33	27	25	33	42	23	28	40	21	31	47
Denmark	na	49	54	43	43	50	51	48	56	46	37	53	57	44	51	41
Dominican Rep.	na	na	na	na	na	na	na	na	na	na	na	na	na	na	na	na
Egypt	na	na	na	na	na	na	na	na	na	na	na	na	na	na	na	na
El Salvador	na	na	na	na	na	na	na	na	na	na	na	na	na	na	na	na
Estonia	na	27	32	24	32	30	23	25	25	38	19	23	33	22	30	27
Finland	na	50	54	46	51	51	49	45	56	59	42	50	55	48	52	44
France	na	44	46	42	44	44	44	42	45	48	38	40	54	40	50	33
Georgia	na	na	na	na	na	na	na	na	na	na	na	na	na	na	na	na
Germany	na	52	54	51	46	53	55	51	54	51	52	55	57	63	50	45
Great Britain	na	40	40	39	36	41	41	37	40	46	37	39	43	na	na	na
Greece	na	31	33	29	29	34	29	23	33	30	30	28	34	37	29	32
Hungary	na	21	21	21	23	22	19	16	28	34	15	20	26	18	23	18
Iceland	na	71	75	66	70	76	64	65	76	71	63	71	77	71	71	65
India	na	na	na	na	na	na	na	na	na	na	na	na	na	na	na	na
Indonesia	na	na	na	na	na	na	na	na	na	na	na	na	na	na	na	na
Iran	na	na	na	na	na	na	na	na	na	na	na	na	na	na	na	na
Ireland	na	40	42	38	41	40	40	38	42	38	36	37	43	29	44	41
Israel	na	na	na	na	na	na	na	na	na	na	na	na	na	na	na	na
Italy	na	46	51	41	48	46	44	42	47	52	40	43	56	37	46	48
Japan	na	na	na	na	na	na	na	na	na	na	na	na	na	na	na	na
Jordan	na	na	na	na	na	na	na	na	na	na	na	na	na	na	na	na
Korea, South	na	na	na	na	na	na	na	na	na	na	na	na	na	na	na	na
Latvia	na	15	16	14	21	16	13	12	16	17	12	14	22	11	17	17
Lithuania	na	50	51	50	58	50	44	43	50	60	46	47	54	52	49	62
Luxembourg	na	21	23	18	23	19	21	20	20	23	17	24	23	18	21	26
Macedonia	na	na	na	na	na	na	na	na	na	na	na	na	na	na	na	na
Malta	na	44	48	40	50	43	41	33	43	59	34	40	61	36	46	64
Mexico	na	na	na	na	na	na	na	na	na	na	na	na	na	na	na	na
Moldova	na	na	na	na	na	na	na	na	na	na	na	na	na	na	na	na
Montenegro	na	na	na	na	na	na	na	na	na	na	na	na	na	na	na	na
Morocco	na	na	na	na	na	na	na	na	na	na	na	na	na	na	na	na
Netherlands	na	30	37	24	27	33	30	26	30	35	25	31	37	24	32	29
New Zealand	na	na	na	na	na	na	na	na	na	na	na	na	na	na	na	na
Nigeria	na	na	na	na	na	na	na	na	na	na	na	na	na	na	na	na
Northern Ireland	na	49	52	47	51	40	57	49	47	53	51	42	45	51	50	50
Norway	na	na	na	na	na	na	na	na	na	na	na	na	na	na	na	na
Pakistan	na	na	na	na	na	na	na	na	na	na	na	na	na	na	na	na
Peru	na	na	na	na	na	na	na	na	na	na	na	na	na	na	na	na
Philippines	na	na	na	na	na	na	na	na	na	na	na	na	na	na	na	na
Poland	na	22	24	21	32	21	18	20	24	28	18	23	31	20	23	34
Portugal	na	31	32	30	30	33	30	30	35	30	29	31	36	30	31	34
Puerto Rico	na	na	na	na	na	na	na	na	na	na	na	na	na	na	na	na
Romania	na	36	42	30	42	41	27	23	38	53	26	31	49	29	40	62
Russian Fed.	na	30	33	27	39	32	22	19	29	37	26	26	35	26	34	44
Serbia	na	na	na	na	na	na	na	na	na	na	na	na	na	na	na	na
Singapore	na	na	na	na	na	na	na	na	na	na	na	na	na	na	na	na
Slovakia	na	15	19	10	18	15	11	11	14	28	11	14	17	10	17	30
Slovenia	na	39	44	34	46	40	32	30	41	45	32	34	45	31	39	40
South Africa	na	na	na	na	na	na	na	na	na	na	na	na	na	na	na	na
Spain	na	29	31	28	29	30	29	29	29	32	27	32	40	31	29	25
Sweden	na	61	65	58	64	61	60	52	64	65	54	62	69	62	63	56
Switzerland	na	na	na	na	na	na	na	na	na	na	na	na	na	na	na	na
Taiwan	na	na	na	na	na	na	na	na	na	na	na	na	na	na	na	na
Tanzania	na	na	na	na	na	na	na	na	na	na	na	na	na	na	na	na
Turkey	na	25	25	25	24	29	16	26	22	37	27	21	30	24	26	25
Uganda	na	na	na	na	na	na	na	na	na	na	na	na	na	na	na	na
Ukraine	na	40	46	36	49	48	27	13	42	50	28	42	52	33	43	58
United States	na	na	na	na	na	na	na	na	na	na	na	na	na	na	na	na
Uruguay	na	na	na	na	na	na	na	na	na	na	na	na	na	na	na	na
Venezuela	na	na	na	na	na	na	na	na	na	na	na	na	na	na	na	na
Vietnam	na	na	na	na	na	na	na	na	na	na	na	na	na	na	na	na
Zimbabwe	na	na	na	na	na	na	na	na	na	na	na	na	na	na	na	na
Total	na	39	42	35	41	40	36	34	40	44	32	37	45	32	41	44

RANKING

Country	2000
Iceland	71
Sweden	61
Austria	59
Germany	52
Lithuania	50
Finland	50
Northern Ireland	49
Belarus	49
Denmark	49
Italy	46
France	44
Malta	44
Ukraine	40
Bulgaria	40
Ireland	40
Croatia	40
Great Britain	40
Slovenia	39
Romania	36
Belgium	32
Portugal	31
Greece	31
Netherlands	30
Russian Fed.	30
Czech Republic	30
Spain	29
Estonia	27
Turkey	25
Poland	22
Hungary	21
Luxembourg	21
Latvia	15
Slovakia	15
Total	39

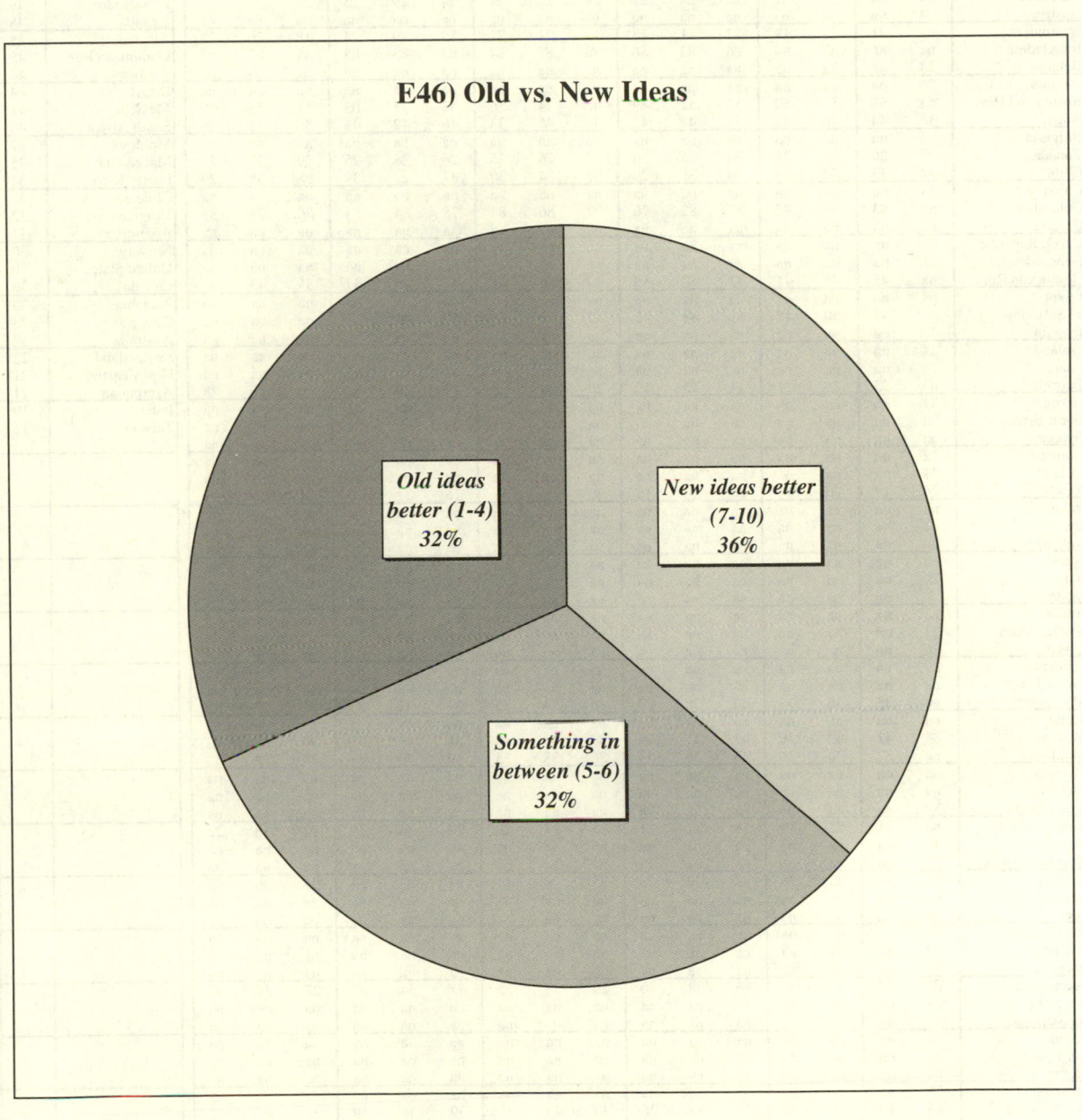
E46) Old vs. New Ideas

E046A) NEW IDEAS ARE BETTER THAN OLD ONES

Now I'd like you to tell me your views on various issues. How would you place your views on this scale?

% New ideas are better than old ones (codes 7 to 10)

(WVS: V145)

Country	Wave 1990	Wave 2000	Gender Male	Gender Female	Age 16-29	Age 30-49	Age 50+	Education Lower	Education Middle	Education Upper	Income Lower	Income Middle	Income Upper	Values Mat	Values Mixed	Values Postm.
Albania	na	45	45	45	51	47	37	42	46	52	42	48	46	41	48	47
Algeria	na	na	na	na	na	na	na	na	na	na	na	na	na	na	na	na
Argentina	32	31	33	29	39	29	25	33	29	24	31	32	29	31	35	23
Armenia	na	25	27	23	29	26	16	21	24	28	33	16	22	22	26	36
Australia	na	22	24	21	22	24	21	24	22	21	24	19	25	27	22	22
Austria	24	na	na	na	na	na	na	na	na	na	na	na	na	na	na	na
Azerbaijan	na	21	22	19	22	21	18	13	21	21	19	19	24	18	26	25
Bangladesh	na	86	87	84	86	85	86	86	87	84	85	85	88	89	83	87
Belarus	28	na	na	na	na	na	na	na	na	na	na	na	na	na	na	na
Belgium	26	na	na	na	na	na	na	na	na	na	na	na	na	na	na	na
Bosnia and Herz.	na	52	55	50	57	51	49	42	54	56	52	47	63	51	53	60
Brazil	38	44	46	42	45	44	42	46	45	33	46	42	43	50	42	38
Bulgaria	40	na	na	na	na	na	na	na	na	na	na	na	na	na	na	na
Canada	30	26	28	24	30	25	26	29	26	25	26	28	25	29	27	25
Chile	42	33	32	33	40	31	29	32	34	30	37	27	34	28	35	29
China	14	na	na	na	na	na	na	na	na	na	na	na	na	na	na	na
Colombia	na	83	84	82	87	82	76	77	86	84	78	84	84	80	78	83
Croatia	na	na	na	na	na	na	na	na	na	na	na	na	na	na	na	na
Czech Republic	30	na	na	na	na	na	na	na	na	na	na	na	na	na	na	na
Denmark	31	na	na	na	na	na	na	na	na	na	na	na	na	na	na	na
Dominican Rep.	na	45	51	41	42	50	55	47	56	41	47	45	47	55	43	35
Egypt	na	na	na	na	na	na	na	na	na	na	na	na	na	na	na	na
El Salvador	na	49	50	48	55	48	42	47	52	51	52	49	51	na	na	na
Estonia	33	na	na	na	na	na	na	na	na	na	na	na	na	na	na	na
Finland	24	na	na	na	na	na	na	na	na	na	na	na	na	na	na	na
France	21	na	na	na	na	na	na	na	na	na	na	na	na	na	na	na
Georgia	na	23	25	21	33	23	13	20	24	23	19	20	32	20	25	28
Germany	31	na	na	na	na	na	na	na	na	na	na	na	na	na	na	na
Great Britain	23	na	na	na	na	na	na	na	na	na	na	na	na	na	na	na
Greece	na	na	na	na	na	na	na	na	na	na	na	na	na	na	na	na
Hungary	22	na	na	na	na	na	na	na	na	na	na	na	na	na	na	na
Iceland	21	na	na	na	na	na	na	na	na	na	na	na	na	na	na	na
India	26	19	20	19	20	20	18	20	20	18	16	21	20	14	23	28
Indonesia	na	na	na	na	na	na	na	na	na	na	na	na	na	na	na	na
Iran	na	na	na	na	na	na	na	na	na	na	na	na	na	na	na	na
Ireland	29	na	na	na	na	na	na	na	na	na	na	na	na	na	na	na
Israel	na	na	na	na	na	na	na	na	na	na	na	na	na	na	na	na
Italy	29	na	na	na	na	na	na	na	na	na	na	na	na	na	na	na
Japan	5	na	na	na	na	na	na	na	na	na	na	na	na	na	na	na
Jordan	na	na	na	na	na	na	na	na	na	na	na	na	na	na	na	na
Korea, South	23	na	na	na	na	na	na	na	na	na	na	na	na	na	na	na
Latvia	26	na	na	na	na	na	na	na	na	na	na	na	na	na	na	na
Lithuania	29	na	na	na	na	na	na	na	na	na	na	na	na	na	na	na
Luxembourg	na	na	na	na	na	na	na	na	na	na	na	na	na	na	na	na
Macedonia	na	35	36	33	42	36	27	36	34	35	33	37	35	40	33	35
Malta	na	na	na	na	na	na	na	na	na	na	na	na	na	na	na	na
Mexico	34	41	42	40	47	41	29	39	43	44	36	41	46	39	42	42
Moldova	na	37	38	36	43	36	33	36	38	35	39	30	37	36	38	52
Montenegro	na	na	na	na	na	na	na	na	na	na	na	na	na	na	na	na
Morocco	na	na	na	na	na	na	na	na	na	na	na	na	na	na	na	na
Netherlands	32	na	na	na	na	na	na	na	na	na	na	na	na	na	na	na
New Zealand	na	21	22	19	18	21	21	23	17	20	24	16	21	22	16	22
Nigeria	40	na	na	na	na	na	na	na	na	na	na	na	na	na	na	na
Northern Ireland	24	na	na	na	na	na	na	na	na	na	na	na	na	na	na	na
Norway	33	30	32	28	32	30	28	35	30	24	na	na	na	36	30	22
Pakistan	na	na	na	na	na	na	na	na	na	na	na	na	na	na	na	na
Peru	na	na	na	na	na	na	na	na	na	na	na	na	na	na	na	na
Philippines	na	na	na	na	na	na	na	na	na	na	na	na	na	na	na	na
Poland	40	na	na	na	na	na	na	na	na	na	na	na	na	na	na	na
Portugal	37	na	na	na	na	na	na	na	na	na	na	na	na	na	na	na
Puerto Rico	na	34	32	35	36	38	30	29	34	35	31	34	37	27	34	37
Romania	25	na	na	na	na	na	na	na	na	na	na	na	na	na	na	na
Russian Fed.	19	na	na	na	na	na	na	na	na	na	na	na	na	na	na	na
Serbia	na	na	na	na	na	na	na	na	na	na	na	na	na	na	na	na
Singapore	na	na	na	na	na	na	na	na	na	na	na	na	na	na	na	na
Slovakia	na	na	na	na	na	na	na	na	na	na	na	na	na	na	na	na
Slovenia	25	na	na	na	na	na	na	na	na	na	na	na	na	na	na	na
South Africa	46	40	41	39	51	35	26	40	40	41	39	45	39	38	43	32
Spain	37	na	na	na	na	na	na	na	na	na	na	na	na	na	na	na
Sweden	36	na	na	na	na	na	na	na	na	na	na	na	na	na	na	na
Switzerland	na	22	25	20	31	23	16	22	23	20	22	21	21	17	21	30
Taiwan	na	12	12	11	13	10	14	12	14	9	15	11	9	9	13	24
Tanzania	na	na	na	na	na	na	na	na	na	na	na	na	na	na	na	na
Turkey	44	na	na	na	na	na	na	na	na	na	na	na	na	na	na	na
Uganda	na	48	47	48	55	42	31	42	51	37	42	49	46	50	46	49
Ukraine	na	na	na	na	na	na	na	na	na	na	na	na	na	na	na	na
United States	20	30	28	31	35	29	27	37	33	25	36	27	27	31	31	27
Uruguay	na	32	34	30	45	30	27	33	31	25	33	37	25	31	32	32
Venezuela	na	50	52	49	55	48	47	47	53	49	51	49	54	51	50	51
Vietnam	na	na	na	na	na	na	na	na	na	na	na	na	na	na	na	na
Zimbabwe	na	44	49	40	51	41	33	40	50	44	45	47	44	44	44	53
Total	29	36	38	35	43	36	29	38	37	33	36	37	37	35	36	33

RANKING

Country	2000
Bangladesh	86
Colombia	83
Bosnia and Herz.	52
Venezuela	50
El Salvador	49
Uganda	48
Albania	45
Dominican Rep.	45
Zimbabwe	44
Brazil	44
Mexico	41
South Africa	40
Moldova	37
Macedonia	35
Puerto Rico	34
Chile	33
Uruguay	32
Argentina	31
Norway	30
United States	30
Canada	26
Armenia	25
Georgia	23
Australia	22
Switzerland	22
New Zealand	21
Azerbaijan	21
India	19
Taiwan	12
Total	36

E046B) OLD IDEAS ARE BETTER THAN NEW ONES

Now I'd like you to tell me your views on various issues. How would you place your views on this scale?

% Ideas that have stood the test of time are generally best (code 1 to 4)

(WVS: V145)

Country	Wave 1990	Wave 2000	Gender Male	Gender Female	Age 16-29	Age 30-49	Age 50+	Education Lower	Education Middle	Education Upper	Income Lower	Income Middle	Income Upper	Values Mat	Values Mixed	Values Postm.
Albania	na	33	35	31	31	30	39	35	32	29	34	32	33	35	30	45
Algeria	na	na	na	na	na	na	na	na	na	na	na	na	na	na	na	na
Argentina	32	32	34	31	27	30	41	37	28	25	39	34	25	42	31	27
Armenia	na	38	36	39	25	38	58	59	36	34	28	43	45	39	38	25
Australia	na	31	34	27	25	29	37	36	29	29	35	28	28	35	32	27
Austria	24	na	na	na	na	na	na	na	na	na	na	na	na	na	na	na
Azerbaijan	na	62	60	64	61	61	68	74	64	57	71	66	53	68	54	50
Bangladesh	na	3	3	3	3	3	5	3	3	5	4	2	4	2	4	1
Belarus	28	na	na	na	na	na	na	na	na	na	na	na	na	na	na	na
Belgium	26	na	na	na	na	na	na	na	na	na	na	na	na	na	na	na
Bosnia and Herz.	na	14	12	15	13	12	16	19	13	12	15	15	12	14	14	9
Brazil	38	36	32	39	35	34	42	37	34	37	38	34	35	35	37	34
Bulgaria	40	na	na	na	na	na	na	na	na	na	na	na	na	na	na	na
Canada	30	24	24	24	16	24	28	32	22	21	32	22	19	22	26	20
Chile	42	33	32	34	27	33	38	37	32	27	33	36	28	38	31	32
China	14	na	na	na	na	na	na	na	na	na	na	na	na	na	na	na
Colombia	na	8	8	8	5	9	12	14	6	6	13	7	6	10	13	10
Croatia	na	na	na	na	na	na	na	na	na	na	na	na	na	na	na	na
Czech Republic	30	na	na	na	na	na	na	na	na	na	na	na	na	na	na	na
Denmark	31	na	na	na	na	na	na	na	na	na	na	na	na	na	na	na
Dominican Rep.	na	24	21	25	24	23	9	31	22	23	22	23	20	27	22	23
Egypt	na	na	na	na	na	na	na	na	na	na	na	na	na	na	na	na
El Salvador	na	34	31	37	29	38	37	38	32	28	34	36	29	na	na	na
Estonia	33	na	na	na	na	na	na	na	na	na	na	na	na	na	na	na
Finland	24	na	na	na	na	na	na	na	na	na	na	na	na	na	na	na
France	21	na	na	na	na	na	na	na	na	na	na	na	na	na	na	na
Georgia	na	51	49	53	40	51	64	55	52	47	58	54	39	55	49	47
Germany	31	na	na	na	na	na	na	na	na	na	na	na	na	na	na	na
Great Britain	23	na	na	na	na	na	na	na	na	na	na	na	na	na	na	na
Greece	na	na	na	na	na	na	na	na	na	na	na	na	na	na	na	na
Hungary	22	na	na	na	na	na	na	na	na	na	na	na	na	na	na	na
Iceland	21	na	na	na	na	na	na	na	na	na	na	na	na	na	na	na
India	26	61	59	64	61	59	64	65	60	56	70	60	58	67	56	54
Indonesia	na	na	na	na	na	na	na	na	na	na	na	na	na	na	na	na
Iran	na	na	na	na	na	na	na	na	na	na	na	na	na	na	na	na
Ireland	29	na	na	na	na	na	na	na	na	na	na	na	na	na	na	na
Israel	na	na	na	na	na	na	na	na	na	na	na	na	na	na	na	na
Italy	29	na	na	na	na	na	na	na	na	na	na	na	na	na	na	na
Japan	5	na	na	na	na	na	na	na	na	na	na	na	na	na	na	na
Jordan	na	na	na	na	na	na	na	na	na	na	na	na	na	na	na	na
Korea, South	23	na	na	na	na	na	na	na	na	na	na	na	na	na	na	na
Latvia	26	na	na	na	na	na	na	na	na	na	na	na	na	na	na	na
Lithuania	29	na	na	na	na	na	na	na	na	na	na	na	na	na	na	na
Luxembourg	na	na	na	na	na	na	na	na	na	na	na	na	na	na	na	na
Macedonia	na	34	35	33	26	32	43	39	34	27	40	34	26	31	35	46
Malta	na	na	na	na	na	na	na	na	na	na	na	na	na	na	na	na
Mexico	34	35	34	35	27	35	46	42	28	21	39	35	28	39	34	27
Moldova	na	31	31	31	27	30	35	33	31	30	31	32	31	30	29	32
Montenegro	na	na	na	na	na	na	na	na	na	na	na	na	na	na	na	na
Morocco	na	na	na	na	na	na	na	na	na	na	na	na	na	na	na	na
Netherlands	32	na	na	na	na	na	na	na	na	na	na	na	na	na	na	na
New Zealand	na	27	29	25	16	25	33	29	28	24	32	26	24	35	25	22
Nigeria	40	na	na	na	na	na	na	na	na	na	na	na	na	na	na	na
Northern Ireland	24	na	na	na	na	na	na	na	na	na	na	na	na	na	na	na
Norway	33	22	26	18	21	20	25	22	21	23	na	na	na	20	22	21
Pakistan	na	na	na	na	na	na	na	na	na	na	na	na	na	na	na	na
Peru	na	na	na	na	na	na	na	na	na	na	na	na	na	na	na	na
Philippines	na	na	na	na	na	na	na	na	na	na	na	na	na	Mat	Mixed	Postm.
Poland	40	na	na	na	na	na	na	na	na	na	na	na	na	na	na	na
Portugal	37	na	na	na	na	na	na	na	na	na	na	na	na	na	na	na
Puerto Rico	na	17	16	18	15	11	23	43	21	11	25	14	13	27	15	16
Romania	25	na	na	na	na	na	na	na	na	na	na	na	na	na	na	na
Russian Fed.	19	na	na	na	na	na	na	na	na	na	na	na	na	na	na	na
Serbia	na	na	na	na	na	na	na	na	na	na	na	na	na	na	na	na
Singapore	na	na	na	na	na	na	na	na	na	na	na	na	na	na	na	na
Slovakia	na	na	na	na	na	na	na	na	na	na	na	na	na	na	na	na
Slovenia	25	na	na	na	na	na	na	na	na	na	na	na	na	na	na	na
South Africa	46	30	29	30	22	33	38	31	28	26	29	34	28	32	27	35
Spain	37	na	na	na	na	na	na	na	na	na	na	na	na	na	na	na
Sweden	36	na	na	na	na	na	na	na	na	na	na	na	na	na	na	na
Switzerland	na	38	38	38	27	36	48	48	36	31	41	44	36	47	39	27
Taiwan	na	55	60	51	46	57	57	57	49	58	53	54	59	56	53	62
Tanzania	na	na	na	na	na	na	na	na	na	na	na	na	na	na	na	na
Turkey	44	na	na	na	na	na	na	na	na	na	na	na	na	na	na	na
Uganda	na	27	23	30	22	30	39	36	23	33	32	33	24	26	28	26
Ukraine	na	na	na	na	na	na	na	na	na	na	na	na	na	na	na	na
United States	20	23	25	21	21	24	23	23	24	22	22	25	22	19	23	25
Uruguay	na	30	27	33	19	24	40	34	25	27	29	34	27	40	28	25
Venezuela	na	25	25	26	21	26	33	34	23	21	31	28	18	29	24	21
Vietnam	na	na	na	na	na	na	na	na	na	na	na	na	na	na	na	na
Zimbabwe	na	36	33	38	31	40	40	40	30	18	32	36	36	33	37	35
Total	29	32	31	32	27	32	38	36	31	28	35	32	29	38	30	26

RANKING

Country	2000
Azerbaijan	62
India	61
Taiwan	55
Georgia	51
Switzerland	38
Armenia	38
Zimbabwe	36
Brazil	36
Mexico	35
El Salvador	34
Macedonia	34
Chile	33
Albania	33
Argentina	32
Moldova	31
Australia	31
Uruguay	30
South Africa	30
Uganda	27
New Zealand	27
Venezuela	25
Canada	24
Dominican Rep.	24
United States	23
Norway	22
Puerto Rico	17
Bosnia and Herz.	14
Colombia	8
Bangladesh	3
Total	32

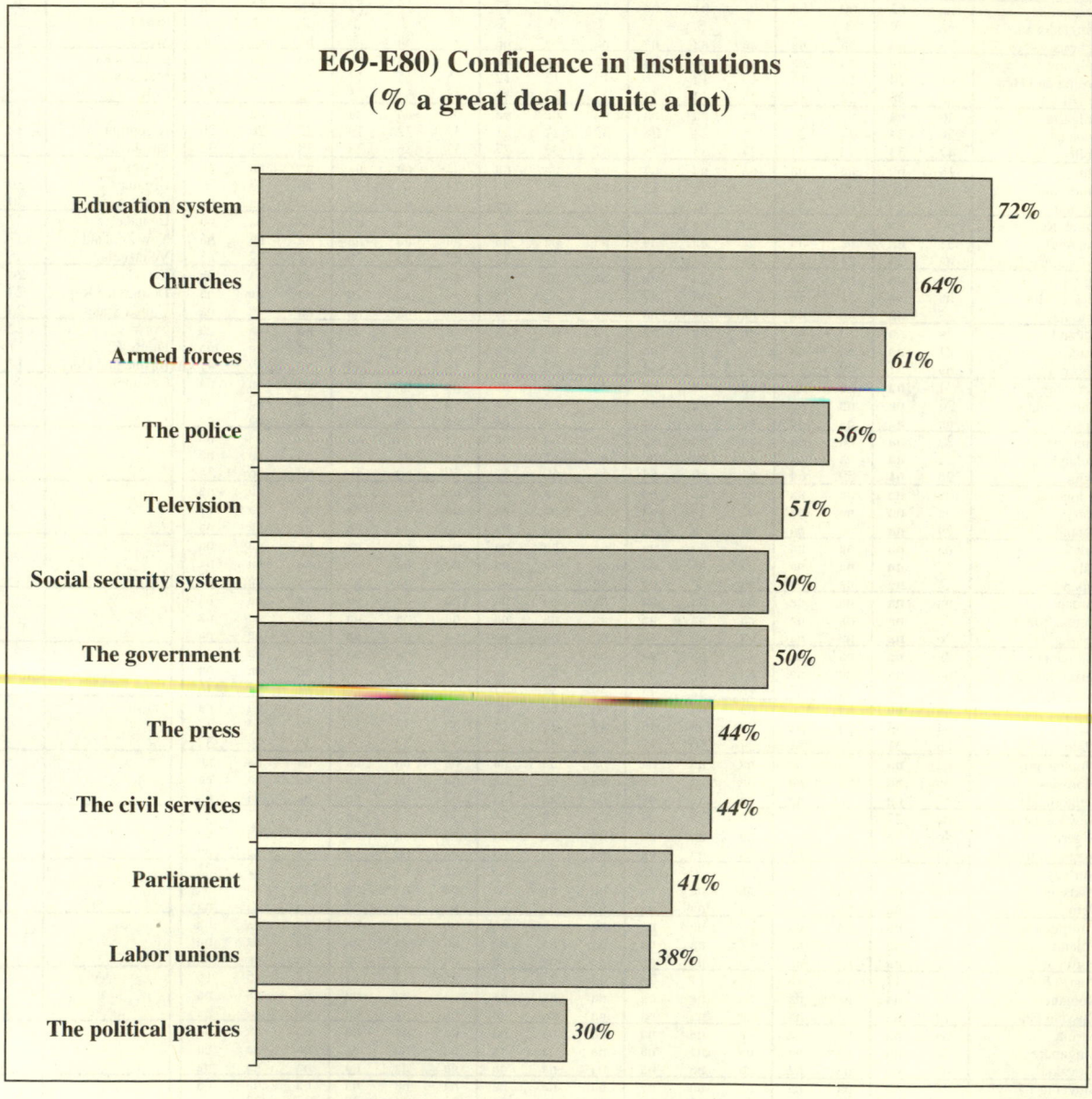

E69-E80) Confidence in Institutions
(% a great deal / quite a lot)

Institution	%
Education system	72%
Churches	64%
Armed forces	61%
The police	56%
Television	51%
Social security system	50%
The government	50%
The press	44%
The civil services	44%
Parliament	41%
Labor unions	38%
The political parties	30%

E069) CONFIDENCE: CHURCHES

I am going to name a number of organizations. For each one, could you tell me how much confidence you have in them: is it a great deal of confidence, quite a lot of confidence, not very much confidence or none at all? The churches.

A great deal / Quite a lot (%)   (WVS: V147; EVS: V200)

Country	Wave		Gender		Age			Education			Income			Values			RANKING Country	2000
	1990	2000	Male	Female	16-29	30-49	50+	Lower	Middle	Upper	Lower	Middle	Upper	Mat	Mixed	Postm.		
Albania	na	67	61	72	64	63	74	67	68	63	66	68	66	65	66	76	Bangladesh	99
Algeria	na	89	90	89	90	86	91	91	89	87	92	91	81	92	87	86	Morocco	97
Argentina	45	60	56	63	54	58	67	63	54	57	69	60	51	68	62	47	Indonesia	96
Armenia	na	68	60	75	67	68	69	70	69	65	68	68	70	68	69	61	Nigeria	95
Australia	na	43	38	47	39	41	48	48	39	42	45	42	39	45	46	36	Tanzania	93
Austria	50	39	36	42	27	35	49	44	33	37	48	41	34	46	40	34	Philippines	92
Azerbaijan	na	72	74	71	70	71	79	91	73	68	71	75	70	73	70	72	Jordan	91
Bangladesh	na	99	98	100	98	99	99	100	98	97	99	98	99	99	98	99	Uganda	89
Belarus	53	71	56	81	65	67	79	81	69	56	77	68	64	73	69	54	Algeria	89
Belgium	50	40	34	46	32	32	51	50	36	38	52	38	35	45	40	35	Pakistan	88
Bosnia and Herz.	na	50	45	54	54	46	50	63	47	48	49	47	56	57	46	42	Iran	86
Brazil	75	74	72	77	74	73	77	75	75	72	76	75	71	77	75	67	Zimbabwe	85
Bulgaria	30	36	28	42	31	27	45	50	28	27	47	29	31	38	32	33	Egypt	84
Canada	64	59	54	63	49	57	66	65	59	54	62	58	57	58	63	51	Puerto Rico	83
Chile	76	78	73	83	73	77	84	82	75	77	79	75	81	80	78	74	South Africa	83
China	5	na	na	na	na	na	na	na	na	na	na	na	na	na	na	na	Romania	83
Colombia	na	82	79	85	80	83	85	84	82	79	83	82	79	84	82	80	Malta	82
Croatia	na	64	59	70	60	65	67	71	62	57	72	62	63	71	67	52	India	82
Czech Republic	43	20	17	22	15	13	28	22	17	16	27	18	13	21	19	22	Colombia	82
Denmark	47	59	56	62	50	58	65	57	56	65	60	58	62	56	60	57	Moldova	82
Dominican Rep.	na	72	72	72	71	73	82	72	72	72	74	73	69	72	72	72	Mexico	82
Egypt	na	84	82	86	85	84	83	87	84	76	87	86	79	87	82	77	Georgia	80
El Salvador	na	63	64	62	63	59	68	58	64	72	62	61	67	na	na	na	Portugal	80
Estonia	54	44	38	49	37	39	53	49	42	41	53	48	38	47	42	40	Chile	78
Finland	32	58	52	64	53	54	65	56	57	70	60	49	63	59	59	52	Venezuela	77
France	50	46	41	50	37	41	55	49	40	43	46	43	45	53	47	32	United States	75
Georgia	na	80	77	83	84	81	76	78	80	83	79	81	82	79	82	84	Brazil	74
Germany	43	39	35	43	32	29	54	46	33	41	44	40	41	46	40	32	Azerbaijan	72
Great Britain	43	34	30	39	31	31	40	33	34	36	33	33	37	na	na	na	Dominican Rep.	72
Greece	na	55	50	58	49	58	63	71	59	48	61	54	50	69	56	35	Turkey	71
Hungary	56	48	39	55	35	41	61	53	37	37	57	47	43	53	42	44	Lithuania	71
Iceland	68	65	59	70	54	63	76	69	62	61	66	66	61	72	65	42	Peru	71
India	85	82	79	86	81	81	86	88	81	70	86	87	76	86	75	76	Belarus	71
Indonesia	na	96	96	98	95	97	98	97	97	96	97	96	98	97	97	93	Poland	69
Iran	na	86	86	87	85	87	90	92	86	80	84	88	85	92	84	71	Slovakia	69
Ireland	72	52	48	56	30	48	72	66	44	46	64	50	44	54	53	43	Armenia	68
Israel	na	na	na	na	na	na	na	na	na	na	na	na	na	na	na	na	Italy	67
Italy	63	67	61	73	55	65	75	72	65	61	74	65	63	79	68	59	Latvia	67
Japan	11	10	9	10	5	10	12	9	11	7	11	9	9	11	9	10	Albania	67
Jordan	na	91	87	95	92	90	90	94	90	87	93	92	86	92	91	81	Ukraine	66
Korea, South	58	49	46	52	46	49	52	45	51	47	47	46	53	51	48	42	Iceland	65
Latvia	64	67	59	73	60	64	72	73	64	68	70	62	67	67	67	60	Croatia	64
Lithuania	73	71	60	79	58	61	88	88	65	66	83	65	67	77	71	55	Northern Ireland	64
Luxembourg	na	48	46	50	38	43	59	56	44	43	46	46	38	51	48	42	El Salvador	63
Macedonia	na	46	43	50	46	44	50	55	44	36	55	43	40	48	46	30	Taiwan	62
Malta	na	82	78	87	69	80	94	90	81	74	86	84	79	84	83	71	Russian Fed.	61
Mexico	76	82	78	85	80	81	85	84	80	73	86	79	77	84	81	76	Argentina	60
Moldova	na	82	74	89	75	81	89	86	82	78	87	77	79	83	81	72	Denmark	59
Montenegro	na	48	43	53	41	47	53	56	46	36	48	48	45	48	47	42	Canada	59
Morocco	na	97	96	98	97	98	98	98	97	93	100	96	96	97	97	94	Finland	58
Netherlands	31	29	26	32	20	23	39	35	28	24	30	29	24	46	28	21	Uruguay	56
New Zealand	na	39	37	41	38	32	45	36	40	40	41	38	35	46	40	35	Greece	55
Nigeria	88	95	93	96	95	95	97	95	95	93	94	96	95	95	95	95	Norway	54
Northern Ireland	80	64	59	68	58	52	76	73	54	59	65	63	60	64	64	62	Serbia	53
Norway	45	54	48	59	44	51	64	57	55	49	na	na	na	59	54	41	Ireland	52
Pakistan	na	88	90	86	89	86	92	88	89	86	88	88	87	90	87	83	Bosnia and Herz.	50
Peru	na	71	64	78	67	74	71	73	73	66	74	71	67	74	70	70	Korea, South	49
Philippines	na	92	89	94	92	92	90	94	91	90	89	93	92	93	90	91	Montenegro	48
Poland	84	69	64	74	69	63	77	75	65	56	73	69	62	77	66	59	Luxembourg	48
Portugal	56	80	72	87	68	85	83	84	72	68	83	81	76	83	80	71	Hungary	48
Puerto Rico	na	83	82	84	78	82	87	89	82	84	86	85	83	80	84	83	Macedonia	46
Romania	72	83	76	89	72	81	90	92	81	69	91	85	76	87	81	61	France	46
Russian Fed.	65	61	50	70	58	58	66	73	60	58	68	60	55	64	58	44	Sweden	45
Serbia	na	53	50	56	53	50	56	64	47	48	58	51	51	54	51	44	Estonia	44
Singapore	na	na	na	na	na	na	na	na	na	na	na	na	na	na	na	na	Australia	43
Slovakia	na	69	61	76	59	64	81	76	66	59	78	68	65	73	67	59	Spain	42
Slovenia	39	35	35	36	29	30	46	51	32	21	46	37	24	42	35	31	Belgium	40
South Africa	83	83	78	90	87	79	86	85	82	73	82	91	78	84	82	84	Germany	39
Spain	46	42	33	50	24	35	59	52	32	31	54	42	34	52	42	23	New Zealand	39
Sweden	38	45	44	47	43	44	48	51	43	45	43	47	47	55	46	41	Switzerland	39
Switzerland	na	39	34	44	24	36	51	47	36	41	45	46	31	48	39	33	Austria	39
Taiwan	na	62	59	66	67	60	65	67	59	61	59	67	60	66	58	53	Bulgaria	36
Tanzania	na	93	92	94	91	93	94	92	92	95	93	94	94	92	94	92	Slovenia	35
Turkey	66	71	70	73	67	71	82	77	67	57	75	71	63	82	72	55	Great Britain	34
Uganda	na	89	85	93	87	92	90	84	92	89	88	95	89	90	90	85	Netherlands	29
Ukraine	na	66	54	75	61	64	70	79	64	61	67	64	66	69	61	60	Vietnam	23
United States	68	75	69	81	70	75	78	76	75	74	75	75	73	84	76	68	Czech Republic	20
Uruguay	na	56	52	59	50	47	65	62	48	47	60	52	54	64	58	42	Japan	10
Venezuela	na	77	73	81	75	75	81	76	77	76	76	76	76	82	75	72		
Vietnam	na	23	19	26	19	23	25	29	14	12	18	22	25	19	24	21		
Zimbabwe	na	85	76	92	86	83	84	88	80	31	86	87	76	84	83	92		
Total	56	64	60	68	64	62	67	69	61	61	68	64	61	71	63	53	Total	64

E070) CONFIDENCE: ARMED FORCES

I am going to name a number of organizations. For each one, could you tell me how much confidence you have in them: is it a great deal of confidence, quite a lot of confidence, not very much confidence or none at all? The armed forces.

A great deal / Quite a lot (%)   (WVS: V148; EVS: V201)

Country	Wave 1990	Wave 2000	Gender Male	Gender Female	Age 16-29	Age 30-49	Age 50+	Education Lower	Education Middle	Education Upper	Income Lower	Income Middle	Income Upper	Values Mat	Values Mixed	Values Postm.	RANKING Country	RANKING 2000
Albania	na	57	54	59	54	54	64	61	54	54	60	57	51	60	54	50	China	97
Algeria	na	67	69	65	64	66	76	79	67	58	69	67	58	76	65	45	Vietnam	96
Argentina	28	27	34	21	24	28	28	29	25	17	32	26	23	32	28	19	Jordan	92
Armenia	na	72	71	73	71	71	76	73	72	71	72	71	70	73	71	81	India	92
Australia	na	68	66	70	67	65	72	74	69	62	69	65	66	70	70	63	Tanzania	91
Austria	29	39	35	43	37	36	44	46	35	29	44	39	37	46	42	34	Pakistan	86
Azerbaijan	na	56	60	52	57	53	61	60	55	57	53	57	57	55	57	57	Turkey	86
Bangladesh	na	74	74	76	74	73	85	81	67	68	82	69	76	75	75	60	Finland	84
Belarus	61	70	67	72	59	65	84	82	68	55	80	66	60	77	66	40	Great Britain	84
Belgium	33	37	36	39	41	32	41	38	41	31	38	38	37	45	36	32	Romania	83
Bosnia and Herz.	na	61	59	62	59	58	67	77	59	52	61	65	58	65	59	55	United States	82
Brazil	67	71	79	64	69	70	81	71	71	75	70	70	73	72	72	69	Slovakia	77
Bulgaria	69	58	58	58	49	53	66	67	52	56	65	53	55	59	58	36	Taiwan	76
Canada	57	63	60	66	61	60	67	68	65	55	65	66	59	68	65	57	Uganda	76
Chile	41	48	45	50	43	47	54	51	48	40	50	45	49	58	46	36	Bangladesh	74
China	90	97	98	95	94	98	100	98	97	98	97	98	97	97	98	97	Philippines	74
Colombia	na	61	65	57	59	62	64	57	62	65	56	62	67	61	60	60	Serbia	74
Croatia	na	66	61	70	65	64	69	77	62	49	76	65	60	79	66	58	Indonesia	74
Czech Republic	39	25	23	27	26	23	27	29	24	14	29	28	19	26	25	23	Norway	73
Denmark	46	61	61	62	68	56	63	61	62	61	59	59	65	63	63	53	Armenia	72
Dominican Rep.	na	30	35	26	29	30	36	41	32	27	33	27	31	33	30	25	Malta	72
Egypt	na	57	57	57	57	56	60	58	57	54	59	56	56	56	59	55	Brazil	71
El Salvador	na	45	47	44	40	45	55	52	39	37	56	42	40	na	na	na	Portugal	71
Estonia	23	35	36	34	29	26	46	39	32	34	35	40	33	33	37	30	Morocco	71
Finland	57	84	84	85	83	82	88	84	86	85	83	82	90	86	86	77	Belarus	70
France	56	63	62	64	60	58	69	67	57	58	61	64	63	73	64	46	Ukraine	69
Georgia	na	52	58	48	50	53	53	52	53	51	52	52	52	50	54	50	Greece	68
Germany	14	55	63	49	46	52	62	62	50	48	54	60	51	61	56	45	Australia	68
Great Britain	81	84	83	84	74	84	88	89	82	74	84	84	82	na	na	na	Poland	68
Greece	na	68	70	67	62	68	82	82	68	66	68	70	67	73	70	61	Japan	67
Hungary	52	46	46	47	42	45	49	47	44	45	50	44	48	46	48	40	Algeria	67
Iceland	24	40	40	40	54	37	32	43	41	34	38	39	43	43	41	29	Russian Fed.	67
India	93	92	92	92	95	91	90	90	94	93	89	93	92	96	90	88	Croatia	66
Indonesia	na	74	72	76	62	73	80	80	77	67	77	70	76	75	74	61	Korea, South	64
Iran	na	na	na	na	na	na	na	na	na	na	na	na	na	na	na	na	Venezuela	64
Ireland	61	59	56	62	45	56	72	65	59	47	64	65	51	69	56	57	Canada	63
Israel	na	na	na	na	na	na	na	na	na	na	na	na	na	na	na	na	France	63
Italy	48	52	50	53	47	46	59	59	49	39	55	52	45	66	53	41	Zimbabwe	62
Japan	24	67	68	67	61	63	74	71	68	62	72	66	63	81	67	50	Denmark	61
Jordan	na	92	92	93	89	94	96	95	92	87	96	91	88	96	92	75	Colombia	61
Korea, South	80	64	67	62	48	65	81	72	70	55	64	63	66	67	65	41	Bosnia and Herz.	61
Latvia	25	48	43	52	40	40	59	58	45	43	53	45	45	51	47	38	New Zealand	60
Lithuania	22	50	48	52	46	38	64	66	46	39	63	47	45	53	50	37	Ireland	59
Luxembourg	na	54	55	54	57	50	57	60	54	43	53	55	41	58	56	45	Bulgaria	58
Macedonia	na	55	56	53	47	53	64	48	59	57	54	55	58	58	56	17	Moldova	57
Malta	na	72	71	73	63	69	81	70	71	61	77	75	64	76	71	66	Egypt	57
Mexico	47	54	57	51	53	54	54	54	52	57	48	55	55	56	53	30	Albania	57
Moldova	na	57	54	60	50	55	66	65	60	44	64	55	51	57	59	41	Northern Ireland	56
Montenegro	na	51	50	51	37	46	65	59	45	45	57	58	42	55	47	51	Azerbaijan	56
Morocco	na	71	72	70	61	76	85	75	55	61	77	63	67	75	68	57	Germany	55
Netherlands	32	40	44	36	54	35	38	39	46	35	42	41	35	41	42	35	South Africa	55
New Zealand	na	60	60	60	59	56	64	64	60	56	65	62	53	67	62	54	Macedonia	55
Nigeria	61	47	50	43	48	47	38	52	43	44	47	45	49	46	47	46	Luxembourg	54
Northern Ireland	79	56	53	59	43	52	66	56	55	61	54	58	61	66	60	34	Mexico	54
Norway	65	73	68	78	70	71	77	74	73	71	na	na	na	74	75	57	Puerto Rico	53
Pakistan	na	86	85	88	85	84	93	87	85	83	87	84	86	88	84	82	Georgia	52
Peru	na	22	24	20	23	21	23	26	23	17	26	20	18	26	21	20	Italy	52
Philippines	na	74	76	72	71	74	79	77	75	70	75	71	78	78	72	70	Montenegro	51
Poland	65	68	67	68	46	67	82	74	60	57	72	68	58	71	68	56	Lithuania	50
Portugal	47	71	75	67	70	69	73	72	67	77	70	74	64	71	69	74	Switzerland	50
Puerto Rico	na	53	56	51	37	51	62	67	52	51	55	52	56	63	53	51	Chile	48
Romania	82	83	81	84	71	82	89	89	80	76	86	85	78	86	82	65	Latvia	48
Russian Fed.	69	67	65	69	61	63	75	80	68	55	70	69	62	71	64	56	Nigeria	47
Serbia	na	74	72	76	63	68	85	84	71	65	80	77	71	81	70	51	Hungary	46
Singapore	na	na	na	na	na	na	na	na	na	na	na	na	na	na	na	na	El Salvador	45
Slovakia	na	77	74	80	70	77	82	79	77	71	82	74	78	78	76	70	Sweden	44
Slovenia	45	42	44	39	35	39	50	52	41	25	46	46	37	48	41	41	Spain	42
South Africa	61	55	56	54	56	53	60	62	49	22	64	58	39	58	54	52	Slovenia	42
Spain	37	42	42	43	32	36	55	48	37	36	54	41	38	52	43	25	Netherlands	40
Sweden	49	44	46	43	47	40	47	39	45	48	41	46	46	59	45	39	Iceland	40
Switzerland	na	50	49	51	42	43	62	55	49	46	47	53	49	63	54	29	Austria	39
Taiwan	na	76	76	77	62	77	84	87	73	69	79	79	71	82	71	69	Uruguay	38
Tanzania	na	91	90	93	90	91	96	94	89	87	94	91	88	91	93	79	Belgium	37
Turkey	91	86	85	87	83	87	91	87	85	81	84	87	85	91	87	77	Estonia	35
Uganda	na	76	78	73	72	81	69	70	77	84	78	83	80	79	75	70	Dominican Rep.	30
Ukraine	na	69	68	70	58	67	76	74	71	62	72	67	67	68	69	61	Argentina	27
United States	48	82	80	83	76	83	85	80	79	84	79	82	86	86	84	74	Czech Republic	25
Uruguay	na	38	37	39	27	27	52	46	29	23	46	36	31	56	40	20	Peru	22
Venezuela	na	64	68	60	58	65	74	66	64	61	61	61	66	65	63	64		
Vietnam	na	96	97	96	94	97	98	96	97	94	95	97	96	96	97	91		
Zimbabwe	na	62	60	64	61	62	66	71	51	17	72	63	46	64	61	60		
Total	52	61	62	61	57	60	66	66	60	56	64	61	59	67	61	49	Total	61

E071_1) CONFIDENCE: EDUCATION SYSTEM

Please look at this card and tell me, for each item listed, how much confidence you have in them, is it a great deal, quite a lot, not very much or none at all? The education system.

A great deal / Quite a lot (%)

(EVS: V202)

Country	Wave 1990	Wave 2000	Gender Male	Gender Female	Age 16-29	Age 30-49	Age 50+	Education Lower	Education Middle	Education Upper	Income Lower	Income Middle	Income Upper	Values Mat	Values Mixed	Values Postm.
Albania	na	na	na	na	na	na	na	na	na	na	na	na	na	na	na	na
Algeria	na	na	na	na	na	na	na	na	na	na	na	na	na	na	na	na
Argentina	38	na	na	na	na	na	na	na	na	na	na	na	na	na	na	na
Armenia	na	na	na	na	na	na	na	na	na	na	na	na	na	na	na	na
Australia	na	na	na	na	na	na	na	na	na	na	na	na	na	na	na	na
Austria	65	86	85	88	84	87	87	87	86	84	80	89	87	86	88	84
Azerbaijan	na	na	na	na	na	na	na	na	na	na	na	na	na	na	na	na
Bangladesh	na	na	na	na	na	na	na	na	na	na	na	na	na	na	na	na
Belarus	43	84	84	84	78	82	92	93	83	74	89	81	81	89	82	70
Belgium	73	80	79	82	80	80	81	81	81	78	76	81	80	82	81	78
Bosnia and Herz.	na	na	na	na	na	na	na	na	na	na	na	na	na	na	na	na
Brazil	67	na	na	na	na	na	na	na	na	na	na	na	na	na	na	na
Bulgaria	53	58	55	60	51	57	62	62	54	58	60	54	58	52	61	66
Canada	73	na	na	na	na	na	na	na	na	na	na	na	na	na	na	na
Chile	73	na	na	na	na	na	na	na	na	na	na	na	na	na	na	na
China	93	na	na	na	na	na	na	na	na	na	na	na	na	na	na	na
Colombia	na	na	na	na	na	na	na	na	na	na	na	na	na	na	na	na
Croatia	na	64	62	67	56	65	70	75	61	46	67	65	63	79	65	52
Czech Republic	61	55	52	57	52	50	60	57	53	47	58	55	50	56	54	54
Denmark	81	75	75	75	73	72	79	74	77	77	74	76	75	73	75	78
Dominican Rep.	na	na	na	na	na	na	na	na	na	na	na	na	na	na	na	na
Egypt	na	na	na	na	na	na	na	na	na	na	na	na	na	na	na	na
El Salvador	na	na	na	na	na	na	na	na	na	na	na	na	na	na	na	na
Estonia	48	74	72	76	70	69	81	78	73	71	72	81	72	75	75	63
Finland	78	89	88	90	90	88	89	88	92	84	86	90	91	92	89	83
France	66	68	67	70	68	69	68	69	62	73	68	69	70	71	67	71
Georgia	na	na	na	na	na	na	na	na	na	na	na	na	na	na	na	na
Germany	40	73	74	72	71	71	75	76	70	72	73	74	73	76	73	69
Great Britain	47	66	68	65	67	68	64	67	67	64	67	70	65	na	na	na
Greece	na	29	29	29	22	30	41	44	26	29	33	28	27	33	29	22
Hungary	61	64	64	65	66	64	64	66	60	61	61	65	67	66	63	72
Iceland	80	82	81	83	77	84	85	85	80	81	83	84	81	87	83	68
India	73	na	na	na	na	na	na	na	na	na	na	na	na	na	na	na
Indonesia	na	na	na	na	na	na	na	na	na	na	na	na	na	na	na	na
Iran	na	na	na	na	na	na	na	na	na	na	na	na	na	na	na	na
Ireland	73	86	84	89	84	86	88	84	87	89	86	84	88	89	86	84
Israel	na	na	na	na	na	na	na	na	na	na	na	na	na	na	na	na
Italy	48	53	51	55	42	52	60	65	45	44	62	53	47	71	52	47
Japan	46	na	na	na	na	na	na	na	na	na	na	na	na	na	na	na
Jordan	na	na	na	na	na	na	na	na	na	na	na	na	na	na	na	na
Korea, South	64	na	na	na	na	na	na	na	na	na	na	na	na	na	na	na
Latvia	53	74	71	76	77	70	76	80	74	68	77	71	73	78	72	75
Lithuania	57	67	64	69	61	56	81	86	61	58	72	69	63	73	66	46
Luxembourg	na	68	69	67	62	67	72	74	60	74	70	64	68	71	69	61
Macedonia	na	na	na	na	na	na	na	na	na	na	na	na	na	na	na	na
Malta	na	84	83	86	80	81	91	90	83	80	88	83	84	85	84	86
Mexico	76	na	na	na	na	na	na	na	na	na	na	na	na	na	na	na
Moldova	na	na	na	na	na	na	na	na	na	na	na	na	na	na	na	na
Montenegro	na	na	na	na	na	na	na	na	na	na	na	na	na	na	na	na
Morocco	na	na	na	na	na	na	na	na	na	na	na	na	na	na	na	na
Netherlands	67	73	76	69	84	71	68	71	74	73	72	76	71	77	72	73
New Zealand	na	na	na	na	na	na	na	na	na	na	na	na	na	na	na	na
Nigeria	84	na	na	na	na	na	na	na	na	na	na	na	na	na	na	na
Northern Ireland	66	83	82	83	79	81	85	83	82	82	85	85	85	84	84	78
Norway	79	na	na	na	na	na	na	na	na	na	na	na	na	na	na	na
Pakistan	na	na	na	na	na	na	na	na	na	na	na	na	na	na	na	na
Peru	na	na	na	na	na	na	na	na	na	na	na	na	na	na	na	na
Philippines	na	na	na	na	na	na	na	na	na	na	na	na	na	na	na	na
Poland	75	81	81	82	76	79	87	87	79	63	85	82	70	82	80	89
Portugal	51	60	56	63	59	56	64	61	54	65	72	58	54	59	60	64
Puerto Rico	na	na	na	na	na	na	na	na	na	na	na	na	na	na	na	na
Romania	79	79	77	82	73	77	85	85	77	74	84	81	76	83	77	69
Russian Fed.	55	71	70	72	67	69	77	82	70	70	74	71	68	74	69	62
Serbia	na	na	na	na	na	na	na	na	na	na	na	na	na	na	na	na
Singapore	na	na	na	na	na	na	na	na	na	na	na	na	na	na	na	na
Slovakia	na	76	73	80	73	75	81	79	76	70	80	78	75	79	75	72
Slovenia	67	80	80	80	79	77	85	84	80	77	82	80	82	81	80	81
South Africa	77	na	na	na	na	na	na	na	na	na	na	na	na	na	na	na
Spain	67	68	63	72	66	61	74	76	64	56	75	68	58	70	70	56
Sweden	70	68	67	69	71	72	63	64	68	71	66	72	65	59	67	71
Switzerland	na	na	na	na	na	na	na	na	na	na	na	na	na	na	na	na
Taiwan	na	na	na	na	na	na	na	na	na	na	na	na	na	na	na	na
Tanzania	na	na	na	na	na	na	na	na	na	na	na	na	na	na	na	na
Turkey	65	57	50	65	54	58	71	69	45	29	66	58	41	69	57	45
Uganda	na	na	na	na	na	na	na	na	na	na	na	na	na	na	na	na
Ukraine	na	72	69	74	61	69	80	83	71	69	72	71	72	70	72	67
United States	55	na	na	na	na	na	na	na	na	na	na	na	na	na	na	na
Uruguay	na	na	na	na	na	na	na	na	na	na	na	na	na	na	na	na
Venezuela	na	na	na	na	na	na	na	na	na	na	na	na	na	na	na	na
Vietnam	na	na	na	na	na	na	na	na	na	na	na	na	na	na	na	na
Zimbabwe	na	na	na	na	na	na	na	na	na	na	na	na	na	na	na	na
Total	64	72	70	73	67	70	76	76	70	67	74	72	70	74	72	68

RANKING

Country	2000
Finland	89
Ireland	86
Austria	86
Malta	84
Belarus	84
Northern Ireland	83
Iceland	82
Poland	81
Slovenia	80
Belgium	80
Romania	79
Slovakia	76
Denmark	75
Estonia	74
Latvia	74
Netherlands	73
Germany	73
Ukraine	72
Russian Fed.	71
France	68
Sweden	68
Luxembourg	68
Spain	68
Lithuania	67
Great Britain	66
Croatia	64
Hungary	64
Portugal	60
Bulgaria	58
Turkey	57
Czech Republic	55
Italy	53
Greece	29
Total	72

E072) CONFIDENCE: THE PRESS

I am going to name a number of organizations. For each one, could you tell me how much confidence you have in them: is it a great deal of confidence, quite a lot of confidence, not very much confidence or none at all? The press.

A great deal / Quite a lot (%)

(WVS: V149; EVS: V203)

Country	Wave		Gender		Age			Education			Income			Values			RANKING Country	2000
	1990	2000	Male	Female	16-29	30-49	50+	Lower	Middle	Upper	Lower	Middle	Upper	Mat	Mixed	Postm.		
Albania	na	35	39	31	32	34	40	33	37	37	33	41	32	37	33	50	Bangladesh	93
Algeria	na	48	45	51	49	45	50	47	50	46	49	46	48	53	45	46	Vietnam	84
Argentina	27	38	37	39	32	42	41	37	42	35	45	35	37	40	36	42	Lithuania	77
Armenia	na	34	34	34	34	35	33	33	34	34	34	35	30	37	34	15	Tanzania	76
Australia	na	17	18	16	20	16	15	16	16	19	17	14	18	19	17	16	Japan	73
Austria	18	32	32	32	34	31	31	31	33	32	35	30	32	35	31	33	India	70
Azerbaijan	na	32	36	27	37	29	27	33	29	36	28	32	34	30	34	50	Egypt	69
Bangladesh	na	93	92	95	93	92	98	94	92	92	93	92	95	93	94	93	China	69
Belarus	25	41	38	43	40	38	45	48	40	31	44	37	41	43	39	28	Philippines	67
Belgium	44	37	39	36	38	41	33	30	36	45	32	36	41	31	37	46	Uganda	67
Bosnia and Herz.	na	25	26	24	26	19	32	30	25	21	25	26	23	23	24	40	Korea, South	66
Brazil	55	61	65	58	61	62	63	64	59	58	60	66	61	56	63	67	Portugal	66
Bulgaria	35	26	26	26	31	24	26	25	24	33	24	26	29	20	31	34	South Africa	65
Canada	46	35	36	34	33	34	37	34	36	34	36	34	37	37	35	35	Venezuela	65
Chile	43	48	45	51	43	48	53	48	48	46	43	51	56	48	48	46	Nigeria	64
China	55	69	70	69	65	67	78	76	65	65	73	69	62	67	68	71	Brazil	61
Colombia	na	45	47	44	47	45	43	43	47	47	43	44	50	46	47	47	Slovenia	61
Croatia	na	18	23	14	13	18	22	20	18	14	21	15	19	23	18	15	Uruguay	61
Czech Republic	43	38	38	38	43	36	36	38	37	38	37	37	40	36	37	46	Georgia	60
Denmark	31	33	35	31	38	29	34	31	33	39	34	30	35	29	34	30	Jordan	59
Dominican Rep.	na	33	35	31	35	27	50	19	33	35	30	37	34	32	32	35	Netherlands	56
Egypt	na	69	66	73	68	68	74	72	68	67	70	71	69	73	68	59	Indonesia	55
El Salvador	na	46	47	46	48	44	48	47	41	50	50	48	47	na	na	na	Zimbabwe	54
Estonia	64	42	44	40	47	39	42	43	43	39	39	44	43	38	45	40	Pakistan	53
Finland	38	36	37	36	38	36	37	31	43	47	34	32	44	33	39	35	Slovakia	49
France	38	36	35	36	39	36	34	32	36	44	33	36	38	34	34	44	Algeria	48
Georgia	na	60	63	58	62	60	58	60	60	60	56	62	63	61	60	61	Chile	48
Germany	21	36	36	36	40	33	38	36	36	32	38	38	38	43	36	27	Poland	47
Great Britain	14	16	17	15	14	14	19	15	17	17	17	22	12	na	na	na	Ukraine	47
Greece	na	31	25	35	33	29	30	31	29	32	31	31	32	35	31	29	El Salvador	46
Hungary	40	31	32	30	24	35	31	32	27	33	28	32	32	29	32	53	Luxembourg	46
Iceland	20	39	40	39	48	37	35	33	43	44	39	37	42	33	41	42	Sweden	46
India	66	70	71	70	76	66	72	66	72	75	64	69	74	76	71	52	Colombia	45
Indonesia	na	55	56	54	58	56	56	50	56	57	51	58	52	52	57	50	Latvia	45
Iran	na	36	36	37	34	38	40	40	37	31	34	33	39	39	33	39	Moldova	44
Ireland	36	35	34	36	26	38	37	36	29	45	35	32	31	33	35	35	Estonia	42
Israel	na	na	na	na	na	na	na	na	na	na	na	na	na	na	na	na	Mexico	42
Italy	39	35	33	38	40	32	35	34	37	34	36	35	34	37	33	38	Spain	41
Japan	56	73	69	76	78	71	73	71	75	69	74	74	70	73	76	61	Taiwan	41
Jordan	na	59	53	65	60	60	55	66	60	46	70	53	53	65	57	43	Belarus	41
Korea, South	66	66	62	70	62	66	69	72	71	58	64	68	66	67	66	56	Puerto Rico	41
Latvia	60	45	44	46	45	41	48	57	42	40	46	44	43	46	44	45	Iceland	39
Lithuania	68	77	76	78	74	71	84	86	74	74	80	75	76	80	77	72	Romania	39
Luxembourg	na	46	46	46	43	45	49	46	46	47	43	43	46	47	49	40	Argentina	38
Macedonia	na	20	18	21	20	18	21	23	17	21	19	20	20	18	20	20	Czech Republic	38
Malta	na	36	38	35	37	31	41	36	37	37	35	30	37	27	37	33	Belgium	37
Mexico	49	42	44	39	43	41	40	42	38	53	33	45	49	42	42	41	Morocco	37
Moldova	na	44	42	45	39	42	50	49	45	35	45	45	44	44	45	39	Malta	36
Montenegro	na	24	27	20	25	22	25	19	25	31	14	23	29	20	27	32	Finland	36
Morocco	na	37	34	40	32	39	50	41	24	29	41	27	36	40	36	29	Iran	36
Netherlands	34	56	57	55	60	59	51	42	59	67	50	56	67	41	57	62	Germany	36
New Zealand	na	33	35	31	33	31	35	35	31	33	32	30	36	37	34	30	France	36
Nigeria	71	64	67	62	64	66	57	63	63	69	63	64	68	61	65	70	Albania	35
Northern Ireland	16	18	18	19	14	14	24	20	14	23	18	15	19	17	18	21	Italy	35
Norway	43	33	30	35	32	32	33	35	32	32	na	na	na	33	33	34	Canada	35
Pakistan	na	53	52	54	52	55	47	50	54	59	49	52	58	48	60	83	Ireland	35
Peru	na	23	25	21	22	25	21	23	24	22	26	21	21	29	22	21	Turkey	35
Philippines	na	67	68	66	72	67	61	68	68	64	62	67	72	67	68	61	Armenia	34
Poland	47	47	46	47	40	46	52	50	43	44	48	46	45	44	48	54	Denmark	33
Portugal	36	66	63	68	71	62	65	66	68	59	68	62	67	69	64	73	Dominican Rep.	33
Puerto Rico	na	41	44	39	30	40	46	57	37	39	44	41	38	37	42	40	New Zealand	33
Romania	28	39	40	37	33	37	44	42	34	43	43	36	38	38	37	49	Norway	33
Russian Fed.	44	30	28	31	30	27	33	37	29	29	33	31	28	30	30	33	Austria	32
Serbia	na	29	31	27	32	26	31	34	26	27	27	29	32	29	28	36	Azerbaijan	32
Singapore	na	na	na	na	na	na	na	na	na	na	na	na	na	na	na	na	Greece	31
Slovakia	na	49	48	50	52	49	47	47	50	50	46	47	53	45	52	53	Hungary	31
Slovenia	50	61	61	62	59	56	68	68	60	53	63	64	66	66	61	59	Russian Fed.	30
South Africa	58	65	67	63	71	62	60	64	67	61	67	75	55	62	67	66	Serbia	29
Spain	45	41	40	42	40	42	41	40	43	39	40	43	40	37	42	41	United States	27
Sweden	33	46	47	45	54	42	45	43	46	49	53	45	39	51	45	48	Bulgaria	26
Switzerland	na	22	23	21	23	22	21	21	22	27	18	25	25	27	22	20	Bosnia and Herz.	25
Taiwan	na	41	38	44	36	41	44	44	40	39	45	39	41	42	40	32	Montenegro	24
Tanzania	na	76	73	81	78	74	76	80	72	72	79	73	73	73	78	83	Peru	23
Turkey	42	35	32	37	33	34	39	37	31	28	38	32	31	35	34	32	Switzerland	22
Uganda	na	67	70	64	70	69	49	56	71	73	67	72	67	61	69	74	Macedonia	20
Ukraine	na	47	46	47	48	44	53	51	48	42	50	43	45	44	50	39	Northern Ireland	18
United States	56	27	28	25	28	27	26	26	30	25	27	29	21	37	26	26	Croatia	18
Uruguay	na	61	61	61	55	58	66	63	56	63	63	61	59	68	60	58	Australia	17
Venezuela	na	65	64	65	66	62	68	62	66	65	63	66	64	70	64	63	Great Britain	16
Vietnam	na	84	87	82	81	86	84	83	85	90	77	87	86	80	87	77		
Zimbabwe	na	54	51	58	57	48	58	59	48	52	64	54	43	47	59	66		
Total	42	44	45	44	46	44	44	46	44	43	45	44	45	46	45	41	Total	44

E073) CONFIDENCE: LABOR UNIONS

I am going to name a number of organizations. For each one, could you tell me how much confidence you have in them: is it a great deal of confidence, quite a lot of confidence, not very much confidence or none at all? Labor unions.

A great deal / Quite a lot (%)

(WVS: V151; EVS: V204)

Country	Wave 1990	Wave 2000	Gender Male	Gender Female	Age 16-29	Age 30-49	Age 50+	Education Lower	Education Middle	Education Upper	Income Lower	Income Middle	Income Upper	Values Mat	Values Mixed	Values Postm.
Albania	na	33	36	29	30	34	32	32	32	35	26	38	34	27	38	29
Algeria	na	29	26	33	25	31	34	33	28	28	29	29	23	30	28	34
Argentina	8	12	13	11	13	14	9	13	10	9	14	13	9	22	9	11
Armenia	na	19	17	21	18	17	25	22	19	18	18	20	18	20	20	9
Australia	na	26	28	23	30	25	22	24	25	28	26	27	25	25	25	27
Austria	35	31	32	31	39	27	32	36	27	25	37	32	27	36	32	30
Azerbaijan	na	30	32	28	26	32	31	27	27	36	25	33	34	29	32	40
Bangladesh	na	72	71	73	71	72	78	76	71	63	76	70	71	70	73	74
Belarus	25	28	32	24	38	29	18	15	31	38	23	27	39	21	31	54
Belgium	37	37	36	37	46	37	32	36	38	35	36	39	35	37	37	36
Bosnia and Herz.	na	23	22	23	18	22	29	26	21	27	26	25	18	27	21	22
Brazil	48	55	56	55	57	52	59	55	54	60	57	55	52	51	57	58
Bulgaria	32	15	12	19	14	17	14	18	13	19	13	16	18	11	18	16
Canada	35	36	36	36	47	34	32	33	38	34	42	35	33	38	35	38
Chile	47	46	44	47	47	43	48	43	47	47	44	48	45	38	49	49
China	42	73	69	79	63	75	79	80	72	62	78	76	68	73	74	52
Colombia	na	35	33	36	38	33	33	31	35	39	32	35	37	34	36	42
Croatia	na	29	33	26	20	29	35	31	30	21	35	28	28	36	29	25
Czech Republic	27	22	23	21	23	20	24	25	20	15	24	25	19	26	22	14
Denmark	46	48	44	52	54	48	45	48	44	52	52	47	43	53	48	47
Dominican Rep.	na	19	22	18	19	20	10	23	16	21	25	21	16	21	17	20
Egypt	na	68	66	70	70	67	65	70	70	60	71	70	64	66	70	57
El Salvador	na	18	18	18	20	16	16	16	19	20	17	18	19	na	na	na
Estonia	27	33	30	35	32	26	39	32	34	30	31	38	33	32	33	32
Finland	32	54	50	57	62	52	52	57	50	45	57	51	53	57	52	52
France	32	35	35	35	38	34	34	32	37	41	31	36	37	28	36	45
Georgia	na	28	28	29	23	27	35	30	28	28	31	26	27	30	27	20
Germany	28	38	39	37	43	35	39	37	40	32	39	39	39	43	37	33
Great Britain	26	28	30	26	33	28	26	26	28	36	29	30	27	na	na	na
Greece	na	14	13	15	14	15	14	13	14	15	14	14	15	14	13	17
Hungary	30	24	26	21	24	22	26	25	21	20	15	24	28	20	28	31
Iceland	51	49	44	54	53	44	52	55	47	40	54	50	42	47	51	44
India	52	48	51	43	51	45	53	51	49	43	52	52	44	51	46	33
Indonesia	na	38	38	38	29	42	39	45	39	34	37	40	31	36	40	35
Iran	na	37	37	38	36	38	41	44	37	31	34	34	38	37	36	45
Ireland	43	46	46	47	46	44	49	45	46	50	43	52	46	49	45	49
Israel	na	na	na	na	na	na	na	na	na	na	na	na	na	na	na	na
Italy	34	29	28	30	31	26	30	31	28	26	33	29	25	34	28	29
Japan	26	43	39	47	48	44	40	41	45	39	39	49	41	48	44	28
Jordan	na	51	41	62	55	48	53	60	45	43	63	43	44	57	49	39
Korea, South	67	52	49	56	52	54	49	66	55	47	52	50	54	48	56	61
Latvia	24	32	27	37	34	32	32	47	29	29	34	34	29	35	32	23
Lithuania	27	40	37	43	35	32	52	55	36	37	50	37	38	38	42	43
Luxembourg	na	52	54	51	50	52	54	57	52	44	50	48	45	46	56	46
Macedonia	na	13	13	13	10	12	16	13	12	15	13	13	14	11	15	9
Malta	na	49	50	48	48	39	59	53	47	47	53	52	42	51	50	34
Mexico	38	29	28	29	30	28	28	30	24	38	26	29	31	30	29	28
Moldova	na	33	31	35	26	32	41	36	32	32	41	32	30	31	35	37
Montenegro	na	20	22	18	20	20	20	18	23	17	17	17	25	21	20	19
Morocco	na	22	20	24	20	19	37	24	14	23	22	15	23	24	20	19
Netherlands	54	58	59	56	68	56	54	53	59	61	60	64	50	51	57	64
New Zealand	na	22	20	23	35	22	18	19	20	27	26	23	20	21	22	23
Nigeria	66	65	68	62	63	68	62	65	63	69	64	64	70	63	67	62
Northern Ireland	24	38	39	37	37	34	41	39	36	39	39	35	36	28	39	47
Norway	59	66	61	71	74	66	61	62	65	72	na	na	na	63	66	70
Pakistan	na	26	25	27	26	22	35	28	22	25	29	26	20	26	26	14
Peru	na	22	24	20	23	21	24	23	24	20	24	23	17	25	22	18
Philippines	na	54	54	55	53	58	50	54	55	54	55	51	58	50	57	60
Poland	23	34	35	33	28	33	39	39	31	21	36	36	29	30	36	35
Portugal	29	47	42	52	50	45	47	47	48	46	49	48	43	50	44	51
Puerto Rico	na	42	43	41	50	40	39	46	42	41	48	38	41	40	43	40
Romania	30	27	28	26	25	26	30	31	27	21	29	25	27	30	25	24
Russian Fed.	47	31	27	34	29	30	35	45	31	23	36	31	27	32	30	22
Serbia	na	23	25	22	20	20	28	27	23	20	25	29	20	23	24	22
Singapore	na	na	na	na	na	na	na	na	na	na	na	na	na	na	na	na
Slovakia	na	43	42	44	42	44	43	44	45	35	43	41	46	42	44	45
Slovenia	27	31	30	32	27	29	37	41	30	22	41	34	29	41	29	30
South Africa	61	52	54	48	48	55	52	59	46	20	58	56	36	48	55	48
Spain	40	30	31	30	33	30	28	30	30	31	31	35	29	29	30	36
Sweden	40	43	43	42	50	39	42	47	43	38	46	46	33	45	41	43
Switzerland	na	37	38	37	46	36	34	41	37	33	43	35	36	43	34	43
Taiwan	na	58	56	60	53	58	61	64	60	52	56	58	57	58	56	64
Tanzania	na	70	67	73	67	71	72	74	67	67	69	73	69	67	72	63
Turkey	40	52	50	55	53	51	55	56	50	43	56	52	44	50	53	54
Uganda	na	58	64	51	60	56	52	48	60	69	56	65	65	46	62	69
Ukraine	na	38	35	40	28	34	47	50	36	35	39	37	38	37	40	31
United States	33	38	37	40	49	35	35	50	42	32	42	43	31	45	39	35
Uruguay	na	39	40	38	38	38	40	37	39	52	39	37	41	36	38	42
Venezuela	na	23	24	22	24	22	23	23	25	18	24	27	21	25	21	29
Vietnam	na	80	80	80	74	80	83	78	82	79	80	82	77	80	81	81
Zimbabwe	na	63	60	66	60	64	70	70	54	92	68	67	50	61	63	69
Total	37	38	38	38	39	38	38	41	37	36	40	39	37	38	40	38

RANKING

Country	2000
Vietnam	80
China	73
Bangladesh	72
Tanzania	70
Egypt	68
Norway	66
Nigeria	65
Zimbabwe	63
Taiwan	58
Netherlands	58
Uganda	58
Brazil	55
Philippines	54
Finland	54
Korea, South	52
Turkey	52
Luxembourg	52
South Africa	52
Jordan	51
Iceland	49
Malta	49
India	48
Denmark	48
Portugal	47
Ireland	46
Chile	46
Slovakia	43
Japan	43
Sweden	43
Puerto Rico	42
Lithuania	40
Uruguay	39
United States	38
Germany	38
Indonesia	38
Ukraine	38
Northern Ireland	38
Iran	37
Switzerland	37
Belgium	37
Canada	36
France	35
Colombia	35
Poland	34
Moldova	33
Albania	33
Estonia	33
Latvia	32
Austria	31
Slovenia	31
Russian Fed.	31
Spain	30
Azerbaijan	30
Algeria	29
Croatia	29
Italy	29
Mexico	29
Georgia	28
Great Britain	28
Belarus	28
Romania	27
Pakistan	26
Australia	26
Hungary	24
Serbia	23
Venezuela	23
Bosnia and Herz.	23
Peru	22
Morocco	22
Czech Republic	22
New Zealand	22
Montenegro	20
Armenia	19
Dominican Rep.	19
El Salvador	18
Bulgaria	15
Greece	14
Macedonia	13
Argentina	12
Total	38

E074) CONFIDENCE: THE POLICE

I am going to name a number of organizations. For each one, could you tell me how much confidence you have in them: is it a great deal of confidence, quite a lot of confidence, not very much confidence or none at all? The police.

A great deal / Quite a lot (%)

(WVS: V152; EVS: V205)

Country	Wave 1990	Wave 2000	Gender Male	Gender Female	Age 16-29	Age 30-49	Age 50+	Education Lower	Education Middle	Education Upper	Income Lower	Income Middle	Income Upper	Values Mat	Values Mixed	Values Postm.
Albania	na	65	63	67	62	64	70	69	62	62	70	66	58	69	62	67
Algeria	na	67	64	69	64	65	75	73	65	64	69	68	59	74	65	53
Argentina	26	24	29	20	19	25	29	28	20	17	31	25	17	32	25	17
Armenia	na	32	32	32	32	32	32	30	33	28	34	28	31	34	30	41
Australia	na	76	73	78	72	78	77	75	77	76	76	78	76	76	78	73
Austria	68	76	74	77	72	73	80	79	74	66	74	78	75	81	79	67
Azerbaijan	na	41	44	38	44	40	38	44	41	42	37	42	43	41	40	59
Bangladesh	na	53	53	54	49	57	49	56	52	47	50	57	52	49	57	49
Belarus	22	40	35	44	30	34	56	53	36	34	45	38	37	44	39	19
Belgium	51	56	52	59	56	54	57	54	58	54	55	58	57	56	58	48
Bosnia and Herz.	na	64	65	63	62	60	70	73	63	57	69	63	63	69	60	76
Brazil	38	45	48	43	43	42	56	49	43	42	46	51	41	45	47	40
Bulgaria	46	47	44	50	42	44	51	52	45	44	49	47	47	47	47	31
Canada	84	79	75	82	70	81	81	78	80	77	76	78	82	78	82	72
Chile	59	55	55	55	56	51	61	56	54	58	57	53	57	55	57	51
China	68	73	68	77	64	73	80	80	69	56	75	77	64	72	70	66
Colombia	na	50	51	48	48	51	50	47	50	53	48	49	53	48	49	44
Croatia	na	53	48	58	45	52	60	62	52	33	65	54	46	66	53	45
Czech Republic	32	33	32	34	36	28	36	33	34	32	34	34	34	34	33	28
Denmark	89	91	89	92	92	88	93	90	95	90	88	91	93	91	93	81
Dominican Rep.	na	13	15	11	11	16	30	17	7	14	15	12	11	21	12	6
Egypt	na	87	88	87	87	88	88	88	87	85	89	85	87	89	86	90
El Salvador	na	49	50	48	50	44	56	55	43	43	60	45	47	na	na	na
Estonia	19	34	32	36	34	28	40	38	33	32	37	37	32	34	34	42
Finland	76	90	87	93	89	90	91	88	95	91	87	91	93	91	90	88
France	67	66	64	69	63	60	74	68	64	64	63	67	65	71	67	59
Georgia	na	38	38	38	34	38	42	41	39	32	38	39	37	40	37	37
Germany	39	74	72	75	60	73	80	74	73	70	75	74	72	81	73	64
Great Britain	77	70	68	71	61	72	74	70	69	71	70	73	71	na	na	na
Greece	na	28	27	29	21	30	38	53	26	26	29	27	32	37	28	19
Hungary	51	45	44	47	45	40	50	47	39	51	45	45	49	47	44	34
Iceland	85	83	78	88	78	86	83	84	81	85	81	85	84	85	84	72
India	39	38	37	40	35	35	47	39	40	34	45	37	36	35	41	28
Indonesia	na	52	52	52	40	51	59	59	53	46	50	50	57	52	52	61
Iran	na	61	61	60	59	62	61	65	61	55	57	61	61	67	56	62
Ireland	86	84	82	85	77	83	89	81	85	84	82	86	84	90	82	79
Israel	na	na	na	na	na	na	na	na	na	na	na	na	na	na	na	na
Italy	67	67	66	69	62	65	72	72	64	62	70	68	65	73	67	64
Japan	59	50	52	49	40	49	57	54	49	52	53	49	49	61	50	34
Jordan	na	91	89	92	91	90	93	94	92	83	94	91	86	94	90	78
Korea, South	53	50	49	52	42	49	64	67	55	42	48	50	53	53	50	37
Latvia	20	40	37	42	42	33	45	48	37	39	42	35	41	40	41	28
Lithuania	29	26	24	29	23	18	37	38	22	24	41	26	20	24	26	34
Luxembourg	na	72	70	75	68	70	79	74	73	67	72	71	71	75	74	65
Macedonia	na	51	53	49	42	49	61	41	56	56	49	54	54	53	53	16
Malta	na	67	65	69	64	62	73	65	67	71	66	69	64	68	67	59
Mexico	32	30	29	30	28	30	31	35	23	25	31	29	29	32	28	28
Moldova	na	35	34	35	27	33	43	42	33	31	38	36	32	41	29	29
Montenegro	na	40	41	39	39	39	41	41	41	35	47	37	44	42	38	38
Morocco	na	53	48	58	44	55	71	57	34	42	55	49	49	57	48	51
Netherlands	73	64	67	62	62	65	64	62	68	62	61	68	65	60	65	63
New Zealand	na	79	78	80	72	76	84	80	80	78	79	80	77	81	81	74
Nigeria	44	35	36	34	34	36	31	40	32	31	36	35	35	32	36	39
Northern Ireland	80	63	56	69	50	62	71	62	64	64	57	62	71	70	67	44
Norway	88	86	82	89	84	85	87	81	86	90	na	na	na	86	86	81
Pakistan	na	29	28	30	31	26	34	30	28	27	32	27	29	26	32	33
Peru	na	16	18	15	16	16	18	17	15	15	16	16	17	18	17	14
Philippines	na	61	61	61	61	62	59	67	64	50	62	61	60	60	63	49
Poland	30	55	56	55	54	52	59	58	55	43	56	54	58	54	57	56
Portugal	44	66	62	69	61	66	68	67	62	69	71	64	62	69	62	70
Puerto Rico	na	56	57	56	47	56	62	79	58	52	63	53	57	62	55	60
Romania	45	45	43	48	44	39	52	58	39	36	57	41	38	49	44	25
Russian Fed.	35	29	24	33	26	25	35	44	28	24	32	30	25	30	28	24
Serbia	na	47	46	49	44	40	56	57	45	38	54	44	43	56	40	25
Singapore	na	na	na	na	na	na	na	na	na	na	na	na	na	na	na	na
Slovakia	na	45	44	45	41	45	46	48	43	41	45	45	47	47	43	37
Slovenia	52	50	47	53	46	47	57	57	47	48	55	54	47	50	52	42
South Africa	64	57	59	54	56	57	57	65	48	31	66	55	45	56	56	63
Spain	58	59	55	63	47	54	70	65	53	51	65	61	55	68	60	44
Sweden	75	76	73	78	73	80	74	73	73	82	73	76	82	72	76	77
Switzerland	na	69	66	72	67	70	68	69	69	66	66	70	70	81	71	57
Taiwan	na	59	56	62	49	58	70	71	54	53	67	57	54	63	56	46
Tanzania	na	67	61	75	66	64	78	74	62	58	71	68	65	66	69	67
Turkey	63	71	68	74	68	71	77	78	65	50	76	71	55	81	71	56
Uganda	na	55	56	55	56	59	40	53	56	58	65	61	55	48	60	53
Ukraine	na	33	30	34	26	26	42	44	31	30	33	31	33	33	33	15
United States	75	71	69	74	66	71	77	67	69	75	67	74	75	77	74	65
Uruguay	na	53	53	53	42	46	64	60	47	36	61	53	46	69	52	48
Venezuela	na	41	45	38	40	40	47	42	43	36	45	39	43	44	40	43
Vietnam	na	93	93	94	90	93	95	94	93	91	89	93	95	94	93	86
Zimbabwe	na	64	60	68	64	63	67	71	55	17	71	73	44	60	65	78
Total	55	56	55	57	51	55	62	61	53	52	57	55	54	55	57	54

RANKING

Country	2000
Vietnam	93
Denmark	91
Jordan	91
Finland	90
Egypt	87
Norway	86
Ireland	84
Iceland	83
New Zealand	79
Canada	79
Australia	76
Austria	76
Sweden	76
Germany	74
China	73
Luxembourg	72
United States	71
Turkey	71
Great Britain	70
Switzerland	69
Italy	67
Tanzania	67
Malta	67
Algeria	67
France	66
Portugal	66
Albania	65
Netherlands	64
Zimbabwe	64
Bosnia and Herz.	64
Northern Ireland	63
Philippines	61
Iran	61
Taiwan	59
Spain	59
South Africa	57
Puerto Rico	56
Belgium	56
Uganda	55
Chile	55
Poland	55
Bangladesh	53
Uruguay	53
Croatia	53
Morocco	53
Indonesia	52
Macedonia	51
Japan	50
Korea, South	50
Slovenia	50
Colombia	50
El Salvador	49
Serbia	47
Bulgaria	47
Romania	45
Brazil	45
Hungary	45
Slovakia	45
Venezuela	41
Azerbaijan	41
Belarus	40
Latvia	40
Montenegro	40
Georgia	38
India	38
Nigeria	35
Moldova	35
Estonia	34
Czech Republic	33
Ukraine	33
Armenia	32
Mexico	30
Russian Fed.	29
Pakistan	29
Greece	28
Lithuania	26
Argentina	24
Peru	16
Dominican Rep.	13
Total	56

E075) CONFIDENCE: PARLIAMENT

I am going to name a number of organizations. For each one, could you tell me how much confidence you have in them: is it a great deal of confidence, quite a lot of confidence, not very much confidence or none at all? Parliament.

A great deal / Quite a lot (%)

(WVS: V155; EVS: V206)

Country	Wave 1990	Wave 2000	Gender Male	Gender Female	Age 16-29	Age 30-49	Age 50+	Education Lower	Education Middle	Education Upper	Income Lower	Income Middle	Income Upper	Values Mat	Values Mixed	Values Postm.	RANKING Country	RANKING 2000
Albania	na	45	47	44	36	45	54	47	42	47	51	45	40	48	42	49	Vietnam	97
Algeria	na	33	32	34	28	35	41	40	31	32	35	37	27	35	35	23	China	95
Argentina	17	11	14	9	8	14	12	11	12	14	10	12	12	13	12	10	Bangladesh	89
Armenia	na	30	29	32	33	28	30	25	33	24	32	28	29	36	25	29	Tanzania	79
Australia	na	31	36	25	28	31	33	25	26	41	28	32	34	27	31	31	Uganda	77
Austria	41	41	46	36	41	37	45	38	44	41	42	38	42	40	42	38	Pakistan	76
Azerbaijan	na	74	77	71	74	73	75	81	72	77	68	75	80	72	75	74	Azerbaijan	74
Bangladesh	na	89	87	91	89	87	94	91	88	84	89	87	91	91	88	84	Iceland	72
Belarus	29	38	37	38	26	30	56	53	33	26	42	36	31	41	37	9	Iran	70
Belgium	43	36	39	33	36	38	34	22	35	47	29	32	44	23	37	45	Norway	70
Bosnia and Herz.	na	20	19	21	17	20	24	31	18	19	21	21	19	19	21	23	Egypt	68
Brazil	24	34	35	32	30	35	38	35	33	34	34	35	32	33	33	37	Jordan	65
Bulgaria	49	27	27	27	30	25	28	25	27	33	28	23	30	22	32	17	Luxembourg	63
Canada	38	41	45	37	39	41	43	38	37	51	38	38	47	47	41	41	Philippines	62
Chile	63	35	33	37	34	35	36	35	37	30	33	35	38	33	37	32	South Africa	60
China	81	95	94	96	91	96	96	96	95	88	95	97	92	95	93	93	Netherlands	55
Colombia	na	25	25	25	25	24	26	25	24	24	26	23	25	25	29	25	India	55
Croatia	na	23	23	22	19	22	25	26	20	22	30	19	22	23	24	15	Malta	52
Czech Republic	44	12	11	13	15	10	12	11	14	13	14	11	14	14	12	12	Sweden	51
Denmark	42	49	53	45	53	44	51	42	55	56	47	47	57	41	49	50	Zimbabwe	50
Dominican Rep.	na	12	15	11	13	12	20	10	15	11	13	11	12	18	12	6	Portugal	49
Egypt	na	68	67	69	67	68	67	70	68	61	71	70	63	68	69	58	Denmark	49
El Salvador	na	31	32	30	32	28	35	32	29	31	35	31	29	na	na	na	Spain	48
Estonia	69	27	27	27	24	23	32	31	24	29	25	27	30	23	30	22	Taiwan	46
Finland	34	44	40	47	42	39	48	38	47	64	47	39	45	41	44	44	Albania	45
France	48	41	42	38	41	42	42	37	41	50	35	38	47	40	40	47	Nigeria	45
Georgia	na	41	39	42	38	40	44	46	41	37	40	40	42	42	40	34	Switzerland	44
Germany	41	36	36	36	30	33	41	36	34	42	39	34	37	47	35	23	Finland	44
Great Britain	46	36	38	33	36	36	35	27	39	50	33	39	36	na	na	na	Turkey	43
Greece	na	24	24	25	20	24	35	27	19	28	19	21	32	28	26	16	Indonesia	43
Hungary	40	34	33	35	31	35	35	34	31	40	30	34	36	34	35	20	Slovakia	43
Iceland	54	72	71	73	65	73	76	70	71	77	72	70	73	73	72	64	Uruguay	42
India	67	55	58	50	56	53	58	53	57	57	58	53	56	62	52	45	Canada	41
Indonesia	na	43	44	42	31	45	47	46	47	38	41	44	43	43	43	32	Austria	41
Iran	na	70	70	69	68	69	76	75	68	67	68	68	70	75	64	75	France	41
Ireland	50	31	32	30	25	31	37	30	27	42	31	30	30	37	30	27	Georgia	41
Israel	na	na	na	na	na	na	na	na	na	na	na	na	na	na	na	na	Northern Ireland	40
Italy	32	34	36	32	28	34	38	33	34	36	35	36	36	41	32	36	United States	38
Japan	29	22	24	20	14	15	31	34	20	21	24	23	20	32	21	12	Belarus	38
Jordan	na	65	58	72	67	63	67	70	67	55	74	60	58	72	61	62	Belgium	36
Korea, South	34	11	10	12	6	10	19	25	13	6	10	11	11	11	11	6	Germany	36
Latvia	73	28	25	30	32	20	31	33	25	30	28	24	30	28	28	23	Great Britain	36
Lithuania	66	11	10	11	11	7	14	15	9	13	16	7	9	13	9	10	Chile	35
Luxembourg	na	63	63	62	58	62	67	60	61	69	56	62	64	62	63	61	Moldova	35
Macedonia	na	7	8	6	3	6	12	7	7	7	7	7	6	7	7	8	Venezuela	34
Malta	na	52	52	52	44	46	63	52	51	57	51	54	53	52	52	51	Italy	34
Mexico	35	23	26	20	20	23	28	27	16	28	22	23	25	25	22	25	Hungary	34
Moldova	na	35	33	36	26	31	46	44	36	24	39	32	29	38	34	26	Brazil	34
Montenegro	na	33	32	34	21	31	43	38	29	32	31	41	26	35	30	38	Algeria	33
Morocco	na	22	18	28	19	22	33	25	10	21	28	16	22	26	19	21	Poland	33
Netherlands	52	55	58	53	64	56	50	42	60	63	52	55	61	46	55	60	Montenegro	33
New Zealand	na	15	17	13	12	15	15	11	10	21	13	11	20	18	15	15	Ireland	31
Nigeria	54	45	49	40	44	48	40	48	42	45	47	43	47	44	45	52	El Salvador	31
Northern Ireland	46	40	34	46	30	37	46	40	37	48	35	34	47	41	41	37	Australia	31
Norway	59	70	73	66	69	73	65	59	71	77	na	na	na	58	70	77	Armenia	30
Pakistan	na	76	77	74	74	76	80	76	75	77	77	76	77	76	77	82	Puerto Rico	28
Peru	na	10	10	9	9	10	9	10	9	11	11	8	9	11	10	6	Latvia	28
Philippines	na	62	62	61	61	64	57	69	60	55	60	60	65	59	63	60	Bulgaria	27
Poland	79	33	35	31	27	30	40	34	32	28	32	33	33	29	36	37	Estonia	27
Portugal	34	49	45	54	44	48	54	51	44	53	50	48	40	59	42	50	Ukraine	27
Puerto Rico	na	28	28	28	24	25	32	39	31	24	33	28	23	35	28	25	Slovenia	25
Romania	21	19	19	20	20	16	22	26	15	17	25	16	17	19	18	23	Colombia	25
Russian Fed.	47	19	17	21	18	17	24	25	19	18	24	19	17	19	20	26	Greece	24
Serbia	na	23	24	23	21	20	27	26	23	21	23	25	23	25	21	18	Serbia	23
Singapore	na	na	na	na	na	na	na	na	na	na	na	na	na	na	na	na	Mexico	23
Slovakia	na	43	39	47	41	42	45	42	42	51	40	39	49	40	44	49	Croatia	23
Slovenia	36	25	25	25	17	24	32	34	23	17	34	23	24	31	26	18	Morocco	22
South Africa	66	60	60	59	65	57	55	68	52	26	74	67	37	62	58	62	Japan	22
Spain	32	48	47	49	38	46	56	51	43	47	56	50	45	51	49	42	Bosnia and Herz.	20
Sweden	47	51	54	49	52	48	54	49	47	60	49	53	54	59	49	57	Russian Fed.	19
Switzerland	na	44	41	47	49	42	43	44	43	48	41	42	49	56	45	34	Romania	19
Taiwan	na	46	41	51	43	45	53	57	45	38	52	45	42	47	45	49	New Zealand	15
Tanzania	na	79	77	81	78	77	86	85	73	75	84	75	77	80	80	75	Dominican Rep.	12
Turkey	58	43	39	48	40	44	47	47	38	32	46	43	36	46	43	36	Czech Republic	12
Uganda	na	77	85	69	79	78	60	69	78	88	86	80	85	74	78	76	Argentina	11
Ukraine	na	27	25	29	23	24	32	36	26	25	28	24	28	24	28	42	Korea, South	11
United States	46	38	40	37	41	35	40	37	37	39	36	40	40	48	39	32	Lithuania	11
Uruguay	na	42	42	42	34	37	49	41	41	47	41	43	41	56	39	39	Peru	10
Venezuela	na	34	39	30	34	32	39	35	36	30	34	37	35	32	35	35	Macedonia	7
Vietnam	na	97	97	96	94	98	97	96	98	96	94	98	97	98	97	94		
Zimbabwe	na	50	46	54	48	49	57	57	41	16	59	51	37	47	51	60		
Total	46	41	41	40	39	40	42	44	38	39	41	40	40	43	40	36	Total	41

E076) CONFIDENCE: THE CIVIL SERVICES

I am going to name a number of organizations. For each one, could you tell me how much confidence you have in them: is it a great deal of confidence, quite a lot of confidence, not very much confidence or none at all? The Civil Service.

A great deal / Quite a lot (%)

(WVS: V156; EVS: V207)

Country	Wave 1990	Wave 2000	Gender Male	Gender Female	Age 16-29	Age 30-49	Age 50+	Education Lower	Education Middle	Education Upper	Income Lower	Income Middle	Income Upper	Values Mat	Values Mixed	Values Postm.
Albania	na	40	41	38	36	40	43	44	37	39	43	38	38	41	38	47
Algeria	na	58	55	62	55	62	57	61	59	54	56	57	55	69	51	59
Argentina	7	7	8	6	5	6	10	8	5	6	7	6	6	11	7	5
Armenia	na	37	35	38	36	39	34	28	39	33	36	33	41	39	35	33
Australia	na	38	38	38	44	35	36	38	35	42	36	37	43	34	39	38
Austria	42	42	45	40	39	41	45	43	41	46	46	42	45	41	44	38
Azerbaijan	na	44	45	42	45	42	45	47	43	44	43	44	44	41	47	56
Bangladesh	na	96	95	97	96	96	96	97	96	92	97	96	96	96	96	95
Belarus	20	23	22	24	15	18	35	37	18	17	26	22	20	25	22	2
Belgium	43	45	48	43	41	47	45	42	47	45	45	47	46	40	45	49
Bosnia and Herz.	na	30	31	29	29	29	33	34	30	27	27	33	31	33	29	32
Brazil	49	59	61	57	62	56	59	59	59	58	58	64	57	60	60	57
Bulgaria	30	24	20	28	20	19	31	33	19	22	30	18	22	25	23	16
Canada	50	50	51	49	51	50	50	54	46	54	49	48	53	55	51	48
Chile	49	40	39	42	38	39	44	41	40	41	39	43	41	35	43	41
China	59	66	65	67	57	68	72	70	64	67	67	70	61	64	68	56
Colombia	na	32	34	31	33	32	31	31	33	33	33	30	34	33	35	35
Croatia	na	35	34	36	37	30	40	44	32	23	46	30	36	40	37	26
Czech Republic	32	22	20	24	23	19	24	23	21	21	24	20	21	22	22	18
Denmark	51	55	53	57	63	50	56	50	60	63	55	55	57	57	56	55
Dominican Rep.	na	10	11	9	9	11	30	7	14	9	12	7	12	15	9	5
Egypt	na	63	66	61	64	63	64	66	64	55	66	66	58	60	66	63
El Salvador	na	na	na	na	na	na	na	na	na	na	na	na	na	na	na	na
Estonia	39	40	40	41	41	37	43	39	41	41	38	40	44	40	42	29
Finland	33	41	39	43	41	35	45	35	47	55	43	38	42	35	43	40
France	49	46	47	45	40	44	50	44	47	49	39	49	48	46	48	43
Georgia	na	56	55	58	50	58	60	59	56	55	54	58	59	60	55	45
Germany	18	39	39	39	35	35	45	42	35	37	42	35	37	44	38	34
Great Britain	44	46	48	44	52	42	47	45	46	53	46	46	42	na	na	na
Greece	na	14	11	17	11	16	20	17	15	14	13	13	18	16	14	11
Hungary	50	50	48	51	51	47	51	49	47	57	42	51	53	47	53	49
Iceland	46	56	52	60	52	53	63	56	54	59	58	55	55	57	56	52
India	74	49	49	48	47	48	52	46	52	48	49	48	49	50	49	45
Indonesia	na	59	60	59	44	61	65	65	64	52	56	63	67	61	59	52
Iran	na	44	43	46	43	44	48	49	44	40	38	49	47	51	41	40
Ireland	59	59	60	59	58	55	65	59	60	58	61	60	60	64	58	58
Israel	na	na	na	na	na	na	na	na	na	na	na	na	na	na	na	na
Italy	27	33	33	33	28	33	36	38	32	21	39	32	29	43	33	28
Japan	34	32	33	31	19	25	44	46	30	32	33	33	31	44	31	23
Jordan	na	66	60	72	68	61	71	73	69	50	78	61	56	74	62	52
Korea, South	61	67	64	69	67	70	59	77	67	65	65	67	69	64	69	72
Latvia	34	49	45	53	52	46	51	53	47	50	50	44	54	51	49	39
Lithuania	52	21	20	21	22	16	24	23	19	23	32	12	20	25	19	12
Luxembourg	na	60	62	57	53	57	67	60	59	60	59	57	63	63	60	54
Macedonia	na	17	17	17	13	18	19	14	18	19	18	16	18	18	18	10
Malta	na	49	46	51	42	46	56	54	48	42	52	52	41	49	50	38
Mexico	28	22	24	20	23	20	27	23	20	27	21	22	23	22	23	24
Moldova	na	47	46	49	42	46	54	50	50	41	48	48	43	51	45	35
Montenegro	na	29	29	29	29	28	29	22	31	36	19	27	36	26	33	28
Morocco	na	41	36	48	36	46	46	44	28	46	37	35	43	45	39	36
Netherlands	46	37	38	37	45	34	37	33	36	43	33	41	38	40	37	39
New Zealand	na	28	28	28	36	26	28	27	24	32	34	24	27	37	25	31
Nigeria	76	71	72	70	69	73	68	72	68	72	70	69	75	69	72	71
Northern Ireland	58	52	45	59	46	48	59	53	50	54	50	48	55	50	55	47
Norway	44	51	49	53	56	49	50	42	52	58	na	na	na	48	51	52
Pakistan	na	50	51	49	43	52	58	50	52	47	51	49	49	51	48	73
Peru	na	9	10	8	9	9	11	11	10	6	12	8	6	12	8	8
Philippines	na	71	70	72	72	73	65	73	70	70	72	69	73	70	71	74
Poland	79	33	34	31	41	28	33	35	31	25	33	33	33	30	34	39
Portugal	32	54	49	58	60	48	54	52	56	57	49	51	52	57	50	61
Puerto Rico	na	27	28	26	21	23	32	42	29	23	33	29	20	40	26	22
Romania	31	27	25	29	32	23	29	31	25	25	35	27	24	32	25	20
Russian Fed.	48	38	34	42	38	37	39	40	37	38	34	38	42	40	36	35
Serbia	na	29	30	28	27	25	34	34	25	29	32	31	25	32	26	22
Singapore	na	na	na	na	na	na	na	na	na	na	na	na	na	na	na	na
Slovakia	na	39	35	42	38	35	44	39	38	40	37	40	40	39	38	40
Slovenia	40	25	24	26	18	24	32	34	24	16	34	25	24	31	25	20
South Africa	60	58	58	58	59	58	53	61	56	38	59	73	49	62	54	68
Spain	34	41	38	45	32	37	50	46	35	39	51	40	43	47	42	31
Sweden	44	49	51	46	50	48	49	48	45	55	47	51	49	52	47	53
Switzerland	na	46	43	49	45	43	49	47	46	45	44	46	47	57	47	38
Taiwan	na	60	60	60	54	58	69	69	55	54	61	60	58	60	59	56
Tanzania	na	71	70	73	67	72	79	76	66	70	70	72	75	72	72	58
Turkey	50	60	57	64	58	61	65	63	56	54	62	63	52	62	61	56
Uganda	na	69	73	65	67	73	60	64	71	70	71	70	77	69	70	68
Ukraine	na	39	36	41	36	40	40	38	40	38	35	40	43	39	38	38
United States	59	55	55	55	60	52	55	52	56	56	53	56	56	61	54	57
Uruguay	na	45	46	44	35	39	54	46	42	50	47	45	42	46	44	46
Venezuela	na	38	41	34	40	33	42	39	40	30	36	43	36	40	36	42
Vietnam	na	79	82	77	79	79	79	79	81	73	77	84	75	83	80	75
Zimbabwe	na	59	56	62	58	59	63	66	50	40	69	58	46	58	58	75
Total	44	44	44	44	44	44	46	47	43	42	45	44	44	47	44	40

RANKING

Country	2000
Bangladesh	96
Vietnam	79
Tanzania	71
Philippines	71
Nigeria	71
Uganda	69
Korea, South	67
China	66
Jordan	66
Egypt	63
Turkey	60
Taiwan	60
Luxembourg	60
Ireland	59
Indonesia	59
Brazil	59
Zimbabwe	59
Algeria	58
South Africa	58
Georgia	56
Iceland	56
Denmark	55
United States	55
Portugal	54
Northern Ireland	52
Norway	51
Canada	50
Pakistan	50
Hungary	50
Latvia	49
Sweden	49
Malta	49
India	49
Moldova	47
France	46
Great Britain	46
Switzerland	46
Belgium	45
Uruguay	45
Iran	44
Azerbaijan	44
Austria	42
Morocco	41
Spain	41
Finland	41
Chile	40
Estonia	40
Albania	40
Ukraine	39
Germany	39
Slovakia	39
Australia	38
Russian Fed.	38
Venezuela	38
Netherlands	37
Armenia	37
Croatia	35
Italy	33
Poland	33
Colombia	32
Japan	32
Bosnia and Herz.	30
Serbia	29
Montenegro	29
New Zealand	28
Romania	27
Puerto Rico	27
Slovenia	25
Bulgaria	24
Belarus	23
Mexico	22
Czech Republic	22
Lithuania	21
Macedonia	17
Greece	14
Dominican Rep.	10
Peru	9
Argentina	7
Total	44

E077_1) CONFIDENCE: SOCIAL SECURITY SYSTEM

Please look at this card and tell me, for each item listed, how much confidence you have in them, is it a great deal, quite a lot, not very much or none at all? The social security.

A great deal / Quite a lot (%)

(EVS: V208)

Country	Wave 1990	Wave 2000	Gender Male	Gender Female	Age 16-29	Age 30-49	Age 50+	Education Lower	Education Middle	Education Upper	Income Lower	Income Middle	Income Upper	Values Mat	Values Mixed	Values Postm.
Albania	na	na	na	na	na	na	na	na	na	na	na	na	na	na	na	na
Algeria	na	na	na	na	na	na	na	na	na	na	na	na	na	na	na	na
Argentina	20	na	na	na	na	na	na	na	na	na	na	na	na	na	na	na
Armenia	na	na	na	na	na	na	na	na	na	na	na	na	na	na	na	na
Australia	na	na	na	na	na	na	na	na	na	na	na	na	na	na	na	na
Austria	68	67	66	67	65	60	74	72	63	57	70	70	64	74	66	67
Azerbaijan	na	na	na	na	na	na	na	na	na	na	na	na	na	na	na	na
Bangladesh	na	na	na	na	na	na	na	na	na	na	na	na	na	na	na	na
Belarus	32	56	55	57	46	52	69	66	54	45	58	55	54	60	54	31
Belgium	67	69	70	68	66	64	75	70	69	68	68	71	70	66	69	69
Bosnia and Herz.	na	na	na	na	na	na	na	na	na	na	na	na	na	na	na	na
Brazil	32	na	na	na	na	na	na	na	na	na	na	na	na	na	na	na
Bulgaria	36	26	21	30	27	25	25	28	22	29	24	27	28	23	28	21
Canada	61	na	na	na	na	na	na	na	na	na	na	na	na	na	na	na
Chile	54	na	na	na	na	na	na	na	na	na	na	na	na	na	na	na
China	81	na	na	na	na	na	na	na	na	na	na	na	na	na	na	na
Colombia	na	na	na	na	na	na	na	na	na	na	na	na	na	na	na	na
Croatia	na	32	31	33	32	30	34	40	29	23	42	29	28	45	33	16
Czech Republic	42	34	31	35	33	30	37	37	30	31	35	34	34	36	32	35
Denmark	69	67	67	67	76	63	67	61	73	74	68	66	69	66	70	59
Dominican Rep.	na	na	na	na	na	na	na	na	na	na	na	na	na	na	na	na
Egypt	na	na	na	na	na	na	na	na	na	na	na	na	na	na	na	na
El Salvador	na	na	na	na	na	na	na	na	na	na	na	na	na	na	na	na
Estonia	46	51	45	56	38	44	64	54	50	46	56	52	49	50	53	39
Finland	75	71	69	72	72	68	72	72	69	71	70	70	73	74	71	61
France	70	67	69	65	61	64	72	65	66	72	66	67	69	67	66	72
Georgia	na	na	na	na	na	na	na	na	na	na	na	na	na	na	na	na
Germany	58	44	42	46	41	39	51	51	39	38	46	41	38	48	47	32
Great Britain	34	36	37	36	34	36	39	37	38	35	43	38	28	na	na	na
Greece	na	19	16	21	14	18	32	24	19	17	17	18	22	21	19	15
Hungary	50	42	39	45	45	38	44	44	39	42	35	45	43	40	46	51
Iceland	69	50	49	51	44	41	66	55	43	49	55	50	43	48	49	53
India	67	na	na	na	na	na	na	na	na	na	na	na	na	na	na	na
Indonesia	na	na	na	na	na	na	na	na	na	na	na	na	na	na	na	na
Iran	na	na	na	na	na	na	na	na	na	na	na	na	na	na	na	na
Ireland	59	56	53	58	48	51	67	62	53	51	62	56	51	52	58	50
Israel	na	na	na	na	na	na	na	na	na	na	na	na	na	na	na	na
Italy	38	34	35	33	30	29	41	40	32	23	42	31	30	46	34	27
Japan	44	na	na	na	na	na	na	na	na	na	na	na	na	na	na	na
Jordan	na	na	na	na	na	na	na	na	na	na	na	na	na	na	na	na
Korea, South	98	na	na	na	na	na	na	na	na	na	na	na	na	na	na	na
Latvia	37	57	54	60	60	52	61	65	57	49	62	49	58	58	59	43
Lithuania	53	32	28	36	28	23	45	50	27	22	47	33	22	39	30	23
Luxembourg	na	79	77	80	70	81	82	79	79	79	74	83	84	79	78	83
Macedonia	na	na	na	na	na	na	na	na	na	na	na	na	na	na	na	na
Malta	na	76	74	78	67	75	84	81	75	71	81	83	70	79	76	66
Mexico	48	na	na	na	na	na	na	na	na	na	na	na	na	na	na	na
Moldova	na	na	na	na	na	na	na	na	na	na	na	na	na	na	na	na
Montenegro	na	na	na	na	na	na	na	na	na	na	na	na	na	na	na	na
Morocco	na	na	na	na	na	na	na	na	na	na	na	na	na	na	na	na
Netherlands	68	65	68	62	66	63	66	59	65	71	68	63	63	58	65	69
New Zealand	na	na	na	na	na	na	na	na	na	na	na	na	na	na	na	na
Nigeria	65	na	na	na	na	na	na	na	na	na	na	na	na	na	na	na
Northern Ireland	48	54	50	58	49	47	62	56	52	50	50	49	54	56	55	46
Norway	48	na	na	na	na	na	na	na	na	na	na	na	na	na	na	na
Pakistan	na	na	na	na	na	na	na	na	na	na	na	na	na	na	na	na
Peru	na	na	na	na	na	na	na	na	na	na	na	na	na	na	na	na
Philippines	na	na	na	na	na	na	na	na	na	na	na	na	na	na	na	na
Poland	43	39	40	38	43	35	41	43	37	26	39	39	39	39	38	48
Portugal	47	51	48	53	54	46	53	53	49	40	48	55	48	50	48	60
Puerto Rico	na	na	na	na	na	na	na	na	na	na	na	na	na	na	na	na
Romania	36	31	31	30	35	25	33	37	28	24	39	33	24	36	27	21
Russian Fed.	67	45	41	49	40	41	53	55	46	40	45	46	45	46	45	39
Serbia	na	na	na	na	na	na	na	na	na	na	na	na	na	na	na	na
Singapore	na	na	na	na	na	na	na	na	na	na	na	na	na	na	na	na
Slovakia	na	37	33	40	39	32	41	40	34	42	40	36	35	35	39	37
Slovenia	40	47	44	49	45	44	51	56	43	46	53	46	47	50	48	43
South Africa	60	na	na	na	na	na	na	na	na	na	na	na	na	na	na	na
Spain	50	63	60	65	58	56	71	68	58	61	69	65	57	68	64	54
Sweden	46	51	50	51	51	48	54	54	46	56	49	53	50	54	51	52
Switzerland	na	na	na	na	na	na	na	na	na	na	na	na	na	na	na	na
Taiwan	na	na	na	na	na	na	na	na	na	na	na	na	na	na	na	na
Tanzania	na	na	na	na	na	na	na	na	na	na	na	na	na	na	na	na
Turkey	75	66	61	70	62	67	72	69	62	55	66	69	58	72	66	57
Uganda	na	na	na	na	na	na	na	na	na	na	na	na	na	na	na	na
Ukraine	na	44	38	49	40	42	48	51	43	43	44	42	49	43	46	42
United States	53	na	na	na	na	na	na	na	na	na	na	na	na	na	na	na
Uruguay	na	na	na	na	na	na	na	na	na	na	na	na	na	na	na	na
Venezuela	na	na	na	na	na	na	na	na	na	na	na	na	na	na	na	na
Vietnam	na	na	na	na	na	na	na	na	na	na	na	na	na	na	na	na
Zimbabwe	na	na	na	na	na	na	na	na	na	na	na	na	na	na	na	na
Total	54	50	48	51	46	46	56	54	47	48	52	49	47	50	51	49

RANKING

Country	2000
Luxembourg	79
Malta	76
Finland	71
Belgium	69
Denmark	67
France	67
Austria	67
Turkey	66
Netherlands	65
Spain	63
Latvia	57
Belarus	56
Ireland	56
Northern Ireland	54
Sweden	51
Estonia	51
Portugal	51
Iceland	50
Slovenia	47
Russian Fed.	45
Germany	44
Ukraine	44
Hungary	42
Poland	39
Slovakia	37
Great Britain	36
Italy	34
Czech Republic	34
Lithuania	32
Croatia	32
Romania	31
Bulgaria	26
Greece	19
Total	50

E078) CONFIDENCE: TELEVISION

I am going to name a number of organizations. For each one, could you tell me how much confidence you have in them: is it a great deal of confidence, quite a lot of confidence, not very much confidence or none at all? Television

A great deal / Quite a lot (%)

(WVS: V150)

Country	Wave 1990	Wave 2000	Gender Male	Gender Female	Age 16-29	Age 30-49	Age 50+	Education Lower	Education Middle	Education Upper	Income Lower	Income Middle	Income Upper	Values Mat	Values Mixed	Values Postm.
Albania	na	54	53	55	52	51	60	56	53	52	52	60	51	52	54	61
Algeria	na	45	42	49	47	41	51	50	48	39	49	41	45	55	40	37
Argentina	na	33	33	32	32	34	32	35	32	22	41	32	25	40	32	30
Armenia	na	45	43	47	47	42	48	50	46	42	46	45	43	48	44	33
Australia	na	26	25	27	31	22	25	34	26	18	32	22	21	26	29	21
Austria	na	na	na	na	na	na	na	na	na	na	na	na	na	na	na	na
Azerbaijan	na	42	46	38	45	40	39	35	42	42	44	42	40	41	43	48
Bangladesh	na	84	80	89	83	84	83	88	82	75	88	83	81	84	84	78
Belarus	na	na	na	na	na	na	na	na	na	na	na	na	na	na	na	na
Belgium	66	na	na	na	na	na	na	na	na	na	na	na	na	na	na	na
Bosnia and Herz.	na	35	33	37	35	31	41	43	36	26	34	35	37	37	33	47
Brazil	38	57	60	55	58	54	61	57	58	57	54	62	58	52	59	61
Bulgaria	50	na	na	na	na	na	na	na	na	na	na	na	na	na	na	na
Canada	50	38	37	39	33	36	43	44	39	30	46	37	32	43	40	32
Chile	32	53	48	57	50	51	58	56	51	50	54	51	55	53	54	47
China	30	75	74	75	69	74	80	81	70	67	77	76	67	72	75	65
Colombia	na	50	50	50	52	49	48	51	51	47	51	48	51	53	52	53
Croatia	na	na	na	na	na	na	na	na	na	na	na	na	na	na	na	na
Czech Republic	66	na	na	na	na	na	na	na	na	na	na	na	na	na	na	na
Denmark	39	na	na	na	na	na	na	na	na	na	na	na	na	na	na	na
Dominican Rep.	na	38	44	34	44	29	30	20	39	40	34	43	42	45	35	34
Egypt	na	68	61	75	67	69	68	72	66	62	71	70	65	70	67	61
El Salvador	na	49	48	50	48	48	50	52	42	51	56	48	46	na	na	na
Estonia	na	na	na	na	na	na	na	na	na	na	na	na	na	na	na	na
Finland	47	na	na	na	na	na	na	na	na	na	na	na	na	na	na	na
France	73	na	na	na	na	na	na	na	na	na	na	na	na	na	na	na
Georgia	na	61	62	60	64	60	59	62	61	60	58	63	63	63	60	55
Germany	64	na	na	na	na	na	na	na	na	na	na	na	na	na	na	na
Great Britain	47	na	na	na	na	na	na	na	na	na	na	na	na	na	na	na
Greece	na	na	na	na	na	na	na	na	na	na	na	na	na	na	na	na
Hungary	63	na	na	na	na	na	na	na	na	na	na	na	na	na	na	na
Iceland	36	na	na	na	na	na	na	na	na	na	na	na	na	na	na	na
India	33	72	72	71	78	69	71	68	75	75	66	72	75	75	73	63
Indonesia	na	61	59	64	54	64	62	63	61	61	60	61	62	59	63	57
Iran	na	50	47	52	48	47	57	61	49	38	48	49	51	60	43	37
Ireland	71	na	na	na	na	na	na	na	na	na	na	na	na	na	na	na
Israel	na	na	na	na	na	na	na	na	na	na	na	na	na	na	na	na
Italy	74	na	na	na	na	na	na	na	na	na	na	na	na	na	na	na
Japan	27	68	62	73	71	65	69	70	71	59	68	70	65	72	70	48
Jordan	na	59	52	65	58	59	56	68	56	44	69	53	48	64	55	53
Korea, South	na	63	61	66	58	65	67	78	70	53	62	63	66	64	64	54
Latvia	na	na	na	na	na	na	na	na	na	na	na	na	na	na	na	na
Lithuania	na	na	na	na	na	na	na	na	na	na	na	na	na	na	na	na
Luxembourg	na	na	na	na	na	na	na	na	na	na	na	na	na	na	na	na
Macedonia	na	22	21	27	20	22	24	28	19	21	25	22	19	18	24	23
Malta	na	na	na	na	na	na	na	na	na	na	na	na	na	na	na	na
Mexico	27	47	47	47	49	45	48	49	44	48	44	50	49	48	48	42
Moldova	na	49	47	51	47	46	55	57	51	39	49	51	49	48	51	47
Montenegro	na	37	40	35	42	34	37	36	38	39	37	34	41	36	37	41
Morocco	na	30	25	35	27	30	38	33	16	25	34	21	33	31	29	24
Netherlands	58	na	na	na	na	na	na	na	na	na	na	na	na	na	na	na
New Zealand	na	36	37	36	43	36	35	41	35	33	37	33	38	52	38	26
Nigeria	69	72	74	71	74	72	60	70	73	75	71	72	76	73	73	67
Northern Ireland	49	na	na	na	na	na	na	na	na	na	na	na	na	na	na	na
Norway	40	49	46	52	50	52	44	52	50	45	na	na	na	54	49	46
Pakistan	na	57	55	59	55	58	58	58	59	49	60	56	57	56	58	83
Peru	na	25	27	24	23	28	25	28	28	19	30	22	21	31	25	17
Philippines	na	71	73	70	74	70	70	72	71	70	66	71	76	70	73	71
Poland	na	na	na	na	na	na	na	na	na	na	na	na	na	na	na	na
Portugal	57	na	na	na	na	na	na	na	na	na	na	na	na	na	na	na
Puerto Rico	na	26	27	26	30	26	26	33	29	24	33	24	24	29	29	17
Romania	na	na	na	na	na	na	na	na	na	na	na	na	na	na	na	na
Russian Fed.	56	na	na	na	na	na	na	na	na	na	na	na	na	na	na	na
Serbia	na	29	28	30	33	24	32	37	26	24	30	26	29	29	28	33
Singapore	na	na	na	na	na	na	na	na	na	na	na	na	na	na	na	na
Slovakia	na	na	na	na	na	na	na	na	na	na	na	na	na	na	na	na
Slovenia	46	na	na	na	na	na	na	na	na	na	na	na	na	na	na	na
South Africa	na	77	79	74	82	75	68	80	74	61	79	87	64	77	76	84
Spain	48	39	38	39	36	38	40	43	37	25	44	40	34	40	40	31
Sweden	58	na	na	na	na	na	na	na	na	na	na	na	na	na	na	na
Switzerland	na	31	30	32	35	29	31	35	31	23	28	37	30	45	32	22
Taiwan	na	51	49	52	46	51	54	56	55	44	51	50	50	54	48	38
Tanzania	na	80	77	83	83	77	80	83	76	75	85	76	75	83	78	88
Turkey	37	37	34	41	37	37	39	39	37	31	38	38	36	36	38	38
Uganda	na	67	69	64	72	61	58	55	71	60	66	66	68	63	68	68
Ukraine	na	na	na	na	na	na	na	na	na	na	na	na	na	na	na	na
United States	45	25	25	25	25	25	25	32	26	21	28	25	20	40	25	18
Uruguay	na	57	57	57	51	52	63	64	48	47	65	58	48	73	56	47
Venezuela	na	64	63	65	66	60	67	63	65	62	62	65	64	71	62	61
Vietnam	na	93	94	92	89	94	94	93	93	90	91	92	94	92	94	91
Zimbabwe	na	59	54	63	64	55	50	65	51	53	67	59	49	54	60	76
Total	49	51	51	52	53	51	50	56	51	43	53	51	51	55	51	40

RANKING

Country	2000
Vietnam	93
Bangladesh	84
Tanzania	80
South Africa	77
China	75
Nigeria	72
India	72
Philippines	71
Egypt	68
Japan	68
Uganda	67
Venezuela	64
Korea, South	63
Indonesia	61
Georgia	61
Zimbabwe	59
Jordan	59
Brazil	57
Pakistan	57
Uruguay	57
Albania	54
Chile	53
Taiwan	51
Colombia	50
Iran	50
Moldova	49
Norway	49
El Salvador	49
Mexico	47
Algeria	45
Armenia	45
Azerbaijan	42
Spain	39
Canada	38
Dominican Rep.	38
Turkey	37
Montenegro	37
New Zealand	36
Bosnia and Herz.	35
Argentina	33
Switzerland	31
Morocco	30
Serbia	29
Puerto Rico	26
Australia	26
Peru	25
United States	25
Macedonia	22
Total	51

E079) CONFIDENCE: THE GOVERNMENT

I am going to name a number of organizations. For each one, could you tell me how much confidence you have in them: is it a great deal of confidence, quite a lot of confidence, not very much confidence or none at all? The government.

A great deal / Quite a lot (%)

(WVS: V153)

Country	Wave		Gender		Age			Education			Income			Values			RANKING Country	2000
	1990	2000	Male	Female	16-29	30-49	50+	Lower	Middle	Upper	Lower	Middle	Upper	Mat	Mixed	Postm.		
Albania	na	58	57	59	51	59	64	64	53	56	66	58	50	65	53	55	Vietnam	98
Algeria	na	54	53	56	50	53	64	64	55	45	59	56	47	64	52	28	China	97
Argentina	7	19	23	17	15	20	23	21	17	20	23	19	17	21	22	13	Azerbaijan	92
Armenia	na	42	42	42	46	40	41	38	45	36	44	42	39	45	39	57	Bangladesh	87
Australia	na	26	30	22	26	30	23	22	23	34	21	30	30	23	27	27	Jordan	83
Austria	42	na	na	na	na	na	na	na	na	na	na	na	na	na	na	na	Tanzania	83
Azerbaijan	na	92	94	91	93	92	91	93	94	90	93	93	89	92	92	92	Uganda	78
Bangladesh	na	87	85	91	87	87	87	91	86	82	89	87	85	91	85	84	Taiwan	70
Belarus	20	na	na	na	na	na	na	na	na	na	na	na	na	na	na	na	Iran	69
Belgium	43	na	na	na	na	na	na	na	na	na	na	na	na	na	na	na	Norway	66
Bosnia and Herz.	na	30	29	30	25	28	36	39	28	26	30	32	26	34	28	37	South Africa	61
Brazil	49	49	51	47	41	48	66	53	45	46	50	50	46	48	50	44	Egypt	61
Bulgaria	30	na	na	na	na	na	na	na	na	na	na	na	na	na	na	na	Morocco	59
Canada	50	42	43	41	39	41	45	40	39	50	40	39	45	51	43	40	Albania	58
Chile	49	58	56	59	56	55	64	60	55	61	58	59	57	55	58	63	Chile	58
China	59	97	97	97	93	97	98	98	96	93	97	97	97	98	95	100	India	56
Colombia	na	37	37	36	37	36	36	36	37	35	38	33	36	35	38	34	Venezuela	56
Croatia	na	na	na	na	na	na	na	na	na	na	na	na	na	na	na	na	Algeria	54
Czech Republic	32	na	na	na	na	na	na	na	na	na	na	na	na	na	na	na	Switzerland	52
Denmark	51	na	na	na	na	na	na	na	na	na	na	na	na	na	na	na	Indonesia	52
Dominican Rep.	na	13	18	9	11	14	27	16	13	12	19	8	11	22	12	5	Georgia	51
Egypt	na	61	58	64	61	62	60	65	61	50	65	63	55	61	61	51	Philippines	51
El Salvador	na	41	40	41	39	37	49	46	36	34	49	38	32	na	na	na	Zimbabwe	51
Estonia	39	na	na	na	na	na	na	na	na	na	na	na	na	na	na	na	Brazil	49
Finland	33	na	na	na	na	na	na	na	na	na	na	na	na	na	na	na	Nigeria	48
France	49	na	na	na	na	na	na	na	na	na	na	na	na	na	na	na	Turkey	46
Georgia	na	51	52	51	48	51	55	58	51	46	52	51	51	52	50	50	Spain	44
Germany	18	na	na	na	na	na	na	na	na	na	na	na	na	na	na	na	Puerto Rico	44
Great Britain	44	na	na	na	na	na	na	na	na	na	na	na	na	na	na	na	Armenia	42
Greece	na	na	na	na	na	na	na	na	na	na	na	na	na	na	na	na	Canada	42
Hungary	50	na	na	na	na	na	na	na	na	na	na	na	na	na	na	na	Uruguay	42
Iceland	46	na	na	na	na	na	na	na	na	na	na	na	na	na	na	na	El Salvador	41
India	74	56	58	53	56	55	58	56	57	55	59	57	54	61	54	39	Pakistan	39
Indonesia	na	52	52	53	36	54	58	61	55	44	55	51	44	52	51	54	United States	38
Iran	na	69	68	69	67	69	73	73	67	66	64	69	70	74	64	63	Moldova	38
Ireland	59	na	na	na	na	na	na	na	na	na	na	na	na	na	na	na	Mexico	37
Israel	na	na	na	na	na	na	na	na	na	na	na	na	na	na	na	na	Colombia	37
Italy	27	na	na	na	na	na	na	na	na	na	na	na	na	na	na	na	Montenegro	34
Japan	34	27	30	25	14	22	38	40	25	26	31	26	26	36	27	16	Serbia	31
Jordan	na	83	80	87	83	83	85	87	86	74	91	79	78	90	80	69	Korea, South	30
Korea, South	61	30	28	32	21	29	45	44	34	23	27	31	33	33	29	25	Bosnia and Herz.	30
Latvia	34	na	na	na	na	na	na	na	na	na	na	na	na	na	na	na	Japan	27
Lithuania	52	na	na	na	na	na	na	na	na	na	na	na	na	na	na	na	Australia	26
Luxembourg	na	na	na	na	na	na	na	na	na	na	na	na	na	na	na	na	Argentina	19
Macedonia	na	11	12	10	7	9	18	12	11	8	13	10	10	10	12	7	Peru	19
Malta	na	na	na	na	na	na	na	na	na	na	na	na	na	na	na	na	New Zealand	16
Mexico	28	37	39	35	35	36	43	42	29	40	43	36	37	39	36	36	Dominican Rep.	13
Moldova	na	38	37	38	27	34	50	47	39	26	43	32	33	42	35	25	Macedonia	11
Montenegro	na	34	32	36	21	32	45	41	29	32	33	41	27	37	31	40		
Morocco	na	59	53	64	52	60	75	64	37	45	63	52	57	67	52	47		
Netherlands	46	na	na	na	na	na	na	na	na	na	na	na	na	na	na	na		
New Zealand	na	16	17	15	14	17	15	14	11	20	13	13	20	18	15	13		
Nigeria	76	48	49	47	48	50	43	53	46	43	50	46	50	49	48	47		
Northern Ireland	58	na	na	na	na	na	na	na	na	na	na	na	na	na	na	na		
Norway	44	66	68	64	65	72	59	55	69	74	na	na	na	59	66	78		
Pakistan	na	39	37	42	43	38	36	39	39	38	39	42	33	37	42	36		
Peru	na	19	21	18	17	20	23	20	19	20	19	19	22	21	18	21		
Philippines	na	51	51	51	54	52	45	51	53	48	54	46	55	48	52	55		
Poland	79	na	na	na	na	na	na	na	na	na	na	na	na	na	na	na		
Portugal	32	na	na	na	na	na	na	na	na	na	na	na	na	na	na	na		
Puerto Rico	na	44	46	43	33	39	54	67	45	41	55	45	36	51	45	39		
Romania	31	na	na	na	na	na	na	na	na	na	na	na	na	na	na	na		
Russian Fed.	48	na	na	na	na	na	na	na	na	na	na	na	na	na	na	na		
Serbia	na	31	32	31	31	26	36	36	28	32	31	32	30	33	30	23		
Singapore	na	na	na	na	na	na	na	na	na	na	na	na	na	na	na	na		
Slovakia	na	na	na	na	na	na	na	na	na	na	na	na	na	na	na	na		
Slovenia	40	na	na	na	na	na	na	na	na	na	na	na	na	na	na	na		
South Africa	60	61	61	61	60	61	62	68	53	43	72	68	39	58	64	53		
Spain	34	44	43	45	31	43	54	47	41	38	50	47	38	52	44	29		
Sweden	44	na	na	na	na	na	na	na	na	na	na	na	na	na	na	na		
Switzerland	na	52	50	55	53	49	55	51	51	65	49	50	58	56	55	43		
Taiwan	na	70	68	72	63	69	77	76	64	67	73	66	69	72	70	51		
Tanzania	na	83	81	85	80	82	92	87	78	78	85	83	81	84	85	78		
Turkey	50	46	40	53	44	47	51	52	39	36	48	46	43	50	47	33		
Uganda	na	78	84	72	78	80	67	76	77	88	88	84	83	76	78	81		
Ukraine	na	na	na	na	na	na	na	na	na	na	na	na	na	na	na	na		
United States	59	38	37	39	43	33	41	36	40	38	36	40	38	50	39	30		
Uruguay	na	42	44	40	28	34	53	45	36	38	46	42	37	52	42	32		
Venezuela	na	56	60	52	50	57	67	65	55	49	58	58	57	59	55	54		
Vietnam	na	98	98	98	97	98	98	98	98	97	97	98	98	99	98	94		
Zimbabwe	na	51	46	55	51	49	52	58	42	na	60	53	36	50	49	65		
Total	44	50	50	49	48	50	52	56	48	43	51	49	47	55	49	40	Total	50

E080) CONFIDENCE: THE POLITICAL PARTIES

I am going to name a number of organizations. For each one, could you tell me how much confidence you have in them: is it a great deal of confidence, quite a lot of confidence, not very much confidence or none at all? Political parties

A great deal / Quite a lot (%)

(WVS: V154)

Country	Wave 1990	Wave 2000	Gender Male	Gender Female	Age 16-29	Age 30-49	Age 50+	Education Lower	Education Middle	Education Upper	Income Lower	Income Middle	Income Upper	Values Mat	Values Mixed	Values Postm.
Albania	na	29	36	23	24	29	34	30	30	27	28	30	30	32	28	26
Algeria	na	19	19	19	16	21	23	20	17	21	22	18	16	19	19	19
Argentina	na	7	7	7	5	8	9	7	6	11	7	7	8	8	7	7
Armenia	na	16	16	16	14	17	16	13	17	13	15	13	19	16	16	11
Australia	na	16	19	13	17	14	17	16	14	18	16	15	18	18	16	15
Austria	na	na	na	na	na	na	na	na	na	na	na	na	na	na	na	na
Azerbaijan	na	54	56	52	57	52	51	53	50	61	45	58	54	51	56	75
Bangladesh	na	79	78	81	78	80	80	82	80	72	83	75	80	82	77	75
Belarus	23	na	na	na	na	na	na	na	na	na	na	na	na	na	na	na
Belgium	na	na	na	na	na	na	na	na	na	na	na	na	na	na	na	na
Bosnia and Herz.	na	15	16	14	12	14	18	20	14	12	10	16	16	15	15	19
Brazil	na	33	35	30	33	29	38	34	30	34	35	35	28	28	34	35
Bulgaria	29	na	na	na	na	na	na	na	na	na	na	na	na	na	na	na
Canada	38	23	25	21	23	22	25	22	23	24	23	21	26	30	23	22
Chile	50	28	28	28	25	27	32	26	29	28	23	27	35	29	29	23
China	80	93	93	93	84	95	95	95	93	79	93	92	93	94	91	84
Colombia	na	17	18	17	17	17	17	19	16	15	19	15	18	20	21	19
Croatia	na	na	na	na	na	na	na	na	na	na	na	na	na	na	na	na
Czech Republic	44	na	na	na	na	na	na	na	na	na	na	na	na	na	na	na
Denmark	na	na	na	na	na	na	na	na	na	na	na	na	na	na	na	na
Dominican Rep.	na	9	12	7	9	8	10	10	11	8	7	9	10	11	8	10
Egypt	na	51	50	52	50	50	52	52	50	48	50	54	49	51	51	47
El Salvador	na	17	17	16	18	16	17	18	15	17	19	16	18	na	na	na
Estonia	17	na	na	na	na	na	na	na	na	na	na	na	na	na	na	na
Finland	na	na	na	na	na	na	na	na	na	na	na	na	na	na	na	na
France	na	na	na	na	na	na	na	na	na	na	na	na	na	na	na	na
Georgia	na	34	35	33	34	33	34	35	35	28	32	35	34	33	34	41
Germany	na	na	na	na	na	na	na	na	na	na	na	na	na	na	na	na
Great Britain	na	na	na	na	na	na	na	na	na	na	na	na	na	na	na	na
Greece	na	na	na	na	na	na	na	na	na	na	na	na	na	na	na	na
Hungary	na	na	na	na	na	na	na	na	na	na	na	na	na	na	na	na
Iceland	na	na	na	na	na	na	na	na	na	na	na	na	na	na	na	na
India	55	34	37	29	35	29	40	36	33	30	40	32	32	38	33	22
Indonesia	na	33	34	32	24	36	35	43	33	27	29	35	32	36	30	32
Iran	na	34	34	34	33	33	42	35	36	31	30	35	40	31	34	40
Ireland	na	na	na	na	na	na	na	na	na	na	na	na	na	na	na	na
Israel	na	na	na	na	na	na	na	na	na	na	na	na	na	na	na	na
Italy	na	na	na	na	na	na	na	na	na	na	na	na	na	na	na	na
Japan	na	18	20	17	10	14	26	35	16	16	20	20	16	24	18	13
Jordan	na	26	19	35	28	25	26	30	24	23	32	25	21	26	26	37
Korea, South	na	11	9	13	6	11	16	29	13	6	12	12	9	11	12	5
Latvia	18	na	na	na	na	na	na	na	na	na	na	na	na	na	na	na
Lithuania	13	na	na	na	na	na	na	na	na	na	na	na	na	na	na	na
Luxembourg	na	na	na	na	na	na	na	na	na	na	na	na	na	na	na	na
Macedonia	na	10	10	9	10	9	10	12	8	9	10	10	9	8	9	27
Malta	na	na	na	na	na	na	na	na	na	na	na	na	na	na	na	na
Mexico	30	25	27	23	22	25	29	30	15	30	27	27	24	28	22	27
Moldova	na	24	24	25	16	22	34	32	24	17	30	23	22	27	22	19
Montenegro	na	26	27	24	23	26	28	22	28	30	21	25	32	22	32	26
Morocco	na	19	17	20	18	18	24	20	11	21	17	15	17	21	16	21
Netherlands	na	na	na	na	na	na	na	na	na	na	na	na	na	na	na	na
New Zealand	na	6	6	6	5	6	6	6	5	7	7	4	7	8	5	5
Nigeria	38	44	49	39	43	47	38	49	41	41	46	42	46	44	44	47
Northern Ireland	na	na	na	na	na	na	na	na	na	na	na	na	na	na	na	na
Norway	na	33	32	34	34	33	31	25	35	38	na	na	na	25	33	40
Pakistan	na	28	31	25	25	29	32	27	27	34	28	26	32	27	30	42
Peru	na	8	10	6	7	9	8	9	7	8	8	8	7	11	8	4
Philippines	na	46	44	48	48	49	37	45	50	40	45	41	53	41	48	54
Poland	9	na	na	na	na	na	na	na	na	na	na	na	na	na	na	na
Portugal	na	na	na	na	na	na	na	na	na	na	na	na	na	na	na	na
Puerto Rico	na	20	19	20	14	15	26	32	22	16	25	23	12	36	19	16
Romania	na	na	na	na	na	na	na	na	na	na	na	na	na	na	na	na
Russian Fed.	46	na	na	na	na	na	na	na	na	na	na	na	na	na	na	na
Serbia	na	15	15	14	17	14	14	14	14	17	16	14	14	15	13	17
Singapore	na	na	na	na	na	na	na	na	na	na	na	na	na	na	na	na
Slovakia	na	na	na	na	na	na	na	na	na	na	na	na	na	na	na	na
Slovenia	na	na	na	na	na	na	na	na	na	na	na	na	na	na	na	na
South Africa	58	44	47	41	44	45	45	52	36	22	54	47	30	43	46	45
Spain	23	27	27	28	22	24	33	29	24	27	37	30	25	32	28	15
Sweden	na	na	na	na	na	na	na	na	na	na	na	na	na	na	na	na
Switzerland	na	27	27	27	31	25	28	27	26	34	24	26	29	36	27	20
Taiwan	na	36	32	39	26	35	44	44	38	27	42	38	28	35	35	40
Tanzania	na	59	58	62	56	58	71	66	52	53	66	55	57	55	62	63
Turkey	49	29	27	31	28	28	33	33	25	21	32	29	24	30	29	25
Uganda	na	41	50	32	39	44	36	36	42	45	45	45	38	32	44	50
Ukraine	na	na	na	na	na	na	na	na	na	na	na	na	na	na	na	na
United States	55	23	22	23	24	21	24	26	24	21	24	23	22	25	23	22
Uruguay	na	37	40	34	27	34	42	35	37	44	34	38	37	46	33	37
Venezuela	na	20	23	17	19	20	24	21	23	13	21	22	20	23	20	16
Vietnam	na	92	92	91	89	91	94	92	91	94	92	92	91	90	92	92
Zimbabwe	na	29	29	30	29	30	31	35	22	na	42	28	14	29	29	32
Total	37	30	32	29	29	31	31	35	30	25	31	31	30	33	30	25

RANKING

Country	2000
China	93
Vietnam	92
Bangladesh	79
Tanzania	59
Azerbaijan	54
Egypt	51
Philippines	46
Nigeria	44
South Africa	44
Uganda	41
Uruguay	37
Taiwan	36
Iran	34
Georgia	34
India	34
Indonesia	33
Norway	33
Brazil	33
Albania	29
Zimbabwe	29
Turkey	29
Pakistan	28
Chile	28
Spain	27
Switzerland	27
Jordan	26
Montenegro	26
Mexico	25
Moldova	24
Canada	23
United States	23
Venezuela	20
Puerto Rico	20
Algeria	19
Morocco	19
Japan	18
Colombia	17
El Salvador	17
Australia	16
Armenia	16
Bosnia and Herz.	15
Serbia	15
Korea, South	11
Macedonia	10
Dominican Rep.	9
Peru	8
Argentina	7
New Zealand	6
Total	30

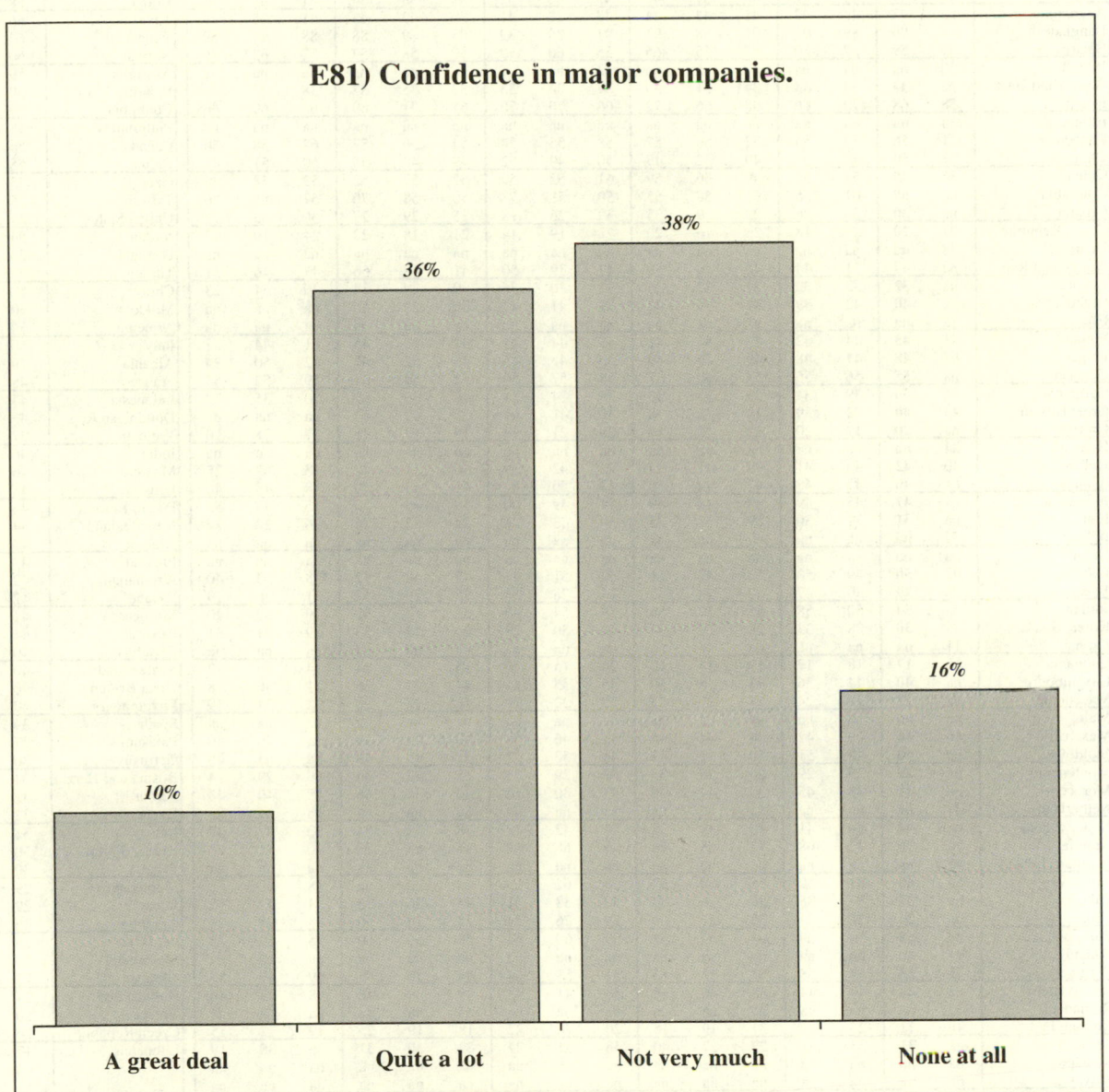

E81) Confidence in major companies.

10% — A great deal
36% — Quite a lot
38% — Not very much
16% — None at all

E081) CONFIDENCE: MAJOR COMPANIES

I am going to name a number of organizations. For each one, could you tell me how much confidence you have in them: is it a great deal of confidence, quite a lot of confidence, not very much confidence or none at all? Major companies.

A great deal / Quite a lot (%)

(WVS: V157; EVS: o27)

Country	Wave 1990	Wave 2000	Gender Male	Gender Female	Age 16-29	Age 30-49	Age 50+	Education Lower	Education Middle	Education Upper	Income Lower	Income Middle	Income Upper	Values Mat	Values Mixed	Values Postm.	RANKING Country	RANKING 2000
Albania	na	49	52	47	52	49	47	51	48	48	47	51	51	53	49	39	Bangladesh	90
Algeria	na	43	42	45	44	44	40	41	43	44	41	44	43	47	41	41	Zimbabwe	77
Argentina	25	26	33	20	28	25	25	27	26	25	26	27	25	32	26	22	South Africa	74
Armenia	na	50	50	50	50	48	51	45	51	47	55	45	45	53	47	43	Nigeria	70
Australia	na	59	62	56	66	57	54	56	60	60	51	63	66	62	61	55	Uganda	70
Austria	42	41	41	42	48	37	42	43	42	32	38	38	44	41	42	39	Brazil	68
Azerbaijan	na	42	43	42	41	43	44	47	42	41	39	43	43	41	45	49	Tanzania	66
Bangladesh	na	90	89	91	91	88	91	91	88	89	93	89	88	88	91	89	Venezuela	64
Belarus	37	59	57	60	57	55	65	55	60	59	60	58	57	57	62	46	Norway	60
Belgium	50	na	na	na	na	na	na	na	na	na	na	na	na	na	na	na	Australia	59
Bosnia and Herz.	na	34	34	34	34	31	39	37	34	33	32	35	37	38	33	33	Belarus	59
Brazil	58	68	70	66	68	66	72	66	70	70	65	71	69	68	69	66	Colombia	59
Bulgaria	34	na	na	na	na	na	na	na	na	na	na	na	na	na	na	na	Philippines	58
Canada	51	56	57	54	52	56	57	58	55	54	54	56	57	62	58	50	Canada	56
Chile	53	50	49	51	49	52	49	50	49	52	49	49	55	50	51	47	China	55
China	36	55	54	57	49	56	59	61	52	59	57	57	52	52	58	46	Georgia	55
Colombia	na	59	61	56	61	58	55	50	58	73	50	58	70	57	55	56	Taiwan	55
Croatia	na	30	33	26	23	29	35	39	26	18	35	29	27	30	33	19	United States	54
Czech Republic	27	20	21	18	26	16	20	22	19	14	21	18	22	24	19	15	Jordan	54
Denmark	38	na	na	na	na	na	na	na	na	na	na	na	na	na	na	na	Portugal	53
Dominican Rep.	na	47	51	44	48	44	50	47	39	50	41	48	56	47	46	51	Turkey	51
Egypt	na	32	32	32	31	31	35	31	30	36	30	29	34	30	34	23	Chile	50
El Salvador	na	40	42	39	41	39	42	38	41	47	39	39	50	na	na	na	Moldova	50
Estonia	15	na	na	na	na	na	na	na	na	na	na	na	na	na	na	na	Armenia	50
Finland	41	43	44	42	47	42	41	42	44	45	42	42	45	41	44	37	Italy	50
France	67	48	47	48	49	46	49	50	43	45	46	52	47	52	50	34	Albania	49
Georgia	na	55	56	55	53	56	57	58	57	50	52	54	61	59	52	54	France	48
Germany	46	36	39	34	33	34	40	39	34	34	40	33	37	50	35	23	Indonesia	47
Great Britain	48	40	42	39	48	38	38	36	41	44	38	42	41	na	na	na	Dominican Rep.	47
Greece	na	20	19	20	22	18	17	20	21	19	19	17	26	27	21	10	Vietnam	47
Hungary	34	na	na	na	na	na	na	na	na	na	na	na	na	na	na	na	India	46
Iceland	40	42	43	41	49	41	37	42	42	39	40	37	47	48	42	25	Mexico	46
India	61	46	45	48	47	43	50	43	50	46	41	43	50	48	48	40	Uruguay	45
Indonesia	na	47	45	49	39	48	49	54	49	40	48	45	50	45	48	52	Puerto Rico	44
Iran	na	31	31	30	29	32	35	30	33	28	24	32	36	30	28	34	New Zealand	44
Ireland	52	na	na	na	na	na	na	na	na	na	na	na	na	na	na	na	Algeria	43
Israel	na	na	na	na	na	na	na	na	na	na	na	na	na	na	na	na	Finland	43
Italy	62	50	49	50	52	47	51	50	51	45	47	48	52	58	53	40	Azerbaijan	42
Japan	28	29	30	27	32	23	32	24	28	33	25	29	32	31	30	19	Iceland	42
Jordan	na	54	50	58	55	52	58	59	54	46	63	47	52	59	52	40	Morocco	41
Korea, South	35	30	28	33	28	29	34	40	30	28	26	32	33	29	31	31	Austria	41
Latvia	11	na	na	na	na	na	na	na	na	na	na	na	na	na	na	na	El Salvador	40
Lithuania	16	17	18	17	17	17	18	20	15	20	15	11	24	14	18	22	Switzerland	40
Luxembourg	na	40	44	36	43	38	40	45	35	41	44	37	36	41	40	38	Great Britain	40
Macedonia	na	23	22	24	24	22	23	20	22	29	19	24	28	22	24	19	Luxembourg	40
Malta	na	na	na	na	na	na	na	na	na	na	na	na	na	na	na	na	Spain	39
Mexico	46	46	49	42	48	44	45	43	46	50	40	43	59	44	46	50	Pakistan	37
Moldova	na	50	48	51	50	52	47	44	52	52	51	49	49	48	55	16	Germany	36
Montenegro	na	29	29	29	26	26	35	32	29	25	25	32	30	29	29	24	Bosnia and Herz.	34
Morocco	na	41	38	45	37	44	48	43	30	50	40	30	46	42	40	43	Serbia	32
Netherlands	48	na	na	na	na	na	na	na	na	na	na	na	na	na	na	na	Egypt	32
New Zealand	na	44	48	41	49	49	37	41	42	48	38	44	54	52	47	39	Iran	31
Nigeria	76	70	72	68	71	68	76	73	68	69	71	68	73	70	71	67	Korea, South	30
Northern Ireland	47	na	na	na	na	na	na	na	na	na	na	na	na	na	na	na	Croatia	30
Norway	53	60	61	59	65	60	57	56	62	63	na	na	na	58	62	52	Montenegro	29
Pakistan	na	37	37	38	36	36	44	40	38	31	45	36	36	34	41	55	Japan	29
Peru	na	26	28	24	25	27	26	29	26	24	25	24	30	28	26	21	Argentina	26
Philippines	na	58	56	60	64	57	51	59	60	54	58	56	60	55	59	72	Peru	26
Poland	71	na	na	na	na	na	na	na	na	na	na	na	na	na	na	na	Macedonia	23
Portugal	45	53	48	58	52	54	53	51	53	64	44	50	45	59	49	53	Ukraine	21
Puerto Rico	na	44	44	44	38	46	46	58	41	43	49	39	46	48	43	46	Russian Fed.	21
Romania	35	na	na	na	na	na	na	na	na	na	na	na	na	na	na	na	Greece	20
Russian Fed.	46	21	23	19	31	19	15	20	20	22	18	19	25	19	22	15	Czech Republic	20
Serbia	na	32	33	31	27	27	40	38	31	27	37	30	31	36	30	19	Lithuania	17
Singapore	na	na	na	na	na	na	na	na	na	na	na	na	na	na	na	na		
Slovakia	na	na	na	na	na	na	na	na	na	na	na	na	na	na	na	na		
Slovenia	33	na	na	na	na	na	na	na	na	na	na	na	na	na	na	na		
South Africa	76	74	76	71	76	73	70	73	74	74	70	79	74	75	74	64		
Spain	43	39	37	41	34	37	45	43	35	39	41	42	39	45	42	25		
Sweden	53	na	na	na	na	na	na	na	na	na	na	na	na	na	na	na		
Switzerland	na	40	43	38	45	40	37	36	40	47	36	36	49	49	43	27		
Taiwan	na	55	55	55	49	57	54	58	53	53	55	56	56	54	56	44		
Tanzania	na	66	62	72	72	61	72	69	63	64	65	64	68	62	68	63		
Turkey	29	51	48	54	53	51	50	53	48	53	50	52	54	51	52	46		
Uganda	na	70	76	64	71	69	63	72	68	79	73	69	74	64	72	72		
Ukraine	na	21	22	21	32	20	15	14	21	24	15	23	27	19	23	29		
United States	51	54	58	50	53	53	56	54	54	54	48	55	61	57	57	47		
Uruguay	na	45	47	43	39	42	49	45	43	46	44	44	47	52	45	37		
Venezuela	na	64	66	63	65	65	60	54	66	72	56	67	69	64	63	74		
Vietnam	na	47	48	46	47	47	47	50	45	41	38	50	48	42	49	43		
Zimbabwe	na	77	75	79	77	75	81	81	72	58	80	71	74	78	76	77		
Total	44	46	47	45	48	45	44	49	45	45	45	45	48	48	47	41	Total	46

E082) CONFIDENCE: THE ENVIRONMENTAL PROTECTION MOVEMENT

I am going to name a number of organizations. For each one, could you tell me how much confidence you have in them: is it a great deal of confidence, quite a lot of confidence, not very much confidence or none at all? Environmental Protection

A great deal / Quite a lot (%)   (WVS: V158)

Country	Wave		Gender		Age			Education			Income			Values		
	1990	2000	Male	Female	16-29	30-49	50+	Lower	Middle	Upper	Lower	Middle	Upper	Mat	Mixed	Postm.
Albania	na	38	38	38	40	39	35	34	37	48	34	40	41	34	43	27
Algeria	na	na	na	na	na	na	na	na	na	na	na	na	na	na	na	na
Argentina	na	67	69	66	68	66	67	64	72	69	66	66	69	61	65	74
Armenia	na	47	42	51	49	44	47	42	48	45	55	36	44	45	47	53
Australia	na	56	52	61	66	60	43	46	57	64	47	62	62	50	54	63
Austria	na	na	na	na	na	na	na	na	na	na	na	na	na	na	na	na
Azerbaijan	na	14	15	13	13	15	16	13	14	14	11	14	19	13	15	26
Bangladesh	na	83	82	85	84	82	87	83	86	79	81	81	89	84	84	76
Belarus	na	na	na	na	na	na	na	na	na	na	na	na	na	na	na	na
Belgium	na	na	na	na	na	na	na	na	na	na	na	na	na	na	na	na
Bosnia and Herz.	na	52	52	53	53	47	58	50	51	59	52	51	55	54	52	69
Brazil	na	80	82	79	84	78	78	76	84	83	75	84	83	76	82	87
Bulgaria	na	na	na	na	na	na	na	na	na	na	na	na	na	na	na	na
Canada	na	68	68	68	66	69	67	66	69	67	70	69	66	71	66	71
Chile	na	65	65	66	70	66	60	61	66	72	63	67	69	57	66	77
China	na	88	87	89	86	88	90	91	87	75	90	91	82	86	88	90
Colombia	na	70	71	69	73	70	65	59	71	85	63	68	81	66	70	76
Croatia	na	na	na	na	na	na	na	na	na	na	na	na	na	na	na	na
Czech Republic	na	na	na	na	na	na	na	na	na	na	na	na	na	na	na	na
Denmark	na	na	na	na	na	na	na	na	na	na	na	na	na	na	na	na
Dominican Rep.	na	64	66	63	65	63	60	42	58	69	63	68	67	61	65	63
Egypt	na	77	76	78	79	75	77	79	76	73	80	76	75	77	77	73
El Salvador	na	38	38	38	39	36	40	35	38	44	37	37	44	na	na	na
Estonia	na	na	na	na	na	na	na	na	na	na	na	na	na	na	na	na
Finland	na	na	na	na	na	na	na	na	na	na	na	na	na	na	na	na
France	na	na	na	na	na	na	na	na	na	na	na	na	na	na	na	na
Georgia	na	42	39	45	38	44	44	45	42	41	40	42	46	43	42	42
Germany	na	na	na	na	na	na	na	na	na	na	na	na	na	na	na	na
Great Britain	na	na	na	na	na	na	na	na	na	na	na	na	na	na	na	na
Greece	na	na	na	na	na	na	na	na	na	na	na	na	na	na	na	na
Hungary	na	na	na	na	na	na	na	na	na	na	na	na	na	na	na	na
Iceland	na	na	na	na	na	na	na	na	na	na	na	na	na	na	na	na
India	na	52	52	51	55	49	55	43	56	58	42	51	57	51	54	58
Indonesia	na	55	56	54	53	56	54	53	56	56	55	57	49	52	57	59
Iran	na	55	55	55	54	55	58	59	54	51	50	53	56	54	52	62
Ireland	na	na	na	na	na	na	na	na	na	na	na	na	na	na	na	na
Israel	na	na	na	na	na	na	na	na	na	na	na	na	na	na	na	na
Italy	na	na	na	na	na	na	na	na	na	na	na	na	na	na	na	na
Japan	na	57	52	62	59	56	57	56	56	61	57	58	53	54	59	57
Jordan	na	69	60	77	71	65	72	71	72	61	79	60	65	72	67	61
Korea, South	na	75	73	76	75	76	71	71	76	73	71	74	79	72	76	85
Latvia	na	na	na	na	na	na	na	na	na	na	na	na	na	na	na	na
Lithuania	na	na	na	na	na	na	na	na	na	na	na	na	na	na	na	na
Luxembourg	na	na	na	na	na	na	na	na	na	na	na	na	na	na	na	na
Macedonia	na	42	43	41	38	43	44	35	44	47	36	42	48	40	45	31
Malta	na	na	na	na	na	na	na	na	na	na	na	na	na	na	na	na
Mexico	na	54	56	52	60	52	49	49	58	64	47	55	62	53	54	58
Moldova	na	52	52	52	54	51	52	45	53	56	58	51	49	54	53	40
Montenegro	na	34	32	37	38	35	31	31	34	42	34	34	34	33	36	40
Morocco	na	66	63	69	63	65	74	67	59	64	69	57	64	63	67	65
Netherlands	na	na	na	na	na	na	na	na	na	na	na	na	na	na	na	na
New Zealand	na	46	40	52	46	53	42	39	45	54	46	48	47	46	43	59
Nigeria	na	61	60	62	62	60	58	64	58	60	61	62	62	60	61	67
Northern Ireland	na	na	na	na	na	na	na	na	na	na	na	na	na	na	na	na
Norway	na	63	57	68	67	68	52	55	63	69	na	na	na	56	62	74
Pakistan	na	36	35	37	37	31	46	41	33	29	44	31	33	34	37	22
Peru	na	48	49	46	48	47	49	49	44	51	45	45	56	42	49	50
Philippines	na	74	74	75	75	77	69	76	75	71	75	75	72	72	76	72
Poland	na	na	na	na	na	na	na	na	na	na	na	na	na	na	na	na
Portugal	na	na	na	na	na	na	na	na	na	na	na	na	na	na	na	na
Puerto Rico	na	69	74	67	68	71	68	55	67	73	67	66	75	61	69	77
Romania	na	na	na	na	na	na	na	na	na	na	na	na	na	na	na	na
Russian Fed.	na	na	na	na	na	na	na	na	na	na	na	na	na	na	na	na
Serbia	na	44	45	42	43	41	47	40	42	51	42	42	50	41	44	50
Singapore	na	na	na	na	na	na	na	na	na	na	na	na	na	na	na	na
Slovakia	na	na	na	na	na	na	na	na	na	na	na	na	na	na	na	na
Slovenia	na	na	na	na	na	na	na	na	na	na	na	na	na	na	na	na
South Africa	na	61	61	62	61	60	64	67	54	61	66	60	56	62	60	69
Spain	na	61	57	65	68	60	57	59	65	61	56	63	63	55	63	65
Sweden	na	na	na	na	na	na	na	na	na	na	na	na	na	na	na	na
Switzerland	na	44	39	48	56	45	35	36	44	52	37	39	52	38	40	57
Taiwan	na	79	77	81	77	79	81	80	79	79	79	78	80	79	80	70
Tanzania	na	61	61	62	66	55	70	66	57	56	65	54	61	56	65	57
Turkey	na	70	67	73	70	70	67	69	70	67	67	72	68	67	71	69
Uganda	na	76	82	70	75	77	73	74	76	78	83	72	79	70	77	83
Ukraine	na	na	na	na	na	na	na	na	na	na	na	na	na	na	na	na
United States	na	60	59	61	65	57	60	60	61	60	59	62	56	62	58	65
Uruguay	na	69	68	70	68	69	70	66	75	73	69	64	77	68	69	74
Venezuela	na	68	69	67	71	67	66	61	69	75	65	68	74	61	70	75
Vietnam	na	79	80	79	80	78	81	79	81	82	78	84	76	83	81	80
Zimbabwe	na	69	67	72	74	63	71	70	69	52	74	68	63	63	72	83
Total	na	60	59	61	62	60	58	60	59	62	59	59	62	57	61	67

RANKING

Country	2000
China	88
Bangladesh	83
Brazil	80
Vietnam	79
Taiwan	79
Egypt	77
Uganda	76
Korea, South	75
Philippines	74
Colombia	70
Turkey	70
Zimbabwe	69
Uruguay	69
Puerto Rico	69
Jordan	69
Venezuela	68
Canada	68
Argentina	67
Morocco	66
Chile	65
Dominican Rep.	64
Norway	63
Tanzania	61
South Africa	61
Spain	61
Nigeria	61
United States	60
Japan	57
Australia	56
Iran	55
Indonesia	55
Mexico	54
Bosnia and Herz.	52
India	52
Moldova	52
Peru	48
Armenia	47
New Zealand	46
Serbia	44
Switzerland	44
Georgia	42
Macedonia	42
Albania	38
El Salvador	38
Pakistan	36
Montenegro	34
Azerbaijan	14
Total	60

E083) CONFIDENCE: THE WOMEN'S MOVEMENT

I am going to name a number of organizations. For each one, could you tell me how much confidence you have in them: is it a great deal of confidence, quite a lot of confidence, not very much confidence or none at all? The women's movement

A great deal / Quite a lot (%)

(WVS: V159)

Country	Wave 1990	Wave 2000	Gender Male	Gender Female	Age 16-29	Age 30-49	Age 50+	Education Lower	Education Middle	Education Upper	Income Lower	Income Middle	Income Upper	Values Mat	Values Mixed	Values Postm.
Albania	na	38	30	46	42	39	34	34	39	47	36	40	39	37	40	27
Algeria	na	30	17	43	31	29	28	30	30	29	30	27	25	34	26	36
Argentina	na	36	39	33	37	36	35	38	34	30	40	37	31	35	37	33
Armenia	na	29	22	36	31	28	27	22	30	31	30	26	30	29	30	22
Australia	na	43	38	49	53	42	36	44	40	47	42	45	40	33	41	51
Austria	na	na	na	na	na	na	na	na	na	na	na	na	na	na	na	na
Azerbaijan	na	20	13	26	19	20	20	11	19	22	18	19	23	18	22	31
Bangladesh	na	80	78	83	81	80	79	82	81	75	83	75	84	82	79	76
Belarus	na	na	na	na	na	na	na	na	na	na	na	na	na	na	na	na
Belgium	na	na	na	na	na	na	na	na	na	na	na	na	na	na	na	na
Bosnia and Herz.	na	45	36	53	47	40	50	43	46	45	45	46	46	49	45	54
Brazil	na	69	68	70	73	66	67	70	70	63	67	77	65	68	69	74
Bulgaria	na	na	na	na	na	na	na	na	na	na	na	na	na	na	na	na
Canada	na	63	60	65	65	64	60	60	65	60	66	63	59	59	61	67
Chile	na	47	40	53	53	46	42	43	48	52	41	52	50	45	47	50
China	na	92	90	94	88	93	93	92	92	90	90	94	91	92	90	96
Colombia	na	52	51	54	56	51	48	48	52	58	51	50	57	52	55	63
Croatia	na	na	na	na	na	na	na	na	na	na	na	na	na	na	na	na
Czech Republic	na	na	na	na	na	na	na	na	na	na	na	na	na	na	na	na
Denmark	na	na	na	na	na	na	na	na	na	na	na	na	na	na	na	na
Dominican Rep.	na	52	52	52	51	54	50	54	45	54	54	45	63	54	49	59
Egypt	na	74	63	86	76	72	74	75	72	73	73	73	75	76	73	69
El Salvador	na	na	na	na	na	na	na	na	na	na	na	na	na	na	na	na
Estonia	na	na	na	na	na	na	na	na	na	na	na	na	na	na	na	na
Finland	na	na	na	na	na	na	na	na	na	na	na	na	na	na	na	na
France	na	na	na	na	na	na	na	na	na	na	na	na	na	na	na	na
Georgia	na	41	35	45	37	43	43	45	40	40	38	43	42	41	41	40
Germany	na	na	na	na	na	na	na	na	na	na	na	na	na	na	na	na
Great Britain	na	na	na	na	na	na	na	na	na	na	na	na	na	na	na	na
Greece	na	na	na	na	na	na	na	na	na	na	na	na	na	na	na	na
Hungary	na	na	na	na	na	na	na	na	na	na	na	na	na	na	na	na
Iceland	na	na	na	na	na	na	na	na	na	na	na	na	na	na	na	na
India	na	53	48	60	54	52	53	48	53	57	46	52	55	57	50	49
Indonesia	na	51	44	58	47	49	55	54	58	41	52	51	49	50	51	50
Iran	na	43	38	49	42	45	41	42	45	41	39	39	46	36	43	56
Ireland	na	na	na	na	na	na	na	na	na	na	na	na	na	na	na	na
Israel	na	na	na	na	na	na	na	na	na	na	na	na	na	na	na	na
Italy	na	na	na	na	na	na	na	na	na	na	na	na	na	na	na	na
Japan	na	45	39	50	51	40	46	42	45	45	47	41	43	42	46	46
Jordan	na	53	37	68	53	53	52	56	50	50	60	41	53	55	51	52
Korea, South	na	71	63	78	74	72	64	69	72	68	65	71	76	68	72	79
Latvia	na	na	na	na	na	na	na	na	na	na	na	na	na	na	na	na
Lithuania	na	na	na	na	na	na	na	na	na	na	na	na	na	na	na	na
Luxembourg	na	na	na	na	na	na	na	na	na	na	na	na	na	na	na	na
Macedonia	na	45	38	52	45	46	44	42	43	53	39	47	50	44	47	43
Malta	na	na	na	na	na	na	na	na	na	na	na	na	na	na	na	na
Mexico	na	39	35	42	42	36	38	37	39	44	39	36	42	36	39	42
Moldova	na	47	42	51	44	46	50	44	49	45	54	46	45	48	46	45
Montenegro	na	29	18	40	32	31	25	26	29	36	28	29	24	28	30	37
Morocco	na	41	25	58	42	39	43	41	38	51	39	36	42	38	41	49
Netherlands	na	na	na	na	na	na	na	na	na	na	na	na	na	na	na	na
New Zealand	na	36	26	44	35	39	34	36	33	40	39	36	34	39	34	43
Nigeria	na	54	44	63	53	56	52	57	53	49	52	55	54	53	55	49
Northern Ireland	na	na	na	na	na	na	na	na	na	na	na	na	na	na	na	na
Norway	na	43	37	49	46	42	43	40	45	44	na	na	na	40	41	62
Pakistan	na	29	21	37	34	26	25	27	31	27	29	27	32	25	33	56
Peru	na	36	30	42	32	36	46	42	36	33	41	30	37	33	38	35
Philippines	na	77	74	80	76	79	74	79	75	77	78	77	76	75	79	77
Poland	na	na	na	na	na	na	na	na	na	na	na	na	na	na	na	na
Portugal	na	na	na	na	na	na	na	na	na	na	na	na	na	na	na	na
Puerto Rico	na	56	59	54	62	54	54	48	54	58	53	54	61	57	55	60
Romania	na	na	na	na	na	na	na	na	na	na	na	na	na	na	na	na
Russian Fed.	na	na	na	na	na	na	na	na	na	na	na	na	na	na	na	na
Serbia	na	39	36	42	37	35	44	37	39	42	42	39	39	37	41	41
Singapore	na	na	na	na	na	na	na	na	na	na	na	na	na	na	na	na
Slovakia	na	na	na	na	na	na	na	na	na	na	na	na	na	na	na	na
Slovenia	na	na	na	na	na	na	na	na	na	na	na	na	na	na	na	na
South Africa	na	63	58	69	66	59	63	61	65	60	59	77	54	60	66	57
Spain	na	48	43	53	56	49	42	47	49	53	43	52	52	44	50	51
Sweden	na	na	na	na	na	na	na	na	na	na	na	na	na	na	na	na
Switzerland	na	39	31	46	47	38	35	33	40	40	38	36	45	34	36	54
Taiwan	na	76	72	80	77	77	74	81	77	71	76	75	77	75	78	75
Tanzania	na	80	76	85	81	78	84	83	78	75	82	78	77	76	83	68
Turkey	na	65	56	75	64	66	68	66	65	59	63	69	64	62	65	70
Uganda	na	75	72	78	74	78	71	74	75	81	79	79	74	73	75	79
Ukraine	na	na	na	na	na	na	na	na	na	na	na	na	na	na	na	na
United States	na	59	57	62	69	54	58	60	63	56	62	62	54	61	58	63
Uruguay	na	49	48	50	45	46	53	49	51	45	48	51	51	42	50	53
Venezuela	na	50	44	56	53	50	43	44	53	50	46	52	55	47	50	56
Vietnam	na	85	83	87	81	84	90	83	89	82	86	89	80	89	85	82
Zimbabwe	na	61	45	73	63	59	56	66	54	22	67	62	49	59	61	69
Total	na	53	47	58	54	53	50	55	52	51	53	53	54	52	53	55

RANKING

Country	2000
China	92
Vietnam	85
Bangladesh	80
Tanzania	80
Philippines	77
Taiwan	76
Uganda	75
Egypt	74
Korea, South	71
Brazil	69
Turkey	65
South Africa	63
Canada	63
Zimbabwe	61
United States	59
Puerto Rico	56
Nigeria	54
Jordan	53
India	53
Colombia	52
Dominican Rep.	52
Indonesia	51
Venezuela	50
Uruguay	49
Spain	48
Chile	47
Moldova	47
Bosnia and Herz.	45
Macedonia	45
Japan	45
Australia	43
Norway	43
Iran	43
Georgia	41
Morocco	41
Serbia	39
Mexico	39
Switzerland	39
Albania	38
New Zealand	36
Peru	36
Argentina	36
Algeria	30
Armenia	29
Montenegro	29
Pakistan	29
Azerbaijan	20
Total	53

E084_1) CONFIDENCE: HEALTH CARE SYSTEM

Please look at this card and tell me, for each item listed, how much confidence you have in them, is it a great deal, quite a lot, not very much or none at all? Health care system

A great deal / Quite a lot (%)

(EVS: V211)

Country	Wave		Gender		Age			Education			Income			Values				Country	2000
	1990	2000	Male	Female	16-29	30-49	50+	Lower	Middle	Upper	Lower	Middle	Upper	Mat	Mixed	Postm.			
Albania	na	na	na	na	na	na	na	na	na	na	na	na	na	na	na	na		Malta	86
Algeria	na	na	na	na	na	na	na	na	na	na	na	na	na	na	na	na		Austria	86
Argentina	na	na	na	na	na	na	na	na	na	na	na	na	na	na	na	na		Iceland	85
Armenia	na	na	na	na	na	na	na	na	na	na	na	na	na	na	na	na		Finland	84
Australia	na	na	na	na	na	na	na	na	na	na	na	na	na	na	na	na		Belgium	83
Austria	na	86	87	86	86	84	88	89	86	80	84	89	86	90	86	86		Luxembourg	78
Azerbaijan	na	na	na	na	na	na	na	na	na	na	na	na	na	na	na	na		France	77
Bangladesh	na	na	na	na	na	na	na	na	na	na	na	na	na	na	na	na		Sweden	76
Belarus	na	67	68	67	61	64	76	78	66	51	69	65	71	74	62	61		Netherlands	76
Belgium	na	83	84	83	84	81	85	84	82	85	83	84	86	83	83	83		Denmark	70
Bosnia and Herz.	na	na	na	na	na	na	na	na	na	na	na	na	na	na	na	na		Slovenia	68
Brazil	na	na	na	na	na	na	na	na	na	na	na	na	na	na	na	na		Northern Ireland	68
Bulgaria	na	34	30	38	35	35	33	36	32	35	35	36	34	33	34	15		Belarus	67
Canada	na	na	na	na	na	na	na	na	na	na	na	na	na	na	na	na		Latvia	67
Chile	na	na	na	na	na	na	na	na	na	na	na	na	na	na	na	na		Spain	66
China	na	na	na	na	na	na	na	na	na	na	na	na	na	na	na	na		Estonia	62
Colombia	na	na	na	na	na	na	na	na	na	na	na	na	na	na	na	na		Romania	59
Croatia	na	44	44	44	47	39	47	53	40	30	57	40	39	46	47	32		Great Britain	59
Czech Republic	na	43	44	42	47	39	44	48	38	38	50	41	41	47	40	50		Ireland	58
Denmark	na	70	75	64	77	67	68	67	76	72	70	70	70	70	70	71		Poland	57
Dominican Rep.	na	na	na	na	na	na	na	na	na	na	na	na	na	na	na	na		Russian Fed.	56
Egypt	na	na	na	na	na	na	na	na	na	na	na	na	na	na	na	na		Turkey	56
El Salvador	na	na	na	na	na	na	na	na	na	na	na	na	na	na	na	na		Germany	53
Estonia	na	62	60	63	70	53	66	65	62	57	59	64	62	62	63	64		Slovakia	51
Finland	na	84	86	83	90	84	82	85	85	82	85	86	85	85	85	82		Ukraine	48
France	na	77	77	78	75	75	81	78	77	77	78	78	77	81	76	78		Portugal	44
Georgia	na	na	na	na	na	na	na	na	na	na	na	na	na	na	na	na		Croatia	44
Germany	na	53	52	54	53	49	57	56	49	56	59	48	56	53	53	55		Hungary	44
Great Britain	na	59	62	56	57	59	60	60	57	60	59	69	50	na	na	na		Czech Republic	43
Greece	na	26	25	27	20	25	38	32	26	25	23	24	30	30	27	19		Lithuania	37
Hungary	na	44	43	45	49	40	45	49	32	42	39	43	48	45	44	36		Italy	37
Iceland	na	85	86	84	82	84	88	86	84	84	84	88	84	87	86	76		Bulgaria	34
India	na	na	na	na	na	na	na	na	na	na	na	na	na	na	na	na		Greece	26
Indonesia	na	na	na	na	na	na	na	na	na	na	na	na	na	na	na	na			
Iran	na	na	na	na	na	na	na	na	na	na	na	na	na	na	na	na			
Ireland	na	58	58	57	61	52	62	62	55	55	64	56	50	59	56	61			
Israel	na	na	na	na	na	na	na	na	na	na	na	na	na	na	na	na			
Italy	na	37	38	36	34	35	40	39	34	36	43	33	37	42	38	32			
Japan	na	na	na	na	na	na	na	na	na	na	na	na	na	na	na	na			
Jordan	na	na	na	na	na	na	na	na	na	na	na	na	na	na	na	na			
Korea, South	na	na	na	na	na	na	na	na	na	na	na	na	na	na	na	na			
Latvia	na	67	67	67	74	61	70	78	68	52	70	68	63	72	65	57			
Lithuania	na	37	36	38	37	31	42	46	34	35	48	33	34	39	36	34			
Luxembourg	na	78	81	75	75	75	83	78	78	79	74	80	78	78	78	80			
Macedonia	na	na	na	na	na	na	na	na	na	na	na	na	na	na	na	na			
Malta	na	86	88	85	81	86	91	89	86	83	89	90	86	92	83	85			
Mexico	na	na	na	na	na	na	na	na	na	na	na	na	na	na	na	na			
Moldova	na	na	na	na	na	na	na	na	na	na	na	na	na	na	na	na			
Montenegro	na	na	na	na	na	na	na	na	na	na	na	na	na	na	na	na			
Morocco	na	na	na	na	na	na	na	na	na	na	na	na	na	na	na	na			
Netherlands	na	76	80	72	80	75	74	70	79	78	76	72	82	80	76	74			
New Zealand	na	na	na	na	na	na	na	na	na	na	na	na	na	na	na	na			
Nigeria	na	na	na	na	na	na	na	na	na	na	na	na	na	na	na	na			
Northern Ireland	na	68	68	68	66	64	74	70	65	68	74	65	69	72	68	56			
Norway	na	na	na	na	na	na	na	na	na	na	na	na	na	na	na	na			
Pakistan	na	na	na	na	na	na	na	na	na	na	na	na	na	na	na	na			
Peru	na	na	na	na	na	na	na	na	na	na	na	na	na	na	na	na			
Philippines	na	na	na	na	na	na	na	na	na	na	na	na	na	na	na	na			
Poland	na	57	54	59	58	53	60	62	53	40	61	54	56	58	56	56			
Portugal	na	44	43	45	51	41	42	44	44	42	46	49	41	39	45	53			
Puerto Rico	na	na	na	na	na	na	na	na	na	na	na	na	na	na	na	na			
Romania	na	59	58	60	57	54	65	71	54	49	70	61	49	65	55	42			
Russian Fed.	na	56	55	57	58	52	60	69	55	52	58	57	53	58	55	52			
Serbia	na	na	na	na	na	na	na	na	na	na	na	na	na	na	na	na			
Singapore	na	na	na	na	na	na	na	na	na	na	na	na	na	na	na	na			
Slovakia	na	51	48	55	53	51	50	53	51	47	55	50	51	52	51	52			
Slovenia	na	68	68	69	72	66	69	71	68	68	70	69	66	73	67	74			
South Africa	na	na	na	na	na	na	na	na	na	na	na	na	na	na	na	na			
Spain	na	66	61	70	60	61	73	70	63	59	72	68	63	71	67	58			
Sweden	na	76	81	72	80	79	72	72	75	82	75	78	77	69	77	77			
Switzerland	na	na	na	na	na	na	na	na	na	na	na	na	na	na	na	na			
Taiwan	na	na	na	na	na	na	na	na	na	na	na	na	na	na	na	na			
Tanzania	na	na	na	na	na	na	na	na	na	na	na	na	na	na	na	na			
Turkey	na	56	51	60	52	58	63	65	46	37	64	56	42	60	56	49			
Uganda	na	na	na	na	na	na	na	na	na	na	na	na	na	na	na	na			
Ukraine	na	48	46	49	48	43	52	48	49	44	46	49	49	44	51	54			
United States	na	na	na	na	na	na	na	na	na	na	na	na	na	na	na	na			
Uruguay	na	na	na	na	na	na	na	na	na	na	na	na	na	na	na	na			
Venezuela	na	na	na	na	na	na	na	na	na	na	na	na	na	na	na	na			
Vietnam	na	na	na	na	na	na	na	na	na	na	na	na	na	na	na	na			
Zimbabwe	na	na	na	na	na	na	na	na	na	na	na	na	na	na	na	na			
Total	na	61	61	61	61	58	64	64	59	59	63	60	59	61	62	62		Total	61

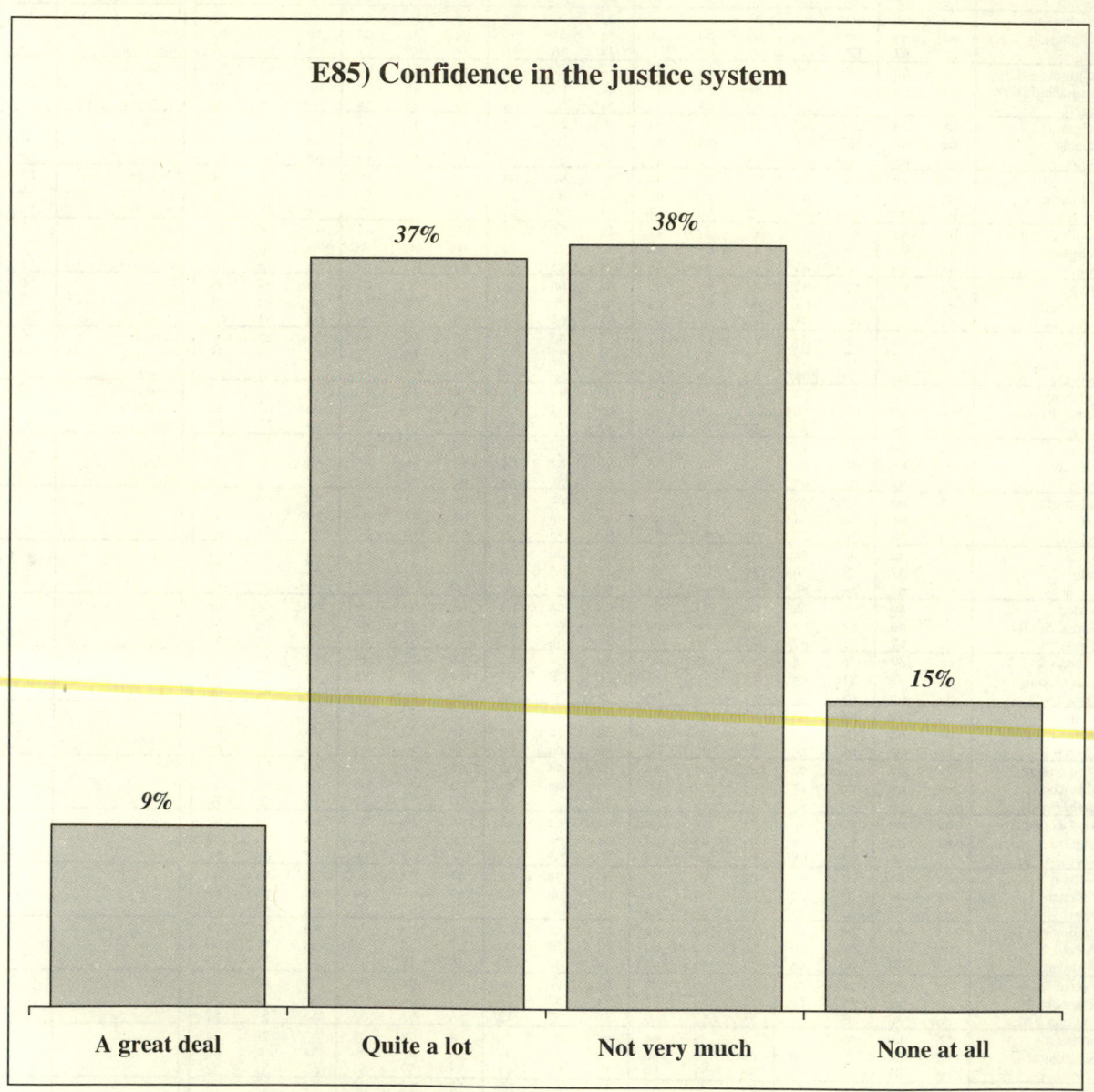

E85) Confidence in the justice system

A great deal	Quite a lot	Not very much	None at all
9%	37%	38%	15%

E085_1) CONFIDENCE: JUSTICE SYSTEM

Please look at this card and tell me, for each item listed, how much confidence you have in them, is it a great deal, quite a lot, not very much or none at all? The justice system

A great deal / Quite a lot (%)

(EVS: V212)

Country	Wave 1990	Wave 2000	Gender Male	Gender Female	Age 16-29	Age 30-49	Age 50+	Education Lower	Education Middle	Education Upper	Income Lower	Income Middle	Income Upper	Values Mat	Values Mixed	Values Postm.
Albania	na	na	na	na	na	na	na	na	na	na	na	na	na	na	na	na
Algeria	na	na	na	na	na	na	na	na	na	na	na	na	na	na	na	na
Argentina	23	na	na	na	na	na	na	na	na	na	na	na	na	na	na	na
Armenia	na	31	30	33	31	31	32	26	33	28	32	29	31	33	28	45
Australia	na	35	35	35	38	34	33	31	32	41	34	34	36	35	35	35
Austria	58	69	71	68	73	68	68	66	71	75	65	67	75	70	70	67
Azerbaijan	na	47	51	42	50	45	45	48	44	51	40	45	54	45	49	52
Bangladesh	na	na	na	na	na	na	na	na	na	na	na	na	na	na	na	na
Belarus	26	46	45	48	44	40	55	59	43	37	51	43	48	49	46	24
Belgium	45	34	32	36	35	34	35	33	33	38	32	34	36	31	35	34
Bosnia and Herz.	na	na	na	na	na	na	na	na	na	na	na	na	na	na	na	na
Brazil	44	55	57	53	53	54	61	58	53	51	59	56	49	56	56	49
Bulgaria	46	28	25	31	31	28	26	30	26	28	30	28	28	25	29	20
Canada	54	na	na	na	na	na	na	na	na	na	na	na	na	na	na	na
Chile	45	na	na	na	na	na	na	na	na	na	na	na	na	na	na	na
China	76	na	na	na	na	na	na	na	na	na	na	na	na	na	na	na
Colombia	na	48	51	45	44	51	48	42	48	57	43	45	58	46	48	48
Croatia	na	35	33	38	35	35	36	44	32	21	44	30	35	40	38	23
Czech Republic	43	23	21	26	31	21	22	25	22	20	26	23	23	27	21	28
Denmark	79	79	79	78	77	79	79	76	85	83	79	76	85	75	78	79
Dominican Rep.	na	15	20	12	16	14	9	17	18	14	15	16	18	17	13	22
Egypt	na	na	na	na	na	na	na	na	na	na	na	na	na	na	na	na
El Salvador	na	41	40	41	39	39	46	46	37	34	53	37	33	na	na	na
Estonia	33	32	31	34	38	27	35	35	32	27	29	35	33	30	35	35
Finland	66	66	64	68	75	65	61	61	74	68	67	63	70	64	67	61
France	58	46	45	46	49	47	43	45	42	51	43	47	47	49	45	45
Georgia	na	46	45	46	45	45	48	51	45	44	44	46	47	46	46	40
Germany	41	62	62	61	59	59	65	61	62	64	63	54	63	71	58	57
Great Britain	54	49	49	49	47	50	51	47	47	58	45	56	50	na	na	na
Greece	na	44	41	46	41	42	54	55	40	45	45	42	48	49	46	35
Hungary	60	45	43	48	47	45	45	46	39	53	42	45	47	45	46	38
Iceland	67	74	74	73	66	78	75	69	74	83	68	76	76	76	73	69
India	64	na	na	na	na	na	na	na	na	na	na	na	na	na	na	na
Indonesia	na	na	na	na	na	na	na	na	na	na	na	na	na	na	na	na
Iran	na	na	na	na	na	na	na	na	na	na	na	na	na	na	na	na
Ireland	47	55	50	59	55	50	60	53	53	61	53	50	57	55	54	54
Israel	na	na	na	na	na	na	na	na	na	na	na	na	na	na	na	na
Italy	32	32	32	32	28	33	32	34	31	27	37	30	28	38	32	27
Japan	62	na	na	na	na	na	na	na	na	na	na	na	na	na	na	na
Jordan	na	na	na	na	na	na	na	na	na	na	na	na	na	na	na	na
Korea, South	67	na	na	na	na	na	na	na	na	na	na	na	na	na	na	na
Latvia	36	47	42	52	50	44	49	59	45	39	51	45	45	52	45	38
Lithuania	39	19	19	19	21	13	25	29	17	15	34	12	18	20	19	15
Luxembourg	na	59	60	58	57	57	62	64	55	59	55	57	55	63	59	53
Macedonia	na	na	na	na	na	na	na	na	na	na	na	na	na	na	na	na
Malta	na	45	43	47	49	37	50	44	45	47	43	49	44	47	46	33
Mexico	53	na	na	na	na	na	na	na	na	na	na	na	na	na	na	na
Moldova	na	na	na	na	na	na	na	na	na	na	na	na	na	na	na	na
Montenegro	na	na	na	na	na	na	na	na	na	na	na	na	na	na	na	na
Morocco	na	na	na	na	na	na	na	na	na	na	na	na	na	na	na	na
Netherlands	64	49	48	50	59	45	47	42	49	54	48	47	54	49	45	58
New Zealand	na	45	44	47	47	46	45	41	42	55	42	44	50	54	47	41
Nigeria	64	na	na	na	na	na	na	na	na	na	na	na	na	na	na	na
Northern Ireland	56	48	46	50	44	43	54	47	43	61	47	49	52	51	50	34
Norway	75	70	70	70	71	74	63	55	73	80	na	na	na	65	70	74
Pakistan	na	na	na	na	na	na	na	na	na	na	na	na	na	na	na	na
Peru	na	na	na	na	na	na	na	na	na	na	na	na	na	na	na	na
Philippines	na	na	na	na	na	na	na	na	na	na	na	na	na	na	na	na
Poland	48	42	38	46	48	40	40	45	41	32	41	42	45	41	43	37
Portugal	41	41	38	44	36	41	44	42	37	38	42	41	38	43	37	51
Puerto Rico	na	na	na	na	na	na	na	na	na	na	na	na	na	na	na	na
Romania	48	40	38	42	46	36	40	50	37	32	50	41	31	45	37	30
Russian Fed.	38	36	34	38	37	33	40	45	36	34	38	37	34	38	35	30
Serbia	na	na	na	na	na	na	na	na	na	na	na	na	na	na	na	na
Singapore	na	na	na	na	na	na	na	na	na	na	na	na	na	na	na	na
Slovakia	na	36	32	38	41	33	34	35	36	35	35	34	37	37	34	40
Slovenia	51	44	41	46	45	44	43	48	43	38	52	45	42	46	44	44
South Africa	74	na	na	na	na	na	na	na	na	na	na	na	na	na	na	na
Spain	49	42	38	47	38	39	47	47	39	38	48	39	39	48	46	31
Sweden	56	61	62	60	67	62	57	54	61	66	57	59	69	59	59	69
Switzerland	na	66	65	67	70	64	66	58	67	76	65	62	72	74	65	67
Taiwan	na	59	53	66	57	57	67	67	57	55	58	59	59	61	57	68
Tanzania	na	na	na	na	na	na	na	na	na	na	na	na	na	na	na	na
Turkey	64	57	53	62	58	56	62	63	52	42	64	58	45	62	59	46
Uganda	na	na	na	na	na	na	na	na	na	na	na	na	na	na	na	na
Ukraine	na	32	29	35	31	27	38	39	31	33	31	30	35	29	33	51
United States	58	na	na	na	na	na	na	na	na	na	na	na	na	na	na	na
Uruguay	na	60	62	58	44	52	72	62	55	62	57	58	62	68	60	55
Venezuela	na	na	na	na	na	na	na	na	na	na	na	na	na	na	na	na
Vietnam	na	na	na	na	na	na	na	na	na	na	na	na	na	na	na	na
Zimbabwe	na	na	na	na	na	na	na	na	na	na	na	na	na	na	na	na
Total	52	46	46	47	45	45	48	49	44	46	46	45	47	46	47	46

RANKING

Country	2000
Denmark	79
Iceland	74
Norway	70
Austria	69
Switzerland	66
Finland	66
Germany	62
Sweden	61
Uruguay	60
Taiwan	59
Luxembourg	59
Turkey	57
Brazil	55
Ireland	55
Great Britain	49
Netherlands	49
Northern Ireland	48
Colombia	48
Latvia	47
Azerbaijan	47
Belarus	46
France	46
Georgia	46
New Zealand	45
Hungary	45
Malta	45
Greece	44
Slovenia	44
Spain	42
Poland	42
El Salvador	41
Portugal	41
Romania	40
Russian Fed.	36
Slovakia	36
Croatia	35
Australia	35
Belgium	34
Estonia	32
Ukraine	32
Italy	32
Armenia	31
Bulgaria	28
Czech Republic	23
Lithuania	19
Dominican Rep.	15
Total	46

E88) IN CONFIDENCE: THE E.U. SYSTEM

Please look at this card and tell me, for each item listed, how much confidence you have in them, is it a great deal, quite a lot, not very much or none at all? Just to recap:

A great deal/Quite a lot

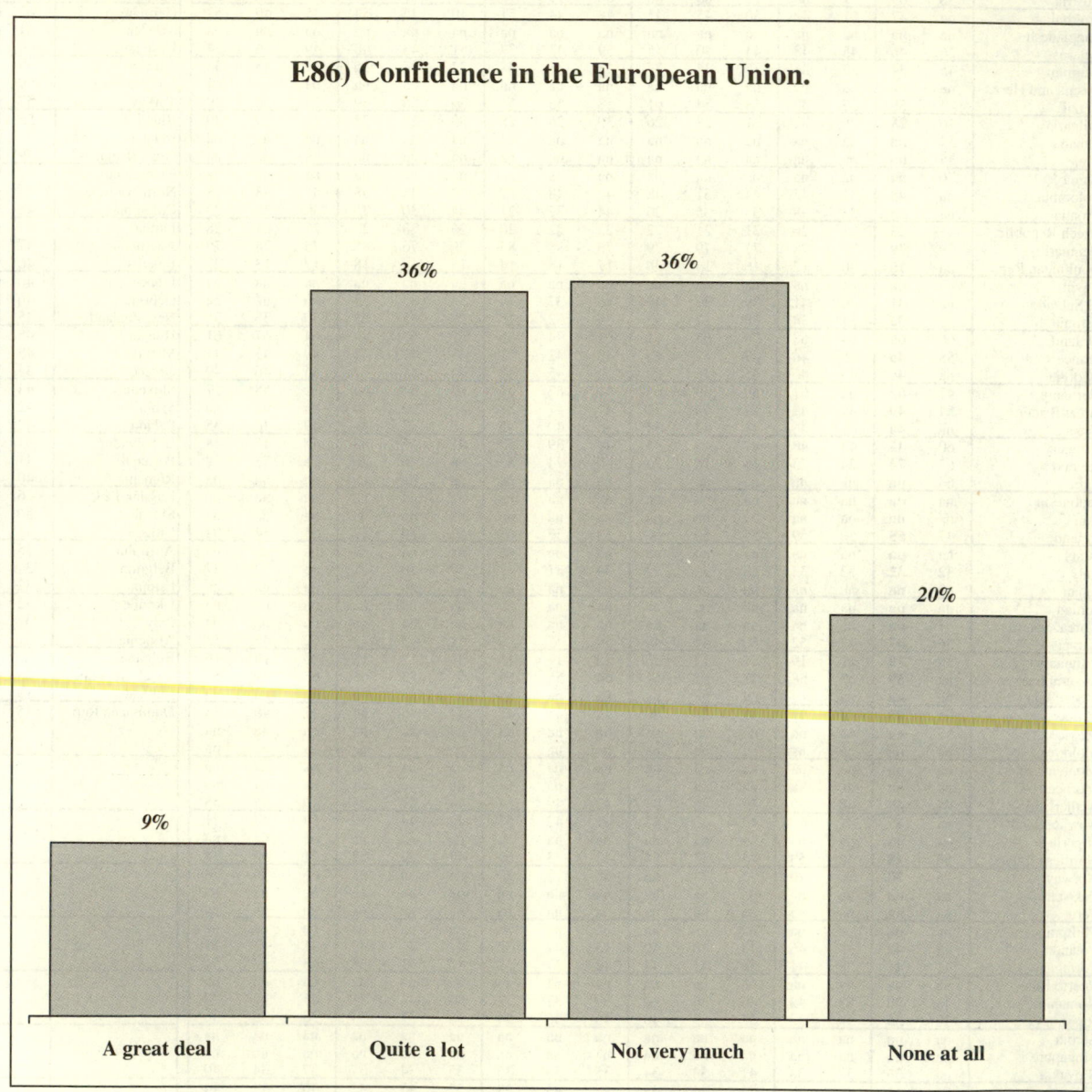

E86) Confidence in the European Union.

9%   A great deal
36%   Quite a lot
36%   Not very much
20%   None at all

E086) CONFIDENCE: THE EUROPEAN UNION

I am going to name a number of organizations. For each one, could you tell me how much confidence you have in them: is it a great deal of confidence, quite a lot of confidence, not very much confidence or none at all? The European Union.

(WVS: V160; EVS: V209)

A great deal / Quite a lot (%)

Country	Wave		Gender		Age			Education			Income			Values				RANKING Country	2000
	1990	2000	Male	Female	16-29	30-49	50+	Lower	Middle	Upper	Lower	Middle	Upper	Mat	Mixed	Postm.			
Albania	na	84	85	83	79	85	86	85	83	85	83	85	85	84	85	82		Albania	84
Algeria	na	16	17	14	18	15	12	14	16	17	16	16	14	18	15	14		Moldova	75
Argentina	na	na	na	na	na	na	na	na	na	na	na	na	na	na	na	na		Italy	69
Armenia	na	60	56	63	63	56	60	55	59	64	64	57	53	60	61	43		Portugal	69
Australia	na	na	na	na	na	na	na	na	na	na	na	na	na	na	na	na		Taiwan	64
Austria	na	38	42	33	42	36	37	33	41	45	34	37	45	40	36	40		Ireland	60
Azerbaijan	na	28	30	25	24	31	27	24	24	35	15	29	37	26	28	42		Georgia	60
Bangladesh	na	na	na	na	na	na	na	na	na	na	na	na	na	na	na	na		Armenia	60
Belarus	na	47	45	49	52	46	43	48	46	50	48	43	56	51	44	46		Hungary	59
Belgium	66	47	49	46	59	48	42	35	47	57	41	42	55	41	48	55		Luxembourg	58
Bosnia and Herz.	na	48	48	49	47	46	53	54	47	46	46	47	54	49	49	57		Malta	56
Brazil	38	na	na	na	na	na	na	na	na	na	na	na	na	na	na	na		Slovakia	55
Bulgaria	50	43	43	44	47	42	43	42	43	47	41	47	46	42	43	40		Spain	53
Canada	50	na	na	na	na	na	na	na	na	na	na	na	na	na	na	na		Montenegro	51
Chile	32	na	na	na	na	na	na	na	na	na	na	na	na	na	na	na		France	48
China	30	39	32	54	33	45	31	43	39	33	46	37	36	34	44	36		Bosnia and Herz.	48
Colombia	na	na	na	na	na	na	na	na	na	na	na	na	na	na	na	na		Belgium	47
Croatia	na	44	47	40	48	39	47	49	42	34	46	42	45	51	43	42		Belarus	47
Czech Republic	66	43	44	42	55	42	36	40	44	54	32	46	48	33	44	54		Ukraine	45
Denmark	39	27	31	23	41	18	29	24	32	28	29	25	26	23	30	14		Iceland	45
Dominican Rep.	na	na	na	na	na	na	na	na	na	na	na	na	na	na	na	na		Croatia	44
Egypt	na	na	na	na	na	na	na	na	na	na	na	na	na	na	na	na		Bulgaria	43
El Salvador	na	na	na	na	na	na	na	na	na	na	na	na	na	na	na	na		Poland	43
Estonia	na	31	33	30	39	26	32	28	31	39	19	32	36	25	35	51		Czech Republic	43
Finland	47	25	26	24	32	23	22	21	28	30	26	21	26	20	27	20		Switzerland	43
France	73	48	49	48	54	48	46	42	51	61	43	47	56	47	48	54		Turkey	40
Georgia	na	60	59	61	59	61	58	62	60	59	56	63	63	61	59	59		Northern Ireland	40
Germany	64	37	38	37	38	36	38	35	39	44	37	35	36	45	38	24		China	39
Great Britain	47	26	28	24	35	28	20	20	29	39	24	30	28	na	na	na		Romania	39
Greece	na	25	25	26	26	21	33	25	21	29	22	23	33	32	26	12		Austria	38
Hungary	63	59	59	58	68	58	52	54	64	70	47	57	66	53	64	75		Germany	37
Iceland	36	45	41	50	55	43	39	41	49	44	42	45	47	42	46	46		Slovenia	37
India	33	na	na	na	na	na	na	na	na	na	na	na	na	na	na	na		Latvia	35
Indonesia	na	na	na	na	na	na	na	na	na	na	na	na	na	na	na	na		Netherlands	33
Iran	na	na	na	na	na	na	na	na	na	na	na	na	na	na	na	na		Macedonia	33
Ireland	71	60	63	57	62	61	59	54	59	73	53	57	68	63	59	62		Estonia	31
Israel	na	na	na	na	na	na	na	na	na	na	na	na	na	na	na	na		Lithuania	31
Italy	74	69	70	68	73	69	66	66	70	72	65	66	76	66	68	70		Norway	29
Japan	27	na	na	na	na	na	na	na	na	na	na	na	na	na	na	na		Sweden	29
Jordan	na	na	na	na	na	na	na	na	na	na	na	na	na	na	na	na		Azerbaijan	28
Korea, South	na	na	na	na	na	na	na	na	na	na	na	na	na	na	na	na		Serbia	27
Latvia	na	35	33	37	46	29	35	38	33	37	33	36	38	32	36	42		Denmark	27
Lithuania	na	31	29	33	38	26	30	32	30	31	30	27	31	35	27	42		Great Britain	26
Luxembourg	na	58	59	57	61	56	58	64	52	59	59	59	54	60	58	49		Russian Fed.	26
Macedonia	na	33	33	33	39	34	27	45	25	33	33	33	30	29	33	56		Greece	25
Malta	na	56	59	53	60	53	56	42	57	82	47	55	68	43	60	80		Finland	25
Mexico	27	na	na	na	na	na	na	na	na	na	na	na	na	na	na	na		Morocco	24
Moldova	na	75	73	78	76	77	72	69	75	81	72	78	76	72	78	83		Algeria	16
Montenegro	na	51	53	50	59	51	46	45	51	65	44	49	58	46	58	60			
Morocco	na	24	22	27	27	23	17	22	25	33	21	20	29	18	24	36			
Netherlands	58	33	32	35	44	33	27	32	32	37	31	32	37	31	35	29			
New Zealand	na	na	na	na	na	na	na	na	na	na	na	na	na	na	na	na			
Nigeria	69	na	na	na	na	na	na	na	na	na	na	na	na	na	na	na			
Northern Ireland	49	40	36	44	43	41	38	32	42	53	35	35	44	31	40	49			
Norway	40	29	32	26	28	29	29	22	30	34	na	na	na	25	29	31			
Pakistan	na	na	na	na	na	na	na	na	na	na	na	na	na	na	na	na			
Peru	na	na	na	na	na	na	na	na	na	na	na	na	na	na	na	na			
Philippines	na	na	na	na	na	na	na	na	na	na	na	na	na	na	na	na			
Poland	na	43	42	44	50	38	45	39	49	48	38	43	54	41	45	48			
Portugal	57	69	64	74	77	64	67	66	71	81	58	65	71	67	69	68			
Puerto Rico	na	na	na	na	na	na	na	na	na	na	na	na	na	na	na	na			
Romania	na	39	41	37	46	36	38	38	40	38	38	37	40	37	39	44			
Russian Fed.	56	26	24	27	32	25	22	20	24	32	21	25	30	25	27	30			
Serbia	na	27	30	23	35	27	23	18	30	32	26	21	30	22	30	42			
Singapore	na	na	na	na	na	na	na	na	na	na	na	na	na	na	na	na			
Slovakia	na	55	56	53	63	53	49	50	55	67	47	55	59	46	60	72			
Slovenia	46	37	37	37	39	32	41	39	35	37	37	38	41	37	38	37			
South Africa	na	na	na	na	na	na	na	na	na	na	na	na	na	na	na	na			
Spain	48	53	53	53	52	52	54	51	55	54	52	55	58	51	54	53			
Sweden	58	29	34	24	31	27	30	20	27	39	24	29	35	38	28	30			
Switzerland	na	43	38	47	54	39	40	35	44	45	41	42	47	42	43	42			
Taiwan	na	64	63	65	62	62	70	69	62	60	67	59	64	65	62	58			
Tanzania	na	na	na	na	na	na	na	na	na	na	na	na	na	na	na	na			
Turkey	37	40	36	45	39	43	37	41	38	41	39	38	47	41	40	39			
Uganda	na	na	na	na	na	na	na	na	na	na	na	na	na	na	na	na			
Ukraine	na	45	44	47	55	47	37	22	46	51	36	45	56	42	48	63			
United States	45	na	na	na	na	na	na	na	na	na	na	na	na	na	na	na			
Uruguay	na	na	na	na	na	na	na	na	na	na	na	na	na	na	na	na			
Venezuela	na	na	na	na	na	na	na	na	na	na	na	na	na	na	na	na			
Vietnam	na	na	na	na	na	na	na	na	na	na	na	na	na	na	na	na			
Zimbabwe	na	na	na	na	na	na	na	na	na	na	na	na	na	na	na	na			
Total	49	44	44	44	48	43	43	43	44	47	41	44	49	44	45	45		Total	44

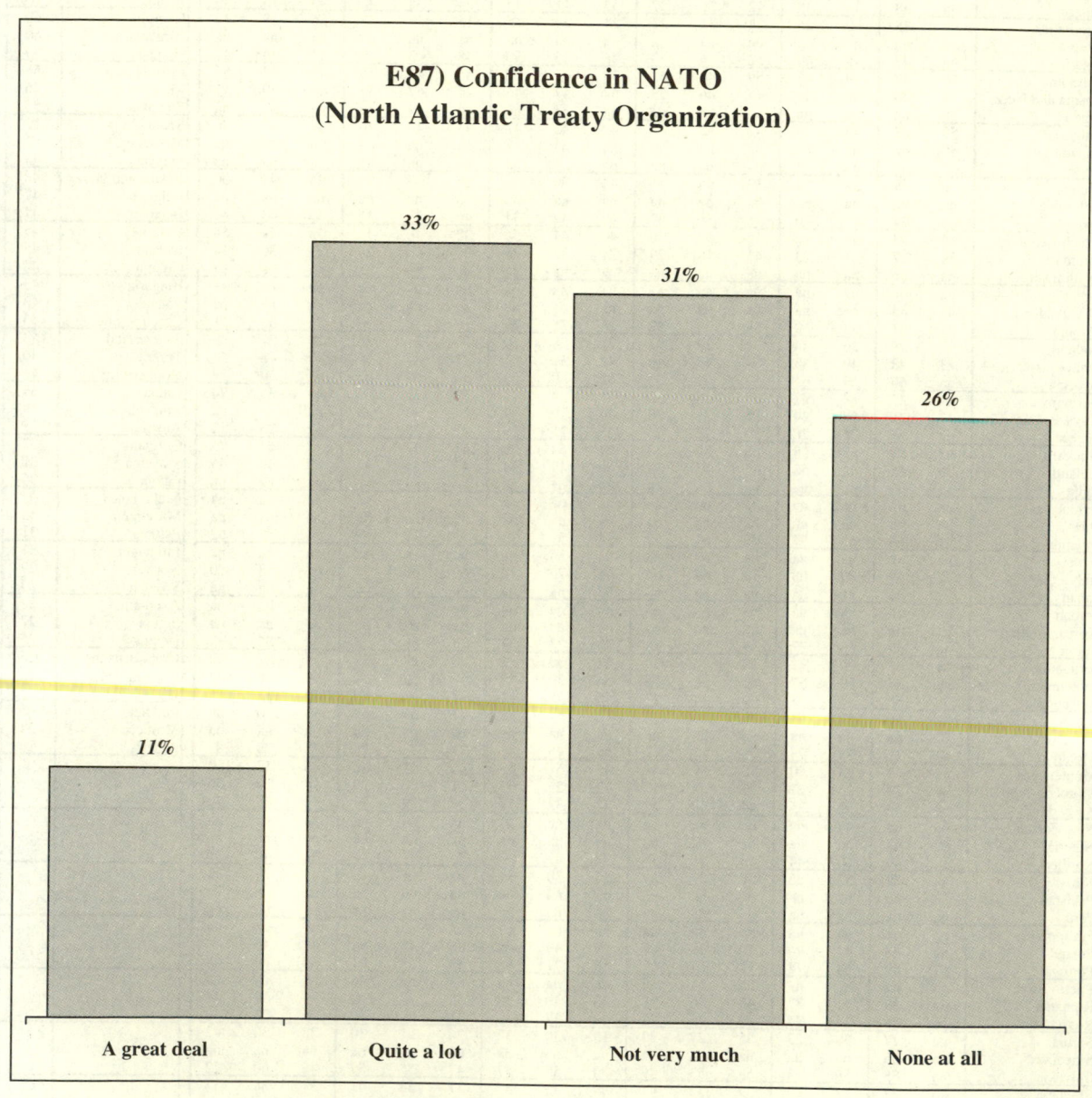

E87) Confidence in NATO
(North Atlantic Treaty Organization)

33%

31%

26%

11%

A great deal   Quite a lot   Not very much   None at all

E087) CONFIDENCE: NATO

I am going to name a number of organizations. For each one, could you tell me how much confidence you have in them: is it a great deal of confidence, quite a lot of confidence, not very much confidence or none at all? NATO (North Atlantic Treaty A great deal / Quite a lot (%)

(WVS: V161; EVS: o26)

Country	Wave 1990	Wave 2000	Gender Male	Gender Female	Age 16-29	Age 30-49	Age 50+	Education Lower	Education Middle	Education Upper	Income Lower	Income Middle	Income Upper	Values Mat	Values Mixed	Values Postm.	RANKING Country	2000
Albania	na	86	88	85	86	87	86	86	86	87	86	87	87	85	88	82	Bangladesh	89
Algeria	na	6	7	5	7	6	5	11	6	5	7	4	6	9	6	1	Albania	86
Argentina	na	na	na	na	na	na	na	na	na	na	na	na	na	na	na	na	Portugal	68
Armenia	na	na	na	na	na	na	na	na	na	na	na	na	na	na	na	na	Moldova	66
Australia	na	na	na	na	na	na	na	na	na	na	na	na	na	na	na	na	Philippines	63
Austria	na	28	28	28	31	27	27	24	31	32	21	31	32	21	29	27	Luxembourg	62
Azerbaijan	na	na	na	na	na	na	na	na	na	na	na	na	na	na	na	na	South Africa	60
Bangladesh	na	89	90	87	87	90	92	88	88	91	89	88	90	87	91	80	Denmark	59
Belarus	na	21	18	24	25	21	19	20	21	24	19	20	28	22	22	18	Great Britain	59
Belgium	46	44	46	42	50	45	41	34	43	53	34	42	51	42	45	47	Canada	57
Bosnia and Herz.	na	38	40	37	36	37	42	45	39	30	38	39	42	40	39	44	Poland	57
Brazil	na	na	na	na	na	na	na	na	na	na	na	na	na	na	na	na	Italy	56
Bulgaria	28	na	na	na	na	na	na	na	na	na	na	na	na	na	na	na	Croatia	56
Canada	50	57	62	51	57	57	57	47	60	59	49	60	61	61	57	55	Uganda	53
Chile	29	50	49	52	53	49	49	49	52	51	47	52	54	48	52	50	United States	53
China	22	26	23	32	21	32	18	29	28	12	27	24	25	25	25	39	Malta	52
Colombia	na	na	na	na	na	na	na	na	na	na	na	na	na	na	na	na	Netherlands	52
Croatia	na	56	58	53	59	54	55	62	54	42	60	57	52	63	57	47	Germany	51
Czech Republic	35	44	45	43	53	42	40	41	45	54	36	46	47	29	47	54	Chile	50
Denmark	52	59	64	54	64	56	60	57	73	58	61	59	62	56	62	44	Venezuela	49
Dominican Rep.	na	na	na	na	na	na	na	na	na	na	na	na	na	na	na	na	Iceland	47
Egypt	na	na	na	na	na	na	na	na	na	na	na	na	na	na	na	na	Belgium	44
El Salvador	na	na	na	na	na	na	na	na	na	na	na	na	na	na	na	na	Czech Republic	44
Estonia	na	37	43	31	41	34	38	34	36	41	24	37	42	26	44	51	Sweden	41
Finland	29	na	na	na	na	na	na	na	na	na	na	na	na	na	na	na	Turkey	39
France	60	na	na	na	na	na	na	na	na	na	na	na	na	na	na	na	Bosnia and Herz.	38
Georgia	na	na	na	na	na	na	na	na	na	na	na	na	na	na	na	na	Zimbabwe	38
Germany	18	51	57	47	44	53	53	49	53	55	48	51	54	59	50	46	Estonia	37
Great Britain	60	59	64	53	57	57	62	57	61	62	56	62	62	na	na	na	Slovenia	37
Greece	na	7	6	7	6	6	11	8	7	7	7	4	11	12	7	1	Latvia	36
Hungary	42	na	na	na	na	na	na	na	na	na	na	na	na	na	na	na	Lithuania	36
Iceland	35	47	50	44	52	45	46	45	51	44	42	45	53	49	49	33	Slovakia	36
India	35	na	na	na	na	na	na	na	na	na	na	na	na	na	na	na	Romania	35
Indonesia	na	na	na	na	na	na	na	na	na	na	na	na	na	na	na	na	Spain	33
Iran	na	na	na	na	na	na	na	na	na	na	na	na	na	na	na	na	Mexico	32
Ireland	59	na	na	na	na	na	na	na	na	na	na	na	na	na	na	na	Ukraine	32
Israel	na	na	na	na	na	na	na	na	na	na	na	na	na	na	na	na	Austria	28
Italy	54	56	57	54	61	52	56	56	59	49	56	56	55	60	59	49	Macedonia	27
Japan	27	na	na	na	na	na	na	na	na	na	na	na	na	na	na	na	China	26
Jordan	na	na	na	na	na	na	na	na	na	na	na	na	na	na	na	na	Belarus	21
Korea, South	na	na	na	na	na	na	na	na	na	na	na	na	na	na	na	na	Montenegro	19
Latvia	na	36	36	35	40	32	38	35	35	38	34	38	37	30	38	49	Morocco	11
Lithuania	na	36	38	34	46	30	33	31	37	36	32	32	40	39	33	40	Russian Fed.	8
Luxembourg	na	62	65	59	66	61	61	65	59	64	62	59	55	66	65	51	Greece	7
Macedonia	na	27	30	25	34	30	18	41	19	25	27	28	23	23	27	54	Algeria	6
Malta	na	52	53	51	53	47	56	45	51	74	43	50	65	45	55	66	Serbia	6
Mexico	27	32	35	29	34	30	34	30	32	40	30	29	39	31	32	36		
Moldova	na	66	63	68	67	66	63	61	65	71	64	67	65	59	70	84		
Montenegro	na	19	21	16	25	17	16	17	20	20	8	17	24	12	25	24		
Morocco	na	11	11	11	10	12	15	11	8	15	15	6	11	13	10	11		
Netherlands	50	52	55	48	60	52	47	47	59	47	51	50	55	51	55	42		
New Zealand	na	na	na	na	na	na	na	na	na	na	na	na	na	na	na	na		
Nigeria	55	na	na	na	na	na	na	na	na	na	na	na	na	na	na	na		
Northern Ireland	53	na	na	na	na	na	na	na	na	na	na	na	na	na	na	na		
Norway	67	na	na	na	na	na	na	na	na	na	na	na	na	na	na	na		
Pakistan	na	na	na	na	na	na	na	na	na	na	na	na	na	na	na	na		
Peru	na	na	na	na	na	na	na	na	na	na	na	na	na	na	na	na		
Philippines	na	63	66	61	65	61	65	65	62	64	59	65	65	67	62	58		
Poland	na	57	61	52	63	52	59	53	61	61	50	60	62	55	60	52		
Portugal	35	68	70	65	71	66	67	65	71	73	58	69	61	67	68	67		
Puerto Rico	na	na	na	na	na	na	na	na	na	na	na	na	na	na	na	na		
Romania	47	35	38	32	42	32	33	30	38	34	35	33	36	33	37	43		
Russian Fed.	68	8	8	8	10	10	5	6	7	12	8	7	9	8	9	3		
Serbia	na	6	7	4	8	6	5	5	6	6	5	4	7	4	7	11		
Singapore	na	na	na	na	na	na	na	na	na	na	na	na	na	na	na	na		
Slovakia	na	36	36	35	42	37	29	31	36	48	27	34	42	26	42	59		
Slovenia	25	37	38	36	41	32	40	39	36	34	37	37	38	42	36	39		
South Africa	na	60	62	56	61	60	53	68	54	26	66	65	51	55	63	66		
Spain	19	33	33	34	30	32	37	34	32	33	35	34	35	36	36	22		
Sweden	36	41	43	39	43	40	41	30	44	46	34	44	47	49	44	33		
Switzerland	na	na	na	na	na	na	na	na	na	na	na	na	na	na	na	na		
Taiwan	na	na	na	na	na	na	na	na	na	na	na	na	na	na	na	na		
Tanzania	na	na	na	na	na	na	na	na	na	na	na	na	na	na	na	na		
Turkey	47	39	35	43	38	38	42	37	43	34	36	40	42	42	39	34		
Uganda	na	53	60	45	53	51	64	42	56	63	43	55	56	56	48	76		
Ukraine	na	32	31	33	41	32	26	22	30	39	24	32	41	30	33	52		
United States	52	53	56	50	52	51	58	46	53	57	45	54	63	62	54	50		
Uruguay	na	na	na	na	na	na	na	na	na	na	na	na	na	na	na	na		
Venezuela	na	49	50	47	49	51	44	39	50	56	44	47	55	40	51	55		
Vietnam	na	na	na	na	na	na	na	na	na	na	na	na	na	na	na	na		
Zimbabwe	na	38	35	42	37	40	35	43	34	47	49	36	32	29	41	42		
Total	41	44	46	41	46	43	43	45	42	43	40	45	46	40	45	43	Total	44

E088) CONFIDENCE: THE UNITED NATIONS

I am going to name a number of organizations. For each one, could you tell me how much confidence you have in them: is it a great deal of confidence, quite a lot of confidence, not very much confidence or none at all? United Nations.

A great deal / Quite a lot (%)

(WVS: V162; EVS: V210)

Country	Wave 1990	Wave 2000	Male	Female	16-29	30-49	50+	Educ. Lower	Educ. Middle	Educ. Upper	Income Lower	Income Middle	Income Upper	Mat	Mixed	Postm.	RANKING Country	2000
Albania	na	86	87	84	85	87	85	85	86	86	84	87	87	85	87	86	Bangladesh	93
Algeria	na	15	12	18	13	20	8	16	16	12	15	14	14	17	13	12	Uganda	87
Argentina	na	42	45	38	42	42	41	36	47	51	37	40	47	42	42	40	Albania	86
Armenia	na	70	66	73	76	63	69	70	70	70	74	65	67	69	70	74	Tanzania	82
Australia	na	50	50	51	56	48	47	47	52	51	50	54	46	47	52	49	Philippines	77
Austria	na	42	42	41	48	40	40	38	44	50	37	42	46	31	41	46	Moldova	74
Azerbaijan	na	33	35	31	30	36	29	32	30	38	20	33	44	31	33	48	Sweden	74
Bangladesh	na	93	93	94	94	93	94	94	90	95	94	92	94	93	93	88	Norway	73
Belarus	na	53	51	55	56	53	52	54	54	51	53	51	59	51	54	62	Iceland	72
Belgium	na	45	47	43	54	46	40	34	44	54	37	42	51	38	47	50	Portugal	71
Bosnia and Herz.	na	39	38	40	37	37	44	44	39	36	39	40	42	39	40	42	Zimbabwe	70
Brazil	na	70	74	66	73	68	69	64	73	79	63	72	76	66	70	81	Brazil	70
Bulgaria	na	40	39	42	44	37	41	37	38	49	37	42	44	39	42	25	Nigeria	70
Canada	na	65	67	63	70	65	63	60	66	68	59	66	67	59	65	68	Armenia	70
Chile	na	58	57	59	57	57	60	54	60	58	52	62	63	55	58	62	China	69
China	na	69	67	73	62	70	76	79	67	55	78	73	56	67	70	77	Italy	68
Colombia	na	na	na	na	na	na	na	na	na	na	na	na	na	na	na	na	South Africa	67
Croatia	na	47	47	47	48	44	49	54	45	33	52	45	45	53	47	43	Puerto Rico	67
Czech Republic	na	48	49	47	57	47	45	44	52	53	39	50	53	37	51	56	Canada	65
Denmark	na	64	66	62	67	61	66	62	72	65	65	65	65	53	65	60	Luxembourg	65
Dominican Rep.	na	44	46	42	47	34	80	22	39	48	36	44	65	44	43	48	Denmark	64
Egypt	na	32	27	37	34	32	29	32	34	29	33	31	31	30	34	27	Malta	63
El Salvador	na	51	53	50	51	48	57	48	53	57	52	49	59	na	na	na	Ireland	63
Estonia	na	43	47	40	50	43	40	37	47	51	26	45	51	40	46	59	Korea, South	62
Finland	na	44	42	47	56	46	36	41	51	44	50	41	43	43	45	43	Japan	61
France	na	54	52	56	56	54	53	52	52	60	48	55	56	58	54	52	Vietnam	61
Georgia	na	61	59	62	61	62	58	62	61	59	57	63	65	61	60	60	Georgia	61
Germany	na	52	54	51	50	52	53	50	55	50	48	56	50	59	53	38	Great Britain	60
Great Britain	na	60	61	59	66	56	62	59	64	56	64	64	57	na	na	na	Hungary	59
Greece	na	19	16	21	20	15	24	16	19	19	18	16	23	25	20	10	Poland	58
Hungary	na	59	59	59	65	61	52	54	67	68	50	57	66	55	63	72	Chile	58
Iceland	na	72	72	73	77	70	72	70	74	74	70	75	72	65	75	68	United States	57
India	na	47	50	41	52	43	48	37	47	56	37	44	51	54	45	43	Uruguay	56
Indonesia	na	48	47	50	45	49	49	51	51	44	51	43	46	45	50	50	Ukraine	55
Iran	na	36	37	35	35	39	34	36	38	34	33	36	36	30	38	41	Netherlands	55
Ireland	na	63	61	64	65	64	59	56	65	66	56	64	65	62	63	60	New Zealand	54
Israel	na	na	na	na	na	na	na	na	na	na	na	na	na	na	na	na	France	54
Italy	na	68	66	70	72	67	66	66	71	66	68	66	70	68	68	68	Belarus	53
Japan	na	61	59	64	64	58	63	54	60	68	58	62	63	70	63	49	Northern Ireland	53
Jordan	na	36	24	50	38	37	32	39	36	31	46	30	32	41	33	35	Slovakia	52
Korea, South	na	62	61	63	53	64	69	63	65	58	60	63	64	64	62	52	Venezuela	52
Latvia	na	48	50	45	51	44	50	45	46	56	45	46	54	44	49	54	Germany	52
Lithuania	na	47	49	45	53	47	42	38	49	52	39	41	52	45	47	60	El Salvador	51
Luxembourg	na	65	65	65	66	65	65	66	64	65	68	62	61	69	64	62	Australia	50
Macedonia	na	37	41	33	42	39	30	49	28	38	37	37	34	34	36	58	Taiwan	49
Malta	na	63	62	64	67	58	66	51	64	84	56	64	71	56	66	77	Slovenia	49
Mexico	na	46	48	43	47	44	45	41	46	60	43	45	55	42	47	50	Spain	49
Moldova	na	74	71	77	76	74	71	70	73	79	72	73	75	68	78	84	Czech Republic	48
Montenegro	na	44	49	40	55	44	39	38	44	61	26	42	57	35	55	50	Latvia	48
Morocco	na	13	11	16	12	15	12	13	11	18	11	12	12	12	12	18	Indonesia	48
Netherlands	na	55	58	53	61	55	52	50	62	53	53	53	62	50	58	51	Lithuania	47
New Zealand	na	54	53	55	64	57	50	51	52	59	52	55	57	65	56	55	India	47
Nigeria	na	70	72	68	71	70	67	64	74	74	68	73	69	71	70	70	Croatia	47
Northern Ireland	na	53	49	57	51	56	51	47	54	63	49	53	55	51	51	59	Turkey	46
Norway	na	73	73	74	77	73	72	72	76	72	na	na	na	68	74	76	Mexico	46
Pakistan	na	22	22	22	22	23	19	22	25	18	22	22	25	23	21	50	Belgium	45
Peru	na	44	47	41	44	44	44	39	42	50	38	43	55	36	46	45	Montenegro	44
Philippines	na	77	80	73	79	75	75	73	77	79	75	77	77	77	77	69	Romania	44
Poland	na	58	61	55	60	55	61	54	63	61	56	58	63	58	59	58	Finland	44
Portugal	na	71	74	68	74	70	70	69	75	78	59	71	67	70	72	73	Peru	44
Puerto Rico	na	67	70	65	61	64	73	70	67	67	69	67	66	68	67	68	Dominican Rep.	44
Romania	na	44	48	40	51	44	41	41	46	46	41	40	49	40	45	61	Estonia	43
Russian Fed.	na	27	28	25	35	26	22	21	26	33	23	25	30	25	30	22	Switzerland	43
Serbia	na	17	18	16	23	14	17	17	16	19	15	15	16	15	18	23	Austria	42
Singapore	na	na	na	na	na	na	na	na	na	na	na	na	na	na	na	na	Argentina	42
Slovakia	na	52	55	50	59	52	47	46	53	63	43	51	60	46	56	72	Bulgaria	40
Slovenia	na	49	47	51	52	42	55	54	49	40	48	53	47	54	50	46	Bosnia and Herz.	39
South Africa	na	67	71	63	72	65	63	70	65	61	66	75	61	68	67	65	Macedonia	37
Spain	na	49	47	51	51	45	51	49	49	50	48	54	52	50	51	45	Jordan	36
Sweden	na	74	72	76	77	75	71	73	76	71	70	80	72	76	74	71	Iran	36
Switzerland	na	43	42	44	55	43	37	39	43	49	40	36	49	45	42	46	Azerbaijan	33
Taiwan	na	49	47	52	45	48	56	61	54	37	57	48	45	52	47	42	Egypt	32
Tanzania	na	82	78	86	83	79	86	84	81	76	83	79	86	81	84	71	Russian Fed.	27
Turkey	na	46	42	51	46	45	49	47	46	46	46	45	49	44	47	43	Pakistan	22
Uganda	na	87	91	84	89	85	92	86	87	90	85	85	86	88	87	89	Greece	19
Ukraine	na	55	56	55	63	56	49	30	56	63	50	50	66	52	58	66	Serbia	17
United States	na	57	55	60	60	55	59	55	57	59	54	58	62	66	57	54	Algeria	15
Uruguay	na	56	60	53	53	53	59	54	57	62	52	59	58	60	58	52	Morocco	13
Venezuela	na	52	52	52	54	52	49	41	54	59	47	52	58	50	52	57		
Vietnam	na	61	60	62	60	61	62	54	70	57	68	60	59	75	58	68		
Zimbabwe	na	70	65	76	68	72	72	76	66	52	71	71	70	69	71	74		
Total	na	54	54	54	56	53	53	53	55	54	52	53	56	52	55	54	Total	54

E110) SATISFACTION WITH DEMOCRACY

On the whole are you very satisfied, rather satisfied, not very satisfied or not at all satisfied with the way democracy is developing in our country?

Very satisfied / Rather satisfied (%)

(WVS: V168; EVS: V213)

Country	Wave 1990	Wave 2000	Gender Male	Gender Female	Age 16-29	Age 30-49	Age 50+	Education Lower	Education Middle	Education Upper	Income Lower	Income Middle	Income Upper	Values Mat	Values Mixed	Values Postm.
Albania	na	27	27	27	28	27	25	23	29	32	22	32	28	25	27	39
Algeria	na	41	40	43	40	41	44	43	41	39	44	45	37	40	45	25
Argentina	na	44	44	44	42	49	41	42	48	45	45	44	44	39	48	40
Armenia	na	na	na	na	na	na	na	na	na	na	na	na	na	na	na	na
Australia	na	na	na	na	na	na	na	na	na	na	na	na	na	na	na	na
Austria	na	77	79	75	77	75	78	77	77	76	77	78	81	67	80	73
Azerbaijan	na	na	na	na	na	na	na	na	na	na	na	na	na	na	na	na
Bangladesh	na	77	73	83	78	76	80	81	76	70	84	75	74	81	74	76
Belarus	na	33	33	33	21	28	53	54	29	22	36	34	26	38	32	8
Belgium	na	49	48	50	57	45	50	45	48	53	41	49	55	53	48	46
Bosnia and Herz.	na	34	37	32	34	34	34	37	33	33	33	34	40	33	34	37
Brazil	na	na	na	na	na	na	na	na	na	na	na	na	na	na	na	na
Bulgaria	na	28	28	27	34	28	24	20	30	35	22	25	33	22	33	42
Canada	na	67	69	66	68	67	67	62	68	71	60	66	74	73	67	66
Chile	na	60	59	60	60	61	57	56	59	69	55	64	63	55	62	60
China	na	88	86	91	85	88	90	92	87	76	90	89	85	89	87	77
Colombia	na	na	na	na	na	na	na	na	na	na	na	na	na	na	na	na
Croatia	na	17	17	17	13	19	18	18	16	19	26	17	12	22	18	8
Czech Republic	na	37	39	36	43	39	33	34	39	47	29	36	47	33	38	47
Denmark	na	67	68	66	70	69	64	60	77	74	66	68	70	63	68	63
Dominican Rep.	na	na	na	na	na	na	na	na	na	na	na	na	na	na	na	na
Egypt	na	95	96	94	94	95	95	95	95	94	95	94	94	94	95	97
El Salvador	na	na	na	na	na	na	na	na	na	na	na	na	na	na	na	na
Estonia	na	36	40	32	47	32	33	33	35	41	27	33	43	30	41	30
Finland	na	57	57	56	74	51	53	50	62	72	51	56	62	60	56	52
France	na	49	52	47	44	50	51	47	51	55	45	46	59	46	52	49
Georgia	na	na	na	na	na	na	na	na	na	na	na	na	na	na	na	na
Germany	na	75	75	76	80	74	75	74	77	74	72	77	81	77	74	76
Great Britain	na	54	54	53	57	58	49	51	54	66	52	57	59	na	na	na
Greece	na	55	57	54	55	55	59	53	51	59	52	58	59	60	59	46
Hungary	na	33	33	33	34	29	36	33	29	38	24	30	44	32	35	16
Iceland	na	65	68	62	78	64	57	62	70	65	60	66	67	68	67	46
India	na	63	64	62	67	62	63	63	65	62	65	64	62	66	63	56
Indonesia	na	29	33	25	20	30	32	29	29	29	30	28	34	27	29	30
Iran	na	67	66	67	67	67	67	67	66	65	63	71	68	73	63	67
Ireland	na	64	61	66	64	63	63	62	61	70	63	62	64	64	65	58
Israel	na	na	na	na	na	na	na	na	na	na	na	na	na	na	na	na
Italy	na	36	37	35	35	38	35	34	38	36	32	38	40	37	36	35
Japan	na	41	43	40	31	39	47	44	41	41	42	41	42	57	40	29
Jordan	na	72	70	74	73	71	74	75	75	63	76	66	73	78	70	53
Korea, South	na	33	33	33	30	32	36	52	35	27	29	32	37	37	30	27
Latvia	na	30	31	30	33	29	30	30	29	36	27	27	37	26	32	21
Lithuania	na	26	24	27	29	20	29	26	25	27	20	29	29	24	24	31
Luxembourg	na	83	83	84	84	81	86	83	84	80	82	83	84	89	85	77
Macedonia	na	18	18	17	18	16	20	15	20	15	17	18	18	18	18	4
Malta	na	78	79	77	78	76	80	73	79	85	73	82	83	74	79	85
Mexico	na	41	41	42	41	40	45	43	40	37	45	44	42	44	41	41
Moldova	na	10	11	10	11	9	12	13	11	8	8	9	13	10	12	9
Montenegro	na	33	34	32	41	31	29	27	35	37	20	25	47	27	40	35
Morocco	na	44	39	50	40	45	55	50	30	27	53	34	42	51	41	28
Netherlands	na	74	75	73	78	73	73	66	80	74	68	74	79	73	74	75
New Zealand	na	na	na	na	na	na	na	na	na	na	na	na	na	na	na	na
Nigeria	na	60	60	60	59	60	59	63	57	58	59	58	61	58	61	58
Northern Ireland	na	29	30	27	29	26	32	27	26	38	25	29	30	34	28	23
Norway	na	na	na	na	na	na	na	na	na	na	na	na	na	na	na	na
Pakistan	na	18	16	21	23	16	15	11	28	21	10	21	23	14	24	27
Peru	na	35	37	33	33	36	38	30	36	37	31	34	42	34	36	34
Philippines	na	45	46	44	48	44	44	46	45	44	41	44	50	44	46	51
Poland	na	45	47	43	58	44	39	39	49	64	33	50	60	41	47	42
Portugal	na	77	78	75	76	77	77	76	74	88	82	73	78	81	74	73
Puerto Rico	na	54	62	49	50	53	56	53	51	55	54	56	53	53	56	49
Romania	na	21	22	19	24	18	22	22	19	22	24	15	23	19	21	31
Russian Fed.	na	7	7	7	11	7	5	7	7	7	6	7	8	6	8	8
Serbia	na	45	45	46	53	46	41	43	45	49	41	45	48	46	45	45
Singapore	na	na	na	na	na	na	na	na	na	na	na	na	na	na	na	na
Slovakia	na	23	23	24	30	22	21	22	23	32	19	22	28	20	26	39
Slovenia	na	45	46	44	46	44	46	42	44	53	44	40	60	42	47	46
South Africa	na	61	63	59	61	63	54	59	64	52	66	64	56	60	61	71
Spain	na	66	66	67	63	65	70	67	64	69	63	73	66	71	67	60
Sweden	na	60	61	59	58	60	61	63	60	58	59	57	65	63	63	52
Switzerland	na	na	na	na	na	na	na	na	na	na	na	na	na	na	na	na
Taiwan	na	na	na	na	na	na	na	na	na	na	na	na	na	na	na	na
Tanzania	na	76	75	77	76	74	79	77	76	71	76	74	77	78	77	57
Turkey	na	24	21	27	23	22	34	25	22	24	24	24	24	33	23	18
Uganda	na	68	64	71	69	67	66	63	70	64	67	68	63	69	66	70
Ukraine	na	16	17	14	17	18	12	13	13	23	11	16	20	14	17	19
United States	na	65	66	64	66	60	69	61	61	68	60	65	72	72	66	58
Uruguay	na	na	na	na	na	na	na	na	na	na	na	na	na	na	na	na
Venezuela	na	62	65	60	58	63	70	69	62	56	63	63	61	64	62	62
Vietnam	na	97	97	96	96	97	96	97	97	94	98	94	98	90	99	96
Zimbabwe	na	30	29	31	32	28	28	32	28	na	35	36	20	30	29	38
Total	na	49	50	49	51	49	48	51	48	50	47	49	52	46	51	51

RANKING

Country	2000
Vietnam	97
Egypt	95
China	88
Luxembourg	83
Malta	78
Bangladesh	77
Austria	77
Portugal	77
Tanzania	76
Germany	75
Netherlands	74
Jordan	72
Uganda	68
Canada	67
Denmark	67
Iran	67
Spain	66
Iceland	65
United States	65
Ireland	64
India	63
Venezuela	62
South Africa	61
Sweden	60
Nigeria	60
Chile	60
Finland	57
Greece	55
Great Britain	54
Puerto Rico	54
France	49
Belgium	49
Serbia	45
Poland	45
Philippines	45
Slovenia	45
Argentina	44
Morocco	44
Japan	41
Mexico	41
Algeria	41
Czech Republic	37
Italy	36
Estonia	36
Peru	35
Bosnia and Herz.	34
Belarus	33
Hungary	33
Montenegro	33
Korea, South	33
Latvia	30
Zimbabwe	30
Indonesia	29
Northern Ireland	29
Bulgaria	28
Albania	27
Lithuania	26
Turkey	24
Slovakia	23
Romania	21
Pakistan	18
Macedonia	18
Croatia	17
Ukraine	16
Moldova	10
Russian Fed.	7
Total	49

E111A) RATE POLITICAL SYSTEM TODAY

People have different views about the system for governing this country. Here is a scale for rating how well things are going?
(1 = very bad; 10 = very good)
% Very good (codes 7 to 10)

(WVS: V163A; EVS: V214)

Country	Wave 1990	Wave 2000	Male	Female	16-29	30-49	50+	Lower	Middle	Upper	Lower	Middle	Upper	Mat	Mixed	Postm.
	Wave		Gender		Age			Education			Income			Values		
Albania	na	26	27	26	27	28	24	23	28	30	26	27	27	27	27	15
Algeria	na	23	20	26	17	26	28	28	22	19	21	29	25	25	23	11
Argentina	na	25	27	24	22	28	25	25	24	31	26	25	25	22	28	21
Armenia	na	14	14	13	15	14	11	12	15	11	17	11	12	13	13	27
Australia	na	18	22	13	18	20	15	16	16	20	14	20	19	19	17	19
Austria	na	39	43	35	41	39	37	36	39	47	37	38	45	33	39	39
Azerbaijan	na	54	56	53	59	51	52	60	48	65	42	53	73	52	57	60
Bangladesh	na	na	na	na	na	na	na	na	na	na	na	na	na	na	na	na
Belarus	na	18	18	18	11	13	30	28	16	9	21	16	18	19	18	10
Belgium	na	22	26	18	19	21	24	19	23	23	20	19	29	20	23	20
Bosnia and Herz.	na	11	11	11	9	10	14	13	11	9	11	12	10	10	12	4
Brazil	na	18	22	14	16	16	25	19	17	17	22	16	15	18	19	13
Bulgaria	na	21	23	20	25	21	20	12	25	27	18	18	27	20	22	23
Canada	na	na	na	na	na	na	na	na	na	na	na	na	na	na	na	na
Chile	na	na	na	na	na	na	na	na	na	na	na	na	na	na	na	na
China	na	na	na	na	na	na	na	na	na	na	na	na	na	na	na	na
Colombia	na	na	na	na	na	na	na	na	na	na	na	na	na	na	na	na
Croatia	na	7	7	7	5	9	6	5	8	7	11	6	5	5	7	4
Czech Republic	na	12	13	11	13	12	11	11	11	19	9	12	15	9	12	16
Denmark	na	28	29	26	30	29	25	24	34	31	27	28	30	26	27	32
Dominican Rep.	na	15	16	14	16	14	9	20	11	16	17	15	13	16	16	11
Egypt	na	na	na	na	na	na	na	na	na	na	na	na	na	na	na	na
El Salvador	na	25	24	25	29	22	21	23	26	26	26	22	25	na	na	na
Estonia	na	15	18	12	21	12	15	14	13	22	10	14	17	11	16	11
Finland	na	41	43	38	51	38	37	34	46	56	37	39	44	41	40	40
France	na	16	19	13	13	18	15	12	16	26	11	14	25	11	16	25
Georgia	na	15	18	12	16	13	15	15	16	12	13	18	15	13	17	12
Germany	na	46	47	45	44	44	49	45	48	44	46	52	52	58	45	36
Great Britain	na	23	25	20	24	24	22	17	24	37	17	22	28	na	na	na
Greece	na	20	24	18	16	23	26	21	18	22	18	22	26	23	22	13
Hungary	na	9	9	8	6	5	13	8	8	16	7	6	13	9	9	na
Iceland	na	45	51	40	45	49	41	38	48	56	39	47	51	43	47	42
India	na	28	28	29	26	28	31	33	26	21	38	30	22	34	24	17
Indonesia	na	23	29	17	21	22	25	30	22	19	18	23	35	24	23	7
Iran	na	38	37	39	36	40	37	36	40	36	31	32	41	35	38	46
Ireland	na	36	40	33	32	35	40	36	33	43	37	34	38	42	36	30
Israel	na	na	na	na	na	na	na	na	na	na	na	na	na	na	na	na
Italy	na	11	14	8	8	11	12	10	10	13	9	12	14	11	10	12
Japan	na	na	na	na	na	na	na	na	na	na	na	na	na	na	na	na
Jordan	na	39	34	43	40	38	38	43	41	28	40	37	36	42	36	39
Korea, South	na	na	na	na	na	na	na	na	na	na	na	na	na	na	na	na
Latvia	na	9	9	9	11	7	10	9	9	11	10	6	11	10	9	6
Lithuania	na	7	8	7	7	7	8	6	7	12	8	5	9	10	5	15
Luxembourg	na	49	53	46	45	49	51	43	50	60	53	49	58	51	52	48
Macedonia	na	8	7	8	9	6	9	7	8	7	6	9	8	5	10	4
Malta	na	60	62	58	59	57	64	60	60	59	50	62	65	59	60	65
Mexico	na	na	na	na	na	na	na	na	na	na	na	na	na	na	na	na
Moldova	na	21	22	19	16	18	28	26	20	16	19	25	20	19	23	12
Montenegro	na	na	na	na	na	na	na	na	na	na	na	na	na	na	na	na
Morocco	na	31	27	35	27	31	43	34	17	21	36	21	27	37	26	24
Netherlands	na	52	58	46	59	53	47	39	53	63	47	53	59	47	53	51
New Zealand	na	7	8	6	9	6	7	4	7	10	7	7	6	4	6	12
Nigeria	na	na	na	na	na	na	na	na	na	na	na	na	na	na	na	na
Northern Ireland	na	31	34	29	18	28	42	31	29	39	27	35	36	35	34	20
Norway	na	51	59	42	56	53	44	43	51	57	na	na	na	44	51	56
Pakistan	na	8	8	8	9	8	7	6	10	10	8	8	8	6	11	17
Peru	na	36	35	37	36	36	36	35	37	36	34	36	39	38	35	37
Philippines	na	na	na	na	na	na	na	na	na	na	na	na	na	na	na	na
Poland	na	11	12	10	17	10	8	10	11	12	8	10	19	9	12	13
Portugal	na	36	35	37	35	30	41	37	35	28	45	34	33	38	34	33
Puerto Rico	na	31	29	32	27	29	34	36	31	30	38	32	25	40	30	29
Romania	na	13	13	13	16	11	14	15	12	14	19	11	12	13	12	18
Russian Fed.	na	3	2	3	4	2	3	3	3	3	2	2	4	3	2	na
Serbia	na	na	na	na	na	na	na	na	na	na	na	na	na	na	na	na
Singapore	na	na	na	na	na	na	na	na	na	na	na	na	na	na	na	na
Slovakia	na	8	7	9	8	8	7	8	7	13	8	7	9	7	9	6
Slovenia	na	13	17	9	12	12	14	10	12	20	12	14	17	8	14	8
South Africa	na	37	36	38	41	36	30	38	37	19	43	48	22	34	39	37
Spain	na	33	32	35	28	33	37	33	33	37	34	36	36	39	33	28
Sweden	na	27	33	21	26	26	28	22	24	35	24	26	33	32	25	33
Switzerland	na	24	26	23	32	20	25	24	24	27	21	25	28	27	24	23
Taiwan	na	28	30	27	19	31	28	30	29	27	30	29	26	24	30	42
Tanzania	na	54	59	48	56	53	55	51	60	52	53	52	54	55	55	50
Turkey	na	6	5	6	5	6	7	6	5	3	6	4	8	6	6	4
Uganda	na	na	na	na	na	na	na	na	na	na	na	na	na	na	na	na
Ukraine	na	7	10	6	7	11	4	3	8	8	5	6	12	6	9	6
United States	na	na	na	na	na	na	na	na	na	na	na	na	na	na	na	na
Uruguay	na	14	15	13	9	7	21	17	7	15	16	11	13	21	13	11
Venezuela	na	na	na	na	na	na	na	na	na	na	na	na	na	na	na	na
Vietnam	na	91	90	91	88	90	94	91	92	84	82	94	92	94	91	83
Zimbabwe	na	na	na	na	na	na	na	na	na	na	na	na	na	na	na	na
Total	na	26	27	24	25	25	26	26	24	27	24	25	27	24	26	25

RANKING

Country	2000
Vietnam	91
Malta	60
Azerbaijan	54
Tanzania	54
Netherlands	52
Norway	51
Luxembourg	49
Germany	46
Iceland	45
Finland	41
Austria	39
Jordan	39
Iran	38
South Africa	37
Ireland	36
Peru	36
Portugal	36
Spain	33
Northern Ireland	31
Morocco	31
Puerto Rico	31
Taiwan	28
India	28
Denmark	28
Sweden	27
Albania	26
Argentina	25
El Salvador	25
Switzerland	24
Indonesia	23
Great Britain	23
Algeria	23
Belgium	22
Bulgaria	21
Moldova	21
Greece	20
Brazil	18
Belarus	18
Australia	18
France	16
Estonia	15
Dominican Rep.	15
Georgia	15
Armenia	14
Uruguay	14
Romania	13
Slovenia	13
Czech Republic	12
Italy	11
Bosnia and Herz.	11
Poland	11
Latvia	9
Hungary	9
Pakistan	8
Slovakia	8
Macedonia	8
Lithuania	7
Ukraine	7
New Zealand	7
Croatia	7
Turkey	6
Russian Fed.	3
Total	26

E111B) RATE POLITICAL SYSTEM TODAY
People have different views about the system for governing this country. Here is a scale for rating how well things are going?
(1 = very bad; 10 = very good)

% Bad (codes 1 to 4)

(WVS: V163A; EVS: V214)

Country	Wave 1990	Wave 2000	Gender Male	Gender Female	Age 16-29	Age 30-49	Age 50+	Education Lower	Education Middle	Education Upper	Income Lower	Income Middle	Income Upper	Values Mat	Values Mixed	Values Postm.	RANKING Country	RANKING 2000
Albania	na	51	51	50	51	51	50	51	52	47	52	49	49	49	52	64	Russian Fed.	83
Algeria	na	52	55	48	56	50	45	45	51	58	50	49	52	49	51	68	Macedonia	76
Argentina	na	37	35	40	35	35	41	38	35	35	40	38	33	40	36	39	Turkey	75
Armenia	na	62	63	62	55	65	70	62	62	65	52	71	69	64	63	52	Lithuania	73
Australia	na	50	47	53	47	48	56	55	52	44	56	48	46	50	51	49	New Zealand	72
Austria	na	21	21	22	22	23	20	21	21	21	24	20	18	30	19	23	Ukraine	70
Azerbaijan	na	2	2	2	2	2	3	2	2	2	2	2	2	2	2	na	Croatia	67
Bangladesh	na	na	na	na	na	na	na	na	na	na	na	na	na	na	na	na	Romania	65
Belarus	na	55	58	52	61	59	44	43	56	66	50	55	61	50	58	78	Slovakia	64
Belgium	na	36	37	35	39	40	31	42	37	30	46	36	31	38	35	38	Uruguay	63
Bosnia and Herz.	na	60	62	58	61	61	58	52	60	65	63	57	60	57	60	71	Pakistan	63
Brazil	na	52	48	56	55	55	41	50	54	50	48	55	55	49	52	56	Armenia	62
Bulgaria	na	49	48	50	44	46	53	60	46	38	58	46	42	54	43	50	Dominican Rep.	61
Canada	na	na	na	na	na	na	na	na	na	na	na	na	na	na	na	na	Bosnia and Herz.	60
Chile	na	na	na	na	na	na	na	na	na	na	na	na	na	na	na	na	Hungary	57
China	na	na	na	na	na	na	na	na	na	na	na	na	na	na	na	na	Georgia	55
Colombia	na	na	na	na	na	na	na	na	na	na	na	na	na	na	na	na	Poland	55
Croatia	na	67	67	67	76	67	61	63	69	73	62	65	72	64	64	83	Belarus	55
Czech Republic	na	53	56	50	46	58	52	55	51	50	56	53	50	60	51	45	Moldova	54
Denmark	na	36	35	37	36	36	35	38	36	33	33	35	40	35	37	32	Czech Republic	53
Dominican Rep.	na	61	57	64	65	57	27	53	65	61	57	62	59	66	59	64	Algeria	52
Egypt	na	na	na	na	na	na	na	na	na	na	na	na	na	na	na	na	Brazil	52
El Salvador	na	44	45	44	37	49	49	46	43	42	43	46	44	na	na	na	Italy	51
Estonia	na	43	40	45	34	46	44	42	45	38	49	39	41	49	38	56	Albania	51
Finland	na	22	23	20	15	24	23	24	20	13	25	22	17	21	21	24	Australia	50
France	na	40	36	44	42	42	38	44	38	33	48	40	33	41	41	38	Bulgaria	49
Georgia	na	55	52	57	53	57	54	58	53	57	58	53	51	57	52	64	Slovenia	48
Germany	na	23	26	22	28	23	22	24	23	23	23	22	19	21	26	22	Latvia	46
Great Britain	na	32	31	33	30	31	33	35	31	25	38	29	27	na	na	na	El Salvador	44
Greece	na	43	42	43	47	41	33	41	46	40	47	41	40	35	40	57	Estonia	43
Hungary	na	57	58	55	55	61	53	57	58	53	68	58	47	52	59	87	Greece	43
Iceland	na	18	17	20	17	18	21	21	18	15	24	18	16	18	17	27	France	40
India	na	24	25	23	23	26	24	23	27	25	24	22	27	22	28	37	Sweden	37
Indonesia	na	37	36	37	46	34	36	32	36	42	42	33	35	36	38	46	Argentina	37
Iran	na	23	24	21	24	22	19	20	22	28	28	22	20	20	24	28	Indonesia	37
Ireland	na	24	23	24	23	29	19	28	25	16	22	25	22	19	26	23	Belgium	36
Israel	na	na	na	na	na	na	na	na	na	na	na	na	na	na	na	na	Denmark	36
Italy	na	51	51	51	57	46	51	52	51	47	51	48	49	49	52	51	South Africa	34
Japan	na	na	na	na	na	na	na	na	na	na	na	na	na	na	na	na	Switzerland	33
Jordan	na	17	20	14	15	19	19	16	13	23	18	16	17	15	17	29	Northern Ireland	33
Korea, South	na	na	na	na	na	na	na	na	na	na	na	na	na	na	na	na	Great Britain	32
Latvia	na	46	48	45	48	51	42	44	46	52	47	48	43	47	45	53	Morocco	30
Lithuania	73	73	75	72	70	76	73	71	76	68	77	76	71	70	75	67	Peru	27
Luxembourg	na	12	13	12	11	13	12	12	13	11	14	11	13	12	10	19	Puerto Rico	25
Macedonia	na	76	75	77	75	77	77	80	75	71	80	74	73	79	74	81	Taiwan	25
Malta	na	12	12	13	12	14	11	16	11	9	16	9	11	14	12	10	India	24
Mexico	na	na	na	na	na	na	na	na	na	na	na	na	na	na	na	na	Ireland	24
Moldova	na	54	56	52	64	53	46	46	53	62	50	52	58	53	52	62	Germany	23
Montenegro	na	na	na	na	na	na	na	na	na	na	na	na	na	na	na	na	Tanzania	23
Morocco	na	30	37	24	35	27	25	28	42	37	30	39	32	24	34	44	Spain	23
Netherlands	na	11	11	12	8	14	10	12	11	11	11	11	10	14	10	12	Iran	23
New Zealand	na	72	71	73	61	73	76	80	75	61	75	73	69	79	75	61	Finland	22
Nigeria	na	na	na	na	na	na	na	na	na	na	na	na	na	na	na	na	Austria	21
Northern Ireland	na	33	34	32	39	40	23	34	35	22	36	29	32	28	29	51	Iceland	18
Norway	na	13	14	13	11	13	16	19	11	10	na	na	na	16	13	10	Jordan	17
Pakistan	na	63	63	63	63	64	61	66	60	61	66	59	58	66	59	58	Portugal	16
Peru	na	27	27	27	27	28	25	27	29	25	33	25	20	26	27	31	Norway	13
Philippines	na	na	na	na	na	na	na	na	na	na	na	na	na	na	na	na	Malta	12
Poland	na	55	54	55	45	55	60	56	53	52	61	54	43	59	52	56	Luxembourg	12
Portugal	na	16	13	19	17	19	14	17	14	20	14	18	16	13	18	21	Netherlands	11
Puerto Rico	na	25	28	24	29	27	23	30	27	24	28	20	28	20	26	24	Azerbaijan	2
Romania	na	65	65	65	62	67	64	65	67	60	62	69	65	67	65	58	Vietnam	1
Russian Fed.	na	83	83	84	82	83	85	86	84	81	87	85	79	84	84	72		
Serbia	na	na	na	na	na	na	na	na	na	na	na	na	na	na	na	na		
Singapore	na	na	na	na	na	na	na	na	na	na	na	na	na	na	na	na		
Slovakia	na	64	66	62	59	65	66	66	63	58	68	63	60	68	61	33		
Slovenia	na	48	46	50	51	53	40	49	50	40	47	49	41	51	45	56		
South Africa	na	34	34	33	29	36	38	32	34	52	26	27	48	37	31	35		
Spain	na	23	24	22	28	22	21	24	20	25	25	23	25	17	23	35		
Sweden	na	37	34	41	34	40	37	35	39	36	39	37	35	22	39	35		
Switzerland	na	33	31	34	28	35	33	40	31	29	37	35	29	31	32	40		
Taiwan	na	25	23	27	33	26	17	24	18	30	26	20	29	27	25	8		
Tanzania	23	23	19	28	24	21	24	30	17	12	30	24	10	23	23	25		
Turkey	na	75	78	73	79	74	70	75	76	78	75	75	76	73	75	81		
Uganda	na	na	na	na	na	na	na	na	na	na	na	na	na	na	na	na		
Ukraine	na	70	69	70	66	64	77	76	70	65	77	71	59	71	70	59		
United States	na	na	na	na	na	na	na	na	na	na	na	na	na	na	na	na		
Uruguay	na	63	66	61	67	72	56	61	70	58	60	67	63	57	63	66		
Venezuela	na	na	na	na	na	na	na	na	na	na	na	na	na	na	na	na		
Vietnam	na	1	1	1	na	1	na	1	1	na	2	1	na	1	1	na		
Zimbabwe	na	na	na	na	na	na	na	na	na	na	na	na	na	na	na	na		
Total	na	41	41	42	42	42	40	41	43	40	45	42	41	43	40	43	Total	41

E112A) RATE POLITICAL SYSTEM TEN YEARS AGO

Where on this scale would you put the political system as it was ten years ago (1 = very bad; 10 = very good)

% Very good (codes 7 to 10)

(WVS: V163; EVS: V215)

Country	Wave 1990	Wave 2000	Gender Male	Gender Female	Age 16-29	Age 30-49	Age 50+	Education Lower	Education Middle	Education Upper	Income Lower	Income Middle	Income Upper	Values Mat	Values Mixed	Values Postm.
Albania	na	11	11	10	10	8	15	12	9	11	13	8	11	11	11	5
Algeria	na	na	na	na	na	na	na	na	na	na	na	na	na	na	na	na
Argentina	na	15	17	15	17	13	17	16	15	10	16	17	13	18	15	16
Armenia	na	43	43	44	32	46	56	56	44	37	34	50	49	47	42	25
Australia	na	31	34	29	25	32	35	36	30	31	31	32	31	29	34	28
Austria	na	48	50	46	47	45	52	52	43	46	50	47	50	46	51	41
Azerbaijan	na	58	54	62	55	59	63	53	60	56	58	57	59	59	57	65
Bangladesh	na	26	25	27	24	25	32	28	23	23	24	23	30	32	20	26
Belarus	na	36	33	38	19	32	54	52	31	29	43	33	30	43	32	14
Belgium	na	26	25	26	21	23	30	30	27	20	29	27	23	25	27	24
Bosnia and Herz.	na	54	51	57	47	54	61	60	53	52	61	56	42	52	54	52
Brazil	na	25	28	22	21	24	35	31	21	19	30	23	21	28	24	23
Bulgaria	na	31	28	35	11	28	43	57	20	15	48	31	16	43	20	21
Canada	na	32	31	32	30	29	36	37	26	36	35	28	31	34	33	29
Chile	na	23	25	21	22	22	25	22	21	28	20	23	26	21	24	22
China	na	64	65	64	69	61	68	70	60	61	59	66	69	66	61	58
Colombia	na	na	na	na	na	na	na	na	na	na	na	na	na	na	na	na
Croatia	na	17	17	17	17	19	14	27	10	11	20	18	13	12	18	15
Czech Republic	na	14	15	13	10	12	18	21	8	6	23	14	7	27	11	5
Denmark	na	35	38	32	37	31	39	33	43	35	30	34	41	36	40	20
Dominican Rep.	na	12	13	12	14	9	na	10	7	14	14	12	15	18	11	8
Egypt	na	68	68	68	67	69	68	67	70	67	69	68	67	68	69	67
El Salvador	na	39	37	40	38	39	39	45	35	29	40	43	31	na	na	na
Estonia	na	21	21	22	17	22	22	24	22	16	19	27	18	21	22	13
Finland	na	36	39	34	36	33	39	35	39	40	37	37	34	34	37	32
France	na	23	24	22	22	23	24	23	26	22	26	26	20	21	23	26
Georgia	na	41	36	44	32	38	53	43	44	29	49	33	34	43	39	34
Germany	na	47	47	48	42	46	51	51	43	51	48	48	55	58	45	40
Great Britain	na	25	27	24	20	22	31	24	27	22	25	22	30	na	na	na
Greece	na	23	22	23	21	23	26	34	24	19	27	20	22	25	24	18
Hungary	na	33	33	34	31	30	37	34	36	24	36	34	30	38	27	39
Iceland	na	25	25	25	17	25	29	24	24	29	28	25	23	28	24	25
India	na	na	na	na	na	na	na	na	na	na	na	na	na	na	na	na
Indonesia	na	na	na	na	na	na	na	na	na	na	na	na	na	na	na	na
Iran	na	na	na	na	na	na	na	na	na	na	na	na	na	na	na	na
Ireland	na	27	29	25	19	25	33	34	25	20	30	25	24	38	25	20
Israel	na	na	na	na	na	na	na	na	na	na	na	na	na	na	na	na
Italy	na	18	18	19	15	17	21	22	17	13	23	18	15	29	17	16
Japan	na	11	13	9	4	7	16	15	10	11	12	10	11	17	10	8
Jordan	na	na	na	na	na	na	na	na	na	na	na	na	na	na	na	na
Korea, South	na	8	8	8	4	10	10	8	10	6	6	10	10	9	8	5
Latvia	na	19	18	20	19	18	19	24	19	11	23	19	14	22	17	17
Lithuania	na	38	34	42	22	34	52	56	36	14	48	46	26	36	41	18
Luxembourg	na	46	49	42	34	42	54	43	45	55	49	44	58	52	43	47
Macedonia	na	17	15	19	34	44	62	48	50	38	52	45	45	55	44	19
Malta	na	46	48	44	42	46	48	48	45	47	43	44	55	47	46	45
Mexico	na	37	36	38	36	35	42	42	34	26	42	39	30	40	36	34
Moldova	na	22	23	20	23	17	27	26	21	18	24	22	21	23	22	16
Montenegro	na	19	18	19	9	18	25	24	16	16	19	22	20	23	16	10
Morocco	na	na	na	na	na	na	na	na	na	na	na	na	na	na	na	na
Netherlands	na	44	47	42	41	44	46	43	44	46	41	44	46	44	48	33
New Zealand	na	38	40	37	38	38	39	38	38	40	32	39	44	37	42	28
Nigeria	na	na	na	na	na	na	na	na	na	na	na	na	na	na	na	na
Northern Ireland	na	27	28	27	19	22	34	28	24	32	26	27	27	26	31	17
Norway	na	36	43	29	31	39	34	29	34	46	na	na	na	34	35	42
Pakistan	na	na	na	na	na	na	na	na	na	na	na	na	na	na	na	na
Peru	na	na	na	na	na	na	na	na	na	na	na	na	na	na	na	na
Philippines	na	27	26	28	24	30	26	33	26	21	27	22	34	25	27	41
Poland	na	24	21	26	14	23	29	30	18	11	31	19	17	30	19	23
Portugal	na	19	20	18	16	22	19	19	18	21	18	18	24	16	22	20
Puerto Rico	na	na	na	na	na	na	na	na	na	na	na	na	na	na	na	na
Romania	na	30	27	32	18	28	37	43	25	18	46	29	21	38	24	10
Russian Fed.	na	41	37	45	26	37	54	63	42	25	53	44	27	46	36	48
Serbia	na	10	10	9	1	8	15	13	9	6	11	8	9	13	7	4
Singapore	na	na	na	na	na	na	na	na	na	na	na	na	na	na	na	na
Slovakia	na	33	32	34	23	36	37	39	32	18	38	35	29	39	30	8
Slovenia	na	23	22	23	18	23	25	29	22	14	29	22	17	22	22	23
South Africa	na	13	13	14	12	13	18	12	16	12	8	12	23	17	12	7
Spain	na	25	24	26	21	27	26	24	26	27	22	26	29	24	25	27
Sweden	na	39	41	36	34	35	44	40	36	42	42	33	41	57	36	42
Switzerland	na	46	48	44	40	43	52	50	45	45	42	48	50	50	49	36
Taiwan	na	34	30	39	35	35	31	34	32	36	33	37	32	39	32	31
Tanzania	na	51	46	58	50	48	60	60	39	40	61	49	38	54	49	50
Turkey	na	51	50	52	50	50	60	60	40	32	60	51	33	49	53	44
Uganda	na	31	37	26	30	28	49	28	31	41	26	37	27	26	32	42
Ukraine	na	33	29	36	19	28	44	53	33	19	43	29	24	37	33	19
United States	na	39	41	37	36	37	45	43	35	40	38	39	41	53	40	33
Uruguay	na	22	23	22	17	15	31	27	14	20	27	21	20	32	24	14
Venezuela	na	23	22	23	25	21	22	24	25	17	26	27	16	24	23	21
Vietnam	na	71	71	70	68	74	68	73	68	64	63	70	75	77	69	53
Zimbabwe	na	52	54	51	48	56	55	54	49	85	58	54	44	53	52	56
Total	na	32	32	32	28	31	36	36	31	28	34	33	30	36	32	26

RANKING

Country	2000
Vietnam	71
Egypt	68
China	64
Azerbaijan	58
Bosnia and Herz.	54
Zimbabwe	52
Turkey	51
Tanzania	51
Austria	48
Germany	47
Macedonia	47
Switzerland	46
Malta	46
Luxembourg	46
Netherlands	44
Armenia	43
Russian Fed.	41
Georgia	41
United States	39
Sweden	39
El Salvador	39
Lithuania	38
New Zealand	38
Mexico	37
Finland	36
Belarus	36
Norway	36
Denmark	35
Taiwan	34
Hungary	33
Slovakia	33
Ukraine	33
Canada	32
Australia	31
Bulgaria	31
Uganda	31
Romania	30
Northern Ireland	27
Philippines	27
Ireland	27
Belgium	26
Bangladesh	26
Spain	25
Great Britain	25
Brazil	25
Iceland	25
Poland	24
France	23
Chile	23
Slovenia	23
Venezuela	23
Greece	23
Uruguay	22
Moldova	22
Estonia	21
Portugal	19
Latvia	19
Montenegro	19
Italy	18
Croatia	17
Argentina	15
Czech Republic	14
South Africa	13
Dominican Rep.	12
Albania	11
Japan	11
Serbia	10
Korea, South	8
Total	32

E112B) RATE POLITICAL SYSTEM TEN YEARS AGO

Where on this scale would you put the political system as it was ten years ago (1 = very bad; 10 = very good)

% Bad (codes 1 to 4) (WVS: V163; EVS: V215)

Country	Wave 1990	Wave 2000	Male	Female	16-29	30-49	50+	Lower	Middle	Upper	Lower	Middle	Upper	Mat	Mixed	Postm.	RANKING Country	2000
Albania	na	74	72	76	76	76	68	69	77	79	70	75	77	71	77	77	Albania	74
Algeria	na	na	na	na	na	na	na	na	na	na	na	na	na	na	na	na	Dominican Rep.	73
Argentina	na	62	62	63	61	63	62	60	63	74	58	63	66	58	63	62	Serbia	72
Armenia	na	26	28	24	28	27	21	17	24	35	32	24	21	22	28	37	South Africa	69
Australia	na	27	26	27	29	28	24	29	28	24	28	26	24	23	26	30	Korea, South	69
Austria	na	17	17	16	15	18	16	13	20	19	22	18	12	24	15	19	Montenegro	68
Azerbaijan	na	25	28	23	30	24	20	27	26	25	27	23	26	23	30	30	Czech Republic	65
Bangladesh	na	29	34	23	31	28	30	27	31	35	20	31	36	27	31	32	Argentina	62
Belarus	na	38	39	36	57	40	19	23	41	51	31	39	45	33	39	65	Croatia	56
Belgium	na	30	34	26	29	33	27	27	31	31	28	29	35	25	29	40	Poland	53
Bosnia and Herz.	na	23	25	21	28	23	18	23	22	24	16	21	33	25	22	17	Venezuela	53
Brazil	na	48	45	51	50	51	37	44	49	59	44	47	55	45	48	53	Japan	53
Bulgaria	na	47	52	43	66	50	36	23	55	70	33	50	59	37	57	63	Estonia	53
Canada	na	29	34	23	33	32	23	26	29	29	26	33	27	28	27	32	Latvia	52
Chile	na	37	38	37	41	37	33	41	35	34	43	31	37	37	37	37	Romania	51
China	na	12	11	12	7	14	10	10	13	7	15	11	8	10	14	13	Moldova	51
Colombia	na	na	na	na	na	na	na	na	na	na	na	na	na	na	na	na	Italy	49
Croatia	na	56	58	55	59	55	56	46	61	67	55	54	60	68	52	61	Brazil	48
Czech Republic	na	65	66	65	72	67	60	56	72	83	56	65	74	44	70	83	Bulgaria	47
Denmark	na	30	28	32	21	37	26	29	27	36	35	29	31	30	23	57	Uganda	46
Dominican Rep.	na	73	71	74	70	75	100	67	77	73	66	78	69	65	72	83	Ukraine	44
Egypt	na	10	10	9	10	10	10	10	10	10	10	9	11	10	10	10	Slovenia	44
El Salvador	na	34	35	34	31	35	38	30	34	44	33	30	38	na	na	na	Uruguay	43
Estonia	na	53	54	51	60	50	52	53	51	57	51	47	58	48	54	66	Northern Ireland	43
Finland	na	24	27	22	23	29	21	24	26	23	24	23	27	25	23	29	Ireland	40
France	na	30	29	30	32	29	30	29	30	33	28	29	32	25	31	33	Greece	38
Georgia	na	36	40	33	46	35	29	33	32	52	29	40	46	34	38	45	Lithuania	38
Germany	na	23	23	22	31	23	19	20	25	21	21	25	17	22	25	18	Belarus	38
Great Britain	na	34	32	37	37	37	30	31	34	42	38	32	33	na	na	na	Slovakia	37
Greece	na	38	41	36	39	35	39	28	39	39	38	36	37	29	37	46	Chile	37
Hungary	na	31	33	28	33	33	26	26	35	50	23	33	32	27	34	42	Georgia	36
Iceland	na	29	31	26	28	30	27	29	29	26	28	29	29	28	28	35	Mexico	36
India	na	na	na	na	na	na	na	na	na	na	na	na	na	na	na	na	Portugal	36
Indonesia	na	na	na	na	na	na	na	na	na	na	na	na	na	na	na	na	El Salvador	34
Iran	na	na	na	na	na	na	na	na	na	na	na	na	na	na	na	na	Great Britain	34
Ireland	na	40	39	42	43	44	35	33	43	49	37	43	43	33	41	48	Zimbabwe	33
Israel	na	na	na	na	na	na	na	na	na	na	na	na	na	na	na	na	Spain	32
Italy	na	49	51	47	53	51	46	44	51	58	46	51	50	35	49	56	Hungary	31
Japan	na	53	52	54	63	62	40	48	53	55	52	54	50	40	56	58	New Zealand	30
Jordan	na	na	na	na	na	na	na	na	na	na	na	na	na	na	na	na	Philippines	30
Korea, South	na	69	68	70	73	68	66	73	68	71	72	68	67	67	70	77	Belgium	30
Latvia	na	52	54	51	54	51	52	46	51	63	48	47	61	49	54	57	Denmark	30
Lithuania	na	38	41	35	54	39	28	22	40	61	31	30	48	40	33	67	France	30
Luxembourg	na	11	10	13	11	13	10	13	11	10	11	12	11	9	11	16	Russian Fed.	30
Macedonia	na	30	32	27	40	32	18	36	26	27	27	31	28	20	33	56	Macedonia	30
Malta	na	18	21	15	20	19	15	15	18	24	18	19	18	13	19	27	Bangladesh	29
Mexico	na	36	39	34	39	40	26	30	41	50	33	37	46	35	37	44	Iceland	29
Moldova	na	51	54	48	54	53	45	43	50	59	43	53	53	49	49	62	Canada	29
Montenegro	na	68	69	66	77	69	60	64	70	72	68	64	64	62	72	77	Turkey	28
Morocco	na	na	na	na	na	na	na	na	na	na	na	na	na	na	na	na	Australia	27
Netherlands	na	10	12	9	8	12	10	13	9	10	13	9	10	13	8	15	Tanzania	27
New Zealand	na	30	32	30	29	30	31	30	32	30	37	27	27	26	27	41	Armenia	26
Nigeria	na	na	na	na	na	na	na	na	na	na	na	na	na	na	na	na	Azerbaijan	25
Northern Ireland	na	43	44	41	54	46	38	42	46	36	52	42	42	40	40	58	Taiwan	25
Norway	na	18	20	16	19	18	17	20	18	15	na	na	na	19	17	21	United States	25
Pakistan	na	na	na	na	na	na	na	na	na	na	na	na	na	na	na	na	Finland	24
Peru	na	na	na	na	na	na	na	na	na	na	na	na	na	na	na	na	Bosnia and Herz.	23
Philippines	na	30	30	30	33	28	31	26	31	34	33	31	26	30	31	24	Germany	23
Poland	na	53	57	50	68	52	47	43	62	74	45	55	70	45	58	62	Sweden	23
Portugal	na	36	36	36	34	33	39	36	34	35	37	34	28	39	33	36	Malta	18
Puerto Rico	na	na	na	na	na	na	na	na	na	na	na	na	na	na	na	na	Norway	18
Romania	na	51	54	48	65	55	40	36	54	69	37	48	64	41	55	83	Austria	17
Russian Fed.	na	30	34	26	40	33	20	16	27	46	21	25	43	25	34	24	China	12
Serbia	na	72	74	70	90	77	59	58	75	86	62	74	78	65	77	94	Switzerland	12
Singapore	na	na	na	na	na	na	na	na	na	na	na	na	na	na	na	na	Luxembourg	11
Slovakia	na	37	39	36	46	33	36	32	37	57	33	35	42	31	40	69	Netherlands	10
Slovenia	na	44	45	42	50	42	41	40	45	46	37	42	48	43	45	43	Egypt	10
South Africa	na	69	71	67	72	69	65	72	66	70	76	71	59	68	70	69	Vietnam	6
Spain	na	32	35	29	32	34	30	31	31	34	31	31	36	26	35	31		
Sweden	na	23	22	23	20	25	22	24	23	21	20	27	21	13	23	25		
Switzerland	na	12	13	10	14	13	9	10	12	12	15	10	10	7	11	19		
Taiwan	na	25	31	20	27	25	26	21	30	27	22	25	31	21	30	29		
Tanzania	na	27	31	21	31	25	25	23	34	25	24	28	24	26	28	29		
Turkey	na	28	31	25	30	28	21	20	37	49	20	27	45	24	25	39		
Uganda	na	46	35	56	45	49	36	53	43	45	52	45	44	51	46	30		
Ukraine	na	44	49	39	61	48	31	25	43	57	33	46	54	37	46	64		
United States	na	25	25	26	26	27	23	22	27	26	28	24	23	17	24	33		
Uruguay	na	43	45	42	47	51	37	37	53	50	38	43	48	39	42	49		
Venezuela	na	53	55	51	52	55	50	51	53	55	51	50	58	56	52	51		
Vietnam	na	6	6	7	9	6	6	6	7	6	6	6	5	7	6	13		
Zimbabwe	na	33	32	33	35	31	32	34	32	15	32	30	36	30	34	38		
Total	na	37	38	37	43	38	33	34	38	42	36	37	41	36	38	42	Total	37

E114A) HAVING A STRONG LEADER

I'm going to describe various types of political systems and ask what you think about each as a way of governing this country.
Having a strong leader who does not have to bother with parliament and elections
Very good / Fairly good (%)

(WVS: V164; EVS: V216)

Country	Wave 1990	Wave 2000	Gender Male	Female	Age 16-29	30-49	50+	Education Lower	Middle	Upper	Income Lower	Middle	Upper	Values Mat	Mixed	Postm.
Albania	na	17	18	16	16	15	22	20	17	13	17	17	18	16	18	19
Algeria	na	39	35	43	40	37	41	47	40	32	43	40	39	44	38	27
Argentina	na	42	43	41	43	42	40	52	30	22	49	47	29	50	45	29
Armenia	na	53	52	55	49	54	61	65	55	44	49	57	60	61	48	36
Australia	na	25	25	24	32	22	22	37	26	14	29	21	20	32	28	19
Austria	na	16	15	17	18	13	18	21	13	4	24	15	12	34	16	11
Azerbaijan	na	7	8	6	5	7	11	6	7	7	6	7	7	6	8	9
Bangladesh	na	12	10	13	14	10	10	7	17	15	11	15	7	11	11	21
Belarus	na	40	39	41	28	40	52	52	39	27	42	44	27	46	37	15
Belgium	na	33	32	35	31	30	37	48	34	23	39	34	28	50	34	18
Bosnia and Herz.	na	37	36	37	37	34	40	40	37	32	35	39	37	32	38	48
Brazil	na	61	58	63	62	60	57	68	58	42	67	64	52	68	59	51
Bulgaria	na	48	49	46	44	50	47	52	51	35	53	49	43	54	45	31
Canada	na	23	22	24	26	24	21	30	25	14	34	22	17	31	25	19
Chile	na	43	43	43	46	43	40	43	46	35	44	40	45	42	47	31
China	na	19	16	21	21	18	18	16	20	18	15	19	21	19	16	31
Colombia	na	54	54	53	57	51	53	61	52	44	60	50	49	61	62	63
Croatia	na	12	9	15	14	12	11	16	11	5	17	14	8	14	13	7
Czech Republic	na	17	17	16	16	14	17	21	14	7	21	17	14	22	15	12
Denmark	na	14	15	13	12	13	16	17	10	9	16	13	13	19	16	7
Dominican Rep.	na	28	30	27	28	28	20	36	36	25	28	26	26	32	28	21
Egypt	na	8	9	7	7	8	8	8	7	8	9	7	7	7	8	6
El Salvador	na	59	59	60	64	55	59	59	64	53	61	60	56	na	na	na
Estonia	na	18	21	16	26	15	17	20	19	13	17	17	18	22	15	15
Finland	na	27	27	26	21	25	30	35	19	11	34	28	20	32	25	26
France	na	35	32	38	32	33	39	41	31	24	42	37	31	44	37	20
Georgia	na	66	65	67	66	62	72	65	68	62	71	63	61	68	65	59
Germany	na	16	17	15	17	15	17	21	12	10	21	18	10	21	17	8
Great Britain	na	25	24	26	28	26	23	31	22	19	36	23	20	na	na	na
Greece	na	9	11	7	6	10	12	13	11	6	9	8	7	8	12	6
Hungary	na	22	21	22	16	23	23	28	10	10	26	21	21	25	19	1
Iceland	na	11	8	14	12	9	13	18	8	2	19	8	6	19	10	3
India	na	59	61	55	64	57	55	66	56	52	73	57	55	62	56	58
Indonesia	na	19	18	21	18	21	19	19	19	20	17	19	21	20	20	18
Iran	na	39	38	41	42	38	33	35	38	43	38	39	42	40	38	41
Ireland	na	27	22	31	24	24	32	36	25	14	37	28	18	30	26	20
Israel	na	na	na	na	na	na	na	na	na	na	na	na	na	na	na	na
Italy	na	16	17	15	14	14	18	21	13	8	15	14	12	22	17	9
Japan	na	28	30	27	28	25	31	46	28	20	31	27	26	28	28	21
Jordan	na	42	42	42	41	42	44	45	39	41	40	43	47	48	37	40
Korea, South	na	28	33	24	16	29	43	50	32	21	35	23	25	32	27	16
Latvia	na	58	55	60	54	55	62	63	60	46	62	58	51	62	58	38
Lithuania	na	56	56	56	58	55	55	65	57	38	64	50	55	61	54	46
Luxembourg	na	45	45	45	47	42	47	50	46	35	55	49	34	53	45	31
Macedonia	na	74	76	73	77	70	76	79	72	71	74	76	70	75	73	74
Malta	na	19	21	17	25	15	19	17	21	16	17	15	10	20	19	15
Mexico	na	56	53	59	54	56	60	64	52	38	65	55	49	57	57	49
Moldova	na	62	63	62	64	57	67	70	64	53	62	61	63	62	62	63
Montenegro	na	15	15	15	11	13	20	21	15	4	18	16	13	17	12	8
Morocco	na	18	19	17	16	19	22	17	21	14	24	14	23	20	18	16
Netherlands	na	27	25	29	17	24	35	43	26	13	31	27	21	40	28	18
New Zealand	na	19	18	19	23	15	21	25	19	11	25	17	13	22	18	10
Nigeria	na	43	41	45	41	45	44	49	39	39	40	43	46	41	42	45
Northern Ireland	na	19	19	20	27	17	15	22	19	14	19	20	19	17	19	19
Norway	na	14	15	13	14	13	15	20	13	9	na	na	na	25	13	6
Pakistan	na	34	33	35	33	33	38	35	34	29	36	34	28	36	31	50
Peru	na	39	38	39	39	37	41	48	39	32	41	38	36	42	38	37
Philippines	na	63	65	60	65	60	63	69	61	57	62	64	61	61	64	53
Poland	na	22	27	17	21	23	22	28	17	15	23	24	17	25	21	21
Portugal	na	36	36	35	29	39	37	33	39	41	47	37	27	36	37	25
Puerto Rico	na	33	31	35	40	32	31	38	40	28	39	33	29	36	33	31
Romania	na	67	61	73	61	62	74	82	64	48	78	71	56	74	63	39
Russian Fed.	na	49	50	48	47	49	50	60	51	39	53	50	44	51	47	45
Serbia	na	19	18	21	17	16	24	31	17	9	25	21	16	25	16	4
Singapore	na	23	21	25	25	20	22	21	25	16	24	21	23	15	25	22
Slovakia	na	20	19	20	18	18	23	23	19	12	25	22	15	24	16	17
Slovenia	na	24	23	25	22	21	29	33	24	8	34	21	16	34	23	14
South Africa	na	34	33	36	34	34	35	37	31	35	32	35	35	34	31	56
Spain	na	21	21	21	19	16	27	22	21	18	23	19	22	28	22	12
Sweden	na	22	24	19	16	20	26	37	20	11	24	26	14	33	24	10
Switzerland	na	31	32	30	27	34	31	36	31	25	37	30	29	43	32	26
Taiwan	na	41	38	44	44	38	48	52	38	34	43	43	36	42	41	32
Tanzania	na	3	2	3	3	2	4	4	1	2	4	2	1	2	3	na
Turkey	na	71	68	75	70	71	74	76	68	59	75	70	64	75	73	60
Uganda	na	30	39	22	25	36	33	30	26	67	37	44	28	29	29	39
Ukraine	na	60	60	59	52	60	64	68	61	52	62	59	57	65	58	43
United States	na	30	30	29	37	29	25	43	33	22	35	29	24	37	31	24
Uruguay	na	27	29	26	28	25	29	34	19	17	31	30	21	38	28	18
Venezuela	na	48	49	46	50	46	47	51	48	45	55	46	45	51	48	42
Vietnam	na	99	99	99	99	100	99	99	100	100	100	99	99	99	100	100
Zimbabwe	na	27	26	27	32	24	20	26	28	30	28	30	23	27	27	23
Total	na	33	33	33	34	32	34	37	34	26	37	34	31	37	32	24

RANKING

Country	2000
Vietnam	99
Macedonia	74
Turkey	71
Romania	67
Georgia	66
Philippines	63
Moldova	62
Brazil	61
Ukraine	60
El Salvador	59
India	59
Latvia	58
Mexico	56
Lithuania	56
Colombia	54
Armenia	53
Russian Fed.	49
Venezuela	48
Bulgaria	48
Luxembourg	45
Chile	43
Nigeria	43
Jordan	42
Argentina	42
Taiwan	41
Belarus	40
Algeria	39
Iran	39
Peru	39
Bosnia and Herz.	37
Portugal	36
France	35
South Africa	34
Pakistan	34
Belgium	33
Puerto Rico	33
Switzerland	31
Uganda	30
United States	30
Korea, South	28
Japan	28
Dominican Rep.	28
Uruguay	27
Netherlands	27
Zimbabwe	27
Ireland	27
Finland	27
Australia	25
Great Britain	25
Slovenia	24
Canada	23
Singapore	23
Poland	22
Hungary	22
Sweden	22
Spain	21
Slovakia	20
Serbia	19
Indonesia	19
Northern Ireland	19
Malta	19
New Zealand	19
China	19
Estonia	18
Morocco	18
Albania	17
Czech Republic	17
Germany	16
Austria	16
Italy	16
Montenegro	15
Denmark	14
Norway	14
Croatia	12
Bangladesh	12
Iceland	11
Greece	9
Egypt	8
Azerbaijan	7
Tanzania	3
Total	33

E115) HAVING EXPERTS MAKE DECISIONS

I'm going to describe various types of political systems and ask what you think about each as a way of governing this country.
Having experts, not government, make decisions according to what they think is best for the country

Very good / Fairly good (%)   (WVS: V165; EVS: V217)

Country	Wave 1990	Wave 2000	Gender Male	Gender Female	Age 16-29	Age 30-49	Age 50+	Education Lower	Education Middle	Education Upper	Income Lower	Income Middle	Income Upper	Values Mat	Values Mixed	Values Postm.
Albania	na	88	90	86	87	88	89	90	86	89	88	87	87	90	86	77
Algeria	na	81	80	81	80	82	80	77	81	81	79	86	80	78	82	81
Argentina	na	54	54	55	54	54	55	61	48	42	56	58	48	59	56	47
Armenia	na	55	55	55	57	55	52	57	55	55	56	54	50	47	62	54
Australia	na	42	42	43	49	38	41	47	44	37	46	38	41	50	43	39
Austria	na	61	59	62	59	61	61	62	62	51	63	60	59	62	61	60
Azerbaijan	na	2	1	2	3	1	1	1	1	3	1	2	3	1	3	2
Bangladesh	na	77	75	79	78	77	68	76	78	76	72	82	73	78	75	89
Belarus	na	79	75	83	83	80	74	77	80	80	80	79	78	76	79	88
Belgium	na	58	56	61	64	56	58	60	59	56	58	56	58	67	60	48
Bosnia and Herz.	na	74	71	76	74	73	75	75	72	79	77	72	76	76	74	75
Brazil	na	83	85	81	80	87	82	84	83	82	80	87	83	84	83	82
Bulgaria	na	82	78	87	77	84	84	86	82	80	89	78	80	83	81	81
Canada	na	44	41	47	53	43	40	48	47	36	49	42	44	51	46	41
Chile	na	59	60	57	66	57	54	59	60	53	60	58	58	62	60	48
China	na	30	31	30	34	32	19	27	31	46	22	33	33	31	30	36
Colombia	na	71	72	70	72	70	72	73	73	65	72	71	69	73	74	71
Croatia	na	88	88	88	86	92	85	88	89	86	85	89	90	93	89	84
Czech Republic	na	63	63	63	65	68	58	64	63	58	60	64	65	69	62	56
Denmark	na	30	27	32	37	29	27	33	25	25	35	29	22	36	32	19
Dominican Rep.	na	49	47	51	47	55	46	62	51	47	56	47	35	40	51	55
Egypt	na	67	70	64	66	66	72	68	65	69	67	66	71	68	66	70
El Salvador	na	69	69	68	71	68	66	70	70	63	70	70	61	na	na	na
Estonia	na	57	55	59	60	55	56	55	59	52	59	58	57	58	56	62
Finland	na	59	56	61	62	57	57	59	61	51	65	56	56	57	58	61
France	na	51	48	55	55	51	49	56	45	44	58	53	44	58	53	38
Georgia	na	58	61	56	59	61	54	60	57	60	58	57	59	54	61	62
Germany	na	56	57	55	53	56	57	57	56	50	62	61	57	60	53	58
Great Britain	na	47	45	49	54	48	43	49	50	37	57	44	41	na	na	na
Greece	na	13	18	10	8	15	20	16	16	11	15	15	12	20	12	8
Hungary	na	85	85	85	85	86	85	85	86	84	79	87	87	88	83	77
Iceland	na	42	35	49	46	41	40	48	39	35	46	41	39	46	43	29
India	na	68	67	69	69	67	67	69	69	65	72	73	63	73	65	76
Indonesia	na	48	51	44	40	55	44	45	49	50	48	47	50	39	54	58
Iran	na	27	30	23	24	29	32	32	23	27	31	27	23	25	29	26
Ireland	na	38	35	42	43	40	35	37	39	37	37	38	41	30	40	34
Israel	na	na	na	na	na	na	na	na	na	na	na	na	na	na	na	na
Italy	na	51	48	54	47	49	55	59	47	39	55	48	45	60	51	46
Japan	na	58	52	65	74	64	47	64	60	55	59	58	58	57	60	61
Jordan	na	88	88	89	88	88	89	89	89	87	90	87	89	92	86	85
Korea, South	na	53	54	51	55	55	46	51	49	59	51	53	55	53	51	66
Latvia	na	61	59	62	61	61	60	59	60	65	64	59	58	60	61	65
Lithuania	na	57	55	59	57	56	59	61	57	54	55	57	58	62	57	43
Luxembourg	na	46	45	47	51	44	46	53	44	40	53	46	38	39	50	33
Macedonia	na	84	84	84	86	83	83	88	84	79	86	85	80	81	85	84
Malta	na	34	35	33	40	33	31	31	35	40	29	35	37	32	36	28
Mexico	na	66	67	66	68	65	66	69	64	65	76	68	64	67	67	60
Moldova	na	51	50	52	54	51	48	50	49	53	62	46	48	50	57	29
Montenegro	na	89	89	89	87	89	91	90	88	90	92	90	85	91	87	86
Morocco	na	70	70	68	74	69	71	65	71	80	67	62	70	71	67	
Netherlands	na	40	38	42	46	38	39	47	42	31	41	44	37	46	43	31
New Zealand	na	42	40	43	49	46	35	44	41	39	42	42	40	53	40	37
Nigeria	na	73	71	75	74	72	77	74	74	72	73	71	75	72	75	68
Northern Ireland	na	38	36	40	47	40	31	39	38	35	35	40	46	38	38	35
Norway	na	34	34	34	43	34	28	35	35	32	na	na	na	41	34	27
Pakistan	na	19	19	19	24	17	16	17	24	16	16	20	18	20	17	20
Peru	na	63	63	63	63	62	65	67	65	58	64	62	62	67	62	63
Philippines	1990	62	61	63	64	59	67	62	63	62	56	63	68	59	65	61
Poland	na	88	88	88	96	86	85	87	87	93	86	89	89	87	89	88
Portugal	na	47	47	48	43	50	48	45	50	56	46	52	46	43	50	49
Puerto Rico	na	42	41	43	47	40	42	58	47	38	47	43	39	45	42	41
Romania	na	85	85	85	81	85	87	89	83	82	89	87	81	88	81	85
Russian Fed.	na	52	51	53	60	50	48	51	53	49	53	51	51	49	56	44
Serbia	na	88	85	92	88	88	89	88	87	90	87	88	89	90	86	86
Singapore	na	40	41	39	46	33	36	35	42	43	37	41	41	38	40	48
Slovakia	na	86	86	85	85	86	86	87	86	78	85	84	86	83	88	71
Slovenia	na	81	83	80	81	77	87	80	83	77	82	82	79	82	82	81
South Africa	na	52	47	58	52	52	50	53	50	58	47	57	55	50	53	55
Spain	na	44	44	45	43	40	49	42	46	45	49	41	40	47	43	43
Sweden	na	41	40	42	48	37	42	49	45	30	45	45	34	56	45	27
Switzerland	na	46	43	50	48	50	42	39	49	41	49	50	44	54	46	48
Taiwan	na	60	59	61	48	61	65	63	60	57	60	59	61	61	59	66
Tanzania	na	30	31	28	29	31	29	32	28	28	34	31	24	30	27	30
Turkey	na	74	72	76	77	73	70	75	73	69	76	74	72	75	74	74
Uganda	na	36	54	19	35	35	41	38	32	55	47	36	26	34	35	43
Ukraine	na	50	47	54	50	54	47	50	53	45	51	46	55	52	49	41
United States	na	44	42	46	50	48	33	53	46	40	46	42	43	52	45	40
Uruguay	na	40	41	39	43	37	41	46	34	29	43	39	36	42	41	36
Venezuela	na	69	69	68	69	68	69	69	69	68	69	68	70	66	68	74
Vietnam	na	98	98	98	99	98	98	99	98	97	97	98	98	100	97	98
Zimbabwe	na	69	71	67	69	71	68	69	70	70	69	70	73	72	69	53
Total	na	58	57	58	59	58	56	61	58	52	59	59	58	60	58	51

RANKING

Country	2000
Vietnam	98
Montenegro	89
Jordan	88
Croatia	88
Serbia	88
Poland	88
Albania	88
Slovakia	86
Hungary	85
Romania	85
Macedonia	84
Brazil	83
Bulgaria	82
Slovenia	81
Algeria	81
Belarus	79
Bangladesh	77
Turkey	74
Bosnia and Herz.	74
Nigeria	73
Colombia	71
Morocco	70
Zimbabwe	69
El Salvador	69
Venezuela	69
India	68
Egypt	67
Mexico	66
Czech Republic	63
Peru	63
Philippines	62
Austria	61
Latvia	61
Taiwan	60
Chile	59
Finland	59
Japan	58
Georgia	58
Belgium	58
Lithuania	57
Estonia	57
Germany	56
Armenia	55
Argentina	54
Korea, South	53
South Africa	52
Russian Fed.	52
France	51
Italy	51
Moldova	51
Ukraine	50
Dominican Rep.	49
Indonesia	48
Portugal	47
Great Britain	47
Luxembourg	46
Switzerland	46
Canada	44
Spain	44
United States	44
Puerto Rico	42
Australia	42
Iceland	42
New Zealand	42
Sweden	41
Netherlands	40
Singapore	40
Uruguay	40
Ireland	38
Northern Ireland	38
Uganda	36
Malta	34
Norway	34
China	30
Tanzania	30
Denmark	30
Iran	27
Pakistan	19
Greece	13
Azerbaijan	2
Total	58

E116) HAVING THE ARMY RULE

I'm going to describe various types of political systems and ask what you think about each as a way of governing this country.

Having the army rule

Very good / Fairly good (%)

(WVS: V166; EVS: V218)

Country	Wave		Gender		Age			Education			Income			Values		
	1990	2000	Male	Female	16-29	30-49	50+	Lower	Middle	Upper	Lower	Middle	Upper	Mat	Mixed	Postm.
Albania	na	12	12	11	15	11	9	11	12	13	11	13	11	10	9	40
Algeria	na	19	21	18	16	19	29	30	19	13	21	19	18	20	20	12
Argentina	na	18	19	16	15	18	20	23	11	7	22	20	10	28	17	10
Armenia	na	19	17	20	18	18	21	24	20	13	15	20	26	15	22	22
Australia	na	7	6	8	10	6	6	10	8	3	10	5	5	11	8	4
Austria	na	2	1	2	3	1	2	3	1	na	4	1	2	14	1	na
Azerbaijan	na	2	3	2	2	2	4	2	2	2	2	2	4	2	3	na
Bangladesh	na	19	17	21	19	20	15	22	16	16	18	22	15	17	19	26
Belarus	na	20	20	20	15	18	26	27	19	12	18	21	17	25	17	14
Belgium	na	5	3	6	5	4	5	7	5	2	6	5	3	8	5	1
Bosnia and Herz.	na	9	7	11	10	8	10	15	9	5	10	11	7	10	9	10
Brazil	na	45	44	47	46	45	45	60	39	20	57	44	35	63	41	26
Bulgaria	na	12	13	11	9	11	15	18	12	7	15	11	11	14	10	9
Canada	na	6	4	8	6	6	6	8	6	3	9	6	3	6	7	3
Chile	na	24	25	24	24	22	28	28	24	17	26	25	20	31	24	15
China	na	45	39	52	37	48	43	59	40	18	55	46	31	44	44	32
Colombia	na	34	33	35	37	30	36	39	36	23	39	33	28	43	39	34
Croatia	na	6	5	6	8	4	6	11	3	3	9	5	5	9	6	1
Czech Republic	na	2	2	3	2	1	3	3	2	na	3	3	1	3	2	2
Denmark	na	1	1	1	1	1	1	1	na	na	1	1	1	1	1	na
Dominican Rep.	na	6	6	7	7	6	na	7	4	7	9	4	8	14	5	2
Egypt	na	na	na	na	na	na	na	na	na	na	na	na	na	na	na	na
El Salvador	na	39	33	45	38	40	40	51	31	23	51	36	19	na	na	na
Estonia	na	3	3	3	4	3	3	4	4	2	4	2	3	3	3	3
Finland	na	6	7	5	5	5	7	9	4	na	10	5	4	8	5	6
France	na	4	3	5	6	3	4	5	4	1	6	3	2	6	4	1
Georgia	na	11	13	10	13	10	12	9	13	7	13	10	10	10	13	7
Germany	na	2	2	1	2	1	2	2	2	1	3	2	1	1	2	1
Great Britain	na	7	7	7	11	6	6	10	5	6	14	4	4	na	na	na
Greece	na	10	11	9	10	9	11	12	14	6	9	10	10	12	9	7
Hungary	na	3	3	3	4	1	5	4	2	1	6	2	3	4	3	na
Iceland	na	1	1	na	na	1	1	1	1	na	1	na	na	1	1	na
India	na	20	20	20	19	21	21	22	22	15	32	22	14	20	21	14
Indonesia	na	96	95	98	97	95	97	97	95	98	96	96	96	95	98	89
Iran	na	84	84	84	84	83	84	84	84	83	83	85	82	91	80	82
Ireland	na	5	4	6	5	4	5	7	4	1	6	6	2	5	3	6
Israel	na	na	na	na	na	na	na	na	na	na	na	na	na	na	na	na
Italy	na	4	3	5	4	3	6	7	3	1	7	3	3	5	5	2
Japan	na	2	2	1	2	2	2	4	2	1	2	1	2	1	2	na
Jordan	na	58	48	67	62	57	51	59	62	51	64	53	55	62	55	48
Korea, South	na	4	4	4	1	4	6	10	4	3	5	2	4	4	4	na
Latvia	na	5	5	6	8	4	6	11	4	4	7	5	4	5	6	2
Lithuania	na	4	4	4	3	4	5	5	4	2	4	4	3	4	4	2
Luxembourg	na	7	9	5	9	6	6	8	7	3	11	4	5	10	6	3
Macedonia	na	26	20	20	29	23	27	31	25	19	28	28	21	22	28	20
Malta	na	4	4	4	4	3	5	7	3	2	4	3	3	6	4	1
Mexico	na	35	32	39	36	33	39	43	31	17	41	35	29	37	36	29
Moldova	na	14	15	13	13	15	13	13	17	9	18	16	11	15	12	12
Montenegro	na	7	7	7	2	7	10	11	6	2	12	8	5	10	4	na
Morocco	na	15	16	15	14	15	19	18	7	6	17	7	14	18	14	9
Netherlands	na	1	1	2	2	1	1	3	1	na	2	1	na	5	na	2
New Zealand	na	2	3	2	4	2	2	3	2	1	5	1	1	2	2	1
Nigeria	na	26	25	27	26	26	24	32	23	22	28	21	29	24	28	20
Northern Ireland	na	2	2	2	2	2	2	3	1	2	2	3	1	3	2	1
Norway	na	5	4	6	7	3	4	9	5	1	na	na	na	9	4	2
Pakistan	na	4	3	5	6	3	4	5	5	2	5	5	2	5	4	8
Peru	na	15	16	14	17	13	12	18	15	12	18	13	11	20	13	14
Philippines	na	49	49	50	51	49	48	55	49	42	48	50	50	47	52	46
Poland	na	17	16	18	20	16	16	22	13	7	19	18	12	18	17	15
Portugal	na	9	9	10	6	10	11	10	8	11	11	13	7	8	11	7
Puerto Rico	na	11	12	10	10	9	12	18	15	8	14	10	8	10	10	12
Romania	na	28	23	33	24	21	37	44	22	17	40	28	20	30	27	15
Russian Fed.	na	19	22	17	20	17	21	27	21	11	21	20	17	17	21	23
Serbia	na	10	10	11	11	6	14	17	9	4	16	12	4	15	7	1
Singapore	na	13	11	15	19	8	7	17	12	6	20	13	9	8	15	18
Slovakia	na	7	6	8	7	8	8	9	7	4	10	8	5	9	7	2
Slovenia	na	5	4	5	4	5	5	9	3	1	9	3	2	7	4	5
South Africa	na	22	23	20	20	23	20	26	17	19	26	24	14	17	23	32
Spain	na	7	7	7	5	7	9	7	8	6	9	6	9	10	8	3
Sweden	na	7	7	7	7	4	9	12	6	4	10	6	3	13	8	2
Switzerland	na	5	5	5	6	2	8	10	4	1	4	8	3	7	6	2
Taiwan	na	16	11	20	11	16	17	23	14	11	21	16	10	17	14	15
Tanzania	na	14	12	16	20	11	8	16	13	8	19	11	8	13	14	9
Turkey	na	29	25	33	28	29	30	35	25	10	33	27	22	34	29	21
Uganda	na	34	32	36	32	37	28	38	32	40	39	39	29	32	32	46
Ukraine	na	13	13	13	10	11	16	21	14	9	18	12	10	14	13	10
United States	na	9	8	9	11	8	8	18	8	6	11	9	5	17	9	5
Uruguay	na	8	6	10	7	8	9	11	4	6	12	7	7	16	5	6
Venezuela	na	23	24	21	25	18	27	25	25	14	26	25	19	25	22	21
Vietnam	na	99	99	99	100	99	98	99	98	99	99	99	99	99	99	100
Zimbabwe	na	12	11	13	17	9	5	12	13	na	13	13	9	10	13	21
Total	na	16	16	17	19	16	15	21	15	12	20	17	14	19	16	10

RANKING

Country	2000
Vietnam	99
Indonesia	96
Iran	84
Jordan	58
Philippines	49
Brazil	45
China	45
El Salvador	39
Mexico	35
Uganda	34
Colombia	34
Turkey	29
Romania	28
Nigeria	26
Macedonia	26
Chile	24
Venezuela	23
South Africa	22
India	20
Belarus	20
Algeria	19
Russian Fed.	19
Bangladesh	19
Armenia	19
Argentina	18
Poland	17
Taiwan	16
Morocco	15
Peru	15
Tanzania	14
Moldova	14
Singapore	13
Ukraine	13
Bulgaria	12
Zimbabwe	12
Albania	12
Georgia	11
Puerto Rico	11
Serbia	10
Greece	10
Portugal	9
Bosnia and Herz.	9
United States	9
Uruguay	8
Slovakia	7
Spain	7
Australia	7
Great Britain	7
Luxembourg	7
Sweden	7
Montenegro	7
Dominican Rep.	6
Finland	6
Canada	6
Croatia	6
Latvia	5
Switzerland	5
Ireland	5
Norway	5
Slovenia	5
Belgium	5
Italy	4
Pakistan	4
Malta	4
France	4
Korea, South	4
Lithuania	4
Estonia	3
Hungary	3
Azerbaijan	2
Czech Republic	2
New Zealand	2
Northern Ireland	2
Austria	2
Japan	2
Germany	2
Netherlands	1
Denmark	1
Iceland	1
Total	16

E117) HAVING A DEMOCRATIC POLITICAL SYSTEM

I'm going to describe various types of political systems and ask what you think about each as a way of governing this country.

Having a democratic political system

Very good / Fairly good (%)

(WVS: V167; EVS: V219)

Country	Wave		Gender		Age			Education			Income			Values			RANKING	
	1990	2000	Male	Female	16-29	30-49	50+	Lower	Middle	Upper	Lower	Middle	Upper	Mat	Mixed	Postm.	Country	2000
Albania	na	98	98	97	98	98	96	97	97	100	97	98	98	99	97	97	Egypt	99
Algeria	na	93	92	93	92	93	93	95	91	93	92	95	91	93	92	96	Bangladesh	98
Argentina	na	91	90	91	88	91	93	86	97	97	86	90	96	85	90	95	Denmark	98
Armenia	na	85	86	84	87	87	78	77	84	91	89	85	76	79	90	90	Greece	98
Australia	na	87	90	85	80	90	90	80	85	96	86	88	91	81	86	90	Iceland	98
Austria	na	96	97	96	97	96	97	95	97	98	95	97	96	89	96	98	Albania	98
Azerbaijan	na	98	98	97	98	97	97	99	98	96	98	96	97	98	97	97	Croatia	98
Bangladesh	na	98	98	99	99	98	98	98	98	100	98	99	98	98	99	97	Azerbaijan	98
Belarus	na	88	89	88	90	89	86	84	89	93	90	87	88	88	89	92	Sweden	97
Belgium	na	89	91	88	92	88	89	79	89	97	87	87	93	80	89	97	Italy	97
Bosnia and Herz.	na	92	92	92	94	92	90	92	92	94	93	91	93	94	91	98	Netherlands	97
Brazil	na	85	85	85	84	86	85	80	87	96	84	83	87	79	87	87	China	96
Bulgaria	na	86	89	84	93	86	83	82	85	93	80	89	89	82	89	94	Norway	96
Canada	na	88	90	87	86	86	93	81	87	97	83	86	93	89	86	93	Austria	96
Chile	na	85	85	84	84	85	85	84	84	89	82	87	87	80	86	90	Uruguay	96
China	na	96	97	95	95	97	96	95	97	95	96	97	96	96	97	93	Morocco	96
Colombia	na	85	86	85	86	86	84	80	85	95	82	86	90	80	84	88	Indonesia	96
Croatia	na	98	98	98	97	98	98	97	99	98	96	98	98	100	97	99	Vietnam	96
Czech Republic	na	93	92	93	92	93	92	89	96	98	89	93	95	87	94	97	Nigeria	95
Denmark	na	98	98	98	96	99	98	97	100	99	97	98	99	92	98	100	Germany	95
Dominican Rep.	na	91	93	90	90	93	91	90	93	91	93	92	93	84	91	99	Spain	95
Egypt	na	99	99	98	99	98	99	99	98	99	98	99	99	98	99	98	Montenegro	95
El Salvador	na	86	88	83	82	86	91	83	86	90	82	86	90	na	na	na	Jordan	94
Estonia	na	87	84	90	84	86	89	82	87	92	84	86	89	85	88	89	Serbia	94
Finland	na	87	88	87	89	91	83	83	92	96	85	86	92	83	89	85	Singapore	94
France	na	89	90	89	87	89	91	86	90	97	89	89	93	87	89	93	Malta	94
Georgia	na	91	91	91	91	91	90	92	90	93	88	93	93	90	91	93	Venezuela	94
Germany	na	95	95	95	93	96	95	94	95	98	95	96	94	96	94	97	Switzerland	93
Great Britain	na	88	89	87	83	88	90	84	89	94	85	91	86	na	na	na	Taiwan	93
Greece	na	98	98	98	97	98	98	96	98	98	99	97	98	99	98	99	Peru	93
Hungary	na	87	90	84	84	88	89	84	93	96	83	87	89	86	88	88	Uganda	93
Iceland	na	98	98	98	97	98	99	97	98	100	97	99	99	95	99	100	Tanzania	93
India	na	93	93	93	95	92	92	91	93	96	89	93	94	95	93	92	India	93
Indonesia	na	96	97	95	95	96	97	97	96	95	95	96	97	96	96	96	Algeria	93
Iran	na	86	87	83	82	88	93	86	85	88	84	88	84	83	86	91	Czech Republic	93
Ireland	na	91	92	90	89	90	93	87	91	98	91	87	93	88	90	96	Bosnia and Herz.	92
Israel	na	na	na	na	na	na	na	na	na	na	na	na	na	na	na	na	Northern Ireland	92
Italy	na	97	97	97	94	97	98	96	97	98	96	98	98	96	97	96	Japan	92
Japan	na	92	92	92	94	92	91	90	92	94	91	91	94	92	92	98	Luxembourg	92
Jordan	na	94	95	94	95	94	93	93	96	96	94	95	94	96	94	89	Turkey	92
Korea, South	na	85	85	84	81	86	87	80	85	84	84	87	84	86	84	86	Macedonia	91
Latvia	na	88	87	89	80	89	91	83	88	95	87	87	91	89	88	87	Dominican Rep.	91
Lithuania	na	86	84	88	90	86	83	82	86	91	82	83	90	81	86	97	Puerto Rico	91
Luxembourg	na	92	91	93	91	94	90	87	94	98	90	92	94	91	93	92	Ireland	91
Macedonia	na	91	93	90	92	91	92	88	92	95	90	90	95	90	92	95	Argentina	91
Malta	na	94	94	93	95	92	94	90	94	100	90	97	94	93	94	98	Georgia	91
Mexico	na	86	87	86	85	85	89	85	85	92	87	87	88	84	85	89	Portugal	91
Moldova	na	75	74	75	79	79	66	66	73	83	70	72	79	70	80	78	South Africa	90
Montenegro	na	95	94	95	96	95	93	93	94	98	93	95	98	93	97	94	Slovenia	90
Morocco	na	96	96	96	96	96	93	95	98	97	96	94	95	96	95	97	France	89
Netherlands	na	97	97	96	96	96	97	91	99	99	94	97	98	92	97	97	Belgium	89
New Zealand	na	87	90	85	81	90	89	84	84	95	87	87	91	88	88	94	United States	89
Nigeria	na	95	96	95	95	96	93	93	96	97	94	96	97	95	95	97	Romania	89
Northern Ireland	na	92	93	91	88	92	94	91	93	93	92	92	91	95	92	88	Belarus	88
Norway	na	96	96	96	94	97	98	94	96	99	na	na	na	90	97	99	Canada	88
Pakistan	na	88	89	88	89	88	86	89	88	86	88	89	89	88	88	91	Latvia	88
Peru	na	93	93	94	93	94	93	92	92	95	92	93	95	92	93	94	Pakistan	88
Philippines	na	82	83	82	84	82	80	81	81	86	79	84	84	81	84	81	Zimbabwe	88
Poland	na	84	84	83	86	82	84	79	87	94	78	88	82	81	85	89	Great Britain	88
Portugal	na	91	89	92	92	87	93	89	93	96	89	86	93	91	90	92	Finland	87
Puerto Rico	na	91	91	92	85	92	94	89	90	92	92	92	91	96	90	93	Australia	87
Romania	na	89	89	89	92	89	87	83	90	94	86	89	91	86	90	96	New Zealand	87
Russian Fed.	na	63	65	62	75	64	53	43	59	81	53	59	74	56	69	66	Hungary	87
Serbia	na	94	95	93	95	96	92	88	95	99	90	94	97	92	96	99	Estonia	87
Singapore	na	94	94	94	94	94	95	95	92	98	90	93	96	95	94	94	Bulgaria	86
Slovakia	na	84	84	84	90	84	80	80	85	92	78	85	89	83	85	98	Lithuania	86
Slovenia	na	90	92	88	89	88	92	83	90	97	86	89	95	81	91	92	Mexico	86
South Africa	na	90	88	92	94	86	91	90	90	93	91	92	88	91	89	93	Iran	86
Spain	na	95	95	95	95	95	95	96	94	95	94	94	94	95	94	97	El Salvador	86
Sweden	na	97	97	98	96	98	98	97	96	100	96	98	99	92	98	98	Colombia	85
Switzerland	na	93	92	94	90	93	95	90	94	94	92	91	95	90	94	94	Armenia	85
Taiwan	na	93	95	91	92	93	94	90	93	96	89	95	95	92	95	92	Brazil	85
Tanzania	na	93	95	90	94	93	92	88	98	99	88	94	99	96	92	100	Chile	85
Turkey	na	92	92	92	91	92	94	90	92	97	91	92	94	91	91	94	Korea, South	85
Uganda	na	93	98	89	94	94	84	85	96	94	96	97	94	94	93	89	Ukraine	85
Ukraine	na	85	85	84	85	89	79	70	85	89	79	86	90	83	85	87	Slovakia	84
United States	na	89	91	88	85	88	94	80	87	94	86	90	93	85	89	91	Poland	84
Uruguay	na	96	96	96	95	96	97	95	99	96	97	94	98	95	97	98	Philippines	82
Venezuela	na	94	94	93	91	95	95	91	93	97	91	92	96	93	93	97	Moldova	75
Vietnam	na	96	95	96	96	96	95	97	93	99	97	96	93	91	96	93	Russian Fed.	63
Zimbabwe	na	88	90	87	86	90	90	88	88	100	86	89	94	91	87	84		
Total	na	91	92	91	91	91	91	89	91	94	89	91	93	89	92	94	Total	91

E120) IN DEMOCRACY, THE ECONOMIC SYSTEM RUNS BADLY

I'm going to read off some things that people sometimes say about a democratic political system. In democracy, the economic system runs badly

Disagree / Strongly disagree (%)

(WVS: V169; EVS: V221)

Country	Wave 1990	Wave 2000	Gender Male	Gender Female	Age 16-29	Age 30-49	Age 50+	Education Lower	Education Middle	Education Upper	Income Lower	Income Middle	Income Upper	Values Mat	Values Mixed	Values Postm.	RANKING Country	2000
Albania	na	79	82	76	87	75	78	77	76	90	76	77	85	82	78	77	Netherlands	92
Algeria	na	69	68	70	64	72	75	81	65	68	61	73	72	70	69	68	Sweden	90
Argentina	na	55	58	52	53	56	55	47	62	76	47	53	65	45	54	64	Bangladesh	90
Armenia	na	58	61	55	64	58	47	52	55	69	67	55	46	50	62	83	Germany	88
Australia	na	70	69	71	62	74	73	55	67	85	64	73	78	68	70	71	Malta	88
Austria	na	87	88	86	85	89	86	85	88	95	83	85	90	70	87	91	Iceland	88
Azerbaijan	na	84	84	83	87	83	80	81	83	85	82	84	85	82	86	91	Austria	87
Bangladesh	na	90	89	90	91	89	87	91	89	87	91	90	89	91	89	92	Denmark	85
Belarus	na	69	73	64	80	70	54	55	70	79	65	66	78	63	71	91	Azerbaijan	84
Belgium	na	67	70	64	67	68	65	51	65	79	57	63	75	61	67	74	Vietnam	82
Bosnia and Herz.	na	75	75	76	77	75	74	75	74	81	72	75	79	76	75	75	Korea, South	82
Brazil	na	30	34	25	27	31	32	29	25	48	32	21	34	25	32	28	Egypt	82
Bulgaria	na	60	61	59	77	61	49	38	63	79	45	60	70	49	69	81	Uruguay	81
Canada	na	73	76	69	69	74	73	58	69	89	62	69	84	65	70	79	Uganda	80
Chile	na	63	65	61	58	65	64	62	64	63	60	65	64	66	60	70	Ireland	80
China	na	74	78	70	76	72	78	73	75	75	76	71	75	75	74	65	Finland	80
Colombia	na	na	na	na	na	na	na	na	na	na	na	na	na	na	na	na	Montenegro	80
Croatia	na	71	73	69	73	72	69	67	70	85	69	67	77	66	69	81	Japan	79
Czech Republic	na	63	66	60	67	68	57	53	70	85	54	62	72	51	65	76	Luxembourg	79
Denmark	na	85	86	84	81	86	86	80	92	89	81	84	91	70	85	92	Northern Ireland	79
Dominican Rep.	na	73	72	74	72	75	90	71	61	78	69	74	82	63	74	81	Albania	79
Egypt	na	82	81	83	80	82	86	85	79	80	83	85	82	84	82	73	Indonesia	78
El Salvador	na	na	na	na	na	na	na	na	na	na	na	na	na	na	na	na	United States	78
Estonia	na	69	72	66	75	70	65	64	70	72	65	63	72	65	71	83	Switzerland	78
Finland	na	80	80	80	83	82	76	75	85	87	76	83	82	76	82	80	Spain	76
France	na	50	52	48	43	54	49	41	57	67	44	47	60	41	50	65	Bosnia and Herz.	75
Georgia	na	69	70	68	71	71	65	70	67	76	63	71	77	69	69	73	China	74
Germany	na	88	89	88	85	89	89	87	88	94	83	88	89	87	88	91	Taiwan	74
Great Britain	na	71	69	73	66	73	73	74	68	69	71	70	76	na	na	na	Dominican Rep.	73
Greece	na	58	60	57	60	56	55	37	51	68	53	56	62	52	61	60	Tanzania	73
Hungary	na	61	63	58	64	64	55	51	72	84	51	59	66	59	62	72	Canada	73
Iceland	na	88	88	87	88	92	82	82	90	94	83	90	91	83	88	94	New Zealand	72
India	na	57	57	56	60	56	55	49	60	64	50	57	59	63	54	40	Great Britain	71
Indonesia	na	78	79	78	76	78	81	76	80	79	73	83	82	78	79	82	Croatia	71
Iran	na	67	69	65	68	67	64	68	67	67	64	70	68	70	67	70	Australia	70
Ireland	na	80	83	78	84	81	77	72	83	89	71	79	88	83	79	86	Zimbabwe	70
Israel	na	na	na	na	na	na	na	na	na	na	na	na	na	na	na	na	Serbia	70
Italy	na	67	70	64	68	71	62	55	71	87	58	69	75	59	66	71	Georgia	69
Japan	na	79	80	79	75	86	75	68	77	89	72	82	83	81	80	86	Algeria	69
Jordan	na	67	71	64	63	69	74	65	70	67	71	71	59	63	69	76	Estonia	69
Korea, South	na	82	81	83	86	82	76	75	79	86	77	86	85	80	83	88	Turkey	69
Latvia	na	52	56	49	58	52	50	42	50	70	46	49	62	47	55	60	Belarus	69
Lithuania	na	60	62	59	70	63	49	47	60	75	50	52	69	59	58	79	Iran	67
Luxembourg	na	79	78	81	77	81	79	76	77	88	74	78	83	71	81	86	Jordan	67
Macedonia	na	55	55	55	60	57	48	51	55	62	44	61	60	52	56	71	Belgium	67
Malta	na	88	87	89	86	89	88	84	89	95	84	87	87	87	87	97	Italy	67
Mexico	na	45	46	43	46	43	46	42	41	64	42	44	52	44	46	40	Norway	66
Moldova	na	58	61	54	58	64	50	48	58	64	51	57	61	52	64	69	Morocco	65
Montenegro	na	80	81	80	86	83	74	75	79	90	73	79	87	79	81	89	Ukraine	64
Morocco	na	65	67	61	66	65	59	63	66	73	52	69	72	64	64	73	Czech Republic	63
Netherlands	na	92	93	90	93	93	89	82	94	97	88	93	95	82	92	95	Nigeria	63
New Zealand	na	72	76	69	61	82	66	61	73	84	63	73	83	74	74	80	Chile	63
Nigeria	na	63	64	62	62	65	60	56	68	67	56	69	68	63	64	61	Pakistan	61
Northern Ireland	na	79	78	81	72	80	81	78	77	85	76	79	83	78	80	77	Portugal	61
Norway	na	66	72	61	64	68	66	58	65	77	na	na	na	54	67	79	Hungary	61
Pakistan	na	61	66	56	57	62	68	60	58	71	60	63	63	61	61	71	Lithuania	60
Peru	na	45	44	46	43	47	44	44	43	49	44	41	51	43	45	45	Bulgaria	60
Philippines	na	48	49	47	47	50	47	45	50	49	48	48	48	46	49	61	Greece	58
Poland	na	53	54	52	54	56	50	42	62	75	44	56	66	47	58	52	Armenia	58
Portugal	na	61	63	58	60	59	63	58	64	67	54	55	64	63	61	52	Moldova	58
Puerto Rico	na	51	61	45	49	48	55	41	47	55	48	56	50	58	49	53	India	57
Romania	na	44	48	40	56	45	36	30	46	63	30	36	58	35	49	76	Venezuela	56
Russian Fed.	na	45	48	43	58	49	32	18	43	65	36	42	56	38	51	61	South Africa	56
Serbia	na	70	71	68	73	73	63	57	70	81	57	70	79	66	71	78	Macedonia	55
Singapore	na	na	na	na	na	na	na	na	na	na	na	na	na	na	na	na	Argentina	55
Slovakia	na	52	52	51	55	54	46	46	52	66	40	50	61	47	56	59	Poland	53
Slovenia	na	53	60	47	62	58	41	33	56	77	36	55	76	44	55	57	Slovenia	53
South Africa	na	56	56	56	57	56	56	46	68	62	53	50	68	62	53	49	Latvia	52
Spain	na	76	76	77	76	78	75	75	76	82	71	79	80	70	79	76	Slovakia	52
Sweden	na	90	90	90	93	90	88	78	91	97	87	87	98	80	90	95	Puerto Rico	51
Switzerland	na	78	78	77	79	76	78	69	78	86	72	72	88	73	76	85	France	50
Taiwan	na	74	75	73	77	76	63	66	76	78	70	77	74	69	78	77	Philippines	48
Tanzania	na	73	79	65	72	74	72	67	79	81	69	75	78	74	74	65	Russian Fed.	45
Turkey	na	69	71	66	68	70	66	64	71	87	66	68	74	66	68	74	Peru	45
Uganda	na	80	77	84	85	79	67	67	87	69	71	79	81	80	82	75	Mexico	45
Ukraine	na	64	69	58	73	68	53	38	63	75	56	65	70	56	67	82	Romania	44
United States	na	78	80	75	72	78	82	61	76	86	74	79	83	74	78	80	Brazil	30
Uruguay	na	81	86	77	80	81	81	79	83	86	79	83	81	79	80	84		
Venezuela	na	56	55	57	55	54	59	54	53	67	51	56	60	56	57	58		
Vietnam	na	82	85	80	83	82	82	81	84	82	75	86	82	74	84	88		
Zimbabwe	na	70	72	68	68	73	69	70	70	85	67	70	75	78	65	60		
Total	na	68	70	66	68	70	66	63	68	76	63	68	73	64	69	74	Total	68

E121) DEMOCRACIES ARE INDECISIVE

I'm going to read off some things that people sometimes say about a democratic political system. Democracies are indecisive and have too much quibbling

Disagree / Strongly disagree (%)

(WVS: V170; EVS: V222)

Country	Wave 1990	Wave 2000	Gender Male	Gender Female	Age 16-29	Age 30-49	Age 50+	Education Lower	Education Middle	Education Upper	Income Lower	Income Middle	Income Upper	Values Mat	Values Mixed	Values Postm.
Albania	na	72	71	72	74	72	69	68	72	78	67	71	79	74	72	62
Algeria	na	37	37	37	33	41	38	43	36	34	32	37	41	39	35	46
Argentina	na	33	33	34	32	31	37	26	40	55	25	33	42	30	31	41
Armenia	na	42	44	41	52	37	34	43	39	52	50	37	34	34	47	69
Australia	na	50	51	49	42	54	53	37	46	65	44	49	61	48	48	55
Austria	na	60	56	64	63	62	56	56	61	71	56	57	64	41	60	63
Azerbaijan	na	81	81	80	83	81	75	76	81	81	80	80	80	79	84	91
Bangladesh	na	87	86	88	86	87	87	92	84	82	88	88	87	88	87	83
Belarus	na	60	64	57	67	59	54	49	62	65	56	60	68	56	62	77
Belgium	na	40	43	36	47	43	33	27	37	52	28	36	48	32	39	50
Bosnia and Herz.	na	55	54	55	56	54	56	56	53	59	54	56	56	53	56	51
Brazil	na	16	19	14	15	16	19	17	13	23	18	11	18	14	17	18
Bulgaria	na	58	58	57	71	60	48	38	62	70	46	57	65	49	64	70
Canada	na	50	51	49	47	49	53	37	46	66	41	47	60	45	47	57
Chile	na	56	55	56	54	57	56	50	58	63	48	64	58	54	53	68
China	na	65	66	64	63	64	71	68	63	73	72	65	58	66	64	71
Colombia	na	na	na	na	na	na	na	na	na	na	na	na	na	na	na	na
Croatia	na	74	75	73	82	75	68	69	74	86	76	71	75	71	72	83
Czech Republic	na	49	49	49	57	54	40	39	57	66	41	47	58	39	49	67
Denmark	na	57	59	55	59	62	50	46	69	67	48	58	71	32	55	73
Dominican Rep.	na	61	58	63	62	57	78	46	51	66	47	67	71	51	60	71
Egypt	na	71	70	72	67	72	75	77	68	64	72	75	69	74	70	61
El Salvador	na	na	na	na	na	na	na	na	na	na	na	na	na	na	na	na
Estonia	na	54	56	54	61	59	47	49	56	59	53	44	61	48	57	70
Finland	na	53	49	56	58	54	47	48	59	57	50	54	53	52	53	48
France	na	26	27	26	26	29	24	18	30	43	19	24	35	16	26	41
Georgia	na	52	54	51	55	53	49	54	51	55	46	55	60	50	54	54
Germany	na	66	65	67	67	68	64	63	68	74	62	64	68	64	67	68
Great Britain	na	55	55	56	51	58	55	55	53	59	56	50	60	na	na	na
Greece	na	49	46	52	52	52	39	32	46	56	45	44	55	47	50	55
Hungary	na	38	39	36	45	41	29	31	44	58	26	33	46	37	38	32
Iceland	na	82	81	82	82	86	75	77	83	86	76	82	85	75	84	80
India	na	34	34	33	34	34	35	35	29	37	40	35	31	39	32	27
Indonesia	na	75	78	73	66	75	80	74	75	76	69	79	81	74	77	79
Iran	na	72	72	72	71	75	67	65	74	74	71	74	71	70	75	75
Ireland	na	60	62	58	60	59	63	54	60	72	52	62	66	61	60	63
Israel	na	na	na	na	na	na	na	na	na	na	na	na	na	na	na	na
Italy	na	48	49	46	52	53	41	34	53	71	41	49	56	34	47	56
Japan	na	57	58	55	46	62	56	49	54	64	53	61	60	52	55	74
Jordan	na	56	58	54	54	58	56	55	60	53	60	58	47	54	57	58
Korea, South	na	62	58	66	66	62	56	58	61	64	57	67	64	60	63	75
Latvia	na	30	32	28	35	31	27	23	29	40	24	31	35	27	29	41
Lithuania	na	37	43	32	43	45	24	24	37	52	23	33	45	37	33	68
Luxembourg	na	47	45	49	50	53	39	42	47	54	42	42	49	44	46	56
Macedonia	na	59	60	58	65	58	54	57	56	68	51	61	66	58	58	70
Malta	na	80	79	81	78	79	83	77	80	86	77	81	80	77	81	87
Mexico	na	38	40	37	39	37	40	38	35	50	38	39	42	36	41	36
Moldova	na	58	61	55	58	65	48	48	57	67	46	59	65	54	61	69
Montenegro	na	73	73	74	76	77	66	68	71	84	63	74	79	71	75	81
Morocco	na	29	30	27	32	27	20	29	29	28	18	25	37	28	30	32
Netherlands	na	58	57	58	58	65	50	44	59	68	50	61	66	45	56	67
New Zealand	na	53	54	53	41	60	52	44	54	64	48	53	64	46	55	67
Nigeria	na	45	45	44	44	47	36	38	50	47	40	46	51	48	44	43
Northern Ireland	na	67	66	68	58	67	71	65	67	71	61	64	72	73	66	66
Norway	na	42	41	42	45	44	36	33	43	49	na	na	na	30	42	55
Pakistan	na	71	73	69	71	70	76	68	74	78	64	72	79	71	72	75
Peru	na	42	43	41	42	44	40	45	41	42	43	42	41	43	43	39
Philippines	na	43	44	41	37	46	45	46	43	40	46	44	38	42	44	40
Poland	na	20	20	21	21	24	16	14	25	35	16	23	24	22	19	26
Portugal	na	40	41	39	37	47	35	37	46	41	31	38	45	38	42	35
Puerto Rico	na	44	51	40	40	43	46	30	35	50	42	48	44	47	43	46
Romania	na	27	31	24	34	28	22	18	27	45	18	23	38	19	32	51
Russian Fed.	na	28	30	26	37	31	18	10	25	45	20	25	35	21	33	47
Serbia	na	51	56	46	57	56	44	34	56	62	41	51	58	46	54	64
Singapore	na	na	na	na	na	na	na	na	na	na	na	na	na	na	na	na
Slovakia	na	45	46	44	48	47	40	37	45	67	35	42	55	39	48	66
Slovenia	na	31	33	29	36	36	22	13	32	59	18	35	46	17	32	39
South Africa	na	48	49	48	55	42	52	43	54	58	48	55	46	50	48	46
Spain	na	64	62	66	67	68	58	61	65	69	57	68	65	56	67	64
Sweden	na	52	51	54	55	58	45	37	50	67	47	51	60	43	48	68
Switzerland	na	25	24	25	24	27	23	22	27	17	25	27	24	32	24	22
Taiwan	na	39	42	36	33	40	42	43	38	38	43	37	38	35	42	53
Tanzania	na	51	55	48	38	55	62	49	48	63	45	55	63	53	51	46
Turkey	na	43	44	42	44	44	40	41	41	58	44	42	46	39	42	51
Uganda	na	55	41	69	56	53	53	51	58	35	40	44	56	59	53	49
Ukraine	na	46	49	43	57	48	37	26	44	59	35	46	57	36	49	77
United States	na	61	62	60	53	60	69	46	56	69	54	59	72	61	61	60
Uruguay	na	58	58	58	55	60	58	56	59	64	59	60	56	61	59	56
Venezuela	na	45	44	45	45	43	48	42	42	54	41	43	46	47	43	46
Vietnam	na	70	71	67	77	67	68	69	71	69	66	73	68	54	73	71
Zimbabwe	na	63	66	61	62	66	62	64	62	70	65	61	66	75	57	42
Total	na	52	52	51	53	54	48	47	52	59	47	52	56	50	52	57

RANKING Country	2000
Bangladesh	87
Iceland	82
Azerbaijan	81
Malta	80
Indonesia	75
Croatia	74
Montenegro	73
Iran	72
Albania	72
Pakistan	71
Egypt	71
Vietnam	70
Northern Ireland	67
Germany	66
China	65
Spain	64
Zimbabwe	63
Korea, South	62
Dominican Rep.	61
United States	61
Ireland	60
Belarus	60
Austria	60
Macedonia	59
Uruguay	58
Bulgaria	58
Moldova	58
Netherlands	58
Denmark	57
Japan	57
Jordan	56
Chile	56
Great Britain	55
Bosnia and Herz.	55
Uganda	55
Estonia	54
New Zealand	53
Finland	53
Georgia	52
Sweden	52
Serbia	51
Tanzania	51
Australia	50
Canada	50
Greece	49
Czech Republic	49
South Africa	48
Italy	48
Luxembourg	47
Ukraine	46
Nigeria	45
Slovakia	45
Venezuela	45
Puerto Rico	44
Turkey	43
Philippines	43
Armenia	42
Peru	42
Norway	42
Portugal	40
Belgium	40
Taiwan	39
Mexico	38
Hungary	38
Lithuania	37
Algeria	37
India	34
Argentina	33
Slovenia	31
Latvia	30
Morocco	29
Russian Fed.	28
Romania	27
France	26
Switzerland	25
Poland	20
Brazil	16
Total	52

E122) DEMOCRACIES AREN'T GOOD AT MAINTAINING ORDER

I'm going to read off some things that people sometimes say about a democratic political system. Democracies aren't good at maintaining order

Disagree / Strongly disagree (%) (WVS: V171; EVS: V223)

Country	Wave 1990	Wave 2000	Gender Male	Gender Female	Age 16-29	Age 30-49	Age 50+	Education Lower	Education Middle	Education Upper	Income Lower	Income Middle	Income Upper	Values Mat	Values Mixed	Values Postm.	RANKING Country	RANKING 2000
Albania	na	71	73	70	79	70	67	65	74	80	70	70	75	77	69	62	Iceland	89
Algeria	na	68	67	68	64	71	71	72	65	69	62	70	73	65	69	71	Bangladesh	88
Argentina	na	65	65	64	65	66	63	55	75	84	51	66	76	48	65	78	Malta	87
Armenia	na	49	50	49	57	48	39	49	47	57	57	45	41	40	55	78	Austria	87
Australia	na	71	73	69	67	76	69	58	67	86	63	74	79	65	69	76	El Salvador	85
Austria	na	87	86	88	88	90	84	85	87	93	82	92	89	67	87	93	Sweden	85
Azerbaijan	na	79	79	79	81	78	75	78	78	81	75	78	83	77	82	90	Germany	84
Bangladesh	na	88	87	89	89	87	85	91	86	83	88	88	88	89	88	92	Denmark	84
Belarus	na	59	60	58	68	61	45	52	59	67	59	57	62	52	63	78	Bosnia and Herz.	82
Belgium	na	62	65	58	66	66	55	44	60	77	48	58	71	54	61	74	China	82
Bosnia and Herz.	na	82	81	82	82	83	80	74	82	87	82	81	81	83	82	80	Spain	81
Brazil	na	44	47	40	43	42	48	36	44	66	41	38	50	34	47	51	Finland	81
Bulgaria	na	65	66	64	76	71	53	40	72	80	52	65	74	56	72	90	Croatia	81
Canada	na	71	74	67	75	71	68	54	68	89	60	68	81	70	67	78	Montenegro	81
Chile	na	64	65	64	62	65	65	61	65	70	58	68	68	62	63	73	Japan	80
China	na	82	84	79	83	80	84	81	81	91	86	78	82	83	81	81	Italy	80
Colombia	na	na	na	na	na	na	na	na	na	na	na	na	na	na	na	na	Egypt	80
Croatia	na	81	80	82	84	82	78	76	82	91	80	77	86	78	78	92	Uganda	79
Czech Republic	na	46	47	45	55	49	37	39	51	61	43	44	51	35	46	68	Luxembourg	79
Denmark	na	84	85	82	86	90	75	77	94	91	77	84	93	71	83	91	Tanzania	79
Dominican Rep.	na	64	62	66	63	68	67	43	61	69	57	69	71	54	65	72	Azerbaijan	79
Egypt	na	80	80	80	78	80	82	83	78	77	81	81	81	81	79	79	Uruguay	79
El Salvador	na	85	87	83	83	85	88	87	82	86	86	85	87	na	na	na	Netherlands	78
Estonia	na	70	68	71	75	72	64	63	70	77	65	66	71	66	71	77	United States	78
Finland	na	81	84	79	87	83	76	75	87	95	77	83	85	75	83	83	Ireland	77
France	na	45	45	45	44	50	40	34	48	67	36	42	53	34	43	63	Indonesia	77
Georgia	na	55	57	53	57	55	51	58	52	60	49	55	63	54	54	62	Korea, South	77
Germany	na	84	84	85	83	85	84	83	85	92	83	86	84	82	85	85	Northern Ireland	75
Great Britain	na	67	65	68	64	69	66	65	64	72	68	60	71	na	na	na	Vietnam	75
Greece	na	67	68	67	71	67	59	46	60	77	61	66	72	59	67	76	Switzerland	73
Hungary	na	61	63	59	68	64	52	54	67	81	46	60	67	59	61	65	Albania	71
Iceland	na	89	90	89	90	91	85	83	92	96	84	91	93	84	90	93	Australia	71
India	na	59	59	58	59	60	56	54	61	62	57	58	60	62	59	57	Canada	71
Indonesia	na	77	79	75	66	82	78	75	78	78	77	79	74	77	77	78	Estonia	70
Iran	na	69	69	68	67	71	69	62	72	69	69	71	67	65	70	75	New Zealand	69
Ireland	na	77	81	74	75	82	74	72	78	86	67	77	85	74	78	80	Serbia	69
Israel	na	na	na	na	na	na	na	na	na	na	na	na	na	na	na	na	Iran	69
Italy	na	80	79	81	83	83	75	70	85	93	75	82	84	70	79	87	Zimbabwe	68
Japan	na	80	80	81	78	85	77	66	78	90	75	82	84	78	81	92	Algeria	68
Jordan	na	66	68	64	67	67	61	63	70	66	71	68	56	62	67	74	Norway	68
Korea, South	na	77	75	78	85	75	71	70	72	83	73	81	77	73	79	88	Greece	67
Latvia	na	56	58	55	67	57	51	41	57	73	49	53	67	54	56	74	Great Britain	67
Lithuania	na	50	51	49	62	51	38	36	51	58	37	51	53	50	46	71	Taiwan	66
Luxembourg	na	79	78	79	76	82	77	76	77	88	78	74	83	79	78	87	Jordan	66
Macedonia	na	59	60	59	62	59	55	58	56	66	48	62	64	60	58	58	Bulgaria	65
Malta	na	87	86	88	85	86	90	85	87	94	85	91	90	86	87	94	Argentina	65
Mexico	na	49	52	46	53	47	46	44	49	67	47	52	54	46	51	48	Turkey	65
Moldova	na	57	59	54	60	60	49	46	58	61	44	63	58	53	60	72	Chile	64
Montenegro	na	81	80	81	84	84	74	74	80	92	71	81	86	79	82	90	Dominican Rep.	64
Morocco	na	59	60	58	62	56	53	57	60	66	48	58	68	61	57	70	Venezuela	64
Netherlands	na	78	77	80	83	82	72	67	81	85	78	78	84	68	76	90	Belgium	62
New Zealand	na	69	73	66	66	77	64	57	68	83	62	70	80	67	71	78	South Africa	61
Nigeria	na	55	53	56	56	55	47	47	59	59	51	56	61	54	55	59	Hungary	61
Northern Ireland	na	75	75	76	69	76	77	72	74	84	69	75	79	76	74	78	Portugal	59
Norway	na	68	67	68	72	72	58	55	68	79	na	na	na	51	68	86	Belarus	59
Pakistan	na	47	51	43	42	50	49	43	49	57	39	46	58	50	44	20	Morocco	59
Peru	na	52	55	50	50	55	52	48	52	56	48	52	61	49	54	50	India	59
Philippines	na	50	51	49	49	52	48	47	50	53	52	52	45	50	49	53	Macedonia	59
Poland	na	32	33	31	35	33	29	25	36	53	28	34	38	25	36	34	Slovakia	58
Portugal	na	59	60	58	56	60	61	58	59	71	57	56	62	58	59	57	Moldova	57
Puerto Rico	na	55	63	51	54	55	57	43	47	61	51	58	59	59	55	58	Latvia	56
Romania	na	49	53	45	60	52	40	36	51	64	35	47	59	40	54	69	Puerto Rico	55
Russian Fed.	na	35	35	34	43	37	25	17	32	50	28	32	43	28	39	56	Georgia	55
Serbia	na	69	73	64	74	76	59	53	72	80	57	69	77	61	73	86	Nigeria	55
Singapore	na	na	na	na	na	na	na	na	na	na	na	na	na	na	na	na	Slovenia	54
Slovakia	na	58	57	58	61	58	55	56	56	73	49	55	67	52	61	73	Peru	52
Slovenia	na	54	59	50	57	59	47	39	54	81	41	56	72	42	55	63	Philippines	50
South Africa	na	61	63	59	65	60	58	54	69	78	61	62	66	66	60	46	Ukraine	50
Spain	na	81	81	82	85	84	77	78	83	88	79	81	81	74	82	88	Lithuania	50
Sweden	na	85	85	86	89	89	80	73	85	93	81	84	92	74	85	91	Armenia	49
Switzerland	na	73	74	73	79	72	71	62	75	85	67	68	81	69	71	81	Mexico	49
Taiwan	na	66	71	61	71	68	59	61	69	70	69	60	69	60	71	76	Romania	49
Tanzania	na	79	83	73	79	79	78	72	86	89	71	82	86	76	81	83	Pakistan	47
Turkey	na	65	65	64	65	65	62	60	64	83	62	65	71	63	64	70	Czech Republic	46
Uganda	na	79	78	81	84	76	68	70	83	75	69	78	83	77	81	76	France	45
Ukraine	na	50	51	49	55	55	41	36	48	61	42	52	57	43	51	68	Brazil	44
United States	na	78	79	77	76	77	80	62	76	85	72	79	84	76	77	80	Russian Fed.	35
Uruguay	na	79	81	77	78	80	78	74	84	87	74	80	81	70	78	88	Poland	32
Venezuela	na	64	62	65	62	64	67	63	60	72	60	64	63	66	62	67		
Vietnam	na	75	79	70	74	76	74	73	77	75	64	78	76	54	81	72		
Zimbabwe	na	68	72	65	66	72	70	70	66	78	68	64	73	77	64	52		
Total	na	67	68	66	68	69	64	62	67	75	62	67	72	62	68	76	Total	67

E123) DEMOCRACY MAY HAVE PROBLEMS BUT IS BETTER

I'm going to read off some things that people sometimes say about a democratic political system. Democracy may have problems but it's better than any other form of government

Agree strongly / Agree (%)

(WVS: V172; EVS: V220)

Country	Wave 1990	Wave 2000	Gender Male	Gender Female	Age 16-29	Age 30-49	Age 50+	Education Lower	Education Middle	Education Upper	Income Lower	Income Middle	Income Upper	Values Mat	Values Mixed	Values Postm.
Albania	na	95	95	95	96	96	92	91	96	98	92	96	97	94	96	97
Algeria	na	88	86	91	88	89	87	90	88	88	88	91	89	86	92	88
Argentina	na	91	89	93	91	92	91	89	96	93	87	92	95	86	92	94
Armenia	na	73	71	75	76	75	66	68	73	77	75	70	71	69	75	86
Australia	na	87	89	84	80	89	89	82	83	95	86	87	89	80	86	89
Austria	na	97	97	98	98	96	98	97	97	98	97	97	98	91	98	98
Azerbaijan	na	96	97	95	97	96	96	98	97	94	97	96	95	96	98	92
Bangladesh	na	98	98	99	98	98	99	99	99	97	98	98	99	99	98	100
Belarus	na	87	87	87	91	87	83	82	87	89	86	87	87	84	89	98
Belgium	na	92	92	92	89	92	93	88	90	97	90	89	95	90	91	96
Bosnia and Herz.	na	92	92	92	94	92	90	92	91	93	92	91	93	91	93	92
Brazil	na	83	83	83	83	81	89	81	84	89	83	82	86	80	84	87
Bulgaria	na	84	85	82	92	89	74	71	86	93	75	82	91	79	87	92
Canada	na	87	88	86	81	87	91	82	86	93	83	86	90	85	87	88
Chile	na	82	83	80	80	82	82	79	82	86	78	83	87	77	82	89
China	na	90	90	90	85	92	90	89	90	90	92	88	91	92	89	88
Colombia	na	na	na	na	na	na	na	na	na	na	na	na	na	na	na	na
Croatia	na	96	96	96	95	95	97	95	96	96	97	94	97	96	96	96
Czech Republic	na	93	92	93	94	94	91	90	94	98	88	93	95	87	94	96
Denmark	na	99	99	99	97	100	99	98	99	100	98	99	100	93	99	99
Dominican Rep.	na	93	93	93	91	96	100	97	90	93	91	93	95	81	95	100
Egypt	na	98	97	98	96	98	99	98	96	99	98	98	98	98	97	97
El Salvador	na	na	na	na	na	na	na	na	na	na	na	na	na	na	na	na
Estonia	na	90	90	91	87	92	91	91	89	93	91	91	90	88	92	85
Finland	na	91	92	89	89	91	91	88	93	97	87	89	94	91	91	91
France	na	94	95	92	92	94	94	91	94	99	92	94	97	92	93	98
Georgia	na	86	86	86	86	88	82	87	84	91	82	90	89	85	87	83
Germany	na	97	97	97	96	97	97	96	97	99	97	96	97	97	96	97
Great Britain	na	78	82	74	74	79	79	71	82	88	69	84	85	na	na	na
Greece	na	97	96	97	97	96	97	97	97	97	97	97	97	98	97	97
Hungary	na	81	81	82	83	82	79	75	89	97	71	81	86	80	83	77
Iceland	na	97	97	97	95	98	99	97	97	100	95	98	99	93	90	97
India	na	92	92	91	93	91	91	90	91	95	84	93	93	93	90	97
Indonesia	na	71	72	71	62	72	76	68	70	74	74	73	66	69	73	75
Iran	na	69	70	68	65	74	74	71	68	71	70	73	65	68	72	60
Ireland	na	92	93	92	89	93	93	87	93	99	88	90	96	92	92	95
Israel	na	na	na	na	na	na	na	na	na	na	na	na	na	na	na	na
Italy	na	94	94	95	92	95	95	93	95	98	94	95	96	92	95	95
Japan	na	92	91	93	87	91	95	91	92	94	92	91	93	93	91	99
Jordan	na	89	92	87	90	90	86	89	90	90	87	89	92	91	90	87
Korea, South	na	91	90	92	92	91	89	86	91	92	88	94	92	92	90	92
Latvia	na	89	88	89	85	90	90	85	89	93	88	87	92	87	90	93
Lithuania	na	88	88	88	89	90	85	78	89	97	84	90	89	87	88	91
Luxembourg	na	96	96	95	94	96	97	94	97	96	96	94	98	93	97	97
Macedonia	na	81	79	84	86	80	79	83	78	87	77	80	88	81	82	86
Malta	na	94	94	94	95	93	95	93	94	98	93	95	94	94	94	94
Mexico	na	80	82	78	78	79	84	79	79	86	77	80	81	78	81	78
Moldova	na	78	82	74	79	78	77	81	75	81	76	79	80	77	83	82
Montenegro	na	92	91	93	96	92	89	90	91	98	88	91	96	90	94	94
Morocco	na	96	96	96	96	97	98	97	95	95	96	97	96	97	96	94
Netherlands	na	96	97	96	97	95	98	92	97	99	96	96	98	92	97	97
New Zealand	na	83	86	82	79	86	83	76	87	91	81	82	89	89	84	88
Nigeria	na	45	47	44	44	45	53	53	41	41	50	45	39	46	45	42
Northern Ireland	na	93	94	93	92	92	95	91	97	93	94	93	90	96	93	91
Norway	na	95	95	95	92	95	97	93	94	98	na	na	na	94	95	96
Pakistan	na	82	83	81	82	83	81	80	85	85	78	83	88	81	84	83
Peru	na	89	88	90	89	89	91	88	88	91	87	89	93	89	89	92
Philippines	na	80	79	80	81	80	79	80	79	80	77	81	80	78	81	86
Poland	na	90	92	88	91	91	88	88	90	98	86	92	92	87	92	87
Portugal	na	93	94	92	89	93	95	94	91	91	92	91	93	96	90	96
Puerto Rico	na	90	89	92	84	90	95	86	93	91	92	93	88	90	92	89
Romania	na	78	81	76	82	78	76	66	80	90	70	78	85	72	81	97
Russian Fed.	na	63	62	64	71	67	53	42	60	79	52	60	76	59	67	67
Serbia	na	89	89	89	91	92	85	80	92	95	84	90	92	86	92	93
Singapore	na	na	na	na	na	na	na	na	na	na	na	na	na	na	na	na
Slovakia	na	84	84	85	87	84	83	79	85	94	79	85	88	82	86	98
Slovenia	na	90	93	88	88	90	92	85	91	98	84	94	96	89	90	92
South Africa	na	84	85	83	85	83	84	85	82	92	85	82	83	86	84	78
Spain	na	93	93	93	93	93	93	93	93	93	93	93	91	92	93	95
Sweden	na	94	94	94	93	95	95	91	93	99	91	95	97	90	94	95
Switzerland	na	91	90	92	92	89	94	89	91	96	92	88	93	88	90	96
Taiwan	na	84	85	82	86	82	86	78	84	87	83	82	85	83	86	78
Tanzania	na	88	91	85	89	88	91	85	91	93	85	90	92	87	89	92
Turkey	na	88	88	89	87	89	91	87	89	92	88	88	89	88	88	89
Uganda	na	92	97	87	94	93	79	84	95	93	94	93	95	93	91	91
Ukraine	na	83	83	82	82	88	77	65	83	88	76	83	89	80	83	90
United States	na	88	87	88	80	87	95	78	86	92	84	88	92	85	88	88
Uruguay	na	96	98	95	95	97	97	96	98	95	97	96	97	97	96	98
Venezuela	na	93	91	94	92	93	93	93	92	95	89	95	94	92	93	93
Vietnam	na	72	71	74	68	75	72	71	75	68	74	70	73	68	76	71
Zimbabwe	na	88	86	89	85	89	92	88	87	100	86	87	90	88	88	86
Total	na	88	88	88	87	89	89	87	88	91	86	88	90	86	89	92

RANKING

Country	2000
Denmark	99
Bangladesh	98
Egypt	98
Iceland	97
Austria	97
Germany	97
Greece	97
Netherlands	96
Morocco	96
Uruguay	96
Azerbaijan	96
Croatia	96
Luxembourg	96
Norway	95
Albania	95
Italy	94
Sweden	94
Malta	94
France	94
Northern Ireland	93
Spain	93
Dominican Rep.	93
Portugal	93
Czech Republic	93
Venezuela	93
Ireland	92
Bosnia and Herz.	92
Japan	92
Uganda	92
Montenegro	92
Belgium	92
India	92
Argentina	91
Switzerland	91
Korea, South	91
Finland	91
Estonia	90
Puerto Rico	90
Slovenia	90
China	90
Poland	90
Jordan	89
Serbia	89
Peru	89
Latvia	89
Algeria	88
Tanzania	88
Turkey	88
Lithuania	88
Zimbabwe	88
United States	88
Canada	87
Belarus	87
Australia	87
Georgia	86
Slovakia	84
South Africa	84
Bulgaria	84
Taiwan	84
Brazil	83
New Zealand	83
Ukraine	83
Pakistan	82
Chile	82
Macedonia	81
Hungary	81
Philippines	80
Mexico	80
Romania	78
Moldova	78
Great Britain	78
Armenia	73
Vietnam	72
Indonesia	71
Iran	69
Russian Fed.	63
Nigeria	45
Total	88

E124) RESPECT FOR INDIVIDUAL HUMAN RIGHTS

How much respect is there for individual human rights nowadays (in our country)? Do you feel there is ...

A lot of respect for / Some respect (%)

(WVS: V173; EVS: V224)

Country	Wave 1990	Wave 2000	Gender Male	Gender Female	Age 16-29	Age 30-49	Age 50+	Education Lower	Education Middle	Education Upper	Income Lower	Income Middle	Income Upper	Values Mat	Values Mixed	Values Postm.
Albania	na	37	38	37	38	38	36	35	38	42	37	41	35	34	41	45
Algeria	na	36	35	37	34	37	37	41	34	34	36	38	31	40	35	27
Argentina	na	22	27	17	19	22	24	20	23	33	24	20	22	24	23	20
Armenia	na	23	24	22	27	19	22	24	24	21	28	14	22	25	21	19
Australia	na	na	na	na	na	na	na	na	na	na	na	na	na	na	na	na
Austria	na	76	78	74	75	76	77	75	76	79	71	75	81	76	79	70
Azerbaijan	na	61	62	61	57	63	67	66	62	59	59	60	66	64	57	50
Bangladesh	na	73	72	76	75	72	71	73	75	71	77	73	70	75	71	79
Belarus	na	36	33	40	23	30	56	57	31	25	42	36	28	43	34	15
Belgium	na	63	67	59	65	61	63	52	61	73	54	60	74	59	62	71
Bosnia and Herz.	na	35	36	33	31	34	39	37	34	34	30	35	40	36	34	43
Brazil	na	na	na	na	na	na	na	na	na	na	na	na	na	na	na	na
Bulgaria	na	34	38	31	37	36	32	30	34	42	33	29	38	26	41	52
Canada	na	84	86	81	82	85	83	75	83	92	77	86	88	84	84	85
Chile	na	57	57	56	55	56	58	54	57	62	53	58	64	53	59	58
China	na	88	88	87	87	88	88	88	88	88	85	89	89	89	87	83
Colombia	na	na	na	na	na	na	na	na	na	na	na	na	na	na	na	na
Croatia	na	58	59	56	60	57	56	61	56	55	58	57	57	64	58	49
Czech Republic	na	65	65	64	68	61	65	61	66	76	57	65	72	57	66	74
Denmark	na	88	90	85	94	90	82	82	95	96	83	88	98	82	86	94
Dominican Rep.	na	na	na	na	na	na	na	na	na	na	na	na	na	na	na	na
Egypt	na	72	68	76	69	71	77	75	70	65	72	74	69	74	72	51
El Salvador	na	na	na	na	na	na	na	na	na	na	na	na	na	na	na	na
Estonia	na	54	55	54	54	52	57	52	54	61	50	53	60	48	60	57
Finland	na	88	89	87	95	87	86	85	92	95	84	90	92	89	89	85
France	na	60	65	55	55	60	62	54	63	73	47	63	70	54	63	62
Georgia	na	25	26	24	27	24	23	25	25	23	22	27	27	25	24	27
Germany	na	79	79	79	77	79	80	75	81	83	75	80	87	82	78	76
Great Britain	na	66	68	65	69	68	65	57	69	85	52	75	73	na	na	na
Greece	na	63	68	59	57	66	69	55	60	67	59	64	65	66	65	59
Hungary	na	57	60	54	56	61	54	52	61	75	52	55	63	55	60	53
Iceland	na	86	87	85	85	87	85	80	89	93	81	88	88	81	87	91
India	na	75	73	78	79	74	71	74	75	76	81	77	72	76	76	68
Indonesia	na	62	64	60	50	67	62	70	63	55	59	65	63	59	63	68
Iran	na	73	71	75	72	73	76	75	74	67	72	72	73	78	72	71
Ireland	na	76	78	75	75	83	71	70	78	85	70	72	83	72	77	80
Israel	na	na	na	na	na	na	na	na	na	na	na	na	na	na	na	na
Italy	na	62	68	57	59	66	61	56	64	78	57	64	72	54	61	69
Japan	na	62	64	61	56	58	68	58	60	70	61	61	68	72	64	47
Jordan	na	74	67	80	73	74	74	76	75	69	80	69	73	78	71	61
Korea, South	na	47	49	45	44	45	56	56	51	41	46	48	48	51	46	30
Latvia	na	52	51	54	46	49	58	52	52	54	54	47	54	57	51	47
Lithuania	na	23	24	22	28	17	26	20	22	34	19	25	24	22	23	19
Luxembourg	na	91	92	89	90	88	94	88	91	96	89	93	93	91	92	88
Macedonia	na	32	34	30	30	31	36	25	35	37	28	30	41	32	34	24
Malta	na	75	76	75	76	74	70	71	75	87	71	80	79	71	78	77
Mexico	na	48	46	49	45	47	52	51	44	43	48	48	48	48	47	40
Moldova	na	21	22	20	20	19	26	23	22	19	18	19	21	20	25	27
Montenegro	na	40	40	41	46	38	39	35	41	50	30	36	50	34	45	41
Morocco	na	42	38	47	39	43	50	45	32	35	40	37	42	52	37	28
Netherlands	na	80	83	76	85	81	75	67	83	88	74	82	88	70	80	83
New Zealand	na	na	na	na	na	na	na	na	na	na	na	na	na	na	na	na
Nigeria	na	63	65	61	63	64	63	64	62	63	58	65	67	63	64	60
Northern Ireland	na	70	71	70	65	70	73	66	71	80	64	69	70	69	73	64
Norway	na	na	na	na	na	na	na	na	na	na	na	na	na	na	na	na
Pakistan	na	54	54	54	55	55	53	57	52	52	56	55	52	54	56	50
Peru	na	45	47	43	44	47	43	40	47	46	43	44	52	46	45	46
Philippines	na	79	79	79	82	78	78	78	80	79	78	79	80	77	82	77
Poland	na	57	56	57	64	57	51	50	61	75	46	59	74	54	58	57
Portugal	na	62	65	59	66	62	60	59	65	76	56	64	68	65	59	68
Puerto Rico	na	56	61	53	54	60	54	41	51	61	52	57	60	56	58	51
Romania	na	24	24	23	24	24	23	19	24	30	23	23	26	23	23	27
Russian Fed.	na	16	16	16	20	16	15	14	16	18	15	17	17	16	17	17
Serbia	na	49	51	46	45	51	49	50	48	48	45	47	52	49	49	44
Singapore	na	na	na	na	na	na	na	na	na	na	na	na	na	na	na	na
Slovakia	na	59	59	59	68	57	55	52	61	70	51	57	66	54	63	71
Slovenia	na	41	47	36	42	42	40	29	42	61	33	44	60	36	43	39
South Africa	na	56	57	54	58	54	57	55	56	71	59	56	54	52	58	58
Spain	na	63	63	63	63	66	61	59	65	72	60	64	67	65	64	63
Sweden	na	75	82	69	77	75	74	66	77	80	71	76	83	66	76	76
Switzerland	na	na	na	na	na	na	na	na	na	na	na	na	na	na	na	na
Taiwan	na	na	na	na	na	na	na	na	na	na	na	na	na	na	na	na
Tanzania	na	70	71	68	58	74	80	73	63	70	70	72	73	68	72	63
Turkey	na	26	26	26	24	27	29	28	24	24	28	26	23	31	26	18
Uganda	na	70	76	66	73	66	76	65	72	73	67	75	71	73	68	74
Ukraine	na	23	21	25	22	23	23	15	22	28	18	23	28	23	22	31
United States	na	74	76	72	70	72	81	69	70	78	67	77	80	70	77	71
Uruguay	na	na	na	na	na	na	na	na	na	na	na	na	na	na	na	na
Venezuela	na	49	51	46	48	50	46	54	46	48	51	45	51	53	48	43
Vietnam	na	95	96	94	95	95	95	95	96	94	94	95	95	96	95	93
Zimbabwe	na	32	32	33	36	27	33	33	32	9	37	30	33	34	31	30
Total	na	57	58	56	55	57	58	57	55	61	53	57	60	53	58	60

RANKING Country	2000
Vietnam	95
Luxembourg	91
Finland	88
Denmark	88
China	88
Iceland	86
Canada	84
Netherlands	80
Philippines	79
Germany	79
Ireland	76
Austria	76
Malta	75
Sweden	75
India	75
United States	74
Jordan	74
Bangladesh	73
Iran	73
Egypt	72
Uganda	70
Northern Ireland	70
Tanzania	70
Great Britain	66
Czech Republic	65
Spain	63
Nigeria	63
Greece	63
Belgium	63
Japan	62
Italy	62
Portugal	62
Indonesia	62
Azerbaijan	61
France	60
Slovakia	59
Croatia	58
Hungary	57
Chile	57
Poland	57
Puerto Rico	56
South Africa	56
Estonia	54
Pakistan	54
Latvia	52
Serbia	49
Venezuela	49
Mexico	48
Korea, South	47
Peru	45
Morocco	42
Slovenia	41
Montenegro	40
Albania	37
Belarus	36
Algeria	36
Bosnia and Herz.	35
Bulgaria	34
Zimbabwe	32
Macedonia	32
Turkey	26
Georgia	25
Romania	24
Armenia	23
Lithuania	23
Ukraine	23
Argentina	22
Moldova	21
Russian Fed.	16
Total	57

E125) SATISFACTION WITH GOVERNMENT

How satisfied are you with the way the people now in national office are handling the country's affairs? Would you say you are very satisfied, fairly satisfied, fairly dissatisfied or very dissatisfied?

Very satisfied / Fairly satisfied (%)

(WVS: V174)

Country	Wave 1990	Wave 2000	Gender Male	Gender Female	Age 16-29	Age 30-49	Age 50+	Education Lower	Education Middle	Education Upper	Income Lower	Income Middle	Income Upper	Values Mat	Values Mixed	Values Postm.
Albania	na	19	20	19	19	20	18	17	20	23	19	22	17	19	18	28
Algeria	na	28	26	31	26	30	31	28	30	26	29	31	28	30	28	16
Argentina	na	27	32	23	24	31	26	28	26	28	31	25	27	29	30	22
Armenia	na	15	14	16	19	12	13	12	16	14	15	9	18	17	14	9
Australia	na	45	48	42	54	45	37	44	44	47	40	50	46	44	44	48
Austria	na	na	na	na	na	na	na	na	na	na	na	na	na	na	na	na
Azerbaijan	na	26	29	23	24	26	29	30	25	26	23	27	28	26	25	20
Bangladesh	na	76	72	81	74	77	80	81	70	71	84	77	69	76	75	81
Belarus	na	na	na	na	na	na	na	na	na	na	na	na	na	na	na	na
Belgium	na	na	na	na	na	na	na	na	na	na	na	na	na	na	na	na
Bosnia and Herz.	na	24	27	22	19	26	28	31	23	22	23	26	26	25	24	21
Brazil	na	57	65	50	53	55	71	59	56	57	60	55	56	55	58	62
Bulgaria	na	na	na	na	na	na	na	na	na	na	na	na	na	na	na	na
Canada	na	65	67	63	66	63	68	65	65	67	62	63	68	73	66	62
Chile	na	66	66	67	68	65	68	66	66	68	61	72	70	63	69	65
China	na	73	72	74	66	75	74	77	71	66	68	78	73	75	71	61
Colombia	na	28	27	30	28	28	29	34	30	22	35	28	24	28	30	33
Croatia	na	na	na	na	na	na	na	na	na	na	na	na	na	na	na	na
Czech Republic	na	na	na	na	na	na	na	na	na	na	na	na	na	na	na	na
Denmark	na	na	na	na	na	na	na	na	na	na	na	na	na	na	na	na
Dominican Rep.	na	6	8	5	7	6	na	22	4	5	9	5	6	12	6	5
Egypt	na	92	93	92	92	93	93	92	92	92	93	91	92	92	93	92
El Salvador	na	na	na	na	na	na	na	na	na	na	na	na	na	na	na	na
Estonia	na	na	na	na	na	na	na	na	na	na	na	na	na	na	na	na
Finland	na	na	na	na	na	na	na	na	na	na	na	na	na	na	na	na
France	na	na	na	na	na	na	na	na	na	na	na	na	na	na	na	na
Georgia	na	23	24	23	24	23	22	23	23	25	20	25	26	23	23	19
Germany	na	na	na	na	na	na	na	na	na	na	na	na	na	na	na	na
Great Britain	na	na	na	na	na	na	na	na	na	na	na	na	na	na	na	na
Greece	na	na	na	na	na	na	na	na	na	na	na	na	na	na	na	na
Hungary	na	na	na	na	na	na	na	na	na	na	na	na	na	na	na	na
Iceland	na	na	na	na	na	na	na	na	na	na	na	na	na	na	na	na
India	na	60	62	57	61	61	57	62	60	56	67	61	56	64	59	49
Indonesia	na	23	26	19	14	22	28	27	24	18	21	23	27	23	21	29
Iran	na	71	70	73	70	74	72	73	71	69	67	70	74	76	69	66
Ireland	na	na	na	na	na	na	na	na	na	na	na	na	na	na	na	na
Israel	na	na	na	na	na	na	na	na	na	na	na	na	na	na	na	na
Italy	na	na	na	na	na	na	na	na	na	na	na	na	na	na	na	na
Japan	na	8	10	7	7	5	12	11	7	10	9	6	9	13	7	7
Jordan	na	77	72	82	78	76	78	77	82	72	82	70	79	79	76	71
Korea, South	na	31	30	33	27	31	38	42	35	25	33	29	31	38	27	22
Latvia	na	na	na	na	na	na	na	na	na	na	na	na	na	na	na	na
Lithuania	na	na	na	na	na	na	na	na	na	na	na	na	na	na	na	na
Luxembourg	na	na	na	na	na	na	na	na	na	na	na	na	na	na	na	na
Macedonia	na	19	21	16	19	16	22	18	19	18	20	18	18	19	20	na
Malta	na	na	na	na	na	na	na	na	na	na	na	na	na	na	na	na
Mexico	na	48	46	50	47	48	49	51	45	41	52	50	44	51	47	43
Moldova	na	21	21	21	17	21	24	22	26	11	25	20	18	25	19	18
Montenegro	na	28	26	30	33	27	25	24	30	31	16	22	41	25	33	22
Morocco	na	49	46	52	43	51	58	53	31	31	53	40	45	58	43	36
Netherlands	na	na	na	na	na	na	na	na	na	na	na	na	na	na	na	na
New Zealand	na	26	28	26	25	30	23	23	25	31	20	26	33	29	27	25
Nigeria	na	72	73	72	73	72	65	75	69	73	69	71	77	72	72	76
Northern Ireland	na	na	na	na	na	na	na	na	na	na	na	na	na	na	na	na
Norway	na	86	85	86	86	89	82	81	88	89	na	na	na	85	86	82
Pakistan	na	43	44	42	43	42	46	40	47	47	40	46	44	42	44	42
Peru	na	35	36	33	33	36	36	33	33	38	32	35	39	36	34	37
Philippines	na	51	55	48	55	50	48	50	52	52	46	51	56	49	55	41
Poland	na	na	na	na	na	na	na	na	na	na	na	na	na	na	na	na
Portugal	na	na	na	na	na	na	na	na	na	na	na	na	na	na	na	na
Puerto Rico	na	42	42	42	39	40	46	49	44	40	48	45	36	49	41	44
Romania	na	na	na	na	na	na	na	na	na	na	na	na	na	na	na	na
Russian Fed.	na	na	na	na	na	na	na	na	na	na	na	na	na	na	na	na
Serbia	na	38	39	37	45	37	35	33	39	42	32	40	41	35	40	45
Singapore	na	92	89	94	92	90	92	94	90	90	93	91	91	95	91	81
Slovakia	na	na	na	na	na	na	na	na	na	na	na	na	na	na	na	na
Slovenia	na	na	na	na	na	na	na	na	na	na	na	na	na	na	na	na
South Africa	na	57	58	56	57	57	57	60	53	58	65	64	40	50	61	68
Spain	na	46	47	45	37	41	56	48	41	46	44	49	44	51	46	35
Sweden	na	44	48	41	48	43	44	46	45	42	43	48	45	44	43	48
Switzerland	na	65	63	68	70	62	66	66	64	67	67	63	66	73	66	59
Taiwan	na	38	36	40	25	35	56	50	38	28	40	40	35	37	38	44
Tanzania	na	60	57	62	60	58	62	60	60	57	59	56	62	59	61	50
Turkey	na	28	25	30	27	28	29	29	27	22	27	29	28	31	28	23
Uganda	na	68	63	72	69	67	62	63	69	73	65	77	61	67	68	71
Ukraine	na	na	na	na	na	na	na	na	na	na	na	na	na	na	na	na
United States	na	67	68	67	68	67	66	68	67	67	62	71	72	74	69	60
Uruguay	na	31	33	29	22	21	42	34	27	27	34	26	30	44	28	25
Venezuela	na	62	67	56	59	64	64	70	61	55	63	61	63	63	61	64
Vietnam	na	94	95	94	93	95	94	96	92	94	91	95	95	95	94	93
Zimbabwe	na	32	31	32	33	30	30	34	29	17	37	32	26	30	31	46
Total	na	47	48	46	48	47	46	52	46	42	45	46	48	47	48	45

RANKING

Country	2000
Vietnam	94
Egypt	92
Singapore	92
Norway	86
Jordan	77
Bangladesh	76
China	73
Nigeria	72
Iran	71
Uganda	68
United States	67
Chile	66
Canada	65
Switzerland	65
Venezuela	62
India	60
Tanzania	60
Brazil	57
South Africa	57
Philippines	51
Morocco	49
Mexico	48
Spain	46
Australia	45
Sweden	44
Pakistan	43
Puerto Rico	42
Taiwan	38
Serbia	38
Peru	35
Zimbabwe	32
Korea, South	31
Uruguay	31
Algeria	28
Colombia	28
Montenegro	28
Turkey	28
Argentina	27
New Zealand	26
Azerbaijan	26
Bosnia and Herz.	24
Georgia	23
Indonesia	23
Moldova	21
Albania	19
Macedonia	19
Armenia	15
Japan	8
Dominican Rep.	6
Total	47

E128) COUNTRY IS RUN BY BIG INTEREST

Generally speaking, would you say that this country is run by a few big interests looking out for themselves, or that it is run for the benefit of all the people?

Run by few big interests (%)

(WVS: V175)

Country	Wave 1990	Wave 2000	Gender Male	Gender Female	Age 16-29	Age 30-49	Age 50+	Education Lower	Education Middle	Education Upper	Income Lower	Income Middle	Income Upper	Values Mat	Values Mixed	Values Postm.
Albania	na	65	70	61	62	66	67	59	68	71	67	56	72	67	64	66
Algeria	na	87	89	85	87	87	88	88	86	89	88	87	82	83	88	96
Argentina	na	90	90	90	87	92	91	87	95	91	88	89	94	86	90	92
Armenia	na	96	97	96	97	97	95	94	96	98	97	98	95	97	97	98
Australia	na	68	65	71	65	67	72	72	72	60	72	68	62	66	67	69
Austria	na	na	na	na	na	na	na	na	na	na	na	na	na	na	na	na
Azerbaijan	na	78	76	80	80	79	72	66	78	81	79	76	79	77	79	91
Bangladesh	na	56	60	52	57	56	54	48	65	66	43	58	65	54	59	62
Belarus	na	na	na	na	na	na	na	na	na	na	na	na	na	na	na	na
Belgium	na	na	na	na	na	na	na	na	na	na	na	na	na	na	na	na
Bosnia and Herz.	na	81	80	82	86	80	78	74	82	82	82	80	81	83	79	90
Brazil	na	75	71	80	75	77	74	66	81	88	69	76	82	69	77	85
Bulgaria	na	na	na	na	na	na	na	na	na	na	na	na	na	na	na	na
Canada	70	52	50	54	51	53	51	56	52	48	58	53	48	42	52	56
Chile	45	65	68	63	67	64	65	67	66	60	71	62	60	68	65	63
China	8	17	17	16	19	17	12	14	19	8	18	17	16	16	18	20
Colombia	na	79	82	76	80	79	75	69	76	90	72	77	86	76	73	81
Croatia	na	na	na	na	na	na	na	na	na	na	na	na	na	na	na	na
Czech Republic	67	na	na	na	na	na	na	na	na	na	na	na	na	na	na	na
Denmark	na	na	na	na	na	na	na	na	na	na	na	na	na	na	na	na
Dominican Rep.	na	92	90	93	90	94	100	84	91	93	91	89	93	84	92	98
Egypt	na	69	69	68	69	70	65	66	69	74	68	69	71	72	66	72
El Salvador	na	74	77	72	71	76	78	65	81	89	59	76	90	na	na	na
Estonia	54	na	na	na	na	na	na	na	na	na	na	na	na	na	na	na
Finland	na	na	na	na	na	na	na	na	na	na	na	na	na	na	na	na
France	na	na	na	na	na	na	na	na	na	na	na	na	na	na	na	na
Georgia	na	94	93	94	94	94	92	93	93	95	93	94	94	94	93	97
Germany	na	na	na	na	na	na	na	na	na	na	na	na	na	na	na	na
Great Britain	na	na	na	na	na	na	na	na	na	na	na	na	na	na	na	na
Greece	na	na	na	na	na	na	na	na	na	na	na	na	na	na	na	na
Hungary	na	na	na	na	na	na	na	na	na	na	na	na	na	na	na	na
Iceland	na	na	na	na	na	na	na	na	na	na	na	na	na	na	na	na
India	55	66	65	68	64	67	66	71	64	60	70	64	66	66	64	71
Indonesia	na	70	71	69	78	70	65	62	69	76	63	74	76	69	69	80
Iran	na	49	48	49	49	49	47	45	50	50	53	49	44	47	45	53
Ireland	na	na	na	na	na	na	na	na	na	na	na	na	na	na	na	na
Israel	na	na	na	na	na	na	na	na	na	na	na	na	na	na	na	na
Italy	na	na	na	na	na	na	na	na	na	na	na	na	na	na	na	na
Japan	na	84	83	84	91	87	78	74	85	84	83	86	83	80	84	90
Jordan	na	69	74	64	68	70	68	66	71	72	63	74	69	63	72	81
Korea, South	na	88	88	89	92	90	80	73	86	93	87	88	89	85	90	94
Latvia	35	na	na	na	na	na	na	na	na	na	na	na	na	na	na	na
Lithuania	50	na	na	na	na	na	na	na	na	na	na	na	na	na	na	na
Luxembourg	na	na	na	na	na	na	na	na	na	na	na	na	na	na	na	na
Macedonia	na	93	92	93	94	93	91	94	92	93	93	93	93	93	93	93
Malta	na	na	na	na	na	na	na	na	na	na	na	na	na	na	na	na
Mexico	81	72	73	70	71	70	75	65	76	87	62	74	80	67	74	72
Moldova	na	91	89	92	89	92	90	93	87	94	96	90	87	90	91	88
Montenegro	na	74	75	73	67	75	78	80	70	69	87	79	62	78	67	82
Morocco	na	76	79	73	79	76	71	73	88	88	76	84	77	71	81	81
Netherlands	na	na	na	na	na	na	na	na	na	na	na	na	na	na	na	na
New Zealand	na	76	74	79	82	74	76	76	81	74	82	80	68	77	75	78
Nigeria	78	72	72	73	72	73	72	74	71	71	77	72	67	74	72	71
Northern Ireland	na	na	na	na	na	na	na	na	na	na	na	na	na	na	na	na
Norway	na	28	26	31	32	23	32	34	27	24	na	na	na	37	27	26
Pakistan	na	89	87	92	88	88	94	93	87	79	97	91	77	90	88	58
Peru	na	57	58	56	58	56	55	53	56	61	52	59	63	51	58	59
Philippines	na	60	61	60	57	63	60	60	61	60	60	59	64	60	61	60
Poland	na	na	na	na	na	na	na	na	na	na	na	na	na	na	na	na
Portugal	na	na	na	na	na	na	na	na	na	na	na	na	na	na	na	na
Puerto Rico	na	52	52	52	63	53	47	42	50	55	43	55	56	43	51	58
Romania	na	na	na	na	na	na	na	na	na	na	na	na	na	na	na	na
Russian Fed.	na	na	na	na	na	na	na	na	na	na	na	na	na	na	na	na
Serbia	na	69	69	70	63	69	72	76	66	66	72	68	70	75	63	75
Singapore	na	22	25	19	25	21	16	15	27	21	16	23	25	15	22	47
Slovakia	na	na	na	na	na	na	na	na	na	na	na	na	na	na	na	na
Slovenia	na	na	na	na	na	na	na	na	na	na	na	na	na	na	na	na
South Africa	na	60	62	58	59	62	54	54	66	71	49	54	79	61	61	48
Spain	51	60	60	60	61	63	56	60	61	58	64	58	58	55	60	63
Sweden	na	na	na	na	na	na	na	na	na	na	na	na	na	na	na	na
Switzerland	na	61	66	55	61	66	56	56	62	63	63	67	59	60	60	66
Taiwan	na	52	53	51	67	52	41	37	53	64	39	57	57	56	49	48
Tanzania	na	48	51	44	53	46	44	43	61	43	48	47	47	51	46	48
Turkey	53	82	84	80	83	82	79	79	86	87	82	82	82	82	82	83
Uganda	na	51	44	58	52	50	52	53	51	54	51	39	48	46	51	68
Ukraine	na	na	na	na	na	na	na	na	na	na	na	na	na	na	na	na
United States	68	63	65	62	65	63	62	61	67	62	65	61	62	56	63	69
Uruguay	na	76	74	78	83	86	66	71	84	82	72	78	79	68	76	84
Venezuela	na	37	34	41	40	38	29	24	37	52	27	37	45	34	37	40
Vietnam	na	9	8	10	7	10	9	9	7	7	14	7	8	9	8	11
Zimbabwe	na	82	84	81	81	85	82	81	85	91	79	80	86	84	83	67
Total	55	67	67	67	68	67	65	63	68	71	68	68	68	68	65	70

RANKING

Country	2000
Armenia	96
Georgia	94
Macedonia	93
Dominican Rep.	92
Moldova	91
Argentina	90
Pakistan	89
Korea, South	88
Algeria	87
Japan	84
Zimbabwe	82
Turkey	82
Bosnia and Herz.	81
Colombia	79
Azerbaijan	78
Morocco	76
Uruguay	76
New Zealand	76
Brazil	75
El Salvador	74
Montenegro	74
Nigeria	72
Mexico	72
Indonesia	70
Serbia	69
Jordan	69
Egypt	69
Australia	68
India	66
Chile	65
Albania	65
United States	63
Switzerland	61
Philippines	60
South Africa	60
Spain	60
Peru	57
Bangladesh	56
Canada	52
Puerto Rico	52
Taiwan	52
Uganda	51
Iran	49
Tanzania	48
Venezuela	37
Norway	28
Singapore	22
China	17
Vietnam	9
Total	67

E129) ECONOMIC AID

Some people favor, and others are against, having this country provide economic aid to poorer countries. Do you think that this country should provide more or less economic aid to poorer countries? Would you say we should give …

Provide a lot more that we do / Somewhat more than we do (%)

(WVS: V176)

Country	Wave 1990	Wave 2000	Gender Male	Gender Female	Age 16-29	Age 30-49	Age 50+	Education Lower	Education Middle	Education Upper	Income Lower	Income Middle	Income Upper	Values Mat	Values Mixed	Values Postm.
Albania	na	43	41	46	36	45	46	33	46	65	36	49	47	37	49	25
Algeria	na	39	38	40	41	35	42	40	37	41	39	40	36	41	36	42
Argentina	na	4	4	3	4	3	4	3	5	1	5	4	2	3	3	5
Armenia	na	63	63	63	64	61	64	66	55	64	66	55	64	61	65	67
Australia	na	75	75	75	76	77	72	68	72	85	69	75	82	75	74	76
Austria	na	na	na	na	na	na	na	na	na	na	na	na	na	na	na	na
Azerbaijan	na	57	59	55	61	55	54	55	54	63	52	60	63	53	62	72
Bangladesh	na	63	64	62	64	62	65	61	61	70	65	59	68	67	61	59
Belarus	na	na	na	na	na	na	na	na	na	na	na	na	na	na	na	na
Belgium	na	na	na	na	na	na	na	na	na	na	na	na	na	na	na	na
Bosnia and Herz.	na	49	47	50	49	46	52	45	48	54	44	48	57	48	48	65
Brazil	na	65	66	64	66	63	67	66	67	56	69	66	59	68	64	62
Bulgaria	na	na	na	na	na	na	na	na	na	na	na	na	na	na	na	na
Canada	na	56	58	54	66	54	51	44	55	67	50	53	65	50	54	62
Chile	na	50	50	51	54	48	49	50	50	51	50	52	46	43	53	54
China	na	69	64	74	77	68	65	70	69	64	65	74	66	64	72	79
Colombia	na	na	na	na	na	na	na	na	na	na	na	na	na	na	na	na
Croatia	na	na	na	na	na	na	na	na	na	na	na	na	na	na	na	na
Czech Republic	na	na	na	na	na	na	na	na	na	na	na	na	na	na	na	na
Denmark	na	na	na	na	na	na	na	na	na	na	na	na	na	na	na	na
Dominican Rep.	na	68	65	69	64	73	82	68	72	66	71	68	59	73	68	63
Egypt	na	na	na	na	na	na	na	na	na	na	na	na	na	na	na	na
El Salvador	na	na	na	na	na	na	na	na	na	na	na	na	na	na	na	na
Estonia	na	na	na	na	na	na	na	na	na	na	na	na	na	na	na	na
Finland	na	na	na	na	na	na	na	na	na	na	na	na	na	na	na	na
France	na	na	na	na	na	na	na	na	na	na	na	na	na	na	na	na
Georgia	na	56	59	55	54	58	56	56	56	58	58	59	54	55	58	71
Germany	na	na	na	na	na	na	na	na	na	na	na	na	na	na	na	na
Great Britain	na	na	na	na	na	na	na	na	na	na	na	na	na	na	na	na
Greece	na	na	na	na	na	na	na	na	na	na	na	na	na	na	na	na
Hungary	na	na	na	na	na	na	na	na	na	na	na	na	na	na	na	na
Iceland	na	na	na	na	na	na	na	na	na	na	na	na	na	na	na	na
India	na	55	55	54	54	56	52	54	57	54	62	52	53	53	58	45
Indonesia	na	na	na	na	na	na	na	na	na	na	na	na	na	na	na	na
Iran	na	na	na	na	na	na	na	na	na	na	na	na	na	na	na	na
Ireland	na	na	na	na	na	na	na	na	na	na	na	na	na	na	na	na
Israel	na	na	na	na	na	na	na	na	na	na	na	na	na	na	na	na
Italy	na	na	na	na	na	na	na	na	na	na	na	na	na	na	na	na
Japan	na	45	47	44	60	48	37	40	43	56	40	45	49	42	46	51
Jordan	na	na	na	na	na	na	na	na	na	na	na	na	na	na	na	na
Korea, South	na	na	na	na	na	na	na	na	na	na	na	na	na	na	na	na
Latvia	na	na	na	na	na	na	na	na	na	na	na	na	na	na	na	na
Lithuania	na	na	na	na	na	na	na	na	na	na	na	na	na	na	na	na
Luxembourg	na	na	na	na	na	na	na	na	na	na	na	na	na	na	na	na
Macedonia	na	20	21	20	23	22	16	26	16	23	22	16	21	19	22	23
Malta	na	na	na	na	na	na	na	na	na	na	na	na	na	na	na	na
Mexico	na	68	65	71	68	67	70	71	67	59	70	71	65	70	68	69
Moldova	na	63	65	62	55	68	65	60	67	59	67	68	57	60	67	60
Montenegro	na	48	46	51	53	46	45	46	48	51	65	47	36	43	52	64
Morocco	na	62	58	67	64	60	63	66	53	39	54	51	44	69	60	46
Netherlands	na	na	na	na	na	na	na	na	na	na	na	na	na	na	na	na
New Zealand	na	68	69	68	69	68	68	58	70	79	63	70	72	68	67	73
Nigeria	na	na	na	na	na	na	na	na	na	na	na	na	na	na	na	na
Northern Ireland	na	na	na	na	na	na	na	na	na	na	na	na	na	na	na	na
Norway	na	82	79	84	83	83	80	77	78	91	na	na	na	70	82	92
Pakistan	na	na	na	na	na	na	na	na	na	na	na	na	na	na	na	na
Peru	1990	94	93	94	94	93	94	93	95	92	95	92	94	92	94	93
Philippines	na	36	33	39	43	34	30	33	39	35	35	32	41	37	36	35
Poland	na	na	na	na	na	na	na	na	na	na	na	na	na	na	na	na
Portugal	na	na	na	na	na	na	na	na	na	na	na	na	na	na	na	na
Puerto Rico	na	84	84	85	86	81	86	91	84	84	87	85	82	80	86	82
Romania	na	na	na	na	na	na	na	na	na	na	na	na	na	na	na	na
Russian Fed.	na	na	na	na	na	na	na	na	na	na	na	na	na	na	na	na
Serbia	na	26	25	28	27	25	28	25	25	31	29	25	25	25	24	47
Singapore	na	68	67	68	75	61	59	67	67	72	70	65	68	63	70	69
Slovakia	na	na	na	na	na	na	na	na	na	na	na	na	na	na	na	na
Slovenia	na	na	na	na	na	na	na	na	na	na	na	na	na	na	na	na
South Africa	na	45	46	43	42	48	42	50	39	37	49	45	40	37	49	56
Spain	na	83	81	85	86	82	82	82	83	87	78	86	86	82	83	84
Sweden	na	40	37	42	47	43	31	27	37	53	37	34	50	18	35	58
Switzerland	na	na	na	na	na	na	na	na	na	na	na	na	na	na	na	na
Taiwan	na	76	74	77	78	75	74	72	81	76	74	73	80	72	80	81
Tanzania	na	40	37	45	40	40	42	44	34	42	44	43	35	36	42	32
Turkey	na	na	na	na	na	na	na	na	na	na	na	na	na	na	na	na
Uganda	na	37	38	37	45	32	21	40	35	39	39	43	26	33	39	39
Ukraine	na	na	na	na	na	na	na	na	na	na	na	na	na	na	na	na
United States	na	44	47	41	52	40	43	45	38	47	41	46	47	41	44	46
Uruguay	na	62	66	60	67	59	63	60	65	68	58	59	72	55	67	63
Venezuela	na	66	66	66	67	65	65	68	70	53	73	67	60	70	64	67
Vietnam	na	74	77	70	75	69	79	75	70	84	75	71	75	61	76	78
Zimbabwe	na	54	48	59	58	50	49	58	50	19	59	55	46	52	55	63
Total	na	57	56	58	59	57	55	55	55	63	56	56	57	53	58	61

RANKING

Country	2000
Peru	94
Puerto Rico	84
Spain	83
Norway	82
Taiwan	76
Australia	75
Vietnam	74
China	69
Mexico	68
New Zealand	68
Dominican Rep.	68
Singapore	68
Venezuela	66
Brazil	65
Bangladesh	63
Armenia	63
Moldova	63
Morocco	62
Uruguay	62
Azerbaijan	57
Georgia	56
Canada	56
India	55
Zimbabwe	54
Chile	50
Bosnia and Herz.	49
Montenegro	48
Japan	45
South Africa	45
United States	44
Albania	43
Tanzania	40
Sweden	40
Algeria	39
Uganda	37
Philippines	36
Serbia	26
Macedonia	20
Argentina	4
Total	57

E135) WHO SHOULD DECIDE: INTERNATIONAL PEACEKEEPING

Who could better handle certain kinds of problems: the United Nations, the respective national governments, or the national governments together with the United Nations?

National governments (%)

(WVS: V177)

Country	Wave 1990	Wave 2000	Gender Male	Gender Female	Age 16-29	Age 30-49	Age 50+	Education Lower	Education Middle	Education Upper	Income Lower	Income Middle	Income Upper	Values Mat	Values Mixed	Values Postm.
Albania	na	60	60	59	61	60	59	54	63	65	56	62	62	58	61	54
Algeria	na	49	48	50	51	46	52	49	50	47	54	44	48	52	47	51
Argentina	na	2	2	3	1	2	3	2	2	3	2	2	2	2	2	3
Armenia	na	na	na	na	na	na	na	na	na	na	na	na	na	na	na	na
Australia	na	na	na	na	na	na	na	na	na	na	na	na	na	na	na	na
Austria	na	na	na	na	na	na	na	na	na	na	na	na	na	na	na	na
Azerbaijan	na	na	na	na	na	na	na	na	na	na	na	na	na	na	na	na
Bangladesh	na	43	42	44	46	43	32	41	45	45	40	42	50	43	44	51
Belarus	na	na	na	na	na	na	na	na	na	na	na	na	na	na	na	na
Belgium	na	na	na	na	na	na	na	na	na	na	na	na	na	na	na	na
Bosnia and Herz.	na	56	56	55	56	57	53	49	56	61	53	56	55	53	57	53
Brazil	na	na	na	na	na	na	na	na	na	na	na	na	na	na	na	na
Bulgaria	na	na	na	na	na	na	na	na	na	na	na	na	na	na	na	na
Canada	na	62	55	69	60	62	63	59	65	59	62	61	61	56	63	62
Chile	na	51	54	50	55	54	45	43	54	61	40	57	62	48	53	54
China	na	46	45	46	48	44	47	43	47	48	49	42	48	46	47	30
Colombia	na	na	na	na	na	na	na	na	na	na	na	na	na	na	na	na
Croatia	na	na	na	na	na	na	na	na	na	na	na	na	na	na	na	na
Czech Republic	na	na	na	na	na	na	na	na	na	na	na	na	na	na	na	na
Denmark	na	na	na	na	na	na	na	na	na	na	na	na	na	na	na	na
Dominican Rep.	na	na	na	na	na	na	na	na	na	na	na	na	na	na	na	na
Egypt	na	48	44	52	52	46	45	47	49	50	52	46	46	47	49	45
El Salvador	na	na	na	na	na	na	na	na	na	na	na	na	na	na	na	na
Estonia	na	na	na	na	na	na	na	na	na	na	na	na	na	na	na	na
Finland	na	na	na	na	na	na	na	na	na	na	na	na	na	na	na	na
France	na	na	na	na	na	na	na	na	na	na	na	na	na	na	na	na
Georgia	na	na	na	na	na	na	na	na	na	na	na	na	na	na	na	na
Germany	na	na	na	na	na	na	na	na	na	na	na	na	na	na	na	na
Great Britain	na	na	na	na	na	na	na	na	na	na	na	na	na	na	na	na
Greece	na	na	na	na	na	na	na	na	na	na	na	na	na	na	na	na
Hungary	na	na	na	na	na	na	na	na	na	na	na	na	na	na	na	na
Iceland	na	na	na	na	na	na	na	na	na	na	na	na	na	na	na	na
India	na	56	59	50	56	57	52	45	59	67	41	53	63	64	54	58
Indonesia	na	57	55	60	57	61	54	52	57	62	58	59	55	61	55	46
Iran	na	59	60	58	58	58	62	58	56	63	60	58	60	59	61	52
Ireland	na	na	na	na	na	na	na	na	na	na	na	na	na	na	na	na
Israel	na	na	na	na	na	na	na	na	na	na	na	na	na	na	na	na
Italy	na	na	na	na	na	na	na	na	na	na	na	na	na	na	na	na
Japan	na	39	38	39	29	40	42	28	40	42	41	40	36	41	39	40
Jordan	na	67	63	71	66	69	64	65	66	71	71	63	70	63	69	65
Korea, South	na	65	61	70	76	64	56	52	62	72	63	65	68	64	66	77
Latvia	na	na	na	na	na	na	na	na	na	na	na	na	na	na	na	na
Lithuania	na	na	na	na	na	na	na	na	na	na	na	na	na	na	na	na
Luxembourg	na	na	na	na	na	na	na	na	na	na	na	na	na	na	na	na
Macedonia	na	29	29	29	25	30	30	26	30	28	29	29	30	30	28	24
Malta	na	na	na	na	na	na	na	na	na	na	na	na	na	na	na	na
Mexico	na	47	45	48	49	47	43	42	50	56	33	50	54	43	47	52
Moldova	na	66	63	68	70	65	64	61	64	74	73	68	60	66	66	53
Montenegro	na	42	39	44	45	43	40	38	44	46	41	41	44	40	44	39
Morocco	na	45	44	46	46	45	41	49	37	33	49	45	39	49	45	37
Netherlands	na	na	na	na	na	na	na	na	na	na	na	na	na	na	na	na
New Zealand	na	na	na	na	na	na	na	na	na	na	na	na	na	na	na	na
Nigeria	na	37	37	38	39	37	27	38	35	40	39	36	35	36	38	36
Northern Ireland	na	na	na	na	na	na	na	na	na	na	na	na	na	na	na	na
Norway	na	na	na	na	na	na	na	na	na	na	na	na	na	na	na	na
Pakistan	na	na	na	na	na	na	na	na	na	na	na	na	na	na	na	na
Peru	na	na	na	na	na	na	na	na	na	na	na	na	na	na	na	na
Philippines	na	36	36	35	33	37	38	35	36	36	40	36	32	36	36	31
Poland	na	na	na	na	na	na	na	na	na	na	na	na	na	na	na	na
Portugal	na	na	na	na	na	na	na	na	na	na	na	na	na	na	na	na
Puerto Rico	na	na	na	na	na	na	na	na	na	na	na	na	na	na	na	na
Romania	na	na	na	na	na	na	na	na	na	na	na	na	na	na	na	na
Russian Fed.	na	na	na	na	na	na	na	na	na	na	na	na	na	na	na	na
Serbia	na	52	51	53	58	53	48	44	52	61	47	52	55	47	55	60
Singapore	na	na	na	na	na	na	na	na	na	na	na	na	na	na	na	na
Slovakia	na	na	na	na	na	na	na	na	na	na	na	na	na	na	na	na
Slovenia	na	na	na	na	na	na	na	na	na	na	na	na	na	na	na	na
South Africa	na	44	43	46	41	48	42	46	41	42	49	45	36	42	46	44
Spain	na	65	66	65	66	66	64	64	67	67	64	66	63	65	64	72
Sweden	na	67	62	71	66	70	65	64	68	67	66	68	66	67	66	67
Switzerland	na	na	na	na	na	na	na	na	na	na	na	na	na	na	na	na
Taiwan	na	na	na	na	na	na	na	na	na	na	na	na	na	na	na	na
Tanzania	na	28	30	26	28	28	29	27	28	33	27	32	28	31	27	17
Turkey	na	na	na	na	na	na	na	na	na	na	na	na	na	na	na	na
Uganda	na	38	39	37	42	34	34	36	40	25	40	30	45	35	41	33
Ukraine	na	na	na	na	na	na	na	na	na	na	na	na	na	na	na	na
United States	na	59	55	62	54	59	63	52	60	61	52	63	61	52	59	61
Uruguay	na	na	na	na	na	na	na	na	na	na	na	na	na	na	na	na
Venezuela	na	na	na	na	na	na	na	na	na	na	na	na	na	na	na	na
Vietnam	na	40	40	40	37	41	41	35	48	39	39	38	43	42	42	51
Zimbabwe	na	27	27	27	29	25	26	28	27	30	31	28	25	32	25	20
Total	na	48	46	49	47	48	47	42	49	55	47	47	49	47	48	48

RANKING

Country	2000
Jordan	67
Sweden	67
Moldova	66
Korea, South	65
Spain	65
Canada	62
Albania	60
Iran	59
United States	59
Indonesia	57
Bosnia and Herz.	56
India	56
Serbia	52
Chile	51
Algeria	49
Egypt	48
Mexico	47
China	46
Morocco	45
South Africa	44
Bangladesh	43
Montenegro	42
Vietnam	40
Japan	39
Uganda	38
Nigeria	37
Philippines	36
Macedonia	29
Tanzania	28
Zimbabwe	27
Argentina	2
Total	48

E136) WHO SHOULD DECIDE: PROTECTION OF THE ENVIRONMENT

Who could better handle certain kinds of problems: the United Nations, the respective national governments, or the national governments together with the United Nations?

National governments (%)

(WVS: V178)

Country	Wave 1990	Wave 2000	Gender Male	Gender Female	Age 16-29	Age 30-49	Age 50+	Education Lower	Education Middle	Education Upper	Income Lower	Income Middle	Income Upper	Values Mat	Values Mixed	Values Postm.	RANKING Country	RANKING 2000
Albania	na	56	55	56	54	59	52	53	59	54	57	55	54	58	52	64	Uganda	72
Algeria	na	28	27	29	29	25	30	29	27	29	29	27	25	24	32	19	Indonesia	71
Argentina	na	67	65	69	64	67	71	72	60	66	77	66	60	78	68	56	Zimbabwe	69
Armenia	na	na	na	na	na	na	na	na	na	na	na	na	na	na	na	na	Argentina	67
Australia	na	na	na	na	na	na	na	na	na	na	na	na	na	na	na	na	Macedonia	63
Austria	na	na	na	na	na	na	na	na	na	na	na	na	na	na	na	na	Tanzania	63
Azerbaijan	na	na	na	na	na	na	na	na	na	na	na	na	na	na	na	na	Montenegro	59
Bangladesh	na	47	49	45	47	45	60	50	46	42	46	42	57	52	46	25	Nigeria	57
Belarus	na	na	na	na	na	na	na	na	na	na	na	na	na	na	na	na	Albania	56
Belgium	na	na	na	na	na	na	na	na	na	na	na	na	na	na	na	na	South Africa	55
Bosnia and Herz.	na	55	52	57	57	58	49	56	55	54	56	56	54	51	58	55	Bosnia and Herz.	55
Brazil	na	na	na	na	na	na	na	na	na	na	na	na	na	na	na	na	Philippines	55
Bulgaria	na	na	na	na	na	na	na	na	na	na	na	na	na	na	na	na	Serbia	54
Canada	na	37	35	39	38	35	38	41	37	34	38	39	34	48	39	30	China	53
Chile	na	40	37	43	41	38	44	48	37	34	47	37	36	41	39	43	Jordan	53
China	na	53	51	56	52	55	50	54	54	38	60	54	44	52	55	48	India	51
Colombia	na	na	na	na	na	na	na	na	na	na	na	na	na	na	na	na	Korea, South	49
Croatia	na	na	na	na	na	na	na	na	na	na	na	na	na	na	na	na	Egypt	48
Czech Republic	na	na	na	na	na	na	na	na	na	na	na	na	na	na	na	na	Bangladesh	47
Denmark	na	na	na	na	na	na	na	na	na	na	na	na	na	na	na	na	Mexico	47
Dominican Rep.	na	na	na	na	na	na	na	na	na	na	na	na	na	na	na	na	Morocco	47
Egypt	na	48	48	48	46	50	47	50	50	38	50	52	43	48	47	49	Vietnam	43
El Salvador	na	na	na	na	na	na	na	na	na	na	na	na	na	na	na	na	Chile	40
Estonia	na	na	na	na	na	na	na	na	na	na	na	na	na	na	na	na	United States	38
Finland	na	na	na	na	na	na	na	na	na	na	na	na	na	na	na	na	Canada	37
France	na	na	na	na	na	na	na	na	na	na	na	na	na	na	na	na	Moldova	36
Georgia	na	na	na	na	na	na	na	na	na	na	na	na	na	na	na	na	Sweden	28
Germany	na	na	na	na	na	na	na	na	na	na	na	na	na	na	na	na	Algeria	28
Great Britain	na	na	na	na	na	na	na	na	na	na	na	na	na	na	na	na	Japan	28
Greece	na	na	na	na	na	na	na	na	na	na	na	na	na	na	na	na	Iran	26
Hungary	na	na	na	na	na	na	na	na	na	na	na	na	na	na	na	na	Spain	24
Iceland	na	na	na	na	na	na	na	na	na	na	na	na	na	na	na	na		
India	na	51	49	54	48	52	50	56	52	43	54	54	47	47	50	61		
Indonesia	na	71	71	70	76	72	68	75	67	74	76	68	69	72	70	75		
Iran	na	26	25	28	28	25	22	28	26	25	27	25	25	23	29	28		
Ireland	na	na	na	na	na	na	na	na	na	na	na	na	na	na	na	na		
Israel	na	na	na	na	na	na	na	na	na	na	na	na	na	na	na	na		
Italy	na	na	na	na	na	na	na	na	na	na	na	na	na	na	na	na		
Japan	na	28	25	30	26	26	30	36	27	28	30	28	25	26	27	25		
Jordan	na	53	54	52	53	52	57	54	56	48	53	54	54	58	53	31		
Korea, South	na	49	49	50	41	53	52	64	52	44	55	48	44	50	51	32		
Latvia	na	na	na	na	na	na	na	na	na	na	na	na	na	na	na	na		
Lithuania	na	na	na	na	na	na	na	na	na	na	na	na	na	na	na	na		
Luxembourg	na	na	na	na	na	na	na	na	na	na	na	na	na	na	na	na		
Macedonia	na	63	59	67	59	64	65	54	68	63	63	62	64	63	66	49		
Malta	na	na	na	na	na	na	na	na	na	na	na	na	na	na	na	na		
Mexico	na	47	48	47	47	47	48	50	44	46	53	42	47	49	46	45		
Moldova	na	36	34	38	35	38	35	38	37	32	30	33	38	38	34	37		
Montenegro	na	59	59	58	55	59	60	60	58	58	70	62	52	62	55	58		
Morocco	na	47	47	46	44	52	43	49	43	32	43	43	48	54	42	46		
Netherlands	na	na	na	na	na	na	na	na	na	na	na	na	na	na	na	na		
New Zealand	na	na	na	na	na	na	na	na	na	na	na	na	na	na	na	na		
Nigeria	na	57	56	57	57	56	56	58	56	55	54	58	60	58	56	58		
Northern Ireland	na	na	na	na	na	na	na	na	na	na	na	na	na	na	na	na		
Norway	na	na	na	na	na	na	na	na	na	na	na	na	na	na	na	na		
Pakistan	na	na	na	na	na	na	na	na	na	na	na	na	na	na	na	na		
Peru	na	na	na	na	na	na	na	na	na	na	na	na	na	na	na	na		
Philippines	na	55	53	56	60	53	51	48	53	66	49	56	58	50	58	59		
Poland	na	na	na	na	na	na	na	na	na	na	na	na	na	na	na	na		
Portugal	na	na	na	na	na	na	na	na	na	na	na	na	na	na	na	na		
Puerto Rico	na	na	na	na	na	na	na	na	na	na	na	na	na	na	na	na		
Romania	na	na	na	na	na	na	na	na	na	na	na	na	na	na	na	na		
Russian Fed.	na	na	na	na	na	na	na	na	na	na	na	na	na	na	na	na		
Serbia	na	54	52	56	53	54	55	55	57	50	56	58	55	58	52	46		
Singapore	na	na	na	na	na	na	na	na	na	na	na	na	na	na	na	na		
Slovakia	na	na	na	na	na	na	na	na	na	na	na	na	na	na	na	na		
Slovenia	na	na	na	na	na	na	na	na	na	na	na	na	na	na	na	na		
South Africa	na	55	55	56	58	50	64	53	58	65	50	60	57	55	55	57		
Spain	na	24	24	24	21	25	26	26	21	25	28	20	30	28	25	17		
Sweden	na	28	27	30	31	24	31	35	29	22	29	29	25	38	30	21		
Switzerland	na	na	na	na	na	na	na	na	na	na	na	na	na	na	na	na		
Taiwan	na	na	na	na	na	na	na	na	na	na	na	na	na	na	na	na		
Tanzania	na	63	63	63	68	60	61	63	68	52	62	64	54	62	64	63		
Turkey	na	na	na	na	na	na	na	na	na	na	na	na	na	na	na	na		
Uganda	na	72	68	75	68	75	74	74	70	75	70	65	68	78	68	72		
Ukraine	na	na	na	na	na	na	na	na	na	na	na	na	na	na	na	na		
United States	na	38	36	39	36	39	38	41	40	35	39	34	41	42	38	37		
Uruguay	na	na	na	na	na	na	na	na	na	na	na	na	na	na	na	na		
Venezuela	na	na	na	na	na	na	na	na	na	na	na	na	na	na	na	na		
Vietnam	na	43	43	44	46	43	41	46	39	48	38	49	41	55	38	36		
Zimbabwe	na	69	70	68	68	70	69	68	70	62	66	71	72	69	69	64		
Total	na	50	48	51	50	50	49	53	50	44	51	50	47	53	49	42	Total	50

E137) WHO SHOULD DECIDE: AID TO DEVELOPING COUNTRIES

Who could better handle certain kinds of problems: the United Nations, the respective national governments, or the national governments together with the United Nations?

National governments (%)

(WVS: V179)

Country	Wave 1990	Wave 2000	Gender Male	Gender Female	Age 16-29	Age 30-49	Age 50+	Education Lower	Education Middle	Education Upper	Income Lower	Income Middle	Income Upper	Values Mat	Values Mixed	Values Postm.
Albania	na	48	48	47	48	46	50	48	47	49	48	47	48	46	50	44
Algeria	na	46	47	44	49	43	45	42	46	47	49	46	44	47	46	44
Argentina	na	3	3	2	2	3	2	1	4	5	1	3	4	2	2	5
Armenia	na	na	na	na	na	na	na	na	na	na	na	na	na	na	na	na
Australia	na	na	na	na	na	na	na	na	na	na	na	na	na	na	na	na
Austria	na	na	na	na	na	na	na	na	na	na	na	na	na	na	na	na
Azerbaijan	na	na	na	na	na	na	na	na	na	na	na	na	na	na	na	na
Bangladesh	na	43	43	43	45	41	41	42	42	43	42	43	42	45	42	47
Belarus	na	na	na	na	na	na	na	na	na	na	na	na	na	na	na	na
Belgium	na	na	na	na	na	na	na	na	na	na	na	na	na	na	na	na
Bosnia and Herz.	na	56	57	55	57	55	56	53	56	56	57	55	55	57	55	53
Brazil	na	na	na	na	na	na	na	na	na	na	na	na	na	na	na	na
Bulgaria	na	na	na	na	na	na	na	na	na	na	na	na	na	na	na	na
Canada	na	58	54	62	56	60	58	56	59	60	57	61	58	60	58	61
Chile	na	54	54	53	59	52	51	50	56	55	45	59	59	50	54	58
China	na	33	29	38	37	31	36	31	32	52	30	30	38	35	30	39
Colombia	na	na	na	na	na	na	na	na	na	na	na	na	na	na	na	na
Croatia	na	na	na	na	na	na	na	na	na	na	na	na	na	na	na	na
Czech Republic	na	na	na	na	na	na	na	na	na	na	na	na	na	na	na	na
Denmark	na	na	na	na	na	na	na	na	na	na	na	na	na	na	na	na
Dominican Rep.	na	na	na	na	na	na	na	na	na	na	na	na	na	na	na	na
Egypt	na	32	29	36	33	32	32	36	30	27	39	32	28	32	33	27
El Salvador	na	na	na	na	na	na	na	na	na	na	na	na	na	na	na	na
Estonia	na	na	na	na	na	na	na	na	na	na	na	na	na	na	na	na
Finland	na	na	na	na	na	na	na	na	na	na	na	na	na	na	na	na
France	na	na	na	na	na	na	na	na	na	na	na	na	na	na	na	na
Georgia	na	na	na	na	na	na	na	na	na	na	na	na	na	na	na	na
Germany	na	na	na	na	na	na	na	na	na	na	na	na	na	na	na	na
Great Britain	na	na	na	na	na	na	na	na	na	na	na	na	na	na	na	na
Greece	na	na	na	na	na	na	na	na	na	na	na	na	na	na	na	na
Hungary	na	na	na	na	na	na	na	na	na	na	na	na	na	na	na	na
Iceland	na	na	na	na	na	na	na	na	na	na	na	na	na	na	na	na
India	na	50	51	48	53	49	48	39	50	62	33	44	60	56	48	53
Indonesia	na	52	50	54	46	51	57	49	56	49	53	54	43	51	55	36
Iran	na	52	53	51	53	53	50	51	52	56	49	55	54	57	48	57
Ireland	na	na	na	na	na	na	na	na	na	na	na	na	na	na	na	na
Israel	na	na	na	na	na	na	na	na	na	na	na	na	na	na	na	na
Italy	na	na	na	na	na	na	na	na	na	na	na	na	na	na	na	na
Japan	na	42	39	44	39	40	45	44	42	39	43	44	38	39	41	45
Jordan	na	54	47	60	54	54	54	53	52	57	57	52	51	49	55	70
Korea, South	na	62	59	65	67	63	55	52	61	64	64	60	62	61	62	71
Latvia	na	na	na	na	na	na	na	na	na	na	na	na	na	na	na	na
Lithuania	na	na	na	na	na	na	na	na	na	na	na	na	na	na	na	na
Luxembourg	na	na	na	na	na	na	na	na	na	na	na	na	na	na	na	na
Macedonia	na	31	32	31	32	31	31	26	32	37	28	33	33	33	30	34
Malta	na	na	na	na	na	na	na	na	na	na	na	na	na	na	na	na
Mexico	na	49	47	51	52	48	47	48	48	57	44	51	53	45	51	53
Moldova	na	62	59	64	61	61	63	63	59	65	65	64	58	59	63	67
Montenegro	na	41	38	43	44	40	40	38	42	43	29	39	44	33	48	45
Morocco	na	44	41	48	44	46	39	46	41	38	51	46	36	45	46	34
Netherlands	na	na	na	na	na	na	na	na	na	na	na	na	na	na	na	na
New Zealand	na	na	na	na	na	na	na	na	na	na	na	na	na	na	na	na
Nigeria	na	33	35	31	34	32	31	33	33	33	32	33	34	34	32	33
Northern Ireland	na	na	na	na	na	na	na	na	na	na	na	na	na	na	na	na
Norway	na	na	na	na	na	na	na	na	na	na	na	na	na	na	na	na
Pakistan	na	na	na	na	na	na	na	na	na	na	na	na	na	na	na	na
Peru	na	na	na	na	na	na	na	na	na	na	na	na	na	na	na	na
Philippines	na	32	31	32	30	33	32	30	31	35	34	33	29	31	32	38
Poland	na	na	na	na	na	na	na	na	na	na	na	na	na	na	na	na
Portugal	na	na	na	na	na	na	na	na	na	na	na	na	na	na	na	na
Puerto Rico	na	na	na	na	na	na	na	na	na	na	na	na	na	na	na	na
Romania	na	na	na	na	na	na	na	na	na	na	na	na	na	na	na	na
Russian Fed.	na	na	na	na	na	na	na	na	na	na	na	na	na	na	na	na
Serbia	na	41	38	44	44	42	39	37	41	46	39	40	41	35	45	53
Singapore	na	na	na	na	na	na	na	na	na	na	na	na	na	na	na	na
Slovakia	na	na	na	na	na	na	na	na	na	na	na	na	na	na	na	na
Slovenia	na	na	na	na	na	na	na	na	na	na	na	na	na	na	na	na
South Africa	na	44	44	43	42	44	46	43	45	33	46	40	44	41	47	37
Spain	na	73	71	74	75	73	70	72	72	77	69	73	70	71	71	81
Sweden	na	64	62	66	60	67	64	64	63	66	65	63	66	64	62	71
Switzerland	na	na	na	na	na	na	na	na	na	na	na	na	na	na	na	na
Taiwan	na	na	na	na	na	na	na	na	na	na	na	na	na	na	na	na
Tanzania	na	35	38	30	30	37	34	34	31	43	30	38	44	34	35	39
Turkey	na	na	na	na	na	na	na	na	na	na	na	na	na	na	na	na
Uganda	na	39	50	30	40	37	45	31	42	53	36	40	43	37	39	48
Ukraine	na	na	na	na	na	na	na	na	na	na	na	na	na	na	na	na
United States	na	53	50	56	47	54	57	49	56	53	49	57	53	48	54	54
Uruguay	na	na	na	na	na	na	na	na	na	na	na	na	na	na	na	na
Venezuela	na	na	na	na	na	na	na	na	na	na	na	na	na	na	na	na
Vietnam	na	34	37	31	34	34	34	32	35	46	33	29	39	35	36	43
Zimbabwe	na	34	32	35	34	33	33	33	33	53	36	30	40	36	33	22
Total	na	45	44	45	44	44	46	41	45	50	44	44	45	43	45	48

RANKING

Country	2000
Spain	73
Sweden	64
Korea, South	62
Moldova	62
Canada	58
Bosnia and Herz.	56
Chile	54
Jordan	54
United States	53
Iran	52
Indonesia	52
India	50
Mexico	49
Albania	48
Algeria	46
Morocco	44
South Africa	44
Bangladesh	43
Japan	42
Serbia	41
Montenegro	41
Uganda	39
Tanzania	35
Vietnam	34
Zimbabwe	34
China	33
Nigeria	33
Egypt	32
Philippines	32
Macedonia	31
Argentina	3
Total	45

E138) WHO SHOULD DECIDE: REFUGEES
Who could better handle certain kinds of problems: the United Nations, the respective national governments, or the national governments together with the United Nations?

National governments (%)

(WVS: V180)

Country	Wave 1990	Wave 2000	Gender Male	Gender Female	Age 16-29	Age 30-49	Age 50+	Education Lower	Education Middle	Education Upper	Income Lower	Income Middle	Income Upper	Values Mat	Values Mixed	Values Postm.
Albania	na	55	54	57	55	55	55	55	56	56	54	57	56	58	53	49
Algeria	na	41	42	40	45	37	42	38	38	47	43	40	41	42	41	43
Argentina	na	1	1	1	1	1	na	na	1	1	na	na	2	1	1	1
Armenia	na	na	na	na	na	na	na	na	na	na	na	na	na	na	na	na
Australia	na	na	na	na	na	na	na	na	na	na	na	na	na	na	na	na
Austria	na	na	na	na	na	na	na	na	na	na	na	na	na	na	na	na
Azerbaijan	na	na	na	na	na	na	na	na	na	na	na	na	na	na	na	na
Bangladesh	na	42	43	42	46	42	34	42	42	44	40	42	46	40	46	41
Belarus	na	na	na	na	na	na	na	na	na	na	na	na	na	na	na	na
Belgium	na	na	na	na	na	na	na	na	na	na	na	na	na	na	na	na
Bosnia and Herz.	na	64	65	63	63	63	66	64	64	63	66	64	61	67	63	64
Brazil	na	na	na	na	na	na	na	na	na	na	na	na	na	na	na	na
Bulgaria	na	na	na	na	na	na	na	na	na	na	na	na	na	na	na	na
Canada	na	53	48	59	52	55	53	53	51	57	52	54	54	49	53	56
Chile	na	49	48	50	52	50	44	45	50	53	40	57	51	44	50	54
China	na	31	29	33	32	28	37	27	30	51	32	29	32	34	29	9
Colombia	na	na	na	na	na	na	na	na	na	na	na	na	na	na	na	na
Croatia	na	na	na	na	na	na	na	na	na	na	na	na	na	na	na	na
Czech Republic	na	na	na	na	na	na	na	na	na	na	na	na	na	na	na	na
Denmark	na	na	na	na	na	na	na	na	na	na	na	na	na	na	na	na
Dominican Rep.	na	na	na	na	na	na	na	na	na	na	na	na	na	na	na	na
Egypt	na	33	29	37	32	33	34	37	30	28	38	32	31	34	33	27
El Salvador	na	na	na	na	na	na	na	na	na	na	na	na	na	na	na	na
Estonia	na	na	na	na	na	na	na	na	na	na	na	na	na	na	na	na
Finland	na	na	na	na	na	na	na	na	na	na	na	na	na	na	na	na
France	na	na	na	na	na	na	na	na	na	na	na	na	na	na	na	na
Georgia	na	na	na	na	na	na	na	na	na	na	na	na	na	na	na	na
Germany	na	na	na	na	na	na	na	na	na	na	na	na	na	na	na	na
Great Britain	na	na	na	na	na	na	na	na	na	na	na	na	na	na	na	na
Greece	na	na	na	na	na	na	na	na	na	na	na	na	na	na	na	na
Hungary	na	na	na	na	na	na	na	na	na	na	na	na	na	na	na	na
Iceland	na	na	na	na	na	na	na	na	na	na	na	na	na	na	na	na
India	na	46	49	40	47	45	46	37	46	55	30	43	53	52	44	53
Indonesia	na	50	57	44	45	54	49	39	57	49	51	54	43	54	50	39
Iran	na	50	49	51	50	50	49	49	48	56	48	50	54	54	50	42
Ireland	na	na	na	na	na	na	na	na	na	na	na	na	na	na	na	na
Israel	na	na	na	na	na	na	na	na	na	na	na	na	na	na	na	na
Italy	na	na	na	na	na	na	na	na	na	na	na	na	na	na	na	na
Japan	na	46	46	46	43	48	46	48	46	47	45	48	44	38	49	46
Jordan	na	53	47	59	52	53	54	52	50	57	57	49	51	54	50	57
Korea, South	na	62	58	65	65	60	60	56	59	66	59	61	64	59	64	62
Latvia	na	na	na	na	na	na	na	na	na	na	na	na	na	na	na	na
Lithuania	na	na	na	na	na	na	na	na	na	na	na	na	na	na	na	na
Luxembourg	na	na	na	na	na	na	na	na	na	na	na	na	na	na	na	na
Macedonia	na	29	30	28	27	31	28	29	28	32	28	28	33	32	27	25
Malta	na	na	na	na	na	na	na	na	na	na	na	na	na	na	na	na
Mexico	na	46	43	48	45	46	45	48	43	46	38	51	47	44	46	46
Moldova	na	57	54	60	60	56	56	54	55	64	59	62	53	55	60	60
Montenegro	na	51	51	52	57	49	50	47	50	62	61	48	48	48	55	53
Morocco	na	41	38	44	41	42	35	42	38	36	48	41	31	40	42	38
Netherlands	na	na	na	na	na	na	na	na	na	na	na	na	na	na	na	na
New Zealand	na	na	na	na	na	na	na	na	na	na	na	na	na	na	na	na
Nigeria	na	37	37	37	39	34	29	32	38	41	37	36	36	35	37	41
Northern Ireland	na	na	na	na	na	na	na	na	na	na	na	na	na	na	na	na
Norway	na	na	na	na	na	na	na	na	na	na	na	na	na	na	na	na
Pakistan	na	na	na	na	na	na	na	na	na	na	na	na	na	na	na	na
Peru	na	na	na	na	na	na	na	na	na	na	na	na	na	na	na	na
Philippines	na	25	26	25	24	28	22	25	24	27	26	28	21	22	27	27
Poland	na	na	na	na	na	na	na	na	na	na	na	na	na	na	na	na
Portugal	na	na	na	na	na	na	na	na	na	na	na	na	na	na	na	na
Puerto Rico	na	na	na	na	na	na	na	na	na	na	na	na	na	na	na	na
Romania	na	na	na	na	na	na	na	na	na	na	na	na	na	na	na	na
Russian Fed.	na	na	na	na	na	na	na	na	na	na	na	na	na	na	na	na
Serbia	na	48	47	49	54	50	44	43	47	54	44	49	48	44	51	58
Singapore	na	na	na	na	na	na	na	na	na	na	na	na	na	na	na	na
Slovakia	na	na	na	na	na	na	na	na	na	na	na	na	na	na	na	na
Slovenia	na	na	na	na	na	na	na	na	na	na	na	na	na	na	na	na
South Africa	na	39	40	39	42	37	41	36	46	32	37	41	38	37	41	39
Spain	na	67	66	69	70	67	64	65	66	74	66	66	68	68	65	73
Sweden	na	62	61	63	53	66	63	58	58	71	60	62	68	62	59	72
Switzerland	na	na	na	na	na	na	na	na	na	na	na	na	na	na	na	na
Taiwan	na	na	na	na	na	na	na	na	na	na	na	na	na	na	na	na
Tanzania	na	35	35	34	36	34	32	37	34	29	34	43	30	38	34	48
Turkey	na	na	na	na	na	na	na	na	na	na	na	na	na	na	na	na
Uganda	na	33	42	25	35	33	23	20	39	36	26	38	42	27	38	27
Ukraine	na	na	na	na	na	na	na	na	na	na	na	na	na	na	na	na
United States	na	54	52	56	49	55	57	49	59	53	52	58	53	51	54	56
Uruguay	na	na	na	na	na	na	na	na	na	na	na	na	na	na	na	na
Venezuela	na	na	na	na	na	na	na	na	na	na	na	na	na	na	na	na
Vietnam	na	34	37	32	32	34	37	30	40	40	35	31	39	28	39	41
Zimbabwe	na	30	31	29	31	31	28	28	33	22	31	27	32	32	30	25
Total	na	44	43	44	43	44	45	39	45	50	43	44	44	43	44	45

RANKING

Country	2000
Spain	67
Bosnia and Herz.	64
Sweden	62
Korea, South	62
Moldova	57
Albania	55
United States	54
Canada	53
Jordan	53
Montenegro	51
Indonesia	50
Iran	50
Chile	49
Serbia	48
Japan	46
India	46
Mexico	46
Bangladesh	42
Algeria	41
Morocco	41
South Africa	39
Nigeria	37
Tanzania	35
Vietnam	34
Uganda	33
Egypt	33
China	31
Zimbabwe	30
Macedonia	29
Philippines	25
Argentina	1
Total	44

E139) WHO SHOULD DECIDE: HUMAN RIGHTS

Who could better handle certain kinds of problems: the United Nations, the respective national governments, or the national governments together with the United Nations?

National governments (%)

(WVS: V181)

Country	Wave 1990	Wave 2000	Gender Male	Gender Female	Age 16-29	Age 30-49	Age 50+	Education Lower	Education Middle	Education Upper	Income Lower	Income Middle	Income Upper	Values Mat	Values Mixed	Values Postm.
Albania	na	57	54	60	50	60	58	61	52	59	58	56	57	58	56	59
Algeria	na	51	53	50	53	47	57	54	48	55	53	53	49	50	53	49
Argentina	na	1	1	1	1	2	1	1	2	3	na	1	3	2	1	2
Armenia	na	na	na	na	na	na	na	na	na	na	na	na	na	na	na	na
Australia	na	na	na	na	na	na	na	na	na	na	na	na	na	na	na	na
Austria	na	na	na	na	na	na	na	na	na	na	na	na	na	na	na	na
Azerbaijan	na	na	na	na	na	na	na	na	na	na	na	na	na	na	na	na
Bangladesh	na	38	37	39	36	41	30	39	34	44	46	35	36	36	41	25
Belarus	na	na	na	na	na	na	na	na	na	na	na	na	na	na	na	na
Belgium	na	na	na	na	na	na	na	na	na	na	na	na	na	na	na	na
Bosnia and Herz.	na	66	67	64	66	65	66	66	66	65	68	65	62	67	66	62
Brazil	na	na	na	na	na	na	na	na	na	na	na	na	na	na	na	na
Bulgaria	na	na	na	na	na	na	na	na	na	na	na	na	na	na	na	na
Canada	na	55	50	60	56	54	54	50	54	59	49	56	58	50	54	59
Chile	na	43	44	43	45	46	38	36	48	46	33	50	50	45	43	43
China	na	20	18	22	24	18	19	20	19	33	18	19	22	21	17	15
Colombia	na	na	na	na	na	na	na	na	na	na	na	na	na	na	na	na
Croatia	na	na	na	na	na	na	na	na	na	na	na	na	na	na	na	na
Czech Republic	na	na	na	na	na	na	na	na	na	na	na	na	na	na	na	na
Denmark	na	na	na	na	na	na	na	na	na	na	na	na	na	na	na	na
Dominican Rep.	na	na	na	na	na	na	na	na	na	na	na	na	na	na	na	na
Egypt	na	37	33	41	39	35	38	39	36	34	39	37	36	38	37	32
El Salvador	na	na	na	na	na	na	na	na	na	na	na	na	na	na	na	na
Estonia	na	na	na	na	na	na	na	na	na	na	na	na	na	na	na	na
Finland	na	na	na	na	na	na	na	na	na	na	na	na	na	na	na	na
France	na	na	na	na	na	na	na	na	na	na	na	na	na	na	na	na
Georgia	na	na	na	na	na	na	na	na	na	na	na	na	na	na	na	na
Germany	na	na	na	na	na	na	na	na	na	na	na	na	na	na	na	na
Great Britain	na	na	na	na	na	na	na	na	na	na	na	na	na	na	na	na
Greece	na	na	na	na	na	na	na	na	na	na	na	na	na	na	na	na
Hungary	na	na	na	na	na	na	na	na	na	na	na	na	na	na	na	na
Iceland	na	na	na	na	na	na	na	na	na	na	na	na	na	na	na	na
India	na	42	45	37	44	41	40	33	44	51	28	39	48	45	43	33
Indonesia	na	40	43	37	35	40	42	34	41	40	40	41	41	39	42	36
Iran	na	56	57	55	58	54	54	56	56	57	58	54	56	57	55	61
Ireland	na	na	na	na	na	na	na	na	na	na	na	na	na	na	na	na
Israel	na	na	na	na	na	na	na	na	na	na	na	na	na	na	na	na
Italy	na	na	na	na	na	na	na	na	na	na	na	na	na	na	na	na
Japan	na	34	34	34	28	34	36	38	34	31	36	33	31	36	33	35
Jordan	na	52	44	59	53	52	48	49	51	55	53	52	52	51	51	59
Korea, South	na	42	43	42	52	39	40	35	39	48	38	44	46	41	43	52
Latvia	na	na	na	na	na	na	na	na	na	na	na	na	na	na	na	na
Lithuania	na	na	na	na	na	na	na	na	na	na	na	na	na	na	na	na
Luxembourg	na	na	na	na	na	na	na	na	na	na	na	na	na	na	na	na
Macedonia	na	20	20	20	29	30	26	26	28	33	24	32	31	27	29	29
Malta	na	na	na	na	na	na	na	na	na	na	na	na	na	na	na	na
Mexico	na	42	40	44	43	39	45	40	41	51	30	47	47	39	42	47
Moldova	na	58	56	59	63	57	54	54	55	66	61	61	54	56	59	57
Montenegro	na	50	52	48	60	48	46	42	52	60	50	49	55	51	50	45
Morocco	na	37	37	38	40	37	31	36	38	51	40	40	31	31	41	38
Netherlands	na	na	na	na	na	na	na	na	na	na	na	na	na	na	na	na
New Zealand	na	na	na	na	na	na	na	na	na	na	na	na	na	na	na	na
Nigeria	na	27	27	26	28	26	23	22	29	31	25	28	27	27	28	21
Northern Ireland	na	na	na	na	na	na	na	na	na	na	na	na	na	na	na	na
Norway	na	na	na	na	na	na	na	na	na	na	na	na	na	na	na	na
Pakistan	na	na	na	na	na	na	na	na	na	na	na	na	na	na	na	na
Peru	na	na	na	na	na	na	na	na	na	na	na	na	na	na	na	na
Philippines	na	20	20	20	21	21	18	19	20	22	18	22	19	21	20	21
Poland	na	na	na	na	na	na	na	na	na	na	na	na	na	na	na	na
Portugal	na	na	na	na	na	na	na	na	na	na	na	na	na	na	na	na
Puerto Rico	na	na	na	na	na	na	na	na	na	na	na	na	na	na	na	na
Romania	na	na	na	na	na	na	na	na	na	na	na	na	na	na	na	na
Russian Fed.	na	na	na	na	na	na	na	na	na	na	na	na	na	na	na	na
Serbia	na	47	49	46	53	48	44	43	47	54	43	45	49	45	50	45
Singapore	na	na	na	na	na	na	na	na	na	na	na	na	na	na	na	na
Slovakia	na	na	na	na	na	na	na	na	na	na	na	na	na	na	na	na
Slovenia	na	na	na	na	na	na	na	na	na	na	na	na	na	na	na	na
South Africa	na	34	31	38	33	36	33	34	35	38	36	30	37	35	33	36
Spain	na	72	71	73	75	72	68	69	73	77	70	71	71	71	72	74
Sweden	na	50	45	56	44	53	52	48	50	53	51	50	50	51	48	55
Switzerland	na	na	na	na	na	na	na	na	na	na	na	na	na	na	na	na
Taiwan	na	na	na	na	na	na	na	na	na	na	na	na	na	na	na	na
Tanzania	na	35	36	35	33	37	34	35	34	35	32	42	34	36	35	39
Turkey	na	na	na	na	na	na	na	na	na	na	na	na	na	na	na	na
Uganda	na	29	39	19	33	26	23	16	35	23	23	32	38	25	32	23
Ukraine	na	na	na	na	na	na	na	na	na	na	na	na	na	na	na	na
United States	na	53	55	52	50	53	57	44	52	58	50	55	58	52	52	57
Uruguay	na	na	na	na	na	na	na	na	na	na	na	na	na	na	na	na
Venezuela	na	na	na	na	na	na	na	na	na	na	na	na	na	na	na	na
Vietnam	na	27	26	28	26	27	28	26	27	31	28	28	26	23	31	29
Zimbabwe	na	29	31	27	29	30	27	27	32	32	25	28	36	31	29	14
Total	na	41	40	41	41	40	41	36	41	48	39	41	42	40	41	42

RANKING

Country	2000
Spain	72
Bosnia and Herz.	66
Moldova	58
Albania	57
Iran	56
Canada	55
United States	53
Jordan	52
Algeria	51
Sweden	50
Montenegro	50
Serbia	47
Chile	43
Korea, South	42
India	42
Mexico	42
Indonesia	40
Bangladesh	38
Morocco	37
Egypt	37
Tanzania	35
South Africa	34
Japan	34
Zimbabwe	29
Uganda	29
Macedonia	28
Vietnam	27
Nigeria	27
Philippines	20
China	20
Argentina	1
Total	41

E143) IMMIGRANT POLICY

How about people from other countries coming here to work.

Which one of the following do you think the government should do?

Let people come as long as there are jobs available (%)

(WVS: V146; EVS: V258)

Country	Wave 1990	Wave 2000	Gender Male	Gender Female	Age 16-29	Age 30-49	Age 50+	Education Lower	Education Middle	Education Upper	Income Lower	Income Middle	Income Upper	Values Mat	Values Mixed	Values Postm	RANKING Country	RANKING 2000
Albania	na	45	44	45	40	46	48	47	41	48	44	44	47	49	42	23	Portugal	61
Algeria	na	45	45	46	43	48	45	36	49	47	42	53	51	48	42	51	Azerbaijan	60
Argentina	na	45	41	48	51	43	41	41	51	47	44	42	49	34	45	52	Iceland	59
Armenia	na	51	47	54	57	46	47	43	50	54	55	48	47	49	51	53	Korea, South	58
Australia	na	52	52	53	48	55	53	49	48	59	49	52	56	52	51	55	Spain	58
Austria	na	52	52	51	52	53	50	43	58	67	46	53	54	41	50	56	New Zealand	56
Azerbaijan	na	60	61	58	56	62	62	54	61	58	63	60	59	64	53	51	Bosnia and Herz.	55
Bangladesh	na	50	49	51	49	51	48	47	53	53	58	46	50	56	46	47	Uruguay	55
Belarus	na	35	35	34	38	37	29	27	38	36	30	38	35	30	39	41	Vietnam	55
Belgium	na	31	31	31	34	29	32	26	31	35	29	33	31	27	30	41	Switzerland	55
Bosnia and Herz.	na	55	57	53	56	58	51	51	55	60	49	58	54	55	56	53	Sweden	55
Brazil	na	37	38	35	39	36	34	29	41	47	33	40	41	31	39	41	Moldova	54
Bulgaria	na	31	31	31	29	33	30	28	29	39	28	32	32	29	33	49	Zimbabwe	53
Canada	na	49	52	47	55	46	50	42	46	62	39	48	60	40	48	57	Georgia	53
Chile	na	48	46	49	50	47	47	43	49	55	48	45	50	41	50	53	Australia	52
China	na	48	47	49	58	48	37	37	54	56	38	50	57	47	50	55	Japan	52
Colombia	na	na	na	na	na	na	na	na	na	na	na	na	na	na	na	na	Luxembourg	52
Croatia	na	28	27	28	26	32	25	22	28	43	24	23	36	27	26	31	Austria	52
Czech Republic	na	30	30	31	31	29	32	27	30	45	27	30	35	24	32	39	Armenia	51
Denmark	na	24	26	22	25	25	22	21	23	30	25	24	27	12	25	27	Bangladesh	50
Dominican Rep.	na	37	37	37	37	39	36	32	30	40	27	41	43	30	41	33	Venezuela	50
Egypt	na	43	42	43	41	43	46	44	42	43	42	44	46	46	42	35	Canada	49
El Salvador	na	na	na	na	na	na	na	na	na	na	na	na	na	na	na	na	Slovenia	48
Estonia	na	37	34	39	48	36	31	38	37	35	42	32	35	35	38	38	Chile	48
Finland	na	35	34	35	30	34	39	32	38	36	31	38	35	27	38	35	China	48
France	na	34	35	32	34	36	32	28	38	45	29	32	42	23	34	50	Italy	47
Georgia	na	53	55	51	53	55	49	50	52	59	50	55	58	53	53	59	Ireland	47
Germany	na	33	32	33	35	34	29	27	36	43	27	38	36	24	33	45	Russian Fed.	46
Great Britain	na	34	32	36	37	34	31	24	40	44	30	35	38	na	na	na	Algeria	45
Greece	na	45	43	46	43	50	40	42	44	47	40	48	46	41	45	49	Greece	45
Hungary	na	12	12	13	11	11	14	10	18	15	11	12	13	11	13	4	Argentina	45
Iceland	na	59	58	61	67	57	56	55	64	61	58	62	57	56	60	64	United States	45
India	na	19	20	19	16	23	18	17	20	24	14	16	25	16	24	21	Albania	45
Indonesia	na	23	27	19	17	25	23	24	23	23	20	22	30	24	22	35	Uganda	45
Iran	na	28	29	27	28	25	33	30	29	26	30	31	26	29	27	33	Ukraine	44
Ireland	na	47	45	49	49	45	46	39	46	62	37	44	56	43	47	49	Pakistan	43
Israel	na	na	na	na	na	na	na	na	na	na	na	na	na	na	na	na	Egypt	43
Italy	na	47	47	48	42	51	47	44	47	57	47	49	51	36	46	56	Norway	43
Japan	na	52	53	51	63	58	42	39	50	64	48	50	57	49	52	68	Peru	42
Jordan	na	31	29	34	30	30	38	29	32	35	32	29	30	31	32	33	Mexico	42
Korea, South	na	58	58	58	71	54	53	36	53	68	53	62	61	57	57	81	Nigeria	41
Latvia	na	27	29	25	38	28	22	21	28	31	25	29	28	24	30	18	Romania	39
Lithuania	na	37	33	39	44	35	33	29	38	43	32	37	39	37	37	34	Morocco	38
Luxembourg	na	52	51	53	49	54	52	51	52	54	47	58	57	54	51	58	Dominican Rep.	37
Macedonia	na	20	20	19	23	22	14	19	19	22	15	21	23	18	20	25	Turkey	37
Malta	na	30	31	29	33	27	31	23	31	43	25	31	31	22	33	46	Brazil	37
Mexico	na	42	43	41	43	41	41	37	45	55	33	46	50	37	43	50	Estonia	37
Moldova	na	54	54	55	51	57	54	54	56	52	56	52	53	55	54	40	Lithuania	37
Montenegro	na	27	30	24	34	28	22	18	30	43	15	25	35	18	37	35	Serbia	36
Morocco	na	38	40	36	37	38	41	37	41	44	42	42	37	36	40	44	Netherlands	35
Netherlands	na	35	37	35	32	38	35	26	38	41	32	35	41	28	34	45	Northern Ireland	35
New Zealand	na	56	58	54	47	54	61	48	54	65	53	59	58	51	56	63	Finland	35
Nigeria	na	41	42	41	42	42	36	41	41	42	43	42	38	36	45	45	Belarus	35
Northern Ireland	na	35	34	37	36	37	36	30	39	41	32	38	42	32	37	37	Great Britain	34
Norway	na	43	40	45	46	42	41	34	38	57	na	na	na	31	43	56	France	34
Pakistan	na	43	40	46	40	46	41	37	48	53	35	38	61	41	45	58	Germany	33
Peru	na	42	42	42	41	41	46	43	39	44	39	43	45	39	43	43	Taiwan	32
Philippines	na	18	18	19	18	17	21	20	20	14	21	19	15	19	19	9	Jordan	31
Poland	na	19	19	18	19	21	15	14	22	28	15	20	22	16	19	23	Belgium	31
Portugal	na	61	61	61	56	56	69	64	57	49	64	59	58	66	59	56	Bulgaria	31
Puerto Rico	na	30	29	31	41	28	27	34	28	31	28	29	34	29	29	35	Czech Republic	30
Romania	na	39	38	39	44	42	33	31	43	41	32	40	42	41	37	45	Puerto Rico	30
Russian Fed.	na	46	44	48	52	48	39	35	44	58	41	45	53	44	48	42	Malta	30
Serbia	na	36	38	34	37	39	33	26	37	49	32	38	40	32	41	41	Iran	28
Singapore	na	24	28	20	29	19	22	23	22	33	23	19	29	21	24	34	Croatia	28
Slovakia	na	27	26	28	30	25	28	28	26	37	27	28	28	23	31	32	Slovakia	27
Slovenia	na	48	45	51	43	50	50	42	48	61	42	52	58	42	48	55	Montenegro	27
South Africa	na	27	28	25	23	29	27	22	31	50	21	24	37	20	32	22	Latvia	27
Spain	na	58	58	58	54	59	59	59	55	61	57	58	59	55	61	52	South Africa	27
Sweden	na	55	58	51	62	50	55	55	55	54	55	55	55	55	54	57	Singapore	24
Switzerland	na	55	54	55	60	53	53	41	56	76	50	53	58	48	52	72	Denmark	24
Taiwan	na	32	34	29	46	31	24	28	26	39	27	34	35	27	36	31	Indonesia	23
Tanzania	na	19	20	18	17	23	17	18	21	23	17	23	16	22	18	26	Macedonia	20
Turkey	na	37	37	38	40	36	33	34	38	45	36	37	40	33	38	41	India	19
Uganda	na	45	44	46	46	47	31	50	41	54	52	45	50	39	45	60	Tanzania	19
Ukraine	na	44	44	45	48	47	40	28	44	54	43	44	47	41	50	47	Poland	19
United States	na	45	45	45	46	40	50	34	45	49	42	43	53	43	44	49	Philippines	18
Uruguay	na	55	54	56	55	55	55	51	62	54	52	51	64	51	53	64	Hungary	12
Venezuela	na	50	51	48	50	47	54	48	51	48	49	48	52	52	49	49		
Vietnam	na	55	56	54	51	53	61	59	49	62	57	53	56	57	54	58		
Zimbabwe	na	53	52	55	50	54	63	57	50	23	58	54	47	57	52	45		
Total	na	40	40	40	41	41	39	36	42	45	38	40	43	37	41	48	Total	40

E145_2) IMMIGRANTS

Which of these statements is the nearest to your opinion? For the greater good of society it is better if immigrants: A) maintain their distinct customs and traditions; or B) take over the customs of the country

Take over the custom (%)   (EVS: V259)

Country	Wave		Gender		Age			Education			Income			Values		
	1990	2000	Male	Female	16-29	30-49	50+	Lower	Middle	Upper	Lower	Middle	Upper	Mat	Mixed	Postm.
Albania	na	na	na	na	na	na	na	na	na	na	na	na	na	na	na	na
Algeria	na	na	na	na	na	na	na	na	na	na	na	na	na	na	na	na
Argentina	na	na	na	na	na	na	na	na	na	na	na	na	na	na	na	na
Armenia	na	na	na	na	na	na	na	na	na	na	na	na	na	na	na	na
Australia	na	na	na	na	na	na	na	na	na	na	na	na	na	na	na	na
Austria	na	82	82	81	75	80	86	86	78	72	83	83	80	92	85	72
Azerbaijan	na	na	na	na	na	na	na	na	na	na	na	na	na	na	na	na
Bangladesh	na	na	na	na	na	na	na	na	na	na	na	na	na	na	na	na
Belarus	na	52	53	51	42	58	54	53	54	41	54	48	56	55	49	46
Belgium	na	75	74	76	68	72	81	81	78	66	75	75	74	86	75	62
Bosnia and Herz.	na	na	na	na	na	na	na	na	na	na	na	na	na	na	na	na
Brazil	na	na	na	na	na	na	na	na	na	na	na	na	na	na	na	na
Bulgaria	na	40	41	38	30	40	44	52	37	32	43	35	38	44	34	42
Canada	na	na	na	na	na	na	na	na	na	na	na	na	na	na	na	na
Chile	na	na	na	na	na	na	na	na	na	na	na	na	na	na	na	na
China	na	na	na	na	na	na	na	na	na	na	na	na	na	na	na	na
Colombia	na	na	na	na	na	na	na	na	na	na	na	na	na	na	na	na
Croatia	na	44	44	44	34	47	47	53	39	36	52	40	45	45	47	33
Czech Republic	na	69	69	70	67	69	71	71	68	66	69	70	70	79	68	51
Denmark	na	77	76	77	77	70	83	83	74	63	80	78	65	88	80	54
Dominican Rep.	na	na	na	na	na	na	na	na	na	na	na	na	na	na	na	na
Egypt	na	na	na	na	na	na	na	na	na	na	na	na	na	na	na	na
El Salvador	na	na	na	na	na	na	na	na	na	na	na	na	na	na	na	na
Estonia	na	48	50	46	53	41	50	59	46	33	48	46	50	48	48	39
Finland	na	68	72	64	64	66	73	73	64	57	70	69	66	73	68	50
France	na	73	71	75	67	71	78	79	70	61	75	76	66	83	73	55
Georgia	na	na	na	na	na	na	na	na	na	na	na	na	na	na	na	na
Germany	na	76	79	74	68	75	81	78	75	75	74	74	80	77	77	72
Great Britain	na	55	58	53	42	55	62	61	55	40	49	55	52	na	na	na
Greece	na	23	23	22	21	21	29	35	26	18	24	22	25	29	23	17
Hungary	na	67	64	68	64	66	68	73	58	49	68	71	61	69	65	50
Iceland	na	73	71	75	69	75	74	69	76	72	71	70	76	73	75	57
India	na	na	na	na	na	na	na	na	na	na	na	na	na	na	na	na
Indonesia	na	na	na	na	na	na	na	na	na	na	na	na	na	na	na	na
Iran	na	na	na	na	na	na	na	na	na	na	na	na	na	na	na	na
Ireland	na	43	46	41	38	44	47	45	46	34	41	47	39	45	44	36
Israel	na	na	na	na	na	na	na	na	na	na	na	na	na	na	na	na
Italy	na	40	41	40	30	37	49	49	34	33	43	39	37	56	43	30
Japan	na	na	na	na	na	na	na	na	na	na	na	na	na	na	na	na
Jordan	na	na	na	na	na	na	na	na	na	na	na	na	na	na	na	na
Korea, South	na	na	na	na	na	na	na	na	na	na	na	na	na	na	na	na
Latvia	na	53	50	55	47	50	58	59	54	42	57	50	53	57	52	47
Lithuania	na	64	66	61	62	62	67	73	64	50	68	70	58	63	65	40
Luxembourg	na	43	43	43	40	39	48	42	43	42	40	48	45	40	44	36
Macedonia	na	na	na	na	na	na	na	na	na	na	na	na	na	na	na	na
Malta	na	44	45	44	41	43	48	48	45	31	52	47	57	45	16	70
Mexico	na	na	na	na	na	na	na	na	na	na	na	na	na	na	na	na
Moldova	na	na	na	na	na	na	na	na	na	na	na	na	na	na	na	na
Montenegro	na	na	na	na	na	na	na	na	na	na	na	na	na	na	na	na
Morocco	na	na	na	na	na	na	na	na	na	na	na	na	na	na	na	na
Netherlands	na	70	69	71	68	67	74	75	74	61	68	69	71	85	70	61
New Zealand	na	na	na	na	na	na	na	na	na	na	na	na	na	na	na	na
Nigeria	na	na	na	na	na	na	na	na	na	na	na	na	na	na	na	na
Northern Ireland	na	46	48	44	33	40	56	52	42	40	47	39	40	50	47	37
Norway	na	na	na	na	na	na	na	na	na	na	na	na	na	na	na	na
Pakistan	na	na	na	na	na	na	na	na	na	na	na	na	na	na	na	na
Peru	na	na	na	na	na	na	na	na	na	na	na	na	na	na	na	na
Philippines	na	na	na	na	na	na	na	na	na	na	na	na	na	Mat	na	na
Poland	na	53	52	53	52	49	57	56	49	49	53	55	44	56	50	57
Portugal	na	51	50	52	48	52	52	51	54	39	41	53	58	52	53	49
Puerto Rico	na	na	na	na	na	na	na	na	na	na	na	na	na	na	na	na
Romania	na	38	37	39	29	34	48	53	32	28	47	41	31	41	39	15
Russian Fed.	na	57	58	56	51	57	60	67	58	49	62	56	53	59	54	74
Serbia	na	na	na	na	na	na	na	na	na	na	na	na	na	na	na	na
Singapore	na	na	na	na	na	na	na	na	na	na	na	na	na	na	na	na
Slovakia	na	60	58	62	61	59	61	65	60	49	64	59	58	66	56	46
Slovenia	na	69	70	69	66	68	72	71	69	68	71	68	68	73	69	65
South Africa	na	na	na	na	na	na	na	na	na	na	na	na	na	na	na	na
Spain	na	48	50	47	35	46	58	52	49	33	46	49	47	56	49	35
Sweden	na	64	64	64	57	63	68	70	65	58	60	69	65	60	70	49
Switzerland	na	na	na	na	na	na	na	na	na	na	na	na	na	na	na	na
Taiwan	na	na	na	na	na	na	na	na	na	na	na	na	na	na	na	na
Tanzania	na	na	na	na	na	na	na	na	na	na	na	na	na	na	na	na
Turkey	na	na	na	na	na	na	na	na	na	na	na	na	na	na	na	na
Uganda	na	na	na	na	na	na	na	na	na	na	na	na	na	na	na	na
Ukraine	na	54	54	54	46	51	61	62	56	45	57	56	47	55	53	49
United States	na	na	na	na	na	na	na	na	na	na	na	na	na	na	na	na
Uruguay	na	na	na	na	na	na	na	na	na	na	na	na	na	na	na	na
Venezuela	na	na	na	na	na	na	na	na	na	na	na	na	na	na	na	na
Vietnam	na	na	na	na	na	na	na	na	na	na	na	na	na	na	na	na
Zimbabwe	na	na	na	na	na	na	na	na	na	na	na	na	na	na	na	na
Total	na	57	58	57	51	56	63	64	55	47	59	58	55	60	58	48

RANKING

Country	2000
Austria	82
Denmark	77
Germany	76
Belgium	75
France	73
Iceland	73
Netherlands	70
Slovenia	69
Czech Republic	69
Finland	68
Hungary	67
Sweden	64
Lithuania	64
Slovakia	60
Russian Fed.	57
Great Britain	55
Ukraine	54
Latvia	53
Poland	53
Belarus	52
Portugal	51
Spain	48
Estonia	48
Northern Ireland	46
Malta	44
Croatia	44
Ireland	43
Luxembourg	43
Italy	40
Bulgaria	40
Romania	38
Greece	23
Total	57

E146_1) ELIMINATING INEQUALITIES

In order to be considered "just", what should a society provide? Please tell me for each statement if it is important or unimportant to you. 1 means very important; 5 means not important at all.

% Important / very important (codes 1 to 2)

(EVS: V260)

Country	Wave		Gender		Age			Education			Income			Values		
	1990	2000	Male	Female	16-29	30-49	50+	Lower	Middle	Upper	Lower	Middle	Upper	Mat	Mixed	Postm.
Albania	na	na	na	na	na	na	na	na	na	na	na	na	na	na	na	na
Algeria	na	na	na	na	na	na	na	na	na	na	na	na	na	na	na	na
Argentina	na	na	na	na	na	na	na	na	na	na	na	na	na	na	na	na
Armenia	na	na	na	na	na	na	na	na	na	na	na	na	na	na	na	na
Australia	na	na	na	na	na	na	na	na	na	na	na	na	na	na	na	na
Austria	na	58	58	58	49	58	62	62	57	43	70	59	49	64	60	55
Azerbaijan	na	na	na	na	na	na	na	na	na	na	na	na	na	na	na	na
Bangladesh	na	na	na	na	na	na	na	na	na	na	na	na	na	na	na	na
Belarus	na	59	52	65	45	57	74	74	56	47	68	56	49	68	54	31
Belgium	na	63	61	65	53	62	69	72	63	56	73	66	53	63	61	66
Bosnia and Herz.	na	na	na	na	na	na	na	na	na	na	na	na	na	na	na	na
Brazil	na	na	na	na	na	na	na	na	na	na	na	na	na	na	na	na
Bulgaria	na	65	62	67	56	61	72	77	61	51	80	67	50	74	58	27
Canada	na	na	na	na	na	na	na	na	na	na	na	na	na	na	na	na
Chile	na	na	na	na	na	na	na	na	na	na	na	na	na	na	na	na
China	na	na	na	na	na	na	na	na	na	na	na	na	na	na	na	na
Colombia	na	na	na	na	na	na	na	na	na	na	na	na	na	na	na	na
Croatia	na	84	80	87	77	83	89	93	79	73	88	86	79	86	85	79
Czech Republic	na	56	55	57	54	49	64	67	49	31	69	60	40	70	53	44
Denmark	na	28	30	26	28	27	30	29	22	30	33	27	26	25	28	35
Dominican Rep.	na	na	na	na	na	na	na	na	na	na	na	na	na	na	na	na
Egypt	na	na	na	na	na	na	na	na	na	na	na	na	na	na	na	na
El Salvador	na	na	na	na	na	na	na	na	na	na	na	na	na	na	na	na
Estonia	na	61	56	64	49	56	72	65	61	53	72	62	56	64	59	52
Finland	na	67	64	70	62	70	68	73	62	50	74	69	59	73	64	70
France	na	70	68	73	69	71	71	72	69	68	73	71	68	73	69	72
Georgia	na	na	na	na	na	na	na	na	na	na	na	na	na	na	na	na
Germany	na	60	58	61	55	60	61	63	60	47	66	61	56	66	59	53
Great Britain	na	56	54	58	59	53	57	57	56	51	61	58	43	na	na	na
Greece	na	81	81	81	79	82	84	82	82	81	84	81	80	72	83	86
Hungary	na	86	84	88	84	84	90	91	84	62	92	87	81	88	85	83
Iceland	na	71	65	77	62	71	80	80	68	60	78	77	58	73	70	74
India	na	na	na	na	na	na	na	na	na	na	na	na	na	na	na	na
Indonesia	na	na	na	na	na	na	na	na	na	na	na	na	na	na	na	na
Iran	na	na	na	na	na	na	na	na	na	na	na	na	na	na	na	na
Ireland	na	69	71	66	59	70	73	73	68	64	77	69	62	66	70	63
Israel	na	na	na	na	na	na	na	na	na	na	na	na	na	na	na	na
Italy	na	61	59	63	58	58	66	67	59	51	67	68	54	63	61	61
Japan	na	na	na	na	na	na	na	na	na	na	na	na	na	na	na	na
Jordan	na	na	na	na	na	na	na	na	na	na	na	na	na	na	na	na
Korea, South	na	na	na	na	na	na	na	na	na	na	na	na	na	na	na	na
Latvia	na	82	78	85	71	80	87	85	83	73	86	85	74	80	84	65
Lithuania	na	68	67	68	56	62	82	84	65	49	80	77	58	75	67	52
Luxembourg	na	64	62	67	61	65	66	71	66	49	70	66	55	67	63	68
Macedonia	na	na	na	na	na	na	na	na	na	na	na	na	na	na	na	na
Malta	na	36	36	35	33	32	41	39	35	29	40	34	29	34	39	18
Mexico	na	na	na	na	na	na	na	na	na	na	na	na	na	na	na	na
Moldova	na	na	na	na	na	na	na	na	na	na	na	na	na	na	na	na
Montenegro	na	na	na	na	na	na	na	na	na	na	na	na	na	na	na	na
Morocco	na	na	na	na	na	na	na	na	na	na	na	na	na	na	na	na
Netherlands	na	41	39	44	39	38	46	44	39	40	49	41	32	46	37	51
New Zealand	na	na	na	na	na	na	na	na	na	na	na	na	na	na	na	na
Nigeria	na	na	na	na	na	na	na	na	na	na	na	na	na	na	na	na
Northern Ireland	na	62	62	63	58	64	63	68	59	55	67	55	60	62	61	70
Norway	na	na	na	na	na	na	na	na	na	na	na	na	na	na	na	na
Pakistan	na	na	na	na	na	na	na	na	na	na	na	na	na	na	na	na
Peru	na	na	na	na	na	na	na	na	na	na	na	na	na	na	na	na
Philippines	na	na	na	na	na	na	na	na	na	na	na	na	na	na	na	na
Poland	na	75	71	79	69	70	86	81	71	62	85	69	66	76	75	70
Portugal	na	87	86	88	82	85	91	89	82	80	89	82	87	86	88	78
Puerto Rico	na	na	na	na	na	na	na	na	na	na	na	na	na	na	na	na
Romania	na	85	84	86	80	83	90	88	88	73	90	91	80	89	84	62
Russian Fed.	na	59	55	63	46	56	71	70	60	52	67	62	51	64	55	54
Serbia	na	na	na	na	na	na	na	na	na	na	na	na	na	na	na	na
Singapore	na	na	na	na	na	na	na	na	na	na	na	na	na	na	na	na
Slovakia	na	86	84	89	82	85	92	92	87	66	92	89	81	92	84	58
Slovenia	na	67	65	69	58	63	79	83	66	41	77	76	48	78	66	64
South Africa	na	na	na	na	na	na	na	na	na	na	na	na	na	na	na	na
Spain	na	83	82	84	84	83	83	83	82	85	84	82	80	82	82	88
Sweden	na	45	42	47	37	47	48	58	42	38	53	46	32	57	42	49
Switzerland	na	na	na	na	na	na	na	na	na	na	na	na	na	na	na	na
Taiwan	na	na	na	na	na	na	na	na	na	na	na	na	na	na	na	na
Tanzania	na	na	na	na	na	na	na	na	na	na	na	na	na	na	na	na
Turkey	na	86	85	87	86	86	86	86	86	87	84	87	87	83	85	92
Uganda	na	na	na	na	na	na	na	na	na	na	na	na	na	na	na	na
Ukraine	na	na	na	na	na	na	na	na	na	na	na	na	na	na	na	na
United States	na	na	na	na	na	na	na	na	na	na	na	na	na	na	na	na
Uruguay	na	na	na	na	na	na	na	na	na	na	na	na	na	na	na	na
Venezuela	na	na	na	na	na	na	na	na	na	na	na	na	na	na	na	na
Vietnam	na	na	na	na	na	na	na	na	na	na	na	na	na	na	na	na
Zimbabwe	na	na	na	na	na	na	na	na	na	na	na	na	na	na	na	na
Total	na	66	63	68	61	64	71	72	64	56	72	67	59	72	64	62

RANKING

Country	2000
Portugal	87
Slovakia	86
Hungary	86
Turkey	86
Romania	85
Croatia	84
Spain	83
Latvia	82
Greece	81
Poland	75
Iceland	71
France	70
Ireland	69
Lithuania	68
Slovenia	67
Finland	67
Bulgaria	65
Luxembourg	64
Belgium	63
Northern Ireland	62
Italy	61
Estonia	61
Germany	60
Russian Fed.	59
Belarus	59
Austria	58
Czech Republic	56
Great Britain	56
Sweden	45
Netherlands	41
Malta	36
Denmark	28
Total	66

E147_1) BASIC NEEDS FOR ALL

In order to be considered "just", what should a society provide? Please tell me for each statement if it is important or unimportant to you. 1 means very important; 5 means not important at all.

% Important / very important (codes 1 to 2)

(EVS: V261)

Country	Wave		Gender		Age			Education			Income			Values				RANKING Country	2000
	1990	2000	Male	Female	16-29	30-49	50+	Lower	Middle	Upper	Lower	Middle	Upper	Mat	Mixed	Postm.			
Albania	na	na	na	na	na	na	na	na	na	na	na	na	na	na	na	na		Greece	84
Algeria	na	na	na	na	na	na	na	na	na	na	na	na	na	na	na	na		Latvia	84
Argentina	na	na	na	na	na	na	na	na	na	na	na	na	na	na	na	na		Belarus	83
Armenia	na	na	na	na	na	na	na	na	na	na	na	na	na	na	na	na		Portugal	81
Australia	na	na	na	na	na	na	na	na	na	na	na	na	na	na	na	na		Lithuania	79
Austria	na	63	62	64	62	65	61	62	63	66	63	63	62	64	64	62		Turkey	79
Azerbaijan	na	na	na	na	na	na	na	na	na	na	na	na	na	na	na	na		Poland	79
Bangladesh	na	na	na	na	na	na	na	na	na	na	na	na	na	na	na	na		Iceland	78
Belarus	na	83	81	85	83	82	84	79	84	83	85	83	79	86	81	66		Slovakia	78
Belgium	na	74	72	76	70	74	76	74	73	76	76	75	71	73	74	78		Russian Fed.	77
Bosnia and Herz.	na	na	na	na	na	na	na	na	na	na	na	na	na	na	na	na		Northern Ireland	77
Brazil	na	na	na	na	na	na	na	na	na	na	na	na	na	na	na	na		France	77
Bulgaria	na	72	70	73	71	68	75	79	67	71	80	66	68	76	69	59		Ireland	76
Canada	na	na	na	na	na	na	na	na	na	na	na	na	na	na	na	na		Hungary	75
Chile	na	na	na	na	na	na	na	na	na	na	na	na	na	na	na	na		Belgium	74
China	na	na	na	na	na	na	na	na	na	na	na	na	na	na	na	na		Malta	74
Colombia	na	na	na	na	na	na	na	na	na	na	na	na	na	na	na	na		Slovenia	72
Croatia	na	66	65	66	62	69	65	65	67	65	69	70	62	63	67	67		Bulgaria	72
Czech Republic	na	53	50	56	58	47	55	58	49	41	56	54	49	63	51	45		Sweden	71
Denmark	na	48	48	48	55	50	43	41	54	60	48	45	56	35	49	59		Great Britain	71
Dominican Rep.	na	na	na	na	na	na	na	na	na	na	na	na	na	na	na	na		Spain	71
Egypt	na	na	na	na	na	na	na	na	na	na	na	na	na	na	na	na		Italy	70
El Salvador	na	na	na	na	na	na	na	na	na	na	na	na	na	na	na	na		Netherlands	70
Estonia	na	63	56	68	53	62	69	64	64	56	70	62	60	70	59	55		Finland	69
Finland	na	69	65	72	74	71	65	72	65	64	72	71	65	73	66	72		Croatia	66
France	na	77	73	79	75	79	74	77	73	78	79	79	71	76	76	79		Austria	63
Georgia	na	na	na	na	na	na	na	na	na	na	na	na	na	na	na	na		Estonia	63
Germany	na	61	58	64	64	63	58	58	64	66	61	59	57	57	61	67		Germany	61
Great Britain	na	71	70	72	70	74	70	74	68	75	70	77	69	na	na	na		Romania	61
Greece	na	84	81	86	84	85	83	85	83	85	85	83	81	79	85	86		Luxembourg	60
Hungary	na	75	75	75	77	76	73	76	75	66	74	78	72	78	71	77		Czech Republic	53
Iceland	na	78	72	84	71	81	80	77	75	85	80	80	75	75	79	78		Denmark	48
India	na	na	na	na	na	na	na	na	na	na	na	na	na	na	na	na			
Indonesia	na	na	na	na	na	na	na	na	na	na	na	na	na	na	na	na			
Iran	na	na	na	na	na	na	na	na	na	na	na	na	na	na	na	na			
Ireland	na	76	77	76	74	78	78	80	72	82	80	72	74	77	75	81			
Israel	na	na	na	na	na	na	na	na	na	na	na	na	na	na	na	na			
Italy	na	70	68	73	72	71	69	71	70	70	72	75	67	68	69	74			
Japan	na	na	na	na	na	na	na	na	na	na	na	na	na	na	na	na			
Jordan	na	na	na	na	na	na	na	na	na	na	na	na	na	na	na	na			
Korea, South	na	na	na	na	na	na	na	na	na	na	na	na	na	na	na	na			
Latvia	na	84	82	85	78	85	85	82	85	83	85	82	81	86	83	75			
Lithuania	na	79	79	80	78	81	78	81	80	76	78	79	81	79	80	77			
Luxembourg	na	60	57	63	56	63	61	56	62	66	56	59	66	56	61	71			
Macedonia	na	na	na	na	na	na	na	na	na	na	na	na	na	na	na	na			
Malta	na	74	74	74	69	78	74	77	73	74	74	71	77	73	75	77			
Mexico	na	na	na	na	na	na	na	na	na	na	na	na	na	na	na	na			
Moldova	na	na	na	na	na	na	na	na	na	na	na	na	na	na	na	na			
Montenegro	na	na	na	na	na	na	na	na	na	na	na	na	na	na	na	na			
Morocco	na	na	na	na	na	na	na	na	na	na	na	na	na	na	na	na			
Netherlands	na	70	68	72	70	71	68	64	71	74	70	74	65	68	67	77			
New Zealand	na	na	na	na	na	na	na	na	na	na	na	na	na	na	na	na			
Nigeria	na	na	na	na	na	na	na	na	na	na	na	na	na	na	na	na			
Northern Ireland	na	77	78	76	77	75	79	79	76	71	75	78	75	79	73	88			
Norway	na	na	na	na	na	na	na	na	na	na	na	na	na	na	na	na			
Pakistan	na	na	na	na	na	na	na	na	na	na	na	na	na	na	na	na			
Peru	na	na	na	na	na	na	na	na	na	na	na	na	na	na	na	na			
Philippines	na	na	na	na	na	na	na	na	na	na	na	na	na	na	na	na			
Poland	na	79	76	81	79	77	80	84	75	64	85	74	73	82	78	64			
Portugal	na	81	80	81	80	75	85	82	78	76	82	76	76	80	80	86			
Puerto Rico	na	na	na	na	na	na	na	na	na	na	na	na	na	na	na	na			
Romania	na	61	59	63	56	63	63	59	64	60	62	66	61	64	61	58			
Russian Fed.	na	77	75	80	72	78	80	80	78	75	78	80	76	79	76	65			
Serbia	na	na	na	na	na	na	na	na	na	na	na	na	na	na	na	na			
Singapore	na	na	na	na	na	na	na	na	na	na	na	na	na	na	na	na			
Slovakia	na	78	78	78	75	78	79	79	79	65	78	80	76	83	75	68			
Slovenia	na	72	67	77	68	74	73	75	74	58	79	72	70	75	71	76			
South Africa	na	na	na	na	na	na	na	na	na	na	na	na	na	na	na	na			
Spain	na	71	70	71	72	71	70	68	70	79	70	72	71	67	68	83			
Sweden	na	71	68	74	72	73	69	68	72	74	73	69	71	62	70	80			
Switzerland	na	na	na	na	na	na	na	na	na	na	na	na	na	na	na	na			
Taiwan	na	na	na	na	na	na	na	na	na	na	na	na	na	na	na	na			
Tanzania	na	na	na	na	na	na	na	na	na	na	na	na	na	na	na	na			
Turkey	na	79	78	80	79	79	81	80	77	82	78	80	81	83	77	86			
Uganda	na	na	na	na	na	na	na	na	na	na	na	na	na	na	na	na			
Ukraine	na	na	na	na	na	na	na	na	na	na	na	na	na	na	na	na			
United States	na	na	na	na	na	na	na	na	na	na	na	na	na	na	na	na			
Uruguay	na	na	na	na	na	na	na	na	na	na	na	na	na	na	na	na			
Venezuela	na	na	na	na	na	na	na	na	na	na	na	na	na	na	na	na			
Vietnam	na	na	na	na	na	na	na	na	na	na	na	na	na	na	na	na			
Zimbabwe	na	na	na	na	na	na	na	na	na	na	na	na	na	na	na	na			
Total	na	72	69	74	71	72	71	71	72	72	74	72	70	74	70	73		Total	72

E148_1) RECOGNIZING MERITS

In order to be considered "just", what should a society provide? Please tell me for each statement if it is important or unimportant to you. 1 means very important; 5 means not important at all.

% Important / very important (codes 1 to 2)

(EVS: V262)

Country	Wave 1990	Wave 2000	Gender Male	Gender Female	Age 16-29	Age 30-49	Age 50+	Education Lower	Education Middle	Education Upper	Income Lower	Income Middle	Income Upper	Values Mat	Values Mixed	Values Postm.
Albania	na	na	na	na	na	na	na	na	na	na	na	na	na	na	na	na
Algeria	na	na	na	na	na	na	na	na	na	na	na	na	na	na	na	na
Argentina	na	na	na	na	na	na	na	na	na	na	na	na	na	na	na	na
Armenia	na	na	na	na	na	na	na	na	na	na	na	na	na	na	na	na
Australia	na	na	na	na	na	na	na	na	na	na	na	na	na	na	na	na
Austria	na	44	41	47	39	39	51	46	41	41	46	42	43	50	45	41
Azerbaijan	na	na	na	na	na	na	na	na	na	na	na	na	na	na	na	na
Bangladesh	na	na	na	na	na	na	na	na	na	na	na	na	na	na	na	na
Belarus	na	78	73	82	75	79	79	75	78	81	75	80	79	81	75	84
Belgium	na	51	52	51	44	47	58	50	53	49	58	52	45	51	49	58
Bosnia and Herz.	na	na	na	na	na	na	na	na	na	na	na	na	na	na	na	na
Brazil	na	na	na	na	na	na	na	na	na	na	na	na	na	na	na	na
Bulgaria	na	67	67	66	67	65	68	66	66	70	69	65	66	67	68	63
Canada	na	na	na	na	na	na	na	na	na	na	na	na	na	na	na	na
Chile	na	na	na	na	na	na	na	na	na	na	na	na	na	na	na	na
China	na	na	na	na	na	na	na	na	na	na	na	na	na	na	na	na
Colombia	na	na	na	na	na	na	na	na	na	na	na	na	na	na	na	na
Croatia	na	47	42	52	45	47	48	53	44	41	56	47	44	57	46	45
Czech Republic	na	65	64	66	58	65	69	64	67	65	66	66	65	61	66	68
Denmark	na	39	43	34	32	37	44	40	36	39	37	38	45	27	39	39
Dominican Rep.	na	na	na	na	na	na	na	na	na	na	na	na	na	na	na	na
Egypt	na	na	na	na	na	na	na	na	na	na	na	na	na	na	na	na
El Salvador	na	na	na	na	na	na	na	na	na	na	na	na	na	na	na	na
Estonia	na	41	43	40	33	42	45	42	39	46	39	42	43	42	43	46
Finland	na	39	35	43	30	36	47	44	33	34	43	44	34	46	36	45
France	na	54	53	55	46	50	62	61	46	43	58	55	47	60	55	40
Georgia	na	na	na	na	na	na	na	na	na	na	na	na	na	na	na	na
Germany	na	44	41	47	41	43	48	44	45	45	46	46	44	48	41	48
Great Britain	na	50	54	47	41	50	56	48	49	52	47	50	51	na	na	na
Greece	na	57	52	61	53	58	63	68	58	54	63	53	57	51	58	58
Hungary	na	64	64	63	62	65	63	66	59	59	65	64	61	63	65	68
Iceland	na	68	65	71	48	74	78	70	65	71	71	68	67	65	69	74
India	na	na	na	na	na	na	na	na	na	na	na	na	na	na	na	na
Indonesia	na	na	na	na	na	na	na	na	na	na	na	na	na	na	na	na
Iran	na	na	na	na	na	na	na	na	na	na	na	na	na	na	na	na
Ireland	na	54	55	53	45	58	57	58	52	53	59	49	50	56	54	48
Israel	na	na	na	na	na	na	na	na	na	na	na	na	na	na	na	na
Italy	na	43	44	41	36	43	46	44	40	46	44	40	41	45	43	41
Japan	na	na	na	na	na	na	na	na	na	na	na	na	na	na	na	na
Jordan	na	na	na	na	na	na	na	na	na	na	na	na	na	na	na	na
Korea, South	na	na	na	na	na	na	na	na	na	na	na	na	na	na	na	na
Latvia	na	52	52	53	49	51	55	52	51	58	55	53	49	53	52	46
Lithuania	na	36	35	38	32	39	37	38	36	36	32	38	36	35	37	42
Luxembourg	na	56	59	54	50	52	65	57	58	53	63	60	54	61	59	44
Macedonia	na	na	na	na	na	na	na	na	na	na	na	na	na	na	na	na
Malta	na	64	63	64	55	69	65	63	63	68	67	67	65	62	65	63
Mexico	na	na	na	na	na	na	na	na	na	na	na	na	na	na	na	na
Moldova	na	na	na	na	na	na	na	na	na	na	na	na	na	na	na	na
Montenegro	na	na	na	na	na	na	na	na	na	na	na	na	na	na	na	na
Morocco	na	na	na	na	na	na	na	na	na	na	na	na	na	na	na	na
Netherlands	na	44	41	46	34	39	54	41	44	46	49	43	37	38	40	58
New Zealand	na	na	na	na	na	na	na	na	na	na	na	na	na	na	na	na
Nigeria	na	na	na	na	na	na	na	na	na	na	na	na	na	na	na	na
Northern Ireland	na	49	51	47	42	48	54	52	45	51	52	46	41	55	45	56
Norway	na	na	na	na	na	na	na	na	na	na	na	na	na	na	na	na
Pakistan	na	na	na	na	na	na	na	na	na	na	na	na	na	na	na	na
Peru	na	na	na	na	na	na	na	na	na	na	na	na	na	na	na	na
Philippines	na	na	na	na	na	na	na	na	na	na	na	na	na	na	na	na
Poland	na	74	73	75	73	72	76	77	71	63	78	72	68	73	74	78
Portugal	na	65	65	64	61	64	67	68	59	57	62	59	66	63	66	62
Puerto Rico	na	na	na	na	na	na	na	na	na	na	na	na	na	na	na	na
Romania	na	65	67	63	62	68	65	53	69	77	55	66	76	63	67	71
Russian Fed.	na	57	56	58	48	58	62	58	56	60	59	56	57	58	57	48
Serbia	na	na	na	na	na	na	na	na	na	na	na	na	na	na	na	na
Singapore	na	na	na	na	na	na	na	na	na	na	na	na	na	na	na	na
Slovakia	na	55	54	56	56	54	56	54	55	60	59	53	56	54	55	58
Slovenia	na	51	50	51	42	53	54	49	52	45	55	48	49	48	51	51
South Africa	na	na	na	na	na	na	na	na	na	na	na	na	na	na	na	na
Spain	na	47	48	46	44	46	49	49	46	44	44	51	44	44	47	49
Sweden	na	42	41	44	34	39	50	46	41	42	46	38	41	43	40	48
Switzerland	na	na	na	na	na	na	na	na	na	na	na	na	na	na	na	na
Taiwan	na	na	na	na	na	na	na	na	na	na	na	na	na	na	na	na
Tanzania	na	na	na	na	na	na	na	na	na	na	na	na	na	na	na	na
Turkey	na	69	69	68	70	68	67	64	74	77	65	69	76	67	68	78
Uganda	na	na	na	na	na	na	na	na	na	na	na	na	na	na	na	na
Ukraine	na	na	na	na	na	na	na	na	na	na	na	na	na	na	na	na
United States	na	na	na	na	na	na	na	na	na	na	na	na	na	na	na	na
Uruguay	na	na	na	na	na	na	na	na	na	na	na	na	na	na	na	na
Venezuela	na	na	na	na	na	na	na	na	na	na	na	na	na	na	na	na
Vietnam	na	na	na	na	na	na	na	na	na	na	na	na	na	na	na	na
Zimbabwe	na	na	na	na	na	na	na	na	na	na	na	na	na	na	na	na
Total	na	54	53	54	49	53	58	55	53	53	56	54	53	57	53	52

RANKING

Country	2000
Belarus	78
Poland	74
Turkey	69
Iceland	68
Bulgaria	67
Czech Republic	65
Romania	65
Portugal	65
Malta	64
Hungary	64
Russian Fed.	57
Greece	57
Luxembourg	56
Slovakia	55
France	54
Ireland	54
Latvia	52
Belgium	51
Slovenia	51
Great Britain	50
Northern Ireland	49
Croatia	47
Spain	47
Germany	44
Austria	44
Netherlands	44
Italy	43
Sweden	42
Estonia	41
Finland	39
Denmark	39
Lithuania	36
Total	54

E150) HOW OFTEN FOLLOWS POLITICS IN THE NEWS

How often do you follow politics in the news on television or on the radio or in the daily papers?

Every day (%)

(WVS: V217; EVS: V263)

Country	Wave 1990	Wave 2000	Gender Male	Gender Female	Age 16-29	Age 30-49	Age 50+	Education Lower	Education Middle	Education Upper	Income Lower	Income Middle	Income Upper	Values Mat	Values Mixed	Values Postm.
Albania	na	31	41	22	16	31	45	26	34	38	30	33	32	30	32	43
Algeria	na	na	na	na	na	na	na	na	na	na	na	na	na	na	na	na
Argentina	na	48	50	46	34	48	61	46	48	57	49	46	48	42	48	50
Armenia	na	na	na	na	na	na	na	na	na	na	na	na	na	na	na	na
Australia	na	na	na	na	na	na	na	na	na	na	na	na	na	na	na	na
Austria	na	57	60	55	34	55	72	54	57	71	57	58	66	49	58	60
Azerbaijan	na	na	na	na	na	na	na	na	na	na	na	na	na	na	na	na
Bangladesh	na	35	39	29	38	33	34	19	51	57	19	36	49	34	37	32
Belarus	na	34	40	30	27	36	39	22	36	49	28	36	42	31	37	44
Belgium	na	47	52	41	27	42	59	36	42	60	43	47	51	42	44	58
Bosnia and Herz.	na	30	37	24	20	29	43	26	29	38	32	28	35	27	31	32
Brazil	na	na	na	na	na	na	na	na	na	na	na	na	na	na	na	na
Bulgaria	na	41	44	39	22	40	52	34	41	56	40	49	40	36	50	39
Canada	na	34	39	29	13	29	52	37	27	44	30	38	34	21	33	39
Chile	na	27	30	24	20	27	33	26	24	38	25	24	35	25	27	32
China	na	46	54	37	43	44	52	36	51	71	37	48	55	49	45	66
Colombia	na	na	na	na	na	na	na	na	na	na	na	na	na	na	na	na
Croatia	na	53	62	44	33	52	66	49	55	51	55	47	56	47	53	53
Czech Republic	na	60	60	60	34	58	75	55	62	74	65	59	57	55	61	65
Denmark	na	64	69	59	44	61	77	59	65	73	65	63	70	44	65	73
Dominican Rep.	na	na	na	na	na	na	na	na	na	na	na	na	na	na	na	na
Egypt	na	na	na	na	na	na	na	na	na	na	na	na	na	na	na	na
El Salvador	na	na	na	na	na	na	na	na	na	na	na	na	na	na	na	na
Estonia	na	48	52	45	24	44	65	48	43	62	47	52	49	45	51	52
Finland	na	39	42	37	21	36	51	37	40	53	33	39	47	35	41	40
France	na	58	61	54	36	52	73	57	55	60	55	60	64	56	59	53
Georgia	na	na	na	na	na	na	na	na	na	na	na	na	na	na	na	na
Germany	na	61	68	56	42	62	68	54	64	86	55	62	66	62	60	66
Great Britain	na	24	26	21	8	21	35	22	22	34	20	24	26	na	na	na
Greece	na	53	58	49	38	60	76	67	47	56	55	54	53	50	53	56
Hungary	na	48	54	44	29	52	56	45	51	66	44	52	48	46	52	53
Iceland	na	45	47	44	21	46	65	41	45	57	42	46	49	39	46	55
India	na	34	40	26	38	34	31	18	37	64	24	25	48	32	43	52
Indonesia	na	na	na	na	na	na	na	na	na	na	na	na	na	na	na	na
Iran	na	na	na	na	na	na	na	na	na	na	na	na	na	na	na	na
Ireland	na	30	34	26	15	30	40	26	28	39	25	32	37	23	31	37
Israel	na	80	82	78	69	81	93	81	78	84	83	82	81	76	82	79
Italy	na	50	56	44	37	49	58	46	49	64	48	52	55	46	51	52
Japan	na	37	44	32	17	26	56	44	34	43	40	36	42	40	36	51
Jordan	na	na	na	na	na	na	na	na	na	na	na	na	na	na	na	na
Korea, South	na	52	63	41	35	54	69	46	55	50	50	55	53	52	53	45
Latvia	na	64	66	62	44	64	73	57	65	72	64	65	65	61	66	70
Lithuania	na	68	69	68	49	74	76	66	69	70	74	67	71	67	70	70
Luxembourg	na	46	47	44	23	46	60	39	47	58	36	54	59	46	45	52
Macedonia	na	56	63	48	30	50	68	51	57	65	55	54	62	58	57	43
Malta	na	34	37	32	17	34	46	47	29	32	43	32	32	33	33	37
Mexico	na	30	30	31	25	32	34	27	31	42	27	32	35	31	33	34
Moldova	na	45	53	38	37	49	47	31	49	51	44	46	43	37	51	55
Montenegro	na	28	37	20	14	27	38	26	27	38	33	26	32	30	29	22
Morocco	na	19	25	13	21	19	16	14	31	62	15	21	33	11	25	35
Netherlands	na	51	54	48	28	49	65	45	49	59	46	53	56	41	50	58
New Zealand	na	na	na	na	na	na	na	na	na	na	na	na	na	na	na	na
Nigeria	na	na	na	na	na	na	na	na	na	na	na	na	na	na	na	na
Northern Ireland	na	32	38	27	24	32	36	33	30	38	28	26	37	30	33	43
Norway	na	na	na	na	na	na	na	na	na	na	na	na	na	na	na	na
Pakistan	na	na	na	na	na	na	na	na	na	na	na	na	na	na	na	na
Peru	na	58	61	55	51	61	68	49	58	64	54	61	61	51	59	64
Philippines	na	28	30	25	27	28	28	22	28	34	26	26	32	26	29	31
Poland	na	53	56	50	28	54	66	49	53	70	55	52	52	51	54	55
Portugal	na	36	41	32	35	41	34	33	40	58	20	38	47	33	37	50
Puerto Rico	na	46	49	45	24	47	56	54	45	45	49	48	44	39	48	46
Romania	na	43	49	37	28	46	48	31	43	69	31	46	52	39	50	48
Russian Fed.	na	67	72	63	51	70	74	64	66	74	65	68	70	68	68	67
Serbia	na	45	54	38	27	41	58	40	45	55	44	45	53	43	48	50
Singapore	na	29	33	25	22	36	33	28	27	41	27	28	29	27	30	26
Slovakia	na	41	46	36	27	40	53	35	42	53	40	41	42	39	42	57
Slovenia	na	44	46	42	17	40	68	41	41	59	46	47	53	48	42	43
South Africa	na	24	29	17	17	30	21	21	25	43	18	31	25	23	25	17
Spain	na	44	50	38	35	46	47	41	43	53	35	48	49	41	44	50
Sweden	na	72	75	69	52	71	86	82	63	79	69	74	76	69	71	76
Switzerland	na	na	na	na	na	na	na	na	na	na	na	na	na	na	na	na
Taiwan	na	na	na	na	na	na	na	na	na	na	na	na	na	na	na	na
Tanzania	na	39	41	35	33	39	45	39	35	43	38	41	40	36	40	50
Turkey	na	49	61	37	44	54	53	42	55	71	42	49	63	46	48	58
Uganda	na	29	33	25	30	26	34	28	28	33	35	30	29	24	28	49
Ukraine	na	62	65	59	49	63	68	50	63	66	59	61	67	59	66	80
United States	na	34	37	31	17	31	54	28	33	38	32	34	38	24	34	40
Uruguay	na	na	na	na	na	na	na	na	na	na	na	na	na	na	na	na
Venezuela	na	32	36	29	27	33	40	32	31	37	29	31	36	28	33	35
Vietnam	na	59	69	49	49	58	68	48	72	78	53	57	65	59	64	67
Zimbabwe	na	15	21	11	14	18	15	11	21	52	7	14	32	10	18	30
Total	na	44	49	40	30	44	56	39	44	54	42	45	49	40	46	50

RANKING

Country	2000
Israel	80
Sweden	72
Lithuania	68
Russian Fed.	67
Latvia	64
Denmark	64
Ukraine	62
Germany	61
Czech Republic	60
Vietnam	59
Peru	58
France	58
Austria	57
Macedonia	56
Greece	53
Poland	53
Croatia	53
Korea, South	52
Netherlands	51
Italy	50
Turkey	49
Hungary	48
Estonia	48
Argentina	48
Belgium	47
Puerto Rico	46
China	46
Luxembourg	46
Iceland	45
Serbia	45
Moldova	45
Slovenia	44
Spain	44
Romania	43
Bulgaria	41
Slovakia	41
Finland	39
Tanzania	39
Japan	37
Portugal	36
Bangladesh	35
Belarus	34
Malta	34
United States	34
India	34
Canada	34
Venezuela	32
Northern Ireland	32
Albania	31
Bosnia and Herz.	30
Mexico	30
Ireland	30
Singapore	29
Uganda	29
Montenegro	28
Philippines	28
Chile	27
Great Britain	24
South Africa	24
Morocco	19
Zimbabwe	15
Total	44

E151_1) INFORMATION TO HELP JUSTICE

Can you tell me your opinion on each of the following statements? If someone has information that may help justice be done, generally he or she should give it to authorities

Strongly agree (%)

(EVS: V264)

Country	Wave		Gender		Age			Education			Income			Values				RANKING Country	2000
	1990	2000	Male	Female	16-29	30-49	50+	Lower	Middle	Upper	Lower	Middle	Upper	Mat	Mixed	Postm.			
Albania	na	na	na	na	na	na	na	na	na	na	na	na	na	na	na	na		France	60
Algeria	na	na	na	na	na	na	na	na	na	na	na	na	na	na	na	na		Belgium	55
Argentina	na	na	na	na	na	na	na	na	na	na	na	na	na	na	na	na		Slovakia	53
Armenia	na	na	na	na	na	na	na	na	na	na	na	na	na	na	na	na		Bulgaria	50
Australia	na	na	na	na	na	na	na	na	na	na	na	na	na	na	na	na		Iceland	49
Austria	na	33	37	30	27	33	38	33	35	30	30	32	37	39	36	28		Finland	49
Azerbaijan	na	na	na	na	na	na	na	na	na	na	na	na	na	na	na	na		Ireland	49
Bangladesh	na	na	na	na	na	na	na	na	na	na	na	na	na	na	na	na		Romania	48
Belarus	na	43	41	44	35	44	48	49	39	46	45	42	39	44	42	44		Portugal	47
Belgium	na	55	55	54	43	53	61	53	55	54	59	54	54	55	56	54		Luxembourg	47
Bosnia and Herz.	na	na	na	na	na	na	na	na	na	na	na	na	na	na	na	na		Slovenia	46
Brazil	na	na	na	na	na	na	na	na	na	na	na	na	na	na	na	na		Denmark	46
Bulgaria	na	50	47	53	36	49	59	55	46	53	56	52	45	52	51	45		Poland	45
Canada	na	na	na	na	na	na	na	na	na	na	na	na	na	na	na	na		Croatia	45
Chile	na	na	na	na	na	na	na	na	na	na	na	na	na	na	na	na		Great Britain	45
China	na	na	na	na	na	na	na	na	na	na	na	na	na	na	na	na		Malta	43
Colombia	na	na	na	na	na	na	na	na	na	na	na	na	na	na	na	na		Belarus	43
Croatia	na	45	43	46	34	47	50	46	46	38	49	42	47	45	45	43		Czech Republic	42
Czech Republic	na	42	41	43	38	38	47	40	44	42	45	39	42	42	41	44		Italy	41
Denmark	na	46	45	47	50	43	47	48	45	43	44	49	46	48	47	35		Spain	38
Dominican Rep.	na	na	na	na	na	na	na	na	na	na	na	na	na	na	na	na		Northern Ireland	38
Egypt	na	na	na	na	na	na	na	na	na	na	na	na	na	na	na	na		Ukraine	37
El Salvador	na	na	na	na	na	na	na	na	na	na	na	na	na	na	na	na		Latvia	37
Estonia	na	33	29	37	25	30	40	32	34	32	34	39	31	31	36	29		Hungary	36
Finland	na	49	44	53	43	44	57	49	45	56	51	47	50	46	51	48		Greece	35
France	na	60	59	60	54	57	65	64	54	54	58	60	59	66	59	51		Austria	33
Georgia	na	na	na	na	na	na	na	na	na	na	na	na	na	na	na	na		Estonia	33
Germany	na	25	27	23	23	21	30	28	21	30	24	26	18	27	23	26		Netherlands	31
Great Britain	na	45	44	46	35	46	49	40	48	51	38	44	53	na	na	na		Russian Fed.	29
Greece	na	35	35	35	30	34	48	52	34	32	38	33	33	36	36	32		Sweden	27
Hungary	na	36	34	37	36	27	43	38	30	31	37	35	35	35	37	12		Lithuania	25
Iceland	na	49	50	49	41	52	53	50	49	48	50	50	48	51	50	41		Germany	25
India	na	na	na	na	na	na	na	na	na	na	na	na	na	na	na	na			
Indonesia	na	na	na	na	na	na	na	na	na	na	na	na	na	na	na	na			
Iran	na	na	na	na	na	na	na	na	na	na	na	na	na	na	na	na			
Ireland	na	49	47	51	39	51	53	51	46	50	51	52	44	43	49	54			
Israel	na	na	na	na	na	na	na	na	na	na	na	na	na	na	na	na			
Italy	na	41	44	38	38	42	41	36	42	51	37	43	43	35	41	44			
Japan	na	na	na	na	na	na	na	na	na	na	na	na	na	na	na	na			
Jordan	na	na	na	na	na	na	na	na	na	na	na	na	na	na	na	na			
Korea, South	na	na	na	na	na	na	na	na	na	na	na	na	na	na	na	na			
Latvia	na	37	33	40	25	34	43	34	37	40	38	37	35	38	36	28			
Lithuania	na	25	23	28	20	23	32	24	25	29	23	30	26	25	26	26			
Luxembourg	na	47	50	44	41	47	51	47	45	52	43	51	54	48	47	54			
Macedonia	na	na	na	na	na	na	na	na	na	na	na	na	na	na	na	na			
Malta	na	43	44	43	43	41	46	46	42	48	39	45	44	45	45	30			
Mexico	na	na	na	na	na	na	na	na	na	na	na	na	na	na	na	na			
Moldova	na	na	na	na	na	na	na	na	na	na	na	na	na	na	na	na			
Montenegro	na	na	na	na	na	na	na	na	na	na	na	na	na	na	na	na			
Morocco	na	na	na	na	na	na	na	na	na	na	na	na	na	na	na	na			
Netherlands	na	31	35	27	24	27	38	34	32	26	27	32	30	37	30	30			
New Zealand	na	na	na	na	na	na	na	na	na	na	na	na	na	na	na	na			
Nigeria	na	na	na	na	na	na	na	na	na	na	na	na	na	na	na	na			
Northern Ireland	na	38	35	40	34	36	41	36	38	42	31	38	52	43	37	29			
Norway	na	na	na	na	na	na	na	na	na	na	na	na	na	na	na	na			
Pakistan	na	na	na	na	na	na	na	na	na	na	na	na	na	na	na	na			
Peru	na	na	na	na	na	na	na	na	na	na	na	na	na	na	na	na			
Philippines	na	na	na	na	na	na	na	na	na	na	na	na	na	na	na	na			
Poland	na	45	46	45	40	46	49	46	49	34	45	47	43	46	46	39			
Portugal	na	47	51	44	48	44	50	49	46	43	46	44	52	46	51	44			
Puerto Rico	na	na	na	na	na	na	na	na	na	na	na	na	na	na	na	na			
Romania	na	48	49	46	41	50	49	46	50	48	45	51	50	48	47	55			
Russian Fed.	na	29	26	31	21	27	36	34	27	29	32	31	24	29	28	29			
Serbia	na	na	na	na	na	na	na	na	na	na	na	na	na	na	na	na			
Singapore	na	na	na	na	na	na	na	na	na	na	na	na	na	na	na	na			
Slovakia	na	53	52	55	52	50	58	56	52	50	55	52	55	53	53	58			
Slovenia	na	46	46	47	44	45	49	50	44	47	45	48	47	51	45	46			
South Africa	na	na	na	na	na	na	na	na	na	na	na	na	na	na	na	na			
Spain	na	38	36	40	31	39	41	40	34	44	36	43	43	41	36	40			
Sweden	na	27	29	24	22	26	30	27	26	27	25	27	28	40	25	27			
Switzerland	na	na	na	na	na	na	na	na	na	na	na	na	na	na	na	na			
Taiwan	na	na	na	na	na	na	na	na	na	na	na	na	na	na	na	na			
Tanzania	na	na	na	na	na	na	na	na	na	na	na	na	na	na	na	na			
Turkey	na	na	na	na	na	na	na	na	na	na	na	na	na	na	na	na			
Uganda	na	na	na	na	na	na	na	na	na	na	na	na	na	na	na	na			
Ukraine	na	37	37	38	31	38	40	39	37	38	38	37	39	34	42	32			
United States	na	na	na	na	na	na	na	na	na	na	na	na	na	na	na	na			
Uruguay	na	na	na	na	na	na	na	na	na	na	na	na	na	na	na	na			
Venezuela	na	na	na	na	na	na	na	na	na	na	na	na	na	na	na	na			
Vietnam	na	na	na	na	na	na	na	na	na	na	na	na	na	na	na	na			
Zimbabwe	na	na	na	na	na	na	na	na	na	na	na	na	na	na	na	na			
Total	na	42	41	42	36	40	46	43	40	41	41	42	42	42	42	39		Total	42

E152_1) STICK TO OWN AFFAIRS

Can you tell me your opinion on each of the following statements? People should stick to their own affairs and not show too much interest in what others say or do

Strongly agree / Agree (%)

(EVS: V265)

Country	Wave 1990	Wave 2000	Gender Male	Gender Female	Age 16-29	Age 30-49	Age 50+	Education Lower	Education Middle	Education Upper	Income Lower	Income Middle	Income Upper	Values Mat	Values Mixed	Values Postm.
Albania	na	na	na	na	na	na	na	na	na	na	na	na	na	na	na	na
Algeria	na	na	na	na	na	na	na	na	na	na	na	na	na	na	na	na
Argentina	na	na	na	na	na	na	na	na	na	na	na	na	na	na	na	na
Armenia	na	na	na	na	na	na	na	na	na	na	na	na	na	na	na	na
Australia	na	na	na	na	na	na	na	na	na	na	na	na	na	na	na	na
Austria	na	60	57	62	54	54	69	68	51	53	69	61	51	72	60	58
Azerbaijan	na	na	na	na	na	na	na	na	na	na	na	na	na	na	na	na
Bangladesh	na	na	na	na	na	na	na	na	na	na	na	na	na	na	na	na
Belarus	na	47	47	48	44	48	49	49	46	49	48	47	47	51	44	37
Belgium	na	50	48	53	43	46	58	65	53	37	61	54	43	63	50	37
Bosnia and Herz.	na	na	na	na	na	na	na	na	na	na	na	na	na	na	na	na
Brazil	na	na	na	na	na	na	na	na	na	na	na	na	na	na	na	na
Bulgaria	na	46	48	45	51	43	47	48	47	42	49	46	44	45	46	41
Canada	na	na	na	na	na	na	na	na	na	na	na	na	na	na	na	na
Chile	na	na	na	na	na	na	na	na	na	na	na	na	na	na	na	na
China	na	na	na	na	na	na	na	na	na	na	na	na	na	na	na	na
Colombia	na	na	na	na	na	na	na	na	na	na	na	na	na	na	na	na
Croatia	na	64	62	67	60	62	70	71	63	48	74	63	61	73	64	60
Czech Republic	na	31	33	30	29	31	33	40	23	19	38	33	22	37	30	22
Denmark	na	35	37	33	32	28	43	46	23	18	40	33	27	61	34	20
Dominican Rep.	na	na	na	na	na	na	na	na	na	na	na	na	na	na	na	na
Egypt	na	na	na	na	na	na	na	na	na	na	na	na	na	na	na	na
El Salvador	na	na	na	na	na	na	na	na	na	na	na	na	na	na	na	na
Estonia	na	65	61	68	60	65	69	67	65	63	68	65	65	66	67	67
Finland	na	62	62	62	62	57	66	67	59	49	70	60	57	66	63	55
France	na	62	61	63	61	57	67	72	55	43	71	61	50	73	62	46
Georgia	na	na	na	na	na	na	na	na	na	na	na	na	na	na	na	na
Germany	na	41	41	41	42	41	40	45	39	27	48	47	34	40	41	38
Great Britain	na	38	34	41	33	32	43	49	28	29	47	35	31	49	28	45
Greece	na	47	48	47	40	49	61	64	53	39	56	47	39	49	48	45
Hungary	na	54	53	54	51	56	53	56	50	48	54	51	57	53	54	37
Iceland	na	55	55	55	51	51	64	62	54	43	61	57	47	60	55	44
India	na	na	na	na	na	na	na	na	na	na	na	na	na	na	na	na
Indonesia	na	na	na	na	na	na	na	na	na	na	na	na	na	na	na	na
Iran	na	na	na	na	na	na	na	na	na	na	na	na	na	na	na	na
Ireland	na	43	43	43	42	40	47	54	42	27	54	45	34	51	40	45
Israel	na	na	na	na	na	na	na	na	na	na	na	na	na	na	na	na
Italy	na	29	27	31	25	24	35	38	23	18	30	28	23	45	29	21
Japan	na	na	na	na	na	na	na	na	na	na	na	na	na	na	na	na
Jordan	na	na	na	na	na	na	na	na	na	na	na	na	na	na	na	na
Korea, South	na	na	na	na	na	na	na	na	na	na	na	na	na	na	na	na
Latvia	na	66	66	66	60	66	68	66	64	69	67	61	67	67	66	66
Lithuania	na	57	56	57	60	55	56	54	59	49	60	56	50	59	56	44
Luxembourg	na	64	64	65	63	63	67	67	67	52	67	64	54	69	64	57
Macedonia	na	na	na	na	na	na	na	na	na	na	na	na	na	na	na	na
Malta	na	63	62	64	58	64	65	71	61	53	62	66	66	68	61	51
Mexico	na	na	na	na	na	na	na	na	na	na	na	na	na	na	na	na
Moldova	na	na	na	na	na	na	na	na	na	na	na	na	na	na	na	na
Montenegro	na	na	na	na	na	na	na	na	na	na	na	na	na	na	na	na
Morocco	na	na	na	na	na	na	na	na	na	na	na	na	na	na	na	na
Netherlands	na	29	25	33	21	25	39	42	27	19	34	30	23	48	29	22
New Zealand	na	na	na	na	na	na	na	na	na	na	na	na	na	na	na	na
Nigeria	na	na	na	na	na	na	na	na	na	na	na	na	na	na	na	na
Northern Ireland	na	39	40	39	38	41	40	44	38	31	46	33	30	44	37	40
Norway	na	na	na	na	na	na	na	na	na	na	na	na	na	na	na	na
Pakistan	na	na	na	na	na	na	na	na	na	na	na	na	na	na	na	na
Peru	na	na	na	na	na	na	na	na	na	na	na	na	na	na	na	na
Philippines	na	na	na	na	na	na	na	na	na	na	na	na	na	na	na	na
Poland	na	63	66	60	68	64	58	64	62	58	66	59	64	64	63	65
Portugal	na	69	68	70	68	66	73	71	68	59	72	69	64	71	69	71
Puerto Rico	na	na	na	na	na	na	na	na	na	na	na	na	na	na	na	na
Romania	na	59	58	61	60	54	64	68	56	52	66	60	54	66	53	55
Russian Fed.	na	63	65	61	60	63	64	62	63	61	60	67	61	63	62	60
Serbia	na	na	na	na	na	na	na	na	na	na	na	na	na	na	na	na
Singapore	na	na	na	na	na	na	na	na	na	na	na	na	na	na	na	na
Slovakia	na	27	27	27	29	27	26	29	28	16	31	28	23	27	27	23
Slovenia	na	71	66	75	70	71	72	77	70	65	76	72	61	70	73	61
South Africa	na	na	na	na	na	na	na	na	na	na	na	na	na	na	na	na
Spain	na	53	51	54	50	50	57	60	52	36	61	50	41	54	56	41
Sweden	na	28	31	25	22	22	37	44	28	15	31	33	18	40	30	19
Switzerland	na	na	na	na	na	na	na	na	na	na	na	na	na	na	na	na
Taiwan	na	na	na	na	na	na	na	na	na	na	na	na	na	na	na	na
Tanzania	na	na	na	na	na	na	na	na	na	na	na	na	na	na	na	na
Turkey	na	na	na	na	na	na	na	na	na	na	na	na	na	na	na	na
Uganda	na	na	na	na	na	na	na	na	na	na	na	na	na	na	na	na
Ukraine	na	58	55	59	56	57	59	58	59	55	60	57	54	56	57	59
United States	na	na	na	na	na	na	na	na	na	na	na	na	na	na	na	na
Uruguay	na	na	na	na	na	na	na	na	na	na	na	na	na	na	na	na
Venezuela	na	na	na	na	na	na	na	na	na	na	na	na	na	na	na	na
Vietnam	na	na	na	na	na	na	na	na	na	na	na	na	na	na	na	na
Zimbabwe	na	na	na	na	na	na	na	na	na	na	na	na	na	na	na	na
Total	na	51	50	52	49	49	55	57	50	42	55	51	46	57	51	42

RANKING

Country	2000
Slovenia	71
Portugal	69
Latvia	66
Estonia	65
Luxembourg	64
Croatia	64
Malta	63
Poland	63
Russian Fed.	63
Finland	62
France	62
Austria	60
Romania	59
Ukraine	58
Lithuania	57
Iceland	55
Hungary	54
Spain	53
Belgium	50
Belarus	47
Greece	47
Bulgaria	46
Ireland	43
Germany	41
Northern Ireland	39
Great Britain	38
Denmark	35
Czech Republic	31
Netherlands	29
Italy	29
Sweden	28
Slovakia	27
Total	51

E153_1) CONCERNED WITH IMMEDIATE FAMILY

To what extent do you feel concerned about the living conditions of: Your immediate family

Very much / Much (%)

(EVS: V266)

Country	Wave 1990	Wave 2000	Gender Male	Gender Female	Age 16-29	Age 30-49	Age 50+	Education Lower	Education Middle	Education Upper	Income Lower	Income Middle	Income Upper	Values Mat	Values Mixed	Values Postm.
Albania	na	na	na	na	na	na	na	na	na	na	na	na	na	na	na	na
Algeria	na	na	na	na	na	na	na	na	na	na	na	na	na	na	na	na
Argentina	na	na	na	na	na	na	na	na	na	na	na	na	na	na	na	na
Armenia	na	na	na	na	na	na	na	na	na	na	na	na	na	na	na	na
Australia	na	na	na	na	na	na	na	na	na	na	na	na	na	na	na	na
Austria	na	76	74	78	72	76	78	79	76	64	76	80	73	70	78	74
Azerbaijan	na	na	na	na	na	na	na	na	na	na	na	na	na	na	na	na
Bangladesh	na	na	na	na	na	na	na	na	na	na	na	na	na	na	na	na
Belarus	na	96	96	97	94	98	96	97	96	94	97	96	95	97	95	98
Belgium	na	93	91	94	94	92	92	90	93	94	87	93	96	94	92	92
Bosnia and Herz.	na	na	na	na	na	na	na	na	na	na	na	na	na	na	na	na
Brazil	na	na	na	na	na	na	na	na	na	na	na	na	na	na	na	na
Bulgaria	na	97	96	97	97	98	96	97	95	99	95	97	98	97	98	100
Canada	na	na	na	na	na	na	na	na	na	na	na	na	na	na	na	na
Chile	na	na	na	na	na	na	na	na	na	na	na	na	na	na	na	na
China	na	na	na	na	na	na	na	na	na	na	na	na	na	na	na	na
Colombia	na	na	na	na	na	na	na	na	na	na	na	na	na	na	na	na
Croatia	na	73	68	77	67	75	74	75	74	61	84	75	62	84	72	68
Czech Republic	na	30	28	32	29	28	33	34	27	23	33	33	26	40	27	23
Denmark	na	34	34	35	48	35	27	36	36	30	34	35	31	43	34	35
Dominican Rep.	na	na	na	na	na	na	na	na	na	na	na	na	na	na	na	na
Egypt	na	na	na	na	na	na	na	na	na	na	na	na	na	na	na	na
El Salvador	na	na	na	na	na	na	na	na	na	na	na	na	na	na	na	na
Estonia	na	88	85	91	86	91	87	84	89	92	84	90	90	88	88	89
Finland	na	34	36	33	25	38	36	37	27	35	35	36	31	36	34	30
France	na	89	87	90	91	87	89	86	89	96	85	89	89	89	89	87
Georgia	na	na	na	na	na	na	na	na	na	na	na	na	na	na	na	na
Germany	na	98	98	98	97	98	98	98	98	98	96	99	97	99	97	98
Great Britain	na	72	72	71	75	73	68	69	71	74	68	75	72	na	na	na
Greece	na	96	96	96	98	95	96	97	96	97	97	97	95	98	96	96
Hungary	na	97	96	97	99	98	94	96	98	98	95	97	97	97	97	100
Iceland	na	93	90	96	92	92	95	92	92	97	93	92	93	93	94	88
India	na	na	na	na	na	na	na	na	na	na	na	na	na	na	na	na
Indonesia	na	na	na	na	na	na	na	na	na	na	na	na	na	na	na	na
Iran	na	na	na	na	na	na	na	na	na	na	na	na	na	na	na	na
Ireland	na	81	81	81	80	81	81	79	81	84	83	81	83	81	81	82
Israel	na	na	na	na	na	na	na	na	na	na	na	na	na	na	na	na
Italy	na	83	79	87	79	86	83	82	81	93	82	85	86	84	83	84
Japan	na	na	na	na	na	na	na	na	na	na	na	na	na	na	na	na
Jordan	na	na	na	na	na	na	na	na	na	na	na	na	na	na	na	na
Korea, South	na	na	na	na	na	na	na	na	na	na	na	na	na	na	na	na
Latvia	na	86	88	86	83	91	84	80	87	93	86	86	88	87	86	77
Lithuania	na	99	98	100	98	100	99	98	99	99	97	100	98	98	99	100
Luxembourg	na	88	87	89	88	88	88	86	89	90	86	87	91	83	89	90
Macedonia	na	na	na	na	na	na	na	na	na	na	na	na	na	na	na	na
Malta	na	96	97	96	96	95	98	98	96	93	95	99	95	98	96	94
Mexico	na	na	na	na	na	na	na	na	na	na	na	na	na	na	na	na
Moldova	na	na	na	na	na	na	na	na	na	na	na	na	na	na	na	na
Montenegro	na	na	na	na	na	na	na	na	na	na	na	na	na	na	na	na
Morocco	na	na	na	na	na	na	na	na	na	na	na	na	na	na	na	na
Netherlands	na	94	92	96	93	95	94	93	95	95	88	96	99	94	94	96
New Zealand	na	na	na	na	na	na	na	na	na	na	na	na	na	na	na	na
Nigeria	na	na	na	na	na	na	na	na	na	na	na	na	na	na	na	na
Northern Ireland	na	74	75	73	73	72	75	73	75	73	76	74	79	78	73	73
Norway	na	na	na	na	na	na	na	na	na	na	na	na	na	na	na	na
Pakistan	na	na	na	na	na	na	na	na	na	na	na	na	na	na	na	na
Peru	na	na	na	na	na	na	na	na	na	na	na	na	na	na	na	na
Philippines	na	na	na	na	na	na	na	na	na	na	na	na	na	na	na	na
Poland	na	95	93	96	96	95	93	94	96	96	94	95	95	95	95	96
Portugal	na	95	94	95	94	92	97	95	92	97	95	94	96	96	95	92
Puerto Rico	na	na	na	na	na	na	na	na	na	na	na	na	na	na	na	na
Romania	na	89	88	90	85	92	88	88	90	86	89	91	88	93	88	83
Russian Fed.	na	87	86	88	83	92	85	81	89	87	88	88	86	89	87	87
Serbia	na	na	na	na	na	na	na	na	na	na	na	na	na	na	na	na
Singapore	na	na	na	na	na	na	na	na	na	na	na	na	na	na	na	na
Slovakia	na	89	86	91	89	88	89	86	90	91	88	91	90	89	87	98
Slovenia	na	86	83	87	83	87	86	88	85	85	88	87	82	87	85	85
South Africa	na	na	na	na	na	na	na	na	na	na	na	na	na	na	na	na
Spain	na	92	92	92	91	93	92	93	91	93	90	94	91	94	91	90
Sweden	na	98	97	99	95	99	98	98	97	98	95	98	99	92	99	96
Switzerland	na	na	na	na	na	na	na	na	na	na	na	na	na	na	na	na
Taiwan	na	na	na	na	na	na	na	na	na	na	na	na	na	na	na	na
Tanzania	na	na	na	na	na	na	na	na	na	na	na	na	na	na	na	na
Turkey	na	na	na	na	na	na	na	na	na	na	na	na	na	na	na	na
Uganda	na	na	na	na	na	na	na	na	na	na	na	na	na	na	na	na
Ukraine	na	96	95	96	95	98	95	95	96	97	96	95	96	97	95	92
United States	na	na	na	na	na	na	na	na	na	na	na	na	na	na	na	na
Uruguay	na	na	na	na	na	na	na	na	na	na	na	na	na	na	na	na
Venezuela	na	na	na	na	na	na	na	na	na	na	na	na	na	na	na	na
Vietnam	na	na	na	na	na	na	na	na	na	na	na	na	na	na	na	na
Zimbabwe	na	na	na	na	na	na	na	na	na	na	na	na	na	na	na	na
Total	na	83	82	85	83	84	83	80	86	85	83	84	83	88	83	81

RANKING

Country	2000
Lithuania	99
Germany	98
Sweden	98
Bulgaria	97
Hungary	97
Greece	96
Belarus	96
Malta	96
Ukraine	96
Poland	95
Portugal	95
Netherlands	94
Iceland	93
Belgium	93
Spain	92
Romania	89
Slovakia	89
France	89
Estonia	88
Luxembourg	88
Russian Fed.	87
Latvia	86
Slovenia	86
Italy	83
Ireland	81
Austria	76
Northern Ireland	74
Croatia	73
Great Britain	72
Denmark	34
Finland	34
Czech Republic	30
Total	83

E154_1) CONCERNED WITH PEOPLE NEIGHBORHOOD

To what extent do you feel concerned about the living conditions of: People in your neighborhood

Very much / Much (%)

(EVS: V267)

Country	Wave 1990	Wave 2000	Gender Male	Gender Female	Age 16-29	Age 30-49	Age 50+	Education Lower	Education Middle	Education Upper	Income Lower	Income Middle	Income Upper	Values Mat	Values Mixed	Values Postm.
Albania	na	na	na	na	na	na	na	na	na	na	na	na	na	na	na	na
Algeria	na	na	na	na	na	na	na	na	na	na	na	na	na	na	na	na
Argentina	na	na	na	na	na	na	na	na	na	na	na	na	na	na	na	na
Armenia	na	na	na	na	na	na	na	na	na	na	na	na	na	na	na	na
Australia	na	na	na	na	na	na	na	na	na	na	na	na	na	na	na	na
Austria	na	27	26	27	22	27	29	29	26	19	28	26	29	21	27	27
Azerbaijan	na	na	na	na	na	na	na	na	na	na	na	na	na	na	na	na
Bangladesh	na	na	na	na	na	na	na	na	na	na	na	na	na	na	na	na
Belarus	na	38	35	41	27	35	50	53	34	26	44	35	33	41	38	24
Belgium	na	36	35	37	32	34	39	36	36	35	32	43	33	42	35	31
Bosnia and Herz.	na	na	na	na	na	na	na	na	na	na	na	na	na	na	na	na
Brazil	na	na	na	na	na	na	na	na	na	na	na	na	na	na	na	na
Bulgaria	na	31	33	29	20	31	36	41	25	26	37	28	25	32	30	31
Canada	na	na	na	na	na	na	na	na	na	na	na	na	na	na	na	na
Chile	na	na	na	na	na	na	na	na	na	na	na	na	na	na	na	na
China	na	na	na	na	na	na	na	na	na	na	na	na	na	na	na	na
Colombia	na	na	na	na	na	na	na	na	na	na	na	na	na	na	na	na
Croatia	na	37	38	36	21	39	44	42	34	32	47	36	32	44	37	29
Czech Republic	na	12	10	13	11	11	13	13	11	7	12	11	11	14	11	14
Denmark	na	11	11	10	11	11	10	11	10	9	9	12	10	14	10	15
Dominican Rep.	na	na	na	na	na	na	na	na	na	na	na	na	na	na	na	na
Egypt	na	na	na	na	na	na	na	na	na	na	na	na	na	na	na	na
El Salvador	na	na	na	na	na	na	na	na	na	na	na	na	na	na	na	na
Estonia	na	22	18	26	19	19	27	23	21	25	21	26	21	21	24	15
Finland	na	8	8	7	4	6	12	9	5	9	7	9	6	6	8	11
France	na	32	29	34	26	29	36	28	32	40	27	36	33	27	31	39
Georgia	na	na	na	na	na	na	na	na	na	na	na	na	na	na	na	na
Germany	na	55	52	57	48	52	60	55	56	50	52	59	62	54	55	58
Great Britain	na	32	31	33	34	35	26	28	33	36	29	31	34	na	na	na
Greece	na	26	26	26	21	27	38	38	25	25	28	24	25	27	25	25
Hungary	na	24	23	26	18	23	29	24	22	29	25	26	22	25	24	27
Iceland	na	25	24	26	20	23	31	25	23	26	23	26	23	21	25	28
India	na	na	na	na	na	na	na	na	na	na	na	na	na	na	na	na
Indonesia	na	na	na	na	na	na	na	na	na	na	na	na	na	na	na	na
Iran	na	na	na	na	na	na	na	na	na	na	na	na	na	na	na	na
Ireland	na	52	55	50	45	52	57	53	51	53	57	53	57	48	52	59
Israel	na	na	na	na	na	na	na	na	na	na	na	na	na	na	na	na
Italy	na	25	22	28	19	23	31	28	23	23	28	27	24	25	24	28
Japan	na	na	na	na	na	na	na	na	na	na	na	na	na	na	na	na
Jordan	na	na	na	na	na	na	na	na	na	na	na	na	na	na	na	na
Korea, South	na	na	na	na	na	na	na	na	na	na	na	na	na	na	na	na
Latvia	na	10	9	11	6	9	12	12	9	11	13	8	7	10	11	2
Lithuania	na	24	20	26	12	25	30	34	22	22	30	21	21	26	24	18
Luxembourg	na	32	31	34	25	31	39	34	31	35	31	37	32	35	31	33
Macedonia	na	na	na	na	na	na	na	na	na	na	na	na	na	na	na	na
Malta	na	44	42	46	28	42	55	54	41	33	52	45	40	49	41	38
Mexico	na	na	na	na	na	na	na	na	na	na	na	na	na	na	na	na
Moldova	na	na	na	na	na	na	na	na	na	na	na	na	na	na	na	na
Montenegro	na	na	na	na	na	na	na	na	na	na	na	na	na	na	na	na
Morocco	na	na	na	na	na	na	na	na	na	na	na	na	na	na	na	na
Netherlands	na	34	31	36	21	35	40	35	32	35	30	34	37	32	35	33
New Zealand	na	na	na	na	na	na	na	na	na	na	na	na	na	na	na	na
Nigeria	na	na	na	na	na	na	na	na	na	na	na	na	na	na	na	na
Northern Ireland	na	40	40	40	38	37	43	41	39	39	43	46	46	38	38	47
Norway	na	na	na	na	na	na	na	na	na	na	na	na	na	na	na	na
Pakistan	na	na	na	na	na	na	na	na	na	na	na	na	na	na	na	na
Peru	na	na	na	na	na	na	na	na	na	na	na	na	na	na	na	na
Philippines	na	na	na	na	na	na	na	na	na	na	na	na	na	na	na	na
Poland	na	37	36	37	30	36	42	38	36	34	38	37	35	35	36	45
Portugal	na	31	31	31	24	27	39	34	29	19	38	34	34	39	26	28
Puerto Rico	na	na	na	na	na	na	na	na	na	na	na	na	na	na	na	na
Romania	na	27	29	26	19	26	33	31	25	24	31	29	25	29	27	23
Russian Fed.	na	15	13	16	9	14	20	17	16	11	21	16	8	14	15	24
Serbia	na	na	na	na	na	na	na	na	na	na	na	na	na	na	na	na
Singapore	na	na	na	na	na	na	na	na	na	na	na	na	na	na	na	na
Slovakia	na	47	43	51	43	46	51	48	46	49	46	49	49	46	49	48
Slovenia	na	23	26	21	17	22	29	26	23	18	29	26	18	25	22	29
South Africa	na	na	na	na	na	na	na	na	na	na	na	na	na	na	na	na
Spain	na	42	42	41	35	41	47	42	42	40	43	45	38	45	39	41
Sweden	na	28	27	29	12	30	36	39	24	26	25	31	29	33	28	28
Switzerland	na	na	na	na	na	na	na	na	na	na	na	na	na	na	na	na
Taiwan	na	na	na	na	na	na	na	na	na	na	na	na	na	na	na	na
Tanzania	na	na	na	na	na	na	na	na	na	na	na	na	na	na	na	na
Turkey	na	7	8	6	9	4	4	4	11	7	4	6	11	6	6	9
Uganda	na	na	na	na	na	na	na	na	na	na	na	na	na	na	na	na
Ukraine	na	21	20	22	16	20	24	25	20	22	24	19	19	20	24	16
United States	na	na	na	na	na	na	na	na	na	na	na	na	na	na	na	na
Uruguay	na	na	na	na	na	na	na	na	na	na	na	na	na	na	na	na
Venezuela	na	na	na	na	na	na	na	na	na	na	na	na	na	na	na	na
Vietnam	na	na	na	na	na	na	na	na	na	na	na	na	na	na	na	na
Zimbabwe	na	na	na	na	na	na	na	na	na	na	na	na	na	na	na	na
Total	na	29	28	30	23	28	34	31	28	28	30	30	28	30	28	31

RANKING

Country	2000
Germany	55
Ireland	52
Slovakia	47
Malta	44
Spain	42
Northern Ireland	40
Belarus	38
Croatia	37
Poland	37
Belgium	36
Netherlands	34
Luxembourg	32
Great Britain	32
France	32
Portugal	31
Bulgaria	31
Sweden	28
Romania	27
Austria	27
Greece	26
Italy	25
Iceland	25
Hungary	24
Lithuania	24
Slovenia	23
Estonia	22
Ukraine	21
Russian Fed.	15
Czech Republic	12
Denmark	11
Latvia	10
Finland	8
Turkey	7
Total	29

E155_1) CONCERNED WITH PEOPLE OWN REGION

To what extent do you feel concerned about the living conditions of: The people of the region you live in

Very much / Much (%)

(EVS: V268)

Country	Wave		Gender		Age			Education			Income			Values				RANKING Country	2000
	1990	2000	Male	Female	16-29	30-49	50+	Lower	Middle	Upper	Lower	Middle	Upper	Mat	Mixed	Postm.		Country	2000
Albania	na	na	na	na	na	na	na	na	na	na	na	na	na	na	na	na		Ireland	37
Algeria	na	na	na	na	na	na	na	na	na	na	na	na	na	na	na	na		Belarus	36
Argentina	na	na	na	na	na	na	na	na	na	na	na	na	na	na	na	na		Romania	34
Armenia	na	na	na	na	na	na	na	na	na	na	na	na	na	na	na	na		Slovakia	34
Australia	na	na	na	na	na	na	na	na	na	na	na	na	na	na	na	14		Germany	33
Austria	na	15	16	14	11	15	17	17	13	12	18	14	14	18	15	15		Malta	33
Azerbaijan	na	na	na	na	na	na	na	na	na	na	na	na	na	na	na	na		Croatia	33
Bangladesh	na	na	na	na	na	na	na	na	na	na	na	na	na	na	na	na		Spain	30
Belarus	na	36	36	36	30	35	42	41	35	29	39	36	31	38	36	35		Northern Ireland	26
Belgium	na	17	17	16	12	12	23	19	17	14	20	17	14	18	16	18		Portugal	24
Bosnia and Herz.	na	na	na	na	na	na	na	na	na	na	na	na	na	na	na	na		Great Britain	23
Brazil	na	na	na	na	na	na	na	na	na	na	na	na	na	na	na	na		Ukraine	21
Bulgaria	na	21	21	20	14	18	26	26	18	17	28	16	15	19	23	18		Bulgaria	21
Canada	na	na	na	na	na	na	na	na	na	na	na	na	na	na	na	na		Poland	20
Chile	na	na	na	na	na	na	na	na	na	na	na	na	na	na	na	na		Greece	20
China	na	na	na	na	na	na	na	na	na	na	na	na	na	na	na	na		Italy	20
Colombia	na	na	na	na	na	na	na	na	na	na	na	na	na	na	na	na		Lithuania	19
Croatia	na	33	36	30	21	34	39	40	27	35	42	32	27	32	35	29		Luxembourg	19
Czech Republic	na	12	10	13	11	12	12	11	13	12	9	13	12	11	11	14		Sweden	19
Denmark	na	8	9	8	7	8	9	9	8	8	8	8	10	13	8	13		Iceland	18
Dominican Rep.	na	na	na	na	na	na	na	na	na	na	na	na	na	na	na	na		France	17
Egypt	na	na	na	na	na	na	na	na	na	na	na	na	na	na	na	na		Belgium	17
El Salvador	na	na	na	na	na	na	na	na	na	na	na	na	na	na	na	na		Russian Fed.	16
Estonia	na	12	9	14	11	8	16	14	11	11	13	15	10	12	12	8		Austria	15
Finland	na	9	9	8	5	8	11	10	5	11	9	9	7	5	10	12		Slovenia	15
France	na	17	18	17	13	16	21	16	17	22	16	19	18	15	17	22		Hungary	13
Georgia	na	na	na	na	na	na	na	na	na	na	na	na	na	na	na	na		Estonia	12
Germany	na	33	31	35	22	32	39	32	34	36	32	37	39	34	34	33		Czech Republic	12
Great Britain	na	23	21	24	23	24	20	23	20	27	21	20	23	na	na	na		Turkey	10
Greece	na	20	21	19	16	18	33	26	20	19	19	21	18	17	19	23		Finland	9
Hungary	na	13	12	14	8	12	18	15	9	12	15	14	11	16	11	14		Netherlands	8
Iceland	na	18	16	19	11	18	23	19	14	22	18	17	18	13	18	25		Denmark	8
India	na	na	na	na	na	na	na	na	na	na	na	na	na	na	na	na		Latvia	8
Indonesia	na	na	na	na	na	na	na	na	na	na	na	na	na	na	na	na			
Iran	na	na	na	na	na	na	na	na	na	na	na	na	na	na	na	na			
Ireland	na	37	41	34	31	38	42	41	35	36	40	37	41	37	36	47			
Israel	na	na	na	na	na	na	na	na	na	na	na	na	na	na	na	na			
Italy	na	20	19	20	17	19	21	20	18	24	18	24	19	16	18	26			
Japan	na	na	na	na	na	na	na	na	na	na	na	na	na	na	na	na			
Jordan	na	na	na	na	na	na	na	na	na	na	na	na	na	na	na	na			
Korea, South	na	na	na	na	na	na	na	na	na	na	na	na	na	na	na	na			
Latvia	na	8	9	7	7	6	10	11	7	10	10	8	7	9	9	5			
Lithuania	na	19	14	24	11	17	27	22	17	23	23	23	16	21	20	16			
Luxembourg	na	19	19	19	15	18	23	20	17	22	18	22	17	18	18	25			
Macedonia	na	na	na	na	na	na	na	na	na	na	na	na	na	na	na	na			
Malta	na	33	33	33	18	33	44	45	29	24	43	30	31	39	30	33			
Mexico	na	na	na	na	na	na	na	na	na	na	na	na	na	na	na	na			
Moldova	na	na	na	na	na	na	na	na	na	na	na	na	na	na	na	na			
Montenegro	na	na	na	na	na	na	na	na	na	na	na	na	na	na	na	na			
Morocco	na	na	na	na	na	na	na	na	na	na	na	na	na	na	na	na			
Netherlands	na	8	7	9	5	7	12	13	6	6	12	8	5	10	9	7			
New Zealand	na	na	na	na	na	na	na	na	na	na	na	na	na	na	na	na			
Nigeria	na	na	na	na	na	na	na	na	na	na	na	na	na	na	na	na			
Northern Ireland	na	26	27	25	27	25	27	25	24	33	30	27	31	21	25	37			
Norway	na	na	na	na	na	na	na	na	na	na	na	na	na	na	na	na			
Pakistan	na	na	na	na	na	na	na	na	na	na	na	na	na	na	na	na			
Peru	na	na	na	na	na	na	na	na	na	na	na	na	na	na	na	na			
Philippines	na	na	na	na	na	na	na	na	na	na	na	na	na	na	na	na			
Poland	na	20	23	17	16	21	20	20	20	19	23	21	11	17	20	31			
Portugal	na	24	23	25	15	24	29	25	21	22	26	26	21	29	20	22			
Puerto Rico	na	na	na	na	na	na	na	na	na	na	na	na	na	na	na	na			
Romania	na	34	36	32	23	36	38	37	30	40	35	37	34	35	33	33			
Russian Fed.	na	16	15	17	11	17	19	14	17	16	18	18	14	15	18	19			
Serbia	na	na	na	na	na	na	na	na	na	na	na	na	na	na	na	na			
Singapore	na	na	na	na	na	na	na	na	na	na	na	na	na	na	na	na			
Slovakia	na	34	31	36	32	33	35	32	34	36	32	36	35	33	33	37			
Slovenia	na	15	18	12	10	14	19	15	15	13	19	18	12	14	15	20			
South Africa	na	na	na	na	na	na	na	na	na	na	na	na	na	na	na	na			
Spain	na	30	30	31	22	32	34	29	31	35	32	30	30	33	29	32			
Sweden	na	19	18	19	8	23	22	23	17	19	20	20	16	22	18	21			
Switzerland	na	na	na	na	na	na	na	na	na	na	na	na	na	na	na	na			
Taiwan	na	na	na	na	na	na	na	na	na	na	na	na	na	na	na	na			
Tanzania	na	na	na	na	na	na	na	na	na	na	na	na	na	na	na	na			
Turkey	na	10	11	10	14	8	5	7	16	13	7	10	17	11	10	10			
Uganda	na	na	na	na	na	na	na	na	na	na	na	na	na	na	na	na			
Ukraine	na	21	23	19	18	22	22	19	21	22	24	20	19	21	23	22			
United States	na	na	na	na	na	na	na	na	na	na	na	na	na	na	na	na			
Uruguay	na	na	na	na	na	na	na	na	na	na	na	na	na	na	na	na			
Venezuela	na	na	na	na	na	na	na	na	na	na	na	na	na	na	na	na			
Vietnam	na	na	na	na	na	na	na	na	na	na	na	na	na	na	na	na			
Zimbabwe	na	na	na	na	na	na	na	na	na	na	na	na	na	na	na	na			
Total	na	21	21	21	16	20	24	21	20	21	22	21	19	22	20	23		Total	21

E156_1) CONCERNED WITH FELLOW COUNTRYMEN

To what extent do you feel concerned about the living conditions of: Your fellow countrymen

Very much / Much (%)

(EVS: V269)

Country	Wave 1990	Wave 2000	Male	Female	16-29	30-49	50+	Lower	Middle	Upper	Lower	Middle	Upper	Mat	Mixed	Postm.
Albania	na	na	na	na	na	na	na	na	na	na	na	na	na	na	na	na
Algeria	na	na	na	na	na	na	na	na	na	na	na	na	na	na	na	na
Argentina	na	na	na	na	na	na	na	na	na	na	na	na	na	na	na	na
Armenia	na	na	na	na	na	na	na	na	na	na	na	na	na	na	na	na
Australia	na	na	na	na	na	na	na	na	na	na	na	na	na	na	na	na
Austria	na	16	17	15	10	14	21	17	15	15	20	17	15	11	17	15
Azerbaijan	na	na	na	na	na	na	na	na	na	na	na	na	na	na	na	na
Bangladesh	na	na	na	na	na	na	na	na	na	na	na	na	na	na	na	na
Belarus	na	51	52	50	49	53	50	45	53	53	49	52	51	47	55	59
Belgium	na	14	16	11	15	12	15	17	12	13	16	15	10	12	14	16
Bosnia and Herz.	na	na	na	na	na	na	na	na	na	na	na	na	na	na	na	na
Brazil	na	na	na	na	na	na	na	na	na	na	na	na	na	na	na	na
Bulgaria	na	30	30	31	22	30	35	29	30	34	30	28	33	27	34	40
Canada	na	na	na	na	na	na	na	na	na	na	na	na	na	na	na	na
Chile	na	na	na	na	na	na	na	na	na	na	na	na	na	na	na	na
China	na	na	na	na	na	na	na	na	na	na	na	na	na	na	na	na
Colombia	na	na	na	na	na	na	na	na	na	na	na	na	na	na	na	na
Croatia	na	35	36	34	20	37	42	41	29	38	46	30	34	39	36	28
Czech Republic	na	17	16	19	17	17	18	17	18	21	18	18	16	17	18	17
Denmark	na	12	12	12	14	11	12	12	11	11	13	11	11	17	11	13
Dominican Rep.	na	na	na	na	na	na	na	na	na	na	na	na	na	na	na	na
Egypt	na	na	na	na	na	na	na	na	na	na	na	na	na	na	na	na
El Salvador	na	na	na	na	na	na	na	na	na	na	na	na	na	na	na	na
Estonia	na	13	12	14	13	8	17	12	12	18	11	14	14	12	13	12
Finland	na	15	15	15	11	14	20	17	12	15	18	15	13	12	16	17
France	na	19	20	17	17	18	20	15	16	28	18	18	20	14	18	27
Georgia	na	na	na	na	na	na	na	na	na	na	na	na	na	na	na	na
Germany	na	30	30	31	27	29	34	30	30	35	29	37	30	26	32	34
Great Britain	na	21	23	19	22	20	21	20	19	27	16	20	20	na	na	na
Greece	na	31	32	30	31	30	36	37	31	30	29	29	32	31	30	37
Hungary	na	20	18	22	16	19	23	18	19	35	16	18	23	20	22	29
Iceland	na	27	25	29	19	28	31	26	24	34	28	25	29	19	27	39
India	na	na	na	na	na	na	na	na	na	na	na	na	na	na	na	na
Indonesia	na	na	na	na	na	na	na	na	na	na	na	na	na	na	na	na
Iran	na	na	na	na	na	na	na	na	na	na	na	na	na	na	na	na
Ireland	na	35	40	31	29	35	41	39	31	38	38	34	38	34	34	42
Israel	na	na	na	na	na	na	na	na	na	na	na	na	na	na	na	na
Italy	na	25	24	25	22	26	25	23	24	33	22	30	24	18	23	33
Japan	na	na	na	na	na	na	na	na	na	na	na	na	na	na	na	na
Jordan	na	na	na	na	na	na	na	na	na	na	na	na	na	na	na	na
Korea, South	na	na	na	na	na	na	na	na	na	na	na	na	na	na	na	na
Latvia	na	10	10	10	11	7	11	10	9	12	10	9	10	8	11	11
Lithuania	na	32	30	34	23	36	35	28	31	46	30	36	30	28	33	52
Luxembourg	na	21	23	19	15	19	26	18	21	26	17	27	22	22	20	25
Macedonia	na	na	na	na	na	na	na	na	na	na	na	na	na	na	na	na
Malta	na	40	40	39	29	40	46	43	37	47	30	10	45	41	39	38
Mexico	na	na	na	na	na	na	na	na	na	na	na	na	na	na	na	na
Moldova	na	na	na	na	na	na	na	na	na	na	na	na	na	na	na	na
Montenegro	na	na	na	na	na	na	na	na	na	na	na	na	na	na	na	na
Morocco	na	na	na	na	na	na	na	na	na	na	na	na	na	na	na	na
Netherlands	na	11	11	11	7	9	15	15	9	9	16	9	7	9	12	10
New Zealand	na	na	na	na	na	na	na	na	na	na	na	na	na	na	na	na
Nigeria	na	na	na	na	na	na	na	na	na	na	na	na	na	na	na	na
Northern Ireland	na	23	25	22	26	22	23	21	23	31	29	22	27	14	24	32
Norway	na	na	na	na	na	na	na	na	na	na	na	na	na	na	na	na
Pakistan	na	na	na	na	na	na	na	na	na	na	na	na	na	na	na	na
Peru	na	na	na	na	na	na	na	na	na	na	na	na	na	na	na	na
Philippines	na	na	na	na	na	na	na	na	na	na	na	na	na	na	na	na
Poland	na	30	33	26	23	31	32	29	29	34	31	30	25	24	33	36
Portugal	na	32	33	31	28	33	33	32	32	31	28	34	27	31	32	30
Puerto Rico	na	na	na	na	na	na	na	na	na	na	na	na	na	na	na	na
Romania	na	44	46	42	40	42	48	43	42	52	44	45	46	42	47	44
Russian Fed.	na	21	20	21	17	21	23	15	21	22	21	23	19	17	25	26
Serbia	na	na	na	na	na	na	na	na	na	na	na	na	na	na	na	na
Singapore	na	na	na	na	na	na	na	na	na	na	na	na	na	na	na	na
Slovakia	na	29	28	31	24	32	31	30	29	31	29	33	29	28	31	30
Slovenia	na	33	34	32	28	34	36	29	35	31	36	37	32	38	32	38
South Africa	na	na	na	na	na	na	na	na	na	na	na	na	na	na	na	na
Spain	na	28	28	28	23	28	31	26	27	36	29	26	33	28	26	34
Sweden	na	28	30	26	25	27	32	31	23	35	30	31	23	29	27	32
Switzerland	na	na	na	na	na	na	na	na	na	na	na	na	na	na	na	na
Taiwan	na	na	na	na	na	na	na	na	na	na	na	na	na	na	na	na
Tanzania	na	na	na	na	na	na	na	na	na	na	na	na	na	na	na	na
Turkey	na	8	8	7	10	7	4	6	11	10	7	9	8	6	8	10
Uganda	na	na	na	na	na	na	na	na	na	na	na	na	na	na	na	na
Ukraine	na	24	26	22	17	26	25	23	23	26	27	22	23	22	26	32
United States	na	na	na	na	na	na	na	na	na	na	na	na	na	na	na	na
Uruguay	na	na	na	na	na	na	na	na	na	na	na	na	na	na	na	na
Venezuela	na	na	na	na	na	na	na	na	na	na	na	na	na	na	na	na
Vietnam	na	na	na	na	na	na	na	na	na	na	na	na	na	na	na	na
Zimbabwe	na	na	na	na	na	na	na	na	na	na	na	na	na	na	na	na
Total	na	25	26	25	22	25	28	24	25	28	26	26	25	25	26	28

RANKING

Country	2000
Belarus	51
Romania	44
Malta	40
Ireland	35
Croatia	35
Slovenia	33
Lithuania	32
Portugal	32
Greece	31
Bulgaria	30
Germany	30
Poland	30
Slovakia	29
Sweden	28
Spain	28
Iceland	27
Italy	25
Ukraine	24
Northern Ireland	23
Luxembourg	21
Great Britain	21
Russian Fed.	21
Hungary	20
France	19
Czech Republic	17
Austria	16
Finland	15
Belgium	14
Estonia	13
Denmark	12
Netherlands	11
Latvia	10
Turkey	8
Total	25

E157_1) CONCERNED WITH EUROPEANS

To what extent do you feel concerned about the living conditions of: European

Very much / Much (%)

(EVS: V270)

Country	Wave 1990	Wave 2000	Gender Male	Gender Female	Age 16-29	Age 30-49	Age 50+	Education Lower	Education Middle	Education Upper	Income Lower	Income Middle	Income Upper	Values Mat	Values Mixed	Values Postm.
Albania	na	na	na	na	na	na	na	na	na	na	na	na	na	na	na	na
Algeria	na	na	na	na	na	na	na	na	na	na	na	na	na	na	na	na
Argentina	na	na	na	na	na	na	na	na	na	na	na	na	na	na	na	na
Armenia	na	na	na	na	na	na	na	na	na	na	na	na	na	na	na	na
Australia	na	na	na	na	na	na	na	na	na	na	na	na	na	na	na	na
Austria	na	8	8	8	7	6	11	7	9	9	9	10	8	7	7	10
Azerbaijan	na	na	na	na	na	na	na	na	na	na	na	na	na	na	na	na
Bangladesh	na	na	na	na	na	na	na	na	na	na	na	na	na	na	na	na
Belarus	na	31	32	31	33	34	26	22	33	41	28	32	35	26	36	45
Belgium	na	9	11	7	7	8	11	6	9	11	10	9	8	5	9	15
Bosnia and Herz.	na	na	na	na	na	na	na	na	na	na	na	na	na	na	na	na
Brazil	na	na	na	na	na	na	na	na	na	na	na	na	na	na	na	na
Bulgaria	na	13	11	14	12	12	13	11	13	15	12	10	15	9	15	27
Canada	na	na	na	na	na	na	na	na	na	na	na	na	na	na	na	na
Chile	na	na	na	na	na	na	na	na	na	na	na	na	na	na	na	na
China	na	na	na	na	na	na	na	na	na	na	na	na	na	na	na	na
Colombia	na	na	na	na	na	na	na	na	na	na	na	na	na	na	na	na
Croatia	na	16	19	14	7	17	22	20	14	15	20	14	17	27	15	12
Czech Republic	na	11	10	12	10	12	11	11	11	9	11	12	10	10	11	12
Denmark	na	10	10	10	10	8	11	10	11	8	10	8	12	7	10	12
Dominican Rep.	na	na	na	na	na	na	na	na	na	na	na	na	na	na	na	na
Egypt	na	na	na	na	na	na	na	na	na	na	na	na	na	na	na	na
El Salvador	na	na	na	na	na	na	na	na	na	na	na	na	na	na	na	na
Estonia	na	5	4	5	5	3	7	6	4	7	3	6	5	5	5	12
Finland	na	7	7	7	6	6	9	9	5	6	9	8	5	6	8	10
France	na	14	15	13	13	14	13	11	13	21	14	13	15	9	13	21
Georgia	na	na	na	na	na	na	na	na	na	na	na	na	na	na	na	na
Germany	na	18	17	20	17	18	20	16	20	23	16	22	25	15	19	23
Great Britain	na	10	10	10	14	9	8	8	11	14	8	11	11	na	na	na
Greece	na	12	12	12	11	12	19	13	10	14	12	14	10	12	11	17
Hungary	na	9	9	10	6	9	12	9	8	13	8	8	11	10	8	19
Iceland	na	13	12	14	6	14	17	12	10	21	14	12	13	7	13	23
India	na	na	na	na	na	na	na	na	na	na	na	na	na	na	na	na
Indonesia	na	na	na	na	na	na	na	na	na	na	na	na	na	na	na	na
Iran	na	na	na	na	na	na	na	na	na	na	na	na	na	na	na	na
Ireland	na	20	22	18	12	21	25	24	17	21	22	18	22	21	19	23
Israel	na	na	na	na	na	na	na	na	na	na	na	na	na	na	na	na
Italy	na	18	18	18	16	19	17	15	19	23	15	20	19	12	16	25
Japan	na	na	na	na	na	na	na	na	na	na	na	na	na	na	na	na
Jordan	na	na	na	na	na	na	na	na	na	na	na	na	na	na	na	na
Korea, South	na	na	na	na	na	na	na	na	na	na	na	na	na	na	na	na
Latvia	na	3	4	3	3	3	4	5	3	2	4	3	3	4	4	2
Lithuania	na	11	10	13	8	12	13	7	12	15	9	12	10	12	11	9
Luxembourg	na	17	18	16	15	15	20	15	16	22	16	20	19	17	14	27
Macedonia	na	na	na	na	na	na	na	na	na	na	na	na	na	na	na	na
Malta	na	27	28	25	25	25	29	21	27	41	23	29	32	24	28	38
Mexico	na	na	na	na	na	na	na	na	na	na	na	na	na	na	na	na
Moldova	na	na	na	na	na	na	na	na	na	na	na	na	na	na	na	na
Montenegro	na	na	na	na	na	na	na	na	na	na	na	na	na	na	na	na
Morocco	na	na	na	na	na	na	na	na	na	na	na	na	na	na	na	na
Netherlands	na	6	6	6	4	5	7	6	4	8	7	7	5	5	5	8
New Zealand	na	na	na	na	na	na	na	na	na	na	na	na	na	na	na	na
Nigeria	na	na	na	na	na	na	na	na	na	na	na	na	na	na	na	na
Northern Ireland	na	13	12	14	12	13	13	12	13	16	17	12	13	9	12	19
Norway	na	na	na	na	na	na	na	na	na	na	na	na	na	na	na	na
Pakistan	na	na	na	na	na	na	na	na	na	na	na	na	na	na	na	na
Peru	na	na	na	na	na	na	na	na	na	na	na	na	na	na	na	na
Philippines	na	na	na	na	na	na	na	na	na	na	na	na	Mat	na	na	na
Poland	na	12	14	10	11	13	12	13	11	11	13	11	12	10	14	12
Portugal	na	18	19	17	14	20	18	18	17	14	13	20	17	17	17	18
Puerto Rico	na	na	na	na	na	na	na	na	na	na	na	na	na	na	na	na
Romania	na	17	18	17	16	18	17	17	16	20	15	19	18	16	18	18
Russian Fed.	na	6	6	6	4	6	8	6	6	6	8	7	5	5	6	9
Serbia	na	na	na	na	na	na	na	na	na	na	na	na	na	na	na	na
Singapore	na	na	na	na	na	na	na	na	na	na	na	na	na	na	na	na
Slovakia	na	16	15	16	15	16	16	14	16	20	15	15	18	14	16	24
Slovenia	na	11	12	10	8	11	13	9	13	9	12	13	9	9	12	12
South Africa	na	na	na	na	na	na	na	na	na	na	na	na	na	na	na	na
Spain	na	18	17	18	14	20	18	16	18	23	18	17	22	19	15	23
Sweden	na	16	15	18	13	17	17	16	13	22	17	17	14	22	15	20
Switzerland	na	na	na	na	na	na	na	na	na	na	na	na	na	na	na	na
Taiwan	na	na	na	na	na	na	na	na	na	na	na	na	na	na	na	na
Tanzania	na	na	na	na	na	na	na	na	na	na	na	na	na	na	na	na
Turkey	na	60	59	61	62	58	63	60	61	59	58	62	61	65	61	56
Uganda	na	na	na	na	na	na	na	na	na	na	na	na	na	na	na	na
Ukraine	na	6	6	7	7	7	5	4	6	8	7	4	8	6	7	9
United States	na	na	na	na	na	na	na	na	na	na	na	na	na	na	na	na
Uruguay	na	na	na	na	na	na	na	na	na	na	na	na	na	na	na	na
Venezuela	na	na	na	na	na	na	na	na	na	na	na	na	na	na	na	na
Vietnam	na	na	na	na	na	na	na	na	na	na	na	na	na	na	na	na
Zimbabwe	na	na	na	na	na	na	na	na	na	na	na	na	na	na	na	na
Total	na	14	14	13	12	14	14	13	13	16	13	14	14	12	13	18

RANKING

Country	2000
Turkey	60
Belarus	31
Malta	27
Ireland	20
Germany	18
Italy	18
Portugal	18
Spain	18
Romania	17
Luxembourg	17
Croatia	16
Sweden	16
Slovakia	16
France	14
Iceland	13
Northern Ireland	13
Bulgaria	13
Greece	12
Poland	12
Lithuania	11
Slovenia	11
Czech Republic	11
Denmark	10
Great Britain	10
Hungary	9
Belgium	9
Austria	8
Finland	7
Ukraine	6
Russian Fed.	6
Netherlands	6
Estonia	5
Latvia	3
Total	14

E158_1) CONCERNED WITH HUMAN KIND

To what extent do you feel concerned about the living conditions of: Human kind

Very much / Much (%)

(EVS: V271)

Country	Wave 1990	Wave 2000	Gender Male	Gender Female	Age 16-29	Age 30-49	Age 50+	Education Lower	Education Middle	Education Upper	Income Lower	Income Middle	Income Upper	Values Mat	Values Mixed	Values Postm.
Albania	na	na	na	na	na	na	na	na	na	na	na	na	na	na	na	na
Algeria	na	na	na	na	na	na	na	na	na	na	na	na	na	na	na	na
Argentina	na	na	na	na	na	na	36	na	na	na	na	na	na	na	na	na
Armenia	na	na	na	na	na	na	na	na	na	na	na	na	na	na	na	na
Australia	na	na	na	na	na	na	na	na	na	na	na	na	na	na	na	na
Austria	na	17	16	18	17	18	17	13	20	24	17	19	19	14	15	23
Azerbaijan	na	na	na	na	na	na	na	na	na	na	na	na	na	na	na	na
Bangladesh	na	na	na	na	na	na	na	na	na	na	na	na	na	na	na	na
Belarus	na	34	34	35	39	37	29	23	36	48	29	35	41	31	38	43
Belgium	na	22	25	20	19	26	21	15	23	27	25	19	22	15	22	34
Bosnia and Herz.	na	na	na	na	na	na	na	na	na	na	na	na	na	na	na	na
Brazil	na	na	na	na	na	na	na	na	na	na	na	na	na	na	na	na
Bulgaria	na	24	22	26	26	25	23	19	26	29	23	24	28	19	30	40
Canada	na	na	na	na	na	na	na	na	na	na	na	na	na	na	na	na
Chile	na	na	na	na	na	na	na	na	na	na	na	na	na	na	na	na
China	na	na	na	na	na	na	na	na	na	na	na	na	na	na	na	na
Colombia	na	na	na	na	na	na	na	na	na	na	na	na	na	na	na	na
Croatia	na	34	33	35	33	33	36	32	33	43	33	33	34	38	31	43
Czech Republic	na	29	26	32	29	29	28	24	31	41	29	27	30	23	31	37
Denmark	na	36	37	36	34	37	36	30	40	44	34	35	42	23	35	54
Dominican Rep.	na	na	na	na	na	na	na	na	na	na	na	na	na	na	na	na
Egypt	na	na	na	na	na	na	na	na	na	na	na	na	na	na	na	na
El Salvador	na	na	na	na	na	na	na	na	na	na	na	na	na	na	na	na
Estonia	na	13	12	13	17	9	13	13	12	13	11	14	13	13	13	12
Finland	na	36	32	40	35	34	39	34	38	43	38	31	38	25	39	51
France	na	24	25	22	25	25	22	19	24	36	26	23	24	15	24	35
Georgia	na	na	na	na	na	na	na	na	na	na	na	na	na	na	na	na
Germany	na	23	21	24	20	23	23	19	25	29	19	28	26	17	24	28
Great Britain	na	29	29	29	36	28	28	24	35	31	27	29	28	na	na	na
Greece	na	46	42	48	47	44	49	52	46	45	46	43	46	40	45	53
Hungary	na	23	22	23	25	25	19	21	26	26	20	22	24	22	23	40
Iceland	na	20	20	21	18	20	23	22	15	26	24	18	19	13	21	32
India	na	na	na	na	na	na	na	na	na	na	na	na	na	na	na	na
Indonesia	na	na	na	na	na	na	na	na	na	na	na	na	na	na	na	na
Iran	na	na	na	na	na	na	na	na	na	na	na	na	na	na	na	na
Ireland	na	35	36	34	28	37	38	36	32	40	30	38	38	33	35	38
Israel	na	na	na	na	na	na	na	na	na	na	na	na	na	na	na	na
Italy	na	29	29	29	28	31	27	25	29	37	27	31	29	21	27	36
Japan	na	na	na	na	na	na	na	na	na	na	na	na	na	na	na	na
Jordan	na	na	na	na	na	na	na	na	na	na	na	na	na	na	na	na
Korea, South	na	na	na	na	na	na	na	na	na	na	na	na	na	na	na	na
Latvia	na	9	na	na	13	10	7	10	10	8	9	9	10	7	10	18
Lithuania	na	16	13	19	15	16	17	10	17	24	14	18	19	11	18	17
Luxembourg	na	29	29	29	28	29	30	26	28	38	25	34	30	22	27	46
Macedonia	na	na	na	na	na	na	na	na	na	na	na	na	na	na	na	na
Malta	na	36	37	34	32	36	38	34	34	36	33	39	47	35	37	37
Mexico	na	na	na	na	na	na	na	na	na	na	na	na	na	na	na	na
Moldova	na	na	na	na	na	na	na	na	na	na	na	na	na	na	na	na
Montenegro	na	na	na	na	na	na	na	na	na	na	na	na	na	na	na	na
Morocco	na	na	na	na	na	na	na	na	na	na	na	na	na	na	na	na
Netherlands	na	33	32	33	27	34	34	30	31	37	36	33	32	25	32	39
New Zealand	na	na	na	na	na	na	na	na	na	na	na	na	na	na	na	na
Nigeria	na	na	na	na	na	na	na	na	na	na	na	na	na	na	na	na
Northern Ireland	na	25	25	25	24	27	24	21	27	31	32	25	26	18	23	37
Norway	na	na	na	na	na	na	na	na	na	na	na	na	na	na	na	na
Pakistan	na	na	na	na	na	na	na	na	na	na	na	na	na	na	na	na
Peru	na	na	na	na	na	na	na	na	na	na	na	na	na	na	na	na
Philippines	na	na	na	na	na	na	na	na	na	na	na	na	na	na	na	na
Poland	na	14	16	12	15	12	15	13	15	15	15	13	13	12	16	14
Portugal	na	40	41	38	50	38	35	37	43	49	29	42	40	36	40	48
Puerto Rico	na	na	na	na	na	na	na	na	na	na	na	na	na	na	na	na
Romania	na	20	20	20	20	20	20	19	19	25	18	22	21	20	21	18
Russian Fed.	na	19	17	20	18	18	20	14	20	18	20	22	16	16	22	19
Serbia	na	na	na	na	na	na	na	na	na	na	na	na	na	na	na	na
Singapore	na	na	na	na	na	na	na	na	na	na	na	na	na	na	na	na
Slovakia	na	20	18	22	19	20	21	20	19	25	22	17	22	19	20	29
Slovenia	na	25	22	27	24	24	26	23	26	22	27	26	23	25	25	27
South Africa	na	na	na	na	na	na	na	na	na	na	na	na	na	na	na	na
Spain	na	35	35	35	31	38	35	32	34	47	37	34	39	30	34	43
Sweden	na	34	30	38	36	34	33	32	32	39	39	35	25	41	31	43
Switzerland	na	na	na	na	na	na	na	na	na	na	na	na	na	na	na	na
Taiwan	na	na	na	na	na	na	na	na	na	na	na	na	na	na	na	na
Tanzania	na	na	na	na	na	na	na	na	na	na	na	na	na	na	na	na
Turkey	na	16	16	17	20	13	14	15	18	17	17	16	13	16	17	15
Uganda	na	na	na	na	na	na	na	na	na	na	na	na	na	na	na	na
Ukraine	na	18	17	20	21	18	16	15	18	20	17	17	21	18	19	32
United States	na	na	na	na	na	na	na	na	na	na	na	na	na	na	na	na
Uruguay	na	na	na	na	na	na	na	na	na	na	na	na	na	na	na	na
Venezuela	na	na	na	na	na	na	na	na	na	na	na	na	na	na	na	na
Vietnam	na	na	na	na	na	na	na	na	na	na	na	na	na	na	na	na
Zimbabwe	na	na	na	na	na	na	na	na	na	na	na	na	na	na	na	na
Total	na	26	26	27	27	26	26	24	26	32	26	27	27	21	27	36

RANKING

Country	2000
Greece	46
Portugal	40
Finland	36
Denmark	36
Malta	36
Spain	35
Ireland	35
Belarus	34
Croatia	34
Sweden	34
Netherlands	33
Great Britain	29
Luxembourg	29
Czech Republic	29
Italy	29
Northern Ireland	25
Slovenia	25
Bulgaria	24
France	24
Germany	23
Hungary	23
Belgium	22
Iceland	20
Romania	20
Slovakia	20
Russian Fed.	19
Ukraine	18
Austria	17
Lithuania	16
Turkey	16
Poland	14
Estonia	13
Latvia	9
Total	26

E159_1) CONCERNED WITH ELDERLY

To what extent do you feel concerned about the living conditions of: Elderly people in your country

Very much / Much (%)

(EVS: V272)

Country	Wave 1990	Wave 2000	Gender Male	Gender Female	Age 16-29	Age 30-49	Age 50+	Education Lower	Education Middle	Education Upper	Income Lower	Income Middle	Income Upper	Values Mat	Values Mixed	Values Postm.
Albania	na	na	na	na	na	na	na	na	na	na	na	na	na	na	na	na
Algeria	na	na	na	na	na	na	na	na	na	na	na	na	na.	na	na	na
Argentina	na	na	na	na	na	na	na	na	na	na	na	na	na	na	na	na
Armenia	na	na	na	na	na	na	na	na	na	na	na	na	na	na	na	na
Australia	na	na	na	na	na	na	na	na	na	na	na	na	na	na	na	na
Austria	na	49	47	51	40	46	57	52	47	43	50	51	48	41	53	43
Azerbaijan	na	na	na	na	na	na	na	na	na	na	na	na	na	na	na	na
Bangladesh	na	na	na	na	na	na	na	na	na	na	na	na	na	na	na	na
Belarus	na	51	46	55	37	50	64	56	49	51	56	51	43	54	51	45
Belgium	na	58	54	62	38	50	75	66	56	56	69	61	53	61	58	56
Bosnia and Herz.	na	na	na	na	na	na	na	na	na	na	na	na	na	na	na	na
Brazil	na	na	na	na	na	na	na	na	na	na	na	na	na	na	na	na
Bulgaria	na	70	66	74	50	66	84	78	65	67	74	68	70	72	70	84
Canada	na	na	na	na	na	na	na	na	na	na	na	na	na	na	na	na
Chile	na	na	na	na	na	na	na	na	na	na	na	na	na	na	na	na
China	na	na	na	na	na	na	na	na	na	na	na	na	na	na	na	na
Colombia	na	na	na	na	na	na	na	na	na	na	na	na	na	na	na	na
Croatia	na	68	63	72	56	68	76	67	66	75	77	67	66	74	67	65
Czech Republic	na	47	44	50	44	42	55	48	47	46	58	44	44	51	48	41
Denmark	na	53	48	58	57	56	49	56	54	51	52	51	56	61	53	56
Dominican Rep.	na	na	na	na	na	na	na	na	na	na	na	na	na	na	na	na
Egypt	na	na	na	na	na	na	na	na	na	na	na	na	na	na	na	na
El Salvador	na	na	na	na	na	na	na	na	na	na	na	na	na	na	na	na
Estonia	na	48	39	55	28	44	61	46	46	54	54	51	45	51	46	42
Finland	na	62	57	67	45	61	73	66	54	61	64	61	62	57	65	59
France	na	67	63	70	56	61	77	70	58	66	66	69	65	65	71	58
Georgia	na	na	na	na	na	na	na	na	na	na	na	na	na	na	na	na
Germany	na	64	63	65	55	61	72	67	60	74	63	67	67	66	64	65
Great Britain	na	70	67	73	60	68	77	69	71	65	68	76	70	na	na	na
Greece	na	68	64	71	60	69	83	80	70	65	73	68	64	67	68	69
Hungary	na	57	53	61	37	52	73	56	58	61	57	57	57	60	55	51
Iceland	na	62	54	70	48	64	72	68	57	60	65	61	60	62	62	65
India	na	na	na	na	na	na	na	na	na	na	na	na	na	na	na	na
Indonesia	na	na	na	na	na	na	na	na	na	na	na	na	na	na	na	na
Iran	na	na	na	na	na	na	na	na	na	na	na	na	na	na	na	na
Ireland	na	81	78	83	76	80	84	82	79	80	80	83	84	81	79	84
Israel	na	na	na	na	na	na	na	na	na	na	na	na	na	na	na	na
Italy	na	76	72	79	62	74	84	80	72	76	81	77	71	74	76	76
Japan	na	na	na	na	na	na	na	na	na	na	na	na	na	na	na	na
Jordan	na	na	na	na	na	na	na	na	na	na	na	na	na	na	na	na
Korea, South	na	na	na	na	na	na	na	na	na	na	na	na	na	na	na	na
Latvia	na	38	36	40	35	37	41	36	39	40	38	44	36	34	40	47
Lithuania	na	76	70	82	58	73	91	86	72	77	85	78	69	78	77	79
Luxembourg	na	44	41	47	26	39	60	42	45	44	43	50	44	39	44	51
Macedonia	na	na	na	na	na	na	na	na	na	na	na	na	na	na	na	na
Malta	na	79	76	83	63	83	88	89	76	74	84	79	76	82	79	70
Mexico	na	na	na	na	na	na	na	na	na	na	na	na	na	na	na	na
Moldova	na	na	na	na	na	na	na	na	na	na	na	na	na	na	na	na
Montenegro	na	na	na	na	na	na	na	na	na	na	na	na	na	na	na	na
Morocco	na	na	na	na	na	na	na	na	na	na	na	na	na	na	na	na
Netherlands	na	53	47	58	39	46	67	60	51	48	53	56	45	57	54	47
New Zealand	na	na	na	na	na	na	na	na	na	na	na	na	na	na	na	na
Nigeria	na	na	na	na	na	na	na	na	na	na	na	na	na	na	na	na
Northern Ireland	na	69	69	69	62	68	72	68	67	74	70	71	80	67	69	76
Norway	na	na	na	na	na	na	na	na	na	na	na	na	na	na	na	na
Pakistan	na	na	na	na	na	na	na	na	na	na	na	na	na	na	na	na
Peru	na	na	na	na	na	na	na	na	na	na	na	na	na	na	na	na
Philippines	na	na	na	na	na	na	na	na	na	na	na	na	na	na	na	na
Poland	na	72	71	73	59	74	78	73	72	73	74	72	70	70	75	68
Portugal	na	83	81	85	74	82	89	86	75	82	85	86	79	88	80	82
Puerto Rico	na	na	na	na	na	na	na	na	na	na	na	na	na	na	na	na
Romania	na	67	62	71	56	65	74	68	64	72	66	68	66	71	65	61
Russian Fed.	na	70	66	74	51	69	84	72	70	70	74	74	66	70	71	63
Serbia	na	na	na	na	na	na	na	na	na	na	na	na	na	na	na	na
Singapore	na	na	na	na	na	na	na	na	na	na	na	na	na	na	na	na
Slovakia	na	69	65	72	59	64	82	73	66	71	74	70	68	71	68	69
Slovenia	na	46	43	48	29	40	64	51	44	41	54	50	40	51	45	43
South Africa	na	na	na	na	na	na	na	na	na	na	na	na	na	na	na	na
Spain	na	63	61	65	50	64	71	68	59	62	68	68	62	69	61	67
Sweden	na	68	61	74	53	66	77	74	62	71	68	67	67	62	66	73
Switzerland	na	na	na	na	na	na	na	na	na	na	na	na	na	na	na	na
Taiwan	na	na	na	na	na	na	na	na	na	na	na	na	na	na	na	na
Tanzania	na	na	na	na	na	na	na	na	na	na	na	na	na	na	na	na
Turkey	na	6	7	4	8	3	4	5	8	4	5	6	5	7	5	8
Uganda	na	na	na	na	na	na	na	na	na	na	na	na	na	na	na	na
Ukraine	na	72	67	77	54	70	84	88	69	71	80	69	67	71	75	77
United States	na	na	na	na	na	na	na	na	na	na	na	na	na	na	na	na
Uruguay	na	na	na	na	na	na	na	na	na	na	na	na	na	na	na	na
Venezuela	na	na	na	na	na	na	na	na	na	na	na	na	na	na	na	na
Vietnam	na	na	na	na	na	na	na	na	na	na	na	na	na	na	na	na
Zimbabwe	na	na	na	na	na	na	na	na	na	na	na	na	na	na	na	na
Total	na	63	59	66	50	60	73	65	61	63	65	63	61	65	62	61

RANKING

Country	2000
Portugal	83
Ireland	81
Malta	79
Lithuania	76
Italy	76
Poland	72
Ukraine	72
Russian Fed.	70
Bulgaria	70
Great Britain	70
Northern Ireland	69
Slovakia	69
Greece	68
Croatia	68
Sweden	68
Romania	67
France	67
Germany	64
Spain	63
Iceland	62
Finland	62
Belgium	58
Hungary	57
Denmark	53
Netherlands	53
Belarus	51
Austria	49
Estonia	48
Czech Republic	47
Slovenia	46
Luxembourg	44
Latvia	38
Turkey	6
Total	63

E160_1) CONCERNED WITH UNEMPLOYED

To what extent do you feel concerned about the living conditions of: Unemployed people in your country

Very much / Much (%)

(EVS: V273)

Country	Wave		Gender		Age			Education			Income			Values		
	1990	2000	Male	Female	16-29	30-49	50+	Lower	Middle	Upper	Lower	Middle	Upper	Mat	Mixed	Postm.
Albania	na	na	na	na	na	na	na	na	na	na	na	na	na	na	na	na
Algeria	na	na	na	na	na	na	na	na	na	na	na	na	na	na	na	na
Argentina	na	na	na	na	na	na	na	na	na	na	na	na	na	na	na	na
Armenia	na	na	na	na	na	na	na	na	na	na	na	na	na	na	na	na
Australia	na	na	na	na	na	na	na	na	na	na	na	na	na	na	na	na
Austria	na	32	32	32	22	30	40	30	31	43	33	33	32	21	33	35
Azerbaijan	na	na	na	na	na	na	na	na	na	na	na	na	na	na	na	na
Bangladesh	na	na	na	na	na	na	na	na	na	na	na	na	na	na	na	na
Belarus	na	27	25	29	25	27	30	28	27	28	29	29	20	29	28	20
Belgium	na	32	33	31	26	28	39	35	31	31	41	38	25	30	31	36
Bosnia and Herz.	na	na	na	na	na	na	na	na	na	na	na	na	na	na	na	na
Brazil	na	na	na	na	na	na	na	na	na	na	na	na	na	na	na	na
Bulgaria	na	57	51	63	40	58	65	65	53	55	62	56	59	58	59	63
Canada	na	na	na	na	na	na	na	na	na	na	na	na	na	na	na	na
Chile	na	na	na	na	na	na	na	na	na	na	na	na	na	na	na	na
China	na	na	na	na	na	na	na	na	na	na	na	na	na	na	na	na
Colombia	na	na	na	na	na	na	na	na	na	na	na	na	na	na	na	na
Croatia	na	69	67	70	59	71	72	66	70	71	77	69	64	71	68	71
Czech Republic	na	44	39	48	37	39	51	45	44	35	54	43	36	46	45	39
Denmark	na	24	24	24	18	24	28	25	30	23	27	23	25	29	23	32
Dominican Rep.	na	na	na	na	na	na	na	na	na	na	na	na	na	na	na	na
Egypt	na	na	na	na	na	na	na	na	na	na	na	na	na	na	na	na
El Salvador	na	na	na	na	na	na	na	na	na	na	na	na	na	na	na	na
Estonia	na	38	32	43	27	37	46	38	38	37	46	40	33	39	38	34
Finland	na	47	44	51	37	47	54	53	40	40	55	48	43	47	48	51
France	na	54	52	56	49	53	59	52	52	62	55	56	54	48	56	58
Georgia	na	na	na	na	na	na	na	na	na	na	na	na	na	na	na	na
Germany	na	34	33	35	29	34	37	31	35	44	32	37	38	27	36	39
Great Britain	na	34	32	35	31	31	38	32	34	36	35	36	32	na	na	na
Greece	na	53	51	53	47	51	71	68	54	48	57	50	49	45	53	58
Hungary	na	30	28	31	21	29	34	32	25	26	34	32	25	30	29	50
Iceland	na	36	34	37	21	36	48	39	32	36	42	36	30	36	34	42
India	na	na	na	na	na	na	na	na	na	na	na	na	na	na	na	na
Indonesia	na	na	na	na	na	na	na	na	na	na	na	na	na	na	na	na
Iran	na	na	na	na	na	na	na	na	na	na	na	na	na	na	na	na
Ireland	na	50	49	50	38	54	54	52	46	54	52	44	58	47	52	45
Israel	na	na	na	na	na	na	na	na	na	na	na	na	na	na	na	na
Italy	na	60	58	63	54	61	64	61	58	65	64	63	56	59	59	67
Japan	na	na	na	na	na	na	na	na	na	na	na	na	na	na	na	na
Jordan	na	na	na	na	na	na	na	na	na	na	na	na	na	na	na	na
Korea, South	na	na	na	na	na	na	na	na	na	na	na	na	na	na	na	na
Latvia	na	23	24	22	20	18	27	21	23	25	26	21	20	22	22	30
Lithuania	na	63	59	67	51	60	74	66	62	61	70	67	56	66	63	67
Luxembourg	na	24	23	24	18	22	29	20	25	26	19	29	22	16	25	30
Macedonia	na	na	na	na	na	na	na	na	na	na	na	na	na	na	na	na
Malta	na	46	47	46	36	49	51	51	44	50	51	51	17	50	45	36
Mexico	na	na	na	na	na	na	na	na	na	na	na	na	na	na	na	na
Moldova	na	na	na	na	na	na	na	na	na	na	na	na	na	na	na	na
Montenegro	na	na	na	na	na	na	na	na	na	na	na	na	na	na	na	na
Morocco	na	na	na	na	na	na	na	na	na	na	na	na	na	na	na	na
Netherlands	na	21	20	21	9	18	30	27	17	19	22	22	17	23	19	26
New Zealand	na	na	na	na	na	na	na	na	na	na	na	na	na	na	na	na
Nigeria	na	na	na	na	na	na	na	na	na	na	na	na	na	na	na	na
Northern Ireland	na	33	35	31	28	32	35	33	29	39	40	31	36	27	32	46
Norway	na	na	na	na	na	na	na	na	na	na	na	na	na	na	na	na
Pakistan	na	na	na	na	na	na	na	na	na	na	na	na	na	na	na	na
Peru	na	na	na	na	na	na	na	na	na	na	na	na	na	na	na	na
Philippines	na	na	na	na	na	na	na	na	na	na	na	na	na	na	na	na
Poland	na	51	48	53	39	55	53	53	51	41	59	46	41	47	53	49
Portugal	na	49	48	49	48	43	54	51	44	39	53	46	55	50	48	52
Puerto Rico	na	na	na	na	na	na	na	na	na	na	na	na	na	na	na	na
Romania	na	58	55	60	53	56	62	59	57	57	56	62	56	63	56	53
Russian Fed.	na	53	46	58	34	52	65	55	53	51	57	56	48	54	53	49
Serbia	na	na	na	na	na	na	na	na	na	na	na	na	na	na	na	na
Singapore	na	na	na	na	na	na	na	na	na	na	na	na	na	na	na	na
Slovakia	na	49	46	53	43	49	54	50	49	49	54	53	46	51	50	39
Slovenia	na	48	45	51	38	46	58	53	47	42	56	50	42	54	47	50
South Africa	na	na	na	na	na	na	na	na	na	na	na	na	na	na	na	na
Spain	na	53	50	55	46	55	56	52	52	58	52	59	54	57	50	57
Sweden	na	36	31	40	26	32	46	45	31	37	40	35	32	35	33	46
Switzerland	na	na	na	na	na	na	na	na	na	na	na	na	na	na	na	na
Taiwan	na	na	na	na	na	na	na	na	na	na	na	na	na	na	na	na
Tanzania	na	na	na	na	na	na	na	na	na	na	na	na	na	na	na	na
Turkey	na	5	5	5	6	4	5	5	6	5	4	6	4	8	4	5
Uganda	na	na	na	na	na	na	na	na	na	na	na	na	na	na	na	na
Ukraine	na	59	52	66	45	57	69	69	58	56	69	55	55	59	63	57
United States	na	na	na	na	na	na	na	na	na	na	na	na	na	na	na	na
Uruguay	na	na	na	na	na	na	na	na	na	na	na	na	na	na	na	na
Venezuela	na	na	na	na	na	na	na	na	na	na	na	na	na	na	na	na
Vietnam	na	na	na	na	na	na	na	na	na	na	na	na	na	na	na	na
Zimbabwe	na	na	na	na	na	na	na	na	na	na	na	na	na	na	na	na
Total	na	43	41	45	35	42	49	44	43	42	47	43	41	44	43	45

RANKING	
Country	2000
Croatia	69
Lithuania	63
Italy	60
Ukraine	59
Romania	58
Bulgaria	57
France	54
Spain	53
Russian Fed.	53
Greece	53
Poland	51
Ireland	50
Slovakia	49
Portugal	49
Slovenia	48
Finland	47
Malta	46
Czech Republic	44
Estonia	38
Sweden	36
Iceland	36
Germany	34
Great Britain	34
Northern Ireland	33
Austria	32
Belgium	32
Hungary	30
Belarus	27
Denmark	24
Luxembourg	24
Latvia	23
Netherlands	21
Turkey	5
Total	43

E161_1) CONCERNED WITH IMMIGRANTS

To what extent do you feel concerned about the living conditions of: Immigrants in your country

Very much / Much (%)

(EVS: V274)

Country	Wave 1990	Wave 2000	Gender Male	Gender Female	Age 16-29	Age 30-49	Age 50+	Education Lower	Education Middle	Education Upper	Income Lower	Income Middle	Income Upper	Values Mat	Values Mixed	Values Postm.
Albania	na	na	na	na	na	na	na	na	na	na	na	na	na	na	na	na
Algeria	na	na	na	na	na	na	na	na	na	na	na	na	na	na	na	na
Argentina	na	na	na	na	na	na	na	na	na	na	na	na	na	na	na	na
Armenia	na	na	na	na	na	na	na	na	na	na	na	na	na	na	na	na
Australia	na	na	na	na	na	na	na	na	na	na	na	na	na	na	na	na
Austria	na	16	15	17	14	15	18	11	19	24	18	15	14	10	13	23
Azerbaijan	na	na	na	na	na	na	na	na	na	na	na	na	na	na	na	na
Bangladesh	na	na	na	na	na	na	na	na	na	na	na	na	na	na	na	na
Belarus	na	9	9	10	8	9	11	7	10	10	8	11	9	10	10	5
Belgium	na	16	16	15	17	16	15	9	13	24	15	16	16	7	15	27
Bosnia and Herz.	na	na	na	na	na	na	na	na	na	na	na	na	na	na	na	na
Brazil	na	na	na	na	na	na	na	na	na	na	na	na	na	na	na	na
Bulgaria	na	9	8	10	5	9	11	8	8	13	9	8	11	8	11	9
Canada	na	na	na	na	na	na	na	na	na	na	na	na	na	na	na	na
Chile	na	na	na	na	na	na	na	na	na	na	na	na	na	na	na	na
China	na	na	na	na	na	na	na	na	na	na	na	na	na	na	na	na
Colombia	na	na	na	na	na	na	na	na	na	na	na	na	na	na	na	na
Croatia	na	20	20	21	12	28	18	21	20	21	25	18	22	18	21	21
Czech Republic	na	13	10	16	14	12	14	13	14	10	13	13	13	14	13	17
Denmark	na	15	15	15	16	16	14	10	21	21	13	15	21	5	14	27
Dominican Rep.	na	na	na	na	na	na	na	na	na	na	na	na	na	na	na	na
Egypt	na	na	na	na	na	na	na	na	na	na	na	na	na	na	na	na
El Salvador	na	na	na	na	na	na	na	na	na	na	na	na	na	na	na	na
Estonia	na	11	9	13	8	12	12	9	11	15	10	13	10	14	10	16
Finland	na	15	15	16	13	18	14	14	15	20	18	15	13	10	17	20
France	na	27	26	27	29	28	25	21	29	41	24	25	32	16	27	43
Georgia	na	na	na	na	na	na	na	na	na	na	na	na	na	na	na	na
Germany	na	22	21	23	24	22	21	18	24	30	17	25	23	13	23	34
Great Britain	na	15	15	14	16	16	13	8	17	27	10	19	17	na	na	na
Greece	na	27	24	29	28	24	31	22	25	29	28	24	25	18	26	40
Hungary	na	5	6	5	3	5	7	6	3	5	5	7	3	6	5	8
Iceland	na	21	18	23	17	20	25	21	16	29	23	20	20	13	21	34
India	na	na	na	na	na	na	na	na	na	na	na	na	na	na	na	na
Indonesia	na	na	na	na	na	na	na	na	na	na	na	na	na	na	na	na
Iran	na	na	na	na	na	na	na	na	na	na	na	na	na	na	na	na
Ireland	na	28	30	27	21	32	30	25	26	40	22	28	37	28	29	30
Israel	na	na	na	na	na	na	na	na	na	na	na	na	na	na	na	na
Italy	na	35	32	37	30	40	32	30	35	46	34	37	37	24	33	44
Japan	na	na	na	na	na	na	na	na	na	na	na	na	na	na	na	na
Jordan	na	na	na	na	na	na	na	na	na	na	na	na	na	na	na	na
Korea, South	na	na	na	na	na	na	na	na	na	na	na	na	na	na	na	na
Latvia	na	5	6	5	4	6	5	6	5	7	5	6	4	4	5	9
Lithuania	na	7	6	9	9	8	6	5	7	13	8	7	8	6	8	8
Luxembourg	na	23	22	24	22	24	22	20	24	27	21	27	27	19	22	32
Macedonia	na	na	na	na	na	na	na	na	na	na	na	na	na	na	na	na
Malta	na	21	20	22	22	22	20	15	23	28	18	21	26	21	22	22
Mexico	na	na	na	na	na	na	na	na	na	na	na	na	na	na	na	na
Moldova	na	na	na	na	na	na	na	na	na	na	na	na	na	na	na	na
Montenegro	na	na	na	na	na	na	na	na	na	na	na	na	na	na	na	na
Morocco	na	na	na	na	na	na	na	na	na	na	na	na	na	na	na	na
Netherlands	na	16	15	16	13	16	16	11	14	22	16	16	15	7	14	23
New Zealand	na	na	na	na	na	na	na	na	na	na	na	na	na	na	na	na
Nigeria	na	na	na	na	na	na	na	na	na	na	na	na	na	na	na	na
Northern Ireland	na	18	17	19	15	20	17	14	17	29	19	15	22	13	18	27
Norway	na	na	na	na	na	na	na	na	na	na	na	na	na	na	na	na
Pakistan	na	na	na	na	na	na	na	na	na	na	na	na	na	na	na	na
Peru	na	na	na	na	na	na	na	na	na	na	na	na	na	na	na	na
Philippines	na	na	na	na	na	na	na	na	na	na	na	na	na	na	na	na
Poland	na	9	10	8	7	8	11	9	7	10	9	8	10	7	10	9
Portugal	na	24	25	23	21	25	25	26	23	17	27	24	26	28	20	29
Puerto Rico	na	na	na	na	na	na	na	na	na	na	na	na	na	na	na	na
Romania	na	20	19	20	18	18	22	20	19	18	21	21	18	19	20	19
Russian Fed.	na	11	10	12	7	11	14	11	10	13	13	11	9	11	12	15
Serbia	na	na	na	na	na	na	na	na	na	na	na	na	na	na	na	na
Singapore	na	na	na	na	na	na	na	na	na	na	na	na	na	na	na	na
Slovakia	na	12	10	13	11	11	13	12	11	13	12	11	14	11	12	12
Slovenia	na	13	12	14	11	13	15	18	12	7	15	15	9	11	13	17
South Africa	na	na	na	na	na	na	na	na	na	na	na	na	na	na	na	na
Spain	na	31	28	33	24	35	31	29	31	36	29	36	33	28	27	41
Sweden	na	30	25	34	35	27	29	25	28	37	30	27	30	26	25	44
Switzerland	na	na	na	na	na	na	na	na	na	na	na	na	na	na	na	na
Taiwan	na	na	na	na	na	na	na	na	na	na	na	na	na	na	na	na
Tanzania	na	na	na	na	na	na	na	na	na	na	na	na	na	na	na	na
Turkey	na	33	33	33	38	29	28	31	36	34	30	35	34	38	32	31
Uganda	na	na	na	na	na	na	na	na	na	na	na	na	na	na	na	na
Ukraine	na	9	8	9	8	10	8	8	8	10	11	4	10	6	10	12
United States	na	na	na	na	na	na	na	na	na	na	na	na	na	na	na	na
Uruguay	na	na	na	na	na	na	na	na	na	na	na	na	na	na	na	na
Venezuela	na	na	na	na	na	na	na	na	na	na	na	na	na	na	na	na
Vietnam	na	na	na	na	na	na	na	na	na	na	na	na	na	na	na	na
Zimbabwe	na	na	na	na	na	na	na	na	na	na	na	na	na	na	na	na
Total	na	17	16	18	16	18	17	16	16	22	17	17	18	13	17	28

RANKING

Country	2000
Italy	35
Turkey	33
Spain	31
Sweden	30
Ireland	28
France	27
Greece	27
Portugal	24
Luxembourg	23
Germany	22
Malta	21
Iceland	21
Croatia	20
Romania	20
Northern Ireland	18
Austria	16
Belgium	16
Netherlands	16
Denmark	15
Finland	15
Great Britain	15
Czech Republic	13
Slovenia	13
Slovakia	12
Estonia	11
Russian Fed.	11
Belarus	9
Bulgaria	9
Poland	9
Ukraine	9
Lithuania	7
Latvia	5
Hungary	5
Total	17

E162_1) CONCERNED WITH SICK AND DISABLED

To what extent do you feel concerned about the living conditions of: Sick and disabled people in your country

Very much / Much (%)

(EVS: V275)

Country	Wave 1990	Wave 2000	Gender Male	Gender Female	Age 16-29	Age 30-49	Age 50+	Education Lower	Education Middle	Education Upper	Income Lower	Income Middle	Income Upper	Values Mat	Values Mixed	Values Postm.
Albania	na	na	na	na	na	na	na	na	na	na	na	na	na	na	na	na
Algeria	na	na	na	na	na	na	na	na	na	na	na	na	na	na	na	na
Argentina	na	na	na	na	na	na	na	na	na	na	na	na	na	na	na	na
Armenia	na	na	na	na	na	na	na	na	na	na	na	na	na	na	na	na
Australia	na	na	na	na	na	na	na	na	na	na	na	na	na	na	na	na
Austria	na	49	48	51	40	49	55	50	50	46	49	50	49	41	51	48
Azerbaijan	na	na	na	na	na	na	na	na	na	na	na	na	na	na	na	na
Bangladesh	na	na	na	na	na	na	na	na	na	na	na	na	na	na	na	na
Belarus	na	35	33	37	32	33	41	36	35	35	37	37	28	36	37	29
Belgium	na	51	49	54	43	46	60	56	51	50	60	56	47	53	51	53
Bosnia and Herz.	na	na	na	na	na	na	na	na	na	na	na	na	na	na	na	na
Brazil	na	na	na	na	na	na	na	na	na	na	na	na	na	na	na	na
Bulgaria	na	60	55	65	49	55	69	65	57	59	59	63	63	59	65	55
Canada	na	na	na	na	na	na	na	na	na	na	na	na	na	na	na	na
Chile	na	na	na	na	na	na	na	na	na	na	na	na	na	na	na	na
China	na	na	na	na	na	na	na	na	na	na	na	na	na	na	na	na
Colombia	na	na	na	na	na	na	na	na	na	na	na	na	na	na	na	na
Croatia	na	69	66	71	61	71	71	66	69	73	79	69	66	71	69	65
Czech Republic	na	65	60	69	64	62	67	64	64	69	68	64	64	66	64	70
Denmark	na	54	49	58	55	56	50	55	57	53	53	52	55	58	55	57
Dominican Rep.	na	na	na	na	na	na	na	na	na	na	na	na	na	na	na	na
Egypt	na	na	na	na	na	na	na	na	na	na	na	na	na	na	na	na
El Salvador	na	na	na	na	na	na	na	na	na	na	na	na	na	na	na	na
Estonia	na	42	36	47	37	37	49	42	42	40	47	43	40	42	42	53
Finland	na	56	53	60	41	55	66	60	49	55	61	56	56	55	58	55
France	na	61	60	61	53	58	66	62	52	63	62	62	61	58	61	61
Georgia	na	na	na	na	na	na	na	na	na	na	na	na	na	na	na	na
Germany	na	53	49	55	41	54	56	49	53	68	49	56	57	50	53	55
Great Britain	na	64	59	70	51	62	76	67	65	60	66	69	61	na	na	na
Greece	na	69	64	72	66	67	78	81	70	65	73	70	64	66	68	74
Hungary	na	46	40	52	35	46	53	47	45	40	48	47	44	47	48	32
Iceland	na	65	58	71	56	64	73	72	57	65	73	65	58	62	65	67
India	na	na	na	na	na	na	na	na	na	na	na	na	na	na	na	na
Indonesia	na	na	na	na	na	na	na	na	na	na	na	na	na	na	na	na
Iran	na	na	na	na	na	na	na	na	na	na	na	na	na	na	na	na
Ireland	na	79	76	82	70	80	85	83	75	82	79	82	82	74	79	85
Israel	na	na	na	na	na	na	na	na	na	na	na	na	na	na	na	na
Italy	na	74	69	77	64	75	78	76	71	73	75	73	73	71	73	78
Japan	na	na	na	na	na	na	na	na	na	na	na	na	na	na	na	na
Jordan	na	na	na	na	na	na	na	na	na	na	na	na	na	na	na	na
Korea, South	na	na	na	na	na	na	na	na	na	na	na	na	na	na	na	na
Latvia	na	34	29	37	33	30	37	31	34	36	36	32	33	31	35	41
Lithuania	na	64	56	70	55	62	71	66	62	67	69	64	62	58	67	64
Luxembourg	na	39	36	42	28	35	50	37	41	40	39	43	36	34	37	50
Macedonia	na	na	na	na	na	na	na	na	na	na	na	na	na	na	na	na
Malta	na	79	78	80	71	83	82	82	70	79	87	84	76	82	79	70
Mexico	na	na	na	na	na	na	na	na	na	na	na	na	na	na	na	na
Moldova	na	na	na	na	na	na	na	na	na	na	na	na	na	na	na	na
Montenegro	na	na	na	na	na	na	na	na	na	na	na	na	na	na	na	na
Morocco	na	na	na	na	na	na	na	na	na	na	na	na	na	na	na	na
Netherlands	na	50	45	54	42	44	59	55	47	47	48	50	47	48	50	49
New Zealand	na	na	na	na	na	na	na	na	na	na	na	na	na	na	na	na
Nigeria	na	na	na	na	na	na	na	na	na	na	na	na	na	na	na	na
Northern Ireland	na	61	63	60	53	60	66	61	58	65	66	65	70	57	61	72
Norway	na	na	na	na	na	na	na	na	na	na	na	na	na	na	na	na
Pakistan	na	na	na	na	na	na	na	na	na	na	na	na	na	na	na	na
Peru	na	na	na	na	na	na	na	na	na	na	na	na	na	na	na	na
Philippines	na	na	na	na	na	na	na	na	na	na	na	na	na	na	na	na
Poland	na	65	63	66	61	66	65	64	68	61	65	65	60	63	66	61
Portugal	na	73	71	76	72	75	73	75	69	77	73	75	70	74	73	71
Puerto Rico	na	na	na	na	na	na	na	na	na	na	na	na	na	na	na	na
Romania	na	65	62	68	60	63	70	66	63	63	63	68	63	67	66	63
Russian Fed.	na	62	56	68	44	63	73	60	63	62	65	64	60	63	62	60
Serbia	na	na	na	na	na	na	na	na	na	na	na	na	na	na	na	na
Singapore	na	na	na	na	na	na	na	na	na	na	na	na	na	na	na	na
Slovakia	na	61	57	65	55	57	70	64	61	55	62	63	62	62	61	61
Slovenia	na	53	47	57	43	47	65	58	50	50	61	54	46	59	52	53
South Africa	na	na	na	na	na	na	na	na	na	na	na	na	na	na	na	na
Spain	na	52	49	55	44	52	56	53	51	51	53	56	52	55	50	58
Sweden	na	60	53	67	57	57	66	65	57	63	66	58	56	56	58	69
Switzerland	na	na	na	na	na	na	na	na	na	na	na	na	na	na	na	na
Taiwan	na	na	na	na	na	na	na	na	na	na	na	na	na	na	na	na
Tanzania	na	na	na	na	na	na	na	na	na	na	na	na	na	na	na	na
Turkey	na	3	3	2	3	2	3	2	4	na	2	3	4	3	2	4
Uganda	na	na	na	na	na	na	na	na	na	na	na	na	na	na	na	na
Ukraine	na	65	59	69	51	60	77	82	62	62	74	60	61	65	66	71
United States	na	na	na	na	na	na	na	na	na	na	na	na	na	na	na	na
Uruguay	na	na	na	na	na	na	na	na	na	na	na	na	na	na	na	na
Venezuela	na	na	na	na	na	na	na	na	na	na	na	na	na	na	na	na
Vietnam	na	na	na	na	na	na	na	na	na	na	na	na	na	na	na	na
Zimbabwe	na	na	na	na	na	na	na	na	na	na	na	na	na	na	na	na
Total	na	58	54	62	51	57	64	60	57	59	60	59	57	57	59	60

RANKING

Country	2000
Malta	79
Ireland	79
Italy	74
Portugal	73
Croatia	69
Greece	69
Romania	65
Iceland	65
Czech Republic	65
Poland	65
Ukraine	65
Great Britain	64
Lithuania	64
Russian Fed.	62
Slovakia	61
Northern Ireland	61
France	61
Sweden	60
Bulgaria	60
Finland	56
Denmark	54
Germany	53
Slovenia	53
Spain	52
Belgium	51
Netherlands	50
Austria	49
Hungary	46
Estonia	42
Luxembourg	39
Belarus	35
Latvia	34
Turkey	3
Total	58

E163_1) PREPARED TO HELP IMMEDIATE FAMILY

Would you be prepared to actually do something to improve the conditions of: Your immediate family

Absolutely yes / Yes (%)   (EVS: V276)

Country	Wave		Gender		Age			Education			Income			Values			RANKING Country	2000
	1990	2000	Male	Female	16-29	30-49	50+	Lower	Middle	Upper	Lower	Middle	Upper	Mat	Mixed	Postm.		
Albania	na	na	na	na	na	na	na	na	na	na	na	na	na	na	na	na	Malta	99
Algeria	na	na	na	na	na	na	na	na	na	na	na	na	na	na	na	na	Iceland	99
Argentina	na	na	na	na	na	na	na	na	na	na	na	na	na	na	na	na	Croatia	99
Armenia	na	na	na	na	na	na	na	na	na	na	na	na	na	na	na	na	Germany	98
Australia	na	na	na	na	na	na	na	na	na	na	na	na	na	na	na	na	Sweden	98
Austria	na	97	97	97	98	98	96	96	98	98	94	97	99	91	97	98	Slovenia	98
Azerbaijan	na	na	na	na	na	na	na	na	na	na	na	na	na	na	na	na	Bulgaria	98
Bangladesh	na	na	na	na	na	na	na	na	na	na	na	na	na	na	na	na	Hungary	98
Belarus	na	66	73	60	69	73	55	52	69	76	56	67	81	67	65	75	Greece	98
Belgium	na	96	95	97	96	96	96	93	96	98	92	97	98	97	96	97	Austria	97
Bosnia and Herz.	na	na	na	na	na	na	na	na	na	na	na	na	na	na	na	na	Portugal	96
Brazil	na	na	na	na	na	na	na	na	na	na	na	na	na	na	na	na	Belgium	96
Bulgaria	na	98	98	98	98	99	97	97	98	99	96	99	98	98	98	100	Poland	96
Canada	na	na	na	na	na	na	na	na	na	na	na	na	na	na	na	na	Ireland	96
Chile	na	na	na	na	na	na	na	na	na	na	na	na	na	na	na	na	France	95
China	na	na	na	na	na	na	na	na	na	na	na	na	na	na	na	na	Netherlands	95
Colombia	na	na	na	na	na	na	na	na	na	na	na	na	na	na	na	na	Northern Ireland	95
Croatia	na	99	98	99	99	98	99	97	100	99	99	98	99	100	98	100	Latvia	95
Czech Republic	na	91	88	94	89	92	92	89	93	96	88	93	92	92	91	92	Spain	95
Denmark	na	89	90	88	88	90	88	86	94	93	85	89	94	81	89	95	Romania	95
Dominican Rep.	na	na	na	na	na	na	na	na	na	na	na	na	na	na	na	na	Luxembourg	95
Egypt	na	na	na	na	na	na	na	na	na	na	na	na	na	na	na	na	Slovakia	94
El Salvador	na	na	na	na	na	na	na	na	na	na	na	na	na	na	na	na	Italy	92
Estonia	na	89	87	90	88	92	86	82	92	92	85	86	94	89	90	89	Czech Republic	91
Finland	na	91	90	92	96	94	86	89	94	91	92	91	91	89	92	92	Finland	91
France	na	95	94	96	95	93	97	95	94	96	94	94	97	96	95	93	Great Britain	91
Georgia	na	na	na	na	na	na	na	na	na	na	na	na	na	na	na	na	Estonia	89
Germany	na	98	99	98	96	99	98	98	98	99	97	99	97	98	98	98	Denmark	89
Great Britain	na	91	93	90	88	93	91	92	89	95	87	94	94	na	na	na	Lithuania	88
Greece	na	98	97	98	98	97	98	98	97	98	97	98	97	96	98	99	Ukraine	88
Hungary	na	98	97	99	98	99	97	97	98	99	96	99	98	98	99	97	Russian Fed.	85
Iceland	na	99	98	99	98	99	99	98	100	100	98	99	99	100	98	99	Belarus	66
India	na	na	na	na	na	na	na	na	na	na	na	na	na	na	na	na		
Indonesia	na	na	na	na	na	na	na	na	na	na	na	na	na	na	na	na		
Iran	na	na	na	na	na	na	na	na	na	na	na	na	na	na	na	na		
Ireland	na	96	96	96	95	97	94	93	96	99	93	96	97	95	96	95		
Israel	na	na	na	na	na	na	na	na	na	na	na	na	na	na	na	na		
Italy	na	92	91	93	89	93	92	91	91	98	90	94	94	91	92	93		
Japan	na	na	na	na	na	na	na	na	na	na	na	na	na	na	na	na		
Jordan	na	na	na	na	na	na	na	na	na	na	na	na	na	na	na	na		
Korea, South	na	na	na	na	na	na	na	na	na	na	na	na	na	na	na	na		
Latvia	na	95	95	95	98	98	92	91	96	98	92	95	99	93	96	98		
Lithuania	na	88	86	91	87	92	86	86	89	90	80	90	93	85	90	97		
Luxembourg	na	95	94	95	95	95	94	93	95	97	90	95	97	91	95	95		
Macedonia	na	na	na	na	na	na	na	na	na	na	na	na	na	na	na	na		
Malta	na	99	99	100	99	100	99	99	100	97	99	100	99	100	99	99		
Mexico	na	na	na	na	na	na	na	na	na	na	na	na	na	na	na	na		
Moldova	na	na	na	na	na	na	na	na	na	na	na	na	na	na	na	na		
Montenegro	na	na	na	na	na	na	na	na	na	na	na	na	na	na	na	na		
Morocco	na	na	na	na	na	na	na	na	na	na	na	na	na	na	na	na		
Netherlands	na	95	95	95	96	97	93	92	97	97	91	96	98	94	95	96		
New Zealand	na	na	na	na	na	na	na	na	na	na	na	na	na	na	na	na		
Nigeria	na	na	na	na	na	na	na	na	na	na	na	na	na	na	na	na		
Northern Ireland	na	95	96	95	93	95	96	95	95	96	92	98	97	96	95	95		
Norway	na	na	na	na	na	na	na	na	na	na	na	na	na	na	na	na		
Pakistan	na	na	na	na	na	na	na	na	na	na	na	na	na	na	na	na		
Peru	na	na	na	na	na	na	na	na	na	na	na	na	na	na	na	na		
Philippines	na	na	na	na	na	na	na	na	na	na	na	na	na	Mat	na	na		
Poland	na	96	97	95	95	97	96	95	98	97	95	97	97	95	97	99		
Portugal	na	96	97	96	96	97	96	96	96	99	91	97	97	97	97	99		
Puerto Rico	na	na	na	na	na	na	na	na	na	na	na	na	na	na	na	na		
Romania	na	95	96	94	94	98	93	90	97	99	92	95	97	94	97	96		
Russian Fed.	na	85	87	83	88	92	75	74	85	91	78	88	90	83	88	80		
Serbia	na	na	na	na	na	na	na	na	na	na	na	na	na	na	na	na		
Singapore	na	na	na	na	na	na	na	na	na	na	na	na	na	na	na	na		
Slovakia	na	94	91	96	95	92	94	91	95	94	92	95	94	93	94	96		
Slovenia	na	98	97	99	99	97	98	97	98	99	98	98	98	97	99	97		
South Africa	na	na	na	na	na	na	na	na	na	na	na	na	na	na	na	na		
Spain	na	95	95	95	96	95	95	96	94	97	95	95	93	96	95	96		
Sweden	na	98	97	99	98	99	97	98	99	97	98	98	98	98	98	99		
Switzerland	na	na	na	na	na	na	na	na	na	na	na	na	na	na	na	na		
Taiwan	na	na	na	na	na	na	na	na	na	na	na	na	na	na	na	na		
Tanzania	na	na	na	na	na	na	na	na	na	na	na	na	na	na	na	na		
Turkey	na	na	na	na	na	na	na	na	na	na	na	na	na	na	na	na		
Uganda	na	na	na	na	na	na	na	na	na	na	na	na	na	na	na	na		
Ukraine	na	88	92	85	93	94	80	76	90	90	82	90	94	85	93	90		
United States	na	na	na	na	na	na	na	na	na	na	na	na	na	na	na	na		
Uruguay	na	na	na	na	na	na	na	na	na	na	na	na	na	na	na	na		
Venezuela	na	na	na	na	na	na	na	na	na	na	na	na	na	na	na	na		
Vietnam	na	na	na	na	na	na	na	na	na	na	na	na	na	na	na	na		
Zimbabwe	na	na	na	na	na	na	na	na	na	na	na	na	na	na	na	na		
Total	na	94	94	94	94	95	92	92	94	96	90	94	96	92	94	96	**Total**	**94**

E164_1) PREPARED TO HELP PEOPLE NEIGHBORHOOD

Would you be prepared to actually do something to improve the conditions of: People in your neighborhood / community

Absolutely yes / Yes (%)

(EVS: V277)

Country	Wave 1990	Wave 2000	Gender Male	Gender Female	Age 16-29	Age 30-49	Age 50+	Education Lower	Education Middle	Education Upper	Income Lower	Income Middle	Income Upper	Values Mat	Values Mixed	Values Postm.
Albania	na	na	na	na	na	na	na	na	na	na	na	na	na	na	na	na
Algeria	na	na	na	na	na	na	na	na	na	na	na	na	na	na	na	na
Argentina	na	na	na	na	na	na	na	na	na	na	na	na	na	na	na	na
Armenia	na	na	na	na	na	na	na	na	na	na	na	na	na	na	na	na
Australia	na	na	na	na	na	na	na	na	na	na	na	na	na	na	na	na
Austria	na	69	69	69	58	74	70	69	70	68	63	73	72	59	72	68
Azerbaijan	na	na	na	na	na	na	na	na	na	na	na	na	na	na	na	na
Bangladesh	na	na	na	na	na	na	na	na	na	na	na	na	na	na	na	na
Belarus	na	10	11	10	9	9	13	13	10	9	12	10	8	11	11	5
Belgium	na	66	64	68	56	66	70	60	67	69	64	65	69	65	66	67
Bosnia and Herz.	na	na	na	na	na	na	na	na	na	na	na	na	na	na	na	na
Brazil	na	na	na	na	na	na	na	na	na	na	na	na	na	na	na	na
Bulgaria	na	43	45	41	33	47	44	47	39	44	42	47	38	42	44	56
Canada	na	na	na	na	na	na	na	na	na	na	na	na	na	na	na	na
Chile	na	na	na	na	na	na	na	na	na	na	na	na	na	na	na	na
China	na	na	na	na	na	na	na	na	na	na	na	na	na	na	na	na
Colombia	na	na	na	na	na	na	na	na	na	na	na	na	na	na	na	na
Croatia	na	68	68	69	58	76	67	67	68	75	80	63	71	65	68	70
Czech Republic	na	51	45	55	43	47	57	49	52	54	51	52	48	49	51	59
Denmark	na	47	48	46	37	48	51	44	51	50	42	51	51	49	45	58
Dominican Rep.	na	na	na	na	na	na	na	na	na	na	na	na	na	na	na	na
Egypt	na	na	na	na	na	na	na	na	na	na	na	na	na	na	na	na
El Salvador	na	na	na	na	na	na	na	na	na	na	na	na	na	na	na	na
Estonia	na	34	31	37	26	31	42	34	34	36	34	35	38	32	39	28
Finland	na	46	43	49	38	49	47	46	44	49	46	46	46	45	45	50
France	na	49	45	52	41	45	56	46	49	55	47	49	49	48	48	51
Georgia	na	na	na	na	na	na	na	na	na	na	na	na	na	na	na	na
Germany	na	60	58	61	53	58	65	58	61	62	56	62	64	54	61	68
Great Britain	na	40	37	43	33	42	41	38	38	47	39	34	43	na	na	na
Greece	na	42	40	43	35	41	58	50	41	40	42	38	41	37	42	45
Hungary	na	53	50	56	49	52	56	51	56	60	44	59	52	51	56	71
Iceland	na	51	47	55	49	54	50	50	52	52	49	53	51	51	51	56
India	na	na	na	na	na	na	na	na	na	na	na	na	na	na	na	na
Indonesia	na	na	na	na	na	na	na	na	na	na	na	na	na	na	na	na
Iran	na	na	na	na	na	na	na	na	na	na	na	na	na	na	na	na
Ireland	na	72	74	71	63	75	75	71	71	77	69	73	80	72	72	73
Israel	na	na	na	na	na	na	na	na	na	na	na	na	na	na	na	na
Italy	na	49	45	52	39	50	54	49	48	53	50	52	51	47	48	53
Japan	na	na	na	na	na	na	na	na	na	na	na	na	na	na	na	na
Jordan	na	na	na	na	na	na	na	na	na	na	na	na	na	na	na	na
Korea, South	na	na	na	na	na	na	na	na	na	na	na	na	na	na	na	na
Latvia	na	30	29	31	25	26	35	29	31	29	33	28	29	29	32	17
Lithuania	na	21	17	25	14	21	26	28	18	20	24	24	16	25	20	12
Luxembourg	na	62	61	64	63	58	67	57	66	65	62	64	68	61	62	68
Macedonia	na	na	na	na	na	na	na	na	na	na	na	na	na	na	na	na
Malta	na	55	54	56	39	58	63	58	54	53	56	57	57	56	56	50
Mexico	na	na	na	na	na	na	na	na	na	na	na	na	na	na	na	na
Moldova	na	na	na	na	na	na	na	na	na	na	na	na	na	na	na	na
Montenegro	na	na	na	na	na	na	na	na	na	na	na	na	na	na	na	na
Morocco	na	na	na	na	na	na	na	na	na	na	na	na	na	na	na	na
Netherlands	na	68	65	71	55	70	72	69	70	64	62	70	68	73	67	66
New Zealand	na	na	na	na	na	na	na	na	na	na	na	na	na	na	na	na
Nigeria	na	na	na	na	na	na	na	na	na	na	na	na	na	na	na	na
Northern Ireland	na	57	58	56	57	58	57	54	56	68	54	59	68	53	57	69
Norway	na	na	na	na	na	na	na	na	na	na	na	na	na	na	na	na
Pakistan	na	na	na	na	na	na	na	na	na	na	na	na	na	na	na	na
Peru	na	na	na	na	na	na	na	na	na	na	na	na	na	na	na	na
Philippines	na	na	na	na	na	na	na	na	na	na	na	na	na	na	na	na
Poland	na	55	56	54	38	59	62	58	51	54	61	53	49	51	57	62
Portugal	na	44	40	48	36	44	49	45	42	44	42	47	49	47	42	51
Puerto Rico	na	na	na	na	na	na	na	na	na	na	na	na	na	na	na	na
Romania	na	48	50	46	41	52	48	46	46	54	45	51	49	49	50	45
Russian Fed.	na	26	24	28	20	29	28	29	26	26	29	28	24	25	28	26
Serbia	na	na	na	na	na	na	na	na	na	na	na	na	na	na	na	na
Singapore	na	na	na	na	na	na	na	na	na	na	na	na	na	na	na	na
Slovakia	na	72	68	75	69	68	78	74	70	76	72	72	74	70	74	75
Slovenia	na	66	66	66	52	68	74	66	65	69	65	71	72	68	66	68
South Africa	na	na	na	na	na	na	na	na	na	na	na	na	na	na	na	na
Spain	na	52	48	56	51	50	55	51	50	63	53	54	53	58	48	61
Sweden	na	67	65	69	57	73	67	67	66	68	61	68	75	69	65	70
Switzerland	na	na	na	na	na	na	na	na	na	na	na	na	na	na	na	na
Taiwan	na	na	na	na	na	na	na	na	na	na	na	na	na	na	na	na
Tanzania	na	na	na	na	na	na	na	na	na	na	na	na	na	na	na	na
Turkey	na	na	na	na	na	na	na	na	na	na	na	na	na	na	na	na
Uganda	na	na	na	na	na	na	na	na	na	na	na	na	na	na	na	na
Ukraine	na	29	29	29	22	32	31	29	28	32	30	26	33	27	32	24
United States	na	na	na	na	na	na	na	na	na	na	na	na	na	na	na	na
Uruguay	na	na	na	na	na	na	na	na	na	na	na	na	na	na	na	na
Venezuela	na	na	na	na	na	na	na	na	na	na	na	na	na	na	na	na
Vietnam	na	na	na	na	na	na	na	na	na	na	na	na	na	na	na	na
Zimbabwe	na	na	na	na	na	na	na	na	na	na	na	na	na	na	na	na
Total	na	50	49	51	42	51	54	51	49	52	48	51	52	46	52	59

RANKING

Country	2000
Ireland	72
Slovakia	72
Austria	69
Croatia	68
Netherlands	68
Sweden	67
Slovenia	66
Belgium	66
Luxembourg	62
Germany	60
Northern Ireland	57
Poland	55
Malta	55
Hungary	53
Spain	52
Iceland	51
Czech Republic	51
Italy	49
France	49
Romania	48
Denmark	47
Finland	46
Portugal	44
Bulgaria	43
Greece	42
Great Britain	40
Estonia	34
Latvia	30
Ukraine	29
Russian Fed.	26
Lithuania	21
Belarus	10
Total	50

E165_1) PREPARED TO HELP ELDERLY

Would you be prepared to actually do something to improve the conditions of: Elderly people in your country

Absolutely yes / Yes (%)

(EVS: V278)

Country	Wave 1990	Wave 2000	Male	Female	16-29	30-49	50+	Education Lower	Middle	Upper	Income Lower	Middle	Upper	Mat	Mixed	Postm
Albania	na	na	na	na	na	na	na	na	na	na	na	na	na	na	na	na
Algeria	na	na	na	na	na	na	na	na	na	na	na	na	na	na	na	na
Argentina	na	na	na	na	na	na	na	na	na	na	na	na	na	na	na	na
Armenia	na	na	na	na	na	na	na	na	na	na	na	na	na	na	na	na
Australia	na	na	na	na	na	na	na	na	na	na	na	na	na	na	na	na
Austria	na	58	58	58	52	59	60	60	56	56	51	63	60	50	58	61
Azerbaijan	na	na	na	na	na	na	na	na	na	na	na	na	na	na	na	na
Bangladesh	na	na	na	na	na	na	na	na	na	na	na	na	na	na	na	na
Belarus	na	7	8	7	7	8	8	5	9	7	6	9	6	5	10	11
Belgium	na	67	65	69	55	64	76	69	68	66	69	68	68	68	66	69
Bosnia and Herz.	na	na	na	na	na	na	na	na	na	na	na	na	na	na	na	na
Brazil	na	na	na	na	na	na	na	na	na	na	na	na	na	na	na	na
Bulgaria	na	58	55	61	44	64	61	62	55	60	53	60	63	53	63	83
Canada	na	na	na	na	na	na	na	na	na	na	na	na	na	na	na	na
Chile	na	na	na	na	na	na	na	na	na	na	na	na	na	na	na	na
China	na	na	na	na	na	na	na	na	na	na	na	na	na	na	na	na
Colombia	na	na	na	na	na	na	na	na	na	na	na	na	na	na	na	na
Croatia	na	76	73	80	72	81	74	77	75	80	87	74	74	76	76	74
Czech Republic	na	63	58	67	53	60	70	62	64	62	66	61	61	59	64	65
Denmark	na	67	64	69	62	68	68	65	71	70	65	68	67	63	67	74
Dominican Rep.	na	na	na	na	na	na	na	na	na	na	na	na	na	na	na	na
Egypt	na	na	na	na	na	na	na	na	na	na	na	na	na	na	na	na
El Salvador	na	na	na	na	na	na	na	na	na	na	na	na	na	na	na	na
Estonia	na	33	29	36	24	35	37	31	34	35	36	28	37	30	37	27
Finland	na	72	66	78	61	73	78	73	73	67	75	70	73	65	75	79
France	na	59	56	61	49	58	64	62	52	57	63	59	56	59	59	57
Georgia	na	na	na	na	na	na	na	na	na	na	na	na	na	na	na	na
Germany	na	50	48	52	41	48	56	48	49	63	48	49	57	44	53	54
Great Britain	na	54	50	58	37	54	63	57	50	55	54	52	57	na	na	na
Greece	na	66	63	68	58	69	78	76	67	63	69	66	60	67	64	71
Hungary	na	57	51	63	46	59	62	54	62	67	46	61	59	54	62	58
Iceland	na	73	67	79	63	77	76	76	69	73	77	73	70	66	75	78
India	na	na	na	na	na	na	na	na	na	na	na	na	na	na	na	na
Indonesia	na	na	na	na	na	na	na	na	na	na	na	na	na	na	na	na
Iran	na	na	na	na	na	na	na	na	na	na	na	na	na	na	na	na
Ireland	na	81	80	81	76	81	83	82	80	80	79	80	86	77	81	82
Israel	na	na	na	na	na	na	na	na	na	na	na	na	na	na	na	na
Italy	na	80	77	83	74	81	83	81	80	81	81	81	78	75	81	84
Japan	na	na	na	na	na	na	na	na	na	na	na	na	na	na	na	na
Jordan	na	na	na	na	na	na	na	na	na	na	na	na	na	na	na	na
Korea, South	na	na	na	na	na	na	na	na	na	na	na	na	na	na	na	na
Latvia	na	56	56	55	59	56	54	46	57	64	54	54	63	51	58	68
Lithuania	35	na	29	40	23	39	40	37	33	38	29	40	35	35	36	28
Luxembourg	na	61	59	62	47	60	71	56	62	65	55	69	63	64	57	72
Macedonia	na	na	na	na	na	na	na	na	na	na	na	na	na	na	na	na
Malta	na	76	77	76	65	79	81	81	74	78	77	79	77	75	79	66
Mexico	na	na	na	na	na	na	na	na	na	na	na	na	na	na	na	na
Moldova	na	na	na	na	na	na	na	na	na	na	na	na	na	na	na	na
Montenegro	na	na	na	na	na	na	na	na	na	na	na	na	na	na	na	na
Morocco	na	na	na	na	na	na	na	na	na	na	na	na	na	na	na	na
Netherlands	na	62	59	66	54	62	67	69	65	53	62	66	57	67	62	60
New Zealand	na	na	na	na	na	na	na	na	na	na	na	na	na	na	na	na
Nigeria	na	na	na	na	na	na	na	na	na	na	na	na	na	na	na	na
Northern Ireland	na	62	64	61	61	64	62	59	63	71	66	66	69	52	65	72
Norway	na	na	na	na	na	na	na	na	na	na	na	na	na	na	na	na
Pakistan	na	na	na	na	na	na	na	na	na	na	na	na	na	na	na	na
Peru	na	na	na	na	na	na	na	na	na	na	na	na	na	na	na	na
Philippines	na	na	na	na	na	na	na	na	na	na	na	na	na	na	na	na
Poland	na	67	67	68	55	71	70	66	70	67	70	66	65	63	69	77
Portugal	na	59	55	61	56	59	60	58	58	68	52	57	59	62	55	62
Puerto Rico	na	na	na	na	na	na	na	na	na	na	na	na	na	na	na	na
Romania	na	67	65	68	59	71	66	62	65	80	61	67	71	66	70	55
Russian Fed.	na	50	50	50	48	54	45	39	50	54	47	51	53	46	55	47
Serbia	na	na	na	na	na	na	na	na	na	na	na	na	na	na	na	na
Singapore	na	na	na	na	na	na	na	na	na	na	na	na	na	na	na	na
Slovakia	na	69	67	71	65	66	77	70	67	80	67	71	73	68	71	75
Slovenia	na	65	62	67	49	65	76	68	64	63	73	69	66	66	64	68
South Africa	na	na	na	na	na	na	na	na	na	na	na	na	na	na	na	na
Spain	na	57	55	59	52	59	58	55	55	69	60	57	55	58	55	65
Sweden	na	85	83	87	82	85	87	88	85	85	86	86	87	84	85	88
Switzerland	na	na	na	na	na	na	na	na	na	na	na	na	na	na	na	na
Taiwan	na	na	na	na	na	na	na	na	na	na	na	na	na	na	na	na
Tanzania	na	na	na	na	na	na	na	na	na	na	na	na	na	na	na	na
Turkey	na	na	na	na	na	na	na	na	na	na	na	na	na	na	na	na
Uganda	na	na	na	na	na	na	na	na	na	na	na	na	na	na	na	na
Ukraine	na	40	36	43	31	42	43	46	38	42	44	37	38	38	44	36
United States	na	na	na	na	na	na	na	na	na	na	na	na	na	na	na	na
Uruguay	na	na	na	na	na	na	na	na	na	na	na	na	na	na	na	na
Venezuela	na	na	na	na	na	na	na	na	na	na	na	na	na	na	na	na
Vietnam	na	na	na	na	na	na	na	na	na	na	na	na	na	na	na	na
Zimbabwe	na	na	na	na	na	na	na	na	na	na	na	na	na	na	na	na
Total	na	61	58	63	53	62	64	61	59	63	60	61	62	55	63	68

RANKING

Country	2000
Sweden	85
Ireland	81
Italy	80
Croatia	76
Malta	76
Iceland	73
Finland	72
Slovakia	69
Belgium	67
Poland	67
Denmark	67
Romania	67
Greece	66
Slovenia	65
Czech Republic	63
Northern Ireland	62
Netherlands	62
Luxembourg	61
France	59
Portugal	59
Bulgaria	58
Austria	58
Hungary	57
Spain	57
Latvia	56
Great Britain	54
Germany	50
Russian Fed.	50
Ukraine	40
Lithuania	35
Estonia	33
Belarus	7
Total	61

E166_1) PREPARED TO HELP IMMIGRANTS

Would you be prepared to actually do something to improve the conditions of: Immigrants in your country

Absolutely yes / Yes (%)

(EVS: V279)

Country	Wave 1990	Wave 2000	Gender Male	Gender Female	Age 16-29	Age 30-49	Age 50+	Education Lower	Education Middle	Education Upper	Income Lower	Income Middle	Income Upper	Values Mat	Values Mixed	Values Postm.	RANKING Country	2000
Albania	na	na	na	na	na	na	na	na	na	na	na	na	na	na	na	na	Sweden	68
Algeria	na	na	na	na	na	na	na	na	na	na	na	na	na	na	na	na	Italy	46
Argentina	na	na	na	na	na	na	na	na	na	na	na	na	na	na	na	na	Luxembourg	41
Armenia	na	na	na	na	na	na	na	na	na	na	na	na	na	na	na	na	Spain	35
Australia	na	na	na	na	na	na	na	na	na	na	na	na	na	na	na	na	Iceland	35
Austria	na	20	20	20	21	22	17	15	21	32	17	19	23	12	17	28	Ireland	35
Azerbaijan	na	na	na	na	na	na	na	na	na	na	na	na	na	na	na	na	Netherlands	34
Bangladesh	na	na	na	na	na	na	na	na	na	na	na	na	na	na	na	na	Croatia	32
Belarus	na	1	2	1	1	2	1	na	2	1	1	2	1	1	2	2	Denmark	30
Belgium	na	29	31	27	31	30	28	18	27	40	25	29	31	19	27	45	Belgium	29
Bosnia and Herz.	na	na	na	na	na	na	na	na	na	na	na	na	na	na	na	na	Greece	29
Brazil	na	na	na	na	na	na	na	na	na	na	na	na	na	na	na	na	Slovenia	28
Bulgaria	na	16	14	18	10	21	15	11	16	22	12	16	19	12	20	18	Malta	26
Canada	na	na	na	na	na	na	na	na	na	na	na	na	na	na	na	na	France	25
Chile	na	na	na	na	na	na	na	na	na	na	na	na	na	na	na	na	Northern Ireland	24
China	na	na	na	na	na	na	na	na	na	na	na	na	na	na	na	na	Germany	24
Colombia	na	na	na	na	na	na	na	na	na	na	na	na	na	na	na	na	Finland	23
Croatia	na	32	30	34	26	35	33	32	30	41	39	26	37	26	34	31	Romania	22
Czech Republic	na	15	13	17	16	12	17	13	17	19	15	13	17	11	15	24	Slovakia	21
Denmark	na	30	31	30	28	33	28	21	36	46	28	29	40	13	28	53	Portugal	20
Dominican Rep.	na	na	na	na	na	na	na	na	na	na	na	na	na	na	na	na	Austria	20
Egypt	na	na	na	na	na	na	na	na	na	na	na	na	na	na	na	na	Poland	16
El Salvador	na	na	na	na	na	na	na	na	na	na	na	na	na	na	na	na	Bulgaria	16
Estonia	na	9	8	10	7	13	7	7	10	10	8	8	10	9	9	9	Czech Republic	15
Finland	na	23	20	26	26	23	22	19	27	29	25	22	23	17	23	36	Great Britain	14
France	na	25	25	26	24	27	24	20	24	39	23	24	31	15	25	42	Latvia	12
Georgia	na	na	na	na	na	na	na	na	na	na	na	na	na	na	na	na	Russian Fed.	11
Germany	na	24	23	25	26	23	23	19	26	33	20	25	26	15	24	37	Estonia	9
Great Britain	na	14	13	14	13	16	11	9	15	23	11	15	17	na	na	na	Ukraine	9
Greece	na	29	27	30	27	30	30	23	27	32	30	24	31	19	27	43	Hungary	8
Hungary	na	8	6	9	5	7	9	6	12	8	6	8	8	6	9	18	Lithuania	4
Iceland	na	35	28	41	32	37	34	31	31	50	35	34	37	22	36	47	Belarus	1
India	na	na	na	na	na	na	na	na	na	na	na	na	na	na	na	na		
Indonesia	na	na	na	na	na	na	na	na	na	na	na	na	na	na	na	na		
Iran	na	na	na	na	na	na	na	na	na	na	na	na	na	na	na	na		
Ireland	na	35	36	33	29	38	35	29	35	44	29	32	46	30	34	43		
Israel	na	na	na	na	na	na	na	na	na	na	na	na	na	na	na	na		
Italy	na	46	45	47	42	51	44	41	48	58	45	51	47	34	45	57		
Japan	na	na	na	na	na	na	na	na	na	na	na	na	na	na	na	na		
Jordan	na	na	na	na	na	na	na	na	na	na	na	na	na	na	na	na		
Korea, South	na	na	na	na	na	na	na	na	na	na	na	na	na	na	na	na		
Latvia	na	12	14	11	15	11	12	13	11	14	12	10	14	10	13	17		
Lithuania	na	4	3	5	6	4	4	3	4	6	3	4	4	5	4	3		
Luxembourg	na	41	40	43	36	44	42	38	38	54	35	45	48	40	38	60		
Macedonia	na	na	na	na	na	na	na	na	na	na	na	na	na	na	na	na		
Malta	na	26	27	26	22	26	30	24	27	28	25	27	29	28	25	20		
Mexico	na	na	na	na	na	na	na	na	na	na	na	na	na	na	na	na		
Moldova	na	na	na	na	na	na	na	na	na	na	na	na	na	na	na	na		
Montenegro	na	na	na	na	na	na	na	na	na	na	na	na	na	na	na	na		
Morocco	na	na	na	na	na	na	na	na	na	na	na	na	na	na	na	na		
Netherlands	na	34	32	35	29	39	31	26	37	38	33	35	32	24	33	41		
New Zealand	na	na	na	na	na	na	na	na	na	na	na	na	na	na	na	na		
Nigeria	na	na	na	na	na	na	na	na	na	na	na	na	na	na	na	na		
Northern Ireland	na	24	25	23	24	26	23	20	24	36	21	23	31	18	26	31		
Norway	na	na	na	na	na	na	na	na	na	na	na	na	na	na	na	na		
Pakistan	na	na	na	na	na	na	na	na	na	na	na	na	na	na	na	na		
Peru	na	na	na	na	na	na	na	na	na	na	na	na	na	na	na	na		
Philippines	na	na	na	na	na	na	na	na	na	na	na	na	na	na	na	na		
Poland	na	16	17	15	10	17	19	16	14	22	15	18	12	13	17	24		
Portugal	na	20	18	23	22	21	19	18	23	30	18	21	23	20	17	27		
Puerto Rico	na	na	na	na	na	na	na	na	na	na	na	na	na	na	na	na		
Romania	na	22	24	20	28	21	19	17	22	29	19	20	26	19	26	23		
Russian Fed.	na	11	11	12	10	11	12	10	10	15	13	11	10	10	13	9		
Serbia	na	na	na	na	na	na	na	na	na	na	na	na	na	na	na	na		
Singapore	na	na	na	na	na	na	na	na	na	na	na	na	na	na	na	na		
Slovakia	na	21	18	23	20	21	21	19	21	24	20	19	25	18	21	35		
Slovenia	na	28	24	32	21	32	30	30	26	31	30	29	37	28	26	36		
South Africa	na	na	na	na	na	na	na	na	na	na	na	na	na	na	na	na		
Spain	na	35	33	37	37	40	30	26	38	50	33	35	42	26	33	51		
Sweden	na	68	65	70	68	71	65	63	66	74	66	64	74	63	63	84		
Switzerland	na	na	na	na	na	na	na	na	na	na	na	na	na	na	na	na		
Taiwan	na	na	na	na	na	na	na	na	na	na	na	na	na	na	na	na		
Tanzania	na	na	na	na	na	na	na	na	na	na	na	na	na	na	na	na		
Turkey	na	na	na	na	na	na	na	na	na	na	na	na	na	na	na	na		
Uganda	na	na	na	na	na	na	na	na	na	na	na	na	na	na	na	na		
Ukraine	na	9	8	9	8	9	8	9	7	11	11	5	9	7	10	10		
United States	na	na	na	na	na	na	na	na	na	na	na	na	na	na	na	na		
Uruguay	na	na	na	na	na	na	na	na	na	na	na	na	na	na	na	na		
Venezuela	na	na	na	na	na	na	na	na	na	na	na	na	na	na	na	na		
Vietnam	na	na	na	na	na	na	na	na	na	na	na	na	na	na	na	na		
Zimbabwe	na	na	na	na	na	na	na	na	na	na	na	na	na	na	na	na		
Total	na	24	23	25	22	25	23	20	23	32	23	23	26	16	25	40	Total	24

E167_1) PREPARED TO HELP SICK AND DISABLED

Would you be prepared to actually do something to improve the conditions of: Sick and disabled people in your country

Absolutely yes / Yes (%)

(EVS: V280)

Country	Wave 1990	Wave 2000	Male	Female	16-29	30-49	50+	Lower	Middle	Upper	Lower	Middle	Upper	Mat	Mixed	Postm.	RANKING Country	2000
Albania	na	na	na	na	na	na	na	na	na	na	na	na	na	na	na	na	Sweden	88
Algeria	na	na	na	na	na	na	na	na	na	na	na	na	na	na	na	na	Iceland	83
Argentina	na	na	na	na	na	na	na	na	na	na	na	na	na	na	na	na	Italy	82
Armenia	na	na	na	na	na	na	na	na	na	na	na	na	na	na	na	na	Malta	82
Australia	na	na	na	na	na	na	na	na	na	na	na	na	na	na	na	na	Ireland	81
Austria	na	57	56	58	52	59	59	57	58	57	53	60	60	55	56	62	Croatia	79
Azerbaijan	na	na	na	na	na	na	na	na	na	na	na	na	na	na	na	na	Czech Republic	76
Bangladesh	na	na	na	na	na	na	na	na	na	na	na	na	na	na	na	na	Finland	73
Belarus	na	10	9	10	10	10	9	5	11	10	8	11	10	7	12	13	Slovakia	72
Belgium	na	68	67	69	58	67	74	71	68	67	70	69	68	72	66	70	Poland	72
Bosnia and Herz.	na	na	na	na	na	na	na	na	na	na	na	na	na	na	na	na	Greece	71
Brazil	na	na	na	na	na	na	na	na	na	na	na	na	na	na	na	na	Slovenia	71
Bulgaria	na	65	61	69	55	69	67	68	62	68	58	69	71	58	72	74	Denmark	70
Canada	na	na	na	na	na	na	na	na	na	na	na	na	na	na	na	na	Belgium	68
Chile	na	na	na	na	na	na	na	na	na	na	na	na	na	na	na	na	Northern Ireland	66
China	na	na	na	na	na	na	na	na	na	na	na	na	na	na	na	na	Netherlands	66
Colombia	na	na	na	na	na	na	na	na	na	na	na	na	na	na	na	na	Luxembourg	66
Croatia	na	79	76	83	78	82	78	80	78	84	92	76	76	75	79	80	Portugal	65
Czech Republic	na	76	74	79	75	76	77	76	77	79	75	78	75	73	78	79	Bulgaria	65
Denmark	na	70	69	71	63	69	75	69	69	73	68	72	72	63	72	76	Romania	64
Dominican Rep.	na	na	na	na	na	na	na	na	na	na	na	na	na	na	na	na	France	62
Egypt	na	na	na	na	na	na	na	na	na	na	na	na	na	na	na	na	Hungary	60
El Salvador	na	na	na	na	na	na	na	na	na	na	na	na	na	na	na	na	Latvia	59
Estonia	na	40	37	42	33	40	43	36	41	41	39	36	43	36	44	36	Great Britain	58
Finland	na	73	69	78	68	71	79	74	76	66	77	73	74	68	75	78	Austria	57
France	na	62	61	63	59	59	66	63	57	62	66	62	60	63	60	63	Spain	55
Georgia	na	na	na	na	na	na	na	na	na	na	na	na	na	na	na	na	Russian Fed.	49
Germany	na	49	44	52	42	49	51	43	50	61	44	48	55	43	50	54	Germany	49
Great Britain	na	58	56	61	46	58	65	58	57	56	62	57	59	na	na	na	Ukraine	41
Greece	na	71	69	72	66	71	82	76	72	69	72	71	68	68	70	75	Estonia	40
Hungary	na	60	54	64	59	60	59	58	63	63	48	62	63	55	65	65	Lithuania	35
Iceland	na	83	80	86	77	84	87	83	82	83	87	81	82	80	84	84	Belarus	10
India	na	na	na	na	na	na	na	na	na	na	na	na	na	na	na	na		
Indonesia	na	na	na	na	na	na	na	na	na	na	na	na	na	na	na	na		
Iran	na	na	na	na	na	na	na	na	na	na	na	na	na	na	na	na		
Ireland	na	81	80	82	78	82	83	82	82	79	83	80	85	74	83	82		
Israel	na	na	na	na	na	na	na	na	na	na	na	na	na	na	na	na		
Italy	na	82	79	85	78	83	83	82	83	83	81	83	83	79	82	85		
Japan	na	na	na	na	na	na	na	na	na	na	na	na	na	na	na	na		
Jordan	na	na	na	na	na	na	na	na	na	na	na	na	na	na	na	na		
Korea, South	na	na	na	na	na	na	na	na	na	na	na	na	na	na	na	na		
Latvia	na	59	58	59	65	58	57	53	59	64	56	58	66	53	62	70		
Lithuania	na	35	30	39	29	35	40	36	34	40	28	37	34	38	34	29		
Luxembourg	na	66	63	68	56	65	72	61	67	70	60	69	69	65	62	79		
Macedonia	na	na	na	na	na	na	na	na	na	na	na	na	na	na	na	na		
Malta	na	82	83	81	78	84	84	82	82	85	83	88	81	80	84	78		
Mexico	na	na	na	na	na	na	na	na	na	na	na	na	na	na	na	na		
Moldova	na	na	na	na	na	na	na	na	na	na	na	na	na	na	na	na		
Montenegro	na	na	na	na	na	na	na	na	na	na	na	na	na	na	na	na		
Morocco	na	na	na	na	na	na	na	na	na	na	na	na	na	na	na	na		
Netherlands	na	66	61	70	68	61	69	71	69	58	64	70	60	71	67	60		
New Zealand	na	na	na	na	na	na	na	na	na	na	na	na	na	na	na	na		
Nigeria	na	na	na	na	na	na	na	na	na	na	na	na	na	na	na	na		
Northern Ireland	na	66	69	64	64	67	67	63	66	74	68	68	75	62	67	74		
Norway	na	na	na	na	na	na	na	na	na	na	na	na	na	na	na	na		
Pakistan	na	na	na	na	na	na	na	na	na	na	na	na	na	na	na	na		
Peru	na	na	na	na	na	na	na	na	na	na	na	na	na	na	na	na		
Philippines	na	na	na	na	na	na	na	na	na	na	na	na	na	na	na	na		
Poland	na	72	73	70	69	73	71	70	75	72	70	73	71	68	72	78		
Portugal	na	65	61	70	67	65	64	63	68	81	58	62	67	60	66	77		
Puerto Rico	na	na	na	na	na	na	na	na	na	na	na	na	na	na	na	na		
Romania	na	64	62	66	65	64	63	59	62	78	58	64	69	64	66	62		
Russian Fed.	na	49	48	49	47	53	45	36	49	54	44	51	52	46	52	57		
Serbia	na	na	na	na	na	na	na	na	na	na	na	na	na	na	na	na		
Singapore	na	na	na	na	na	na	na	na	na	na	na	na	na	na	na	na		
Slovakia	na	72	70	74	71	68	77	73	70	78	70	73	75	69	75	77		
Slovenia	na	71	69	72	61	71	77	73	69	72	76	73	74	69	71	78		
South Africa	na	na	na	na	na	na	na	na	na	na	na	na	na	na	na	na		
Spain	na	55	52	57	55	56	53	51	55	65	58	54	55	53	54	62		
Sweden	na	88	87	89	85	88	89	89	88	86	87	88	90	86	87	91		
Switzerland	na	na	na	na	na	na	na	na	na	na	na	na	na	na	na	na		
Taiwan	na	na	na	na	na	na	na	na	na	na	na	na	na	na	na	na		
Tanzania	na	na	na	na	na	na	na	na	na	na	na	na	na	na	na	na		
Turkey	na	na	na	na	na	na	na	na	na	na	na	na	na	na	na	na		
Uganda	na	na	na	na	na	na	na	na	na	na	na	na	na	na	na	na		
Ukraine	na	41	39	42	33	43	43	50	39	41	44	39	40	40	44	48		
United States	na	na	na	na	na	na	na	na	na	na	na	na	na	na	na	na		
Uruguay	na	na	na	na	na	na	na	na	na	na	na	na	na	na	na	na		
Venezuela	na	na	na	na	na	na	na	na	na	na	na	na	na	na	na	na		
Vietnam	na	na	na	na	na	na	na	na	na	na	na	na	na	na	na	na		
Zimbabwe	na	na	na	na	na	na	na	na	na	na	na	na	na	na	na	na		
Total	na	64	62	65	60	64	66	64	63	67	63	64	65	57	66	71	Total	64

E188_1) WATCH TV

Do you ever watch television? If yes: How much time do you usually spend watching television on an average weekday (NOT WEEKENDS)?

Less than 3 hours per day (%)

(WVS: V237B)

Country	Wave		Gender		Age			Education			Income			Values		
	1990	2000	Male	Female	16-29	30-49	50+	Lower	Middle	Upper	Lower	Middle	Upper	Mat	Mixed	Postm.
Albania	na	na	na	na	na	na	na	na	na	na	na	na	na	na	na	na
Algeria	na	70	76	64	64	72	80	73	68	70	70	71	75	72	70	69
Argentina	na	77	79	75	66	83	81	77	74	83	77	74	80	76	74	82
Armenia	na	42	46	38	41	43	42	48	40	45	41	46	35	46	39	28
Australia	na	70	72	68	70	77	62	60	66	84	56	75	83	59	69	73
Austria	na	na	na	na	na	na	na	na	na	na	na	na	na	na	na	na
Azerbaijan	na	48	48	48	42	48	61	62	47	48	44	55	49	49	47	47
Bangladesh	na	94	94	94	94	94	95	96	92	91	92	94	96	95	94	88
Belarus	na	na	na	na	na	na	na	na	na	na	na	na	na	na	na	na
Belgium	na	na	na	na	na	na	na	na	na	na	na	na	na	na	na	na
Bosnia and Herz.	na	na	na	na	na	na	na	na	na	na	na	na	na	na	na	na
Brazil	na	70	72	69	65	75	71	73	66	76	71	69	70	68	73	65
Bulgaria	na	na	na	na	na	na	na	na	na	na	na	na	na	na	na	na
Canada	na	na	na	na	na	na	na	na	na	na	na	na	na	na	na	na
Chile	na	na	na	na	na	na	na	na	na	na	na	na	na	na	na	na
China	na	na	na	na	na	na	na	na	na	na	na	na	na	na	na	na
Colombia	na	85	86	83	79	87	88	86	80	89	87	82	87	84	83	78
Croatia	na	na	na	na	na	na	na	na	na	na	na	na	na	na	na	na
Czech Republic	na	na	na	na	na	na	na	na	na	na	na	na	na	na	na	na
Denmark	na	na	na	na	na	na	na	na	na	na	na	na	na	na	na	na
Dominican Rep.	na	85	87	84	82	91	91	78	76	89	86	85	89	87	85	85
Egypt	na	78	87	69	68	83	84	82	75	76	82	78	76	82	77	68
El Salvador	na	81	80	82	77	83	83	84	77	76	87	78	75	na	na	na
Estonia	na	na	na	na	na	na	na	na	na	na	na	na	na	na	na	na
Finland	na	na	na	na	na	na	na	na	na	na	na	na	na	na	na	na
France	na	na	na	na	na	na	na	na	na	na	na	na	na	na	na	na
Georgia	na	100	100	100	100	100	100	100	100	100	100	100	100	100	100	100
Germany	na	na	na	na	na	na	na	na	na	na	na	na	na	na	na	na
Great Britain	na	na	na	na	na	na	na	na	na	na	na	na	na	na	na	na
Greece	na	na	na	na	na	na	na	na	na	na	na	na	na	na	na	na
Hungary	na	na	na	na	na	na	na	na	na	na	na	na	na	na	na	na
Iceland	na	na	na	na	na	na	na	na	na	na	na	na	na	na	na	na
India	na	na	na	na	na	na	na	na	na	na	na	na	na	na	na	na
Indonesia	na	76	84	68	67	79	77	73	73	81	75	76	75	75	75	89
Iran	na	na	na	na	na	na	na	na	na	na	na	na	na	na	na	na
Ireland	na	na	na	na	na	na	na	na	na	na	na	na	na	na	na	na
Israel	na	na	na	na	na	na	na	na	na	na	na	na	na	na	na	na
Italy	na	na	na	na	na	na	na*	na	na	na	na	na	na	na	na	na
Japan	na	na	na	na	na	na	na	na	na	na	na	na	na	na	na	na
Jordan	na	73	76	71	63	78	84	79	66	70	78	74	66	74	74	60
Korea, South	na	na	na	na	na	na	na	na	na	na	na	na	na	na	na	na
Latvia	na	na	na	na	na	na	na	na	na	na	na	na	na	na	na	na
Lithuania	na	na	na	na	na	na	na	na	na	na	na	na	na	na	na	na
Luxembourg	na	na	na	na	na	na	na	na	na	na	na	na	na	na	na	na
Macedonia	na	na	na	na	na	na	na	na	na	na	na	na	na	na	na	na
Malta	na	na	na	na	na	na	na	na	na	na	na	na	na	na	na	na
Mexico	na	na	na	na	na	na	na	na	na	na	na	na	na	na	na	na
Moldova	na	na	na	na	na	na	na	na	na	na	na	na	na	na	na	na
Montenegro	na	na	na	na	na	na	na	na	na	na	na	na	na	na	na	na
Morocco	na	78	85	71	75	81	79	76	86	86	93	84	74	80	77	78
Netherlands	na	na	na	na	na	na	na	na	na	na	na	na	na	na	na	na
New Zealand	na	78	80	77	79	83	73	71	81	85	69	80	89	77	80	79
Nigeria	na	75	75	75	70	81	86	86	72	63	84	74	65	79	74	71
Northern Ireland	na	na	na	na	na	na	na	na	na	na	na	na	na	na	na	na
Norway	na	87	86	87	85	89	85	81	87	92	na	na	na	80	87	93
Pakistan	na	93	92	93	88	94	99	95	88	94	95	92	91	94	91	91
Peru	na	80	80	79	73	83	86	83	78	80	83	76	79	80	79	79
Philippines	na	na	na	na	na	na	na	na	na	na	na	na	na	na	na	na
Poland	na	na	na	na	na	na	na	na	na	na	na	na	na	na	na	na
Portugal	na	na	na	na	na	na	na	na	na	na	na	na	na	na	na	na
Puerto Rico	na	78	80	77	77	80	77	72	72	82	70	80	83	74	78	80
Romania	na	na	na	na	na	na	na	na	na	na	na	na	na	na	na	na
Russian Fed.	na	na	na	na	na	na	na	na	na	na	na	na	na	na	na	na
Serbia	na	na	na	na	na	na	na	na	na	na	na	na	na	na	na	na
Singapore	na	na	na	na	na	na	na	na	na	na	na	na	na	na	na	na
Slovakia	na	na	na	na	na	na	na	na	na	na	na	na	na	na	na	na
Slovenia	na	na	na	na	na	na	na	na	na	na	na	na	na	na	na	na
South Africa	na	68	69	67	57	77	72	72	62	79	74	61	72	67	69	66
Spain	na	79	78	80	85	84	71	72	87	94	62	81	86	78	79	83
Sweden	na	na	na	na	na	na	na	na	na	na	na	na	na	na	na	na
Switzerland	na	93	93	93	94	94	92	89	94	98	87	94	96	92	93	94
Taiwan	na	76	80	73	64	78	79	75	68	82	75	74	78	76	76	83
Tanzania	na	na	na	na	na	na	na	na	na	na	na	na	na	na	na	na
Turkey	na	na	na	na	na	na	na	na	na	na	na	na	na	na	na	na
Uganda	na	88	95	81	82	93	99	91	86	96	93	96	89	87	88	90
Ukraine	na	na	na	na	na	na	na	na	na	na	na	na	na	na	na	na
United States	na	na	na	na	na	na	na	na	na	na	na	na	na	na	na	na
Uruguay	na	70	72	69	73	76	65	67	71	88	72	70	72	68	70	76
Venezuela	na	na	na	na	na	na	na	na	na	na	na	na	na	na	na	na
Vietnam	na	na	na	na	na	na	na	na	na	na	na	na	na	na	na	na
Zimbabwe	na	88	88	87	83	90	93	94	79	62	95	91	73	86	89	92
Total	na	78	80	76	73	81	78	80	74	80	77	78	78	77	78	78

RANKING

Country	2000
Georgia	100
Bangladesh	94
Switzerland	93
Pakistan	93
Uganda	88
Zimbabwe	88
Norway	87
Dominican Rep.	85
Colombia	85
El Salvador	81
Peru	80
Spain	79
Egypt	78
Morocco	78
New Zealand	78
Puerto Rico	78
Argentina	77
Taiwan	76
Indonesia	76
Nigeria	75
Jordan	73
Algeria	70
Brazil	70
Uruguay	70
Australia	70
South Africa	68
Azerbaijan	48
Armenia	42
Total	78

E189) TV MOST IMPORTANT ENTERTAINMENT

Do you agree strongly, agree, disagree or disagree strongly with the following statement: "Television is my most important form of entertainment."

Strongly agree / Agree (%)

(WVS: V237)

Country	Wave 1990	Wave 2000	Gender Male	Gender Female	Age 16-29	Age 30-49	Age 50+	Education Lower	Education Middle	Education Upper	Income Lower	Income Middle	Income Upper	Values Mat	Values Mixed	Values Postm.
Albania	na	57	54	61	50	55	67	67	54	42	65	55	51	57	55	51
Algeria	na	42	37	47	41	41	47	56	43	31	47	44	30	47	40	29
Argentina	na	na	na	na	na	na	na	na	na	na	na	na	na	na	na	na
Armenia	na	na	na	na	na	na	na	na	na	na	na	na	na	na	na	na
Australia	na	na	na	na	na	na	na	na	na	na	na	na	na	na	na	na
Austria	na	na	na	na	na	na	na	na	na	na	na	na	na	na	na	na
Azerbaijan	na	na	na	na	na	na	na	na	na	na	na	na	na	na	na	na
Bangladesh	na	89	91	86	85	90	96	92	86	84	98	90	79	87	89	88
Belarus	na	na	na	na	na	na	na	na	na	na	na	na	na	na	na	na
Belgium	na	na	na	na	na	na	na	na	na	na	na	na	na	na	na	na
Bosnia and Herz.	na	39	37	41	31	35	53	56	40	22	46	39	32	40	39	43
Brazil	na	na	na	na	na	na	na	na	na	na	na	na	na	na	na	na
Bulgaria	na	na	na	na	na	na	na	na	na	na	na	na	na	na	na	na
Canada	na	33	35	31	27	29	41	45	34	21	42	36	22	43	36	26
Chile	na	52	54	50	48	51	58	63	49	38	61	45	50	52	53	46
China	na	62	60	64	54	63	67	63	62	48	60	65	62	63	62	42
Colombia	na	na	na	na	na	na	na	na	na	na	na	na	na	na	na	na
Croatia	na	na	na	na	na	na	na	na	na	na	na	na	na	na	na	na
Czech Republic	na	na	na	na	na	na	na	na	na	na	na	na	na	na	na	na
Denmark	na	na	na	na	na	na	na	na	na	na	na	na	na	na	na	na
Dominican Rep.	na	na	na	na	na	na	na	na	na	na	na	na	na	na	na	na
Egypt	na	61	52	70	62	62	58	65	59	52	61	66	58	63	61	54
El Salvador	na	na	na	na	na	na	na	na	na	na	na	na	na	na	na	na
Estonia	na	na	na	na	na	na	na	na	na	na	na	na	na	na	na	na
Finland	na	na	na	na	na	na	na	na	na	na	na	na	na	na	na	na
France	na	na	na	na	na	na	na	na	na	na	na	na	na	na	na	na
Georgia	na	na	na	na	na	na	na	na	na	na	na	na	na	na	na	na
Germany	na	na	na	na	na	na	na	na	na	na	na	na	na	na	na	na
Great Britain	na	na	na	na	na	na	na	na	na	na	na	na	na	na	na	na
Greece	na	na	na	na	na	na	na	na	na	na	na	na	na	na	na	na
Hungary	na	na	na	na	na	na	na	na	na	na	na	na	na	na	na	na
Iceland	na	na	na	na	na	na	na	na	na	na	na	na	na	na	na	na
India	na	63	63	64	70	64	54	54	75	69	52	61	70	66	63	67
Indonesia	na	69	67	71	65	69	71	82	71	57	73	69	60	77	64	57
Iran	na	na	na	na	na	na	na	na	na	na	na	na	na	na	na	na
Ireland	na	na	na	na	na	na	na	na	na	na	na	na	na	na	na	na
Israel	na	na	na	na	na	na	na	na	na	na	na	na	na	na	na	na
Italy	na	na	na	na	na	na	na	na	na	na	na	na	na	na	na	na
Japan	na	69	67	71	72	63	73	82	70	57	76	67	62	73	68	58
Jordan	na	41	34	47	44	37	41	44	40	36	35	44	47	40	41	38
Korea, South	na	na	na	na	na	na	na	na	na	na	na	na	na	na	na	na
Latvia	na	na	na	na	na	na	na	na	na	na	na	na	na	na	na	na
Lithuania	na	na	na	na	na	na	na	na	na	na	na	na	na	na	na	na
Luxembourg	na	na	na	na	na	na	na	na	na	na	na	na	na	na	na	na
Macedonia	na	52	51	54	46	45	68	71	46	39	63	50	40	54	51	52
Malta	na	na	na	na	na	na	na	na	na	na	na	na	na	na	na	na
Mexico	na	52	51	53	47	55	54	61	44	33	54	48	48	59	50	41
Moldova	na	55	58	53	46	54	64	59	63	38	62	55	52	57	55	48
Montenegro	na	44	44	45	32	40	56	59	38	30	59	45	36	48	39	40
Morocco	na	48	41	55	46	50	52	54	30	20	47	40	52	49	48	45
Netherlands	na	na	na	na	na	na	na	na	na	na	na	na	na	na	na	na
New Zealand	na	na	na	na	na	na	na	na	na	na	na	na	na	na	na	na
Nigeria	na	76	77	75	80	72	65	71	79	78	73	76	79	73	77	82
Northern Ireland	na	na	na	na	na	na	na	na	na	na	na	na	na	na	na	na
Norway	na	na	na	na	na	na	na	na	na	na	na	na	na	na	na	na
Pakistan	na	na	na	na	na	na	na	na	na	na	na	na	na	na	na	na
Peru	na	na	na	na	na	na	na	na	na	na	na	na	na	na	na	na
Philippines	na	64	63	65	66	64	62	61	66	64	61	61	71	66	63	60
Poland	na	na	na	na	na	na	na	na	na	na	na	na	na	na	na	na
Portugal	na	na	na	na	na	na	na	na	na	na	na	na	na	na	na	na
Puerto Rico	na	na	na	na	na	na	na	na	na	na	na	na	na	na	na	na
Romania	na	na	na	na	na	na	na	na	na	na	na	na	na	na	na	na
Russian Fed.	na	na	na	na	na	na	na	na	na	na	na	na	na	na	na	na
Serbia	na	44	41	47	32	38	55	66	38	25	53	39	38	55	35	23
Singapore	na	54	50	59	52	53	69	64	53	35	66	56	45	56	54	44
Slovakia	na	na	na	na	na	na	na	na	na	na	na	na	na	na	na	na
Slovenia	na	na	na	na	na	na	na	na	na	na	na	na	na	na	na	na
South Africa	na	na	na	na	na	na	na	na	na	na	na	na	na	na	na	na
Spain	na	na	na	na	na	na	na	na	na	na	na	na	na	na	na	na
Sweden	na	29	31	26	23	24	36	43	25	22	33	28	23	37	30	19
Switzerland	na	na	na	na	na	na	na	na	na	na	na	na	na	na	na	na
Taiwan	na	na	na	na	na	na	na	na	na	na	na	na	na	na	na	na
Tanzania	na	55	54	57	59	52	57	62	54	39	61	54	51	58	53	70
Turkey	na	na	na	na	na	na	na	na	na	na	na	na	na	na	na	na
Uganda	na	45	44	45	53	39	23	30	52	36	36	48	56	46	45	39
Ukraine	na	na	na	na	na	na	na	na	na	na	na	na	na	na	na	na
United States	na	28	30	25	23	26	33	35	29	24	33	25	24	35	28	23
Uruguay	na	na	na	na	na	na	na	na	na	na	na	na	na	na	na	na
Venezuela	na	52	52	52	51	51	56	59	54	38	61	50	47	57	51	46
Vietnam	na	93	94	91	94	91	91	92	95	85	90	93	94	95	93	93
Zimbabwe	na	50	49	51	59	43	38	43	59	31	41	51	63	45	53	60
Total	na	54	53	55	53	53	57	61	54	42	57	55	52	58	53	42

RANKING

Country	2000
Vietnam	93
Bangladesh	89
Nigeria	76
Japan	69
Indonesia	69
Philippines	64
India	63
China	62
Egypt	61
Albania	57
Tanzania	55
Moldova	55
Singapore	54
Macedonia	52
Chile	52
Mexico	52
Venezuela	52
Zimbabwe	50
Morocco	48
Uganda	45
Serbia	44
Montenegro	44
Algeria	42
Jordan	41
Bosnia and Herz.	39
Canada	33
Sweden	29
United States	28
Total	54

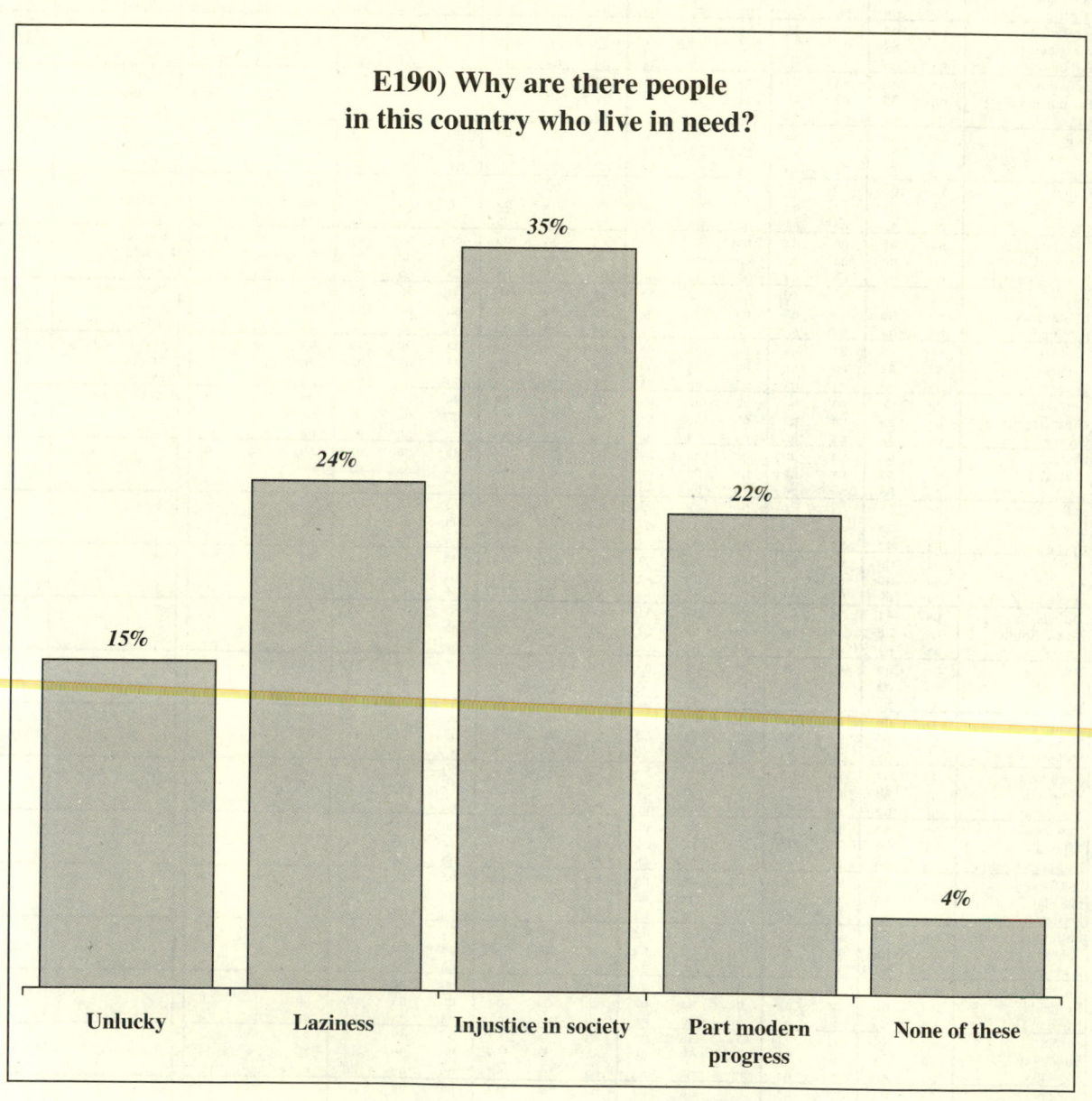

**E190) Why are there people
in this country who live in need?**

15%	24%	35%	22%	4%
Unlucky	Laziness	Injustice in society	Part modern progress	None of these

E190_3) WHY ARE THERE PEOPLE LIVING IN NEED: FIRST
Why are there people in this country who live in need? Here are four possible reasons. Which one reason do you consider to be most important?

Injustice in society (%)

(EVS: V69)

Country	Wave 1990	Wave 2000	Gender Male	Gender Female	Age 16-29	Age 30-49	Age 50+	Education Lower	Education Middle	Education Upper	Income Lower	Income Middle	Income Upper	Values Mat	Values Mixed	Values Postm.
Albania	na	na	na	na	na	na	na	na	na	na	na	na	na	na	na	na
Algeria	na	na	na	na	na	na	na	na	na	na	na	na	na	na	na	na
Argentina	49	na	na	na	na	na	na	na	na	na	na	na	na	na	na	na
Armenia	na	na	na	na	na	na	na	na	na	na	na	na	na	na	na	na
Australia	na	na	na	na	na	na	na	na	na	na	na	na	na	na	na	na
Austria	25	22	20	23	20	25	20	19	22	32	22	24	23	14	21	25
Azerbaijan	na	na	na	na	na	na	na	na	na	na	na	na	na	na	na	na
Bangladesh	na	na	na	na	na	na	na	na	na	na	na	na	na	na	na	na
Belarus	60	46	43	48	42	49	46	48	47	39	51	44	40	49	46	40
Belgium	33	34	33	35	41	37	27	30	36	34	32	35	34	31	30	48
Bosnia and Herz.	na	na	na	na	na	na	na	na	na	na	na	na	na	na	na	na
Brazil	40	na	na	na	na	na	na	na	na	na	na	na	na	na	na	na
Bulgaria	52	50	47	53	46	45	56	59	46	44	58	49	46	60	41	31
Canada	32	na	na	na	na	na	na	na	na	na	na	na	na	na	na	na
Chile	41	na	na	na	na	na	na	na	na	na	na	na	na	na	na	na
China	36	na	na	na	na	na	na	na	na	na	na	na	na	na	na	na
Colombia	na	na	na	na	na	na	na	na	na	na	na	na	na	na	na	na
Croatia	na	70	69	71	68	68	72	74	67	64	79	72	63	60	70	78
Czech Republic	27	19	19	18	16	17	22	20	18	16	23	20	13	23	18	14
Denmark	29	17	15	19	15	19	16	16	17	18	18	16	16	17	15	28
Dominican Rep.	na	na	na	na	na	na	na	na	na	na	na	na	na	na	na	na
Egypt	na	na	na	na	na	na	na	na	na	na	na	na	na	na	na	na
El Salvador	na	na	na	na	na	na	na	na	na	na	na	na	na	na	na	na
Estonia	57	42	39	44	30	41	49	46	41	37	51	47	34	48	39	39
Finland	20	24	20	27	25	25	22	26	22	19	26	25	24	23	24	35
France	42	44	41	47	46	47	41	43	42	50	45	46	44	40	44	52
Georgia	na	na	na	na	na	na	na	na	na	na	na	na	na	na	na	na
Germany	47	37	38	36	35	40	34	34	39	44	43	34	34	38	34	47
Great Britain	34	31	29	32	37	33	24	25	35	35	29	33	32	na	na	na
Greece	na	24	24	24	26	24	20	16	29	22	28	21	21	21	25	25
Hungary	39	38	38	37	34	42	36	39	40	24	42	41	32	38	38	34
Iceland	27	30	27	32	28	30	31	31	25	34	35	30	25	29	27	47
India	33	na	na	na	na	na	na	na	na	na	na	na	na	na	na	na
Indonesia	na	na	na	na	na	na	na	na	na	na	na	na	na	na	na	na
Iran	na	na	na	na	na	na	na	na	na	na	na	na	na	na	na	na
Ireland	36	33	30	36	35	31	32	26	35	41	31	37	35	28	33	39
Israel	na	na	na	na	na	na	na	na	na	na	na	na	na	na	na	na
Italy	43	38	36	39	40	39	35	35	40	40	35	40	39	30	37	45
Japan	29	na	na	na	na	na	na	na	na	na	na	na	na	na	na	na
Jordan	na	na	na	na	na	na	na	na	na	na	na	na	na	na	na	na
Korea, South	35	na	na	na	na	na	na	na	na	na	na	na	na	na	na	na
Latvia	65	32	34	31	27	33	34	35	33	29	36	34	26	34	32	33
Lithuania	51	50	50	50	43	53	52	48	53	38	64	48	47	49	54	35
Luxembourg	na	23	21	26	25	24	21	21	23	28	20	25	26	16	22	35
Macedonia	na	na	na	na	na	na	na	na	na	na	na	na	na	na	na	na
Malta	na	24	25	23	28	22	23	24	24	24	26	23	19	22	24	29
Mexico	32	na	na	na	na	na	na	na	na	na	na	na	na	na	na	na
Moldova	na	na	na	na	na	na	na	na	na	na	na	na	na	na	na	na
Montenegro	na	na	na	na	na	na	na	na	na	na	na	na	na	na	na	na
Morocco	na	na	na	na	na	na	na	na	na	na	na	na	na	na	na	na
Netherlands	39	25	22	28	22	26	26	28	23	25	27	30	15	23	23	35
New Zealand	na	na	na	na	na	na	na	na	na	na	na	na	na	na	na	na
Nigeria	48	na	na	na	na	na	na	na	na	na	na	na	na	na	na	na
Northern Ireland	25	28	25	31	32	32	21	27	28	29	21	25	29	21	28	40
Norway	49	na	na	na	na	na	na	na	na	na	na	na	na	na	na	na
Pakistan	na	na	na	na	na	na	na	na	na	na	na	na	na	na	na	na
Peru	na	na	na	na	na	na	na	na	na	na	na	na	na	na	na	na
Philippines	na	na	na	na	na	na	na	na	na	na	na	na	na	na	na	na
Poland	59	50	52	49	50	52	50	53	49	43	58	46	46	49	52	48
Portugal	39	22	21	22	26	23	18	17	33	24	14	23	22	18	22	32
Puerto Rico	na	na	na	na	na	na	na	na	na	na	na	na	na	na	na	na
Romania	36	43	44	43	40	46	42	40	47	41	40	46	46	44	44	37
Russian Fed.	50	22	22	22	16	19	30	30	23	17	25	25	17	26	19	9
Serbia	na	na	na	na	na	na	na	na	na	na	na	na	na	na	na	na
Singapore	na	na	na	na	na	na	na	na	na	na	na	na	na	na	na	na
Slovakia	na	37	40	35	35	39	36	35	40	29	40	37	34	41	36	34
Slovenia	44	35	37	34	37	35	35	36	39	20	42	37	25	37	35	37
South Africa	58	na	na	na	na	na	na	na	na	na	na	na	na	na	na	na
Spain	44	48	47	50	56	50	43	44	50	57	47	44	48	40	50	58
Sweden	35	50	46	53	51	46	51	55	47	50	51	49	48	40	47	61
Switzerland	na	na	na	na	na	na	na	na	na	na	na	na	na	na	na	na
Taiwan	na	na	na	na	na	na	na	na	na	na	na	na	na	na	na	na
Tanzania	na	na	na	na	na	na	na	na	na	na	na	na	na	na	na	na
Turkey	37	67	68	66	70	66	57	64	70	69	67	66	69	64	66	74
Uganda	na	na	na	na	na	na	na	na	na	na	na	na	na	na	na	na
Ukraine	na	26	24	27	24	24	29	34	26	22	30	27	21	28	25	29
United States	33	na	na	na	na	na	na	na	na	na	na	na	na	na	na	na
Uruguay	na	na	na	na	na	na	na	na	na	na	na	na	na	na	na	na
Venezuela	na	na	na	na	na	na	na	na	na	na	na	na	na	na	na	na
Vietnam	na	na	na	na	na	na	na	na	na	na	na	na	na	na	na	na
Zimbabwe	na	na	na	na	na	na	na	na	na	na	na	na	na	na	na	na
Total	40	35	34	36	34	36	34	35	36	32	38	36	32	36	34	41

RANKING

Country	2000
Croatia	70
Turkey	67
Poland	50
Lithuania	50
Bulgaria	50
Sweden	50
Spain	48
Belarus	46
France	44
Romania	43
Estonia	42
Italy	38
Hungary	38
Slovakia	37
Germany	37
Slovenia	35
Belgium	34
Ireland	33
Latvia	32
Great Britain	31
Iceland	30
Northern Ireland	28
Ukraine	26
Netherlands	25
Greece	24
Finland	24
Malta	24
Luxembourg	23
Russian Fed.	22
Austria	22
Portugal	22
Czech Republic	19
Denmark	17
Total	35

E190_2) WHY ARE THERE PEOPLE LIVING IN NEED: FIRST

Why are there people in this country who live in need? Here are four possible reasons. Which one reason do you consider to be most important?

Laziness or lack of willpower (%)

(EVS: V69)

Country	Wave 1990	Wave 2000	Gender Male	Gender Female	Age 16-29	Age 30-49	Age 50+	Education Lower	Education Middle	Education Upper	Income Lower	Income Middle	Income Upper	Values Mat	Values Mixed	Values Postm.	RANKING Country	RANKING 2000
Albania	na	na	na	na	na	na	na	na	na	na	na	na	na	na	na	na	Malta	50
Algeria	na	na	na	na	na	na	na	na	na	na	na	na	na	na	na	na	Czech Republic	43
Argentina	34	na	na	na	na	na	na	na	na	na	na	na	na	na	na	na	Portugal	42
Armenia	na	na	na	na	na	na	na	na	na	na	na	na	na	na	na	na	Slovenia	33
Australia	na	na	na	na	na	na	na	na	na	na	na	na	na	na	na	na	Austria	32
Austria	37	32	34	31	33	27	37	40	29	14	35	33	31	42	35	25	Slovakia	31
Azerbaijan	na	na	na	na	na	na	na	na	na	na	na	na	na	na	na	na	Romania	30
Bangladesh	na	na	na	na	na	na	na	na	na	na	na	na	na	na	na	na	Latvia	29
Belarus	27	21	26	18	24	20	21	19	22	22	14	21	34	19	22	40	Northern Ireland	29
Belgium	22	18	18	17	17	15	21	24	18	13	25	16	13	21	19	7	Germany	28
Bosnia and Herz.	na	na	na	na	na	na	na	na	na	na	na	na	na	na	na	na	Hungary	28
Brazil	27	na	na	na	na	na	na	na	na	na	na	na	na	na	na	na	Great Britain	25
Bulgaria	27	15	17	14	13	15	16	14	16	15	14	13	17	13	18	17	Finland	23
Canada	32	na	na	na	na	na	na	na	na	na	na	na	na	na	na	na	Italy	23
Chile	35	na	na	na	na	na	na	na	na	na	na	na	na	na	na	na	Russian Fed.	23
China	12	na	na	na	na	na	na	na	na	na	na	na	na	na	na	na	Greece	23
Colombia	na	na	na	na	na	na	na	na	na	na	na	na	na	na	na	na	Poland	23
Croatia	na	12	11	12	10	12	14	11	13	10	10	9	15	18	12	7	Luxembourg	23
Czech Republic	43	43	45	42	42	43	43	44	41	45	41	43	44	47	44	34	Turkey	23
Denmark	14	17	21	13	25	16	15	21	15	12	16	18	18	28	19	5	Iceland	22
Dominican Rep.	na	na	na	na	na	na	na	na	na	na	na	na	na	na	na	na	Belarus	21
Egypt	na	na	na	na	na	na	na	na	na	na	na	na	na	na	na	na	Ireland	21
El Salvador	na	na	na	na	na	na	na	na	na	na	na	na	na	na	na	na	Spain	20
Estonia	24	15	15	15	15	16	15	16	15	14	10	16	17	16	14	19	Belgium	18
Finland	26	23	25	21	27	17	27	25	23	14	21	26	20	29	21	18	Denmark	17
France	15	11	14	9	11	8	15	13	11	7	13	11	12	13	13	5	Ukraine	17
Georgia	na	na	na	na	na	na	na	na	na	na	na	na	na	na	na	na	Estonia	15
Germany	29	28	30	27	19	28	33	33	25	22	28	30	25	33	31	15	Bulgaria	15
Great Britain	27	25	28	22	17	20	34	29	21	21	24	24	17	na	na	na	Netherlands	15
Greece	na	23	24	22	15	25	34	36	26	18	24	24	21	29	22	19	Croatia	12
Hungary	34	28	25	30	26	21	34	30	23	26	28	29	25	32	25	5	France	11
Iceland	23	22	29	16	30	20	19	22	26	16	24	20	24	28	22	14	Lithuania	10
India	40	na	na	na	na	na	na	na	na	na	na	na	na	na	na	na	Sweden	7
Indonesia	na	na	na	na	na	na	na	na	na	na	na	na	na	na	na	na		
Iran	na	na	na	na	na	na	na	na	na	na	na	na	na	na	na	na		
Ireland	21	21	22	20	17	20	25	26	18	16	22	23	19	22	21	19		
Israel	na	na	na	na	na	na	na	na	na	na	na	na	na	na	na	na		
Italy	30	23	24	22	19	21	27	27	22	16	24	24	20	32	24	16		
Japan	33	na	na	na	na	na	na	na	na	na	na	na	na	na	na	na		
Jordan	na	na	na	na	na	na	na	na	na	na	na	na	na	na	na	na		
Korea, South	36	na	na	na	na	na	na	na	na	na	na	na	na	na	na	na		
Latvia	17	29	30	29	33	27	29	30	30	25	28	32	29	26	30	31		
Lithuania	25	10	11	9	10	8	12	13	9	11	8	12	9	11	9	12		
Luxembourg	na	23	23	22	23	20	25	26	24	12	25	22	17	29	23	14		
Macedonia	na	na	na	na	na	na	na	na	na	na	na	na	na	na	na	na		
Malta	na	50	50	51	49	53	49	48	52	46	51	52	58	34	48	52		
Mexico	39	na	na	na	na	na	na	na	na	na	na	na	na	na	na	na		
Moldova	na	na	na	na	na	na	na	na	na	na	na	na	na	na	na	na		
Montenegro	na	na	na	na	na	na	na	na	na	na	na	na	na	na	na	na		
Morocco	na	na	na	na	na	na	na	na	na	na	na	na	na	na	na	na		
Netherlands	14	15	18	12	25	12	12	19	16	9	19	13	10	24	16	7		
New Zealand	na	na	na	na	na	na	na	na	na	na	na	na	na	na	na	na		
Nigeria	24	na	na	na	na	na	na	na	na	na	na	na	na	na	na	na		
Northern Ireland	32	29	29	29	31	25	32	30	29	27	29	31	25	37	29	16		
Norway	11	na	na	na	na	na	na	na	na	na	na	na	na	na	na	na		
Pakistan	na	na	na	na	na	na	na	na	na	na	na	na	na	na	na	na		
Peru	na	na	na	na	na	na	na	na	na	na	na	na	na	na	na	na		
Philippines	na	na	na	na	na	na	na	na	na	na	na	na	na	na	na	na		
Poland	20	23	23	22	24	19	27	24	20	22	19	24	27	26	20	26		
Portugal	24	42	45	40	37	44	44	45	37	28	48	37	42	45	42	35		
Puerto Rico	na	na	na	na	na	na	na	na	na	na	na	na	na	na	na	na		
Romania	34	30	31	29	22	26	38	38	27	24	35	33	25	33	28	20		
Russian Fed.	34	23	25	22	27	23	20	23	23	24	17	23	27	22	24	29		
Serbia	na	na	na	na	na	na	na	na	na	na	na	na	na	na	na	na		
Singapore	na	na	na	na	na	na	na	na	na	na	na	na	na	na	na	na		
Slovakia	na	31	30	33	28	30	35	33	30	31	31	30	34	33	31	29		
Slovenia	24	33	33	33	31	33	35	35	33	30	29	34	35	35	35	25		
South Africa	22	na	na	na	na	na	na	na	na	na	na	na	na	na	na	na		
Spain	24	20	20	19	20	16	23	23	17	17	22	22	18	23	20	14		
Sweden	16	7	10	4	8	9	5	5	8	7	7	9	6	15	8	2		
Switzerland	na	na	na	na	na	na	na	na	na	na	na	na	na	na	na	na		
Taiwan	na	na	na	na	na	na	na	na	na	na	na	na	na	na	na	na		
Tanzania	na	na	na	na	na	na	na	na	na	na	na	na	na	na	na	na		
Turkey	39	23	23	22	21	22	30	23	21	22	21	23	23	24	24	18		
Uganda	na	na	na	na	na	na	na	na	na	na	na	na	na	na	na	na		
Ukraine	na	17	16	18	19	17	16	17	17	17	15	14	23	16	19	23		
United States	40	na	na	na	na	na	na	na	na	na	na	na	na	na	na	na		
Uruguay	na	na	na	na	na	na	na	na	na	na	na	na	na	na	na	na		
Venezuela	na	na	na	na	na	na	na	na	na	na	na	na	na	na	na	na		
Vietnam	na	na	na	na	na	na	na	na	na	na	na	na	na	na	na	na		
Zimbabwe	na	na	na	na	na	na	na	na	na	na	na	na	na	na	na	na		
Total	27	24	25	23	23	22	26	27	23	18	23	23	23	27	24	17	Total	24

E191_1) WHY ARE THERE PEOPLE LIVING IN NEED: SECOND

And which reason do you consider to be the second most important?

Unlucky (%)

(EVS: V70)

Country	Wave 1990	Wave 2000	Gender Male	Gender Female	Age 16-29	Age 30-49	Age 50+	Education Lower	Education Middle	Education Upper	Income Lower	Income Middle	Income Upper	Values Mat	Values Mixed	Values Postm.
Albania	na	na	na	na	na	na	na	na	na	na	na	na	na	na	na	na
Algeria	na	na	na	na	na	na	na	na	na	na	na	na	na	na	na	na
Argentina	na	na	na	na	na	na	na	na	na	na	na	na	na	na	na	na
Armenia	na	na	na	na	na	na	na	na	na	na	na	na	na	na	na	na
Australia	na	na	na	na	na	na	na	na	na	na	na	na	na	na	na	na
Austria	na	16	17	16	14	16	18	17	16	17	19	15	16	16	18	14
Azerbaijan	na	na	na	na	na	na	na	na	na	na	na	na	na	na	na	na
Bangladesh	na	na	na	na	na	na	na	na	na	na	na	na	na	na	na	na
Belarus	na	18	18	18	14	19	19	23	17	13	20	18	14	20	17	19
Belgium	na	30	31	29	30	28	32	31	29	30	27	29	31	28	32	29
Bosnia and Herz.	na	na	na	na	na	na	na	na	na	na	na	na	na	na	na	na
Brazil	na	na	na	na	na	na	na	na	na	na	na	na	na	na	na	na
Bulgaria	na	21	17	25	20	18	25	32	17	14	29	21	17	27ʳ	16	17
Canada	na	na	na	na	na	na	na	na	na	na	na	na	na	na	na	na
Chile	na	na	na	na	na	na	na	na	na	na	na	na	na	na	na	na
China	na	na	na	na	na	na	na	na	na	na	na	na	na	na	na	na
Colombia	na	na	na	na	na	na	na	na	na	na	na	na	na	na	na	na
Croatia	na	13	11	16	8	13	18	13	13	14	13	14	12	20	12	13
Czech Republic	na	27	29	26	27	23	32	28	27	27	26	30	26	27	26	34
Denmark	na	23	23	23	24	17	28	24	23	22	24	24	21	31	23	21
Dominican Rep.	na	na	na	na	na	na	na	na	na	na	na	na	na	na	na	na
Egypt	na	na	na	na	na	na	na	na	na	na	na	na	na	na	na	na
El Salvador	na	na	na	na	na	na	na	na	na	na	na	na	na	na	na	na
Estonia	na	24	25	23	20	24	26	26	22	25	27	28	19	26	22	28
Finland	na	23	22	25	23	20	26	24	23	23	29	20	20	23	23	28
France	na	21	19	23	19	20	23	21	21	21	21	23	21	21	21	21
Georgia	na	na	na	na	na	na	na	na	na	na	na	na	na	na	na	na
Germany	na	22	20	24	24	22	21	23	23	15	25	20	20	24	22	21
Great Britain	na	20	22	19	24	19	19	18	19	26	17	19	23	na	na	na
Greece	na	15	15	15	15	16	13	18	14	16	14	14	15	19	14	15
Hungary	na	24	27	23	24	24	26	25	23	25	26	25	23	28	22	14
Iceland	na	28	28	29	20	29	34	28	28	28	30	28	26	35	26	30
India	na	na	na	na	na	na	na	na	na	na	na	na	na	na	na	na
Indonesia	na	na	na	na	na	na	na	na	na	na	na	na	na	na	na	na
Iran	na	na	na	na	na	na	na	na	na	na	na	na	na	na	na	na
Ireland	na	25	27	24	23	26	25	27	24	24	27	23	25	24	28	16
Israel	na	na	na	na	na	na	na	na	na	na	na	na	na	na	na	na
Italy	na	22	20	24	20	21	25	25	20	19	21	26	19	27	24	17
Japan	na	na	na	na	na	na	na	na	na	na	na	na	na	na	na	na
Jordan	na	na	na	na	na	na	na	na	na	na	na	na	na	na	na	na
Korea, South	na	na	na	na	na	na	na	na	na	na	na	na	na	na	na	na
Latvia	na	19	20	18	18	19	19	19	19	21	20	18	18	22	17	21
Lithuania	na	21	23	19	23	21	20	22	22	16	21	15	24	23	20	25
Luxembourg	na	26	26	26	23	26	27	27	24	28	27	29	26	28	24	32
Macedonia	na	na	na	na	na	na	na	na	na	na	na	na	na	na	na	na
Malta	na	18	18	17	18	17	17	18	19	8	18	12	18	21	16	13
Mexico	na	na	na	na	na	na	na	na	na	na	na	na	na	na	na	na
Moldova	na	na	na	na	na	na	na	na	na	na	na	na	na	na	na	na
Montenegro	na	na	na	na	na	na	na	na	na	na	na	na	na	na	na	na
Morocco	na	na	na	na	na	na	na	na	na	na	na	na	na	na	na	na
Netherlands	na	31	32	29	30	30	31	30	32	29	31	32	27	33	30	30
New Zealand	na	na	na	na	na	na	na	na	na	na	na	na	na	na	na	na
Nigeria	na	na	na	na	na	na	na	na	na	na	na	na	na	na	na	na
Northern Ireland	na	19	19	20	17	17	22	20	18	20	26	17	20	21	17	26
Norway	na	na	na	na	na	na	na	na	na	na	na	na	na	na	na	na
Pakistan	na	na	na	na	na	na	na	na	na	na	na	na	na	na	na	na
Peru	na	na	na	na	na	na	na	na	na	na	na	na	na	na	na	na
Philippines	na	na	na	na	na	na	na	na	na	na	na	na	na	na	na	na
Poland	na	21	21	20	23	18	23	24	19	11	23	18	21	22	19	22
Portugal	na	31	33	30	23	32	36	36	26	12	34	37	25	32	30	22
Puerto Rico	na	na	na	na	na	na	na	na	na	na	na	na	na	na	na	na
Romania	na	18	16	20	12	18	21	25	15	13	24	19	14	20	16	14
Russian Fed.	na	19	18	20	17	20	19	28	20	12	21	21	14	21	17	10
Serbia	na	na	na	na	na	na	na	na	na	na	na	na	na	na	na	na
Singapore	na	na	na	na	na	na	na	na	na	na	na	na	na	na	na	na
Slovakia	na	18	19	18	16	18	20	22	17	11	22	17	15	21	17	10
Slovenia	na	14	14	13	12	12	16	18	13	6	13	14	14	16	13	13
South Africa	na	na	na	na	na	na	na	na	na	na	na	na	na	na	na	na
Spain	na	25	25	25	26	21	27	26	25	24	24	25	21	32	25	18
Sweden	na	22	20	24	22	21	22	20	21	24	22	19	25	18	21	23
Switzerland	na	na	na	na	na	na	na	na	na	na	na	na	na	na	na	na
Taiwan	na	na	na	na	na	na	na	na	na	na	na	na	na	na	na	na
Tanzania	na	na	na	na	na	na	na	na	na	na	na	na	na	na	na	na
Turkey	na	11	10	12	10	10	17	13	8	7	13	11	7	15	11	7
Uganda	na	na	na	na	na	na	na	na	na	na	na	na	na	na	na	na
Ukraine	na	19	20	18	20	21	17	20	20	18	16	21	21	19	19	10
United States	na	na	na	na	na	na	na	na	na	na	na	na	na	na	na	na
Uruguay	na	na	na	na	na	na	na	na	na	na	na	na	na	na	na	na
Venezuela	na	na	na	na	na	na	na	na	na	na	na	na	na	na	na	na
Vietnam	na	na	na	na	na	na	na	na	na	na	na	na	na	na	na	na
Zimbabwe	na	na	na	na	na	na	na	na	na	na	na	na	na	na	na	na
Total	na	22	22	22	20	21	24	24	20	20	23	22	20	24	21	21

RANKING

Country	2000
Portugal	31
Netherlands	31
Belgium	30
Iceland	28
Czech Republic	27
Luxembourg	26
Ireland	25
Spain	25
Hungary	24
Estonia	24
Finland	23
Denmark	23
Germany	22
Italy	22
Sweden	22
Bulgaria	21
France	21
Lithuania	21
Poland	21
Great Britain	20
Northern Ireland	19
Ukraine	19
Latvia	19
Russian Fed.	19
Slovakia	18
Belarus	18
Romania	18
Malta	18
Austria	16
Greece	15
Slovenia	14
Croatia	13
Turkey	11
Total	22

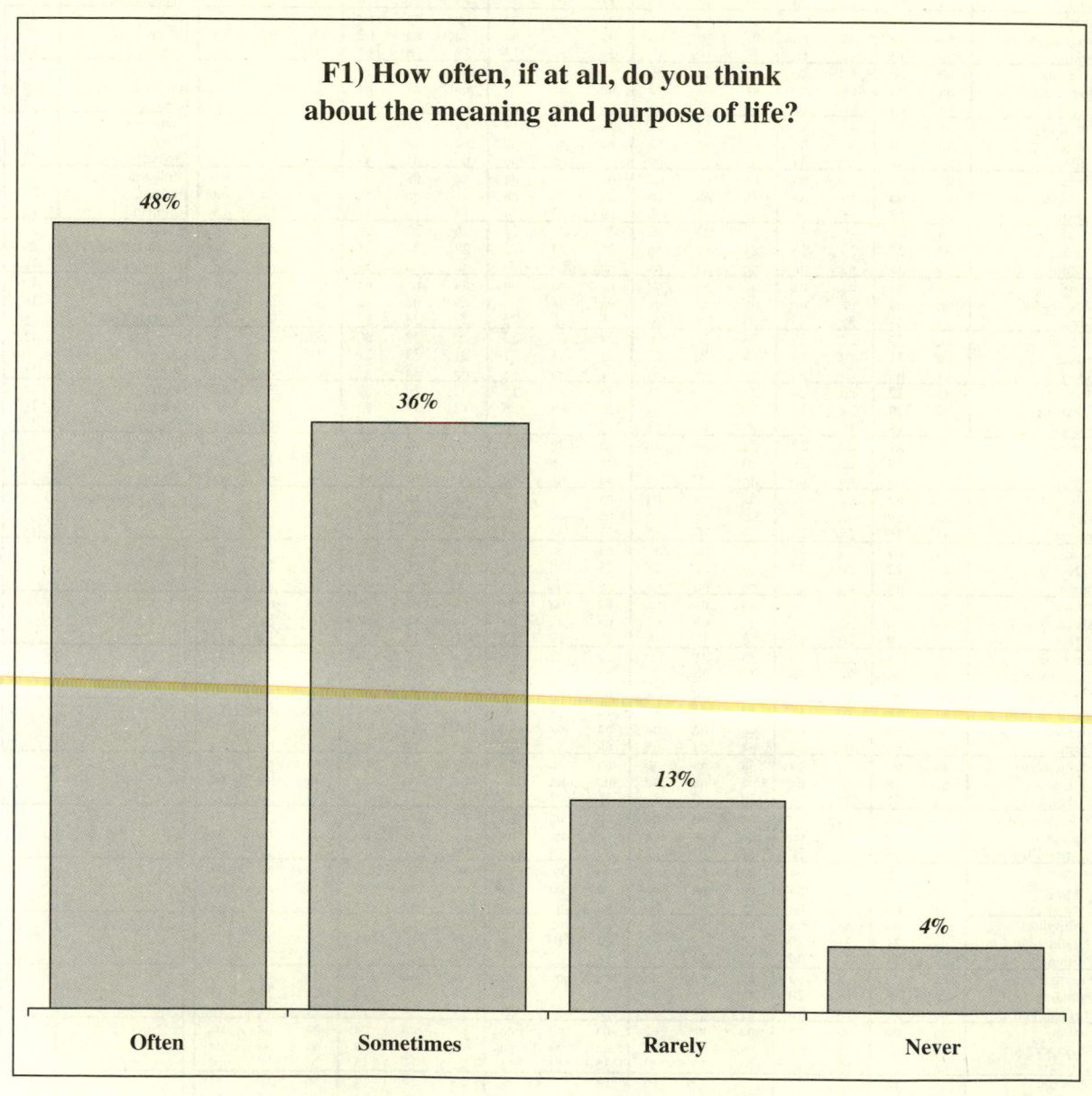

F1) How often, if at all, do you think about the meaning and purpose of life?

48%

36%

13%

4%

Often   Sometimes   Rarely   Never

F001) THINKING ABOUT MEANING AND PURPOSE OF LIFE

How often, if at all, do you think about the meaning and purpose of life?

Often (%)

(WVS: V182; EVS: o6)

Country	Wave 1990	Wave 2000	Gender Male	Gender Female	Age 16-29	Age 30-49	Age 50+	Education Lower	Education Middle	Education Upper	Income Lower	Income Middle	Income Upper	Values Mat	Values Mixed	Values Postm.
Albania	na	53	53	54	61	54	46	49	53	65	54	55	51	55	50	49
Algeria	na	50	47	52	48	49	54	53	48	49	49	50	49	51	49	54
Argentina	57	51	46	56	46	56	51	46	57	66	50	48	57	44	52	58
Armenia	na	60	55	65	58	58	68	65	60	60	61	54	69	55	64	73
Australia	na	44	39	50	41	45	46	42	41	50	48	45	42	33	45	45
Austria	28	34	30	38	28	32	38	33	33	38	35	34	30	33	32	37
Azerbaijan	na	42	44	41	40	43	44	48	39	48	43	39	47	43	41	42
Bangladesh	na	47	53	40	44	45	64	44	47	56	43	43	55	50	43	49
Belarus	35	36	32	39	40	33	35	31	37	40	35	35	37	33	39	36
Belgium	29	na	na	na	na	na	na	na	na	na	na	na	na	na	na	na
Bosnia and Herz.	na	41	42	41	44	40	40	40	42	40	44	39	43	43	40	53
Brazil	44	37	36	38	36	37	41	35	36	49	36	33	41	33	37	44
Bulgaria	44	46	40	51	44	50	43	38	49	53	46	50	43	38	56	44
Canada	43	52	49	54	50	54	49	51	54	48	58	53	48	49	51	55
Chile	53	50	49	52	58	49	45	48	50	57	50	50	54	45	48	68
China	32	32	37	28	42	32	26	27	36	35	30	36	31	31	38	47
Colombia	na	70	70	71	68	72	69	61	66	83	62	68	79	67	66	62
Croatia	na	41	38	44	39	46	37	42	40	44	49	39	37	29	43	42
Czech Republic	31	na	na	na	na	na	na	na	na	na	na	na	na	na	na	na
Denmark	29	37	32	41	36	38	35	33	34	44	43	32	34	25	36	41
Dominican Rep.	na	56	52	59	59	49	73	50	50	59	59	50	60	59	55	56
Egypt	na	52	55	49	53	52	49	46	56	61	53	52	54	51	53	55
El Salvador	na	54	55	52	52	54	55	47	60	62	48	55	63	na	na	na
Estonia	35	40	31	47	41	40	39	36	40	44	45	40	41	41	40	50
Finland	38	42	31	53	37	38	49	42	42	46	54	40	35	35	43	56
France	39	na	na	na	na	na	na	na	na	na	na	na	na	na	na	na
Georgia	na	73	69	76	69	77	72	76	72	73	77	74	67	73	73	76
Germany	40	22	21	23	17	23	23	19	23	33	17	27	23	16	24	27
Great Britain	36	24	23	26	24	19	29	22	24	29	24	23	22	na	na	na
Greece	na	na	na	na	na	na	na	na	na	na	na	na	na	na	na	na
Hungary	45	na	na	na	na	na	na	na	na	na	na	na	na	na	na	na
Iceland	36	na	na	na	na	na	na	na	na	na	na	na	na	na	na	na
India	34	36	37	35	37	36	36	32	34	46	28	32	43	38	39	44
Indonesia	na	58	58	59	65	59	55	50	58	67	51	60	73	59	60	71
Iran	na	46	46	46	44	44	54	48	41	49	48	43	46	44	47	56
Ireland	34	na	na	na	na	na	na	na	na	na	na	na	na	na	na	na
Israel	na	na	na	na	na	na	na	na	na	na	na	na	na	na	na	na
Italy	47	50	43	57	47	53	50	46	53	56	51	50	50	46	50	53
Japan	21	26	27	25	30	23	27	25	24	32	28	24	26	25	25	34
Jordan	na	60	57	64	60	65	50	56	60	69	61	61	62	60	61	62
Korea, South	39	41	40	43	52	40	33	29	37	49	41	43	41	34	48	50
Latvia	36	na	na	na	na	na	na	na	na	na	na	na	na	na	na	na
Lithuania	41	40	32	46	31	40	45	42	38	44	48	43	31	39	41	42
Luxembourg	na	36	32	40	27	36	42	34	35	43	37	42	39	30	35	47
Macedonia	na	50	48	53	57	51	44	46	52	55	54	48	50	47	52	64
Malta	na	na	na	na	na	na	na	na	na	na	na	na	na	na	na	na
Mexico	40	44	46	43	50	44	36	37	50	64	35	45	58	43	43	57
Moldova	na	57	55	59	50	60	61	57	55	62	61	56	57	58	58	50
Montenegro	na	37	34	40	43	36	34	30	38	50	41	38	37	37	39	27
Morocco	na	75	77	73	75	76	73	75	72	77	68	71	77	75	77	64
Netherlands	30	na	na	na	na	na	na	na	na	na	na	na	na	na	na	na
New Zealand	na	43	38	48	38	45	45	41	44	46	48	43	39	48	42	44
Nigeria	59	56	59	53	55	58	52	50	58	61	55	55	58	60	54	54
Northern Ireland	33	na	na	na	na	na	na	na	na	na	na	na	na	na	na	na
Norway	31	32	27	37	30	32	33	31	30	35	na	na	na	27	31	42
Pakistan	na	36	34	37	28	34	52	34	37	37	35	34	40	32	40	27
Peru	na	54	55	53	51	54	58	44	54	60	53	52	58	43	55	64
Philippines	na	64	62	66	62	65	64	60	66	66	65	62	65	65	62	71
Poland	34	na	na	na	na	na	na	na	na	na	na	na	na	na	na	na
Portugal	43	na	na	na	na	na	na	na	na	na	na	na	na	na	na	na
Puerto Rico	na	76	77	76	77	83	71	57	75	80	68	79	80	74	76	81
Romania	45	na	na	na	na	na	na	na	na	na	na	na	na	na	na	na
Russian Fed.	41	49	37	40	45	49	50	47	50	47	49	52	45	50	48	47
Serbia	na	39	37	40	43	42	33	34	39	45	40	41	38	32	43	49
Singapore	na	32	34	30	41	26	18	22	36	44	28	32	36	22	35	41
Slovakia	na	na	na	na	na	na	na	na	na	na	na	na	na	na	na	na
Slovenia	37	na	na	na	na	na	na	na	na	na	na	na	na	na	na	na
South Africa	57	56	56	57	58	56	52	49	66	72	49	58	63	52	62	42
Spain	26	22	20	24	22	22	23	21	22	27	24	21	25	19	22	29
Sweden	24	37	32	41	27	40	39	36	34	42	39	39	31	32	34	47
Switzerland	44	43	38	47	40	43	44	42	43	45	47	47	39	36	42	51
Taiwan	na	28	29	28	33	29	23	19	32	35	23	26	36	24	33	38
Tanzania	na	84	84	85	84	84	87	84	84	88	83	83	87	81	87	83
Turkey	38	na	na	na	na	na	na	na	na	na	na	na	na	na	na	na
Uganda	na	59	57	61	63	54	64	62	60	41	53	45	55	61	58	60
Ukraine	na	51	46	54	47	47	56	51	51	51	59	47	46	48	51	64
United States	48	58	54	62	56	59	60	60	58	58	61	58	54	61	55	65
Uruguay	na	42	38	45	48	46	36	36	50	54	36	41	49	32	41	53
Venezuela	na	66	64	67	65	69	60	56	68	71	64	64	66	60	68	66
Vietnam	na	58	63	54	55	59	59	47	73	72	61	53	63	47	66	69
Zimbabwe	na	70	69	70	67	75	67	69	70	92	70	69	77	73	66	76
Total	38	48	46	49	49	48	46	44	48	54	49	47	49	46	49	52

RANKING

Country	2000
Tanzania	84
Puerto Rico	76
Morocco	75
Georgia	73
Colombia	70
Zimbabwe	70
Venezuela	66
Philippines	64
Armenia	60
Jordan	60
Uganda	59
Vietnam	58
Indonesia	58
United States	58
Moldova	57
South Africa	56
Dominican Rep.	56
Nigeria	56
Peru	54
El Salvador	54
Albania	53
Egypt	52
Canada	52
Argentina	51
Ukraine	51
Chile	50
Italy	50
Macedonia	50
Algeria	50
Russian Fed.	49
Bangladesh	47
Iran	46
Bulgaria	46
Australia	44
Mexico	44
New Zealand	43
Switzerland	43
Finland	42
Azerbaijan	42
Uruguay	42
Korea, South	41
Bosnia and Herz.	41
Croatia	41
Estonia	40
Lithuania	40
Serbia	39
Brazil	37
Montenegro	37
Sweden	37
Denmark	37
India	36
Luxembourg	36
Belarus	36
Pakistan	36
Austria	34
China	32
Norway	32
Singapore	32
Taiwan	28
Japan	26
Great Britain	24
Spain	22
Germany	22
Total	48

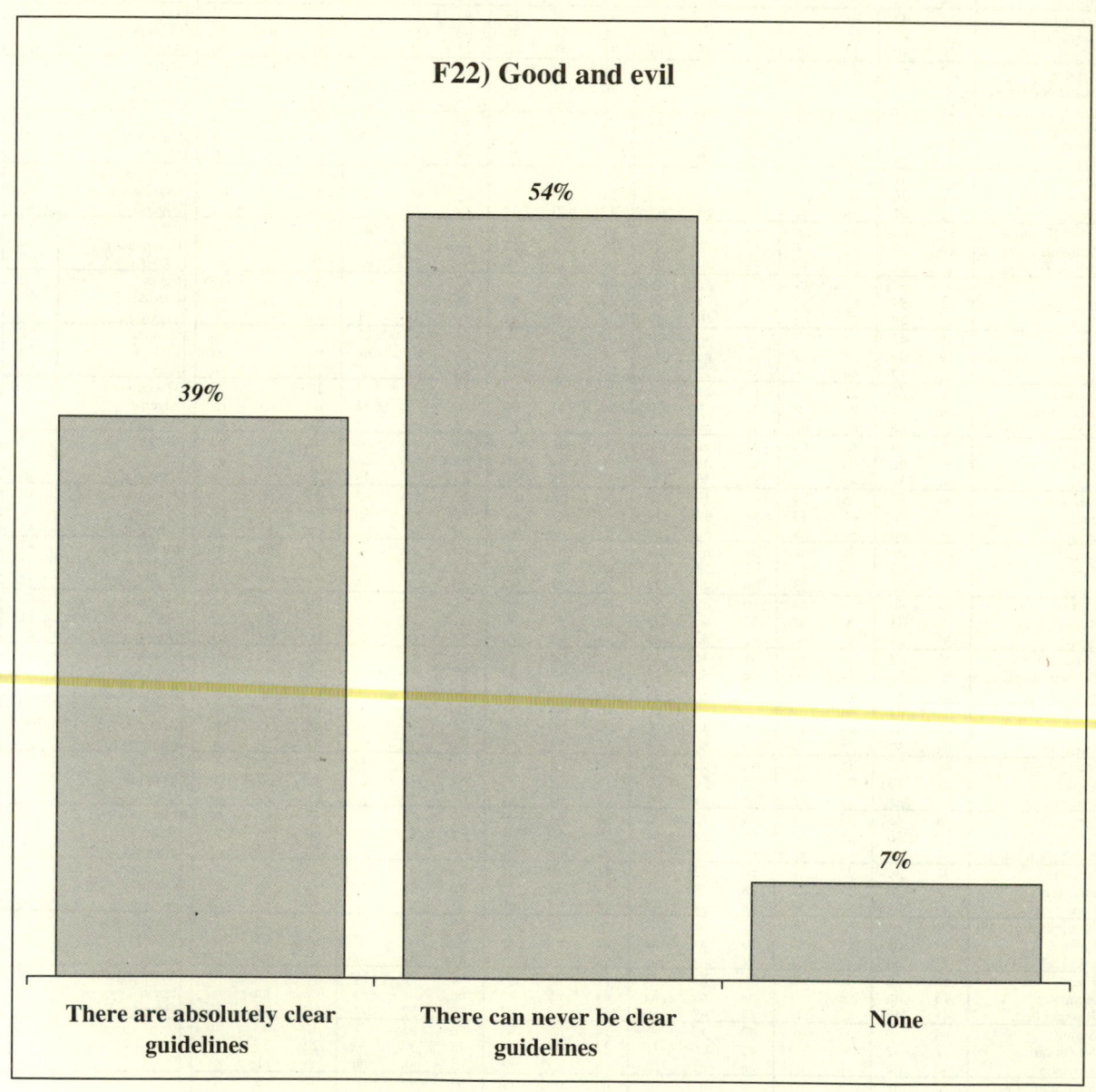

F22) Good and evil

54%

39%

7%

There are absolutely clear
guidelines

There can never be clear
guidelines

None

F022) GOOD AND EVIL

Here are two statements which people sometimes make when discussing good and evil.

Which one comes closest to your own point of view?

There are absolutely clear guidelines about what is good and evil (%)

(WVS: V183; EVS: V100)

Country	Wave 1990	Wave 2000	Gender Male	Gender Female	Age 16-29	Age 30-49	Age 50+	Education Lower	Education Middle	Education Upper	Income Lower	Income Middle	Income Upper	Values Mat	Values Mixed	Values Postm.
Albania	na	49	48	50	50	49	49	52	47	49	47	51	50	44	52	58
Algeria	na	na	na	na	na	na	na	na	na	na	na	na	na	na	na	na
Argentina	33	39	39	39	36	40	40	39	39	38	44	34	40	43	40	32
Armenia	na	41	41	41	39	40	45	45	43	32	38	46	38	43	42	24
Australia	na	42	42	41	33	43	48	44	44	37	45	44	36	57	43	37
Austria	28	20	21	20	15	16	28	23	18	18	25	20	18	28	22	15
Azerbaijan	na	57	58	56	57	55	60	53	55	60	57	53	62	59	52	62
Bangladesh	na	48	48	48	43	49	61	51	44	44	55	48	42	49	47	40
Belarus	26	25	21	28	17	24	32	34	24	15	32	22	20	26	25	15
Belgium	33	31	31	30	22	29	37	39	31	25	37	28	26	38	32	21
Bosnia and Herz.	na	54	56	52	50	56	55	59	53	52	50	54	57	55	53	56
Brazil	46	49	50	48	48	50	50	49	51	47	52	48	47	49	50	44
Bulgaria	47	33	32	34	24	32	39	41	31	27	37	35	30	31	36	41
Canada	31	42	41	44	35	46	43	46	44	37	40	46	40	46	44	38
Chile	35	53	54	52	47	54	57	57	52	47	56	53	47	60	53	41
China	35	36	37	36	29	36	45	47	32	20	34	40	34	37	33	35
Colombia	na	38	37	39	35	39	41	38	38	37	36	39	38	42	42	32
Croatia	na	35	37	34	23	37	41	40	31	36	54	28	33	35	38	23
Czech Republic	na	24	24	23	17	21	29	26	20	24	30	21	20	28	22	18
Denmark	10	10	13	8	10	9	13	11	6	8	16	8	7	12	10	5
Dominican Rep.	na	35	40	31	32	40	55	34	38	34	40	35	32	30	36	36
Egypt	na	na	na	na	na	na	na	na	na	na	na	na	na	na	na	na
El Salvador	na	49	49	48	48	48	53	49	50	49	50	47	52	na	na	na
Estonia	23	30	32	28	24	24	39	34	27	33	37	32	26	30	30	43
Finland	26	29	27	32	21	26	37	29	27	34	31	26	33	35	28	28
France	24	25	28	23	16	23	33	30	20	19	24	26	24	30	28	13
Georgia	na	60	61	60	55	59	66	59	61	59	61	59	59	61	60	52
Germany	23	35	35	34	34	31	40	43	27	29	41	36	30	38	34	32
Great Britain	36	42	41	42	30	40	49	47	38	39	47	33	41	na	na	na
Greece	na	16	18	15	11	20	19	25	17	13	16	17	15	18	15	15
Hungary	17	15	16	15	15	13	18	15	14	19	14	18	13	18	14	5
Iceland	11	9	9	9	7	9	10	8	10	9	12	8	8	10	9	7
India	45	30	30	30	32	29	31	30	27	32	34	31	27	30	31	22
Indonesia	na	na	na	na	na	na	na	na	na	na	na	na	na	na	na	na
Iran	na	na	na	na	na	na	na	na	na	na	na	na	na	na	na	na
Ireland	42	39	37	40	33	36	45	40	39	36	42	38	32	43	40	29
Israel	na	na	na	na	na	na	na	na	na	na	na	na	na	na	na	na
Italy	45	36	37	36	24	37	43	40	33	36	40	36	36	39	37	32-
Japan	15	19	21	18	8	17	26	27	19	16	19	18	22	18	19	16
Jordan	na	na	na	na	na	na	na	na	na	na	na	na	na	na	na	na
Korea, South	23	37	37	37	26	38	48	45	40	32	39	37	35	40	34	32
Latvia	27	41	40	42	38	37	46	42	41	41	43	43	38	47	38	40
Lithuania	23	35	31	38	23	31	47	55	30	22	49	39	26	48	29	34
Luxembourg	na	23	24	22	19	20	30	25	20	28	28	21	20	18	25	23
Macedonia	na	55	54	57	57	53	56	62	54	49	60	51	52	57	54	50
Malta	na	48	48	48	41	48	54	57	47	37	59	56	45	56	45	39
Mexico	38	41	42	40	37	42	45	45	36	35	45	36	38	48	39	29
Moldova	na	39	37	41	30	39	48	47	40	32	47	40	38	37	41	40
Montenegro	na	49	48	49	33	48	60	61	43	36	62	55	39	59	42	24
Morocco	na	79	79	78	74	81	87	81	71	66	91	79	71	78	79	79
Netherlands	23	27	28	25	20	27	29	35	24	21	30	27	22	37	28	17
New Zealand	na	42	41	43	29	41	47	45	49	35	47	40	39	46	42	35
Nigeria	60	na	na	na	na	na	na	na	na	na	na	na	na	na	na	na
Northern Ireland	51	47	46	48	42	41	52	52	46	37	50	47	39	52	45	49
Norway	32	29	31	27	24	30	32	31	26	31	na	na	na	34	29	21
Pakistan	na	na	na	na	na	na	na	na	na	na	na	na	na	na	na	na
Peru	na	53	55	51	51	53	58	53	52	54	54	51	53	53	53	52
Philippines	na	55	56	55	53	56	57	54	55	57	58	54	54	58	53	53
Poland	33	51	52	49	42	50	58	50	50	54	51	50	53	55	50	44
Portugal	31	39	38	40	36	40	40	39	43	27	43	40	32	44	36	37
Puerto Rico	na	45	46	45	44	47	44	34	50	44	41	49	42	39	47	42
Romania	23	40	37	42	35	33	49	49	38	27	45	47	32	42	38	21
Russian Fed.	31	39	37	40	27	39	46	44	38	38	43	39	33	39	39	39
Serbia	na	47	46	47	38	44	53	55	43	41	48	48	45	50	44	39
Singapore	na	38	38	38	36	41	38	40	36	40	44	36	34	39	38	33
Slovakia	na	36	36	37	29	36	43	42	34	32	38	39	35	40	35	28
Slovenia	21	22	23	21	18	20	27	21	23	18	24	20	17	20	24	15
South Africa	52	63	62	64	58	65	66	60	66	78	60	64	70	68	59	63
Spain	34	39	38	40	32	34	48	46	34	30	42	42	39	52	39	25
Sweden	19	16	19	13	10	15	21	21	13	16	15	19	14	30	16	13
Switzerland	22	28	29	27	18	27	36	32	26	31	33	31	25	35	29	15
Taiwan	na	28	28	28	23	29	30	25	37	26	26	26	31	28	29	17
Tanzania	na	69	68	70	68	68	74	73	65	64	71	64	68	67	69	63
Turkey	34	35	38	33	32	39	37	37	32	38	39	34	32	33	37	31
Uganda	na	59	58	60	57	61	60	59	59	63	55	59	52	63	57	58
Ukraine	na	43	42	43	32	44	48	47	45	36	50	39	40	44	41	41
United States	50	49	46	52	41	56	47	51	49	49	50	49	49	54	53	41
Uruguay	na	32	33	31	27	29	36	34	29	29	34	34	29	39	35	20
Venezuela	na	41	42	40	41	38	46	47	43	30	46	41	37	48	40	32
Vietnam	na	58	57	60	57	56	63	60	58	53	64	63	51	64	58	50
Zimbabwe	na	57	59	56	56	56	64	58	56	62	58	54	53	60	55	58
Total	31	39	40	39	36	39	43	43	38	35	43	39	36	44	38	31

RANKING

Country	2000
Morocco	79
Tanzania	69
South Africa	63
Georgia	60
Uganda	59
Vietnam	58
Zimbabwe	57
Azerbaijan	57
Philippines	55
Macedonia	55
Bosnia and Herz.	54
Chile	53
Peru	53
Poland	51
Brazil	49
United States	49
Albania	49
Montenegro	49
El Salvador	49
Malta	48
Bangladesh	48
Northern Ireland	47
Serbia	47
Puerto Rico	45
Ukraine	43
Canada	42
Australia	42
New Zealand	42
Great Britain	42
Armenia	41
Latvia	41
Mexico	41
Venezuela	41
Romania	40
Moldova	39
Portugal	39
Spain	39
Ireland	39
Argentina	39
Russian Fed.	39
Colombia	38
Singapore	38
Korea, South	37
Italy	36
Slovakia	36
China	36
Turkey	35
Croatia	35
Lithuania	35
Dominican Rep.	35
Germany	35
Bulgaria	33
Uruguay	32
Belgium	31
India	30
Estonia	30
Finland	29
Norway	29
Taiwan	28
Switzerland	28
Netherlands	27
France	25
Belarus	25
Czech Republic	24
Luxembourg	23
Slovenia	22
Austria	20
Japan	19
Greece	16
Sweden	16
Hungary	15
Denmark	10
Iceland	9
Total	39

F024) BELONG TO RELIGIOUS DENOMINATION

Do you belong to a religious denomination?

Yes (%)   (WVS: *V184; EVS: V101)

Country	Wave 1990	Wave 2000	Gender Male	Gender Female	Age 16-29	Age 30-49	Age 50+	Edu Lower	Edu Middle	Edu Upper	Inc Lower	Inc Middle	Inc Upper	Val Mat	Val Mixed	Val Postm.
Albania	na	87	85	89	85	84	93	89	84	89	89	88	84	91	83	92
Algeria	na	na	na	na	na	na	na	na	na	na	na	na	na	na	na	na
Argentina	84	87	84	90	83	87	91	87	87	89	90	85	87	87	89	82
Armenia	na	87	82	91	86	88	85	88	86	86	85	86	88	87	88	75
Australia	na	81	77	85	77	78	89	86	82	76	85	81	76	85	84	76
Austria	86	88	86	90	91	88	86	88	88	88	86	88	89	89	89	86
Azerbaijan	na	94	94	94	93	95	94	97	96	90	97	97	86	95	91	94
Bangladesh	na	100	100	100	100	100	100	100	100	100	100	100	100	100	100	100
Belarus	30	52	41	61	51	49	57	61	51	43	61	49	43	54	51	50
Belgium	68	64	59	68	53	57	74	72	61	61	66	63	60	72	64	54
Bosnia and Herz.	na	75	75	76	79	74	73	83	75	69	74	75	77	79	73	79
Brazil	88	88	84	92	83	90	94	88	88	89	89	89	86	91	87	89
Bulgaria	34	70	65	75	62	64	79	81	64	65	79	66	65	72	70	71
Canada	74	69	64	73	55	67	79	75	68	65	72	71	62	71	74	59
Chile	82	66	60	72	65	61	75	72	63	63	69	65	63	73	67	53
China	4	6	5	7	6	6	6	5	7	9	5	6	8	5	7	3
Colombia	na	92	89	95	88	94	95	93	92	90	92	93	90	91	93	87
Croatia	na	89	87	90	88	89	90	97	85	80	88	89	89	94	91	78
Czech Republic	56	34	28	39	21	23	50	35	34	25	43	32	25	39	31	36
Denmark	92	90	88	92	90	88	92	92	90	87	91	91	88	94	93	78
Dominican Rep.	na	76	71	80	75	78	91	74	70	79	77	76	76	77	74	85
Egypt	na	100	100	100	100	100	100	100	100	100	100	100	100	100	100	100
El Salvador	na	84	82	86	81	83	90	83	85	86	82	83	88	na	na	na
Estonia	13	25	18	30	14	23	33	29	22	25	30	30	18	28	23	20
Finland	89	88	84	91	92	85	88	88	88	89	90	85	88	92	89	80
France	62	58	55	60	46	54	67	60	53	55	54	61	54	65	59	43
Georgia	na	94	93	95	94	95	92	92	94	94	93	94	94	94	93	100
Germany	35	77	73	79	73	72	83	83	73	67	76	76	83	78	77	75
Great Britain	58	83	80	87	76	84	89	83	86	78	82	83	86	na	na	na
Greece	na	96	94	97	95	96	97	98	97	95	97	96	95	98	97	92
Hungary	58	57	53	61	43	54	68	61	48	54	61	59	53	64	51	46
Iceland	98	96	96	95	93	95	99	97	98	90	97	96	95	98	96	89
India	99	93	94	92	95	93	92	94	92	93	90	94	94	94	92	93
Indonesia	na	100	100	100	100	100	100	100	100	100	100	100	100	100	100	100
Iran	na	99	99	99	99	99	99	99	99	99	99	99	99	100	99	100
Ireland	96	91	88	93	86	89	96	89	92	92	91	92	90	91	91	87
Israel	na	100	100	100	100	100	100	100	100	100	100	100	100	100	100	100
Italy	85	82	78	87	80	80	86	88	79	74	83	82	78	90	82	79
Japan	na	41	43	39	19	32	59	56	42	34	45	46	37	43	41	36
Jordan	na	100	100	100	100	100	100	100	100	100	100	100	100	100	100	100
Korea, South	72	63	57	69	60	63	69	64	65	60	60	63	68	63	63	62
Latvia	37	59	53	64	44	54	70	67	54	66	63	60	54	63	59	57
Lithuania	63	81	72	89	72	75	94	92	77	81	88	79	78	83	82	74
Luxembourg	na	72	70	74	59	71	82	78	69	72	69	77	71	76	73	63
Macedonia	na	86	88	84	85	86	86	92	85	79	89	83	85	89	85	90
Malta	na	99	97	100	97	99	100	99	99	96	100	99	98	98	99	97
Mexico	85	81	78	83	76	80	88	85	76	72	83	80	77	84	80	67
Moldova	na	100	100	100	100	100	100	100	100	100	100	100	100	100	100	100
Montenegro	na	97	97	98	97	97	97	98	96	97	97	99	99	98	97	93
Morocco	na	100	100	100	100	100	100	100	100	100	100	100	100	100	100	100
Netherlands	51	45	42	48	34	38	58	49	44	43	43	45	43	58	46	34
New Zealand	na	82	80	84	64	80	90	86	83	76	84	80	82	78	84	77
Nigeria	95	99	99	99	99	99	99	99	99	99	99	99	99	98	100	100
Northern Ireland	91	86	83	89	81	78	95	91	81	84	88	86	85	88	86	87
Norway	90	91	89	93	90	89	93	92	93	86	na	na	na	95	92	78
Pakistan	na	71	69	73	69	71	74	79	70	41	78	70	63	73	68	67
Peru	na	95	94	97	93	97	97	95	97	94	96	96	94	96	95	97
Philippines	na	90	92	89	89	90	92	89	89	92	92	90	90	88	92	91
Poland	na	96	95	97	95	96	97	98	95	87	97	96	94	98	95	92
Portugal	72	89	84	94	82	93	91	93	82	79	94	92	85	92	89	75
Puerto Rico	na	88	87	90	83	86	93	90	90	88	89	90	88	88	90	85
Romania	94	98	97	99	98	97	98	99	97	97	97	98	97	98	98	92
Russian Fed.	37	51	39	60	43	46	61	62	49	50	61	50	42	55	46	36
Serbia	na	94	93	95	94	95	94	97	93	91	96	93	94	96	93	87
Singapore	na	80	78	82	78	79	92	87	79	67	92	80	73	88	78	69
Slovakia	na	77	71	82	66	74	88	83	76	65	85	78	73	79	76	69
Slovenia	74	70	69	71	65	66	78	82	70	50	76	71	59	78	68	70
South Africa	na	86	79	94	85	84	96	85	87	88	85	92	80	86	87	86
Spain	85	83	77	89	74	81	91	88	78	77	87	81	81	90	84	68
Sweden	82	76	74	78	76	73	78	79	74	76	75	76	78	70	77	74
Switzerland	92	100	100	100	100	100	100	100	100	100	100	100	100	100	100	100
Taiwan	na	79	72	86	67	81	83	89	79	70	82	82	72	81	79	62
Tanzania	na	98	99	99	99	99	99	99	99	98	98	99	99	100	99	100
Turkey	97	98	98	98	97	98	100	99	98	90	99	98	94	99	98	94
Uganda	na	99	98	100	100	99	97	98	99	100	99	99	99	99	99	99
Ukraine	na	56	43	67	53	53	62	77	53	52	59	56	55	57	53	64
United States	77	79	73	84	65	80	88	70	75	84	74	78	85	84	80	73
Uruguay	na	52	40	61	43	47	60	57	45	48	55	51	50	61	54	42
Venezuela	na	73	69	77	65	76	83	76	70	78	71	70	73	76	72	70
Vietnam	na	54	50	58	54	51	57	62	43	45	48	57	52	62	49	40
Zimbabwe	na	100	100	100	100	100	100	100	100	100	100	100	100	100	100	100
Total	70	80	78	83	79	79	83	84	78	79	81	80	78	82	80	75

RANKING

Country	2000
Jordan	100
Moldova	100
Morocco	100
Zimbabwe	100
Switzerland	100
Egypt	100
Bangladesh	100
Israel	100
Indonesia	100
Nigeria	99
Uganda	99
Iran	99
Malta	99
Tanzania	98
Turkey	98
Romania	98
Montenegro	97
Greece	96
Iceland	96
Poland	96
Peru	95
Azerbaijan	94
Serbia	94
Georgia	94
India	93
Colombia	92
Ireland	91
Norway	91
Philippines	90
Denmark	90
Portugal	89
Croatia	89
Puerto Rico	88
Austria	88
Finland	88
Brazil	88
Albania	87
Argentina	87
Armenia	87
South Africa	86
Northern Ireland	86
Macedonia	86
El Salvador	84
Great Britain	83
Spain	83
Italy	82
New Zealand	82
Lithuania	81
Australia	81
Mexico	81
Singapore	80
Taiwan	79
United States	79
Slovakia	77
Germany	77
Dominican Rep.	76
Sweden	76
Bosnia and Herz.	75
Venezuela	73
Luxembourg	72
Pakistan	71
Bulgaria	70
Slovenia	70
Canada	69
Chile	66
Belgium	64
Korea, South	63
Latvia	59
France	58
Hungary	57
Ukraine	56
Vietnam	54
Belarus	52
Uruguay	52
Russian Fed.	51
Netherlands	45
Japan	41
Czech Republic	34
Estonia	25
China	6
Total	80

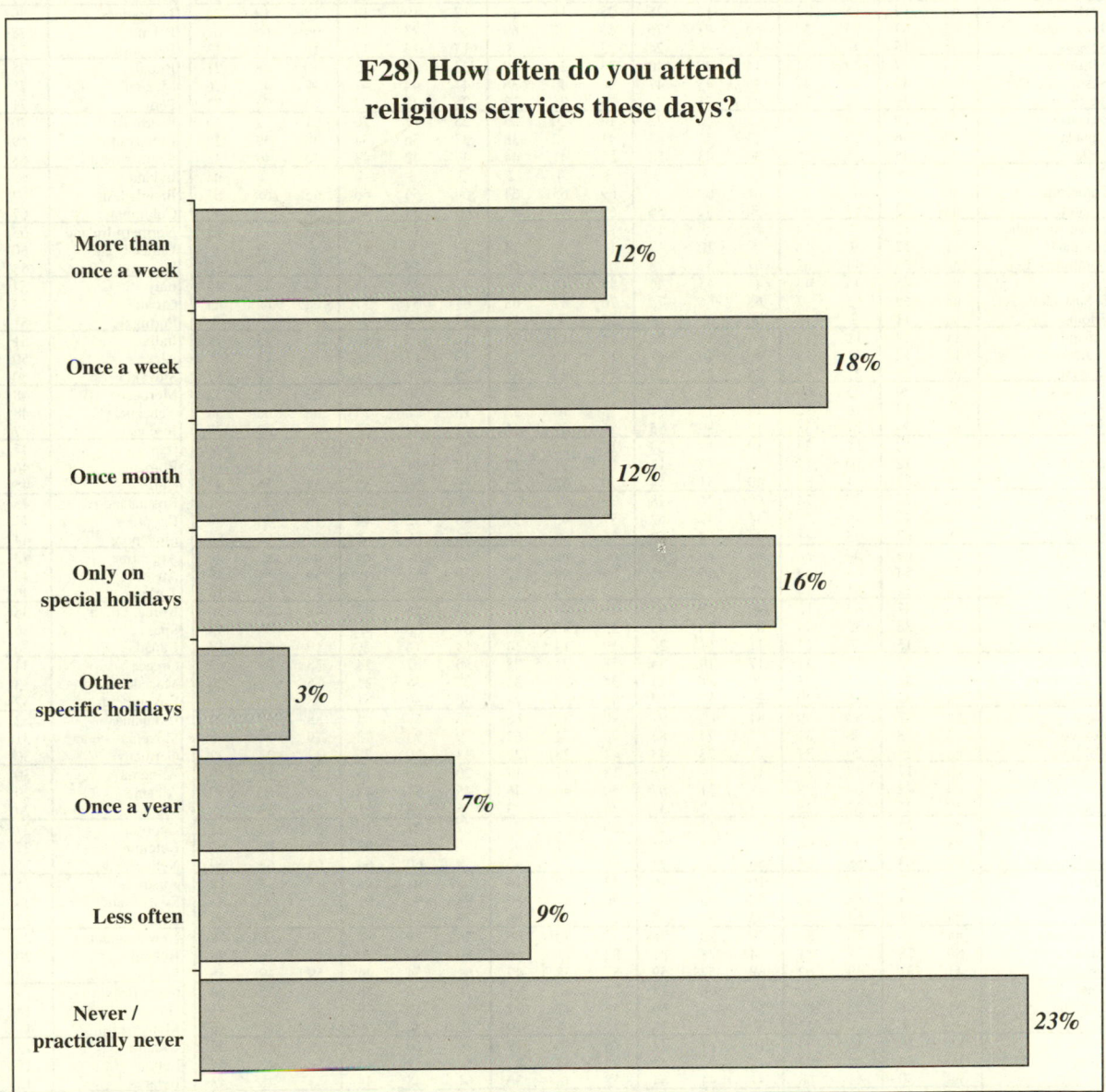

F28) How often do you attend religious services these days?

- More than once a week — 12%
- Once a week — 18%
- Once month — 12%
- Only on special holidays — 16%
- Other specific holidays — 3%
- Once a year — 7%
- Less often — 9%
- Never / practically never — 23%

F028) HOW OFTEN DO YOU ATTEND RELIGIOUS SERVICES

Apart from weddings, funerals and christenings, about how often do you attend religious services these days

Once a month or more (%) (WVS: V185; EVS: V105)

Country	Wave 1990	Wave 2000	Gender Male	Gender Female	Age 16-29	Age 30-49	Age 50+	Education Lower	Education Middle	Education Upper	Income Lower	Income Middle	Income Upper	Values Mat	Values Mixed	Values Postm.
Albania	na	29	25	34	25	27	37	34	27	24	33	30	26	28	29	39
Algeria	na	50	73	27	43	50	65	58	49	46	53	50	50	50	52	47
Argentina	55	43	33	52	34	44	50	44	40	44	46	44	39	42	45	38
Armenia	na	30	21	37	32	29	28	30	30	28	27	32	31	31	28	25
Australia	na	25	21	29	23	23	30	28	22	27	26	26	20	29	28	19
Austria	44	42	40	45	25	43	51	44	40	44	47	42	40	38	45	39
Azerbaijan	na	14	15	13	11	13	25	28	13	14	12	19	14	12	17	24
Bangladesh	na	67	75	57	60	71	76	63	75	69	66	73	61	66	68	61
Belarus	6	15	6	21	10	9	24	22	13	8	17	13	12	18	11	13
Belgium	31	27	23	31	14	20	40	33	23	29	33	28	23	30	28	21
Bosnia and Herz.	na	45	44	47	46	43	47	60	44	36	47	44	47	47	46	26
Brazil	50	75	72	78	74	75	77	75	75	73	76	79	73	74	76	71
Bulgaria	9	20	16	24	23	16	22	18	20	25	23	17	20	21	22	16
Canada	40	36	30	41	23	33	47	41	32	38	37	36	34	38	39	28
Chile	47	45	35	55	36	43	58	51	41	44	47	42	48	46	49	33
China	1	3	2	4	3	3	3	3	4	2	3	3	4	3	4	na
Colombia	na	67	61	72	61	69	73	69	65	64	68	66	66	65	68	65
Croatia	na	53	44	61	50	52	56	62	47	47	62	54	47	58	55	40
Czech Republic	21	12	10	14	10	5	18	13	10	11	17	10	7	15	10	14
Denmark	11	12	9	15	5	10	18	11	8	14	17	8	12	6	12	9
Dominican Rep.	na	55	44	63	57	51	73	61	53	56	58	59	49	61	53	58
Egypt	na	45	45	45	44	45	46	45	44	44	47	45	45	44	45	46
El Salvador	na	69	65	72	68	66	75	70	67	68	67	67	71	na	na	na
Estonia	na	11	7	15	5	8	18	15	9	11	17	14	6	14	9	4
Finland	11	14	11	17	7	11	21	14	12	20	18	12	15	12	15	12
France	17	12	11	13	5	10	17	12	10	13	13	11	12	13	13	7
Georgia	na	27	22	32	36	26	20	24	26	35	25	28	31	26	28	37
Germany	20	30	25	34	20	22	43	34	27	28	31	30	33	29	31	32
Great Britain	24	19	16	22	12	17	24	15	18	25	13	22	25	na	na	na
Greece	na	34	27	38	19	39	55	51	39	26	41	33	27	43	32	27
Hungary	34	18	11	23	10	12	27	18	15	18	21	18	15	20	15	9
Iceland	9	12	10	15	5	12	18	10	11	17	13	11	10	11	12	11
India	71	51	51	52	49	51	54	50	52	54	46	50	55	54	54	47
Indonesia	na	75	77	74	69	76	78	78	77	71	70	82	76	76	76	71
Iran	na	47	49	43	41	47	62	57	43	39	48	52	44	49	45	39
Ireland	88	67	63	71	44	64	89	75	63	66	76	69	62	73	67	58
Israel	na	na	na	na	na	na	na	na	na	na	na	na	na	na	na	na
Italy	53	54	44	63	40	50	65	59	49	52	59	53	49	59	54	49
Japan	14	12	11	14	2	12	17	13	14	7	14	15	11	13	12	14
Jordan	na	47	83	12	40	45	66	49	47	41	43	56	42	48	48	36
Korea, South	64	38	32	44	34	38	43	35	40	36	34	38	43	38	38	43
Latvia	9	15	7	22	11	11	20	19	14	14	19	14	9	19	13	13
Lithuania	na	32	20	41	17	19	54	58	21	28	50	32	24	38	29	23
Luxembourg	na	32	31	33	20	24	47	34	29	35	27	35	31	35	32	26
Macedonia	na	33	36	29	20	33	37	44	27	28	36	30	31	38	29	40
Malta	na	87	83	90	81	86	91	90	85	88	85	89	83	80	87	70
Mexico	63	75	68	81	71	74	83	79	71	67	79	73	72	79	74	68
Moldova	na	29	20	37	21	23	43	44	23	27	38	30	25	33	23	22
Montenegro	na	17	17	17	15	17	19	18	17	17	20	15	15	16	18	19
Morocco	na	48	69	28	38	51	67	50	40	46	45	54	48	45	50	50
Netherlands	30	25	22	28	13	17	39	30	24	23	25	25	21	38	25	19
New Zealand	na	22	17	26	18	17	28	20	22	23	27	21	16	25	22	15
Nigeria	88	95	96	94	95	95	94	93	97	97	96	96	93	95	95	97
Northern Ireland	69	63	58	68	56	55	74	69	56	65	58	60	64	63	63	69
Norway	13	12	10	15	10	11	16	12	10	16	na	na	na	15	12	12
Pakistan	na	91	88	95	87	93	95	94	87	89	94	90	91	92	90	83
Peru	na	71	64	79	63	77	78	73	74	66	73	71	69	77	70	69
Philippines	na	79	76	83	79	80	78	73	80	86	78	79	82	79	80	78
Poland	85	78	75	81	74	78	81	82	75	69	80	80	70	84	76	73
Portugal	41	51	39	62	38	52	59	57	38	42	61	54	45	59	49	36
Puerto Rico	na	70	65	73	61	66	78	73	68	71	70	76	66	72	72	66
Romania	31	46	33	60	34	40	59	58	41	37	53	49	39	50	44	33
Russian Fed.	6	9	5	13	7	7	13	15	8	10	12	9	7	10	8	16
Serbia	na	20	16	24	19	17	23	26	16	19	24	20	19	19	20	23
Singapore	na	44	44	44	42	46	47	45	43	47	46	44	44	50	43	34
Slovakia	na	50	41	58	41	44	64	58	48	36	61	48	44	53	48	43
Slovenia	35	31	27	34	24	27	39	41	29	19	40	30	20	38	30	27
South Africa	na	68	59	79	67	67	77	69	67	65	67	66	70	71	65	76
Spain	39	36	24	47	16	29	54	44	27	30	48	33	30	47	35	18
Sweden	10	9	8	11	7	6	14	12	7	12	11	8	8	11	9	9
Switzerland	43	25	22	27	9	19	40	38	21	25	31	28	16	30	25	20
Taiwan	na	15	12	17	17	10	24	21	10	11	17	13	12	15	12	3
Tanzania	na	87	86	88	85	88	87	86	89	86	87	88	84	87	87	92
Turkey	38	40	71	8	37	38	51	40	41	39	45	38	31	40	41	40
Uganda	na	88	84	92	86	93	82	84	90	91	89	85	92	86	89	92
Ukraine	na	17	12	21	12	17	20	30	16	13	17	18	15	17	15	16
United States	58	60	54	67	47	64	66	54	59	63	58	63	59	69	61	56
Uruguay	na	23	14	30	18	20	28	27	18	21	28	21	22	32	21	19
Venezuela	na	48	39	57	38	52	62	52	45	49	49	51	45	54	46	44
Vietnam	na	13	9	17	11	10	18	16	8	10	10	14	13	19	12	12
Zimbabwe	na	81	68	93	83	82	76	82	80	47	75	87	84	80	81	93
Total	36	41	39	43	40	39	45	46	38	40	44	42	38	43	41	37

RANKING

Country	2000
Nigeria	95
Pakistan	91
Uganda	88
Malta	87
Tanzania	87
Zimbabwe	81
Philippines	79
Poland	78
Indonesia	75
Brazil	75
Mexico	75
Peru	71
Puerto Rico	70
El Salvador	69
South Africa	68
Ireland	67
Bangladesh	67
Colombia	67
Northern Ireland	63
United States	60
Dominican Rep.	55
Italy	54
Croatia	53
Portugal	51
India	51
Algeria	50
Slovakia	50
Morocco	48
Venezuela	48
Jordan	47
Iran	47
Romania	46
Chile	45
Bosnia and Herz.	45
Egypt	45
Singapore	44
Argentina	43
Austria	42
Turkey	40
Korea, South	38
Spain	36
Canada	36
Greece	34
Macedonia	33
Luxembourg	32
Lithuania	32
Slovenia	31
Germany	30
Armenia	30
Albania	29
Moldova	29
Georgia	27
Belgium	27
Netherlands	25
Australia	25
Switzerland	25
Uruguay	23
New Zealand	22
Bulgaria	20
Serbia	20
Great Britain	19
Hungary	18
Montenegro	17
Ukraine	17
Latvia	15
Belarus	15
Taiwan	15
Finland	14
Azerbaijan	14
Vietnam	13
Japan	12
Norway	12
Iceland	12
Denmark	12
France	12
Czech Republic	12
Estonia	11
Sweden	9
Russian Fed.	9
China	3
Total	41

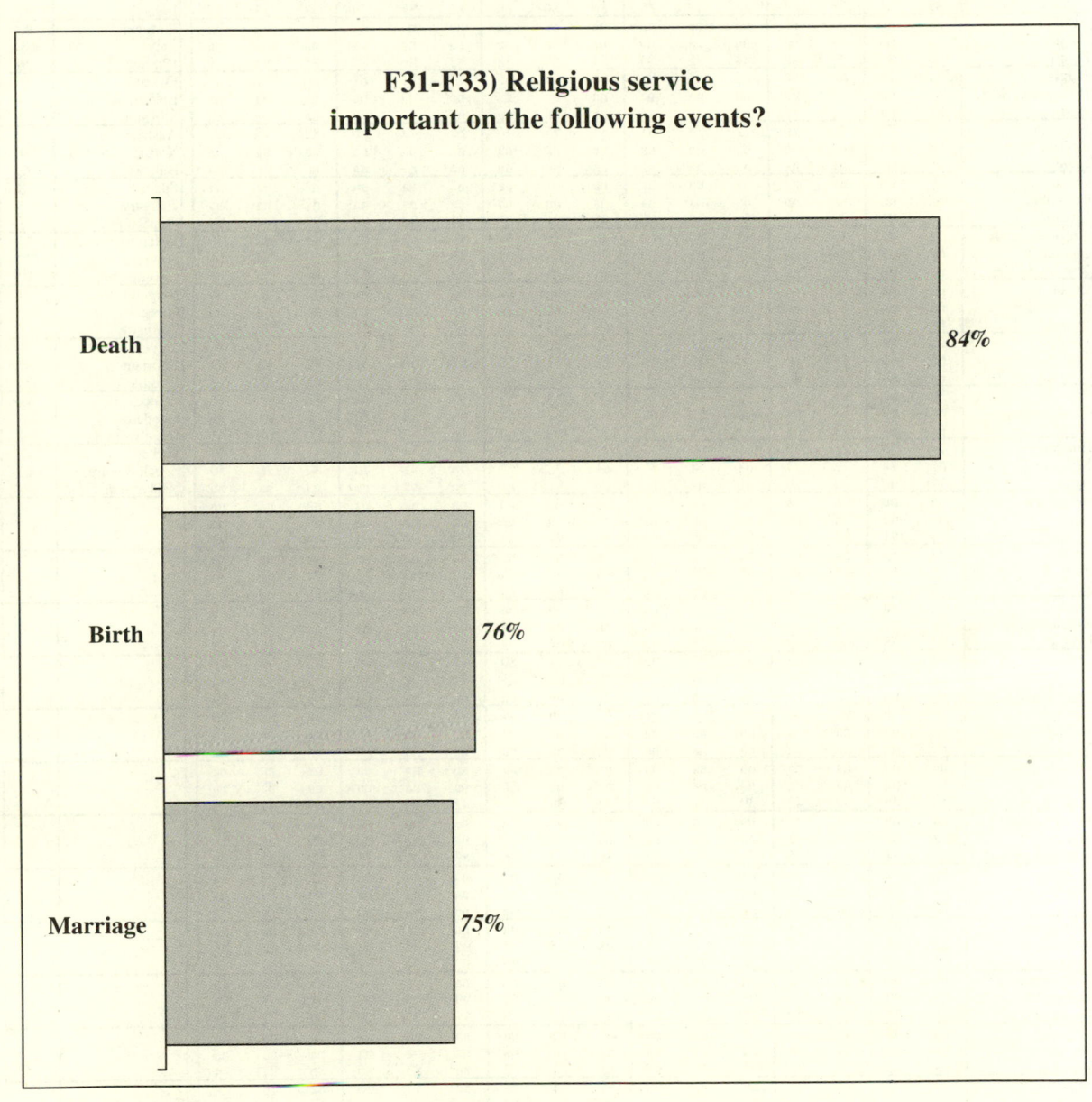

F31-F33) Religious service
important on the following events?

Death   *84%*

Birth   *76%*

Marriage   *75%*

F031_1) RELIGIOUS SERVICE BIRTH

Do you personally think it is important to hold a religious service for any of the following events? Birth

Yes (%)

(EVS: V107)

Country	Wave 1990	Wave 2000	Gender Male	Gender Female	Age 16-29	Age 30-49	Age 50+	Education Lower	Education Middle	Education Upper	Income Lower	Income Middle	Income Upper	Values Mat	Values Mixed	Values Postm.
Albania	na	na	na	na	na	na	na	na	na	na	na	na	na	na	na	na
Algeria	na	na	na	na	na	na	na	na	na	na	na	na	na	na	na	na
Argentina	67	na	na	na	na	na	na	na	na	na	na	na	na	na	na	na
Armenia	na	na	na	na	na	na	na	na	na	na	na	na	na	na	na	na
Australia	na	na	na	na	na	na	na	na	na	na	na	na	na	na	na	na
Austria	87	81	78	84	81	78	85	86	80	69	82	82	79	88	83	77
Azerbaijan	na	na	na	na	na	na	na	na	na	na	na	na	na	na	na	na
Bangladesh	na	na	na	na	na	na	na	na	na	na	na	na	na	na	na	na
Belarus	83	84	77	88	81	85	84	84	85	78	82	86	81	85	83	79
Belgium	74	70	66	74	65	63	79	78	69	65	71	71	67	80	71	56
Bosnia and Herz.	na	na	na	na	na	na	na	na	na	na	na	na	na	na	na	na
Brazil	81	na	na	na	na	na	na	na	na	na	na	na	na	na	na	na
Bulgaria	78	78	77	79	79	74	81	84	75	76	82	77	76	82	75	72
Canada	68	na	na	na	na	na	na	na	na	na	na	na	na	na	na	na
Chile	77	na	na	na	na	na	na	na	na	na	na	na	na	na	na	na
China	4	na	na	na	na	na	na	na	na	na	na	na	na	na	na	na
Colombia	na	na	na	na	na	na	na	na	na	na	na	na	na	na	na	na
Croatia	na	91	89	93	89	93	90	95	91	81	91	92	90	92	94	84
Czech Republic	52	42	36	47	35	34	52	46	40	30	49	43	31	45	41	39
Denmark	69	65	64	66	63	62	70	70	60	59	66	64	67	62	68	55
Dominican Rep.	na	na	na	na	na	na	na	na	na	na	na	na	na	na	na	na
Egypt	na	na	na	na	na	na	na	na	na	na	na	na	na	na	na	na
El Salvador	na	na	na	na	na	na	na	na	na	na	na	na	na	na	na	na
Estonia	66	64	56	69	57	61	69	69	63	57	66	68	57	67	62	53
Finland	58	84	82	86	81	81	89	86	82	84	84	80	87	88	85	76
France	65	61	57	64	60	52	70	66	57	50	64	60	54	72	62	41
Georgia	na	na	na	na	na	na	na	na	na	na	na	na	na	na	na	na
Germany	39	64	58	68	52	59	74	70	59	57	62	63	66	73	63	56
Great Britain	66	59	55	63	50	53	69	67	54	44	63	58	55	na	na	na
Greece	na	67	65	68	63	68	71	75	69	64	68	64	66	70	67	61
Hungary	79	75	71	79	65	69	88	79	67	70	81	74	74	81	70	64
Iceland	67	74	72	77	68	74	81	81	73	65	78	75	70	82	76	50
India	74	na	na	na	na	na	na	na	na	na	na	na	na	na	na	na
Indonesia	na	na	na	na	na	na	na	na	na	na	na	na	na	na	na	na
Iran	na	na	na	na	na	na	na	na	na	na	na	na	na	na	na	na
Ireland	94	91	88	93	88	89	94	92	91	88	90	94	88	93	92	82
Israel	na	na	na	na	na	na	na	na	na	na	na	na	na	na	na	na
Italy	86	89	85	93	88	86	93	94	88	79	92	88	85	94	91	83
Japan	36	na	na	na	na	na	na	na	na	na	na	na	na	na	na	na
Jordan	na	na	na	na	na	na	na	na	na	na	na	na	na	na	na	na
Korea, South	na	na	na	na	na	na	na	na	na	na	na	na	na	na	na	na
Latvia	84	65	60	69	62	65	66	69	64	62	66	63	65	68	64	59
Lithuania	87	93	87	98	91	92	96	98	92	89	97	89	93	93	96	75
Luxembourg	na	70	67	74	68	64	79	79	67	63	75	72	58	77	72	54
Macedonia	na	na	na	na	na	na	na	na	na	na	na	na	na	na	na	na
Malta	na	96	95	98	96	95	90	97	96	97	98	95	96	96	97	93
Mexico	76	na	na	na	na	na	na	na	na	na	na	na	na	na	na	na
Moldova	na	na	na	na	na	na	na	na	na	na	na	na	na	na	na	na
Montenegro	na	na	na	na	na	na	na	na	na	na	na	na	na	na	na	na
Morocco	na	na	na	na	na	na	na	na	na	na	na	na	na	na	na	na
Netherlands	48	40	39	42	39	31	51	42	39	41	42	40	36	48	41	35
New Zealand	na	na	na	na	na	na	na	na	na	na	na	na	na	na	na	na
Nigeria	92	na	na	na	na	na	na	na	na	na	na	na	na	na	na	na
Northern Ireland	83	81	77	85	79	79	84	86	77	76	83	78	78	80	83	79
Norway	66	na	na	na	na	na	na	na	na	na	na	na	na	na	na	na
Pakistan	na	na	na	na	na	na	na	na	na	na	na	na	na	na	na	na
Peru	na	na	na	na	na	na	na	na	na	na	na	na	na	na	na	na
Philippines	na	na	na	na	na	na	na	na	na	na	na	na	na	na	na	na
Poland	95	96	95	97	97	95	97	98	95	91	97	97	94	98	95	95
Portugal	75	90	88	93	84	90	95	94	85	75	97	92	83	95	90	81
Puerto Rico	na	na	na	na	na	na	na	na	na	na	na	na	na	na	na	na
Romania	86	98	97	98	95	98	99	99	97	97	99	97	97	98	98	96
Russian Fed.	78	75	67	81	75	73	77	85	75	70	79	77	69	79	72	57
Serbia	na	na	na	na	na	na	na	na	na	na	na	na	na	na	na	na
Singapore	na	na	na	na	na	na	na	na	na	na	na	na	na	na	na	na
Slovakia	na	83	79	86	77	78	91	88	81	72	88	83	80	86	81	74
Slovenia	79	73	73	73	66	73	78	87	71	54	86	72	60	82	73	64
South Africa	78	na	na	na	na	na	na	na	na	na	na	na	na	na	na	na
Spain	74	78	72	83	67	74	87	87	72	68	81	78	68	90	80	53
Sweden	56	60	58	62	54	58	65	67	59	56	59	63	55	65	62	52
Switzerland	na	na	na	na	na	na	na	na	na	na	na	na	na	na	na	na
Taiwan	na	na	na	na	na	na	na	na	na	na	na	na	na	na	na	na
Tanzania	na	na	na	na	na	na	na	na	na	na	na	na	na	na	na	na
Turkey	42	42	37	47	40	41	51	47	37	29	44	42	35	55	40	32
Uganda	na	na	na	na	na	na	na	na	na	na	na	na	na	na	na	na
Ukraine	na	86	79	91	83	85	88	90	85	84	86	87	85	87	85	75
United States	57	na	na	na	na	na	na	na	na	na	na	na	na	na	na	na
Uruguay	na	na	na	na	na	na	na	na	na	na	na	na	na	na	na	na
Venezuela	na	na	na	na	na	na	na	na	na	na	na	na	na	na	na	na
Vietnam	na	na	na	na	na	na	na	na	na	na	na	na	na	na	na	na
Zimbabwe	na	na	na	na	na	na	na	na	na	na	na	na	na	na	na	na
Total	70	76	72	79	72	73	81	80	75	68	77	75	73	82	76	65

RANKING

Country	2000
Romania	98
Malta	96
Poland	96
Lithuania	93
Croatia	91
Ireland	91
Portugal	90
Italy	89
Ukraine	86
Finland	84
Belarus	84
Slovakia	83
Austria	81
Northern Ireland	81
Bulgaria	78
Spain	78
Hungary	75
Russian Fed.	75
Iceland	74
Slovenia	73
Luxembourg	70
Belgium	70
Greece	67
Denmark	65
Latvia	65
Germany	64
Estonia	64
France	61
Sweden	60
Great Britain	59
Turkey	42
Czech Republic	42
Netherlands	40
Total	76

F032_1) RELIGIOUS SERVICE MARRIAGE

Do you personally think it is important to hold a religious service for any of the following events? Marriage

Yes (%)

(EVS: V108)

Country	Wave 1990	Wave 2000	Gender Male	Gender Female	Age 16-29	Age 30-49	Age 50+	Education Lower	Education Middle	Education Upper	Income Lower	Income Middle	Income Upper	Values Mat	Values Mixed	Values Postm.
Albania	na	na	na	na	na	na	na	na	na	na	na	na	na	na	na	na
Algeria	na	na	na	na	na	na	na	na	na	na	na	na	na	na	na	na
Argentina	73	na	na	na	na	na	na	na	na	na	na	na	na	na	na	na
Armenia	na	na	na	na	na	na	na	na	na	na	na	na	na	na	na	na
Australia	na	na	na	na	na	na	na	na	na	na	na	na	na	na	na	na
Austria	85	76	74	79	71	73	82	82	73	64	77	79	72	89	79	68
Azerbaijan	na	na	na	na	na	na	na	na	na	na	na	na	na	na	na	na
Bangladesh	na	na	na	na	na	na	na	na	na	na	na	na	na	na	na	na
Belarus	62	61	54	67	59	57	68	70	58	59	63	59	63	63	59	49
Belgium	76	70	66	73	70	60	79	79	69	65	73	69	66	77	71	55
Bosnia and Herz.	na	na	na	na	na	na	na	na	na	na	na	na	na	na	na	na
Brazil	82	na	na	na	na	na	na	na	na	na	na	na	na	na	na	na
Bulgaria	81	83	82	84	84	81	85	86	82	79	86	82	83	86	80	79
Canada	82	na	na	na	na	na	na	na	na	na	na	na	na	na	na	na
Chile	87	na	na	na	na	na	na	na	na	na	na	na	na	na	na	na
China	13	na	na	na	na	na	na	na	na	na	na	na	na	na	na	na
Colombia	na	na	na	na	na	na	na	na	na	na	na	na	na	na	na	na
Croatia	na	95	94	96	95	97	94	98	95	88	92	97	96	95	96	94
Czech Republic	50	40	35	45	40	30	50	44	38	31	47	40	31	44	39	42
Denmark	64	63	62	64	66	57	68	68	54	57	66	63	57	70	65	49
Dominican Rep.	na	na	na	na	na	na	na	na	na	na	na	na	na	na	na	na
Egypt	na	na	na	na	na	na	na	na	na	na	na	na	na	na	na	na
El Salvador	na	na	na	na	na	na	na	na	na	na	na	na	na	na	na	na
Estonia	64	65	61	68	67	57	71	77	61	55	67	68	59	65	66	50
Finland	64	83	80	86	80	79	88	83	81	84	84	78	84	87	83	71
France	68	66	64	67	66	58	73	71	63	54	72	65	57	77	66	44
Georgia	na	na	na	na	na	na	na	na	na	na	na	na	na	na	na	na
Germany	46	68	63	72	63	61	78	74	63	63	67	67	70	71	68	64
Great Britain	80	69	62	76	65	63	75	74	66	57	74	65	66	na	na	na
Greece	na	83	80	85	83	82	84	96	88	76	86	84	81	90	85	71
Hungary	76	75	71	79	73	66	86	79	72	60	80	73	74	82	69	77
Iceland	66	67	64	71	65	65	71	73	68	56	66	68	66	76	68	42
India	79	na	na	na	na	na	na	na	na	na	na	na	na	na	na	na
Indonesia	na	na	na	na	na	na	na	na	na	na	na	na	na	na	na	na
Iran	na	na	na	na	na	na	na	na	na	na	na	na	na	na	na	na
Ireland	94	92	90	94	92	88	96	94	92	89	92	93	91	96	93	83
Israel	na	na	na	na	na	na	na	na	na	na	na	na	na	na	na	na
Italy	83	85	82	88	83	81	90	91	82	76	89	84	81	92	86	77
Japan	56	na	na	na	na	na	na	na	na	na	na	na	na	na	na	na
Jordan	na	na	na	na	na	na	na	na	na	na	na	na	na	na	na	na
Korea, South	na	na	na	na	na	na	na	na	na	na	na	na	na	na	na	na
Latvia	79	78	74	81	78	76	79	81	77	76	77	77	82	82	76	76
Lithuania	84	89	83	93	83	86	95	97	86	85	96	84	88	90	92	67
Luxembourg	na	66	64	67	63	59	75	75	63	57	71	68	52	75	67	47
Macedonia	na	na	na	na	na	na	na	na	na	na	na	na	na	na	na	na
Malta	na	96	94	98	94	95	98	98	95	94	98	96	95	96	97	89
Mexico	82	na	na	na	na	na	na	na	na	na	na	na	na	na	na	na
Moldova	na	na	na	na	na	na	na	na	na	na	na	na	na	na	na	na
Montenegro	na	na	na	na	na	na	na	na	na	na	na	na	na	na	na	na
Morocco	na	na	na	na	na	na	na	na	na	na	na	na	na	na	na	na
Netherlands	52	46	44	47	45	33	59	53	42	43	49	45	39	61	45	37
New Zealand	na	na	na	na	na	na	na	na	na	na	na	na	na	na	na	na
Nigeria	95	na	na	na	na	na	na	na	na	na	na	na	na	na	na	na
Northern Ireland	93	90	87	93	88	86	94	94	86	88	90	92	86	88	91	91
Norway	70	na	na	na	na	na	na	na	na	na	na	na	na	na	na	na
Pakistan	na	na	na	na	na	na	na	na	na	na	na	na	na	na	na	na
Peru	na	na	na	na	na	na	na	na	na	na	na	na	na	na	na	na
Philippines	na	na	na	na	na	na	na	na	na	na	na	na	na	Mat	na	na
Poland	97	95	94	95	91	95	96	97	94	87	96	95	90	96	94	93
Portugal	79	89	86	91	76	91	94	94	79	73	98	91	79	92	90	76
Puerto Rico	na	na	na	na	na	na	na	na	na	na	na	na	na	na	na	na
Romania	92	98	97	99	96	99	99	99	98	99	99	99	98	99	98	96
Russian Fed.	62	54	45	60	52	46	63	71	53	47	59	56	46	56	51	38
Serbia	na	na	na	na	na	na	na	na	na	na	na	na	na	na	na	na
Singapore	na	na	na	na	na	na	na	na	na	na	na	na	na	na	na	na
Slovakia	na	80	76	84	75	76	89	87	78	72	87	80	78	82	80	70
Slovenia	76	70	71	70	64	69	76	85	68	51	79	74	54	75	70	66
South Africa	93	na	na	na	na	na	na	na	na	na	na	na	na	na	na	na
Spain	74	75	71	80	62	69	88	87	68	62	79	77	65	87	78	48
Sweden	59	62	64	61	64	58	66	70	62	58	62	64	59	72	65	50
Switzerland	na	na	na	na	na	na	na	na	na	na	na	na	na	na	na	na
Taiwan	na	na	na	na	na	na	na	na	na	na	na	na	na	na	na	na
Tanzania	na	na	na	na	na	na	na	na	na	na	na	na	na	na	na	na
Turkey	76	82	79	84	81	81	87	89	76	54	92	79	68	88	82	72
Uganda	na	na	na	na	na	na	na	na	na	na	na	na	na	na	na	na
Ukraine	na	69	61	74	64	69	71	81	66	67	67	75	65	69	67	68
United States	86	na	na	na	na	na	na	na	na	na	na	na	na	na	na	na
Uruguay	na	na	na	na	na	na	na	na	na	na	na	na	na	na	na	na
Venezuela	na	na	na	na	na	na	na	na	na	na	na	na	na	na	na	na
Vietnam	na	na	na	na	na	na	na	na	na	na	na	na	na	na	na	na
Zimbabwe	na	na	na	na	na	na	na	na	na	na	na	na	na	na	na	na
Total	73	75	72	78	73	71	81	81	73	68	77	75	72	80	76	65

RANKING

Country	2000
Romania	98
Malta	96
Croatia	95
Poland	95
Ireland	92
Northern Ireland	90
Lithuania	89
Portugal	89
Italy	85
Bulgaria	83
Greece	83
Finland	83
Turkey	82
Slovakia	80
Latvia	78
Austria	76
Hungary	75
Spain	75
Slovenia	70
Belgium	70
Ukraine	69
Great Britain	69
Germany	68
Iceland	67
Luxembourg	66
France	66
Estonia	65
Denmark	63
Sweden	62
Belarus	61
Russian Fed.	54
Netherlands	46
Czech Republic	40
Total	75

F033_1) RELIGIOUS SERVICE DEATH

Do you personally think it is important to hold a religious service for any of the following events? Death

Yes (%)

(EVS: V109)

Country	Wave 1990	Wave 2000	Gender Male	Gender Female	Age 16-29	Age 30-49	Age 50+	Education Lower	Education Middle	Education Upper	Income Lower	Income Middle	Income Upper	Values Mat	Values Mixed	Values Postm.
Albania	na	na	na	na	na	na	na	na	na	na	na	na	na	na	na	na
Algeria	na	na	na	na	na	na	na	na	na	na	na	na	na	na	na	na
Argentina	67	na	na	na	na	na	na	na	na	na	na	na	na	na	na	na
Armenia	na	na	na	na	na	na	na	na	na	na	na	na	na	na	na	na
Australia	na	na	na	na	na	na	na	na	na	na	na	na	na	na	na	na
Austria	88	85	83	87	83	84	87	88	83	79	85	85	84	89	86	81
Azerbaijan	na	na	na	na	na	na	na	na	na	na	na	na	na	na	na	na
Bangladesh	na	na	na	na	na	na	na	na	na	na	na	na	na	na	na	na
Belarus	76	88	84	91	85	90	88	89	88	86	90	87	86	90	86	88
Belgium	79	74	71	77	76	66	81	80	75	70	75	75	72	83	75	61
Bosnia and Herz.	na	na	na	na	na	na	na	na	na	na	na	na	na	na	na	na
Brazil	76	na	na	na	na	na	na	na	na	na	na	na	na	na	na	na
Bulgaria	87	89	88	89	92	86	90	92	87	87	90	89	89	91	86	85
Canada	84	na	na	na	na	na	na	na	na	na	na	na	na	na	na	na
Chile	82	na	na	na	na	na	na	na	na	na	na	na	na	na	na	na
China	11	na	na	na	na	na	na	na	na	na	na	na	na	na	na	na
Colombia	na	na	na	na	na	na	na	na	na	na	na	na	na	na	na	na
Croatia	na	96	95	96	94	97	94	98	95	89	94	97	95	98	96	92
Czech Republic	62	50	46	54	50	46	54	55	48	39	54	50	43	53	50	49
Denmark	80	80	77	83	81	77	83	83	76	77	82	79	79	81	83	68
Dominican Rep.	na	na	na	na	na	na	na	na	na	na	na	na	na	na	na	na
Egypt	na	na	na	na	na	na	na	na	na	na	na	na	na	na	na	na
El Salvador	na	na	na	na	na	na	na	na	na	na	na	na	na	na	na	na
Estonia	72	76	72	78	72	73	79	80	75	70	80	77	69	78	75	63
Finland	83	90	87	93	88	86	95	90	89	90	90	89	91	92	91	80
France	73	73	71	75	77	68	76	78	68	64	77	73	67	81	75	55
Georgia	na	na	na	na	na	na	na	na	na	na	na	na	na	na	na	na
Germany	61	74	69	77	67	69	81	79	69	68	70	73	77	77	74	68
Great Britain	86	79	72	85	77	76	81	83	78	65	84	79	73	na	na	na
Greece	na	87	83	90	85	88	91	95	92	82	91	87	84	90	89	78
Hungary	86	82	78	86	78	77	89	85	76	75	86	80	81	86	78	77
Iceland	93	91	91	92	87	90	96	94	91	84	91	91	91	97	92	77
India	75	na	na	na	na	na	na	na	na	na	na	na	na	na	na	na
Indonesia	na	na	na	na	na	na	na	na	na	na	na	na	na	na	na	na
Iran	na	na	na	na	na	na	na	na	na	na	na	na	na	na	na	na
Ireland	97	96	94	97	96	93	98	97	96	93	94	96	96	98	96	88
Israel	na	na	na	na	na	na	na	na	na	na	na	na	na	na	na	na
Italy	87	89	86	93	89	86	92	92	89	83	91	88	87	92	91	84
Japan	87	na	na	na	na	na	na	na	na	na	na	na	na	na	na	na
Jordan	na	na	na	na	na	na	na	na	na	na	na	na	na	na	na	na
Korea, South	na	na	na	na	na	na	na	na	na	na	na	na	na	na	na	na
Latvia	85	88	86	90	88	86	90	90	87	88	87	88	90	88	89	86
Lithuania	89	95	93	98	94	94	98	98	95	93	98	94	95	96	97	88
Luxembourg	na	77	73	80	78	71	82	84	73	71	81	75	65	83	78	58
Macedonia	na	na	na	na	na	na	na	na	na	na	na	na	na	na	na	na
Malta	na	97	96	98	95	96	99	99	96	97	99	97	97	96	98	92
Mexico	81	na	na	na	na	na	na	na	na	na	na	na	na	na	na	na
Moldova	na	na	na	na	na	na	na	na	na	na	na	na	na	na	na	na
Montenegro	na	na	na	na	na	na	na	na	na	na	na	na	na	na	na	na
Morocco	na	na	na	na	na	na	na	na	na	na	na	na	na	na	na	na
Netherlands	62	56	54	57	54	48	64	62	52	53	57	55	52	67	57	47
New Zealand	na	na	na	na	na	na	na	na	na	na	na	na	na	na	na	na
Nigeria	90	na	na	na	na	na	na	na	na	na	na	na	na	na	na	na
Northern Ireland	96	93	91	95	92	90	95	96	90	92	92	93	91	93	94	91
Norway	81	na	na	na	na	na	na	na	na	na	na	na	na	na	na	na
Pakistan	na	na	na	na	na	na	na	na	na	na	na	na	na	na	na	na
Peru	na	na	na	na	na	na	na	na	na	na	na	na	na	na	na	na
Philippines	na	na	na	na	na	na	na	na	na	na	na	na	na	na	na	na
Poland	95	96	95	97	93	97	97	98	96	89	97	97	92	98	95	94
Portugal	79	92	91	94	84	96	95	97	87	73	97	96	85	96	93	81
Puerto Rico	na	na	na	na	na	na	na	na	na	na	na	na	na	na	na	na
Romania	89	98	97	99	96	98	99	99	97	97	99	98	97	98	98	96
Russian Fed.	74	79	71	85	79	78	80	88	79	74	81	80	75	81	76	67
Serbia	na	na	na	na	na	na	na	na	na	na	na	na	na	na	na	na
Singapore	na	na	na	na	na	na	na	na	na	na	na	na	na	na	na	na
Slovakia	na	85	82	87	81	82	90	89	83	78	90	85	83	85	84	87
Slovenia	81	77	79	76	77	75	80	89	76	59	88	78	61	82	77	73
South Africa	86	na	na	na	na	na	na	na	na	na	na	na	na	na	na	na
Spain	75	80	75	85	70	77	88	89	75	71	82	78	75	91	83	57
Sweden	80	78	76	79	80	72	81	82	79	72	79	77	76	80	80	70
Switzerland	na	na	na	na	na	na	na	na	na	na	na	na	na	na	na	na
Taiwan	na	na	na	na	na	na	na	na	na	na	na	na	na	na	na	na
Tanzania	na	na	na	na	na	na	na	na	na	na	na	na	na	na	na	na
Turkey	95	95	94	96	94	96	97	97	93	89	96	97	90	98	94	93
Uganda	na	na	na	na	na	na	na	na	na	na	na	na	na	na	na	na
Ukraine	na	85	78	91	84	86	85	94	83	84	84	86	86	86	84	82
United States	87	na	na	na	na	na	na	na	na	na	na	na	na	na	na	na
Uruguay	na	na	na	na	na	na	na	na	na	na	na	na	na	na	na	na
Venezuela	na	na	na	na	na	na	na	na	na	na	na	na	na	na	na	na
Vietnam	na	na	na	na	na	na	na	na	na	na	na	na	na	na	na	na
Zimbabwe	na	na	na	na	na	na	na	na	na	na	na	na	na	na	na	na
Total	80	84	81	86	83	81	87	88	83	78	85	84	82	88	84	75

RANKING

Country	2000
Romania	98
Malta	97
Poland	96
Croatia	96
Ireland	96
Lithuania	95
Turkey	95
Northern Ireland	93
Portugal	92
Iceland	91
Finland	90
Italy	89
Bulgaria	89
Belarus	88
Latvia	88
Greece	87
Austria	85
Ukraine	85
Slovakia	85
Hungary	82
Spain	80
Denmark	80
Russian Fed.	79
Great Britain	79
Sweden	78
Slovenia	77
Luxembourg	77
Estonia	76
Belgium	74
Germany	74
France	73
Netherlands	56
Czech Republic	50
Total	84

F34) Independently of whether you go to church or not, would you say you are…

A convinced atheist
4%

Not a religious
person
24%

A religious person
72%

F034) RELIGIOUS PERSON

Independently of whether you go to church or not, would you say you are...

A religious person (%) (WVS: V186; EVS: V110)

Country	Wave 1990	Wave 2000	Male	Female	16-29	30-49	50+	Education Lower	Education Middle	Education Upper	Income Lower	Income Middle	Income Upper	Mat	Mixed	Postm.
Albania	na	68	63	74	67	65	75	72	69	58	69	70	66	70	66	64
Algeria	na	59	60	58	53	58	74	68	56	56	62	64	50	57	60	59
Argentina	73	84	80	88	79	84	90	86	83	80	89	85	79	89	86	77
Armenia	na	75	66	82	78	73	73	74	76	71	75	73	77	73	78	65
Australia	na	59	52	66	48	59	70	67	54	58	63	57	54	63	61	54
Austria	81	80	75	84	71	79	84	82	79	72	82	80	76	78	81	77
Azerbaijan	na	88	86	90	87	89	90	92	89	86	90	87	87	89	86	88
Bangladesh	na	97	96	98	94	98	99	99	95	94	99	95	97	98	96	96
Belarus	41	28	17	36	23	20	40	43	22	18	35	26	18	30	26	15
Belgium	68	67	62	72	55	63	78	74	66	64	71	66	63	81	68	52
Bosnia and Herz.	na	74	71	77	84	72	69	83	75	65	75	74	74	75	74	69
Brazil	88	85	84	87	81	87	91	84	87	87	83	88	87	85	86	84
Bulgaria	36	52	42	61	43	43	63	65	44	45	62	47	45	51	53	52
Canada	71	74	67	80	59	71	85	82	73	67	77	75	68	76	77	67
Chile	77	71	62	79	64	69	79	80	66	65	71	71	68	70	73	65
China	5	15	12	17	16	15	14	14	15	21	9	14	24	14	15	17
Colombia	na	85	82	89	82	85	92	87	85	83	86	86	84	88	86	88
Croatia	na	85	78	91	77	89	86	91	84	74	88	86	84	94	85	75
Czech Republic	46	43	36	50	34	35	55	44	43	41	50	42	36	45	42	47
Denmark	73	77	69	84	60	78	84	81	65	73	78	78	73	72	78	72
Dominican Rep.	na	76	75	77	77	76	82	74	69	79	81	77	75	75	76	77
Egypt	na	99	98	99	98	99	100	99	98	99	99	99	99	99	99	96
El Salvador	na	70	67	73	66	67	79	68	71	74	68	68	72	na	na	na
Estonia	21	42	32	50	34	34	52	47	40	37	51	45	36	44	40	31
Finland	59	67	56	76	50	64	78	69	62	69	68	64	67	64	69	62
France	51	47	41	52	35	42	56	51	39	43	50	47	41	56	47	31
Georgia	na	89	86	93	93	90	84	90	90	88	88	90	90	90	89	96
Germany	38	56	48	62	43	51	66	60	52	50	55	60	59	57	57	51
Great Britain	56	42	37	46	26	37	53	41	43	32	39	41	43	na	na	na
Greece	na	80	74	84	76	82	84	90	86	73	81	78	80	88	81	67
Hungary	57	59	48	69	47	53	72	66	46	43	70	59	53	64	55	47
Iceland	75	74	68	80	60	76	83	81	72	65	76	76	68	83	74	51
India	84	79	78	82	77	81	80	82	78	75	77	82	78	83	73	73
Indonesia	na	84	83	87	80	83	88	85	86	82	83	86	83	82	86	87
Iran	na	95	94	96	94	95	97	96	94	94	95	96	94	97	94	94
Ireland	72	74	70	78	68	71	84	77	72	74	79	69	74	79	74	69
Israel	na	na	na	na	na	na	na	na	na	na	na	na	na	na	na	na
Italy	86	86	80	91	82	85	89	90	83	80	89	85	82	94	88	77
Japan	26	27	23	30	15	24	33	33	28	19	31	26	23	26	26	27
Jordan	na	86	76	95	81	88	93	87	83	87	90	85	84	87	86	76
Korea, South	na	31	27	35	25	32	37	36	33	28	27	29	36	31	30	35
Latvia	54	77	65	86	71	75	81	81	76	76	79	80	73	80	76	77
Lithuania	55	84	72	94	76	79	94	93	80	87	83	83	79	85	86	70
Luxembourg	na	63	58	68	51	59	76	71	62	55	62	69	60	62	64	58
Macedonia	na	84	84	84	86	84	82	93	80	77	90	81	80	86	82	85
Malta	na	75	69	80	64	72	85	85	71	71	81	75	67	77	74	66
Mexico	75	77	74	80	74	76	85	80	75	74	85	75	73	70	78	73
Moldova	na	91	86	95	87	92	93	94	92	86	94	90	89	93	88	86
Montenegro	na	73	67	80	67	72	78	83	68	62	73	76	70	78	70	53
Morocco	na	95	93	97	92	96	100	95	96	92	93	95	92	97	93	92
Netherlands	61	62	54	69	54	55	72	67	61	59	60	63	57	76	61	55
New Zealand	na	51	45	56	38	49	57	49	54	51	56	52	46	50	55	43
Nigeria	93	97	96	97	96	97	99	97	97	96	96	97	97	96	97	97
Northern Ireland	72	62	56	68	53	57	72	69	55	62	63	58	61	62	63	68
Norway	48	47	37	56	35	46	57	48	42	51	na	na	na	47	47	46
Pakistan	na	91	87	94	87	94	88	95	87	85	96	89	88	93	88	91
Peru	na	88	85	91	85	90	93	89	89	87	87	91	87	91	87	90
Philippines	na	80	78	81	72	82	85	82	76	81	82	80	76	77	81	82
Poland	95	94	93	96	94	95	95	98	93	83	97	94	90	98	93	85
Portugal	69	88	81	94	78	93	90	93	80	74	91	91	85	91	89	77
Puerto Rico	na	82	77	86	76	80	88	90	81	82	81	86	80	84	82	84
Romania	75	85	78	92	77	81	92	92	83	75	90	87	78	89	84	57
Russian Fed.	56	66	52	77	64	62	71	73	65	65	71	64	64	70	60	52
Serbia	na	75	67	82	76	76	72	81	72	72	78	77	69	77	73	63
Singapore	na	na	na	na	na	na	na	na	na	na	na	na	na	na	na	na
Slovakia	na	82	76	87	74	79	90	85	82	69	82	83	79	83	80	83
Slovenia	73	70	65	74	66	67	76	86	69	47	82	68	51	80	68	66
South Africa	83	79	71	88	77	77	90	76	82	87	74	81	83	80	78	79
Spain	70	61	50	72	46	57	74	69	53	54	68	61	59	74	61	43
Sweden	31	39	32	46	26	35	51	43	34	44	40	38	37	46	38	37
Switzerland	74	57	51	64	41	58	66	65	55	61	61	57	54	54	56	59
Taiwan	na	75	70	80	65	77	78	81	73	72	75	80	71	76	75	59
Tanzania	na	94	93	96	93	95	96	94	94	97	94	95	93	94	95	91
Turkey	75	80	75	84	76	81	84	87	74	59	84	79	68	84	80	69
Uganda	na	94	95	94	95	94	89	93	95	95	98	94	94	91	96	97
Ukraine	na	75	62	86	77	71	78	83	73	78	76	76	74	74	74	83
United States	84	83	77	88	75	84	87	82	83	83	83	80	86	87	83	80
Uruguay	na	55	42	64	47	47	64	60	48	46	59	51	55	60	57	47
Venezuela	na	79	75	82	73	83	82	78	77	84	72	80	81	81	78	80
Vietnam	na	38	31	46	33	36	46	46	29	27	42	38	36	45	37	39
Zimbabwe	na	89	82	95	89	90	86	89	89	70	85	93	93	87	90	93
Total	63	72	66	77	69	70	75	76	69	69	74	72	69	75	72	66

RANKING

Country	2000
Egypt	99
Bangladesh	97
Nigeria	97
Iran	95
Morocco	95
Poland	94
Tanzania	94
Uganda	94
Moldova	91
Pakistan	91
Georgia	89
Zimbabwe	89
Azerbaijan	88
Peru	88
Portugal	88
Jordan	86
Italy	86
Brazil	85
Croatia	85
Colombia	85
Romania	85
Argentina	84
Lithuania	84
Indonesia	84
Macedonia	84
United States	83
Puerto Rico	82
Slovakia	82
Greece	80
Austria	80
Philippines	80
Turkey	80
India	79
South Africa	79
Venezuela	79
Mexico	77
Latvia	77
Denmark	77
Dominican Rep.	76
Ukraine	75
Taiwan	75
Malta	75
Armenia	75
Serbia	75
Bosnia and Herz.	74
Ireland	74
Iceland	74
Canada	71
Montenegro	73
Chile	71
Slovenia	70
El Salvador	70
Albania	68
Belgium	67
Finland	67
Russian Fed.	66
Luxembourg	63
Northern Ireland	62
Netherlands	62
Spain	61
Algeria	59
Hungary	59
Australia	59
Switzerland	57
Germany	56
Uruguay	55
Bulgaria	52
New Zealand	51
France	47
Norway	47
Czech Republic	43
Estonia	42
Great Britain	42
Sweden	39
Vietnam	38
Korea, South	31
Belarus	28
Japan	27
China	15
Total	72

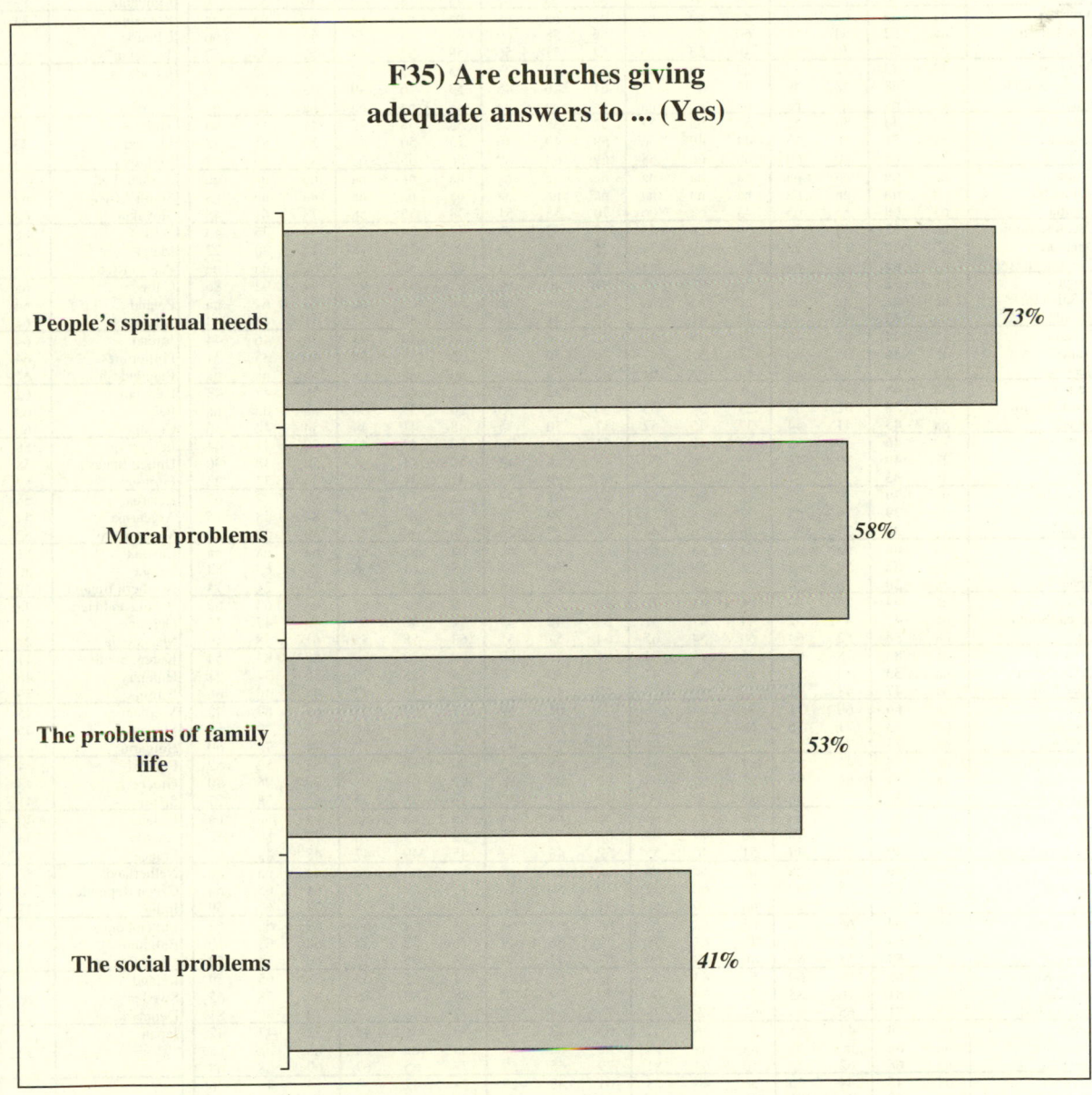

**F35) Are churches giving
adequate answers to ... (Yes)**

People's spiritual needs — 73%

Moral problems — 58%

The problems of family
life — 53%

The social problems — 41%

F035) CHURCHES GIVE ANSWERS: MORAL PROBLEMS

Generally speaking, do you think that the churches in your country are giving adequate answers to ...

The moral problems and needs of the individual

Yes (%)

(WVS: V187; EVS: V111)

Country	Wave 1990	Wave 2000	Gender Male	Gender Female	Age 16-29	Age 30-49	Age 50+	Education Lower	Education Middle	Education Upper	Income Lower	Income Middle	Income Upper	Values Mat	Values Mixed	Values Postm.
Albania	na	64	61	67	60	61	71	71	60	59	65	66	62	65	63	54
Algeria	na	91	92	89	90	89	96	95	89	89	92	90	86	95	89	90
Argentina	42	54	49	58	47	53	61	59	46	48	62	56	44	66	57	38
Armenia	na	na	na	na	na	na	na	na	na	na	na	na	na	na	na	na
Australia	na	na	na	na	na	na	na	na	na	na	na	na	na	na	na	na
Austria	47	38	37	38	29	37	43	38	35	42	43	38	37	30	37	38
Azerbaijan	na	na	na	na	na	na	na	na	na	na	na	na	na	na	na	na
Bangladesh	na	62	64	57	60	63	64	66	58	60	65	64	57	65	60	66
Belarus	83	56	46	63	48	53	66	67	51	56	58	57	49	57	53	52
Belgium	42	33	32	34	29	26	41	42	32	28	43	33	27	39	32	26
Bosnia and Herz.	na	48	48	49	47	47	51	61	46	46	53	46	49	43	51	49
Brazil	44	na	na	na	na	na	na	na	na	na	na	na	na	na	na	na
Bulgaria	49	44	36	52	37	38	52	57	37	42	55	38	42	41	45	45
Canada	55	51	48	53	44	49	56	59	49	46	55	50	47	55	55	42
Chile	77	65	60	69	60	66	68	69	63	60	66	65	62	65	65	63
China	na	na	na	na	na	na	na	na	na	na	na	na	na	na	na	na
Colombia	na	na	na	na	na	na	na	na	na	na	na	na	na	na	na	na
Croatia	na	60	55	65	45	63	66	70	55	51	78	55	58	73	61	48
Czech Republic	na	35	32	38	30	28	45	37	32	38	42	34	28	33	35	43
Denmark	20	20	17	23	14	19	24	21	17	22	20	23	18	15	20	22
Dominican Rep.	na	na	na	na	na	na	na	na	na	na	na	na	na	na	na	na
Egypt	na	92	89	95	90	93	95	94	90	90	92	93	92	94	92	86
El Salvador	na	na	na	na	na	na	na	na	na	na	na	na	na	na	na	na
Estonia	na	45	41	49	33	41	55	52	41	46	54	50	37	51	41	44
Finland	25	44	41	46	37	38	51	42	44	52	43	40	44	38	46	44
France	38	36	35	36	33	31	41	36	30	41	36	35	38	40	35	31
Georgia	na	na	na	na	na	na	na	na	na	na	na	na	na	na	na	na
Germany	58	48	43	52	38	42	60	53	43	50	52	47	51	56	47	43
Great Britain	34	33	32	34	29	34	33	30	34	33	36	33	36	na	na	na
Greece	na	43	41	44	37	45	52	57	50	35	48	41	44	54	42	36
Hungary	79	46	39	53	33	40	60	51	39	36	53	47	42	50	42	44
Iceland	37	40	39	42	33	38	50	43	36	44	40	41	41	50	38	30
India	38	33	31	37	32	33	34	36	29	33	31	31	35	33	33	23
Indonesia	na	79	77	83	67	80	84	87	81	72	81	77	79	84	77	67
Iran	na	79	76	83	77	78	88	87	79	72	78	81	78	84	78	75
Ireland	42	30	27	33	16	26	44	42	25	20	38	30	23	33	30	21
Israel	na	na	na	na	na	na	na	na	na	na	na	na	na	na	na	na
Italy	55	62	58	65	53	59	69	67	58	57	68	61	56	70	63	54
Japan	28	20	16	24	21	22	17	15	23	16	20	18	19	21	21	14
Jordan	na	64	54	74	64	61	70	69	63	56	69	61	62	65	63	69
Korea, South	na	47	43	52	44	47	51	53	48	45	44	46	52	48	47	35
Latvia	88	58	52	64	50	54	65	64	57	55	63	58	55	61	58	49
Lithuania	na	83	78	85	75	75	91	94	77	80	90	79	80	88	83	54
Luxembourg	na	33	34	32	27	29	41	38	30	34	39	28	25	32	34	31
Macedonia	na	47	48	47	48	47	47	62	41	37	52	45	42	44	46	66
Malta	na	66	60	71	49	64	78	79	61	59	71	60	55	68	67	42
Mexico	65	73	71	76	68	73	82	79	68	63	79	72	66	75	73	65
Moldova	na	73	71	75	60	76	81	83	75	63	81	65	73	74	76	60
Montenegro	na	52	47	58	44	50	60	62	48	42	50	56	49	52	52	52
Morocco	na	97	96	98	95	97	98	97	98	88	97	97	95	98	96	90
Netherlands	36	36	33	38	33	32	40	42	34	32	33	39	35	45	38	27
New Zealand	na	na	na	na	na	na	na	na	na	na	na	na	na	na	na	na
Nigeria	86	79	78	79	78	79	84	83	77	75	79	79	78	77	80	78
Northern Ireland	55	49	49	49	51	40	55	52	48	43	45	49	47	48	49	51
Norway	41	na	na	na	na	na	na	na	na	na	na	na	na	na	na	na
Pakistan	na	62	58	67	61	60	72	70	57	47	71	63	52	61	65	64
Peru	na	68	63	72	66	70	66	71	71	61	73	68	57	73	67	59
Philippines	na	64	66	62	65	63	65	64	64	64	64	64	64	62	65	62
Poland	na	64	63	66	49	61	78	73	56	49	70	62	59	69	63	60
Portugal	57	57	53	60	46	49	69	63	43	49	68	55	52	60	54	52
Puerto Rico	na	65	59	69	51	63	73	82	64	63	71	65	63	73	65	59
Romania	62	81	76	85	73	79	86	89	79	70	88	83	75	85	78	65
Russian Fed.	88	71	65	75	62	69	78	75	69	72	72	73	67	72	69	81
Serbia	na	50	44	55	52	46	52	63	43	43	53	51	45	52	47	42
Singapore	na	na	na	na	na	na	na	na	na	na	na	na	na	na	na	na
Slovakia	na	68	62	75	59	63	81	79	65	59	77	65	67	69	68	68
Slovenia	64	45	44	46	36	40	58	61	42	29	54	47	38	53	45	36
South Africa	na	69	64	75	66	69	77	73	67	38	73	68	64	78	65	55
Spain	40	41	33	48	26	33	56	50	32	29	53	42	31	53	40	20
Sweden	19	26	25	28	21	25	31	36	21	27	27	28	23	33	28	18
Switzerland	na	na	na	na	na	na	na	na	na	na	na	na	na	na	na	na
Taiwan	na	na	na	na	na	na	na	na	na	na	na	na	na	na	na	na
Tanzania	na	80	76	85	79	82	74	78	80	85	78	81	82	82	79	71
Turkey	50	76	76	76	77	74	82	83	69	61	87	74	62	78	76	71
Uganda	na	89	90	88	90	90	85	86	90	93	92	96	92	88	90	90
Ukraine	na	80	72	86	68	81	85	91	78	77	83	80	74	80	78	83
United States	68	58	55	60	54	61	56	64	57	55	60	59	51	63	61	49
Uruguay	na	na	na	na	na	na	na	na	na	na	na	na	na	na	na	na
Venezuela	na	na	na	na	na	na	na	na	na	na	na	na	na	na	na	na
Vietnam	na	45	41	49	40	46	47	50	39	42	41	43	49	45	45	48
Zimbabwe	na	87	80	93	86	88	88	92	81	62	88	89	78	90	85	83
Total	53	58	54	61	56	56	61	64	55	52	62	57	54	64	57	47

RANKING

Country	2000
Morocco	97
Egypt	92
Algeria	91
Uganda	89
Zimbabwe	87
Lithuania	83
Romania	81
Ukraine	80
Tanzania	80
Indonesia	79
Iran	79
Nigeria	79
Turkey	76
Mexico	73
Moldova	73
Russian Fed.	71
South Africa	69
Slovakia	68
Peru	68
Malta	66
Puerto Rico	65
Chile	65
Poland	64
Albania	64
Jordan	64
Philippines	64
Bangladesh	62
Pakistan	62
Italy	62
Croatia	60
Latvia	58
United States	58
Portugal	57
Belarus	56
Argentina	54
Montenegro	52
Canada	51
Serbia	50
Northern Ireland	49
Bosnia and Herz.	48
Germany	48
Macedonia	47
Korea, South	47
Hungary	46
Estonia	45
Vietnam	45
Slovenia	45
Bulgaria	44
Finland	44
Greece	43
Spain	41
Iceland	40
Austria	38
France	36
Netherlands	36
Czech Republic	35
India	33
Luxembourg	33
Belgium	33
Great Britain	33
Ireland	30
Sweden	26
Denmark	20
Japan	20
Total	58

F036) CHURCHES GIVE ANSWERS: THE PROBLEMS OF FAMILY LIFE

Generally speaking, do you think that the churches in your country are giving adequate answers to ...

The problems of family life.

Yes (%)

(WVS: V188; EVS: V112)

Country	Wave 1990	Wave 2000	Male	Female	Age 16-29	Age 30-49	Age 50+	Educ. Lower	Educ. Middle	Educ. Upper	Income Lower	Income Middle	Income Upper	Values Mat	Values Mixed	Values Postm.	RANKING Country	RANKING 2000
Albania	na	53	53	54	47	51	61	58	48	54	54	55	51	53	53	51	Morocco	97
Algeria	na	90	90	89	92	88	88	91	88	90	92	85	88	95	86	92	Algeria	90
Argentina	49	59	55	62	55	58	63	63	52	52	68	59	49	69	61	46	Zimbabwe	88
Armenia	na	na	na	na	na	na	na	na	na	na	na	na	na	na	na	na	Egypt	87
Australia	na	na	na	na	na	na	na	na	na	na	na	na	na	na	na	na	Uganda	84
Austria	34	29	28	30	26	28	31	27	28	38	33	29	29	30	29	29	Lithuania	81
Azerbaijan	na	na	na	na	na	na	na	na	na	na	na	na	na	na	na	na	Tanzania	81
Bangladesh	na	54	54	54	52	54	61	61	44	50	60	57	46	55	53	58	Nigeria	79
Belarus	83	36	29	42	27	32	49	50	33	27	39	35	33	40	33	24	Romania	79
Belgium	37	30	29	31	25	25	37	38	28	27	36	28	26	36	30	21	Indonesia	77
Bosnia and Herz.	na	34	33	34	34	31	37	43	31	33	37	29	39	28	35	26	Peru	76
Brazil	51	na	na	na	na	na	na	na	na	na	na	na	na	na	na	na	Malta	74
Bulgaria	38	29	25	34	22	23	39	45	22	23	40	25	26	28	30	21	Mexico	74
Canada	56	48	45	50	39	48	52	57	48	40	48	48	44	53	50	42	Iran	73
Chile	83	68	66	70	67	68	71	75	66	62	69	70	64	69	65	77	South Africa	73
China	na	na	na	na	na	na	na	na	na	na	na	na	na	na	na	na	Puerto Rico	72
Colombia	na	na	na	na	na	na	na	na	na	na	na	na	na	na	na	na	Chile	68
Croatia	na	59	51	66	50	58	65	67	55	51	77	57	52	70	59	48	Turkey	67
Czech Republic	na	30	26	35	25	23	40	32	28	32	36	28	24	28	32	23	Moldova	67
Denmark	13	15	14	17	13	12	20	18	12	13	15	16	14	12	16	13	Poland	64
Dominican Rep.	na	na	na	na	na	na	na	na	na	na	na	na	na	na	na	na	Slovakia	64
Egypt	na	87	84	91	85	88	90	90	84	88	88	89	87	90	87	81	Ukraine	63
El Salvador	na	na	na	na	na	na	na	na	na	na	na	na	na	na	na	na	Philippines	63
Estonia	na	31	29	32	23	27	38	37	26	32	36	35	25	33	28	20	Jordan	61
Finland	27	42	35	48	32	38	51	43	42	42	45	36	42	37	44	45	United States	61
France	28	28	26	29	22	23	36	29	25	27	30	26	30	31	28	23	Croatia	59
Georgia	na	na	na	na	na	na	na	na	na	na	na	na	na	na	na	na	Argentina	59
Germany	43	39	35	42	34	32	48	44	35	34	39	41	48	46	38	33	Russian Fed.	55
Great Britain	36	30	28	32	25	29	33	29	31	25	33	36	30	na	na	na	Bangladesh	54
Greece	na	31	30	30	24	29	46	53	35	23	38	27	28	39	30	21	Albania	53
Hungary	70	41	31	49	29	33	54	46	30	34	47	40	39	44	37	24	Pakistan	49
Iceland	40	45	41	49	35	45	54	50	42	41	44	47	45	52	45	28	Latvia	48
India	28	27	24	32	25	28	28	30	22	27	26	27	27	26	27	30	Italy	48
Indonesia	na	77	73	83	68	81	79	88	76	71	77	79	72	83	74	71	Northern Ireland	48
Iran	na	73	71	76	74	69	80	79	72	68	75	73	72	77	70	70	Canada	48
Ireland	36	27	25	29	20	23	37	34	22	25	31	26	23	33	27	14	Portugal	46
Israel	na	na	na	na	na	na	na	na	na	na	na	na	na	na	na	na	Iceland	45
Italy	47	48	43	52	34	46	57	54	43	41	56	44	43	61	48	40	Slovenia	43
Japan	22	16	12	20	10	17	18	16	19	9	20	14	13	15	17	11	Finland	42
Jordan	na	61	54	68	61	59	66	65	58	57	64	58	64	63	59	63	Hungary	41
Korea, South	na	39	34	44	34	41	41	40	42	34	35	42	40	41	38	31	Germany	39
Latvia	63	48	43	52	35	44	56	55	44	50	53	45	44	50	47	37	Korea, South	39
Lithuania	na	81	75	85	71	72	93	95	77	70	88	76	78	87	81	57	Serbia	39
Luxembourg	na	24	26	23	19	18	34	26	23	24	22	22	22	29	24	19	Spain	37
Macedonia	na	31	30	32	32	29	33	44	25	24	37	30	25	30	29	45	Belarus	36
Malta	na	74	72	76	61	69	87	84	72	60	75	75	71	76	75	55	Montenegro	34
Mexico	64	74	71	76	71	74	79	78	71	66	80	74	64	73	74	70	Bosnia and Herz.	34
Moldova	na	67	61	71	56	69	73	80	66	55	78	60	60	66	67	70	Netherlands	31
Montenegro	na	34	30	39	26	34	40	41	32	26	34	38	28	32	35	36	Macedonia	31
Morocco	na	97	97	97	96	97	99	97	97	94	97	97	96	97	97	92	Greece	31
Netherlands	34	31	29	33	29	27	36	41	27	26	35	32	23	46	33	20	Estonia	31
New Zealand	na	na	na	na	na	na	na	na	na	na	na	na	na	na	na	na	Czech Republic	30
Nigeria	86	79	78	80	79	79	81	82	78	74	80	78	78	77	80	77	Vietnam	30
Northern Ireland	59	48	47	49	47	37	56	52	45	42	48	48	42	47	47	51	Great Britain	30
Norway	29	na	na	na	na	na	na	na	na	na	na	na	na	na	na	na	Belgium	30
Pakistan	na	49	47	51	45	46	63	53	43	43	51	49	44	52	44	55	Bulgaria	29
Peru	na	76	71	80	75	76	78	79	80	67	80	76	67	80	76	67	Austria	29
Philippines	na	63	60	65	64	63	61	67	60	61	61	61	67	63	62	67	France	28
Poland	na	64	62	66	53	62	73	71	57	49	67	63	59	70	63	50	India	27
Portugal	56	46	42	50	43	36	56	51	32	47	52	44	45	52	43	37	Ireland	27
Puerto Rico	na	72	64	77	65	69	78	88	71	70	78	73	69	79	72	67	Luxembourg	24
Romania	53	79	74	82	71	75	86	88	77	63	85	80	72	83	75	60	Sweden	18
Russian Fed.	74	55	47	61	50	50	64	65	53	55	60	60	46	55	55	54	Japan	16
Serbia	na	39	35	42	43	32	43	49	31	37	43	36	36	40	37	32	Denmark	15
Singapore	na	na	na	na	na	na	na	na	na	na	na	na	na	na	na	na		
Slovakia	na	64	57	71	55	58	77	75	60	58	74	65	58	65	63	64		
Slovenia	54	43	42	43	40	35	54	55	42	26	53	45	34	50	43	37		
South Africa	na	73	66	81	66	77	78	77	70	54	75	72	72	80	71	59		
Spain	42	37	31	42	20	31	52	46	29	24	49	36	28	48	35	21		
Sweden	14	18	17	20	11	15	25	31	13	17	19	19	16	32	19	13		
Switzerland	na	na	na	na	na	na	na	na	na	na	na	na	na	na	na	na		
Taiwan	na	na	na	na	na	na	na	na	na	na	na	na	na	na	na	na		
Tanzania	na	81	78	84	86	79	77	80	82	80	81	83	81	83	80	87		
Turkey	34	67	66	69	66	66	76	77	56	47	77	68	49	72	69	58		
Uganda	na	84	88	80	84	84	85	80	85	91	86	91	86	82	85	86		
Ukraine	na	63	54	70	50	63	71	76	61	62	66	64	59	61	61	75		
United States	69	61	59	63	61	62	59	66	63	58	65	59	58	59	63	57		
Uruguay	na	na	na	na	na	na	na	na	na	na	na	na	na	na	na	na		
Venezuela	na	na	na	na	na	na	na	na	na	na	na	na	na	na	na	na		
Vietnam	na	30	28	33	28	31	32	36	25	21	26	24	38	22	31	38		
Zimbabwe	na	88	83	93	89	87	89	90	86	60	87	90	86	90	87	87		
Total	48	53	49	56	52	50	56	59	50	47	57	51	49	58	52	44	Total	53

F037) CHURCHES GIVE ANSWERS: PEOPLE'S SPIRITUAL NEEDS

Generally speaking, do you think that the churches in your country are giving adequate answers to ...
People's spiritual needs.

Yes (%)

(WVS: V189; EVS: V113)

Country	Wave		Gender		Age			Education			Income			Values				RANKING	
	1990	2000	Male	Female	16-29	30-49	50+	Lower	Middle	Upper	Lower	Middle	Upper	Mat	Mixed	Postm.		Country	2000
Albania	na	79	75	82	81	76	81	83	76	75	79	80	78	75	81	75		Algeria	98
Algeria	na	98	99	97	97	98	98	98	97	98	98	98	96	98	97	97		Morocco	97
Argentina	59	68	64	72	68	65	73	71	67	59	75	67	63	75	71	58		Uganda	93
Armenia	na	na	na	na	na	na	na	na	na	na	na	na	na	na	na	na		Egypt	93
Australia	na	na	na	na	na	na	na	na	na	na	na	na	na	na	na	na		Zimbabwe	91
Austria	68	60	58	62	55	61	62	59	60	68	58	62	60	47	62	59		Tanzania	91
Azerbaijan	na	na	na	na	na	na	na	na	na	na	na	na	na	na	na	na		Romania	89
Bangladesh	na	78	80	73	76	78	84	79	76	77	88	76	72	81	76	78		Croatia	87
Belarus	83	70	63	76	64	67	78	81	66	68	71	70	69	71	68	72		Lithuania	87
Belgium	58	49	47	52	50	43	55	48	49	50	50	45	52	49	50	47		Malta	85
Bosnia and Herz.	na	67	65	68	66	68	65	76	66	61	67	64	70	69	66	61		Nigeria	85
Brazil	57	na	na	na	na	na	na	na	na	na	na	na	na	na	na	na		Indonesia	84
Bulgaria	56	55	43	66	50	50	61	65	50	51	63	49	54	52	55	48		Mexico	83
Canada	75	72	69	75	69	73	73	72	73	70	72	70	73	70	74	69		Slovakia	83
Chile	86	83	80	86	83	80	88	89	80	78	86	82	79	83	83	82		Turkey	83
China	na	na	na	na	na	na	na	na	na	na	na	na	na	na	na	na		Chile	83
Colombia	na	na	na	na	na	na	na	na	na	na	na	na	na	na	na	na		Poland	83
Croatia	na	87	84	90	81	89	89	92	85	83	89	85	87	96	87	79		South Africa	83
Czech Republic	na	69	64	74	71	67	70	71	68	63	68	68	67	67	70	71		Ukraine	82
Denmark	49	51	46	55	47	48	57	57	46	48	51	52	51	56	52	42		Moldova	82
Dominican Rep.	na	na	na	na	na	na	na	na	na	na	na	na	na	na	na	na		Latvia	81
Egypt	na	93	92	94	91	93	94	95	90	92	94	95	92	95	92	89		Philippines	81
El Salvador	na	na	na	na	na	na	na	na	na	na	na	na	na	na	na	na		Peru	80
Estonia	na	73	66	79	64	70	80	78	69	74	78	73	70	75	73	73		Albania	79
Finland	51	68	60	76	67	65	71	70	66	71	73	61	68	69	68	72		Bangladesh	78
France	59	55	54	57	56	53	58	52	53	67	51	55	63	55	55	55		Northern Ireland	77
Georgia	na	na	na	na	na	na	na	na	na	na	na	na	na	na	na	na		Puerto Rico	76
Germany	64	56	51	59	51	49	64	60	51	57	53	59	56	58	55	54		Macedonia	75
Great Britain	63	58	57	60	55	61	56	55	57	71	59	59	62	na	na	na		Montenegro	75
Greece	na	62	59	64	59	63	68	81	65	56	63	62	64	71	63	50		Iran	75
Hungary	90	67	57	76	60	63	76	71	62	55	74	65	68	69	65	68		United States	75
Iceland	58	54	51	57	47	51	65	60	50	50	54	56	49	63	54	32		Russian Fed.	74
India	59	43	39	49	40	45	44	47	41	40	35	45	45	46	40	48		Estonia	73
Indonesia	na	84	82	87	74	84	90	91	84	80	83	85	83	87	82	74		Serbia	73
Iran	na	75	73	77	71	77	81	83	73	66	75	76	70	81	73	59		Portugal	73
Ireland	71	64	60	67	60	60	70	69	62	60	68	63	62	74	62	54		Italy	72
Israel	na	na	na	na	na	na	na	na	na	na	na	na	na	na	na	na		Canada	72
Italy	72	72	69	75	67	70	78	77	68	70	79	70	69	81	72	69		Slovenia	70
Japan	42	34	29	39	48	35	27	24	36	34	36	33	32	40	34	21		Belarus	70
Jordan	na	64	58	71	63	63	73	69	60	61	66	64	64	68	61	62		Czech Republic	69
Korea, South	na	59	53	65	54	58	67	63	61	55	54	63	61	61	58	46		Argentina	68
Latvia	87	81	75	86	76	78	86	88	79	76	84	80	80	81	81	86		Finland	68
Lithuania	na	87	81	91	86	77	95	97	84	78	94	86	83	92	88	65		Hungary	67
Luxembourg	na	46	45	47	43	45	49	46	44	50	42	41	42	40	46	49		Bosnia and Herz.	67
Macedonia	na	75	76	75	76	74	76	82	72	72	82	73	68	77	73	82		Pakistan	65
Malta	na	85	83	88	83	81	90	90	83	84	83	86	83	80	86	70		Jordan	64
Mexico	80	83	82	84	80	85	86	86	81	78	88	81	81	85	83	78		Ireland	64
Moldova	na	82	78	86	73	83	88	91	82	75	87	80	78	84	80	85		Greece	62
Montenegro	na	75	71	79	74	72	78	81	71	72	74	76	70	74	75	81		Vietnam	60
Morocco	na	97	97	97	96	98	99	98	97	92	98	98	96	98	97	97		Austria	60
Netherlands	55	49	46	53	55	48	49	50	50	48	49	49	48	62	53	35		Korea, South	59
New Zealand	na	na	na	na	na	na	na	na	na	na	na	na	na	na	na	na		Great Britain	58
Nigeria	89	85	85	85	85	84	92	86	85	86	86	84	86	86	85	81		Sweden	57
Northern Ireland	80	77	73	80	80	68	82	80	74	73	73	81	77	75	77	76		Germany	56
Norway	55	na	na	na	na	na	na	na	na	na	na	na	na	na	na	na		France	55
Pakistan	na	65	62	69	61	66	72	71	62	51	71	67	57	64	68	91		Bulgaria	55
Peru	na	80	78	83	80	79	83	84	84	72	84	82	72	85	81	69		Spain	55
Philippines	na	81	80	81	82	80	80	79	79	85	77	82	83	79	82	85		Iceland	54
Poland	na	83	83	83	79	83	86	87	79	74	84	84	80	87	82	75		Denmark	51
Portugal	62	73	65	80	68	68	79	77	62	65	77	72	67	76	71	68		Netherlands	49
Puerto Rico	na	76	70	80	67	73	83	90	74	75	82	76	74	78	78	71		Belgium	49
Romania	78	89	88	90	85	90	91	89	90	85	90	91	86	90	89	80		Luxembourg	46
Russian Fed.	92	74	67	81	74	73	77	80	75	71	77	76	69	76	73	66		India	43
Serbia	na	73	69	77	77	69	74	80	68	72.	74	74	71	74	73	56		Japan	34
Singapore	na	na	na	na	na	na	na	na	na	na	na	na	na	na	na	na			
Slovakia	na	83	80	86	79	80	89	88	82	77	90	84	80	86	81	82			
Slovenia	77	70	69	72	70	69	72	78	70	58	75	71	62	78	70	65			
South Africa	na	83	78	88	81	82	86	83	82	74	84	81	78	85	81	79			
Spain	54	55	48	61	44	47	67	62	48	48	66	54	47	63	55	39			
Sweden	51	57	55	58	55	53	61	66	56	51	53	61	53	64	60	46			
Switzerland	na	na	na	na	na	na	na	na	na	na	na	na	na	na	na	na			
Taiwan	na	na	na	na	na	na	na	na	na	na	na	na	na	na	na	na			
Tanzania	na	91	91	90	88	93	90	89	91	93	88	92	92	94	90	82			
Turkey	59	83	82	85	83	82	87	87	78	77	87	84	75	83	85	78			
Uganda	na	93	93	93	94	95	83	93	92	99	92	96	93	92	94	94			
Ukraine	na	82	74	88	77	82	85	90	79	86	81	83	82	80	82	95			
United States	84	75	73	76	74	75	74	75	75	74	74	75	75	79	75	73			
Uruguay	na	na	na	na	na	na	na	na	na	na	na	na	na	na	na	na			
Venezuela	na	na	na	na	na	na	na	na	na	na	na	na	na	na	na	na			
Vietnam	na	60	59	62	57	61	63	66	54	56	56	55	68	56	61	63			
Zimbabwe	na	91	86	95	90	91	95	94	88	70	91	93	89	93	89	91			
Total	68	73	69	76	72	71	75	76	71	69	75	72	71	76	72	65		Total	73

F038) CHURCHES GIVE ANSWERS: THE SOCIAL PROBLEMS

Generally speaking, do you think that the churches in your country are giving adequate answers to ...

The social problems facing our country today.

Yes (%) (WVS: V190; EVS: V114)

Country	Wave 1990	Wave 2000	Male	Female	16-29	30-49	50+	Education Lower	Middle	Upper	Income Lower	Middle	Upper	Mat	Mixed	Postm.	RANKING Country	2000
Albania	na	33	32	34	28	28	43	40	26	33	36	27	35	39	31	12	Morocco	91
Algeria	na	77	81	72	79	75	75	83	75	75	81	72	71	84	72	76	Egypt	83
Argentina	37	50	47	52	43	47	58	53	45	42	57	51	41	59	52	37	Algeria	77
Armenia	na	na	na	na	na	na	na	na	na	na	na	na	na	na	na	na	Tanzania	74
Australia	na	na	na	na	na	na	na	na	na	na	na	na	na	na	na	na	Nigeria	73
Austria	39	30	27	33	20	30	35	27	31	38	30	30	29	28	29	34	Zimbabwe	72
Azerbaijan	na	na	na	na	na	na	na	na	na	na	na	na	na	na	na	na	Uganda	70
Bangladesh	na	58	59	55	57	57	65	62	50	57	58	59	56	62	55	59	Puerto Rico	65
Belarus	83	23	18	27	18	19	33	36	20	15	26	22	19	26	20	11	Jordan	65
Belgium	29	27	28	26	22	24	33	32	25	27	33	25	26	31	28	20	Peru	64
Bosnia and Herz.	na	27	26	28	27	26	27	32	26	26	28	23	31	23	28	26	Indonesia	64
Brazil	42	na	na	na	na	na	na	na	na	na	na	na	na	na	na	na	South Africa	62
Bulgaria	23	15	12	18	12	13	18	24	12	10	25	12	9	12	16	12	Iran	62
Canada	44	35	32	38	27	35	40	42	34	31	39	37	31	37	38	31	Lithuania	61
Chile	76	50	47	53	44	50	55	59	46	40	54	49	46	55	51	38	Bangladesh	58
China	na	na	na	na	na	na	na	na	na	na	na	na	na	na	na	na	Malta	56
Colombia	na	na	na	na	na	na	na	na	na	na	na	na	na	na	na	na	Mexico	54
Croatia	na	44	39	49	38	44	48	49	43	35	56	40	42	59	45	29	Philippines	52
Czech Republic	na	15	12	19	10	11	23	17	13	17	22	15	9	16	15	19	Romania	52
Denmark	8	12	11	12	9	12	13	14	10	10	12	11	12	8	12	13	Chile	50
Dominican Rep.	na	na	na	na	na	na	na	na	na	na	na	na	na	na	na	na	Argentina	50
Egypt	na	83	80	86	81	82	86	84	80	84	83	82	84	86	81	76	United States	46
El Salvador	na	na	na	na	na	na	na	na	na	na	na	na	na	na	na	na	Pakistan	45
Estonia	na	14	11	16	15	10	17	17	13	14	17	16	12	17	12	5	Croatia	44
Finland	12	31	26	36	23	27	40	34	24	37	33	29	31	31	30	37	Turkey	44
France	24	21	19	23	15	20	26	23	18	21	22	21	21	24	22	15	Italy	44
Georgia	na	na	na	na	na	na	na	na	na	na	na	na	na	na	na	na	Poland	39
Germany	58	32	29	34	22	26	42	37	27	30	33	34	35	39	30	25	Moldova	39
Great Britain	29	27	25	29	23	25	30	27	27	21	33	31	28	na	na	na	Netherlands	37
Greece	na	31	30	31	26	31	42	51	37	22	37	30	27	37	31	23	Portugal	36
Hungary	55	25	20	30	12	23	35	29	16	19	32	24	24	25	24	23	Northern Ireland	36
Iceland	24	28	26	30	23	26	35	36	23	21	34	24	26	31	28	17	Canada	35
India	24	29	26	33	28	29	29	33	24	26	26	28	29	29	27	32	Slovenia	34
Indonesia	na	64	64	65	56	66	59	76	62	59	61	64	70	70	60	52	Albania	33
Iran	na	62	58	66	58	62	72	75	59	49	61	60	61	68	58	51	Germany	32
Ireland	33	27	28	25	18	24	36	32	25	22	29	28	24	31	27	19	Greece	31
Israel	na	na	na	na	na	na	na	na	na	na	na	na	na	na	na	na	Finland	31
Italy	43	44	40	46	30	42	53	50	39	39	50	42	41	52	43	40	Spain	31
Japan	7	7	5	9	4	7	9	13	8	4	9	4	7	7	6	3	Ukraine	30
Jordan	na	65	57	72	65	63	68	67	65	60	65	67	60	68	61	64	Austria	30
Korea, South	na	23	23	23	15	23	34	23	26	18	22	23	24	24	22	19	Slovakia	30
Latvia	42	26	22	30	23	21	32	32	24	27	31	23	22	26	27	19	India	29
Lithuania	na	61	57	65	46	50	77	85	52	46	77	57	52	69	62	35	Iceland	28
Luxembourg	na	24	25	24	14	22	34	27	20	29	20	25	25	25	24	25	Serbia	28
Macedonia	na	22	23	20	23	19	24	29	19	16	24	23	15	19	22	23	Belgium	27
Malta	na	56	51	61	40	52	69	67	53	45	63	57	49	61	55	43	Great Britain	27
Mexico	47	54	49	59	49	53	63	64	44	36	65	51	40	60	51	44	Bosnia and Herz.	27
Moldova	na	39	34	43	27	41	48	54	39	28	46	37	33	40	40	38	Ireland	27
Montenegro	na	22	21	22	12	24	25	23	21	20	21	24	17	21	21	18	Latvia	26
Morocco	na	91	91	92	89	92	96	93	87	77	95	88	89	92	91	84	Hungary	25
Netherlands	33	37	35	39	34	35	40	37	37	36	35	37	36	49	38	29	Russian Fed.	25
New Zealand	na	na	na	na	na	na	na	na	na	na	na	na	na	na	na	na	Luxembourg	24
Nigeria	83	73	72	74	73	72	75	75	72	69	72	75	70	72	74	66	Belarus	23
Northern Ireland	52	36	34	39	36	26	45	41	33	30	34	33	32	36	36	38	Korea, South	23
Norway	19	na	na	na	na	na	na	na	na	na	na	na	na	na	na	na	Montenegro	22
Pakistan	na	45	44	46	44	45	47	51	40	34	52	44	35	46	44	36	Macedonia	22
Peru	na	64	59	70	64	65	66	70	68	55	70	63	55	70	64	56	France	21
Philippines	na	52	52	53	52	51	56	55	49	54	51	55	49	49	55	53	Vietnam	18
Poland	na	39	36	43	28	37	50	45	35	28	46	38	29	43	39	36	Sweden	17
Portugal	44	36	31	41	30	30	47	41	25	31	43	37	36	42	32	30	Czech Republic	15
Puerto Rico	na	65	61	69	53	63	74	79	67	63	74	64	64	75	66	59	Bulgaria	15
Romania	32	52	46	59	39	46	65	69	48	34	65	52	43	58	49	33	Estonia	14
Russian Fed.	60	25	19	30	19	22	33	37	24	23	31	27	18	26	25	23	Denmark	12
Serbia	na	28	24	32	26	25	31	35	26	24	33	30	21	29	27	25	Japan	7
Singapore	na	na	na	na	na	na	na	na	na	na	na	na	na	na	na	na		
Slovakia	na	30	23	37	20	24	45	46	24	20	43	28	24	33	28	24		
Slovenia	49	34	32	36	28	35	48	45	30	26	45	38	21	39	33	31		
South Africa	na	62	56	69	60	61	70	62	64	53	60	70	58	72	55	66		
Spain	33	31	26	35	15	25	46	39	22	25	40	29	27	41	30	15		
Sweden	12	17	16	18	11	16	22	25	15	16	17	20	14	16	18	15		
Switzerland	na	na	na	na	na	na	na	na	na	na	na	na	na	na	na	na		
Taiwan	na	na	na	na	na	na	na	na	na	na	na	na	na	na	na	na		
Tanzania	na	74	71	77	77	73	69	72	77	73	73	77	72	73	75	70		
Turkey	29	44	45	42	40	45	54	50	36	34	47	45	34	47	44	39		
Uganda	na	70	78	63	72	67	72	68	70	83	76	84	67	67	69	84		
Ukraine	na	30	22	37	25	32	32	41	30	25	31	31	28	25	31	52		
United States	57	46	42	49	40	48	46	49	47	44	52	42	42	52	48	37		
Uruguay	na	na	na	na	na	na	na	na	na	na	na	na	na	na	na	na		
Venezuela	na	na	na	na	na	na	na	na	na	na	na	na	na	na	na	na		
Vietnam	na	18	16	20	12	18	22	22	14	13	21	15	21	16	19	19		
Zimbabwe	na	72	63	81	70	71	82	80	63	48	79	70	67	76	70	63		
Total	40	41	39	44	41	39	44	48	38	37	46	40	37	45	41	35	Total	41

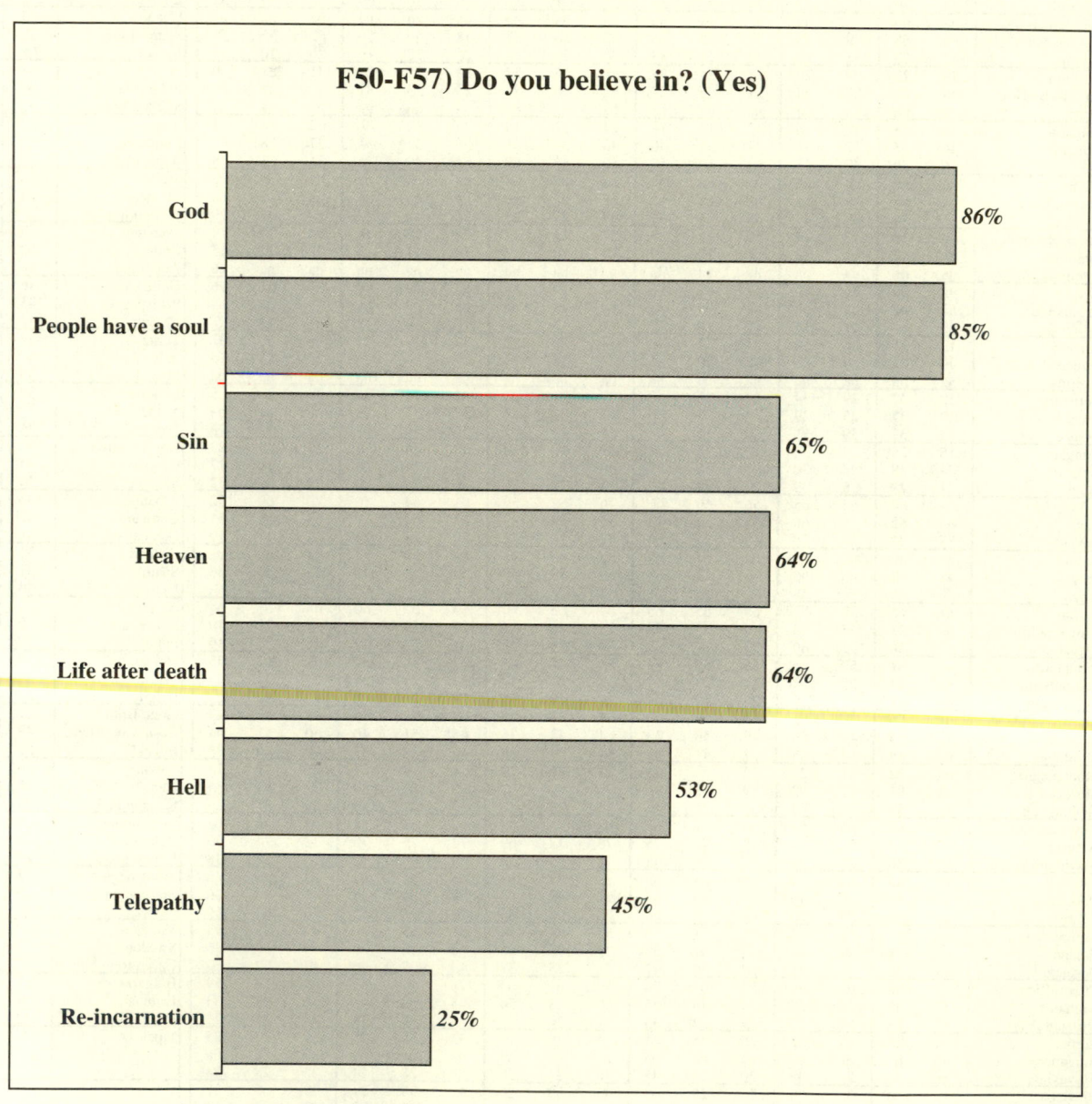

F50-F57) Do you believe in? (Yes)

- God — 86%
- People have a soul — 85%
- Sin — 65%
- Heaven — 64%
- Life after death — 64%
- Hell — 53%
- Telepathy — 45%
- Re-incarnation — 25%

F050) BELIEVE IN GOD

Which, if any, of the following do you believe in? Believe in God.

Yes (%)

(WVS: V191; EVS: V115)

Country	Wave		Gender		Age			Education			Income			Values			RANKING Country	2000
	1990	2000	Male	Female	16-29	30-49	50+	Lower	Middle	Upper	Lower	Middle	Upper	Mat	Mixed	Postm.		
Albania	na	92	88	96	90	93	92	94	91	88	92	91	92	91	92	87	Morocco	100
Algeria	na	100	100	100	100	99	100	100	100	99	100	100	99	99	97	93	Pakistan	100
Argentina	92	96	94	98	95	97	97	98	95	91	98	97	94	99	97	93	Egypt	100
Armenia	na	86	80	91	89	84	82	83	87	83	84	86	88	85	88	70	Algeria	100
Australia	na	80	75	86	79	77	85	86	78	78	84	80	73	83	82	76	Jordan	100
Austria	87	87	83	90	80	87	91	87	88	83	86	88	86	90	88	82	Nigeria	100
Azerbaijan	na	98	97	99	98	98	97	97	99	96	99	99	95	98	98	97	Bangladesh	100
Bangladesh	na	100	99	100	99	100	100	100	99	99	100	99	100	100	99	100	Indonesia	100
Belarus	43	83	72	91	79	82	86	90	82	73	86	83	75	85	82	69	Malta	100
Belgium	69	71	65	76	56	67	81	79	69	69	76	71	66	79	71	62	El Salvador	99
Bosnia and Herz.	na	88	86	90	93	90	81	94	90	78	88	88	87	90	87	88	Iran	99
Brazil	99	99	99	100	99	99	100	100	99	98	99	100	99	99	99	99	Philippines	99
Bulgaria	40	66	60	72	66	61	71	77	61	59	73	68	60	68	64	67	Zimbabwe	99
Canada	89	89	86	93	84	88	94	92	91	85	92	90	86	94	92	82	Uganda	99
Chile	95	97	96	98	97	97	97	98	97	93	99	97	94	98	98	91	Tanzania	99
China	na	na	na	na	na	na	na	na	na	na	na	na	na	na	na	na	Brazil	99
Colombia	na	99	99	100	99	99	99	100	99	98	100	100	98	100	99	98	Colombia	99
Croatia	na	93	92	95	89	96	93	96	94	85	93	94	92	98	93	89	South Africa	99
Czech Republic	na	39	32	46	34	31	49	40	38	40	46	36	32	43	37	40	Puerto Rico	99
Denmark	64	69	61	77	55	67	79	74	55	64	72	70	63	64	71	59	Peru	99
Dominican Rep.	na	93	95	91	95	89	91	87	94	93	90	93	95	92	93	92	Mexico	98
Egypt	na	100	100	100	100	100	100	100	100	100	100	100	100	100	100	100	Turkey	98
El Salvador	na	99	99	100	99	100	99	100	99	99	100	99	100	na	na	na	Azerbaijan	98
Estonia	na	51	40	61	43	46	61	58	49	45	61	58	44	54	51	31	Poland	97
Finland	76	83	73	91	73	79	91	83	83	83	83	75	89	81	85	74	Chile	97
France	62	62	58	64	53	60	67	63	59	60	61	61	61	67	63	48	Argentina	96
Georgia	na	93	90	96	96	94	89	92	94	93	92	94	94	94	92	99	Portugal	96
Germany	36	68	61	73	56	63	78	74	62	66	64	70	71	68	69	65	Romania	96
Great Britain	78	72	63	80	64	71	76	74	71	62	68	74	67	na	na	na	Moldova	96
Greece	na	91	88	93	90	91	95	97	95	87	93	91	89	96	93	80	United States	96
Hungary	65	68	56	79	53	63	82	74	57	52	76	71	62	75	62	54	Ireland	96
Iceland	85	84	78	90	76	86	89	87	84	80	85	87	82	88	85	73	India	95
India	94	95	94	96	94	96	94	95	93	94	93	96	95	96	93	93	Italy	94
Indonesia	na	100	100	100	99	100	100	100	100	100	100	100	99	100	100	100	Croatia	93
Iran	na	99	99	100	99	100	99	100	100	99	99	100	99	100	100	99	Georgia	93
Ireland	98	96	93	98	93	94	98	95	95	97	96	96	95	99	95	90	Northern Ireland	93
Israel	na	na	na	na	na	na	na	na	na	na	na	na	na	na	na	na	Dominican Rep.	93
Italy	91	94	90	97	94	92	95	96	92	90	94	94	90	97	94	89	Albania	92
Japan	65	53	46	59	47	55	53	56	53	49	55	55	49	54	52	51	Greece	91
Jordan	na	100	100	100	100	100	100	100	100	99	100	100	100	100	100	100	Macedonia	91
Korea, South	na	na	na	na	na	na	na	na	na	na	na	na	na	na	na	na	Canada	89
Latvia	58	80	67	90	75	79	82	83	78	80	82	80	76	80	80	80	Bosnia and Herz.	88
Lithuania	na	87	75	95	80	83	93	95	83	85	95	82	86	88	87	68	Singapore	87
Luxembourg	na	73	67	79	63	73	81	73	74	73	70	74	71	75	73	67	Austria	87
Macedonia	na	91	89	92	91	92	88	98	87	86	96	89	85	92	90	89	Uruguay	87
Malta	na	100	99	100	100	99	100	100	99	100	99	100	99	98	98	97	Lithuania	87
Mexico	93	98	98	98	98	98	99	99	97	97	99	98	97	99	98	96	Armenia	86
Moldova	na	96	94	98	94	97	97	98	97	92	97	96	95	97	96	96	Spain	85
Montenegro	na	83	80	86	77	84	86	89	80	75	84	87	83	85	83	72	Iceland	84
Morocco	na	100	100	100	100	100	100	100	100	100	100	100	100	100	100	100	Switzerland	83
Netherlands	64	60	55	64	50	54	70	66	58	56	58	62	52	76	57	58	Montenegro	83
New Zealand	na	78	74	81	76	73	83	77	82	77	79	79	74	84	80	71	Belarus	83
Nigeria	100	100	100	100	100	100	100	100	100	100	100	100	100	100	100	99	Slovakia	83
Northern Ireland	97	93	90	96	89	94	95	95	92	92	95	94	92	96	92	92	Finland	83
Norway	65	69	60	77	55	68	80	74	68	65	na	na	na	75	70	53	Serbia	83
Pakistan	na	100	100	100	100	100	100	100	100	100	100	100	100	100	100	100	Ukraine	80
Peru	na	99	98	100	98	99	99	98	99	97	99	99	97	99	99	98	Australia	80
Philippines	na	99	99	100	100	99	99	99	100	99	100	99	99	99	100	100	Latvia	80
Poland	97	97	97	98	97	98	97	99	96	93	98	97	95	99	96	95	New Zealand	78
Portugal	86	96	94	98	92	98	98	99	94	82	100	97	94	99	97	90	Taiwan	76
Puerto Rico	na	99	99	99	99	99	99	100	99	99	99	100	99	99	99	99	Luxembourg	73
Romania	94	96	94	99	94	98	97	98	96	94	97	97	96	96	97	92	Great Britain	72
Russian Fed.	44	70	57	81	70	66	75	80	69	68	76	68	66	75	66	55	Belgium	71
Serbia	na	83	76	88	86	82	81	90	78	79	86	83	78	85	81	75	Russian Fed.	70
Singapore	na	87	84	90	84	89	94	90	86	83	89	89	84	92	86	76	Denmark	69
Slovakia	na	83	77	88	76	80	91	87	82	72	89	85	78	84	82	85	Norway	69
Slovenia	63	65	61	69	59	64	71	81	64	41	76	62	50	81	62	62	Hungary	68
South Africa	98	99	98	100	99	99	99	99	99	99	99	100	98	99	99	99	Germany	68
Spain	86	85	79	90	73	84	93	91	80	75	89	83	81	92	84	72	Bulgaria	66
Sweden	45	53	46	61	43	50	63	61	49	54	52	57	50	58	54	47	Slovenia	65
Switzerland	na	83	78	89	66	85	91	86	82	85	84	86	82	89	83	82	France	62
Taiwan	na	76	70	83	79	74	82	81	76	72	77	78	71	78	75	68	Netherlands	60
Tanzania	na	99	99	99	100	99	100	99	100	99	99	100	99	100	100	100	Sweden	53
Turkey	na	98	97	99	97	98	99	100	97	91	99	98	94	100	98	94	Japan	53
Uganda	na	99	99	100	99	100	97	98	100	100	100	100	100	99	100	99	Estonia	51
Ukraine	na	80	68	90	80	81	80	85	79	80	82	81	79	81	77	83	Czech Republic	39
United States	96	96	94	98	93	97	96	94	97	95	96	95	96	97	96	95	Vietnam	19
Uruguay	na	87	81	91	81	83	92	91	83	71	91	85	86	87	89	80		
Venezuela	na	na	na	na	na	na	na	na	na	na	na	na	na	na	na	na		
Vietnam	na	19	14	24	22	19	17	25	10	15	15	19	20	32	15	17		
Zimbabwe	na	99	100	99	99	100	100	99	99	100	99	99	100	99	100	100		
Total	76	86	83	89	86	85	87	89	85	84	88	87	84	89	85	81	Total	86

F051) BELIEVE IN LIFE AFTER DEATH

Which, if any, of the following do you believe in? Believe in life after death

Yes (%) (WVS: V192; EVS: V116)

Country	Wave 1990	Wave 2000	Gender Male	Gender Female	Age 16-29	Age 30-49	Age 50+	Education Lower	Education Middle	Education Upper	Income Lower	Income Middle	Income Upper	Values Mat	Values Mixed	Values Postm.
Albania	na	47	41	54	47	42	56	55	42	40	43	51	49	45	48	39
Algeria	na	100	100	100	100	99	100	100	100	99	100	100	99	100	100	99
Argentina	65	63	56	70	64	67	59	60	69	67	59	64	67	62	64	63
Armenia	na	36	30	42	41	36	29	36	37	35	40	37	29	33	41	32
Australia	na	64	55	73	69	63	60	67	64	62	66	64	57	59	66	62
Austria	56	59	53	65	62	61	56	55	65	59	59	61	56	44	58	65
Azerbaijan	na	56	50	61	58	51	64	69	53	57	55	59	49	52	60	70
Bangladesh	na	56	55	57	53	56	68	61	50	49	73	50	46	60	51	51
Belarus	18	41	30	50	43	36	45	45	40	40	39	39	48	42	40	39
Belgium	44	44	40	48	45	41	45	39	42	50	48	44	40	42	45	42
Bosnia and Herz.	na	60	56	64	68	57	57	73	59	54	67	58	61	62	60	57
Brazil	74	71	70	71	73	68	71	64	76	76	72	65	74	64	73	77
Bulgaria	18	36	30	42	40	30	39	46	31	32	42	29	34	35	35	49
Canada	69	73	67	78	74	71	73	68	76	71	71	77	70	70	74	72
Chile	70	82	75	87	84	81	81	80	82	85	81	80	85	86	82	75
China	na	na	na	na	na	na	na	na	na	na	na	na	na	na	na	na
Colombia	na	70	68	71	70	68	76	73	66	72	74	68	70	67	70	62
Croatia	na	68	62	73	72	71	62	71	66	64	63	64	75	74	68	64
Czech Republic	na	36	30	42	48	30	35	36	36	35	36	36	31	33	36	42
Denmark	34	38	28	49	49	39	32	36	35	42	41	37	35	31	38	39
Dominican Rep.	na	72	72	72	75	66	82	62	68	75	66	75	77	58	74	81
Egypt	na	100	100	100	100	100	100	100	100	100	100	100	100	100	100	100
El Salvador	na	83	80	86	84	83	84	84	82	84	87	81	83	na	na	na
Estonia	na	36	29	43	43	38	31	36	35	40	36	33	40	32	39	38
Finland	60	57	44	68	50	54	62	57	55	62	60	49	59	55	57	63
France	44	45	35	54	49	48	39	43	49	45	44	47	41	46	44	44
Georgia	na	58	54	60	68	56	48	52	56	66	52	57	67	56	59	62
Germany	21	39	34	43	38	38	40	41	37	35	33	40	42	36	40	45
Great Britain	52	58	48	68	58	58	58	54	62	57	55	61	60	na	na	na
Greece	na	61	57	63	62	61	58	62	65	56	61	60	59	67	61	49
Hungary	26	33	24	41	37	31	32	31	36	37	35	32	34	31	36	44
Iceland	81	78	72	85	79	77	79	83	79	69	80	79	75	85	78	65
India	41	66	63	69	63	67	67	70	62	59	67	65	65	75	52	66
Indonesia	na	99	100	99	99	99	100	100	99	100	100	99	99	100	99	100
Iran	na	98	97	98	98	97	99	98	97	98	98	99	97	99	98	97
Ireland	83	79	75	83	67	80	86	80	77	82	82	78	82	76	81	75
Israel	na	na	na	na	na	na	na	na	na	na	na	na	na	na	na	na
Italy	68	73	63	81	74	74	71	70	75	76	73	72	72	75	73	71
Japan	54	51	41	60	61	61	35	48	54	46	52	56	43	48	53	48
Jordan	na	98	98	97	97	97	99	97	99	98	97	99	97	97	98	95
Korea, South	na	na	na	na	na	na	na	na	na	na	na	na	na	na	na	na
Latvia	30	45	30	59	53	44	43	52	42	48	47	47	43	47	44	50
Lithuania	na	79	66	88	77	72	85	95	72	73	91	70	77	85	77	64
Luxembourg	na	54	47	61	54	50	59	54	54	54	57	50	57	57	51	57
Macedonia	na	47	43	50	61	17	26	63	39	39	47	47	45	43	47	69
Malta	na	86	84	89	85	86	87	87	85	93	86	89	87	83	80	81
Mexico	61	76	73	78	72	76	80	75	77	76	75	76	77	78	75	77
Moldova	na	59	52	65	62	55	63	68	57	55	66	54	58	61	59	48
Montenegro	na	23	18	28	16	24	27	34	18	13	29	20	20	22	21	24
Morocco	na	100	100	100	100	100	100	100	99	100	100	100	100	100	100	98
Netherlands	47	51	46	55	54	51	49	49	53	49	51	49	48	57	51	46
New Zealand	na	64	53	73	77	64	60	58	67	69	65	67	61	63	65	62
Nigeria	82	88	88	87	87	88	88	89	86	88	88	87	87	86	89	83
Northern Ireland	78	75	70	80	66	73	83	78	69	82	77	80	75	78	76	71
Norway	45	47	37	58	47	47	48	47	47	49	na	na	na	42	49	44
Pakistan	na	100	100	100	100	100	100	100	100	100	100	100	100	100	100	100
Peru	na	72	68	76	70	74	72	75	71	72	70	74	74	71	73	69
Philippines	na	86	87	86	86	87	86	85	85	90	87	87	86	86	87	84
Poland	78	80	74	86	85	80	79	81	81	75	83	79	79	85	77	81
Portugal	39	47	41	54	43	47	50	46	50	46	54	42	41	52	44	47
Puerto Rico	na	78	76	80	74	82	78	86	71	80	74	79	81	73	80	76
Romania	58	68	61	75	79	66	64	70	68	63	68	67	68	71	64	72
Russian Fed.	21	37	26	46	47	31	36	42	36	36	40	34	35	36	36	33
Serbia	na	27	23	32	38	25	24	32	21	31	30	24	26	22	32	34
Singapore	na	74	71	77	72	76	76	76	74	69	79	74	72	79	72	73
Slovakia	na	68	62	74	62	64	78	73	68	58	73	68	67	69	67	76
Slovenia	28	32	28	36	37	27	34	39	30	29	38	30	24	29	32	37
South Africa	78	73	64	83	71	71	83	70	77	64	66	74	78	76	70	77
Spain	52	53	43	63	47	50	59	56	48	54	59	52	51	61	51	44
Sweden	38	46	32	59	53	46	42	40	48	48	51	47	37	45	46	44
Switzerland	64	64	57	70	68	64	60	65	63	64	61	62	63	68	62	70
Taiwan	na	61	55	66	71	60	55	61	54	64	55	63	61	64	59	39
Tanzania	na	87	88	86	84	89	90	86	87	92	87	86	90	90	86	82
Turkey	80	90	89	91	90	89	93	93	88	77	94	90	80	94	90	84
Uganda	na	85	83	87	82	90	79	80	87	86	82	92	85	84	85	87
Ukraine	na	40	30	49	48	37	38	48	37	43	40	40	38	35	41	50
United States	78	81	79	84	77	83	83	77	83	82	81	81	83	83	81	80
Uruguay	na	45	37	51	48	44	45	43	47	51	42	45	50	43	45	49
Venezuela	na	na	na	na	na	na	na	na	na	na	na	na	na	na	na	na
Vietnam	na	16	11	20	18	15	16	20	10	13	14	14	19	15	16	15
Zimbabwe	na	75	73	76	72	75	80	73	76	100	67	77	77	77	73	71
Total	53	64	59	69	69	63	60	66	62	65	66	63	63	64	63	63

RANKING

Country	2000
Pakistan	100
Egypt	100
Algeria	100
Morocco	100
Indonesia	99
Iran	98
Jordan	98
Turkey	90
Nigeria	88
Tanzania	87
Philippines	86
Malta	86
Uganda	85
El Salvador	83
Chile	82
United States	81
Poland	80
Ireland	79
Lithuania	79
Iceland	78
Puerto Rico	78
Mexico	76
Northern Ireland	75
Zimbabwe	75
Singapore	74
Italy	73
South Africa	73
Canada	73
Dominican Rep.	72
Peru	72
Brazil	71
Colombia	70
Slovakia	68
Croatia	68
Romania	68
India	66
Australia	64
New Zealand	64
Switzerland	64
Argentina	63
Taiwan	61
Greece	61
Bosnia and Herz.	60
Moldova	59
Austria	59
Great Britain	58
Georgia	58
Finland	57
Bangladesh	56
Azerbaijan	56
Luxembourg	54
Spain	53
Japan	51
Netherlands	51
Norway	47
Portugal	47
Albania	47
Macedonia	47
Sweden	46
Latvia	45
Uruguay	45
France	45
Belgium	44
Belarus	41
Ukraine	40
Germany	39
Denmark	38
Russian Fed.	37
Armenia	36
Estonia	36
Czech Republic	36
Bulgaria	36
Hungary	33
Slovenia	32
Serbia	27
Montenegro	23
Vietnam	16
Total	64

F052) BELIEVE IN PEOPLE HAVE A SOUL

Which, if any, of the following do you believe in? Do you believe people have a soul?.

Yes (%)

(WVS: V193)

Country	Wave 1990	Wave 2000	Gender Male	Gender Female	Age 16-29	Age 30-49	Age 50+	Education Lower	Education Middle	Education Upper	Income Lower	Income Middle	Income Upper	Values Mat	Values Mixed	Values Postm.
Albania	na	75	69	81	74	74	78	80	72	68	75	77	73	73	75	72
Algeria	na	99	100	99	99	99	99	99	100	99	100	99	98	100	99	99
Argentina	81	85	82	88	83	88	86	84	89	85	86	85	86	88	86	83
Armenia	na	65	59	70	69	65	58	56	64	71	70	62	59	59	71	65
Australia	na	85	77	93	87	85	83	88	83	85	86	85	84	85	86	85
Austria	73	na	na	na	na	na	na	na	na	na	na	na	na	na	na	na
Azerbaijan	na	69	62	76	70	67	76	79	70	67	75	72	58	67	72	81
Bangladesh	na	99	99	99	100	99	100	100	99	99	100	99	99	100	99	100
Belarus	45	na	na	na	na	na	na	na	na	na	na	na	na	na	na	na
Belgium	60	na	na	na	na	na	na	na	na	na	na	na	na	na	na	na
Bosnia and Herz.	na	85	83	87	90	84	81	89	85	82	91	84	82	85	85	90
Brazil	84	82	81	84	83	81	83	78	85	86	82	81	83	76	85	88
Bulgaria	38	na	na	na	na	na	na	na	na	na	na	na	na	na	na	na
Canada	85	91	86	96	92	90	92	92	92	88	93	93	88	92	92	89
Chile	81	89	85	93	90	89	89	90	89	89	90	89	89	91	91	82
China	na	na	na	na	na	na	na	na	na	na	na	na	na	na	na	na
Colombia	na	87	85	89	87	87	88	89	85	89	88	87	88	89	87	76
Croatia	na	na	na	na	na	na	na	na	na	na	na	na	na	na	na	na
Czech Republic	na	na	na	na	na	na	na	na	na	na	na	na	na	na	na	na
Denmark	47	na	na	na	na	na	na	na	na	na	na	na	na	na	na	na
Dominican Rep.	na	89	88	90	91	84	91	86	91	88	84	87	95	88	87	95
Egypt	na	100	100	100	100	100	100	100	100	100	100	100	100	100	100	100
El Salvador	na	94	93	95	95	92	94	94	93	94	95	93	93	na	na	na
Estonia	na	na	na	na	na	na	na	na	na	na	na	na	na	na	na	na
Finland	73	na	na	na	na	na	na	na	na	na	na	na	na	na	na	na
France	55	na	na	na	na	na	na	na	na	na	na	na	na	na	na	na
Georgia	na	76	71	81	83	78	66	73	75	83	73	76	82	76	75	79
Germany	37	na	na	na	na	na	na	na	na	na	na	na	na	na	na	na
Great Britain	70	na	na	na	na	na	na	na	na	na	na	na	na	na	na	na
Greece	na	na	na	na	na	na	na	na	na	na	na	na	na	na	na	na
Hungary	14	na	na	na	na	na	na	na	na	na	na	na	na	na	na	na
Iceland	88	na	na	na	na	na	na	na	na	na	na	na	na	na	na	na
India	75	81	79	83	78	83	82	82	81	80	80	81	82	88	74	71
Indonesia	na	99	99	99	98	99	100	98	99	100	99	100	99	99	99	100
Iran	na	99	99	99	98	99	99	99	99	98	99	99	98	99	99	98
Ireland	88	na	na	na	na	na	na	na	na	na	na	na	na	na	na	na
Israel	na	na	na	na	na	na	na	na	na	na	na	na	na	na	na	na
Italy	78	na	na	na	na	na	na	na	na	na	na	na	na	na	na	na
Japan	75	71	63	78	80	78	60	71	73	68	72	75	64	71	73	63
Jordan	na	100	99	100	100	100	99	99	100	99	100	100	99	100	99	100
Korea, South	na	na	na	na	na	na	na	na	na	na	na	na	na	na	na	na
Latvia	78	na	na	na	na	na	na	na	na	na	na	na	na	na	na	na
Lithuania	na	na	na	na	na	na	na	na	na	na	na	na	na	na	na	na
Luxembourg	na	na	na	na	na	na	na	na	na	na	na	na	na	na	na	na
Macedonia	na	80	77	84	86	81	74	87	75	80	82	78	80	78	80	89
Malta	na	na	na	na	na	na	na	na	na	na	na	na	na	na	na	na
Mexico	72	93	92	94	93	93	94	94	93	89	94	93	91	93	93	95
Moldova	na	81	75	86	83	78	82	83	80	81	82	77	81	82	81	69
Montenegro	na	35	30	39	28	36	37	41	31	29	40	34	28	35	33	29
Morocco	na	100	100	100	100	100	100	100	100	100	100	100	100	100	100	100
Netherlands	75	na	na	na	na	na	na	na	na	na	na	na	na	na	na	na
New Zealand	na	84	78	90	92	87	80	79	88	88	84	86	84	88	84	87
Nigeria	92	97	97	97	97	97	96	95	98	97	96	97	97	98	96	97
Northern Ireland	92	na	na	na	na	na	na	na	na	na	na	na	na	na	na	na
Norway	54	60	49	70	62	57	61	57	59	63	na	na	na	50	61	62
Pakistan	na	100	100	100	100	100	100	100	100	100	100	100	100	100	100	100
Peru	na	89	87	91	87	91	90	90	89	89	90	88	89	91	89	89
Philippines	na	96	96	96	97	96	96	97	96	96	96	97	95	98	96	90
Poland	86	na	na	na	na	na	na	na	na	na	na	na	na	na	na	na
Portugal	66	na	na	na	na	na	na	na	na	na	na	na	na	na	na	na
Puerto Rico	na	96	94	97	95	96	97	99	94	97	96	95	97	96	96	98
Romania	76	na	na	na	na	na	na	na	na	na	na	na	na	na	na	na
Russian Fed.	54	na	na	na	na	na	na	na	na	na	na	na	na	na	na	na
Serbia	na	34	28	40	46	31	32	37	28	42	32	34	35	30	38	35
Singapore	na	92	89	93	91	92	95	91	93	90	95	90	90	96	90	93
Slovakia	na	na	na	na	na	na	na	na	na	na	na	na	na	na	na	na
Slovenia	46	na	na	na	na	na	na	na	na	na	na	na	na	na	na	na
South Africa	91	94	93	95	95	93	94	92	96	96	90	96	96	94	94	92
Spain	65	72	61	81	66	69	78	75	66	70	82	70	67	78	71	61
Sweden	58	na	na	na	na	na	na	na	na	na	na	na	na	na	na	na
Switzerland	81	89	86	93	89	87	93	94	89	87	91	90	87	90	88	93
Taiwan	na	77	70	84	83	76	77	78	71	81	78	76	76	80	76	68
Tanzania	na	98	98	98	97	98	99	98	98	99	98	99	97	99	98	100
Turkey	87	91	92	91	92	91	92	94	90	79	95	90	84	95	92	83
Uganda	na	92	94	91	91	94	91	86	94	95	91	94	93	90	94	90
Ukraine	na	na	na	na	na	na	na	na	na	na	na	na	na	na	na	na
United States	93	96	94	97	95	97	95	96	95	96	96	95	95	97	95	97
Uruguay	na	61	53	67	57	60	63	62	61	58	62	61	62	69	58	64
Venezuela	na	na	na	na	na	na	na	na	na	na	na	na	na	na	na	na
Vietnam	na	38	31	45	43	38	35	40	37	31	44	33	41	38	40	41
Zimbabwe	na	93	91	95	92	94	94	93	94	57	91	94	94	94	92	94
Total	70	85	82	87	88	84	81	86	83	86	86	85	83	84	84	85

RANKING

Country	2000
Morocco	100
Pakistan	100
Egypt	100
Jordan	100
Bangladesh	99
Algeria	99
Indonesia	99
Iran	99
Tanzania	98
Nigeria	97
Philippines	96
Puerto Rico	96
United States	96
South Africa	94
El Salvador	94
Mexico	93
Zimbabwe	93
Uganda	92
Singapore	92
Turkey	91
Canada	91
Chile	89
Switzerland	89
Peru	89
Dominican Rep.	89
Colombia	87
Argentina	85
Australia	85
Bosnia and Herz.	85
New Zealand	84
Brazil	82
India	81
Moldova	81
Macedonia	80
Taiwan	77
Georgia	76
Albania	75
Spain	72
Japan	71
Azerbaijan	69
Armenia	65
Uruguay	61
Norway	60
Vietnam	38
Montenegro	35
Serbia	34
Total	85

F053) BELIEVE IN HELL

Which, if any, of the following do you believe in? Believe in hell

Yes (%)

(WVS: V194; EVS: V117)

Country	Wave		Gender		Age			Education			Income			Values			RANKING Country	2000
	1990	2000	Male	Female	16-29	30-49	50+	Lower	Middle	Upper	Lower	Middle	Upper	Mat	Mixed	Postm.		
Albania	na	41	34	48	38	36	51	52	35	31	41	40	43	39	45	13	Pakistan	100
Algeria	na	99	99	98	99	98	99	98	99	99	99	99	99	99	99	98	Egypt	100
Argentina	41	44	40	47	42	46	42	42	46	46	44	44	44	46	45	39	Morocco	100
Armenia	na	36	31	41	41	34	33	37	37	33	41	35	30	31	43	28	Indonesia	100
Australia	na	41	36	46	46	39	39	46	41	36	43	42	35	45	45	33	Jordan	99
Austria	20	18	16	20	14	18	21	21	16	16	22	19	15	18	20	15	Algeria	99
Azerbaijan	na	59	54	63	60	56	66	69	57	60	60	61	55	55	64	76	Iran	98
Bangladesh	na	95	96	95	96	95	94	98	93	92	98	95	93	91	99	96	Tanzania	96
Belarus	9	35	24	45	30	30	45	47	33	20	41	30	34	39	32	22	Bangladesh	95
Belgium	17	16	15	17	18	14	17	16	17	15	20	16	12	15	19	11	Nigeria	94
Bosnia and Herz.	na	60	56	64	68	58	55	72	59	53	67	60	58	57	62	57	Turkey	94
Brazil	39	49	49	49	49	50	47	52	48	42	56	50	42	51	50	38	Philippines	93
Bulgaria	11	30	25	35	34	24	33	42	25	22	38	23	27	31	29	39	Malta	81
Canada	42	50	48	53	58	49	47	52	54	42	53	53	44	53	54	43	Zimbabwe	79
Chile	45	65	59	71	62	65	69	71	64	58	70	65	58	70	68	49	Singapore	79
China	na	na	na	na	na	na	na	na	na	na	na	na	na	na	na	na	Uganda	77
Colombia	na	40	38	43	46	37	40	39	42	39	40	42	39	45	42	29	El Salvador	76
Croatia	na	57	49	64	57	59	55	61	57	46	58	53	59	64	58	49	Mexico	75
Czech Republic	na	13	12	14	17	9	15	16	10	12	16	12	9	14	12	14	United States	75
Denmark	8	10	8	11	10	8	11	9	8	9	13	8	6	8	10	6	Northern Ireland	74
Dominican Rep.	na	68	67	69	70	64	55	85	71	66	71	63	63	59	66	79	Puerto Rico	73
Egypt	na	100	100	100	100	100	100	100	100	100	100	100	100	100	100	100	Romania	71
El Salvador	na	76	74	79	76	78	75	79	76	70	79	76	72	na	na	na	India	69
Estonia	na	16	14	18	17	17	15	20	15	15	15	20	15	18	15	11	Lithuania	68
Finland	27	31	25	38	27	28	37	33	26	36	31	33	30	32	31	30	Dominican Rep.	68
France	17	20	17	22	23	20	18	21	17	18	20	21	17	23	20	13	Poland	66
Georgia	na	59	55	63	70	57	50	54	58	66	56	57	67	59	59	57	Chile	65
Germany	9	20	17	22	17	17	25	23	19	10	20	20	21	19	22	17	Peru	65
Great Britain	28	35	32	38	33	39	33	34	38	36	30	43	36	na	na	na	Moldova	65
Greece	na	41	38	42	40	40	40	57	46	32	44	39	37	45	43	27	Taiwan	62
Hungary	16	20	13	27	21	15	25	20	20	21	24	20	18	20	20	26	South Africa	61
Iceland	12	18	21	14	21	18	14	18	18	15	19	19	13	20	17	15	Bosnia and Herz.	60
India	39	69	65	73	65	69	72	74	65	59	72	71	64	78	57	54	Georgia	59
Indonesia	na	100	100	100	99	100	100	100	100	100	100	100	99	100	100	100	Azerbaijan	59
Iran	na	98	98	98	98	98	99	99	98	97	98	99	98	100	98	97	Croatia	57
Ireland	53	53	50	57	43	49	66	63	48	49	65	52	45	54	54	49	Ireland	53
Israel	na	na	na	na	na	na	na	na	na	na	na	na	na	na	na	na	Canada	50
Italy	42	49	44	54	45	45	56	55	47	40	54	50	44	53	50	44	Brazil	49
Japan	32	30	24	36	32	39	21	36	32	25	29	36	27	27	31	27	Italy	49
Jordan	na	99	99	99	99	99	99	99	100	99	100	100	98	99	99	100	Macedonia	47
Korea, South	na	na	na	na	na	na	na	na	na	na	na	na	na	na	na	na	Slovakia	46
Latvia	7	28	19	37	34	26	28	32	29	23	29	29	27	31	27	32	Argentina	44
Lithuania	na	68	52	81	60	54	82	90	61	43	88	60	58	72	68	48	Australia	41
Luxembourg	na	22	21	23	20	19	25	26	20	15	27	21	18	23	22	19	Albania	41
Macedonia	na	47	44	49	61	46	36	66	37	35	49	48	38	45	43	76	Greece	41
Malta	na	81	76	85	77	72	91	87	78	82	82	82	77	78	82	80	Colombia	40
Mexico	48	75	72	77	74	74	76	77	74	65	75	77	71	79	73	72	Ukraine	38
Moldova	na	65	55	72	66	59	70	77	63	56	73	59	61	66	63	63	Portugal	38
Montenegro	na	21	17	24	16	21	23	29	18	9	29	22	13	24	16	17	Spain	37
Morocco	na	100	100	100	100	100	100	100	100	98	100	100	100	100	100	100	Armenia	36
Netherlands	13	14	14	13	16	14	12	15	14	12	16	13	11	22	14	10	Russian Fed.	36
New Zealand	na	33	33	34	42	35	29	29	40	34	36	38	27	39	36	22	Great Britain	35
Nigeria	51	94	93	94	94	94	91	93	93	96	93	93	95	93	94	95	Belarus	35
Northern Ireland	73	74	72	76	67	72	79	78	72	68	74	76	67	76	74	71	New Zealand	33
Norway	19	20	18	21	21	19	20	23	18	19	na	na	na	23	20	16	Finland	31
Pakistan	na	100	100	100	100	100	100	100	100	100	100	100	100	100	100	100	Japan	30
Peru	na	65	62	68	62	69	64	66	64	66	67	64	63	63	66	66	Bulgaria	30
Philippines	na	93	91	94	91	93	94	94	92	92	92	93	92	92	94	83	Latvia	28
Poland	54	66	56	74	72	64	64	66	70	53	68	65	61	71	61	66	Uruguay	25
Portugal	25	38	30	44	25	36	47	42	29	30	46	41	24	45	35	30	Luxembourg	22
Puerto Rico	na	73	71	75	75	76	71	68	68	77	70	75	75	76	74	72	Montenegro	21
Romania	43	71	63	79	73	66	76	86	69	49	81	73	63	77	66	57	Switzerland	21
Russian Fed.	16	36	24	46	39	30	40	51	35	30	41	35	31	38	33	19	Slovenia	20
Serbia	na	18	16	20	24	14	19	23	14	20	17	17	19	15	21	22	Hungary	20
Singapore	na	79	77	81	78	80	83	79	80	77	83	81	75	88	76	72	Germany	20
Slovakia	na	46	38	53	34	42	60	57	43	31	55	44	42	50	44	45	Norway	20
Slovenia	17	20	16	24	16	19	25	33	17	11	27	20	11	24	20	21	France	20
South Africa	52	61	53	70	55	63	67	57	67	52	54	56	71	61	62	48	Austria	18
Spain	30	37	29	44	25	32	48	45	28	29	44	35	31	45	36	22	Serbia	18
Sweden	8	10	10	9	9	8	11	12	8	10	12	8	8	13	9	9	Iceland	18
Switzerland	24	21	19	22	18	20	22	28	18	23	24	25	17	27	21	16	Vietnam	17
Taiwan	na	62	52	72	73	60	58	67	56	60	62	67	56	65	60	41	Estonia	16
Tanzania	na	96	96	95	93	97	97	96	94	98	96	95	95	97	95	96	Belgium	16
Turkey	85	94	93	95	93	93	94	97	92	75	97	94	84	97	94	85	Netherlands	14
Uganda	na	77	79	74	74	84	61	75	76	90	83	87	83	69	81	77	Czech Republic	13
Ukraine	na	38	26	49	38	36	41	53	36	34	43	34	37	39	35	31	Denmark	10
United States	71	75	72	77	77	78	68	84	74	71	77	76	72	73	77	69	Sweden	10
Uruguay	na	25	22	28	22	25	27	27	23	20	27	21	29	29	24	22		
Venezuela	na	na	na	na	na	na	na	na	na	na	na	na	na	na	na	na		
Vietnam	na	17	12	22	20	17	15	22	13	5	20	15	17	18	17	19		
Zimbabwe	na	79	73	85	76	79	89	83	74	100	83	77	79	76	81	85		
Total	31	53	50	56	58	52	48	57	50	51	57	53	49	58	52	43	Total	53

F054) BELIEVE IN HEAVEN

Which, if any, of the following do you believe in? Believe in heaven

Yes (%)

(WVS: V195; EVS: V118)

Country	Wave		Gender		Age			Education			Income			Values		
	1990	2000	Male	Female	16-29	30-49	50+	Lower	Middle	Upper	Lower	Middle	Upper	Mat	Mixed	Postm
Albania	na	48	41	56	49	43	56	57	44	37	48	50	47	43	50	42
Algeria	na	100	100	100	100	99	100	100	100	99	100	100	99	100	100	99
Argentina	69	81	76	85	82	80	80	84	77	73	84	83	75	85	83	72
Armenia	na	41	36	46	48	38	36	42	42	37	46	38	36	34	50	31
Australia	na	64	53	73	67	60	64	75	64	53	67	63	54	71	66	57
Austria	47	41	35	48	41	39	44	45	38	39	43	43	35	46	42	40
Azerbaijan	na	61	57	66	63	58	67	72	60	61	62	62	58	58	65	76
Bangladesh	na	100	99	100	99	100	100	100	99	99	100	100	99	100	100	99
Belarus	12	37	25	47	30	33	45	45	35	26	38	36	34	38	34	36
Belgium	34	31	27	35	34	28	32	35	30	29	37	33	25	33	33	24
Bosnia and Herz.	na	62	58	66	71	59	57	75	61	55	68	61	61	58	64	61
Brazil	76	82	82	83	86	80	80	87	83	65	88	86	73	90	83	65
Bulgaria	16	33	28	37	39	27	34	42	29	25	41	28	29	34	32	41
Canada	72	74	67	80	74	72	76	81	77	61	78	75	68	84	78	63
Chile	77	80	70	88	80	79	81	87	76	75	85	78	72	86	81	67
China	na	na	na	na	na	na	na	na	na	na	na	na	na	na	na	na
Colombia	na	82	77	87	86	78	86	93	86	69	93	85	71	89	84	74
Croatia	na	64	58	70	65	69	58	69	64	50	65	61	65	68	65	55
Czech Republic	na	21	19	23	22	15	25	25	15	17	27	20	13	23	19	22
Denmark	19	18	13	24	22	15	20	20	13	17	22	16	15	19	19	11
Dominican Rep.	na	81	80	82	83	79	70	89	83	80	84	76	81	80	80	85
Egypt	na	100	100	100	100	100	100	100	100	100	100	100	100	100	100	100
El Salvador	na	86	82	90	88	84	87	90	84	79	92	84	81	na	na	na
Estonia	na	19	16	22	19	20	19	26	16	18	21	22	16	20	18	10
Finland	55	61	47	74	54	59	68	62	60	63	63	55	66	65	61	59
France	32	31	25	37	34	30	31	34	28	27	34	32	26	40	30	20
Georgia	na	63	59	66	73	61	53	57	62	68	59	61	69	61	64	63
Germany	25	31	25	36	28	27	36	36	27	21	30	33	33	26	35	28
Great Britain	59	56	44	67	50	53	60	64	53	43	60	58	50	na	na	na
Greece	na	47	45	48	48	45	47	64	53	38	51	47	43	50	49	34
Hungary	27	29	21	37	28	24	34	32	23	29	36	29	26	30	29	42
Iceland	57	59	54	63	53	59	63	67	60	41	63	60	51	72	57	36
India	43	72	69	76	69	72	75	77	69	64	75	73	69	80	62	56
Indonesia	na	100	100	100	99	100	100	100	100	100	100	100	99	100	100	100
Iran	na	98	98	99	98	98	100	99	98	98	98	99	98	100	98	99
Ireland	90	85	81	89	80	82	93	91	84	79	91	85	82	88	86	78
Israel	na	na	na	na	na	na	na	na	na	na	na	na	na	na	na	na
Italy	54	59	52	65	55	54	65	65	56	49	64	59	52	67	60	53
Japan	43	38	28	46	43	46	27	46	39	33	37	40	35	33	40	35
Jordan	na	100	99	100	100	100	99	99	100	100	100	100	99	100	99	100
Korea, South	na	na	na	na	na	na	na	na	na	na	na	na	na	na	na	na
Latvia	12	33	22	44	41	30	33	41	32	27	34	37	29	35	32	33
Lithuania	na	71	53	83	61	57	84	92	63	49	89	64	60	76	70	50
Luxembourg	na	33	30	35	34	31	34	40	30	24	39	33	24	39	32	30
Macedonia	na	50	47	54	63	50	40	69	42	40	54	51	41	49	48	76
Malta	na	88	82	93	83	82	96	93	86	85	90	90	83	88	87	88
Mexico	70	88	85	91	87	88	90	92	87	75	93	90	83	91	88	85
Moldova	na	68	58	76	71	63	71	76	66	62	75	59	65	69	67	63
Montenegro	na	19	17	20	13	20	20	26	16	7	28	20	12	21	14	12
Morocco	na	100	100	100	100	100	100	100	99	98	100	100	100	100	100	98
Netherlands	37	38	31	45	42	35	38	45	38	31	37	39	32	54	38	28
New Zealand	na	61	53	68	66	60	61	61	68	56	66	64	52	74	63	47
Nigeria	96	99	99	99	99	99	100	99	100	100	99	99	100	99	99	99
Northern Ireland	90	87	83	90	83	84	91	90	83	84	86	88	81	88	87	85
Norway	44	47	38	55	42	45	53	54	45	42	na	na	na	49	49	31
Pakistan	na	100	100	100	100	100	100	100	100	100	100	100	100	100	100	100
Peru	na	85	81	88	82	87	85	89	87	77	88	83	80	88	84	82
Philippines	na	96	95	98	96	96	97	98	96	96	97	97	95	97	97	91
Poland	80	80	74	85	86	77	79	83	80	63	82	79	74	87	75	76
Portugal	56	60	53	67	48	58	69	67	46	38	66	66	43	65	58	48
Puerto Rico	na	91	88	93	93	92	90	90	90	92	89	92	90	88	92	92
Romania	58	75	67	83	78	70	78	87	75	54	82	78	68	80	71	62
Russian Fed.	18	36	24	47	38	30	41	51	35	30	42	35	30	38	33	22
Serbia	na	17	16	19	25	13	18	24	13	17	19	17	17	15	19	25
Singapore	na	81	77	85	79	82	83	83	80	79	85	81	77	88	79	71
Slovakia	na	55	46	63	44	50	70	65	53	37	66	55	49	59	53	53
Slovenia	30	28	25	30	25	23	34	45	23	14	38	26	16	34	27	26
South Africa	91	91	87	96	90	91	93	90	91	90	88	95	89	90	91	91
Spain	52	51	40	61	38	45	64	61	40	43	62	49	43	62	50	33
Sweden	31	31	24	38	25	29	37	41	30	26	35	34	21	38	32	26
Switzerland	44	45	37	52	37	44	51	62	41	35	51	49	36	56	44	36
Taiwan	na	62	52	71	68	60	60	66	56	60	64	64	55	64	60	43
Tanzania	na	93	93	92	91	94	93	92	92	96	92	93	94	93	93	91
Turkey	87	94	93	95	94	94	95	98	93	76	97	94	84	98	95	85
Uganda	na	92	90	94	91	97	84	90	93	98	92	96	95	91	94	90
Ukraine	na	40	28	51	41	37	43	58	38	35	45	38	36	40	37	38
United States	87	88	84	91	87	90	85	92	89	85	89	88	85	91	89	83
Uruguay	na	51	39	60	42	46	58	58	43	34	56	48	49	67	47	43
Venezuela	na	na	na	na	na	na	na	na	na	na	na	na	na	na	na	na
Vietnam	na	17	12	21	20	17	14	21	11	7	18	15	16	17	16	17
Zimbabwe	na	93	91	95	93	92	96	94	91	100	92	94	92	93	93	96
Total	51	64	60	69	69	63	61	70	61	61	69	65	60	68	64	56

RANKING

Country	2000
Pakistan	100
Egypt	100
Algeria	100
Morocco	100
Jordan	100
Bangladesh	100
Indonesia	100
Nigeria	99
Iran	98
Philippines	96
Turkey	94
Zimbabwe	93
Tanzania	93
Uganda	92
Puerto Rico	91
South Africa	91
Mexico	88
Malta	88
United States	88
Northern Ireland	87
El Salvador	86
Ireland	85
Peru	85
Brazil	82
Colombia	82
Dominican Rep.	81
Singapore	81
Argentina	81
Chile	80
Poland	80
Romania	75
Canada	74
India	72
Lithuania	71
Moldova	68
Croatia	64
Australia	64
Georgia	63
Bosnia and Herz.	62
Taiwan	62
Azerbaijan	61
Finland	61
New Zealand	61
Portugal	60
Iceland	59
Italy	59
Great Britain	56
Slovakia	55
Uruguay	51
Spain	51
Macedonia	50
Albania	48
Greece	47
Norway	47
Switzerland	45
Austria	41
Armenia	41
Ukraine	40
Netherlands	38
Japan	38
Belarus	37
Russian Fed.	36
Latvia	33
Luxembourg	33
Bulgaria	33
France	31
Sweden	31
Germany	31
Belgium	31
Hungary	29
Slovenia	28
Czech Republic	21
Estonia	19
Montenegro	19
Denmark	18
Serbia	17
Vietnam	17
Total	64

F055_1) BELIEVE IN SIN

Which, if any, of the following do you believe in? Sin.

Yes (%)

(EVS: V119)

Country	Wave		Gender		Age			Education			Income			Values		
	1990	2000	Male	Female	16-29	30-49	50+	Lower	Middle	Upper	Lower	Middle	Upper	Mat	Mixed	Postm.
Albania	na	na	na	na	na	na	na	na	na	na	na	na	na	na	na	na
Algeria	na	na	na	na	na	na	na	na	na	na	na	na	na	na	na	na
Argentina	72	na	na	na	na	na	na	na	na	na	na	na	na	na	na	na
Armenia	na	65	60	70	68	64	64	61	64	71	72	58	62	59	72	65
Australia	na	74	73	75	74	74	75	73	75	73	72	79	74	73	76	72
Austria	66	61	58	64	56	59	67	63	61	57	63	62	56	66	64	54
Azerbaijan	na	75	75	76	71	75	84	85	73	78	77	75	75	73	77	85
Bangladesh	na	na	na	na	na	na	na	na	na	na	na	na	na	na	na	na
Belarus	48	59	46	70	49	58	68	68	56	53	62	58	56	60	59	41
Belgium	45	43	43	43	41	39	47	44	42	44	47	42	42	42	47	35
Bosnia and Herz.	na	na	na	na	na	na	na	na	na	na	na	na	na	na	na	na
Brazil	82	89	89	89	88	90	89	93	90	74	93	94	82	95	90	71
Bulgaria	30	53	44	61	49	47	59	58	50	49	58	51	51	58	50	54
Canada	74	na	na	na	na	na	na	na	na	na	na	na	na	na	na	na
Chile	88	na	na	na	na	na	na	na	na	na	na	na	na	na	na	na
China	na	na	na	na	na	na	na	na	na	na	na	na	na	na	na	na
Colombia	na	85	84	87	89	84	85	89	89	78	88	89	79	89	88	83
Croatia	na	76	70	82	76	79	74	82	74	67	84	76	73	78	77	71
Czech Republic	na	59	52	65	54	56	64	56	60	68	61	58	55	52	60	65
Denmark	24	21	20	21	20	16	26	23	15	20	30	15	16	19	22	12
Dominican Rep.	na	84	82	84	86	81	64	90	86	82	89	74	81	81	83	86
Egypt	na	na	na	na	na	na	na	na	na	na	na	na	na	na	na	na
El Salvador	na	95	95	95	94	96	96	96	95	93	95	96	95	na	na	na
Estonia	na	52	48	56	46	53	56	53	51	56	53	55	50	52	52	38
Finland	66	67	62	72	56	65	75	69	63	72	73	62	67	58	72	64
France	43	40	36	43	35	36	46	42	37	38	43	40	37	45	40	29
Georgia	na	84	81	87	88	85	79	82	83	89	82	84	87	83	85	92
Germany	37	41	36	45	35	37	49	46	39	31	39	42	48	41	42	42
Great Britain	72	67	66	68	61	67	71	65	67	71	65	63	71	na	na	na
Greece	na	74	69	77	69	75	82	90	80	65	75	74	71	81	76	59
Hungary	39	46	36	54	44	39	52	45	45	48	52	46	41	47	45	39
Iceland	70	64	66	63	55	63	76	69	62	59	68	68	58	67	66	45
India	67	na	na	na	na	na	na	na	na	na	na	na	na	na	na	na
Indonesia	na	na	na	na	na	na	na	na	na	na	na	na	na	na	na	na
Iran	na	na	na	na	na	na	na	na	na	na	na	na	na	na	na	na
Ireland	87	86	86	86	85	85	88	85	86	85	85	85	87	89	85	84
Israel	na	na	na	na	na	na	na	na	na	na	na	na	na	na	na	na
Italy	73	73	66	79	70	70	78	79	71	63	80	69	67	80	75	65
Japan	28	na	na	na	na	na	na	na	na	na	na	na	na	na	na	na
Jordan	na	na	na	na	na	na	na	na	na	na	na	na	na	na	na	na
Korea, South	na	na	na	na	na	na	na	na	na	na	na	na	na	na	na	na
Latvia	51	74	63	83	74	75	72	74	72	78	74	71	75	75	72	90
Lithuania	na	91	83	96	85	89	95	96	88	88	95	89	90	90	91	96
Luxembourg	na	47	43	51	42	45	54	50	45	48	49	46	48	54	47	38
Macedonia	na	na	na	na	na	na	na	na	na	na	na	na	na	na	na	na
Malta	na	93	90	96	89	91	97	94	92	97	93	93	91	92	93	96
Mexico	74	na	na	na	na	na	na	na	na	na	na	na	na	na	na	na
Moldova	na	na	na	na	na	na	na	na	na	na	na	na	na	na	na	na
Montenegro	na	na	na	na	na	na	na	na	na	na	na	na	na	na	na	na
Morocco	na	na	na	na	na	na	na	na	na	na	na	na	na	na	na	na
Netherlands	43	40	40	40	33	32	52	46	37	36	44	37	34	56	38	36
New Zealand	na	66	65	68	73	70	61	60	71	71	65	68	68	70	68	63
Nigeria	62	na	na	na	na	na	na	na	na	na	na	na	na	na	na	na
Northern Ireland	91	90	88	93	88	87	93	92	90	87	91	91	87	92	91	89
Norway	44	45	42	49	37	42	57	53	42	42	na	na	na	53	46	33
Pakistan	na	na	na	na	na	na	na	na	na	na	na	na	na	na	na	na
Peru	na	na	na	na	na	na	na	na	na	na	na	na	na	na	na	na
Philippines	na	na	na	na	na	na	na	na	na	na	na	na	na	na	na	na
Poland	91	90	87	93	92	90	90	92	89	85	90	91	88	95	88	85
Portugal	68	71	63	78	59	73	77	77	62	55	79	74	58	76	70	67
Puerto Rico	na	na	na	na	na	na	na	na	na	na	na	na	na	na	na	na
Romania	77	91	87	95	89	90	93	95	91	81	93	93	87	93	90	77
Russian Fed.	47	68	56	77	71	64	72	72	67	70	68	68	68	68	68	62
Serbia	na	na	na	na	na	na	na	na	na	na	na	na	na	na	na	na
Singapore	na	na	na	na	na	na	na	na	na	na	na	na	na	na	na	na
Slovakia	na	76	70	81	66	74	86	80	74	70	84	75	72	77	76	69
Slovenia	47	43	39	47	39	40	49	56	41	32	51	47	31	52	42	43
South Africa	69	na	na	na	na	na	na	na	na	na	na	na	na	na	na	na
Spain	56	51	40	62	33	43	68	65	40	44	61	50	45	69	49	31
Sweden	31	26	25	27	21	18	36	36	23	22	31	24	20	36	26	20
Switzerland	64	57	54	60	48	54	66	70	55	52	60	60	52	60	58	52
Taiwan	na	46	38	53	51	44	45	53	42	42	49	45	42	48	45	33
Tanzania	na	na	na	na	na	na	na	na	na	na	na	na	na	na	na	na
Turkey	91	96	95	96	94	97	99	99	94	82	98	97	88	98	97	90
Uganda	na	na	na	na	na	na	na	na	na	na	na	na	na	na	na	na
Ukraine	na	74	65	81	77	74	73	74	73	76	75	73	74	76	72	83
United States	89	na	na	na	na	na	na	na	na	na	na	na	na	na	na	na
Uruguay	na	53	42	60	46	45	61	60	44	37	58	50	50	64	52	44
Venezuela	na	na	na	na	na	na	na	na	na	na	na	na	na	na	na	na
Vietnam	na	na	na	na	na	na	na	na	na	na	na	na	na	na	na	na
Zimbabwe	na	na	na	na	na	na	na	na	na	na	na	na	na	na	na	na
Total	61	65	61	69	65	63	68	68	65	63	69	65	64	69	64	56

RANKING

Country	2000
Turkey	96
El Salvador	95
Malta	93
Romania	91
Lithuania	91
Poland	90
Northern Ireland	90
Brazil	89
Ireland	86
Colombia	85
Georgia	84
Dominican Rep.	84
Croatia	76
Slovakia	76
Azerbaijan	75
Australia	74
Ukraine	74
Greece	74
Latvia	74
Italy	73
Portugal	71
Russian Fed.	68
Finland	67
Great Britain	67
New Zealand	66
Armenia	65
Iceland	64
Austria	61
Belarus	59
Czech Republic	59
Switzerland	57
Bulgaria	53
Uruguay	53
Estonia	52
Spain	51
Luxembourg	47
Taiwan	46
Hungary	46
Norway	45
Slovenia	43
Belgium	43
Germany	41
France	40
Netherlands	40
Sweden	26
Denmark	21
Total	65

F056_1) BELIEVE IN TELEPATHY

Which, if any, of the following do you believe in? Telepathy

Yes (%)

(EVS: V120)

Country	Wave 1990	Wave 2000	Gender Male	Gender Female	Age 16-29	Age 30-49	Age 50+	Education Lower	Education Middle	Education Upper	Income Lower	Income Middle	Income Upper	Values Mat	Values Mixed	Values Postm.
Albania	na	na	na	na	na	na	na	na	na	na	na	na	na	na	na	na
Algeria	na	na	na	na	na	na	na	na	na	na	na	na	na	na	na	na
Argentina	na	na	na	na	na	na	na	na	na	na	na	na	na	na	na	na
Armenia	na	na	na	na	na	na	na	na	na	na	na	na	na	na	na	na
Australia	na	na	na	na	na	na	na	na	na	na	na	na	na	na	na	na
Austria	na	48	41	55	51	52	43	43	53	53	41	50	50	45	46	55
Azerbaijan	na	na	na	na	na	na	na	na	na	na	na	na	na	na	na	na
Bangladesh	na	na	na	na	na	na	na	na	na	na	na	na	na	na	na	na
Belarus	na	32	29	34	43	32	21	27	33	33	29	30	39	27	37	26
Belgium	na	38	33	43	39	41	35	30	41	39	38	35	41	37	40	38
Bosnia and Herz.	na	na	na	na	na	na	na	na	na	na	na	na	na	na	na	na
Brazil	na	na	na	na	na	na	na	na	na	na	na	na	na	na	na	na
Bulgaria	na	45	37	52	46	56	34	29	47	62	30	45	56	43	46	62
Canada	na	na	na	na	na	na	na	na	na	na	na	na	na	na	na	na
Chile	na	na	na	na	na	na	na	na	na	na	na	na	na	na	na	na
China	na	na	na	na	na	na	na	na	na	na	na	na	na	na	na	na
Colombia	na	na	na	na	na	na	na	na	na	na	na	na	na	na	na	na
Croatia	na	39	41	37	47	42	30	32	42	46	29	37	47	26	40	45
Czech Republic	na	73	70	76	80	76	67	68	78	77	64	73	79	69	75	72
Denmark	na	36	29	43	34	40	32	35	38	38	39	34	30	31	36	41
Dominican Rep.	na	na	na	na	na	na	na	na	na	na	na	na	na	na	na	na
Egypt	na	na	na	na	na	na	na	na	na	na	na	na	na	na	na	na
El Salvador	na	na	na	na	na	na	na	na	na	na	na	na	na	na	na	na
Estonia	na	55	51	58	55	62	48	41	61	60	42	53	64	53	56	71
Finland	na	46	34	57	41	48	46	45	50	44	51	41	45	47	45	49
France	na	40	35	44	44	43	34	38	43	41	39	41	38	39	39	42
Georgia	na	na	na	na	na	na	na	na	na	na	na	na	na	na	na	na
Germany	na	29	22	34	37	31	22	24	32	27	26	28	34	25	28	33
Great Britain	na	45	40	50	50	45	43	43	46	46	43	46	42	na	na	na
Greece	na	55	53	56	62	49	50	43	56	56	52	56	58	50	55	54
Hungary	na	46	40	52	51	52	37	39	59	56	44	48	46	43	50	56
Iceland	na	61	56	66	43	60	79	65	60	56	64	61	56	61	61	58
India	na	na	na	na	na	na	na	na	na	na	na	na	na	na	na	na
Indonesia	na	na	na	na	na	na	na	na	na	na	na	na	na	na	na	na
Iran	na	na	na	na	na	na	na	na	na	na	na	na	na	na	na	na
Ireland	na	42	38	45	47	42	36	37	42	49	35	39	48	39	43	42
Israel	na	na	na	na	na	na	na	na	na	na	na	na	na	na	na	na
Italy	na	37	32	42	41	41	32	31	42	43	31	39	39	34	36	42
Japan	na	na	na	na	na	na	na	na	na	na	na	na	na	na	na	na
Jordan	na	na	na	na	na	na	na	na	na	na	na	na	na	na	na	na
Korea, South	na	na	na	na	na	na	na	na	na	na	na	na	na	na	na	na
Latvia	na	52	49	55	57	58	46	41	52	66	45	49	66	49	53	66
Lithuania	na	79	69	87	82	82	74	79	78	86	77	74	83	83	78	90
Luxembourg	na	38	34	43	39	45	31	35	43	35	43	39	39	39	37	45
Macedonia	na	na	na	na	na	na	na	na	na	na	na	na	na	na	na	na
Malta	na	34	31	36	39	33	31	29	34	44	27	28	45	34	35	19
Mexico	na	na	na	na	na	na	na	na	na	na	na	na	na	na	na	na
Moldova	na	na	na	na	na	na	na	na	na	na	na	na	na	na	na	na
Montenegro	na	na	na	na	na	na	na	na	na	na	na	na	na	na	na	na
Morocco	na	na	na	na	na	na	na	na	na	na	na	na	na	na	na	na
Netherlands	na	50	45	55	56	58	39	42	52	56	44	57	51	47	49	54
New Zealand	na	na	na	na	na	na	na	na	na	na	na	na	na	na	na	na
Nigeria	na	na	na	na	na	na	na	na	na	na	na	na	na	na	na	na
Northern Ireland	na	38	34	41	38	41	37	32	40	49	33	33	45	35	40	37
Norway	na	na	na	na	na	na	na	na	na	na	na	na	na	na	na	na
Pakistan	na	na	na	na	na	na	na	na	na	na	na	na	na	na	na	na
Peru	na	na	na	na	na	na	na	na	na	na	na	na	na	na	na	na
Philippines	na	na	na	na	na	na	na	na	na	na	na	na	na	na	na	na
Poland	na	40	35	44	46	41	34	30	48	57	30	44	50	36	42	44
Portugal	na	35	33	37	45	33	30	31	40	46	17	38	33	36	32	45
Puerto Rico	na	na	na	na	na	na	na	na	na	na	na	na	na	na	na	na
Romania	na	67	63	70	73	66	62	54	67	78	51	64	75	64	69	75
Russian Fed.	na	59	55	63	68	62	47	40	57	70	50	58	67	57	61	46
Serbia	na	na	na	na	na	na	na	na	na	na	na	na	na	na	na	na
Singapore	na	na	na	na	na	na	na	na	na	na	na	na	na	na	na	na
Slovakia	na	53	50	56	56	56	46	42	56	60	46	53	57	51	53	63
Slovenia	na	27	27	28	35	31	18	19	28	40	24	29	37	30	27	30
South Africa	na	na	na	na	na	na	na	na	na	na	na	na	na	na	na	na
Spain	na	27	24	30	30	32	21	21	30	33	27	22	38	26	25	29
Sweden	na	48	40	57	52	45	49	44	54	43	53	45	45	51	48	49
Switzerland	na	na	na	na	na	na	na	na	na	na	na	na	na	na	na	na
Taiwan	na	na	na	na	na	na	na	na	na	na	na	na	na	na	na	na
Tanzania	na	na	na	na	na	na	na	na	na	na	na	na	na	na	na	na
Turkey	na	8	7	9	8	9	7	8	10	8	8	8	9	7	8	10
Uganda	na	na	na	na	na	na	na	na	na	na	na	na	na	na	na	na
Ukraine	na	57	58	56	65	61	46	29	57	68	52	56	64	58	57	52
United States	na	na	na	na	na	na	na	na	na	na	na	na	na	na	na	na
Uruguay	na	na	na	na	na	na	na	na	na	na	na	na	na	na	na	na
Venezuela	na	na	na	na	na	na	na	na	na	na	na	na	na	na	na	na
Vietnam	na	na	na	na	na	na	na	na	na	na	na	na	na	na	na	na
Zimbabwe	na	na	na	na	na	na	na	na	na	na	na	na	na	na	na	na
Total	na	45	41	49	49	48	40	38	48	51	41	45	51	44	46	46

RANKING

Country	2000
Lithuania	79
Czech Republic	73
Romania	67
Iceland	61
Russian Fed.	59
Ukraine	57
Estonia	55
Greece	55
Slovakia	53
Latvia	52
Netherlands	50
Austria	48
Sweden	48
Hungary	46
Finland	46
Great Britain	45
Bulgaria	45
Ireland	42
France	40
Poland	40
Croatia	39
Luxembourg	38
Belgium	38
Northern Ireland	38
Italy	37
Denmark	36
Portugal	35
Malta	34
Belarus	32
Germany	29
Slovenia	27
Spain	27
Turkey	8
Total	45

F057_1) BELIEVE IN RE-INCARNATION

Do you believe in re-incarnation, that is, that we are born into this world again?

Yes (%)

(EVS: V121)

Country	Wave 1990	Wave 2000	Gender Male	Gender Female	Age 16-29	Age 30-49	Age 50+	Education Lower	Education Middle	Education Upper	Income Lower	Income Middle	Income Upper	Values Mat	Values Mixed	Values Postm.
Albania	na	na	na	na	na	na	na	na	na	na	na	na	na	na	na	na
Algeria	na	na	na	na	na	na	na	na	na	na	na	na	na	na	na	na
Argentina	39	na	na	na	na	na	na	na	na	na	na	na	na	na	na	na
Armenia	na	na	na	na	na	na	na	na	na	na	na	na	na	na	na	na
Australia	na	na	na	na	na	na	na	na	na	na	na	na	na	na	na	na
Austria	29	23	20	26	27	26	18	20	27	22	24	21	24	22	22	24
Azerbaijan	na	na	na	na	na	na	na	na	na	na	na	na	na	na	na	na
Bangladesh	na	na	na	na	na	na	na	na	na	na	na	na	na	na	na	na
Belarus	24	33	27	37	41	31	27	29	34	31	30	29	44	34	30	33
Belgium	16	17	13	21	29	18	11	15	19	16	22	20	12	15	18	20
Bosnia and Herz.	na	na	na	na	na	na	na	na	na	na	na	na	na	na	na	na
Brazil	57	na	na	na	na	na	na	na	na	na	na	na	na	na	na	na
Bulgaria	25	30	24	37	43	31	22	19	32	45	22	29	37	26	33	49
Canada	31	na	na	na	na	na	na	na	na	na	na	na	na	na	na	na
Chile	49	na	na	na	na	na	na	na	na	na	na	na	na	na	na	na
China	na	na	na	na	na	na	na	na	na	na	na	na	na	na	na	na
Colombia	na	na	na	na	na	na	na	na	na	na	na	na	na	na	na	na
Croatia	na	23	22	24	38	23	14	21	25	22	17	21	28	7	25	31
Czech Republic	na	23	20	26	36	25	15	24	24	19	16	27	23	22	24	22
Denmark	17	17	11	24	24	20	11	17	20	17	19	15	16	17	18	18
Dominican Rep.	na	na	na	na	na	na	na	na	na	na	na	na	na	na	na	na
Egypt	na	na	na	na	na	na	na	na	na	na	na	na	na	na	na	na
El Salvador	na	na	na	na	na	na	na	na	na	na	na	na	na	na	na	na
Estonia	na	37	30	43	49	43	25	33	39	37	34	30	44	34	38	57
Finland	34	18	12	25	19	19	17	22	16	7	23	13	17	16	20	17
France	28	29	23	35	36	34	20	29	30	26	31	31	26	28	28	32
Georgia	na	na	na	na	na	na	na	na	na	na	na	na	na	na	na	na
Germany	13	19	15	22	23	21	16	19	22	10	16	21	26	22	18	20
Great Britain	29	na	na	na	na	na	na	na	na	na	na	na	na	na	na	na
Greece	na	26	27	25	32	26	15	25	28	25	26	26	26	27	27	20
Hungary	23	20	17	23	28	23	12	19	24	18	17	18	23	17	22	34
Iceland	40	41	34	49	47	45	31	49	41	27	47	41	35	51	39	33
India	91	na	na	na	na	na	na	na	na	na	na	na	na	na	na	na
Indonesia	na	na	na	na	na	na	na	na	na	na	na	na	na	na	na	na
Iran	na	na	na	na	na	na	na	na	na	na	na	na	na	na	na	na
Ireland	20	23	19	27	25	26	18	26	23	17	26	24	18	17	24	28
Israel	na	na	na	na	na	na	na	na	na	na	na	na	na	na	na	na
Italy	27	18	15	21	24	19	14	17	21	14	17	20	14	13	19	18
Japan	50	na	na	na	na	na	na	na	na	na	na	na	na	na	na	na
Jordan	na	na	na	na	na	na	na	na	na	na	na	na	na	na	na	na
Korea, South	na	na	na	na	na	na	na	na	na	na	na	na	na	na	na	na
Latvia	45	33	26	41	42	38	25	28	34	39	29	36	38	33	34	33
Lithuania	na	44	37	50	47	43	43	44	43	46	46	40	43	38	48	31
Luxembourg	na	24	21	27	30	25	19	25	25	17	23	25	22	21	25	24
Macedonia	na	na	na	na	na	na	na	na	na	na	na	na	na	na	na	na
Malta	na	12	11	13	14	12	11	10	13	9	12	11	10	11	13	10
Mexico	43	na	na	na	na	na	na	na	na	na	na	na	na	na	na	na
Moldova	na	na	na	na	na	na	na	na	na	na	na	na	na	na	na	na
Montenegro	na	na	na	na	na	na	na	na	na	na	na	na	na	na	na	na
Morocco	na	na	na	na	na	na	na	na	na	na	na	na	na	na	na	na
Netherlands	22	22	16	28	27	27	14	20	24	22	22	22	24	25	21	23
New Zealand	na	na	na	na	na	na	na	na	na	na	na	na	na	na	na	na
Nigeria	39	na	na	na	na	na	na	na	na	na	na	na	na	na	na	na
Northern Ireland	33	17	16	18	24	21	11	15	19	17	18	20	20	12	16	25
Norway	15	na	na	na	na	na	na	na	na	na	na	na	na	na	na	na
Pakistan	na	na	na	na	na	na	na	na	na	na	na	na	na	na	na	na
Peru	na	na	na	na	na	na	na	na	na	na	na	na	na	na	na	na
Philippines	na	na	na	na	na	na	na	na	na	na	na	na	na	na	na	na
Poland	26	25	20	29	32	27	19	26	24	18	26	25	22	22	26	33
Portugal	29	29	24	35	34	24	31	29	31	32	19	29	25	31	30	27
Puerto Rico	na	na	na	na	na	na	na	na	na	na	na	na	na	na	na	na
Romania	24	28	24	33	34	27	25	24	27	34	25	23	31	27	29	31
Russian Fed.	22	32	24	39	45	31	25	28	32	35	29	32	35	31	33	39
Serbia	na	na	na	na	na	na	na	na	na	na	na	na	na	na	na	na
Singapore	na	na	na	na	na	na	na	na	na	na	na	na	na	na	na	na
Slovakia	na	20	20	20	25	21	14	16	22	20	15	20	23	16	20	36
Slovenia	17	17	16	17	30	17	7	12	18	21	14	11	22	14	17	20
South Africa	43	na	na	na	na	na	na	na	na	na	na	na	na	na	na	na
Spain	28	20	18	23	21	21	19	18	23	18	21	18	23	23	20	18
Sweden	20	22	15	29	27	24	18	19	26	18	27	19	17	36	21	23
Switzerland	36	na	na	na	na	na	na	na	na	na	na	na	na	na	na	na
Taiwan	na	na	na	na	na	na	na	na	na	na	na	na	na	na	na	na
Tanzania	na	na	na	na	na	na	na	na	na	na	na	na	na	na	na	na
Turkey	54	33	32	34	31	34	38	33	35	28	28	39	29	35	36	24
Uganda	na	na	na	na	na	na	na	na	na	na	na	na	na	na	na	na
Ukraine	na	28	25	32	37	28	24	27	26	35	30	27	30	26	31	35
United States	26	na	na	na	na	na	na	na	na	na	na	na	na	na	na	na
Uruguay	na	na	na	na	na	na	na	na	na	na	na	na	na	na	na	na
Venezuela	na	na	na	na	na	na	na	na	na	na	na	na	na	na	na	na
Vietnam	na	na	na	na	na	na	na	na	na	na	na	na	na	na	na	na
Zimbabwe	na	na	na	na	na	na	na	na	na	na	na	na	na	na	na	na
Total	32	25	20	29	32	26	18	23	26	24	24	24	26	24	25	24

RANKING

Country	2000
Lithuania	44
Iceland	41
Estonia	37
Latvia	33
Turkey	33
Belarus	33
Russian Fed.	32
Bulgaria	30
Portugal	29
France	29
Ukraine	28
Romania	28
Greece	26
Poland	25
Luxembourg	24
Croatia	23
Czech Republic	23
Ireland	23
Austria	23
Netherlands	22
Sweden	22
Spain	20
Hungary	20
Slovakia	20
Germany	19
Finland	18
Italy	18
Denmark	17
Belgium	17
Slovenia	17
Northern Ireland	17
Malta	12
Total	25

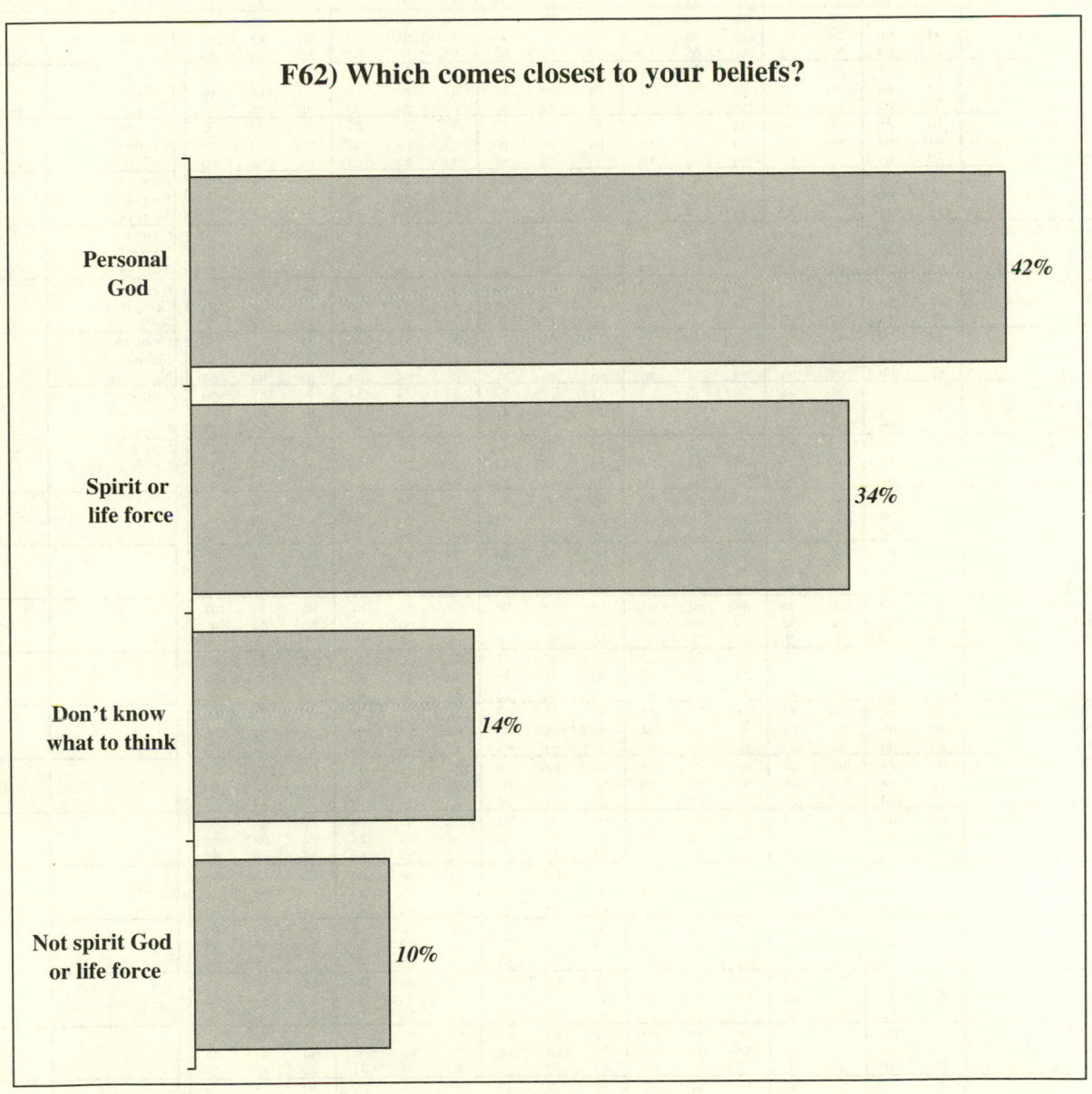

F62) Which comes closest to your beliefs?

Personal God — 42%

Spirit or life force — 34%

Don't know what to think — 14%

Not spirit God or life force — 10%

F062_1) STATEMENT OF YOUR BELIEF

Which of these statements comes closest to your beliefs?

Personal God (%)

(EVS: V122)

Country	Wave		Gender		Age			Education			Income			Values				Country	2000
	1990	2000	Male	Female	16-29	30-49	50+	Lower	Middle	Upper	Lower	Middle	Upper	Mat	Mixed	Postm.		**RANKING**	
Albania	na	na	na	na	na	na	na	na	na	na	na	na	na	na	na	na		Poland	83
Algeria	na	na	na	na	na	na	na	na	na	na	na	na	na	na	na	na		Portugal	79
Argentina	58	na	na	na	na	na	na	na	na	na	na	na	na	na	na	na		Malta	78
Armenia	na	na	na	na	na	na	na	na	na	na	na	na	na	na	na	na		Italy	71
Australia	na	na	na	na	na	na	na	na	na	na	na	na	na	na	na	na		Greece	66
Austria	29	32	29	34	28	31	34	33	29	34	35	33	29	32	32	28		Ireland	64
Azerbaijan	na	na	na	na	na	na	na	na	na	na	na	na	na	na	na	na		Belarus	64
Bangladesh	na	na	na	na	na	na	na	na	na · na			na	na	na	na	na	na		Northern Ireland	61
Belarus	6	64	54	71	60	65	65	67	62	66	63	65	61	65	64	68		Iceland	51
Belgium	32	29	26	31	20	21	40	40	24	27	37	27	23	37	27	24		Lithuania	51
Bosnia and Herz.	na	na	na	na	na	na	na	na	na	na	na	na	na	na	na	na		Finland	50
Brazil	56	na	na	na	na	na	na	na	na	na	na	na	na	na	na	na		Spain	49
Bulgaria	10	36	32	39	34	28	43	50	29	25	50	30	25	37	33	32		Hungary	45
Canada	44	na	na	na	na	na	na	na	na	na	na	na	na	na	na	na		Ukraine	42
Chile	52	na	na	na	na	na	na	na	na	na	na	na	na	na	na	na		Croatia	41
China	3	na	na	na	na	na	na	na	na	na	na	na	na	na	na	na		Romania	37
Colombia	na	na	na	na	na	na	na	na	na	na	na	na	na	na	na	na		Bulgaria	36
Croatia	na	41	35	47	30	41	50	42	44	30	45	41	40	45	44	29		Slovakia	35
Czech Republic	na	7	6	7	5	5	9	9	4	6	8	6	4	9	5	8		Germany	35
Denmark	20	25	23	27	22	22	29	28	19	21	27	25	23	23	26	18		Luxembourg	33
Dominican Rep.	na	na	na	na	na	na	na	na	na	na	na	na	na	na	na	na		Russian Fed.	32
Egypt	na	na	na	na	na	na	na	na	na	na	na	na	na	na	na	na		Austria	32
El Salvador	na	na	na	na	na	na	na	na	na	na	na	na	na	na	na	na		Great Britain	31
Estonia	7	16	12	19	13	12	21	22	15	9	25	16	12	18	15	9		Belgium	29
Finland	29	50	43	56	38	46	59	53	44	51	51	51	46	51	51	38		Denmark	25
France	22	22	19	25	16	23	24	22	22	23	21	22	24	27	22	13		Slovenia	24
Georgia	na	na	na	na	na	na	na	na	na	na	na	na	na	na	na	na		Netherlands	24
Germany	17	35	31	38	28	30	44	41	31	32	33	34	34	39	35	30		France	22
Great Britain	33	31	25	36	27	30	34	30	32	27	29	33	33	na	na	na		Sweden	16
Greece	na	66	61	69	62	68	71	76	73	58	68	66	66	75	67	55		Estonia	16
Hungary	40	45	35	53	37	37	57	50	35	35	58	44	38	50	41	26		Latvia	8
Iceland	51	51	48	55	40	53	58	54	53	42	52	51	49	61	50	35		Czech Republic	7
India	30	na	na	na	na	na	na	na	na	na	na	na	na	na	na	na			
Indonesia	na	na	na	na	na	na	na	na	na	na	na	na	na	na	na	na			
Iran	na	na	na	na	na	na	na	na	na	na	na	na	na	na	na	na			
Ireland	67	64	60	68	49	60	79	75	57	60	70	66	57	69	65	48			
Israel	na	na	na	na	na	na	na	na	na	na	na	na	na	na	na	na			
Italy	67	71	65	76	64	67	78	76	67	65	78	70	65	78	72	63			
Japan	5	na	na	na	na	na	na	na	na	na	na	na	na	na	na	na			
Jordan	na	na	na	na	na	na	na	na	na	na	na	na	na	na	na	na			
Korea, South	na	na	na	na	na	na	na	na	na	na	na	na	na	na	na	na			
Latvia	10	8	7	9	6	7	9	11	8	4	9	9	5	7	7	16			
Lithuania	21	51	40	60	36	38	72	74	43	41	71	46	43	55	49	39			
Luxembourg	na	33	31	35	20	28	48	40	31	25	30	35	30	35	35	21			
Macedonia	na	na	na	na	na	na	na	na	na	na	na	na	na	na	na	na			
Malta	na	78	72	83	68	77	86	89	75	67	78	78	74	83	76	66			
Mexico	56	na	na	na	na	na	na	na	na	na	na	na	na	na	na	na			
Moldova	na	na	na	na	na	na	na	na	na	na	na	na	na	na	na	na			
Montenegro	na	na	na	na	na	na	na	na	na	na	na	na	na	na	na	na			
Morocco	na	na	na	na	na	na	na	na	na	na	na	na	na	na	na	na			
Netherlands	27	24	20	27	16	19	32	28	21	22	25	23	19	38	24	14			
New Zealand	na	na	na	na	na	na	na	na	na	na	na	na	na	na	na	na			
Nigeria	68	na	na	na	na	na	na	na	na	na	na	na	na	na	na	na			
Northern Ireland	66	61	58	65	52	53	72	72	49	60	62	59	56	67	60	61			
Norway	30	na	na	na	na	na	na	na	na	na	na	na	na	na	na	na			
Pakistan	na	na	na	na	na	na	na	na	na	na	na	na	na	na	na	na			
Peru	na	na	na	na	na	na	na	na	na	na	na	na	na	na	na	na			
Philippines	na	na	na	na	na	na	na	na	na	na	na	na	na	na	na	na			
Poland	na	83	78	87	82	81	85	89	79	64	86	82	75	89	79	78			
Portugal	62	79	72	84	66	76	89	84	72	55	91	80	70	87	76	66			
Puerto Rico	na	na	na	na	na	na	na	na	na	na	na	na	na	na	na	na			
Romania	36	37	34	40	30	33	45	47	35	25	49	34	34	41	35	25			
Russian Fed.	8	32	23	40	24	27	43	50	32	23	41	30	25	37	26	16			
Serbia	na	na	na	na	na	na	na	na	na	na	na	na	na	na	na	na			
Singapore	na	na	na	na	na	na	na	na	na	na	na	na	na	na	na	na			
Slovakia	na	35	30	40	23	33	48	45	32	24	46	33	31	40	32	29			
Slovenia	22	24	24	24	22	21	30	32	22	17	29	21	20	30	23	20			
South Africa	na	na	na	na	na	na	na	na	na	na	na	na	na	na	na	na			
Spain	49	49	42	56	29	44	64	61	41	38	56	46	44	60	48	34			
Sweden	16	16	14	19	13	13	21	19	14	17	17	17	14	13	16	13			
Switzerland	23	na	na	na	na	na	na	na	na	na	na	na	na	na	na	na			
Taiwan	na	na	na	na	na	na	na	na	na	na	na	na	na	na	na	na			
Tanzania	na	na	na	na	na	na	na	na	na	na	na	na	na	na	na	na			
Turkey	na	na	na	na	na	na	na	na	na	na	na	na	na	na	na	na			
Uganda	na	na	na	na	na	na	na	na	na	na	na	na	na	na	na	na			
Ukraine	na	42	30	51	39	39	46	64	41	30	45	41	38	43	37	46			
United States	69	na	na	na	na	na	na	na	na	na	na	na	na	na	na	na			
Uruguay	na	na	na	na	na	na	na	na	na	na	na	na	na	na	na	na			
Venezuela	na	na	na	na	na	na	na	na	na	na	na	na	na	na	na	na			
Vietnam	na	na	na	na	na	na	na	na	na	na	na	na	na	na	na	na			
Zimbabwe	na	na	na	na	na	na	na	na	na	na	na	na	na	na	na	na			
Total	34	42	37	46	36	38	49	49	39	36	45	42	37	48	41	34		Total	42

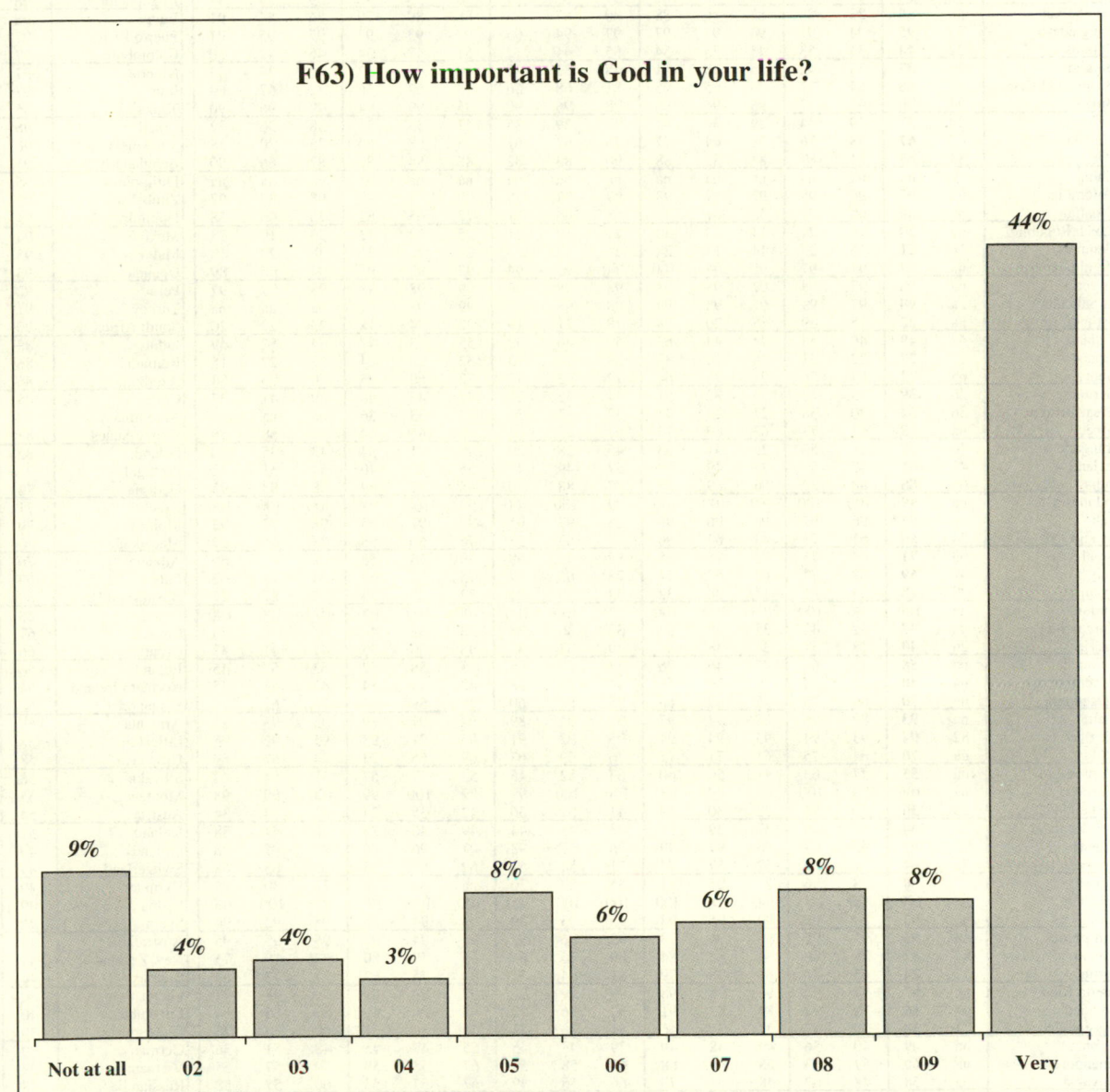

F63) How important is God in your life?

Not at all	02	03	04	05	06	07	08	09	Very
9%	4%	4%	3%	8%	6%	6%	8%	8%	44%

F063) HOW IMPORTANT IS GOD IN YOUR LIFE

How important is God in your life? Please use this scale to indicate.

(10 means very important and 1 means not at all important)

% Important (codes 7 to 10)

(WVS: V196; EVS: V123)

Country	Wave		Gender		Age			Education			Income			Values				RANKING	
	1990	2000	Male	Female	16-29	30-49	50+	Lower	Middle	Upper	Lower	Middle	Upper	Mat	Mixed	Postm.		Country	2000
Albania	na	70	64	75	68	66	76	75	68	61	72	70	67	72	68	63		Pakistan	100
Algeria	na	98	98	99	99	98	98	97	98	99	98	99	98	99	98	98		Jordan	100
Argentina	74	83	78	87	76	85	87	88	77	73	89	84	76	87	85	75		Morocco	100
Armenia	na	59	49	67	61	56	59	63	59	57	59	55	63	56	63	48		Indonesia	99
Australia	na	45	39	51	38	42	55	51	42	43	48	46	37	49	46	41		Algeria	98
Austria	41	54	45	62	47	50	62	57	51	51	58	53	48	59	54	51		El Salvador	98
Azerbaijan	na	86	83	88	85	86	88	90	87	83	88	89	79	86	84	91		Egypt	98
Bangladesh	na	95	94	97	94	97	97	97	94	93	97	93	97	97	95	91		Puerto Rico	97
Belarus	22	44	31	53	43	35	54	55	41	32	51	42	34	46	42	30		Colombia	97
Belgium	39	37	33	42	26	28	51	48	32	37	49	35	32	40	38	33		Nigeria	97
Bosnia and Herz.	na	68	64	72	76	65	65	81	68	56	73	67	66	72	67	60		Iran	97
Brazil	94	96	95	97	96	96	96	98	96	90	95	99	94	99	96	90		Tanzania	96
Bulgaria	20	37	29	44	29	34	44	49	29	35	47	33	31	38	36	22		Brazil	96
Canada	62	67	58	76	58	64	77	75	67	61	73	68	60	75	70	58		Venezuela	96
Chile	84	85	81	89	83	85	88	90	83	82	88	84	82	87	86	80		Bangladesh	95
China	3	na	na	na	na	na	na	na	na	na	na	na	na	na	na	na		Philippines	95
Colombia	na	97	96	98	97	97	98	99	97	95	99	97	95	98	97	97		Zimbabwe	95
Croatia	na	66	60	72	58	67	71	68	66	61	77	65	62	75	66	58		Dominican Rep.	94
Czech Republic	na	20	16	25	14	13	30	21	19	21	25	22	13	23	19	23		Mexico	94
Denmark	18	21	16	25	14	17	28	21	13	23	24	16	21	9	22	19		Malta	93
Dominican Rep.	na	94	91	97	95	93	100	100	95	94	97	92	91	94	96	89		Uganda	93
Egypt	na	98	97	98	97	98	98	98	98	96	99	98	98	98	97	97		Peru	92
El Salvador	na	98	97	99	97	98	99	98	98	96	99	98	97	na	na	na		Turkey	91
Estonia	na	22	15	29	15	20	28	28	21	19	32	24	18	23	22	20		South Africa	90
Finland	42	49	40	58	34	43	62	50	46	52	55	43	47	44	52	49		India	88
France	27	27	22	31	16	26	33	29	24	23	32	26	24	33	27	15		Romania	86
Georgia	na	72	67	76	77	73	64	72	72	72	72	69	75	70	73	84		Azerbaijan	86
Germany	26	39	35	42	30	32	51	44	35	35	41	43	40	39	41	37		Chile	85
Great Britain	36	34	30	38	27	28	43	32	33	36	33	33	36	na	na	na		Argentina	83
Greece	na	68	61	73	63	69	75	81	73	61	73	65	64	74	68	58		United States	83
Hungary	40	39	28	50	29	31	53	45	28	29	48	41	33	43	35	30		Poland	82
Iceland	47	51	42	59	35	49	68	57	49	43	55	53	40	54	51	42		Portugal	74
India	68	88	88	87	86	89	88	87	88	90	88	87	89	88	88	93		Georgia	72
Indonesia	na	99	100	100	100	100	100	99	100	100	99	100	100	100	100	100		Israel	71
Iran	na	97	96	97	96	96	99	98	97	95	97	97	95	98	97	93		Moldova	70
Ireland	74	66	61	71	43	64	86	77	63	53	76	66	58	73	65	60		Macedonia	70
Israel	na	71	66	75	72	75	65	85	72	59	79	75	58	68	71	69		Albania	70
Italy	65	69	59	77	60	67	74	73	65	64	75	70	63	74	71	62		Italy	69
Japan	20	28	24	31	17	28	32	34	29	21	32	27	24	25	27	27		Bosnia and Herz.	68
Jordan	na	100	100	100	100	100	100	100	100	100	100	100	100	100	100	100		Greece	68
Korea, South	na	37	32	42	35	38	37	32	36	38	33	32	44	35	38	43		Canada	67
Latvia	26	40	28	51	34	38	45	49	38	37	48	36	33	41	41	37		Croatia	66
Lithuania	na	58	45	68	47	46	76	78	50	55	75	58	52	63	57	45		Ireland	66
Luxembourg	na	40	36	44	29	36	53	47	36	38	42	44	34	42	41	35		Northern Ireland	64
Macedonia	na	70	67	73	73	69	66	86	67	60	75	69	61	72	67	75		Singapore	60
Malta	na	93	89	96	85	94	97	97	92	89	94	97	89	95	93	83		Armenia	59
Mexico	82	94	93	94	93	94	94	95	92	91	95	91	93	95	92	96		Lithuania	58
Moldova	na	70	64	75	63	71	75	76	69	67	69	65	73	74	67	69		Uruguay	58
Montenegro	na	55	47	63	47	56	60	63	52	45	53	57	54	57	54	44		Slovakia	58
Morocco	na	100	99	100	99	99	100	100	100	99	99	100	99	100	99	98		Montenegro	55
Netherlands	33	36	30	42	22	30	49	41	31	36	42	35	24	51	34	34		Austria	54
New Zealand	na	44	38	49	37	39	51	43	45	44	49	46	35	46	44	38		Iceland	51
Nigeria	98	97	97	97	96	97	99	96	97	98	97	96	98	97	97	98		Finland	49
Northern Ireland	73	64	57	69	52	57	75	71	54	62	62	64	55	64	63	68		Switzerland	49
Norway	27	30	23	36	23	25	41	35	27	30	na	na	na	31	30	25		Ukraine	49
Pakistan	na	100	100	100	100	100	100	100	100	100	100	100	100	100	100	100		Serbia	49
Peru	na	92	89	96	90	95	93	95	93	89	93	94	89	95	92	90		Spain	46
Philippines	na	95	95	95	96	96	93	92	96	97	95	94	97	95	95	95		Australia	45
Poland	87	82	77	86	80	80	84	89	76	64	85	79	80	87	79	75		New Zealand	44
Portugal	57	74	63	84	61	78	79	81	64	51	81	75	67	77	73	68		Belarus	44
Puerto Rico	na	97	97	98	96	98	98	99	99	97	97	99	97	99	98	97		Latvia	40
Romania	67	86	79	92	83	82	91	92	86	72	92	86	81	89	85	66		Luxembourg	40
Russian Fed.	21	38	27	47	31	34	46	51	36	35	44	38	31	40	34	23		Hungary	39
Serbia	na	49	40	56	49	48	49	59	43	45	55	47	45	48	51	36		Germany	39
Singapore	na	60	57	63	58	60	68	64	58	59	67	58	59	70	57	55		Vietnam	39
Slovakia	na	58	48	67	48	53	70	66	55	49	67	57	53	60	57	58		Russian Fed.	38
Slovenia	30	35	30	38	23	31	47	52	29	22	49	29	27	40	34	34		Belgium	37
South Africa	88	90	87	93	91	88	90	91	88	89	89	88	94	90	89	85		Bulgaria	37
Spain	48	46	34	57	32	43	58	54	38	39	58	43	43	54	45	34		Korea, South	37
Sweden	19	23	18	28	15	20	31	26	20	25	24	24	18	31	21	24		Netherlands	36
Switzerland	56	49	43	55	29	46	64	58	45	55	56	51	45	49	48	49		Slovenia	35
Taiwan	na	31	25	36	19	28	45	43	28	21	37	28	22	33	27	24		Great Britain	34
Tanzania	na	96	96	96	97	96	96	97	96	95	97	96	95	98	96	100		Taiwan	31
Turkey	86	91	89	94	90	91	94	96	90	75	95	90	84	95	92	83		Norway	30
Uganda	na	93	90	95	95	92	83	89	95	87	90	89	93	91	94	93		Japan	28
Ukraine	na	49	38	58	39	48	55	62	47	46	55	47	44	48	46	62		France	27
United States	77	83	78	88	76	86	85	84	84	82	85	80	85	85	84	80		Sweden	23
Uruguay	na	58	48	65	52	53	65	63	55	40	63	57	54	54	60	55		Estonia	22
Venezuela	na	96	94	98	96	96	94	96	96	93	95	95	96	95	96	96		Denmark	21
Vietnam	na	39	37	40	38	39	38	43	35	19	39	35	42	27	40	40		Czech Republic	20
Zimbabwe	na	95	93	96	95	94	94	94	96	100	95	94	94	92	96	100			
Total	50	66	61	70	68	64	66	71	63	63	71	66	62	70	65	59		Total	66

F064) COMFORT AND STRENGTH FROM RELIGION

Do you find that you get comfort and strength from religion?

Yes (%) (WVS: V197; EVS: V124)

Country	Wave 1990	Wave 2000	Gender Male	Gender Female	Age 16-29	Age 30-49	Age 50+	Education Lower	Education Middle	Education Upper	Income Lower	Income Middle	Income Upper	Values Mat	Values Mixed	Values Postm.
Albania	na	73	69	77	67	73	78	75	73	68	72	75	72	72	74	73
Algeria	na	99	99	99	99	99	99	100	99	98	100	99	98	100	99	98
Argentina	66	77	70	84	66	80	86	82	71	72	84	80	68	84	79	68
Armenia	na	70	59	79	74	67	68	70	72	63	66	72	73	69	73	61
Australia	na	49	41	57	41	48	58	56	46	47	54	49	42	54	51	43
Austria	61	62	54	69	53	59	69	65	60	58	67	62	56	65	64	55
Azerbaijan	na	88	86	89	86	88	91	92	87	88	88	89	84	88	87	92
Bangladesh	na	99	98	100	98	99	99	100	100	95	100	99	98	100	98	99
Belarus	31	54	38	67	47	48	67	69	50	44	64	51	46	61	49	31
Belgium	47	49	41	56	35	42	62	58	45	47	59	48	43	56	49	40
Bosnia and Herz.	na	72	67	77	80	70	68	82	73	62	74	71	73	74	71	65
Brazil	86	89	86	92	85	90	94	91	89	84	91	89	87	91	89	86
Bulgaria	33	45	34	55	34	36	57	61	34	40	58	37	37	43	44	53
Canada	62	63	54	72	47	60	76	76	61	56	69	66	53	69	67	54
Chile	83	75	66	83	66	74	85	86	68	69	81	72	69	78	75	69
China	4	na	na	na	na	na	na	na	na	na	na	na	na	na	na	na
Colombia	na	91	89	93	89	90	95	96	92	85	96	92	86	94	94	92
Croatia	na	82	76	87	77	83	85	85	82	78	86	82	81	89	82	74
Czech Republic	na	26	20	32	21	18	35	27	25	24	33	24	20	30	24	28
Denmark	27	33	24	41	25	31	39	34	24	36	39	27	35	23	36	24
Dominican Rep.	na	81	75	85	79	83	91	88	84	79	86	78	77	84	82	76
Egypt	na	100	100	100	100	100	100	100	100	100	100	100	100	100	100	99
El Salvador	na	89	86	90	86	89	91	89	90	86	91	87	88	na	na	na
Estonia	na	36	23	46	22	29	49	43	33	33	45	44	28	40	33	26
Finland	49	59	46	71	42	55	71	60	56	64	64	52	57	59	59	59
France	36	35	28	41	24	32	43	36	32	33	39	34	34	40	37	21
Georgia	na	83	78	88	87	85	78	84	83	85	81	82	87	82	84	96
Germany	31	50	41	57	35	43	63	56	45	44	53	51	52	53	50	46
Great Britain	45	37	30	44	28	31	48	37	37	35	37	36	40	na	na	na
Greece	na	76	70	81	71	78	84	91	82	68	77	77	75	86	77	64
Hungary	49	49	35	63	33	43	65	55	39	37	58	50	44	55	45	23
Iceland	75	75	68	81	59	76	86	81	72	69	79	76	67	80	76	56
India	81	85	83	87	82	84	88	87	85	79	82	87	84	87	81	78
Indonesia	na	100	100	100	100	100	100	100	100	100	100	100	100	100	100	100
Iran	na	96	96	97	95	96	99	98	97	93	97	97	95	99	95	94
Ireland	83	75	67	83	56	73	90	82	71	73	82	76	68	78	75	69
Israel	na	na	na	na	na	na	na	na	na	na	na	na	na	na	na	na
Italy	71	72	62	80	57	71	81	80	65	64	81	69	63	82	73	61
Japan	42	35	31	38	10	31	49	46	37	26	42	35	31	37	33	38
Jordan	na	100	100	100	100	100	100	100	99	100	100	100	100	100	100	99
Korea, South	na	67	58	75	63	68	69	68	67	68	62	66	73	67	67	65
Latvia	37	63	48	76	53	62	69	70	61	62	70	62	57	66	62	61
Lithuania	na	72	57	83	61	62	87	91	63	70	86	69	66	77	71	59
Luxembourg	na	49	44	54	34	45	63	56	45	47	50	51	45	51	48	45
Macedonia	na	71	70	72	76	71	67	84	66	61	75	68	67	72	69	78
Malta	na	93	89	95	85	92	98	98	91	87	95	95	88	96	92	82
Mexico	77	89	86	93	87	89	94	92	87	80	94	89	85	93	89	82
Moldova	na	92	87	96	83	94	96	96	93	85	95	91	89	93	90	89
Montenegro	na	66	57	74	57	67	70	74	62	53	60	66	67	70	62	55
Morocco	na	100	100	100	100	100	100	100	100	99	100	100	100	100	100	99
Netherlands	45	43	37	49	39	38	51	47	41	42	49	40	36	58	42	38
New Zealand	na	50	45	54	39	43	61	49	51	49	57	49	42	53	50	43
Nigeria	96	98	98	98	98	98	100	99	98	97	98	98	98	98	99	98
Northern Ireland	77	69	62	75	56	61	80	75	61	68	71	66	64	71	68	71
Norway	36	40	31	48	28	36	53	43	37	41	na	na	na	39	40	33
Pakistan	na	96	95	97	95	96	98	96	96	94	96	96	96	97	94	92
Peru	na	91	87	95	87	93	94	92	93	86	93	92	86	92	91	88
Philippines	na	91	91	92	90	92	91	90	93	90	91	91	91	93	90	91
Poland	90	82	75	88	80	81	85	89	77	66	84	81	80	89	78	82
Portugal	67	80	69	89	66	82	85	87	66	59	83	84	72	85	77	73
Puerto Rico	na	86	79	91	80	83	93	97	89	84	90	90	81	89	88	83
Romania	76	87	79	93	79	84	93	94	87	74	92	90	80	91	84	67
Russian Fed.	35	57	42	69	49	53	66	69	55	56	63	57	50	59	54	44
Serbia	na	63	53	72	63	64	63	76	56	58	71	60	59	66	63	45
Singapore	na	77	73	81	71	80	87	83	74	71	82	80	71	83	76	60
Slovakia	na	64	54	72	52	59	77	72	61	56	74	60	61	66	62	63
Slovenia	51	48	42	54	37	44	60	64	45	32	59	48	35	59	47	45
South Africa	89	89	83	96	88	89	92	92	85	83	90	92	86	88	90	88
Spain	56	54	41	66	32	50	72	65	43	44	67	53	45	65	55	32
Sweden	27	33	26	40	23	30	43	38	30	34	36	33	27	38	32	34
Switzerland	na	55	47	63	36	55	66	64	53	52	66	57	49	59	53	56
Taiwan	na	68	58	78	70	68	67	72	65	66	69	68	65	67	70	52
Tanzania	88	96	95	97	95	97	96	94	97	100	93	97	99	96	97	96
Turkey	88	92	90	95	91	93	95	97	89	76	96	91	84	96	93	83
Uganda	na	95	93	98	95	95	95	95	95	99	98	94	93	93	96	96
Ukraine	na	65	49	77	58	62	71	81	61	63	68	65	62	64	63	66
United States	80	80	72	87	68	82	85	82	80	79	82	77	80	85	81	75
Uruguay	na	55	42	65	45	49	64	61	49	43	61	48	56	64	56	47
Venezuela	na	na	na	na	na	na	na	na	na	na	na	na	na	na	na	na
Vietnam	na	27	17	37	24	26	32	34	18	21	23	24	32	34	26	18
Zimbabwe	na	93	87	98	93	94	91	93	93	70	91	97	92	93	92	100
Total	57	71	65	77	70	70	74	76	68	68	76	71	68	77	70	61

RANKING

Country	2000
Egypt	100
Jordan	100
Morocco	100
Indonesia	100
Algeria	99
Bangladesh	99
Nigeria	98
Iran	96
Tanzania	96
Pakistan	96
Uganda	95
Zimbabwe	93
Malta	93
Turkey	92
Moldova	92
Philippines	91
Peru	91
Colombia	91
Mexico	89
South Africa	89
Brazil	89
El Salvador	89
Azerbaijan	88
Romania	87
Puerto Rico	86
India	85
Georgia	83
Croatia	82
Poland	82
Dominican Rep.	81
Portugal	80
United States	80
Argentina	77
Singapore	77
Greece	76
Chile	75
Ireland	75
Iceland	75
Albania	73
Lithuania	72
Bosnia and Herz.	72
Italy	72
Macedonia	71
Armenia	70
Northern Ireland	69
Taiwan	68
Korea, South	67
Montenegro	66
Ukraine	65
Slovakia	64
Serbia	63
Latvia	63
Canada	63
Austria	62
Finland	59
Russian Fed.	57
Uruguay	55
Switzerland	55
Belarus	54
Spain	54
New Zealand	50
Germany	50
Hungary	49
Australia	49
Luxembourg	49
Belgium	49
Slovenia	48
Bulgaria	45
Netherlands	43
Norway	40
Great Britain	37
Estonia	36
Japan	35
France	35
Sweden	33
Denmark	33
Vietnam	27
Czech Republic	26
Total	71

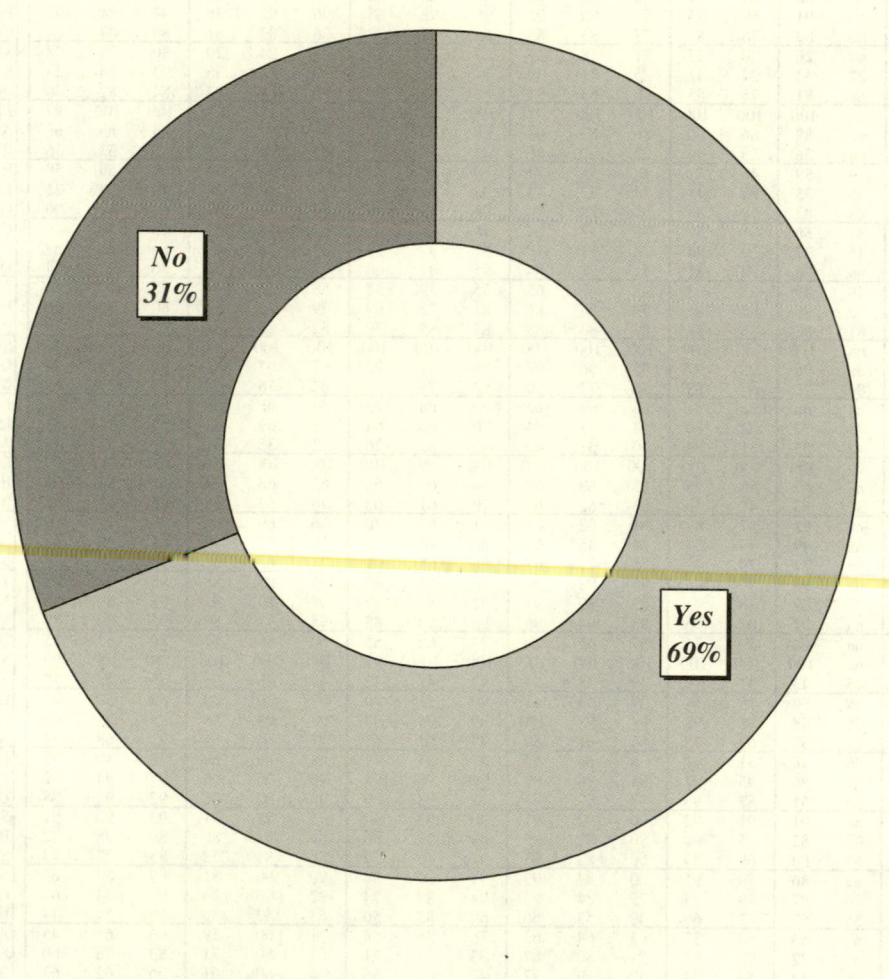

F65) Do you take some moments of prayer, meditation or contemplation or something like that?

No 31%

Yes 69%

F065) MOMENTS OF PRAYER, MEDITATION...

Do you take some moments of prayer, meditation or contemplation or something like that?

Yes (%)

(WVS: V198; EVS: V125)

Country	Wave 1990	Wave 2000	Gender Male	Gender Female	Age 16-29	Age 30-49	Age 50+	Education Lower	Education Middle	Education Upper	Income Lower	Income Middle	Income Upper	Values Mat	Values Mixed	Values Postm.	RANKING Country	RANKING 2000
Albania	na	81	75	87	78	81	85	81	81	83	79	83	82	79	82	78	Philippines	97
Algeria	na	na	na	na	na	na	na	na	na	na	na	na	na	na	na	na	Tanzania	97
Argentina	75	78	69	86	70	82	82	79	77	80	81	78	75	81	79	74	Bangladesh	96
Armenia	na	na	na	na	na	na	na	na	na	na	na	na	na	na	na	na	Uganda	95
Australia	72	69	60	77	55	68	78	67	68	77	71	71	67	65	70	68	Romania	94
Austria	na	na	na	na	na	na	na	na	na	na	na	na	na	na	na	na	Turkey	93
Azerbaijan	na	na	na	na	na	na	na	na	na	na	na	na	na	na	na	na	Zimbabwe	92
Bangladesh	na	96	95	97	94	96	99	98	94	89	95	95	97	98	94	94	Malta	91
Belarus	40	71	54	84	68	67	79	79	70	61	73	71	67	72	70	68	Puerto Rico	90
Belgium	55	62	55	68	51	57	71	65	56	69	71	58	60	65	61	64	United States	89
Bosnia and Herz.	na	80	77	83	86	80	76	87	80	77	82	80	79	80	80	84	South Africa	89
Brazil	89	na	na	na	na	na	na	na	na	na	na	na	na	na	na	na	Moldova	88
Bulgaria	36	34	22	45	33	22	44	46	25	30	45	31	23	33	34	30	India	88
Canada	74	80	73	86	73	79	84	82	79	79	83	81	76	85	79	79	Mexico	87
Chile	85	82	76	88	79	82	86	86	80	82	84	80	82	85	81	83	Poland	87
China	20	na	na	na	na	na	na	na	na	na	na	na	na	na	na	na	Chile	82
Colombia	na	na	na	na	na	na	na	na	na	na	na	na	na	na	na	na	Ireland	82
Croatia	na	75	67	82	68	76	77	80	72	68	81	77	68	84	75	65	Albania	81
Czech Republic	na	37	32	43	34	30	46	34	38	51	42	33	37	35	37	47	Bosnia and Herz.	80
Denmark	43	51	39	63	42	48	59	48	48	56	54	48	54	36	52	55	Canada	80
Dominican Rep.	na	na	na	na	na	na	na	na	na	na	na	na	na	na	na	na	Peru	80
Egypt	na	na	na	na	na	na	na	na	na	na	na	na	na	na	na	na	Italy	79
El Salvador	na	na	na	na	na	na	na	na	na	na	na	na	na	na	na	na	Argentina	78
Estonia	na	51	39	60	46	46	58	51	51	49	51	53	54	49	53	46	Croatia	75
Finland	22	75	63	86	65	73	82	73	75	85	79	70	75	73	75	78	Finland	75
France	46	41	34	48	35	40	46	39	38	49	43	37	44	41	42	38	Portugal	73
Georgia	na	na	na	na	na	na	na	na	na	na	na	na	na	na	na	na	Northern Ireland	73
Germany	53	54	44	62	46	50	63	58	51	53	53	52	57	56	54	54	Belarus	71
Great Britain	54	50	44	56	45	46	56	43	52	57	49	49	53	na	na	na	Singapore	70
Greece	na	61	50	69	61	59	65	72	62	58	66	62	55	64	61	55	Austria	69
Hungary	58	61	47	73	45	57	74	63	58	55	66	61	58	64	59	40	Netherlands	69
Iceland	46	54	45	63	46	55	60	54	53	54	58	52	51	48	56	53	Slovakia	66
India	85	88	85	91	86	89	88	90	85	85	89	89	86	89	87	73	Latvia	65
Indonesia	na	na	na	na	na	na	na	na	na	na	na	na	na	na	na	na	Macedonia	62
Iran	na	na	na	na	na	na	na	na	na	na	na	na	na	na	na	na	Belgium	62
Ireland	84	82	76	88	76	80	89	83	81	85	89	78	79	84	83	76	Lithuania	62
Israel	na	na	na	na	na	na	na	na	na	na	na	na	na	na	na	na	Greece	61
Italy	76	79	70	87	71	80	83	80	77	83	83	78	77	80	80	77	Hungary	61
Japan	41	40	38	41	19	36	52	49	41	32	44	42	36	41	39	38	Serbia	59
Jordan	na	na	na	na	na	na	na	na	na	na	na	na	na	na	na	na	Korea, South	59
Korea, South	na	59	51	66	54	62	58	66	58	59	57	55	64	59	59	53	Montenegro	58
Latvia	66	65	52	75	63	64	66	64	63	72	67	63	64	63	66	63	Luxembourg	58
Lithuania	na	62	45	75	52	48	81	83	52	66	82	56	55	66	60	47	Spain	55
Luxembourg	na	58	52	64	41	57	71	63	56	59	57	61	57	55	58	59	Germany	54
Macedonia	na	62	59	65	70	61	57	76	54	55	65	59	59	61	60	71	Iceland	54
Malta	na	91	87	95	85	91	95	96	89	90	93	91	86	92	91	86	Denmark	51
Mexico	82	87	84	91	85	87	91	89	85	85	88	86	86	89	87	87	Estonia	51
Moldova	na	88	81	94	78	91	93	94	85	87	93	88	83	88	87	85	Great Britain	50
Montenegro	na	58	50	66	49	57	66	67	53	52	56	56	60	61	56	51	Ukraine	49
Morocco	na	na	na	na	na	na	na	na	na	na	na	na	na	na	na	na	Slovenia	46
Netherlands	68	69	65	73	63	69	72	59	70	77	67	67	74	76	65	76	Sweden	44
New Zealand	na	na	na	na	na	na	na	na	na	na	na	na	na	na	na	na	France	41
Nigeria	99	na	na	na	na	na	na	na	na	na	na	na	na	na	na	na	Japan	40
Northern Ireland	76	73	65	79	65	69	80	79	65	71	74	70	69	74	72	78	Czech Republic	37
Norway	64	na	na	na	na	na	na	na	na	na	na	na	na	na	na	na	Bulgaria	34
Pakistan	na	na	na	na	na	na	na	na	na	na	na	na	na	na	na	na	Russian Fed.	33
Peru	na	80	76	83	75	82	85	79	83	75	85	77	75	80	78	85	Vietnam	30
Philippines	na	97	96	99	96	98	98	97	98	97	97	97	97	97	98	95		
Poland	89	87	82	92	85	87	89	88	88	84	90	85	88	89	87	87		
Portugal	61	73	60	84	59	73	80	79	59	63	74	80	68	75	72	70		
Puerto Rico	na	90	85	94	84	87	97	96	87	92	92	91	90	94	90	90		
Romania	86	94	89	98	88	92	97	97	93	90	97	94	91	94	92	93		
Russian Fed.	37	33	18	46	26	27	45	52	31	31	42	31	26	36	29	29		
Serbia	na	59	49	68	52	60	62	68	52	59	66	55	58	58	61	53		
Singapore	na	70	65	74	66	70	83	75	68	63	72	72	67	78	67	64		
Slovakia	na	66	55	77	57	62	79	73	63	65	75	68	61	70	64	69		
Slovenia	45	46	36	55	39	43	55	62	40	40	59	40	40	53	45	46		
South Africa	86	89	85	94	88	90	91	90	88	89	89	91	87	90	90	84		
Spain	62	55	42	67	38	49	70	62	48	48	69	49	48	64	54	40		
Sweden	34	44	36	52	37	40	52	38	40	56	45	42	43	43	42	49		
Switzerland	na	na	na	na	na	na	na	na	na	na	na	na	na	na	na	na		
Taiwan	na	na	na	na	na	na	na	na	na	na	na	na	na	na	na	na		
Tanzania	na	97	96	99	96	98	97	96	99	99	95	98	98	97	97	100		
Turkey	90	93	90	96	92	94	95	96	90	82	96	94	87	95	94	88		
Uganda	na	95	92	98	95	95	96	95	95	97	97	93	91	94	96	96		
Ukraine	na	49	32	64	43	46	56	73	45	46	54	47	47	51	47	57		
United States	84	89	85	94	83	92	91	85	91	90	90	90	90	92	89	91		
Uruguay	na	na	na	na	na	na	na	na	na	na	na	na	na	na	na	na		
Venezuela	na	na	na	na	na	na	na	na	na	na	na	na	na	na	na	na		
Vietnam	na	30	20	39	25	30	33	37	20	24	26	27	33	41	27	25		
Zimbabwe	na	92	85	97	91	93	91	93	89	100	90	95	92	90	92	97		
Total	63	69	61	76	66	68	73	73	66	69	72	68	67	71	69	69	Total	69

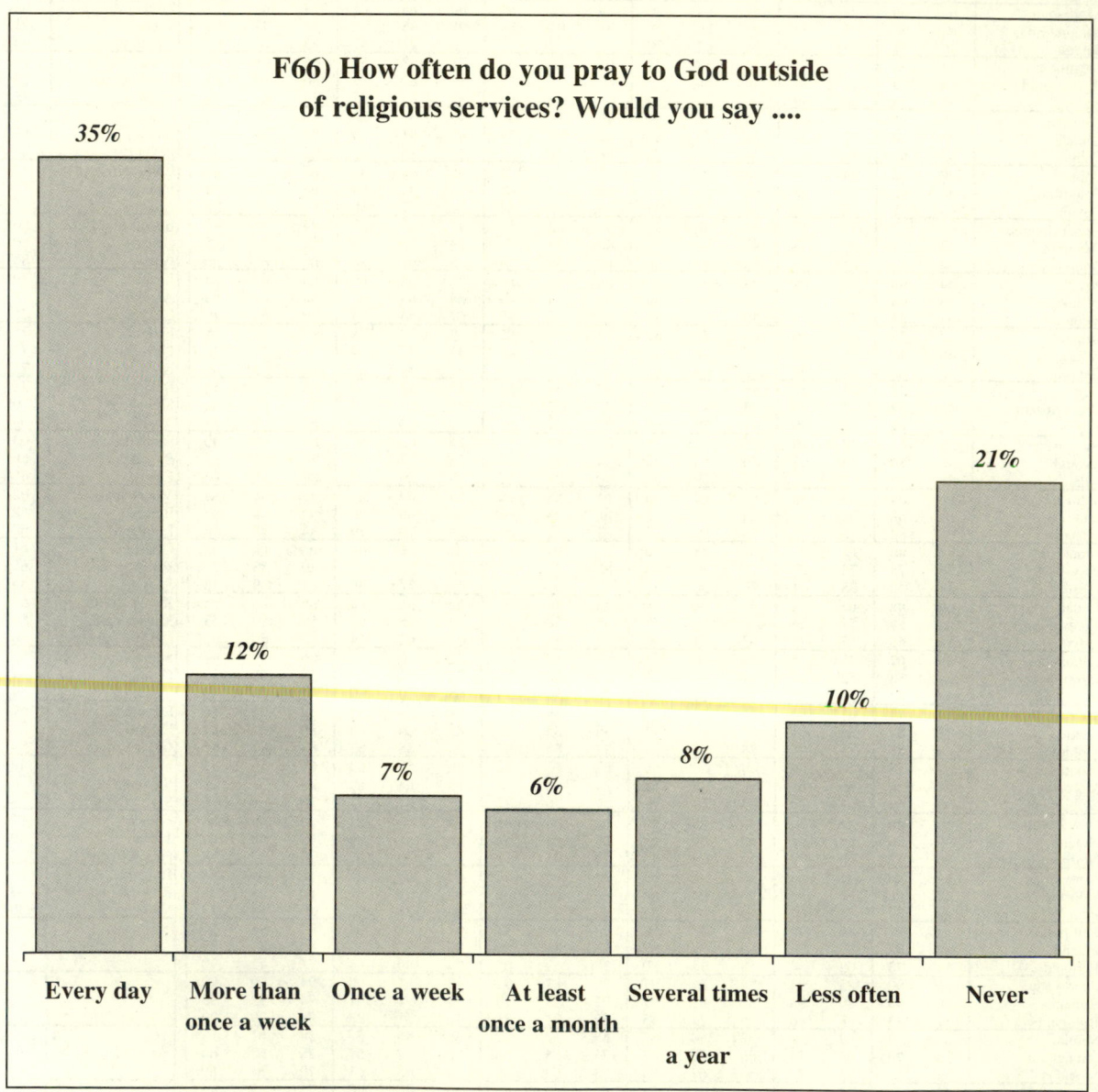

F66) How often do you pray to God outside of religious services? Would you say ....

35%

21%

12%

10%

8%

7%

6%

Every day | More than once a week | Once a week | At least once a month | Several times a year | Less often | Never

How often do you pray to God outside of religious services? Would you say...

Every day / More than once a week (%)   (WVS: V199; EVS: V126)

Country	Wave 1990	Wave 2000	Male	Female	16-29	30-49	50+	Educ. Lower	Educ. Middle	Educ. Upper	Income Lower	Income Middle	Income Upper	Mat	Mixed	Postm.	RANKING Country	2000
Albania	na	48	38	57	46	43	57	51	47	40	49	52	43	49	45	50	Tanzania	87
Algeria	na	na	na	na	na	na	na	na	na	na	na	na	na	na	na	na	Puerto Rico	86
Argentina	66	51	36	64	35	56	60	53	48	47	55	52	45	54	51	48	Philippines	86
Armenia	na	na	na	na	na	na	na	na	na	na	na	na	na	na	na	na	Uganda	83
Australia	na	na	na	na	na	na	na	na	na	na	na	na	na	na	na	na	Turkey	82
Austria	57	34	26	42	19	30	46	37	30	33	39	34	28	33	35	31	Bangladesh	81
Azerbaijan	na	na	na	na	na	na	na	na	na	na	na	na	na	na	na	na	Malta	80
Bangladesh	na	81	79	83	77	82	89	81	83	77	78	84	78	83	78	87	Zimbabwe	78
Belarus	6	27	11	39	21	17	41	41	22	20	33	27	16	28	24	25	South Africa	76
Belgium	41	27	20	33	15	18	40	38	22	25	42	26	17	27	27	25	Peru	75
Bosnia and Herz.	na	40	34	46	45	35	43	53	38	36	45	38	40	36	42	33	Morocco	74
Brazil	87	na	na	na	na	na	na	na	na	na	na	na	na	na	na	na	Venezuela	72
Bulgaria	21	20	10	29	13	14	27	29	13	18	30	18	11	20	20	7	United States	71
Canada	62	49	38	60	35	45	62	58	48	43	56	48	40	55	51	43	Romania	70
Chile	76	55	44	65	47	55	64	60	53	51	61	48	55	61	53	52	Poland	68
China	6	na	na	na	na	na	na	na	na	na	na	na	na	na	na	na	Mexico	66
Colombia	na	na	na	na	na	na	na	na	na	na	na	na	na	na	na	na	India	62
Croatia	na	53	39	65	49	52	56	62	47	47	65	51	48	60	54	39	Iran	60
Czech Republic	na	15	10	18	10	7	23	15	14	15	23	11	10	17	14	15	Ireland	60
Denmark	25	17	11	22	7	13	25	18	10	17	24	12	15	9	18	10	Moldova	60
Dominican Rep.	na	na	na	na	na	na	na	na	na	na	na	na	na	na	na	na	Chile	55
Egypt	na	na	na	na	na	na	na	na	na	na	na	na	na	na	na	na	Northern Ireland	55
El Salvador	na	na	na	na	na	na	na	na	na	na	na	na	na	na	na	na	Italy	55
Estonia	na	15	7	21	9	11	22	16	15	12	26	15	10	17	13	9	Portugal	53
Finland	53	35	24	45	23	29	47	36	33	41	42	30	33	34	35	42	Croatia	53
France	34	15	11	18	7	13	21	16	14	13	20	14	12	18	15	10	Argentina	51
Georgia	na	na	na	na	na	na	na	na	na	na	na	na	na	na	na	na	Slovakia	50
Germany	28	27	20	33	17	22	38	32	24	25	25	30	32	28	26	32	Canada	49
Great Britain	43	24	17	31	15	19	34	23	24	23	21	26	25	na	na	na	Greece	48
Greece	na	48	38	55	43	50	54	68	51	42	52	47	41	54	48	40	Albania	48
Hungary	38	30	16	42	17	19	47	33	22	25	41	31	23	32	29	14	Singapore	45
Iceland	51	37	25	48	21	35	52	41	30	38	46	33	29	34	38	30	Macedonia	44
India	73	62	57	69	61	62	63	63	60	62	54	62	65	61	60	42	Bosnia and Herz.	40
Indonesia	na	na	na	na	na	na	na	na	na	na	na	na	na	na	na	na	Korea, South	40
Iran	na	60	61	60	62	58	60	61	59	60	63	59	60	61	61	60	Iceland	37
Ireland	81	60	51	68	35	55	84	73	55	49	77	60	49	62	60	56	Finland	35
Israel	na	na	na	na	na	na	na	na	na	na	na	na	na	na	na	na	Ukraine	35
Italy	67	55	38	70	44	51	64	60	51	51	62	53	48	60	55	51	Austria	34
Japan	38	20	15	24	5	17	28	20	22	12	24	20	17	21	20	18	Spain	33
Jordan	na	na	na	na	na	na	na	na	na	na	na	na	na	na	na	na	Lithuania	32
Korea, South	na	40	35	45	33	43	41	33	42	39	42	34	43	42	38	45	Hungary	30
Latvia	28	27	12	39	18	20	35	35	25	21	34	21	19	28	26	24	Serbia	30
Lithuania	na	32	16	44	17	22	52	54	23	31	55	33	21	38	29	27	Netherlands	29
Luxembourg	na	25	21	29	16	20	37	32	19	27	29	24	25	23	25	23	Germany	27
Macedonia	na	44	40	48	49	43	40	64	34	33	48	41	39	41	42	68	Belarus	27
Malta	na	80	73	88	67	77	92	89	78	74	85	80	75	85	79	70	Belgium	27
Mexico	71	66	58	74	56	68	78	72	57	67	66	65	63	65	68	64	Latvia	27
Moldova	na	60	46	72	45	60	71	75	57	50	68	58	52	66	52	51	Luxembourg	25
Montenegro	na	19	15	23	13	18	23	25	15	15	21	21	18	22	16	8	Great Britain	24
Morocco	na	74	67	81	64	80	87	76	67	70	74	75	72	76	71	68	Russian Fed.	22
Netherlands	46	29	23	35	20	21	42	33	27	28	34	28	21	42	28	24	Japan	20
New Zealand	na	na	na	na	na	na	na	na	na	na	na	na	na	na	na	na	Bulgaria	20
Nigeria	97	na	na	na	na	na	na	na	na	na	na	na	na	na	na	na	Montenegro	19
Northern Ireland	75	55	49	61	42	47	69	63	45	55	60	53	46	61	54	57	Denmark	17
Norway	36	na	na	na	na	na	na	na	na	na	na	na	na	na	na	na	France	15
Pakistan	na	na	na	na	na	na	na	na	na	na	na	na	na	na	na	na	Estonia	15
Peru	na	75	66	83	66	78	85	79	75	71	77	73	73	76	74	77	Czech Republic	15
Philippines	na	86	82	90	83	86	90	84	86	88	85	86	86	84	87	85	Vietnam	9
Poland	na	68	57	77	61	61	80	71	67	56	73	66	58	75	64	60		
Portugal	58	53	38	67	38	51	64	61	36	39	70	60	44	59	51	47		
Puerto Rico	na	86	77	92	76	86	92	92	80	89	88	86	86	89	87	85		
Romania	72	70	58	81	58	62	82	84	64	56	82	69	60	74	67	41		
Russian Fed.	17	22	10	33	13	16	35	42	19	19	30	20	15	25	18	14		
Serbia	na	30	20	38	26	25	36	40	23	27	37	29	26	31	29	19		
Singapore	na	45	42	48	39	51	49	46	44	47	51	48	43	52	42	44		
Slovakia	na	50	37	62	39	45	64	63	45	39	64	48	43	54	47	41		
Slovenia	38	na	na	na	na	na	na	na	na	na	na	na	na	na	na	na		
South Africa	na	76	68	85	75	74	84	76	76	84	74	73	80	75	76	80		
Spain	56	33	19	45	17	28	46	40	25	27	41	30	30	42	31	19		
Sweden	25	na	na	na	na	na	na	na	na	na	na	na	na	na	na	na		
Switzerland	na	na	na	na	na	na	na	na	na	na	na	na	na	na	na	na		
Taiwan	na	na	na	na	na	na	na	na	na	na	na	na	na	na	na	na		
Tanzania	na	87	84	89	85	86	90	84	88	92	85	90	84	88	86	92		
Turkey	na	82	76	87	77	84	90	90	72	62	87	82	71	82	83	73		
Uganda	na	83	81	84	82	84	83	81	83	86	87	79	86	78	83	95		
Ukraine	na	35	20	47	21	31	46	63	30	30	39	34	30	37	32	27		
United States	78	71	62	80	57	75	78	70	69	73	72	72	69	85	72	66		
Uruguay	na	na	na	na	na	na	na	na	na	na	na	na	na	na	na	na		
Venezuela	na	72	63	81	63	75	84	77	70	71	72	73	67	76	72	66		
Vietnam	na	9	8	10	7	9	10	12	5	5	6	7	12	6	9	11		
Zimbabwe	na	78	65	90	76	82	77	80	76	60	74	87	80	77	79	93		
Total	49	48	39	55	44	46	53	53	43	46	53	47	43	50	47	45	Total	48

F102) POLITICIANS WHO DON'T BELIEVE IN GOD UNFIT FOR PUBLIC OFFICE

How much do you agree or disagree with each of the following statements:

Politicians who do not believe in God are unfit for public office

Disagree / Strongly disagree (%)

(WVS: V200; EVS: V129)

Country	Wave 1990	Wave 2000	Gender Male	Gender Female	Age 16-29	Age 30-49	Age 50+	Education Lower	Education Middle	Education Upper	Income Lower	Income Middle	Income Upper	Values Mat	Values Mixed	Values Postm.	RANKING Country	RANKING 2000
Albania	na	29	31	26	28	29	29	26	29	35	29	26	31	29	30	27	Netherlands	94
Algeria	na	13	12	14	13	14	11	13	12	14	14	12	16	11	14	14	Denmark	92
Argentina	na	46	49	43	52	44	42	38	54	68	37	45	56	38	43	60	Sweden	85
Armenia	na	na	na	na	na	na	na	na	na	na	na	na	na	na	na	na	Belgium	82
Australia	na	na	na	na	na	na	na	na	na	na	na	na	na	na	na	na	Czech Republic	80
Austria	na	69	71	66	73	73	62	64	71	82	62	69	74	55	69	72	Iceland	79
Azerbaijan	na	na	na	na	na	na	na	na	na	na	na	na	na	na	na	na	France	78
Bangladesh	na	24	25	22	27	23	10	16	30	33	15	31	22	16	28	38	Slovenia	74
Belarus	na	55	64	48	63	58	45	51	57	56	55	54	60	56	55	60	Great Britain	71
Belgium	na	82	86	79	84	88	77	73	83	89	74	83	89	76	84	89	Ireland	70
Bosnia and Herz.	na	51	53	49	46	51	57	43	52	57	51	52	52	51	52	48	Spain	69
Brazil	na	na	na	na	na	na	na	na	na	na	na	na	na	na	na	na	Austria	69
Bulgaria	na	52	56	49	63	53	47	42	58	55	43	58	56	55	51	58	Northern Ireland	68
Canada	na	59	64	53	63	61	53	50	56	70	52	56	69	55	54	69	Luxembourg	67
Chile	na	55	57	53	58	54	54	48	59	59	48	60	63	56	52	63	Germany	67
China	na	na	na	na	na	na	na	na	na	na	na	na	na	na	na	na	Portugal	66
Colombia	na	na	na	na	na	na	na	na	na	na	na	na	na	na	na	na	Hungary	66
Croatia	na	57	64	51	66	54	55	48	61	69	56	53	61	53	55	68	Finland	65
Czech Republic	na	80	82	79	85	84	75	76	85	86	75	80	87	73	82	85	Italy	64
Denmark	na	92	93	90	93	94	89	89	95	96	89	94	94	94	91	94	Poland	64
Dominican Rep.	na	na	na	na	na	na	na	na	na	na	na	na	na	na	na	na	Vietnam	62
Egypt	na	10	10	9	9	11	9	10	9	11	9	11	10	9	10	9	Latvia	59
El Salvador	na	na	na	na	na	na	na	na	na	na	na	na	na	na	na	na	Korea, South	59
Estonia	na	59	64	55	70	60	52	49	64	61	57	53	65	55	61	71	Estonia	59
Finland	na	65	67	63	71	71	56	61	68	74	63	68	68	58	68	72	Canada	59
France	na	78	82	75	78	80	77	75	84	80	73	79	82	73	78	87	Russian Fed.	58
Georgia	na	na	na	na	na	na	na	na	na	na	na	na	na	na	na	na	Serbia	57
Germany	na	67	72	63	75	73	57	61	71	76	66	66	66	63	66	72	Croatia	57
Great Britain	na	71	73	70	73	75	69	70	73	75	67	65	78	na	na	na	Belarus	55
Greece	na	37	42	33	42	34	32	22	30	45	32	36	39	34	35	46	Chile	55
Hungary	na	66	70	62	72	72	55	61	73	76	58	64	71	61	70	79	Montenegro	55
Iceland	na	79	81	78	87	84	66	74	81	88	72	78	87	75	79	89	Slovakia	53
India	na	44	49	36	50	44	38	32	43	63	37	35	55	44	48	55	Bulgaria	52
Indonesia	na	9	9	10	6	10	10	11	11	7	12	6	7	6	12	4	Bosnia and Herz.	51
Iran	na	na	na	na	na	na	na	na	na	na	na	na	na	na	na	na	Lithuania	51
Ireland	na	70	74	67	78	75	60	60	74	80	58	74	78	67	71	77	Mexico	49
Israel	na	na	na	na	na	na	na	na	na	na	na	na	na	na	na	na	Macedonia	47
Italy	na	64	68	61	71	70	55	53	72	75	55	68	73	48	64	74	Argentina	46
Japan	na	41	43	40	59	44	31	24	38	59	35	40	50	39	45	43	Ukraine	46
Jordan	na	17	16	18	16	16	21	19	14	15	15	17	18	16	18	14	India	44
Korea, South	na	59	61	57	69	57	52	45	57	63	59	60	59	57	61	61	Malta	43
Latvia	na	59	65	54	73	62	51	52	63	58	55	58	65	54	62	64	Japan	41
Lithuania	na	51	61	42	65	57	35	32	56	59	34	58	54	49	48	74	Zimbabwe	37
Luxembourg	na	67	67	68	67	68	66	57	68	81	53	74	81	56	68	78	Greece	37
Macedonia	na	47	17	17	40	50	49	33	54	52	44	44	58	50	48	29	United States	36
Malta	na	43	46	40	58	46	29	30	45	63	34	41	49	30	45	51	Moldova	32
Mexico	na	49	50	48	54	49	41	41	56	62	45	47	60	43	51	60	Venezuela	32
Moldova	na	32	34	30	40	29	29	24	33	38	27	39	34	35	26	35	South Africa	29
Montenegro	na	55	60	50	63	57	47	45	58	68	45	58	60	54	58	47	Albania	29
Morocco	na	9	10	8	11	8	7	8	15	17	5	13	16	6	11	11	Turkey	28
Netherlands	na	94	96	93	96	95	92	92	94	97	92	95	97	86	95	97	Bangladesh	24
New Zealand	na	na	na	na	na	na	na	na	na	na	na	na	na	na	na	na	Puerto Rico	23
Nigeria	na	11	11	11	10	11	10	10	11	10	8	11	13	12	10	9	Romania	23
Northern Ireland	na	68	73	64	71	77	61	61	73	77	58	72	78	59	69	81	Tanzania	23
Norway	na	na	na	na	na	na	na	na	na	na	na	na	na	na	na	na	Uganda	22
Pakistan	na	1	1	1	1	1	1	2	na	na	1	1	na	1	1	na	Jordan	17
Peru	na	na	na	na	na	na	na	na	na	na	na	na	na	na	na	na	Philippines	14
Philippines	na	14	15	13	13	15	12	13	16	11	21	12	10	14	15	11	Algeria	13
Poland	na	64	66	63	62	71	58	55	73	79	59	68	70	56	69	68	Nigeria	11
Portugal	na	66	71	62	78	64	61	61	77	81	47	61	77	62	66	77	Egypt	10
Puerto Rico	na	23	26	22	26	23	22	25	21	24	23	21	26	21	21	30	Indonesia	9
Romania	na	23	27	19	32	27	15	13	28	30	16	24	29	19	26	37	Morocco	9
Russian Fed.	na	58	65	52	60	60	54	48	57	65	52	57	64	56	59	65	Pakistan	1
Serbia	na	57	62	52	56	58	57	45	62	64	53	58	63	53	60	66		
Singapore	na	na	na	na	na	na	na	na	na	na	na	na	na	na	na	na		
Slovakia	na	53	58	48	61	54	44	43	55	68	42	52	60	47	57	65		
Slovenia	na	74	73	75	76	78	68	63	76	86	63	77	82	72	73	81		
South Africa	na	29	35	22	29	30	23	29	29	32	30	25	33	28	30	27		
Spain	na	69	73	64	77	73	59	62	75	76	59	70	73	57	71	81		
Sweden	na	85	84	85	89	88	78	78	82	93	81	85	88	79	84	88		
Switzerland	na	na	na	na	na	na	na	na	na	na	na	na	na	na	na	na		
Taiwan	na	na	na	na	na	na	na	na	na	na	na	na	na	na	na	na		
Tanzania	na	23	22	24	20	23	27	24	19	25	24	21	27	24	21	26		
Turkey	na	28	27	29	31	27	23	19	33	57	19	29	46	18	28	44		
Uganda	na	22	22	22	23	20	26	22	22	16	14	20	29	27	21	14		
Ukraine	na	46	54	38	60	42	41	33	48	47	40	48	51	44	47	50		
United States	na	36	42	30	39	33	37	32	33	39	35	36	37	25	35	43		
Uruguay	na	na	na	na	na	na	na	na	na	na	na	na	na	na	na	na		
Venezuela	na	32	32	32	39	27	28	28	34	34	29	34	35	28	35	28		
Vietnam	na	62	71	52	65	62	60	57	66	66	59	61	64	42	68	61		
Zimbabwe	na	37	37	38	41	36	31	38	38	10	38	38	32	37	38	40		
Total	na	49	51	47	48	50	49	43	51	54	43	49	54	41	50	61	Total	49

F103) RELIGIOUS LEADERS SHOULD NOT INFLUENCE PEOPLE VOTE

How much do you agree or disagree with each of the following statements:

Religious leaders should not influence how people vote in elections

Agree strongly / Agree (%)

(WVS: V201; EVS: V130)

Country	Wave		Gender		Age			Education			Income			Values			RANKING Country	2000
	1990	2000	Male	Female	16-29	30-49	50+	Lower	Middle	Upper	Lower	Middle	Upper	Mat	Mixed	Postm.		
Albania	na	77	77	77	74	78	78	77	75	81	78	75	78	82	73	68	Malta	90
Algeria	na	38	34	42	40	37	36	34	38	41	42	39	34	32	43	29	Indonesia	86
Argentina	na	75	76	74	74	75	75	74	77	76	74	74	77	69	73	82	France	86
Armenia	na	na	na	na	na	na	na	na	na	na	na	na	na	na	na	na	Poland	86
Australia	na	na	na	na	na	na	na	na	na	na	na	na	na	na	na	na	Serbia	85
Austria	na	85	83	86	82	84	86	84	85	85	79	87	86	84	84	88	Denmark	85
Azerbaijan	na	na	na	na	na	na	na	na	na	na	na	na	na	na	na	na	Austria	85
Bangladesh	na	75	73	76	77	74	63	73	75	77	79	71	75	78	72	73	Estonia	84
Belarus	na	82	86	79	86	84	77	79	83	85	82	83	82	82	82	91	Croatia	84
Belgium	na	79	80	79	80	79	79	77	79	81	81	79	83	75	81	83	Latvia	84
Bosnia and Herz.	na	76	76	77	75	75	79	71	76	82	77	74	79	80	76	77	Montenegro	83
Brazil	na	na	na	na	na	na	na	na	na	na	na	na	na	na	na	na	Bulgaria	83
Bulgaria	na	83	84	82	79	87	82	78	86	83	80	82	86	83	84	86	Ukraine	83
Canada	na	77	78	77	78	78	77	79	78	76	76	78	79	84	76	78	Belarus	82
Chile	na	69	70	68	68	71	68	68	70	71	67	71	70	74	68	65	Luxembourg	82
China	na	na	na	na	na	na	na	na	na	na	na	na	na	na	na	na	Russian Fed.	82
Colombia	na	na	na	na	na	na	na	na	na	na	na	na	na	na	na	na	Iceland	81
Croatia	na	84	82	86	88	85	80	87	81	87	87	81	86	84	84	86	Lithuania	81
Czech Republic	na	81	83	78	81	80	81	80	82	78	81	83	80	81	81	79	Czech Republic	81
Denmark	na	85	83	86	84	82	88	87	83	80	85	88	77	89	87	84	Portugal	80
Dominican Rep.	na	na	na	na	na	na	na	na	na	na	na	na	na	na	na	na	Macedonia	80
Egypt	na	57	60	54	53	58	60	56	56	61	59	58	57	58	56	54	Belgium	79
El Salvador	na	na	na	na	na	na	na	na	na	na	na	na	na	na	na	na	Turkey	79
Estonia	na	84	82	86	87	84	84	80	86	87	83	85	84	85	85	74	Italy	79
Finland	na	68	70	65	67	69	67	71	64	58	67	71	65	73	68	59	Ireland	79
France	na	86	87	85	87	87	85	87	88	84	88	87	84	87	85	89	Greece	78
Georgia	na	na	na	na	na	na	na	na	na	na	na	na	na	na	na	na	Romania	78
Germany	na	75	76	74	81	78	68	69	79	84	74	72	71	69	73	88	Slovenia	78
Great Britain	na	70	69	70	70	68	72	70	71	69	71	67	68	na	na	na	Canada	77
Greece	na	78	80	77	81	79	72	74	79	78	80	81	77	77	79	79	Albania	77
Hungary	na	77	79	75	78	79	73	74	82	83	69	77	80	74	79	89	Hungary	77
Iceland	na	81	81	82	81	82	80	83	81	78	83	80	80	83	81	79	Bosnia and Herz.	76
India	na	68	67	70	69	68	67	66	69	70	63	70	69	61	75	69	Northern Ireland	76
Indonesia	na	86	87	86	81	90	86	86	89	85	88	87	87	90	86	75	Morocco	76
Iran	na	na	na	na	na	na	na	na	na	na	na	na	na	na	na	na	Jordan	75
Ireland	na	79	78	79	82	78	77	78	80	74	77	82	78	76	79	79	Philippines	75
Israel	na	na	na	na	na	na	na	na	na	na	na	na	na	na	na	na	Germany	75
Italy	na	79	80	77	82	80	76	78	81	76	74	83	80	70	79	83	Argentina	75
Japan	na	74	78	71	73	73	76	62	74	80	68	77	80	75	78	74	Bangladesh	75
Jordan	na	75	74	76	74	74	76	73	78	77	76	73	76	78	73	74	Pakistan	74
Korea, South	na	69	73	66	74	66	71	53	69	72	71	67	69	66	73	67	Japan	74
Latvia	na	84	87	82	80	85	85	78	87	83	80	88	86	84	84	84	Slovakia	74
Lithuania	na	81	82	79	83	87	73	74	84	80	68	88	79	76	82	91	Nigeria	73
Luxembourg	na	82	82	82	82	83	81	80	83	85	72	85	85	81	82	82	Puerto Rico	70
Macedonia	na	80	79	82	79	79	83	75	82	85	81	79	82	81	81	78	Tanzania	70
Malta	na	90	88	91	92	90	88	92	90	86	91	88	88	87	91	92	Great Britain	70
Mexico	na	64	62	66	63	66	61	62	65	71	60	63	66	62	63	64	Korea, South	69
Moldova	na	69	68	69	73	68	65	64	68	73	62	68	70	69	64	75	Chile	69
Montenegro	na	83	85	82	90	84	78	77	86	91	81	84	89	85	84	76	Moldova	69
Morocco	na	76	74	77	72	75	87	80	63	53	87	64	72	77	76	64	Vietnam	69
Netherlands	na	66	66	65	58	65	71	68	64	65	63	67	68	60	65	73	India	68
New Zealand	na	na	na	na	na	na	na	na	na	na	na	na	na	na	na	na	Sweden	68
Nigeria	na	73	73	72	72	74	68	73	73	72	73	74	72	74	72	75	Finland	68
Northern Ireland	na	76	73	78	75	79	75	76	81	65	75	79	77	80	74	75	Spain	67
Norway	na	na	na	na	na	na	na	na	na	na	na	na	na	na	na	na	Netherlands	66
Pakistan	na	74	73	76	85	74	55	66	83	87	69	72	86	70	80	100	South Africa	65
Peru	na	na	na	na	na	na	na	na	na	na	na	na	na	na	na	na	United States	64
Philippines	na	75	77	73	79	73	73	72	74	80	75	75	75	76	75	71	Mexico	64
Poland	na	86	87	85	89	86	83	84	88	85	87	86	83	84	86	89	Zimbabwe	63
Portugal	na	80	84	77	86	79	78	78	87	83	72	80	79	79	81	79	Uganda	63
Puerto Rico	na	70	71	69	68	72	70	68	70	71	73	70	72	59	72	70	Egypt	57
Romania	na	78	79	77	81	81	74	72	80	83	75	79	80	73	81	87	Venezuela	56
Russian Fed.	na	82	84	81	84	84	79	76	82	87	76	82	88	82	84	74	Algeria	38
Serbia	na	85	86	85	82	86	86	80	88	88	84	85	88	83	89	81		
Singapore	na	na	na	na	na	na	na	na	na	na	na	na	na	na	na	na		
Slovakia	na	74	75	73	79	76	68	72	76	72	70	75	77	73	77	66		
Slovenia	na	78	77	78	73	81	78	74	78	82	76	79	85	83	78	75		
South Africa	na	65	63	66	62	68	63	62	69	57	60	71	64	59	69	60		
Spain	na	67	69	64	72	69	61	61	71	72	62	65	72	57	69	78		
Sweden	na	68	67	69	63	67	72	79	69	58	69	73	62	64	70	65		
Switzerland	na	na	na	na	na	na	na	na	na	na	na	na	na	na	na	na		
Taiwan	na	na	na	na	na	na	na	na	na	na	na	na	na	na	na	na		
Tanzania	na	70	69	71	69	68	77	71	69	66	72	70	64	69	71	67		
Turkey	na	79	80	78	79	79	78	76	82	88	76	81	82	77	80	81		
Uganda	na	63	61	65	62	62	68	62	63	66	69	61	65	61	63	69		
Ukraine	na	83	84	81	88	84	78	76	82	86	83	85	79	82	83	88		
United States	na	64	66	61	67	61	65	73	69	57	72	60	59	68	62	65		
Uruguay	na	na	na	na	na	na	na	na	na	na	na	na	na	na	na	na		
Venezuela	na	56	55	58	53	59	59	61	52	61	55	59	57	55	58	55		
Vietnam	na	69	76	61	65	70	69	64	73	75	71	66	71	68	70	65		
Zimbabwe	na	63	64	62	63	62	65	63	64	78	59	64	69	65	62	65		
Total	na	75	76	75	74	75	75	74	76	75	74	76	76	75	76	76	Total	75

F104) PEOPLE WITH STRONG RELIGIOUS BELIEFS SHOULD HELD PUBLIC OFFICE

How much do you agree or disagree with each of the following statements: It would be better for [country] if more people with strong religious beliefs held public office

Disagree / Strongly disagree (%)

(WVS: V202; EVS: V131)

Country	Wave 1990	Wave 2000	Gender Male	Gender Female	Age 16-29	Age 30-49	Age 50+	Education Lower	Education Middle	Education Upper	Income Lower	Income Middle	Income Upper	Values Mat	Values Mixed	Values Postm.
Albania	na	32	35	30	34	33	29	30	33	35	33	30	33	33	32	32
Algeria	na	30	28	33	27	34	28	23	33	31	28	27	40	27	31	38
Argentina	na	44	45	44	51	40	43	36	55	57	34	44	54	33	43	56
Armenia	na	na	na	na	na	na	na	na	na	na	na	na	na	na	na	na
Australia	na	na	na	na	na	na	na	na	na	na	na	na	na	na	na	na
Austria	na	49	51	47	58	51	43	45	51	57	44	47	55	41	46	58
Azerbaijan	na	na	na	na	na	na	na	na	na	na	na	na	na	na	na	na
Bangladesh	na	54	57	50	55	54	50	47	59	66	57	51	57	55	53	60
Belarus	na	36	44	29	39	38	31	29	38	36	37	34	37	38	33	42
Belgium	na	66	67	64	71	71	58	57	67	70	61	65	71	58	65	77
Bosnia and Herz.	na	41	45	38	37	41	45	32	42	46	43	41	39	38	43	46
Brazil	na	na	na	na	na	na	na	na	na	na	na	na	na	na	na	na
Bulgaria	na	42	45	39	46	43	38	30	49	41	30	46	49	42	44	32
Canada	na	50	54	45	55	53	43	47	49	54	46	48	55	48	46	58
Chile	na	49	51	47	48	50	47	43	52	53	39	53	58	48	47	57
China	na	na	na	na	na	na	na	na	na	na	na	na	na	na	na	na
Colombia	na	na	na	na	na	na	na	na	na	na	na	na	na	na	na	na
Croatia	na	29	32	27	32	31	25	23	32	38	21	30	33	23	28	40
Czech Republic	na	72	73	71	73	76	67	70	74	70	69	73	75	69	72	73
Denmark	na	88	88	88	89	93	82	87	91	88	86	90	90	92	87	93
Dominican Rep.	na	na	na	na	na	na	na	na	na	na	na	na	na	na	na	na
Egypt	na	4	4	4	5	4	4	3	5	7	3	3	6	4	4	7
El Salvador	na	na	na	na	na	na	na	na	na	na	na	na	na	na	na	na
Estonia	na	42	46	39	51	41	39	39	43	44	43	36	48	42	40	70
Finland	na	58	61	55	65	67	47	57	60	57	58	61	58	54	59	58
France	na	68	70	65	68	71	64	67	69	69	68	68	68	62	67	77
Georgia	na	na	na	na	na	na	na	na	na	na	na	na	na	na	na	na
Germany	na	48	54	43	60	53	36	39	53	58	49	45	42	42	49	49
Great Britain	na	54	56	52	51	56	55	55	53	56	50	55	55	na	na	na
Greece	na	31	35	27	31	30	29	21	28	35	27	31	31	20	30	45
Hungary	na	50	58	43	57	56	40	45	60	59	48	46	56	45	56	53
Iceland	na	59	60	58	65	63	48	53	62	65	53	55	70	60	57	72
India	na	49	52	44	51	49	48	42	51	58	43	44	57	50	50	71
Indonesia	na	na	na	na	na	na	na	na	na	na	na	na	na	na	na	na
Iran	na	na	na	na	na	na	na	na	na	na	na	na	na	na	na	na
Ireland	na	60	63	57	72	64	46	50	64	66	49	65	67	49	63	64
Israel	na	na	na	na	na	na	na	na	na	na	na	na	na	na	na	na
Italy	na	49	53	46	57	53	42	41	57	53	42	51	55	38	48	57
Japan	na	63	66	61	71	67	56	59	61	69	55	65	69	63	66	64
Jordan	na	25	28	22	27	26	19	17	30	33	24	17	34	23	26	30
Korea, South	na	40	44	35	42	40	35	28	37	44	44	42	34	40	38	50
Latvia	na	33	39	28	42	37	27	24	37	33	28	36	40	31	32	43
Lithuania	na	26	37	18	34	34	15	10	31	37	18	34	22	22	25	46
Luxembourg	na	53	50	55	57	58	45	45	55	60	43	58	64	45	53	66
Macedonia	na	51	51	51	46	53	55	38	57	58	49	49	59	55	51	38
Malta	na	21	24	18	32	24	11	12	24	29	19	19	24	18	21	35
Mexico	na	40	44	37	45	39	35	31	50	56	34	40	53	39	41	32
Moldova	na	11	13	9	17	8	10	5	12	15	10	11	13	12	11	16
Montenegro	na	38	43	32	43	37	34	32	38	48	27	42	41	37	40	30
Morocco	na	24	24	24	25	26	18	20	40	38	15	26	47	24	24	30
Netherlands	na	73	73	73	74	79	67	67	74	78	66	79	76	61	73	79
New Zealand	na	na	na	na	na	na	na	na	na	na	na	na	na	na	na	na
Nigeria	na	5	5	5	5	4	4	3	6	5	3	5	7	5	4	8
Northern Ireland	na	59	63	56	58	65	55	56	59	70	55	63	66	52	61	66
Norway	na	na	na	na	na	na	na	na	na	na	na	na	na	na	na	na
Pakistan	na	50	48	52	57	52	32	38	60	71	38	53	61	45	56	67
Peru	na	na	na	na	na	na	na	na	na	na	na	na	na	na	na	na
Philippines	na	7	9	5	8	7	6	7	7	7	8	9	5	6	8	6
Poland	na	45	46	43	39	50	42	37	56	54	42	49	40	40	47	55
Portugal	na	47	50	44	56	47	42	45	50	60	35	47	50	43	47	55
Puerto Rico	na	34	39	32	35	37	33	24	34	37	32	32	42	20	35	43
Romania	na	13	17	9	18	15	8	5	15	21	5	15	16	10	14	22
Russian Fed.	na	25	32	20	28	27	22	16	26	27	22	24	30	23	27	46
Serbia	na	37	45	29	29	39	39	29	41	39	30	37	43	34	39	46
Singapore	na	na	na	na	na	na	na	na	na	na	na	na	na	na	na	na
Slovakia	na	35	42	29	40	40	26	28	38	46	25	36	40	33	36	39
Slovenia	na	71	70	71	70	76	65	58	73	82	64	72	80	67	72	70
South Africa	na	16	23	8	18	14	14	12	19	37	14	14	21	15	16	19
Spain	na	56	60	51	64	61	45	50	59	63	46	59	59	42	57	72
Sweden	na	70	68	72	66	73	69	68	67	75	67	70	74	62	70	76
Switzerland	na	na	na	na	na	na	na	na	na	na	na	na	na	na	na	na
Taiwan	na	na	na	na	na	na	na	na	na	na	na	na	na	na	na	na
Tanzania	na	25	25	26	26	26	24	26	22	27	24	23	30	25	24	38
Turkey	na	27	27	28	28	29	21	17	36	53	18	29	48	19	27	40
Uganda	na	10	9	11	10	9	15	10	11	5	10	5	12	11	10	10
Ukraine	na	22	29	16	27	20	22	16	23	23	22	21	24	21	23	26
United States	na	25	30	20	28	24	24	20	24	28	23	25	27	19	23	33
Uruguay	na	na	na	na	na	na	na	na	na	na	na	na	na	na	na	na
Venezuela	na	27	28	25	30	26	21	22	27	31	24	24	33	22	29	27
Vietnam	na	46	53	38	50	45	43	39	51	65	50	46	44	39	49	49
Zimbabwe	na	24	27	22	27	22	22	24	23	70	26	26	23	20	26	37
Total	na	41	44	38	41	43	39	37	42	46	36	42	45	34	42	53

RANKING

Country	2000
Denmark	88
Netherlands	73
Czech Republic	72
Slovenia	71
Sweden	70
France	68
Belgium	66
Japan	63
Ireland	60
Northern Ireland	59
Iceland	59
Finland	58
Spain	56
Bangladesh	54
Great Britain	54
Luxembourg	53
Macedonia	51
Hungary	50
Pakistan	50
Canada	50
Italy	49
India	49
Austria	49
Chile	49
Germany	48
Portugal	47
Vietnam	46
Poland	45
Argentina	44
Estonia	42
Bulgaria	42
Bosnia and Herz.	41
Mexico	40
Korea, South	40
Montenegro	38
Serbia	37
Belarus	36
Slovakia	35
Puerto Rico	34
Latvia	33
Albania	32
Greece	31
Algeria	30
Croatia	29
Turkey	27
Venezuela	27
Lithuania	26
Russian Fed.	25
Tanzania	25
Jordan	25
United States	25
Zimbabwe	24
Morocco	24
Ukraine	22
Malta	21
South Africa	16
Romania	13
Moldova	11
Uganda	10
Philippines	7
Nigeria	5
Egypt	4
Total	41

F105) RELIGIOUS LEADERS SHOULD NOT INFLUENCE GOVERNMENT

How much do you agree or disagree with each of the following statements.

Religious leaders should not influence government

Agree strongly / Agree (%)

(WVS: V203; EVS: V132)

Country	Wave 1990	Wave 2000	Gender Male	Gender Female	Age 16-29	Age 30-49	Age 50+	Education Lower	Education Middle	Education Upper	Income Lower	Income Middle	Income Upper	Values Mat	Values Mixed	Values Postm.
Albania	na	76	77	74	71	76	79	74	75	83	74	75	79	79	74	73
Algeria	na	40	39	40	43	37	37	37	40	41	45	40	38	37	40	43
Argentina	na	65	65	64	61	65	68	64	66	63	63	64	68	60	64	70
Armenia	na	na	na	na	na	na	na	na	na	na	na	na	na	na	na	na
Australia	na	na	na	na	na	na	na	na	na	na	na	na	na	na	na	na
Austria	na	80	80	79	80	79	80	80	80	76	78	81	78	82	79	80
Azerbaijan	na	na	na	na	na	na	na	na	na	na	na	na	na	na	na	na
Bangladesh	na	71	69	73	73	70	61	66	75	75	77	69	66	71	69	75
Belarus	na	73	76	71	75	76	67	68	75	74	73	73	73	73	73	74
Belgium	na	74	74	73	75	74	72	73	73	75	76	73	77	69	73	79
Bosnia and Herz.	na	72	71	72	70	71	75	67	72	76	73	71	74	76	71	71
Brazil	na	na	na	na	na	na	na	na	na	na	na	na	na	na	na	na
Bulgaria	na	80	80	79	77	81	79	74	82	82	74	80	81	80	79	89
Canada	na	67	68	67	67	68	67	69	67	66	67	68	68	75	64	72
Chile	na	68	69	66	64	69	69	67	67	72	63	74	70	68	67	69
China	na	na	na	na	na	na	na	na	na	na	na	na	na	na	na	na
Colombia	na	na	na	na	na	na	na	na	na	na	na	na	na	na	na	na
Croatia	na	79	83	76	81	80	77	82	78	77	76	80	80	82	81	75
Czech Republic	na	74	77	71	70	74	76	73	75	77	74	72	78	73	75	71
Denmark	na	85	82	89	83	85	87	88	84	80	87	89	77	93	86	83
Dominican Rep.	na	na	na	na	na	na	na	na	na	na	na	na	na	na	na	na
Egypt	na	na	na	na	na	na	na	na	na	na	na	na	na	na	na	na
El Salvador	na	na	na	na	na	na	na	na	na	na	na	na	na	na	na	na
Estonia	na	75	74	75	73	75	76	74	74	77	79	75	71	76	74	51
Finland	na	58	61	55	56	65	52	61	57	47	54	62	61	65	57	50
France	na	82	81	82	82	83	80	81	85	81	80	83	83	81	80	88
Georgia	na	na	na	na	na	na	na	na	na	na	na	na	na	na	na	na
Germany	na	71	74	69	75	75	65	68	74	77	72	68	70	71	68	82
Great Britain	na	65	67	64	62	64	70	69	66	60	68	63	63	na	na	na
Greece	na	59	65	55	55	62	62	59	59	60	56	60	63	54	60	63
Hungary	na	70	73	67	71	70	69	68	76	69	64	70	72	67	72	63
Iceland	na	70	71	69	72	70	69	68	75	67	71	72	67	74	68	72
India	na	71	73	68	72	71	72	66	72	79	63	69	77	67	75	81
Indonesia	na	91	89	93	86	91	93	91	92	90	89	94	92	89	92	86
Iran	na	na	na	na	na	na	na	na	na	na	na	na	na	na	na	na
Ireland	na	73	74	72	78	71	72	72	76	68	73	70	74	76	73	73
Israel	na	na	na	na	na	na	na	na	na	na	na	na	na	na	na	na
Italy	na	68	70	66	64	70	68	67	69	67	64	72	70	59	68	73
Japan	na	72	78	68	71	73	72	62	71	81	66	74	80	76	75	74
Jordan	na	na	na	na	na	na	na	na	na	na	na	na	na	na	na	na
Korea, South	na	57	61	53	55	58	59	53	57	58	61	54	56	57	59	47
Latvia	na	73	75	71	67	74	75	68	77	69	71	77	73	75	71	81
Lithuania	na	76	81	71	81	82	66	65	80	78	67	83	76	70	77	88
Luxembourg	na	77	78	75	77	78	76	73	79	78	68	76	79	76	78	77
Macedonia	na	74	72	75	69	74	76	66	77	77	69	76	77	73	73	79
Malta	na	78	77	80	81	80	74	79	79	73	82	77	72	77	78	80
Mexico	na	65	67	63	64	65	65	65	64	68	62	65	66	63	64	64
Moldova	na	58	56	60	59	58	59	56	57	62	56	65	56	66	48	55
Montenegro	na	78	79	75	83	78	74	72	80	86	76	79	81	78	79	78
Morocco	na	65	62	68	66	63	65	63	72	61	71	63	65	67	64	58
Netherlands	na	60	61	59	57	60	62	57	63	59	59	60	64	50	60	65
New Zealand	na	na	na	na	na	na	na	na	na	na	na	na	na	na	na	na
Nigeria	na	na	na	na	na	na	na	na	na	na	na	na	na	na	na	na
Northern Ireland	na	66	63	68	65	70	64	67	68	57	65	67	62	68	64	70
Norway	na	na	na	na	na	na	na	na	na	na	na	na	na	na	na	na
Pakistan	na	na	na	na	na	na	na	na	na	na	na	na	na	na	na	na
Peru	na	na	na	na	na	na	na	na	na	na	na	na	na	na	na	na
Philippines	na	76	78	74	80	74	74	73	78	77	77	76	74	78	75	68
Poland	na	81	82	80	79	83	80	80	83	81	82	84	73	78	82	85
Portugal	na	80	82	77	84	78	78	79	79	83	73	78	84	76	81	82
Puerto Rico	na	59	63	57	65	56	59	60	61	58	61	60	56	53	59	63
Romania	na	78	80	75	78	78	76	73	80	79	76	78	78	75	78	85
Russian Fed.	na	68	72	65	68	69	67	67	67	71	63	68	72	68	68	61
Serbia	na	82	84	80	78	83	83	78	84	83	79	85	82	82	82	81
Singapore	na	na	na	na	na	na	na	na	na	na	na	na	na	na	na	na
Slovakia	na	71	72	69	72	73	67	69	72	72	65	71	74	71	71	68
Slovenia	na	73	75	72	69	77	72	71	73	77	72	77	78	75	74	74
South Africa	na	52	54	51	49	57	48	52	55	32	49	60	51	51	54	51
Spain	na	69	72	65	75	71	63	63	74	75	67	67	71	59	70	82
Sweden	na	52	53	50	49	53	52	55	55	45	54	53	48	50	53	52
Switzerland	na	na	na	na	na	na	na	na	na	na	na	na	na	na	na	na
Taiwan	na	na	na	na	na	na	na	na	na	na	na	na	na	na	na	na
Tanzania	na	69	68	70	71	66	74	74	69	51	77	66	57	70	69	65
Turkey	na	72	71	73	73	72	72	69	73	84	68	73	76	72	74	72
Uganda	na	55	52	58	53	57	58	55	54	65	64	53	45	51	55	65
Ukraine	na	72	78	67	76	73	69	63	74	72	73	73	71	70	74	82
United States	na	51	55	47	55	47	53	56	53	48	52	54	48	52	50	53
Uruguay	na	na	na	na	na	na	na	na	na	na	na	na	na	na	na	na
Venezuela	na	57	58	56	55	58	58	55	56	60	55	58	60	60	57	53
Vietnam	na	67	72	61	63	67	70	60	75	69	74	66	64	67	69	62
Zimbabwe	na	52	51	52	53	50	53	53	51	10	51	56	51	53	51	44
Total	na	69	71	68	68	70	70	69	70	68	68	71	69	70	69	70

RANKING

Country	2000
Indonesia	91
Denmark	85
Serbia	82
France	82
Poland	81
Austria	80
Bulgaria	80
Portugal	80
Croatia	79
Malta	78
Romania	78
Montenegro	78
Luxembourg	77
Philippines	76
Lithuania	76
Albania	76
Estonia	75
Czech Republic	74
Macedonia	74
Belgium	74
Slovenia	73
Latvia	73
Belarus	73
Ireland	73
Japan	72
Turkey	72
Ukraine	72
Bosnia and Herz.	72
India	71
Germany	71
Slovakia	71
Bangladesh	71
Iceland	70
Hungary	70
Spain	69
Tanzania	69
Russian Fed.	68
Italy	68
Chile	68
Canada	67
Vietnam	67
Northern Ireland	66
Great Britain	65
Argentina	65
Mexico	65
Morocco	65
Netherlands	60
Greece	59
Puerto Rico	59
Moldova	58
Finland	58
Korea, South	57
Venezuela	57
Uganda	55
South Africa	52
Sweden	52
Zimbabwe	52
United States	51
Algeria	40
Total	69

F105) RELIGIOUS FAILURES SHOULD NOT INFLUENCE GOVERNMENT
How much do you agree or disagree with each of the following statements.
Religious leaders should not influence government...
Agree strongly (A)

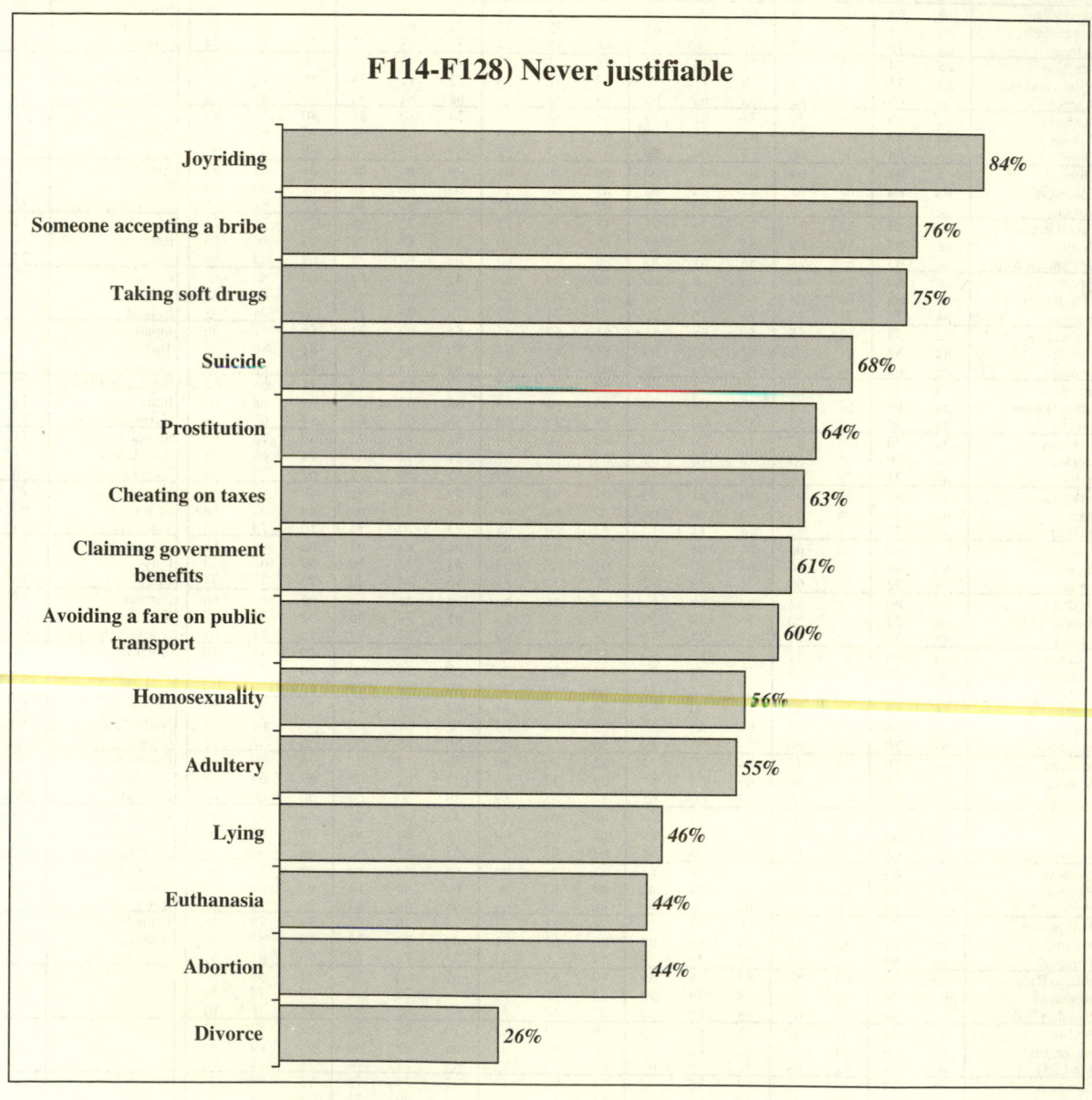

F114-F128) Never justifiable

Joyriding	84%
Someone accepting a bribe	76%
Taking soft drugs	75%
Suicide	68%
Prostitution	64%
Cheating on taxes	63%
Claiming government benefits	61%
Avoiding a fare on public transport	60%
Homosexuality	56%
Adultery	55%
Lying	46%
Euthanasia	44%
Abortion	44%
Divorce	26%

F114) JUSTIFIABLE: CLAIMING GOVERNMENT BENEFITS

Please tell me for each of the following statements whether you think it can always be justified, never be justified, or something in between: Claiming government benefits to which you have no right

Never justifiable (%) (WVS: V204; EVS: V225)

Country	Wave 1990	Wave 2000	Male	Female	16-29	30-49	50+	Educ. Lower	Educ. Middle	Educ. Upper	Income Lower	Income Middle	Income Upper	Mat	Mixed	Postm.	RANKING Country	2000
Albania	na	58	56	61	52	59	63	54	59	70	54	58	64	60	58	56	Bangladesh	92
Algeria	na	51	49	53	51	49	54	53	48	53	55	45	47	51	49	60	Turkey	90
Argentina	79	64	63	66	55	66	72	65	61	72	62	66	65	62	65	65	Tanzania	87
Armenia	na	44	43	44	40	45	47	43	43	47	43	40	46	39	49	35	Morocco	86
Australia	na	73	71	75	53	77	87	71	74	74	72	74	76	77	75	69	Malta	85
Austria	69	58	56	59	39	58	67	63	52	53	56	58	57	69	62	48	Denmark	83
Azerbaijan	na	62	61	64	61	62	64	69	65	55	74	60	57	66	57	52	Jordan	80
Bangladesh	na	92	90	94	92	92	95	94	89	90	95	89	94	95	90	91	Zimbabwe	80
Belarus	58	35	33	37	24	38	42	38	33	38	38	35	30	35	37	27	Uruguay	79
Belgium	52	57	56	58	37	56	69	57	56	59	58	56	60	55	61	51	Croatia	78
Bosnia and Herz.	na	76	77	74	73	73	81	80	73	79	79	76	71	77	75	74	Pakistan	77
Brazil	72	55	55	55	48	55	67	54	55	66	52	47	62	49	55	64	Netherlands	77
Bulgaria	69	70	68	71	56	67	78	76	66	66	75	73	62	70	69	81	Bosnia and Herz.	76
Canada	70	71	69	73	56	69	81	78	68	71	70	69	72	77	72	68	India	75
Chile	51	47	45	50	46	46	51	48	48	44	48	45	51	58	44	41	Hungary	74
China	76	62	64	60	56	62	68	66	60	55	61	65	62	61	59	71	El Salvador	74
Colombia	na	72	70	74	67	74	77	75	67	75	74	70	72	76	73	73	Egypt	73
Croatia	na	78	72	82	72	78	81	81	76	75	79	77	80	84	76	80	Vietnam	73
Czech Republic	2	64	63	65	47	64	73	63	65	66	69	66	59	62	66	61	Australia	73
Denmark	81	83	82	85	71	85	88	84	81	84	79	85	86	78	85	85	Uganda	72
Dominican Rep.	na	70	71	69	68	71	100	78	75	68	69	69	71	71	70	69	Colombia	72
Egypt	na	73	72	75	72	74	74	73	72	77	76	69	75	75	73	65	Canada	71
El Salvador	na	74	75	73	68	79	75	76	72	70	75	75	73	na	na	na	Norway	71
Estonia	63	36	35	37	25	34	45	34	38	36	41	37	37	33	39	31	Puerto Rico	71
Finland	13	51	48	54	31	54	60	50	52	61	45	49	57	50	52	47	Dominican Rep.	70
France	40	41	40	41	26	36	52	42	38	39	43	39	41	47	41	30	Romania	70
Georgia	na	47	48	47	41	49	51	49	48	45	54	52	33	46	48	44	Bulgaria	70
Germany	74	63	60	65	49	60	71	66	57	77	65	58	58	68	61	62	New Zealand	69
Great Britain	70	67	65	69	45	66	79	69	63	67	69	63	70	na	na	na	Iceland	68
Greece	na	24	26	23	18	27	33	36	25	21	29	24	20	26	24	21	Iran	67
Hungary	67	74	70	77	64	69	85	74	75	73	76	77	71	77	70	74	Great Britain	67
Iceland	73	68	64	72	50	71	79	73	64	68	65	66	72	76	68	52	Ireland	67
India	77	75	77	73	77	74	76	72	76	81	66	73	81	78	75	72	Switzerland	67
Indonesia	na	42	39	45	28	45	46	53	44	31	47	36	41	44	39	19	Northern Ireland	66
Iran	na	67	65	70	64	69	74	72	71	56	65	70	64	77	64	58	Italy	65
Ireland	69	67	62	71	54	65	78	72	64	63	71	67	66	64	68	60	Argentina	64
Israel	na	na	na	na	na	na	na	na	na	na	na	na	na	na	na	na	Japan	64
Italy	68	65	65	65	46	67	73	67	63	67	67	65	63	60	66	66	Czech Republic	64
Japan	67	64	66	63	42	62	76	78	64	59	69	65	60	69	64	55	United States	64
Jordan	na	80	84	76	74	80	92	82	79	76	73	87	79	78	81	78	Germany	63
Korea, South	78	na	na	na	na	na	na	na	na	na	na	na	na	na	na	na	Latvia	62
Latvia	75	62	60	64	48	65	66	64	60	67	63	59	65	65	60	58	Nigeria	62
Lithuania	61	54	51	57	45	49	66	64	50	53	54	62	51	52	54	66	Azerbaijan	62
Luxembourg	na	46	44	48	31	47	55	46	44	51	43	46	52	41	47	52	China	62
Macedonia	na	47	49	45	41	45	55	48	45	52	47	44	52	51	46	43	Serbia	61
Malta	na	85	83	86	75	86	90	88	83	83	85	87	85	86	84	84	Portugal	59
Mexico	25	45	46	45	37	47	56	48	42	43	44	44	43	46	45	37	Albania	58
Moldova	na	28	26	30	23	32	27	24	27	33	35	28	25	27	30	19	Russian Fed.	58
Montenegro	na	42	43	41	33	39	52	45	40	41	44	43	45	45	39	42	Austria	58
Morocco	na	84	86	89	84	88	91	87	84	81	89	86	81	87	85	88	Belgium	57
Netherlands	71	77	76	78	62	75	87	79	80	72	71	79	81	76	80	70	Spain	56
New Zealand	na	69	67	72	48	67	81	76	75	60	68	69	71	71	70	64	Sweden	55
Nigeria	69	62	60	64	61	62	70	62	64	59	61	63	61	59	64	65	Brazil	55
Northern Ireland	77	66	63	70	62	60	75	66	66	67	68	66	65	73	67	53	Taiwan	55
Norway	80	71	68	74	43	75	86	76	68	71	na	na	na	70	72	64	Lithuania	54
Pakistan	na	77	79	76	72	76	90	78	75	79	78	79	78	74	81	80	Venezuela	54
Peru	na	44	42	46	39	46	48	38	44	48	40	40	56	34	47	46	Poland	53
Philippines	na	28	27	29	23	29	33	31	25	28	34	31	18	30	26	27	Finland	51
Poland	65	53	54	52	40	55	59	52	53	61	52	57	44	51	54	55	Algeria	51
Portugal	58	59	59	59	57	59	60	61	54	61	52	57	58	57	60	60	South Africa	50
Puerto Rico	na	71	69	73	51	70	81	76	67	72	72	71	70	74	72	71	Slovenia	49
Romania	71	70	70	70	62	67	77	72	67	74	72	71	71	72	67	76	Singapore	48
Russian Fed.	66	58	55	61	46	57	66	67	56	58	62	59	53	57	59	60	Ukraine	48
Serbia	na	61	59	62	42	61	68	62	59	61	61	66	61	64	55	68	Chile	47
Singapore	na	48	49	47	38	58	57	50	46	54	49	47	50	52	49	31	Georgia	47
Slovakia	na	37	34	40	31	37	43	38	37	37	37	39	37	37	38	28	Macedonia	47
Slovenia	51	49	47	52	29	53	60	49	48	55	48	53	52	50	51	44	Luxembourg	46
South Africa	77	50	48	51	51	46	59	42	60	62	39	53	59	56	49	27	Mexico	45
Spain	70	56	52	60	48	53	64	62	50	49	61	58	53	63	56	49	Peru	44
Sweden	75	55	53	58	38	57	64	64	48	60	55	55	55	65	56	49	Armenia	44
Switzerland	75	67	63	70	53	66	76	67	67	67	66	64	68	68	68	63	Montenegro	42
Taiwan	na	55	57	52	53	56	52	49	56	59	53	54	58	57	53	49	Indonesia	42
Tanzania	na	87	89	85	87	87	92	86	88	92	86	86	90	88	88	87	France	41
Turkey	84	90	89	91	88	92	90	90	89	94	88	92	90	88	92	92	Slovakia	37
Uganda	na	72	76	68	68	77	72	72	71	86	75	68	76	71	71	78	Estonia	36
Ukraine	na	48	43	52	32	46	59	58	46	47	57	45	40	50	46	50	Belarus	35
United States	69	64	60	67	48	66	74	58	66	65	61	65	67	56	63	68	Moldova	28
Uruguay	na	79	77	80	69	77	84	80	78	72	84	79	75	89	78	73	Philippines	28
Venezuela	na	54	53	54	53	57	47	50	54	58	45	52	63	48	56	54	Greece	24
Vietnam	na	73	76	70	72	72	76	76	72	58	70	76	72	79	70	63		
Zimbabwe	na	80	77	82	77	83	81	81	79	62	82	76	83	81	79	81		
Total	64	61	60	62	53	62	68	65	58	61	61	61	61	61	61	59	Total	61

F115) JUSTIFIABLE: AVOIDING A FARE ON PUBLIC TRANSPORT

Please tell me for each of the following statements whether you think it can always be justified, never be justified, or something in between: Avoiding a fare on public transport

Never justifiable (%)

(WVS: V205; EVS: o33)

Country	Wave 1990	Wave 2000	Gender Male	Gender Female	Age 16-29	Age 30-49	Age 50+	Education Lower	Education Middle	Education Upper	Income Lower	Income Middle	Income Upper	Values Mat	Values Mixed	Values Postm.	RANKING Country	RANKING 2000
Albania	na	47	46	49	38	46	58	44	47	55	43	45	54	46	49	51	Bangladesh	96
Algeria	na	64	63	65	61	65	70	62	62	68	66	65	62	60	65	72	Tanzania	90
Argentina	73	67	66	67	56	68	76	68	64	71	66	67	67	65	69	63	Vietnam	89
Armenia	na	37	34	40	34	39	39	37	35	44	36	34	38	35	40	26	Jordan	89
Australia	na	63	60	66	41	64	82	69	65	56	70	59	59	71	65	57	Pakistan	87
Austria	66	53	49	57	39	49	64	64	47	33	57	54	48	71	58	40	Indonesia	87
Azerbaijan	na	49	47	50	49	50	46	56	52	42	54	46	50	50	48	44	Iran	84
Bangladesh	na	96	95	98	96	97	97	98	95	96	98	94	99	98	95	97	China	83
Belarus	50	21	20	22	13	19	30	30	18	19	23	22	15	21	21	20	Zimbabwe	83
Belgium	59	61	56	64	43	58	71	66	61	56	66	64	59	65	58	60	Morocco	82
Bosnia and Herz.	na	73	73	72	66	71	82	81	71	71	76	74	66	75	72	70	Puerto Rico	80
Brazil	67	56	56	55	51	55	66	54	55	64	50	55	62	53	56	58	India	80
Bulgaria	65	na	na	na	na	na	na	na	na	na	na	na	na	na	na	na	Japan	77
Canada	63	63	60	67	45	60	78	75	61	58	67	65	57	63	66	58	Egypt	74
Chile	60	47	45	48	43	44	53	43	48	50	42	46	54	53	44	49	Bosnia and Herz.	73
China	80	83	83	84	77	85	84	84	82	88	83	83	86	82	83	78	Uruguay	72
Colombia	na	49	50	49	42	52	56	50	44	55	43	48	53	49	46	45	Dominican Rep.	71
Croatia	na	56	55	58	36	58	68	66	53	42	66	54	55	59	57	53	Denmark	71
Czech Republic	na	41	36	46	23	35	57	45	39	31	54	40	32	42	42	38	Norway	70
Denmark	75	71	68	74	47	68	86	78	61	62	75	71	63	65	74	65	Macedonia	69
Dominican Rep.	na	71	72	70	68	75	82	81	72	70	70	72	72	69	73	66	Argentina	67
Egypt	na	74	72	76	72	75	75	72	74	80	73	70	79	76	73	74	Uganda	66
El Salvador	na	na	na	na	na	na	na	na	na	na	na	na	na	na	na	na	Algeria	64
Estonia	61	na	na	na	na	na	na	na	na	na	na	na	na	na	na	na	New Zealand	64
Finland	54	50	43	57	25	43	71	58	41	42	53	50	47	53	50	47	Canada	63
France	55	54	53	54	32	50	68	60	46	44	54	54	54	63	56	35	Australia	63
Georgia	na	47	46	48	39	49	53	49	47	47	53	48	38	46	48	47	Belgium	61
Germany	73	54	54	54	39	50	64	57	49	59	57	51	48	57	53	50	Italy	61
Great Britain	60	48	42	53	30	43	59	48	46	42	54	47	46	na	na	na	Taiwan	60
Greece	na	36	37	36	23	43	56	58	40	29	43	33	29	37	38	31	Switzerland	59
Hungary	59	na	na	na	na	na	na	na	na	na	na	na	na	na	na	na	Serbia	59
Iceland	56	na	na	na	na	na	na	na	na	na	na	na	na	na	na	na	Spain	57
India	84	80	80	79	79	81	79	75	82	88	70	77	87	82	82	80	Croatia	56
Indonesia	na	87	84	90	83	87	89	92	86	84	87	85	89	91	84	68	Venezuela	56
Iran	na	84	83	84	80	89	86	84	83	83	82	84	84	90	79	85	Brazil	56
Ireland	58	na	na	na	na	na	na	na	na	na	na	na	na	na	na	na	Nigeria	56
Israel	na	na	na	na	na	na	na	na	na	na	na	na	na	na	na	na	Singapore	55
Italy	67	61	59	62	35	60	75	70	54	51	69	56	55	65	63	55	South Africa	54
Japan	79	77	77	78	59	75	87	86	79	69	80	79	76	80	77	73	Peru	54
Jordan	na	89	91	86	87	88	92	89	90	87	89	91	88	88	89	85	Germany	54
Korea, South	69	41	44	38	25	43	56	64	44	34	44	43	37	42	41	38	France	54
Latvia	61	na	na	na	na	na	na	na	na	na	na	na	na	na	na	na	Austria	53
Lithuania	56	38	37	39	24	37	49	45	36	33	47	38	34	35	39	43	Luxembourg	51
Luxembourg	na	51	49	53	31	52	63	55	50	46	45	61	52	54	52	43	Finland	50
Macedonia	na	69	67	71	62	68	76	73	68	66	74	66	68	72	68	59	United States	50
Malta	na	na	na	na	na	na	na	na	na	na	na	na	na	na	na	na	Colombia	49
Mexico	32	49	52	46	40	52	55	52	46	44	47	48	47	52	47	44	Mexico	49
Moldova	na	22	23	20	16	28	20	18	21	25	29	20	19	20	22	22	Azerbaijan	49
Montenegro	na	42	43	42	32	39	53	45	40	40	47	38	48	43	41	48	Great Britain	48
Morocco	na	82	79	86	77	84	90	84	76	75	87	80	78	81	82	83	Albania	47
Netherlands	56	44	40	48	26	36	62	57	45	32	43	47	39	60	44	36	Georgia	47
New Zealand	na	64	61	67	37	58	80	74	66	52	70	63	59	68	64	60	Chile	47
Nigeria	61	56	54	58	54	57	63	56	56	53	55	57	53	53	57	62	Netherlands	44
Northern Ireland	72	na	na	na	na	na	na	na	na	na	na	na	na	na	na	na	Montenegro	42
Norway	76	70	68	72	44	73	86	77	70	64	na	na	na	70	71	64	Czech Republic	41
Pakistan	na	87	89	85	83	85	99	86	87	89	86	87	89	85	89	83	Korea, South	41
Peru	na	54	51	57	49	56	60	52	54	56	49	55	61	44	57	58	Lithuania	38
Philippines	na	35	33	36	30	38	34	33	33	39	38	37	28	37	33	37	Armenia	37
Poland	na	na	na	na	na	na	na	na	na	na	na	na	na	na	na	na	Greece	36
Portugal	57	na	na	na	na	na	na	na	na	na	na	na	na	na	na	na	Philippines	35
Puerto Rico	na	80	79	81	66	78	89	93	78	79	87	75	79	81	82	77	Ukraine	34
Romania	64	na	na	na	na	na	na	na	na	na	na	na	na	na	na	na	Russian Fed.	33
Russian Fed.	54	33	31	34	22	29	43	47	32	26	39	32	27	33	32	37	Moldova	22
Serbia	na	59	58	60	38	57	72	60	61	56	61	66	57	61	57	60	Belarus	21
Singapore	na	55	57	52	45	64	63	54	55	59	56	53	58	57	56	37		
Slovakia	na	na	na	na	na	na	na	na	na	na	na	na	na	na	na	na		
Slovenia	63	na	na	na	na	na	na	na	na	na	na	na	na	na	na	na		
South Africa	na	54	53	56	54	53	60	48	63	63	46	55	63	58	56	31		
Spain	68	57	53	61	46	54	68	62	51	52	67	53	56	64	56	49		
Sweden	68	na	na	na	na	na	na	na	na	na	na	na	na	na	na	na		
Switzerland	79	59	56	62	37	57	76	65	58	59	63	59	59	63	61	52		
Taiwan	na	60	59	61	58	62	57	59	60	61	58	65	60	64	60	49		
Tanzania	na	90	91	88	89	89	93	88	91	92	89	88	91	91	90	92		
Turkey	76	na	na	na	na	na	na	na	na	na	na	na	na	na	na	na		
Uganda	na	66	75	58	63	70	64	67	64	82	76	60	75	60	68	76		
Ukraine	na	34	33	34	17	33	43	43	30	37	40	30	30	34	35	37		
United States	62	50	49	51	32	51	63	43	53	51	49	52	50	48	51	49		
Uruguay	na	72	71	72	60	69	78	73	71	63	72	75	70	79	71	65		
Venezuela	na	56	58	54	55	58	55	53	56	59	44	54	60	50	59	57		
Vietnam	na	89	90	87	88	87	91	89	88	85	90	93	83	91	87	87		
Zimbabwe	na	83	82	85	78	89	86	85	81	83	86	81	83	86	82	83		
Total	63	60	59	60	52	60	68	65	56	57	61	60	58	60	61	55	Total	60

F116) JUSTIFIABLE: CHEATING ON TAXES

Please tell me for each of the following statements whether you think it can always be justified, never be justified, or something in between: Cheating on taxes if you have a chance

Never justifiable (%)

(WVS: V206; EVS: V226)

Country	Wave 1990	Wave 2000	Gender Male	Gender Female	Age 16-29	Age 30-49	Age 50+	Education Lower	Education Middle	Education Upper	Income Lower	Income Middle	Income Upper	Values Mat	Values Mixed	Values Postm.
Albania	na	59	56	61	54	57	65	55	59	67	60	55	60	58	61	51
Algeria	na	76	73	80	72	79	81	75	77	76	79	79	73	76	77	75
Argentina	81	77	73	81	71	77	83	78	75	79	77	77	78	74	79	75
Armenia	na	41	38	44	37	42	46	42	40	44	42	35	46	41	42	32
Australia	na	62	57	67	47	62	76	68	63	58	69	60	55	67	63	59
Austria	63	58	54	62	47	58	64	65	55	42	59	55	55	65	61	53
Azerbaijan	na	48	44	51	49	47	49	40	50	45	53	46	51	50	46	41
Bangladesh	na	99	98	99	98	99	98	99	98	97	100	98	99	99	98	97
Belarus	47	26	22	30	17	26	35	33	23	27	30	26	22	27	28	14
Belgium	38	38	33	43	28	34	46	45	38	32	49	40	30	37	38	33
Bosnia and Herz.	na	77	75	79	72	76	83	86	75	75	84	78	68	78	77	74
Brazil	65	47	47	47	40	47	61	47	47	49	45	47	48	44	47	54
Bulgaria	60	67	63	71	52	59	81	75	65	58	76	68	58	65	70	67
Canada	61	67	61	73	58	66	74	76	66	62	73	67	60	66	69	63
Chile	78	70	70	70	68	71	70	67	73	68	66	71	74	72	67	78
China	82	77	78	77	71	78	80	81	75	70	78	79	72	76	76	78
Colombia	na	72	70	74	68	74	77	78	67	71	78	68	70	78	75	76
Croatia	na	61	57	65	48	63	68	69	58	50	73	57	61	65	62	56
Czech Republic	na	59	55	63	49	53	70	61	58	53	69	61	48	60	60	56
Denmark	59	66	57	74	64	61	72	69	59	63	69	64	63	70	66	71
Dominican Rep.	na	70	70	71	69	72	80	86	64	71	74	68	64	66	73	65
Egypt	na	80	76	84	78	80	82	79	81	80	80	77	82	81	79	74
El Salvador	na	81	81	81	78	83	83	82	80	81	81	79	85	na	na	na
Estonia	66	40	38	42	24	32	56	41	39	41	49	43	37	40	41	20
Finland	42	53	45	60	38	49	64	57	47	54	56	50	51	53	53	52
France	48	48	46	51	33	47	57	53	36	46	54	49	47	55	49	37
Georgia	na	53	53	52	46	54	58	57	52	53	56	56	45	52	53	53
Germany	68	57	53	60	46	55	64	58	53	70	60	51	53	64	53	57
Great Britain	55	56	51	61	33	56	67	58	51	56	58	55	58	na	na	na
Greece	na	37	38	37	32	39	46	49	40	33	43	36	30	39	36	40
Hungary	62	66	63	67	52	57	82	71	60	47	69	70	60	71	62	50
Iceland	59	58	52	63	48	55	70	66	54	51	62	59	52	64	57	50
India	82	80	80	81	80	81	79	75	85	87	71	78	86	83	82	80
Indonesia	na	79	76	83	79	78	82	85	77	78	79	77	82	82	78	68
Iran	na	89	89	90	87	91	92	91	89	87	87	91	89	92	87	89
Ireland	50	58	53	62	48	56	68	67	50	58	66	53	53	56	58	57
Israel	na	na	na	na	na	na	na	na	na	na	na	na	na	na	na	na
Italy	57	57	55	58	44	56	64	57	56	55	59	58	52	53	58	57
Japan	82	84	80	87	74	83	89	90	85	79	86	85	81	86	84	82
Jordan	na	84	85	82	79	84	93	89	83	76	84	85	83	85	83	84
Korea, South	91	75	72	77	71	75	79	82	77	71	77	75	72	76	74	71
Latvia	68	60	56	63	39	59	69	66	57	59	62	63	54	63	59	47
Lithuania	58	39	37	41	27	33	53	48	36	37	42	48	38	39	39	47
Luxembourg	na	41	38	44	30	44	44	49	37	37	43	43	45	42	42	38
Macedonia	na	68	67	69	57	67	79	70	67	69	74	65	67	72	68	44
Malta	na	80	75	84	71	80	86	87	77	77	85	80	76	81	80	80
Mexico	41	69	67	71	62	71	78	73	65	67	68	68	71	75	66	66
Moldova	na	26	27	25	21	30	26	22	25	31	37	25	20	22	30	21
Montenegro	na	46	43	48	37	40	57	50	41	47	50	46	46	48	43	50
Morocco	na	96	94	98	94	96	99	96	95	92	96	95	95	97	95	96
Netherlands	44	46	42	51	34	41	59	52	48	39	49	49	39	54	46	45
New Zealand	na	59	52	66	41	57	69	65	60	53	61	59	57	57	60	55
Nigeria	64	58	57	59	59	56	67	56	59	60	59	56	57	57	58	64
Northern Ireland	71	59	52	65	54	53	67	61	57	59	61	56	55	69	58	47
Norway	45	48	38	57	43	40	60	54	43	47	na	na	na	50	47	44
Pakistan	na	91	91	91	91	89	97	91	92	88	92	91	91	90	92	83
Peru	na	64	61	67	63	64	68	62	64	65	62	62	71	53	68	65
Philippines	na	41	38	44	37	44	41	39	40	45	45	42	35	42	39	49
Poland	51	60	61	59	46	61	67	62	56	58	62	60	53	58	62	52
Portugal	45	55	55	55	56	50	59	57	48	61	59	48	57	52	58	53
Puerto Rico	na	77	76	78	65	75	85	85	77	76	83	76	74	80	79	71
Romania	69	57	56	59	44	54	67	61	53	61	61	55	59	57	56	58
Russian Fed.	56	46	42	49	29	43	60	60	45	40	52	46	40	49	41	50
Serbia	na	64	63	65	51	60	73	61	64	69	67	68	64	64	62	80
Singapore	na	68	66	69	60	74	73	71	67	63	69	68	65	67	70	46
Slovakia	na	59	55	64	54	58	65	60	60	56	60	61	60	60	60	53
Slovenia	70	60	56	63	48	61	67	61	61	53	61	63	55	69	60	53
South Africa	68	55	52	59	56	50	68	49	62	73	51	55	57	54	58	42
Spain	65	57	53	60	48	53	65	63	49	52	66	56	56	64	56	51
Sweden	58	51	47	55	45	47	57	60	45	53	54	48	50	52	51	51
Switzerland	66	54	48	59	40	48	69	59	53	48	57	55	49	52	58	43
Taiwan	na	64	67	62	62	64	67	65	63	65	63	64	66	67	63	60
Tanzania	na	85	86	84	86	83	89	86	84	85	85	84	84	88	86	75
Turkey	90	92	91	93	91	94	92	91	93	95	91	93	93	91	93	92
Uganda	na	58	62	55	54	64	56	61	55	77	65	58	68	53	59	71
Ukraine	na	41	38	43	26	36	54	51	40	38	47	38	36	43	39	45
United States	69	62	55	69	53	61	71	64	62	61	63	63	59	60	63	60
Uruguay	na	80	79	81	77	77	84	82	78	75	82	80	79	84	79	77
Venezuela	na	70	70	70	70	71	69	69	70	72	60	69	79	60	73	75
Vietnam	na	88	90	86	90	85	91	88	89	83	89	91	83	87	87	86
Zimbabwe	na	84	79	87	82	86	82	85	82	83	84	84	81	85	81	91
Total	61	63	60	65	58	62	69	68	60	61	66	63	61	63	63	59

RANKING

Country	2000
Bangladesh	99
Morocco	96
Turkey	92
Pakistan	91
Iran	89
Vietnam	88
Tanzania	85
Jordan	84
Japan	84
Zimbabwe	84
El Salvador	81
India	80
Uruguay	80
Malta	80
Egypt	80
Indonesia	79
Argentina	77
China	77
Bosnia and Herz.	77
Puerto Rico	77
Algeria	76
Korea, South	75
Colombia	72
Dominican Rep.	70
Venezuela	70
Chile	70
Mexico	69
Macedonia	68
Singapore	68
Canada	67
Bulgaria	67
Denmark	66
Hungary	66
Taiwan	64
Peru	64
Serbia	64
Australia	62
United States	62
Croatia	61
Slovenia	60
Latvia	60
Poland	60
Slovakia	59
New Zealand	59
Czech Republic	59
Northern Ireland	59
Albania	59
Austria	58
Nigeria	58
Uganda	58
Iceland	58
Ireland	58
Germany	57
Romania	57
Spain	57
Italy	57
Great Britain	56
South Africa	55
Portugal	55
Switzerland	54
Finland	53
Georgia	53
Sweden	51
France	48
Azerbaijan	48
Norway	48
Brazil	47
Netherlands	46
Russian Fed.	46
Montenegro	46
Armenia	41
Philippines	41
Luxembourg	41
Ukraine	41
Estonia	40
Lithuania	39
Belgium	38
Greece	37
Belarus	26
Moldova	26
Total	63

F117) JUSTIFIABLE: SOMEONE ACCEPTING A BRIBE

Please tell me for each of the following statements whether you think it can always be justified, never be justified, or something in between: Someone accepting a bribe in the course of his / her duties

Never justifiable (%)

(WVS: V207; EVS: V231)

Country	Wave 1990	Wave 2000	Gender Male	Gender Female	Age 16-29	Age 30-49	Age 50+	Education Lower	Education Middle	Education Upper	Income Lower	Income Middle	Income Upper	Values Mat	Values Mixed	Values Postm.
Albania	na	53	51	55	50	51	60	50	53	61	52	52	56	54	52	59
Algeria	na	89	88	89	87	90	89	84	90	90	91	90	84	88	89	89
Argentina	95	92	90	94	87	93	96	92	92	95	93	91	94	89	91	95
Armenia	na	63	60	66	56	64	72	69	63	62	59	65	66	63	66	43
Australia	na	86	83	88	72	88	95	88	85	85	89	83	84	87	88	82
Austria	72	72	69	76	66	72	77	77	70	63	72	75	70	83	72	71
Azerbaijan	na	53	55	52	55	50	61	60	53	54	57	59	52	50	58	61
Bangladesh	na	99	98	100	98	100	99	99	99	98	100	98	100	99	99	99
Belarus	75	39	35	43	24	40	52	49	36	36	50	37	26	43	39	18
Belgium	61	68	65	70	52	68	75	69	67	68	74	69	66	65	67	72
Bosnia and Herz.	na	86	85	86	80	87	89	90	83	89	89	84	83	84	86	89
Brazil	88	46	43	49	39	48	56	41	48	60	39	47	54	47	44	52
Bulgaria	81	78	77	78	64	76	86	86	73	74	86	75	71	80	77	93
Canada	77	80	77	84	66	81	88	83	80	79	79	81	81	79	81	78
Chile	85	71	71	71	71	70	72	67	73	72	66	73	75	76	67	75
China	87	83	84	83	79	85	83	85	83	74	83	86	80	83	83	90
Colombia	na	81	81	82	76	84	85	83	77	85	81	80	82	84	79	79
Croatia	na	79	76	82	66	81	86	84	76	76	87	77	80	83	79	75
Czech Republic	57	51	47	56	37	47	63	50	53	52	60	52	43	48	52	52
Denmark	91	93	90	96	86	94	95	94	92	92	92	94	92	91	93	94
Dominican Rep.	na	76	78	74	72	81	91	87	73	76	82	73	71	71	76	80
Egypt	na	94	93	95	93	94	96	95	93	93	94	93	95	95	93	96
El Salvador	na	89	88	90	86	90	93	89	88	91	90	88	92	na	na	na
Estonia	70	67	62	71	57	63	77	67	67	67	71	68	66	67	68	52
Finland	74	80	76	83	71	82	83	81	76	82	81	78	80	81	79	82
France	64	67	63	71	53	68	73	69	62	68	69	70	64	70	67	65
Georgia	na	73	71	74	63	76	78	77	73	70	77	75	63	73	72	77
Germany	64	67	62	70	61	64	72	70	62	73	66	64	67	68	66	67
Great Britain	75	67	65	69	50	67	77	67	67	65	66	68	73	na	na	na
Greece	na	64	61	67	59	66	78	81	66	60	70	62	58	60	65	70
Hungary	70	53	47	59	45	44	67	55	49	56	52	55	54	54	53	54
Iceland	84	87	82	92	75	89	95	90	84	88	86	87	88	90	86	85
India	86	85	85	85	85	85	84	81	89	91	75	85	90	89	84	84
Indonesia	na	82	79	86	81	81	85	87	81	81	84	81	78	84	82	71
Iran	na	93	93	94	92	95	96	95	93	91	93	96	92	96	93	90
Ireland	85	83	79	87	77	83	88	86	79	88	83	84	80	79	85	81
Israel	na	86	83	88	79	88	92	91	83	86	84	80	89	83	86	88
Italy	77	79	76	82	67	82	83	81	76	83	84	78	77	77	79	82
Japan	71	83	80	86	73	83	87	85	84	81	86	84	79	85	83	83
Jordan	na	96	98	95	96	96	98	97	96	96	97	96	97	98	96	95
Korea, South	85	80	77	83	79	79	85	91	81	77	84	78	78	81	80	81
Latvia	76	74	72	77	62	74	79	81	73	72	79	76	69	76	73	68
Lithuania	60	67	60	73	53	61	81	80	62	62	78	69	60	64	68	64
Luxembourg	na	71	69	73	57	75	76	67	72	77	62	75	83	71	71	70
Macedonia	na	87	86	87	84	83	92	85	87	90	86	86	89	88	87	74
Malta	na	94	93	96	91	96	95	96	94	94	95	95	92	95	95	91
Mexico	55	73	73	72	65	76	80	75	69	75	68	74	71	74	71	71
Moldova	na	49	46	52	39	54	53	55	47	48	67	54	34	51	50	33
Montenegro	na	84	81	88	79	82	91	89	78	88	90	87	82	86	84	82
Morocco	na	98	97	99	97	98	100	98	97	96	98	97	97	98	97	97
Netherlands	68	73	69	76	57	73	80	77	73	68	73	71	76	70	73	73
New Zealand	na	81	80	84	56	83	90	85	84	78	82	81	83	79	82	83
Nigeria	66	64	63	64	63	62	69	59	66	65	63	64	62	64	63	65
Northern Ireland	85	78	75	80	72	74	86	81	77	73	85	78	73	90	76	71
Norway	80	85	83	86	73	86	91	87	83	85	na	na	na	82	85	86
Pakistan	na	92	91	93	91	90	97	90	94	93	90	93	93	91	93	91
Peru	na	73	71	75	70	75	74	72	73	73	74	68	77	63	76	74
Philippines	na	40	39	41	36	41	41	36	40	44	39	44	34	40	39	42
Poland	83	77	75	79	65	77	84	79	74	73	78	77	69	77	77	73
Portugal	74	74	71	77	74	69	78	74	71	76	72	69	74	75	72	75
Puerto Rico	na	89	89	90	83	92	91	90	84	93	92	87	90	92	90	90
Romania	68	80	79	82	71	80	86	83	79	80	83	80	80	81	78	81
Russian Fed.	85	70	66	74	52	69	83	84	70	64	76	70	66	71	69	74
Serbia	na	86	84	89	78	86	91	86	85	89	89	87	88	88	84	87
Singapore	na	77	77	76	75	80	73	74	78	77	75	79	76	77	78	66
Slovakia	na	39	36	43	29	41	46	43	38	34	41	40	39	39	41	34
Slovenia	81	74	69	77	59	76	81	76	73	71	77	76	71	80	72	75
South Africa	80	61	58	65	65	56	66	55	69	76	54	63	67	62	63	47
Spain	83	72	69	75	67	70	77	76	68	68	78	70	73	74	72	69
Sweden	74	69	65	72	65	67	72	75	66	68	70	69	67	69	68	68
Switzerland	84	79	72	86	66	80	85	80	80	69	82	78	76	80	79	79
Taiwan	na	75	75	74	73	74	77	72	77	76	73	74	77	77	74	70
Tanzania	na	92	93	91	93	90	96	90	94	95	91	91	94	94	93	88
Turkey	92	94	93	95	92	96	95	93	94	98	92	95	95	94	95	95
Uganda	na	73	78	68	70	75	76	75	71	86	79	77	79	68	73	85
Ukraine	na	64	61	67	44	64	76	76	63	62	76	57	57	68	62	72
United States	80	80	77	83	68	81	89	77	80	82	79	79	82	75	81	82
Uruguay	na	91	90	92	90	91	91	90	93	90	93	88	91	88	91	90
Venezuela	na	75	75	75	73	76	78	74	74	78	64	74	83	72	77	76
Vietnam	na	94	93	94	93	93	95	94	94	85	96	96	90	94	93	93
Zimbabwe	na	92	92	92	89	94	96	94	89	100	91	92	92	93	91	92
Total	76	76	74	78	70	76	81	79	74	76	77	76	75	75	76	77

RANKING

Country	2000
Bangladesh	99
Morocco	98
Jordan	96
Malta	94
Egypt	94
Vietnam	94
Turkey	94
Iran	93
Denmark	93
Tanzania	92
Argentina	92
Pakistan	92
Zimbabwe	92
Uruguay	91
Puerto Rico	89
El Salvador	89
Algeria	89
Iceland	87
Macedonia	87
Serbia	86
Israel	86
Australia	86
Bosnia and Herz.	86
India	85
Norway	85
Montenegro	84
China	83
Ireland	83
Japan	83
Indonesia	82
New Zealand	81
Colombia	81
Canada	80
Korea, South	80
Romania	80
United States	80
Finland	80
Italy	79
Croatia	79
Switzerland	79
Northern Ireland	78
Bulgaria	78
Poland	77
Singapore	77
Dominican Rep.	76
Venezuela	75
Taiwan	75
Latvia	74
Portugal	74
Slovenia	74
Peru	73
Georgia	73
Netherlands	73
Uganda	73
Mexico	73
Austria	72
Spain	72
Chile	71
Luxembourg	71
Russian Fed.	70
Sweden	69
Belgium	68
Great Britain	67
France	67
Estonia	67
Lithuania	67
Germany	67
Greece	64
Ukraine	64
Nigeria	63
Armenia	63
South Africa	61
Azerbaijan	53
Hungary	53
Albania	53
Czech Republic	51
Moldova	49
Brazil	46
Philippines	40
Slovakia	39
Belarus	39
Total	76

F118) JUSTIFIABLE: HOMOSEXUALITY

Please tell me for each of the following statements whether you think it can always be justified, never be justified, or something in between: Homosexuality

Never justifiable (%)

(WVS: V208; EVS: V232)

Country	Wave 1990	Wave 2000	Gender Male	Female	Age 16-29	30-49	50+	Education Lower	Middle	Upper	Income Lower	Middle	Upper	Values Mat	Mixed	Postm.	RANKING Country	2000
Albania	na	81	81	81	70	83	88	82	82	74	84	79	80	83	80	74	Egypt	100
Algeria	na	93	93	94	92	93	96	95	93	92	94	94	91	95	92	95	Bangladesh	99
Argentina	63	40	45	35	32	37	52	50	28	23	49	41	30	53	42	27	Jordan	98
Armenia	na	71	75	68	60	75	83	87	71	67	68	73	75	74	70	58	Pakistan	96
Australia	na	31	38	25	23	25	46	49	30	17	40	33	16	51	32	24	Zimbabwe	96
Austria	52	26	30	23	13	22	37	37	19	5	36	27	21	54	26	19	Indonesia	95
Azerbaijan	na	89	90	88	86	90	93	94	90	85	93	91	80	91	85	95	Tanzania	94
Bangladesh	na	99	99	99	98	100	99	100	98	98	100	98	100	99	99	99	Iran	94
Belarus	84	57	57	58	39	59	72	73	53	50	62	58	48	66	51	40	Algeria	93
Belgium	46	27	31	23	19	20	36	41	26	16	37	30	16	34	26	17	China	92
Bosnia and Herz.	na	72	76	69	63	72	82	85	72	63	80	75	64	74	72	60	Uganda	91
Brazil	73	56	62	50	54	55	61	63	52	46	61	56	51	67	52	45	Azerbaijan	89
Bulgaria	81	60	64	56	49	55	70	75	57	42	74	61	45	67	53	61	Hungary	88
Canada	40	27	29	24	21	22	35	42	26	15	32	28	17	31	29	18	Montenegro	86
Chile	78	37	41	34	33	34	46	45	36	24	43	38	25	44	38	22	Turkey	85
China	93	92	93	91	87	93	96	93	93	86	88	95	94	92	92	88	Georgia	82
Colombia	na	61	62	60	54	63	72	72	59	48	69	62	51	67	60	51	Vietnam	82
Croatia	na	70	71	69	54	69	81	78	68	53	78	68	67	77	71	61	El Salvador	81
Czech Republic	39	27	31	23	18	21	37	33	21	15	32	28	19	36	25	19	Albania	81
Denmark	44	21	27	15	6	12	39	31	9	6	29	17	12	41	22	6	Romania	80
Dominican Rep.	na	53	57	50	49	58	70	77	63	46	62	50	38	53	52	49	Lithuania	78
Egypt	na	100	100	100	100	100	100	100	100	100	100	100	100	100	100	100	Nigeria	78
El Salvador	na	81	83	79	75	83	88	86	79	69	87	80	76	na	na	na	Latvia	77
Estonia	78	57	60	54	42	51	71	61	56	53	62	64	51	59	55	49	Macedonia	76
Finland	36	29	38	20	17	21	44	38	19	15	32	31	22	33	28	25	Serbia	75
France	42	23	28	18	12	17	35	30	15	12	29	23	20	33	22	11	Bosnia and Herz.	72
Georgia	na	82	84	80	79	81	87	87	83	76	88	84	71	80	83	80	Armenia	71
Germany	50	19	21	17	10	12	29	27	11	16	25	17	12	27	17	10	Ukraine	71
Great Britain	42	25	30	19	12	20	33	28	20	21	24	28	17	na	na	na	India	71
Greece	na	24	29	20	13	24	51	60	27	15	33	24	19	30	24	18	Russian Fed.	71
Hungary	85	88	89	88	86	87	91	91	86	76	89	87	87	89	88	78	Croatia	70
Iceland	30	12	17	7	3	11	23	15	13	3	16	12	9	15	11	7	Taiwan	65
India	94	71	71	70	66	74	70	67	75	74	70	67	73	76	72	83	Moldova	65
Indonesia	na	95	94	96	91	95	97	97	95	93	97	94	94	97	94	89	Venezuela	62
Iran	na	94	94	94	92	96	96	95	95	92	95	95	92	97	93	92	Colombia	61
Ireland	52	37	39	35	20	26	62	64	26	15	60	34	21	46	38	19	Malta	61
Israel	na	38	39	37	32	36	46	61	37	23	51	39	19	51	34	35	Poland	60
Italy	49	30	35	26	17	22	44	45	19	16	43	26	19	49	30	18	Bulgaria	60
Japan	61	30	33	27	12	18	49	50	30	21	36	26	30	35	27	22	Belarus	57
Jordan	na	98	99	98	98	98	99	99	99	96	98	100	97	99	97	96	Estonia	57
Korea, South	91	53	56	50	29	58	69	79	59	41	56	53	49	56	52	34	Peru	57
Latvia	84	77	81	74	64	73	86	85	75	70	83	76	70	82	75	64	Brazil	56
Lithuania	89	78	79	77	61	76	92	92	73	72	89	77	73	81	78	76	Singapore	55
Luxembourg	na	20	23	18	12	18	29	32	15	14	22	26	15	26	21	12	Mexico	53
Macedonia	na	76	80	71	66	78	80	89	72	62	87	73	65	72	76	78	Dominican Rep.	53
Malta	na	61	61	61	44	57	76	77	57	39	74	59	51	69	59	37	Korea, South	53
Mexico	58	53	57	49	40	56	66	65	43	29	59	52	44	64	51	33	Puerto Rico	50
Moldova	na	65	66	63	51	68	73	74	65	57	81	66	49	66	65	43	South Africa	48
Montenegro	na	86	88	83	81	82	93	93	85	71	93	86	83	92	81	73	Uruguay	46
Morocco	na	na	na	na	na	na	na	na	na	na	na	na	na	na	na	na	Portugal	43
Netherlands	20	7	9	5	6	5	9	14	5	3	11	5	3	12	7	5	Northern Ireland	42
New Zealand	na	30	39	22	18	21	42	40	32	17	38	28	21	41	30	18	Slovenia	42
Nigeria	73	78	78	77	78	78	74	75	79	80	79	76	76	76	79	78	Argentina	40
Northern Ireland	65	42	46	39	31	33	55	52	38	26	49	41	26	56	43	26	Israel	38
Norway	53	27	36	19	18	22	41	39	26	18	na	na	na	36	28	9	Chile	37
Pakistan	na	96	96	97	94	97	99	98	94	95	99	96	94	97	96	92	Ireland	37
Peru	na	57	55	58	53	60	59	62	59	50	65	51	49	57	56	59	United States	32
Philippines	na	29	28	30	28	29	32	26	30	32	31	31	24	29	30	24	Australia	31
Poland	81	60	65	55	38	59	74	72	50	34	67	55	54	64	57	64	Italy	30
Portugal	67	43	43	44	30	41	55	50	35	22	54	42	37	49	42	32	Japan	30
Puerto Rico	na	50	55	48	36	46	61	67	56	45	60	52	43	61	51	45	New Zealand	30
Romania	87	80	81	78	70	75	91	92	75	71	88	83	73	86	77	57	Philippines	29
Russian Fed.	89	71	73	69	56	69	83	80	71	64	77	72	63	73	68	70	Finland	29
Serbia	na	75	77	73	60	70	87	86	77	55	84	74	68	81	71	56	Norway	27
Singapore	na	55	58	52	48	62	61	58	56	41	59	59	50	58	54	48	Czech Republic	27
Slovakia	na	24	23	25	18	21	33	33	22	9	32	26	18	27	21	14	Canada	27
Slovenia	66	42	47	37	26	42	53	59	40	18	54	43	25	59	39	33	Belgium	27
South Africa	78	48	51	43	51	45	46	48	46	60	47	48	47	52	47	30	Austria	26
Spain	46	17	18	16	7	10	28	24	10	9	25	12	13	25	16	5	Great Britain	25
Sweden	45	9	12	5	5	5	15	21	5	4	10	12	4	17	10	3	Greece	24
Switzerland	49	17	20	15	11	14	25	25	16	13	23	19	11	21	19	8	Slovakia	24
Taiwan	na	65	66	65	52	66	74	70	72	58	68	67	63	66	65	65	France	23
Tanzania	na	94	95	94	96	93	96	93	97	95	93	96	93	96	95	96	Denmark	21
Turkey	85	85	84	86	79	89	91	91	80	59	90	88	69	87	86	80	Luxembourg	20
Uganda	na	91	92	90	90	92	94	93	90	93	92	94	90	91	92	86	Germany	19
Ukraine	na	71	74	68	53	71	82	81	72	65	78	67	65	73	68	69	Switzerland	17
United States	57	32	34	30	28	35	31	45	33	26	36	29	29	38	33	27	Spain	17
Uruguay	na	46	49	44	35	38	57	55	33	32	49	47	41	56	46	33	Iceland	12
Venezuela	na	62	63	60	59	62	66	69	64	47	64	60	62	66	62	52	Sweden	9
Vietnam	na	82	83	81	83	78	87	82	83	76	80	86	79	90	79	83	Netherlands	7
Zimbabwe	na	96	95	97	95	97	97	98	94	92	98	95	92	98	95	99		
Total	63	56	59	53	52	55	61	63	55	46	63	57	50	68	53	36	Total	56

F119) JUSTIFIABLE: PROSTITUTION

Please tell me for each of the following statements whether you think it can always be justified, never be justified, or something in between: Prostitution

Never justifiable (%)

(WVS: V209; EVS: o35)

Country	Wave 1990	Wave 2000	Gender Male	Gender Female	Age 16-29	Age 30-49	Age 50+	Education Lower	Education Middle	Education Upper	Income Lower	Income Middle	Income Upper	Values Mat	Values Mixed	Values Postm.	RANKING Country	2000
Albania	na	80	78	82	69	81	88	85	77	75	83	80	77	83	79	71	Jordan	98
Algeria	na	93	93	93	91	94	96	92	94	93	94	94	92	95	93	93	Pakistan	96
Argentina	75	51	46	57	45	48	62	60	41	32	60	54	40	61	52	41	Iran	95
Armenia	na	65	62	68	58	64	78	78	67	53	59	67	74	72	62	41	Bangladesh	95
Australia	na	29	26	32	26	22	41	43	29	18	36	29	17	43	31	23	Zimbabwe	94
Austria	49	36	35	36	28	32	44	47	29	15	44	35	33	56	37	28	Indonesia	94
Azerbaijan	na	85	85	84	80	86	91	90	87	79	90	88	75	87	80	83	Algeria	93
Bangladesh	na	95	94	96	93	96	99	98	94	88	98	92	97	97	95	87	Tanzania	93
Belarus	73	49	38	57	28	48	66	64	44	39	56	48	35	54	46	25	China	93
Belgium	48	na	na	na	na	na	na	na	na	na	na	na	na	na	na	na	Egypt	93
Bosnia and Herz.	na	76	71	80	70	72	85	86	74	73	82	78	66	74	77	70	Vietnam	92
Brazil	75	68	69	67	69	66	70	74	65	59	73	68	63	77	65	63	El Salvador	85
Bulgaria	72	na	na	na	na	na	na	na	na	na	na	na	na	na	na	na	Azerbaijan	85
Canada	44	44	38	49	40	39	52	60	42	33	50	44	34	45	48	34	Croatia	82
Chile	78	48	47	50	47	46	54	56	47	37	53	51	36	58	47	34	Macedonia	81
China	92	93	92	93	89	94	92	91	94	93	89	94	96	93	91	97	Montenegro	81
Colombia	na	64	63	66	61	65	71	76	65	56	73	66	57	64	58	57	Albania	80
Croatia	na	82	75	88	70	82	90	90	78	73	86	80	84	87	84	72	Uganda	78
Czech Republic	43	45	34	55	33	34	60	50	42	29	55	46	33	48	44	41	Nigeria	77
Denmark	45	na	na	na	na	na	na	na	na	na	na	na	na	na	na	na	Bosnia and Herz.	76
Dominican Rep.	na	55	58	52	52	58	73	68	66	49	53	58	45	55	55	48	Serbia	75
Egypt	na	93	92	94	93	93	92	93	92	93	92	93	94	92	93	94	India	74
El Salvador	na	85	86	85	81	86	91	91	83	74	92	84	79	na	na	na	Romania	74
Estonia	63	na	na	na	na	na	na	na	na	na	na	na	na	na	na	na	Georgia	74
Finland	31	45	32	56	28	37	60	51	35	41	52	42	37	48	45	43	Northern Ireland	69
France	48	na	na	na	na	na	na	na	na	na	na	na	na	na	na	na	Brazil	68
Georgia	na	74	69	77	68	73	81	80	74	68	81	74	62	74	74	68	Ukraine	67
Germany	53	35	30	39	23	31	44	41	30	25	39	32	27	41	34	26	Taiwan	66
Great Britain	43	42	36	48	32	33	54	49	36	27	47	44	34	na	na	na	Peru	66
Greece	na	41	34	46	31	44	61	70	46	32	48	40	37	40	43	37	Venezuela	66
Hungary	78	na	na	na	na	na	na	na	na	na	na	na	na	na	na	na	Armenia	65
Iceland	54	50	35	64	39	45	66	62	44	37	60	47	42	64	48	28	Lithuania	65
India	84	74	73	75	71	75	74	72	76	75	75	75	72	82	71	84	Colombia	64
Indonesia	na	94	94	94	94	94	95	96	94	93	94	95	93	94	94	89	Japan	64
Iran	na	95	95	96	95	95	98	96	96	93	96	97	94	98	94	95	Russian Fed.	61
Ireland	61	58	51	64	49	51	73	71	52	48	71	57	46	63	59	46	Moldova	61
Israel	na	48	41	54	43	49	54	64	50	34	57	47	31	52	47	58	Mexico	61
Italy	60	57	50	64	45	52	69	69	49	45	65	55	47	68	58	49	Korea, South	59
Japan	71	64	53	74	40	64	76	71	68	51	69	63	63	67	64	57	Ireland	58
Jordan	na	98	99	98	98	98	99	99	99	97	98	99	98	99	98	97	South Africa	58
Korea, South	79	59	53	65	44	63	67	75	65	48	59	63	55	62	58	44	Italy	57
Latvia	68	na	na	na	na	na	na	na	na	na	na	na	na	na	na	na	Dominican Rep.	55
Lithuania	78	65	56	73	44	58	87	90	57	54	84	69	57	71	63	57	Singapore	54
Luxembourg	na	45	43	48	38	42	55	58	38	40	48	48	31	50	46	35	Argentina	51
Macedonia	na	81	80	83	77	81	86	92	77	74	88	79	74	80	82	86	Iceland	50
Malta	na	na	na	na	na	na	na	na	na	na	na	na	na	na	na	na	Slovenia	50
Mexico	52	61	60	62	51	61	74	71	51	39	65	61	53	70	56	52	Belarus	49
Moldova	na	61	57	64	47	65	68	73	57	56	79	63	45	64	59	48	Chile	48
Montenegro	na	81	80	81	73	77	88	89	79	65	85	82	77	87	75	71	Israel	48
Morocco	na	na	na	na	na	na	na	na	na	na	na	na	na	na	na	na	United States	47
Netherlands	21	na	na	na	na	na	na	na	na	na	na	na	na	na	na	na	Luxembourg	45
New Zealand	na	29	23	33	20	18	43	37	29	19	41	25	18	33	30	15	Czech Republic	45
Nigeria	68	77	77	77	76	77	81	75	78	79	76	78	76	78	77	76	Finland	45
Northern Ireland	65	69	62	75	63	61	80	79	64	55	79	68	59	81	67	57	Uruguay	44
Norway	66	43	40	46	35	36	58	56	39	37	na	na	na	51	44	30	Canada	44
Pakistan	na	96	96	96	95	96	98	99	94	90	100	96	91	97	95	82	Norway	43
Peru	na	66	60	72	62	69	69	71	67	62	71	62	63	64	66	68	Philippines	43
Philippines	na	43	40	47	41	44	45	39	44	47	47	44	38	45	43	34	Great Britain	42
Poland	76	na	na	na	na	na	na	na	na	na	na	na	na	na	na	na	Greece	41
Portugal	68	na	na	na	na	na	na	na	na	na	na	na	na	na	na	na	Austria	36
Puerto Rico	na	na	na	na	na	na	na	na	na	na	na	na	na	na	na	na	Germany	35
Romania	80	74	66	81	62	68	85	89	69	58	85	76	64	81	70	43	Spain	30
Russian Fed.	78	61	53	68	39	60	76	76	62	51	71	62	50	66	57	47	Australia	29
Serbia	na	75	72	78	60	71	87	82	79	60	81	75	70	81	71	62	New Zealand	29
Singapore	na	54	54	55	51	59	53	57	55	45	59	57	51	56	54	45	Switzerland	22
Slovakia	na	na	na	na	na	na	na	na	na	na	na	na	na	na	na	na		
Slovenia	63	50	40	57	34	47	63	72	46	23	63	50	29	63	49	38		
South Africa	81	58	57	59	61	54	61	57	59	55	59	53	57	59	57	49		
Spain	50	30	27	34	21	26	40	36	25	24	42	25	26	40	29	19		
Sweden	66	na	na	na	na	na	na	na	na	na	na	na	na	na	na	na		
Switzerland	45	22	21	22	18	17	30	29	20	21	26	25	14	25	22	14		
Taiwan	na	66	62	70	69	60	65	67	70	64	65	67	69	67	66	61		
Tanzania	na	93	93	93	95	90	95	93	93	92	93	94	89	96	93	88		
Turkey	83	na	na	na	na	na	na	na	na	na	na	na	na	na	na	na		
Uganda	na	78	79	78	77	78	89	85	75	82	78	80	76	80	77	80		
Ukraine	na	67	58	75	39	66	84	86	66	60	75	64	61	71	63	70		
United States	61	47	40	55	47	46	49	55	50	43	52	44	45	45	50	41		
Uruguay	na	44	43	46	34	33	58	52	34	33	49	42	41	57	44	33		
Venezuela	na	66	63	68	64	66	69	69	66	60	65	63	68	68	67	57		
Vietnam	na	92	93	92	92	91	96	92	94	85	96	95	87	96	90	94		
Zimbabwe	na	94	91	96	91	95	99	97	90	92	95	95	91	95	93	97		
Total	62	64	61	67	60	63	70	72	62	56	70	65	59	73	62	47	Total	64

F120) JUSTIFIABLE: ABORTION

Please tell me for each of the following statements whether you think it can always be justified, never be justified, or something in between: Abortion.

Never justifiable (%)   (WVS: V210; EVS: V233)

Country	Wave		Gender		Age			Education			Income			Values			RANKING Country	2000
	1990	2000	Male	Female	16-29	30-49	50+	Lower	Middle	Upper	Lower	Middle	Upper	Mat	Mixed	Postm.		
Albania	na	26	25	27	24	25	30	28	26	23	25	30	24	22	29	23	Zimbabwe	92
Algeria	na	79	78	80	76	80	84	83	79	76	82	79	74	78	80	78	El Salvador	91
Argentina	48	66	64	67	63	66	68	74	56	47	76	67	54	73	68	55	Tanzania	90
Armenia	na	23	26	20	23	20	28	33	23	18	19	22	28	24	23	18	Bangladesh	90
Australia	na	24	22	25	20	20	32	38	22	14	30	22	14	31	25	18	Malta	89
Austria	34	24	22	25	17	19	32	28	23	10	28	22	22	32	24	21	Indonesia	88
Azerbaijan	na	30	34	26	39	22	31	44	29	29	27	30	36	29	32	35	Jordan	85
Bangladesh	na	90	89	90	86	92	96	95	86	82	96	88	86	94	88	76	Morocco	84
Belarus	28	18	16	19	12	14	26	27	15	13	22	18	8	21	15	7	Algeria	79
Belgium	24	30	29	31	27	23	39	47	29	19	36	32	21	41	29	21	Iran	77
Bosnia and Herz.	na	35	35	35	32	34	40	43	35	27	45	33	30	30	37	32	Uganda	76
Brazil	66	75	74	76	76	74	76	80	73	64	82	79	67	82	73	67	Brazil	75
Bulgaria	29	20	21	19	16	16	27	30	16	13	28	20	12	22	20	7	Colombia	74
Canada	23	30	26	33	25	27	36	46	28	18	36	29	21	40	32	22	Nigeria	74
Chile	76	67	66	68	64	66	72	72	66	60	69	68	60	76	66	54	Peru	74
China	16	56	53	59	54	58	53	56	59	29	56	56	55	52	57	58	Puerto Rico	74
Colombia	na	74	72	77	73	73	81	82	76	59	82	75	63	79	76	75	Venezuela	71
Croatia	na	44	44	44	27	46	52	50	43	28	52	42	42	55	43	34	Mexico	69
Czech Republic	9	14	13	14	11	10	18	17	10	7	21	12	9	16	13	9	Chile	67
Denmark	na	13	10	16	10	11	17	18	4	8	19	11	7	25	13	6	Argentina	66
Dominican Rep.	na	59	60	59	59	58	90	77	64	55	64	58	47	60	61	55	India	65
Egypt	na	57	62	51	55	56	59	59	55	54	61	52	55	55	57	59	Turkey	64
El Salvador	na	91	90	92	89	91	93	94	89	83	96	92	84	na	na	na	Vietnam	61
Estonia	15	21	23	19	20	15	26	27	19	14	26	22	18	24	19	8	Pakistan	60
Finland	14	11	11	12	7	7	17	15	8	6	15	11	8	11	11	15	Dominican Rep.	59
France	20	14	15	14	13	11	19	19	9	8	20	14	9	21	14	5	Egypt	57
Georgia	na	29	36	24	32	26	32	35	30	23	35	29	21	29	30	36	China	56
Germany	21	27	26	27	14	20	39	36	19	18	30	27	23	34	26	17	Philippines	55
Great Britain	19	26	22	29	18	19	34	35	19	11	33	25	15	na	na	na	South Africa	53
Greece	na	18	18	19	11	18	39	41	21	12	26	18	13	18	19	13	Ireland	51
Hungary	27	33	32	35	34	24	42	37	27	24	38	33	30	33	34	30	Uruguay	48
Iceland	12	12	11	12	8	9	18	19	9	2	17	8	8	15	12	4	Taiwan	46
India	39	65	66	65	63	66	67	67	67	61	66	67	64	75	61	59	Northern Ireland	46
Indonesia	na	88	90	86	83	88	91	94	87	85	87	89	88	90	87	86	Poland	44
Iran	na	77	77	77	76	75	83	82	75	71	77	76	74	82	72	79	Croatia	44
Ireland	53	51	49	53	29	44	74	69	44	35	70	49	38	62	49	39	Moldova	42
Israel	na	27	26	27	26	28	26	41	29	14	34	29	10	38	23	23	Singapore	41
Italy	26	32	28	36	20	28	42	41	25	25	44	26	24	44	33	22	Macedonia	40
Japan	29	15	16	13	8	13	19	20	15	10	17	15	12	14	15	10	Romania	40
Jordan	na	85	86	84	85	83	88	87	82	84	84	85	84	87	84	83	Korea, South	37
Korea, South	40	37	41	32	26	37	48	54	42	28	41	39	31	40	35	31	Latvia	37
Latvia	27	37	37	36	37	27	45	53	33	28	43	36	31	40	34	33	Portugal	36
Lithuania	31	33	28	37	19	21	54	65	22	20	53	33	20	39	31	28	Bosnia and Herz.	35
Luxembourg	na	18	19	17	12	16	24	28	13	10	25	19	10	19	19	11	Hungary	33
Macedonia	na	40	43	38	44	39	40	56	37	24	48	38	31	38	40	54	Lithuania	33
Malta	na	89	86	92	78	90	95	97	88	77	97	91	82	90	90	76	Ukraine	33
Mexico	43	69	68	71	62	71	77	77	63	52	71	70	64	78	66	59	Montenegro	32
Moldova	na	42	41	42	35	40	50	51	39	37	57	42	30	47	38	23	Italy	32
Montenegro	na	32	32	32	21	26	46	45	25	20	33	28	24	41	25	15	Belgium	30
Morocco	na	84	85	84	80	86	93	89	69	56	87	79	83	89	82	70	Azerbaijan	30
Netherlands	13	15	15	15	10	13	20	28	12	7	23	12	8	28	16	7	Canada	30
New Zealand	na	18	16	20	16	14	23	23	17	12	29	15	11	25	19	8	United States	30
Nigeria	53	74	74	74	73	75	79	75	74	72	73	75	73	77	73	72	Georgia	29
Northern Ireland	41	46	45	48	40	34	59	58	40	30	54	48	30	52	45	45	Spain	28
Norway	16	15	15	15	14	11	20	23	15	6	na	na	na	27	14	4	Israel	27
Pakistan	na	60	66	53	61	57	65	57	60	65	58	59	58	60	60	9	Germany	27
Peru	na	74	70	77	71	76	75	78	75	68	77	71	71	71	75	72	Albania	26
Philippines	na	55	52	59	55	55	57	47	59	60	60	57	48	57	55	50	Great Britain	26
Poland	43	44	42	46	35	39	55	53	36	27	49	42	37	50	40	41	Slovakia	25
Portugal	28	36	32	39	25	32	44	40	27	29	52	32	33	43	34	24	Austria	24
Puerto Rico	na	74	71	76	68	67	82	90	77	70	85	73	65	82	74	70	Australia	24
Romania	25	40	40	40	34	33	49	54	36	23	52	39	31	45	35	26	Armenia	23
Russian Fed.	20	17	18	16	14	13	23	30	16	12	24	15	12	18	15	18	Switzerland	22
Serbia	na	20	25	16	19	16	25	28	18	14	27	20	13	21	18	22	Estonia	21
Singapore	na	41	41	41	37	45	44	47	39	33	47	40	39	40	42	32	Bulgaria	20
Slovakia	na	25	22	29	18	20	38	38	21	15	37	25	19	28	23	20	Serbia	20
Slovenia	19	20	20	19	14	18	26	34	16	6	29	17	10	30	17	17	Slovenia	20
South Africa	66	53	55	50	53	51	57	55	51	49	52	51	55	55	52	45	Greece	18
Spain	33	28	24	32	15	19	44	39	17	15	43	22	23	39	26	13	New Zealand	18
Sweden	15	5	6	5	1	5	8	10	4	4	8	5	2	11	6	2	Luxembourg	18
Switzerland	56	22	20	25	13	19	31	32	20	20	31	25	14	23	24	14	Belarus	18
Taiwan	na	46	44	48	39	47	51	53	50	39	52	43	44	48	44	44	Russian Fed.	17
Tanzania	na	90	90	90	94	88	92	91	92	84	91	91	82	92	91	92	Netherlands	15
Turkey	40	64	68	61	61	65	73	73	57	39	74	65	46	69	64	59	Norway	15
Uganda	na	76	78	74	73	75	91	85	71	83	80	75	76	75	77	74	Japan	15
Ukraine	na	33	36	31	24	30	41	52	30	30	41	29	28	34	33	29	France	14
United States	35	30	27	33	26	28	35	41	33	24	36	28	23	31	31	26	Czech Republic	14
Uruguay	na	48	43	51	41	37	59	59	33	30	53	48	39	60	48	32	Denmark	13
Venezuela	na	71	69	73	71	72	72	77	71	66	72	72	70	73	72	69	Iceland	12
Vietnam	na	61	59	63	67	61	57	69	52	45	56	68	55	58	61	54	Finland	11
Zimbabwe	na	92	89	95	90	92	98	96	87	44	96	92	84	94	90	99	Sweden	5
Total	31	44	44	44	45	42	46	54	40	36	50	44	38	49	42	34	Total	44

F121) JUSTIFIABLE: DIVORCE

Please tell me for each of the following statements whether you think it can always be justified, never be justified, or something in between: Divorce.

Never justifiable (%)

(WVS: V211; EVS: V234)

Country	Wave 1990	Wave 2000	Gender Male	Gender Female	Age 16-29	Age 30-49	Age 50+	Education Lower	Education Middle	Education Upper	Income Lower	Income Middle	Income Upper	Values Mat	Values Mixed	Values Postm.
Albania	na	18	19	17	17	18	20	19	18	17	16	21	18	16	19	18
Algeria	na	26	25	27	22	26	33	35	25	20	32	23	19	27	26	16
Argentina	32	25	24	25	19	24	31	32	16	12	30	28	15	37	26	14
Armenia	na	18	18	18	16	16	26	31	19	11	12	20	24	21	17	11
Australia	na	10	12	8	9	8	13	17	8	6	13	8	6	19	11	6
Austria	19	11	12	10	8	8	16	15	8	3	15	9	11	25	10	10
Azerbaijan	na	27	29	24	29	24	28	35	27	25	32	29	22	28	24	29
Bangladesh	na	82	78	87	80	83	86	88	80	69	88	80	80	86	80	68
Belarus	22	9	7	10	5	6	14	12	7	10	11	8	5	8	9	5
Belgium	18	14	14	13	10	10	19	24	13	7	18	17	7	21	12	6
Bosnia and Herz.	na	15	15	15	9	17	18	26	14	11	21	16	12	13	16	8
Brazil	39	30	32	29	29	30	35	38	27	16	37	34	21	39	29	20
Bulgaria	33	18	19	18	13	14	25	28	15	9	27	16	11	20	17	21
Canada	15	11	11	10	9	8	15	22	8	5	16	8	8	13	12	7
Chile	49	27	26	28	23	22	37	36	24	16	34	23	18	38	25	15
China	16	57	53	61	48	61	57	64	54	26	57	60	53	54	54	66
Colombia	na	34	33	35	30	33	43	53	34	20	47	37	21	41	37	26
Croatia	na	31	28	33	16	33	37	36	29	21	36	28	31	32	31	25
Czech Republic	8	7	6	8	4	5	10	10	5	2	11	7	3	9	6	5
Denmark	17	7	8	7	5	5	10	11	4	2	12	4	4	17	7	1
Dominican Rep.	na	27	29	25	27	24	60	47	34	22	37	18	17	22	28	25
Egypt	na	16	18	14	15	16	17	16	17	13	18	13	13	16	15	19
El Salvador	na	57	58	56	52	58	64	64	53	45	58	60	47	na	na	na
Estonia	12	11	11	11	10	8	14	18	10	5	17	11	9	12	10	na
Finland	7	3	4	3	2	3	4	4	2	2	5	3	3	3	4	1
France	13	7	8	7	5	6	10	10	4	3	9	9	4	12	7	3
Georgia	na	21	22	21	21	20	25	27	23	13	27	21	12	20	23	20
Germany	14	13	12	14	5	9	21	19	8	8	16	13	7	15	13	11
Great Britain	12	12	13	11	6	10	14	13	9	11	16	11	10	13	12	12
Greece	na	7	8	6	3	8	14	19	6	5	9	6	5	6	7	5
Hungary	26	24	21	28	15	22	32	29	16	15	28	24	22	25	24	34
Iceland	5	4	4	4	2	2	8	7	3	na	8	3	2	5	4	1
India	52	51	49	54	47	51	55	54	52	45	54	55	46	57	47	47
Indonesia	na	54	53	56	41	61	53	61	57	46	55	53	51	56	53	39
Iran	na	55	55	55	52	56	62	65	54	42	55	56	50	62	47	46
Ireland	31	26	24	26	15	15	46	42	19	13	41	23	16	37	23	19
Israel	na	12	14	10	12	11	12	20	12	5	14	13	3	19	10	10
Italy	21	19	16	21	8	13	29	28	12	10	30	14	11	31	20	9
Japan	19	6	6	5	2	3	9	11	6	2	8	3	5	5	6	3
Jordan	na	42	33	51	38	43	50	44	38	44	46	36	47	46	39	39
Korea, South	40	21	24	18	10	21	34	46	23	15	26	20	16	22	21	16
Latvia	20	25	26	25	20	19	32	45	20	15	29	29	18	30	22	19
Lithuania	25	20	17	23	8	13	35	44	11	15	32	25	12	21	20	13
Luxembourg	na	10	10	9	6	10	12	18	7	4	11	13	5	11	10	5
Macedonia	na	36	37	35	35	36	37	52	32	20	44	35	27	35	35	51
Malta	na	59	56	62	41	53	77	76	55	41	69	62	46	65	57	44
Mexico	29	40	41	40	29	42	53	51	30	17	50	39	30	49	36	31
Moldova	na	29	28	30	18	32	35	42	26	22	45	30	18	34	24	18
Montenegro	na	9	9	10	3	6	18	16	6	3	14	9	3	11	8	6
Morocco	na	44	40	47	38	46	52	47	37	11	44	39	37	45	43	28
Netherlands	7	5	5	4	4	3	6	9	2	3	6	5	2	11	5	1
New Zealand	na	6	7	6	1	5	9	8	7	3	11	4	3	10	5	2
Nigeria	44	55	51	58	55	53	55	52	57	54	54	58	49	53	55	59
Northern Ireland	28	24	22	25	19	17	31	28	23	12	28	28	11	32	22	18
Norway	16	7	8	5	5	4	11	10	7	3	na	na	na	13	6	1
Pakistan	na	67	68	65	67	65	70	62	70	74	64	67	70	65	69	33
Peru	na	42	37	46	37	43	52	49	46	31	49	38	35	42	43	38
Philippines	na	43	38	47	43	41	46	39	46	43	46	46	36	47	40	37
Poland	33	26	27	25	18	22	37	33	19	15	28	25	22	31	25	18
Portugal	20	17	15	19	10	14	24	20	13	7	31	14	16	21	17	6
Puerto Rico	na	35	35	35	24	29	45	56	42	28	46	36	25	46	34	30
Romania	25	33	31	34	26	25	43	49	26	19	46	30	23	37	28	12
Russian Fed.	18	11	12	10	6	9	16	22	10	6	16	10	7	11	10	7
Serbia	na	13	15	12	8	10	18	20	12	6	18	15	7	14	13	4
Singapore	na	31	31	31	26	35	36	34	31	23	34	26	33	30	32	20
Slovakia	na	14	11	16	7	12	20	20	12	4	20	15	9	14	13	10
Slovenia	20	14	14	14	10	13	19	26	12	1	23	11	5	20	12	17
South Africa	53	32	33	30	30	32	35	31	32	43	30	35	30	36	31	18
Spain	25	12	11	13	4	7	21	17	6	4	17	10	10	20	10	3
Sweden	9	2	3	1	2	1	3	5	2	1	3	3	na	4	2	na
Switzerland	26	9	9	8	5	6	15	16	7	6	14	13	3	11	10	4
Taiwan	na	33	31	36	19	33	44	44	37	21	38	32	29	33	33	42
Tanzania	na	53	54	53	52	54	57	52	57	53	54	53	47	55	53	57
Turkey	27	42	43	41	36	45	55	53	29	20	55	41	23	48	43	34
Uganda	na	62	67	58	57	64	77	65	59	81	63	76	62	62	62	63
Ukraine	na	24	22	25	15	22	30	40	22	19	31	19	20	26	23	21
United States	20	8	9	6	9	7	8	13	10	4	10	7	6	8	8	6
Uruguay	na	22	21	23	16	15	30	29	11	17	23	22	19	27	22	13
Venezuela	na	30	27	32	25	29	41	39	30	18	31	31	27	32	30	25
Vietnam	na	50	48	53	54	49	49	54	49	33	45	62	40	46	51	50
Zimbabwe	na	74	69	79	75	72	77	79	68	44	80	77	59	75	72	87
Total	23	26	26	26	25	25	29	34	24	18	31	27	21	31	24	16

RANKING

Country	2000
Bangladesh	82
Zimbabwe	74
Pakistan	67
Uganda	62
Malta	59
China	57
El Salvador	57
Iran	55
Nigeria	55
Indonesia	54
Tanzania	53
India	51
Vietnam	50
Morocco	44
Philippines	43
Turkey	42
Jordan	42
Peru	42
Mexico	40
Macedonia	36
Puerto Rico	35
Colombia	34
Taiwan	33
Romania	33
South Africa	32
Singapore	31
Croatia	31
Brazil	30
Venezuela	30
Moldova	29
Chile	27
Azerbaijan	27
Dominican Rep.	27
Poland	26
Algeria	26
Ireland	26
Latvia	25
Argentina	25
Hungary	24
Ukraine	24
Northern Ireland	24
Uruguay	22
Georgia	21
Korea, South	21
Lithuania	20
Italy	19
Albania	18
Bulgaria	18
Armenia	18
Portugal	17
Egypt	16
Bosnia and Herz.	15
Slovenia	14
Slovakia	14
Belgium	14
Serbia	13
Germany	13
Great Britain	12
Spain	12
Israel	12
Austria	11
Estonia	11
Russian Fed.	11
Canada	11
Australia	10
Luxembourg	10
Montenegro	9
Switzerland	9
Belarus	9
United States	8
France	7
Denmark	7
Czech Republic	7
Greece	7
Norway	7
New Zealand	6
Japan	6
Netherlands	5
Iceland	4
Finland	3
Sweden	2
Total	26

F122) JUSTIFIABLE: EUTHANASIA

Please tell me for each of the following statements whether you think it can always be justified, never be justified, or something in between: Euthanasia - ending the life of the incurably sick

Never justifiable (%)

(WVS: V212; EVS: V235)

Country	Wave		Gender		Age			Education			Income			Values			RANKING Country	2000
	1990	2000	Male	Female	16-29	30-49	50+	Lower	Middle	Upper	Lower	Middle	Upper	Mat	Mixed	Postm.		
Albania	na	47	46	49	43	47	50	49	44	49	46	48	47	47	47	43	Pakistan	100
Algeria	na	86	85	86	84	86	88	87	88	81	91	84	78	90	83	82	Bangladesh	97
Argentina	61	49	45	52	42	50	54	58	37	32	59	47	42	62	47	42	Morocco	93
Armenia	na	39	39	39	37	37	45	45	39	35	38	34	44	41	38	32	Zimbabwe	90
Australia	na	15	16	15	11	12	23	24	13	11	22	12	9	17	16	13	Jordan	90
Austria	42	31	28	33	22	26	40	35	27	27	35	31	31	36	31	29	Tanzania	89
Azerbaijan	na	47	47	47	46	46	49	54	45	49	48	41	52	51	42	29	Algeria	86
Bangladesh	na	97	96	97	96	97	97	99	96	92	99	96	95	97	96	93	Indonesia	84
Belarus	40	20	17	22	13	19	26	27	18	13	26	18	13	21	18	11	El Salvador	83
Belgium	23	12	12	12	11	8	16	19	10	10	19	11	6	14	12	10	Uganda	83
Bosnia and Herz.	na	43	43	43	37	42	51	56	42	37	44	45	40	45	43	32	Egypt	78
Brazil	71	61	59	63	57	65	61	67	58	47	71	61	51	69	58	55	Iran	76
Bulgaria	52	45	45	45	40	38	54	60	42	28	58	44	34	52	41	39	Malta	69
Canada	25	20	16	23	14	15	28	31	18	12	26	21	11	22	22	14	Puerto Rico	68
Chile	68	45	42	48	42	40	55	55	41	36	49	44	41	55	44	33	Turkey	65
China	24	53	51	54	46	53	58	63	49	21	62	54	38	50	50	45	Nigeria	64
Colombia	na	45	43	48	45	43	54	64	48	29	63	49	30	53	49	34	India	63
Croatia	na	45	40	50	22	47	59	55	40	36	54	45	41	58	43	40	Brazil	61
Czech Republic	na	18	16	19	11	11	27	21	15	11	25	17	13	21	16	18	Mexico	59
Denmark	26	12	11	13	8	9	17	14	10	9	16	11	6	21	12	6	Georgia	57
Dominican Rep.	na	53	52	53	53	51	70	70	60	48	62	53	36	51	49	61	Romania	56
Egypt	na	78	77	78	77	78	78	77	78	80	76	78	80	78	78	71	Macedonia	56
El Salvador	na	83	81	85	81	84	83	87	81	73	89	85	74	na	na	na	Venezuela	55
Estonia	40	23	18	27	15	18	32	30	21	18	34	23	17	25	21	8	China	53
Finland	14	18	16	19	6	12	30	23	11	14	22	16	13	18	18	13	Dominican Rep.	53
France	24	12	11	14	13	10	14	15	10	9	15	13	9	15	12	9	Vietnam	51
Georgia	na	57	55	58	53	55	62	61	58	50	63	57	47	55	58	49	Poland	50
Germany	43	28	28	28	21	22	38	36	22	21	32	25	24	29	27	29	Philippines	50
Great Britain	23	21	20	22	15	16	26	25	16	16	26	21	16	na	na	na	Moldova	50
Greece	na	30	27	32	23	31	43	49	34	22	35	29	25	30	30	25	Argentina	49
Hungary	48	44	42	46	39	36	54	50	35	29	47	44	44	48	42	11	Ireland	49
Iceland	22	18	16	19	12	15	28	26	14	8	22	20	11	22	17	11	Albania	47
India	57	63	63	64	62	63	66	64	66	60	67	63	62	69	62	57	Azerbaijan	47
Indonesia	na	84	83	85	67	85	90	92	86	75	83	84	83	87	82	71	Colombia	45
Iran	na	76	73	80	73	78	83	83	76	68	78	79	72	83	73	69	Chile	45
Ireland	56	49	46	52	32	41	69	62	43	38	63	46	39	58	48	38	Croatia	45
Israel	na	na	na	na	na	na	na	na	na	na	na	na	na	na	na	na	Bulgaria	45
Italy	47	40	38	42	27	35	52	51	32	31	52	39	31	50	41	32	Hungary	44
Japan	21	10	10	11	3	5	19	20	10	6	13	10	8	10	11	7	Bosnia and Herz.	43
Jordan	na	90	88	91	87	91	93	91	88	89	93	91	88	92	89	87	Portugal	41
Korea, South	na	24	26	23	14	24	36	52	27	17	27	27	19	26	23	19	Northern Ireland	41
Latvia	48	30	27	32	18	25	40	44	27	23	38	30	19	34	28	16	Singapore	40
Lithuania	45	26	23	28	16	18	40	46	19	18	39	21	17	28	23	22	South Africa	40
Luxembourg	na	19	22	16	15	17	24	29	14	13	21	21	14	18	21	13	Italy	40
Macedonia	na	56	56	56	50	58	58	68	54	43	64	54	47	55	55	63	Uruguay	40
Malta	na	69	64	74	50	67	84	87	64	54	78	67	56	74	69	48	Armenia	39
Mexico	38	59	59	58	53	58	68	67	54	33	62	55	51	71	54	44	Serbia	35
Moldova	na	50	47	53	35	53	59	63	48	43	68	50	37	54	49	22	Montenegro	35
Montenegro	na	35	33	38	30	33	41	46	30	26	52	40	25	43	30	16	Austria	31
Morocco	na	93	92	94	91	94	96	94	90	83	95	88	92	95	91	92	Ukraine	30
Netherlands	13	8	9	8	6	6	12	15	5	5	15	5	3	16	8	5	Latvia	30
New Zealand	na	12	11	12	8	9	15	12	14	10	16	9	8	19	11	8	Greece	30
Nigeria	56	64	63	65	65	62	65	65	63	64	66	66	57	63	63	72	Germany	28
Northern Ireland	43	41	38	43	29	31	55	49	34	30	46	36	26	48	41	33	Slovenia	28
Norway	32	18	15	21	9	14	31	26	14	16	na	na	na	24	18	12	Taiwan	27
Pakistan	na	100	100	100	100	100	100	100	100	100	100	100	100	100	100	100	Lithuania	26
Peru	na	na	na	na	na	na	na	na	na	na	na	na	na	na	na	na	Slovakia	25
Philippines	na	50	47	54	46	51	56	48	50	53	53	52	45	53	49	40	Korea, South	24
Poland	67	50	51	50	38	45	65	61	42	30	55	50	40	53	49	49	United States	24
Portugal	53	41	40	43	34	36	50	46	34	28	55	36	38	49	38	34	Spain	24
Puerto Rico	na	68	62	72	55	64	78	83	72	64	74	70	62	69	69	70	Estonia	23
Romania	54	56	54	58	39	51	71	70	52	45	66	63	47	63	51	41	Russian Fed.	23
Russian Fed.	54	23	21	25	15	20	32	38	22	17	29	22	18	24	21	20	Great Britain	21
Serbia	na	35	34	37	21	33	45	47	33	26	46	35	29	39	33	27	Canada	20
Singapore	na	40	40	41	36	44	46	51	38	22	51	40	35	46	39	30	Belarus	20
Slovakia	na	25	22	27	18	22	34	34	22	16	31	25	21	26	23	35	Luxembourg	19
Slovenia	51	28	28	27	17	26	38	41	25	14	36	27	20	33	28	21	Norway	18
South Africa	61	40	40	41	39	40	46	42	38	35	38	44	37	43	39	31	Iceland	18
Spain	45	24	20	27	12	15	38	33	14	14	35	21	18	36	21	10	Czech Republic	18
Sweden	21	10	10	11	6	9	14	17	7	10	12	10	8	7	11	8	Finland	18
Switzerland	32	15	13	16	11	10	22	25	11	18	20	15	13	14	16	9	Australia	15
Taiwan	na	27	23	30	15	28	31	37	30	16	33	25	22	25	28	28	Switzerland	15
Tanzania	na	89	88	90	91	87	92	90	88	86	92	88	83	90	90	88	France	12
Turkey	70	65	62	69	58	71	75	77	53	36	75	67	45	65	66	61	Denmark	12
Uganda	na	83	89	77	78	88	81	85	81	90	89	82	86	82	84	82	Belgium	12
Ukraine	na	30	26	33	13	30	40	44	30	23	33	29	28	29	27	36	New Zealand	12
United States	34	24	21	27	19	23	30	33	22	22	29	21	19	23	26	20	Japan	10
Uruguay	na	40	39	41	29	33	50	51	25	24	47	40	31	50	41	28	Sweden	10
Venezuela	na	55	53	58	51	58	60	63	56	44	61	54	53	57	57	46	Netherlands	8
Vietnam	na	51	47	55	52	53	47	51	54	28	43	55	50	51	50	55		
Zimbabwe	na	90	86	93	89	91	92	93	86	82	93	90	82	91	89	93		
Total	42	44	43	45	43	42	47	54	40	36	50	44	38	52	42	32	Total	44

F123) JUSTIFIABLE: SUICIDE

Please tell me for each of the following statements whether you think it can always be justified, never be justified, or something in between: Suicide

Never justifiable (%)

(WVS: V213; EVS: V236)

Country	Wave 1990	Wave 2000	Gender Male	Gender Female	Age 16-29	Age 30-49	Age 50+	Education Lower	Education Middle	Education Upper	Income Lower	Income Middle	Income Upper	Values Mat	Values Mixed	Values Postm.
Albania	na	68	67	69	66	69	69	67	69	70	62	73	70	68	68	72
Algeria	na	94	94	94	93	94	95	93	94	94	95	93	91	95	93	96
Argentina	83	78	76	79	71	79	82	81	76	66	84	77	73	81	78	74
Armenia	na	60	61	59	52	64	66	68	59	62	58	58	63	58	63	51
Australia	na	48	49	46	41	46	55	59	50	36	54	46	40	57	51	40
Austria	50	47	44	49	35	42	57	59	39	25	56	47	41	58	47	42
Azerbaijan	na	73	75	71	65	77	77	76	74	70	75	67	71	76	68	55
Bangladesh	na	99	99	100	99	100	100	100	100	98	100	99	100	99	99	100
Belarus	64	50	42	56	37	53	57	56	47	49	59	46	41	54	47	36
Belgium	51	45	45	44	35	37	57	56	48	32	52	49	36	51	47	29
Bosnia and Herz.	na	80	79	81	78	78	86	88	80	76	83	82	75	80	82	64
Brazil	90	87	88	87	87	88	89	87	87	88	88	90	85	87	87	87
Bulgaria	68	71	70	71	61	67	78	80	67	63	78	66	66	74	68	91
Canada	53	52	49	54	44	50	59	68	52	38	57	55	43	60	52	48
Chile	82	71	71	72	70	70	75	76	72	61	73	72	69	79	69	65
China	55	83	83	83	76	86	82	83	85	63	80	88	82	82	83	81
Colombia	na	82	81	83	79	83	88	89	83	76	87	83	78	82	79	72
Croatia	na	84	81	86	75	83	90	89	83	74	89	84	82	85	84	84
Czech Republic	na	48	46	51	36	44	59	56	42	33	56	53	37	57	46	43
Denmark	60	51	54	48	47	48	57	61	46	34	55	51	42	63	52	42
Dominican Rep.	na	76	77	76	73	80	100	90	81	73	78	76	70	76	76	74
Egypt	na	95	96	94	92	96	96	95	93	97	94	93	96	96	93	93
El Salvador	na	94	94	94	91	96	96	97	91	90	98	92	93	na	na	na
Estonia	59	62	58	64	53	60	68	60	63	60	62	64	61	62	62	51
Finland	33	41	38	44	25	35	56	48	31	34	43	43	36	42	42	38
France	34	26	27	26	24	26	28	30	22	21	28	29	24	34	25	18
Georgia	na	79	77	80	77	78	82	76	80	76	82	78	74	77	80	75
Germany	56	54	51	56	40	51	63	62	44	57	58	52	47	64	52	43
Great Britain	40	39	39	40	31	39	43	47	34	26	39	45	32	na	na	na
Greece	na	53	51	55	47	57	64	70	58	47	62	50	47	55	56	48
Hungary	73	81	81	80	78	79	84	83	78	70	79	82	80	81	81	72
Iceland	57	63	61	65	54	62	74	72	63	46	66	65	55	67	64	52
India	82	72	74	70	69	74	72	70	74	76	70	72	73	77	72	80
Indonesia	na	97	97	98	97	96	99	100	97	97	98	96	99	98	97	93
Iran	na	95	94	95	93	96	97	96	95	91	94	95	94	97	93	92
Ireland	63	69	67	70	57	67	80	80	67	53	78	63	60	74	68	63
Israel	na	na	na	na	na	na	na	na	na	na	na	na	na	na	na	na
Italy	70	62	62	63	52	59	71	72	57	49	71	63	54	73	63	56
Japan	58	48	45	51	37	47	55	59	52	35	54	52	40	54	46	40
Jordan	na	97	99	96	95	98	99	97	97	98	97	98	97	98	97	91
Korea, South	66	51	52	50	35	53	63	70	56	41	56	51	45	51	52	37
Latvia	64	76	72	78	70	76	78	78	76	69	78	77	74	76	76	78
Lithuania	70	76	69	81	67	74	84	89	71	71	86	72	70	79	74	81
Luxembourg	na	38	38	39	30	35	47	50	35	21	47	39	25	42	40	24
Macedonia	na	85	84	85	80	84	84	90	81	79	87	81	81	82	84	82
Malta	na	93	92	95	88	95	96	96	94	82	97	93	80	95	94	79
Mexico	51	82	82	83	76	84	88	87	79	74	82	82	78	86	80	76
Moldova	na	67	63	71	56	71	72	73	65	66	81	69	54	71	66	43
Montenegro	na	53	51	55	45	50	61	60	50	41	70	51	44	60	47	46
Morocco	na	98	98	99	98	99	99	98	98	98	99	98	97	99	98	99
Netherlands	32	28	27	28	26	21	35	43	28	13	36	25	17	40	29	18
New Zealand	na	47	46	48	35	44	54	55	53	34	51	47	42	55	45	41
Nigeria	74	76	75	77	75	78	75	74	77	78	78	77	72	76	76	79
Northern Ireland	58	68	65	71	53	62	81	79	63	50	78	67	54	78	67	57
Norway	58	52	57	48	43	51	61	68	51	38	na	na	na	65	53	34
Pakistan	na	97	96	97	95	97	98	99	94	92	99	96	94	97	96	83
Peru	na	75	72	78	70	78	79	76	76	73	78	72	75	68	78	73
Philippines	na	57	55	60	55	58	59	52	58	63	60	59	52	60	57	45
Poland	75	64	63	65	47	63	74	72	54	48	66	63	57	67	60	65
Portugal	72	63	58	67	63	60	66	66	55	61	71	55	56	66	60	59
Puerto Rico	na	90	89	92	79	93	94	92	91	90	95	88	88	92	92	89
Romania	77	87	85	90	82	86	91	92	86	83	90	87	86	89	87	76
Russian Fed.	68	67	65	69	58	66	73	73	68	61	73	66	63	69	65	63
Serbia	na	73	72	75	65	71	79	75	75	69	78	74	70	74	73	69
Singapore	na	69	69	68	61	77	73	73	69	55	73	70	66	68	70	57
Slovakia	na	37	36	38	28	31	51	46	34	24	45	39	31	39	34	46
Slovenia	59	47	48	46	32	47	57	59	45	31	56	52	31	59	46	39
South Africa	78	65	67	63	70	62	62	61	72	49	54	72	70	64	68	50
Spain	72	52	47	56	42	45	64	61	45	37	61	49	44	64	50	38
Sweden	47	29	31	27	25	32	28	41	29	19	28	33	25	31	30	23
Switzerland	58	38	38	38	33	37	43	48	37	28	45	37	33	40	39	35
Taiwan	na	63	63	63	59	61	71	69	68	56	69	61	59	65	62	50
Tanzania	na	96	97	96	95	95	97	95	96	96	95	96	96	97	96	96
Turkey	81	90	89	90	86	93	93	92	87	82	91	90	85	91	91	87
Uganda	na	93	95	92	92	95	93	94	93	95	96	92	95	92	93	96
Ukraine	na	73	70	76	62	72	81	82	73	70	76	69	76	76	71	75
United States	62	57	55	59	57	57	57	68	62	50	64	55	51	58	60	51
Uruguay	na	71	70	71	61	68	78	77	63	56	74	71	66	78	71	61
Venezuela	na	80	78	81	78	82	80	79	80	80	77	78	84	75	81	82
Vietnam	na	86	86	86	82	87	87	86	86	79	82	90	83	84	88	87
Zimbabwe	na	93	91	95	91	95	94	95	90	100	95	92	87	93	92	98
Total	62	68	68	69	66	68	71	75	67	61	72	69	64	74	68	57

RANKING

Country	2000
Bangladesh	99
Morocco	98
Indonesia	97
Jordan	97
Pakistan	97
Tanzania	96
Egypt	95
Iran	95
El Salvador	94
Algeria	94
Malta	93
Uganda	93
Zimbabwe	93
Puerto Rico	90
Turkey	90
Brazil	87
Romania	87
Vietnam	86
Croatia	84
Macedonia	83
China	83
Mexico	82
Colombia	82
Hungary	81
Bosnia and Herz.	80
Venezuela	80
Georgia	79
Argentina	78
Nigeria	76
Dominican Rep.	76
Lithuania	76
Latvia	76
Peru	75
Ukraine	73
Serbia	73
Azerbaijan	73
India	72
Chile	71
Uruguay	71
Bulgaria	71
Ireland	69
Singapore	69
Albania	68
Northern Ireland	68
Moldova	67
Russian Fed.	67
South Africa	65
Poland	64
Iceland	63
Taiwan	63
Portugal	63
Italy	62
Estonia	62
Armenia	60
Philippines	57
United States	57
Germany	54
Greece	53
Montenegro	53
Norway	52
Canada	52
Spain	52
Denmark	51
Korea, South	51
Belarus	50
Czech Republic	48
Japan	48
Australia	48
Austria	47
New Zealand	47
Slovenia	47
Belgium	45
Finland	41
Great Britain	39
Luxembourg	38
Switzerland	38
Slovakia	37
Sweden	29
Netherlands	28
France	26
Total	68

F125_1) JUSTIFIABLE: JOYRIDING

Please tell me for each of the following statements whether you think it can always be justified, never be justified, or something in between: Taking and driving away a car belonging to someone else (joyriding)

Never justifiable (%)

(EVS: V227)

Country	Wave 1990	Wave 2000	Gender Male	Gender Female	Age 16-29	Age 30-49	Age 50+	Education Lower	Education Middle	Education Upper	Income Lower	Income Middle	Income Upper	Values Mat	Values Mixed	Values Postm.
Albania	na	na	na	na	na	na	na	na	na	na	na	na	na	na	na	na
Algeria	na	na	na	na	na	na	na	na	na	na	na	na	na	na	na	na
Argentina	95	na	na	na	na	na	na	na	na	na	na	na	na	na	na	na
Armenia	na	na	na	na	na	na	na	na	na	na	na	na	na	na	na	na
Australia	na	na	na	na	na	na	na	na	na	na	na	na	na	na	na	na
Austria	94	92	90	93	87	92	94	93	91	90	88	93	92	90	93	89
Azerbaijan	na	na	na	na	na	na	na	na	na	na	na	na	na	na	na	na
Bangladesh	na	na	na	na	na	na	na	na	na	na	na	na	na	na	na	na
Belarus	75	67	60	72	55	67	75	72	63	72	70	66	61	70	65	52
Belgium	83	93	92	94	84	94	95	93	93	93	93	93	93	94	93	90
Bosnia and Herz.	na	na	na	na	na	na	na	na	na	na	na	na	na	na	na	na
Brazil	90	na	na	na	na	na	na	na	na	na	na	na	na	na	na	na
Bulgaria	86	90	90	91	82	89	95	95	88	87	92	93	86	92	89	96
Canada	83	na	na	na	na	na	na	na	na	na	na	na	na	na	na	na
Chile	88	na	na	na	na	na	na	na	na	na	na	na	na	na	na	na
China	85	na	na	na	na	na	na	na	na	na	na	na	na	na	na	na
Colombia	na	na	na	na	na	na	na	na	na	na	na	na	na	na	na	na
Croatia	na	91	91	92	89	90	94	95	89	88	93	93	90	91	92	92
Czech Republic	na	67	65	69	54	62	78	66	67	66	75	66	59	69	65	63
Denmark	96	97	97	96	95	96	97	97	99	95	96	96	97	96	97	95
Dominican Rep.	na	na	na	na	na	na	na	na	na	na	na	na	na	na	na	na
Egypt	na	na	na	na	na	na	na	na	na	na	na	na	na	na	na	na
El Salvador	na	na	na	na	na	na	na	na	na	na	na	na	na	na	na	na
Estonia	93	83	80	85	79	82	86	78	85	88	83	84	85	85	82	80
Finland	78	82	82	83	66	82	91	86	75	81	80	85	82	85	82	76
France	84	86	86	86	76	87	90	87	85	83	84	85	89	88	87	80
Georgia	na	na	na	na	na	na	na	na	na	na	na	na	na	na	na	na
Germany	93	88	88	88	80	90	89	88	87	91	86	86	84	93	87	83
Great Britain	89	89	86	92	75	92	94	89	89	85	86	91	92	na	na	na
Greece	na	74	73	75	70	76	83	88	76	70	80	73	70	75	76	67
Hungary	85	93	92	94	88	93	95	91	96	96	91	94	93	93	92	87
Iceland	72	75	73	77	64	76	84	84	73	61	77	74	73	85	74	61
India	84	na	na	na	na	na	na	na	na	na	na	na	na	na	na	na
Indonesia	na	na	na	na	na	na	na	na	na	na	na	na	na	na	na	na
Iran	na	na	na	na	na	na	na	na	na	na	na	na	na	na	na	na
Ireland	95	96	96	96	94	96	97	97	95	96	96	96	95	96	96	93
Israel	na	na	na	na	na	na	na	na	na	na	na	na	na	na	na	na
Italy	83	80	78	82	69	79	87	83	78	79	85	78	78	78	82	78
Japan	91	na	na	na	na	na	na	na	na	na	na	na	na	na	na	na
Jordan	na	na	na	na	na	na	na	na	na	na	na	na	na	na	na	na
Korea, South	83	na	na	na	na	na	na	na	na	na	na	na	na	na	na	na
Latvia	92	92	92	92	84	94	94	90	92	94	92	93	92	92	93	83
Lithuania	94	93	92	94	88	94	97	97	92	92	95	96	93	96	93	94
Luxembourg	na	77	74	80	64	81	82	79	75	79	70	83	86	76	78	77
Macedonia	na	na	na	na	na	na	na	na	na	na	na	na	na	na	na	na
Malta	na	93	91	96	89	96	94	95	93	91	95	94	91	94	94	87
Mexico	56	na	na	na	na	na	na	na	na	na	na	na	na	na	na	na
Moldova	na	na	na	na	na	na	na	na	na	na	na	na	na	na	na	na
Montenegro	na	na	na	na	na	na	na	na	na	na	na	na	na	na	na	na
Morocco	na	na	na	na	na	na	na	na	na	na	na	na	na	na	na	na
Netherlands	80	82	79	85	76	81	87	84	82	81	83	83	79	85	83	78
New Zealand	na	na	na	na	na	na	na	na	na	na	na	na	na	na	na	na
Nigeria	63	na	na	na	na	na	na	na	na	na	na	na	na	na	na	na
Northern Ireland	98	93	93	93	90	92	97	94	92	93	94	97	96	97	93	85
Norway	89	na	na	na	na	na	na	na	na	na	na	na	na	na	na	na
Pakistan	na	na	na	na	na	na	na	na	na	na	na	na	na	na	na	na
Peru	na	na	na	na	na	na	na	na	na	na	na	na	na	na	na	na
Philippines	na	na	na	na	na	na	na	na	na	na	na	na	Mat	na	na	
Poland	na	91	91	90	86	91	93	89	91	94	91	90	90	89	91	94
Portugal	87	79	76	81	80	73	83	80	75	81	84	72	78	81	78	75
Puerto Rico	na	na	na	na	na	na	na	na	na	na	na	na	na	na	na	na
Romania	87	93	92	94	89	93	94	94	91	95	94	91	94	94	94	85
Russian Fed.	93	85	84	86	76	86	91	90	85	85	86	86	83	85	86	89
Serbia	na	na	na	na	na	na	na	na	na	na	na	na	na	na	na	na
Singapore	na	na	na	na	na	na	na	na	na	na	na	na	na	na	na	na
Slovakia	na	42	40	44	35	42	49	43	41	47	43	41	46	42	43	39
Slovenia	90	78	75	81	67	80	84	80	77	78	80	82	77	80	78	78
South Africa	na	na	na	na	na	na	na	na	na	na	na	na	na	na	na	na
Spain	84	71	69	74	64	68	78	78	67	64	77	69	67	76	72	65
Sweden	97	87	86	89	81	88	90	93	86	85	85	90	88	88	90	79
Switzerland	85	na	na	na	na	na	na	na	na	na	na	na	na	na	na	na
Taiwan	na	na	na	na	na	na	na	na	na	na	na	na	na	na	na	na
Tanzania	na	na	na	na	na	na	na	na	na	na	na	na	na	na	na	na
Turkey	88	92	91	93	91	93	92	90	94	96	89	94	93	91	93	94
Uganda	na	na	na	na	na	na	na	na	na	na	na	na	na	na	na	na
Ukraine	na	82	80	84	72	84	87	87	81	83	85	80	81	84	81	83
United States	88	na	na	na	na	na	na	na	na	na	na	na	na	na	na	na
Uruguay	na	na	na	na	na	na	na	na	na	na	na	na	na	na	na	na
Venezuela	na	na	na	na	na	na	na	na	na	na	na	na	na	na	na	na
Vietnam	na	na	na	na	na	na	na	na	na	na	na	na	na	na	na	na
Zimbabwe	na	na	na	na	na	na	na	na	na	na	na	na	na	na	na	na
Total	86	84	83	85	76	84	89	86	82	84	85	84	84	85	85	81

RANKING

Country	2000
Denmark	97
Ireland	96
Lithuania	93
Malta	93
Romania	93
Northern Ireland	93
Hungary	93
Belgium	93
Latvia	92
Turkey	92
Austria	92
Croatia	91
Poland	91
Bulgaria	90
Great Britain	89
Germany	88
Sweden	87
France	86
Russian Fed.	85
Estonia	83
Finland	82
Ukraine	82
Netherlands	82
Italy	80
Portugal	79
Slovenia	78
Luxembourg	77
Iceland	75
Greece	74
Spain	71
Belarus	67
Czech Republic	67
Slovakia	42
Total	84

F126_1) JUSTIFIABLE: TAKING SOFT DRUGS

Please tell me for each of the following statements whether you think it can always be justified, never be justified, or something in between: Taking the drug marijuana or hashish

Never justifiable (%)

(EVS: V228)

Country	Wave 1990	Wave 2000	Gender Male	Gender Female	Age 16-29	Age 30-49	Age 50+	Education Lower	Education Middle	Education Upper	Income Lower	Income Middle	Income Upper	Values Mat	Values Mixed	Values Postm.
Albania	na	na	na	na	na	na	na	na	na	na	na	na	na	na	na	na
Algeria	na	na	na	na	na	na	na	na	na	na	na	na	na	na	na	na
Argentina	95	na	na	na	na	na	na	na	na	na	na	na	na	na	na	na
Armenia	na	na	na	na	na	na	na	na	na	na	na	na	na	na	na	na
Australia	na	na	na	na	na	na	na	na	na	na	na	na	na	na	na	na
Austria	86	75	73	77	57	73	87	85	70	52	77	77	74	85	81	62
Azerbaijan	na	na	na	na	na	na	na	na	na	na	na	na	na	na	na	na
Bangladesh	na	na	na	na	na	na	na	na	na	na	na	na	na	na	na	na
Belarus	85	76	71	80	64	75	87	84	72	77	80	76	68	79	74	71
Belgium	85	80	77	84	66	76	91	90	82	71	86	83	75	89	83	63
Bosnia and Herz.	na	na	na	na	na	na	na	na	na	na	na	na	na	na	na	na
Brazil	91	na	na	na	na	na	na	na	na	na	na	na	na	na	na	na
Bulgaria	88	84	84	85	69	84	92	91	81	81	92	86	77	86	83	93
Canada	65	na	na	na	na	na	na	na	na	na	na	na	na	na	na	na
Chile	90	na	na	na	na	na	na	na	na	na	na	na	na	na	na	na
China	96	na	na	na	na	na	na	na	na	na	na	na	na	na	na	na
Colombia	na	na	na	na	na	na	na	na	na	na	na	na	na	na	na	na
Croatia	na	87	82	92	74	89	95	94	83	82	93	88	83	94	88	82
Czech Republic	77	77	75	79	58	75	88	80	75	67	85	79	67	85	75	67
Denmark	73	62	57	67	42	55	82	75	46	44	70	59	52	74	66	43
Dominican Rep.	na	na	na	na	na	na	na	na	na	na	na	na	na	na	na	na
Egypt	na	na	na	na	na	na	na	na	na	na	na	na	na	na	na	na
El Salvador	na	na	na	na	na	na	na	na	na	na	na	na	na	na	na	na
Estonia	89	81	76	86	69	82	88	80	83	81	83	86	79	85	79	77
Finland	79	79	76	82	54	78	94	85	71	72	77	82	78	84	79	63
France	83	69	67	72	55	63	82	80	61	50	73	71	66	81	70	53
Georgia	na	na	na	na	na	na	na	na	na	na	na	na	na	na	na	na
Germany	95	68	68	69	48	65	80	75	61	70	71	69	64	80	67	54
Great Britain	77	52	48	56	28	46	69	63	45	32	59	50	44	na	na	na
Greece	na	51	45	55	37	56	77	81	59	39	58	50	44	57	53	41
Hungary	90	91	89	92	84	88	97	93	89	85	94	89	91	93	89	81
Iceland	80	72	67	78	52	72	91	82	66	63	73	76	66	78	72	58
India	91	na	na	na	na	na	na	na	na	na	na	na	na	na	na	na
Indonesia	na	na	na	na	na	na	na	na	na	na	na	na	na	na	na	na
Iran	na	na	na	na	na	na	na	na	na	na	na	na	na	na	na	na
Ireland	88	72	68	76	51	70	89	87	69	55	86	70	61	80	72	61
Israel	na	na	na	na	na	na	na	na	na	na	na	na	na	na	na	na
Italy	85	71	66	76	50	67	87	83	64	54	81	71	59	84	73	62
Japan	92	na	na	na	na	na	na	na	na	na	na	na	na	na	na	na
Jordan	na	na	na	na	na	na	na	na	na	na	na	na	na	na	na	na
Korea, South	94	na	na	na	na	na	na	na	na	na	na	na	na	na	na	na
Latvia	92	93	91	94	78	95	96	93	92	93	95	92	91	94	93	83
Lithuania	94	88	86	89	78	89	93	94	85	88	92	89	85	91	86	90
Luxembourg	na	67	66	68	52	64	80	76	64	59	62	76	63	71	71	47
Macedonia	na	na	na	na	na	na	na	na	na	na	na	na	na	na	na	na
Malta	na	96	95	96	90	98	98	97	96	91	97	97	93	98	95	90
Mexico	69	na	na	na	na	na	na	na	na	na	na	na	na	na	na	na
Moldova	na	na	na	na	na	na	na	na	na	na	na	na	na	na	na	na
Montenegro	na	na	na	na	na	na	na	na	na	na	na	na	na	na	na	na
Morocco	na	na	na	na	na	na	na	na	na	na	na	na	na	na	na	na
Netherlands	66	47	42	51	31	39	63	69	45	27	53	48	35	69	49	31
New Zealand	na	na	na	na	na	na	na	na	na	na	na	na	na	na	na	na
Nigeria	71	na	na	na	na	na	na	na	na	na	na	na	na	na	na	na
Northern Ireland	91	69	64	74	54	62	83	81	61	53	79	68	55	80	70	49
Norway	91	na	na	na	na	na	na	na	na	na	na	na	na	na	na	na
Pakistan	na	na	na	na	na	na	na	na	na	na	na	na	na	na	na	na
Peru	na	na	na	na	na	na	na	na	na	na	na	na	na	na	na	na
Philippines	na	na	na	na	na	na	na	na	na	na	na	na	na	na	na	na
Poland	91	84	81	86	73	84	91	88	80	76	87	84	75	86	83	78
Portugal	82	70	64	75	54	67	82	77	55	60	84	67	58	73	71	52
Puerto Rico	na	na	na	na	na	na	na	na	na	na	na	na	na	na	na	na
Romania	91	95	94	95	90	96	97	96	95	94	96	94	95	96	95	89
Russian Fed.	94	88	85	91	74	90	95	93	88	85	90	90	84	90	87	87
Serbia	na	na	na	na	na	na	na	na	na	na	na	na	na	na	na	na
Singapore	na	na	na	na	na	na	na	na	na	na	na	na	na	na	na	na
Slovakia	na	51	47	55	39	52	60	56	50	44	54	53	50	55	50	47
Slovenia	88	68	63	72	41	72	83	79	65	57	80	75	53	80	66	60
South Africa	84	na	na	na	na	na	na	na	na	na	na	na	na	na	na	na
Spain	82	66	61	72	46	60	83	82	54	53	73	66	50	83	66	47
Sweden	93	72	70	75	58	70	83	88	72	60	69	79	69	81	76	59
Switzerland	79	na	na	na	na	na	na	na	na	na	na	na	na	na	na	na
Taiwan	na	na	na	na	na	na	na	na	na	na	na	na	na	na	na	na
Tanzania	na	na	na	na	na	na	na	na	na	na	na	na	na	na	na	na
Turkey	93	93	92	95	91	96	94	93	95	92	91	95	94	94	95	94
Uganda	na	na	na	na	na	na	na	na	na	na	na	na	na	na	na	na
Ukraine	na	87	83	90	73	89	93	90	87	86	91	84	87	89	86	86
United States	74	na	na	na	na	na	na	na	na	na	na	na	na	na	na	na
Uruguay	na	na	na	na	na	na	na	na	na	na	na	na	na	na	na	na
Venezuela	na	na	na	na	na	na	na	na	na	na	na	na	na	na	na	na
Vietnam	na	na	na	na	na	na	na	na	na	na	na	na	na	na	na	na
Zimbabwe	na	na	na	na	na	na	na	na	na	na	na	na	na	na	na	na
Total	85	75	72	78	59	73	86	82	73	65	80	76	71	84	76	60

RANKING

Country	2000
Malta	96
Romania	95
Turkey	93
Latvia	93
Hungary	91
Russian Fed.	88
Lithuania	88
Croatia	87
Ukraine	87
Bulgaria	84
Poland	84
Estonia	81
Belgium	80
Finland	79
Czech Republic	77
Belarus	76
Austria	75
Iceland	72
Sweden	72
Ireland	72
Italy	71
Portugal	70
France	69
Northern Ireland	69
Germany	68
Slovenia	68
Luxembourg	67
Spain	66
Denmark	62
Great Britain	52
Slovakia	51
Greece	51
Netherlands	47
Total	75

F127_1) JUSTIFIABLE: LYING

Please tell me for each of the following statements whether you think it can always be justified, never be justified, or something in between: Lying in your own interest

Never justifiable (%)

(EVS: V229)

Country	Wave 1990	Wave 2000	Gender Male	Gender Female	Age 16-29	Age 30-49	Age 50+	Education Lower	Education Middle	Education Upper	Income Lower	Income Middle	Income Upper	Values Mat	Values Mixed	Values Postm.
Albania	na	na	na	na	na	na	na	na	na	na	na	na	na	na	na	na
Algeria	na	na	na	na	na	na	na	na	na	na	na	na	na	na	na	na
Argentina	65	na	na	na	na	na	na	na	na	na	na	na	na	na	na	na
Armenia	na	na	na	na	na	na	na	na	na	na	na	na	na	na	na	na
Australia	na	na	na	na	na	na	na	na	na	na	na	na	na	na	na	na
Austria	39	33	30	36	28	30	39	37	31	25	39	32	29	49	35	26
Azerbaijan	na	na	na	na	na	na	na	na	na	na	na	na	na	na	na	na
Bangladesh	na	na	na	na	na	na	na	na	na	na	na	na	na	na	na	na
Belarus	47	20	16	22	10	17	30	29	16	18	26	16	16	21	19	11
Belgium	30	31	30	32	16	30	39	36	30	28	36	36	24	33	30	31
Bosnia and Herz.	na	na	na	na	na	na	na	na	na	na	na	na	na	na	na	na
Brazil	63	na	na	na	na	na	na	na	na	na	na	na	na	na	na	na
Bulgaria	70	80	80	79	64	78	88	88	75	76	88	77	71	80	78	83
Canada	46	na	na	na	na	na	na	na	na	na	na	na	na	na	na	na
Chile	64	na	na	na	na	na	na	na	na	na	na	na	na	na	na	na
China	34	na	na	na	na	na	na	na	na	na	na	na	na	na	na	na
Colombia	na	na	na	na	na	na	na	na	na	na	na	na	na	na	na	na
Croatia	na	56	50	60	39	56	66	57	55	51	64	54	53	60	55	50
Czech Republic	29	34	31	37	22	29	44	38	30	25	45	33	23	38	33	24
Denmark	59	61	57	64	45	60	70	68	52	49	65	59	55	67	62	55
Dominican Rep.	na	na	na	na	na	na	na	na	na	na	na	na	na	na	na	na
Egypt	na	na	na	na	na	na	na	na	na	na	na	na	na	na	na	na
El Salvador	na	na	na	na	na	na	na	na	na	na	na	na	na	na	na	na
Estonia	47	36	34	38	27	32	45	34	36	41	41	37	34	40	33	17
Finland	31	40	35	46	21	36	55	46	32	37	44	39	37	36	42	38
France	34	34	32	37	20	31	44	40	24	28	40	33	31	42	33	28
Georgia	na	na	na	na	na	na	na	na	na	na	na	na	na	na	na	na
Germany	37	30	27	32	17	27	39	34	26	32	35	27	25	32	28	33
Great Britain	40	40	36	43	19	37	51	43	34	37	43	39	35	33	32	38
Greece	na	33	33	33	22	38	49	57	37	26	43	30	25	33	32	38
Hungary	40	48	49	48	35	38	66	52	42	37	47	49	48	52	45	51
Iceland	69	69	65	73	51	72	81	77	68	55	73	72	61	73	70	54
India	58	na	na	na	na	na	na	na	na	na	na	na	na	na	na	na
Indonesia	na	na	na	na	na	na	na	na	na	na	na	na	na	na	na	na
Iran	na	na	na	na	na	na	na	na	na	na	na	na	na	na	na	na
Ireland	52	54	48	60	37	52	71	67	47	50	67	53	43	54	56	49
Israel	na	na	na	na	na	na	na	na	na	na	na	na	na	na	na	na
Italy	50	51	46	55	30	49	63	59	45	44	59	46	45	57	51	48
Japan	55	na	na	na	na	na	na	na	na	na	na	na	na	na	na	na
Jordan	na	na	na	na	na	na	na	na	na	na	na	na	na	na	na	na
Korea, South	70	na	na	na	na	na	na	na	na	na	na	na	na	na	na	na
Latvia	61	60	53	65	38	56	71	68	57	57	65	61	51	64	58	38
Lithuania	58	35	29	40	23	32	46	45	31	33	47	40	28	35	34	36
Luxembourg	na	40	40	41	24	42	50	46	39	36	40	47	40	39	43	36
Macedonia	na	na	na	na	na	na	na	na	na	na	na	na	na	na	na	na
Malta	na	76	73	79	64	79	82	84	74	67	81	79	67	76	76	76
Mexico	31	na	na	na	na	na	na	na	na	na	na	na	na	na	na	na
Moldova	na	na	na	na	na	na	na	na	na	na	na	na	na	na	na	na
Montenegro	na	na	na	na	na	na	na	na	na	na	na	na	na	na	na	na
Morocco	na	na	na	na	na	na	na	na	na	na	na	na	na	na	na	na
Netherlands	25	27	22	32	13	24	38	34	28	20	25	29	26	30	29	22
New Zealand	na	na	na	na	na	na	na	na	na	na	na	na	na	na	na	na
Nigeria	45	na	na	na	na	na	na	na	na	na	na	na	na	na	na	na
Northern Ireland	60	54	48	59	46	48	65	59	51	49	59	54	51	65	53	44
Norway	56	na	na	na	na	na	na	na	na	na	na	na	na	na	na	na
Pakistan	na	na	na	na	na	na	na	na	na	na	na	na	na	na	na	na
Peru	na	na	na	na	na	na	na	na	na	na	na	na	na	na	na	na
Philippines	na	na	na	na	na	na	na	na	na	na	na	na	na	na	na	na
Poland	63	59	58	61	43	60	69	62	56	55	60	61	52	58	61	52
Portugal	38	56	53	59	48	51	65	60	48	50	68	49	48	57	55	57
Puerto Rico	na	na	na	na	na	na	na	na	na	na	na	na	na	na	na	na
Romania	38	51	47	55	36	48	62	63	44	47	58	51	46	53	49	45
Russian Fed.	50	32	30	34	19	30	43	42	33	25	38	34	26	34	30	32
Serbia	na	na	na	na	na	na	na	na	na	na	na	na	na	na	na	na
Singapore	na	na	na	na	na	na	na	na	na	na	na	na	na	na	na	na
Slovakia	na	31	29	32	24	28	39	33	30	27	39	31	27	29	31	38
Slovenia	67	56	53	58	31	60	69	63	54	50	65	58	47	64	55	50
South Africa	62	na	na	na	na	na	na	na	na	na	na	na	na	na	na	na
Spain	52	41	37	44	30	35	52	51	35	29	52	42	32	49	42	29
Sweden	55	41	38	45	27	38	53	60	37	34	42	44	39	42	43	38
Switzerland	51	na	na	na	na	na	na	na	na	na	na	na	na	na	na	na
Taiwan	na	na	na	na	na	na	na	na	na	na	na	na	na	na	na	na
Tanzania	na	na	na	na	na	na	na	na	na	na	na	na	na	na	na	na
Turkey	67	84	81	87	78	89	87	87	78	86	83	87	79	81	84	87
Uganda	na	na	na	na	na	na	na	na	na	na	na	na	na	na	na	na
Ukraine	na	44	41	46	25	42	56	55	40	45	53	37	40	45	44	62
United States	56	na	na	na	na	na	na	na	na	na	na	na	na	na	na	na
Uruguay	na	na	na	na	na	na	na	na	na	na	na	na	na	na	na	na
Venezuela	na	na	na	na	na	na	na	na	na	na	na	na	na	na	na	na
Vietnam	na	na	na	na	na	na	na	na	na	na	na	na	na	na	na	na
Zimbabwe	na	na	na	na	na	na	na	na	na	na	na	na	na	na	na	na
Total	**50**	**46**	**43**	**49**	**32**	**44**	**57**	**53**	**42**	**40**	**52**	**45**	**40**	**48**	**46**	**40**

RANKING

Country	2000
Turkey	84
Bulgaria	80
Malta	76
Iceland	69
Denmark	61
Latvia	60
Poland	59
Portugal	56
Croatia	56
Slovenia	56
Ireland	54
Northern Ireland	54
Romania	51
Italy	51
Hungary	48
Ukraine	44
Sweden	41
Spain	41
Finland	40
Luxembourg	40
Great Britain	40
Estonia	36
Lithuania	35
France	34
Czech Republic	34
Austria	33
Greece	33
Russian Fed.	32
Belgium	31
Slovakia	31
Germany	30
Netherlands	27
Belarus	20
Total	**46**

F128_1) JUSTIFIABLE: ADULTERY

Please tell me for each of the following statements whether you think it can always be justified, never be justified, or something in between: Married men/women having an affair

Never justifiable (%)

(EVS: V230)

Country	Wave 1990	Wave 2000	Gender Male	Gender Female	Age 16-29	Age 30-49	Age 50+	Education Lower	Education Middle	Education Upper	Income Lower	Income Middle	Income Upper	Values Mat	Values Mixed	Values Postm.
Albania	na	na	na	na	na	na	na	na	na	na	na	na	na	na	na	na
Algeria	na	na	na	na	na	na	na	na	na	na	na	na	na	na	na	na
Argentina	72	na	na	na	na	na	na	na	na	na	na	na	na	na	na	na
Armenia	na	na	na	na	na	na	na	na	na	na	na	na	na	na	na	23
Australia	na	na	na	na	na	na	na	na	na	na	na	na	na	na	na	na
Austria	52	50	45	55	44	47	57	58	48	29	55	48	46	69	52	41
Azerbaijan	na	na	na	na	na	na	na	na	na	na	na	na	na	na	na	na
Bangladesh	na	na	na	na	na	na	na	na	na	na	na	na	na	na	na	na
Belarus	45	37	27	45	31	34	45	44	33	43	42	36	30	37	37	26
Belgium	52	54	48	60	48	49	62	68	54	44	57	56	50	62	55	43
Bosnia and Herz.	na	na	na	na	na	na	na	na	na	na	na	na	na	na	na	na
Brazil	68	na	na	na	na	na	na	na	na	na	na	na	na	na	na	na
Bulgaria	49	40	33	47	28	26	58	57	33	26	58	36	27	44	36	43
Canada	55	na	na	na	na	na	na	na	na	na	na	na	na	na	na	na
Chile	63	na	na	na	na	na	na	na	na	na	na	na	na	na	na	na
China	72	na	na	na	na	na	na	na	na	na	na	na	na	na	na	na
Colombia	na	na	na	na	na	na	na	na	na	na	na	na	na	na	na	na
Croatia	na	59	52	66	42	61	68	65	55	57	62	57	62	73	59	48
Czech Republic	31	40	36	44	35	32	49	45	36	27	48	41	29	44	40	31
Denmark	67	67	65	69	68	65	69	75	58	58	70	67	56	80	70	49
Dominican Rep.	na	na	na	na	na	na	na	na	na	na	na	na	na	na	na	na
Egypt	na	na	na	na	na	na	na	na	na	na	na	na	na	na	na	na
El Salvador	na	na	na	na	na	na	na	na	na	na	na	na	na	na	na	na
Estonia	31	36	28	41	34	27	44	37	37	29	36	41	34	35	36	13
Finland	42	53	50	55	50	47	59	58	46	45	57	51	49	50	54	50
France	35	38	33	42	36	34	42	42	37	27	45	37	31	48	37	23
Georgia	na	na	na	na	na	na	na	na	na	na	na	na	na	na	na	na
Germany	57	41	36	45	27	39	51	47	36	39	44	41	33	42	43	36
Great Britain	53	55	50	59	39	55	61	57	56	40	53	56	56	na	na	na
Greece	na	43	35	49	36	45	60	79	45	34	48	43	38	48	43	39
Hungary	64	66	55	75	51	62	78	69	62	56	62	71	62	68	64	52
Iceland	72	79	74	84	74	80	82	85	80	64	79	82	75	87	80	55
India	91	na	na	na	na	na	na	na	na	na	na	na	na	na	na	na
Indonesia	na	na	na	na	na	na	na	na	na	na	na	na	na	na	na	na
Iran	na	na	na	na	na	na	na	na	na	na	na	na	na	na	na	na
Ireland	69	73	68	78	61	69	86	82	71	62	84	75	62	80	74	58
Israel	na	na	na	na	na	na	na	na	na	na	na	na	na	na	na	na
Italy	52	51	43	58	39	46	62	62	44	36	61	47	40	64	52	42
Japan	47	na	na	na	na	na	na	na	na	na	na	na	na	na	na	na
Jordan	na	na	na	na	na	na	na	na	na	na	na	na	na	na	na	na
Korea, South	72	na	na	na	na	na	na	na	na	na	na	na	na	na	na	na
Latvia	48	46	41	51	31	42	56	61	43	38	51	48	39	49	44	40
Lithuania	61	60	50	68	45	52	77	80	53	50	70	63	54	61	58	60
Luxembourg	na	56	52	59	45	54	65	61	53	55	50	66	55	58	59	42
Macedonia	na	na	na	na	na	na	na	na	na	na	na	na	na	na	na	na
Malta	na	94	91	97	92	95	95	97	94	89	96	94	90	93	94	91
Mexico	43	na	na	na	na	na	na	na	na	na	na	na	na	na	na	na
Moldova	na	na	na	na	na	na	na	na	na	na	na	na	na	na	na	na
Montenegro	na	na	na	na	na	na	na	na	na	na	na	na	na	na	na	na
Morocco	na	na	na	na	na	na	na	na	na	na	na	na	na	na	na	na
Netherlands	45	49	44	53	51	43	53	65	50	32	50	50	42	62	51	37
New Zealand	na	na	na	na	na	na	na	na	na	na	na	na	na	na	na	na
Nigeria	58	na	na	na	na	na	na	na	na	na	na	na	na	na	na	na
Northern Ireland	78	74	71	76	65	70	84	80	70	66	78	77	63	81	73	69
Norway	62	na	na	na	na	na	na	na	na	na	na	na	na	na	na	na
Pakistan	na	na	na	na	na	na	na	na	na	na	na	na	na	na	na	na
Peru	na	na	na	na	na	na	na	na	na	na	na	na	na	na	na	na
Philippines	na	na	na	na	na	na	na	na	na	na	na	na	na	na	na	na
Poland	69	67	63	71	56	68	73	73	64	47	67	70	59	69	66	60
Portugal	62	59	50	67	50	53	69	64	47	55	66	59	47	60	59	48
Puerto Rico	na	na	na	na	na	na	na	na	na	na	na	na	na	na	na	na
Romania	62	72	65	78	56	69	83	84	67	61	80	73	64	79	66	49
Russian Fed.	51	49	47	51	38	48	58	63	50	38	56	52	41	52	48	39
Serbia	na	na	na	na	na	na	na	na	na	na	na	na	na	na	na	na
Singapore	na	na	na	na	na	na	na	na	na	na	na	na	na	na	na	na
Slovakia	na	36	29	44	28	33	47	47	33	27	44	39	31	41	34	13
Slovenia	43	44	39	49	35	39	57	62	41	24	52	45	31	56	43	37
South Africa	73	na	na	na	na	na	na	na	na	na	na	na	na	na	na	na
Spain	59	54	44	63	37	50	67	69	42	46	63	58	41	68	53	35
Sweden	63	51	53	48	49	47	55	68	50	38	50	55	45	58	53	40
Switzerland	56	na	na	na	na	na	na	na	na	na	na	na	na	na	na	na
Taiwan	na	na	na	na	na	na	na	na	na	na	na	na	na	na	na	na
Tanzania	na	na	na	na	na	na	na	na	na	na	na	na	na	na	na	na
Turkey	87	na	na	na	na	na	na	na	na	na	na	na	na	na	na	na
Uganda	na	na	na	na	na	na	na	na	na	na	na	na	na	na	na	na
Ukraine	na	57	48	64	37	56	68	72	55	51	66	50	51	59	54	61
United States	71	na	na	na	na	na	na	na	na	na	na	na	na	na	na	na
Uruguay	na	na	na	na	na	na	na	na	na	na	na	na	na	na	na	na
Venezuela	na	na	na	na	na	na	na	na	na	na	na	na	na	na	na	na
Vietnam	na	na	na	na	na	na	na	na	na	na	na	na	na	na	na	na
Zimbabwe	na	na	na	na	na	na	na	na	na	na	na	na	na	na	na	na
Total	58	55	49	60	46	51	64	63	51	46	59	56	48	59	55	44

RANKING

Country	2000
Malta	94
Iceland	79
Northern Ireland	74
Ireland	73
Romania	72
Denmark	67
Poland	67
Hungary	66
Lithuania	60
Croatia	59
Portugal	59
Ukraine	57
Luxembourg	56
Great Britain	55
Belgium	54
Spain	54
Finland	53
Italy	51
Sweden	51
Austria	50
Russian Fed.	49
Netherlands	49
Latvia	46
Slovenia	44
Greece	43
Germany	41
Bulgaria	40
Czech Republic	40
France	38
Belarus	37
Slovakia	36
Estonia	36
Total	55

F129_1) JUSTIFIABLE: THROWING AWAY LITTER

Please tell me for each of the following statements whether you think it can always be justified, never be justified, or something in between: Throwing away litter in a public place

Never justifiable (%)

(EVS: V237)

Country	Wave 1990	Wave 2000	Gender Male	Gender Female	Age 16-29	Age 30-49	Age 50+	Education Lower	Education Middle	Education Upper	Income Lower	Income Middle	Income Upper	Values Mat	Values Mixed	Values Postm.
Albania	na	na	na	na	na	na	na	na	na	na	na	na	na	na	na	na
Algeria	na	na	na	na	na	na	na	na	na	na	na	na	na	na	na	na
Argentina	na	na	na	na	na	na	na	na	na	na	na	na	na	na	na	na
Armenia	na	na	na	na	na	na	na	na	na	na	na	na	na	na	na	na
Australia	na	na	na	na	na	na	na	na	na	na	na	na	na	na	na	na
Austria	na	57	55	59	49	55	63	63	54	40	55	59	54	67	61	48
Azerbaijan	na	na	na	na	na	na	na	na	na	na	na	na	na	na	na	na
Bangladesh	na	na	na	na	na	na	na	na	na	na	na	na	na	na	na	na
Belarus	na	44	38	50	33	46	51	44	42	52	49	46	33	46	43	38
Belgium	na	79	77	82	63	78	87	82	82	74	84	83	74	81	79	77
Bosnia and Herz.	na	na	na	na	na	na	na	na	na	na	na	na	na	na	na	na
Brazil	na	na	na	na	na	na	na	na	na	na	na	na	na	na	na	na
Bulgaria	na	76	76	76	62	79	79	77	75	76	77	78	72	76	77	89
Canada	na	na	na	na	na	na	na	na	na	na	na	na	na	na	na	na
Chile	na	na	na	na	na	na	na	na	na	na	na	na	na	na	na	na
China	na	na	na	na	na	na	na	na	na	na	na	na	na	na	na	na
Colombia	na	na	na	na	na	na	na	na	na	na	na	na	na	na	na	na
Croatia	na	90	90	89	89	88	93	95	86	87	90	91	88	91	90	89
Czech Republic	na	68	65	72	55	67	76	69	68	64	75	69	64	69	69	64
Denmark	na	80	77	82	67	80	87	86	77	73	80	79	80	84	80	83
Dominican Rep.	na	na	na	na	na	na	na	na	na	na	na	na	na	na	na	na
Egypt	na	na	na	na	na	na	na	na	na	na	na	na	na	na	na	na
El Salvador	na	na	na	na	na	na	na	na	na	na	na	na	na	na	na	na
Estonia	na	62	56	67	53	60	69	59	63	66	64	64	61	62	62	55
Finland	na	51	48	55	31	46	67	58	42	48	54	52	48	53	52	41
France	na	76	76	76	65	76	82	79	73	72	74	78	78	76	77	75
Georgia	na	na	na	na	na	na	na	na	na	na	na	na	na	na	na	na
Germany	na	52	51	53	41	50	59	57	46	55	54	52	47	51	53	50
Great Britain	na	49	42	56	30	48	58	47	49	45	49	47	51	na	na	na
Greece	na	60	57	62	56	62	65	69	61	57	69	60	50	57	61	61
Hungary	na	68	66	70	60	62	79	70	67	63	72	70	65	70	67	73
Iceland	na	63	58	68	38	65	80	69	57	60	66	63	57	66	63	54
India	na	na	na	na	na	na	na	na	na	na	na	na	na	na	na	na
Indonesia	na	na	na	na	na	na	na	na	na	na	na	na	na	na	na	na
Iran	na	na	na	na	na	na	na	na	na	na	na	na	na	na	na	na
Ireland	na	71	69	72	64	73	75	69	69	77	75	64	73	68	71	71
Israel	na	na	na	na	na	na	na	na	na	na	na	na	na	na	na	na
Italy	na	74	72	76	62	77	78	75	73	73	75	71	71	75	74	74
Japan	na	na	na	na	na	na	na	na	na	na	na	na	na	na	na	na
Jordan	na	na	na	na	na	na	na	na	na	na	na	na	na	na	na	na
Korea, South	na	na	na	na	na	na	na	na	na	na	na	na	na	na	na	na
Latvia	na	84	82	86	69	87	88	84	84	84	87	86	82	87	83	77
Lithuania	na	64	59	67	55	62	71	68	62	60	67	63	62	57	65	73
Luxembourg	na	71	69	73	61	73	75	72	71	70	63	77	76	67	73	68
Macedonia	na	na	na	na	na	na	na	na	na	na	na	na	na	na	na	na
Malta	na	95	93	97	96	96	94	95	95	94	96	94	96	95	96	94
Mexico	na	na	na	na	na	na	na	na	na	na	na	na	na	na	na	na
Moldova	na	na	na	na	na	na	na	na	na	na	na	na	na	na	na	na
Montenegro	na	na	na	na	na	na	na	na	na	na	na	na	na	na	na	na
Morocco	na	na	na	na	na	na	na	na	na	na	na	na	na	na	na	na
Netherlands	na	66	60	72	43	66	80	74	63	63	70	66	63	71	66	66
New Zealand	na	na	na	na	na	na	na	na	na	na	na	na	na	na	na	na
Nigeria	na	na	na	na	na	na	na	na	na	na	na	na	na	na	na	na
Northern Ireland	na	53	49	56	48	46	63	57	47	56	60	49	60	56	53	47
Norway	na	na	na	na	na	na	na	na	na	na	na	na	na	na	na	na
Pakistan	na	na	na	na	na	na	na	na	na	na	na	na	na	na	na	na
Peru	na	na	na	na	na	na	na	na	na	na	na	na	na	na	na	na
Philippines	na	na	na	na	na	na	na	na	na	na	na	na	na	na	na	na
Poland	na	69	69	68	57	70	73	70	68	65	69	69	66	68	68	72
Portugal	na	68	67	69	72	63	69	67	67	77	66	58	73	73	65	69
Puerto Rico	na	na	na	na	na	na	na	na	na	na	na	na	na	na	na	na
Romania	na	86	84	87	79	84	90	88	84	84	89	84	86	84	87	80
Russian Fed.	na	75	70	78	68	76	78	75	75	75	74	77	76	75	75	74
Serbia	na	na	na	na	na	na	na	na	na	na	na	na	na	na	na	na
Singapore	na	na	na	na	na	na	na	na	na	na	na	na	na	na	na	na
Slovakia	na	39	36	42	31	39	45	40	38	45	39	42	39	39	39	48
Slovenia	na	71	65	75	55	74	78	76	70	63	76	76	63	73	71	69
South Africa	na	na	na	na	na	na	na	na	na	na	na	na	na	na	na	na
Spain	na	65	64	66	59	64	70	68	61	67	74	69	59	66	65	66
Sweden	na	44	45	43	31	43	52	59	37	43	48	45	38	56	45	38
Switzerland	na	na	na	na	na	na	na	na	na	na	na	na	na	na	na	na
Taiwan	na	na	na	na	na	na	na	na	na	na	na	na	na	na	na	na
Tanzania	na	na	na	na	na	na	na	na	na	na	na	na	na	na	na	na
Turkey	na	89	87	91	87	91	89	88	89	92	86	89	93	87	90	94
Uganda	na	na	na	na	na	na	na	na	na	na	na	na	na	na	na	na
Ukraine	na	66	63	69	55	67	73	68	66	66	72	63	64	69	66	76
United States	na	na	na	na	na	na	na	na	na	na	na	na	na	na	na	na
Uruguay	na	na	na	na	na	na	na	na	na	na	na	na	na	na	na	na
Venezuela	na	na	na	na	na	na	na	na	na	na	na	na	na	na	na	na
Vietnam	na	na	na	na	na	na	na	na	na	na	na	na	na	na	na	na
Zimbabwe	na	na	na	na	na	na	na	na	na	na	na	na	na	na	na	na
Total	na	67	64	69	57	67	74	70	65	65	69	67	65	68	68	65

RANKING

Country	2000
Malta	95
Croatia	90
Turkey	89
Romania	86
Latvia	84
Denmark	80
Belgium	79
France	76
Bulgaria	76
Russian Fed.	75
Italy	74
Luxembourg	71
Ireland	71
Slovenia	71
Poland	69
Hungary	68
Czech Republic	68
Portugal	68
Ukraine	66
Netherlands	66
Spain	65
Lithuania	64
Iceland	63
Estonia	62
Greece	60
Austria	57
Northern Ireland	53
Germany	52
Finland	51
Great Britain	49
Belarus	44
Sweden	44
Slovakia	39
Total	67

F130_1) JUSTIFIABLE: DRIVING UNDER INFLUENCE OF ALCOHOL

Please tell me for each of the following statements whether you think it can always be justified, never be justified, or something in between: Driving under the influence of alcohol

Never justifiable (%)

(EVS: V238)

Country	Wave 1990	Wave 2000	Gender Male	Gender Female	Age 16-29	Age 30-49	Age 50+	Education Lower	Education Middle	Education Upper	Income Lower	Income Middle	Income Upper	Values Mat	Values Mixed	Values Postm.
Albania	na	na	na	na	na	na	na	na	na	na	na	na	na	na	na	na
Algeria	na	na	na	na	na	na	na	na	na	na	na	na	na	na	na	na
Argentina	na	na	na	na	na	na	na	na	na	na	na	na	na	na	na	na
Armenia	na	na	na	na	na	na	na	na	na	na	na	na	na	na	na	na
Australia	na	na	na	na	na	na	na	na	na	na	na	na	na	na	na	na
Austria	na	75	69	81	69	73	81	78	74	70	73	77	73	85	76	73
Azerbaijan	na	na	na	na	na	na	na	na	na	na	na	na	na	na	na	na
Bangladesh	na	na	na	na	na	na	na	na	na	na	na	na	na	na	na	na
Belarus	na	56	46	63	42	59	63	62	53	53	62	55	44	56	55	48
Belgium	na	74	65	82	67	68	82	80	75	67	78	77	67	81	74	67
Bosnia and Herz.	na	na	na	na	na	na	na	na	na	na	na	na	na	na	na	na
Brazil	na	na	na	na	na	na	na	na	na	na	na	na	na	na	na	na
Bulgaria	na	81	79	83	69	81	88	89	77	77	90	77	76	84	79	81
Canada	na	na	na	na	na	na	na	na	na	na	na	na	na	na	na	na
Chile	na	na	na	na	na	na	na	na	na	na	na	na	na	na	na	na
China	na	na	na	na	na	na	na	na	na	na	na	na	na	na	na	na
Colombia	na	na	na	na	na	na	na	na	na	na	na	na	na	na	na	na
Croatia	na	80	70	89	64	82	88	88	75	76	90	80	76	88	82	68
Czech Republic	na	73	67	80	63	71	81	76	73	64	82	73	66	76	74	66
Denmark	na	93	89	96	92	93	94	94	91	92	95	93	90	93	93	93
Dominican Rep.	na	na	na	na	na	na	na	na	na	na	na	na	na	na	na	na
Egypt	na	na	na	na	na	na	na	na	na	na	na	na	na	na	na	na
El Salvador	na	na	na	na	na	na	na	na	na	na	na	na	na	na	na	na
Estonia	na	75	67	81	69	71	81	75	76	71	80	81	67	79	73	65
Finland	na	82	75	89	69	83	88	85	79	78	80	81	84	80	83	77
France	na	66	59	73	56	64	74	70	62	62	69	67	61	70	68	57
Georgia	na	na	na	na	na	na	na	na	na	na	na	na	na	na	na	na
Germany	na	78	75	81	72	79	80	77	79	84	79	76	75	87	76	76
Great Britain	na	81	76	85	74	80	84	81	84	71	82	75	82	na	na	na
Greece	na	69	66	70	63	73	74	83	70	65	76	70	59	67	69	72
Hungary	na	90	87	93	89	86	95	90	92	86	91	92	89	92	90	82
Iceland	na	78	72	85	72	77	86	87	77	63	83	81	70	83	80	60
India	na	na	na	na	na	na	na	na	na	na	na	na	na	na	na	na
Indonesia	na	na	na	na	na	na	na	na	na	na	na	na	na	na	na	na
Iran	na	na	na	na	na	na	na	na	na	na	na	na	na	na	na	na
Ireland	na	82	78	86	80	81	87	85	80	81	84	82	80	81	82	84
Israel	na	na	na	na	na	na	na	na	na	na	na	na	na	na	na	na
Italy	na	81	76	85	67	82	87	86	76	77	86	81	74	84	82	78
Japan	na	na	na	na	na	na	na	na	na	na	na	na	na	na	na	na
Jordan	na	na	na	na	na	na	na	na	na	na	na	na	na	na	na	na
Korea, South	na	na	na	na	na	na	na	na	na	na	na	na	na	na	na	na
Latvia	na	79	72	85	63	81	84	80	80	75	83	80	76	81	78	72
Lithuania	na	76	67	84	70	72	84	85	73	69	87	77	68	79	74	81
Luxembourg	na	55	51	60	48	54	62	61	55	46	50	59	58	56	57	44
Macedonia	na	na	na	na	na	na	na	na	na	na	na	na	na	na	na	na
Malta	na	95	92	98	93	95	96	97	94	93	95	94	94	95	93	92
Mexico	na	na	na	na	na	na	na	na	na	na	na	na	na	na	na	na
Moldova	na	na	na	na	na	na	na	na	na	na	na	na	na	na	na	na
Montenegro	na	na	na	na	na	na	na	na	na	na	na	na	na	na	na	na
Morocco	na	na	na	na	na	na	na	na	na	na	na	na	na	na	na	na
Netherlands	na	76	67	83	66	77	79	81	76	70	75	79	72	82	76	72
New Zealand	na	na	na	na	na	na	na	na	na	na	na	na	na	na	na	na
Nigeria	na	na	na	na	na	na	na	na	na	na	na	na	na	na	na	na
Northern Ireland	na	87	83	91	89	85	90	87	87	89	92	89	86	89	87	83
Norway	na	na	na	na	na	na	na	na	na	na	na	na	na	na	na	na
Pakistan	na	na	na	na	na	na	na	na	na	na	na	na	na	na	na	na
Peru	na	na	na	na	na	na	na	na	na	na	na	na	na	na	na	na
Philippines	na	na	na	na	na	na	na	na	na	na	na	na	na	na	na	na
Poland	na	90	86	95	87	91	92	89	91	94	90	92	89	92	91	80
Portugal	na	70	65	74	72	64	73	71	65	71	81	65	64	70	69	67
Puerto Rico	na	na	na	na	na	na	na	na	na	na	na	na	na	na	na	na
Romania	na	87	84	91	78	88	92	93	85	83	91	88	86	88	88	76
Russian Fed.	na	77	70	84	63	76	88	86	77	73	80	81	74	78	76	73
Serbia	na	na	na	na	na	na	na	na	na	na	na	na	na	na	na	na
Singapore	na	na	na	na	na	na	na	na	na	na	na	na	na	na	na	na
Slovakia	na	54	45	61	46	53	60	57	52	52	56	58	52	58	50	56
Slovenia	na	68	58	76	53	68	77	76	65	60	73	69	59	77	67	60
South Africa	na	na	na	na	na	na	na	na	na	na	na	na	na	na	na	na
Spain	na	75	70	79	66	72	82	82	69	68	79	80	64	82	74	69
Sweden	na	83	78	88	79	81	88	92	81	79	83	88	78	83	84	81
Switzerland	na	na	na	na	na	na	na	na	na	na	na	na	na	na	na	na
Taiwan	na	na	na	na	na	na	na	na	na	na	na	na	na	na	na	na
Tanzania	na	na	na	na	na	na	na	na	na	na	na	na	na	na	na	na
Turkey	na	93	91	95	91	95	92	93	92	95	92	93	93	92	93	95
Uganda	na	na	na	na	na	na	na	na	na	na	na	na	na	na	na	na
Ukraine	na	74	65	80	56	74	83	83	72	72	80	70	71	73	73	86
United States	na	na	na	na	na	na	na	na	na	na	na	na	na	na	na	na
Uruguay	na	na	na	na	na	na	na	na	na	na	na	na	na	na	na	na
Venezuela	na	na	na	na	na	na	na	na	na	na	na	na	na	na	na	na
Vietnam	na	na	na	na	na	na	na	na	na	na	na	na	na	na	na	na
Zimbabwe	na	na	na	na	na	na	na	na	na	na	na	na	na	na	na	na
Total	na	77	71	82	69	76	83	82	75	73	81	78	73	79	77	72

RANKING

Country	2000
Malta	95
Denmark	93
Turkey	93
Poland	90
Hungary	90
Romania	87
Northern Ireland	87
Sweden	83
Finland	82
Ireland	82
Bulgaria	81
Great Britain	81
Italy	81
Croatia	80
Latvia	79
Germany	78
Iceland	78
Russian Fed.	77
Lithuania	76
Netherlands	76
Austria	75
Estonia	75
Spain	75
Belgium	74
Ukraine	74
Czech Republic	73
Portugal	70
Greece	69
Slovenia	68
France	66
Belarus	56
Luxembourg	55
Slovakia	54
Total	77

F131_1) JUSTIFIABLE: AVOID TAXES

Please tell me for each of the following statements whether you think it can always be justified, never be justified, or something in between: Paying cash for services to avoid taxes

Never justifiable (%)

(EVS: V239)

Country	Wave 1990	Wave 2000	Gender Male	Gender Female	Age 16-29	Age 30-49	Age 50+	Education Lower	Education Middle	Education Upper	Income Lower	Income Middle	Income Upper	Values Mat	Values Mixed	Values Postm.
Albania	na	na	na	na	na	na	na	na	na	na	na	na	na	na	na	na
Algeria	na	na	na	na	na	na	na	na	na	na	na	na	na	na	na	na
Argentina	na	na	na	na	na	na	na	na	na	na	na	na	na	na	na	na
Armenia	na	na	na	na	na	na	na	na	na	na	na	na	na	na	na	na
Australia	na	na	na	na	na	na	na	na	na	na	na	na	na	na	na	na
Austria	na	37	34	40	36	32	43	43	35	21	42	33	34	56	38	31
Azerbaijan	na	na	na	na	na	na	na	na	na	na	na	na	na	na	na	na
Bangladesh	na	na	na	na	na	na	na	na	na	na	na	na	na	na	na	na
Belarus	na	26	23	29	16	27	36	33	23	31	34	24	18	29	25	11
Belgium	na	27	25	29	18	23	35	34	25	24	33	27	23	31	26	27
Bosnia and Herz.	na	na	na	na	na	na	na	na	na	na	na	na	na	na	na	na
Brazil	na	na	na	na	na	na	na	na	na	na	na	na	na	na	na	na
Bulgaria	na	77	75	79	61	73	88	84	73	74	87	76	70	79	76	76
Canada	na	na	na	na	na	na	na	na	na	na	na	na	na	na	na	na
Chile	na	na	na	na	na	na	na	na	na	na	na	na	na	na	na	na
China	na	na	na	na	na	na	na	na	na	na	na	na	na	na	na	na
Colombia	na	na	na	na	na	na	na	na	na	na	na	na	na	na	na	na
Croatia	na	58	53	63	42	60	67	69	53	46	69	56	55	62	58	55
Czech Republic	na	46	39	52	33	41	57	48	45	34	57	45	36	47	46	38
Denmark	na	24	22	26	16	20	32	27	23	16	31	21	21	34	22	25
Dominican Rep.	na	na	na	na	na	na	na	na	na	na	na	na	na	na	na	na
Egypt	na	na	na	na	na	na	na	na	na	na	na	na	na	na	na	na
El Salvador	na	na	na	na	na	na	na	na	na	na	na	na	na	na	na	na
Estonia	na	40	35	45	27	34	53	40	42	35	52	43	35	40	41	20
Finland	na	30	26	33	14	24	43	34	24	24	31	31	24	33	29	26
France	na	32	27	36	23	31	36	35	27	28	35	32	32	36	31	27
Georgia	na	na	na	na	na	na	na	na	na	na	na	na	na	na	na	na
Germany	na	42	41	44	34	39	49	47	36	50	45	38	35	45	40	46
Great Britain	na	34	29	39	20	29	44	35	31	30	38	35	31	na	na	na
Greece	na	34	31	37	29	35	47	50	36	30	41	32	31	34	34	36
Hungary	na	53	51	56	47	43	67	60	41	43	55	59	48	57	50	50
Iceland	na	44	43	46	32	47	51	53	41	35	48	44	40	51	44	32
India	na	na	na	na	na	na	na	na	na	na	na	na	na	na	na	na
Indonesia	na	na	na	na	na	na	na	na	na	na	na	na	na	na	na	na
Iran	na	na	na	na	na	na	na	na	na	na	na	na	na	na	na	na
Ireland	na	48	44	51	47	39	59	55	45	41	61	41	42	48	48	43
Israel	na	na	na	na	na	na	na	na	na	na	na	na	na	na	na	na
Italy	na	54	52	55	43	53	60	59	50	52	58	54	44	53	55	51
Japan	na	na	na	na	na	na	na	na	na	na	na	na	na	na	na	na
Jordan	na	na	na	na	na	na	na	na	na	na	na	na	na	na	na	na
Korea, South	na	na	na	na	na	na	na	na	na	na	na	na	na	na	na	na
Latvia	na	46	39	51	27	40	58	59	44	35	55	51	32	47	46	35
Lithuania	na	30	25	34	15	22	49	46	24	28	37	41	23	27	30	34
Luxembourg	na	29	29	30	19	28	37	38	25	26	32	32	26	29	31	22
Macedonia	na	na	na	na	na	na	na	na	na	na	na	na	na	na	na	na
Malta	na	72	70	74	62	73	77	76	70	70	75	76	68	72	72	70
Mexico	na	na	na	na	na	na	na	na	na	na	na	na	na	na	na	na
Moldova	na	na	na	na	na	na	na	na	na	na	na	na	na	na	na	na
Montenegro	na	na	na	na	na	na	na	na	na	na	na	na	na	na	na	na
Morocco	na	na	na	na	na	na	na	na	na	na	na	na	na	na	na	na
Netherlands	na	16	13	18	6	15	22	25	14	8	17	14	14	23	16	12
New Zealand	na	na	na	na	na	na	na	na	na	na	na	na	na	na	na	na
Nigeria	na	na	na	na	na	na	na	na	na	na	na	na	na	na	na	na
Northern Ireland	na	50	44	56	42	44	60	56	46	46	59	50	42	64	49	39
Norway	na	na	na	na	na	na	na	na	na	na	na	na	na	na	na	na
Pakistan	na	na	na	na	na	na	na	na	na	na	na	na	na	na	na	na
Peru	na	na	na	na	na	na	na	na	na	na	na	na	na	na	na	na
Philippines	na	na	na	na	na	na	na	na	na	na	na	na	na	na	na	na
Poland	na	44	42	47	33	45	52	50	40	33	45	46	39	43	45	47
Portugal	na	57	59	56	53	49	67	60	48	61	69	51	54	57	57	59
Puerto Rico	na	na	na	na	na	na	na	na	na	na	na	na	na	na	na	na
Romania	na	56	49	63	47	49	68	67	50	52	64	57	50	56	54	49
Russian Fed.	na	41	36	45	27	37	56	52	42	32	52	43	31	44	39	40
Serbia	na	na	na	na	na	na	na	na	na	na	na	na	na	na	na	na
Singapore	na	na	na	na	na	na	na	na	na	na	na	na	na	na	na	na
Slovakia	na	24	21	27	18	25	27	29	22	17	26	29	20	23	25	18
Slovenia	na	44	39	48	23	46	57	56	41	33	54	42	34	53	43	36
South Africa	na	na	na	na	na	na	na	na	na	na	na	na	na	na	na	na
Spain	na	41	38	43	29	36	51	54	31	30	51	40	30	52	39	30
Sweden	na	26	23	28	23	22	31	40	21	21	30	26	19	29	26	23
Switzerland	na	na	na	na	na	na	na	na	na	na	na	na	na	na	na	na
Taiwan	na	na	na	na	na	na	na	na	na	na	na	na	na	na	na	na
Tanzania	na	na	na	na	na	na	na	na	na	na	na	na	na	na	na	na
Turkey	na	87	85	89	84	90	88	87	87	88	86	88	87	89	87	90
Uganda	na	na	na	na	na	na	na	na	na	na	na	na	na	na	na	na
Ukraine	na	42	39	45	22	38	57	56	41	37	49	40	35	44	40	50
United States	na	na	na	na	na	na	na	na	na	na	na	na	na	na	na	na
Uruguay	na	na	na	na	na	na	na	na	na	na	na	na	na	na	na	na
Venezuela	na	na	na	na	na	na	na	na	na	na	na	na	na	na	na	na
Vietnam	na	na	na	na	na	na	na	na	na	na	na	na	na	na	na	na
Zimbabwe	na	na	na	na	na	na	na	na	na	na	na	na	na	na	na	na
Total	na	42	38	45	32	38	51	49	39	35	48	41	37	47	41	36

RANKING

Country	2000
Turkey	87
Bulgaria	77
Malta	72
Croatia	58
Portugal	57
Romania	56
Italy	54
Hungary	53
Northern Ireland	50
Ireland	48
Latvia	46
Czech Republic	46
Poland	44
Iceland	44
Slovenia	44
Germany	42
Ukraine	42
Russian Fed.	41
Spain	41
Estonia	40
Austria	37
Greece	34
Great Britain	34
France	32
Finland	30
Lithuania	30
Luxembourg	29
Belgium	27
Belarus	26
Sweden	26
Slovakia	24
Denmark	24
Netherlands	16
Total	42

F132_1) JUSTIFIABLE: HAVING CASUAL SEX

Please tell me for each of the following statements whether you think it can always be justified, never be justified, or something in between: Having casual sex

Never justifiable (%)

(EVS: V240)

Country	Wave 1990	Wave 2000	Gender Male	Gender Female	Age 16-29	Age 30-49	Age 50+	Education Lower	Education Middle	Education Upper	Income Lower	Income Middle	Income Upper	Values Mat	Values Mixed	Values Postm.
Albania	na	na	na	na	na	na	na	na	na	na	na	na	na	na	na	na
Algeria	na	na	na	na	na	na	na	na	na	na	na	na	na	na	na	na
Argentina	na	na	na	na	na	na	na	na	na	na	na	na	na	na	na	na
Armenia	na	na	na	na	na	na	na	na	na	na	na	na	na	na	na	na
Australia	na	na	na	na	na	na	na	na	na	na	na	na	na	na	na	na
Austria	na	46	41	51	28	42	60	56	40	27	56	47	40	68	49	36
Azerbaijan	na	na	na	na	na	na	na	na	na	na	na	na	na	na	na	na
Bangladesh	na	na	na	na	na	na	na	na	na	na	na	na	na	na	na	na
Belarus	na	29	18	37	18	25	42	42	25	22	36	27	20	31	26	20
Belgium	na	54	47	61	33	48	69	68	55	42	61	58	47	65	54	39
Bosnia and Herz.	na	na	na	na	na	na	na	na	na	na	na	na	na	na	na	na
Brazil	na	na	na	na	na	na	na	na	na	na	na	na	na	na	na	na
Bulgaria	na	51	43	59	30	46	66	68	42	43	65	52	40	56	46	51
Canada	na	na	na	na	na	na	na	na	na	na	na	na	na	na	na	na
Chile	na	na	na	na	na	na	na	na	na	na	na	na	na	na	na	na
China	na	na	na	na	na	na	na	na	na	na	na	na	na	na	na	na
Colombia	na	na	na	na	na	na	na	na	na	na	na	na	na	na	na	na
Croatia	na	62	49	73	44	63	72	71	58	51	69	60	61	75	62	52
Czech Republic	na	41	31	51	31	33	53	44	40	29	49	44	30	43	42	32
Denmark	na	46	41	52	27	43	61	56	35	34	50	44	41	59	49	30
Dominican Rep.	na	na	na	na	na	na	na	na	na	na	na	na	na	na	na	na
Egypt	na	na	na	na	na	na	na	na	na	na	na	na	na	na	na	na
El Salvador	na	na	na	na	na	na	na	na	na	na	na	na	na	na	na	na
Estonia	na	42	29	52	29	33	57	42	43	39	48	48	38	42	42	29
Finland	na	34	30	37	18	27	49	40	24	28	37	35	29	32	35	29
France	na	36	29	43	26	32	46	43	29	25	40	40	30	47	37	20
Georgia	na	na	na	na	na	na	na	na	na	na	na	na	na	na	na	na
Germany	na	39	37	41	26	35	49	49	30	33	45	40	35	37	42	36
Great Britain	na	37	32	43	19	31	51	44	31	26	37	34	33	na	na	na
Greece	na	21	16	25	12	25	38	52	22	15	26	21	16	23	22	14
Hungary	na	56	44	67	42	53	69	60	52	42	59	61	50	58	54	56
Iceland	na	21	18	23	7	18	36	24	21	12	22	20	18	26	20	11
India	na	na	na	na	na	na	na	na	na	na	na	na	na	na	na	na
Indonesia	na	na	na	na	na	na	na	na	na	na	na	na	na	na	na	na
Iran	na	na	na	na	na	na	na	na	na	na	na	na	na	na	na	na
Ireland	na	55	50	60	25	52	81	71	50	39	69	56	43	54	55	53
Israel	na	na	na	na	na	na	na	na	na	na	na	na	na	na	na	na
Italy	na	49	38	58	28	44	64	64	39	32	58	47	37	63	51	37
Japan	na	na	na	na	na	na	na	na	na	na	na	na	na	na	na	na
Jordan	na	na	na	na	na	na	na	na	na	na	na	na	na	na	na	na
Korea, South	na	na	na	na	na	na	na	na	na	na	na	na	na	na	na	na
Latvia	na	59	47	68	36	59	68	68	56	55	63	61	55	63	58	37
Lithuania	na	58	44	69	41	49	77	80	50	48	72	61	48	59	57	49
Luxembourg	na	44	40	48	24	44	58	53	41	32	43	57	38	45	47	34
Macedonia	na	na	na	na	na	na	na	na	na	na	na	na	na	na	na	na
Malta	na	94	90	97	88	95	90	97	93	89	97	93	91	93	95	88
Mexico	na	na	na	na	na	na	na	na	na	na	na	na	na	na	na	na
Moldova	na	na	na	na	na	na	na	na	na	na	na	na	na	na	na	na
Montenegro	na	na	na	na	na	na	na	na	na	na	na	na	na	na	na	na
Morocco	na	na	na	na	na	na	na	na	na	na	na	na	na	na	na	na
Netherlands	na	41	35	46	26	32	58	61	41	21	44	41	33	63	41	29
New Zealand	na	na	na	na	na	na	na	na	na	na	na	na	na	na	na	na
Nigeria	na	na	na	na	na	na	na	na	na	na	na	na	na	na	na	na
Northern Ireland	na	51	47	55	31	39	72	61	44	44	60	50	42	59	53	40
Norway	na	na	na	na	na	na	na	na	na	na	na	na	na	na	na	na
Pakistan	na	na	na	na	na	na	na	na	na	na	na	na	na	na	na	na
Peru	na	na	na	na	na	na	na	na	na	na	na	na	na	na	na	na
Philippines	na	na	na	na	na	na	na	na	na	na	na	na	na	na	na	na
Poland	na	61	56	66	38	61	75	66	58	49	66	59	54	66	58	54
Portugal	na	51	38	62	39	47	61	56	39	49	65	49	41	54	50	40
Puerto Rico	na	na	na	na	na	na	na	na	na	na	na	na	na	na	na	na
Romania	na	73	61	83	52	71	85	83	67	68	80	72	69	75	72	47
Russian Fed.	na	45	38	51	27	42	62	63	46	35	54	46	37	47	44	36
Serbia	na	na	na	na	na	na	na	na	na	na	na	na	na	na	na	na
Singapore	na	na	na	na	na	na	na	na	na	na	na	na	na	na	na	na
Slovakia	na	37	28	45	26	33	49	48	33	26	46	36	33	41	33	28
Slovenia	na	38	30	46	20	37	53	55	34	27	49	42	24	50	36	35
South Africa	na	na	na	na	na	na	na	na	na	na	na	na	na	na	na	na
Spain	na	34	22	45	13	28	52	53	19	23	46	35	20	48	32	17
Sweden	na	27	29	24	13	25	37	50	21	17	21	33	26	33	29	17
Switzerland	na	na	na	na	na	na	na	na	na	na	na	na	na	na	na	na
Taiwan	na	na	na	na	na	na	na	na	na	na	na	na	na	na	na	na
Tanzania	na	na	na	na	na	na	na	na	na	na	na	na	na	na	na	na
Turkey	na	79	74	84	72	84	87	86	69	65	84	78	70	84	79	73
Uganda	na	na	na	na	na	na	na	na	na	na	na	na	na	na	na	na
Ukraine	na	50	37	60	27	48	65	65	49	43	61	42	43	53	46	60
United States	na	na	na	na	na	na	na	na	na	na	na	na	na	na	na	na
Uruguay	na	na	na	na	na	na	na	na	na	na	na	na	na	na	na	na
Venezuela	na	na	na	na	na	na	na	na	na	na	na	na	na	na	na	na
Vietnam	na	na	na	na	na	na	na	na	na	na	na	na	na	na	na	na
Zimbabwe	na	na	na	na	na	na	na	na	na	na	na	na	na	na	na	na
Total	na	47	39	53	30	43	61	56	43	36	53	47	41	53	47	35

RANKING

Country	2000
Malta	94
Turkey	79
Romania	73
Croatia	62
Poland	61
Latvia	59
Lithuania	58
Hungary	56
Ireland	55
Belgium	54
Bulgaria	51
Northern Ireland	51
Portugal	51
Ukraine	50
Italy	49
Austria	46
Denmark	46
Russian Fed.	45
Luxembourg	44
Estonia	42
Czech Republic	41
Netherlands	41
Germany	39
Slovenia	38
Great Britain	37
Slovakia	37
France	36
Spain	34
Finland	34
Belarus	29
Sweden	27
Greece	21
Iceland	21
Total	47

F133_1) JUSTIFIABLE: SMOKING IN PUBLIC BUILDINGS

Please tell me for each of the following statements whether you think it can always be justified, never be justified, or something in between: smoking in public buildings

Never justifiable (%)

(EVS: V241)

Country	Wave 1990	Wave 2000	Gender Male	Gender Female	Age 16-29	Age 30-49	Age 50+	Education Lower	Education Middle	Education Upper	Income Lower	Income Middle	Income Upper	Values Mat	Values Mixed	Values Postm.
Albania	na	na	na	na	na	na	na	na	na	na	na	na	na	na	na	na
Algeria	na	na	na	na	na	na	na	na	na	na	na	na	na	na	na	na
Argentina	na	na	na	na	na	na	na	na	na	na	na	na	na	na	na	na
Armenia	na	na	na	na	na	na	na	na	na	na	na	na	na	na	na	na
Australia	na	na	na	na	na	na	na	na	na	na	na	na	na	na	na	na
Austria	na	24	25	23	17	19	33	27	23	16	28	25	21	43	26	16
Azerbaijan	na	na	na	na	na	na	na	na	na	na	na	na	na	na	na	na
Bangladesh	na	na	na	na	na	na	na	na	na	na	na	na	na	na	na	na
Belarus	na	22	17	25	13	21	29	25	20	20	26	21	14	22	20	13
Belgium	na	49	45	52	37	42	60	50	50	45	54	50	44	48	49	46
Bosnia and Herz.	na	na	na	na	na	na	na	na	na	na	na	na	na	na	na	na
Brazil	na	na	na	na	na	na	na	na	na	na	na	na	na	na	na	na
Bulgaria	na	38	34	42	32	30	49	48	35	30	48	35	31	41	36	42
Canada	na	na	na	na	na	na	na	na	na	na	na	na	na	na	na	na
Chile	na	na	na	na	na	na	na	na	na	na	na	na	na	na	na	na
China	na	na	na	na	na	na	na	na	na	na	na	na	na	na	na	na
Colombia	na	na	na	na	na	na	na	na	na	na	na	na	na	na	na	na
Croatia	na	52	48	57	37	52	63	60	48	49	65	50	48	56	54	42
Czech Republic	na	34	33	35	22	29	46	34	36	32	41	35	29	34	36	29
Denmark	na	26	25	26	18	23	32	28	26	21	28	28	19	28	27	19
Dominican Rep.	na	na	na	na	na	na	na	na	na	na	na	na	na	na	na	na
Egypt	na	na	na	na	na	na	na	na	na	na	na	na	na	na	na	na
El Salvador	na	na	na	na	na	na	na	na	na	na	na	na	na	na	na	na
Estonia	na	34	32	36	28	28	43	33	36	31	38	35	34	35	34	29
Finland	na	38	36	40	24	34	50	41	33	38	38	37	37	40	37	37
France	na	42	38	45	29	37	53	45	35	38	42	40	42	46	42	35
Georgia	na	na	na	na	na	na	na	na	na	na	na	na	na	na	na	na
Germany	na	25	24	26	15	22	33	29	22	20	31	24	22	25	25	26
Great Britain	na	31	28	34	16	22	44	33	27	27	37	24	32	na	na	na
Greece	na	22	22	23	13	25	41	44	27	14	29	20	18	23	23	20
Hungary	na	51	48	55	46	43	63	52	55	43	51	52	52	54	51	41
Iceland	na	44	44	44	33	41	57	49	43	37	48	43	41	47	44	32
India	na	na	na	na	na	na	na	na	na	na	na	na	na	na	na	na
Indonesia	na	na	na	na	na	na	na	na	na	na	na	na	na	na	na	na
Iran	na	na	na	na	na	na	na	na	na	na	na	na	na	na	na	na
Ireland	na	43	41	44	36	40	51	41	45	41	45	42	40	44	44	37
Israel	na	na	na	na	na	na	na	na	na	na	na	na	na	na	na	na
Italy	na	39	39	39	21	38	49	46	33	37	46	38	34	47	40	34
Japan	na	na	na	na	na	na	na	na	na	na	na	na	na	na	na	na
Jordan	na	na	na	na	na	na	na	na	na	na	na	na	na	na	na	na
Korea, South	na	na	na	na	na	na	na	na	na	na	na	na	na	na	na	na
Latvia	na	51	43	58	37	45	63	59	49	49	53	53	50	55	51	35
Lithuania	na	32	23	40	19	26	48	46	27	31	44	36	26	25	35	37
Luxembourg	na	25	26	25	19	25	30	32	20	27	29	29	25	30	26	20
Macedonia	na	na	na	na	na	na	na	na	na	na	na	na	na	na	na	na
Malta	na	89	85	92	83	90	91	92	87	88	92	89	87	89	89	84
Mexico	na	na	na	na	na	na	na	na	na	na	na	na	na	na	na	na
Moldova	na	na	na	na	na	na	na	na	na	na	na	na	na	na	na	na
Montenegro	na	na	na	na	na	na	na	na	na	na	na	na	na	na	na	na
Morocco	na	na	na	na	na	na	na	na	na	na	na	na	na	na	na	na
Netherlands	na	31	27	34	15	25	46	38	30	26	35	32	25	34	30	32
New Zealand	na	na	na	na	na	na	na	na	na	na	na	na	na	na	na	na
Nigeria	na	na	na	na	na	na	na	na	na	na	na	na	na	na	na	na
Northern Ireland	na	35	34	36	28	29	45	38	34	32	37	31	38	44	34	30
Norway	na	na	na	na	na	na	na	na	na	na	na	na	na	na	na	na
Pakistan	na	na	na	na	na	na	na	na	na	na	na	na	na	na	na	na
Peru	na	na	na	na	na	na	na	na	na	na	na	na	na	na	na	na
Philippines	na	na	na	na	na	na	na	na	na	na	na	na	na	na	na	na
Poland	na	39	36	42	21	36	53	42	35	38	43	37	34	41	38	33
Portugal	na	36	33	40	26	33	45	40	27	39	54	36	29	40	35	33
Puerto Rico	na	na	na	na	na	na	na	na	na	na	na	na	na	na	na	na
Romania	na	57	51	63	41	52	70	71	52	45	65	57	50	63	52	37
Russian Fed.	na	42	35	47	29	39	53	50	42	35	50	42	34	42	42	37
Serbia	na	na	na	na	na	na	na	na	na	na	na	na	na	na	na	na
Singapore	na	na	na	na	na	na	na	na	na	na	na	na	na	na	na	na
Slovakia	na	32	28	36	25	33	37	35	30	32	37	34	29	32	31	32
Slovenia	na	46	44	47	32	42	61	58	43	34	57	48	32	52	46	36
South Africa	na	na	na	na	na	na	na	na	na	na	na	na	na	na	na	na
Spain	na	33	28	37	23	29	41	41	24	34	41	38	28	39	34	22
Sweden	na	40	42	38	26	40	48	50	39	33	36	47	35	55	40	37
Switzerland	na	na	na	na	na	na	na	na	na	na	na	na	na	na	na	na
Taiwan	na	na	na	na	na	na	na	na	na	na	na	na	na	na	na	na
Tanzania	na	na	na	na	na	na	na	na	na	na	na	na	na	na	na	na
Turkey	na	74	73	75	71	77	78	79	69	67	80	73	67	72	77	71
Uganda	na	na	na	na	na	na	na	na	na	na	na	na	na	na	na	na
Ukraine	na	43	35	49	29	39	54	54	41	40	50	39	39	45	42	59
United States	na	na	na	na	na	na	na	na	na	na	na	na	na	na	na	na
Uruguay	na	na	na	na	na	na	na	na	na	na	na	na	na	na	na	na
Venezuela	na	na	na	na	na	na	na	na	na	na	na	na	na	na	na	na
Vietnam	na	na	na	na	na	na	na	na	na	na	na	na	na	na	na	na
Zimbabwe	na	na	na	na	na	na	na	na	na	na	na	na	na	na	na	na
Total	na	39	37	42	28	36	50	44	38	34	44	39	36	43	40	33

RANKING

Country	2000
Malta	89
Turkey	74
Romania	57
Croatia	52
Hungary	51
Latvia	51
Belgium	49
Slovenia	46
Iceland	44
Ireland	43
Ukraine	43
Russian Fed.	42
France	42
Sweden	40
Italy	39
Poland	39
Bulgaria	38
Finland	38
Portugal	36
Northern Ireland	35
Czech Republic	34
Estonia	34
Spain	33
Lithuania	32
Slovakia	32
Netherlands	31
Great Britain	31
Denmark	26
Luxembourg	25
Germany	25
Austria	24
Greece	22
Belarus	22
Total	39

F134_1) JUSTIFIABLE: SPEEDING OVER LIMIT

Please tell me for each of the following statements whether you think it can always be justified, never be justified, or something in between: Speeding over the limit in built-up areas

Never justifiable (%)

(EVS: V242)

Country	Wave 1990	Wave 2000	Gender Male	Gender Female	Age 16-29	Age 30-49	Age 50+	Education Lower	Education Middle	Education Upper	Income Lower	Income Middle	Income Upper	Values Mat	Values Mixed	Values Postm.
Albania	na	na	na	na	na	na	na	na	na	na	na	na	na	na	na	na
Algeria	na	na	na	na	na	na	na	na	na	na	na	na	na	na	na	na
Argentina	na	na	na	na	na	na	na	na	na	na	na	na	na	na	na	na
Armenia	na	na	na	na	na	na	na	na	na	na	na	na	na	na	na	na
Australia	na	na	na	na	na	na	na	na	na	na	na	na	na	na	na	na
Austria	na	58	53	64	46	57	66	64	56	43	57	60	59	72	62	49
Azerbaijan	na	na	na	na	na	na	na	na	na	na	na	na	na	na	na	na
Bangladesh	na	na	na	na	na	na	na	na	na	na	na	na	na	na	na	na
Belarus	na	22	15	27	12	19	33	32	17	21	28	22	9	23	20	9
Belgium	na	59	53	65	36	54	74	73	59	49	71	62	49	66	58	52
Bosnia and Herz.	na	na	na	na	na	na	na	na	na	na	na	na	na	na	na	na
Brazil	na	na	na	na	na	na	na	na	na	na	na	na	na	na	na	na
Bulgaria	na	68	65	71	56	63	79	79	65	57	77	69	61	74	63	66
Canada	na	na	na	na	na	na	na	na	na	na	na	na	na	na	na	na
Chile	na	na	na	na	na	na	na	na	na	na	na	na	na	na	na	na
China	na	na	na	na	na	na	na	na	na	na	na	na	na	na	na	na
Colombia	na	na	na	na	na	na	na	na	na	na	na	na	na	na	na	na
Croatia	na	78	71	84	62	78	88	84	74	75	87	74	78	87	77	74
Czech Republic	na	50	44	56	39	44	62	55	48	34	62	51	41	57	49	43
Denmark	na	56	49	63	42	50	71	64	43	49	66	51	47	63	58	51
Dominican Rep.	na	na	na	na	na	na	na	na	na	na	na	na	na	na	na	na
Egypt	na	na	na	na	na	na	na	na	na	na	na	na	na	na	na	na
El Salvador	na	na	na	na	na	na	na	na	na	na	na	na	na	na	na	na
Estonia	na	54	44	63	37	51	67	54	57	48	61	61	48	61	49	59
Finland	na	37	30	44	17	33	52	44	27	30	44	34	29	36	37	38
France	na	45	40	50	30	41	56	50	37	38	51	44	40	52	44	36
Georgia	na	na	na	na	na	na	na	na	na	na	na	na	na	na	na	na
Germany	na	56	51	60	43	55	63	60	52	57	58	55	50	64	55	48
Great Britain	na	56	50	63	41	53	67	63	51	43	66	52	45	na	na	na
Greece	na	50	45	54	38	58	65	71	55	43	61	48	43	50	52	47
Hungary	na	67	59	74	57	60	79	72	63	46	74	68	63	76	60	40
Iceland	na	39	31	46	22	37	56	55	31	22	48	37	30	49	39	18
India	na	na	na	na	na	na	na	na	na	na	na	na	na	na	na	na
Indonesia	na	na	na	na	na	na	na	na	na	na	na	na	na	na	na	na
Iran	na	na	na	na	na	na	na	na	na	na	na	na	na	na	na	na
Ireland	na	69	65	73	65	67	77	76	69	57	81	68	57	67	69	69
Israel	na	na	na	na	na	na	na	na	na	na	na	na	na	na	na	na
Italy	na	48	42	54	32	45	59	60	40	35	58	48	33	56	49	43
Japan	na	na	na	na	na	na	na	na	na	na	na	na	na	na	na	na
Jordan	na	na	na	na	na	na	na	na	na	na	na	na	na	na	na	na
Korea, South	na	na	na	na	na	na	na	na	na	na	na	na	na	na	na	na
Latvia	na	66	57	74	41	67	76	72	66	57	74	69	55	75	62	52
Lithuania	na	55	47	62	35	51	73	77	48	45	69	62	45	55	54	68
Luxembourg	na	44	43	46	26	44	57	53	44	32	48	56	45	49	46	36
Macedonia	na	na	na	na	na	na	na	na	na	na	na	na	na	na	na	na
Malta	na	92	88	96	88	94	94	95	92	85	95	92	90	92	93	90
Mexico	na	na	na	na	na	na	na	na	na	na	na	na	na	na	na	na
Moldova	na	na	na	na	na	na	na	na	na	na	na	na	na	na	na	na
Montenegro	na	na	na	na	na	na	na	na	na	na	na	na	na	na	na	na
Morocco	na	na	na	na	na	na	na	na	na	na	na	na	na	na	na	na
Netherlands	na	60	51	68	43	56	73	71	59	51	66	63	49	72	58	61
New Zealand	na	na	na	na	na	na	na	na	na	na	na	na	na	na	na	na
Nigeria	na	na	na	na	na	na	na	na	na	na	na	na	na	na	na	na
Northern Ireland	na	63	58	67	55	56	73	72	55	55	71	64	61	67	61	60
Norway	na	na	na	na	na	na	na	na	na	na	na	na	na	na	na	na
Pakistan	na	na	na	na	na	na	na	na	na	na	na	na	na	na	na	na
Peru	na	na	na	na	na	na	na	na	na	na	na	na	na	na	na	na
Philippines	na	na	na	na	na	na	na	na	na	na	na	na	na	na	na	na
Poland	na	59	55	63	38	60	72	66	55	42	64	59	48	62	58	53
Portugal	na	50	45	54	38	45	61	56	38	40	65	48	44	52	50	44
Puerto Rico	na	na	na	na	na	na	na	na	na	na	na	na	na	na	na	na
Romania	na	68	61	75	50	63	82	81	63	56	78	71	59	74	64	44
Russian Fed.	na	59	51	67	41	56	75	72	59	53	68	62	49	61	57	53
Serbia	na	na	na	na	na	na	na	na	na	na	na	na	na	na	na	na
Singapore	na	na	na	na	na	na	na	na	na	na	na	na	na	na	na	na
Slovakia	na	29	25	33	20	30	36	35	27	23	36	33	23	31	27	22
Slovenia	na	50	44	55	28	48	68	67	47	33	61	53	31	61	48	47
South Africa	na	na	na	na	na	na	na	na	na	na	na	na	na	na	na	na
Spain	na	60	57	63	50	59	67	69	53	58	72	61	54	67	59	58
Sweden	na	39	35	42	23	38	48	54	35	31	43	43	26	41	40	35
Switzerland	na	na	na	na	na	na	na	na	na	na	na	na	na	na	na	na
Taiwan	na	na	na	na	na	na	na	na	na	na	na	na	na	na	na	na
Tanzania	na	na	na	na	na	na	na	na	na	na	na	na	na	na	na	na
Turkey	na	90	89	92	88	93	91	91	89	95	90	91	91	88	91	95
Uganda	na	na	na	na	na	na	na	na	na	na	na	na	na	na	na	na
Ukraine	na	58	48	65	36	57	70	70	56	53	67	53	52	61	54	67
United States	na	na	na	na	na	na	na	na	na	na	na	na	na	na	na	na
Uruguay	na	na	na	na	na	na	na	na	na	na	na	na	na	na	na	na
Venezuela	na	na	na	na	na	na	na	na	na	na	na	na	na	na	na	na
Vietnam	na	na	na	na	na	na	na	na	na	na	na	na	na	na	na	na
Zimbabwe	na	na	na	na	na	na	na	na	na	na	na	na	na	na	na	na
Total	na	55	49	61	41	53	67	63	53	47	63	55	48	60	54	50

RANKING

Country	2000
Malta	92
Turkey	90
Croatia	78
Ireland	69
Bulgaria	68
Romania	68
Hungary	67
Latvia	66
Northern Ireland	63
Spain	60
Netherlands	60
Russian Fed.	59
Poland	59
Belgium	59
Austria	58
Ukraine	58
Denmark	56
Great Britain	56
Germany	56
Lithuania	55
Estonia	54
Greece	50
Czech Republic	50
Slovenia	50
Portugal	50
Italy	48
France	45
Luxembourg	44
Iceland	39
Sweden	39
Finland	37
Slovakia	29
Belarus	22
Total	55

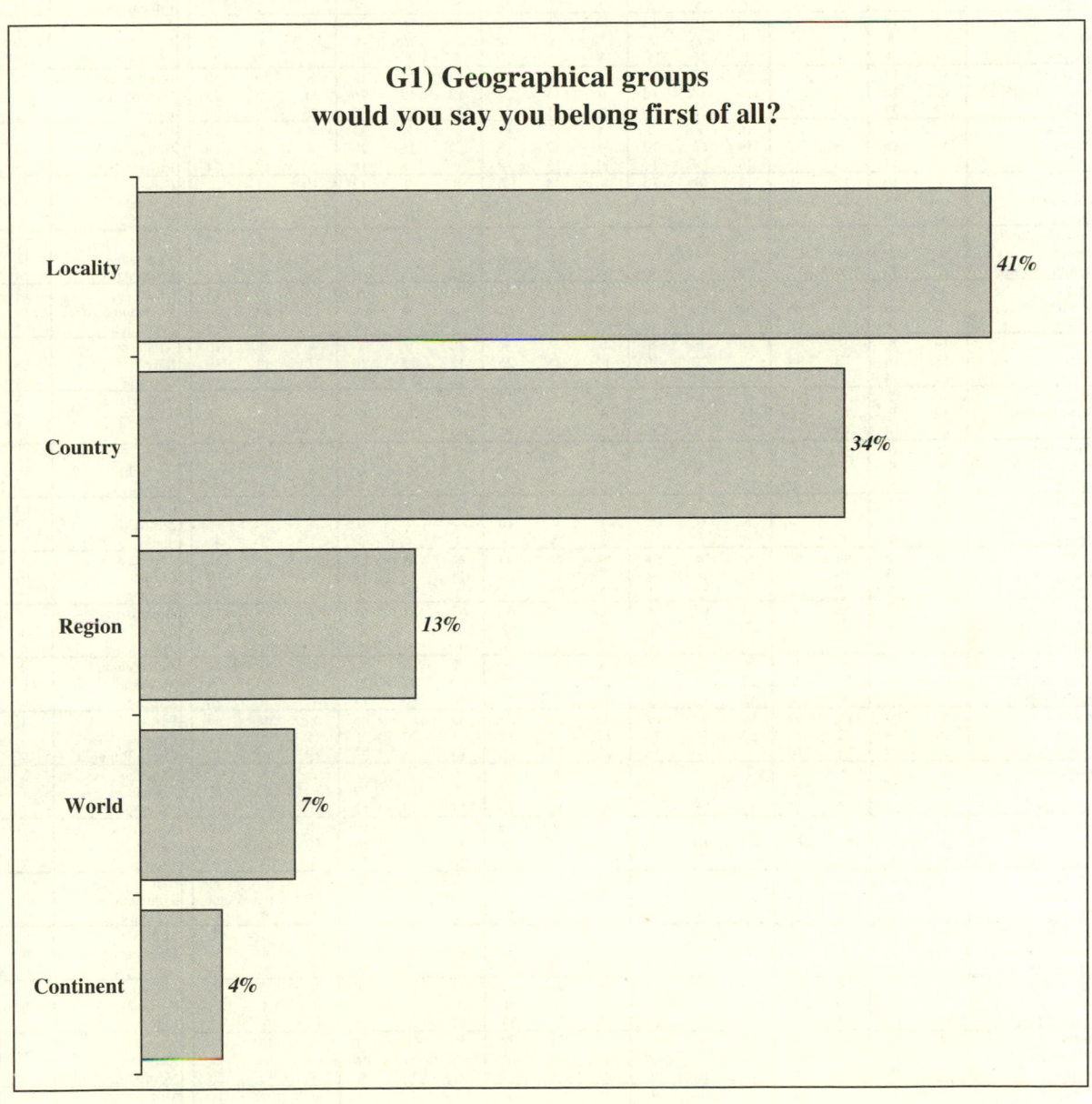

G001) BELONG FIRST TO CONTINENT OR THE WORLD

To which of these geographical groups would you say you belong first of all?

Continent / The world (%)

(WVS: V214; EVS: V251)

Country	Wave 1990	Wave 2000	Gender Male	Gender Female	Age 16-29	Age 30-49	Age 50+	Education Lower	Education Middle	Education Upper	Income Lower	Income Middle	Income Upper	Values Mat	Values Mixed	Values Postm.
Albania	na	2	2	2	4	1	1	1	2	4	1	3	3	1	2	na
Algeria	na	10	10	10	14	8	6	5	10	13	8	14	11	8	10	14
Argentina	11	13	13	13	15	15	9	11	15	22	9	14	15	8	12	19
Armenia	na	11	12	11	13	11	9	5	11	15	12	9	15	9	12	18
Australia	na	11	12	10	15	11	7	6	10	15	10	10	10	6	10	13
Austria	7	7	7	7	6	8	8	7	7	9	6	8	9	6	8	7
Azerbaijan	na	18	19	17	19	19	14	14	18	19	19	16	24	19	17	19
Bangladesh	na	3	4	2	4	2	5	1	4	8	2	2	5	2	4	8
Belarus	6	8	9	7	9	10	5	3	9	13	7	8	10	7	7	21
Belgium	18	17	19	14	20	20	12	8	16	24	17	15	17	8	15	30
Bosnia and Herz.	na	14	16	12	15	14	12	6	13	24	12	12	16	11	15	23
Brazil	22	29	30	28	32	28	26	26	31	31	28	27	30	26	29	34
Bulgaria	11	7	8	7	16	8	3	3	7	17	2	8	11	4	10	12
Canada	13	16	18	13	19	17	12	9	17	18	12	16	18	6	16	19
Chile	13	14	15	13	16	14	11	11	15	18	9	14	18	10	12	24
China	4	10	12	7	13	8	10	4	14	7	8	9	12	10	11	7
Colombia	na	14	14	13	16	13	11	11	14	17	13	12	16	11	15	17
Croatia	na	10	13	8	10	14	7	6	12	17	7	10	13	3	10	16
Czech Republic	13	8	9	7	12	9	5	7	8	13	8	7	9	3	9	14
Denmark	4	3	4	3	5	4	2	3	3	4	2	3	3	na	3	8
Dominican Rep.	na	33	34	32	32	34	36	28	23	37	22	35	44	28	34	35
Egypt	na	9	9	9	13	8	6	8	11	9	9	9	8	7	10	14
El Salvador	na	na	na	na	na	na	na	na	na	na	na	na	na	na	na	na
Estonia	5	5	6	4	8	6	3	2	5	11	3	5	6	5	5	12
Finland	14	8	9	6	10	6	8	6	9	9	10	6	7	4	8	16
France	18	16	18	14	19	20	10	11	18	25	13	15	20	7	12	39
Georgia	na	13	12	13	13	14	10	11	12	15	12	13	13	12	13	17
Germany	10	5	6	4	7	6	4	3	6	13	3	5	5	1	6	8
Great Britain	12	9	12	7	13	10	7	5	11	14	8	9	11	na	na	na
Greece	na	16	17	15	21	14	6	7	16	17	17	16	15	12	14	25
Hungary	9	6	8	5	11	8	2	5	8	11	7	5	8	4	8	26
Iceland	5	5	6	4	8	5	2	4	4	6	5	4	6	3	4	9
India	9	5	5	4	7	4	4	3	4	10	4	3	7	3	7	9
Indonesia	na	3	2	4	9	2	2	2	2	6	3	3	3	3	3	21
Iran	na	7	7	7	8	6	5	4	7	10	7	7	6	5	7	10
Ireland	5	4	4	3	2	5	3	1	5	4	4	4	4	1	3	8
Israel	na	na	na	na	na	na	na	na	na	na	na	na	na	na	na	na
Italy	20	13	14	12	15	16	9	7	15	24	11	13	16	7	11	19
Japan	3	2	2	3	3	2	2	2	2	3	3	1	2	1	2	5
Jordan	na	68	66	69	73	67	60	66	72	67	67	71	68	65	69	75
Korea, South	na	3	4	3	5	3	1	2	3	4	4	4	2	1	5	4
Latvia	5	7	10	5	15	7	4	8	6	9	6	6	8	5	8	9
Lithuania	6	7	8	6	8	8	4	6	6	10	5	7	8	6	6	14
Luxembourg	na	21	23	20	27	26	13	22	16	33	20	21	27	14	20	35
Macedonia	na	9	9	9	12	10	5	6	8	16	5	10	13	7	9	20
Malta	na	na	na	na	na	na	na	na	na	na	na	na	na	na	na	na
Mexico	18	19	22	17	22	20	14	14	24	32	14	20	26	15	20	31
Moldova	na	19	21	16	22	19	16	13	17	26	16	18	23	19	19	23
Montenegro	na	4	5	3	7	4	2	1	5	7	2	2	6	2	5	10
Morocco	na	9	11	6	11	7	7	7	14	17	7	10	15	7	10	15
Netherlands	13	13	14	11	16	15	8	8	12	18	12	13	12	6	13	16
New Zealand	na	9	9	9	13	9	8	5	9	13	10	8	10	4	9	13
Nigeria	20	11	11	11	13	10	7	10	10	15	9	9	16	10	11	13
Northern Ireland	8	4	5	4	7	7	2	3	5	7	3	4	7	5	3	6
Norway	4	6	7	4	9	6	3	4	5	9	na	na	na	6	6	8
Pakistan	na	na	na	na	na	na	na	na	na	na	na	na	na	na	na	na
Peru	na	8	10	7	8	9	7	8	8	9	9	6	10	5	9	8
Philippines	na	4	4	4	5	3	4	3	4	5	3	3	6	5	3	4
Poland	7	3	4	2	3	4	2	3	3	6	3	3	6	1	4	6
Portugal	14	6	7	5	9	8	3	3	11	13	2	7	9	4	6	13
Puerto Rico	na	17	16	18	16	19	17	22	18	17	19	15	18	25	17	17
Romania	5	5	5	5	7	5	4	3	5	9	4	4	6	4	4	18
Russian Fed.	16	16	17	15	21	18	11	12	17	17	14	16	18	13	19	12
Serbia	na	11	13	10	17	14	6	4	11	22	9	10	15	5	14	42
Singapore	na	na	na	na	na	na	na	na	na	na	na	na	na	na	na	na
Slovakia	na	9	10	8	11	10	6	6	9	17	6	8	9	5	11	24
Slovenia	4	6	7	5	8	7	4	5	7	7	4	5	7	3	6	10
South Africa	11	14	13	16	17	14	10	14	13	35	12	20	12	18	11	23
Spain	10	10	12	9	15	13	5	6	14	18	8	9	12	6	10	19
Sweden	7	10	10	10	12	10	7	3	11	13	11	8	6	6	9	13
Switzerland	12	23	24	22	35	26	11	14	24	35	20	19	26	12	21	34
Taiwan	na	15	18	11	12	15	14	11	14	19	13	13	17	12	17	19
Tanzania	na	8	8	8	10	6	8	7	8	11	7	8	11	9	8	17
Turkey	9	11	12	9	13	11	4	7	13	24	7	11	21	7	10	19
Uganda	na	19	14	23	17	20	20	27	16	9	16	12	17	22	19	7
Ukraine	na	17	20	14	25	17	11	10	16	23	15	18	18	13	19	43
United States	19	22	22	23	28	20	21	24	27	19	25	18	25	14	21	29
Uruguay	na	17	16	18	19	19	15	12	23	27	14	11	26	13	13	30
Venezuela	na	15	15	14	17	14	10	10	14	20	12	13	15	14	14	18
Vietnam	na	7	8	6	8	8	5	7	6	11	6	9	6	5	8	9
Zimbabwe	na	10	12	9	13	9	8	8	13	38	9	10	13	9	12	6
Total	11	11	12	11	15	12	8	8	12	16	10	11	13	9	11	18

RANKING

Country	2000
Jordan	68
Dominican Rep.	33
Brazil	29
Switzerland	23
United States	22
Luxembourg	21
Mexico	19
Uganda	19
Moldova	19
Azerbaijan	18
Puerto Rico	17
Uruguay	17
Ukraine	17
Belgium	17
Russian Fed.	16
Greece	16
France	16
Canada	16
Taiwan	15
Venezuela	15
South Africa	14
Chile	14
Bosnia and Herz.	14
Colombia	14
Argentina	13
Italy	13
Georgia	13
Netherlands	13
Armenia	11
Serbia	11
Nigeria	11
Australia	11
Turkey	11
Croatia	10
Zimbabwe	10
Spain	10
Algeria	10
China	10
Sweden	10
Great Britain	9
Egypt	9
Macedonia	9
New Zealand	9
Slovakia	9
Morocco	9
Peru	8
Belarus	8
Czech Republic	8
Tanzania	8
Finland	8
Bulgaria	7
Austria	7
Latvia	7
Vietnam	7
Iran	7
Lithuania	7
Hungary	6
Slovenia	6
Portugal	6
Norway	6
Estonia	5
Germany	5
India	5
Romania	5
Iceland	5
Northern Ireland	4
Montenegro	4
Philippines	4
Ireland	4
Korea, South	3
Bangladesh	3
Denmark	3
Poland	3
Indonesia	3
Japan	2
Albania	2
Total	11

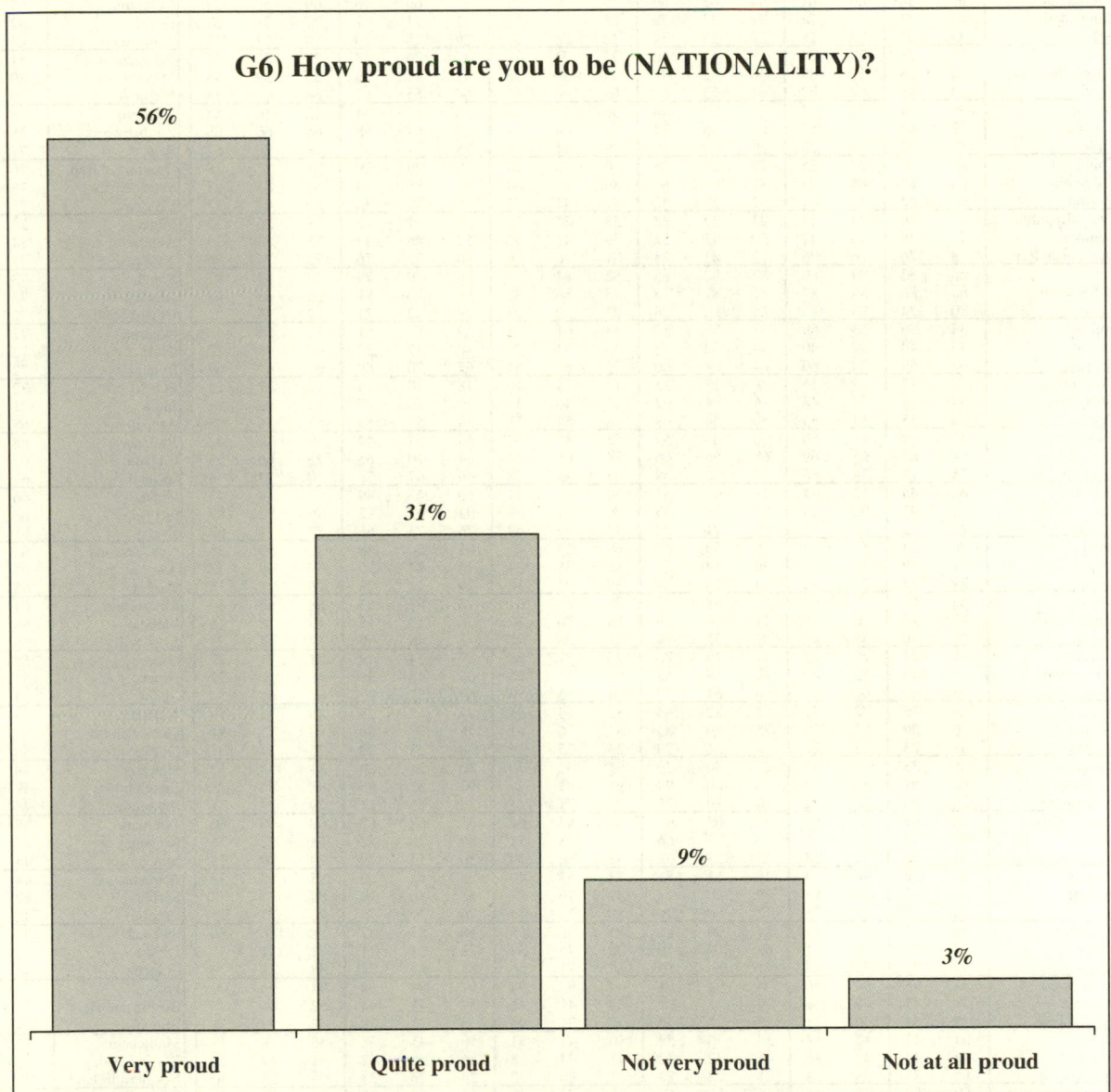

G6) How proud are you to be (NATIONALITY)?

56%

31%

9%

3%

Very proud   Quite proud   Not very proud   Not at all proud

G006) HOW PROUD OF YOUR NATIONALITY

How proud are you to be (NATIONALITY)?

Very proud (%)   (WVS: V216; EVS: V255)

Country	Wave 1990	Wave 2000	Gender Male	Gender Female	Age 16-29	Age 30-49	Age 50+	Education Lower	Education Middle	Education Upper	Income Lower	Income Middle	Income Upper	Values Mat	Values Mixed	Values Postm.
Albania	na	73	74	71	67	71	81	72	73	74	74	65	78	77	71	74
Algeria	na	74	73	74	68	75	83	80	73	71	75	71	72	78	71	71
Argentina	55	68	69	67	65	66	73	72	65	54	74	68	61	69	72	62
Armenia	na	44	46	41	39	48	45	50	44	39	47	36	46	42	44	52
Australia	na	73	73	74	68	72	81	83	74	65	75	72	73	73	75	72
Austria	53	53	52	53	47	49	59	57	52	35	51	50	57	55	59	39
Azerbaijan	na	64	66	61	64	62	66	75	59	71	55	60	76	69	55	57
Bangladesh	na	73	75	71	71	73	79	75	71	72	71	71	77	77	71	67
Belarus	35	27	25	28	22	23	34	32	26	21	29	28	20	29	27	16
Belgium	29	23	23	23	18	17	30	33	24	14	31	26	17	28	22	17
Bosnia and Herz.	na	38	37	39	36	32	47	49	36	33	47	41	29	34	39	33
Brazil	64	65	67	62	64	63	69	66	67	49	68	65	62	68	65	58
Bulgaria	39	34	32	37	28	27	44	36	33	36	36	33	34	32	36	38
Canada	61	67	66	67	62	65	72	74	64	64	64	67	68	68	66	68
Chile	53	72	70	73	69	69	79	79	71	59	75	71	67	78	70	67
China	43	26	27	25	29	25	26	20	30	24	20	29	29	27	27	28
Colombia	na	85	85	85	83	85	87	86	85	84	85	85	84	83	85	87
Croatia	na	42	42	41	31	39	52	47	41	32	56	40	36	50	41	37
Czech Republic	25	26	24	28	23	22	32	28	25	22	29	27	23	28	26	23
Denmark	42	48	49	47	50	43	52	59	41	32	52	48	43	55	50	39
Dominican Rep.	na	76	76	76	72	83	73	81	76	76	80	72	76	72	74	86
Egypt	na	82	84	80	82	82	83	82	84	79	86	79	79	78	84	87
El Salvador	na	86	84	87	82	87	90	87	86	82	89	86	84	na	na	na
Estonia	30	24	23	25	25	20	26	27	20	27	29	22	21	22	25	22
Finland	38	56	53	59	53	58	57	53	61	58	49	61	61	59	56	48
France	35	40	40	40	34	32	49	46	34	29	48	37	32	46	41	27
Georgia	na	65	70	60	64	64	66	73	64	61	65	70	60	67	63	69
Germany	29	17	19	15	9	13	23	19	14	16	18	20	15	18	17	14
Great Britain	54	51	54	48	36	44	62	56	46	43	49	50	47	na	na	na
Greece	na	55	54	55	50	54	68	68	57	51	59	52	53	63	56	48
Hungary	47	49	48	50	40	45	59	53	45	37	50	54	44	50	48	42
Iceland	54	67	65	69	68	66	66	74	65	54	64	70	65	75	66	55
India	75	71	74	66	73	70	69	66	73	78	66	67	76	70	73	76
Indonesia	na	48	53	44	43	48	51	54	48	44	50	47	49	54	47	43
Iran	na	92	92	93	91	93	95	96	91	89	92	92	92	96	92	83
Ireland	77	72	72	71	65	71	79	77	69	69	76	73	65	77	71	63
Israel	na	54	51	57	46	52	66	69	54	45	61	54	48	32	59	56
Italy	41	39	39	40	30	34	50	48	35	24	45	44	29	49	40	33
Japan	29	23	24	22	14	13	34	39	23	16	29	21	20	26	21	15
Jordan	na	68	72	64	65	68	72	73	66	61	73	67	63	68	68	59
Korea, South	45	17	20	15	11	16	29	34	20	12	22	13	15	19	16	15
Latvia	49	40	38	43	21	35	54	41	38	48	43	40	39	37	43	33
Lithuania	41	22	20	23	21	18	26	23	21	21	27	24	18	21	21	27
Luxembourg	na	49	52	47	40	38	63	59	51	25	65	48	35	66	50	27
Macedonia	na	61	60	61	50	61	70	54	65	59	63	57	62	62	61	34
Malta	na	75	72	77	63	72	84	83	74	55	77	75	69	80	74	59
Mexico	56	80	81	79	75	80	85	82	76	81	78	77	80	83	77	84
Moldova	na	23	25	22	18	21	29	23	25	19	26	23	20	25	17	31
Montenegro	na	33	33	32	26	30	39	35	32	30	30	34	29	31	34	52
Morocco	na	89	86	92	86	90	94	91	81	77	93	87	85	93	86	78
Netherlands	21	20	18	22	16	16	26	29	21	11	23	15	21	29	22	11
New Zealand	na	64	64	65	58	63	69	68	64	61	61	62	67	63	65	60
Nigeria	68	72	74	70	73	72	66	71	73	71	69	75	72	71	72	76
Northern Ireland	54	28	31	27	25	23	33	32	30	19	30	32	22	29	30	22
Norway	45	50	48	53	48	51	51	57	53	40	na	na	na	55	53	27
Pakistan	na	81	79	83	79	80	91	87	76	71	85	80	79	84	77	100
Peru	na	77	75	78	72	80	79	79	77	74	76	79	75	77	77	75
Philippines	na	87	87	87	84	90	86	85	90	85	88	87	87	88	86	86
Poland	69	72	72	71	69	67	79	75	73	54	72	71	71	71	71	81
Portugal	42	79	75	83	71	80	83	84	71	56	84	84	74	88	75	70
Puerto Rico	na	95	94	96	94	91	98	94	97	94	97	94	94	94	95	96
Romania	48	47	49	46	29	42	61	58	41	41	57	43	44	52	44	27
Russian Fed.	26	31	30	31	25	28	38	39	31	26	33	31	28	32	29	31
Serbia	na	42	40	44	30	36	53	50	41	31	50	45	38	46	38	38
Singapore	na	44	42	46	45	42	42	45	44	38	46	45	42	41	47	27
Slovakia	na	25	26	24	21	22	32	27	24	22	28	23	23	28	23	20
Slovenia	59	56	53	58	46	52	67	68	53	45	61	54	50	59	56	54
South Africa	64	75	75	75	78	75	68	78	72	67	76	82	67	73	77	74
Spain	45	53	51	56	43	51	61	61	44	47	54	56	53	58	55	40
Sweden	41	41	42	41	38	40	44	52	39	36	43	40	41	42	42	39
Switzerland	38	25	25	25	18	20	36	34	24	12	26	26	24	34	27	13
Taiwan	na	15	14	16	8	16	17	19	17	10	18	16	12	13	15	22
Tanzania	na	82	81	83	78	80	92	85	76	82	87	80	83	83	81	92
Turkey	67	63	60	66	57	65	73	67	61	46	62	65	54	70	65	48
Uganda	na	66	80	54	71	64	57	65	67	70	79	73	70	54	72	78
Ukraine	na	24	25	23	18	23	28	23	25	23	22	17	33	22	25	38
United States	76	72	72	72	61	71	83	76	75	69	71	71	76	74	74	68
Uruguay	na	75	72	77	61	70	84	77	73	66	78	76	71	76	77	70
Venezuela	na	92	92	92	91	92	95	95	91	91	92	93	92	88	93	95
Vietnam	na	78	82	75	76	75	86	76	83	77	81	76	80	79	82	79
Zimbabwe	na	78	78	78	78	78	79	80	76	52	80	77	78	76	79	87
Total	47	56	57	56	56	54	59	63	53	52	59	56	54	56	56	53

RANKING

Country	2000
Puerto Rico	95
Iran	92
Venezuela	92
Morocco	89
Philippines	87
El Salvador	86
Colombia	85
Egypt	82
Tanzania	82
Pakistan	81
Mexico	80
Portugal	79
Vietnam	78
Zimbabwe	78
Peru	77
Dominican Rep.	76
South Africa	75
Uruguay	75
Malta	75
Algeria	74
Australia	73
Bangladesh	73
Albania	73
United States	72
Nigeria	72
Chile	72
Ireland	72
Poland	72
India	71
Argentina	68
Jordan	68
Canada	67
Iceland	67
Uganda	66
Georgia	65
Brazil	65
New Zealand	64
Azerbaijan	64
Turkey	63
Macedonia	61
Finland	56
Slovenia	56
Greece	55
Israel	54
Spain	53
Austria	53
Great Britain	51
Norway	50
Hungary	49
Luxembourg	49
Indonesia	48
Denmark	48
Romania	47
Singapore	44
Armenia	44
Serbia	42
Croatia	42
Sweden	41
Latvia	40
France	40
Italy	39
Bosnia and Herz.	38
Bulgaria	34
Montenegro	33
Russian Fed.	31
Northern Ireland	28
Belarus	27
Czech Republic	26
China	26
Switzerland	25
Slovakia	25
Ukraine	24
Estonia	24
Belgium	23
Moldova	23
Japan	23
Lithuania	22
Netherlands	20
Korea, South	17
Germany	17
Taiwan	15
Total	56

Y002) MATERIALIST

MATERIALIST-POSTMATERIALIST VALUES

% Materialist values

(WVS: V405)

Country	Wave 1990	Wave 2000	Gender Male	Gender Female	Age 16-29	Age 30-49	Age 50+	Education Lower	Education Middle	Education Upper	Income Lower	Income Middle	Income Upper	Values Mat	Values Mixed	Values Postm.
Albania	na	44	40	47	37	44	48	52	39	34	49	47	36	100	na	na
Algeria	na	35	34	37	34	31	47	45	39	23	37	36	30	100	na	na
Argentina	25	18	19	18	16	15	24	24	11	9	25	17	13	100	na	na
Armenia	na	45	41	48	41	46	49	52	47	32	38	51	49	100	na	na
Australia	na	8	9	7	7	7	10	9	9	6	8	9	6	100	na	na
Austria	14	8	7	8	8	5	10	10	6	5	11	8	7	100	na	na
Azerbaijan	na	60	56	64	59	60	62	72	61	57	64	61	56	100	na	na
Bangladesh	na	39	34	45	37	40	40	43	37	30	47	34	37	100	na	na
Belarus	34	50	43	55	38	46	63	66	46	36	59	46	40	100	na	na
Belgium	22	23	18	28	17	21	28	42	21	12	28	26	15	100	na	na
Bosnia and Herz.	na	30	28	33	29	29	34	35	31	23	33	30	27	100	na	na
Brazil	40	31	28	33	26	34	33	39	27	16	37	34	21	100	na	na
Bulgaria	28	49	46	51	41	40	60	67	43	31	62	45	41	100	na	na
Canada	12	8	8	8	6	9	9	12	8	7	7	9	8	100	na	na
Chile	25	28	24	32	22	26	36	32	27	20	32	27	22	100	na	na
China	51	42	45	40	35	45	42	41	44	30	40	42	51	100	na	na
Colombia	na	14	13	15	14	13	16	21	12	6	20	12	9	100	na	na
Croatia	na	15	13	18	7	18	19	18	15	10	12	20	12	100	na	na
Czech Republic	26	25	22	28	22	24	28	32	21	11	31	25	21	100	na	na
Denmark	16	9	9	8	11	5	11	11	6	4	11	9	4	100	na	na
Dominican Rep.	na	19	15	21	20	16	18	28	30	13	25	13	17	100	na	na
Egypt	na	43	38	48	32	47	51	54	36	25	50	45	39	100	na	na
El Salvador	na	na	na	na	na	na	na	na	na	na	na	na	na	na	na	na
Estonia	32	41	34	47	35	38	47	46	41	32	43	44	39	100	na	na
Finland	6	26	24	28	24	28	26	31	20	17	25	26	27	100	na	na
France	21	28	25	30	21	24	35	35	20	15	35	29	17	100	na	na
Georgia	na	46	45	48	40	47	51	52	46	44	47	48	43	100	na	na
Germany	12	28	26	30	13	25	37	36	24	14	33	30	30	100	na	na
Great Britain	20	na	na	na	na	na	na	na	na	na	na	na	na	na	na	na
Greece	na	19	18	20	17	20	21	16	21	18	15	20	22	100	na	na
Hungary	45	51	48	53	45	44	60	57	41	34	55	52	45	100	na	na
Iceland	25	22	19	24	20	23	22	29	20	11	24	20	20	100	na	na
India	40	39	41	36	40	40	34	39	42	36	42	44	34	100	na	na
Indonesia	na	38	35	42	29	36	45	54	41	24	38	39	43	100	na	na
Iran	na	25	25	26	25	26	27	30	26	20	26	27	23	100	na	na
Ireland	24	20	19	20	17	20	22	14	17	26	25	17	16	100	na	na
Israel	na	16	17	14	19	17	10	13	16	16	10	17	17	100	na	na
Italy	25	14	12	16	8	11	20	21	9	9	21	12	8	100	na	na
Japan	29	17	17	16	11	17	19	13	17	18	17	16	19	100	na	na
Jordan	na	40	39	41	32	43	51	47	31	36	43	39	37	100	na	na
Korea, South	46	46	43	50	35	47	57	77	50	37	50	46	43	100	na	na
Latvia	27	35	31	38	20	32	43	39	34	33	42	32	29	100	na	na
Lithuania	27	31	30	32	27	25	39	47	27	17	38	32	25	100	na	na
Luxembourg	na	20	19	22	18	20	22	22	22	16	30	18	13	100	na	na
Macedonia	na	34	33	35	29	33	41	34	34	37	35	35	32	100	na	na
Malta	na	35	30	39	22	37	41	51	31	12	45	33	26	100	na	na
Mexico	25	25	25	26	21	26	31	31	20	13	29	26	19	100	na	na
Moldova	na	46	44	47	41	46	50	52	47	39	49	50	44	100	na	na
Montenegro	na	46	44	49	35	42	58	61	41	28	54	49	42	100	na	na
Morocco	na	39	34	43	36	40	43	42	29	14	32	33	38	100	na	na
Netherlands	10	12	9	15	11	9	16	21	9	6	17	12	4	100	na	na
New Zealand	na	9	10	8	7	10	9	9	11	8	11	7	9	100	na	na
Nigeria	36	35	33	38	33	39	33	39	34	33	33	37	37	100	na	na
Northern Ireland	22	25	23	28	17	25	29	29	25	14	31	25	18	100	na	na
Norway	29	14	12	15	11	10	19	23	11	7	0	0	0	100	na	na
Pakistan	na	58	60	55	53	59	64	69	45	44	70	59	38	100	na	na
Peru	na	21	20	21	20	21	21	28	22	13	24	21	14	100	na	na
Philippines	na	39	38	40	36	39	46	42	40	36	45	36	38	Mat	na	na
Poland	31	37	31	42	35	34	41	44	31	23	42	34	31	100	na	na
Portugal	34	36	30	41	21	28	51	42	25	16	52	33	30	100	na	na
Puerto Rico	na	12	11	12	10	10	14	21	13	10	14	12	10	100	na	na
Romania	44	45	41	50	39	42	52	60	45	22	55	51	35	100	na	na
Russian Fed.	39	52	46	57	41	51	60	66	54	40	59	53	45	100	na	na
Serbia	na	48	45	51	40	42	56	67	44	26	56	53	37	100	na	na
Singapore	na	27	22	31	18	30	49	34	21	32	35	26	23	100	na	na
Slovakia	na	46	41	50	38	42	57	60	41	30	58	49	35	100	na	na
Slovenia	28	17	16	17	11	16	22	24	15	11	23	12	15	100	na	na
South Africa	35	37	35	40	35	36	47	35	41	31	37	35	40	100	na	na
Spain	30	25	21	29	13	20	37	32	18	17	28	26	19	100	na	na
Sweden	14	6	8	5	7	4	8	10	6	4	8	6	5	100	na	na
Switzerland	14	14	12	15	12	14	15	19	14	2	16	16	11	100	na	na
Taiwan	na	45	38	52	41	44	50	50	44	41	46	48	46	100	na	na
Tanzania	na	32	32	32	30	34	27	32	32	28	36	30	28	100	na	na
Turkey	25	22	21	23	18	23	30	26	18	12	23	24	17	100	na	na
Uganda	na	32	28	37	30	32	48	37	32	22	27	27	29	100	na	na
Ukraine	na	46	41	49	40	43	52	61	47	35	54	41	41	100	na	na
United States	16	9	8	11	7	11	9	10	10	9	8	9	10	100	na	na
Uruguay	na	18	17	19	10	12	26	24	10	9	31	13	9	100	na	na
Venezuela	na	25	24	26	25	24	25	31	26	14	28	26	20	100	na	na
Vietnam	na	20	19	21	21	18	22	21	18	24	14	23	20	100	na	na
Zimbabwe	na	41	38	44	37	44	45	46	35	0	46	41	32	100	na	na
Total	27	30	28	32	26	29	34	36	29	21	34	30	26	100	na	na

RANKING

Country	2000
Azerbaijan	60
Pakistan	58
Russian Fed.	52
Hungary	51
Belarus	50
Bulgaria	49
Serbia	48
Montenegro	46
Georgia	46
Korea, South	46
Slovakia	46
Moldova	46
Ukraine	46
Romania	45
Taiwan	45
Armenia	45
Albania	44
Egypt	43
China	42
Estonia	41
Zimbabwe	41
Jordan	40
Philippines	39
India	39
Bangladesh	39
Morocco	39
Indonesia	38
South Africa	37
Poland	37
Portugal	36
Algeria	35
Nigeria	35
Latvia	35
Malta	35
Macedonia	34
Uganda	32
Tanzania	32
Lithuania	31
Brazil	31
Bosnia and Herz.	30
Germany	28
France	28
Chile	28
Singapore	27
Finland	26
Mexico	25
Northern Ireland	25
Czech Republic	25
Iran	25
Spain	25
Venezuela	25
Belgium	23
Turkey	22
Iceland	22
Peru	21
Luxembourg	20
Ireland	20
Vietnam	20
Greece	19
Dominican Rep.	19
Argentina	18
Uruguay	18
Slovenia	17
Japan	17
Israel	16
Croatia	15
Italy	14
Colombia	14
Switzerland	14
Norway	14
Netherlands	12
Puerto Rico	12
United States	9
New Zealand	9
Denmark	9
Canada	8
Australia	8
Austria	8
Sweden	6
Total	30

Y002) POSTMATERIALIST

MATERIALIST-POSTMATERIALIST VALUES

% Postmaterialist

(WVS: V405)

Country	Wave 1990	Wave 2000	Gender Male	Gender Female	Age 16-29	Age 30-49	Age 50+	Education Lower	Education Middle	Education Upper	Income Lower	Income Middle	Income Upper	Values Mat	Values Mixed	Values Postm.
Albania	na	4	5	3	4	4	3	3	4	6	5	4	3	na	na	100
Algeria	na	9	10	9	11	10	5	5	7	15	8	13	12	na	na	100
Argentina	19	25	26	25	29	27	20	17	35	47	16	23	38	na	na	100
Armenia	na	5	5	6	7	4	4	4	5	7	7	4	5	na	na	100
Australia	na	35	34	35	37	36	31	29	33	41	32	34	41	na	na	100
Austria	25	30	29	30	38	32	23	23	33	46	24	30	37	na	na	100
Azerbaijan	na	3	4	3	3	4	3	2	3	5	3	5	3	na	na	100
Bangladesh	na	5	5	5	6	4	4	4	6	5	5	6	4	na	na	100
Belarus	7	6	8	5	8	8	3	2	6	13	3	6	11	na	na	100
Belgium	24	20	24	17	22	24	16	6	19	33	15	19	27	na	na	100
Bosnia and Herz.	na	4	5	4	5	5	3	3	5	5	5	4	5	na	na	100
Brazil	7	12	13	10	14	11	9	6	14	23	6	10	20	na	na	100
Bulgaria	9	3	4	3	6	4	1	2	4	4	2	4	3	na	na	100
Canada	26	29	31	26	34	28	26	23	26	38	24	30	33	na	na	100
Chile	19	17	17	17	20	19	9	10	17	28	13	16	24	na	na	100
China	6	3	2	4	4	4	2	2	4	9	2	4	5	na	na	100
Colombia	na	8	8	8	11	7	5	6	10	8	8	7	9	na	na	100
Croatia	na	19	21	18	27	20	13	13	21	31	14	18	23	na	na	100
Czech Republic	11	10	11	9	13	10	8	7	11	19	7	9	14	na	na	100
Denmark	16	16	15	17	12	23	12	10	19	26	10	18	27	na	na	100
Dominican Rep.	na	16	18	15	17	15	0	6	13	18	16	14	17	na	na	100
Egypt	na	6	6	5	9	4	3	3	7	11	5	5	7	na	na	100
El Salvador	na	na	na	na	na	na	na	na	na	na	na	na	na	na	na	na
Estonia	6	3	3	2	5	2	2	1	3	4	1	2	4	na	na	100
Finland	29	11	11	11	14	10	9	9	11	18	13	9	10	na	na	100
France	25	18	20	16	24	21	13	11	25	31	16	16	25	na	na	100
Georgia	na	4	5	3	4	4	3	2	4	4	4	3	4	na	na	100
Germany	23	17	19	16	27	18	12	9	21	36	13	14	23	na	na	100
Great Britain	20	na	na	na	na	na	na	na	na	na	na	na	na	na	na	na
Greece	na	17	21	14	19	14	17	15	15	18	21	14	15	na	na	100
Hungary	4	2	4	1	4	3	1	2	4	4	2	3	2	na	na	100
Iceland	11	11	11	10	11	11	10	6	9	23	11	10	11	na	na	100
India	6	2	3	2	3	3	1	1	3	4	2	2	3	na	na	100
Indonesia	na	3	4	2	3	4	2	2	2	5	1	4	4	na	na	100
Iran	na	10	11	9	11	9	8	5	10	15	8	9	12	na	na	100
Ireland	19	14	13	15	15	14	13	19	14	11	11	13	17	na	na	100
Israel	na	4	4	3	5	3	3	3	4	3	3	4	4	na	na	100
Italy	22	28	30	27	37	33	20	17	35	41	24	34	35	na	na	100
Japan	10	9	11	8	10	10	9	7	8	15	8	8	13	na	na	100
Jordan	na	6	7	6	8	7	3	5	6	10	5	6	7	na	na	100
Korea, South	11	6	6	6	14	4	1	0	3	10	6	5	6	na	na	100
Latvia	9	5	7	3	10	5	3	3	5	6	4	4	7	na	na	100
Lithuania	13	6	8	5	9	8	3	1	7	11	3	5	9	na	na	100
Luxembourg	na	17	15	18	16	21	13	11	17	27	14	15	24	na	na	100
Macedonia	na	5	5	4	7	5	2	5	5	4	3	6	5	na	na	100
Malta	na	8	9	7	9	9	5	4	8	17	5	5	11	na	na	100
Mexico	12	12	14	11	15	13	7	8	15	25	8	15	17	na	na	100
Moldova	na	5	6	5	7	5	4	4	4	9	2	4	8	na	na	100
Montenegro	na	6	6	6	9	8	2	4	7	9	4	5	7	na	na	100
Morocco	na	6	8	5	8	5	4	4	11	24	6	10	6	na	na	100
Netherlands	36	22	25	19	19	24	22	15	23	29	20	21	26	na	na	100
New Zealand	na	20	22	18	19	23	17	13	18	29	17	20	23	na	na	100
Nigeria	7	9	9	9	9	8	9	6	9	11	10	8	8	na	na	100
Northern Ireland	15	17	19	16	26	20	11	14	20	21	14	14	19	na	na	100
Norway	10	11	12	11	12	14	8	6	10	18	0	0	0	na	na	100
Pakistan	na	1	1	1	1	1	0	0	1	1	0	0	2	na	na	100
Peru	na	14	17	12	17	12	13	8	14	20	13	14	17	na	na	100
Philippines	na	6	4	8	8	6	4	5	6	7	5	5	8	na	na	100
Poland	10	8	10	6	10	7	7	6	8	13	5	8	13	na	na	100
Portugal	12	10	10	10	17	9	7	6	17	20	3	7	14	na	na	100
Puerto Rico	na	22	23	21	29	21	19	13	19	25	14	22	29	na	na	100
Romania	7	7	9	5	12	8	4	1	7	17	5	3	11	na	na	100
Russian Fed.	6	2	3	1	2	2	1	1	1	3	1	2	2	na	na	100
Serbia	na	6	7	5	7	7	4	2	5	15	2	5	10	na	na	100
Singapore	na	7	8	6	11	4	3	6	7	9	7	7	7	na	na	100
Slovakia	na	4	5	3	5	4	3	2	4	12	3	4	5	na	na	100
Slovenia	7	16	17	15	21	16	13	15	16	18	14	17	16	na	na	100
South Africa	8	7	7	7	10	6	3	8	6	11	7	7	6	na	na	100
Spain	21	17	19	15	29	19	8	10	23	28	14	15	22	na	na	100
Sweden	23	22	20	25	28	22	19	9	25	30	23	20	24	na	na	100
Switzerland	24	17	15	19	24	16	15	10	18	24	16	15	19	na	na	100
Taiwan	na	5	5	4	3	5	5	4	5	5	4	6	4	na	na	100
Tanzania	na	2	2	2	3	2	2	2	2	2	3	2	2	na	na	100
Turkey	20	18	21	15	22	17	12	12	23	36	13	20	26	na	na	100
Uganda	na	12	13	10	13	8	19	11	11	22	13	15	13	na	na	100
Ukraine	na	4	4	3	6	2	3	0	2	8	2	2	6	na	na	100
United States	23	25	28	23	28	24	25	22	23	28	25	25	25	na	na	100
Uruguay	na	23	22	24	34	28	14	14	32	47	13	23	35	na	na	100
Venezuela	na	14	14	14	16	15	9	9	15	19	11	16	15	na	na	100
Vietnam	na	8	9	8	12	7	7	8	8	10	9	9	8	na	na	100
Zimbabwe	na	6	6	6	6	5	6	5	6	9	7	6	3	na	na	100
Total	15	11	12	10	13	11	9	7	11	17	9	10	13	na	na	100

RANKING

Country	2000
Australia	35
Austria	30
Canada	29
Italy	28
Argentina	25
United States	25
Uruguay	23
Sweden	22
Netherlands	22
Puerto Rico	22
Belgium	20
New Zealand	20
Croatia	19
Turkey	18
France	18
Switzerland	17
Germany	17
Northern Ireland	17
Spain	17
Chile	17
Greece	17
Luxembourg	17
Denmark	16
Slovenia	16
Dominican Rep.	16
Peru	14
Venezuela	14
Ireland	14
Mexico	12
Brazil	12
Uganda	12
Norway	11
Finland	11
Iceland	11
Portugal	10
Czech Republic	10
Iran	10
Japan	9
Algeria	9
Nigeria	9
Vietnam	8
Colombia	8
Poland	8
Malta	8
South Africa	7
Romania	7
Singapore	7
Jordan	6
Lithuania	6
Philippines	6
Belarus	6
Morocco	6
Serbia	6
Montenegro	6
Korea, South	6
Egypt	6
Zimbabwe	6
Armenia	5
Moldova	5
Bangladesh	5
Latvia	5
Taiwan	5
Macedonia	5
Bosnia and Herz.	4
Slovakia	4
Albania	4
Georgia	4
Israel	4
Ukraine	4
Azerbaijan	3
Bulgaria	3
China	3
Indonesia	3
Estonia	3
Hungary	2
India	2
Tanzania	2
Russian Fed.	2
Pakistan	1
Total	11

Cross-Cultural Comparisons, Survey Methodology and the Values Surveys

Yilmaz Esmer

The Values Surveys, which have produced an enormous and hitherto unmatched database for comparative and longitudinal analyses of the belief and value systems of societies, use the sample survey as its mode of data collection. To gain an understanding of the issues and questions that the Values Surveys aim to address, there is no alternative. If one is interested in finding out what a person thinks or believes one had better ask directly. Trying to infer values from secondary or indirect sources would be a very poor substitute for data collected by survey interviews.

The advantages and pitfalls of the sample survey method are widely known and well documented. A vast literature now exists on survey techniques and numerous methodological experiments have been conducted to help identify potential problem areas. It is not the aim of this chapter to review this literature. Rather, I will limit myself to the issues concerning cross-national and cross-cultural surveys in general and the Values Surveys project in particular.

Questionnaire design, sampling, data collection (in our case, face-to-face interviews) and analysis are the basic stages of a sample survey. These are also the basic sources of error. In a project of the magnitude of the Values Surveys, each one of these stages is more complicated than usual. Additionally, when we consider translation problems and practical problems of all sorts, we can begin to appreciate the enormity and complexity of the task in our hands.

Briefly and succinctly, the sample survey can be defined as "consist[ing] of relatively systematic, standardized approaches to the collection of information on individuals, households, or larger organized entities through the questioning of systematically identified samples of individuals."[1] There are two basic elements in this definition: "systematic" and "standardized." Now let us recall that we are dealing with more than 80 countries, many more languages and hundreds of ethnic groups. Achieving standardization under these circumstances, as anyone who has collected data in a single city alone

---

[1] Rossi, Peter H. et al, "Sample Surveys: History, Current Practice, and Future Prospects" in Rossi, Peter H., James D. Wright and Andy B. Anderson, eds., *Handbook of Survey Research*, San Diego: Academic Press, Inc., 1983, p. 1.

will testify, will have to be "relative" indeed. It is very easy to criticize such an endeavor from the perspective of a methodological purist. One could without much effort find faults with many aspects of the design, that is, the questions, the sampling, the translations, and the interviewing techniques. It would be foolish to deny the well-known difficulties and errors associated with cross-cultural surveys, and the Values Surveys project is not immune to them. But research, in any field and with any method, is an arduous undertaking. The researcher's job is not to throw up his/her hands in despair but to be as meticulous and demanding as he/she possibly can. The road is full of hurdles of all types and sizes but, then, "Fear not [....] your reward shall be very great."[2]

Questionnaire design, sampling, data collection and analysis are the four basic aspects of sample surveys. Beginning with questionnaires, I will comment on each one of these four topics with reference to the Values Surveys.

A question for all cultures?

Writing survey questions and designing a questionnaire even for homogenous populations requires considerable experience and knowledge. Wording, question order, question type, order and nature of response categories, presence or absence of a no answer category can alter both the responses and the response rates. In addition there are problems related to context effects, social desirability effects, need for approval effects, acquiescence effects, to mention but a few examples. Sensitive topics or questions inquiring about illegal behavior comprise another set of challenges for the survey researcher.

The Detroit Area Studies carried out by the University of Michigan have produced a sizeable literature on these issues. These surveys are based on data collected from not a country, not a state but only the city of greater Detroit, Michigan. It goes without saying that multinational, multicultural, multilingual settings can only increase the magnitude and add to the variety of problems. What is sensitive, legal or socially desirable, for example, varies greatly from one country to another. Marijuana for personal use is legal in Amsterdam and is sold in so-called coffee shops but its possession will result in years of imprisonment in some countries. Fully 61 percent of Czech citizens, 49 percent of the Estonians, 39 percent of both the French and the Dutch say they do not believe in God. Daring to say this in public is no less than a capital offense in some Islamic states. Asking a man about his sexual preferences is not much of a problem in San Francisco but may be a cause for murder in a Turkish village. One could think of numerous other examples but there is no need to belabor the point: cultures differ enormously, in many ways that are directly related to the conduct of surveys and cross-cultural researchers must be keenly aware of this fact.

What is a family?

One of the most frequent criticisms that cross-cultural survey researchers hear refers to the different ways a given question is understood in different places. "How can you," the argument goes, "compare 'religiosity' in Poland and Japan when the concept refers

---

[2] Genesis, 15:1.

to very different things in these two countries?" We are, at times, even accused of being unaware that God in monotheist cultures has an entirely different meaning than, say, in Buddhist or Confucian societies.

Cross-cultural survey researchers are very much aware that the same question, based on even rather simple concepts, can be understood differently in different countries. But is this really a problem only when the survey covers more than one society? Do all Americans understand a given question in the same way? Or all New Yorkers? Within Sweden, are the political "left" and "right" interpreted in the same way by a university graduate and a person with no formal education? Better yet, do two Swedish PhD's have the same perception of these and other concepts? Pushed to the extreme, do husbands and wives always agree on the meaning of a word or a sentence? Do you and your daughter understand a phrase from a contemporary television show in exactly the same way? This line of reasoning can easily lead us to the position that since no two individuals' cognitive processes are identical, a question cannot be standardized even for two persons in the same household. Clearly, such a conclusion is not of much help for social science researchers who study shared meanings, and coherent and consistent patterns.

Family is a simple concept and is as universal as one can get. Yet, we know that it refers to a nuclear family in Norway --and a very small one at that-- while in Nigeria it can include a whole village and sometimes two or three. But whatever operational meaning they attach to it, family is very important for people and universally so. So much so that, of the 97,237 respondents from 67 societies who answered the question "how important is family in your life?" in the last round of the Values Surveys, 89.4 percent said "very important." Only 1.1 percent said family was "not important" for them and the proportion of those whose response was "not important at all" was negligible - merely 0.3 percent. This is strong evidence that, despite differences in operational definitions, the concept has a common core meaning in all societies. It is difficult to think of another plausible explanation for this extremely low variance in the responses from almost one hundred thousand respondents scattered all over the globe.

Religion, God and culture

The fact that different societies have different understandings of "religion" and "God," is frequently cited to question the validity of data obtained from standardized questions containing these concepts and asked in widely differing cultures. Let us then try to assess the performance of such questions, using Values Surveys data, which, fortunately, allow us to evaluate the "construct validity"[3] of these concepts.

Being skeptics about the comparability of "religiosity" and "belief in God" across cultures and being particularly concerned with the different understanding of these concepts in East Asian civilizations, we should be able to agree on the following proposition:

---

[3] Babbie (Babbie, Earl R., *The Practice of Social Research*, 9th ed., Belmont: Wadsworth/Thomson Learning, 2001, p. 143) explains construct validity as follows: "We can consider how the variable in question ought, theoretically, to relate to other variables. **Construct validity** [author's emphasis] is based on the logical relationship among variables."

An individual's level of religiosity will have a strong positive correlation with how much importance God has in that individual's life in monotheistic (Christian, Islamic, Judaic) cultures. However, no such correlation will be observed outside of this monotheist cultural zone, since the wordings of these questions have entirely different meanings, for example, in Japan, Korea or China. Therefore, they have no validity in these societies and will probably produce random responses.

We now turn to our data to test these hypotheses. The survey instrument used by Values Surveys included the following two questions:

1. How important is God in your life? (Respondents were shown a 10-point scale.)

2. Independently of whether you go to church (mosque, synagogue, temple), would you say you are a religious person, not a religious person or a convinced atheist?

An examination of 87,931 cases reveals that the mean importance of God score for those who described themselves as religious is 8.63 while the mean score for the non-religious sample is 4.81. Taking into account that the overall standard deviation of the importance of God scale is 3.09, this difference of 3.82 between the group means is of considerable magnitude.

Table 1 gives the mean "importance of God" scores broken down by religion and religiosity. We observe that in all cases, respondents who described themselves as religious attach more importance, on the whole, to God than those who said they were not religious. In Hindu, Buddhist, Muslim, Protestant, Catholic and Jewish cultures, being more religious is linked with attaching more importance of God, regardless of how these different cultures understand and define these concepts. An analysis at the country level yields similar results. For example, in Japan, the mean importance of God score for religious respondents is 6.95 while it is only 4.74 for the non-religious sample. The questions do seem to work in Japan as well.

The next question we ask concerns what is referred to in the literature as "criterion-related validity."[4] In other words, can an outside variable unrelated to the survey that should theoretically be related to the construct in question, be predicted by the latter. It has been frequently argued that decreased levels of religiosity and faith are important components of the "modernization syndrome." Better living conditions and higher levels of education are known to correlate negatively with religiosity. "Thus, according to the dominant view, in modern society religion and church leaders are decreasingly able to dictate people's decisions in everyday life. The taken for granted status in consciousness and beliefs has disappeared and in secularized society, religious and moral beliefs and practices are said to be dependent upon personal desires and preferences and constantly open to debate, reformulation and change."[5] According to this "dominant view," then, the Human Development Index (HDI) published annually by the United Nations Development Program should serve as a good "outside criterion" to test the

---

[4] Babbie, *Ibid.*

[5] Draulans, Veerle and Loek Halman, "Religious and Moral Pluralism in Contemporary Europe" in Arts, Will, Jacques Hagenaars and Loek Halman, eds., *The Cultural Diversity of European Unity*, Leiden-Boston: Brill, 2003, p. 373.

validity of our constructs, since the HDI is a composite index of income, education and life expectancy. Secularization theory implies that as a country's HDI score rises, its level of emphasis on religion should fall significantly. The secularization thesis, as summarized by Draulans and Halman, also suggests that modernization and individualization should decrease people's confidence in organized religion, i.e. the church or its functional equivalent. A number of questions in the instruments used by Values Surveys are appropriate for testing these hypotheses. We will continue to use the "importance of God scale" as an indicator of individual religiosity. If we find that the HDI is a good predictor of how much importance a society attaches to God, and its level of confidence in organized religion, it means that our data from more than 80 societies are behaving according to widely shared theoretical expectations—giving us greater confidence in the cross-cultural validity of our measure.

If we correlate the mean on the importance of God scale, with each country's HDI score[6], we get a Pearson $r = 0.64$ ($N = 60$, sig.$< .000$). This is an impressive correlation coefficient, which translates into an r2 of 0.40, i.e. the HDI scores explain 40 percent of the cross-national variance in the importance of God scale. The corresponding simple regression equation estimates that an increase of one standard deviation in the HDI (0.137 in original units) is expected to produce a decrease of 3 units (for example, from a mean of 9 to a mean of 6 on the ten-point scale) in a country's mean importance of God.

A scatterplot of the mean HDI scores for each country with the Importance of God mean scores reveals two things: (1) the relationship is not linear and a second degree polynomial can improve the fit considerably, and (2) the United States and Vietnam are the two conspicuous outliers (Figure 1). When we modify the equation accordingly, the percentage of explained variance rises to 48 percent. Moreover, if the two outliers, the United States and Vietnam, are omitted from the equation, r^2 increases by another 5 percentage points. When an outside "objective" variable (in our case, the HDI), explains more than half of the cross-national variation in a variable (the importance of God), the argument that the variable lacks criterion-related validity can no longer be entertained.

We repeat the analysis, this time with "confidence in church" as the independent variable. This is important because church organizations are radically different in different countries. The Roman Catholic Church, for example, is a well-defined hierarchical organization. Church membership and church tax are automatic in many Western European countries and a formal petition is required if an individual wishes to rescind his/her membership. In Iran the head of the clergy is also the political authority for all practical purposes while in Turkey, with a 98 percent Muslim population, no clergy, church organization, or formal membership exist. Given such massive contextual variation, can a question like "How much confidence do you have in the church (or functional equivalent)?" have any cross-cultural validity? It turns out that the answer is definitely "yes" and even to a greater degree than with the importance of God question.

A country's score on the HDI explains 51 percent of the cross-national variation in the degree of confidence in the church.[7] Moreover, an examination of the scatterplot

---

[6] UNDP, *Human Development Report 2002*, New York-Oxford: Oxford University Press, 2002.
[7] Coded from 1 (not at all) to 4 (a great deal); country mean scores are used in the analysis.

(Figure 2) reveals a pattern that is very similar to the one observed with the importance of God variable -a curvilinear relationship with the United States and Vietnam being the outliers again. Including the square of the independent variable (mean confidence in the church) in the equation increases the r^2 to 61 percent. And if the United States and Vietnam are removed, we explain two-thirds of the total variance.

It is fair to conclude that, despite the very real and very serious difficulties that critics of cross-cultural research evoke, these data show a high degree of cross-cultural validity.

Religious institutions and worldviews vary immensely from one society to another. Nevertheless, it is clear that a sufficient degree of shared meanings exist that people from widely different cultures understand and respond to such concepts as "God" or "church" in broadly comparable ways.

Sampling for the Values Surveys

It is beyond the scope of this article to discuss the technical issues related to sampling. However, since surveys in some Values Surveys countries have used quota sampling, we should briefly address the arguments against and in defense this method. It should be made clear that the comparison is not between a full probability sample and crude quota designs that are no longer used except by novices.[8] Rather, the case in point is a combination of probability and quota designs. For instance, some surveys used a probability model (area sampling) down to the household level, but switched to a quota design at this last stage. This design is very similar to what Sudman calls "probability sampling with quotas." As he explains, "these quotas are normally determined for the smallest geographic area for which information is available."[9]

There is hardly any disagreement that probability samples —as opposed to nonprobability samples such as quota— have a number of desirable properties. First and foremost, only full probability samples (in which every unit in the population has a known and nonzero probability of selection) allow us to calculate sampling errors and confidence intervals. Furthermore, all significance tests are based on this assumption. But probability sampling is expensive—and often prohibitively expensive. It can multiply the cost of a survey by a factor of three or four.[10] Probability sampling requires repeated callbacks to persons with whom an interview cannot be completed at the first visit for whatever reason. If the mode of data collection is face-to-face interviewing, as is almost exclusively the case with the Values Surveys, this means repeated trips to remote places to complete a single interview. "A researcher must do what a researcher must do" one could say, and this is what the book says should be done. Unfortunately,

---

[8] By "crude quota samples" we are referring to plans that, at their worst, may involve no more than handing the interviewer the quotas for each category and instructing him/her to fill these quotas (e.g. gender and age) in any way he/she can in a given locality which can be as large as an entire city.

[9] Sudman, *op.cit.* p. 193

[10] "Comparing the total costs of probability callback and quota studies, call-back sample costs per case are typically three times higher than the costs per case of quota samples..." Sudman, Seymour, *Applied Sampling,* New York: Academic Press, 1976, p. 199.

many funding agencies are not swayed by this argument— and in many societies, research funding is very limited.

What does one lose by switching to a combination of probability plus quota design? The methodologist's response to this question will be simple: "Sorry to say, we cannot know." As far as sampling error is concerned, this is true. But one must consider the following points as well:

a. Low response rates have become a serious problem for probability designs. To cite one example, the recent European Social Survey project, which made data from 15 countries available in the fall of 2003, reports that the response rate was 33.5 percent in Switzerland, 43.7 percent in Italy, and 53.2 percent in Spain.[11] With such low response rates, which are fast becoming the norm rather than the exception, especially in industrialized Western countries, it is difficult to contend that a probability design still retains its desirable properties.

b. It is well known that sampling error constitutes only a rather small proportion of the total error in a survey. This should especially be true for large scale cross-cultural studies which exacerbate the problems related to questionnaire design and data collection. When resources are scarce, it is necessary to weigh the small reductions in sampling error that an ideal design can offer, against the astronomical increases in cost. In many instances, the researcher is not even in a position to choose. The options are, use a mixed probability/quota design, or give up hope of carrying out the survey. A purist would choose the latter course—which is why survey data from most low-income countries is scarce or non-existent.

c. It is not an easy task, to put it mildly, to come up with a reasonably acceptable sampling frame in some parts of the globe. There are places where there are no addresses, no lists, no registries and where the size of the relevant population is a mystery: a few huts on top of a hill, tents in the middle of a desert or nomads who take to the mountains in the summer. Often there is no record, official or otherwise, of these groups. Under these circumstances, any kind of sampling, let alone probability sampling, is a major challenge. An added complication is the lack of infrastructure. In some instances, the only mode of transportation can be hours of walking or of riding various kinds of animals.

d. Wars, internal strife, terrorism and violence can present insurmountable obstacles both in terms of the preparation of a sampling frame and, of course, interviewer access.

When one or more of these conditions (and more could easily be added to this list) exist, it would be a folly to pretend that one has an ideal sampling design. Imple-

---

[11] ESS (European Social Survey) project is uncompromising with respect to methodological rigor and goes to great lengths to ensure the highest standards and maximum adherence to the rules of good survey practice. They are to be commended for openly sharing full methodological information including response rates with the academic community at large. The above figures on response are from "Round 1 Technical Report, Chapter 6." More information is available on "http://www.europeansocialsurvey.org."

menting the survey instrument in all corners of the globe, the WVS policy with respect to sampling can be summarized as follows:

    a. Encourage full probability sampling whenever feasible.
    b. When this is not feasible or possible, use a combination of probability and refined quota sampling.
    c. In any case, provide a full technical report of all sample properties, problems and deviations. Response rates should be reported when probability sample designs are used.

Known population characteristics can provide a benchmark to assess the performance of a sample. If certain sample statistics are within acceptable error margins with respect to population parameters obtained through, say, an official census of the population, this is strong indication that the sample on the whole is satisfactory.[12] With this criterion, the vast majority of Values Surveys samples perform very well. We should not hesitate to add that there are exceptions; there are countries, which have oversampled certain areas (e.g. urban centers) or certain groups (e.g. the highly educated or a given ethnic group). Some of these deviations from probability proportional to size (PPS) sampling can easily be salvaged by weighting. But, obviously, weighting has its limits too. First, it decreases the effective sample size. Second, weighting assumes that population data are available for the given attributes. Third, weighting cannot compensate for the absence or near absence of certain groups in the sample.

The intellectual costs of limiting Values Research to the roughly 30 countries in which almost all previous social science surveys have been carried out are even greater than the difficulties of dealing with reasonably accurate, but less than optimal data. The problem is not merely that the 30-some societies usually surveyed omit most of the world's population; it is that these societies constitute an extremely skewed sample of the world's societies, omitting most of the cultural, economic and social variation found in the world as a whole. If we are to understand how the world is changing, we need to analyze the much more diverse range of societies included in the Values Surveys. At this point in history, there is a trade-off between methodological purism and broad coverage, and we are keenly aware of it. Many of the participants in the Values Surveys network have devoted much of their professional lives to methodological questions. Hopefully, in the future, as more adequate resources become available for cross-national research, such trade-offs will not be necessary. But when it comes to the choice between methodological purism and being able to analyze the much wider range of variation that actually exists in the world as a whole, Values Surveys have come down on the side of "cautious inclusiveness".

---

[12] Of course, the fact that gender, age and educational level distributions in a sample are close to those given by census data is no way a guarantee that we have a perfect sample but it does help to ease the worries of the researcher.

Comparisons over time

The Values Surveys provide a unique opportunity to assess the performances of various country samples. The second, third and fourth waves of these surveys are approximately five years apart. The basic values and demographic structure in a society should remain fairly stable over such a short period of time, unless there is a traumatic event like a war or severe economic crisis. Thus, it is a rather simple exercise. Select certain variables that are relatively stable against short-term fluctuations, and compare their distributions in successive rounds of surveys.[13] Obviously, this requires country-by-country and variable-by-variable comparisons and assumes highly reliable and valid measurements but is a worthwhile challenge for the meticulous analyst. Clearly, not all differences point to sampling problems. After all, if no change were expected, repeated surveys would be unnecessary. Cultural change is a reality and, therefore, the differences between surveys often indicate genuine change. We know that values related to gender equity or sexual tolerance, for example, have gone through rapid changes in most countries in the last decade or so. But under normal circumstances, mass conversions from one religious faith to another, for example, would not be expected to occur in five years and consequently, if we found major changes in the religious affiliations of a given public, it would send a strong warning signal to the analyst.

We conclude this section by presenting an example of this type of analysis, using data from the third (1995-97) and the fourth (1999-2001) waves of WVS. I have argued elsewhere[14] that responses to a question on the individual's health have a strong cultural component that does not change much over time. Thus a Nigerian and a Japanese, with the same health status from a medical point of view, are likely to offer very different subjective evaluations of their health. If this is true and subjective health is a reasonably enduring cultural trait, a comparison of the distributions should give some clues to the adequacy of given samples. Table 2 compares the percentages of respondents who said the state of their health was good or very good in the two waves of surveys, for the 21 WVS countries for which data are available. The results are encouraging. In 16 out of 21 countries in Table 2, the discrepancy is five percentage points or less —well within acceptable sampling error limits. Nigeria and South Africa show larger shifts from one wave to the next.[15] Nevertheless, 19 of the 21 countries show differences of eight points or less between the two waves and the mean shift from one wave to the next is only 3 percentage points.

---

[13] To cite but one example, Turkish second and third wave surveys produced almost identical distributions for life satisfaction and income satisfaction -both 10-point scales. Household income satisfaction distributions for the second and third waves are given below. The probability of obtaining such similar distributions by chance is infinitesimal.

Score	1	2	3	4	5	6	7	8	9	10	mean
1990-91 %	7	6	9	10	36	14	8	5	1	5	5.02
1996-97 %	8	4	9	8	36	12	9	7	1	5	5.09

[14] Esmer, Yilmaz, *Devrim, Evrim, Statuko*, Istanbul: Tesev, 1999.

[15] Of course, there could be substantive explanations for these significant differences.

Analyzing Values Survey Data

The proof of the pudding is in the eating, as the saying goes. We believe that the ultimate litmus test for any data set is its performance. Do the analyses produce meaningful, coherent, consistent and stable results? Do the findings make theoretical sense? Are there plausible explanations for any deviations or anomalies? Overall, the Values Surveys data provide very satisfactory answers to these questions. Without any question, there are imperfections in the data set. In some cases, errors of various types are of greater magnitude than one would be willing to allow. Nevertheless, analyses of the Values Surveys data since 1981 have produced extremely interesting results with great theoretical import. Moreover, the resulting relationships and patterns have been consistent.

Recent decades have witnessed considerable progress in quantitative data analysis methods in the social sciences. Today's statistical packages contain procedures that were unheard of in the 1960s or even 1970s. Furthermore, with the widespread availability of extremely low cost but high speed and high capacity personal computing, these techniques have become household goods. While writing this article at my home computer, I frequently consulted the almost 200,000 case Values Surveys data file occupying only a fraction of the space on my hard disk. This was not possible on the so-called mainframes at the largest universities 25 or 30 years ago.

The advances in techniques for analysis coupled with the enormous increases in computing capacity and speed, however, can easily make us forget that our subject matter is human beings and that we analyze data provided by them. Surveys collect data from men and women whose basic make-up and reactions remain the same. They still yearn for social desirability; they still cannot remember a dozen response categories in a question; they still can be very inconsistent from the perspective of an outside person; and they still have basic fears. The moral of the story is that social science data usually are approximate, and contain a substantial component of measurement error. We, as social scientists, should recognize this fact and not pretend that our data can match the accuracy of a physicist's data.

We would be well advised to heed Dogan's[16] warning:

"After decades of methodological improvements in comparative research we are today in a situation of imbalance between the level of accurate quantitative data and the technological capacity of statistical treatment. We have arrived at a stage where the available statistical information simply does not match the methodological sophistication achieved.

....

Measurement and statistical evidence are obviously needed in all social sciences. The limits to quantification appear when there is a gap between the amount and quality of data available and the statistical technique adopted for its treatment. In other words, over quantification consists in the treatment of soft data by very sophisticated techniques."

---

[16] Dogan, Mattei, "Use and Misuse of Statistics in Comparative Research" in Dogan, Mattei and Ali Kazancigil, eds., *Comparing Nations*, Oxford: Blackwell, 1994, p. 37.

Perhaps the two graphs presented in the introductory chapter to this sourcebook can better illustrate what I have called the "litmus test of data." They help us to visually grasp the remarkably coherent patterns that are obtained from analysis of the Values Surveys data.

The highly structured patterns and the strong correlations with objective criterion variables that appear in Figures 1 and 2 would not emerge if these data were heavily contaminated by measurement error. When one asks questions that are meaningless in a given cultural context, one obtains a great deal of non-response or random answers; and when one asks questions that are understood in completely different ways in different cultural settings, one obtains weakly-related or unrelated patterns of cross-national response. Both of these problems tend to produce weakly structured or uncorrelated responses. But the findings shown in Figures 1 and 2 in the Introductory Chapter are just the opposite: both the Traditional/Secular-rational and the Survival/Self-expression dimensions show remarkably strong correlations with a country's level of economic development (in Figure 1) and with a society's historic cultural heritage (in Figure 2). Moreover (as is demonstrated in Inglehart and Welzel, 2004), these dimensions show remarkably strong correlations with other criterion variables, such as a society's human fertility rate, or its score on the UN Gender Equality Measure. If low levels of cross-cultural validity (or massive measurement error) were present, we would not find such crisply structured cross-national patterns. Finally, these same highly structured patterns appear in each successive wave of the surveys, with each society generally falling into a position very close to the same relative position that it occupied in previous surveys. This would not happen unless the results for given societies were reasonably accurate.

Despite the very real difficulties linked with cross-cultural survey research, we have learned, and can continue to learn, a great deal about human values and behavior from survey data.

Conclusion

The Values Surveys project is the largest social science data collection effort undertaken to date. It started out with what in retrospect seems to be a modest number of countries (24) in 1981 and has expanded its coverage to over 80 societies. Social scientists now have at their disposal time series cultural values data from all over the world and can analyze it to help answer a wide range of significant questions. These data, to be sure, contain both random and systematic error. They contain sampling error, interviewer error, respondent error and other types of error. They are prone to all types of effects that may produce bias that are cited in the literature. The Values Surveys project faces all the usual difficulties of survey research, plus the additional difficulties of cross-cultural research. In addition, there are a number of practical difficulties that researchers working in the West need not worry about. But in statistical terms, we have every reason to believe that the error sum of squares is only a small proportion of the total sum of squares.

We have discussed at some length the problems of validity in cross-cultural research. Various methodological remedies, some very ingenious,[17] have been proposed

---

[17] The "anchoring vignettes" approach is one interesting example. Gary King's website at http://gking.harvard.edu/vign/ contains detailed information on this approach.

to ameliorate cross-cultural measurement efforts. Some of these techniques will probably be incorporated in future waves of these surveys. Nevertheless, using Values Surveys data, we have tried to demonstrate that some of the most difficult concepts for cross-cultural research have high construct validity and criterion-related validity. With carefully designed questionnaires and carefully worded and constructed questions, reliability and validity problems of cross-cultural research can be minimized.

Commenting on the difficulties of doing research in the Arab world, Saad Eddin Ibrahim wrote that "many problems are associated with the conduct of survey research and other kinds of social inquiry in the Arab world. Among them are such meta-sociological problems as (1) the lack of trained researchers, (2) the lack of research funds, and (3) the absence of academic freedom."[18] The lack of research funds is universal. But the lack of trained researchers and the absence of freedoms are serious problems in many parts of the world. The 2000 WVS was the first national sample survey ever carried out in some countries. We are in complete agreement with Ibrahim that lack of academic freedom in particular, and violations of basic human rights in general, are serious obstacles to all social research, but especially to survey research, which depends on answers from ordinary citizens who cannot be expected to speak their minds under the threat of imprisonment or other severe punishment. Fortunately, there are researchers who are making heroic efforts to conduct surveys under these circumstances and the research community owes much to them.

Table 1
Importance of God by Religiosity and Religion
(mean score)

| | Respondent is | | | | | |
| | Religious | | | Not Religious | | |
	n	Mean	St. Dev.	n	Mean	St. Dev.
Muslim	16,662	9.66	1.15	1,940	8.62	2.50
Roman Catholic	21,526	8.36	2.13	3,614	5.82	3.16
Protestant	7,988	8.22	2.38	2,094	4.12	2.86
Buddhist	422	6.72	2.90	430	4.87	2.37
Hindu	1,286	9.00	1.03	262	7.90	2.53
Jew	218	8.73	2.04	73	5.49	2.80

Note: Table is based on respondents who mentioned these broad religious categories and ignores those who offered finer denominational affiliations.

Table 2
Percent of Respondents Describing their Health as Good or Very Good

	1999-01	1995-97	Difference
Albania	75	73	2
Argentina	65	62	3
Bosnia Herzegovina	64	62	2
Chile	69	61	8
China	61	68	–7
India	63	59	4
Japan	55	56	–1
S Korea	78	76	2
Mexico	61	56	5
Moldova	30	31	–1
Nigeria	90	75	15
Pakistan	66	64	2
Peru	49	50	–1
Philippines	57	52	5
Puerto Rico	73	68	5
S Africa	78	68	10
Spain	76	68	8
Turkey	64	61	3
Macedonia	71	73	–2
USA	84	79	5
Serbia-Montenegro	56	51	5
	mean difference		3.4

Technical Note

Jaime Díez-Medrano and Ruud Luijkx

Questionnaire Development

The 1999-2001 Values Studies build on previous waves of this project that were carried out in 1981-82, 1990-91, and 1995-96. Each successive wave has covered a broader range of societies than the previous one, with the 1981 wave being carried out in 24 countries, the 1990 wave in 43 societies, the 1995 wave in 62 societies and the 2000 wave in 82 societies. Analysis of each successive wave has indicated that certain questions tapped theoretically interesting and substantively important concepts, while others were of little value. This led to the more useful items being replicated in future waves, while the less useful items were dropped, making room to add new items. The current wave added batteries of questions designed to probe into social capital, gender equality, pro-democratic political democracy, feelings of solidarity, and work ethics.

In preparation for the current wave, the WVS group gave special attention to improving our measures of support for gender equality and a democratic political culture, while the EVS group focused on items tapping religion and morality, society and politics, primary relations, and work. Suggestions were solicited from participants throughout the world, and expert groups developed the questionnaires used in the 1999-2001 survey, giving particular attention to issues of comparability between and across countries. An EVS methodology group also developed a methodological questionnaire to be completed by the principal investigators in each country, giving a detailed report on how fieldwork had been carried out in their country. These questionnaires are included in the CD-ROM that accompanies this sourcebook. We will not repeat all of these details here, but will simply give a general description of how fieldwork was conducted.

A final master questionnaire was prepared in English, and it was translated into the various national languages and, in many cases, the translated questionnaire was then independently translated back into English to check the accuracy of the translation. In most countries, the translated questionnaire was then pre-tested to help identify questions or concepts, for which the translation was problematic. In some cases, certain problematic questions were omitted from the national questionnaire.

In many countries, country-specific questions were included; in two-thirds of the countries all core questions were asked and in almost all countries the order of the questions in the master questionnaire was followed.

More details on questionnaire development and fieldwork is available from Halman (2001) and from the methodological questionnaires on the accompanying CD-ROM. The actual questionnaires, in the languages used in the various national surveys, are also available on the accompanying CD-ROM.

Sampling Procedures

In most countries, some form of stratified multistage random sampling was used to obtain representative national samples. In the first stages, a random selection of sampling points was made based on the given society's statistical regions, districts, census units, election sections, electoral registers, or voting stations, and central population registers. In most countries, the population size and/or degree of urbanization of these Primary Sampling Units was taken into account. In some countries, individuals were drawn directly from national registers. When no named individuals were drawn, various methods were used to select respondents, such as the Kish selection grid, the Troldhal and Carter-method, last or next birthday method, quota sampling on the basis of gender and age, and sometimes also on education or profession, and, in a few cases, random routes with age and gender quota. In most countries, substitution of respondents was allowed.

In all countries, samples were drawn from the entire population of 18 years and older. In most countries, no upper age limit was imposed. For a more detailed description of the sampling procedures, see the methodological questionnaires on the accompanying CD-ROM.

Fieldwork

Representative national samples of each country's public were interviewed using uniformly structured questionnaires. Fieldwork for most of the European countries was carried out in 1999; in most of the non-European countries, fieldwork took in 2001, but a few surveys carried over into 2002.

In most countries, the survey was carried out by professional survey organizations, using face-to-face interviews. In Iceland, phone interviews were used for remote areas (constituting 26% of the sample). The response rates varied from a low of 25 percent in Spain to a high of 95 percent in Slovakia.

In most countries, the sample was weighted to correct for deviations from national parameters. This weight factor was not constructed uniformly over countries. The following characteristics were used to construct the weighting factor in various countries: nationality, region, the urban/rural divide, town size, household size, sex, age, occupation, education, marital status, and economic activity.

In Spain, Morocco and Turkey, two surveys were carried out for the fourth wave of the Values Surveys: in Spain, the first was carried out in March-April, 1999 and the second in November, 2000; in Morocco, the first survey was carried out in August, 2001 and the second in February-March, 2002; in Turkey, the first survey was carried out in December 2000 to January 2001 and the second in September-October, 2001.

The tables in this sourcebook show the combined results from the two surveys, since our main interest is in comparing basic values that are relatively stable. But any reader who wishes to compare the results from these two surveys can do so by using the data on the accompanying CD-ROM, using variable S001 to distinguish between the two surveys.

Principal Investigators

Survey organizations, fieldwork dates, sample sizes and the principal investigators for each country are shown below. If not otherwise noted, the investigator is affiliated with the institution that carried out the fieldwork.

ALBANIA — INDEX Albania; February 17 to March 5, 2002. N = 1000. Principal investigator: Kosta Barjaba. A nationally representative multistage random probability sample of the population aged 18 and over.

ALGERIA — University of Algiers; March 1 to May 31, 2002. N = 1282. Principal investigators: Abdallah Bedaida, Mark Tessler. Respondents were selected by quota in each district based on sex and age.

ARGENTINA — Instituto Gallup de Argentina; January 22 to February 9, 1999. N = 1280. Principal investigator: Marita Carballo. A nationally representative sample of the population aged 18 and over. The sample was stratified according to two criteria, using multistage random selection of the sampling units.

ARMENIA — Sociological Research Center, Armenian Academy of Sciences (Yerevan). February, 1997. N = 2000. Principal Investigators, Gevork Pogosian and Hans-Dieter Klingemann, Berlin Science Center for Social Research.

AUSTRALIA — Roy Morgan Research Center (Melbourne); Fall, 1995. N = 2048. Principal investigator, Alan Black, Edith Cowan University.

AUSTRIA — Fessel GfK Austria N = 1522; August-October 1999. Principal investigator, Paul M. Zulehner, Universität Wien, Vienna.

AZERBAIJAN — SIAR (Baku); Nov, 1996. N = 2002. Principal Investigators, Dr. Ali Aliev and Hans-Dieter Klingemann, Berlin Science Center for Social Research.

BANGLADESH — Bangladesh Unnayan Parishad; August 20 to September 15, 2002. N = 1499. Principal investigators: Q. K. Ahmad, Nilufar Banu. Population 18 years old and over, representative of Bangladesh. Stratified random sampling used.

BELARUS — The Centre of Political and Sociological Researches of Belarus State University N = 1000; March-April 2000. Principal investigators, David Rotman and Larissa Titarenko, Belarus State University, Minsk.

BELGIUM — Nationaal Instituut voor Dataverzameling/Dimarso; N = 1912; March-June 1999. Principal investigators, Karel Dobbelaere and Jaak Billiet, Katholieke Universiteit, Leuven, and Bernadette Bawin, Université de Liège.

BOSNIA-HERCEGOVINA — Mareco INDEX Bosnia; December 3 to 10, 2001. N = 1200. Principal investigator: Hans-Dieter Klingemann. The survey interviewed in 16 cantons/regions, ensuring the required ethnic and demographic structure of the sample.

BRAZIL — Instituto Gallup de Opiniao Publico (Sao Paulo); Fall, 1997. N = 1149. Principal investigator, Carlos Matheus.

BULGARIA — Institute of Sociology at the Bulgarian Academy of Sciences N = 1000; June-July 1999. Principal investigators, Georgy Fotev and Mario Marinov, Bulgarian Academy of Sciences, Sofia.

CANADA — Dept. of Political Science, University of Toronto; August 3 to September 24, 2000. N = 1931. Principal investigator: Neil Nevitte. National probability sample of Canadians aged 18 and over.

CHILE — Latinobarómetro / MORI Chile; November 9 to 19, 2000. N = 1791. Principal investigator: Marta Lagos. Modified probabilistic sample, random in the first and second stage, by age and sex quota on the last stage.

CHINA — Research Center for Contemporary China, Peking University. N = 1000. Principal investigator: Shen Mingming. Population 18 years old and over, representative of China.

COLOMBIA — Centro Nacional de Consultoria (Bogota), 1997 and april 1998. n = 6025. Principal Investigators, Dr. Carlos Lemoine, John Sudarsky.

CROATIA — Market Research Agency "Target" N = 1003; March-April 1999. Principal investigator, Josip Baloban, Universitatis Zagrabiensies, Zagreb

CZECH REPUBLIC — SC&C Ltd., Statistical Computations and Computing N = 1908; March-May 1999. Principal investigator, Ladislav Rabušic, Masaryk University, Brno.

DENMARK — SFI, the Danish national institute of social research N = 1023; April-November 1999. Principal investigator, Peter Gundelach, University of Copenhagen, Copenhagen.

DOMINICAN REPUBLIC — Centro POVEDA (Santo Domingo); April, 1996. N = 417. Principal Investigators, Josefina Zaiter, Marcos Villaman and Julio Valeiron.

EL SALVADOR Universidad Centroamericana José Simeón Cañas y FEPADE; September 1999. N = 417. .

ESTONIA — Saar Poll, Ltd. N = 1005; October 1999. Principal investigator, Andrus Saar, Saar Poll, Tallinn.

EGYPT — Emac Research and Training Center in collaboration with Women's College, Ain Shams University; July 1, 2000 to January 1, 2001. N = 3000. Principal investigators: Abdel-Hamid Abdel-Latif, Mansoor Moaddel. A random sample of households in each PSU's was first selected. Eligible individuals who were 16 years old and over with certain educational level were then selected.

FINLAND — Suomen Gallup Oy N = 1038; September-October 2000. Principal investigator, Juhani Pehkonen, Suomen Gallup Oy, Helsinki.

FRANCE — Research International N = 1615; March-April 1999. Principal investigator, Jean-François Tchernia, Tchernia Etudes Conseil, Paris.

GEORGIA — Georgian Institute of Public Opinion, (Tbilisi); December, 1996. N = 2593. Principal Investigator, Merab Pachulia (GIPO) and Hans-Dieter Klingemann, Berlin Science Center for Social Research.

GERMANY — INFASS (Bonn) N = 2036; October-December 1999. Principal investigator, Wolfgang Jagodzinski, Universität zu Köln, Cologne.

GREAT BRITAIN — Quality Fieldwork & Research Services N = 1000; October-November 1999. Principal investigator, Helmut Anheier, London School of Economics and Political Science, London.

GREECE — Department of Psychology, School of Philosophy, the University of Athens N = 1142; March-June 1999. Principal investigators, James Georgas, Kostas Mylonas and Aikaterini Gari, the University of Athens, Athens.

HUNGARY — Szonda-Ipsos Média-, Vélemény- és Piaclutató Intézet (Budapest) N = 1000; November-December 1999. Principal investigator, Miklós Tomka, Hungarian Religious Research Centre, Budapest.

ICELAND — The Institute of Social Research at the University of Iceland N = 968; June-December 1999. Principal investigators, Fridrik H. Jonsson and Stefan Olafsson, University of Iceland, Reykjavik.

INDIA — Political Science Faculty, Bangalore University; August 20 to October 15, 2001. N = 2002. Principal investigators: Sandeep Shastri, Pradeep Chibber. National representative sample of Indians aged 18 and over.

INDONESIA — Institute of Quranic Studies; March 1 to September 30, 2001. N = 1004. Principal investigator: Nadra Muhamad Hosen. Stratified sample.

IRAN — Institute of Social Research and Studies, University of Teheran. N = 2532. Principal investigators: Taghi Azadarmaki, Mansoor Moaddel.

IRELAND — The Survey Unit, The Economic and Social Research Unit (Dublin) N = 1012; October 1999-February 2000. Principal investigators, Tony Fahey, ESRI, Dublin, Bernadette C. Hayes, the Queen's University, Belfast, and Richard Sinnott, Trinity College, Dublin.

ISRAEL — B.I. Cohen Institute for Public Opinion Research; September 1 to November 1, 2001. N = 1199. Principal investigator: Noah Lewin-Epstein. Population 18 years old and over, representative of Israel. Multistage sampling using Kish-grid method.

ITALY — Centro Ricerche Sociali di Moncomo G. e C. SaS (Milan) N = 2000; March-May 1999. Principal investigator, Renzo Gubert, University of Trento, Trento.

JAPAN — Nippon Research Center; July 11 to 26, 2000. N = 1362. Principal investigators: Seiko Yamazaki, Toru Takahashi. Population 17 years old and over, representative of Japan. Stratified multistage sampling.

JORDAN — Center for Strategic Studies, University of Jordan; September 15 to 21, 2001. N = 1223. Principal investigator: Fares al-Braizat, Mustafa Harmaneh. National representative multistage sampling of population 18 years old and over.

LATVIA — Latvia Social Research Centre N = 1013; March 1999. Principal investigator, Brigita Zepa, Baltic Institute of Social Sciences, Riga.

LITHUANIA — Baltic Surveys Ltd. N = 1018; November-December 1999. Principal investigators, Stanislovas Juknevicius, Lithuanian Institute of Culture and Arts, and Rasa Alishauskene, Institute for Social Research, Vilnius.

LUXEMBOURG — ILRES Market Research N = 1211; July-October 1999. Principal investigators, Pol Estgen and Michel Legrand, SeSoPi Centre Intercommunautaire a.s.b.l., Luxembourg.

MALTA — MISCO International N = 1002; March-May 1999. Principal investigator, Anthony M. Abela, University of Malta.

MACEDONIA — BRIMA Skopje; November 28 to December 2, 2001, N = 1055. Principal investigator: Hans-Dieter Klingemann. A nationally representative multistage random probability sample of the population aged 18 and over.

MEXICO — Instituto Tecnológico Autónomo de México; January 28 to February 7, 2000. N = 1535. Principal investigator: Alejandro Moreno. Multistage sampling procedure. Population between 18 and 94 years of age.

MOLDOVA — Institute of Sociology, Moldovan Academy of Sciences (Chisinau), N = 1008. Principal investigators: Ljubov Ishimova, Hans-Dieter Klingemann.

MONTENEGRO — Institute of Social Sciences, Belgrade; November 1 to 17, 2001. N = 1060. Principal investigators: Dragomir Pantic, Hans-Dieter Klingemann, Ronald Inglehart. Three-stage stratified probability sample, 18 years old and over.

MOROCCO 1 — SEREC, Bureau d'études; August 2 to 28, 2001. N = 1247. Principal investigator: Juan Diez-Nicolas (ASEP, Spain). The sampling method is based on sex, age, education level, socio-economic and professional level and place of residence.

MOROCCO 2 — SEREC, Bureau d'études; February 8 to March 7, 2002. N = 1013. Principal investigator: Mansoor Moaddel. The sampling method is based on sex, age, education level, socio-economic and professional level and place of residence.

NETHERLANDS — Survey data (Tilburg) N = 1003; March-August 1999. Principal investigators ,Wil Arts, Jacques Hagenaars, Loek Halman, and Ruud Luijkx, Tilburg University, Tilburg.

NEW ZEALAND — The New Zealand Study of Values Trust in association with The School of Sociology and Women's Studies- Massey University; September, 1998. N = 1201. Principal investigator, Dr. Paul Perry (Massey University), Dr. Alan Webster.

NIGERIA — Research and Marketing Services; October 13 to November 22, 2000. N = 2022. Principal investigators: Bukola Bandele, Kareem Tejumola. Population 18 years old and over, representative of Nigeria. Multi-stage sampling method was observed until the final respondent selection. The final respondent was selected by quota by age and sex in all locations

NORTHERN IRELAND — Research and Evaluation Services (Belfast) N = 1000; July-November 1999. Principal investigators, Bernadette C. Hayes, the Queen's University, Belfast, Tony Fahey, ESRI, Dublin, and Richard Sinnott, Trinity College, Dublin.

NORWAY — Norwegian Central Bureau of Statistics; Fall, 1996. N = 1,127. Principal investigator, Ola Listhaug, University of Trondheim.

PAKISTAN — Faculty of Agricultural, Economics and Rural Sociology, University of Agriculture; August 15, 2001 to February 28, 2002. N = 2000. Principal investigator: Farooq Tanwir. Combination of purposive, random and quota sampling.

PERU — Instituto Bartolomé de las Casas / Datum International; July 19 to 25, 2001. N = 1501. Principal investigator: Catalina Romero. Combination of random and probability sampling method. Kish method used to select final respondent.

PHILIPPINES — Social Weather Stations, July 9 to 27, 2001. N = 1200. Principal investigators: Linda Luz Guerrero, Gerardo Sandoval, Mahar Mangahas. Voting age adults (18 years old and over), representative of Philippines. Multistage probability sampling was used in the selection of sample spots.

POLAND — CBOS- Public Opinion Research Centre N = 1095; February-March 1999. Principal investigators, Aleksandra Jasinska-Kania, Mira Marody and Joanna Konieczna, University of Warsaw, Warsaw.

PORTUGAL — Euroteste-Marketing E Opinião N = 1000; October-December 1999. Principal investigators, Jorge Vala, Alice Ramos and Manuel Villaverde Cabral, Instituto de Cienciais Sociais, Lisbon.

PUERTO RICO — Dept. of Political Science, University of Puerto Rico; April 15 to May 15, 2001. N = 720. Principal investigators: Jorge Benítez-Nazario, Ángel Rivera-Ortiz. National population representative of Puerto Rico, without age cutoffs. Structured random sample.

ROMANIA — The Research Institute for the Quality of Life N = 1146; July 1999. Principal investigators, Malina Voicu, C t lin Zamfir and Lucien Pop, Romanian Academy, Bucharest.

RUSSIA — ROMIR (Moscow) N = 2500; April-June 1999. Principal investigator, Elena Bashkirova, ROMIR Research Group, Moscow.

SERBIA — Institute of Social Sciences, Belgrade; October 29 to November 8, 2001. N = 1200. Principal investigators: Dragomir Pantic, Hans-Dieter Klingemann, Ronald Inglehart. Three-stage stratified probability sample, 18 years old and over.

SINGAPORE — Faculty of Arts and Social Sciences, National University of Singapore with the assistance of Joshua Research Consultants; March 14 to August 7, 2002. N = 1512. Principal investigator: Tan Ern Ser. Stratified, random sample of Singapore citizens.

SLOVAKIA — Agentúra MVK (Bratislava) N = 1331; June-July 1999. Principal investigator, Zuzana Kusá, Slovak Academy of Sciences, Bratislava.

SLOVENIA — Public Opinion and Mass Communications Research Center, Faculty of Social Sciences, University of Ljubljana N = 1006; October 1999. Principal investigators, Niko Tos and Brina Malnar, University of Ljubljana, Ljubljana.

SOUTH AFRICA — Markinor (Stellenbosch); March 1 to May 22, 2001. N = 3000. Principal investigator: Mari Harris, Hennie Kotzé (University of Stellenbosch). National representative sample of South Africa's population aged 16 and over. Random sample according to a selection grid used by Markinor.

SOUTH KOREA — Dpt. of Political Science and Diplomacy, Ewha Women's University; November 10 to 21, 2001. N = 1200. Principal investigator: Soo Young Auh. Population 20 years old and over, representative of the Republic of Korea. Selection of 120 clusters with a sample of 10 chosen from the household of each of the selected clusters.

SPAIN (WVS) — Análisis Sociológicos, Económicos y Políticos, S.A. (ASEP); November 6 to 13, 2000. N = 1209. Principal investigators: Juan Díez-Nicolás, Jose R. Torregrosa, Juan Diez-Medrano. National representative multistage random sample of the Spanish population aged 18 and over. Kish-grid method used.

SPAIN (EVS) — Data SA (Madrid) N = 1200; March-April 1999. Principal investigators, Javier Elzo, Universidad de Deusto, Bilbao, and Francisco Andrés Orizo, DATA, Madrid.

SWEDEN — ARS Research AB, Stockholm; November 15, 1999 to February 13, 2000. N = 1015. Principal investigators: Bi Puranen, Theseus Institute, Sophia Antipolis (France) and Thorleif Pettersson, Uppsala University. A two-stage representative sample of Swedish population aged 18-75 years old.

SWITZERLAND — Geselleschaft fuer Socialforschung; Fall, 1996. N = 1212. Principal investigators, Simon Hug and Pascal Sciarini, University of Geneva.

TAIWAN — Survey Research Center, Academia Sinica (Taipei); summer, 1994 and summer1995. N = 1452. Principal Investigators, Hei-yuan Chiu, Pi-chao Chen, Jin-yun Liu, Ronald Inglehart.

TANZANIA — University of Dar-es-Salaam, Tanzania; May 30 to November 6, 2001. N = 1171. Principal investigator: Prof. G. K. Munishi. Multistage representative sample of Tanzania's population aged 18 and over.

TURKEY (WVS) — Bogazici University (Istanbul) and Birim Arastirma; December 2000 to January 2001. N = 3401. Principal investigator: Yilmaz Esmer. Multistage representative sample of Turkey's population aged 18 and over.

TURKEY (EVS) — Bogazici University (Istanbul) and Birim Arastirma N = 1206; September-October 2001. Principal investigator, Yilmaz Esmer, Multistage representative sample of Turkey's population aged 18 and over.

UKRAINE — Social Monitoring Centre (NGO) and Ukrainian Institute for Social Research N = 1195; December 1999. Principal investigator, Olga N. Balakireva, Ukrainian Institute for Social Research, Kiev.

UGANDA — Markinor (Stellenbosch, South Africa); March 3 to 18, 2001. N = 1002. Principal investigator: Mari Harris (Stellenbosch). National representative sample of Uganda's population aged 18 and over. Random sample according to a selection grid used by Markinor.

URUGUAY — Equipos Consultores Associados (Montevideo). October, 1996. N = 1000. Principal Investigators, Cesar Aguiar, Jose Arocena, Augustin Canzani, Rafael Mendizabal.

USA — Institute for Social Research, University of Michigan; first phase: November 19 to December 23, 1999; second phase: August 4 to September 25, 2000. N = 1200. Principal investigators: Virginia Hodgkinson, Ronald Inglehart and Miguel Basáñez. A nationally representative multistage random probability sample of the population aged 18 and over.

VENEZUELA — Red Interuniversitaria de Cultura Política, Universidad del Zulia; November 30 to December 20, 2000. N = 1200. Principal investigator: Jose Molina. Random sample stratified by States and Municipalities within locations of 5000 inhabitants and over.

VIETNAM — Institute of Human Studies; August 28 to September 30, 2001. N = 995. Principal investigators: Pham Minh Hac, Pham Thanh Nghi, Russell Dalton and Nhu-Ngoc Ong. . Multistage probability sample.

ZIMBABWE — Markinor (Stellenbosch, South Africa); February 2 to March 28, 2001. N = 1002. Principal investigator: Mari Harris (Stellenbosch). National representative sample of Zimbabwe's population aged 18 and over. Random sample according to the traditional Kish-grid method.

Data cleaning and weighting

After the fieldwork, data cleaning was carried out by the principal investigators. Further cleaning for the European surveys was performed at Tilburg University and the Zentralarchiv in Cologne and by JD Systems in Madrid, for the other countries.

Data validation was carried out, using the documentation, statistical data and survey data cleaning software that makes data cleaning more reliable by providing automatic procedures and tests. Validation involved the following steps:

- Comparing the country questionnaire and the official questionnaire.
- Matching identical questions.

- Finding, documenting and correcting differences in the categories.
- Checking for filter inconsistencies
- Validation of the cleaning procedure by the participant country
- Building a final country file after applying the approved cleaning procedures.

Semantic analysis was done in order to identify inconsistencies, suspicious deviations from other country results or incoherencies between different question answers. Deviations from reasonable patterns were noted and if they seemed significant, the principal investigators from the given country were consulted to determine whether these inconsistencies reflected methodological anomalies or errors in the data validation phase.

Creating the Integrated dataset

To combine the various national datasets into one integrated dataset, a master codebook was created, based on the national data sets, the national questionnaires, and the master questionnaire. For the European datasets, this was done at the Zentralarchiv in Cologne, and Tilburg University (in collaboration with the Netherlands Institute for Scientific Information Services); the country data files were then integrated at Tilburg University. In September 2003, Zentralarchiv, in collaboration with Tilburg University, released the CD-ROM "EVS 1999/2000" containing 33 national data sets, the integrated data set and the relevant documentation required for secondary analyses. (see Luijkx, Brislinger, and Zenk-Moeltgen 2003).

The 47 other surveys were cleaned and combined into one integrated dataset by JD Systems in Madrid, which then combined the European and non-European surveys into the dataset on the accompanying CD-ROM. This CD contains a browsing program developed by JD Systems that provides for:

- Simple and extended searches in a user-friendly manner.
- Analyses and the creation of tables or graphs for frequencies, cross-tabulations and comparative analyses.
- The ability to print codebooks, tables and graphs.

In addition, the user can get direct access to the following information:

- The national data sets and the integrated data set (in SPSS-format).
- The original questionnaires and the methodological questionnaires of all participating countries.
- The Master Questionnaire and the summarized information from the methodological questionnaires.
- The List of Country Codes, which also contains the ZA number to identify the data sets and the corresponding documentation, and the internet abbreviations which were used for the names of the country-specific variables.

All documents are available as PDF-files and can be viewed and printed with Adobe Acrobat Reader included on the CD-ROM. The data files are in SPSS-format for analyses using SPSS software

Construction of the independent variables

In this source book, we cross tabulate each question by the following independent variables: gender, age, education, income, and materialist-postmaterialist values.

For gender, we use the obvious categories "female" (51%) and "male" (49%). For age, the following three age groups are used: 15-29 years: 30% / 30-49 years: 41% / 50+ years 29%. The **education** variable (x025) distinguishes the following categories:

1. inadequately completed elementary education
2. completed (compulsory) elementary education
3. (compulsory) elementary education and basic vocational qualification
4. secondary, intermediate vocational qualification
5. secondary, intermediate general qualification
6. full secondary, maturity level certificate
7. higher education - lower-level tertiary certificate
8. higher education - upper-level tertiary certificate

We construct a category "lower" by collapsing categories 1-3; "medium" by collapsing 4-5-6; and "upper" by combining 7 and 8. The marginals for the constructed variable education are:

Lower   38%
Medium   42%
Upper   20%

For income, we used the national income variables, recoded into three categories: 1=Lower, 2=Middle and 3=Upper. As in Inglehart, Basáñez and Moreno (1998), the sample was recoded so that each category would comprise a third of the sample as closely as possible. In the following table the national codes that fall in each of the three categories are indicated:

	Lower	Middle	Upper
Albania	1-4	5,6	7-10
Algeria	1,2	3	4-10
Argentina	1-3	4-7	8-10
Armenia	1,2	3,4	5-10
Australia	1-3	4-7	8-10
Austria	1-3	4-6	7-10
Azerbaijan	1,2	3,4	5-7
Bangladesh	1-3	4,5	6-10
Belarus	1-3	4,5	6-9
Belgium	1-3	4-6	7-10
Bosnia and Herzegovina	1-3	4,5	6-10
Brazil	1	2	3-10
Bulgaria	1,2	3-6	7-10
Canada	1-3	4-6	7-10

	Lower	Middle	Upper
Chile	1,2	3-6	7-10
China	1-5	6,7	8-10
Colombia	1-3	4,5	6-10
Croatia	1,2	3,4	5-10
Czech Republic	1,2	3-5	6-10
Denmark	1-3	4-7	8-10
Dominican Republic	1-3	4-6	7-10
Egypt	1-4	5,6	7-10
El Salvador	1-4	5,6	7-10
Estonia	1,2	3,4	5-10
Finland	1-3	4,5	6-10
France	1,2	3-5	6-10
Georgia	1,2	3	4-10
Germany	1-3	4,5	6-10
Great Britain	1-4	5,6	7-10
Greece	1-4	5,6	7-10
Hungary	1,2	3,4	5-10
Iceland	1-3	4-6	7-10
India	1,2	3	4-10
Indonesia	1-5	6,7	8-10
Iran	1-4	5	6-10
Ireland	1-4	5,6	7-10
Israel	1,2	3,4	5-9
Italy	1-3	4-6	7-10
Japan	1-3	4-6	7-10
Jordan	1,2	3,4	5-10
Korea, South	1-4	5	6-10
Latvia	1,2	3	4-10
Lithuania	1,2	3,4	5-10
Luxembourg	1-3	4-7	8-10
Macedonia	1-3	4,5	6-10
Malta	1-3	4,5	6-10
Mexico	1-3	4-6	7-10
Moldavia	1,2	3,4	5-10
Montenegro	1-4	5-7	8-10
Morocco	1-3	4,5	6-10
Netherlands	1-5	6,7	8-10
New Zealand	1-4	5-7	8-10
Nigeria	1-4	5,6	7-10
Northern Ireland	1-4	5,6	7-10
Pakistan	1-3	4,5	6-10
Peru	1,2	3,4	5-9
Philippines	1-3	4,5	6-10
Poland	1-3	4,5	6-10
Portugal	1,2	3,4	5,6
Puerto Rico	1	2,3	4-10

	Lower	Middle	Upper
Romania	1-3	4-6	7-10
Russian Federation	1-4	5-7	8-10
Serbia	1-3	4-6	7-10
Singapore	1,2	3,4	5-10
Slovakia	1-3	4-6	7-10
Slovenia	1-4	5-7	8-10
South Africa	1-3	4,5	6-10
Spain	1-3	4,5	6-10
Sweden	1-4	5-7	8-10
Switzerland	1-3	4-7	8-10
Taiwan	1-3	4-7	8-10
Tanzania	1,2	3,4	5-10
Turkey	1,2	3,4	5-10
Uganda	1,2	3	4-7
Ukraine	1,2	3,4	5-10
United States	1-4	5-7	8-10
Uruguay	1-3	4,5	6-10
Venezuela	1-3	4-6	7-10
Viet Nam	1-4	5	6-10
Zimbabwe	1,2	3,4	5-9

Not all nations used the full ten-point scale in coding income: in some cases, the scale was shortened, or some codes were missing data.

The **Materialist/Postmaterialist Values** variable measures the extent to which the respondent gives top priority to economic and physical security, on one hand; or to autonomy and self expression. This index is based on the respondent's first and second choices in the original four item Materialist / Postmaterialist values battery, which follows:

"People sometimes talk about what the aims of this country should be for the next ten years. On this card are listed some of the goals which different people would give top priority. Would you please say which one of these you, yourself, consider the most important? And which would be the second most important?"

	1ˢᵗ CHOICE	2ⁿᵈ CHOICE
1. Maintaining order in the nation	1	1
2. Giving people more say in important government decisions	2	2
3. Fighting rising prices	3	3
4. Protecting freedom of speech	4	4

The first and third options tap Materialist priorities, while the second and fourth options tap Postmaterialist priorities. If both Materialist items are given high priority, the score is "1"; if both Postmaterialist items are given high priority, the score is "3" if one Materialist item and one Postmaterialist item are given high priority, the score is "2." If the respondent makes only one or no choices, the result is missing data.

Most samples contain a **weighting** variable. These weighting variables for the European Values Study are described in more detail in Halman (2001). For the present dataset, we have constructed a new weight variable that incorporates the national weights but also gives each country the same weight to offset the fact that some countries used much larger samples than others, which could distort results when two or more samples are analyzed together. When this weighting factor is used, each country has the same weight, regardless of sample size.

REFERENCES

Halman, Loek. 2001. *The European Values Study: A Third Wave. Source book of the 1999/2000 European Values Study Surveys*. Tilburg: EVS/WORC.

Inglehart, Ronald, Miguel Basáñez, and Alejandro Moreno. 1998. *Human Values and Beliefs. A Cross-Cultural Sourcebook*. Ann Arbor (MI): The University of Michigan Press.

Luijkx, Ruud, E. Brislinger, and W. Zenk-Moeltgen. 2003. „European Values Study 1999/2000- A Third Wave: Data, Documentation and Databases on CD-ROM." *ZA-Information* 52:171-183.

World values survey
2000-2001 questionnaire

INTRODUCTION BY INTERVIEWER:

Hello. I am from the [NAME OF ORGANIZATION]. We are carrying out the [NATION] part of a world-wide study of what people value in life. This study will interview samples representing most of the world's people. Your name has been selected at random as part of a representative sample of the [BRAZILIAN] public. I'd like to ask your views on a number of different subjects. Your help will contribute to a better understanding of what people all over the world believe and want out of life.

SHOW CARD A

For each of the following, indicate how important it is in your life. Would you say it is:

		Very important	Rather important	Not very important	Not at all important	DK
v4	Family	1	2	3	4	9
v5	Friends	1	2	3	4	9
v6	Leisure time	1	2	3	4	9
v7	Politics	1	2	3	4	9
v8	Work	1	2	3	4	9
v9	Religion	1	2	3	4	9
v10	Service to others	1	2	3	4	9

V11. Taking all things together, would you say you are:
[READ OUT]

    1. Very happy
    2. Quite happy
    3. Not very happy
    4. Not at all happy
    9.   Don't know [DO NOT READ OUT]

V12. All in all, how would you describe your state of health these days? Would you say it is... (READ OUT REVERSING ORDER FOR ALTERNATE CONTACTS)

1. Very good
2. Good
3. Fair
4. Poor
9.   Don't know [DO NOT READ OUT]

SHOW CARD B

V13. With which of these two statements do you tend to agree? (CODE ONE ANSWER ONLY)

A. Regardless of what the qualities and faults of one's parents are, one must always love and respect them
B. One does not have the duty to respect and love parents who have not earned it by their behavior and attitudes
1. Tend to agree with statement A
2. Tend to agree with statement B
9.   Don't know [DO NOT READ OUT]

SHOW CARD C

V14. Which of the following statements best describes your views about parents' responsibilities to their children? (CODE ONE ONLY)

1 Parents' duty is to do their best for their children even at the expense of their own well-being
2 Parents have a life of their own and should not be asked to sacrifice their own well-being for the sake of their children
3 Neither [IF VOLUNTEERED]
9 Don't know [DO NOT READ OUT]

SHOW CARD D

Here is a list of qualities that children can be encouraged to learn at home. Which, if any, do you consider to be especially important? Please choose up to five.
(CODE FIVE ONLY)

		Important	Not Mentioned
V15	Independence	1	2
V16	Hard work	1	2
V17	Feeling of responsibility	1	2
V18	Imagination	1	2
V19	Tolerance and respect for other people	1	2

		Important	Not Mentioned
V20	Thrift, saving money and things	1	2
V21	Determination, perseverance	1	2
V22	Religious faith	1	2
V23	Unselfishness	1	2
V24	Obedience	1	2

V25. Generally speaking, would you say that most people can be trusted or that you need to be very careful in dealing with people?

    1. Most people can be trusted
    2. Need to be very careful
    9.   Don't know [DO NOT READ OUT]

V26. Do you think most people would try to take advantage of you if they got a chance, or would they try to be fair?

    1. Would take advantage
    2. Would try to be fair
    9.   Don't know [DO NOT READ OUT]

    I'm going to ask how of often you do various things. For each activity, would you say you do them every week or nearly every week; once or twice a month; only a few times a year; or not at all?

		Weekly/ nearly every week	Once or twice a month	Only a few times a year	Not at all	DK
V27	Spend time with parents or other relatives	1	2	3	4	9
V28	Spend time with friends	1	2	3	4	9
V29	Spend time socially with colleagues from work or your profession	1	2	3	4	9
V30	Spend time with people at your church, mosque or synagogue	1	2	3	4	9
V31	Spend time socially with people at sports clubs or voluntary or service organization	1	2	3	4	9

V32. When you get together with your friends, would you say you discuss political matters frequently, occasionally or never?

1. Frequently
2. Occasionally
3. Never
9.   Don't know [DO NOT READ OUT]

SHOW CARD B

I am now going to read out some statements about the environment. For each one read out, can you tell me whether you agree strongly, agree, disagree or strongly disagree? (Read out each statement and code an answer for each)

		Strongly Agree	Agree	Disagree	Strongly Disagree	DK
v33	I would give part of my income if I were certain that the money would be used to prevent environmental pollution	1	2	3	4	9
v34	I would agree to an increase in taxes if the extra money were used to prevent environmental pollution	1	2	3	4	9
v35	The Government should reduce environmental pollution, but it should not cost me any money	1	2	3	4	9

V36. Here are two statements people sometimes make when discussing the environment and economic growth. Which of them comes closer to your own point of view?

1. Protecting the environment should be given priority, even if it causes slower economic growth and some loss of jobs.
2. Economic growth and creating jobs should be the top priority, even if the environment suffers to some extent
3. Other answer (VOLUNTEERED)
9. DK

V37. For each of the following pairs of statements, please tell me which one comes closest to your own views:

1. Human beings should master nature;
        OR
2. Humans should coexist with nature.
9. DK

V38

1. To build good human relationships, it is most important to try to understand others' preferences;
   OR
2. To build good relationships, it is most important to express one's own preferences clearly.
9. DK

SHOW CARD C

Please look carefully at the following list of voluntary organisations and activities and say...

which, if any, do you belong to? (Code all 'yes' answers as 1, if not mentioned code as 2)

		Belong	Not Mentioned
V39	Social welfare services for elderly, handicapped or deprived people	1	2
V40	Religious or church organizations	1	2
V41	Education, arts, music or cultural activities	1	2
V42	Labor unions	1	2
V43	Political parties or groups	1	2
V44	Local community action on issues like poverty, employment, housing, racial equality	1	2
V45	Third world development or human rights	1	2
V46	Conservation, environment, animal rights groups	1	2
V47	Professional associations	1	2
V48	Youth work (e.g. scouts, guides, youth clubs etc.)	1	2
V49	Sports or recreation	1	2
V50	Women's groups	1	2
V51	Peace movement	1	2
V52	Voluntary organizations concerned with health	1	2
V53	Other groups	1	2

B) And for which, if any, are you currently doing unpaid voluntary work?
[Code all 'yes' answers as 1; if not mentioned code as 2]

		Do voluntary work	Not Mentioned
V54	Social welfare services for elderly, handicapped or deprived people	1	2
V55	Religious or church organizations	1	2
V56	Education, arts, music or cultural activities	1	2
V57	Labor unions	1	2
V58	Political parties or groups	1	2

		Do voluntary work	Not Mentioned
V59	Local community action on issues like poverty, employment, housing, racial equality	1	2
V60	Third world development or human rights	1	2
V61	Conservation, environmental, animal rights groups	1	2
V62	Professional associations	1	2
V63	Youth work (scouts, guides, youth clubs, etc.)	1	2
V64	Sports or recreation	1	2
V65	Women's groups	1	2
V66	Peace movement	1	2
V67	Voluntary organizations concerned with health	1	2

SHOW CARD G

On this list are various groups of people. Could you please sort out any that you would not like to have as neighbors? (CODE AN ANSWER FOR EACH)

		Mentioned	Not Mentioned
V68	People with a criminal record	1	2
V69	People of a different race	1	2
V70	Heavy drinkers	1	2
V71	Emotionally unstable people	1	2
V72	Muslims	1	2
V73	Immigrants/foreign workers	1	2
V74	People who have AIDS	1	2
V75	Drug addicts	1	2
V76	Homosexuals	1	2
V77	Jews	1	2

In societies with Islamic majorities, ask about Christians
If Jews are not a salient group in your society, substitute some small but visible minority group

Do you agree or disagree with the following statements?

		Agree	Neither	Disagree	DK
V78	When jobs are scarce, men should have more right to a job than women	1	2	3	4
V79	When jobs are scarce, employers should give priority to [BRITISH] people over immigrants	1	2	3	4

[Substitute your own nationality]

SHOW CARD H

V80. How satisfied are you with the financial situation of your household? If "1" means you are completely dissatisfied on this scale, and "10" means you are completely satisfied, where would you put your satisfaction with your household's financial situation?

Dissatisfied					Satisfied				
1	2	3	4	5	6	7	8	9	10

DK = 99

SHOW CARD H AGAIN

V81. All things considered, how satisfied are you with your life as a whole these days? Please use this card to help with your answer.

Dissatisfied					Satisfied				
1	2	3	4	5	6	7	8	9	10

DK = 99

V82. Some people feel they have completely free choice and control over their lives, while other people feel that what they do has no real effect on what happens to them. Please use this scale where 1 means "none at all" and 10 means "a great deal" to indicate how much freedom of choice and control you feel you have over the way your life turns out.

None at all					A great deal				
1	2	3	4	5	6	7	8	9	10

DK = 99

SHOW CARD I

V83. Which point on this scale most clearly describes how much weight you place on work (including housework and schoolwork), as compared with leisure or recreation?

1. It's leisure that makes life worth living, not work
2.
3.
4.
5. Work is what makes life worth living, not leisure
9. DK

SHOW CARD J

V84. Now I would like to ask you something about the things which would seem to you, personally, most important if you were looking for a job. Here are some of the things many people take into account in relation to their work. Regardless of whether you're actually looking for a job, which one would you, personally, place first if you were looking for a job?

1. A good income so that you do not have any worries about money
2. A safe job with no risk of closing down or unemployment
3. Working with people you like
4. Doing an important job which gives you a feeling of accomplishment
9. DK

V85. And what would be your second choice?

1. A good income so that you do not have any worries about money
2. A safe job with no risk of closing down or unemployment
3. Working with people you like
4. Doing an important job which gives you a feeling of accomplishment
9. DK

SHOW CARD J2

Here are some more aspects of a job that people say are important. Please look at them
and tell me which ones you personally think are important in a job? (CODE ALL MEN-
TIONED)

		Mentioned	Not mentioned
V86	Good pay	1	2
V87	Not too much pressure	1	2
V88	Good job security	1	2
V89	A job respected by people in general	1	2
V90	Good hours	1	2
V91	An opportunity to use initiative	1	2
V92	Generous holidays	1	2
V93	A job in which you feel you can achieve something	1	2
V94	A responsible job	1	2
V95	A job that is interesting	1	2
V96	A job that meets one's abilities	1	2

SHOW CARD L

N2. Do you agree or disagree with the following statements?

		Strongly agree	Agree	Neither agree or disagree	Disagree	Strongly disagree	DK
V97	To fully develop your talents, you need to have a job	1	2	3	4	5	9

		Strongly agree	Agree	Neither agree or disagree	Disagree	Strongly disagree	DK
V98	It is humiliating to receive money without having to work for it	1	2	3	4	5	9
V99	People who don't work turn lazy	1	2	3	4	5	9
V100	Work is a duty towards society	1	2	3	4	5	9
V101	People should not have to work if they don't want to	1	2	3	4	5	9
V102	Work should always come first, even if it means less spare time	1	2	3	4	5	9

V103. Imagine two secretaries, of the same age, doing practically the same job. One finds out that the other earns considerably more than she does. The better paid secretary, however, is quicker, more efficient and more reliable at her job. In your opinion, is it fair or not fair that one secretary is paid more than the other?

    1 Fair
    2 Not fair
    9 Don't know [DO NOT READ OUT]

SHOW CARD K

V104. There is a lot of discussion about how business and industry should be managed. Which of these four statements comes closest to your opinion? (CODE ONE ONLY)

    1 The owners should run their business or appoint the managers
    2 The owners and the employees should participate in the selection of managers
    3 The government should be the owner and appoint the managers
    4 The employees should own the business and should elect the managers
    9 Don't know [DO NOT READ OUT]

V105. People have different ideas about following instructions at work. Some say that one should follow one's superior's instructions even when one does not fully agree with them. Others say that one should follow one's superior's instructions only when one is convinced that they are right. With which of these two opinions do you agree?

    1 Should follow instructions
    2 Must be convinced first
    3 Depends [IF VOLUNTEERED]
    9 Don't know [DO NOT READ OUT]

V106. Are you currently ....(READ OUT AND CODE ONE ONLY)

    1 Married
    2 Living together as married
    3 Divorced
    4 Separated
    5 Widowed
    6 Single

V107. Have you had any children? IF YES, how many?

    0   No child
    1   1 child
    2   2 children
    3   3 children
    4   4 children
    5   5 children
    6   6 children
    7   7 children
    8   8 or more children
    9   No answer

V108. What do you think is the ideal size of the family — how many children, if any?

    0   None
    1   1 child
    2   2 children
    3   3 children
    4   4 children
    5   5 children
    6   6 children
    7   7 children
    8   8 or more children
    9   DK, no answer

V109. If someone says a child needs a home with both a father and a mother to grow up happily, would you tend to agree or disagree?

1 Tend to agree
2 Tend to disagree
9 Don't know [DO NOT READ OUT]

V110. Do you think that a woman has to have children in order to be fulfilled or is this not necessary?

1 Needs children
2 Not necessary
9 Don't know [DO NOT READ OUT]

V111. Do you agree or disagree with the following statement? (READ OUT): "Marriage is an out-dated institution"

1 Agree
2 Disagree
9 Don't know [DO NOT READ OUT]

V112. If a woman wants to have a child as a single parent but she doesn't want to have a stable relationship with a man, do you approve or disapprove?

1 Approve
2 Disapprove
3 Depends [IF VOLUNTEERED]
9 Don't know [DO NOT READ OUT]

For each of the following statements I read out, can you tell me how much you agree with each. Do you agree strongly, agree, disagree, or disagree strongly?

		Agree strongly	Agree	Disagree	Strongly disagree	DK
V113	One of my main goals in life has been to make my parents proud	1	2	3	4	9
V114	I make a lot of effort to live up to what my friends expect	1	2	3	4	9
V115	A working mother can establish just as warm and secure a relationship with her children as a mother who does not work	1	2	3	4	9
V116	Being a housewife is just as fulfilling as working for pay	1	2	3	4	9

		Agree strongly	Agree	Disagree	Strongly disagree	DK
V117	Both the husband and wife should contribute to household income	1	2	3	4	9
V118	On the whole, men make better political leaders than women do	1	2	3	4	9
V119	A university education is more important for a boy than for a girl	1	2	3	4	9

SHOW CARD L

V120. People sometimes talk about what the aims of this country should be for the next ten years. On this card are listed some of the goals which different people would give top priority. Would you please say which one of these you, yourself, consider the most important? CODE ONE ANSWER ONLY UNDER "First Choice."

V121. And which would be the next most important? CODE ONE ANSWER ONLY UNDER "Second Choice."

	1st CHOICE	2nd CHOICE
A high level of economic growth	1	1
Making sure this country has strong defense forces	2	2
Seeing that people have more say about how things are done at their jobs and in their communities	3	3
Trying to make our cities and countryside more beautiful	4	4
Don't know [DO NOT READ OUT]	9	9

SHOW CARD M

V122. If you had to choose, which one of the things on this card would you say is most important? CODE ONE ANSWER ONLY

V123. And which would be the next most important? CODE ONE ANSWER ONLY

	1st CHOICE	2nd CHOICE
Maintaining order in the nation	1	1
Giving people more say in important government decisions	2	2
Fighting rising prices	3	3
Protecting freedom of speech	4	4
Don't know [DO NOT READ OUT]	9	9

SHOW CARD N

V124. Here is another list. In your opinion, which one of these is most important? CODE ONE ANSWER ONLY

V125. And what would be the next most important? CODE ONE ANSWER ONLY

	1st CHOICE	2nd CHOICE
A stable economy	1	1
Progress toward a less impersonal and More humane society	2	2
Progress toward a society in which Ideas count more than money	3	3
The fight against crime	4	4
Don't know [DO NOT READ OUT]	9	9

V126. Of course, we all hope that there will not be another war, but if it were to come to that, would you be willing to fight for your country?

    1 Yes
    2 No
    9 Don't know [DO NOT READ OUT]

I'm going to read out a list of various changes in our way of life that might take place in the near future. Please tell me for each one, if it were to happen, whether you think it would be a good thing, a bad thing, or don't you mind?

		GOOD	Don't Mind	BAD
V127	Less emphasis on money and material possessions	1	2	3
V128	Less importance placed on work in our lives	1	2	3
V129	More emphasis on the development of technology	1	2	3
V130	Greater respect for authority	1	2	3
V131	More emphasis on family life	1	2	3

V132. In the long run, do you think the scientific advances we are making will help or harm mankind?

    1 Will help
    2 Will harm
    3 Some of each
    9 Don't know [DO NOT READ OUT]

V133. How interested would you say you are in politics?

    1 Very interested
    2 Somewhat interested
    3 Not very interested
    4 Not at all interested
    9 Don't know [DO NOT READ OUT]

SHOW CARD O

[WHICH LISTS "HAVE DONE," "MIGHT DO," WOULD NEVER DO]
    Now I'd like you to look at this card. I'm going to read out some different forms
of political action that people can take, and I'd like you to tell me, for each one, whether you have actually done any of these things, whether you might do it or would never,
under any circumstances, do it.

		Have done	Might do	Would never do	DK
V134	Signing a petition	1	2	3	4
V135	Joining in boycotts	1	2	3	4
V136	Attending lawful demonstrations	1	2	3	4
V137	Joining unofficial strikes	1	2	3	4
V138	Occupying buildings or factories	1	2	3	4

SHOW CARD P

V139. In political matters, people talk of "the left" and "the right." How would you place
your views on this scale, generally speaking?

Left   Right
 1   2   3   4   5   6   7   8   9   10
DK = 99

SHOW CARD Q

V140. On this card are three basic kinds of attitudes concerning the society we live in.
Please choose the one which best describes your own opinion. CODE ONE ONLY

    1 The entire way our society is organized must be radically changed by revolu-
       tionary action
    2 Our society must be gradually improved by reforms
    3 Our present society must be valiantly defended against all subversive forces
    9 Don't know [DO NOT READ OUT]

SHOW CARD R

Now I'd like you to tell me your views on various issues. How would you place your
views on this scale? 1 means you agree completely with the statement on the left; 10

means you agree completely with the statement on the right; and if your views fall somewhere in between, you can choose any number in between.

V141

Incomes should be made more equal						We need larger income differences as incentives for individual effort			
1	2	3	4	5	6	7	8	9	10

DK = 99

V142

Private ownership of business and industry should be increased						Government ownership of business and industry should be increased			
1	2	3	4	5	6	7	8	9	10

DK = 99

V143

The government should take more responsibility to ensure that everyone is provided for						People should take more responsibility to provide for themselves			
1	2	3	4	5	6	7	8	9	10

DK = 99

V144

Competition is good. It stimulates people to work hard and develop new ideas						Competition is harmful. It brings out the worst in people			
1	2	3	4	5	6	7	8	9	10

DK = 99

Now I'm going to read you some pairs of contrasting statements. For each pair, do you think that the first statement or the second one best describes the CURRENT SITUATION in this country?

NOTE: The early version of this questionnaire, used in some countries including the U.S., has the following item INSTEAD OF V145A –V145F:

V145

Ideas that have stood the test of time are generally best						New ideas are generally better than old ones			
1	2	3	4	5	6	7	8	9	10

DK = 99

V145A. An egalitarian society where the   A competitive society, where
        gap between rich and poor is small,   wealth is distributed according
        regardless of achievement   to ones' achievement

			somewhat		
closer	somewhat	can't say	closer to	closer to	
to first	closer to first	which	second	second	NA
1	2	3	4	5	9

V145B. A society with extensive social   A society where taxes are low and
        welfare, but high taxes   individuals take responsibility for
                                                   themselves

			somewhat		
closer	somewhat	can't say	closer to	closer to	
to first	closer to first	which	second	second	NA
1	2	3	4	5	9

V145C. A society that assures safety and   A deregulated society where
        stability through appropriate   people are responsible for their
        regulations   own actions

			somewhat		
closer	somewhat	can't say	closer to	closer to	
to first	closer to first	which	second	second	NA
1	2	3	4	5	9

And now, could you please tell me which type of society this country you think
this country SHOULD aim to be in the future. For each pair of statements,
would you prefer being closer to the first or to the second alternative?

V145D. An egalitarian society where the   A competitive society, where
        gap between rich and poor is small,   wealth is distributed according to
        regardless of achievement   ones' achievement

			somewhat		
closer	somewhat	can't say	closer to	closer to	
to first	closer to first	which	second	second	NA
1	2	3	4	5	9

V145E. A society with extensive social   A society where taxes are low
        taxes   welfare, but high individuals take
                                                   responsibility for themselves

			somewhat		
closer	somewhat	can't say	closer to	closer to	
to first	closer to first	which	second	second	NA
1	2	3	4	5	9

V145F. A society that assures safety and   A deregulated society where
        stability through appropriate   people are responsible for their
        regulations   own actions

closer to first	somewhat closer to first	can't say which	somewhat closer to second	closer to second	NA
1	2	3	4	5	9

V146. How about people from other countries coming here to work. Which one of the following do you think the government should do?

1. Let anyone come who wants to?
2. Let people come as long as there are jobs available?
3. Place strict limits on the number of foreigners who can come here?
4. Prohibit people coming here from other countries?
9. DK

I am going to name a number of organizations. For each one, could you tell me how much confidence you have in them: is it a great deal of confidence, quite a lot of confidence, not very much confidence or none at all?

		A great deal	Quite a lot	Not very much	None at all	DK
V147	The churches	1	2	3	4	9
V148	The armed forces	1	2	3	4	9
V149	The press	1	2	3	4	9
V150	Television	1	2	3	4	9
V151	Labor unions	1	2	3	4	9
V152	The police	1	2	3	4	9
V153	The government in [WASHINGTON/ YOUR CAPITAL]	1	2	3	4	9
V154	Political parties	1	2	3	4	9
V155	Parliament	1	2	3	4	9
V156	The Civil service	1	2	3	4	9
V157	Major Companies	1	2	3	4	9
V158	The Environmental Protection movement	1	2	3	4	9
V159	The women's movement	1	2	3	4	9
V160	The European Union*	1	2	3	4	9
V161	NATO (North Atlantic Treaty Organization)	1	2	3	4	9
V162	The United Nations	1	2	3	4	9

   * In non-European countries ask about the most important regional organization (e.g., in North America, NAFTA).

V163. People have different views about the system for governing this country. Here is a scale for rating how well things are going: 1 means very bad; 10 means very good

Where on this scale would you put the political system as it was ....

[*in former communist countries*: under the communist regime]
[*in countries where recently a change of regime has taken place*:
       under the xxx regime;]
[*in countries where no regime change has taken place*: ten years ago]?

1	2	3	4	5	6	7	8	9	10	99
Bad									Very good	Dk

I'm going to describe various types of political systems and ask what you think about each as a way of governing this country. For each one, would you say it is a very good, fairly good, fairly bad or very bad way of governing this country?

		Very good	Fairly good	Bad	Very bad	DK
164	Having a strong leader who does not have to bother with parliament and elections	1	2	3	4	9
165	Having experts, not government, make decisions according to what they think is best for the country	1	2	3	4	9
166	Having the army rule	1	2	3	4	9
167	Having a democratic political system	1	2	3	4	9

V168. On the whole are you very satisfied, rather satisfied, not very satisfied or not at all satisfied with the way democracy is developing in our country?

1 Very satisfied
2 Rather satisfied
3 Not very satisfied
4 Not at all satisfied
9 DK

I'm going to read off some things that people sometimes say about a democratic political system. Could you please tell me if you agree strongly, agree, disagree or disagree strongly, after I read each one of them?

		Agree strongly	Agree	Disagree	Strongly disagree	DK
V169	In democracy, the economic system runs badly	1	2	3	4	9

		Agree strongly	Agree	Disagree	Strongly disagree	DK
V170	Democracies are indecisive and have too much quibbling	1	2	3	4	9
V171	Democracies aren't good at maintaining order	1	2	3	4	9
V172	Democracy may have problems but it's better than any other form of government	1	2	3	4	9

V173. How much respect is there for individual human rights nowadays (in our country)?. Do you feel there is (read out):

1 A lot of respect for individual human rights
2 Some respect
3 Not much respect
4 No respect at all
9 Don't know

V174. How satisfied are you with the way the people now in national office are handling the country's affairs? Would you say you are very satisfied, fairly satisfied, fairly dissatisfied or very dissatisfied?

1 Very satisfied
2 Fairly satisfied
3 Fairly dissatisfied
4 Very dissatisfied
9 DK

V175. Generally speaking, would you say that this country is run by a few big interests looking out for themselves, or that it is run for the benefit of all the people?

1 Run by a few big interests
2 Run for all the people
9 Don't know

V176. Some people favor, and others are against, having this country provide economic aid to poorer countries. Do you think that this country should provide more or less economic aid to poorer countries? Would you say we should give...

1. A lot more than we do now
2. Somewhat more than we do now
3. Somewhat less than we do now
4. A lot less than we do now
9. DK

Some people believe that certain kinds of problems could be better handled by the United Nations than by the various national governments. Others think that these problems should be left entirely to the respective national governments; while others think they would be handled best by the national governments working together with coordination by the United Nations.

I'm going to mention some problems. For each one, would you tell me whether you think that policies in this area should be decided by the national governments, by the United Nations, or by the national governments with UN coordination?

		National Governments	United Nations	National governments, with UN coordination
V177	International peacekeeping	1	2	3
V178	Protection of the environment	1	2	3
V179	Aid to developing countries	1	2	3
V180	Refugees	1	2	3
V181	Human Rights	1	2	3

V182. How often, if at all, do you think about the meaning and purpose of life?
(READ OUT IN REVERSE ORDER FOR ALTERNATE CONTACTS)

1 Often
2 Sometimes
3 Rarely
4 Never
9 Don't know [DO NOT READ OUT]

SHOW CARD T

V183. Here are two statements which people sometimes make when discussing good and evil.
Which one comes closest to your own point of view?

A. There are absolutely clear guidelines about what is good and evil. These always apply to everyone, whatever the circumstances.
B. There can never be absolutely clear guidelines about what is good and evil. What is good and evil depends entirely upon the circumstances at the time.

1 Agree with statement A
2 Agree with statement B
3 Disagree with both [IF VOLUNTEERED]
9 Don't know [DO NOT READ OUT]

V184. Do you belong to a religious denomination?
IF YES: Which one?
[IF NO: CODE 0]

RELIGIOUS DENOMINATION

NO, not a member	0
Roman Catholic	1
Protestant	2
Orthodox (Russian/Greek/etc.)	3
Jews	4
Muslim	5
Hindu	6
Buddhist	7
Other (WRITE IN)	8
No answer	9

NOTE: if your own society does not fit into this coding system, please devise an alternative, following this as closely as possible; point out any variations when sending the data.

ASK ALL

SHOW CARD U

V185. Apart from weddings, funerals and christenings, about how often do you attend religious services these days?

    1 More than once a week
    2 Once a week
    3 Once a month
    4 Only on special holy days
    5 Once a year
    6 Less often
    7 Never, practically never

V186. Independently of whether you go to church or not, would you say you are... (READ OUT)

    1 A religious person
    2 Not a religious person
    3 A convinced atheist
    9 Don't know [DO NOT READ OUT]

Generally speaking, do you think that the churches in your country are giving adequate answers to...

    (Read out and code one answer for each)

    NB: In non-Christian countries, refer to "the religious authorities in your country" or "the religious leaders in your country," instead of "the churches."

		YES	NO	DK
V187	The moral problems and needs of the individual	1	2	9
V188	The problems of family life	1	2	9
V189	People's spiritual needs	1	2	9
V190	The social problems facing our country today	1	2	9

Which, if any, of the following do you believe in? (READ OUT AND CODE ONE ANSWER FOR EACH)

		YES	NO	DK
V191	Do you believe in God?	1	2	9
V192	Do you believe in life after death?	1	2	9
V193	Do you believe people have a soul?	1	2	9
V194	Do you believe in hell?	1	2	9
V195	Do you believe in heaven?	1	2	9

SHOW CARD V

V196. How important is God in your life? Please use this scale to indicate- 10 means very important and 1 means not at all important.

Not at all   Very
1   2   3   4   5   6   7   8   9   10
DK = 99

V197. Do you find that you get comfort and strength from religion?

1 Yes
2 No
9 Don't know [DO NOT READ OUT]

V198. Do you take some moments of prayer, meditation or contemplation or something like that?

1 Yes
2 No
9 Don't know

V199. How often do you pray to God outside of religious services? Would you say...

1 every day
2 more than once a week
3 once a week
4 at least once a month
5 several times a year
6 less often
7 never
9 Don't know

SHOW CARD

How much do you agree or disagree with each of the following

		Agree Strongly	Agree	Neither agree or disagree	Disagree	Strongly disagree	DK
V200	Politicians who do not believe in God are unfit for public office	1	2	3	4	5	9
V201	Religious leaders should not influence how people vote in elections	1	2	3	4	5	9
V202	It would be better for [this country] if more people with strong religious beliefs held public office	1	2	3	4	5	9
V203	Religious leaders should not influence government decisions	1	2	3	4	5	9

SHOW CARD W

Please tell me for each of the following statements whether you think it can always be justified, never be justified, or something in between, using this card. READ OUT STATEMENTS. CODE ONE ANSWER FOR EACH STATEMENT

V204. Claiming government benefits to which you are not entitled

Never Justifiable								Always Justifiable	
1	2	3	4	5	6	7	8	9	10

DK = 99

V205. Avoiding a fare on public transport

Never   Always
Justifiable   Justifiable
1   2   3   4   5   6   7   8   9   10
DK = 99

V206. Cheating on taxes if you have a chance

Never   Always
Justifiable   Justifiable
1   2   3   4   5   6   7   8   9   10
DK = 99

V207. Someone accepting a bribe in the course of their duties

Never   Always
Justifiable   Justifiable
1   2   3   4   5   6   7   8   9   10
DK = 99

V208. Homosexuality

Never   Always
Justifiable   Justifiable
1   2   3   4   5   6   7   8   9   10
DK = 99

V209. Prostitution

Never   Always
Justifiable   Justifiable
1   2   3   4   5   6   7   8   9   10
DK = 99

V210. Abortion

Never   Always
Justifiable   Justifiable
1   2   3   4   5   6   7   8   9   10
DK = 99

V211. Divorce

Never   Always
Justifiable   Justifiable
1   2   3   4   5   6   7   8   9   10
DK = 99

V212. Euthanasia— ending the life of the incurably sick

Never Justifiable									Always Justifiable
1	2	3	4	5	6	7	8	9	10

DK = 99

V213. Suicide

Never Justifiable									Always Justifiable
1	2	3	4	5	6	7	8	9	10

DK = 99

SHOW CARD X

V214. To which of these geographical groups would you say you belong first of all?

V215. And the next?
[substitute your own nation and continent for these]

	FIRST	NEXT
Locality or town where you live	1	1
State or region of country where you live	2	2
[The U.S.] as a whole	3	3
[North America]	4	4
The world as a whole	5	5
Don't know [DO NOT READ OUT]	9	9

V216. How proud are you to be FRENCH? (substitute your own nationality for 'French')

1 Very proud
2 Quite proud
3 Not very proud
4 Not at all proud
5 [IF VOLUNTEERED]: I am not FRENCH
9 Don't know [DO NOT READ OUT]

SHOW CARD N29

V217. How often do you follow politics in the news on television or on the radio or in the daily papers?

1 Every day
2 Several times a week
3 Once or twice a week

4 Less often
5 Never
9 DK

SHOW CARD Y

V218. Which of the following best describes you? Just call out one of the letters on this card.

1 [A] Above all, I am an Hispanic American
2 [B] Above all, I am a Black American
3 [C] Above all, I am a white American
4 [D] Above all, I am an Asian American
5 [E] I am an American first and a member of some ethnic group second

[modify the ethnic groups in this question to fit your own society]

V219. What language do you normally speak at home?

1. English
2. Spanish
3. French
4. Chinese
5. Japanese

[modify the list of languages to fit your own society]

SHOW CARD Z

V220. If there were a national election tomorrow, for which party on this list would you vote? Just call out the number on this card. If DON'T KNOW: Which party appeals to you most?

1. Party 1
2. Party 2
3. Party 3
4. etc.

[use two-column code to cover all major parties in given society; use "01," "02," for first parties]

V221. And which party would be your second choice?

1. Party 1
2. Party 2
3. Party 3
4. etc.

V222. And is there any party on this list that you would never vote for?

    01. Party 1
    02. Party 2
    03. Party 3
    04. etc.

DEMOGRAPHICS

V223. Sex of respondent:

    1 Male
    2 Female

V224. Can you tell me your year of birth, please? 19____
[ENTER ONLY THE LAST TWO DIGITS OF THE YEAR: "19" IS ASSUMED]

V225. This means you are __ __ years old.
[ALSO A TWO DIGIT VARIABLE]

V226. What is the highest educational level that you have attained?
    (use functional equivalent of the following, in given society;
    IF STUDENT, CODE HIGHEST LEVEL HE/SHE EXPECTS TO COM-
PLETE):

    1. No formal education
    2. Incomplete primary school
    3. Complete primary school
    4. Incomplete secondary school: technical/vocational type
    5. Complete secondary school: technical/vocational type
    6. Incomplete secondary: university-preparatory type
    7. Complete secondary: university-preparatory type
    8. Some university-level education, without degree
    9. University-level education, with degree
    0. DK/NA

V227. At what age did you (or will you) complete your full time education, either at
school or at an institution of higher education? Please exclude apprenticeships:
[IF STUDENT, CODE AGE AT WHICH HE/SHE EXPECTS TO COMPLETE EDU-
CATION]
WRITE IN AGE IN YEARS _____
[TWO DIGITS]

V228. Do you live with your parents?

    1 Yes
    2 No

V229. Are you employed now or not?
    IF YES:
    About how many hours a week? If more than one job: only for the main job

    Has paid employment
    Full Time(30 hours a week or more)   1
    Part time (less than 30 hours a week)   2
    Self employed   3
    If no paid employment:
    Retired/pensioned   4
    Housewife not otherwise employed   5
    Student   6
    Unemployed   7
    Other PLEASE SPECIFY   8

V230. In which profession/occupation do you or did you work? If more than one job,
the main job?
    What is/was your job there? WRITE IN AND CODE V230 BELOW
    [THIS IS ASKED SIMPLY IN ORDER TO CODE V230 BELOW]

        1 Employer/manager of establishment with 10 or more employees
        2 Employer/manager of establishment with less than 10 employees
        3 Professional worker lawyer, accountant, teacher, etc
        4 Supervisory - office worker: supervises others.
        5 non-manual - office worker: non-supervisory
        6 Foreman and supervisor
        7 Skilled manual worker
        8 Semi-skilled manual worker
        9 Unskilled manual worker
       10 Farmer: has own farm
       11 Agricultural worker
       12 Member of armed forces, security personnel
       13 Never had a job

V231. Are you the chief wage earner in your household?

        1 Yes - GO TO V234.
        2 No - GO TO V232.

V232. Is the chief wage earner employed now or not?

        1 Yes
        2 No

V233. In which profession/occupation does he/she work? (or did work) If more than one
job, the main job? What is/was his/her job there? WRITE IN AND CODE V233 BE-
LOW

1 Employer/manager of establishment with 10 or more employees
2 Employer/manager of establishment with less than 10 employees
3 Professional worker lawyer, accountant, teacher, etc.
4 Supervisory non-manual - office worker.
5 non-manual - office worker: non-supervisory
6 Foreman and supervisor
7 Skilled manual worker
8 Semi-skilled manual worker
9 Unskilled manual worker
10 Farmer: has own farm
11 Agricultural worker
12 Member of armed forces, security personnel
13 Never had a job

V234. During the past year, did your family:

1. Save money
2. Just get by
3. Spent some savings
4. Spent savings and borrowed money
9. DK, NA

V235. People sometimes describe themselves as belonging to the working class, the middle class, or the upper or lower class. Would you describe yourself as belonging to the:

1. Upper class
2. Upper middle class
3. Lower middle class
4. Working class
5. Lower class
9. Don't know [DO NOT READ OUT]

SHOW INCOME CARD AA

V236. Here is a scale of incomes. We would like to know in what group your household is, counting all wages, salaries, pensions and other incomes that come in. Just give the letter of the group your household falls into, before taxes and other deductions.

1	2	3	4	5	6	7	8	9	10
C	D	E	F	G	H	I	J	k	L

No answer = 99

[CODE INCOME CATEGORIES BY DECILES FOR YOUR SOCIETY, 1=LOWEST DECILE, 10=HIGHEST DECILE]

V237. Do you agree strongly, agree, disagree or disagree strongly with the following statement:
"Television is my most important form of entertainment."

1. Agree strongly
2. Agree
3. Disagree
4. Disagree Strongly
9. DK

V238. Time at the end of the interview: ....

V239. Total length of interview Hours Minute

V240. During the interview the respondent was....

1 Very interested
2 Somewhat interested
3 Not very interested

V241. Size of town:

1 Under 2,000
2 2,000 - 5,000
3 5 - 10,000
4 10 - 20,000
5 20 - 50,000
6 50 - 100,000
7 100   500,000
8 500,000 and more

V242. Ethnic group [code by observation]:

1 Caucasian white
2 Negro Black
3 South Asian Indian, Pakistani, etc.
4 East Asian Chinese, Japanese, etc.
5 Arabic, Central Asian
6 Other write in ....

V243. Region where the interview was conducted:

1 New England
2 Middle Atlantic states
3 South Atlantic
4 East South Central
5 West South Central

 6 East North Central
 7 West North Central
 8 Rocky Mountain states
 9 Northwest
10 California
[use 2-digit regional code appropriate to your own society]

V244. Language in which interview was conducted

1. English
2. French
[IF RELEVANT; use code appropriate to your own society]

V245. Weight variable.

Provide a 4-digit weight variable here to correct your sample to reflect national distributions of key variables. If no weighting is necessary, simply code each case as "1". It is especially important to correct for education. For example, if your sample contains twice as many university-educated respondents as there are in the adult population as a whole, members of this group should be given a weight of .5 (coded as "50").

European values study
1999 questionnaire (February version)

Variable names: v = master / o = optional / c = country-specific - to be included before demographics - / DK = don't know = code –1 / Na = no answer = code –2 / Not applicable = code –3 / caseno = respondent number / country = country code / intno = interviewer number

SHOW CARD 1

1 Please say, for each of the following, how important it is in your life.

			Very important	Quite important	Not important	Not at all important	Dk	Na
v1	A	Work	1	2	3	4	-1	-2
v2	B	Family	1	2	3	4	-1	-2
v3	C	Friends and acquaintances	1	2	3	4	-1	-2
v4	D	Leisure time	1	2	3	4	-1	-2
v5	E	Politics	1	2	3	4	-1	-2
v6	F	Religion	1	2	3	4	-1	-2

2 When you get together with your friends, would you say you discuss political matters frequently, occasionally or never?

v7	A	Frequently	1
	B	Occasionally	2
	C	Never	3
		Don't know	-1
		No answer	-2

SHOW CARD 3

3 I am now going to read out some statements about the environment. For each one read out, can you tell me whether you agree strongly, agree, disagree or strongly disagree? (Read out each statement and code an answer for each)

			Strongly agree	Agree	Disagree	Strongly disagree	Dk	Na
v8	A	I would give part of my income if I were certain that the money would be used to prevent environmental pollution	1	2	3	4	-1	-2
v9	B	I would agree to an increase in taxes if the extra money is used to prevent environmental pollution	1	2	3	4	-1	-2
v10	C	The Government has to reduce environmental pollution but it should not cost me any money	1	2	3	4	-1	-2

SHOW CARD 4

4 Taking all things together, would you say you are:

v11	A	Very happy	1
	B	Quite happy	2
	C	Not very happy	3
	D	Not at all happy	4
		Don't know	-1
		No answer	-2

SHOW CARD 5

5 Please look carefully at the following list of voluntary organisations and activities and say...
   a) which, if any, do you belong to? (Code all mentioned under (a))
   b) which, if any, are you currently doing unpaid voluntary work for? (Code all mentioned under (b))

				a		b	
				mentioned	not mentioned	mentioned	not mentioned
v12	v30	A	Social welfare services for elderly, handicapped or deprived people	1	0	1	0
v13	v31	B	Religious or church organisations	1	0	1	0
v14	v32	C	Education, arts, music or cultural activities	1	0	1	0
v15	v33	D	Trade unions	1	0	1	0
v16	v34	E	Political parties or groups	1	0	1	0
v17	v35	F	Local community action on issues like poverty, employment, housing, racial equality	1	0	1	0
v18	v36	G	Third world development or human rights	1	0		
v19	v37	H	Conservation, the environment, ecology, animal rights	1	0	1	0
v20	v38	I	Professional associations				
v21	v39	J	Youth work (e.g. scouts, guides, youth clubs etc.)	1	0	1	0
v22	v40	K	Sports or recreation	1	0	1	0
v23	v41	L	Women's groups	1	0	1	0
v24	v42	M	Peace movement	1	0	1	0
v25	v43	N	Voluntary organisations concerned with health	1	0	1	0
v26	v44	O	Other groups	1	0	1	0
v27	v45		None	1	0	1	0
v28	v46		Don't know	-1	0	-1	0
v29	v47		No answer	-2	0	-2	0

SHOW CARD 6

6   I'm going to ask how often you do certain things. For each activity, would you say you do them every week or nearly every week; once or twice a month; only a few times a year; or not at all? *(Interviewer: Code 'Not applicable' when respondent is not involved in work, church or club)*

SHOW CARD 13

13   Here are some aspects of a job that people say are important. Please look at them and tell me which ones you personally think are important in a job? (Code all mentioned)

			mentioned	not mentioned
v71	A	Good pay	1	0
v72	B	Pleasant people to work with	1	0
v73	C	Not too much pressure	1	0
v74	D	Good job security	1	0
v75	E	Good chances for promotion	1	0
v76	F	A job respected by people in general	1	0
v77	G	Good hours	1	0
v78	H	An opportunity to use initiative	1	0
v79	I	A useful job for society	1	0
v80	J	Generous holidays	1	0
v81	K	Meeting people	1	0
v82	L	A job in which you feel you can achieve something	1	0
v83	M	A responsible job	1	0
v84	N	A job that is interesting	1	0
v85	O	A job that meets one's abilities	1	0
o2	P	*Good physical working conditions*	*1*	*0*
o3	Q	*To have time off at the weekends*	*1*	*0*
v86		None of these	1	0

v87   14   Are you yourself employed or not?

A   Yes 1 ——→ go to 15
B   No 2 ——→ go to 17

SHOW CARD 15

v88   15   Overall, how satisfied or dissatisfied are you with your job?

1   2   3   4   5   6   7   8   9   10   -1   -2   -3
Dissatisfied   Satisfied   Dk   Na   Nap

SHOW CARD 16

v89   16   How free are you to make decisions in your job? Please use this card to indicate how much decision-making freedom you feel you have.

1   2   3   4   5   6   7   8   9   10   -1   -2   -3
None at all   A great deal   Dk   Na   Nap

SHOW CARD 16a

o4 *16a And how satisfied or dissatisfied are you with your job security? Please use this card to indicate how satisfied or dissatisfied you are.*

1	*2*	*3*	*4*	*5*	*6*	*7*	*8*	*9*	*10*	*-1*	*-2*	*-3*
Dissatisfied								*Satisfied*		*Dk*	*Na*	*Nap*

ASK ALL
SHOW CARD 17

17 Do you agree or disagree with the following statements?

			Agree strongly	Agree	Neither agree nor disagree	Disagree	Disagree strongly	Dk	Na
v90	A	To fully develop your talents, you need to have a job	1	2	3	4	5	-1	-2
v91	B	It is humiliating to receive money without having to work for it	1	2	3	4	5	-1	-2
v92	C	People who don't work turn lazy	1	2	3	4	5	-1	-2
v93	D	Work is a duty towards society	1	2	3	4	5	-1	-2
v94	E	People should not have to work if they don't want to	1	2	3	4	5	-1	-2
v95	F	Work should always come first, even if it means less spare time	1	2	3	4	5	-1	-2

v96 18 Imagine two secretaries, of the same age, doing practically the same job. One finds out that the other earns £ 30 **(Countries other than UK: Please use own currency)** a week more than she does. The better paid secretary, however, is quicker, more efficient and more reliable at her job.

In your opinion is it fair or not fair that one secretary is paid more than the other?

A	Fair	1
B	Unfair	2
	Don't know	-1
	No answer	-2

V64 European Values Study 1999 Questionnaire February 1999

SHOW CARD 24

V101–V104 Which one?

Which one?

NB: PRE-LIST COUNTRY-SPECIFIC LEISURE ORGANISATIONS

Roman Catholic
Church of England (Protestant)
Free Church/Non Conformist
Evangelical
Jew
Muslim
Hindu
Buddhist
Orthodox
Sikh (no V101)
Other/None
Don't know
Not applicable

SHOW CARD 25

V105 Apart from weddings, funerals and christenings, about how often do you attend religious services these days?

A. More than once a week
B. Once a week
C. Once a month
D. Christmas/Easter day
E. Other specific holy days
F. Once a year
G. Less often
H. Never, practically never
Don't know
Not applicable

SHOW CARD 26

V106 Apart from weddings, funerals and christenings, about how often did you attend religious services when you were 12 years old?

A. More than once a week
B. Once a week
C. Once a month

SHOW CARD 24

v104   24b   Which one?

Which one?

NB: PRESENT COUNTRY SPECIFIC LIST! RECODE INTO:

	b
Roman Catholic	1
Church of England (Protestant)	2
Free Church/Non-Conformist/	
Evangelical	3
Jew	4
Muslim	5
Hindu	6
Buddhist	7
Orthodox	8
Other (Write in)	9
Don't know	-1
No answer	-2
Not applicable	-3

SHOW CARD 25

v105   25   Apart from weddings, funerals and christenings, about how often do you attend religious services these days?

A	More than once a week	1
B	Once a week	2
C	Once a month	3
D	Christmas/Easter day	4
E	Other specific holy days	5
F	Once a year	6
G	Less often	7
H	Never, practically never	8
	Don't know	-1
	No answer	-2

SHOW CARD 26

v106   26   Apart from weddings, funerals and christenings, about how often did you attend religious services when you were 12 years old?

A	More than once a week	1
B	Once a week	2
C	Once a month	3

D	Christmas/Easter day	4	
E	Other specific holy days	5	
F	Once a year	6	
G	Less often	7	
H	Never, practically never	8	
	Don't know	-1	
	No answer	-2	

27 Do you personally think it is important to hold a religious service for any of the following events?

			Yes	No	Dk	Na
v107	A	Birth	1	2	-1	-2
v108	B	Marriage	1	2	-1	-2
v109	C	Death	1	2	-1	-2

V110   28 Independently of whether you go to church or not, would you say you are ... (Read out reversing order)

A	A religious person	1
B	Not a religious person	2
C	A convinced atheist	3
	Don't know	-1
	No answer	-2

29 Generally speaking, do you think that your church is/the churches are giving, in your country, adequate answers to ...(Read out and code one answer for each)

NB:For those belonging to a church or a religious community; ask YOUR church/ religious community

For those not belonging to a church or religious community ask: THE churches

			Yes	No	Dk	Na
V111	A	The moral problems and needs of the individual	1	2	-1	-2
V112	B	The problems of family life	1	2	-1	-2
V113	C	People's spiritual needs	1	2	-1	-2
V114	D	The social problems facing our country today	1	2	-1	-2

30 Which, if any, of the following do you believe in? (Read out and code one answer for each)

			Yes	No	Dk	Na
V115	A	God	1	2	-1	-2
V116	B	Life after death	1	2	-1	-2

SHOW CARD 38

V128   38   Do you believe that a lucky charm such as a mascot or a talisman can protect or help you?

1	2	3	4	5	6	7	8	9	10	-1	-2
Definitely not							Definitely yes			Dk	Na

o10   38a   *How often do you consult your horoscope to know about your future?*

A	*every day*	*1*
B	*at least once a week*	*2*
C	*at least once a month*	*3*
D	*less often*	*4*
E	*never*	*5*
	Don't know	*-1*
	No answer	*-2*

o11   38b   *How often do you take this into account in your daily life?*

A	*always*	*1*
B	*most of the time*	*2*
C	*sometimes*	*3*
D	*not very often*	*4*
E	*never*	*5*
	Don't know	*-1*
	No answer	*-2*

SHOW CARD 38

39   How much do you agree or disagree with each of the following:

			Agree strongly	Agree	Neither agree nor disagree	Disagree	Disagree strongly	Dk	Na
v129	A	Politicians who do not believe in God are unfit for public office	1	2	3	4	5	-1	-2
v130	B	Religious leaders should not influence how people vote in elections	1	2	3	4	5	-1	-2

			Agree strongly	Agree	Neither agree nor disagree	Disagree	Disagree strongly	Dk	Na
v131	C	It would be better for [Britain] if more people with strong religious beliefs held public office	1	2	3	4	5	-1	-2
v132	D	Religious leaders should not influence government decisions	1	2	3	4	5	-1	-2
o12	E	*If a nurse were asked to help perform a legal abortion, she should be allowed to refuse on religious grounds*	*1*	*2*	*3*	*4*	*5*	*-1*	*-2*

SHOW CARD 39a

o13 39a *In my opinion, some time should be set aside for prayer, meditation or contemplation in all schools.*

A	*I strongly agree*	*1*
B	*I agree*	*2*
C	*I don't agree nor disagree*	*3*
D	*I strongly disagree*	*4*
	Don't know	*-1*
	No answer	*-2*

SHOW CARD 39b

o14 39B *Should books and films that attack religions be prohibited by law or should they be allowed?*

A	*Definitely should be banned*	*1*
B	*Probably should be banned*	*2*
C	*Probably should be allowed*	*3*
D	*Definitely should be allowed*	*4*
E	*Can't choose*	*5*
	Don't know	*-1*
	No answer	*-2*

			Strongly agree	Agree	Disagree	Strongly disagree	Dk	Na
v154	A	A working mother can establish just as warm and secure a relation-ship with her children as a mother who does not work	1	2	3	4	-1	-2
v155	B	A pre-school child is likely to suffer if his or her mother works	1	2	3	4	-1	-2
v156	C	A job is alright but what most women really want is a home and children	1	2	3	4	-1	-2
v157	D	Being a housewife is just as fulfilling as working for pay	1	2	3	4	-1	-2
v158	E	Having a job is the best way for a woman to be an independent person	1	2	3	4	-1	-2
v159	F	Both the husband and wife should contribute to house-hold income	1	2	3	4	-1	-2
v160	G	In general, fathers are as well suited to look after their children as mothers	1	2	3	4	-1	-2
V161	H	Men are less able to handle emotions in relationships than women	1	2	3	4	-1	-2

SHOW CARD 47

V162   47   Which of these two statements do you tend to agree with? (Code one answer only)

A   Regardless of what the qualities and faults of ones parents are, one must always love and respect them

B   One does not have the duty to respect and love parents who have not earned it by their behaviour and attitudes

A	Tend to agree with statement A	1
B	Tend to agree with statement B	2
	Don't know	-1
	No answer	-2

SHOW CARD 48

V163   48   Which of the following statements best describes your views about parents, responsibilities to their children? (Code one only)

A	Parents' duty is to do their best for their children even at the expense of their own well-being	1
B	Parents have a life of their own and should not be asked to sacrifice their own well-being for the sake of their children	2
		2
C	Neither	3
	Don't know	-1
	No answer	-2

SHOW CARD 49

49   Here is a list of qualities which children can be encouraged to learn at home. Which, if any, do you consider to be especially important? **Please choose up to five? (Code five only)**

			Important	not mentioned
v164	A	Good manners	1	0
v165	B	Independence	1	0
v166	C	Hard work	1	0
v167	D	Feeling of responsibility	1	0
v168	E	Imagination	1	0
v169	F	Tolerance and respect for other people	1	0
v170	G	Thrift, saving money and things	1	0
v171	H	Determination, perseverance	1	0
v172	I	Religious faith	1	0
v173	J	Unselfishness	1	0
v174	K	Obedience	1	0
v175		Don't know	-1	0
v176		No answer	-2	0

SHOW CARD 50

50   Do you approve or disapprove of abortion under the following circumstances?

			Approve	Disapprove	Dk	Na
v177	A	Where the woman is not married	1	2	-1	-2

			Approve	Disapprove	Dk	Na
v178	B	Where a married couple does not want to have any more children	1	2	-1	-2

o17   *51a   How interested would you say you are in politics?*

	A	*Very interested*	*1*
	B	*Somewhat interested*	*2*
	C	*Not very interested*	*3*
	D	*Not at all interested*	*4*
		Don't know	*-1*
		No answer	*-2*

SHOW CARD 51

51   Now I'd like you to look at this card. I'm going to read out some different forms of political action that people can take, and I'd like you to tell me, for each one, whether you have actually <u>done</u> any of these things, whether you might do it or would never, under any circumstances, do it.

			Have Done	Might Do	Would Never do	Dk	Na
v179	A	Signing a petition	1	2	3	-1	-2
v180	B	Joining in boycotts	1	2	3	-1	-2
v181	C	Attending lawful demonstrations	1	2	3	-1	-2
v182	D	Joining unofficial strikes	1	2	3	-1	-2
v183	E	Occupying buildings or factories	1	2	3	-1	-2

SHOW CARD 52

v184   52   Which of these two statements comes closest to your own opinion?

A   I find that both freedom and equality are important. But if I were to choose one or the other, I would consider personal freedom more important, that is, everyone can live in freedom and develop without hinderance

B   Certainly both freedom and equality are important. But if I were to choose one or the other, I would consider equality more important, that is, that nobody is underprivileged and that social class differences are not so strong

	A	Agree with statement A	1
	B	Agree with statement B	2
	C	Neither	3
		Don't know	-1
		No answer	-2

SHOW CARD 53

v185   53   In political matters, people talk of 'the left' and the 'the right'. How would you place your views on this scale, generally speaking?

1	2	3	4	5	6	7	8	9	10	-1	-2
Left									Right	Dk	Na

SHOW CARD 53

54   Now I'd like you to tell me your views on various issues. How would you place yourviews on this scale?

		1	2	3	4	5	6	7	8	9	10	-1	-2
v186	A	Individuals should take more responsibility for providing for themselves					The state should take more responsibility to ensure that everyone is provided for					Dk	Na

		1	2	3	4	5	6	7	8	9	10	-1	-2
v187	B	People who are unemployed should have to take any job available or lose their unemployment benefits					People who are unemployed should have the right to refuse a job they do not want					Dk	Na

		1	2	3	4	5	6	7	8	9	10	-1	-2
v188	C	Competition is good. It stimulates people to work hard and develop new ideas					Competition is harmful, it brings out the worst in people					Dk	Na

		1	2	3	4	5	6	7	8	9	10	-1	-2
v189	D	The state should give more freedom to firms					The state should control firms more effectively					Dk	Na

		1	2	3	4	5	6	7	8	9	10	-1	-2
o18	E	*Incomes should be made more equal*					*There should be greater incentives for individual effort*					*Dk*	*Na*

		1	2	3	4	5	6	7	8	9	10	-1	-2
o19	F	*Private ownership of business and industry should be increased*					*Government ownership of business and industry should be increased*					*Dk*	*Na*

		1	2	3	4	5	6	7	8	9	10	-1	-2
o20	G	*Each individual should be responsible for arranging his or her own pension*					*The state should be responsible for everyone's pension*					*Dk*	*Na*

			1	2	3	4	5	6	7	8	9	10	-1	-2

o21   H   *Each individual should be responsible for arranging his or her own housing*   *The state should be responsible for everyone's housing*   Dk   Na

			1	2	3	4	5	6	7	8	9	10	-1	-2

o22   I   *One should be cautious about making major changes in life*   *You will never achieve much unless you act boldly*   Dk   Na

SHOW CARD 54a

o23   54a   *On this card are three basic kinds of attitudes vis-à-vis the society we live in. Please choose the one which best describes your own opinion. (Code one only)*

    A   *The entire way our society is organised must be radically changed by revolutionary action*   1

    B   *Our society must be gradually improved by reforms*   2

    C   *Our present society must be valiantly defended against all subversive forces*   3

       Don't know   -1

       No answer   -2

SHOW CARD 55

v190   55   There is a lot of talk these days about what the aims of this country should be for the next ten years. On this card are listed some of the goals which different people would give top priority. If you had to choose, which of the things on this card would you say is most important? (Code one answer only)

v191   56   And which would be the next most important? (Code one answer only)

		First Choice	Second Choice
A	Maintaining order in the nation	1	1
B	Giving people more say in important government decisions	2	2
C	Fighting rising prices	3	3
D	Protecting freedom of speech	4	4
	Don't know	-1	-1
	No answer	-2	-2

SHOW CARD 56a

o24   56a   *Of course we all hope that there will not be another war, but if it were to come to that, would you be willing to fight for your country?*

      A   *Yes*   *1*
      B   *No*   *2*
         Don't know   *-1*
         No answer   *-2*

SHOW CARD 57

57   Here is a list of various changes in our way of life that might take place in the near future. Please tell me for each one, if it were to happen whether you think it would be a good thing, a bad thing, or don't you mind?

			Good	Bad	Don't mind	Dk	Na
v192	A	Less emphasis on money and material possessions	1	2	3	-1	-2
v193	B	Decrease in the importance of work in our lives	1	2	3	-1	-2
v194	C	More emphasis on the development of technology	1	2	3	-1	-2
v195	D	Greater emphasis on the development of the individual	1	2	3	-1	-2
v196	E	Greater respect for authority	1	2	3	-1	-2
v197	F	More emphasis on family life	1	2	3	-1	-2
v198	G	A simple and more natural lifestyle	1	2	3	-1	-2
v199	H	More power to local authorities	1	2	3	-1	-2

o25   57a   *In the long run, do you think the scientific advances we are making will help or harm mankind?*

      A   *Will help*   *1*
      B   *Will harm*   *2*
      C   *Some of each*   *3*
         Don't know   *-1*
         No answer   *-2*

SHOW CARD 58

58   Please look at this card and tell me, for each item listed, how much confidence you have in them, is it a great deal, quite a lot, not very much or none at all?
(Code one answer for each item)

			A great deal	Quite a lot	Not very much	None at all	Dk	Na
v200	A	The church	1	2	3	4	-1	-2
v201	B	The armed forces	1	2	3	4	-1	-2
v202	C	The education system	1	2	3	4	-1	-2
v203	D	The press	1	2	3	4	-1	-2
v204	E	Trade unions	1	2	3	4	-1	-2
v205	F	The police	1	2	3	4	-1	-2
v206	G	Parliament	1	2	3	4	-1	-2
v207	H	Civil service	1	2	3	4	-1	-2
v208	I	The social security system	1	2	3	4	-1	-2
v209	J	The European Union	1	2	3	4	-1	-2
o26	K	*NATO*	*1*	*2*	*3*	*4*	*-1*	*-2*
v210	L	United Nations Organization	1	2	3	4	-1	-2
v211	M	Health care system	1	2	3	4	-1	-2
v212	N	The justice system	1	2	3	4	-1	-2
o27	O	*Major companies*	*1*	*2*	*3*	*4*	*-1*	*-2*

58a   *Do you agree or disagree with the following statements on international cooperation?*

			Agree strongly	Agree	Disagree	Strongly disagree	Dk	Na
o28	A	*[Belgium] cannot solve its environmental problems by itself, but needs to collaborate with international organisations on environment protection*	*1*	*2*	*3*	*4*	*-1*	*-2*
o29	B	*[Belgium] cannot solve its problem of criminality by itself, but needs to collaborate with international police organisations*	*1*	*2*	*3*	*4*	*-1*	*-2*

			Agree strongly	Agree	Disagree	Strongly disagree	Dk	Na
o30	C	*[Belgium] cannot solve its problems of unemployment by itself, but needs to collaborate with international orga- nisations on eco- nomic development*	*1*	2	3	4	-1	-2

v213   59   On the whole are you very satisfied, rather satisfied, not very satisfied or not at all satisfied with the way democracy is developing in our country?

A	Very satisfied	1
B	Rather satisfied	2
C	Not very satisfied	3
D	Not at all satisfied	4
	Don't know	-1
	No answer	-2

SHOW CARD 60

v214   60   People have different views about the system for governing this country. Here is a scale for rating how well things are going: 1 means very bad; 10 means very good

1	2	3	4	5	6	7	8	9	10	-1	-2
Bad								Very good		Dk	Na

SHOW CARD 60

v215   61   Where on this scale would you put the political system as it was ....
[in former communist countries: under communist regime]
[in countries where recently a change of regime xx has taken place: under xx regime;]
[in countries where no regime change has taken place: ten years ago]?

1	2	3	4	5	6	7	8	9	10	-1	-2
Bad								Very good		Dk	Na

SHOW CARD 60

62   I'm going to describe various types of political systems and ask what you think about each as a way of governing this country. For each one, would you say it is a very good, fairly good, fairly bad or very bad way of gov- erning this country?

			Very good	Fairly good	Fairly bad	Very bad	Dk	Na
v216	A	Having a strong leader who does not have to bother with parliament and elections	1	2	3	4	-1	-2
v217	B	Having experts, not government, make decisions according to what they think is best for the country	1	2	3	4	-1	-2
v218	C	Having the army rule the country	1	2	3	4	-1	-2
v219	D	Having a democratic political system	1	2	3	4	-1	-2

SHOW CARD 60

63   I'm going to read off some things that people sometimes say about a democratic political system. Could you please tell me if you agree strongly, agree, disagree or disagree strongly, after I read each of them?

			Agree strongly	Agree	Disagree	Disagree strongly	Dk	Na
v220	A	Democracy may have problems but it's better than any other form of government	1	2	3	4	-1	-2
v221	B	In democracy, the economic system runs badly	1	2	3	4	-1	-2
v222	C	Democracies are indecisive and have too much squabbling	1	2	3	4	-1	-2
v223	D	Democracies aren't good at maintaining order	1	2	3	4	-1	-2

v224   64   How much respect is there for individual human rights nowadays (in our country)? Do you feel there is (read out):

A	A lot of respect for individual human rights	1
B	Some respect	2
C	Not much respect	3
D	No respect at all	4
	Don't know	-1
	No answer	-2

o31 64a *In politics, different parties often hold different views. Which do you think is better?*

> A *A party leader should stand firm for what he or she believes, even if others disagree*
> *or*
> B *A party leader should be prepared to cooperate with other groups, even if it means compromising some important beliefs*

> A *Agree most with statement A*   *1*
> B *Agree most with statement B*   *2*
> *Don't know*   *-1*
> *No answer*   *-2*

o32 64b *If you had to choose, which would you say is the most important responsibility of government?*

> A *To maintain order in society*
> *or*
> B *to respect freedom of the individual*

> A *Agree most with statement A*   *1*
> B *Agree most with statement B*   *2*
> *Don't know*   *-1*
> *No answer*   *-2*

SHOW CARD 65

65 Please tell me for each of the following statements whether you think it can always be justified, never be justified, or something in between, using this card. (Read out statements reversing order for alternate contacts. Code one answer for each statement)

1	2	3	4	5	6	7	8	9	10	-1	-2
Never									Always	Dk	Na

v225	A	Claiming state benefits which you are not entitled to
v226	B	Cheating on tax if you have the chance
v227	C	Taking and driving away a car belonging to someone else (joyriding)
v228	D	Taking the drug marijuana or hashish
v229	E	Lying in your own interest
v230	F	Married men/women having an affair
v231	G	Someone accepting a bribe in the course of their duties
v232	H	Homosexuality
v233	I	Abortion
v234	J	Divorce
v235	K	Euthanasia (terminating the life of the incurably sick)

v236	L	Suicide
v237	M	Throwing away litter in a public place
v238	N	Driving under the influence of alcohol
v239	O	Paying cash for services to avoid taxes
v240	P	Having casual sex
v241	Q	Smoking in public buildings
v242	R	Speeding over the limit in built-up areas
o33	S	*Avoiding a fare on public transport*
o34	T	*Sex under the legal age of consent*
o35	U	*Prostitution*
o36	V	*Political assassinations*
o37	W	*Scientific experiments on human embryos*
o38	X	*Genetic manipulation of food stuffs*

SHOW CARD 66

66   According to you, how many of your compatriots do the following?

			Almost all	Many	Some	Almost none	Dk	Na
			1	2	3	4	-1	-2
v243	A	Claiming state benefits to which they are not entitled	1	2	3	4	-1	-2
v244	B	Cheating on tax if they have the chance	1	2	3	4	-1	-2
v245	C	Paying cash for services to avoid taxes	1	2	3	4	-1	-2
v246	D	Taking the drug marijuana or hash	1	2	3	4	-1	-2
v247	E	Throwing away litter in a public place	1	2	3	4	-1	-2
v248	F	Speeding over the limit in built-up areas	1	2	3	4	-1	-2
v249	G	Driving under the influence of alcohol	1	2	3	4	-1	-2
v250	H	Having casual sex	1	2	3	4	-1	-2
o39	*I*	*Avoiding a fare on public transport*	*1*	*2*	*3*	*4*	*-1*	*-2*
o40	*J*	*Lying in their own interest*	*1*	*2*	*3*	*4*	*-1*	*-2*
o41	*K*	*Accepting a bribe in the course of their duties*	*1*	*2*	*3*	*4*	*-1*	*-2*

SHOW CARD 66a

66a *Do you fully agree, agree, disagree, fully disagree with the following state-*
     ments:
     Stealing food in a shop should be punished more severely if:

			Agree strongly	Agree	Agree nor disagree	Disagree	Disagree strongly	Dk	Na
o42	A	*the thief is young*	*1*	*2*	*3*	*4*	*5*	*-1*	*-2*
o43	B	*the thief is poor*	*1*	*2*	*3*	*4*	*5*	*-1*	*-2*
o44	C	*the shop is part of a supermarket chain*	*1*	*2*	*3*	*4*	*5*	*-1*	*-2*

SHOW CARD 67

v251 67 Which of these geographical groups would you say you belong to first of
          all?

v252 68 And the next?

v253 69 And which do you belong to least of all?

		First	Next	The least
A	Locality or town where you live	1	1	1
B	Region of country where you live	2	2	2
C	Your country as a whole	3	3	3
D	Europe	4	4	4
E	The world as a whole	5	5	5
	Don't know	-1	-1	-1
	No answer	-2	-2	-2

**Countries other than UK: Please put in corresponding explanations
if necessary)**

v254 70 Are you a citizen of Britain? (**Countries other than UK: Please substi-
          tute your nation for 'Britain'!**)

     A Yes 1 ⟶ go to 71
     B No 2 ⟶ go to 72

v255 71 How proud are you to be a British citizen? (**Countries other than UK:
          Please substitute your nationality for 'British'!**)

     A Very proud   1
     B Quite proud   2
     C Not very proud   3

D	Not at all proud	4
	Don't know	-1
	No answer	-2
	Not applicable	-3

SHOW CARD 71a

o45   71a   *Using the responses on this card, could you tell me how much you trust* ***[Britisch]*** *people in general? (Countries other than UK: Please substitute your nationality for 'British')*

A	*Trust them completely*	*1*
B	*Trust them a little*	*2*
C	*Neither trust nor distrust them*	*3*
D	*Do not trust them very much*	*4*
E	*Do not trust them at all*	*5*
	Don't know	*-1*
	No answer	*-2*

SHOW CARD 71b

o46   71b   *There is much talk about what the individual member states of the European Community Union have in common and what makes each one distinct. (Interviewer presents illustration with responses and scale from 1 to 7)*

A   *Some people say: If the European member states were truly to be united, this would mean the end of their national, historical and cultural identities. Their national economic interests would also be sacrificed.*

B   *Others say: Only a truly united Europe can protect its states' national, historical and cultural identities and their national economic interests from the challenges of the superpowers.*

Which opinion is closest to your own opinion, the first one or the second one? Please use the scale listed.1 would mean that you agree completely with A and 7 would mean that you agree completely with B. The numbers in between allow you to show which of the opinions you tend to agree with, whether you tend to agree more with the one or with the other.

1	2	3	4	5	6	7	-1	-2
A						B	Dk	Na

SHOW CARD 72

v256   72   If there was a general election tomorrow, which party would you vote for? (Code one answer under (a) below) v257   73   If don't know in (a): And which party appeals to you most?(Code one answer under (b) below)

COUNTRY SPECIFIC LIST OF POLITICAL PARTIES!

	a	b
	..	..
I would not vote	96	96
I would cast a blank ballot	97	97
Response refused	-2	-2
Don't know	-1	-1

SHOW CARD 72

v258   74   How about people from less developed countries coming here to work. Which one of the following do you think the government should do?

A	Let anyone come who wants to	1
B	Let people come as long as there are jobs available	2
C	Put strict limits on the number of foreigners who can come here	3
D	Prohibit people coming here from other countries	4
	Don't know	-1
	No answer	-2

o47   74a   *Do you tend to agree or disagree with the following statement: The future is so uncertain that it is best to live from day to day*

A	*Tend to agree*	*1*
B	*Tend to disagree*	*2*
	Don't know	*-1*
	No answer	*-2*

SHOW CARD 75

v259   75   Which of these statements is the nearest to your opinion?

A	For the greater good of society it is better if immigrants maintain theirdistinct customs and traditions	1
B	For the greater good of society it is better if immigrants do not maintain their distinct customs and traditions but take over the customs of the country	2
	Don't know	-1
	No answer	-2

SHOW CARD 75

76   In order to be considered "just", what should a society provide? Please tell me for each statement if it is important or unimportant to you. 1 means very important; 5 means not important at all.

			Very important	2	3	4	Not at all important	Dk	Na
			1	2	3	4	5	-1	-2
v260	A	Eliminating big inequalities in income between citizens	1	2	3	4	5	-1	-2
v261	B	Guaranteeing that basic needs are met for all, in terms of food, housing, cloths, education, health	1	2	3	4	5	-1	-2
v262	C	Recognizing people on their merits	1	2	3	4	5	-1	-2
o48	D	*Giving young people equal opportunity to pursue their education irrespective of family income*	*1*	*2*	*3*	*4*	*5*	*-1*	*-2*

SHOW CARD 77

v263   77   How often do you follow politics in the news on television or on the radio or in the daily papers?

	A	Every day	1
	B	Several times a week	2
	C	Once or twice a week	3
	D	Less often	4
	E	Never	5
		Don't know	-1
		No answer	-2

SHOW CARD 78

78   Can you tell me your opinion on each of the following statements?

			Agree strongly	Agree	Neither agree nor disagree	Disagree	Disagree strongly	Dk	Na
v264	A	If someone has information that may help justice be done, generally he or she should give it to authorities	1	2	3	4	5	-1	-2

			Agree strongly	Agree	Neither agree nor disagree	Disagree	Disagree strongly	Dk	Na
			1	2	3	4	5	-1	-2
v265	B	People should stick to their own affairs and not show too much interest in what others say or do							

SHOW CARD 79

79   To what extent do you feel concerned about the living conditions of:

			Very much	Much	To a certain extent	Not so much	Not at all	DK	Na
v266	A	Your immediate family	1	2	3	4	5	-1	-2
v267	B	People in your neighbourhood	1	2	3	4	5	-1	-2
v268	C	The people of the region you live in	1	2	3	4	5	-1	-2
v269	D	Your fellow countrymen	1	2	3	4	5	-1	-2
v270	E	Europeans	1	2	3	4	5	-1	-2
v271	F	Human kind	1	2	3	4	5	-1	-2

SHOW CARD 80

80   To what extent do you feel concerned about the living conditions of:

			Very much	Much	To a certain extent	Not so much	Not at all	DK	Na
v272	A	elderly people in your country	1	2	3	4	5	-1	-2
v273	B	unemployed people in your country	1	2	3	4	5	-1	-2
v274	C	immigrants in your country	1	2	3	4	5	-1	-2
v275	D	sick and disabled people in your country	1	2	3	4	5	-1	-2

SHOW CARD 81

81 Would you be prepared to actually do something to improve the conditions of:

			Absolutely yes	Yes	Maybe yes/ maybe no	No	Absolutely no	DK	Na
v276	A	your immediate family	1	2	3	4	5	-1	-2
v277	B	people in your neighbourhood/ community	1	2	3	4	5	-1	-2
v278	C	elderly people in your country	1	2	3	4	5	-1	-2
v279	D	immigrants in your country	1	2	3	4	5	-1	-2
v280	E	sick and disabled people in your country	1	2	3	4	5	-1	-2

INTERVIEWER: ONLY those who have absolutely yes or yes on 81c!

SHOW CARD 82

82 There can be several reasons to do something to help the elderly people your country. Please tell me for each of the reasons I am going to read out, if they apply to you or not. (Code an answer for each reason).

			Very much	Much	To a certain extent	Not so much	Not at all	DK	Na	Nap
v281	A	Because you feel you have a moral duty to help	1	2	3	4	5	-1	-2	-3
v282	B	Because you sympathize with them	1	2	3	4	5	-1	-2	-3
v283	C	Because it is in the interest of society	1	2	3	4	5	-1	-2	-3
v284	D	Because it is in your own interest	1	2	3	4	5	-1	-2	-3
v285	E	To do something in return	1	2	3	4	5	-1	-2	-3

INTERVIEWER: ONLY those who have absolutely yes or yes on 81d!

SHOW CARD 83

83   There can be several reasons to do something to help immigrants in your country. Please tell me for each of the reasons I am going to read out, if they apply to you or not? (Code an answer for each reason)

			Very much	Much	To a certain extent	Not so much	Not at all	DK	Na	Nap
v286	A	Because you feel you have a moral duty to help	1	2	3	4	5	-1	-2	-3
v287	B	Because you sympathize with them	1	2	3	4	5	-1	-2	-3
v288	C	Because it is in the interest of society	1	2	3	4	5	-1	-2	-3
v289	D	Because it is in your own interest	1	2	3	4	5	-1	-2	-3
v290	E	To do something in return	1	2	3	4	5	-1	-2	-3

INCLUDE COUNTRY-SPECIFIC QUESTIONS HERE

ASK ALL
DEMOGRAPHICS

v291   84   Sex of respondent

    A   male   1
    B   female   2

v292   85   Can you tell me your year of birth, please 19..

v293   86   Whether you are married or not: Do you live in a stable relationship with a partner?

    A   Yes   1
    B   No   2 ——→ go to 88

v294   87   Are you legally married to this partner?

    A   Yes   1 ——→ go to 90
    B   No   2 ——→ go to 89
         Not applicable   -3

v295   88   Did you ever live in a stable relationship before, i.e. without being married?

      A Yes   1
      B No   2
      Not applicable   -3

v296   89   What is your current legal marital status?

      A Married   1
      B Widowed   2
      C Divorced   3 ⟶ go to 91
      D Separated   4
      E Never married   5 ⟶ go to 91
      Don't know   -1
      No answer   -2
      Not applicable   -3

v297   90   Have you ever been divorced?

      A Yes   1
      B No   2
      Don't know   -1
      No answer   -2
      Not applicable   -3

v298   91   How many children, including deceased children, have you yourself ever had?

      .... (write in)

        92   How many people, including yourself, are currently living in your household?

v299   A   Aged 18 and over   ......
v300   B   Aged between 13 and 17 ......
v301   C   Aged between 5 and 12   ......
v302   D   Under 5   ......

v303   93   At what age did you (or will you) complete your full time education, either at school or at an institution of higher education? Please exclude apprenticeships. (*Interviewer instruction: If respondent is still at school, ask: at what age do you expect you will have completed your education?*) (Write in age) ....

v304   94   What is the highest level you have reached in your education?
         To be measured as detailed as possible on national level and to be transformed into this variable:

A	Inadequately completed elementary education	1
B	Completed (compulsory) elementary education	2
C	(Compulsory) elementary education and basic vocational qualification	3
D	Secondary, intermediate vocational qualification	4
E	Secondary, intermediate general qualification	5
F	Full secondary, maturity level certificate	6
G	Higher education – lower-level tertiary certificate	7
H	Higher education – upper-level tertiary certificate	8

v305   95   Do you live with your parents?

A	Yes	1
B	No	2

v306   96   Are you yourself employed now or not? If yes: About how many hours a week? (If more than one job: only for the main job)

Has paid employment
    30 hours a week or more   1
    Less than 30 hours a week   2
    Self employed   3 ⟶ go to 100
If no paid employment
    Retired/pensioned   4 ⟶ go to 101
    Housewife not otherwise employed   5 ⟶ go to 105
    Student   6 ⟶ go to 105
    Unemployed   7 ⟶ go to 104
    Other (Please specify) ....   8 ⟶ go to 105

v307   97   In your present job, do you supervise anyone who is directly responsible to you?

A	Yes	1	
B	No	2	→ go to 101
	Don't know	-1	
	No answer	-2	

v308   98   How many people do you supervise? ...... (write in number)

v309   99   How many other people usually work for the organization? .... (write in number)   ⟶ go to 101

v310   100   How many employees do you have? ...... (write in number)

     101   In which profession/industry do you or did you work? (If more than one job: the main job) (Write in) ....

v311   **Code according to ISCO88**

    102   What is/was your job there? (Write in and code below).........................

v312 103 a Employer/manager of establishment with 10 or more employees 1
           b Employer/manager of establishment with less then 10 employees 2
           c professional worker (lawyer, accountant, teacher etc.) 3
           d Middle level non-manual - office worker etc. 4
           e Junior level non-manual - office worker etc. 5
           f Foreman and supervisor 6
           g Skilled manual worker 7
           h Semi-skilled manual worker 8
           i Unskilled manual worker 9
           j Farmer: employer, manager on own account 10
           k Agricultural worker 11
           l Member of armed forces 12
           m Never had a job 13
             Don't know -1
             No answer -2

v313   **Code according to ISCO88** ....

v314 104 And for how long are you unemployed?

       A Less than half a year 1
       B Between half a year and one year 2
       C One year 3
       D Between one and two years 4
       E Two years 5
       F More than two years 6
         Don't know -1
         No answer -2
         Not applicable -3

v315 105 Are you the chief wage earner?

       A Yes 1 ⟶ 110
       B No 2

v316 106 Is the chief wage earner employed now or not?

       A Yes 1
       B No 2
         Don't know -1
         No answer -2
         Not applicable -3

107   In which profession/industry does/did he (she) work? (Write in)
....

v317   **Code according to ISCO88** ....

108   What is/was his/her job? (Write in and code below) ....

v318   109   a   Employer/manager, of establishment with 10 or more employees   1
             b   Employer/manager of establishment with less then 10 employees   2
             c   Professional worker (lawyer, accountant, teacher etc.)   3
             d   Middle level non-manual - office worker etc.   4
             e   Junior level non-manual - office worker etc.   5
             f   Foreman and supervisor   6
             g   Skilled manual worker   7
             h   Semi-skilled manual worker   8
             i   Unskilled manual worker   9
             j   Farmer:employer, manager on own account   10
             k   Agricultural worker   11
             l   Member of armed forces   12
             m   Never had a job   13
             Don't know   -1
             No answer   -2
             Not applicable   -3

v319   **Code according to ISCO88** ....

ASK ALL
SHOW INCOME CARD

v320   110   Here is a scale of incomes and we would like to know in what group your
             household is, counting all wages, salaries, pensions and other incomes that
             come in. Just give the letter of the group your household falls into, after
             taxes and other deductions.

             1   2   3   4   5   6   7   8   9   10   -1   -2

                                                               Dk Na

o49   *110a*   *Interviewer code by yourself*
             Socio-ecomonic status of respondent
      A   *AB (upper, uppr-middle class)*   *1*
      B   *C1 (middle, non-manual workers)*   *2*
      C   *C2 (manual workers -skilled, semi-skilled)*   *3*
      D   *DE (manual workers -unskilled, unemployed)*   *4*

v321   111   Town where the interview was conducted. (Please write in) ....

             NB: ZIP code and/or official statistical code for place of living

v322   112   Size of town

Under 2.000	1	5 - 10.000	2
2 - 5.000	3	10 - 20.000	4
20 - 50.000	5	100 - 500.000	7
50 - 100.000	6	500.000 and more	8

v332   113   Region: (Please write in) .... **(code + label)**

o50   *Date of the interview:.............(day , month)*

              Total length of interview
o51   *...........Hours*
o52   *...........Minutes*

o53   *114   During the interview the respondent was ...*

       A   *Very interested*   *1*
       B   *Somewhat interested*   *2*
       C   *Not very interested*   *3*

Appendix:
list of variables on CD-ROM,
but not in the Source Book

For reasons of space, we haven't included all the existing variables in the present source book. Doing so would have turned an already large book into an immense book. Variables that were not asked in all, or almost all surveys in a given wave, have been omitted. All variables *are* included in the accompanying CD-ROM, however.

The CD-ROM has an auto run feature that will make the program run upon inserting it. If it doesn't start automatically, you may execute JDSSURVEY.EXE from the root directory. The program allows browsing all included documentation, survey results with a select, and click interface. All included documentation can also be found in the \DATA folder of this CD-ROM.

The additional variables that can be found in the CD-ROM are grouped in three categories:

- IVS variables: This is the set of variables included in a special Islamic Values Survey module, integrated within the WVS wave. The detailed variables are:

LABEL	VARIABLE
Government protects freedom	F108
Government protects religion	F109
Laws: people's wishes	F110
Laws of the shari'a	F111
Justifiable: Drinking alcohol	F124
Aggression from neighboring country.	E184
Exploitation of local resources	E185
Cultural invasion by the west	E186
Where R lived after married	X010
Woman wearing weil	D067
Woman good mother	D068
Woman good wife	D069
Woman religious	D070

LABEL	VARIABLE
Woman educated	D071
More than one wife	D076
Wife must obey	D077
Woman being independent	D072
Woman having work outside home	D073
Woman maintaining her family	D074
Woman being sociable	D075

• Country variations of "Neighbours" question:

LABEL	VARIABLE
Neighbours: Evangelists	A134
Neighbours: People of a different religion	A135
Neighbours: People same religion	A136
Neighbours: Militant minority	A137
Neighbours: Zoroastrians	A138
Neighbours: People not from country of origin	A139
Neighbours: Political extremists	A141
Neighbours: trafficants	A142
Neighbours: Indians or Lebanese	A143
Neighbours: Chinese or Philippino-Chinese	A144
Neighbours: Spiritists	A145
Neighbours: Protestants	A146
Neighbours: Christians	A147
Neighbours: Witchdoctors and related labels	A148

• Country variations of "Confidence in institutions" question:

LABEL	VARIABLE
Confidence: the Arab League	E089
Confidence: the Association of South East Asian nations —ASEAN	E090
Confidence: the Organisation for African Unity-OAU	E091
Confidence: the NAFTA	E092
Confidence: the Andean Pact	E093
Confidence: the Mercosur	E094

LABEL	VARIABLE
Confidence: the SAARC	E095
Confidence: the ECO	E096
Confidence: the APEC	E097
Confidence: the Tratado de Libre Comercio	E098
Confidence: the Organización de Estados Unidos Americanos (OEA)	E099
Confidence: the Movimiento en pro de Vieques (Puerto Rico)	E100
Confidence: local/regional government	E101
Confidence: SADC/SADEC	E102
Confidence: East African Cooperation (EAC)	E103
Confidence: the Presidence	E103B
Confidence: the civil society groups	E103C

- WVS-2000 optional questions:

LABEL	VARIABLE
Egalitarian vs. Competitive society	E063
Extensive welfare vs. Low taxes	E064
Regulated vs. Responsible society	E065
Should: egalitarian vs. Competitive	E066
Should: extensive welfare or low taxes	E067
Should: regulated — responsible	E068
Rate political system in 10 years	E113

- Country specific questions:

LABEL	VARIABLE
Which of the following best describes you	G015
Language at home	G016
Party that would never vote	E182
Education (country specific)	X025CS
Size of town (country specific)	X049CS
Ethnic group	X051

Index

Printed by Programas Educativos, S. A. de C. V.
Calz. Chabacano núm. 65 local A, Col. Asturias
06850, México, D. F.
August 2004

Printing house certified by
Instituto Mexicano de Normalización y Certificación, A. C.
followin the ISO-9002: 1994 / NMX-CC-004: 1995
(registration number RSC-048)
and ISO 14000: 1996 NMX-SSA-001: 1998 IMNC
(registration number RSSA-003) standards.